Baseball Weekly
1998 Almanac

Everything the baseball fan needs — all in one book

Edited by
Paul White
Editor, *Baseball Weekly*

With contributions from
the staffs of *Baseball Weekly*
and USA TODAY Sports

Project Editor, John M. Shostrom

A Balliett & Fitzgerald Book

An Owl Book
Henry Holt and Company
New York

Henry Holt and Company, Inc.
Publishers since 1866
115 West 18th Street
New York, New York 10011

Henry Holt® is a registered trademark
of Henry Holt and Company, Inc.

Published in Canada by Fitzhenry & Whiteside Ltd.,
195 Allstate Parkway, Markham, Ontario L3R 4T8.

ISSN: 1091-7071
ISBN: 0-8050-5148-1

Henry Holt books are available for special promotions and premiums.
For details contact: Director, Special Markets.

First Edition—1998

Printed in the United States of America
All first editions are printed on acid-free paper. ∞

10 9 8 7 6 5 4 3 2 1

Produced by Balliett & Fitzgerald, Inc.
Managing editors: Rachel Aydt, Vijay Balakrishnan
Production editor: Sue Canavan
Production staff: Emma Cobb, Peggy Goddard, Beatrice Schafroth, Mike Walters
Copyeditor: Anthony Scheitinger
Proofreader: Kevin Kerr
Editorial assistant: Nathaniel LeClery
Fact checking: Ed H. Foley

Acknowledgments

We would like to thank Paul White and especially Keith Cutler for making this
    possible, as well as Susan Mayoralgo, Russell Beeker, Greg Frazier
    and Michelle Mattox.

Major league statistics provided by Elias Sports Bureau.
Minor league statistics provided by Howe SportsData International.
Record book, historical statistics, and disabled list information provided by
    Pete Palmer and Garry Gillette of Total Sports.
Photographs of Major League Baseball are used with the permission of
    Major League Baseball.

Contents

1998 Baseball Weekly Almanac

Leading off

▶*Baseball Weekly*
editor Paul White:
A modest game of
musical chairs

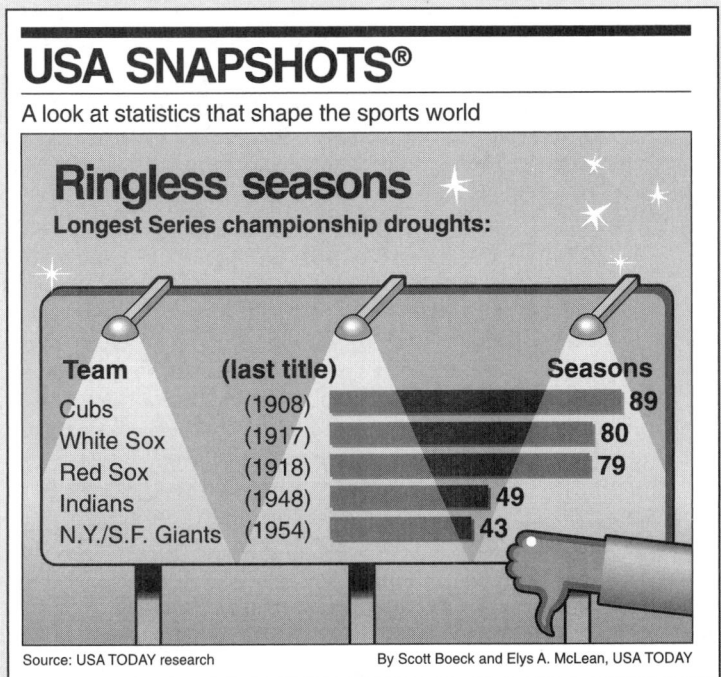

USA SNAPSHOTS®

A look at statistics that shape the sports world

Ringless seasons

Longest Series championship droughts:

Team	(last title)	Seasons
Cubs	(1908)	89
White Sox	(1917)	80
Red Sox	(1918)	79
Indians	(1948)	49
N.Y./S.F. Giants	(1954)	43

Source: USA TODAY research   By Scott Boeck and Elys A. McLean, USA TODAY

A modest game of musical chairs

Another season, another set of rules. Every season, it seems, we need to brush up on what's new. And these days, it's not just players and managers in new uniforms and cities. In getting ready for the 1998 season, your biggest challenge will not be so much the new stuff you need to learn but rather the stuff you need to forget.

Yes, there are more changes in major league baseball for this season. In what may be an experiment in reverse psychology, however, there may not be as many changes as you had been girding yourself for. For much of the summer of 1997, we were regularly teased or frightened with all sorts of radical possibilities for 1998. And that's as if the introduction of interleague play wasn't enough of a jolt—and it did turn out to be a successful jolt, both aesthetically and economically. The "inter" part is back for a second season, and for the most part, so is the "league."

But just when Bud Selig had us convinced that we'd never be able to recognize those leagues, what did we get? It seems the only club Bud Selig could persuade to change leagues was the one he owns, the Milwaukee Brewers. So, National League baseball returns to Milwaukee for the first time since the Braves fled to Atlanta in 1966. And the Brewers, along with the incumbent teams in the new NL Central Division, will get an opportunity to become the first major league team to finish sixth since 1993. Meanwhile, the American League West will remain at four teams for at least another season.

Before you get too lost, here's a quick review of the changes:
• The new Tampa Bay Devil Rays join the high-spending AL East.
• The Detroit Tigers get out of that rat race and into the AL Central, where they easily are as good as anyone except the Cleveland Indians.
• The expansion Arizona Diamondbacks have their wish granted to play in the NL West.

• Milwaukee moves from the AL Central to the NL Central.
• The end result is a 16-team National League, while the American League remains at 14.

Selig reminds us, however, that realignment is a work in progress. Many teams, with the Texas Rangers atop the list, still want it to end up with divisions contained within one time zone as much as possible, so 1999's groupings may be different.

For now, the wild-card playoff structure remains the same—sort of. Owners resisted general managers' recommendations that the first-round Division Series be extended from best-of-five to best-of-seven. But the general managers were able to push through a change in the format of those best-of-fives. Now the team with home advantage will host Games 1, 2 and 5. And home advantage will be earned. The four playoff teams in each league will be seeded by their regular-season records, with the best playing the worst.

Of course, what spurred a lot of these changes was the addition of two new markets: Phoenix and Tampa Bay. Expansion, for the second time in five years, is here again. If the Florida Marlins could win a World Series in five seasons, what could happen with these clubs, especially with the free-spending ways the Diamondbacks displayed as soon they began assembling a roster? If Mark McGwire and Ken Griffey could come oh so close to Roger Maris' single-season home run record, what happens when another 20 or so pitchers are suddenly decreed major leaguers rather than AAA guys?

Those two questions will be answered on the field, along with the merits of realigned divisions, interleague games and wild-card races. Isn't debating the game on the field fun? It's certainly better for us and for baseball than the discussions of some other recent offseasons. What would you rather be talking about, the length of the strike or the size of the strike zone? That's an easy call to make.

—by Paul White, editor

Inside pitch

- ▶Willie Blair's luck
- ▶A car for Castillo
- ▶Reggie strikes out
- ▶Reinsdorf's unscientific poll

- ▶Butler's farewell
- ▶Robb vs. "Rapid Robert"
- ▶and more ...

USA SNAPSHOTS®

A look at statistics that shape the sports world

Armed and dangerous

Three Braves pitchers are among the top eight in career postseason wins:

Pitcher	Wins
Whitey Ford	10
John Smoltz	10
Dave Stewart	10
Tom Glavine	9
Catfish Hunter	9
Orel Hershiser	8
Greg Maddux	8
Jim Palmer	8

Source: Elias Sports Bureau   By Scott Boeck and Elys A. McLean, USA TODAY

An anecdotal review of the 1997 season

Somebody must have called

If you would have called Detroit general manager Randy Smith's spring-training home in Lakeland, Fla., you would have gotten this message from his wife: "Hi, this is Erin and Randy. We can't get to the phone, so please leave a message. If you have any pitching, we'll be sure to get right back to you."

Valetine's day

Mets manager Bobby Valentine found out before New York's home opener that one of his new white uniforms had his name spelled "VALETINE."

Aaron was honored by his hometown of Mobile.

A park for Hank

For years, when it wasn't being called "The Launching Pad," old Atlanta–Fulton County Stadium was informally called "The House That Hank Built." Now, though, Hank Aaron, baseball's career home run leader, really does have a ballpark named after him—even though the new Atlanta stadium was named (Ted) Turner Field. He threw out the ceremonial first ball at Hank Aaron Stadium in his hometown of Mobile, Ala., on April 17. The Mobile BayBears' Southern League opener was sold out as AA ball returned to the city following a 27-year absence.

Aaron recalled going to games as a youngster, back when blacks were forced to sit in the bleachers. "I do have a lot of friends still here," he said. "They're beaming. We used to play in the pecan orchards. This is quite a tribute." Aaron, who began his career with the Mobile Black Shippers of the Negro leagues, was honored in front of his 88-year-old father, Henry Sr.

They're wild about Jose

Jose Canseco was passively effective for the A's early in the season, winning two games in his last plate appearance without even swinging. On April 24, Canseco was at the plate when Minnesota's Rick Aguilera threw a wild pitch to allow the winning run to score in the 11th inning. Two days later he again was up in the 11th, this time in a 6-6 game with the Royals, when Mitch Williams—yes, the Wild Thing—threw a bases-loaded wild pitch. "I'm leading the league in wild pitches with the winning run on third," Canseco crowed.

Even the postman only rings twice

Cleveland rookie Bartolo Colon had a long day on May 10. Starting at 3 a.m., the phone kept ringing in his hotel room in Detroit. The caller said, "I've bet a lot of money on the Cleveland Indians. If you don't pitch good, I'm going to kill you and your family." Colon said he received five calls. "I was scared," said Colon afterward. "I didn't know who the guy was."

Several hours later, he allowed two runs on five hits in six innings in a 6-0 loss to

1998 BASEBALL WEEKLY ALMANAC

By Mike Kittrell, AP/Wide World Photos

the Tigers. It was the best of his four starts before he was optioned to AAA Buffalo. The Indians wouldn't be needing a fifth starter for a while.

It's easy for him to say

Dr. James Christian, chief of oral and facial surgery at Detroit's Henry Ford Hospital, noted how close Tigers right-hander Willie Blair came to a devastating injury when he was hit on May 4 by a 107-mph line shot off the bat of Cleveland's Julio Franco. "By moving his head that split second, the ball hit a muscle instead of his temple or eye socket," Christian said. "He was lucky."

Blair felt a little differently: "If I were lucky, the ball would have missed me."

And neither is a golfer

During a Mets-Rockies series, Bobby Jones started on May 17 for the Mets, and another Bobby Jones started the next day for the Rockies. The New York Jones picked up his seventh win of the season in a 3-1 game, while the Colorado Jones, who was recently called up from the minors, went 5⅓ innings, allowing just two earned runs and not getting a decision in a 10-4 loss.

Book 'em, Cal

Three-year-old Ryan Belton got a Cal Ripken autograph on June 4. That's not so unusual, except that he got it at 3:04 a.m., the last of about 2,200 fans who took advantage of a middle-of-the-night book signing by the Orioles third baseman. After playing in an extra-inning victory against the Yankees on June 3, Ripken went to a bookstore in suburban Towson, Md., and signed his new book, *The Only Way I Know*, for 3½ hours. Proceeds from the book and T-shirts sold that night went to his charity, Baltimore Reads/The Ripken Learning Center. "I haven't stayed up this late in a long time," he said. "It was fun."

Even teammate Brady Anderson was curious enough to check out the event, staying for an hour to pose for pictures. "I told him I'd come to one of his book signings and check it out," Anderson said. "This is amazing." Some of the fans had waited at the store for 20 hours to be at the front of the line.

New meaning for "muscle car"

Who cares that pitcher Frank Castillo hit a batting-practice home run on May 30 while he was with the Cubs? Castillo, now with the Rockies, and former teammate Brian McRae. The center fielder told the pitcher three years ago that if he ever homered in batting practice, McRae, who is now with the New York Mets, would buy him a Mercedes-Benz. If he somehow homered in a game, the car would go to Castillo's wife, Tracy.

"It was a pretty safe bet," McRae said after he lost it, noting that Castillo at the time was a .108 batter (he hit .121 in '97) with nothing close to an extra-base hit. After Castillo homered not once but twice, McRae and Mark Grace ran into the cage to hug a stunned Castillo in mock celebration. Then Cubs shortstop Shawon Dunston suggested that Castillo buy one of the flagship 600 series Mercedes-Benzes priced from $126,000 to $140,000, but McRae reminded everyone that he got to pick the car and added, "He's still the worst hitting pitcher I've ever seen."

All-Star swap

Milwaukee and Boston made a blockbuster trade in July: the All-Star Game. Milwaukee will have the game in the year 2001, with Boston hosting in 1999. The Brewers' new stadium would not have been ready by then.

Baseball's Leiter side

Mark and Al Leiter were scheduled to pitch against each other for the first time in their major league careers in the Philadelphia Phillies–Florida Marlins game on July 12. Some 25 family members were in Miami for the occasion, but the game was rained out. The next day, Marlins manager Jim Leyland bumped Al in favor of Alex Fernandez. The Leiter brothers have missed each other by a single day six times.

Their mother, Maria, made the trip from New Jersey to watch her two sons face each other. Asked jokingly who she was rooting for, Maria Leiter began the standard "I hope they both do well" speech before noting, "Both boys need a win. And the Phillies . . . that whole team needs a win." Philadelphia was 25-62 at the time.

No strikes against Fox

The late Nellie Fox, inducted on Aug. 3 into the Hall of Fame, was the American League MVP in 1959. A superb fielder, he also finished with 2,663 hits and a .288 batting average in 19 seasons. Yet when Fox's election was announced last January, critics—including Hall of Famer Reggie Jackson—lamented that Hall standards had been lowered. "They have been lowered," Lou Gould, a member of the Nellie Fox Society, told *Utica Observer-Dispatch* columnist Mike Sherman. "They let in a guy with [almost] 2,600 strikeouts," a reference to Jackson's 2,597 career K's. Fox never whiffed more than 18 times in a season and had only 216 in his career.

Four of out five Reinsdorfs agree...

Fox baseball analyst Bob Brenly commented on White Sox owner Jerry Reinsdorf's statement that fan reaction was 80% positive after trading pitchers Wilson Alvarez, Roberto Hernandez and Danny Darwin to San Francisco for six minor leaguers, saying, "Of course that 80% was [four of] the five family members he asked." A Baseball Weekly Online survey showed that 85% of fans believed that the White Sox, at three games behind the Indians, were not out of contention in the AL Central when the July 31 trade was made. Chicago finished the season six back of Cleveland.

He couldn't wait for a home run

When the Atlanta Braves displayed the news of four-time Cy Young Award winner Greg Maddux's then record $57.5 million contract renewal on Turner Field's center field screen on Aug. 10, the sellout crowd of 47,649 gave him a standing ovation. The pitcher did not emerge from the dugout, but shortstop Rafael Belliard did and tipped his hat to the crowd.

The Cleveland High Sox

The Cleveland Indians, looking to put some energy in a then-lackluster season, started socking it to their opponents on Aug. 27 in Anaheim Stadium. The Indians' starting position players—prompted by David Justice—decided to wear their uniform socks high in honor of the 27th birthday of first baseman Jim Thome, who always wears his socks high. The Indians, 67-61 at the time, scored 10 runs in the fourth inning to beat the Angels 10-4. "I thought the socks looked good," said third baseman Matt Williams after the game.

The socks stayed up from then until the end of the World Series, and

Thome's style of socks started a Tribe trend.

Cleveland came within two outs of winning the championship.

Could Tarkenton play left?

The Minnesota Twins can now make an unusual claim. Two former draftees started at quarterback for NFL teams on Sept. 7—Rob Johnson of the Jacksonville Jaguars and Tony Banks of the St. Louis Rams. Johnson didn't sign with the Twins out of USC; Banks did sign with the Twins out of Michigan State, but was a flop in the minors.

There'll always be an Englund

The Yankees' intentions were good, even if their spelling left something to be desired. The flags at Yankee Stadium flew at half-mast after Diana's fatal car crash. The team's press notes explained the gesture was in memory of "Diana, Princess of Whales."

Interleague by the numbers

NL vs. AL: 117-97
Best NL record: Marlins, Expos 12-3
Worst NL record: Astros 4-11
Best AL record: Rangers 10-6
Worst NL record: Angels 4-12
AL vs. NL, HRs: 229-220
Most HRs: Mariners 33
Fewest HRs: Yankees 4
AL vs. NL, ERA: 4.23-4.32
Lowest ERA: Braves 2.99
Highest ERA: Mariners 6.20
Attendance vs. regular games: +20.2%

Boomer vs. The Boss

Yankees pitcher David Wells threatened to knock out owner George Steinbrenner during an Aug. 30 clubhouse argument. It began after Wells was pulled from a game in which a fan reached over the wall and pulled in a ball—ruled a home run by the umps. Wells suggested to Steinbrenner that extra security be added in right field, and

Steinbrenner responded by telling Wells he should just worry about his pitching.

Wells told Steinbrenner to trade him if he wasn't satisfied. The Boss responded that no one wanted Wells. At that point, Wells threatened to knock out Steinbrenner. George dared him to do it, and both then stared at each other. By the end of the season, no punches had yet been thrown between the two.

MacPhail takes his medicine

Cubs president Andy MacPhail was roundly booed when he was introduced at Ryne Sandberg's retirement ceremonies at Wrigley Field on Sept. 20. He took it in stride, saying, "Thank you for that warm tribute, which this year I deserve."

A man named Jed

After Royals rookie second baseman Jed Hansen stole third base on Sept. 19, he turned to talk to third base coach Rich Dauer. Enter Indians third baseman Matt Williams.

"[Williams] said, 'Why don't you step off the bag, so I can clean it off?' I was gullible enough to step off," Hansen said. "I was not paying attention and talking to Rich Dauer. I learned something. I didn't expect that"—a polite tag by Williams. Hansen was called out.

Butler bows out

A lengthy standing ovation prompted Brett Butler to doff his helmet and acknowledge the fans at Dodger Stadium on Sept. 24, in his last game there before his retirement. "I lay a piece of my heart here; it's like a second home for me," said Butler, 40. "What more could a person ask than to win the respect of the fans he plays for? They gave me nothing but good memories."

Butler, pinch-hitting in the fifth, reached out and slapped a ball that Padres shortstop Chris Gomez had to backhand. It was the type of hit Butler had legged out for countless singles in his career, but he could not beat the throw. Another ovation and a shower of flashbulbs followed as Butler trotted toward the Dodgers' dugout.

Manipulated milestone

Randy Johnson won 20 games, but it involved some maneuvering. Johnson came out of the bullpen on Sept. 27 to become Seattle's first 20-game winner. It was a gift from manager Lou Piniella, who brought Johnson in to relieve Omar Olivares in the fifth inning with the Mariners leading 7-2. "We wanted to give Randy every opportunity to win 20, and rightfully so," Piniella said. "Randy deserves it. He's been a horse here. His finger prevented him from doing this earlier or he'd have had his 20th a long time ago." Johnson missed four starts in August and September because of finger tendinitis.

Hershiser hex

Cleveland's Orel Hershiser not only lost two World Series games to Florida; he was also the loser in the Marlins' first

By Robert Deutsch, USA TODAY

As a Dodger or an Indian, Orel has helped Florida.

game, dropping a 6-3 decision against knuckleballer Charlie Hough at what was then called Joe Robbie Stadium on Opening Day in 1993. Hershiser, who allowed five runs on 10 hits in five innings in that game, said, "The adrenaline was rushing through everyone's body. Because I was overthrowing, I had great velocity and not much movement. I know I'm up there in their trophy case."

A tale of two heaters

Though Miami's Pro Player Stadium scoreboard credited Florida reliever Robb Nen with throwing a 102-mph fastball in Game 1 of the Series, Indians Hall of Famer Bob Feller wasn't all that impressed. "Rapid Robert" says he has film of himself being clocked in 1946 by a "photo electric cell device" that registered his hard one at 107.9 mph. Feller said of Nen's pitch, "That was my changeup."

Out of the money

On Oct. 25, the day of Game 6 of the Series, a horse named Dutch Daulton finished sixth in a race at Philadelphia Park, and another named Renteria was fourth at Hollywood Park.

Digging up funding

A La Jolla, Calif., marketing consultant has offered a bizarre plan to help finance the Padres' proposed new ballpark. Denis Braun presented a task force that is studying the issue with a model that features a cemetery in the outfield walls. Braun believes that selling space for cremated remains could raise more than $100 million toward the project.

"It gives new meaning to 'dead center,'" cracked Padres president Larry Luchino. No, the idea isn't getting serious consideration.

NL/AL beat

1998 Baseball Weekly Almanac

- Features
- 1997 Hall of Fame inductees
- All-Star Game
- 1997 award winners
- Division wrap-ups
- 1997 league leaders
- Obituaries

USA SNAPSHOTS®

A look at statistics that shape the sports world

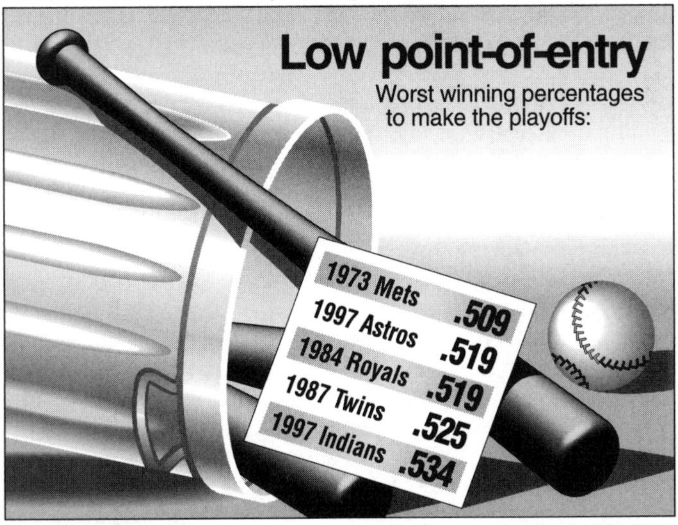

Low point-of-entry
Worst winning percentages to make the playoffs:
1973 Mets .509
1997 Astros .519
1984 Royals .519
1987 Twins .525
1997 Indians .534

Source: USA TODAY research

By Scott Boeck and Gary Visgaitis, USA TODAY

1947: Jackie Robinson rewrote history

By Seth Harrison, Gannett Suburban Newspapers

Jackie and Rachel were a tremendous team.

On April 15, 1997, the baseball world, Rachel Robinson and President Bill Clinton honored the 20th century's first African-American major league ballplayer in a ceremony at a Dodgers-Mets game at Shea Stadium. Fifty years earlier, Hall of Famer Jackie Robinson's ascension to the big leagues had merited a two-sentence press release. The Brooklyn Dodgers were playing their top farm club, the Montreal Royals, in an exhibition game the week before the 1947 season opener. During the sixth inning, Arthur Mann, an assistant to Dodgers president Branch Rickey, handed reporters typed notes. They read: "The Brooklyn Dodgers today purchased the contract of Jackie Roosevelt Robinson from the Montreal Royals. He will report immediately. [Signed] Branch Rickey." Five days later, on April 15 at Ebbets Field, Robinson dug in at home plate against Boston Braves pitcher Johnny Sain for his first major league at-bat.

It was against a backdrop of fear and uncertainty that Robinson made his debut 50 years ago, crossing baseball's racial divide in the process. Opponents taunted him and threatened boycotts. Hotels denied him access.

Robinson's arrival was just a matter of time. The previous year he hit .349 for Montreal, leading the Royals to the International League championship. "We knew he could play," said Dodgers pitcher Ralph Branca, one of several surviving Robinson teammates at the Shea ceremony. That spring of 1947, Rickey set up a series of exhibition games between the Dodgers and the Royals in Cuba and Panama, in less hostile racial climates than Florida's. Still playing for Montreal, Robinson hit .625 and stole seven bases in seven games against the major leaguers.

During this trip several Dodgers players drew up a petition against Robinson and said they wouldn't take the field if he was on the team. Manager Leo Durocher heard about it and called an impromptu team meeting. Players showed up for the bizarre midnight session in pajamas and underwear. Durocher rebuked his players for their attitude and informed them that Robinson was going to be just the first of many black players.

The players backed down, and the Dodgers broke camp and headed to Brooklyn for the season. Jackie's widow, Rachel, said of the subsequent famous Opening Day in her book, *Jackie Robinson: An Intimate Portrait*, "I don't recall ever having been so nervous." In the bottom of the first inning, Robinson stepped in to face Boston's Sain. In his first at-bat, Robinson bounced out to third on a close play in the first inning. Robinson did not—was instructed not to—argue. The trials, and the legend, of Jackie Robinson had begun.

This April 15, Rachel and Jackie Robinson's courage was saluted by President Clinton and acting commissioner Bud Selig when they announced that Jackie's Number 42 would be retired by Major League Baseball forever. Major League Baseball also contributed $1 million to the Jackie Robinson Foundation, started by Rachel, which provides scholarships for minority students.

—by Bill Koenig

Griffey and McGwire pursued Maris' ghost

Griffey watched a lot of balls go deep in 1997.

Roger Maris' record of 61 homers stayed safe for the 36th consecutive season, but Mark McGwire and Ken Griffey Jr. gave the mark a good chase, becoming the first 55-homer men since Maris in 1961. McGwire ended up with a two-league total of 58, and Griffey won the AL home run title with 56. Griffey hit 50 for the first time, while McGwire cranked 52 in 1996. He is the only player besides Babe Ruth to have consecutive 50-homer seasons.

Toward the end of the season, McGwire-Griffey comparisons were inevitable, no matter how dissimilar the players appear. "He's 6-6, 6-7 and 250-plus," said Griffey, exaggerating a bit. (McGwire is listed at 6-5, 245.) "I'm 6-3, 205. It's not fair." Neither player enjoyed talking about the home run race, but both realized such talk was unavoidable. With a lack of late-season team drama for McGwire's Cardinals, who were eliminated from contention early, and Griffey's Seattle Mariners, who clinched in the AL West, the sluggers became the show. Each of their games down the stretch contained a heightened sense of excitement and anticipation. You never knew when McGwire or Griffey might get hold of a couple, bringing his number closer to 61.

McGwire didn't catch Maris, but his name will be in the record book for what he did in 1997. He became the first player to hit 20 homers for two teams in the same season (34 with Oakland, 24 with St. Louis after being traded on July 31), and his two-year total of 110 broke the record for a right-handed batter, 106, set by Jimmie Foxx in 1932-33. It is said that certain players are worth the price of admission. With McGwire's titanic shots, even batting practice is worth the price of admission.

St. Louis fans received an extra treat on Sept. 16—news that McGwire had agreed to a three-year, $28.5 million contract with the Cardinals. In his first at-bat after announcing the signing at Busch Stadium, McGwire was greeted by a prolonged standing ovation. He responded by hitting his 52nd home run, a 517-foot rocket off Los Angeles' Ramon Martinez. "I'm proud to be a Cardinal," McGwire said, adding that he had thought he would try the free-agent market when he was traded.

Griffey had an outstanding all-around season (.304, 147 RBI, 125 runs) and capped it by being unanimously voted the AL's MVP. Griffey already owns more home runs than he ever imagined hitting. He's never looked the part of the muscular slugger, and as a kid, Griffey's role model wasn't Hank Aaron or Willie Mays. He found his example closer to home. "I figured I'd be the same player as my father," said Griffey, whose dad was a .296 hitter who never hit more than 21 homers in a season.

Griffey certainly wouldn't mind breaking Maris' record, but he keeps his eye on something else. "People want to talk about home runs," he says. "But my dad has three things I don't have." He's talking about the things that really count. World Series rings.

—by Deron Snyder and Carrie Muskat

Interleague debut was a hit—and an ordeal

Shrewd innovation or shameless gimmick, baseball's latest wrinkle was unveiled in June to bolstered crowds. Attendance on the first weekend averaged 35,938—an increase of 42.9% from the games leading up to the interleague interlude. Still, players seemed underwhelmed by the historic first weekend of interleague play. "It's just another game for us," White Sox shortstop Ozzie Guillen said of his team's series with the Cubs, unmoved by the crosstown rivalry even after 12 years in Chicago. "It means more for the fans."

All sorts of games from the past were revisited between June 13 and 16. Perhaps you've seen the unofficial video of interleague play: footage of Bill Buckner, Mookie Wilson and Game 6 of the 1986 World Series, shown almost continuously at Shea Stadium as part of the Mets–Red Sox series. No matter that not a single player from either team remained from 11 years ago. "Talk about overkill," said Sox infielder John Valentin.

You want overkill? I killed four days immersing myself in the opening days of interleague play. To fully appreciate interleague, I traveled interstate: 3,152 miles of early-morning flights. All told, I saw eight teams in four cities—New York, Miami, Atlanta and Chicago. It was a search for the answer to a question best posed by Mets manager Bobby Valentine, who, upon losing his interleague opener 8-4 to the Red Sox on Friday the 13th, shook his head and said, "What's the big deal with this interleague play anyway?"

NEW YORK

After much ado was made about 1986, Red Sox fans took a small measure of revenge with their struggling team's victory. Not that those on hand at Shea gloated. Maybe they were reminded of the atmosphere at Yankee Stadium, where cheering for the opposition is akin to inviting suicide. Walking through the upper deck, it was difficult to spot Sox hats, but hard to miss the Boston cynicism. "I get worried

The Mets and the Red Sox collided at Shea.

when they're ahead," said Marc Robbins of Norwalk, Conn., sitting with friends in Section 28.

For a while, it seemed like '86 again. When the Mets loaded the bases for catcher Todd Hundley with two outs in the bottom of the ninth, the crowd erupted. On the mound, Red Sox reliever Kerry Lacy struggled to avoid thoughts of Buckner before getting Hundley to ground out routinely to Valentin. "Of course I thought about it," Lacy said afterward. "When he stepped into the batter's box and the crowd reacted like it did, I got goose bumps." Not everyone did. By the seventh inning, fans apparently already had grown bored with the interleague concept, lofting a squadron of paper airplanes onto the field.

MIAMI

The distance between Queens and New York's unofficial sixth borough is 1,072 miles by air. The Marlins sold out all three of their interleague games against the Yankees in early May, and they could have sold far more than their 40,585 listed capacity had they removed the tarps covering much of the upper deck, which is used for football. But overall attendance has slipped after a quick start in 1993, and even after drawing 127,453 fans, many of them rooting for the Yankees, over the first three interleague games, Marlins owner Wayne Huizenga reiterated over that May weekend that his team's projected loss of $30 million this season might force him to move or sell the team.

The Marlins did not seem to mind playing a home game in a place that seemed more like the Bronx than South Florida. "Why shouldn't they root for the Yankees?" asked manager Jim Leyland. "As long as they're here and rooting for baseball." Many stayed through a four-hour rain delay. At midnight, with only two innings on the scoreboard, I pondered my own options. With a 7 a.m. flight to Atlanta, I could go straight to the airport if the game resumed.

At 12:10, the game was postponed. In the interests of keeping all of the gate for both games, it was decided that a split doubleheader would be played on Sunday. At 1:12, the few hundred fans remaining were finally informed of this. Sitting in the press box, looking at an angry mob of mostly Yankees fans and facing the possibility of two hours of sleep, I still was not sold on interleague play. What was baseball thinking when it came up with this concept? And what was I thinking when I embarked on this grueling odyssey?

ATLANTA

With a three-game sweep of the Braves, the Orioles found many ways to beat the team of the '90s. Baltimore won by outpitching Greg Maddux, John Smoltz and Tom Glavine. They won with improbable hitting from catcher Lenny Webster. And they won with Davey Johnson dusting off his National League managerial skills and pulling off so many double switches that on Sunday, Cal Ripken found himself at shortstop for the first time this season.

The Orioles felt comfortable playing in a new stadium that looks and plays like Camden Yards—minus the warehouse. Webster did his best impersonation of '96 World Series hero Jim Leyritz on Sunday, launching a two-run home run with two outs in the 10th inning off closer Mark Wohlers. For Johnson, who managed for 10 seasons in the NL, Sunday's game allowed him to use 17 players, including four at multiple positions.

CHICAGO

Maybe it was the losing records of the Cubs and the White Sox. Or maybe it was Sox owner Jerry Reinsdorf's insistence that fans purchasing tickets to any of the three interleague contests at Comiskey Park buy a "four-pack" of tickets that included other games—a policy he later revoked. Whatever the reason, fans did not fill Comiskey Park on Monday for the first meaningful game between the teams since the 1906 World Series. The opening game drew 36,213, second largest at Comiskey Park in 1997, but still 8,000 below capacity and hardly a ringing endorsement for interleague play.

Thousands of Cubs fans traveled from the North Side to watch the Cubs win the first game of the three-game series 8-3. By the time Guillen came to bat with two outs in the bottom of the ninth, most of the remaining fans were on their feet rooting for him to strike out. "The only Sox fans left were my wife and three kids," Guillen said. "Everyone else was trying to beat the traffic."

And so I headed to Milwaukee to catch the Brewers and the Cardinals, with a host of events commemorating the 1982 World Series. By journey's end, I will have been to games celebrating more glorious baseball times in 1906, '82 and '86. Two questions: If interleague play is supposed to bring baseball into the present, doesn't the game have something to market besides its past? And if it does not, how long before the fans, like the players, view interleague play as just another game?

—by Pete Williams

Eric Davis' remarkable comeback

On the final weekend of the regular season, outfielder Eric Davis and his Orioles teammates prepared for the playoffs in most diverse ways. At around 2:30 p.m. on Sept. 26, the first players trickled into the cramped visitors clubhouse at Milwaukee's County Stadium to get ready for the last series against the Brewers. Most of the players sat at their lockers, reading or quietly chatting. About five miles away, inside a private room of a medical clinic, Davis reclined in a large chair, his feet propped up. A videocassette of the movie *Hoop Dreams* played on a small TV set in front of him. A blue-and-white IV bottle, suspended from a metal stand over his shoulder, dispensed a clear, powerful elixir through a white tube into his muscular right forearm.

Davis, 35, who underwent successful colon cancer surgery in June, was at the Oncology Center of Wisconsin, in the western Milwaukee suburb of Wauwatosa, to receive the ninth of 18 chemotherapy treatments that, hopefully, will restore him to full health. "You do what you gotta do," he said softly. "It's a little boring. Just knowing you have to let it drip for two hours."

The sessions were literally a shot in the arm for Davis and his team. When, the next week, Seattle started left-hander Randy Johnson in Game 1 of the Division Series, Davis knocked in two crucial runs against the Mariners ace in the fifth inning. In the ALCS against Cleveland, his ninth-inning homer in Game 5 helped keep Baltimore alive. "It's a miracle as far as I'm concerned," then Orioles manager Davey Johnson said shortly after Davis' return. "He has been an inspiration to all of us. I didn't expect him back in uniform at all this season."

Yet this story isn't about circus catches in right field or being penciled into the lineup in the postseason. It is about two girls named Erica, 11, and Sacha, 7, back home in Woodland Hills, Calif. "I'm putting myself in a situation to see my kids, and then to see their kids," Davis said. "To sacrifice 18 weeks for the privilege of having 40 more years with my kids—this isn't tough at all."

There were usually about half a dozen people in the Oncology Center's waiting room. They cut across all lines of gender and race, but they share a sobering common denominator. "I'm no different than those other people," said Davis. "I just happen to be a professional athlete. I'm part of a [population] that cancer has touched."

Adenocarcinoma, or colon cancer, is one of the most common cancers in America. "Generally, it affects an older age group than Eric," said Dr. Keith Lillemoe, Davis' surgeon, a professor of surgery at the Johns Hopkins Medical Institutions in Baltimore. Davis' outlook is good; Lillemoe won't give odds but says, "It is a very favorable prognosis. Eric has done everything within his power to get back."

Davis was running several minutes late when he arrived shortly after noon wearing jeans, athletic shoes and a multicolored sweater. He was immediately ushered back to a room marked "Private Therapy." He was hooked to the IV and the draining process began. "This makes me real tired," he said. "It won't hit me right away. It won't hit me until around six o'clock. So I just go back to the hotel, watch a little TV, then go to bed." Although Davis didn't go to the ballpark on the day of this therapy, he would waste no time getting back into the groove the following evening, when he slugged his first home run since his surgery and went 4-for-5 to help the Orioles beat the Brewers 5-4.

Davis had felt searing pain at the bottom of his rib cage starting in May. At first, no one could diagnose its origin. That's when Eric's wife, Sherrie, was most scared. "They wanted to do exploratory surgery," she says. "At one point, they said it might be an ulcer. Then they said it could be an abscess. But cancer was the furthest thing from my mind."

It wasn't completely out of the question, though. Davis' father had prostate cancer last year, and an uncle had colon cancer when he was in his 40s. Early in June, Davis got a second opinion from Lillemoe, who discovered a mass in the right side of Davis' transverse colon, or large intestine. Davis was scheduled for surgery on June 13, a Friday, the day the Orioles played their first interleague game. Doctors removed a tumor the size of a baseball from Davis' midsection. A subsequent biopsy revealed it was malignant. Doctors also removed three feet—about one-third—of Davis' large intestine.

Eric's mother, Shirley Davis-Frazier, came east to be with her son, but Sherrie stayed home with the children in California. "Erica was having her fifth-grade graduation that week," Davis said with a big smile. "She told her mom she would never speak to her again if she missed it." Once the biopsy revealed the malignancy, however, Sherrie caught a red-eye out of L.A. and showed up at Eric's bedside at 6:30 the next morning.

Following surgery, Davis decided to get chemotherapy. He receives a combination of two drugs. The primary drug is known as 5-FU. "It's a very common drug used to selectively kill cancer cells," Lillemoe says. Davis began the treatments on July 16 at the UCLA Medical Center in Los Angeles, and following the postseason, Davis returned to L.A. for his third and final round of chemo, which was scheduled to end around Dec. 10.

Colon cancer revisited the Orioles family in August. Popular Boog Powell, the AL MVP with Baltimore in 1970, had almost identical surgery on Aug. 25. Powell admits he drew strength from Davis, who visited him in the hospital five days after his surgery. "I just wanted him to know he wasn't alone," Davis said. "I saw his face light up when I walked into his room."

The day after his visit with Powell, however, the light went out of Davis' face. He received news from L.A. that his older brother, Jimmy, had died of a heart attack. He was one year older, and they had talked almost daily on the phone.

Davis made a remarkable comeback in September.

By H. Darr Beiser, USA TODAY

"The way I looked at it, I had 35 wonderful years with him," Davis said. "I dwell on what I had, not what I lost."

Davis has vowed to help the fight against his disease. He held the Eric Davis Golf and Gala to benefit cancer research at Lakewood Country Club in Los Angeles. Davis is also appreciative of the Orioles, who showed good faith by picking up their 1998 option on Davis' $2.2 million contract. Davis, who once retired from baseball, in 1994, because of injuries, says his battle with cancer has taught him that "you shouldn't take anything for granted . . . live one day at a time because the next day isn't promised."

—*by Bill Koenig*

NL / AL BEAT

19

Two strikes on Cuba: Defections, economics

Schoolchildren wearing red bandannas, military personnel in sharply creased brown uniforms and aspiring doctors in white smocks crowded the balconies overlooking a courtyard in Havana. Everyone wanted a glimpse, for below stood 30 of Cuba's finest athletes, including boxer Felix Savon and track star Ana Fidelia Quirot.

Early in 1997 we walked in, uninvited, to a celebration that few foreigners witness. La Premiacion del Atleta, the awards presentation to the island's best athletes, is the annual reaffirmation of how important sport, especially baseball, is to Cuba. Once this country and its leader, one-time pitcher Fidel Castro, were known for exporting revolution. Today, the nation, on its own since the Soviet Union imploded in 1991, survives by selling tourism, sugar and baseball talent. In 1997, more than 50 Cuban baseball stars, mostly veterans, played outside the country, with 80% of their salaries returning to Cuba to fuel its sports program.

Few are satisfied with the new arrangement. Nightly on Radio Rebelde, which first aired almost 40 years ago under the direction of Che Guevara, callers clog the lines to the sports-talk show. Their major complaint? What happened to their baseball heroes. "It was never explained to us," said one caller. "We woke up one day and they were gone."

Since the revolution's success in 1959, baseball in Cuba has enjoyed a rarefied status. In part, this is because Castro played the game while growing up. But the game was established here long before Castro threw a pitch. "In Cuba, baseball is more than a sport. It is part of the culture. It is part of our national pride," said Sigfredo Barros of *Granma*, the nation's official newspaper. Cuba's 16-team winter league, the National Series, was considered one of the top showcases of amateur talent in the world, but this year it saw as many lousy plays as good ones. Baseball, like Cuban society, is in transition.

American dollars are the currency of choice on the street. After a burgeoning black market threatened to stifle the state-run economy, Castro declared dollars legal tender. The result was a fall through the looking glass. In Cuba today, a waiter makes more than a dentist, and a taxi driver is rich compared with a university professor. Tourism recently surpassed sugar as the country's top industry. For years Cuba and Castro could keep the world at an arm's length. Now everybody except Americans, who are forbidden to travel here because of the U.S. embargo, crowd the island's white-sand beaches and sidewalk cafes. In 1992, its capital was a ghost town. On this visit, though, construction cranes rode the Havana skyline. The Castro government would like the tourists to come, spend their money, revive the economy—and have the natives somehow remain unaffected. Of course, things rarely work that way.

Before the courtyard ceremony began, I approached Alberto Juantorena, now Cuba's top sports official, who stunned the world at the 1976 Olympics by winning two gold medals in track. He began telling me how in a few years, perhaps at the next Summer Games in Sydney, he believed his efforts could shock the world again.

Eight of Cuba's top baseball prospects had defected in the last 18 months. While the money was seductive, many Cubans left because they wanted a chance to play—now. Rey Ordonez, the New York Mets' shortstop, defected in large part because a veteran, German Mesa, was a fixture at that position on the Cuban national team. In sending older players to Japan and elsewhere, Cuba has told its remaining top prospects that there will be room for them at home. Juantorena claimed such "adjustments" would also assure that his country's national team could compete against a major league American "Dream Team."

Those who wear the Cuban uniform today don't share Juantorena's bravado. But in talking with them in the quiet moments, before they take the field or accept another award, one cannot overlook a quiet confidence. Osmani Romero, the best young pitcher in Cuba, says his country's teams are "always of good quality" because "there's a discipline. You learn it early on."

Cuba won gold medals in Barcelona (1992) and Atlanta ('96). For almost a decade, the squad has been led by the most complete ballplayer ever in Cuba: third baseman Omar Linares. At La Premiacion del Atleta, the applause grows as he steps forward. Linares says he won't leave his wife or the system that fostered him. That would be a "betrayal," he says. Such loyalty backs up Juantorena's brash talk. Linares, who set a Cuban batting record (.409) in 1985, resembles Brooks Robinson in the field and Albert Belle at the plate. In Atlanta, he led the Cuban regulars with a .476 average and hit eight home runs. When I asked about the possibility of facing major leaguers at the Olympics, he nodded in anticipation. "It would be a series worth waiting for," he says. "We would get a chance to show how good a team we are."

The risk for Cuban baseball is that in focusing so much on the Olympics and on keeping its homegrown talent, will it ultimately lose the fans? After the awards ceremony, we head into a downtown Havana park where Cubans meet daily to discuss baseball. For a population that remains isolated from the rest of the world, with no newspaper, television or radio reports about the major leagues, somehow these fans are as passionate as any in the world. Welcome to the Esquina Caliente (Hot Corner).

Debates about who's the best in Havana or Houston swirl in small groups. The old men, shaky on skinny legs, get off the marble benches to say that Linares will never leave or that Romero is the best young pitcher in Cuba. Word quickly spreads that two Americans are suddenly in their midst. We are greeted with curiosity, never hostility. Nobody speaks of politics, the U.S. trade embargo, the Helms-Burton Act. We are quizzed only about baseball, everything from Roger Clemens' signing with Toronto

By Tim Wendel, Baseball Weekly

Linares has said he will never abandon Cuba.

to what Belle and Frank Thomas could do together on Chicago's South Side. Soon the discussion moves closer to home. What really concerns these diehard fans is their national pastime. To them, it is going downhill in a hurry.

"Baseball was once above politics," one fan says. "But now it has fallen into the great contradiction." By that he means that in a society now powered by dollars, baseball has become like all things here. It will succeed or fail by how well it competes against the rest of the world, rather than by how much it is cherished by its people. Many doubt that Castro can still help Cuban baseball.

Among those in the park is an older man, 69. He sells copies of *Trabajadores*, a Havana newspaper. Stigfredo Medina knows Castro as well as anybody because he used to play baseball against him when both were young men growing up at the eastern end of the island. Medina says of the ex-pitcher, "He had great control. He always had great control." Whether Castro still has great control could well determine the future not only of Cuba but of its national pastime.

—by Tim Wendel, with Milton Jamail

1997 Hall of Fame inductees

By Kathy Willens, AP/Wide World Photos

Phil Niekro's prayers were finally answered.

Phil Niekro

Phil Niekro, who rode the untamed knuckleball taught to him by his father to 318 major league victories, darted and danced into the Hall of Fame on his fifth try. "My mother's rosary beads were worn out, I'm sure," he said with a laugh after his election.

Niekro, 58, is now the general manager of the all-female Colorado Silver Bullets, after managing them from the team's inception in December 1993 until 1997.

Niekro was 318-274 with the Milwaukee and Atlanta Braves, the New York Yankees, the Cleveland Indians and the Toronto Blue Jays in a career that spanned 1964-87. He won 20 games three times and ranks eighth with 3,342 strikeouts in 5,403⅓ innings. He had a lifetime 3.35 ERA and led the NL with a 1.87 mark in '67. He and Cy Young share the major league record with 19 seasons of 200 or more innings. He also led the National League in losses four consecutive seasons (1977-80) and led the league in runs allowed three times—both major league records.

Niekro, a native of Blaine, Ohio, was the last pitcher to win and lose 20 games in the same season, when he went 21-20 in 1979. Phil and Joe Niekro hold the major league records for brothers with a combined 579 victories, 478 losses and 46 years of major league service. They met several times, the most memorable matchup occurring on Sept. 26, 1979, when Phil outdueled Joe 9-4 to win his 20th game of the season. Oddly, Joe was the National League's only other 20-game winner that year, as the Niekros joined Gaylord and Jim Perry as the only brothers to win 20 games in the same season.

Phil Niekro had one of his best seasons in 1982 when, at age 43, he went 17-4 and led the majors in winning percentage. However, after 19 seasons with the Braves, the team did not offer him a contract in 1984, and he signed a two-year deal with the Yankees, where he got his 300th victory on Oct. 6, 1985.

—by Bill Koenig

Tommy Lasorda

As a child, Tommy Lasorda imagined pitching for the New York Yankees. "I dreamed of playing with Dickey, DiMaggio, Gehrig," Lasorda said at his induction in Cooperstown on Aug. 3. "And then my mother would wake me up and say, 'It's time to go to school.' The Hall of Fame is eternity. I only hope somebody doesn't shake me and say, 'Wake up, it's time to go to school.'"

Lasorda, a Norristown, Pa., native who was a career minor leaguer as a left-handed pitcher, mostly in the Dodgers farm system, had a 1,599-1,439 record as the Dodgers manager, with seven NL West championships, four pennants and two World Series titles in his 20-year managerial career. He retired in the middle of the 1996 season and was elected by the Veterans Committee in his first year of eligibility. The 70-year-old Lasorda is the 14th manager elected to the Hall. He has worked as a vice president for the

Dodgers since leaving the dugout.

The gregarious Lasorda is often referred to as one of baseball's top ambassadors. For much of his tenure, Los Angeles was the top-drawing team in baseball, topping the three-million mark in home attendance for a record 11th time in his final season as manager. His devotion to the Dodgers organization is legendary, and he has been with them for 47 of his 51 years in pro baseball.

Nellie Fox

After two of the narrowest misses in Hall of Fame voting history, 12-time All-Star second baseman Nellie Fox finally made it in 1997. Fox, who died in 1975, began his 19-year career with the Philadelphia Athletics but made his reputation during his 14 seasons with the White Sox. He had received 295 votes in the 1985 Hall election, two votes shy of the required 75%. Then, in 1996, he got enough votes from the Veterans Committee, but Jim Bunning was named on one more ballot, and Fox was denied again because of the one-player-per-year rule of the committee.

Fox was the American League MVP in 1959, the year of the last White Sox pennant, and he hit .300 or better six times. A career .288 hitter and a three-time Gold Glove winner, Fox was extremely durable (798 consecutive games played, 12 straight years with more than 600 at-bats) and consistent (10 straight years hitting .285 or better). He lacked power but was a superb bunter and hit-and-run man, and his ability to put the bat on the ball was unparalleled in modern baseball. He struck out only 216 times in 9,232 at-bats, with a career *high* of 18, and led the AL in fewest strikeouts 11 years in a row, from 1952 to '62.

Joanne Fox accepted the honor for her late husband and thanked three Hall of Famers in the audience who were close to Nellie: White Sox double-play partner Luis Aparicio, who played alongside Fox for seven years; Ted Williams, whom Fox coached under in 1968-72 when Williams managed the Washington Senators and

Fox led the AL in putouts a record 10 times.

By AP/Wide World Photos

Texas Rangers; and Joe Morgan, who was a rookie with Houston when Fox was a player-coach and who has often cited Fox as being a key mentor. Morgan replaced Fox as the Astros' second baseman in Fox's last season, 1965.

Willie Wells

Known as "The Devil," Negro leagues shortstop Willie Wells could do it all: He hit for power and average, and was a great defensive player as well. In a quarter-century-long career with 11 teams, Wells, who was born in Austin, Texas, in 1905, batted .331 and three times led the Negro National League in home runs, in 1927, '29 and '30 for the St. Louis Stars. He also won the batting title in the latter year, with a .403 average.

Wells played in eight East-West All-Star Games between 1933 and '45, and when the *Pittsburgh Courier* named its all-time Negro leagues team in 1952, Wells was the second-team shortstop. In the ceremony at Cooperstown, Stella Wells accepted for her father, who died in 1989. Wells was the 14th Negro leagues player to be named to the Hall.

Philly was fanatical about Ashburn

Ashburn was a Philadelphia fixture for 47 years.

A record crowd of more than 25,000 was on hand when Richie Ashburn was inducted into the Hall of Fame in 1995. You only had to hear the roar from the gallery to sense the genuine affection he generated among the Philly faithful.

Ashburn arrived in Philadelphia from Tilden, Neb., in 1948 and stuck around for 47 years as a player and broadcaster. "He was as loyal a friend as a man can have," said Harry Kalas, his broadcast partner since 1971. Ashburn died of a heart attack on Sept. 9 in a New York City hotel room. He was 70.

Youngsters knew him only as a broadcaster, but to old-timers, he was the fleet center fielder who won National League batting titles in 1955 and '58. No National League player had more hits than Ashburn during the decade of the 1950s. He hit .308 lifetime with 2,574 hits in 2,189 games, all but 455 of them singles. Defensively, he was the greatest fly-chaser ever, with an unprecedented four 500-putout seasons and a record nine putout titles.

The consistent and durable "Whitey" was 21 when he came up to the Phillies in 1948. He hit .333 and was named *The Sporting News* Rookie of the Year. He missed just 22 games from 1949 to '58 and hit .300 or better nine times. The play with which Ashburn is most closely identified, however, was a throw at Ebbets Field on the final day of the 1950 season, with the Phillies leading the Dodgers by a game. With the score tied in the ninth inning, Brooklyn had men on first and second with nobody out. Ashburn fielded a hit by Duke Snider and threw out Cal Abrams at the plate. Dick Sisler's three-run homer in the 10th won it 4-1 for the Phils.

Ashburn was traded to the Cubs after the 1959 season and was taken by the Mets in the '62 expansion draft, hitting .306 for a 40-120 team in his final year. "I was voted the Most Valuable Player on the worst team in baseball history," he said. "I wasn't sure what to make of that." The following year, Ashburn began a broadcasting career full of his storytelling. Many dealt with the woeful '62 Mets; among them was Ashburn's favorite: about Mets shortstop Elio Chacon, who didn't understand English. Ashburn, wishing to avoid collisions with his new teammate, acquainted himself with the phrase *"Yo lo tengo"*—Spanish for "I got it."

Sure enough, the next day a batter hit a fly ball to short left-center. "I'm yelling, '*Yo lo tengo! Yo lo tengo!*'" Ashburn said. "And Chacon backs off, just like he's supposed to. But next thing I know, here comes our left fielder, Frank Thomas, who doesn't speak any Spanish, and he bowls me over."

Ashburn concluded his Hall of Fame induction speech with another Mets story: "After the final game of the 1962 Mets season—our 120th loss—Casey Stengel said, 'This was a complete team effort. No one or two people could have done this.' That's how I feel about my induction today. No one or two people could have this. You've made this the greatest day of my life."

—by Bill Koenig

AL pitching stifles NL bats

The 68th edition of major league baseball's All-Star Game, held at Cleveland's Jacobs Field, prominently featured three of the recurring themes of the 1997 season: the resurgence of pitching, the hot hitting of catcher Sandy Alomar and the intrigue of interleague play. The Mariners' Randy Johnson led a parade of eight American League pitchers who held National League batters to just three hits, and with the win, the AL cut the NL's lead in the series to 40-27-1.

Sandy Alomar, who brought a 30-game hitting streak into the All-Star Game, became the first home-team player to hit a home run since Hank Aaron did so in Atlanta in 1972. Alomar's two-run shot, off San Francisco's Shawn Estes in the seventh inning, gave the AL a 3-1 victory and earned Alomar the Most Valuable Player award before a crowd of 44,916.

An award for Least Visible Player could have been given to White Sox left fielder Albert Belle, who, in his visit to his old town, passed on Monday's home run derby, then before the game didn't take batting practice, throw during warm-ups or even show up for the AL team photo. Belle asked AL manager Joe Torre not to play him unless necessary, and Torre didn't use him, making Belle the only position player on either roster not to appear in the game.

ERAs were down through the first half of '97, and nine pitchers came into the break with 10 or more victories. Johnson retired six of the seven batters he faced, allowing only a walk to the left-handed Larry Walker, who in June sat out rather than face Johnson during the first round of interleague play.

Edgar Martinez, AL designated hitter and one of five Mariners in the game, led off the second inning with a home run off NL starter Greg Maddux of Atlanta. Braves catcher Javier Lopez homered in the seventh to tie the score.

Walker and Johnson provided the game's most interesting subplot. When Walker, with a .398 batting average at the All-Star break, stepped to the plate in the second inning, Johnson uncorked a pitch that soared over Walker's head to the backstop. Johnson said the pitch was an accident, caused by humidity making the ball slippery.

"I guess it was kind of apropos that it slipped while Larry Walker was up," joked Johnson, who teamed with Walker in the Montreal farm system. After the wild pitch, Walker stepped across the plate, turned his helmet backward (for use of the protective flap) and batted right-handed for one pitch, a ball. He then returned to the left side and walked on the fifth pitch.

"Randy and I are good friends," Walker said. "It was a fun at-bat. I'm glad it worked out."

—by Pete Williams

All-Star Game

American 3, National 1

National	0	0	0	0	0	0	1	0	0	- 1
American	0	1	0	0	0	0	2	0	x	- 3

National	AB	R	H	BI	BB	SO	AVG
Biggio 2b	3	0	0	0	1	0	.000
Womack 2b	1	0	0	0	0	0	.000
Gwynn dh	3	0	0	0	0	1	.000
a-Galarraga ph-dh	1	0	0	0	0	1	.000
Bonds lf	1	0	0	0	1	0	.000
Finley lf	1	0	0	0	0	1	.000
Piazza c	1	0	0	0	1	0	.000
Lopez c	1	1	1	1	0	0	1.000
Johnson c	1	0	0	0	0	1	.000
Bagwell 1b	3	0	0	0	0	1	.000
Grace 1b	1	0	0	0	0	0	.000
Walker rf	1	0	0	0	1	0	.000
Alou rf	2	0	1	0	0	0	.500
Caminiti 3b	2	0	0	0	0	1	.000
CJones 3b	1	0	0	0	0	1	.000
Lankford cf	2	0	0	0	1	0	.000
Blauser ss	2	0	1	0	0	0	.500
Clayton ss	1	0	0	0	0	2	.000
Totals	29	1	3	1	4	7	7

a-struck out for Gwynn in the 8th. **BATTING— HR:** Lopez (7th inning off Rosado). **RBI:** Lopez. **LOB:** 5. **BASERUNNING—SB:** Bonds **FIELDING—PB:** Lopez.

American	AB	R	H	BI	BB	SO	AVG
Anderson lf-rf	4	0	2	0	0	1	.500
ARodriguez ss	3	0	1	0	0	2	.333
Garciaparra ss	1	0	0	0	0	1	.000
Griffey cf	4	0	0	0	0	3	.000
TMartinez 1b	2	0	0	0	0	1	.000
McGwire 1b	2	0	0	0	2	1	.000
EMartinez dh	2	1	2	1	0	0	1.000
a-Thome ph-dh	1	0	0	0	0	0	.000
O'Neill rf	2	0	0	0	1	0	.000
Williams lf	0	1	0	0	1	0	—
Ripken 3b	2	0	1	0	0	0	.500
Cora pr-2b	1	0	0	0	0	1	.000
Knoblauch 2b	0	0	0	0	0	0	—
IRodriguez c	2	0	0	0	0	0	.000
SAlomar c	1	1	1	2	0	0	1.000
RAlomar 2b	2	0	0	0	0	1	.000
Cirillo 3b	1	0	0	0	1	0	.000
Totals	30	3	7	3	1	8	10

a-grounded to shortstop for EMartinez in the 7th. **BATTING—2B:** Anderson. **HR:** EMartinez (2nd inning off Maddux); SAlomar (7th inning off Estes). **RBI:** EMartinez, SAlomar 2. **LOB:** 4. **BASERUNNING—CS:** EMartinez.

National	IP	H	R	ER	BB	SO	BF	ERA
Maddux	2	2	1	1	0	0	8	4.50
Schilling	2	2	0	0	0	3	7	0.00
Brown	1	1	0	0	0	0	4	0.00
PMartinez	1	0	0	0	0	2	3	0.00
Estes (0-1)	1	1	2	2	1	1	5	18.00
BJones	1	1	0	0	0	2	4	0.00

American	IP	H	R	ER	BB	SO	BF	ERA
Johnson	2	0	0	0	1	2	7	0.00
Clemens	1	1	0	0	0	4	4	0.00
Cone	1	0	0	0	2	0	4	0.00
Thompson	1	0	0	0	0	1	3	0.00
Hentgen	1	0	0	0	0	0	3	0.00
Rosado (1-0)	1	2	1	1	1	1	6	9.00
Myers	1	0	0	0	0	2	3	0.00
Rivera (S)	1	0	0	0	0	1	3	0.00

WP: Estes Schilling . . **GAME DATA—T:** 2:36. **Att:** 44,916.

HOW THEY SCORED

American 2nd: EMartinez homered to left. O'Neill grounded out to pitcher. Ripken grounded out to second. IRodriguez grounded out to pitcher. **American 1, National 0.**

National 7th: Rosado relieved Hentgen. Lopez homered to left. Bagwell lined out to shortstop. Alou singled to right. CJones flied out to right. Lankford walked, Alou to second. Clayton struck out swinging. **National 1, American 1.**

American 7th: Estes relieved PMartinez. Grace at first. Thome hit for EMartinez. Thome grounded out to shortstop. Williams walked. Cora flied out to deep left center. Williams to second on Estes wild pitch. SAlomar homered to left center, Williams scored. Cirillo struck out swinging. **American 3, National 1.**

1997 award winners

AL Most Valuable Player: Ken Griffey

Seattle center fielder Ken Griffey finally won the honor long predicted for him when he was voted the American League's MVP by the Baseball Writers Association of America. Yankees first baseman Tino Martinez finished second. Griffey had an overwhelming season and was the ninth unanimous selection in league history. He led the AL in home runs (56), RBI (147), runs scored (125), total bases (393), extra-base hits (93) and slugging average (.646). Griffey hit .304 and also won his eighth straight Gold Glove. His home run total was the league's highest since Roger Maris' record 61 in 1961, and Griffey set major league marks with 13 homers in April and 24 through May.

Clemens' Canadian debut was a smash.

first AL pitcher since Hal Newhouser in 1945 to win the pitchers Triple Crown, leading in wins (21), ERA (2.05) and strikeouts (292). He was tied for the league lead in innings pitched (264), complete games (nine) and shutouts (three). In winning his fourth Cy Young Award, Clemens set an AL record and tied Steve Carlton's and Greg Maddux's major league mark. Seattle's Randy Johnson finished second in the voting.

NL Most Valuable Player: Larry Walker

The Rockies' Larry Walker beat the long-standing bias against mile-high offensive players to decisively win the National League MVP Award over Dodgers catcher Mike Piazza, who was the runner-up for the second straight year. Right fielder Walker, the first Canadian to win an MVP, batted .346 away from Colorado and slammed 29 homers, nine more than at home. Overall, he had an extraordinary season, leading the NL in home runs and on-base average (.452) and finishing second in batting (.366) and third in RBI (130). He led the majors in slugging average (.720), extra-base hits (99) and total bases (409). Walker wasn't just a slugger, though. He won a Gold Glove and also had 33 steals.

AL Cy Young Award: Roger Clemens

The first year in Toronto for longtime Red Sox ace Roger Clemens was far from the "twilight" that Boston GM Dan Duquette had predicted for him. Clemens became the

NL Cy Young Award: Pedro Martinez

The Expos' Pedro Martinez won't be playing for Montreal in 1998, but the team was delighted with his Cy Young Award–winning performance in 1997. Martinez led the majors in ERA with a 1.90 and finished second in strikeouts with 305. He broke Atlanta's stranglehold on the award by easily beating Braves Greg Maddux and Denny Neagle, who finished second and third, respectively. Martinez won only 17 games due to poor run support, but had 13 complete games to lead the majors. Opponents hit only .184 against him, a major league low.

Martinez's Montreal farewell was memorable.

AL Manager of the Year: Davey Johnson

Former Orioles manager Davey Johnson had a bitter-sweet Nov. 5. He resigned from his job after a long-running feud with Baltimore owner Peter Angelos, and then was named AL Manager of the Year a few hours later. Johnson's team led the AL East from Opening Day to the finish and won a league-high 98 games, but they lost a hard-fought ALCS to the Indians in six games. Johnson, who has a career winning percentage of .575, best among active managers, made the playoffs in both of his seasons with the Orioles and has never finished lower than second in 10 full seasons as a skipper.

NL Manager of the Year: Dusty Baker

The Giants were one of the season's big surprises, going from last to first, and San Francisco's Dusty Baker was rewarded for it by being named NL Manager of the Year for the second time. This occasion was more satisfying, though, because the Giants won the NL West, with a 90-72 record. His first award came in 1993, when San Francisco finished second to Atlanta in the NL West, despite winning 103 games. In 1997, the sum was greater than the parts, as Baker's team won although it was ninth in ERA and 10th in batting average.

AL Jackie Robinson Award: Nomar Garciaparra

Boston's Nomar Garciaparra beat out an accomplished veteran, John Valentin, to win the Red Sox shortstop job, and he went on to have one of the greatest rookie seasons ever. He was unanimously selected for the AL Jackie Robinson Award after setting major league records for homers by a rookie shortstop (30) and RBI by a leadoff hitter (98). He also established a league rookie mark with a 30-game hitting streak and led the AL with 209 hits and 11 triples.

NL Jackie Robinson Award: Scott Rolen

Scott Rolen of the Phillies was a unanimous choice for the National League's Jackie Robinson Award. The Philadelphia third baseman, who was only eligible because he had his season ended by a broken wrist in 1996 when he was at the maximum of 130 at-bats, led the league's rookies in almost all offensive departments, including batting average (.283), home runs (21) and RBI (92). He led his team in the latter two departments.

1997 Gold Glove winners

AMERICAN LEAGUE

P	Mike Mussina	Baltimore
C	Ivan Rodriguez	Texas
1B	Rafael Palmeiro	Baltimore
2B	C. Knoblauch	Minnesota
SS	Omar Vizquel	Cleveland
3B	Matt Williams	Cleveland
OF	Jim Edmonds	Anaheim
OF	Bernie Williams	New York
OF	Ken Griffey Jr.	Seattle

NATIONAL LEAGUE

P	Greg Maddux	Atlanta
C	C. Johnson	Florida
1B	J.T. Snow	SF
2B	Craig Biggio	Houston
SS	Rey Ordonez	New York
3B	Ken Caminiti	San Diego
OF	Barry Bonds	SF
OF	Raul Mondesi	LA
OF	Larry Walker	Colorado

1997 Silver Slugger winners

AMERICAN LEAGUE

C	Ivan Rodriguez	Texas
1B	Tino Martinez	New York
2B	C. Knoblauch	Minnesota
SS	N. Garciaparra	Boston
3B	Matt Williams	Cleveland
OF	Ken Griffey Jr.	Seattle
OF	David Justice	Indians
OF	Juan Gonzalez	Texas
DH	Edgar Martinez	Seattle

NATIONAL LEAGUE

P	John Smoltz	Atlanta
C	Mike Piazza	LA
1B	Jeff Bagwell	Houston
2B	Craig Biggio	Houston
SS	Jeff Blauser	Atlanta
3B	Vinny Castilla	Colorado
OF	Larry Walker	Colorado
OF	Barry Bonds	SF
OF	Tony Gwynn	San Diego

AL East: The Orioles led wire to wire

Baltimore learned last year that it was no fun chasing the Yankees. Their solution: Chase no one. The Orioles won their first three games and became only the third team in American League history to be in first place every day of the season, finishing with the best record in the AL, 98-64.

Baltimore reversed the roles of 1996, when New York won the division and the Orioles got the wild card. In 1997, Baltimore won eight of the 12 meetings between the teams, including the first seven. The Orioles held a 9½-game advantage as late as Sept. 6, after winning three in a row at Yankee Stadium. Baltimore clinched a playoff berth on Sept. 15, the first team in the majors to do so.

STANDINGS AT ALL-STAR BREAK				
	W	L	Pct.	GB
Baltimore	55	30	.647	—
New York	48	37	.565	7
Detroit	41	44	.482	14
Toronto	40	43	.482	14
Boston	38	48	.442	17½

Pitching was the foundation of Baltimore's season. Jimmy Key, pirated away from the Yankees on the free-agent market, won his first eight decisions. He combined with Scott Erickson and Mike Mussina to go 28-4 with a 3.19 ERA through June 15. Randy Myers converted 45 of 46 save opportunities. The Orioles had a balanced offense led by Rafael Palmeiro's 38 home runs and 110 RBI, a .333 performance by Roberto Alomar and Eric Davis' heroic .304 season, during which he returned to the lineup while receiving chemotherapy for colon cancer.

The Yankees led the wild-card race virtually all season, allowing them to let the Hideki Irabu saga play itself out. Irabu, a fine pitcher in the Japanese leagues, was acquired after much negotiation with the San Diego Padres. But Irabu struggled after he joined the New York rotation and was left off the postseason roster. Starters David Cone and Andy Pettitte finished third and fourth in the AL in

ERA, and Mariano Rivera successfully replaced the departed John Wetteland with 43 saves. The offense took up the rest of the slack, led by Tino Martinez, who slugged a career-high 44 home runs and had 141 RBI.

The East was supposed to be a three-team battle. The Toronto Blue Jays signed Roger Clemens and made a multi-player deal with Pittsburgh to presumably become instant contenders. Clemens did his part, leading the AL in wins, ERA and strikeouts, but the offense was woeful. Toronto's .244 batting average was by far the lowest in the league, and manager Cito Gaston paid the price with his job during the season's final week.

The only three-team race the Blue Jays found themselves in was with Boston and Detroit for last place. Toronto did win that race, sinking to last place, two games behind the Red Sox and three back of the rapidly improving Tigers.

After losing 109 games in 1996 and having an AL-record-worst 6.38 ERA, the Tigers went 79-83 and reduced their ERA to 4.56. It was by far the best mark for a team that had lost as many as 109 games the previous season. "The guys I'm most proud of are the guys who were here last year," manager Buddy Bell said. "They really sucked it up."

The Boston Red Sox had little to smile about beyond the Jackie Robinson Award season turned in by rookie shortstop Nomar Garciaparra and another solid year from first baseman Mo Vaughn, as controversy and dissension swirled around general manager Dan Duquette. It was a classic Red Sox team: first in batting average, 12th in ERA.

FINAL STANDINGS				
	W	L	Pct.	GB
Baltimore	98	64	.605	—
New York	96	66	.593	2
Detroit	79	83	.488	19
Boston	78	84	.481	20
Toronto	76	86	.469	22

AL Central: Sox gave up; Tribe gave its all

White Sox owner Jerry Reinsdorf told Chicago fans their team wasn't going to catch the Indians anyway, justifying his July 31 trade of pitchers Wilson Alvarez, Roberto Hernandez and Danny Darwin to the San Francisco Giants.

He should have spoken up sooner. Cleveland fans would just have soon been spared the summer of anguish and concern. It was not until September that Indians general manager John Hart pronounced himself pleased with how his rebuilt team was performing. Reinsdorf got the majority of the preseason attention for signing free-agent outfielder Albert Belle away from the Indians, but the reconstruction that Hart began during 1996 by dumping Carlos Baerga and Eddie Murray continued with an offseason deal for slugging third baseman Matt Williams and the late-March swap of Kenny Lofton to bring in outfielders Marquis Grissom and David Justice from Atlanta.

The 1997 Indians set a franchise home run record with 220. When Chicago lost third baseman Robin Ventura to injury for most of the season, the Central should have been Cleveland's. Justice, catcher Sandy Alomar and first baseman Jim Thome had consistent offensive seasons, but Grissom and Williams struggled early. Closer Jose Mesa had legal problems and wasn't effective until the second half. The starting pitching was decimated by injuries.

STANDINGS AT ALL-STAR BREAK

	W	L	Pct.	GB
Cleveland	44	36	.550	—
Chicago	43	42	.506	3½
Milwaukee	39	44	.470	6½
Kansas City	36	46	.439	9
Minnesota	37	48	.435	9½

Hart's made-over team, with more than half the faces changed between the 1996 and '97 playoff rosters, needed time to jell. Eventually, it worked, but "for the first half of the season," said shortstop Omar Vizquel, "we weren't even sure how to joke with each other." Cleveland took over first place for good on May 18 but never led by more than 5½ games until mid-September,

and as late as Sept. 2, they were only 2½ in front of the Brewers.

Though the White Sox took second place despite an 80-81 record, Milwaukee was the team that wouldn't go away for most of the second half, despite losing pitcher Ben McDonald and offensive forces John Jaha and Marc Newfield to injuries. The Brewers went 10-16 in September to fall out of contention.

The pressure was on the White Sox from the beginning. The $55 million doled out for Belle and the $20 million to pitcher Jaime Navarro ensured that. Navarro went 9-14 and had a 5.79 ERA. Belle had his first sub-.300 season since 1993, and his production fell off by 18 home runs and 32 RBI from '96. But the Sox players thought they had a chance, especially when Ventura returned from his broken ankle. Then came the trade with San Francisco. "Guys were sitting around on couches, looking like their dogs had just been run over," said Ventura. It was small consolation that Frank Thomas (.347) won the first White Sox batting title since Luke Appling's in 1943.

Hopes were dashed earlier in Kansas City, where the Royals spent money on veterans but were fading fast after losing three straight before the All-Star break. That was the end of manager Bob Boone's tenure, with Tony Muser taking over, but the club's record was worse after the change.

Kansas City's struggles were all that spared the Minnesota Twins from finishing last, but only by a half-game. Despite the 20-win season of Brad Radke, the Twins had their fifth consecutive losing season, hit the fewest home runs in the league, struck out a team-record 1,121 times and faced the threat of leaving the Twin Cities over a stadium issue.

FINAL STANDINGS

	W	L	Pct.	GB
Cleveland	86	75	.534	—
Chicago	80	81	.497	6
Milwaukee	78	83	.484	8
Minnesota	68	94	.420	18½
Kansas City	67	94	.416	19

AL West: Seattle had too many weapons

In their first 20 seasons, the Mariners spent a total of 106 days in first place. On Aug. 25, 1997, they spent their 107th day of the season atop the American League West. It was the franchise's best season ever, with a club-record 90 victories and a second division title in three seasons.

As they did in their first championship season two years ago, the Mariners had to hold off the Angels, but this time, the Mariners went into the season expecting to battle the Texas Rangers for the division crown. Anaheim, which was expected to be far less of a factor in the race than the defending champion Rangers, was tied for first place with Seattle as late as Aug. 19, while Texas had long since faded and had begun looking to the future. Texas' starting pitchers' ERA was the third worst in the league, and last year's potent offense was only seventh in runs. "It was a tough season," Rangers manager Johnny Oates said. "We just ran out of firepower."

STANDINGS AT ALL-STAR BREAK

	W	L	Pct.	GB
Seattle	49	39	.563	—
Anaheim	44	42	.512	4
Texas	43	42	.506	4½
Oakland	37	52	.416	12½

The Mariners certainly had the firepower. They set a major league record with 264 home runs, led by Ken Griffey's 56; topped the majors in runs with 925; and had a .485 slugging percentage, the highest in the majors since the 1930 Yankees. What kept the AL West a race was the Seattle bullpen. While left-handers Randy Johnson, Jamie Moyer and Jeff Fassero combined to produce 53 victories, the relievers' incompetence led to a pair of controversial trades. Desperate for a closer, Seattle general manager Woody Woodward sent sensational young left fielder Jose Cruz to the Toronto Blue Jays for relievers Mike Timlin and Paul Spoljaric, and dealt former No. 1 draft pick Jason Varitek to get Boston's Heathcliff Slocumb, who became the closer.

Seattle led the West by a half-game on July 31, when the deals were made. The Mariners and the Angels stayed within 1½ games of each other until Aug. 21, but during that period, the Angels' fortunes took a significant downturn. On Aug. 10, with Anaheim in first place by a half-game, GM Bill Bavasi held a news conference to explain Tony Phillips' absence from the starting lineup that night. Phillips had been arrested in a nearby motel for alleged possession of cocaine.

The Angels lost that night and went into a 3-9 slide. Phillips rejoined the team after a few days, but more went wrong. The Angels lost ace Chuck Finley on Aug. 19. Going for his club-record 11th straight win against the Yankees, Finley was hurt when he slipped and fell on his left hand. That was too much for a rotation that had already lost left-hander Mark Langston. Seattle began September with an 11-6 run to go six games up, and the only drama left was to see how many home runs Griffey would hit.

Fans in Oakland didn't even get a chance at similar drama. As the Athletics stumbled to a 65-97 record, Mark McGwire was traded to St. Louis. McGwire finished with 58 home runs between his two teams, 34 before the trade. "What we tried to do in the month of September, or since the trade of Mark McGwire, is expose our young players to the fans," said Sandy Alderson, who completed the dismantling of the once-powerful club before being replaced as GM.

FINAL STANDINGS

	W	L	Pct.	GB
Seattle	90	72	.556	—
Anaheim	84	78	.519	6
Texas	77	85	.475	13
Oakland	65	97	.401	25

NL East: The playoffs got Atlanta again

The Braves made a sixth consecutive postseason appearance in 1997, having won their division in each of those seasons. They won 101 games, the second-best total in franchise history, and beat the second-best regular-season NL team, the Marlins, by nine games. But the Braves, who were reminded in August just how tough the Marlins could be, found out for sure when Florida knocked them off in the NLCS and went on to win the World Series.

Florida won five of the eight meetings with Atlanta between July 31 and Aug. 11, not enough to alter the shape of the East race but enough to discomfort Atlanta. Marlins owner Wayne Huizenga had shelled out nearly $90 million in free-agent contracts in the offseason in an attempt to catch the Braves. But Atlanta still had the best starting pitching in baseball, and general manager John Schuerholz made the bold move of getting center fielder and leadoff hitter Kenny Lofton in a trade just before Opening Day.

STANDINGS AT ALL-STAR BREAK

	W	L	Pct.	GB
Atlanta	57	30	.655	—
Florida	50	36	.581	6½
New York	48	38	.558	8½
Montreal	47	39	.547	9½
Philadelphia	24	61	.282	32

By April 30, the Braves were already four games ahead of Florida and Lofton was hitting .395. The streaky Braves then kept Florida at bay. The Marlins crept to within 2½ in late June, but the Braves responded by winning 10 of 11. Atlanta polished off the race in the last month with a seven-of-eight streak that ended with the Sept. 22 clincher.

Typically, the Braves' pitching was at the center of their success. Denny Neagle won an NL-high 20 games, and Greg Maddux added 19. Tom Glavine and John Smoltz joined Neagle and Maddux among the league's top 10 in ERA. The offense held its own, finishing third in the league in runs and batting average.

The Marlins didn't get quite the offensive production they expected. Gary Sheffield was pitched around for much of the season, but Moises Alou, one of the free agents, picked up much of the slack with 115 RBI. Starters Alex Fernandez and Kevin Brown combined for 33 victories, and Brown had a 2.69 ERA and threw a no-hitter.

The third-place Mets were the biggest surprise, hanging in the wild-card race deep into September by overcoming key injuries to pitchers. The Mets led the majors with 47 come-from-behind victories and won 88 games. John Olerud had 102 RBI, and Todd Hundley hit 30 homers despite being sidelined with elbow problems.

The rest of the division was a couple of teams trying to remain respectable around one dominant pitcher. Cy Young winner Pedro Martinez was dominant in Montreal, leading the league in ERA, but manager Felipe Alou indeed had run out of miracles. Alou had usually found ways to remain in contention, but this year's group faded after the All-Star break. "The reality is we're last in revenues, last in attendance and last in local television revenues," club president Claude Brochu said.

Philadelphia's star pitcher was Curt Schilling, who with Martinez topped the 300-strikeout plateau. But Phillies fans were feeling a bit more optimistic than their Montreal counterparts by season's end. Even though the Phillies tied the Chicago Cubs for the NL's worst record, at 68-94, Philadelphia's 44-33 mark after the All-Star break was a surprising turnaround for a team that had been threatening the 20th-century record of 120 losses in a season. Another bright spot was third baseman Scott Rolen, who won the Jackie Robinson Award as the league's top rookie.

FINAL STANDINGS

	W	L	Pct.	GB
Atlanta	101	61	.623	—
Florida	92	70	.568	9
New York	88	74	.543	13
Montreal	78	84	.481	23
Philadelphia	68	94	.420	33

NL Central: Astros edged upstart Pirates

The way things have gone for the Astros the last few seasons, it probably was just as well that their final series of the season didn't turn out to decide the National League Central title. The second-place Pirates visited the Astrodome for three games on the final weekend of the season, but on the previous night, Houston clinched its first division championship since winning the NL West in 1986. In '95 and '96 the Astros had finished second in the Central because they couldn't beat the team that eventually won the division. Houston was only 6-6 this year against surprising Pittsburgh, but that was good enough to win in baseball's weakest division.

The Astros won with only 84 victories, and their .519 winning percentage was the second lowest ever for a playoff qualifier. Predictably, Houston was swept in the first round of the playoffs by Atlanta. As usual, the Houston offense centered around first baseman Jeff Bagwell, with 43 home runs and 135 RBI, and leadoff man Craig Biggio, with 22 homers and 47 steals. "It was a lot of fun this season, but I wish it had ended differently," said ace Darryl Kile, who compiled a 19-7 record and a 2.57 ERA. The Astros' nine-game winning streak in late July gave them a five-game lead, a margin that got as high as 6½ games several times. However, the Pirates just wouldn't go away.

STANDINGS AT ALL-STAR BREAK

	W	L	Pct.	GB
Pittsburgh	43	43	.500	—
Houston	43	45	.489	1
St. Louis	41	45	.477	2
Cincinnati	38	48	.442	5
Chicago	37	50	.425	6½

"You've got to remember, everybody said we wouldn't do anything—nothing," said Pittsburgh second baseman Tony Womack, who led the league in stolen bases. "We were disappointed not to win, but we can't be disappointed with the season." The team was happy with its 79-83 finish; consider that the Pirates' entire roster made less money than Albert Belle

did. Management didn't deviate from its plan to let a core of young players develop into a team that could contend in any division within a couple of years, including outfielder Jose Guillen, Womack, closer Rich Loiselle and starters Francisco Cordoba, Esteban Loaiza and Jon Lieber.

St. Louis' veterans, who won this division in 1996, never made a serious run at the Astros. When Houston went on its July streak, the Cardinals were left in the dust and eventually finished behind Cincinnati. By the time St. Louis acquired Mark McGwire for the stretch drive, the Cardinals were too far behind to make a move. They had been irreparably damaged by season-long injuries to right fielder Brian Jordan and catcher Tom Pagnozzi, plus sub-par years from left fielder Ron Gant and third baseman Gary Gaetti. McGwire's addition and another strong season from Ray Lankford were the highlights, plus the emergence of young right-hander Matt Morris.

Cincinnati was never much of a factor, even after Jack McKeon replaced Ray Knight as manager late in the season. Neither Barry Larkin nor Reggie Sanders stayed healthy, and the Reds went through 50 players trying to patch holes. The star for the Reds was new closer Jeff Shaw, who compiled 42 saves behind a starting staff that didn't have anyone win more than 11 times.

The annual "wait till next year" mantra at Wrigley Field began earlier than usual when the Cubs lost their first 14 games, an NL record for the beginning of a season. All that remained was watching the final season of Ryne Sandberg, who retired at the end of the year.

FINAL STANDINGS

	W	L	Pct.	GB
Houston	84	78	.519	—
Pittsburgh	79	83	.488	5
Cincinnati	76	86	.469	8
St. Louis	73	89	.451	11
Chicago	68	94	.420	16

NL West: Giants went from worst to first

The Giants had the National League's biggest turnaround from 1996 to '97, but it took a few extra twists and turns for manager Dusty Baker's team to grab its first playoff berth since 1989. The Giants improved 22 games from their 68-94 record the previous year and built as much as a six-game lead in the division, but they went to the next-to-last day of the season before eliminating the second-place Dodgers. After leading the division for 105 days, from May 11 to Aug. 23, it began to look like San Francisco's last-to-first dream might come unraveled despite the deal on July 31 in which general manager Brian Sabean brought in pitchers Wilson Alvarez, Roberto Hernandez and Danny Darwin from the Chicago White Sox.

But after four consecutive losses in Florida and Atlanta, the Giants came home on Sept. 17 for two games with the Dodgers, who led the division by two games. The Giants won both to pull into a tie for the division lead and then won three of four games at San Diego, while the Dodgers continued a mid-September tailspin that saw them lose 11 of 15 games. Despite excellent pitching, MVP candidate Mike Piazza and four 30-homer men, Los Angeles fell short. "This is the most talented team I've ever been on," said Los Angeles first baseman Eric Karros. "It's a joke to look at this team and think it isn't going to the postseason. It shows you that statistics don't mean everything."

found plenty of production from the middle of the order. Barry Bonds' usual 40-homer season was supplemented by 29 from second baseman Jeff Kent, one of the players acquired from Cleveland in the Williams deal, and 28 from first baseman J.T. Snow.

Injuries had a lot to do with the failure of the division's defending champions, the Padres. San Diego starters Joey Hamilton, Andy Ashby and Sterling Hitchcock all went on the DL, and inspirational third basemen Ken Caminiti, coming off an MVP season and rotator-cuff surgery, played hurt and started slowly. By the time he got going (.290, 26 HRs, 90 RBI), the pitching had collapsed and the Padres were out of contention. Tony Gwynn won his eighth batting title and set career highs in homers (17) and RBI (119).

The Colorado Rockies started quickly (21-9) and were in first place as late as May 12, but losing 15 of 16 games to begin July seemingly knocked them out of the race. The Rockies made one final surge, going 20-5 over the final month to lurk on the fringe of the race. It was a typical Colorado season, with an NL-record 239 home runs and a league-leading .288 batting average. MVP Larry Walker flirted with the Triple Crown, finally winning the home run title with 49 but finishing second in the batting and RBI races. Teammate Andres Galarraga won the latter. It was also a typical season in that the pitching didn't hold up. All five members of the original starting rotation spent time on the disabled list, and the Rockies didn't stabilize their staff until late-season trades for Pedro Astacio and Frank Castillo.

STANDINGS AT ALL-STAR BREAK

	W	L	Pct.	GB
San Francisco	51	36	.586	—
Los Angeles	45	42	.517	6
Colorado	43	45	.489	8½
San Diego	38	49	.437	13

Some do. The Giants were the majors' best in one- and two-run games (43-28) and extra-inning games (11-3), and had 46 come-from-behind triumphs, one fewer than the Mets' major league high. Heavily criticized for trading away Matt Williams in the offseason, the Giants still

FINAL STANDINGS

	W	L	Pct.	GB
San Francisco	90	72	.556	—
Los Angeles	88	74	.543	2
Colorado	83	79	.512	7
San Diego	76	86	.469	14

AL hitting leaders

BATTING AVERAGE

F. Thomas, Chi.	.347
E. Martinez, Sea.	.330
Justice, Cle.	.329
B. Williams, N.Y.	.328
M. Ramirez, Cle.	.328
O'Neill, N.Y.	.324
Greer, Tex.	.321
Jefferson, Bos.	.319
M. Vaughn, Bos.	.315
I. Rodriguez, Tex.	.313

HOME RUNS

Griffey, Sea.	56
T. Martinez, N.Y.	44
J. Gonzalez, Tex.	42
Buhner, Sea.	40
Thome, Cle.	40
R. Palmeiro, Bal.	38
F. Thomas, Chi.	35
M. Vaughn, Bos.	35
McGwire, Oak.	34
Justice, Cle.	33

TRIPLES

Garciaparra, Bos.	11
Knoblauch, Min.	10
Burnitz, Mil.	8
Damon, K.C.	8
Alicea, Ana.	7
B. Anderson, Bal.	7
Hunter, Det.	7
Jeter, N.Y.	7
Stewart, Tor.	7
8 tied	6

DOUBLES

Valentin, Bos.	47
Cirillo, Mil.	46
Belle, Chi.	45
Garciaparra, Bos.	44
Delgado, Tor.	42
Greer, Tex.	42
O'Neill, N.Y.	42
Giambi, Oak.	41
3 tied	40

RUNS BATTED IN

Griffey, Sea.	147
T. Martinez, N.Y.	141
J. Gonzalez, Tex.	131
Salmon, Ana.	129
F. Thomas, Chi.	125
T. Clark, Det.	117
O'Neill, N.Y.	117
Belle, Chi.	116
King, K.C.	112
R. Palmeiro, Bal.	110

RUNS SCORED

Griffey, Sea.	125
Garciaparra, Bos.	122
Knoblauch, Min.	117
Jeter, N.Y.	116
Greer, Tex.	112
Hunter, Det.	112
F. Thomas, Chi.	110
B. Williams, N.Y.	107
Durham, Chi.	106
2 tied	105

HITS

Garciaparra, Bos.	209
Greer, Tex.	193
Jeter, N.Y.	190
G. Anderson, Ana.	189
I. Rodriguez, Tex.	187
Griffey, Sea.	185
M. Ramirez, Cle.	184
F. Thomas, Chi.	184
E. Martinez, Sea.	179
O'Neill, N.Y.	179

BASES ON BALLS

Thome, Cle.	120
Buhner, Sea.	119
E. Martinez, Sea.	119
F. Thomas, Chi.	109
Phillips, Chi.-Ana.	102
Salmon, Ana.	95
T. Clark, Det.	93
King, K.C.	89
M. Vaughn, Bos.	86
C. Davis, K.C.	85

STOLEN BASES

Hunter, Det.	74
Knoblauch, Min.	62
T. Goodwin, K.C.-Tex.	50
Nixon, Tor.	47
Vizquel, Cle.	43
Durham, Chi.	33
I. Rodriguez, Sea.	29
Easley, Det.	28
4 tied	23

SLUGGING PERCENTAGE

Griffey, Sea.	.646
F. Thomas, Chi.	.611
Justice, Cle.	.596
J. Gonzalez, Tex.	.589
Thome, Cle.	.579
T. Martinez, N.Y.	.577
M. Vaughn, Bos.	.560
E. Martinez, Sea.	.554
Burnitz, Mil.	.553
B. Williams, N.Y.	.544

ON-BASE PERCENTAGE

F. Thomas, Chi.	.456
E. Martinez, Sea.	.456
Thome, Cle.	.423
M. Vaughn, Bos.	.420
Justice, Cle.	.418
M. Ramirez, Cle.	.415
B. Williams, N.Y.	.408
Greer, Tex.	.405
O'Neill, N.Y.	.399
Salmon, Ana.	.394

EXTRA-BASE HITS

Griffey, Sea.	93
Garciaparra, Bos.	85
T. Martinez, N.Y.	77
Belle, Chi.	76
Delgado, Tor.	75
Burnitz, Mil.	72
Greer, Tex.	71
F. Thomas, Chi.	70
Valentin, Bos.	70
J. Gonzalez, Tex.	69

SINGLES

G. Anderson, Ana.	142
Jeter, N.Y.	142
Hunter, Det.	137
Knoblauch, Min.	133
Durham, Chi.	129
I. Rodriguez, Tex.	129
Garciaparra, Bos.	124
Vizquel, Cle.	124
Greer, Tex.	122
C. Ripken, Bal.	119

LEAD-ASSUMING RBI

Griffey, Sea.	38
F. Thomas, Chi.	36
Fryman, Det.	34
T. Martinez, N.Y.	34
J. Carter, Tor.	29
Greer, Tex.	29
J. Bell, K.C.	27
O'Neill, N.Y.	27
R. Palmeiro, Bal.	27
2 tied	26

GAME-WINNING RBI

T. Martinez, N.Y.	22
R. Palmeiro, Bal.	17
Fryman, Det.	16
O'Neill, N.Y.	15
Salmon, Ana.	15
F. Thomas, Chi.	15
Burnitz, Mil.	13
J. Carter, Tor.	13
Garciaparra, Bos.	13
Molitor, Min.	13

SACRIFICE HITS

Vizquel, Cle.	16
D. Cruz, Det.	14
Bordick, Bal.	12
J. Gonzalez, Tor.	11
T. Goodwin, K.C.-Tex.	11
Guillen, Chi.	11
Reboulet, Bal.	11
C. Garcia, Tor.	10
Matheny, Mil.	9
5 tied	8

SACRIFICE FLIES

T. Martinez, N.Y.	13
Griffey, Sea.	12
King, K.C.	12
Molitor, Min.	12
Fryman, Det.	11
Salmon, Ana.	11
J. Gonzalez, Tex.	10
Loretta, Mil.	10
C. Ripken, Bal.	10
Surhoff, Bal.	10

INTENTIONAL WALKS

Griffey, Sea.	23
M. Vaughn, Bos.	17
C. Davis, K.C.	16
T. Martinez, N.Y.	14
Surhoff, Bal.	14
T. Clark, Det.	13
Baines, Chi-Bal.	11
W. Clark, Tex.	11
Justice, Cle.	11
E. Martinez, Sea.	11

HIT-BY-PITCH

B. Anderson, Bal.	19
Knoblauch, Min.	17
Easley, Det.	16
Meares, Min.	16
Cirillo, Mil.	14
M. Vaughn, Bos.	12
E. Martinez, Sea.	11
O'Brien, Tor.	11
3 tied	10

GROUND OUTS

Jeter, N.Y.	241
C. Ripken, Bal.	226
DiSarcina, Ana.	219
Hunter, Det.	216
T. Goodwin, K.C.-Tex.	213
G. Anderson, Ana.	206
Durham, Chi.	205
Guillen, Chi.	198
Vizquel, Cle.	196
J. Rodriguez, Tex.	192

AIR OUTS

J. Carter, Tor.	256
King, K.C.	216
Spiezio, Oak.	215
R. Palmeiro, Bal.	212
T. Martinez, N.Y.	203
Garciaparra, Bos.	201
Belle, Chi.	200
Cora, Sea.	198
Fryman, Det.	196
Surhoff, Bal.	195

STRIKEOUTS

Buhner, Sea.	175
Nieves, Det.	157
M. Vaughn, Bos.	154
Thome, Cle.	146
T. Clark, Det.	144
Salmon, Ana.	142
Palmer, Tex.-K.C.	134
Delgado, Tor.	133
Becker, Min.	130
Jeter, N.Y.	125

GROUNDED INTO DP

Belle, Chi.	26
Bordick, Bal.	23
Buhner, Sea.	23
E. Martinez, Sea.	21
Valentin, Bos.	21
G. Anderson, Ana.	20
M. Ramirez, Cle.	19
C. Ripken, Bal.	19
5 tied	18

CAUGHT STEALING

Hunter, Det.	18
Durham, Chi.	16
T. Goodwin, K.C.-Tex.	16
Burnitz, Mil.	13
Easley, Det.	13
Grissom, Cle.	13
B. Anderson, Bal.	12
Jeter, N.Y.	12
Salmon, Ana.	12
Vizquel, Cle.	12

AL pitching leaders

MOST WINS

Clemens, Tor.	21
R. Johnson, Sea.	20
Radke, Min.	20
Pettitte, N.Y.	18
Moyer, Sea.	17
Blair, Det.	16
Erickson, Bal.	16
Fassero, Sea.	16
Key, Bal.	16
Wells, N.Y.	16

MOST LOSSES

Baldwin, Chi.	15
Eldred, Mil.	15
Wakefield, Bos.	15
Navarro, Chi.	14
S. Sanders, Sea.-Det.	14
W. Williams, Tor.	14
Appier, K.C.	13
Karl, Mil.	13
Tewksbury, Min.	13
12 tied	12

MOST STRIKEOUTS

Clemens, Tor.	292
R. Johnson, Sea.	291
Cone, N.Y.	222
Mussina, Bal.	218
Appier, K.C.	196
Fassero, Sea.	189
Radke, Min.	174
Pettitte, N.Y.	166
Hentgen, Tor.	160
Gordon, Bos.	159

MOST COMPLETE GAMES

Clemens, Tor.	9
Hentgen, Tor.	9
R. Johnson, Sea.	5
Tewksbury, Min.	5
Wells, N.Y.	5
6 tied	4

MOST SAVES

R. Myers, Bal.	45
M. Rivera, N.Y.	43
D. Jones, Mil.	36
T. Jones, Det.	31
Wetteland, Tex.	31
R. Hernandez, Chi.	27
Percival, Ana.	27
Slocumb, Bos.-Sea.	27
Aguilera, Min.	26
Taylor, Oak.	23

MOST GAMES STARTED

Fassero, Sea.	35
Hentgen, Tor.	35
Pettitte, N.Y.	35
Radke, Min.	35
Appier, K.C.	34
Clemens, Tor.	34
Eldred, Mil.	34
Key, Bal.	34
Nagy, Cle.	34
Watson, Ana.	34

LOWEST ERA

Clemens, Tor.	2.05
R. Johnson, Sea.	2.28
Cone, N.Y.	2.82
Pettitte, N.Y.	2.88

Thompson, Det.	3.02
Mussina, Bal.	3.20
Appier, K.C.	3.40
Key, Bal.	3.43
Fassero, Sea.	3.61
Hentgen, Tor.	3.68

BATTING AVERAGE AGAINST

R. Johnson, Sea.	.194
Clemens, Tor.	.213
Cone, N.Y.	.218
Gordon, Bos.	.226
Thompson, Det.	.233
Mussina, Bal.	.234
Appier, K.C.	.243
Finley, Ana.	.248
Fassero, Sea.	.249
Hentgen, Tor.	.254

FEWEST HITS PER 9 INNINGS

R. Johnson, Sea.	6.21
Clemens, Tor.	6.95
Cone, N.Y.	7.15
Thompson, Det.	7.58
Gordon, Bos.	7.64
Mussina, Bal.	7.89
Appier, K.C.	8.21
Finley, Ana.	8.34
Hentgen, Tor.	8.63
Wakefield, Bos.	8.63

FEWEST HOME RUNS PER 9 INNINGS

Pettitte, N.Y.	0.26
Clemens, Tor.	0.31
Gordon, Bos.	0.49
Tewksbury, Min.	0.64
Erickson, Bal.	0.65
Cone, N.Y.	0.78
Thompson, Det.	0.81
Fassero, Sea.	0.81
R. Johnson, Sea.	0.85
Baldwin, Chi.	0.86

FEWEST WALKS PER 9 INNINGS

Burkett, Tex.	1.43
Tewksbury, Min.	1.65
Radke, Min.	1.80
Wells, N.Y.	1.86
Moyer, Sea.	2.05
Mussina, Bal.	2.16
Clemens, Tor.	2.32
Blair, Det.	2.37
Hentgen, Tor.	2.42
Pettitte, N.Y.	2.43

MOST STRIKEOUTS PER 9 INNINGS

R. Johnson, Sea.	12.30
Cone, N.Y.	10.25
Clemens, Tor.	9.95
Mussina, Bal.	8.73
Finley, Ana.	8.51
Gordon, Bos.	7.83
Appier, K.C.	7.49
Fassero, Sea.	7.26
Wakefield, Bos.	6.75
Burkett, Tex.	6.61

MOST EXTRA-BASE HITS

Belcher, K.C.	87
Springer, Ana.	86
Radke, Min.	84
Witt, Tex.	84
Wells, N.Y.	82
Hentgen, Tor.	80
Watson, Ana.	80
W. Williams, Tor.	80
Baldwin, Chi.	79
4 tied	78

MOST HOME RUNS

Watson, Ana.	37
Witt, Tex.	33
Dickson, Ana.	32
Springer, Ana.	32
Belcher, K.C.	31
Eldred, Mil.	31
Hentgen, Tor.	31
W. Williams, Tor.	31
Drabek, Chi.	30
S. Sanders, Sea.-Det.	30

MOST HIT-BY-PITCH

Wakefield, Bos.	16
Sele, Bos.	15
Olivares, Det.-Sea.	13
Clemens, Tor.	12
Hershiser, Cle.	11
Oliver, Tex.	11
R. Johnson, Sea.	10
Springer, Ana.	10
Eldred, Mil.	9
Karsay, Oak.	9

MOST GROUNDED INTO DP

Pettitte, N.Y.	36
Erickson, Bal.	33
Hershiser, Cle.	31
Clemens, Tor.	27
Thompson, Det.	24
Key, Bal.	23
Olivares, Det.-Sea.	22
Hentgen, Tor.	21
Mercedes, Mil.	21
4 tied	20

MOST STOLEN BASES

Kamienicki, Bal.	25
Suppan, Bos.	25
Wakefield, Bos.	25
Nagy, Cle.	24
Navarro, Chi.	23
Cone, N.Y.	22
Lira, Det.-Sea.	22
Erickson, Bal.	21
Moehler, Det.	21
4 tied	20

MOST CAUGHT STEALING

Wakefield, Bos.	18
R. Johnson, Sea.	16
Hentgen, Tor.	15
Key, Bal.	13
Fassero, Sea.	11
Springer, Ana.	11
Thompson, Det.	11
Watson, Ana.	11
Nagy, Cle.	10
Oliver, Tex.	10

MOST PICKOFFS

Pettitte, N.Y.	14
Watson, Ana.	10
Thompson, Det.	8
Hentgen, Tor.	7
Key, Bal.	7
Rogers, N.Y.	7
Gooden, N.Y.	6
Kamienicki, Bal.	6
Fassero, Sea.	5
Swindell, Min.	5

MOST BALKS

Baldwin, Chi.	3
Hawkins, Min.	3
Irabu, N.Y.	3
Spoljaric, Tor.-Sea.	3
15 tied	2

MOST WILD PITCHES

Appier, K.C.	14
Baldwin, Chi.	14
Cone, N.Y.	14
Navarro, Chi.	14
Fassero, Sea.	13
Drabek, Chi.	12
Erickson, Bal.	11
Hershiser, Cle.	11
Ritchie, Min.	11
3 tied	10

LOWEST BATTING AVERAGE VS. LEFT-HANDERS

Clemens, Tor.	.205
Cone, N.Y.	.213
Mussina, Bal.	.223
Gordon, Bos.	.231
Hentgen, Tor.	.241
Eldred, Mil.	.245
Erickson, Bal.	.248
Appier, K.C.	.257
Drabek, Chi.	.258
Kamienicki, Bal.	.262

LOWEST BATTING AVERAGE VS. RIGHT-HANDERS

R. Johnson, Sea.	.186
Radke, Min.	.221
Clemens, Tor.	.222
Alvarez, Chi.	.226
Appier, K.C.	.227
Moyer, Sea.	.234
Pettitte, N.Y.	.238
Thompson, Det.	.242
Wakefield, Bos.	.243
Mussina, Bal.	.245

NL hitting leaders

1998 BASEBALL WEEKLY ALMANAC

BATTING AVERAGE

Gwynn, S.D.	.372
L. Walker, Col.	.366
Piazza, L.A.	.362
Lofton, Atl.	.333
Joyner, S.D.	.327
Grace, Chi.	.319
Galarraga, Col.	.318
Alfonzo, N.Y.	.315
Mondesi, L.A.	.310
Biggio, Hou.	.309

HOME RUNS

L. Walker, Col.	49
Bagwell, Hou.	43
Galarraga, Col.	41
Bonds, S.F.	40
Castilla, Col.	40
Piazza, L.A.	40
Sosa, Chi.	36
Burks, Col.	32
Karros, L.A.	31
Lankford, St.L	31

TRIPLES

DeShields, St.L	14
N. Perez, Col.	10
W. Guerrero, L.A.	9
Randa, Pit.	9
Womack, Pit.	9
Biggio, Hou.	8
Daulton, Phi.-Fla.	8
L. Johnson, N.Y.-Chi.	8
E. Young, Col.-L.A.	8
5 tied	7

DOUBLES

Grudzielanek, Mon.	54
Gwynn, S.D.	49
L. Walker, Col.	46
Lansing, Mon.	45
Mondesi, L.A.	42
C. Jones, Atl.	41
Bagwell, Hou.	40
Morandini, Phi.	40
Bonilla, Fla.	39
Clayton, St.L	39

RUNS BATTED IN

Galarraga, Col.	140
Bagwell, Hou.	135
L. Walker, Col.	130
Piazza, L.A.	124
Kent, S.F.	121
Gwynn, S.D.	119
Sosa, Chi.	119
Bichette, Col.	118
Alou, Fla.	115
Castilla, Col.	113

RUNS SCORED

Biggio, Hou.	146
L. Walker, Col.	143
Bonds, S.F.	123
Galarraga, Col.	120
Bagwell, Hou.	109
E. Young, Col.-L.A.	106
Piazza, L.A.	104
Finley, S.D.	101
C. Jones, Atl.	100
Gwynn, S.D.	97

HITS

Gwynn, S.D.	220
L. Walker, Col.	208
Piazza, L.A.	201
Biggio, Hou.	191
Galarraga, Col.	191
Mondesi, L.A.	191
Castilla, Col.	186
Womack, Pit.	178
Grace, Chi.	177
Grudzielanek, Mon.	177

BASES ON BALLS

Bonds, S.F.	145
Bagwell, Hou.	127
Sheffield, Fla.	121
Snow, S.F.	96
Lankford, St.L	95
Grace, Chi.	88
Olerud, N.Y.	85
Zeile, L.A.	85
Biggio, Hou.	84
Hundley, N.Y.	83

STOLEN BASES

Womack, Pit.	60
D. Sanders, Cin.	56
DeShields, St.L	55
Biggio, Hou.	47
E. Young, Col.-L.A.	45
Bonds, S.F.	37
Q. Veras, S.D.	33
L. Walker, Col.	33
3 tied	32

SLUGGING PERCENTAGE

L. Walker, Col.	.720
Piazza, L.A.	.638
Bagwell, Hou.	.592
Galarraga, Col.	.585
Lankford, St.L	.585
Bonds, S.F.	.585
Hundley, N.Y.	.549
Castilla, Col.	.547
Gwynn, S.D.	.547
Mondesi, L.A.	.541

ON-BASE PERCENTAGE

L. Walker, Col.	.452
Bonds, S.F.	.446
Piazza, L.A.	.431
Bagwell, Hou.	.425
Sheffield, Fla.	.424
Biggio, Hou.	.415
Lankford, St.L	.411
Lofton, Atl.	.409
Gwynn, S.D.	.409
Grace, Chi.	.409

EXTRA-BASE HITS

L. Walker, Col.	99
Bagwell, Hou.	85
Mondesi, L.A.	77
Galarraga, Col.	75
Piazza, L.A.	73
Bonds, S.F.	71
Sosa, Chi.	71
Lankford, St.L	70
Kent, S.F.	69
Gwynn, S.D.	68

SINGLES

Gwynn, S.D.	152
Renteria, Fla.	143
Womack, Pit.	137
Lofton, Atl.	133
Piazza, L.A.	128
Grace, Chi.	127
E. Young, Col.-L.A.	125
Alfonzo, N.Y.	124
Biggio, Hou.	124
2 tied	120

LEAD-ASSUMING RBI

Bagwell, Hou.	46
Galarraga, Col.	34
Gwynn, S.D.	34
L. Walker, Col.	34
Kent, S.F.	33
Piazza, L.A.	32
Sheffield, Fla.	32
Karros, L.A.	30
C. Jones, Atl.	29
Sosa, Chi.	27

GAME-WINNING RBI

Bagwell, Hou.	21
Piazza, L.A.	21
C. Jones, Atl.	18
Sheffield, Fla.	17
Karros, L.A.	16
Kent, S.F.	16
Bonds, S.F.	15
W. Greene, Cin.	15
R. White, Mon.	15
4 tied	14

SACRIFICE HITS

Renteria, Fla.	19
Glavine, Atl.	17
Butler, L.A.	15
Ordonez, N.Y.	14
W. Guerrero, L.A.	13
Vizcaino, S.F.	13
Morandini, Phi.	12
Santangelo, Mon.	12
Schilling, Phi.	12
5 tied	11

SACRIFICE FLIES

Gilkey, N.Y.	12
Gwynn, S.D.	12
Joyner, S.D.	10
Kent, S.F.	10
Blauser, Atl.	9
Daulton, Phi.-Fla.	9
Karros, L.A.	9
6 tied	8

INTENTIONAL WALKS

Bonds, S.F.	34
Bagwell, Hou.	27
Hundley, N.Y.	16
L. Walker, Col.	14
Snow, S.F.	13
Gwynn, S.D.	12
Segui, Mon.	12
Piazza, L.A.	11
Sheffield, Fla.	11
2 tied	10

HIT-BY-PITCH

Biggio, Hou.	34
Kendall, Pit.	31
Santangelo, Mon.	25
Blauser, Atl.	20
Galarraga, Col.	17
Bagwell, Hou.	16
Sheffield, Fla.	15
L. Walker, Col.	14
3 tied	13

GROUND OUTS

Grudzielanek, Mon.	233
Vizcaino, S.F.	229
Renteria, Fla.	228
E. Young, Col.-L.A.	222
DeShields, St.L	207
Womack, Pit.	203
McRae, Chi.-N.Y.	199
Q. Veras, S.D.	196
R. White, Mon.	195
2 tied	192

AIR OUTS

Karros, L.A.	210
E. Young, Col.-L.A.	188
Finley, S.D.	187
Kent, S.F.	187
L. Gonzalez, Hou.	186
Mondesi, L.A.	184
Bonds, S.F.	176
Gilkey, N.Y.	173
Gwynn, S.D.	171
Bichette, Col.	170

STRIKEOUTS

Sosa, Chi.	174
Gant, St.L	162
H. Rodriguez, Mon.	149
Galarraga, Col.	141
Rolen, Phi.	138
Kent, S.F.	133
Klesko, Atl.	130
Lankford, St.L	125
Snow, S.F.	124
Bagwell, Hou.	122

GROUNDED INTO DP

McGriff, Atl.	22
Huskey, N.Y.	21
Gaetti, St.L	20
Clayton, St.L	19
C. Jones, Atl.	19
Olerud, N.Y.	19
Piazza, L.A.	19
R. White, Mon.	19
4 tied	18

CAUGHT STEALING

Lofton, Atl.	20
Mondesi, L.A.	15
Renteria, Fla.	15
DeShields, St.L	14
E. Young, Col.-L.A.	14
Goodwin, Cin.	13
Morandini, Phi.	13
D. Sanders, Cin.	13
3 tied	12

NL pitching leaders

MOST WINS

Neagle, Atl.	20
Estes, S.F.	19
Kile, Hou.	19
G. Maddux, Atl.	19
A. Fernandez, Fla.	17
P. Martinez, Mon.	17
Schilling, Phi.	17
K. Brown, Fla.	16
Hampton, Hou.	15
B. Jones, NY	15

MOST LOSSES

M. Leiter, Phi.	17
S. Cooke, Pit.	15
Lieber, Pit.	14
Mulholland, Chi.-S.F.	13
C. Perez, Mon.	13
11 tied	12

MOST STRIKEOUTS

Schilling, Phi.	319
P. Martinez, Mon.	305
Smoltz, Atl.	241
Nomo, L.A.	233
K. Brown, Fla.	205
Kile, Hou.	205
A. Fernandez, Fla.	183
Estes, S.F.	181
G. Maddux, Atl.	177
An. Benes, St.L	175

MOST COMPLETE GAMES

P. Martinez, Mon.	13
C. Perez, Mon.	8
Hampton, Hou.	7
Schilling, Phi.	7
Smoltz, Atl.	7
K. Brown, Fla.	6
Kile, Hou.	6
4 tied	5

MOST SAVES

Shaw, Cin.	42
Beck, S.F.	37
Hoffman, S.D.	37
Eckersley, St.L	36
J. Franco, N.Y.	36
Nen, Fla.	35
T. Worrell, L.A.	35
Bottalico, Phi.	34
Wohlers, Atl.	33
Loiselle, Pit.	29

MOST GAMES STARTED

Schilling, Phi.	35
Smoltz, Atl.	35
Hampton, Hou.	34
Kile, Hou.	34
Neagle, Atl.	34
Trachsel, Chi	34
6 tied	33

LOWEST ERA

Martinez, Mon.	1.90
Maddux, Atl.	2.20
Kile, Hou.	2.57
Valdes, L.A.	2.65
Brown, Fla.	2.69
Reed, NY-N	2.89
Glavine, Atl.	2.96
Neagle, Atl.	2.97
Schilling, Phi.	2.97
Smoltz, Atl.	3.02

BATTING AVERAGE AGAINST

P. Martinez, Mon.	.184
Park, L.A.	.213
Estes, S.F.	.223
Schilling, Phi.	.224
Kile, Hou.	.225
Glavine, Atl.	.226
An. Benes, St.L	.230
Stottlemyre, St.L	.231
Neagle, Atl.	.233
Valdes, L.A.	.234

FEWEST HITS PER 9 INNINGS

P. Martinez, Mon.	5.89
Park, L.A.	6.98
Estes, S.F.	7.25
Kile, Hou.	7.32
Schilling, Phi.	7.36
Glavine, Atl.	7.39
An. Benes, St.L	7.58
Stottlemyre, St.L	7.71
G. Maddux, Atl.	7.74
Valdes, L.A.	7.83

FEWEST HOME RUNS PER 9 INNINNGS

G. Maddux, Atl.	0.35
K. Brown, Fla.	0.38
An. Benes, St.L	0.46
M. Morris, St.L	0.50
Estes, S.F.	0.54
P. Martinez, Mon.	0.60
Hampton, Hou.	0.65
Kile, Hou.	0.67
Neagle, Atl.	0.69
Cordova, Pit.	0.71

FEWEST WALKS PER 9 INNINGS

G. Maddux, Atl.	0.77
R. Reed, N.Y.	1.34
Neagle, Atl.	1.89
Schilling, Phi.	2.05
C. Perez, Mon.	2.09
Valdes, L.A.	2.15
Ashby, S.D.	2.20
Smoltz, Atl.	2.21
Reynolds, Hou.	2.34
Rueter, S.F.	2.41

MOST STRIKEOUTS PER 9 INNINGS

P. Martinez, Mon.	11.37
Schilling, Phi.	11.29
Nomo, L.A.	10.11
An. Benes, St.L	8.90
Smoltz, Atl.	8.47
Estes, S.F.	8.10
Stottlemyre, St.L	7.96
Park, L.A.	7.78
K. Brown, Fla.	7.77
Lieber, Pit.	7.65

MOST EXTRA-BASE HITS

M. Leiter, Phi.	90
C. Perez, Mon.	81
Schilling, Phi.	81
Trachsel, Chi.	81
M. Clark, N.Y.-Chi.	78
Castillo, Chi.-Col.	76
R. Bailey, Col.	75
A. Fernandez, Fla.	74
Mulholland, Chi.-S.F.	71
2 tied	70

MOST HOME RUNS

Trachsel, Chi.	32
Gardner, S.F.	28
R. Bailey, Col.	27
Foster, Chi.	27
Beech, Phi.	25
Castillo, Chi.-Col.	25
A. Fernandez, Fla.	25
M. Leiter, Phi.	25
Schilling, Phi.	25
6 tied	24

MOST HIT-BY-PITCH

K. Brown, Fla.	14
R. Bailey, Col.	13
Bullinger, Mon.	12
Hamilton, S.D.	12
A. Leiter, Fla.	12
Loaiza, Pit.	12
Stottlemyre, St.L	12
Candiotti, L.A.	11
Mulholland, Chi.-S.F.	11
J. Wright, Col.	11

MOST GROUNDED INTO DP

Glavine, Atl.	33
R. Bailey, Col.	27
Hampton, Hou.	27
K. Brown, Fla.	26
M. Morris, St.L	25
Thomson, Col.	25
Kile, Hou.	24
C. Perez, Mon.	24
G. Maddux, Atl.	23
5 tied	21

MOST STOLEN BASES

Juden, Mon.	41
Bullinger, Mon.	34
Ashby, S.D.	30
Trachsel, Chi.	27
Hitchcock, S.D.	26
Mlicki, N.Y.	26
An. Benes, St.L	22
Foster, Chi.	21
5 tied	20

MOST CAUGHT STEALING

Gardner, S.F.	16
A. Leiter, Fla.	16
Castillo, Chi.-Col.	15
Al. Benes, St.L	12
S. Cooke, Pit.	12
Estes, S.F.	12
Hamilton, S.D.	12
Holt, Hou.	12
Trachsel, Chi.	12
2 tied	11

MOST PICKOFFS

R. Bailey, Col.	7
Remlinger, Cin.	7
Rueter, S.F.	7
J. Wright, Col.	7
J. Gonzalez, Chi.	5
Guthrie, L.A.	5
Hitchcock, S.D.	5
Trachsel, Chi.	5
Valenzuela, S.D.-St.L	5
6 tied	4

MOST BALKS

Nomo, L.A.	4
Astacio, L.A.-Col.	3
Gardner, S.F.	3
Loaiza, Pit.	3
M. Morris, St.L	3
Rincon, Pit.	3
P. Smith, S.D.	3
19 tied	2

MOST WILD PITCHES

Remlinger, Cin.	12
M. Leiter, Phi.	11
Estes, S.F.	10
Nomo, L.A.	10
Smoltz, Atl.	10
Al. Benes, St.L	9
A. Fernandez, Fla.	9
VanLandingham, S.F.	9
3 tied	8

LOWEST BATTING AVERAGE VS. LEFT-HANDERS

P. Martinez, Mon.	.183
G. Maddux, Atl.	.213
R. Reed, N.Y.	.231
Kile, Hou.	.231
J. Gonzalez, Chi.	.232
Hermanson, Mon.	.232
Schilling, Phi.	.234
Al. Benes, St.L	.234
B. Jones, N.Y.	.237
Park, L.A.	.237

LOWEST BATTING AVERAGE VS. RIGHT-HANDERS

P. Martinez, Mon.	.184
A. Fernandez, Fla.	.189
Valdes, L.A.	.206
Schilling, Phi.	.214
Remlinger, Cin.	.217
Estes, S.F.	.218
Kile, Hou.	.218
Glavine, Atl.	.224
Holt, Hou.	.226
Neagle, Atl.	.232

Obituaries: selected major leaguers

Cal Abrams: Feb. 25, Fort Lauderdale, Fla.; 1949-56 Dodgers, Reds, Pirates, Orioles, White Sox.

Bobby Adams: Feb. 13, Gig Harbor, Wash.; 1946-59 Reds, White Sox, Orioles, Cubs.

Luis Aloma: April 7, Park Ridge, Ill.; 1950-53 White Sox.

Richie Ashburn: Sept. 9, New York; 1948-62 Phillies, Cubs, Mets.

Rex Barney: Aug. 12, Baltimore; 1943-50 Dodgers.

Ray Benge: June 27, Centerville, Texas; 1925-38 Indians, Phillies, Dodgers, Reds.

Al Blanche: April 2, Melrose, Mass.; 1935-36 Braves.

Roger Bowman: July 21, Los Angeles; 1949-55 Giants, Pirates.

Bill Butland: Sept. 19, Terre Haute, Ind.; 1940-47 Red Sox.

Bob Cain: April 8, Cleveland; 1949-53 White Sox, Tigers, Browns.

Dolph Camilli: Oct. 21, San Mateo, Calif.; 1933-45 Cubs, Phillies, Dodgers, Red Sox.

Fred Chapman: March 27, Kannapolis, N.C.; 1939-41 Athletics.

Joe Coleman: April 9, Fort Myers, Fla.; 1942-55 Athletics, Orioles, Tigers.

Jeff Cross: July 23, Huntsville, Texas; 1942-48 Cardinals, Cubs.

Harry Davis: March 3, Shreveport, La.; 1932-37 Tigers, Browns.

Eddie Delker: May 14, Pottsville, Pa.; 1929-33 Cardinals, Phillies.

Johnny Dickshot: Nov. 4, Waukegan, Ill.; 1936-45 Pirates, Giants, White Sox.

George Dockins: Jan. 22, Clyde, Kan.; 1945-47 Cardinals, Dodgers.

Gus Dugas: April 14, Colchester, Conn.; 1930-34 Pirates, Senators.

Woody English: Sept. 26, Newark, Ohio; 1927-38 Cubs, Dodgers.

Curt Flood: Jan. 20, Los Angeles; 1956-71 Reds, Cardinals, Senators.

Rufe Gentry: July 3, Winston-Salem, N.C.; 1943-48 Tigers.

Buddy Hassett: Aug. 23, Westwood, N.J.; 1936-42 Dodgers, Yankees.

Joe Hauser: July 11, Sheboygan, Wis.; 1922-29 Athletics, Indians.

Jim Hickey: Sept. 20, Manchester, Conn.; 1942-44 Braves.

Duane Josephson: Jan. 30, New Hampton, Iowa; 1965-72 White Sox, Red Sox.

Billy Jurges: March 3, Clearwater, Fla.; 1931-47 Cubs, Giants.

Monte Kennedy: March 1, Midlothian, Va.; 1946-53 Giants.

Alex Konikowski: Sept. 28, Seymour, Conn.; 1948-54 Giants.

Thornton Lee: June 9, Tucson, Ariz.; 1933-48 Indians, White Sox, Giants.

Dwight Lowry: July 10, Jamestown, N.Y.; 1984-88 Tigers, Twins.

Phil Marchildon: Jan. 10, Toronto, Ontario; 1940-50 Athletics, Red Sox.

Stu Martin: Jan. 11, Severn, N.C.; 1936-43 Cardinals, Pirates, Cubs.

Roy McMillan: Nov. 2, Bonham, Texas; 1951-66 Reds, Braves, Mets.

Russ Meyer: Nov. 16, Oglesby, Ill.; 1946-59 Cubs, Phillies, Dodgers, Reds, Red Sox, Athletics.

Eddie Miller: July 31, Lake Worth, Fla.; 1936-50 Reds, Braves, Phillies, Cardinals.

Dee Moore: July 2, Williston, N.D.; 1936-46 Reds, Dodgers, Phillies.

Les Munns: Feb. 28, Cedar Rapids, Iowa; 1934-36 Dodgers, Cardinals.

Don O'Riley: May 2, Kansas City, Mo.; 1969-70 Royals.

Homer Peel: April 8, Shreveport, La.; 1927-34 Cardinals, Phillies, Giants.

Lou Possehl: Oct. 7, Sarasota, Fla.; 1946-52 Phillies.

Stan Rojek: July 9, North Tonawanda, N.Y.; 1942-52 Dodgers, Pirates, Cardinals, Browns.

Manny Salvo: Feb. 7, Vallejo, Calif.; 1939-43 Giants, Red Sox, Phillies.

Bill Smith: March 30, Clinton, Md.; 1958-62 Cardinals, Phillies.

Glen Stewart: Feb. 11, Memphis, Tenn.; 1940-44 Giants, Phillies.

Oad Swigart: Aug. 8, St. Joseph, Mo.; 1939-40 Pirates.

Johnny Vander Meer: Oct. 6, Tampa, Fla.; 1937-51 Reds, Indians.

Jim Walkup: Feb. 7, Danville, Ark.; 1934-39 Browns, Tigers.

Butch Weis: May 4, St. Louis; 1922-25 Cubs.

—compiled by Bill Carle (through Nov. 26)

Postseason

▶AL and NL Division
  Series
▶NLCS and ALCS
  stories and
  composite box
  scores

▶World Series game-
  by-game wrap-ups,
  box scores and
  player statistics

USA SNAPSHOTS®

A look at statistics that shape the sports world

Best match for World Series?

Times American and National league teams with the best
season record have reached the World Series since
divisional play started in 1969:

27

Number
of World
Series
since
1969

17
Best AL
team
reached
Series

15
Best NL
team
reached
Series

Both
best-
record
teams

10

Neither
best-
record
team

6

Source: USA TODAY research   By Scott Boeck and Dave Merrill, USA TODAY

AL Division Series: Player statistics

Cleveland 3, New York 2

SERIES BATTING / NEW YORK

	AVG	G	AB	R	H	2B	3B	HR	RBI	BB	SO
Stanley	.750	2	4	1	3	1	0	0	1	0	1
Boggs	.429	3	7	1	3	0	0	0	2	0	0
O'Neill	.421	5	19	5	8	2	0	2	7	3	0
Jeter	.333	5	21	6	7	1	0	2	2	3	5
Hayes	.333	5	15	0	5	0	0	0	1	0	2
Martinez	.222	5	18	1	4	1	0	1	4	2	4
Raines	.211	5	19	4	4	0	0	1	3	1	1
Sanchez	.200	5	15	1	3	1	0	0	1	1	2
Curtis	.167	4	6	0	1	0	0	0	0	3	1
Girardi	.133	5	15	2	2	0	0	0	0	1	3
Fielder	.125	2	8	0	1	0	0	0	1	0	3
B.Williams	.118	5	17	3	2	1	0	0	1	4	3
Posada	.000	3	2	0	0	0	0	0	0	0	1
Fox	—	2	0	0	0	0	0	0	0	0	0
Pose	—	1	0	0	0	0	0	0	0	0	0

SERIES PITCHING / NEW YORK

	G	CG	W	L	ERA	SV	IP	H	R	ER	HR	BB	SO
Nelson	4	0	0	0	0.00	0	4	4	0	0	0	2	0
Bohrngr	1	0	0	0	0.00	0	1.2	1	0	0	0	1	2
Lloyd	2	0	0	0	0.00	0	1.1	0	0	0	0	0	1
Stanton	3	0	0	0	0.00	0	1	1	0	0	0	1	3
Wells	1	1	1	0	1.00	0	9	5	1	1	0	0	1
Gooden	1	0	0	0	1.59	0	5.2	5	1	1	1	3	5
Mendoza	2	0	1	1	2.45	0	3.2	3	1	1	0	0	2
Rivera	2	0	0	0	4.50	1	2	2	1	1	1	0	1
Pettitte	2	0	0	2	8.49	0	11.2	15	11	11	1	1	5
Cone	1	0	0	0	16.20	0	3.1	7	6	6	1	2	2

SERIES BATTING / CLEVELAND

	AVG	G	AB	R	H	2B	3B	HR	RBI	BB	SO
Vizquel	.500	5	18	3	9	0	0	0	1	2	1
Alomar	.316	5	19	4	6	1	0	2	5	0	2
Roberts	.316	5	19	1	6	0	0	0	1	2	2
Justice	.263	5	19	3	5	2	0	1	2	2	3
M.Williams	.235	5	17	4	4	1	0	1	3	3	3
Grissom	.235	5	17	3	4	0	1	0	0	1	2
Thome	.200	4	15	1	3	0	0	0	1	0	5
Fernandez	.182	4	11	0	2	1	0	0	4	0	0
Ramirez	.143	5	21	3	3	1	0	0	3	0	3
Giles	.143	3	7	0	1	0	0	0	0	0	1
Seltzer	.000	1	4	0	0	0	0	0	0	0	0

SERIES PITCHING / CLEVELAND

	G	CG	W	L	ERA	SV	IP	H	R	ER	HR	BB	SO
Morman	1	0	0	0	—	0	0	0	0	0	0	1	0
Jackson	4	0	1	0	0.00	0	4.1	3	0	0	0	1	5
Ogea	1	0	0	0	1.69	0	5.1	2	1	1	0	1	0
Mesa	2	0	0	0	2.70	1	3.1	5	1	1	1	0	2
Hershiser	2	0	0	0	3.97	0	11.1	14	5	5	1	2	4
Wright	2	0	2	0	3.97	0	11.1	11	6	5	0	7	10
Assnmchr	4	0	0	0	5.40	0	3.1	2	2	2	1	2	2
Nagy	1	0	0	1	9.82	0	3.2	2	5	4	0	6	1
Plunk	1	0	0	1	27.00	0	1.1	4	4	4	2	0	1

Wright was wrong for the Yanks

Rookie right-hander Jaret Wright led the Indians to two of their three victories in the dethroning of the Yankees in the American League Division Series. First, he kept Cleveland's hopes alive by winning Game 2 in the circus atmosphere of Yankee Stadium. Then he came back on three days' rest to finish off the defending world champions in Game 5 in Cleveland.

After watching staff ace David Cone get touched for five runs in the first inning of Game 1, the Yankees knocked out Orel Hershiser and battered the Indians' bullpen to win 8-6. Tim Raines, Derek Jeter and Paul O'Neill walloped back-to-back-to-back home runs—a major league postseason first.

The crowd almost got to Wright in Game 2. At age 21, he became the youngest hurler to start in an AL Division Series game when he took the mound. He couldn't get a breaking ball over for a strike and began to aim his fastball. Somehow he weathered walking three men in a row and falling behind 3-0 in the first inning. Indians manager Mike Hargrove said his young phenom came "within a hitter or two" from being yanked from the ball game. But after requiring 35 pitches to make it through the first, Wright needed only 38 pitches over the next three innings and held the Yankees scoreless before leaving after the fifth.

On this night of a thousand screams, Wright stepped front and center, but Cone found himself undergoing an MRI examination for his injured shoulder at Columbia-Presbyterian Hospital. The results showed only swelling, but the next day Yankees manager Joe Torre announced that Cone would be sidelined for the rest of the series.

With Cone out, Dwight Gooden was chosen to replace him in the New York rotation. Following David Wells' complete-game victory in Game 3, to put New York up 2-1, Gooden had a chance to close out the series for New York. In Game 4, he and Hershiser went at it once more in the glare of prime time. Both were equal to the task. The two starters woke up the echoes: Gooden allowed only one run in 5⅔ innings, and Hershiser just two in seven. After Cleveland catcher Sandy Alomar tied the score with his dramatic solo shot in the eighth inning off Yankees closer Mariano Rivera, the Indians quickly won it in the bottom of the ninth on an Omar Vizquel RBI single off Ramiro Mendoza.

Early on in Game 5, Wright kept the defending champions at bay, holding base runners at third in the first two innings. He didn't tire until the fifth inning, with the Indians holding a 4-3 lead. From there, the Cleveland bullpen, which was embarrassed in Game 1, did its job, and Wright led the charge from the dugout after closer Jose Mesa got the final out.

—by Tim Wendel

The Mariners' Johnson couldn't find an answer against the Orioles.

O's stifled Seattle sluggers

The Mariners, who led baseball with 925 runs and set a major league record with 264 home runs, went out like lambs in losing the Division Series against the Orioles three games to one. Seattle posted a club-record 90 victories this season, but the postseason was a different story. The team hit .218 and scored just 11 runs in the four games, and ace Randy Johnson lost twice.

Center fielder Ken Griffey, right fielder Jay Buhner and DH Edgar Martinez, who combined for 364 RBI during the season, were a collective 8-for-44 (.182) in the series. "We just didn't do what we wanted," Griffey said. He went hitless in three trips in the 3-1 loss in Game 4 against Orioles starter Mike Mussina, who outpitched Johnson and extended his career domination over Griffey. Junior is 4-for-36 against the Orioles' right-hander.

In Game 4, the Mariners managed just two hits, both in the second inning. Still, they had one last gasp in the eighth inning. Pinch-hitter Rick Wilkins drew a leadoff walk against reliever Armando Benitez, and Griffey, who hit 56 homers during the year, came up with two out, representing the tying run. Griffey hit a roller to third on which Cal Ripken made a nice play to throw him out.

The much-maligned Seattle bullpen gave up 15 hits, five walks and 10 earned runs in 8⅓ innings in Games 1 and 2, consecutive 9-3 blowouts. In Game 1 the Orioles got to Johnson for five runs in five innings, then battered reliever Mike Timlin for four more. Bobby Ayala, who hadn't allowed a run since Sept. 4, was torched for six of them in 1⅔ innings in Game 2. The series probably turned when Jamie Moyer, nursing a 2-1 lead, had to leave in the fifth inning with a strained flexor muscle in his left elbow. The Orioles proceeded to score eight runs after he departed. Seattle's Jeff Fassero shut down Baltimore 4-2 in Game 3, but that just delayed the Mariners' vacation plans.

—by Bill Koenig

AL Division Series: Player statistics

Baltimore 3, Seattle 1

SERIES BATTING / BALTIMORE

	AVG	G	AB	R	H	2B	3B	HR	RBI	BB	SO
Ripken	.438	4	16	1	7	2	0	0	1	2	2
Bordick	.400	4	10	4	4	1	0	0	4	4	2
Baines	.400	2	5	2	2	0	0	1	1	1	0
Berroa	.385	4	13	4	5	1	0	2	2	2	2
Anderson	.353	4	17	3	6	1	0	1	4	1	4
Alomar	.300	4	10	1	3	2	0	0	2	1	1
Surhoff	.273	3	11	0	3	1	0	0	2	0	2
Palmeiro	.250	4	12	2	3	2	0	0	0	0	2
Davis	.222	3	9	0	2	0	0	0	2	0	5
Reboulet	.200	2	5	1	1	0	0	1	1	0	2
Webster	.167	3	6	1	1	0	0	0	1	1	0
Hoiles	.143	3	7	1	1	0	0	1	1	2	1
Hammonds	.100	4	10	3	1	1	0	0	2	2	2
Walton	.000	2	4	0	0	0	0	0	0	0	2

SERIES PITCHING / BALTIMORE

	G	CG	W	L	ERA	SV	IP	H	R	ER	HR	BB	SO
Rhodes	1	0	0	0	0.00	0	2.1	0	0	0	0	0	4
Myers	2	0	0	0	0.00	1	2.0	0	0	0	0	0	5
Orosco	2	0	0	0	0.00	0	1.1	1	0	0	0	0	1
Mills	1	0	0	0	0.00	0	1.0	1	0	0	0	0	1
Mussina	2	0	2	0	1.93	0	14.0	7	3	3	3		16
Benitez	3	0	0	0	3.00	0	3.0	3	1	1	1	2	4
Key	1	0	0	1	3.86	0	4.2	8	2	2	0	0	4
Erickson	1	0	1	0	4.05	0	6.2	7	3	3	0	2	6
Mathews	1	0	0	0	18.00	0	1.0	2	2	2	2	0	1

SERIES BATTING / SEATTLE

	AVG	G	AB	R	H	2B	3B	HR	RBI	BB	SO
Amaral	.500	2	4	2	2	0	0	0	0	0	1
Ducey	.500	2	4	0	2	0	0	0	1	0	0
Sheets	.333	2	3	0	1	0	0	0	0	0	2
Rodriguez	.313	4	16	1	5	1	0	1	1	0	5
Kelly	.308	4	13	1	4	3	0	0	1	0	3
Sorrento	.300	4	10	2	3	1	0	1	1	2	3
Buhner	.231	4	13	2	3	0	0	2	2	3	6
Blowers	.200	3	5	0	1	0	0	0	0	0	3
Martinez	.188	4	16	2	3	0	0	2	3	0	3
Cora	.176	4	17	1	3	0	0	0	0	0	4
Griffey	.133	4	15	0	2	0	0	0	2	1	3
Gates	.000	2	4	0	0	0	0	0	0	0	0
Wilson	.000	4	13	0	0	0	0	0	0	0	9
Wilkins	—	1	0	0	0	0	0	0	0	1	0

SERIES PITCHING / SEATTLE

	G	CG	W	L	ERA	SV	IP	H	R	ER	HR	BB	SO
Charlton	2	0	0	0	0.00	0	2.1	2	0	0	0	0	1
Spoljaric	2	0	0	0	0.00	0	1.2	4	0	0	0	0	1
Wells	1	0	0	0	0.00	0	1.1	1	0	0	0	0	1
Fassero	1	0	1	0	1.13	0	8.0	3	1	1	0	4	3
Slocumb	2	0	0	0	4.50	0	2.0	3	1	1	0	1	0
Johnson	2	1	0	2	5.54	0	13.0	14	8	8	3	6	16
Moyer	1	0	0	1	5.79	0	4.2	5	3	3	1	1	2
Ayala	1	0	0	0	40.50	0	1.1	4	6	6	1	3	2
Timlin	1	0	0	0	54.00	0	0.2	3	4	4	1	1	1

NL Division Series: Player statistics

Florida 3, San Francisco 0

SERIES BATTING / FLORIDA

	AVG	G	AB	R	H	2B	3B	HR	RBI	BB	SO
Arias	1.000	1	1	1	0	0	0	0	1	0	0
Sheffield	.556	3	9	3	5	1	0	1	1	5	0
Counsell	.400	3	5	0	2	1	0	0	1	1	0
Conine	.364	3	11	3	4	1	0	0	0	1	0
Bonilla	.333	3	12	1	4	0	0	1	3	2	1
Abbott	.250	3	8	0	2	0	0	0	0	0	0
CJohnson	.250	3	8	5	2	1	0	1	2	3	2
Alou	.214	3	14	1	3	1	0	0	1	0	3
White	.182	3	11	1	2	0	0	1	4	2	3
Renteria	.154	3	13	1	2	0	0	0	1	2	4
Cangelosi	.000	1	1	0	0	0	0	0	0	0	0
Eisenreich	—	2	0	0	0	0	0	0	0	2	0
Wehner	—	1	0	0	0	0	0	0	0	0	0

SERIES PITCHING / FLORIDA

	G	CG	W	L	ERA	SV	IP	H	R	ER	HR	BB	SO
Cook	2	0	1	0	0.00	0	3.0	0	0	0	0	1	3
Nen	2	0	1	0	0.00	0	2.0	1	1	0	0	2	2
Brown	1	0	0	0	1.29	0	7.0	4	1	1	1	0	5
LHrnandz	1	0	0	0	2.25	0	4.0	3	1	1	0	0	3
Fernandez	1	0	1	0	2.57	0	7.0	7	2	2	2	0	5
Leiter	1	0	0	0	9.00	0	4.0	7	4	4	1	3	3

SERIES BATTING / SAN FRANCISCO

	AVG	G	AB	R	H	2B	3B	HR	RBI	BB	SO
Lewis	.600	1	5	0	3	0	0	0	1	0	0
Javier	.417	3	12	2	5	1	0	0	1	0	2
Kent	.300	3	10	2	3	0	0	2	2	2	1
Bonds	.250	3	12	0	3	2	0	0	2	0	3
Mueller	.250	3	12	1	3	0	0	1	1	0	0
Vizcaino	.182	3	11	1	2	1	0	0	0	0	5
Snow	.167	3	6	0	1	0	0	0	0	1	1
BJohnson	.100	3	10	2	1	0	0	1	1	1	4
Benard	.000	2	2	0	0	0	0	0	0	0	1
Berryhill	.000	1	1	0	0	0	0	0	0	0	0
Hamilton	.000	2	5	1	0	0	0	0	0	0	1
Hill	.000	3	7	0	0	0	0	0	0	2	2
Powell	.000	1	0	0	0	0	0	0	0	0	0

SERIES PITCHING / SAN FRANCISCO

	G	CG	W	L	ERA	SV	IP	H	R	ER	HR	BB	SO
Beck	1	0	0	0	0.00	0	1.1	1	0	0	0	0	1
Henry	1	0	0	0	0.00	0	2.0	1	0	0	0	3	2
Rodriguez	2	0	0	0	0.00	0	1.0	1	0	0	0	0	0
Rueter	1	0	0	0	1.29	0	7.0	4	1	1	1	3	5
Tavarez	3	0	0	1	4.50	0	4.0	4	2	2	1	2	0
Alvarez	1	0	0	1	6.00	0	6.0	6	4	4	1	4	4
Estes	1	0	0	0	15.00	0	3.0	5	5	5	1	4	3
RHrnandz	3	0	0	1	20.25	0	1.1	5	3	3	0	3	1

Pricey Marlins swept San Francisco

In sweeping the Giants in three games, the Marlins looked like the best team money could buy. Florida featured free-agent mercenaries Kevin Brown, Alex Fernandez, Moises Alou and Bobby Bonilla; and the Giants folded like so many of Florida owner Wayne Huizenga's business competitors.

The Marlins' two biggest heroes of the Division Series have had precious little contact with their teammates. Several Marlins say they can't recall having a substantive conversation with center fielder Devon White in the two seasons he's been in Florida. And shortstop Edgar Renteria, who speaks little English, says he's kept to himself ever since Opening Day second baseman Luis Castillo was sent to the minors.

No matter. As Huizenga might say, the only thing that matters is the bottom line. Renteria delivered a ninth-inning, game-winning single in Game 1, and White's grand slam off Wilson Alvarez in Game 3 sealed the sweep. Florida manager Jim Leyland broke down and sobbed during the victory celebration. He thought back to Francisco Cabrera's ninth-inning pinch hit for the Braves during the 1992 NLCS, which stole the pennant away from his Pirates. "I'm finally a member of a team that won a playoff series," said Leyland. "I've been dumb for quite a few years because Francisco Cabrera didn't hit the ball right at somebody."

The Division Series provided numerous reunions that served as reminders of the burgeoning gap between baseball's haves and have-nots. There were Leyland, Marlins third baseman Bobby Bonilla and Giants left fielder Barry Bonds, all members of the financially strapped early '90s Pirates. Game 3 was a matchup of the Marlins' Fernandez and left-hander Alvarez, both part of Jerry Reinsdorf's downsizing of the White Sox.

With so much attractive, high-priced talent on display, it was no wonder Marlins president Don Smiley held an open house in Miami during the first two games of the series. Smiley, who hopes to purchase the team from Huizenga, hosted would-be investors. "Winning helps a lot," says Smiley. "They're all potential limited partners."

As Smiley conducted his best sales job on the Marlins, the business side dominated baseball in Florida. Even nine-year-old Marlins fan Ryan Kurlander, better known as "Muscle Boy" for his telescreen posing and flexing to the song *Macho Man* by the Village People, wore a radio-station bumper sticker on his 65-pound frame during Game 1. But when Kurlander removed the sticker for Game 2, it became almost possible to view the Marlins as something other than a high-priced commodity to be packaged and sold to the highest bidder.

—*by Pete Williams*

Leadoff man Lofton got the Braves off to a quick start in Game 1.

Braves stung the Killer B's

The Braves entered the postseason with the same bullpen liabilities that plagued them in previous Octobers, but Atlanta did not need to rely on their relievers in the Division Series against Houston, receiving complete games from Greg Maddux and John Smoltz in Games 1 and 3, respectively, and blowing out the Astros in Game 2.

"They're a better team," Astros first baseman Jeff Bagwell said of the Braves after the three-game sweep. "I'm proud of the guys in this locker room. I'll play with them any time." Some of them, however, won't be back. Darryl Kile has signed a big free-agent contract with Colorado.

Outfielder Luis Gonzalez left as a free agent and will be replaced by Moises Alou. Outfielder Derek Bell has been mentioned as trade bait. Along with fellow "Killer B's" Bagwell and second baseman Craig Biggio, Bell was a key component of the Astros' attack. But the trio lost its sting, going 2-for-37 (.054) in the Division Series.

The Astros had high hopes going into the Division Series. Although Atlanta won seven of 11 regular season games over 84-78 Houston, none was decided by more than two runs. The pattern held through Game 1, a 2-1 hard-luck loss in which Kile's brilliant two-hitter over seven innings was wasted. But the Astros never held a lead in the series, and they batted .167 as a team.
— *by Deron Snyder*

NL Division Series: Player statistics

Atlanta 3, Houston 0

SERIES BATTING / ATLANTA

	AVG	G	AB	R	H	2B	3B	HR	RBI	BB	SO
Colbrunn	1.000	1	1	0	1	0	0	0	2	0	0
C.Jones	.500	3	8	3	4	0	0	1	2	3	2
Bautista	.333	3	3	0	1	0	0	0	2	0	1
Blauser	.300	3	10	2	3	0	0	1	4	2	2
Lopez	.286	2	7	3	2	2	0	0	1	2	1
Klesko	.250	3	8	2	2	1	0	1	1	0	2
McGriff	.222	3	9	4	2	0	0	0	1	3	2
Tucker	.167	2	6	0	1	0	0	0	1	0	1
Lofton	.154	3	13	2	2	1	0	0	0	1	2
Graffanino	.000	3	3	0	0	0	0	0	0	2	1
A.Jones	.000	3	5	1	0	0	0	0	1	1	1
Lockhart	.000	2	6	0	0	0	0	0	0	0	1
Perez	.000	1	3	0	0	0	0	0	0	0	1

SERIES PITCHING / ATLANTA

	G	CG	W	L	ERA	SV	IP	H	R	ER	HR	BB	SO
Cather	1	0	0	0	0.00	0	2.0	0	0	0	0	1	2
Wohlers	1	0	0	0	0.00	0	1.0	1	0	0	0	0	1
Maddux	1	1	1	0	1.00	0	9.0	7	1	1	0	1	6
Smoltz	1	1	1	0	1.00	0	9.0	3	1	1	1	1	11
Glavine	1	0	1	0	4.50	0	6.0	5	3	3	0	5	4

SERIES BATTING / HOUSTON

	AVG	G	AB	R	H	2B	3B	HR	RBI	BB	SO
Eusebio	.667	1	3	1	2	0	0	0	0	0	1
Ausmus	.400	2	5	1	2	1	0	0	2	0	1
Abreu	.333	3	3	0	1	0	0	0	0	0	2
Gonzalez	.333	3	12	0	4	0	0	0	0	0	1
Carr	.250	2	4	1	1	0	0	1	1	1	3
Gutierrez	.125	3	8	0	1	0	0	0	0	2	1
Bagwell	.083	3	12	0	1	0	0	0	0	1	5
Biggio	.083	3	12	0	1	0	0	0	0	1	0
Bell	.000	3	13	0	0	0	0	0	0	0	3
Berry	.000	1	1	0	0	0	0	0	0	0	0
Hidalgo	.000	2	5	1	0	0	0	0	0	1	2
Howard	.000	2	1	0	0	0	0	0	0	1	1
Johnson	.000	1	1	0	0	0	0	0	0	0	1
Spiers	.000	3	11	1	0	0	0	0	0	1	2
Pena	—	2	0	0	0	0	0	0	0	0	0

SERIES PITCHING / HOUSTON

	G	CG	W	L	ERA	SV	IP	H	R	ER	HR	BB	SO
Garcia	2	0	0	0	0.00	0	1.0	1	2	0	0	1	1
Lima	1	0	0	0	0.00	0	1.0	0	0	0	0	1	1
Martin	2	0	0	0	0.00	0	0.2	1	1	0	0	1	0
Kile	1	0	0	1	2.57	0	7.0	2	2	2	1	2	4
Reynolds	1	0	0	1	3.00	0	6.0	5	2	2	1	1	5
Magnante	2	0	0	0	4.50	0	2.0	4	3	1	0	0	2
Springer	2	0	0	0	5.40	0	1.2	2	1	1	0	1	3
Hampton	1	0	0	1	11.57	0	4.2	2	6	6	1	8	2
Wagner	1	0	0	0	18.00	0	1.0	3	2	2	0	0	2

POSTSEASON

43

ALCS: Player statistics

Cleveland 4, Baltimore 2

SERIES BATTING / CLEVELAND

	G	AB	R	H	2B	3B	HR	RBI	BB	SO	AVG
Fernandez 2b	5	14	1	5	1	0	1	2	1	2	.357
Justice dh	6	21	3	7	1	0	0	0	2	4	.333
Ramirez rf	6	21	3	6	1	0	2	3	5	5	.286
Grissom cf	6	23	2	6	0	0	1	4	1	9	.261
Williams 3b	6	23	1	5	1	0	0	2	3	7	.217
Giles lf	6	16	1	3	3	0	0	0	2	6	.188
Roberts 2b-lf	5	20	0	3	1	0	0	0	0	8	.150
SAlomar c	6	24	3	3	0	0	1	4	1	3	.125
Thome 1b	6	14	3	1	0	0	0	0	5	4	.071
Vizquel ss	6	25	1	1	0	0	0	0	2	10	.040
Seitzer 1b	4	4	0	0	0	0	0	0	1	2	.000
Branson dh	1	2	0	0	0	0	0	0	0	2	.000
Totals	6	207	18	40	8	0	5	15	23	62	.193

SERIES PITCHING / CLEVELAND

	G	CG	IP	H	R	ER	BB	SO	W	L	SV	ERA
Hershiser	1	0	7	4	0	0	1	7	0	0	0	0.00
MJackson	5	0	4.1	1	0	0	1	7	0	0	0	0.00
Morman	2	0	1.1	0	0	0	0	1	0	0	0	0.00
Juden	3	0	1	2	0	0	2	2	0	0	0	0.00
Plunk	1	0	.2	1	0	0	0	1	0	0	0	0.00
BnAnderson	3	0	6.1	1	1	1	3	7	1	0	0	1.42
Nagy	2	0	13	17	4	4	5	5	0	0	0	2.77
Ogea	2	0	14	12	5	5	5	7	0	2	0	3.21
Mesa	4	0	5.1	5	2	2	3	5	1	0	2	3.38
Assenmacher	5	0	2	5	2	2	1	3	1	0	0	9.00
Wright	1	0	3	6	5	5	2	3	0	0	0	15.00
Totals	6	0	58	54	19	19	23	47	4	2	2	2.95

SERIES BATTING / BALTIMORE

	G	AB	R	H	2B	3B	HR	RBI	BB	SO	AVG
ByAndrsn cf	6	25	5	9	2	0	2	3	4	4	.360
Baines dh	6	17	1	6	0	0	1	2	2	1	.353
Ripken 3b	6	23	3	8	2	0	1	3	4	6	.348
Berroa rf-dh	6	21	1	6	2	0	0	3	0	3	.286
Palmeiro 1b	6	25	3	7	2	0	1	2	0	10	.280
Webster c	4	9	0	2	0	0	0	0	0	1	.222
Surhoff lf-1b	6	25	1	5	2	0	0	1	2	2	.200
RAlomar 2b	6	22	2	4	0	0	1	2	7	3	.182
Bordick ss	6	19	0	3	1	0	0	2	0	6	.158
Davis rf-dh	6	13	1	2	0	0	1	1	1	3	.154
Hoiles c	4	14	1	2	0	0	0	0	2	5	.143
Hmmnds rf-lf	5	3	0	0	0	0	0	0	1	2	.000
Reboulet ss	1	2	1	0	0	0	0	0	0	1	.000
Walton rf	1	0	0	0	0	0	0	0	0	0	—
Totals	6	218	19	54	11	0	7	19	23	47	.248

SERIES PITCHING / BALTIMORE

	G	CG	IP	H	R	ER	BB	SO	W	L	SV	ERA
Kamieniecki	2	0	8	4	0	0	2	5	1	0	0	0.00
Rhodes	2	0	2.1	2	0	0	3	2	0	0	0	0.00
Orosco	2	0	1.1	0	0	0	1	1	0	0	0	0.00
Mussina	2	0	15	4	1	1	4	25	0	0	0	0.60
Key	2	0	7	5	2	2	3	7	0	0	2	2.57
Mills	3	0	3.1	1	1	1	2	3	0	1	0	2.70
Erickson	2	0	12.2	15	7	6	1	6	1	0	0	4.26
Myers	4	0	5.1	6	3	3	3	7	0	1	1	5.06
ABenitez	4	0	3	3	4	4	4	6	0	2	0	12.00
Totals	6	0	58	40	18	17	23	62	2	4	1	2.64

Mike Mussina performed heroically for Baltimore, but couldn't win.

By H. Darr Beiser, USA TODAY

Indians won the squeakers

Could White Sox owner Jerry Reinsdorf have been the one guy who knew what he was talking about? No sense trying to beat the Cleveland Indians, he said back in July, as he tried to justify trading away the guts of his pitching staff. Everyone else figured the Indians were a nice prize for anyone wanting to advance in the playoffs. What kind of foolish system would reward the wild-card team with the 86-75 Indians in the first round while the division winner got stuck with the 90-win Seattle Mariners? The Indians edged the Yankees, while the division-winning Orioles, second to nobody for all of 1997, steamrollered Seattle but then fell in six to Cleveland, which took all four of their winning games by one run.

It was a tense, wild series that was filled with improbabilities. For instance, Orioles outfielder Eric Davis was getting colon cancer chemotherapy treatments one day and batting third in an American League Championship Series game the next. Even more unlikely was Davis' slamming the ninth-inning home run that ended up being the winning run in Baltimore's backs-to-the-wall victory in Game 5. An ironic twist was that Davis spent his therapy watching *Major League II*, in which the cinematic Cleveland Indians win the World Series. But no screenwriter in his right mind would script the stuff the real-life Tribe did. Winning a game on a home run by a guy who had been so sick he was given fluids intra-venously? Snaring the next game by botching a suicide squeeze? Turning around yet another by scoring twice on a wild pitch that never got 10 feet from home plate? And, finally, winning the series on an 11th-inning homer by a guy who wasn't even supposed to be in the lineup?

Preposterous, but true. Four magical one-run victories turned Cleveland into Believeland. Indians fans had almost expected a ninth-inning rally from four runs down against closer deluxe Randy Myers in Game 5 to cap the miracle, but two runs and two runners in scoring position later, the Orioles were still breathing, if only until Tony Fernandez's pennant-winning dinger in Game 6. Fernandez brought a .172 career Camden Yards average to the plate before going deep on an Armando Benitez breaking ball with two out in the 11th of a scoreless game. In the clincher the Orioles outhit the Indians 10-3 but stranded 14 runners and went 0-for-12 with runners in scoring position.

Cleveland made it to the World Series thanks to guys like Marquis Grissom. There were the Orioles, coming off Scott Erickson's dominating shutout in Game 1, with Game 2 in the hands of their real advantage coming into the series, the bullpen. The Orioles bullpen at Camden Yards is exactly where Grissom, who had received an IV the previous day to combat a virus, deposited Benitez's eighth-inning slider to turn a 4-2 deficit into a 5-4 Cleveland victory.

For the bullpens, it became a battle of attrition. Orioles manager Davey Johnson said before Game 1 he would opt for a 10-man pitching staff instead of the 11 that skipper Mike Hargrove had chosen. Hargrove's 11th was a left-handed kid named Brian Anderson, who mowed down the Orioles for 3⅓ innings through the middle of Game 4 while his teammates came back from being down 5-2. During the rally, ailing Orioles lefty Arthur Rhodes, who couldn't throw his slider, had to be used in relief of Erickson instead of lefty Rick Krivda, who probably would have been Johnson's 11th pitcher.

That was the least of what seemed to conspire against the Orioles:

▶They were certain that the Game 2 batter before Grissom, Jim Thome, swung at strike three for the third out, but third base umpire Larry McCoy ruled it a checked swing.

▶They watched Grissom score the winning run in the 12th inning of Game 3 when Omar Vizquel missed a squeeze bunt; catcher Lenny Webster thought the ball was foul-tipped and didn't chase it.

▶They saw two Indians runs score on a Game 4 wild pitch that got away from Webster, who then made a throwing error after taking a long time to find the ball.

▶Twice they stubbornly got off the mat and tied games in the ninth against Cleveland closer Jose Mesa, but won neither game.

Despite the two runs off Mesa, Baltimore could muster only three off the Indians bullpen in 16⅓ innings during the first four games. Meanwhile, Orioles relievers Benitez, Myers and Alan Mills took consecutive losses, and Benitez then lost the clincher.

Indians catcher Sandy Alomar made a clutch contribution. Before Game 4, Alomar had been feeling the effects of having caught every inning of every game, particularly the 12-inning marathon the day before. After Game 4 ended on his tie-breaking single off Benitez in the bottom of the ninth, he wasn't nearly as tired. Alomar and Grissom led Cleveland with four RBI apiece in the series.

For Baltimore, ace Mike Mussina was the star. In Game 3, which started in the late afternoon, Mussina's missiles in the shadows accounted for 15 strikeouts in seven innings. He was nearly as dominant in Game 6, another twilight game, striking out 10 and allowing one hit in eight innings. Unfortunately for Mussina, the Indians' Charles Nagy kept pace though he allowed nine hits and walked three in 7⅓ innings. Nagy was brilliant with runners on, and the game stayed scoreless through the 10th. Then Fernandez, who was only playing because second baseman Bip Roberts had been injured in batting practice, ended it with one swing.

—by Paul White, with Bill Koenig

NLCS: Player Statistics

Florida 4, Atlanta 2

SERIES BATTING / FLORIDA

	G	AB	R	H	2B	3B	HR	RBI	BB	SO	AVG
Arias 3b	3	1	0	1	0	0	0	0	0	0	1.000
Counsell 2b	5	14	0	6	0	0	0	2	3	3	.429
Abbott 2b	2	8	0	3	1	0	0	0	0	2	.375
Bonilla 3b	6	23	3	6	1	0	0	4	1	6	.261
Daulton 1b	3	4	1	1	1	0	0	1	1	2	.250
Sheffield rf	6	17	6	4	0	0	1	1	7	3	.235
Renteria ss	6	22	4	5	1	0	0	3	6		.227
Cangelosi lf	3	5	0	1	0	0	0	0	1	0	.200
White cf	6	21	4	4	1	0	0	1	2	7	.190
Johnson c	6	17	1	2	2	0	0	5	3	8	.118
Conine 1b	6	18	1	2	0	0	0	1	1	4	.111
Alou lf	5	15	0	1	1	0	0	5	1	3	.067
Fernandez p	1	1	0	0	0	0	0	0	0	1	.000
Leiter p	2	1	0	0	0	0	0	0	0	1	.000
Saunders p	1	2	0	0	0	0	0	0	0	2	.000
Eisenreich lf	1	3	0	0	0	0	0	0	0	0	.000
Hernandez p	2	3	0	0	0	0	0	0	0	1	.000
Brown p	2	6	0	0	0	0	0	0	0	3	.000
Zaun c	1	0	0	0	0	0	0	0	0	0	—
Totals	6	181	20	36	8	0	1	20	23	52	.199

SERIES PITCHING / FLORIDA

	G	CG	IP	H	R	ER	BB	SO	W	L	SV	ERA
Vosberg	2	0	2.2	2	0	0	1	3	0	0	0	0.00
Cook	2	0	2.1	0	0	0	2	0	0	0	0	0.00
Nen	2	0	2	0	0	0	0	1	0	0	2	0.00
Powell	1	0	-2	0	0	0	0	0	0	0	0	0.00
Hernandez	2	1	10.2	5	1	1	2	16	2	0	0	0.84
Saunders	1	0	5.1	4	2	2	3	3	0	0	0	3.38
Brown	2	1	15	16	7	7	5	11	2	0	0	4.20
Leiter	2	0	8.1	13	4	4	2	6	0	1	0	4.32
Heredia	2	0	3.1	3	2	2	2	4	0	0	0	5.40
Fernandez	1	0	2.2	6	5	5	1	3	0	1	0	16.88
Totals	6	2	53	49	21	21	16	49	4	2	2	3.57

SERIES BATTING / ATLANTA

	G	AB	R	H	2B	3B	HR	RBI	BB	SO	AVG
Colbrunn ph	3	3	0	2	0	0	0	0	0	0	.667
Lockhart 2b	5	16	4	8	1	1	0	3	1	1	.500
AJones rf	5	9	0	4	0	0	0	1	1	1	.444
McGriff 1b	6	21	0	7	1	0	0	4	2	7	.333
Glavine p	2	3	0	1	0	0	0	0	0	2	.333
Blauser ss	6	20	5	6	0	0	1	1	3	6	.300
CJones 3b	6	24	5	7	1	0	2	4	2	3	.292
Graffanino 2b	3	8	1	2	1	0	0	0	0	3	.250
Bautista lf	2	4	0	1	0	0	0	0	0	0	.250
Klesko lf	5	17	2	4	0	0	2	4	2	3	.235
Lofton cf	6	27	3	5	0	1	0	1	1	7	.185
Tucker rf	5	10	1	1	0	0	1	1	3	4	.100
Lopez c	5	17	0	1	1	0	0	2	1	7	.059
Smoltz p	2	2	0	0	0	0	0	0	0	1	.000
GMaddux p	2	3	0	0	0	0	0	0	0	2	.000
Neagle p	2	3	0	0	0	0	0	0	0	1	.000
Perez c	3	2	0	0	0	0	0	0	0	0	.000
Gregg ph	4	4	0	0	0	0	0	0	0	1	.000
Totals	6	194	21	49	5	2	6	21	16	49	.253

SERIES PITCHING/ATLANTA

	G	CG	IP	H	R	ER	BB	SO	W	L	SV	ERA
Neagle	2	1	12	5	0	0	1	9	1	0	0	0.00
Ligtenberg	2	0	3	1	0	0	4	0	0	0	0	0.00
Cather	4	0	2.2	3	0	0	3	0	0	0	0	0.00
Embree	1	0	1	0	0	0	1	1	0	0	0	0.00
Wohlers	1	0	1	0	0	0	1	1	0	0	0	0.00
Maddux	2	0	13	9	7	2	4	16	0	2	0	1.38
Glavine	2	0	13.1	13	8	8	11	9	1	1	0	5.40
Smoltz	1	0	6	5	5	5	5	9	0	1	0	7.50
Totals	6	1	52	36	20	15	23	52	2	4	0	2.60

1998 BASEBALL WEEKLY ALMANAC

Livan Hernandez set an NLCS strikeout record and was the series MVP.

By Anne Ryan, USA TODAY

Braves went home early again

Bad news began cascading on the Florida Marlins as if they were under a waterfall. The euphoria of defeating Greg Maddux in Game 1 didn't last long. It ended more quickly than Alex Fernandez's stint in Game 2.

Before Fernandez's start, Florida learned it would be without top RBI man and Game 1 hero Moises Alou, out with a sprained left wrist. His absence was viewed as potentially devastating. Later, ace Kevin Brown was taken ill with a virus, and didn't pitch between Games 1 and 6.

But these were nothing compared with what awaited the Marlins when they arrived at Pro Player Stadium for an off-day workout after Game 2. Fernandez, who lasted just 2⅔ innings in losing Game 2, had a torn rotator cuff and wouldn't be able to pitch for a long, long time. Certainly not in 1997. Maybe not ever again.

Utter silence greeted the announcement. The Braves were trotting out John Smoltz against rookie Tony Saunders in Game 3; and Alou would be missing his second consecutive start. With hearts so heavy they could have been used to drag the infield, the Marlins, amazingly, came out playing with intensity. Florida manager Jim Leyland led the inspirational charge. "He told us to keep playing hard and don't let up, because Atlanta wasn't going to be over there feeling sorry for us," right fielder Gary Sheffield said.

For all their experience, it was the Braves who often looked like first-timers on October's grand stage. They lost Game 1 on two errors and five unearned runs. They lost Game 3 on mistakes that don't appear in box scores, a base running gaffe and a butchered fly ball. But Smoltz contributed as well. Going for a record 11th postseason victory, Smoltz let two leads slip away. Granted, he should have been out of the sixth inning on a Darren Daulton drive that Andruw Jones misplayed, creating a 2-2 tie. But Smoltz then walked Devon White and yielded a two-out, bases-loaded double to catcher Charles Johnson.

Perhaps Smoltz had no one to blame but himself. Conversely, Maddux could point a finger toward almost everyone in the Braves' lineup. He was supposed to have had more to show than two losses, considering he allowed just nine hits and a pair of earned runs in 13 innings. Game 1 was particularly painful for Maddux. Errors by Fred McGriff and Kenny Lofton, and a bouncer down the line that went past a waving Chipper Jones, gave the Marlins a gift-wrapped victory. But Game 5 was more difficult to accept—seven innings, four hits, two earned runs . . . and his second NLCS loss.

That set the stage for Game 6 in Atlanta, where Brown made his illness-delayed start and the Braves' Tom Glavine unexpectedly blew up. Pitching doesn't come much better than Tom Glavine's Game 2 masterpiece—one run and three hits over 7⅔ innings—so it was shocking when he allowed four first-inning runs in the Marlins' clincher. He settled down after that until the sixth, when Florida parlayed four ground-ball singles and two walks into three more runs. Brown, meanwhile, was steady if not brilliant, pitching an 11-hitter in going the distance in the 7-4 win.

Florida had managed to pull out a victory in Game 3 while Brown watched on TV. Brown was still feeling weak for Game 4, and Al Leiter took his place but was hit hard for four runs on 10 hits. Denny Neagle, a 20-game winner in the regular season but the fourth starter in Atlanta's bottomless rotation, pitched a four-hit shutout to even the series.

How much more was Florida supposed to withstand? Surely they couldn't rebound yet again. "It's like when you have a flat tire on the side of the highway," Leyland said. "You can't sit there and pout for an hour. You have to get up and get going."

"It's tough to tell them [teammates] what it's like," said center fielder Devon White of postseason pressure. White, who won two World Series rings with Toronto, added, "You really have to go through it to experience it all. At this point of the season you can't be down over what happens. But it's not time to get too excited either."

He would have had a hard time convincing South Florida of that after the Marlins won Game 5 because of the brilliance of rookie right-hander Livan Hernandez and the generous strike zone of umpire Eric Gregg. Strike-zone complaints are not unusual when Maddux is on the mound. What doesn't happen often is that the gripes emanate from the Braves' clubhouse and focus on the opposing pitcher. Maybe the Braves were starting to feel the pressure. They were becoming adept at making excuses. First they tried to denigrate the quality of Florida's victories in Games 1 and 3, claiming that the Marlins won because of Atlanta's errors afield and on the base paths (as if those mistakes meant that the Braves deserved to win).

Hernandez, the 22-year-old Cuban defector who wasn't included in the postseason rotation until Fernandez and Brown went down, struck out 15 Braves and allowed just three hits in his 2-1 complete-game win. The Braves barely acknowledged his ability. Instead, they blasted Gregg for calling so many outside strikes. (Incidentally, Maddux struck out nine in seven innings, a high total for him.) The Braves failed to score with men on first and third with no outs in the first inning, but they blamed Gregg for their offensive failures. Said manager Bobby Cox, "It was like we had no chance. Some hitters came back saying [pitches] were six to 10 inches outside."

The Marlins—especially Hernandez and Johnson, who called a very smart game—made the adjustments, while the Braves made the complaints and wound up without a world championship for the fifth time in six postseason appearances in the 1990s.
—by Deron Snyder

1997 World Series

▶**Game 1:** Oct. 18
Florida 7, Cleveland 4

▶**Game 2:** Oct. 19
Cleveland 6, Florida 1

▶**Game 3:** Oct. 21
Florida 14, Cleveland 11

▶**Game 4:** Oct. 22
Cleveland 10, Florida 3

▶**Game 5:** Oct. 23
Florida 8, Cleveland 7

▶**Game 6:** Oct. 25
Cleveland 4, Florida 1

▶**Game 7:** Oct. 26
Florida 3, Cleveland 2

Florida wins series 4-3

By Elise Amendola, AP/Wide World Photos

Edgar Renteria got a lift from his teammates after his clinching hit.

'Break up the Marlins!'

The best team money could buy provided the ultimate winning hand for Florida owner Wayne Huizenga on Oct. 26. But very soon after, he started cashing in his player chips in the fastest dismantling of a top team since Connie Mack sold most of his Philadelphia Athletics stars after taking the 1914 American League pennant. The Marlins' inspiring postseason run gave way to the cold economic calculations of 1997 baseball, and before a month had passed, World Series batting star Moises Alou, fireballing closer Robb Nen and center fielder Devon White were all gone, with superstar right fielder Gary Sheffield almost certain to follow. Florida also lost World Series Game 4 starter Tony Saunders, a rookie, as the top pick in the expansion draft, to the Tampa Bay Devil Rays. Never will a defending world champion have been as thoroughly transformed as the 1998 Marlins.

Even the ownership may change, as Huizenga put the club up for sale during the summer and may complete a deal before next season. After the Marlins' NLCS victory over the Braves in Atlanta, the Blockbuster billionaire had taken a spontaneous postgame run around the bases with a few friends in celebration of his team's pennant. It was a wonderful, childlike demonstration of joy, in stark contrast to the bottom-line decisions soon to follow. Huizenga said during the World Series celebration, "I don't want to sell the team," but winning often causes a short-term euphoria that quickly dissipates.

Game 1: Alou's big blow

The first player to go, Alou, was the first Marlins hero in the Series. Alou hit a three-run homer off the Indians' Orel Hershiser in the fourth inning of Game 1, powering the Marlins to a 7-4 victory. Alou reached out to swat an 0-and-2 offspeed pitch. The ball was hooking . . . hooking . . . hooking, but clanked off the foul pole to snap a 1-1 tie. Alou had been just 1-for-12 against Hershiser in their NL matchups when the Bulldog was with the Dodgers. "He's a guy who can get you in a lot of 0-fors," said Alou, who hadn't been having a great postseason until the Series. He hit .138 (4-for-29) in the Division Series against San Francisco and the NLCS against Atlanta.

Following Alou's home run, the Marlins' record crowd of 67,245 settled in with their team in front 4-1. They didn't remain in their seats very long. The next batter, catcher Charles Johnson, slammed a 2-and-1 pitch 10 rows into the upper deck for a 438-foot home run. After the Marlins added two more runs in the fifth inning, Hershiser departed in unusual circumstances. His 4⅓-inning stint was his shortest in five World Series starts; and the seven earned runs he allowed tied a single-game Series mark.

The opening matchup was something of a May-December marriage. While Hershiser (39 years, one month, two days) was the oldest pitcher to start a World Series opener since Early Wynn of the Chicago White Sox in 1959, Florida counterpart Livan Hernandez (22 years, seven months, 28 days) became the youngest pitcher ever to win Game 1. Hernandez went 5⅔ innings before getting relief help from Dennis Cook, Jay Powell and closer Robb Nen.

The sixth Marlins run was driven in by first baseman Jeff Conine, who, along with infielder Alex Arias, was one of two original Marlins remaining from 1993. "Yeah, me and Alex and Billy the Marlin. We have a special bond," Conine said, joking. "This wipes out a lot of losing to be in this situation, to be where we are."

Game 2: Indians on cruise control

A big home run by Sandy Alomar. A clutch hit by Marquis Grissom. Flawless bullpen work. All familiar scenarios. But Game 2 of the World Series was like no other postseason game the Cleveland Indians had

Game 1

Florida 7, Cleveland 4

Cleveland	100 011 010 - 4
Florida	001 420 00X - 7

BATTING

FLORIDA	AB	R	H	RBI	BB	SO	LOB	AVG
White cf	4	0	0	0	1	1	0	.000
Renteria ss	4	0	1	0	0	0	0	.000
Sheffield rf	2	1	0	0	2	1	1	.000
Bonilla 3b	3	2	2	0	1	1	1	.667
Daulton 1b	2	1	1	0	0	0	0	.500
Conine 1b	2	0	1	1	0	0	1	.500
Alou lf	3	1	1	3	1	1	2	.333
Johnson c	3	1	1	1	1	0	1	.333
Counsell 2b	3	1	1	0	1	0	0	.333
Hernandez p	2	0	0	0	0	3	.000
Cook p	0	0	0	0	0	0	0	.000
Powell p	0	0	0	0	0	0	0	.000
a-Cangelosi ph	1	0	0	0	0	1	0	.000
Nen p	0	0	0	0	0	0	0	.000
Totals	29	7	7	6	7	5	9	

a-struck out for Powell in the 8th.
▶**BATTING - 2B:** Counsell (1, Hershiser). **HR:** Alou (1, 4th inning off Hershiser 2 on, 0 out); Johnson (1, 4th inning off Hershiser 0 on, 0 out). **S:** Hernandez. **RBI:** Renteria (1), Alou 3 (3), Johnson (1), Conine (1). **Runners left in scoring position, 2 out:** Sheffield 1, Hernandez 2. **GIDP:** Conine. **LOB:** 6.
▶**FIELDING - E:** Sheffield (1, bobble).

CLEVELAND	AB	R	H	RBI	BB	SO	LOB	AVG
Roberts 2b	4	1	2	0	1	0	2	.500
Vizquel ss	4	0	0	0	0	2	2	.000
Ramirez rf	3	1	1	1	2	0	0	.333
Justice lf	4	0	2	1	1	0	2	.500
Williams 3b	5	0	1	0	0	1	5	.200
Thome 1b	5	1	1	1	0	2	4	.200
Alomar c	5	0	1	0	0	2	2	.200
Grissom cf	3	1	2	0	1	1	0	.667
Hershiser p	2	0	0	0	0	1	1	.000
Juden p	0	0	0	0	0	0	0	.000
a-Branson ph	1	0	0	0	0	1	2	.000
Plunk p	0	0	0	0	0	0	0	.000
b-Giles ph	1	0	1	1	0	0	0	1.000
Assenmacher p	0	0	0	0	0	0	0	.000
Totals	37	4	11	4	5	10	20	

a-struck out for Juden in the 6th; b-doubled for Plunk in the 8th.
▶**BATTING - 2B:** Roberts 2 (2, Hernandez 2); Grissom (1, Hernandez); Giles (1, Powell). **HR:** Ramirez (1, 5th inning off Hernandez 0 on, 2 out). **S:** Vizquel. **RBI:** Justice (1), Ramirez (1), Thome (1), Giles (1). **2-out RBI:** Thome (1, 6th inning off Hernandez 0 on, 1 out). **S:** Vizquel. **RBI:** Justice (1), Ramirez (1), Thome (1), Giles (1). **2-out RBI:** Ramirez, Giles. **Runners left in scoring position, 2 out:** Thome 1, Williams 1, Hershiser 1, Roberts 1, Vizquel 1, Alomar 1. **LOB:** 12.
▶**FIELDING - DP:** 1 (Roberts-Vizquel-Thome).

PITCHING

FLORIDA	IP	H	R	ER	BB	SO	BF	ERA
Hernandez (W, 1-0)	5.2	8	3	3	2	5	27	4.76
Cook (H, 1)	1.2	0	0	0	1	2	6	0.00
Powell	.2	1	1	1	2	1	5	13.50
Nen (S, 1)	1	2	0	0	0	2	5	0.00

CLEVELAND	IP	H	R	ER	BB	SO	BF	ERA
Hershiser (L, 0-1)	4.1	6	7	7	4	2	23	14.54
Juden	.2	0	0	0	2	0	4	0.00
Plunk	2	1	0	0	1	1	7	0.00
Assenmacher	1	0	0	0	0	2	3	0.00

WP: Juden.
▶**UMPIRES - HP:** Ed Montague. **1B:** Dale Ford. **2B:** Joe West. **3B:** Greg Kosc. **LF:** Randy Marsh. **RF:** Ken Kaiser.
▶**GAME DATA - T:** 3:19. **Att:** 67,245. **Weather:** 84 degrees, clear. **Wind:** 8 mph, left to right.

Game 2

Cleveland 6, Florida 1

Cleveland	1 0 0	0 3 2	0 0 0	-	6
Florida	1 0 0	0 0 0	0 0 0	-	1

BATTING

CLEVELAND	AB	R	H	RBI	BB	SO	LOB	AVG
Roberts 2b	3	0	1	2	0	1	0	.429
a-Fernandez ph-2b	2	0	2	0	0	0	0	1.000
Vizquel ss	4	1	2	0	1	0	2	.250
Ramirez rf	5	0	0	0	0	1	5	.125
Justice lf	3	0	1	1	1	1	1	.429
Williams 3b	4	2	2	0	0	0	1	.333
Thome 1b	4	0	1	0	0	1	3	.222
Alomar c	4	2	2	2	0	0	2	.333
Grissom cf	4	1	3	1	0	0	0	.714
Ogea p	2	0	0	0	0	1	1	.000
Jackson p	1	0	0	0	0	0	2	.000
Mesa p	0	0	0	0	0	0	0	.000
Totals	36	6	14	6	2	5	17	

a-doubled for Roberts in the 7th.
▶BATTING - 2B: Vizquel (1, Brown); Fernandez (1, Heredia). HR: Alomar (1, 6th inning off Brown 1 on, 2 out). S: Ogea. RBI: Justice (2), Grissom (1), Roberts 2 (2), Alomar 2 (2). 2-out RBI: Justice, Roberts 2, Alomar 2. Runners left in scoring position, 2 out: Ramirez 1, Justice 1, Jackson 1. GIDP: Alomar, Ramirez 2. LOB: 6.
▶BASERUNNING - CS: Justice (1, 2nd base by Brown/Johnson).
▶FIELDING - DP: 1 (Williams-Roberts-Thome).

FLORIDA	AB	R	H	RBI	BB	SO	LOB	AVG
White cf	5	0	2	0	0	1	1	.222
Renteria ss	4	1	2	0	0	1	2	.250
Sheffield rf	2	0	1	0	1	0	1	.250
Bonilla 3b	4	0	0	0	0	1	5	.286
Conine 1b	3	0	1	1	0	0	2	.400
b-Daulton ph-1b	1	0	0	0	0	0	1	.333
Alou lf	4	0	2	0	0	0	3	.429
Johnson c	3	0	0	0	0	1	1	.167
c-Zaun ph	1	0	0	0	0	0	0	.000
Counsell 2b	3	0	0	0	1	0	1	.167
Brown p	2	0	0	0	0	1	1	.000
Heredia p	0	0	0	0	0	0	0	.000
a-Eisenreich ph	1	0	0	0	0	0	0	.000
Alfonseca p	0	0	0	0	0	0	0	.000
d-Floyd ph	1	0	0	0	0	1	1	.000
Totals	34	1	8	1	2	6	19	

a-grounded to pitcher for Heredia in the 7th; b-flied to left for Conine in the 8th; c-grounded to second for Johnson in the 9th; d-struck out for Alfonseca in the 9th.
▶BATTING - 2B: Renteria (1, Ogea); Alou 2 (2, Ogea 2); White (1, Ogea). RBI: Conine (2). 2-out RBI: Conine. Runners left in scoring position, 2 out: Alou 1, Conine 1, Johnson 1, Renteria 1. GIDP: Sheffield. LOB: 9.
▶FIELDING - DP: 3 (Bonilla-Counsell-Conine, Counsell-Renteria-Conine, Bonilla-Counsell-Daulton).

PITCHING

CLEVELAND	IP	H	R	ER	BB	SO	BF	ERA
Ogea (W, 1-0)	6.2	7	1	1	1	4	28	1.35
Jackson	1.1	1	0	0	0	1	5	0.00
Mesa	1	0	0	0	1	1	4	0.00

FLORIDA	IP	H	R	ER	BB	SO	BF	ERA
Brown (L, 0-1)	6	10	6	6	2	4	27	9.00
Heredia	1	1	0	0	0	1	4	0.00
Alfonseca	2	3	0	0	0	0	8	0.00

HBP: Sheffield (by Ogea).
▶UMPIRES - HP: Dale Ford. 1B: Joe West. 2B: Greg Kosc. 3B: Randy Marsh. LF: Ken Kaiser. RF: Ed Montague.
▶GAME DATA - T: 2:48. Att: 67,025. Weather: 78 degrees, clear. Wind: 6 mph, left to right.

Moises Alou got Florida going with a three-run homer in Game 1.

played in 1997. They won easily. The 6-1 triumph at Florida evened the Series 1-1, but it must have seemed downright boring to the Indians. After all, their last six postseason victories, all four in the ALCS against Baltimore and their final two over the Yankees in the Division Series, had been decided by only a run.

The resilient Indians had lost the first game in the last six series they had played: all three in 1997, their first-round loss to Baltimore in '96 and the '95 ALCS and World Series. "It's all about adjustments," said second baseman Bip Roberts, whose two-out, two-run single completed a three-run fifth inning against Marlins ace Kevin Brown, giving the Indians a 4-1 lead.

Cleveland's game plan was to force Brown into adjustments and not give him a chance to get comfortable. "He didn't get a chance to work fast," said center fielder Grissom. For the most part Brown still was able to pitch his game, using his devastating sinker to get ground balls. But two fifth-inning grounders got through the infield. Grissom bounced one barely to Florida shortstop Edgar Renteria's right, driving in Matt Williams to break a 1-1 tie. Then, with runners on second and third, Roberts' chopper went between Renteria and second baseman Craig Counsell.

The Indians built their lead to five runs in the next inning, when catcher Sandy Alomar hit a two-run home run. Alomar also made a crucial defensive play while the game was still 1-1. After Moises Alou led off Florida's fourth with a double, Alomar scooped up a nubber by catcher Charles Johnson and cut down Alou trying to go to third base.

The cushion must have seemed downright luxurious to Indians starter Chad Ogea, who hadn't received a single run of support in his previous 19⅓ innings over three postseason appearances. This night, the Indians scored all six before Ogea turned the game over in the seventh inning to Mike Jackson and then closer Jose Mesa. They increased the Cleveland bullpen's shutout streak to six innings in the World Series and 10⅔ overall.

Game 3: Sheffield's masterpiece

As Cleveland slugger Jim Thome settled into the batter's box in the seventh inning, right fielder Gary Sheffield peered into the Marlins' dugout. Bench coach Jerry Manuel was waving frantically, motioning for Sheffield to move back and to his right. Moments later, Thome hit a ball in that direction. Sheffield went back and timed his leap perfectly. He hauled in Thome's drive just below the top of the wall, preserving a 7-7 tie.

It was a key moment in the second-highest-scoring World Series game ever, as the Marlins outlasted the Indians 14-11. Some facts and figures:

▶The 25 runs were topped only by Toronto's 15-14 victory against Philadelphia in 1993's Game 4.

▶The combined 11 runs in the ninth inning tied a record last equaled in Game 2 in 1956, when the Yankees and Dodgers scored that many in the second frame.

▶There were 17 walks, two shy of the single-game Series mark.

▶The game time of 4:12 was just two minutes off the mark for the longest nine-inning game, set in the 15-14 game in 1993.

For all the offensive fortitude and defensive ineptitude, the game might have turned on Sheffield's catch. He certainly showed up with his bat for Game 3, too. Sheffield hit a solo home run into the 25-mph wind in the first inning, drew a bases-loaded walk in the third, doubled home a run in the seventh to knot the game 7-7 and then added a two-run single as the Marlins scored seven in the ninth. His five RBI were one shy of Bobby Richardson's single-game Series record, set in 1960.

The game began with a windchill factor of 29 degrees, and it got down to 23 by the ninth inning. Yet Sheffield, a native of Tampa, persevered. "We felt it at first," he said. "But once the game began, you block it out and concentrate on the job. This is the World Series. I was so pumped, I actually started sweating."

The game didn't start out as a special one for Marlins starter Al Leiter, who tied a World Series record with four walks in the fourth inning. Nor did it have an auspicious start for third baseman Bobby Bonilla, who committed two errors in the first four innings. However, he redeemed himself with a defensive gem to rob Matt Williams in the sixth, throwing him out from the seat of his pants. Then Bonilla scored the go-ahead run in the ninth after scampering from first to third on a single despite his bad hamstring.

Game 3

Florida 14, Cleveland 11

Florida	101	102	207 -	14
Cleveland	200	320	004 -	11

BATTING

FLORIDA	AB	R	H	RBI	BB	SO	LOB	AVG
White cf	5	0	1	0	1	1	2	.214
Renteria ss	4	2	2	1	2	0	3	.333
Sheffield rf	5	2	3	5	1	0	4	.444
Bonilla 3b	5	1	1	2	1	1	3	.250
Daulton 1b	4	3	2	1	2	0	1	.429
Conine 1b	0	0	0	0	0	0	0	.000
Alou lf	5	0	0	0	0	3	4	.250
Eisenreich dh	3	1	2	2	0	0	0	.500
a-Abbott ph-dh	1	0	0	0	0	1	0	.000
b-Floyd ph-dh	0	1	0	0	1	0	0	.000
Johnson c	5	2	3	0	0	0	1	.364
Counsell 2b	5	2	2	1	0	2	3	.273
Totals	**42**	**14**	**16**	**12**	**8**	**8**	**21**	

a-struck out for Eisenreich in the 8th; b-intentionally walked for Abbott in the 9th.
▶BATTING - **2B:** Sheffield (1, Jackson). **HR:** Sheffield (1, 1st inning off Nagy 0 on, 2 out); Daulton (1, 4th inning off Nagy 0 on, 0 out); Eisenreich (1, 6th inning off Nagy 1 on, 2 out). **RBI:** Sheffield 5 (5), Daulton (1), Eisenreich 2 (2), Renteria (2), Counsell (1), Bonilla 2 (2). **2-out RBI:** Sheffield 3, Eisenreich 2, Bonilla 2. **Runners left in scoring position, 2 out:** Alou 1, Sheffield 2. **GIDP:** Bonilla, Sheffield. **LOB:** 9.
▶FIELDING - **E:** Leiter (1, bobble); Bonilla 2 (2, ground ball, throw). **DP:** 1 (Counsell-Renteria-Daulton).

CLEVELAND	AB	R	H	RBI	BB	SO	LOB	AVG
Roberts lf	5	1	1	2	0	1	4	.333
Vizquel ss	4	0	0	1	2	1	2	.167
Ramirez rf	5	0	1	1	0	0	3	.154
Justice dh	3	2	0	0	2	0	3	.300
Williams 3b	5	0	1	1	0	2	3	.286
Alomar c	3	2	2	1	1	0	0	.417
a-Giles ph	0	1	0	0	1	0	0	1.000
Thome 1b	4	3	2	2	1	1	2	.308
Fernandez 2b	4	0	1	1	0	0	2	.500
Grissom cf	3	2	2	1	2	0	1	.700
Totals	**36**	**11**	**10**	**10**	**9**	**5**	**20**	

a-walked for Alomar in the 9th.
▶BATTING - **2B:** Roberts (3, Nen). **HR:** Thome (2, 5th inning off Leiter 1 on, 1 out). **S -** Roberts. **SF -** Fernandez. **RBI:** Williams (1), Alomar (3), Vizquel (1), Ramirez (2), Thome 2 (3), Fernandez (1), Grissom (2), Roberts 2 (4). **2-out RBI:** Williams, Alomar, Vizquel, Ramirez, Grissom, Roberts 2. **Runners left in scoring position, 2 out:** Thome 1, Justice 1, Williams 1, Ramirez 1, Vizquel 1. **GIDP:** Grissom. **LOB:** 9.
▶FIELDING - **E:** Grissom (1, throw); Thome (1, catch); Fernandez (1, ground ball). **DP:** 2 (Thome-Vizquel-Nagy, Vizquel-Fernandez-Thome).

PITCHING

FLORIDA	IP	H	R	ER	BB	SO	BF	ERA
Leiter	4.2	6	7	4	6	3	27	7.71
Heredia	2.1	0	0	0	1	0	8	0.00
Cook (W, 1-0)	1	1	0	0	1	1	4	0.00
Nen	1	3	4	4	2	1	8	18.00

CLEVELAND	IP	H	R	ER	BB	SO	BF	ERA
Nagy	6	6	5	5	4	5	26	7.50
Anderson (H, 1	.1	1	1	1	0	0	2	27.00
Jackson (BS, 1)	.2	2	1	1	1	0	5	4.50
Assenmacher	.2	3	0	0	0	1	5	0.00
Plunk (L, 0-1)	.2	2	4	3	2	1	6	10.12
Morman	.1	0	2	0	1	1	3	0.00
Mesa	.1	2	1	1	0	0	3	6.75

WP: Mesa. **IBB:** Daulton (by Jackson); Floyd (by Plunk).
▶UMPIRES - **HP:** Joe West. **1B:** Greg Kosc. **2B:** Randy Marsh. **3B:** Ken Kaiser. **LF:** Ed Montague. **RF:** Dale Ford.
▶GAME DATA - **T:** 4:12. **Att:** 44,880. **Weather:** 49 degrees, cloudy. **Wind:** 25 mph, left to right.

Game 4

Cleveland 10, Florida 3

Florida	000	102	000	-	3
Cleveland	303	001	12X	-	10

BATTING

CLEVELAND	AB	R	H	RBI	BB	SO	LOB	AVG
Roberts lf	4	0	1	0	0	2	3	.313
Giles lf	1	0	1	1	0	0	0	1.000
Vizquel ss	5	2	2	0	0	0	4	.235
Ramirez rf	4	2	1	2	1	1	1	.176
Justice dh	3	2	1	0	2	2	0	.308
Williams 3b	3	3	3	2	2	0	0	.412
Alomar c	5	0	3	3	0	0	3	.471
Thome 1b	4	0	1	0	1	1	5	.294
Fernandez 2b	5	1	2	1	0	0	1	.455
Grissom cf	4	0	0	0	0	1	3	.500
Totals	**38**	**10**	**15**	**9**	**6**	**7**	**20**	

▶**BATTING - 2B:** Alomar (1, Saunders); Roberts (4, Saunders). **HR:** Ramirez (2, 1st inning off Saunders 1 on, 1 out); Williams (1, 8th inning off Powell 1 on, 1 out). **RBI:** Ramirez 2 (4), Alomar 3 (6), Fernandez (2), Giles (2), Williams 2 (3). **2-out RBI:** Alomar. **Runners left in scoring position, 2 out:** Thome 3, Vizquel 3. **LOB:** 10.
▶**BASERUNNING - SB:** Vizquel (1, 2nd base off Vosberg/Johnson). **CS:** Giles (1, 2nd base by Vosberg).
▶**FIELDING - DP:** 2 (Fernandez-Vizquel-Thome, Thome).

FLORIDA	AB	R	H	RBI	BB	SO	LOB	AVG
White cf	4	0	0	0	0	4	1	.167
Renteria ss	4	0	1	0	0	0	0	.313
Sheffield rf	3	0	0	0	1	2	1	.333
Bonilla 3b	4	0	0	0	0	0	2	.188
Daulton 1b	3	2	2	0	1	0	0	.500
Alou lf	3	1	1	2	1	0	1	.267
Eisenreich dh	2	0	2	1	1	0	0	.667
a-Arias ph-dh	1	0	0	0	0	0	0	.000
Johnson c	4	0	0	0	1	4	0	.267
Counsell 2b	2	0	0	0	1	0	2	.231
b-Abbott ph	1	0	0	0	0	0	0	.000
Totals	**31**	**3**	**6**	**3**	**5**	**7**	**11**	

a-popped to second for Eisenreich in the 9th; b-grounded to pitcher for Counsell in the 9th.
▶**BATTING - 2B:** Daulton (1, Wright). **HR:** Alou (2, 6th inning off Wright 1 on, 1 out). **RBI:** Eisenreich (3), Alou 2 (5). **Runners left in scoring position, 2 out:** Johnson 1, Sheffield 1, Counsell 1. **GIDP:** Bonilla **LOB:** 6.
▶**BASERUNNING - SB:** Counsell (1, 2nd base off Wright/Alomar).
▶**FIELDING - E:** Saunders (1, throw); Renteria (1, throw).

PITCHING

CLEVELAND	IP	H	R	ER	BB	SO	BF	ERA
Wright (W, 1-0)	6	5	3	3	5	5	26	4.50
Anderson (S, 1)	3	1	0	0	0	2	10	2.70

FLORIDA	IP	H	R	ER	BB	SO	BF	ERA
Saunders (L, 0-1)	2	7	6	6	3	2	16	27.00
Alfonseca	3	3	0	0	0	4	12	0.00
Vosberg	2	3	2	2	2	1	10	9.00
Powell	1	2	2	2	1	0	6	16.20

Saunders pitched to 5 batters in the 3rd.
WP: Wright.
▶**UMPIRES - HP:** Greg Kosc. **1B:** Randy Marsh. **2B:** Ken Kaiser. **3B:** Ed Montague. **LF:** Dale Ford. **RF:** Joe West.
▶**GAME DATA - T:** 3:15. **Att:** 44,877. **Weather:** 38 degrees, cloudy. **Wind:** 15 mph, left to right.

Meanwhile, the Marlins' bats looked like frozen fish sticks as they fell behind 7-3. But they pecked away, getting two big runs on Jim Eisenreich's two-run home run in the sixth inning, then tying it in the seventh. "That was the biggest hit of the night," Sheffield said of Eisenreich's homer. "It was a real pickup for us."

Game 4: Indians blew off cold

When the Indians' Jaret Wright played linebacker at Katella High School in Anaheim, he had no concept of what Cleveland "football weather" meant. The chilly winds and lake-effect snow squalls in Game 4 were reminiscent of times when Jim Brown won NFL championships, but the 21-year-old Wright fit in fine. "He pitches like a linebacker," said teammate Brian Anderson of Wright, whom Anderson relieved for the final three innings of the Indians' 10-3 Series-tying victory.

Who could tell that the World Series–record 38-degree game-time temperature and 18-degree wind-chill had an effect? Wright held the Marlins to five hits and three runs in six innings. "There's heaters in the dugout and stuff," Wright said. "We can warm up like that. But it was tough to get a grip on the ball." Marlins starter Tony Saunders, also a rookie, couldn't get a grip on the game, leaving after retiring none of the five batters he faced in the third inning, when Cleveland scored three to go up 6-0.

Florida battled back to 6-3 by the sixth inning, but only one call to the Indians bullpen was needed: the one to Anderson. Anderson recalled a day in Buffalo this summer, shortly after Wright had rolled in from AA Akron. "I told Jaret to focus in," Anderson said. "I said, 'With the stuff you have, you'll find yourself in Cleveland this year.' "

The only disappointment in the Indians' Game 4 performance was Marquis Grissom's 0-for-4 night. That ended Grissom's World Series hitting streak at 15 games, second longest ever, to Yankee Hank Bauer's 17 straight in 1956-58. Grissom did hit the ball hard twice, but Devon White caught both in the deepest part of the ballpark.

Game 5: Hernandez hung on

The Marlins capitalized on Orel Hershiser's uncharacteristic October slump and came from behind to win 8-7 and take a 3-2 Series lead. Game 5 was a Series microcosm. Florida's Moises Alou and Cleveland's Sandy Alomar launched key home runs. Livan Hernandez pitched with grit. Both teams' bullpens were shaky. And there was controversial umpiring.

Alou and Hernandez made early bids for MVP honors. Alou, playing with an injured wrist, hit his third

Chad Ogea won Games 2 and 6 over Marlins ace Kevin Brown.

home run of the Series. The three-run shot gave the Marlins a 5-4 lead in the sixth inning. In this game, Hernandez did not have Eric Gregg's massive strike zone for assistance. Home plate umpire Randy Marsh's more reasonable zone seemed stingy, and Hernandez allowed six walks and five hits in the first three innings.

Hernandez was angry when he came off the field after the third inning. Marlins manager Jim Leyland grew concerned that his pitcher would break. "I had [pitching coach Larry] Rothschild and every Spanish-speaking guy I had on the team talk to him when he came into the dugout," Leyland said. "They told him, 'Don't lose your cool, settle down.'"

Hernandez did calm down after the third, allowing only a single and a walk in the next four innings. He left in the ninth after throwing 142 pitches and walking eight, the most in a World Series game in 26 years. Leyland stuck with Hernandez as long as possible before turning to shaky closer Robb Nen. The Marlins held an 8-4 advantage entering the bottom of the ninth, when Bip Roberts led off with a grounder to Jeff Conine. Conine flipped the ball to Hernandez, who appeared to graze first base with his right foot. But umpire Ken Kaiser ruled Roberts safe. After Omar Vizquel singled, Leyland brought in Nen, who struck out Manny Ramirez before allowing David Justice's two-run single. Jim Thome later drove in Matt Williams before Nen finally escaped with his second save.

Game 6: Ogea's dangerous bat

By defeating Kevin Brown 4-1 in Game 6, the Indians improved their postseason record to 7-1 when they faced

Game 5

Florida 8, Cleveland 7

Florida	020 004 011	-	8
Cleveland	013 000 003	-	7

BATTING

FLORIDA	AB	R	H	RBI	BB	SO	LOB	AVG
White cf	4	0	2	2	1	0	0	.227
Renteria ss	5	0	1	0	0	2	5	.286
Sheffield rf	5	1	2	0	0	0	0	.353
Bonilla 3b	4	1	1	0	1	0	1	.200
Arias pr-3b	0	1	0	0	0	0	0	.000
Daulton dh	5	1	2	0	0	0	2	.467
Alou lf	5	2	3	4	0	1	1	.350
Conine 1b	5	1	1	0	0	0	2	.300
Johnson c	5	1	3	2	0	2	2	.350
Counsell 2b	2	0	0	0	2	1	1	.200
Totals	**40**	**8**	**15**	**8**	**4**	**6**	**14**	

▶**BATTING - 2B:** Daulton (2, Hershiser); White 2 (3, Hershiser, Assenmacher); Bonilla (1, Mesa). **HR:** Alou (1, 6th inning off Hershiser 2 on, 2 out). **RBI:** Johnson 2 (3), White 2 (2), Alou 4 (9). **2-out RBI:** Johnson, White 2, Alou 3. **Runners left in scoring position, 2 out:** Renteria 4, Johnson 1. **GIDP:** Bonilla. **LOB:** 9.
▶**BASERUNNING - SB:** Alou (1, 2nd base off Juden/Alomar); Daulton (1, 3rd base off Mesa/Alomar).
▶**FIELDING - E:** Hernandez (1, catch); Counsell (1, throw). **DP:** 2 (Renteria-Counsell-Conine, Hernandez-Renteria-Conine).

CLEVELAND	AB	R	H	RBI	BB	SO	LOB	AVG
Roberts 2b	3	1	0	0	2	0	2	.263
Vizquel ss	4	1	1	0	0	0	3	.238
Ramirez rf	5	0	1	0	0	1	3	.182
Justice dh	5	0	1	2	0	1	2	.278
Williams 3b	3	2	1	0	2	0	1	.400
Thome 1b	4	2	1	1	1	0	2	.333
Alomar c	5	1	2	4	0	0	3	.455
Giles lf	1	0	0	0	3	1	0	.667
Grissom cf	4	0	1	0	0	0	2	.444
Totals	34	7	9	7	8	3	18	

▶**BATTING - 3B:** Thome (1, Hernandez). **HR:** Alomar (2, 3rd inning off Hernandez 2 on, 2 out). **S:** Vizquel. **RBI:** Alomar 4 (10), Justice 2 (4), Thome (4). **2-out RBI:** Alomar 3, Thome. **Runners left in scoring position, 2 out:** Justice 1, Vizquel 2, Roberts 1, Grissom 1. **GIDP:** Alomar, Justice. **LOB:** 9.
▶**FIELDING - Outfield assists:** Ramirez (Counsell at home). **DP:** 1 (Roberts-Vizquel-Thome).

PITCHING

FLORIDA	IP	H	R	ER	BB	SO	BF	ERA
Hernandez (W, 2-0)	8	7	6	5	8	2	38	5.27
Nen (S, 2)	1	2	1	0	0	1	5	12.00

CLEVELAND	IP	H	R	ER	BB	SO	BF	ERA
Hershiser (L, 0-2)	5.2	9	6	6	2	3	26	11.70
Morman	0	0	0	0	1	0	1	0.00
Plunk	.1	0	0	0	1	1	2	9.00
Juden	1.1	2	1	1	0	0	6	4.50
Assenmacher	.2	1	0	0	0	1	3	0.00
Mesa	1	3	1	1	0	1	6	7.71

Morman pitched to 1 batter in the 6th; Hernandez pitched to 2 batters in the 9th.
WP: Hernandez.
▶**UMPIRES: H:** Randy Marsh. **1B:** Ken Kaiser. **2B:** Ed Montague. **3B:** Dale Ford. **LF:** Joe West. **RF:** Greg Kosc.
▶**GAME DATA - T:** 3:39. **Att:** 44,888. **Weather:** 46 degrees, cloudy. **Wind:** 12 mph, left to right.

Game 6

Cleveland 4, Florida 1

```
Cleveland    021 010 000 - 4
Florida      000 010 000 - 1
```

BATTING

CLEVELAND	AB	R	H	RBI	BB	SO	LOB	AVG
Roberts 2b	3	0	1	0	0	1	2	.273
Fernandez 2b	1	0	1	0	0	0	0	.500
Vizquel ss	4	1	1	0	0	3		.240
Ramirez rf	1	0	0	2	1	0	2	.174
Justice lf	4	0	0	0	0	1	2	.227
Williams 3b	4	1	2	0	0	1	0	.417
Thome 1b	3	1	0	0	1	2	1	.292
Alomar c	3	0	0	0	1	0	0	.400
Grissom cf	3	0	0	0	1	1	1	.381
Ogea p	2	1	2	2	0	0	0	.500
Jackson p	1	0	0	0	0	1	0	.000
Assenmacher p	0	0	0	0	0	0	0	.000
a-Seitzer ph	1	0	0	0	0	0	2	.000
Mesa p	0	0	0	0	0	0	0	.000
Totals	**30**	**4**	**7**	**4**	**4**	**8**	**15**	

a-grounded to third for Assenmacher in the 9th.

►**BATTING - 2B:** Vizquel (2, Brown); Ogea (1, Brown); Williams (1, Powell). **SF:** Ramirez 2. **RBI:** Ogea 2 (2), Ramirez 2 (6). **Runners left in scoring position, 2 out:** Justice 1, Seitzer 1. **GIDP:** Roberts. **LOB:** 5.
►**BASERUNNING - SB:** Vizquel 2 (3, 3rd base off Brown/Johnson, 2nd base off Powell/Johnson). **CS:** Roberts (1, 2nd base by Brown).

FLORIDA	AB	R	H	RBI	BB	SO	LOB	AVG
White cf	5	0	3	0	0	1	2	.296
Renteria ss	5	0	0	0	0	2	6	.231
Sheffield rf	3	0	0	0	2	0	1	.300
Bonilla 3b	4	0	0	0	0	0	4	.167
Conine 1b	2	0	0	0	0	0	0	.250
b-Eisenreich ph-1b	1	0	0	0	1	1	0	.571
Alou lf	3	1	1	0	1	0	0	.348
Johnson c	4	0	2	0	0	0	3	.375
Counsell 2b	4	0	1	0	0	1	3	.211
Brown p	1	0	0	0	0	0	0	.000
a-Daulton ph	0	0	0	1	0	0	1	.467
Heredia p	0	0	0	0	0	0	0	.000
c-Cangelosi ph	1	0	1	0	0	0	0	.500
Powell p	0	0	0	0	0	0	0	.000
Vosberg p	0	0	0	0	0	0	0	.000
d-Floyd ph	1	0	0	0	0	0	0	.000
Totals	**34**	**1**	**8**	**1**	**4**	**5**	**20**	

a-hit sacrifice fly to right for Brown in the 5th; b-walked for Conine in the 6th; c-singled for Heredia in the 7th; d-grounded to second for Vosberg in the 9th.

►**BATTING - 3B:** White (1, Mesa). **SF:** Daulton. **RBI:** Daulton (2). **Runners left in scoring position, 2 out:** Renteria 2, Johnson 2, Bonilla 2, Sheffield 1. **LOB:** 11.
►**BASERUNNING - SB:** White (1, 2nd base off Ogea/Alomar).
►**FIELDING - DP:** 1 (Counsell-Renteria-Conine).

PITCHING

CLEVELAND	IP	H	R	ER	BB	SO	BF	ERA
Ogea (W, 2-0)	5	4	1	1	2	1	21	1.54
Jackson (H, 1)	2	2	0	0	2	2	10	2.25
Assenmacher (H, 1)	1	1	0	0	0	1	4	0.00
Mesa (S, 1)	1	1	0	0	0	1	4	5.40

FLORIDA	IP	H	R	ER	BB	SO	BF	ERA
Brown (L, 0-2)	5	5	4	4	3	2	21	8.18
Heredia	2	0	0	0	0	4	6	0.00
Powell	1	2	0	0	0	1	5	0.12
Vosberg	1	0	0	0	1	1	4	6.00

Ogea pitched to 1 batter in the 6th; Powell pitched to 1 batter in the 9th.

IBB: Alomar (by Vosberg).
►**UMPIRES - HP:** Ken Kaiser. **1B:** Ed Montague. **2B:** Dale Ford. **3B:** Joe West. **LF:** Greg Kosc. **RF:** Randy Marsh.
►**GAME DATA - T:** 3:15. **Att:** 67,498. **Weather:** 81 degrees, partly cloudy. **Wind:** 15 mph, out to left center.

a starting pitcher who was in his league's top 10 in ERA this season. Cleveland matched baseball's stars pitch for pitch, even with an unknown like Chad Ogea. But until the World Series, Ogea hadn't gotten to show his batting prowess. As good fortune and the rotation would have it, Ogea's two Series starts were in Florida, under NL rules. The Indians right-hander borrowed Orel Hershiser's bat and got a double, a single and two RBI to stun Brown and set up the first World Series Game 7 since 1991.

Ogea's hitting probably was the least expected of the string of unlikely hits, plays and heroes that peppered the Indians' road through the playoffs. Pardon us, Chad, if everyone just reacts with speechlessness. When was your last hit? "That would have been 1988," he said of his high school days in St. Louis, La., when he also played shortstop. "I know the hitters laughed at me," Ogea said of his first experience against Brown, in Game 2. "I came back [to the dugout] and said I can see the ball good off this guy," said Ogea, explaining what so amused his teammates.

Hershiser had details about Ogea's weapon. "It's a 33-inch, 31-ounce Louisville Slugger, flame-treated," he said. "If you'd like to interview it, I could teach it to speak." It already had told the tale of this game. In the second inning of a scoreless Game 6, Ogea lined a single over first baseman Jeff Conine to drive in two runs. Up 3-0 in the fifth, Ogea led off with a double between Conine and the bag. He eventually moved to third on a single by Roberts and scored on Manny Ramirez's sacrifice fly.

However, Ogea's offensive exploits tired him out. He finally allowed a run in the bottom of the fifth, and after walking Gary Sheffield to lead off the sixth, he turned the game over to Mike Jackson—and Omar Vizquel. Jackson walked another batter, and the Marlins had runners on second and third with two outs. Charles Johnson slapped a ball into the hole between shortstop and third base. Vizquel dove headlong and horizontally to stop the ball, saving one run. "I knew if I dove, I had a good chance to catch it," Vizquel said. "I didn't know if I could throw him out."

He could, and saved another run. While Vizquel threw out Johnson, just as amazing was that Johnson couldn't throw out Vizquel. The Indians' stolen base leader swiped two against the feared arm. Cleveland had run on him only twice in the previous five games, stealing once, but Vizquel raced to third base after doubling to lead off the third inning, stealing as much on the jump he got against Brown as on Johnson's arm. When Ramirez lifted a fly ball to center, Vizquel was able to score.

One other fly ball to center ended the Marlins' last serious threat. Bobby Bonilla harmlessly skied that one against Jackson with two outs and the bases loaded in the seventh.

Omar Vizquel was too stunned to move after Cleveland's narrow loss.

Game 7: Florida's dramatic 11th

The Marlins won a World Series title in just their fifth season by defeating Cleveland 3-2 in an extra-inning Game 7. The win sent South Florida into a sweaty, pulsing frenzy. The Marlins committed $89 million to free agents during the 1996-97 offseason, but this game belonged to the lesser wage earners. Edgar Renteria got the game-winning single in the 11th, scoring rookie second baseman Craig Counsell, who made the major league minimum $150,000 and toiled half the season in the Rockies' farm system. As Counsell leaped into the waiting arms of his teammates at home plate, a teary-eyed Jim Leyland sprinted onto the field, saluting and shouting to the crowd of 67,204, and taking a victory lap around Pro Player Stadium. The manager was quickly joined by Bobby Bonilla, who had shared in Leyland's heartbreaking playoff losses with the Pittsburgh Pirates in the early '90s.

Leyland had never played in the majors and spent 11 seasons managing in the minors before joining the White Sox as a member of Tony La Russa's coaching staff in 1982. He dedicated the title to "guys like me who weren't very good players; guys who think they aren't going anywhere and think they have no chance to get to the major leagues. I finally arrived at the pinnacle of this sport tonight, so there's hope for all those guys out there."

While only two members of the Marlins—Bonilla and reserve outfielder John Cangelosi—had played for Leyland before this season, he commanded respect instantly in the clubhouse with his no-nonsense style and self-effacing manner. "He absolutely willed this team to win," said third base coach Rich Donnelly, a Leyland staff member for 12 seasons.

Game 7

Florida 3, Cleveland 2

Cleveland	002	000	000	00 - 2
Florida	000	000	101	01 - 3

BATTING

CLEVELAND	AB	R	H	RBI	BB	SO	LOB	AVG
Vizquel ss	5	0	1	0	0	2	2	.233
Fernandez 2b	5	0	2	2	0	1	1	.471
Ramirez rf	3	0	0	0	2	2	1	.154
Justice lf	5	0	0	0	0	3	5	.185
Williams 3b	2	0	0	0	3	2	0	.385
Alomar c	5	0	1	0	0	0	3	.367
Thome 1b	4	1	1	0	1	0	3	.286
Grissom cf	4	1	1	0	0	1	2	.360
Wright p	2	0	0	0	0	2	0	.000
Assenmacher p	0	0	0	0	0	0	0	.000
Jackson p	0	0	0	0	0	0	0	.000
Anderson p	0	0	0	0	0	0	0	.000
a-Giles ph	1	0	0	0	0	0	2	.500
Mesa p	0	0	0	0	0	0	0	.000
Nagy p	0	0	0	0	0	0	0	.000
Totals	36	2	6	2	6	13	19	

a-flied to left for Anderson in the 9th.

▶BATTING - S: Wright. RBI: Fernandez 2 (4). **2-out RBI:** Fernandez 2. **Runners left in scoring position, 2 out:** Justice 2, Giles 1. **GIDP:** Thome 2. **LOB:** 8.
▶BASERUNNING - SB: Vizquel 2 (5, 2nd base off Leiter/Johnson, 3rd base off Leiter/Johnson).
▶FIELDING - E: Ramirez (1, fly ball); Fernandez (2, ground ball). DP: 1 (Fernandez-Vizquel-Thome). Two out when winning run scored.

FLORIDA	AB	R	H	RBI	BB	SO	LOB	AVG
White cf	6	0	0	0	0	2	6	.242
Renteria ss	5	0	3	1	1	0	0	.290
Sheffield rf	4	0	1	0	1	2	2	.292
Daulton 1b	3	0	0	0	0	0	2	.389
c-Conine ph-1b	1	0	0	0	0	0	0	.231
Nen p	0	0	0	0	0	0	0	.000
d-Cangelosi ph	1	0	0	0	0	1	2	.333
Powell p	0	0	0	0	0	0	0	.000
Alou lf	5	1	1	0	0	1	3	.321
Bonilla 3b	5	1	2	1	0	2	1	.207
Johnson c	4	0	1	0	0	2	0	.357
Zaun pr-c	1	0	0	0	0	0	1	.000
Counsell 2b	3	1	0	1	1	1	2	.182
Leiter p	2	0	0	0	0	2	0	.000
Cook p	0	0	0	0	0	0	0	.000
a-Floyd ph	0	0	0	0	0	0	0	.000
b-Abbott ph	1	0	0	0	0	0	1	.000
Alfonseca p	0	0	0	0	0	0	0	.000
Heredia p	0	0	0	0	0	0	0	.000
Eisenreich 1b	1	0	0	0	1	0	1	.500
Totals	40	3	8	3	6	11	21	

a-announced for Cook in the 7th; b-flied to right for Floyd in the 7th; c-fouled to left for Daulton in the 8th; d-struck out for Nen in the 10th.
▶BATTING - 2B: Renteria (2, Wright). HR: Bonilla (1, 7th inning off Wright 0 on, 0 out). SF: Counsell. RBI: Bonilla (3), Counsell (2), Renteria (3). **2-out RBI:** Renteria. **Runners left in scoring position, 2 out:** Sheffield 1, Alou 2. **GIDP:** Daulton. **LOB:** 12.
▶FIELDING - DP: 2 (Daulton-Renteria-Daulton, Counsell-Renteria-Eisenreich).

PITCHING

CLEVELAND	IP	H	R	ER	BB	SO	BF	ERA
Wright	6.1	2	1	1	5	7	26	2.92
Assenmacher (H, 2)	.2	0	0	0	0	1	2	0.00
Jackson (H, 2)	.2	0	0	0	0	1	1	1.93
Anderson (H, 2)	.1	0	0	0	0	0	1	2.45
Mesa (BS, 1)	1.2	4	1	1	0	2	9	5.40
Nagy (L, 0-1)	1	2	1	0	1	0	7	6.43

FLORIDA	IP	H	R	ER	BB	SO	BF	ERA
Leiter	6	4	2	2	4	7	25	5.06
Cook	1	0	0	0	2	3	0.00	
Alfonseca	1.1	0	0	0	1	1	5	0.00
Heredia	0	1	0	0	0	0	1	0.00
Nen	1.2	1	0	0	0	3	6	7.71
Powell (W, 1-0)	1	0	0	0	0	3	7.36	

Heredia pitched to 1 batter in the 9th.
IBB: Ramirez (by Leiter); Eisenreich (by Nagy).
▶UMPIRES - HP: Ed Montague. **1B:** Dale Ford. **2B:** Joe West. **3B:** Greg Kosc. **LF:** Randy Marsh. **RF:** Ken Kaiser.
▶GAME DATA - T: 4:10. **Att:** 67,204. **Weather:** 80 degrees, clear. **Wind:** 8 mph, out to left center.

Among the few pitchers not to appear in the finale was Livan Hernandez, the winner of Games 1 and 5, who was named the Series MVP. His mother, Miriam Carreras, secured an 11th-hour visa from Cuban officials and arrived before Game 7. The two had an emotional meeting amid the pregame hoopla. "I am very happy to be here with my son and to see this last game," Carreras said in a statement.

The Marlins were two outs away from defeat before tying the game 2-2 off Jose Mesa on a Counsell sacrifice fly in the bottom of the ninth. In the memorable 11th, Bonilla led off with a single to center field. After Gregg Zaun popped out to pitcher Charles Nagy on a botched bunt attempt, Counsell reached first when Indians second baseman Tony Fernandez failed to come up with a routine ground ball. Jim Eisenreich was walked intentionally to load the bases, and the Indians got a second out when Devon White's ground ball forced Bonilla at home. That brought up Renteria, the 22-year old native of Barranquilla, Colombia, who had emerged in the playoffs as a late-inning offensive threat. This time, he smacked the ball cleanly to center, setting off the Marlins' celebration of what was certainly that group's last hurrah.

—by Paul White, Bill Koenig and Pete Williams

World Series: Composite player statistics

Florida 4, Cleveland 3

CLEVELAND INDIANS

Batting	G	AB	R	H	2B	3B	HR	RBI	SO	BB	AVG
Ogea p	2	4	1	2	1	0	0	2	0	1	.500
Giles ph-lf	5	4	1	2	1	0	0	2	4	1	.500
TFernandez 2b	5	17	1	8	1	0	0	4	0	1	.471
Williams 3b	7	26	8	10	1	0	1	3	7	6	.385
Alomar c	7	30	5	11	1	0	2	10	2	3	.367
Grissom cf	7	25	5	9	1	0	0	2	4	4	.360
Thome 1b	7	28	8	8	0	1	2	4	5	7	.286
Roberts 2b-lf	6	22	3	6	4	0	0	4	3	5	.273
Vizquel ss	7	30	5	7	2	0	0	1	3	5	.233
Justice lf-dh	7	27	4	5	0	0	0	4	6	8	.185
Ramirez rf	7	26	3	4	0	0	2	6	6	5	.154
Branson ph	1	1	0	0	0	0	0	0	0	1	.000
Seitzer ph	1	1	0	0	0	0	0	0	0	0	.000
Hershiser p	1	2	0	0	0	0	0	0	0	1	.000
Wright p	2	2	0	0	0	0	0	0	0	2	.000
Jackson p	3	2	0	0	0	0	0	0	0	1	.000
Assenmacher p	3	0	0	0	0	0	0	0	0	0	—
Nagy p	2	0	0	0	0	0	0	0	0	0	—
Juden p	1	0	0	0	0	0	0	0	0	0	—
Mesa p	2	0	0	0	0	0	0	0	0	0	—
Anderson p	3	0	0	0	0	0	0	0	0	0	—
Plunk p	1	0	0	0	0	0	0	0	0	0	—
Totals	7	247	44	72	12	1	7	42	40	51	.291

Pitching	G	CG	IP	H	R	BB	SO	W	L	SV	ER	ERA
Assenmacher	5	0	4	5	0	0	6	0	0	0	0	0.00
Morman	2	0	.1	0	2	2	1	0	0	0	0	0.00
Ogea	2	0	11.2	11	2	3	5	2	0	0	2	1.54
Jackson	4	0	4.2	5	1	3	4	0	0	1	1	1.93
Anderson	3	0	3.2	2	1	0	2	0	0	1	1	2.45
Wright	2	0	12.1	7	4	10	12	1	0	0	4	2.92
Juden	2	0	2	2	1	2	0	0	0	0	1	4.50
Mesa	5	0	5	10	3	1	5	0	0	1	3	5.40
Nagy	2	0	7	8	6	5	5	0	1	0	5	6.43
Plunk	3	0	3	3	4	4	3	0	1	0	3	9.00
Hershiser	2	0	10	15	13	6	5	0	2	0	13	11.70
Totals	7	0	63.2	68	37	36	48	3	4	2	33	4.66

FLORIDA MARLINS

Batting	G	AB	R	H	2B	3B	HR	RBI	SO	BB	AVG
Eisenreich dh-1b	5	8	1	4	0	0	1	3	3	1	.500
Daulton 1b-dh	7	18	7	7	2	0	1	2	3	0	.389
Johnson c	7	28	4	10	0	0	1	3	1	6	.357
Cangelosi ph	3	3	0	1	0	0	0	0	0	2	.333
Alou lf	7	28	6	9	2	0	3	9	3	6	.321
Sheffield rf	7	24	4	7	1	0	1	5	8	5	.292
Renteria ss	7	31	3	9	2	0	0	3	3	5	.290
White cf	7	33	0	8	3	1	0	2	3	10	.242
Conine 1b	6	13	1	3	0	0	0	2	0	0	.231
Bonilla 3b	7	29	5	6	1	0	1	3	3	5	.207
Counsell 2b	7	22	4	4	1	0	0	2	6	5	.182
Arias ph-pr-3b	2	1	1	0	0	0	0	0	0	0	.000
Hernandez p	1	2	0	0	0	0	0	0	0	0	.000
Zaun ph	2	2	0	0	0	0	0	0	0	0	.000
Floyd dh-ph	4	2	1	0	0	0	0	0	1	1	.000
Abbott dh	3	3	0	0	0	0	0	0	0	1	.000
Brown p	2	3	0	0	0	0	0	0	0	1	.000
Cook p	2	0	0	0	0	0	0	0	0	0	—
Alfonseca p	2	0	0	0	0	0	0	0	0	0	—
Heredia p	3	0	0	0	0	0	0	0	0	0	—
Nen p	2	0	0	0	0	0	0	0	0	0	—
Leiter p	2	0	0	0	0	0	0	0	2	0	—
Saunders p	1	0	0	0	0	0	0	0	0	0	—
Powell p	3	0	0	0	0	0	0	0	0	0	—
Vosberg p	1	0	0	0	0	0	0	0	0	0	—
Totals	7	250	37	68	12	1	8	34	36	48	.272

Pitching	G	CG	IP	H	R	BB	SO	W	L	SV	ER	ERA
Alfonseca	3	0	6.1	6	0	1	5	0	0	0	0	0.00
Heredia	4	0	5.1	2	0	1	5	0	0	0	0	0.00
Cook	3	0	3.2	1	0	1	5	1	0	0	0	0.00
Leiter	2	0	10.2	10	9	10	10	0	0	0	6	5.06
Hernandez	2	0	13.2	15	9	10	7	2	0	0	8	5.27
Vosberg	2	0	3	3	2	3	2	0	0	0	2	6.00
Powell	4	0	3.2	5	3	4	2	1	0	0	3	7.36
Nen	4	0	4.2	8	5	2	7	0	0	2	4	7.71
Brown	2	0	11	15	10	5	6	0	2	0	10	8.18
Saunders	1	0	2	7	6	3	2	0	1	0	6	27.00
Totals	7	0	64	72	44	40	51	4	3	2	39	5.48

SCORE BY INNINGS

Cleveland	739	374	137	00	-	44
Florida	222	638	319	01	-	37

E: Bonilla (2), Sheffield, Leiter, Thome, TFernandez (2), Grissom, Renteria, Saunders, Counsell, Hernandez, Ramirez. **DP:** Cleveland 8, Florida 9. **LOB:** Cleveland 59, Florida 62. **SB:** Counsell, Vizquel (5), Daulton, Alou, DWhite. **CS:** Justice, Giles, Roberts. **S:** Vizquel (2), Hernandez, Ogea, Roberts, Wright. **SF:** TFernandez, Ramirez (2), Daulton, Counsell. **GIDP:** Bonilla 3, Alomar 2, Ramirez 2, Thome 2, Sheffield 2, Grissom, Justice, Roberts, Conine, Daulton. **IBB:** off Plunk (Floyd), off Jackson (Daulton), off Vosberg (Alomar), off Nagy (Eisenreich), off Leiter (Ramirez). **HBP:** Sheffield (by Ogea). **WP:** Juden, Mesa, Wright, Hernandez. **Umpires:** Ed Montague, Dale Ford, Joe West, Greg Kosc, Randy Marsh, Ken Kaiser.

For the record

▶Active-player career records
▶All-time single-season and club records

▶Career records
▶Top fielding marks
▶All no-hitters

Record qualifications

All-time records:
1000 games played minimum for BA, OBA and SA.
1500 innings pitched minimum for ERA.
100 wins minimum for winning percentage.

Active-player records:
One-half of above all-time minimum requirements.

Club records:
Same as active-player records, except pitchers winning percentage (40 wins minimum).

Season records:
3.1 plate appearances per game played by team for BA, OBA and SA.
1 inning pitched per game played by team for ERA.
15 victories for winning percentage.

Active-player records

Players listed through 1997 season.

Hitters

Games played: Most, career

3026	Eddie Murray, 1977-1997
2557	Paul Molitor, 1978-1997
2543	Cal Ripken, 1981-1997
2463	Harold Baines, 1980-1997
2460	Rickey Henderson, 1979-1997
2261	Gary Gaetti, 1981-1997
2255	Chili Davis, 1981-1997
2227	Wade Boggs, 1982-1997
2213	Brett Butler, 1981-1997
2186	Tim Raines, 1979-1997

At-bats: Most, career

11336	Eddie Murray, 1977-1997
10333	Paul Molitor, 1978-1997
9832	Cal Ripken, 1981-1997
8931	Rickey Henderson, 1979-1997
8818	Harold Baines, 1980-1997
8453	Wade Boggs, 1982-1997
8385	Ryne Sandberg, 1981-1997
8238	Tim Raines, 1979-1997
8227	Gary Gaetti, 1981-1997
8187	Tony Gwynn, 1982-1997

Runs: Most, career

1913	Rickey Henderson, 1979-1997
1707	Paul Molitor, 1978-1997
1627	Eddie Murray, 1977-1997
1475	Tim Raines, 1979-1997
1445	Cal Ripken, 1981-1997
1422	Wade Boggs, 1982-1997
1359	Brett Butler, 1981-1997
1318	Ryne Sandberg, 1981-1997
1244	Barry Bonds, 1986-1997
1237	Tony Gwynn, 1982-1997

Hits: Most, career

3255	Eddie Murray, 1977-1997
3178	Paul Molitor, 1978-1997
2800	Wade Boggs, 1982-1997
2780	Tony Gwynn, 1982-1997
2715	Cal Ripken, 1981-1997
2561	Harold Baines, 1980-1997
2550	Rickey Henderson, 1979-1997
2439	Tim Raines, 1979-1997
2386	Ryne Sandberg, 1981-1997
2375	Brett Butler, 1981-1997

Total bases: Most, career

5397	Eddie Murray, 1977-1997
4662	Paul Molitor, 1978-1997
4428	Cal Ripken, 1981-1997
4113	Harold Baines, 1980-1997
3850	Rickey Henderson, 1979-1997
3787	Ryne Sandberg, 1981-1997
3780	Wade Boggs, 1982-1997
3731	Joe Carter, 1983-1997
3729	Tony Gwynn, 1982-1997
3656	Chili Davis, 1981-1997

2B: Most, career

576	Paul Molitor, 1978-1997
560	Eddie Murray, 1977-1997
541	Wade Boggs, 1982-1997
517	Cal Ripken, 1981-1997
460	Tony Gwynn, 1982-1997
439	Harold Baines, 1980-1997
426	Rickey Henderson, 1979-1997
410	Joe Carter, 1983-1997
403	Ryne Sandberg, 1981-1997
401	Tim Raines, 1979-1997

3B: Most, career

131	Brett Butler, 1981-1997
111	Tim Raines, 1979-1997
109	Paul Molitor, 1978-1997
107	Lance Johnson, 1987-1997
102	Juan Samuel, 1983-1997
93	Willie McGee, 1982-1997
90	Tony Fernandez, 1983-1997
89	Vince Coleman, 1985-1997
84	Tony Gwynn, 1982-1997
76	Ryne Sandberg, 1981-1997

HR: Most, career

504	Eddie Murray, 1977-1997
387	Mark McGwire, 1986-1997
378	Joe Carter, 1983-1997
374	Barry Bonds, 1986-1997
370	Cal Ripken, 1981-1997
351	Jose Canseco, 1985-1997
339	Harold Baines, 1980-1997
339	Fred McGriff, 1986-1997
332	Gary Gaetti, 1981-1997
328	Chili Davis, 1981-1997

RBI: Most, career

1917	Eddie Murray, 1977-1997
1453	Cal Ripken, 1981-1997
1423	Harold Baines, 1980-1997
1382	Joe Carter, 1983-1997
1285	Chili Davis, 1981-1997
1238	Paul Molitor, 1978-1997
1224	Gary Gaetti, 1981-1997
1107	Jose Canseco, 1985-1997
1094	Barry Bonds, 1986-1997
1061	Bobby Bonilla, 1986-1997
1061	Ryne Sandberg, 1981-1997

SB: Most, career

1231	Rickey Henderson, 1979-1997
795	Tim Raines, 1979-1997
752	Vince Coleman, 1985-1997
558	Brett Butler, 1981-1997
557	Otis Nixon, 1983-1997
495	Paul Molitor, 1978-1997
417	Barry Bonds, 1986-1997
383	Juan Samuel, 1983-1997
356	Delino DeShields, 1990-1997
354	Kenny Lofton, 1991-1997

BB: Most, career

1772	Rickey Henderson, 1979-1997
1333	Eddie Murray, 1977-1997
1328	Wade Boggs, 1982-1997
1227	Barry Bonds, 1986-1997
1209	Tim Raines, 1979-1997
1201	Tony Phillips, 1982-1997
1129	Brett Butler, 1981-1997
1107	Chili Davis, 1981-1997
1049	Paul Molitor, 1978-1997
1016	Cal Ripken, 1981-1997

HBP: Most, career

119	Craig Biggio, 1988-1997
112	Andres Galarraga, 1985-1997
97	Brady Anderson, 1988-1997
92	Mike Macfarlane, 1987-1997
88	Joe Carter, 1983-1997
84	Gary Gaetti, 1981-1997
79	Rickey Henderson, 1979-1997
75	Jeff Blauser, 1987-1997
74	Chuck Knoblauch, 1991-1997
73	Juan Samuel, 1983-1997

GIDP: Most, career

315	Eddie Murray, 1977-1997
302	Cal Ripken, 1981-1997
257	Harold Baines, 1980-1997
255	Julio Franco, 1982-1997
234	Tony Pena, 1980-1997
225	Tony Gwynn, 1982-1997
219	Gary Gaetti, 1981-1997
214	Chili Davis, 1981-1997
209	Wade Boggs, 1982-1997
190	Paul Molitor, 1978-1997

BA: Highest, career

.340	Tony Gwynn, 1982-1997
.334	Mike Piazza, 1992-1997
.331	Wade Boggs, 1982-1997
.330	Frank Thomas, 1990-1997
.317	Edgar Martinez, 1987-1997
.316	Kenny Lofton, 1991-1997
.312	Rusty Greer, 1994-1997
.310	Mark Grace, 1988-1997
.308	Paul Molitor, 1978-1997
.305	Hal Morris, 1988-1997

On-base avg: Highest, career

.452	Frank Thomas, 1990-1997
.423	Edgar Martinez, 1987-1997
.420	Wade Boggs, 1982-1997
.409	Jeff Bagwell, 1991-1997
.408	Jim Thome, 1991-1997
.408	Barry Bonds, 1986-1997
.406	Rickey Henderson, 1979-1997
.398	Mike Piazza, 1992-1997
.396	John Olerud, 1989-1997
.393	Manny Ramirez, 1993-1997

Slug avg: Highest, career

.600	Frank Thomas, 1990-1997
.576	Mike Piazza, 1992-1997
.566	Albert Belle, 1989-1997

.562	Ken Griffey, 1989-1997
.557	Juan Gonzalez, 1989-1997
.556	Mark McGwire, 1986-1997
.551	Barry Bonds, 1986-1997
.546	Manny Ramirez, 1993-1997
.542	Larry Walker, 1989-1997
.541	Jim Thome, 1991-1997

Extra-base hits: Most, career

1099	Eddie Murray, 1977-1997
930	Cal Ripken, 1981-1997
915	Paul Molitor, 1978-1997
840	Joe Carter, 1983-1997
826	Harold Baines, 1980-1997
789	Barry Bonds, 1986-1997
769	Gary Gaetti, 1981-1997
761	Ryne Sandberg, 1981-1997
749	Chili Davis, 1981-1997
737	Rickey Henderson, 1979-1997

Pitchers

Games: Most, career

1022	Lee Smith, 1980-1997
1021	Dennis Eckersley, 1975-1997
956	Jesse Orosco, 1979-1997
797	Rick Honeycutt, 1977-1997
771	John Franco, 1984-1997
760	Paul Assenmacher, 1986-1997
694	Mike Jackson, 1986-1997
683	Danny Darwin, 1978-1997
680	Dan Plesac, 1986-1997
666	Randy Myers, 1985-1997

Complete games: Most, career

121	Dennis Martinez, 1976-1997
113	Fernando Valenzuela, 1980-1997
109	Roger Clemens, 1984-1997
100	Dennis Eckersley, 1975-1997
81	Mark Langston, 1984-1997
80	Greg Maddux, 1986-1997
76	Bret Saberhagen, 1984-1997
68	Dwight Gooden, 1984-1997
68	Orel Hershiser, 1983-1997
65	Tom Candiotti, 1983-1997

Saves: Most, career

478	Lee Smith, 1980-1997
389	Dennis Eckersley, 1975-1997
359	John Franco, 1984-1997
319	Randy Myers, 1985-1997
278	Doug Jones, 1982-1997
256	Jeff Montgomery, 1987-1997
256	Todd Worrell, 1985-1997
237	Rick Aguilera, 1985-1997
211	John Wetteland, 1989-1997
199	Rod Beck, 1991-1997

Shutouts: Most, career

41	Roger Clemens, 1984-1997
31	Fernando Valenzuela, 1980-1997
29	Dennis Martinez, 1976-1997
25	Orel Hershiser, 1983-1997

24	Dwight Gooden, 1984-1997
23	Greg Maddux, 1986-1997
21	David Cone, 1986-1997
21	Doug Drabek, 1986-1997
20	Dennis Eckersley, 1975-1997
20	Ramon Martinez, 1988-1997

Wins: Most, career

241	Dennis Martinez, 1976-1997
213	Roger Clemens, 1984-1997
193	Dennis Eckersley, 1975-1997
184	Greg Maddux, 1986-1997
180	Jimmy Key, 1984-1997
179	Orel Hershiser, 1983-1997
177	Dwight Gooden, 1984-1997
174	Mark Langston, 1984-1997
173	Fernando Valenzuela, 1980-1997
163	Danny Darwin, 1978-1997

Losses: Most, career

187	Dennis Martinez, 1976-1997
172	Danny Darwin, 1978-1997
170	Dennis Eckersley, 1975-1997
167	Mike Morgan, 1978-1997
158	Kevin Gross, 1983-1997
153	Fernando Valenzuela, 1980-1997
150	Mark Langston, 1984-1997
143	Rick Honeycutt, 1977-1997
142	Tom Candiotti, 1983-1997
136	Mark Gubicza, 1984-1997

HR allowed: Most, career

364	Dennis Martinez, 1976-1997
341	Dennis Eckersley, 1975-1997
298	Danny Darwin, 1978-1997
291	Mark Langston, 1984-1997
249	Jimmy Key, 1984-1997
230	Kevin Gross, 1983-1997
226	Doug Drabek, 1986-1997
226	Fernando Valenzuela, 1980-1997
213	Greg Swindell, 1986-1997
211	Chuck Finley, 1986-1997

BB: Most, career

1219	Mark Langston, 1984-1997
1195	Bobby Witt, 1986-1997
1151	Fernando Valenzuela, 1980-1997
1146	Dennis Martinez, 1976-1997
986	Kevin Gross, 1983-1997
924	Roger Clemens, 1984-1997
915	Chuck Finley, 1986-1997
857	Randy Johnson, 1988-1997
836	David Cone, 1986-1997
831	Orel Hershiser, 1983-1997

K: Most, career

2882	Roger Clemens, 1984-1997
2379	Dennis Eckersley, 1975-1997
2365	Mark Langston, 1984-1997
2087	Dennis Martinez, 1976-1997
2074	Fernando Valenzuela, 1980-1997
2067	Dwight Gooden, 1984-1997

2034	David Cone, 1986-1997
2000	Randy Johnson, 1988-1997
1861	Danny Darwin, 1978-1997
1820	Greg Maddux, 1986-1997

Wild pitches: Most, career

119	Fernando Valenzuela, 1980-1997
116	David Cone, 1986-1997
114	John Smoltz, 1988-1997
112	Bobby Witt, 1986-1997
107	Mark Gubicza, 1984-1997
101	Orel Hershiser, 1983-1997
96	Mike Morgan, 1978-1997
94	Chuck Finley, 1986-1997
93	Tom Candiotti, 1983-1997
84	Mark Langston, 1984-1997

Win pct: Highest, career

.682	Mike Mussina, 1991-1997
.680	Andy Pettitte, 1995-1997
.646	Dwight Gooden, 1984-1997
.646	Randy Johnson, 1988-1997
.643	Roger Clemens, 1984-1997
.632	David Cone, 1986-1997
.630	Greg Maddux, 1986-1997
.625	Pedro Martinez, 1992-1997
.612	Jimmy Key, 1984-1997
.611	Ramon Martinez, 1988-1997

ERA: Lowest, career

2.57	John Franco, 1984-1997
2.81	Greg Maddux, 1986-1997
2.91	Jeff Montgomery, 1987-1997
2.95	Jesse Orosco, 1979-1997
2.97	Roger Clemens, 1984-1997
3.00	Pedro Martinez, 1992-1997
3.03	Lee Smith, 1980-1997
3.08	Randy Myers, 1985-1997
3.10	Doug Jones, 1982-1997
3.13	David Cone, 1986-1997

Innings: Most, career

3908.7	Dennis Martinez, 1976-1997
3246.0	Dennis Eckersley, 1975-1997
3040.0	Roger Clemens, 1984-1997
2930.0	Fernando Valenzuela, 1980-1997
2868.0	Danny Darwin, 1978-1997
2819.7	Mark Langston, 1984-1997
2724.7	Orel Hershiser, 1983-1997
2598.3	Greg Maddux, 1986-1997
2512.3	Jimmy Key, 1984-1997
2487.7	Kevin Gross, 1983-1997

AL single-season records

ACTIVE PLAYERS in caps.

Hitters

At-bats: Most

705	Willie Wilson, KC-1980
692	Bobby Richardson, NY-1962
691	Kirby Puckett, Min-1985
689	Sandy Alomar, Cal-1971

687	TONY FERNANDEZ, Tor-1986
686	Horace Clarke, NY-1970
684	NOMAR GARCIAPARRA, Bos-1997
680	Kirby Puckett, Min-1986
679	Harvey Kuenn, Det-1953
679	Bobby Richardson, NY-1964

Runs: Most

177	Babe Ruth, NY-1921
167	Lou Gehrig, NY-1936
163	Lou Gehrig, NY-1931
163	Babe Ruth, NY-1928
158	Babe Ruth, NY-1920
158	Babe Ruth, NY-1927
152	Al Simmons, Phi-1930
151	Joe DiMaggio, NY-1937
151	Jimmie Foxx, Phi-1932
151	Babe Ruth, NY-1923

Hits: Most

257	George Sisler, StL-1920
253	Al Simmons, Phi-1925
248	Ty Cobb, Det-1911
246	George Sisler, StL-1922
241	Heinie Manush, StL-1928
240	WADE BOGGS, Bos-1985
239	Rod Carew, Min-1977
238	Don Mattingly, NY-1986
237	Harry Heilmann, Det-1921
236	Jack Tobin, StL-1921

Total bases: Most

457	Babe Ruth, NY-1921
447	Lou Gehrig, NY-1927
438	Jimmie Foxx, Phi-1932
419	Lou Gehrig, NY-1930
418	Joe DiMaggio, NY-1937
417	Babe Ruth, NY-1927
410	Lou Gehrig, NY-1931
409	Lou Gehrig, NY-1934
406	Jim Rice, Bos-1978
405	Hal Trosky, Cle-1936

2B: Most

67	Earl Webb, Bos-1931
64	George Burns, Cle-1926
63	Hank Greenberg, Det-1934
60	Charlie Gehringer, Det-1936
59	Tris Speaker, Cle-1923
56	George Kell, Det-1950
55	Gee Walker, Det-1936
54	Hal McRae, KC-1977
54	JOHN OLERUD, Tor-1993
54	ALEX RODRIGUEZ, Sea-1996

3B: Most

26	Sam Crawford, Det-1914
26	Joe Jackson, Cle-1912
25	Sam Crawford, Det-1903
24	Ty Cobb, Det-1911
24	Ty Cobb, Det-1917
23	Ty Cobb, Det-1912
23	Earle Combs, NY-1927
23	Sam Crawford, Det-1913

23	Dale Mitchell, Cle-1949
22	Bill Bradley, Cle-1903
22	Earle Combs, NY-1930
22	Birdie Cree, NY-1911
22	Elmer Flick, Cle-1906
22	Tris Speaker, Bos-1913
22	Snuffy Stirnweiss, NY-1945

HR: Most

61	Roger Maris, NY-1961
60	Babe Ruth, NY-1927
59	Babe Ruth, NY-1921
58	Jimmie Foxx, Phi-1932
58	Hank Greenberg, Det-1938
56	KEN GRIFFEY, Sea-1997
54	Mickey Mantle, NY-1961
54	Babe Ruth, NY-1920
54	Babe Ruth, NY-1928
52	Mickey Mantle, NY-1956
52	MARK McGWIRE, Oak-1996

RBI: Most

184	Lou Gehrig, NY-1931
183	Hank Greenberg, Det-1937
175	Jimmie Foxx, Bos-1938
175	Lou Gehrig, NY-1927
174	Lou Gehrig, NY-1930
171	Babe Ruth, NY-1921
170	Hank Greenberg, Det-1935
169	Jimmie Foxx, Phi-1932
167	Joe DiMaggio, NY-1937
165	Lou Gehrig, NY-1934
165	Al Simmons, Phi-1930

SB: Most

130	RICKEY HENDERSON, Oak-1982
108	RICKEY HENDERSON, Oak-1983
100	RICKEY HENDERSON, Oak-1980
96	Ty Cobb, Det-1915
93	RICKEY HENDERSON, NY-1988
88	Clyde Milan, Was-1912
87	RICKEY HENDERSON, NY-1986
83	Ty Cobb, Det-1911
83	Willie Wilson, KC-1979
81	Eddie Collins, Phi-1910

BB: Most

170	Babe Ruth, NY-1923
162	Ted Williams, Bos-1947
162	Ted Williams, Bos-1949
156	Ted Williams, Bos-1946
151	Eddie Yost, Was-1956
149	Eddie Joost, Phi-1949
148	Babe Ruth, NY-1920
146	Mickey Mantle, NY-1957
145	Harmon Killebrew, Min-1969
145	Ted Williams, Bos-1941
145	Ted Williams, Bos-1942

K: Most

186	Rob Deer, Mil-1987
185	PETE INCAVIGLIA, Tex-1986

182	CECIL FIELDER, Det-1990
179	Rob Deer, Mil-1986
175	JAY BUHNER, Sea-1997
175	JOSE CANSECO, Oak-1986
175	Rob Deer, Det-1991
175	Dave Nicholson, Chi-1963
175	Gorman Thomas, Mil-1979
172	Bo Jackson, KC-1989
172	Jim Presley, Sea-1986

GIDP: Most

36	Jim Rice, Bos-1984
35	Jim Rice, Bos-1985
32	Jackie Jensen, Bos-1954
32	CAL RIPKEN, Bal-1985
31	Tony Armas, Bos-1983
31	Bobby Doerr, Bos-1949
31	Jim Rice, Bos-1983
30	Billy Hitchcock, Phi-1950
30	Dave Winfield, NY-1983
30	Carl Yastrzemski, Bos-1964

BA: Highest

.426	Nap Lajoie, Phi-1901
.420	George Sisler, StL-1922
.420	Ty Cobb, Det-1911
.409	Ty Cobb, Det-1912
.408	Joe Jackson, Cle-1911
.407	George Sisler, StL-1920
.406	Ted Williams, Bos-1941
.403	Harry Heilmann, Det-1923
.401	Ty Cobb, Det-1922
.398	Harry Heilmann, Det-1927

On-base avg: Highest

.551	Ted Williams, Bos-1941
.545	Babe Ruth, NY-1923
.530	Babe Ruth, NY-1920
.526	Ted Williams, Bos-1957
.516	Babe Ruth, NY-1926
.513	Ted Williams, Bos-1954
.513	Babe Ruth, NY-1924
.512	Mickey Mantle, NY-1957
.512	Babe Ruth, NY-1921
.499	Ted Williams, Bos-1942

Slug avg: Highest

.847	Babe Ruth, NY-1920
.846	Babe Ruth, NY-1921
.772	Babe Ruth, NY-1927
.765	Lou Gehrig, NY-1927
.764	Babe Ruth, NY-1923
.749	Jimmie Foxx, Phi-1932
.739	Babe Ruth, NY-1924
.737	Babe Ruth, NY-1926
.735	Ted Williams, Bos-1941
.732	Babe Ruth, NY-1930

Extra-base hits: Most

119	Babe Ruth, NY-1921
117	Lou Gehrig, NY-1927
103	ALBERT BELLE, Cle-1995
103	Hank Greenberg, Det-1937
100	Jimmie Foxx, Phi-1932
100	Lou Gehrig, NY-1930
99	Hank Greenberg, Det-1940
99	Babe Ruth, NY-1920

| 99 | Babe Ruth, NY-1923 |
| 98 | Hank Greenberg, Det-1935 |

Pitchers

Games: Most

90	Mike Marshall, Min-1979
89	Mark Eichhorn, Tor-1987
88	MIKE MYERS, Det-1997
88	Wilbur Wood, Chi-1968
85	MITCH WILLIAMS, Tex-1987
84	Dan Quisenberry, KC-1985
83	EDDIE GUARDADO, Min-1996
83	MIKE MYERS, Det-1996
83	Ken Sanders, Mil-1971
82	Eddie Fisher, Chi-1965

Complete games: Most

48	Jack Chesbro, NY-1904
42	George Mullin, Det-1904
42	Ed Walsh, Chi-1908
41	Cy Young, Bos-1902
40	Cy Young, Bos-1904
39	Bill Dinneen, Bos-1902
39	Joe McGinnity, Bal-1901
39	Rube Waddell, Phi-1904
38	Walter Johnson, Was-1910
38	Jack Powell, NY-1904
38	Cy Young, Bos-1901

Saves: Most

57	Bobby Thigpen, Chi-1990
51	DENNIS ECKERSLEY, Oak-1992
48	DENNIS ECKERSLEY, Oak-1990
46	Bryan Harvey, Cal-1991
46	JOSE MESA, Cle-1995
46	Dave Righetti, NY-1986
45	DENNIS ECKERSLEY Oak-1988
45	JEFF MONTGOMERY, KC-1993
45	RANDY MYERS, Bal-1997
45	Dan Quisenberry, KC-1983
45	Duane Ward, Tor-1993

Shutouts: Most

13	Jack Coombs, Phi-1910
11	Dean Chance, LA-1964
11	Walter Johnson, Was-1913
11	Ed Walsh, Chi-1908
10	Bob Feller, Cle-1946
10	Bob Lemon, Cle-1948
10	Jim Palmer, Bal-1975
10	Ed Walsh, Chi-1906
10	Joe Wood, Bos-1912
10	Cy Young, Bos-1904

Wins: Most

41	Jack Chesbro, NY-1904
40	Ed Walsh, Chi-1908
36	Walter Johnson, Was-1913
34	Joe Wood, Bos-1912
33	Walter Johnson, Was-1912
33	Cy Young, Bos-1901

32	Cy Young, Bos-1902
31	Jim Bagby, Cle-1920
31	Jack Coombs, Phi-1910
31	Lefty Grove, Phi-1931
31	Denny McLain, Det-1968

Losses: Most

26	Pete Dowling, Mil-Cle-1901
26	Bob Groom, Was-1909
26	Happy Townsend, Was-1904
25	Patsy Flaherty, Chi-1903
25	Fred Glade, StL-1905
25	Walter Johnson, Was-1909
25	Scott Perry, Phi-1920
25	Red Ruffing, Bos-1928
24	Joe Bush, Phi-1916
24	Pat Caraway, Chi-1931
24	Dolly Gray, StL-1931
24	Tom Hughes, NY-Was-1904

HR allowed: Most

50	Bert Blyleven, Min-1986
46	Bert Blyleven, Min-1987
43	Pedro Ramos, Was-1957
42	Denny McLain, Det-1966
40	SHAWN BOSKIE, Cal-1996
40	Fergie Jenkins, Tex-1979
40	Jack Morris, Det-1986
40	Orlando Pena, KC-1964
40	BRAD RADKE, Min-1996
40	Ralph Terry, NY-1962

BB: Most

208	Bob Feller, Cle-1938
204	Nolan Ryan, Cal-1977
202	Nolan Ryan, Cal-1974
194	Bob Feller, Cle-1941
192	Bobo Newsom, StL-1938
183	Nolan Ryan, Cal-1976
181	Bob Turley, Bal-1954
179	Tommy Byrne, NY-1949
177	Bob Turley, NY-1955
171	Bump Hadley, Chi-StL-1932

K: Most

383	Nolan Ryan, Cal-1973
367	Nolan Ryan, Cal-1974
349	Rube Waddell, Phi-1904
348	Bob Feller, Cle-1946
341	Nolan Ryan, Cal-1977
329	Nolan Ryan, Cal-1972
327	Nolan Ryan, Cal-1976
325	Sam McDowell, Cle-1965
313	Walter Johnson, Was-1910
308	RANDY JOHNSON, Sea-1993
308	Mickey Lolich, Det-1971

Win pct: Highest

.938	Johnny Allen, Cle-1937
.900	RANDY JOHNSON, Sea-1995
.893	Ron Guidry, NY-1978
.886	Lefty Grove, Phi-1931
.882	Bob Stanley, Bos-1978
.872	Joe Wood, Bos-1912
.862	Whitey Ford, NY-1961
.862	Bill Donovan, Det-1907
.857	ROGER CLEMENS, Bos-1986

| .850 | Chief Bender, Phi-1914 |

ERA: Lowest

0.96	Dutch Leonard, Bos-1914
1.14	Walter Johnson, Was-1913
1.16	Addie Joss, Cle-1908
1.26	Cy Young, Bos-1908
1.27	Ed Walsh, Chi-1910
1.27	Walter Johnson, Was-1918
1.30	Jack Coombs, Phi-1910
1.36	Walter Johnson, Was-1910
1.39	Walter Johnson, Was-1912
1.39	Harry Krause, Phi-1909

Innings: Most

464.0	Ed Walsh, Chi-1908
454.2	Jack Chesbro, NY-1904
422.1	Ed Walsh, Chi-1907
393.0	Ed Walsh, Chi-1912
390.1	Jack Powell, NY-1904
384.2	Cy Young, Bos-1902
383.0	Rube Waddell, Phi-1904
382.1	George Mullin, Det-1904
382.0	Joe McGinnity, Bal-1901
380.0	Cy Young, Bos-1904

AL club records

BA: Highest, season

.316	Detroit, 1921
.313	St. Louis, 1922
.309	New York, 1930
.308	St. Louis, 1920
.308	Cleveland, 1921

BA: Lowest, season

.211	Chicago, 1910
.214	New York, 1968
.217	Texas, 1972
.218	St. Louis, 1910
.221	Chicago, 1909

Slug avg: Highest, season

.489	New York, 1927
.488	New York, 1930
.485	Seattle, 1997
.484	Cleveland, 1994
.484	Seattle, 1996

On base avg: Highest, season

.385	Boston, 1950
.385	Detroit, 1921
.384	New York, 1930
.383	Cleveland, 1921
.383	New York, 1927

Runs: Most, season

1067	New York, 1931
1065	New York, 1936
1062	New York, 1930
1027	Boston, 1950
1002	New York, 1932

HR: Most, season

264	Seattle, 1997
257	Baltimore, 1996
245	Seattle, 1996

243	Oakland, 1996
240	New York, 1961

SB: Most, season

341	Oakland, 1976
288	New York, 1910
287	Washington, 1913
280	Chicago, 1901
280	Detroit, 1909

GIDP: Most, season

174	Boston, 1990
172	Minnesota, 1996
171	Boston, 1982
171	Boston, 1983
170	Philadelphia, 1950

Fielding avg: Highest, season

.986	Baltimore, 1995
.986	Baltimore, 1994
.986	New York, 1995
.986	Toronto, 1990
.986	Baltimore, 1989

Errors: Most, season

410	Detroit, 1901
401	Baltimore, 1901
393	Milwaukee, 1901
385	St. Louis, 1910
382	New York, 1912

Errors: Fewest, season

84	Minnesota, 1988
86	Toronto, 1990
87	Texas, 1996
87	Oakland, 1990
87	Baltimore, 1989

Double plays: Most, season

217	Philadelphia, 1949
214	New York, 1956
208	Philadelphia, 1950
207	Boston, 1949
206	Boston, 1980
206	Toronto, 1980

ERA: Lowest, season

1.78	Philadelphia, 1910
1.93	Philadelphia, 1909
1.99	Chicago, 1905
2.02	Cleveland, 1908
2.03	Chicago, 1910

ERA: Highest, season

6.37	Detroit, 1996
6.24	St. Louis, 1936
6.08	Philadelphia, 1936
6.01	St. Louis, 1939
6.00	St. Louis, 1937

Shutouts: Most, season

32	Chicago, 1906
28	Los Angeles, 1964
27	Cleveland, 1906
27	Philadelphia, 1907
27	Philadelphia, 1909

HR allowed: Most, season

241	Detroit, 1996
233	Minnesota, 1996
226	Baltimore, 1987
220	Kansas City, 1964
219	Cleveland, 1987
219	California, 1996

HR allowed: Fewest, season

6	Boston, 1913
7	St. Louis, 1908
8	Philadelphia, 1910
8	Chicago, 1909
8	Detroit, 1907
8	Cleveland, 1907

Walks allowed: Most, season

827	Philadelphia, 1915
812	New York, 1949
801	St. Louis, 1951
784	Detroit, 1996
779	Washington, 1949

NL single-season records

Hitters

At-bats: Most

701	JUAN SAMUEL, Phi-1984
699	Dave Cash, Phi-1975
698	Matty Alou, Pit-1969
696	Woody Jensen, Pit-1936
695	Omar Moreno, Pit-1979
695	Maury Wills, LA-1962
689	Lou Brock, StL-1967
687	Dave Cash, Phi-1974
682	LANCE JOHNSON, NY-1996
681	Jo-Jo Moore, NY-1935
681	Lloyd Waner, Pit-1931

Runs: Most

192	Billy Hamilton, Phi-1894
166	Billy Hamilton, Phi-1895
165	Willie Keeler, Bal-1894
165	Joe Kelley, Bal-1894
162	Willie Keeler, Bal-1895
160	Jesse Burkett, Cle-1896
160	Hugh Duffy, Bos-1894
159	Hughie Jennings, Bal-1895
158	Chuck Klein, Phi-1930
158	Bobby Lowe, Bos-1894

Hits: Most

254	Lefty O'Doul, Phi-1929
254	Bill Terry, NY-1930
250	Rogers Hornsby, StL-1922
250	Chuck Klein, Phi-1930
241	Babe Herman, Bro-1930
240	Jesse Burkett, Cle-1896
239	Willie Keeler, Bal-1897
238	Ed Delahanty, Phi-1899
237	Hugh Duffy, Bos-1894
237	Joe Medwick, StL-1937
237	Paul Waner, Pit-1927

Total bases: Most

450	Rogers Hornsby, StL-1922
445	Chuck Klein, Phi-1930
429	Stan Musial, StL-1948
423	Hack Wilson, Chi-1930
420	Chuck Klein, Phi-1932
416	Babe Herman, Bro-1930
409	Rogers Hornsby, Chi-1929
409	LARRY WALKER, Col-1997
406	Joe Medwick, StL-1937
405	Chuck Klein, Phi-1929

2B: Most

64	Joe Medwick, StL-1936
62	Paul Waner, Pit-1932
59	Chuck Klein, Phi-1930
57	Billy Herman, Chi-1935
57	Billy Herman, Chi-1936
56	Joe Medwick, StL-1937
55	Ed Delahanty, Phi-1899
54	MARK GRUDZIELANEK, Mon-1997
53	Stan Musial, StL-1953
53	Paul Waner, Pit-1936

3B: Most

36	Chief Wilson, Pit-1912
31	Heinie Reitz, Bal-1894
29	Perry Werden, StL-1893
28	Harry Davis, Pit-1897
27	George Davis, NY-1893
27	Sam Thompson, Phi-1894
27	Jimmy Williams, Pit-1899
26	Kiki Cuyler, Pit-1925
26	John Reilly, Cin-1890
26	George Treadway, Bro-1894

HR: Most

56	Hack Wilson, Chi-1930
54	Ralph Kiner, Pit-1949
52	George Foster, Cin-1977
52	Willie Mays, SF-1965
51	Ralph Kiner, Pit-1947
51	Willie Mays, NY-1955
51	Johnny Mize, NY-1947
49	Andre Dawson, Chi-1987
49	Ted Kluszewski, Cin-1954
49	Willie Mays, SF-1962
49	LARRY WALKER, Col-1997

RBI: Most

190	Hack Wilson, Chi-1930
170	Chuck Klein, Phi-1930
166	Sam Thompson, Det-1887
165	Sam Thompson, Phi-1895
159	Hack Wilson, Chi-1929
154	Joe Medwick, StL-1937
153	Tommy Davis, LA-1962
152	Rogers Hornsby, StL-1922
151	Mel Ott, NY-1929
150	ANDRES GALARRAGA, Col-1996

SB: Most

118	Lou Brock, StL-1974
111	Billy Hamilton, Phi-1891

111 John Ward, NY-1887
110 VINCE COLEMAN, StL-1985
109 VINCE COLEMAN, StL-1987
107 VINCE COLEMAN, StL-1986
104 Maury Wills, LA-1962
102 Jim Fogarty, Phi-1887
102 Billy Hamilton, Phi-1890
99 Jim Fogarty, Phi-1889

BB: Most
151 BARRY BONDS, SF-1996
148 Eddie Stanky, Bro-1945
148 Jim Wynn, Hou-1969
147 Jimmy Sheckard, Chi-1911
145 BARRY BONDS, SF-1997
144 Eddie Stanky, NY-1950
142 GARY SHEFFIELD, Fla-1996
137 Ralph Kiner, Pit-1951
137 Willie McCovey, SF-1970
137 Eddie Stanky, Bro-1946

K: Most
189 Bobby Bonds, SF-1970
187 Bobby Bonds, SF-1969
180 Mike Schmidt, Phi-1975
174 SAMMY SOSA, Chi-1997
169 ANDRES GALARRAGA, Mon-1990
168 JUAN SAMUEL, Phi-1984
163 Donn Clendenon, Pit-1968
162 RON GANT, StL-1997
162 JUAN SAMUEL, Phi-1987
161 Dick Allen, Phi-1968

GIDP: Most
30 Ernie Lombardi, Cin-1938
29 Ted Simmons, StL-1973
28 Sid Gordon, Bos-1951
27 John Bateman, Mon-1971
27 Carl Furillo, Bro-1956
27 ERIC KARROS, LA-1996
27 Ron Santo, Chi-1973
27 Ken Singleton, Mon-1973
26 Sid Gordon, NY-1943
26 Cleon Jones, NY-1970
26 Billy Jurges, NY-1939
26 Ernie Lombardi, Cin-1933
26 Willie Montanez, Phi-SF-1975
26 Willie Montanez, SF-Atl-1976
26 Dave Parker, Cin-1985
26 Joe Torre, Mil-1964

BA: Highest
.440 Hugh Duffy, Bos-1894
.424 Willie Keeler, Bal-1897
.424 Rogers Hornsby, StL-1924
.410 Ed Delahanty, Phi-1899
.410 Jesse Burkett, Cle-1896
.409 Jesse Burkett, Cle-1895
.407 Ed Delahanty, Phi-1894
.404 Billy Hamilton, Phi-1894
.404 Ed Delahanty, Phi-1895
.403 Rogers Hornsby, StL-1925

On-base avg: Highest
.548 John McGraw, Bal-1899
.523 Billy Hamilton, Phi-1894
.507 Rogers Hornsby, StL-1924
.502 Joe Kelley, Bal-1894
.502 Hugh Duffy, Bos-1894
.500 Ed Delahanty, Phi-1895
.498 Rogers Hornsby, Bos-1928
.491 Arky Vaughan, Pit-1935
.490 Billy Hamilton, Phi-1895
.489 Rogers Hornsby, StL-1925

Slug avg: Highest
.756 Rogers Hornsby, StL-1925
.750 JEFF BAGWELL, Hou-1994
.723 Hack Wilson, Chi-1930
.722 Rogers Hornsby, StL-1922
.720 LARRY WALKER, Col-1997
.702 Stan Musial, StL-1948
.696 Rogers Hornsby, StL-1924
.694 Hugh Duffy, Bos-1894
.687 Chuck Klein, Phi-1930
.679 Rogers Hornsby, Chi-1929

Extra-base hits: Most
107 Chuck Klein, Phi-1930
103 Chuck Klein, Phi-1932
103 Stan Musial, StL-1948
102 Rogers Hornsby, StL-1922
99 LARRY WALKER, Col-1997
97 Joe Medwick, StL-1937
97 Hack Wilson, Chi-1930
95 Joe Medwick, StL-1936
94 Babe Herman, Bro-1930
94 Rogers Hornsby, Chi-1929
94 Chuck Klein, Phi-1929

Pitchers

Games: Most
106 Mike Marshall, LA-1974
94 Kent Tekulve, Pit-1979
92 Mike Marshall, Mon-1973
91 Kent Tekulve, Pit-1978
90 Wayne Granger, Cin-1969
90 Kent Tekulve, Phi-1987
89 JULIAN TAVAREZ, SF-1997
87 Rob Murphy, Cin-1987
85 Kent Tekulve, Pit-1982
85 Frank Williams, Cin-1987

Complete games: Most
75 Will White, Cin-1879
73 Charley Radbourn, Pro-1884
72 Pud Galvin, Buf-1883
72 Jim McCormick, Cle-1880
71 Pud Galvin, Buf-1884
68 John Clarkson, Chi-1885
68 John Clarkson, Bos-1889
67 Bill Hutchison, Chi-1892
66 Jim Devlin, Lou-1876
66 Charley Radbourn, Pro-1883

Saves: Most
53 RANDY MYERS, Chi-1993
48 ROD BECK, SF-1993
47 LEE SMITH, StL-1991
45 Bryan Harvey, Fla-1993
45 Bruce Sutter, StL-1984
44 JEFF BRANTLEY, Cin-1996
44 MARK DAVIS, SD-1989
44 TODD WORRELL, LA-1996
43 LEE SMITH, StL-1992
43 LEE SMITH, StL-1993
43 JOHN WETTELAND, Mon-1993
43 MITCH WILLIAMS, Phi-1993

Shutouts: Most
16 Pete Alexander, Phi-1916
16 George Bradley, StL-1876
13 Bob Gibson, StL-1968
12 Pete Alexander, Phi-1915
12 Pud Galvin, Buf-1884
11 Tommy Bond, Bos-1879
11 Sandy Koufax, LA-1963
11 Christy Mathewson, NY-1908
11 Charley Radbourn, Pro-1884
10 John Clarkson, Chi-1885
10 Mort Cooper, StL-1942
10 Carl Hubbell, NY-1933
10 Juan Marichal, SF-1965
10 John Tudor, StL-1985

Wins: Most
59 Charley Radbourn, Pro-1884
53 John Clarkson, Chi-1885
49 John Clarkson, Bos-1889
48 Charlie Buffinton, Bos-1884
48 Charley Radbourn, Pro-1883
47 Al Spalding, Chi-1876
47 John Ward, Pro-1879
46 Pud Galvin, Buf-1883
46 Pud Galvin, Buf-1884
45 George Bradley, StL-1876
45 Jim McCormick, Cle-1880

Losses: Most
48 John Coleman, Phi-1883
42 Will White, Cin-1880
40 George Bradley, Tro-1879
40 Jim McCormick, Cle-1879
37 George Cobb, Bal-1892
36 Bill Hutchison, Chi-1892
36 Stump Wiedman, KC-1886
35 Jim Devlin, Lou-1876
35 Red Donahue, StL-1897
35 Pud Galvin, Buf-1880

HR allowed: Most
46 Robin Roberts, Phi-1956
41 Phil Niekro, Atl-1979
41 Robin Roberts, Phi-1955
40 Phil Niekro, Atl-1970
40 Robin Roberts, Phi-1957
39 Murry Dickson, StL-1948
38 Lew Burdette, Mil-1959
38 Warren Hacker, Chi-1955
38 Don Sutton, LA-1970
37 MARK LEITER, SF-Mon-1996

BB: Most, season
289 Amos Rusie, NY-1890
270 Amos Rusie, NY-1892
262 Amos Rusie, NY-1891

227 Mark Baldwin, Pit-1891
218 Amos Rusie, NY-1893
213 Cy Seymour, NY-1898
203 John Clarkson, Bos-1889
200 Amos Rusie, NY-1894
199 Bill Hutchison, Chi-1890
194 Mark Baldwin, Pit-1892

K: Most
441 Charley Radbourn, Pro-1884
417 Charlie Buffinton, Bos-1884
382 Sandy Koufax, LA-1965
369 Pud Galvin, Buf-1884
345 Mickey Welch, NY-1884
345 Jim Whitney, Bos-1883
341 Amos Rusie, NY-1890
337 Amos Rusie, NY-1891
335 Tim Keefe, NY-1888
323 Lady Baldwin, Det-1886

Win pct: Highest
.947 Roy Face, Pit-1959
.941 Rick Sutcliffe, Chi-1984
.905 GREG MADDUX, Atl-1995
.889 Freddie Fitzsimmons,
     Bro-1940
.880 Preacher Roe, Bro-1951
.875 Fred Goldsmith, Chi-1880
.870 DAVID CONE, NY-1988
.864 OREL HERSHISER, LA-1985
.857 DWIGHT GOODEN,
     NY-1985
.842 Emil Yde, Pit-1924
.842 Ron Perranoski, LA-1963
.842 Tom Hughes, Bos-1916

ERA: Lowest
1.04 Mordecai Brown, Chi-1906
1.12 Bob Gibson, StL-1968
1.14 Christy Mathewson, NY-
     1909
1.15 Jack Pfiester, Chi-1907
1.17 Carl Lundgren, Chi-1907
1.22 Pete Alexander, Phi-1915
1.23 George Bradley, StL-1876
1.28 Christy Mathewson,
     NY-1905
1.31 Mordecai Brown, Chi-1909
1.33 Jack Taylor, Chi-1902

Innings: Most
680.0 Will White, Cin-1879
678.2 Charley Radbourn, Pro-1884
657.2 Jim McCormick, Cle-1880
656.1 Pud Galvin, Buf-1883
636.1 Pud Galvin, Buf-1884
632.1 Charley Radbourn, Pro-1883
623.0 John Clarkson, Chi-1885
622.0 Jim Devlin, Lou-1876
622.0 Bill Hutchison, Chi-1892
620.0 John Clarkson, Bos-1889

NL club records

BA: Highest, season
.349 Philadelphia, 1894
.343 Baltimore, 1894
.337 Chicago, 1876
.331 Boston, 1894
.330 Philadelphia, 1895

BA: Lowest, season
.208 Washington, 1888
.208 Detroit, 1884
.210 Washington, 1886
.213 Brooklyn, 1908
.219 New York, 1963

Slug pct: Highest, season
.484 Boston, 1894
.483 Baltimore, 1894
.481 Chicago, 1930
.478 Colorado, 1997
.476 Philadelphia, 1894

On-base avg: Highest, season
.418 Baltimore, 1894
.414 Philadelphia, 1894
.401 Boston, 1894
.394 Philadelphia, 1895
.394 Baltimore, 1897

Runs: Most, season
1220 Boston, 1894
1171 Baltimore, 1894
1143 Philadelphia, 1894
1068 Philadelphia, 1895
1041 Chicago, 1894

HR: Most, season
239 Colorado, 1997
221 New York, 1947
221 Cincinnati, 1956
221 Colorado, 1996
209 Chicago, 1987

SB: Most, season
441 Baltimore, 1896
415 New York, 1887
409 Brooklyn, 1892
401 Baltimore, 1897
382 Chicago, 1887

GIDP: Most, season
166 St. Louis, 1958
161 Chicago, 1933
161 Cincinnati, 1933
157 Chicago, 1938
154 Atlanta, 1985

Fielding avg: Highest, season
.986 Cincinnati, 1995
.985 St. Louis, 1992
.985 San Francisco, 1994
.984 Pittsburgh, 1992
.984 Cincinnati, 1977

Errors: Most, season
639 Philadelphia, 1883
607 Pittsburgh, 1890

595 Chicago, 1884
584 Baltimore, 1892
565 New York, 1892

Errors: Fewest, season
94 St. Louis, 1992
95 Cincinnati, 1977
96 Cincinnati, 1992
100 Cincinnati, 1958
101 San Francisco, 1993
101 Pittsburgh, 1992

Double plays: Most, season
215 Pittsburgh, 1966
202 Colorado, 1997
198 Los Angeles, 1958
197 Atlanta, 1985
195 Pittsburgh, 1963
195 Pittsburgh, 1970

ERA: Lowest, season
1.22 St. Louis, 1876
1.61 Providence, 1884
1.64 Providence, 1880
1.67 Hartford, 1876
1.69 Louisville, 1876

ERA: Highest, season
6.71 Philadelphia, 1930
6.37 Cleveland, 1899
6.21 St. Louis, 1897
6.13 Philadelphia, 1929
5.99 Cincinnati, 1894

Shutouts: Most, season
32 Chicago, 1907
32 Chicago, 1909
30 Chicago, 1906
30 St. Louis, 1968
29 Chicago, 1908

HR allowed: Most, season
198 Colorado, 1996
196 Colorado, 1997
194 San Francisco, 1996
192 New York, 1962
185 St. Louis, 1955
185 Atlanta, 1970
185 Chicago, 1997

HR allowed: Fewest, season
5 Cincinnati, 1909
6 Chicago, 1909
8 Philadelphia, 1908
11 Chicago, 1907
12 Pittsburgh, 1909
12 Pittsburgh, 1907
12 Chicago, 1906
12 Pittsburgh, 1905

Walks Allowed: Most, season
716 Montreal, 1970
715 San Diego, 1974
702 Montreal, 1969
701 St. Louis, 1911
701 Atlanta, 1977

Career records

ACTIVE PLAYERS in caps.

Hitters

Games played: Most
3562	Pete Rose, 1963-1986
3308	Carl Yastrzemski, 1961-1983
3298	Hank Aaron, 1954-1976
3035	Ty Cobb, 1905-1928
3026	EDDIE MURRAY, 1977-1997
3026	Stan Musial, 1941-1963
2992	Willie Mays, 1951-1973
2973	Dave Winfield, 1973-1995
2951	Rusty Staub, 1963-1985
2896	Brooks Robinson, 1955-1977
2856	Robin Yount, 1974-1993
2834	Al Kaline, 1953-1974
2826	Eddie Collins, 1906-1930
2820	Reggie Jackson, 1967-1987
2808	Frank Robinson, 1956-1976
2792	Honus Wagner, 1897-1917
2789	Tris Speaker, 1907-1928
2777	Tony Perez, 1964-1986
2730	Mel Ott, 1926-1947
2707	George Brett, 1973-1993

At-bats: Most
14053	Pete Rose, 1963-1986
12364	Hank Aaron, 1954-1976
11988	Carl Yastrzemski, 1961-1983
11434	Ty Cobb, 1905-1928
11336	EDDIE MURRAY, 1977-1997
11008	Robin Yount, 1974-1993
11003	Dave Winfield, 1973-1995
10972	Stan Musial, 1941-1963
10881	Willie Mays, 1951-1973
10654	Brooks Robinson, 1955-1977
10430	Honus Wagner, 1897-1917
10349	George Brett, 1973-1993
10333	PAUL MOLITOR, 1978-1997
10332	Lou Brock, 1961-1979
10277	Cap Anson, 1871-1897
10230	Luis Aparicio, 1956-1973
10195	Tris Speaker, 1907-1928
10116	Al Kaline, 1953-1974
10078	Rabbit Maranville, 1912-1935
10006	Frank Robinson, 1956-1976

Runs: Most
2246	Ty Cobb, 1905-1928
2174	Hank Aaron, 1954-1976
2174	Babe Ruth, 1914-1935
2165	Pete Rose, 1963-1986
2062	Willie Mays, 1951-1973
1996	Cap Anson, 1871-1897
1949	Stan Musial, 1941-1963
1913	RICKEY HENDERSON, 1979-1997
1888	Lou Gehrig, 1923-1939
1882	Tris Speaker, 1907-1928
1859	Mel Ott, 1926-1947
1829	Frank Robinson, 1956-1976
1821	Eddie Collins, 1906-1930
1816	Carl Yastrzemski, 1961-1983
1798	Ted Williams, 1939-1960

1774	Charlie Gehringer, 1924-1942
1751	Jimmie Foxx, 1925-1945
1736	Honus Wagner, 1897-1917
1729	Jim O'Rourke, 1872-1904
1720	Jesse Burkett, 1890-1905

Hits: Most
4256	Pete Rose, 1963-1986
4189	Ty Cobb, 1905-1928
3771	Hank Aaron, 1954-1976
3630	Stan Musial, 1941-1963
3514	Tris Speaker, 1907-1928
3419	Carl Yastrzemski, 1961-1983
3418	Cap Anson, 1871-1897
3415	Honus Wagner, 1897-1917
3315	Eddie Collins, 1906-1930
3283	Willie Mays, 1951-1973
3255	EDDIE MURRAY, 1977-1997
3242	Nap Lajoie, 1896-1916
3178	PAUL MOLITOR, 1978-1997
3154	George Brett, 1973-1993
3152	Paul Waner, 1926-1945
3142	Robin Yount, 1974-1993
3110	Dave Winfield, 1973-1995
3053	Rod Carew, 1967-1985
3023	Lou Brock, 1961-1979
3007	Al Kaline, 1953-1974

Total bases: Most
6856	Hank Aaron, 1954-1976
6134	Stan Musial, 1941-1963
6066	Willie Mays, 1951-1973
5854	Ty Cobb, 1905-1928
5793	Babe Ruth, 1914-1935
5752	Pete Rose, 1963-1986
5539	Carl Yastrzemski, 1961-1983
5397	EDDIE MURRAY, 1977-1997
5373	Frank Robinson, 1956-1976
5221	Dave Winfield, 1973-1995
5101	Tris Speaker, 1907-1928
5060	Lou Gehrig, 1923-1939
5044	George Brett, 1973-1993
5041	Mel Ott, 1926-1947
4956	Jimmie Foxx, 1925-1945
4884	Ted Williams, 1939-1960
4862	Honus Wagner, 1897-1917
4852	Al Kaline, 1953-1974
4834	Reggie Jackson, 1967-1987
4787	Andre Dawson, 1976-1996

2B: Most
792	Tris Speaker, 1907-1928
746	Pete Rose, 1963-1986
725	Stan Musial, 1941-1963
724	Ty Cobb, 1905-1928
665	George Brett, 1973-1993
657	Nap Lajoie, 1896-1916
646	Carl Yastrzemski, 1961-1983
640	Honus Wagner, 1897-1917
624	Hank Aaron, 1954-1976
605	Paul Waner, 1926-1945
583	Robin Yount, 1974-1993
581	Cap Anson, 1871-1897
576	PAUL MOLITOR, 1978-1997
574	Charlie Gehringer, 1924-1942
560	EDDIE MURRAY, 1977-1997

542	Harry Heilmann, 1914-1932
541	WADE BOGGS, 1982-1997
541	Rogers Hornsby, 1915-1937
540	Joe Medwick, 1932-1948
540	Dave Winfield, 1973-1995

3B: Most
309	Sam Crawford, 1899-1917
295	Ty Cobb, 1905-1928
252	Honus Wagner, 1897-1917
243	Jake Beckley, 1888-1907
233	Roger Connor, 1880-1897
222	Tris Speaker, 1907-1928
220	Fred Clarke, 1894-1915
205	Dan Brouthers, 1879-1904
194	Joe Kelley, 1891-1908
191	Paul Waner, 1926-1945
188	Bid McPhee, 1882-1899
187	Eddie Collins, 1906-1930
185	Ed Delahanty, 1888-1903
184	Sam Rice, 1915-1934
182	Jesse Burkett, 1890-1905
182	Ed Konetchy, 1907-1921
182	Edd Roush, 1913-1931
178	Buck Ewing, 1880-1897
177	Rabbit Maranville, 1912-1935
177	Stan Musial, 1941-1963

HR: Most
755	Hank Aaron, 1954-1976
714	Babe Ruth, 1914-1935
660	Willie Mays, 1951-1973
586	Frank Robinson, 1956-1976
573	Harmon Killebrew, 1954-1975
563	Reggie Jackson, 1967-1987
548	Mike Schmidt, 1972-1989
536	Mickey Mantle, 1951-1968
534	Jimmie Foxx, 1925-1945
521	Willie McCovey, 1959-1980
521	Ted Williams, 1939-1960
512	Ernie Banks, 1953-1971
512	Eddie Mathews, 1952-1968
511	Mel Ott, 1926-1947
504	EDDIE MURRAY, 1977-1997
493	Lou Gehrig, 1923-1939
475	Stan Musial, 1941-1963
475	Willie Stargell, 1962-1982
465	Dave Winfield, 1973-1995
452	Carl Yastrzemski, 1961-1983

RBI: Most
2297	Hank Aaron, 1954-1976
2213	Babe Ruth, 1914-1935
2076	Cap Anson, 1871-1897
1995	Lou Gehrig, 1923-1939
1951	Stan Musial, 1941-1963
1937	Ty Cobb, 1905-1928
1922	Jimmie Foxx, 1925-1945
1917	EDDIE MURRAY, 1977-1997
1903	Willie Mays, 1951-1973
1860	Mel Ott, 1926-1947
1844	Carl Yastrzemski, 1961-1983
1839	Ted Williams, 1939-1960
1833	Dave Winfield, 1973-1995
1827	Al Simmons, 1924-1944
1812	Frank Robinson, 1956-1976

1732	Honus Wagner, 1897-1917
1702	Reggie Jackson, 1967-1987
1652	Tony Perez, 1964-1986
1636	Ernie Banks, 1953-1971
1609	Goose Goslin, 1921-1938

SB: Most

1231	RICKEY HENDERSON, 1979-1997
938	Lou Brock, 1961-1979
912	Billy Hamilton, 1888-1901
892	Ty Cobb, 1905-1928
795	TIM RAINES, 1979-1997
752	VINCE COLEMAN, 1985-1997
744	Eddie Collins, 1906-1930
739	Arlie Latham, 1880-1909
738	Max Carey, 1910-1929
722	Honus Wagner, 1897-1917
689	Joe Morgan, 1963-1984
668	Willie Wilson, 1976-1994
657	Tom Brown, 1882-1898
649	Bert Campaneris, 1964-1983
616	George Davis, 1890-1909
594	Dummy Hoy, 1888-1902
586	Maury Wills, 1959-1972
583	George Vanhaltren, 1887-1903
580	Ozzie Smith, 1978-1996
574	Hugh Duffy, 1888-1906

BB: Most

2056	Babe Ruth, 1914-1935
2019	Ted Williams, 1939-1960
1865	Joe Morgan, 1963-1984
1845	Carl Yastrzemski, 1961-1983
1772	RICKEY HENDERSON, 1979-1997
1733	Mickey Mantle, 1951-1968
1708	Mel Ott, 1926-1947
1614	Eddie Yost, 1944-1962
1605	Darrell Evans, 1969-1989
1599	Stan Musial, 1941-1963
1566	Pete Rose, 1963-1986
1559	Harmon Killebrew, 1954-1975
1508	Lou Gehrig, 1923-1939
1507	Mike Schmidt, 1972-1989
1499	Eddie Collins, 1906-1930
1464	Willie Mays, 1951-1973
1452	Jimmie Foxx, 1925-1945
1444	Eddie Mathews, 1952-1968
1420	Frank Robinson, 1956-1976
1402	Hank Aaron, 1954-1976

HBP: Most

287	Hughie Jennings, 1891-1918
272	Tommy Tucker, 1887-1899
267	Don Baylor, 1970-1988
243	Ron Hunt, 1963-1974
230	Dan McGann, 1896-1908
198	Frank Robinson, 1956-1976
192	Minnie Minoso, 1949-1980
183	Jake Beckley, 1888-1907
173	Curt Welch, 1884-1893
165	Kid Elberfeld, 1898-1914

153	Fred Clarke, 1894-1915
151	Chet Lemon, 1975-1990
143	Carlton Fisk, 1969-1993
142	Nellie Fox, 1947-1965
141	Art Fletcher, 1909-1922
140	Bill Dahlen, 1891-1911
137	Frank Chance, 1898-1914
134	Dummy Hoy, 1888-1902
134	Nap Lajoie, 1896-1916
134	John McGraw, 1891-1906

K: Most

2597	Reggie Jackson, 1967-1987
1936	Willie Stargell, 1962-1982
1883	Mike Schmidt, 1972-1989
1867	Tony Perez, 1964-1986
1816	Dave Kingman, 1971-1986
1757	Bobby Bonds, 1968-1981
1748	Dale Murphy, 1976-1993
1730	Lou Brock, 1961-1979
1710	Mickey Mantle, 1951-1968
1699	Harmon Killebrew, 1954-1975
1697	Dwight Evans, 1972-1991
1686	Dave Winfield, 1973-1995
1580	CHILI DAVIS, 1981-1997
1570	Lee May, 1965-1982
1556	Dick Allen, 1963-1977
1550	Willie McCovey, 1959-1980
1537	Dave Parker, 1973-1991
1532	Frank Robinson, 1956-1976
1527	Lance Parrish, 1977-1995
1526	Willie Mays, 1951-1973

GIDP: Most

328	Hank Aaron, 1954-1976
323	Carl Yastrzemski, 1961-1983
319	Dave Winfield, 1973-1995
315	EDDIE MURRAY, 1977-1997
315	Jim Rice, 1974-1989
302	CAL RIPKEN, 1981-1997
297	Brooks Robinson, 1955-1977
297	Rusty Staub, 1963-1985
287	Ted Simmons, 1968-1988
284	Joe Torre, 1960-1977
277	George Scott, 1966-1979
275	Roberto Clemente, 1955-1972
271	Al Kaline, 1953-1974
270	Frank Robinson, 1956-1976
268	Tony Perez, 1964-1986
266	Dave Concepcion, 1970-1988
261	Ernie Lombardi, 1931-1947
257	HAROLD BAINES, 1980-1997
256	Ron Santo, 1960-1974
255	Buddy Bell, 1972-1989
255	JULIO FRANCO, 1982-1997

BA: Highest

.366	Ty Cobb, 1905-1928
.359	Rogers Hornsby, 1915-1937
.356	Joe Jackson, 1908-1920
.346	Ed Delahanty, 1888-1903
.345	Tris Speaker, 1907-1928
.344	Ted Williams, 1939-1960
.344	Billy Hamilton, 1888-1901
.342	Dan Brouthers, 1879-1904
.342	Babe Ruth, 1914-1935

.342	Harry Heilmann, 1914-1932
.342	Pete Browning, 1882-1894
.341	Willie Keeler, 1892-1910
.341	Bill Terry, 1923-1936
.340	George Sisler, 1915-1930
.340	Lou Gehrig, 1923-1939
.340	TONY GWYNN, 1982-1997
.338	Jesse Burkett, 1890-1905
.338	Nap Lajoie, 1896-1916
.336	Riggs Stephenson, 1921-1934
.334	Al Simmons, 1924-1944

On-base avg: Highest

.482	Ted Williams, 1939-1960
.474	Babe Ruth, 1914-1935
.466	John McGraw, 1891-1906
.455	Billy Hamilton, 1888-1901
.452	FRANK THOMAS, 1990-1997
.447	Lou Gehrig, 1923-1939
.434	Rogers Hornsby, 1915-1937
.433	Ty Cobb, 1905-1928
.428	Jimmie Foxx, 1925-1945
.428	Tris Speaker, 1907-1928
.424	Eddie Collins, 1906-1930
.424	Ferris Fain, 1947-1955
.423	Dan Brouthers, 1879-1904
.423	EDGAR MARTINEZ, 1987-1997
.423	Joe Jackson, 1908-1920
.423	Max Bishop, 1924-1935
.421	Mickey Mantle, 1951-1968
.420	WADE BOGGS, 1982-1997
.419	Mickey Cochrane, 1925-1937
.417	Stan Musial, 1941-1963

Slug avg: Highest

.690	Babe Ruth, 1914-1935
.634	Ted Williams, 1939-1960
.632	Lou Gehrig, 1923-1939
.609	Jimmie Foxx, 1925-1945
.605	Hank Greenberg, 1930-1947
.600	FRANK THOMAS, 1990-1997
.579	Joe DiMaggio, 1936-1951
.577	Rogers Hornsby, 1915-1937
.566	ALBERT BELLE, 1989-1997
.562	Johnny Mize, 1936-1953
.562	KEN GRIFFEY, 1989-1997
.559	Stan Musial, 1941-1963
.558	Willie Mays, 1951-1973
.557	Mickey Mantle, 1951-1968
.556	MARK McGWIRE, 1986-1997
.554	Hank Aaron, 1954-1976
.551	BARRY BONDS, 1986-1997
.548	Ralph Kiner, 1946-1955
.545	Hack Wilson, 1923-1934
.543	Chuck Klein, 1928-1944

Extra-base hits: Most

1477	Hank Aaron, 1954-1976
1377	Stan Musial, 1941-1963
1356	Babe Ruth, 1914-1935
1323	Willie Mays, 1951-1973
1190	Lou Gehrig, 1923-1939
1186	Frank Robinson, 1956-1976
1157	Carl Yastrzemski, 1961-1983

1136	Ty Cobb, 1905-1928
1131	Tris Speaker, 1907-1928
1119	George Brett, 1973-1993
1117	Jimmie Foxx, 1925-1945
1117	Ted Williams, 1939-1960
1099	EDDIE MURRAY, 1977-1997
1093	Dave Winfield, 1973-1995
1075	Reggie Jackson, 1967-1987
1071	Mel Ott, 1926-1947
1041	Pete Rose, 1963-1986
1039	Andre Dawson, 1976-1996
1015	Mike Schmidt, 1972-1989
1011	Rogers Hornsby, 1915-1937

Pitchers

Games: Most

1070	Hoyt Wilhelm, 1952-1972
1050	Kent Tekulve, 1974-1989
1022	LEE SMITH, 1980-1997
1021	DENNIS ECKERSLEY, 1975-1997
1002	Rich Gossage, 1972-1994
987	Lindy McDaniel, 1955-1975
956	JESSE OROSCO, 1979-1997
944	Rollie Fingers, 1968-1985
931	Gene Garber, 1969-1988
906	Cy Young, 1890-1911
899	Sparky Lyle, 1967-1982
898	Jim Kaat, 1959-1983
880	Jeff Reardon, 1979-1994
874	Don McMahon, 1957-1974
864	Phil Niekro, 1964-1987
858	Charlie Hough, 1970-1994
848	Roy Face, 1953-1969
824	Tug McGraw, 1965-1984
807	Nolan Ryan, 1966-1993
802	Walter Johnson, 1907-1927

Complete games: Most

749	Cy Young, 1890-1911
646	Pud Galvin, 1875-1892
554	Tim Keefe, 1880-1893
531	Walter Johnson, 1907-1927
531	Kid Nichols, 1890-1906
525	Bobby Mathews, 1871-1887
525	Mickey Welch, 1880-1892
489	Charley Radbourn, 1880-1891
485	John Clarkson, 1882-1894
468	Tony Mullane, 1881-1894
466	Jim McCormick, 1878-1887
448	Gus Weyhing, 1887-1901
437	Pete Alexander, 1911-1930
434	Christy Mathewson, 1900-1916
422	Jack Powell, 1897-1912
410	Eddie Plank, 1901-1917
394	Will White, 1877-1886
393	Amos Rusie, 1889-1901
388	Vic Willis, 1898-1910
386	Tommy Bond, 1874-1884

Saves: Most

478	LEE SMITH, 1980-1997
389	DENNIS ECKERSLEY, 1975-1997

367	Jeff Reardon, 1979-1994
359	JOHN FRANCO, 1984-1997
341	Rollie Fingers, 1968-1985
319	RANDY MYERS, 1985-1997
311	Tom Henke, 1982-1995
310	Rich Gossage, 1972-1994
300	Bruce Sutter, 1976-1988
278	DOUG JONES, 1982-1997
256	JEFF MONTGOMERY, 1987-1997
256	TODD WORRELL, 1985-1997
252	Dave Righetti, 1979-1995
244	Dan Quisenberry, 1979-1990
238	Sparky Lyle, 1967-1982
237	RICK AGUILERA, 1985-1997
227	Hoyt Wilhelm, 1952-1972
218	Gene Garber, 1969-1988
216	Dave Smith, 1980-1992
211	JOHN WETTELAND, 1989-1997
201	Bobby Thigpen, 1986-1994
199	ROD BECK, 1991-1997
193	Roy Face, 1953-1969
193	Mike Henneman, 1987-1996
192	MITCH WILLIAMS, 1986-1997
188	Mike Marshall, 1967-1981
186	Jeff Russell, 1983-1996
184	Steve Bedrosian, 1981-1995
184	Kent Tekulve, 1974-1989
180	Tug McGraw, 1965-1984

Shutouts: Most

110	Walter Johnson, 1907-1927
90	Pete Alexander, 1911-1930
79	Christy Mathewson, 1900-1916
76	Cy Young, 1890-1911
69	Eddie Plank, 1901-1917
63	Warren Spahn, 1942-1965
61	Nolan Ryan, 1966-1993
61	Tom Seaver, 1967-1986
60	Bert Blyleven, 1970-1992
58	Don Sutton, 1966-1988
57	Pud Galvin, 1875-1892
57	Ed Walsh, 1904-1917
56	Bob Gibson, 1959-1975
55	Mordecai Brown, 1903-1916
55	Steve Carlton, 1965-1988
53	Jim Palmer, 1965-1984
53	Gaylord Perry, 1962-1983
52	Juan Marichal, 1960-1975
50	Rube Waddell, 1897-1910
50	Vic Willis, 1898-1910

Wins: Most

511	Cy Young, 1890-1911
417	Walter Johnson, 1907-1927
373	Pete Alexander, 1911-1930
373	Christy Mathewson, 1900-1916
364	Pud Galvin, 1875-1892
363	Warren Spahn, 1942-1965
361	Kid Nichols, 1890-1906
342	Tim Keefe, 1880-1893
329	Steve Carlton, 1965-1988

328	John Clarkson, 1882-1894
326	Eddie Plank, 1901-1917
324	Nolan Ryan, 1966-1993
324	Don Sutton, 1966-1988
318	Phil Niekro, 1964-1987
314	Gaylord Perry, 1962-1983
311	Tom Seaver, 1967-1986
309	Charley Radbourn, 1880-1891
307	Mickey Welch, 1880-1892
300	Lefty Grove, 1925-1941
300	Early Wynn, 1939-1963

Losses: Most

316	Cy Young, 1890-1911
310	Pud Galvin, 1875-1892
292	Nolan Ryan, 1966-1993
279	Walter Johnson, 1907-1927
274	Phil Niekro, 1964-1987
265	Gaylord Perry, 1962-1983
256	Don Sutton, 1966-1988
254	Jack Powell, 1897-1912
251	Eppa Rixey, 1912-1933
250	Bert Blyleven, 1970-1992
248	Bobby Mathews, 1871-1887
245	Robin Roberts, 1948-1966
245	Warren Spahn, 1942-1965
244	Steve Carlton, 1965-1988
244	Early Wynn, 1939-1963
237	Jim Kaat, 1959-1983
236	Frank Tanana, 1973-1993
232	Gus Weyhing, 1887-1901
231	Tommy John, 1963-1989
230	Bob Friend, 1951-1966
230	Ted Lyons, 1923-1946

HR allowed: Most

505	Robin Roberts, 1948-1966
484	Fergie Jenkins, 1965-1983
482	Phil Niekro, 1964-1987
472	Don Sutton, 1966-1988
448	Frank Tanana, 1973-1993
434	Warren Spahn, 1942-1965
430	Bert Blyleven, 1970-1992
414	Steve Carlton, 1965-1988
399	Gaylord Perry, 1962-1983
395	Jim Kaat, 1959-1983
389	Jack Morris, 1977-1994
383	Charlie Hough, 1970-1994
380	Tom Seaver, 1967-1986
374	Catfish Hunter, 1965-1979
372	Jim Bunning, 1955-1971
364	DENNIS MARTINEZ, 1976-1997
347	Mickey Lolich, 1963-1979
346	Luis Tiant, 1964-1982
341	DENNIS ECKERSLEY, 1975-1997
338	Early Wynn, 1939-1963

BB: Most

2795	Nolan Ryan, 1966-1993
1833	Steve Carlton, 1965-1988
1809	Phil Niekro, 1964-1987
1775	Early Wynn, 1939-1963
1764	Bob Feller, 1936-1956

1732	Bobo Newsom, 1929-1953
1707	Amos Rusie, 1889-1901
1665	Charlie Hough, 1970-1994
1566	Gus Weyhing, 1887-1901
1541	Red Ruffing, 1924-1947
1442	Bump Hadley, 1926-1941
1434	Warren Spahn, 1942-1965
1431	Earl Whitehill, 1923-1939
1408	Tony Mullane, 1881-1894
1396	Sam Jones, 1914-1935
1390	Jack Morris, 1977-1994
1390	Tom Seaver, 1967-1986
1379	Gaylord Perry, 1962-1983
1371	Mike Torrez, 1967-1984
1363	Walter Johnson, 1907-1927

Hit batsmen: Most

277	Gus Weyhing, 1887-1901
219	Chick Fraser, 1896-1909
210	Pink Hawley, 1892-1901
205	Walter Johnson, 1907-1927
190	Eddie Plank, 1901-1917
185	Tony Mullane, 1881-1894
179	Joe McGinnity, 1899-1908
174	Charlie Hough, 1970-1994
171	Clark Griffith, 1891-1914
163	Cy Young, 1890-1911
160	Jim Bunning, 1955-1971
158	Nolan Ryan, 1966-1993
156	Vic Willis, 1898-1910
155	Bert Blyleven, 1970-1992
154	Don Drysdale, 1956-1969
148	Adonis Terry, 1884-1897
147	Bert Cunningham, 1887-1901
146	Silver King, 1886-1897
144	Win Mercer, 1894-1902
142	Frank Foreman, 1884-1902

K: Most

5714	Nolan Ryan, 1966-1993
4136	Steve Carlton, 1965-1988
3701	Bert Blyleven, 1970-1992
3640	Tom Seaver, 1967-1986
3574	Don Sutton, 1966-1988
3534	Gaylord Perry, 1962-1983
3509	Walter Johnson, 1907-1927
3342	Phil Niekro, 1964-1987
3192	Fergie Jenkins, 1965-1983
3117	Bob Gibson, 1959-1975
2882	ROGER CLEMENS, 1984-1997
2855	Jim Bunning, 1955-1971
2832	Mickey Lolich, 1963-1979
2803	Cy Young, 1890-1911
2773	Frank Tanana, 1973-1993
2583	Warren Spahn, 1942-1965
2581	Bob Feller, 1936-1956
2560	Tim Keefe, 1880-1893
2556	Jerry Koosman, 1967-1985
2502	Christy Mathewson, 1900-1916

Wild pitches: Most

343	Tony Mullane, 1881-1894
277	Nolan Ryan, 1966-1993

274	Mickey Welch, 1880-1892
252	Bobby Mathews, 1871-1887
240	Tim Keefe, 1880-1893
240	Gus Weyhing, 1887-1901
226	Phil Niekro, 1964-1987
221	Mark Baldwin, 1887-1893
221	Pud Galvin, 1875-1892
221	Will White, 1877-1886
214	Charley Radbourn, 1880-1891
214	Jim Whitney, 1881-1890
206	Jack Morris, 1977-1994
206	Adonis Terry, 1884-1897
203	Matt Kilroy, 1886-1898
189	George Bradley, 1875-1888
187	Tommy John, 1963-1989
183	Steve Carlton, 1965-1988
182	John Clarkson, 1882-1894
179	Charlie Hough, 1970-1994
179	Toad Ramsey, 1885-1890

Win pct: Highest

.795	Al Spalding, 1871-1878
.717	Spud Chandler, 1937-1947
.690	Dave Foutz, 1884-1896
.690	Whitey Ford, 1950-1967
.688	Bob Caruthers, 1884-1893
.686	Don Gullett, 1970-1978
.680	Lefty Grove, 1925-1941
.672	Joe Wood, 1908-1922
.667	Vic Raschi, 1946-1955
.665	Larry Corcoran, 1880-1887
.665	Christy Mathewson, 1900-1916
.660	Sam Leever, 1898-1910
.657	Sal Maglie, 1945-1958
.656	Dick McBride, 1871-1876
.655	Sandy Koufax, 1955-1966
.654	Johnny Allen, 1932-1944
.651	Ron Guidry, 1975-1988
.650	Lefty Gomez, 1930-1943
.648	John Clarkson, 1882-1894
.648	Mordecai Brown, 1903-1916

ERA: Lowest

1.82	Ed Walsh, 1904-1917
1.89	Addie Joss, 1902-1910
2.04	Al Spalding, 1871-1878
2.06	Mordecai Brown, 1903-1916
2.10	John Ward, 1878-1894
2.13	Christy Mathewson, 1900-1916
2.14	Tommy Bond, 1874-1884
2.16	Rube Waddell, 1897-1910
2.17	Walter Johnson, 1907-1927
2.23	Orval Overall, 1905-1913
2.28	Will White, 1877-1886
2.28	Ed Reulbach, 1905-1917
2.30	Jim Scott, 1909-1917
2.35	Eddie Plank, 1901-1917
2.35	Larry Corcoran, 1880-1887
2.38	George McQuillan, 1907-1918
2.38	Ed Killian, 1903-1910
2.38	Eddie Cicotte, 1905-1920

2.39	Candy Cummings, 1872-1877
2.39	Doc White, 1901-1913

Innings: Most

7356.0	Cy Young, 1890-1911
6003.1	Pud Galvin, 1875-1892
5914.2	Walter Johnson, 1907-1927
5404.1	Phil Niekro, 1964-1987
5386.0	Nolan Ryan, 1966-1993
5350.1	Gaylord Perry, 1962-1983
5282.1	Don Sutton, 1966-1988
5243.2	Warren Spahn, 1942-1965
5217.1	Steve Carlton, 1965-1988
5190.0	Pete Alexander, 1911-1930
5056.1	Kid Nichols, 1890-1906
5047.2	Tim Keefe, 1880-1893
4970.0	Bert Blyleven, 1970-1992
4956.0	Bobby Mathews, 1871-1887
4802.0	Mickey Welch, 1880-1892
4782.2	Tom Seaver, 1967-1986
4780.2	Christy Mathewson, 1900-1916
4710.1	Tommy John, 1963-1989
4688.2	Robin Roberts, 1948-1966
4564.0	Early Wynn, 1939-1963

General club records

Highest percentage for league champion

.832	St. Louis, UA-1884
.798	Chicago, NL-1880
.788	Chicago, NL-1876
.777	Chicago, NL-1885
.763	Chicago, NL-1906

Lowest percentage for league champion

.509	New York, NL-1973
.525	Minnesota, AL-1987
.534	Cleveland, AL-1997
.551	New York, AL-1981
.556	Philadelphia, NL-1983
.556	Oakland, AL-1974

Most wins

116	Chicago, NL-1906
111	Cleveland, AL-1954
110	Pittsburgh, NL-1909
110	New York, NL-1927
109	New York, NL-1961
109	Baltimore, AL-1969

Fewest wins

36	Philadelphia, AL-1916
38	Washington, AL-1904
38	Boston, NL-1935
40	New York, NL-1962
42	Washington, AL-1909
42	Philadelphia, NL-1942
42	Pittsburgh, NL-1952

Most league championships

34	New York, AL
21	Brooklyn-Los Angeles, NL
19	New York-San Francisco, NL
16	Chicago, NL
15	Phil-KC-Oak, AL
15	St. Louis, NL

Individual fielding records

Gold Gloves: Most, pitcher

16	Jim Kaat
9	Bob Gibson
8	GREG MADDUX
8	Bobby Shantz
7	MARK LANGSTON
5	Ron Guidry
5	Phil Niekro
4	Jim Palmer
3	Harvey Haddix
2	Andy Messersmith
2	MIKE MUSSINA
2	Mike Norris
2	Rick Reuschel

Gold Gloves: Most, catcher

10	Johnny Bench
7	Bob Boone
6	IVAN RODRIGUEZ
6	Jim Sundberg
5	Bill Freehan
4	Del Crandall
4	TONY PENA
3	Earl Battey
3	Gary Carter
3	CHARLES JOHNSON
3	Sherm Lollar
3	Thurman Munson
3	TOM PAGNOZZI
3	Lance Parrish
3	BENITO SANTIAGO

Gold Gloves: Most, first base

11	Keith Hernandez
9	Don Mattingly
8	George Scott
7	Vic Power
7	Bill White
6	Wes Parker
4	Steve Garvey
4	MARK GRACE
3	Gil Hodges
3	EDDIE MURRAY
3	Joe Pepitone
3	J. T. SNOW

Gold Gloves: Most, second base

9	RYNE SANDBERG
8	Bill Mazeroski
8	Frank White
6	ROBERTO ALOMAR
5	Joe Morgan
5	Bobby Richardson
4	CRAIG BIGGIO

4	Bobby Grich
3	Nellie Fox
3	Davey Johnson
3	Bobby Knoop
3	Harold Reynolds
3	Manny Trillo
3	Lou Whitaker

Gold Gloves: Most, third base

16	Brooks Robinson
10	Mike Schmidt
6	Buddy Bell
5	Ken Boyer
5	Doug Rader
5	Ron Santo
4	GARY GAETTI
4	ROBIN VENTURA
4	MATT WILLIAMS
3	KEN CAMINITI
3	TERRY PENDELTON
3	Frank Malzone
3	Tim Wallach

Gold Gloves: Most, shortstop

13	Ozzie Smith
9	Luis Aparicio
8	Mark Belanger
5	Dave Concepcion
5	OMAR VIZQUEL
4	TONY FERNANDEZ
4	Alan Trammell
3	BARRY LARKIN
3	Roy McMillan
2	Gene Alley
2	Larry Bowa
2	Don Kessinger
2	CAL RIPKEN
2	Maury Wills
2	Zoilo Versalles

Gold Gloves: Most, outfield

12	Roberto Clemente
12	Willie Mays
10	Al Kaline
8	Paul Blair
8	Andre Dawson
8	Dwight Evans
8	KEN GRIFFEY JR.
8	Garry Maddox
7	BARRY BONDS
7	Curt Flood
7	Dave Winfield
7	DEVON WHITE
7	Carl Yastrzemski

Assists: Most, pitcher

227	Ed Walsh, Chi/A-1907
223	Will White, Cin/A-1882
190	Ed Walsh, Chi/A-1908
178	Harry Howell, StL/A-1905
177	Tony Mullane, Lou/A-1882
174	John Clarkson, Chi/N-1885
172	John Clarkson, Bos/N-1889
166	Jack Chesbro, NY/A-1904
163	George Mullin, Det/A-1904
160	Ed Walsh, Chi/A-1911

Assists: Most, catcher

238	Bill Rariden, New/F-1915
215	Bill Rariden, Ind/F-1914
214	Pat Moran, Bos/N-1903
212	Oscar Stanage, Det/A-1911
212	Art Wilson, Chi/F-1914
210	Gabby Street, Was/A-1909
204	Frank Snyder, StL/N-1915
203	George Gibson, Pit/N-1910
202	Bill Bergen, Bro/N-1909
202	Claude Berry, Pit/F-1914

Assists: Most, first base

184	Bill Buckner, Bos/A-1985
180	MARK GRACE, Chi/N-1990
167	MARK GRACE, Chi/N-1991
166	Sid Bream, Pit/N-1986
161	Bill Buckner, Chi/N-1983
159	Bill Buckner, Chi/N-1982
157	Bill Buckner, Bos/A-1986
155	Mickey Vernon, Cle/A-1949
152	EDDIE MURRAY, Bal/A-1985
152	Fred Tenney, Bos/N-1905

Assists: Most, second base

641	Frankie Frisch, StL/N-1927
588	Hughie Critz, Cin/N-1926
582	Rogers Hornsby, NY/N-1927
572	Ski Melillo, StL/A-1930
571	RYNE SANDBERG, Chi/N-1983
568	Rabbit Maranville, Pit/N-1924
562	Frank Parkinson, Phi/N-1922
559	Tony Cuccinello, Bos/N-1936
557	Johnny Hodapp, Cle/A-1930
555	Lou Bierbauer, Pit/N-1892

Assists: Most, shortstop

621	Ozzie Smith, SD/N-1980
601	Glenn Wright, Pit/N-1924
598	Dave Bancroft, Phi-NY/N-1920
597	Tommy Thevenow, StL/N-1926
595	Ivan DeJesus, Chi/N-1977
583	CAL RIPKEN, Bal/A-1984
581	Whitey Wietelmann, Bos/N-1943
579	Dave Bancroft, NY/N-1922
574	Rabbit Maranville, Bos/N-1914
573	Don Kessinger, Chi/N-1968

Assists: Most, third base

412	Graig Nettles, Cle/A-1971
410	Graig Nettles, NY/A-1973
410	Brooks Robinson, Bal/A-1974
405	Harlond Clift, StL/A-1937
405	Brooks Robinson, Bal/A-1967
404	Mike Schmidt, Phi/N-1974
399	Doug DeCinces, Cal/A-1982
396	Buddy Bell, Tex/A-1982
396	Clete Boyer, NY/A-1962
396	Mike Schmidt, Phi/N-1977

Assists: Most, outfield

50	Orator Shaffer, Chi/N-1879	
48	Hugh Nicol, StL/A-1884	
45	Hardy Richardson, Buf/N-1881	
44	Chuck Klein, Phi/N-1930	
44	Tommy McCarthy, StL/A-1888	
43	Charlie Duffee, StL/A-1889	
43	Jimmy Bannon, Bos/N-1894	
42	Jim Fogarty, Phi/N-1889	
41	Jim Lillie, Buf/N-1884	
41	Orator Shaffer, Buf/N-1883	

Assists: Most, pitcher, active players

71	Greg Maddux, Atl/N-1996
64	Greg Maddux, Chi/N-1992
64	Fernando Valenzuela LA/N-1982
60	Orel Hershiser, LA/N-1988
59	Dennis Martinez, Bal/A-1979
59	Greg Maddux, Atl/N-1993

Assists: Most, catcher, active players

103	Jason Kendall, Pit/N-1997
100	Tony Pena, Pit/N-1985
100	Benito Santiago, SD/N-1991
99	Tony Pena, Pit/N-1986
99	Mike Piazza, LA/N-1993

Assists: Most, first base, active players

180	Mark Grace, Chi/N-1990
167	Mark Grace, Chi/N-1991
152	Eddie Murray, Bal/A-1985
147	Eric Karros, LA/N-1993
147	Jeff King, KC/A-1997
147	Rafael Palmeiro, Tex/A-1993

Assists: Most, second base, active players

571	Ryne Sandberg, Chi/N-1983
550	Ryne Sandberg, Chi/N-1984
539	Ryne Sandberg, Chi/N-1992
522	Ryne Sandberg, Chi/N-1988
515	Ryne Sandberg, Chi/N-1991

Assists: Most, shortstop, active players

583	Cal Ripken, Bal/A-1984
570	Ozzie Guillen, Chi/A-1988
534	Cal Ripken, Bal/A-1983
531	Cal Ripken, Bal/A-1989
528	Cal Ripken, Bal/A-1991

Assists: Most, third base, active players

389	Vinny Castilla, Col/N-1996
372	Robin Ventura, Chi/N-1992
368	Wade Boggs, Bos/A-1983
360	Gary Gaetti, Min/A-1983
353	Gary Gaetti, Cal/A-1991
353	Jeff King, Pit/N-1993

Assists: Most, outfield, active players

22	Joe Orsulak, Bal/A-1991
21	Tim Raines, Mon/N-1983
20	Bobby Higginson, Det/A-1997
19	Brett Butler, Cle/A-1985
19	Bernard Gilkey, StL/N-1993
19	Tony Gwynn, SD/N-1986
19	Wayne Kirby, Cle/A-1993
19	Manny Ramirez, Cle/A-1996

Putouts: Most, pitcher

57	Dave Foutz, StL/A-1886
54	Tony Mullane, Lou/A-1882
50	George Bradley, StL/N-1876
50	Guy Hecker, Lou/A-1884
49	Mike Boddicker, Bal/A-1984
47	Larry Corcoran, Chi/N-1884
45	Ted Breitenstein, StL/N-1895
45	Al Spalding, Chi/N-1876
44	Jim Devlin, Lou/N-1876
44	Dave Foutz, StL/A-1887
44	Bill Hutchison, Chi/N-1890

Putouts: Most, catcher

1135	Johnny Edwards, Hou/N-1969
1055	MIKE PIAZZA, LA/N-1996
1051	DAN WILSON, Sea/A-1997
1045	MIKE PIAZZA, LA/N-1997
1008	Johnny Edwards, Cin/N-1963
993	JAVY LOPEZ, Atl/N-1996
981	DARREN DAULTON, Phi/N-1993
978	Randy Hundley, Chi/N-1969
976	TONY PENA, Pit/N-1983
971	Bill Freehan, Det/A-1968

Putouts: Most, first base

1846	Jiggs Donahue, Chi/A-1907
1759	George Kelly, NY/N-1920
1755	Phil Todt, Bos/A-1926
1710	Wally Pipp, Cin/N-1926
1697	Jiggs Donahue, Chi/A-1906
1691	Candy LaChance, Bos/A-1904
1687	Tom Jones, StL/A-1907
1682	Ernie Banks, Chi/N-1965
1667	Wally Pipp, NY/A-1922
1662	Lou Gehrig, NY/A-1927

Putouts: Most, second base

529	Bid McPhee, Cin/A-1886
484	Bobby Grich, Bal/A-1974
483	Bucky Harris, Was/A-1922
478	Nellie Fox, Chi/A-1956
472	Lou Bierbauer, Phi/A-1889
466	Billy Herman, Chi/N-1933
463	Bill Wambsganss, Bos/A-1924
461	Cub Stricker, Cle/A-1887
460	Buddy Myer, Was/A-1935
459	Bill Sweeney, Bos/N-1912

Putouts: Most, shortstop

425	Hughie Jennings, Bal/N-1895
425	Donie Bush, Det/A-1914
408	Joe Cassidy, Was/A-1905
407	Rabbit Maranville, Bos/N-1914
405	Dave Bancroft, NY/N-1922
405	Eddie Miller, Bos/N-1940
404	Monte Cross, Phi/N-1898
396	Dave Bancroft, NY/N-1921
395	Mickey Doolan, Phi/N-1906
392	Buck Weaver, Chi/A-1913

Putouts: Most, third base

255	Denny Lyons, Phi/A-1887
251	Jimmy Collins, Bos/N-1900
251	Jimmy Williams, Pit/N-1899
243	Jimmy Collins, Bos/N-1898
243	Willie Kamm, Chi/A-1928
236	Willie Kamm, Chi/A-1927
233	Frank Baker, Phi/A-1913
232	Bill Coughlin, Was/A-1901
229	Ernie Courtney, Phi/N-1905
228	Jimmy Austin, StL/A-1911

Putouts: Most, outfield

547	Taylor Douthit, StL/N-1928
538	Richie Ashburn, Phi/N-1951
514	Richie Ashburn, Phi/N-1949
512	Chet Lemon, Chi/A-1977
507	Dwayne Murphy, Oak/A-1980
503	Richie Ashburn, Phi/N-1956
503	Dom DiMaggio, Bos/A-1948
502	Richie Ashburn, Phi/N-1957
496	Richie Ashburn, Phi/N-1953
495	Richie Ashburn, Phi/N-1958

Putouts: Most, pitcher, active players

40	Kevin Brown, Bal/A-1995
39	Greg Maddux, Chi/N-1990
39	Greg Maddux, Chi/N-1991
39	Greg Maddux, Atl/N-1993
37	Kevin Brown, Tex/A-1992
37	Orel Hershiser, LA/N-1987
37	Greg Maddux, Atl/N-1996

Putouts: Most, catcher, active players

1055	Mike Piazza, LA/N-1996
1051	Dan Wilson, Sea/A-1997
1045	Mike Piazza, LA/N-1997
993	Javy Lopez, Atl/N-1996
981	Darren Daulton, Phi/N-1993

Putouts: Most, first base, active players

1580	Mark Grace, Chi/N-1992
1538	Eddie Murray, Bal/A-1984
1528	Andres Galarraga, Col/N-1996
1520	Mark Grace, Chi/N-1991
1504	Eddie Murray, Bal/A-1978

Putouts: Most, second base, active players

400	Carlos Baerga, Cle/A-1992
389	Juan Samuel, Phi/N-1985
388	Juan Samuel, Phi/N-1984

374	Juan Samuel, Phi/N-1987	33	George Davis, NY/N-1893	77	Lenny Harris, 1988-1997
361	Craig Biggio, Hou/N-1996	33	Rogers Hornsby, StL/N-1922	73	Dave Hansen, 1990-1997

Putouts: Most, shortstop, active players

320	Shawon Dunston, Chi/N-1986
297	Tony Fernandez, Tor/A-1990
297	Cal Ripken, Bal/A-1984
294	Tony Fernandez, Tor/A-1986
287	Cal Ripken, Bal/A-1992

Putouts: Most, third base, active players

146	Gary Gaetti, Min/A-1985
144	Scott Rolen, Phi/N-1997
142	Gary Gaetti, Min/A-1984
141	Wade Boggs, Bos/A-1984
141	Robin Ventura, Chi/A-1992

Putouts: Most, outfield, active players

469	Lenny Dykstra, Phi/N-1993
448	Brett Butler, Cle/A-1984
444	Joe Carter, Cle/A-1988
443	Devon White, Tor/A-1992
439	Rickey Henderson, NY/A-1985
439	Lenny Dykstra, Phi/N-1990
439	Devon White, Tor/A-1991

Individual records

Hitters

Most consecutive games played, career

2478	CAL RIPKEN, 1982-1996
2130	Lou Gehrig, 1925-1939
1307	Everett Scott, 1916-1925
1207	Steve Garvey, 1975-1983
1117	Billy Williams, 1963-1970
1103	Joe Sewell, 1922-1930
895	Stan Musial, 1951-1957
829	Eddie Yost, 1949-1955
822	Gus Suhr, 1931-1937
798	Nellie Fox, 1955-1960

Longest hitting streak, season

56	Joe DiMaggio, NY/A-1941
44	Willie Keeler, Bal/N-1897
44	Pete Rose, Cin/N-1978
42	Bill Dahlen, Chi/N-1894
41	George Sisler, StL/A-1922
40	Ty Cobb, Det/A-1911
39	PAUL MOLITOR, Mil/A-1987
37	Tommy Holmes, Bos/N-1945
36	Billy Hamilton, Phi/N-1894
35	Fred Clarke, Lou/N-1895
35	Ty Cobb, Det/A-1917
34	Dom DiMaggio, Bos/A-1949
34	George McQuinn, StL/A-1938
34	BENITO SANTIAGO, SD/N-1987
34	George Sisler, StL/A-1925
33	Hal Chase, NY/N-1907

33	Heinie Manush, Was/A-1933
31	Rico Carty, Atl/N-1970
31	Willie Davis, LA/N-1969
31	Ed Delahanty, Phi/N-1899
31	Nap Lajoie, Cle/A-1906
31	Ken Landreaux, Min/A-1980
31	Sam Rice, Was/A-1924
30	SANDY ALOMAR, Cle/A-1997
30	George Brett, KC/A-1980
30	NOMAR GARCIAPARRA, Bos/A-1997
30	Goose Goslin, Det/A-1934
30	Ron LeFlore, Det/A-1976
30	Cal McVey, Chi/N-1876
30	Stan Musial, StL/N-1950
30	Elmer Smith, Cin/N-1898
30	Tris Speaker, Bos/A-1912
30	JEROME WALTON Chi/N-1989

Longest hitting streak, season, active players

39	Paul Molitor, Mil/A-1987
34	Benito Santiago, SD/N-1987
30	Sandy Alomar, Cle/A-1997
30	Nomar Garciaparra, Bos/A-1997
30	Jerome Walton, Chi/N-1989
29	Hal Morris, Cin/N-1996
28	Wade Boggs, Bos/A-1985
28	Marquis Grissom, Atl/N-1996
27	Albert Belle, Chi/A-1997
27	John Flaherty, SD/N-1996
26	John Olerud, Tor/A-1993
25	Wade Boggs, Bos/A-1987
25	Tony Gwynn, SD/N-1983
25	Lance Johnson, Chi/A-1992

Most pinch hits, career

150	Manny Mota, 1962-1982
145	Smoky Burgess, 1949-1967
143	Greg Gross, 1973-1989
123	Jose Morales, 1973-1984
116	Jerry Lynch, 1954-1966
114	Red Lucas, 1923-1938
113	Steve Braun, 1971-1985
108	Terry Crowley, 1969-1983
108	Denny Walling, 1975-1992
107	Gates Brown, 1963-1975
103	Mike Lum, 1967-1981
102	Jim Dwyer, 1973-1990
100	Rusty Staub, 1963-1985
95	Larry Biittner, 1970-1983
95	Vic Davalillo, 1963-1980
95	Gerald Perry, 1983-1995
94	Jerry Hairston, 1973-1989
93	Dave Philley, 1941-1962
93	Joel Youngblood, 1976-1989
92	Jay Johnstone, 1966-1985

Most pinch hits, career, active players

82	John Vander Wal, 1991-1997
79	Dave Clark, 1986-1997

66	John Cangelosi, 1985-1997
63	Willie McGee, 1982-1997
63	Joe Orsulak, 1983-1997
62	Thomas Howard, 1990-1997
61	Dave Magadan, 1986-1997
55	Jim Eisenreich, 1982-1997

Most pinch-hit home runs, career

20	Cliff Johnson, 1972-1986
18	Jerry Lynch, 1954-1966
16	Gates Brown, 1963-1975
16	Smoky Burgess, 1949-1967
16	Willie McCovey, 1959-1980
14	George Crowe, 1952-1961
12	Joe Adcock, 1950-1966
12	Bob Cerv, 1951-1962
12	Jose Morales, 1973-1984
12	Graig Nettles, 1967-1988
11	Jeff Burroughs, 1970-1985
11	Jay Johnstone, 1966-1985
11	Candy Maldonado, 1981-1995
11	Fred Whitfield, 1962-1970
11	Cy Williams, 1912-1930
10	Mark Carreon, 1987-1996
10	DAVE CLARK, 1986-1997
10	Jim Dwyer, 1973-1990
10	Mike Lum, 1967-1981
10	Ken McMullen, 1962-1977
10	Don Mincher, 1960-1972
10	Wally Post, 1949-1964
10	Champ Summers, 1974-1984
10	Jerry Turner, 1974-1983
10	JOHN VANDER WAL, 1991-1997
10	Gus Zernial, 1949-1959

Most pinch-hit home runs, career, active players

10	Dave Clark, 1986-1997
10	John Vander Wal, 1991-1997
7	Billy Ashley, 1992-1997
7	Jack Howell, 1985-1997
7	Paul Sorrento, 1989-1997
6	Rex Hudler, 1984-1997
5	Eric Anthony, 1989-1997
5	Chili Davis, 1981-1997
5	Thomas Howard, 1990-1997
5	Mark Johnson, 1995-1997
5	Terry Steinbach, 1986-1997
5	Rick Wilkins, 1991-1997

Pitchers

Most consecutive scoreless innings, season

59	OREL HERSHISER, LA/N - Aug. 30 to Sept. 28, 1988 (end of season; allowed a run in first inning of next start, April 5, 1989)
58	Don Drysdale, LA/N - May 14 to June 8, 1968
55.2	Walter Johnson, Was/A-

	April 10 to May 14, 1913
53	Jack Coombs, Phi/A - Sept. 5 to 25, 1910
47	Bob Gibson, StL/N - June 2 to 26, 1968
45.1	Carl Hubbell, NY/N - July 13 to Aug. 1, 1933 (allowed a run charged to starter in a relief appearance on July 19, after 12 scoreless innings, had a 33-inning string afterwards)
45	Sal Maglie, NY/N - Aug. 16 to Sept. 13, 1950
45	Doc White, Chi/A - Sept. 12 to 30, 1904
45	Cy Young, Bos/A - April 25 to May 17, 1904
44	Ed Reulbach, Chi/N- Sept. 17 to Oct. 3, 1908 (end of season; added 6 more innings on April 17, 1909 for a total of 50 over 2 years)
43.2	Rube Waddell, Phi/A - Aug. 22 to Sept. 5, 1905
42	George "Rube" Foster, Bos/A - May 1 to 26, 1914
41	Grover Cleveland Alexander, Phi/N - Sept. 7 to 24, 1911
41	Jack Chesbro, Pit/N - June 26 to July 16, 1902
41	Art Nehf, Bos/N - Sept. 13 to Oct. 4, 1917
41	Luis Tiant, Cle/A - April 28 to May 17, 1968
40	Walter Johnson, Was/A - May 7 to 26, 1918
40	Gaylord Perry, SF/N - Aug. 28 to Sept. 10, 1967
40	Luis Tiant, Bos/A - Aug. 19 to Sept. 8, 1972
39.2	Mordecai Brown, Chi/N - June 8 to July 8, 1908
39.2	Billy Pierce, Chi/A - Aug. 3 to 19, 1953
39	Ray Culp, Bos/A- Sept.7 to 25, 1968
39	Christy Mathewson, NY/N - May 3 to 21, 1901
39	Don Newcombe, Bro/N - July 25 to Aug. 11, 1956
39	Gaylord Perry, SF/N - Sept. 1 to 23, 1970
39	Ed Walsh, Chi/A - Aug. 10 to 22, 1906
38.1	Bill Lee, Chi/N - Sept. 5 to 26, 1938
38	Jim Bagby, Cle/A - June 30 to July 16, 1917
38	John Clarkson, Chi/N - May 18 to 27, 1885
38	Jim Galvin, Buf/N - Aug. 2 to 8, 1884
38	Ray Herbert, Chi/A - May 1 to 14, 1963

37	George Bradley, StL/N - July 8 to 18, 1876
37	Joel Horlen, Chi/A - May 11 to 29, 1968
37	Walter Johnson, Was/A - June 27 to July 13, 1913
37	Mike Torrez, Oak/A - Aug. 29 to Sept. 15, 1976
37	Ed Walsh, Chi/A - July 31 to Aug. 14, 1910
37	Cy Young, Bos/A - June 13 to July 1, 1903
36	Hal Brown, Bal/A - July 7 to Aug. 8, 1961 (allowed 4 runs on July 17 in a rained out game)
36	Charlie Hough, Tex/A - Aug. 23 to Sept. 14, 1983
36	Jim McGlothlin, Cal/A - May 22 to June 11, 1967 (GREGG OLSON, Bal/A had a streak of 41 scoreless innings over two seasons from Aug. 4, 1989 to May 4, 1990, 26 in 1989 and 15 in 1990)
36	Ed Morris, Pit/N - Sept. 5 to 17, 1888

Most strikeouts, game

21	Tom Cheney, Was/A - Sept. 12, 1962 (16 innings)
20	ROGER CLEMENS, Bos/A - April 29, 1986
20	ROGER CLEMENS, Bos/A - Sept. 18, 1996
19	Steve Carlton, StL/N - Sept. 15, 1969
19	DAVID CONE, NY/N - Oct. 6, 1991
19	Hugh (One Arm) Daily, Chi/UA-July 7, 1884
19	RANDY JOHNSON, Sea/A - June 24, 1997
19	RANDY JOHNSON, Sea/A - Aug. 8, 1997
19	Nolan Ryan, Cal/A - June 14, 1974 (12 innings)
19	Nolan Ryan, Cal/A - Aug. 12, 1974
19	Nolan Ryan, Cal/A - Aug. 20, 1974 (11 innings)
19	Nolan Ryan, Cal/A - June 8, 1977 (10 innings)
19	Tom Seaver, NY/N - April 22, 1970
19	Charlie Sweeney, Pro/N - June 7, 1884
19	Luis Tiant, Cle/A - July 3, 1968 (10 innings)
18	Jack Coombs, Phi/A - Sept. 1, 1906 (24 innings)
18	Bob Feller, Cle/A - Oct. 2, 1938 (1st game)
18	Ron Guidry, NY/A -

	June 17, 1978
18	Bill Gullickson, Mon/N - Sept. 10, 1980
18	RANDY JOHNSON, Sea/A - Sept. 27, 1992
18	Sandy Koufax, LA/N - Aug. 31, 1959
18	Sandy Koufax, LA/N - April 24, 1962
18	Jim Maloney, Cin/N - June 14, 1965 (11 innings)
18	RAMON MARTINEZ, LA/N - June 4, 1990
18	Henry Porter, Mil/UA - Oct. 3, 1884
18	Nolan Ryan, Cal/A - Sept. 10, 1976
18	Dupee Shaw, Bos/UA - July 19, 1884
18	Chris Short, Phi/N - Oct. 2, 1965 (15 innings in an 18 inning game)
18	Warren Spahn, Bos/N - June 14, 1952 (15 innings)
18	Jim Whitney, Bos/N - June 14, 1884 (15 innings)
18	Don Wilson, Hou/N - July 14, 1968

Most bases on balls, game

16	Tommy Byrne, NY/A - Aug. 22, 1951 (13 innings)
16	Bill George, NY/N - May 30, 1887 (1st game)
16	Henry Gruber, Cle/PL - April 19, 1890
16	Bruno Haas, Phi/A - June 23, 1915
16	George Vanhaltren, Chi/N - June 27, 1887
15	Carroll Brown, Phi/A - July 12, 1913
14	Ed Crane, Was/N - Sept. 1, 1886
14	Skipper Friday, Was/A - June 17, 1923
14	Charlie Hickman, Bos/N - Aug. 16, 1899 (2nd game)
14	Henry Mathewson, NY/N - Oct. 5, 1906
13	Tommy Byrne, NY/A - June 8, 1949
13	Mal Eason, Bos/N - Sept. 3, 1902
13	Bill George, NY/N - May 17, 1887
13	John Kirby, Ind/N - June 9, 1887
13	Bud Podbielan, Cin/N - May 18, 1953 (11 innings)
13	Cy Seymour, NY/N - May 24, 1899 (10 innings)
13	Pete Schneider, Cin/N - July 6, 1918
13	George Turbeville, Phi/A -

Aug. 24, 1935 (15 innings)
13 Dick Weik, Was/A - Sept. 1, 1949

No-hit games, nine or more innings (number to left is career total if greater than 1)

Joe Borden, Phi vs Chi NA, 4-0; July 28, 1875.

George Bradley, StL vs Har NL, 2-0; July 15, 1876.

Lee Richmond, Wor vs Cle NL, 1-0; June 12, 1880 (perfect game).

Monte Ward, Pro vs Buf NL, 5-0; June 17, 1880 (perfect game).

Larry Corcoran, Chi vs Bos NL, 6-0; Aug. 19, 1880.

Jim Galvin, Buf at Wor NL, 1-0; Aug. 20, 1880.

Tony Mullane, Lou at Cin AA, 2-0; Sept. 11, 1882.

Guy Hecker, Lou at Pit AA, 3-1; Sept. 19, 1882.

2 Larry Corcoran, Chi vs Wor NL, 5-0; Sept. 20, 1882.

Charley Radbourn, Pro at Cle NL, 8-0; July 25, 1883.

Hugh (One Arm) Daily, Cle at Phi NL, 1-0; Sept. 13, 1883.

Al Atkisson, Phi vs Pit AA, 10-1; May 24, 1884.

Ed Morris, Col at Pit AA, 5-0; May 29, 1884.

Frank Mountain, Col at Was AA, 12-0; June 5, 1884.

3 Larry Corcoran, Chi vs Pro NL, 6-0; June 27, 1884.

2 Jim Galvin, Buf at Det NL, 18-0; Aug. 4, 1884.

Dick Burns, Cin at KC UA, 3-1; Aug. 26, 1884.

Ed Cushman, Mil vs Was UA, 5-0; Sept. 28, 1884.

Sam Kimber, Bro vs Tol AA, 0-0; Oct. 4, 1884 (10 innings, darkness).

John Clarkson, Chi at Pro NL, 4-0; July 27, 1885.

Charlie Ferguson, Phi vs Pro NL, 1-0; Aug. 29, 1885.

2 Al Atkisson, Phi vs NY AA, 3-2; May 1, 1886.

Adonis Terry, Bro vs StL AA, 1-0; July 24, 1886.

Matt Kilroy, Bal at Pit AA, 6-0; Oct. 6, 1886.

2 Adonis Terry, Bro vs Lou AA, 4-0; May 27, 1888.

Henry Porter, KC at Bal AA, 4-0; June 6, 1888.

Ed Seward, Phi vs Cin AA, 12-2; July 26, 1888.

Gus Weyhing, Phi vs KC AA, 4-0; July 31, 1888.

Silver King, Chi vs Bro PL, 0-1;

June 21, 1890, (8 innings, lost the game; bottom of 9th not played).

Cannonball Titcomb, Roch vs Syr AA, 7-0; Sept. 15, 1890.

Tom Lovett, Bro vs NY NL, 4-0; June 22, 1891.

Amos Rusie, NY vs Bro NL, 6-0; July 31, 1891.

Ted Breitenstein, StL vs Lou AA, 8-0; Oct. 4, 1891 (1st game, 1st start in the major leagues).

Jack Stivetts, Bos vs Bro NL, 11-0; Aug. 6, 1892.

Ben Sanders, Lou vs Bal NL, 6-2; Aug. 22, 1892.

Bumpus Jones, Cin vs Pit NL, 7-1; Oct. 15, 1892 (1st game in the major leagues).

Bill Hawke, Bal vs Was NL, 5-0; Aug. 16, 1893.

Cy Young, Cle vs Cin NL, 6-0; Sept. 18, 1897 (1st game).

2 Ted Breitenstein, Cin vs Pit NL, 11-0; April 22, 1898.

Jim Hughes, Bal vs Bos NL, 8-0; April 22, 1898.

Red Donahue, Phi vs Bos NL, 5-0; July 8, 1898.

Walter Thornton, Chi vs Bro NL, 2-0; Aug. 21, 1898 (2nd game).

Deacon Phillippe, Lou vs NY NL, 7-0; May 25, 1899.

Noodles Hahn, Cin vs Phi NL, 4-0; July 12, 1900.

Earl Moore, Cle vs Chi AL, 2-4; May 9, 1901 (lost on two hits in the 10th).

Christy Mathewson, NY at StL NL, 5-0; July 15, 1901.

Nixey Callahan, Chi vs Det AL, 3-0; Sept. 20, 1902 (1st game).

Chick Fraser, Phi at Chi NL; 10-0; Sept. 18, 1903 (2nd game).

2 Cy Young, Bos vs Phi AL, 3-0; May 5, 1904 (perfect game).

Bob Wicker, Chi at NY NL, 1-0; June 11, 1904 (won in 12 innings after allowing one hit in the 10th).

Jesse Tannehill, Bos at Chi AL, 6-0; Aug. 17, 1904.

2 Christy Mathewson, NY at Chi NL, 1-0; June 13, 1905.

Weldon Henley, Phi at StL AL, 6-0; July 22, 1905 (1st game).

Frank Smith, Chi at Det AL, 15-0; Sept. 6, 1905 (2nd game).

Bill Dinneen, Bos vs Chi AL, 2-0; Sept. 27, 1905 (1st game).

Johnny Lush, Phi at Bro NL, 6-0; May 1, 1906.

Mal Eason, Bro at StL NL, 2-0; July 20, 1906.

Harry McIntyre, Bro vs Pit NL, 0-1; Aug. 1, 1906 (lost on four hits in

13 innings after allowing the first hit in the 11th).

Frank (Jeff) Pfeffer, Bos vs Cin NL, 6-0; May 8, 1907.

Nick Maddox, Pit vs Bro NL, 2-1; Sept. 20, 1907.

3 Cy Young, Bos at NY AL, 8-0; June 30, 1908.

Hooks Wiltse, NY vs Phi NL, 1-0; July 4, 1908 (1st game, 10 innings).

Nap Rucker, Bro vs Bos NL, 6-0; Sept. 5, 1908 (2nd game).

Dusty Rhoades, Cle vs Bos AL, 2-1; Sept. 18, 1908.

2 Frank Smith, Chi vs Phi AL, 1-0; Sept. 20, 1908.

Addie Joss, Cle vs Chi AL, 1-0; Oct. 2, 1908 (perfect game).

Red Ames, NY vs Bro NL. 0-3; April 15, 1909 (lost on seven hits in 13 innings after allowing the first hit in the 10th).

2 Addie Joss, Cle at Chi AL, 1-0; April 20, 1910.

Chief Bender, Phi vs Cle AL, 4-0; May 12, 1910.

Tom L. Hughes, NY vs Cle AL, 0-5; Aug. 30, 1910 (2nd game; lost on seven hits in 11 innings after allowing the first hit in the 10th).

Joe Wood, Bos vs StL AL, 5-0; July 29, 1911 (1st game).

Ed Walsh, Chi vs Bos AL, 5-0; Aug. 27, 1911.

George Mullin, Det vs StL AL, 7-0; July 4, 1912 (2nd game).

Earl Hamilton, StL at Det AL, 5-1; Aug. 30, 1912.

Jeff Tesreau, NY at Phi NL, 3-0; Sept. 6, 1912 (1st game).

Jim Scott, Chi at Was AL, 0-1; May 14, 1914 (lost on two hits in the 10th).

Joe Benz, Chi vs Cle AL, 6-1; May 31, 1914.

George Davis, Bos vs Phi NL, 7-0; Sept. 9, 1914 (2nd game).

Ed Lafitte, Bro vs KC FL, 6-2; Sept. 19, 1914.

Rube Marquard, NY vs Bro NL, 2-0; April 15, 1915.

Frank Allen, Pit at StL FL, 2-0; April 24, 1915.

Claude Hendrix, Chi at Pit FL, 10-0; May 15, 1915.

Alex Main, KC at Buf FL, 5-0; Aug. 16, 1915.

Jimmy Lavender, Chi at NY NL, 2-0; Aug. 31, 1915 (1st game).

Dave Davenport, StL vs Chi FL, 3-0; Sept. 7, 1915.

2 Tom L. Hughes, Bos vs Pit NL, 2-0; June 16, 1916.

Rube Foster, Bos vs NY AL, 2-0;

June 21, 1916.
Joe Bush, Phi vs Cle AL, 5-0;
Aug. 26, 1916.
Hubert (Dutch) Leonard, Bos vs StL
AL, 4-0; Aug. 30, 1916.
Eddie Cicotte, Chi at StL AL, 11-0;
April 14, 1917.
George Mogridge, NY at Bos AL, 2-
1; April 24, 1917.
Fred Toney, Cin at Chi NL, 1-0;
May 2, 1917 (10 innings).
Hippo Vaughn, Chi vs Cin NL, 0-1;
May 2, 1917 (lost on two hits in
the 10th, Fred Toney pitched a
no-hitter in this game).
Ernie Koob, StL vs Chi AL, 1-0;
May 5, 1917.
Bob Groom, StL vs Chi AL, 3-0;
May 6, 1917 (2nd game).
Ernie Shore, Bos vs Was AL, 4-0;
June 23, 1917 (1st game, perfect
game. Shore relieved Babe Ruth
in the first inning after Ruth had
been thrown out of the game for
protesting a walk to the first bat-
ter. The runner was caught steal-
ing and Shore retired the remain-
ing 26 batters in order.)
2 Hubert (Dutch) Leonard, Bos at Det
AL, 5-0; June 3, 1918.
Hod Eller, Cin vs StL NL, 6-0;
May 11, 1919.
Ray Caldwell, Cle at NY AL, 3-0;
Sept. 10, 1919 (1st game).
Walter Johnson, Was at Bos AL, 1-0;
July 1, 1920.
Charlie Robertson, Chi at Det AL,
2-0; April 30, 1922 (perfect
game).
Jesse Barnes, NY vs Phi NL, 6-0;
May 7, 1922.
Sam Jones, NY at Phi AL, 2-0;
Sept. 4, 1923.
Howard Ehmke, Bos at Phi AL, 4-0;
Sept. 7, 1923.
Jesse Haines, StL vs Bos NL, 5-0;
July 17, 1924.
Dazzy Vance, Bro vs Phi NL, 10-1;
Sept. 13, 1925 (1st game).
Ted Lyons, Chi at Bos AL, 6-0;
Aug. 21, 1926.
Carl Hubbell, NY at Pit NL, 11-0;
May 8, 1929.
Wes Ferrell, Cle vs StL AL, 9-0;
April 29, 1931.
Bobby Burke, Was vs Bos AL, 5-0;
Aug. 8, 1931.
Bobo Newsom, StL vs Bos AL, 1-2;
Sept. 18, 1934 (lost on one hit in
the 10th).
Paul Dean, StL at Bro NL, 3-0;
Sept. 21, 1934 (2nd game).
Vern Kennedy, Chi vs Cle AL, 5-0;
Aug. 31, 1935.
Bill Dietrich, Chi vs StL AL, 8-0;

June 1, 1937.
Johnny Vander Meer, Cin vs Bos NL,
3-0; June 11, 1938.
2 Johnny Vander Meer, Cin at Bro
NL, 6-0; June 15, 1938 (next
start after June 11).
Monte Pearson, NY vs Cle AL, 13-0;
Aug. 27, 1938 (2nd game).
Bob Feller, Cle at Chi AL, 1-0;
April 16, 1940 (Opening Day).
Tex Carleton, Bro at Cin NL, 3-0;
April 30, 1940.
Lon Warneke, StL at Cin NL, 2-0;
Aug. 30, 1941.
Jim Tobin, Bos vs Bro NL, 2-0;
April 27, 1944.
Clyde Shoun, Cin vs Bos NL, 1-0;
May 15, 1944.
Dick Fowler, Phi vs StL AL, 1-0;
Sept. 9, 1945 (2nd game).
Ed Head, Bro vs Bos NL, 5-0;
April 23, 1946.
2 Bob Feller, Cle at NY AL, 1-0;
April 30, 1946.
Ewell Blackwell, Cin vs Bos NL, 6-0;
June 18, 1947.
Don Black, Cle vs Phi AL, 3-0;
July 10, 1947 (1st game).
Bill McCahan, Phi vs Was AL, 3-0;
Sept. 3, 1947.
Bob Lemon, Cle at Det AL, 2-0;
June 30, 1948.
Rex Barney, Bro at NY NL, 2-0;
Sept. 9, 1948.
Vern Bickford, Bos vs Bro NL, 7-0;
Aug. 11, 1950.
Cliff Chambers, Pit at Bos NL, 3-0;
May 6, 1951 (2nd game).
3 Bob Feller, Cle vs Det AL, 2-1;
July 1, 1951 (1st game).
Allie Reynolds, NY at Cle AL, 1-0;
July 12, 1951.
2 Allie Reynolds, NY vs Bos AL, 8-0;
Sept. 28, 1951 (1st game).
Virgil Trucks, Det vs Was AL, 1-0;
May 15, 1952.
Carl Erskine, Bro vs Chi NL, 5-0;
June 19, 1952.
2 Virgil Trucks, Det at NY AL, 1-0;
Aug. 25, 1952.
Bobo Holloman, StL vs Phi AL, 6-0;
May 6, 1953 (1st start in the
major leagues).
Jim Wilson, Mil vs Phi NL, 2-0;
June 12, 1954.
Sam Jones, Chi vs Pit NL, 4-0;
May 12, 1955.
2 Carl Erskine, Bro vs NY NL, 3-0;
May 12, 1956.
Johnny Klippstein (7 innings),
Hershell Freeman (1 inning) and
Joe Black (3 innings), Cin at Mil
NL, 1-2;
May 26, 1956 (lost on three hits
in 11 innings after allowing the

first hit in the 10th).
Mel Parnell, Bos vs Chi AL, 4-0;
July 14, 1956.
Sal Maglie, Bro vs Phi NL, 5-0;
Sept. 25, 1956.
Don Larsen, NY AL vs Bro NL, 2-0;
Oct. 8, 1956 (World Series, per-
fect game).
Bob Keegan, Chi vs Was AL, 6-0;
Aug. 20, 1957 (2nd game).
Jim Bunning, Det at Bos AL, 3-0;
July 20, 1958 (1st game).
Hoyt Wilhelm, Bal vs NY AL, 1-0;
Sept. 20, 1958.
Harvey Haddix, Pit at Mil NL, 0-1;
May 26, 1959 (lost on one hit in
13 innings after pitching 12 per-
fect innings).
Don Cardwell, Chi vs StL NL, 4-0;
May 15, 1960 (2nd game).
Lew Burdette, Mil vs Phi NL, 1-0;
Aug. 18, 1960.
Warren Spahn, Mil vs Phi NL, 4-0;
Sept. 16, 1960.
2 Warren Spahn, Mil vs SF NL, 1-0;
April 28, 1961.
Bo Belinsky, LA vs Bal AL, 2-0;
May 5, 1962.
Earl Wilson, Bos vs LA AL, 2-0;
June 26, 1962.
Sandy Koufax, LA vs NY NL, 5-0;
June 30, 1962.
Bill Monbouquette, Bos at Chi AL,
1-0; Aug. 1, 1962.
Jack Kralick, Min vs KC AL, 1-0;
Aug. 26, 1962.
2 Sandy Koufax, LA vs SF NL, 8-0;
May 11, 1963.
Don Nottebart, Hou vs Phi NL, 4-1;
May 17, 1963.
Juan Marichal, SF vs Hou NL, 1-0;
June 15, 1963.
Ken T. Johnson, Hou vs Cin NL, 0-1;
April 23, 1964 (lost the game).
3 Sandy Koufax, LA at Phi NL, 3-0;
June 4, 1964.
2 Jim Bunning, Phi at NY NL, 6-0;
June 21, 1964 (1st game, perfect
game).
Jim Maloney, Cin vs NY NL, 0-1;
June 14, 1965 (lost on two hits in
11 innings after pitching 10 hit-
less innings).
2 Jim Maloney, Cin at Chi NL, 1-0;
Aug. 19, 1965 (1st game, 10
innings).
4 Sandy Koufax, LA vs Chi NL, 1-0;
Sept. 9, 1965 (perfect game).
Dave Morehead, Bos vs Cle AL, 2-0;
Sept. 16, 1965.
Sonny Siebert, Cle vs Was AL, 2-0;
June 10, 1966.
Steve D. Barber (8⅔ innings) and
Stu Miller (⅓ inning), Bal vs Det
AL, 1-2; April 30, 1967 (1st

game, lost the game).

Don Wilson, Hou vs Atl NL, 2-0;
June 18, 1967.

Dean Chance, Min at Cle AL, 2-1;
Aug. 25, 1967 (2nd game).

Joe Horlen, Chi vs Det AL, 6-0;
Sept. 10, 1967 (1st game).

Tom Phoebus, Bal vs Bos AL, 6-0;
April 27, 1968.

Catfish Hunter, Oak vs Min AL, 4-0;
May 8, 1968 (perfect game).

George Culver, Cin at Phi NL, 6-1;
July 29, 1968 (2nd game).

Gaylord Perry, SF vs StL NL, 1-0;
Sept. 17, 1968.

Ray Washburn, StL at SF NL, 2-0;
Sept. 18, 1968.

Bill Stoneman, Mon at Phi NL, 7-0;
April 17, 1969.

3 Jim Maloney, Cin vs Hou NL, 10-0;
April 30, 1969.

2 Don Wilson, Hou at Cin NL, 4-0;
May 1, 1969.

Jim Palmer, Bal vs Oak AL, 8-0;
Aug. 13, 1969.

Ken Holtzman, Chi vs Atl NL, 3-0;
Aug. 19, 1969.

Bob Moose, Pit at NY NL, 4-0;
Sept. 20, 1969.

Dock Ellis, Pit at SD NL, 2-0;
June 12, 1970 (1st game).

Clyde Wright, Cal vs Oak AL, 4-0;
July 3, 1970.

Bill Singer, LA vs Phi NL, 5-0;
July 20, 1970.

Vida Blue, Oak vs Min AL, 6-0;
Sept. 21, 1970.

2 Ken Holtzman, Chi at Cin NL, 1-0;
June 3, 1971.

Rick Wise, Phi at Cin NL, 4-0;
June 23, 1971.

Bob Gibson, StL at Pit NL, 11-0;
Aug. 14, 1971.

Burt Hooton, Chi vs Phi NL, 4-0;
April 16, 1972.

Milt Pappas, Chi vs SD NL, 8-0;
Sept. 2, 1972.

2 Bill Stoneman, Mon vs NY NL, 7-0;
Oct. 2, 1972 (1st game).

Steve Busby, KC at Det AL, 3-0;
April 16, 1973.

Nolan Ryan, Cal at KC AL, 3-0;
May 15, 1973.

2 Nolan Ryan, Cal at Det AL, 6-0;
July 15, 1973.

Jim Bibby, Tex at Oak AL, 6-0;
July 30, 1973.

Phil Niekro, Atl vs SD NL, 9-0;
Aug. 5, 1973.

2 Steve Busby, KC at Mil AL, 2-0;
June 19, 1974.

Dick Bosman, Cle vs Oak AL, 4-0;
July 19, 1974.

3 Nolan Ryan, Cal vs Min AL, 4-0;
Sept. 28, 1974.

4 Nolan Ryan, Cal vs Bal AL, 1-0;
June 1, 1975.

Ed Halicki, SF vs NY NL, 6-0;
Aug. 24, 1975 (2nd game).

Vida Blue (5 innings), Glenn Abbott (1 inning), Paul Lindblad (1 inning) and Rollie Fingers (2 innings), Oak vs Cal AL, 5-0; Sept. 28, 1975.

Larry Dierker, Hou vs Mon NL, 6-0;
July 9, 1976.

Blue Moon Odom (5 innings) and Francisco Barrios (4 innings), Chi at Oak AL, 2-1; July 28, 1976.

John Candelaria, Pit vs LA NL, 2-0;
Aug. 9, 1976.

John Montefusco, SF at Atl NL, 9-0;
Sept. 29, 1976.

Jim Colborn, KC vs Tex AL, 6-0;
May 14, 1977.

DENNIS ECKERSLEY, Cle vs Cal AL, 1-0; May 30, 1977.

Bert Blyleven, Tex at Cal AL, 6-0;
Sept. 22, 1977.

Bob Forsch, StL vs Phi NL, 5-0;
April 16, 1978.

Tom Seaver, Cin vs StL NL, 4-0;
June 16, 1978.

Ken Forsch, Hou vs Atl NL, 6-0;
April 7, 1979.

Jerry Reuss, LA at SF NL, 8-0;
June 27, 1980.

Charlie Lea, Mon vs SF NL, 4-0;
May 10, 1981 (2nd game).

Len Barker, Cle vs Tor AL, 3-0;
May 15, 1981 (perfect game).

5 Nolan Ryan, Hou vs LA NL, 5-0;
Sept. 26, 1981.

Dave Righetti, NY vs Bos AL, 4-0;
July 4, 1983.

2 Bob Forsch, StL vs Mon NL, 3-0;
Sept. 26, 1983.

Mike Warren, Oak vs Chi AL, 3-0;
Sept. 29, 1983.

Jack Morris, Det at Chi AL, 4-0;
April 7, 1984.

Mike Witt, Cal at Tex AL, 1-0;
Sept. 30, 1984 (perfect game).

Joe Cowley, Chi at Cal AL, 7-1;
Sept. 19, 1986.

Mike Scott, Hou vs SF NL, 2-0;
Sept. 25, 1986.

Juan Nieves, Mil at Bal AL, 7-0;
April 15, 1987.

Tom Browning, Cin vs LA NL, 1-0;
Sept. 16, 1988 (perfect game).

MARK LANGSTON (7 innings) and Mike Witt (2 innings), Cal vs Sea AL, 1-0; April 11, 1990.

RANDY JOHNSON, Sea vs Det AL, 2-0; June 2, 1990.

6 Nolan Ryan, Tex at Oak AL, 5-0;
June 11, 1990.

Dave Stewart, Oak at Tor AL, 5-0;

June 29, 1990.

FERNANDO VALENZUELA, LA vs StL NL, 6-0; June 29, 1990.

Andy Hawkins, NY at Chi AL, 0-4; July 1, 1990 (8 innings, lost the game; bottom of 9th not played).

TERRY MULHOLLAND, Phi vs SF NL, 6-0; Aug. 15, 1990.

Dave Stieb, Tor at Cle AL, 3-0;
Sept. 2, 1990.

7 Nolan Ryan, Tex vs Tor AL, 3-0;
May 1, 1991.

Tommy Greene, Phi at Mon NL, 2-0;
May 23, 1991.

Bob Milacki (6 innings), Mike Flanagan (1 inning), Mark Williamson, (1 inning) and GREGG OLSON (1 inning), Bal at Oak AL, 2-0; July 13, 1991.

MARK GARDNER, Mon at LA NL, 0-1; July 26, 1991 (9 innings, lost on two hits in 10th; relieved by JEFF FASSERO, who allowed one more hit).

DENNIS MARTINEZ, Mon at LA NL, 2-0; July 28, 1991 (perfect game).

WILSON ALVAREZ, Chi at Bal AL, 7-0; Aug. 11, 1991.

BRET SABERHAGEN, KC vs Chi AL, 7-0; Aug. 26, 1991.

KENT MERCKER (6 innings), MARK WOHLERS (2 innings) and Alejandro Pena (1 inning), Atl at SD NL, 1-0; Sept. 11, 1991.

Matt Young, Bos at Cle AL, 1-2; April 12, 1992 (1st game) (8 innings, lost the game, bottom of 9th not played).

KEVIN GROSS, LA vs SF NL, 2-0;
Aug. 17, 1992.

Chris Bosio, Sea vs Bos AL, 7-0;
April 22, 1993.

Jim Abbott, NY vs Cle AL, 4-0;
Sept. 4, 1993.

DARRYL KILE, Hou vs NY NL, 7-1;
Sept. 8, 1993.

KENT MERCKER, Atl at LA NL, 6-0;
April 8, 1994.

SCOTT ERICKSON, Min vs Mil AL, 6-0; April 27, 1994.

KENNY ROGERS, Tex vs Cal AL, 4-0; July 28, 1994 (perfect game).

PEDRO J. MARTINEZ (9 innings) and MEL ROJAS (1 inning), Mon at SD NL, 1-0; June 3,1995 (Martinez pitched nine perfect innings, but allowed a hit in the 10th; Rojas relieved and finished the game).

RAMON MARTINEZ, LA vs Fla NL, 7-0; July 14, 1995.

AL LEITER, Fla vs Col NL, 11-0;
May 11, 1996.

DWIGHT GOODEN, NY vs Sea AL,

2-0; May 14, 1996.

HIDEO NOMO, LA at Col NL, 9-0; Sept. 17, 1996.

KEVIN BROWN, Fla at SF NL, 9-0; June 10, 1997.

FRANCISCO CORDOVA (9 innings) and RICARDO RINCON (1 inning), Pit vs Hou NL, 3-0; July 12, 1997

No-hit games, less than 9 innings

Larry McKeon, 6 innings, rain, Ind at Cin AA, 0-0; May 6, 1884.

Charlie Gagus, 8 innings, darkness, Was vs Wil UA, 12-1; Aug. 21, 1884.

Charlie Getzien, 6 innings, rain, Det vs Phi NL, 1-0; Oct. 1, 1884.

Charlie Sweeney (2 innings) and Henry Boyle (3 innings), 5 innings, rain, StL vs StP UA, 0-1; Oct. 5,1884.

Dupee Shaw, 5 innings, agreement, Pro at Buf NL, 4-0; Oct. 7, 1885 (1st game).

George Vanhaltren, 6 innings, rain, Chi vs Pit NL, 1-0, June 21,1888.

Ed Crane, 7 innings, darkness, NY vs Was NL, 3-0; Sept. 27, 1888.

Matt Kilroy, 7 innings, darkness, Bal vs StL AA, 0-0; July 29, 1889 (2nd game).

George Nicol, 7 innings, darkness, StL vs Phi AA, 21-2; Sept. 23, 1890.

Hank Gastright, 8 innings, darkness, Col vs Tol AA, 6-0; Oct. 12, 1890.

Jack Stivetts, 5 innings, called so Boston could catch train to Cleveland for Temple Cub play-offs, Bos at Was NL, 6-0; Oct. 15, 1892 (2nd game).

Elton Chamberlain, 7 innings, darkness, Cin vs Bos NL, 6-0; Sept. 23, 1893 (2nd game).

Ed Stein, 6 innings, rain, Bro vs Chi NL, 6-0; June 2, 1894.

Red Ames, 5 innings, darkness, NY at StL NL, 5-0; Sept. 14, 1903 (2nd game, 1st game in the major leagues).

Rube Waddell, 5 innings, rain, Phi vs StL AL, 2-0; Aug. 15, 1905.

Jake Weimer, 7 innings, agreement, Cin vs Bro NL, 1-0; Aug. 24, 1906 (2nd game).

Jimmy Dygert (3 innings) and Rube Waddell (2 innings), 5 innings, rain, Phi vs Chi AL, 4-3; Aug. 29, 1906 (Waddell allowed hit and two runs in 6th, but rain caused game to revert to 5 innings).

Stoney McGlynn, 7 innings, agree-ment, StL at Bro NL, 1-1; Sept. 24, 1906 (2nd game).

Lefty Leifield, 6 innings, darkness, Pit at Phi NL, 8-0; Sept. 26, 1906 (2nd game).

Ed Walsh, 5 innings, rain, Chi vs NY AL, 8-1; May 26, 1907.

Ed Karger, 7 perfect innings, agree-ment, StL vs Bos NL, 4-0; Aug. 11, 1907 (2nd game).

Howie Camnitz, 5 innings, agree-ment, Pit at NY NL, 1-0; Aug. 23, 1907 (2nd game).

Rube Vickers, 5 perfect innings, darkness, Phi at Was AL, 4-0; Oct. 5, 1907 (2nd game).

Johnny Lush, 6 innings, rain, StL at Bro NL, 2-0; Aug. 6, 1908.

King Cole, 7 innings, called so Chicago could catch train, Chi at StL NL, 4-0; July 31, 1910 (2nd game).

Jay Cashion, 6 innings, called so Cleveland could catch train, Was vs Cle AL, 2-0; Aug. 20, 1912 (2nd game).

Walter Johnson, 7 innings, rain, Was vs StL AL, 2-0; Aug. 25, 1924.

Fred Frankhouse, 7⅔ innings, rain, Bro vs Cin NL, 5-0; Aug. 27, 1937.

John Whitehead, 6 innings, rain, StL vs Det AL, 4-0; Aug. 5, 1940 (2nd game).

Jim Tobin, 5 innings, darkness, Bos vs Phi NL, 7-0; June 22, 1944 (2nd game).

Mike McCormick, 5 innings, rain, SF at Phi NL, 3-0; June 12, 1959 (allowed hit in 6th, but rain caused game to revert to 5 innings.

Sam Jones,7 innings, rain, SF at StL NL, 4-0; Sept. 26, 1959.

Dean Chance, 5 perfect innings, rain, Min vs Bos AL, 2-0; Aug. 6, 1967.

David Palmer, 5 perfect innings, rain, Mon at StL NL, 4-0; April 21, 1984 (2nd game).

Pascual Perez, 5 innings, rain, Mon at Phi NL, 1-0; Sept. 24, 1988.

Melido Perez, 6 innings, rain, Chi at NY AL, 8-0; July 12, 1990.

Major league report

1998 Baseball Weekly Almanac

- ▶1997 season wrap-ups
- ▶1997 team MVPs
- ▶Week-by-week season notes
- ▶Quotes of the year
- ▶Team rosters and statistics
- ▶Franchise records

AL East		AL Central		AL West	
Orioles	78	Indians	118	Mariners	158
Yankees	86	White Sox	126	Angels	166
Tigers	94	Brewers	134	Rangers	174
Red Sox	102	Twins	142	Athletics	182
Blue Jays	110	Royals	150		
Devil Rays	190				

NL East		NL Central		NL West	
Braves	194	Astros	234	Giants	274
Marlins	202	Pirates	242	Dodgers	282
Mets	210	Reds	250	Rockies	290
Expos	218	Cardinals	258	Padres	298
Phillies	226	Cubs	266	Diamondbacks	306

Baltimore Orioles

By Russell Beeker, *Baseball Weekly*

A 15-game winner during the regular season, Mike Mussina set a playoff record with 41 strikeouts.

1997 Orioles: AL's best mark wasn't enough

This year the Orioles still felt the sting of having fallen to the Yankees in 1996, but even vanquishing New York didn't quite make this season a success. They won eight of 12 from the Yanks and led the East from wire to wire. Much of that was forgotten, however, in the disappointment of losing to Cleveland in a six-game ALCS. To compound the team's troubles, manager Davey Johnson resigned on Nov. 5 after two years of battles with owner Peter Angelos. Ironically, Johnson was named AL Manager of the Year hours after quitting.

The major difference between 1996 and '97 for Baltimore was the bullpen. The Orioles blew the fewest saves in the majors, and their tandem of setup man Armando Benitez and closer Randy Myers mirrored the success of the Yankees' Mariano Rivera and John Wetteland in '96. Myers was one step from perfect in converting 45 of 46 save opportunities. But Benitez, hailed as the closer of the future in Baltimore, will need to bounce back from his playoff failures. He held leads in 46 of 48 regular-season situations but gave up game-winning home runs in two play-off losses to Cleveland and the winning single in another.

Orioles starting pitchers were particularly hot early in the year, when Baltimore bolted to a 45-19 start and a division lead that reached 9½ games. The big three of Mike Mussina, Scott Erickson and Jimmy Key were a combined 28-4 by June 15. Erickson finished 16-7, and Key ended up 16-10. Mussina, the staff ace, finished 15-8 with a 3.20 ERA. His postseason numbers were staggering: In 29 innings, Mussina allowed 12 hits and four runs, with a postseason-record 41 strikeouts and a 1.24 ERA.

Johnson adroitly managed a team that was burdened by injuries to key players like Brady Anderson, Roberto Alomar, Cal Ripken and Chris Hoiles. Rafael Palmeiro was still a steady force in the balanced offense, with 38 home runs and 110, but his batting average dipped to .254, an

alarming 44 points below his career average. Anderson couldn't disprove the skeptics who said he wouldn't hit 50 homers again, but he was a fine leadoff man, with a .393 on-base average and 18 dingers. Cal Ripken moved from shortstop to third, and despite nagging back problems, he continued his consecutive-game streak. It reached 2,478 by the end of the year. Shortstop Mike Bordick didn't hit (.236) but excelled defensively.

Outfielder Eric Davis carried the team with his bat early in the season and with his courage the rest of the way. He had colon-cancer surgery but returned to the lineup in September while undergoing chemotherapy. The front office didn't tinker too much with the winning formula during the season, but did add proven bats Harold Baines and Geronimo Berroa through trades after Davis' condition was diagnosed.

Beyond the Orioles' stars, this was a team that also relied on the contributions of Lenny Webster, Aaron Ledesma, Jeff Reboulet and pitcher Scott Kamieniecki. Webster hit .300 while filling in when catcher Hoiles went on the DL. Ledesma and Reboulet made up for the frequent absence of second baseman Alomar, who hit .333 but missed time to injuries and his spitting-related suspension. Kamieniecki was invaluable as the fourth starter, winning 10 games despite low run support.

Team MVP

Randy Myers: It was just another off-season through which the whispers followed Randy Myers. How much did the Baltimore closer really have left? The left-hander's answer was to be baseball's best closer in 1997. His 45 saves led baseball, and he only missed converting one of his 46 opportunities. Myers had a 1.51 ERA while allowing just two home runs in 59⅔ innings.

1997 Orioles: Week-by-week notes

These notes were excerpted from the following issues of Baseball Weekly.

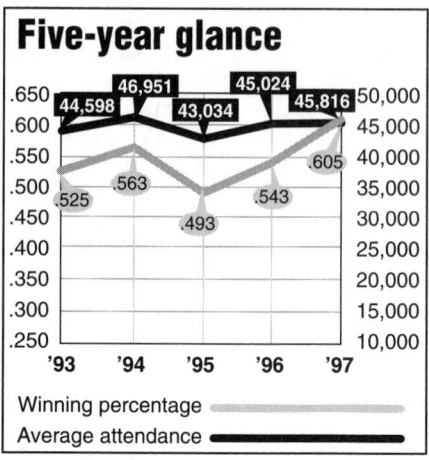

Five-year glance

Winning percentage

Average attendance

▶**April 9:** The Orioles' bullpen has improved so dramatically, it might be one of the best in the AL. In the club's first three games, relievers combined to pitch 10⅓ scoreless innings, allowing only six hits while striking out 16. The Orioles also signed third baseman Cal Ripken to a two-year, $15.1 million contract extension.

▶**April 16:** Right-hander Mike Mussina eased concerns about the calcium deposit in his right elbow, allowing only three hits in seven innings in a 9-3 victory against Texas on April 11. Mussina, rocked by Texas in his first start of 1997, said he does not foresee further problems.

▶**April 23:** Umpire John Hirschbeck declined to participate in a proposed meeting with second baseman Roberto Alomar before the two shared the same field for the first time this season, on April 22. Alomar served a five-game suspension at the start of the season for spitting on Hirschbeck last year. Hirschbeck said he did not believe a meeting was necessary.

▶**April 30:** The Orioles, trying to overcome a series of injuries to their outfielders, placed Jerome Walton on the 15-day DL and recalled Tony Tarasco from AAA Rochester. Brady Anderson aggravated his cracked rib by crashing into the center field wall on April 24, and B.J. Surhoff had a strained left groin. Eric Davis (shoulder) and Jeffrey Hammonds (groin) also missed time with injuries.

▶**May 7:** Closer Randy Myers converted his first 11 save opportunities before blowing one on May 3, when he gave up a two-out, two-run homer to Oakland's Jason Giambi. The runs were the first that Myers had allowed this season.

▶**May 21:** Starters Jimmy Key, Scott Erickson and Mike Mussina continued their dominance of the AL, combining for a 20-2 record through May 18.

▶**June 4:** On May 30, Mike Mussina just missed becoming only the 13th player in this century to pitch a perfect game, retir-

ing the first 25 Indians before Sandy Alomar hit a one-out single in the ninth inning. The 28-year-old right-hander shook off the hit and promptly struck out the next two batters. The team has been nearly perfect as well—their 36-15 record after 51 games matched the best in franchise history.

▶**June 11:** With their 4-0 record against the Yankees after home wins on June 3-4, the Orioles have already exceeded last season's victory total against New York. The Yankees went 9-0 at Camden Yards in 1996, including three victories in the ALCS.

▶**June 18:** Doctors at Johns Hopkins Hospital in Baltimore removed one-third of Eric Davis' colon in a two-hour operation on June 13, then conducted tests to determine if the mass that had caused him abdominal pain was cancerous. General manager Pat Gillick said the Orioles would seek a trade to replace Davis, preferably a slugger who could protect first baseman Rafael Palmeiro in the batting order. The Orioles appeared to focus on Oakland's Geronimo Berroa, a right-handed hitter who hit 36 home runs last season.

▶**July 2:** The Orioles acquired outfielder Geronimo Berroa from Oakland in exchange for AAA right-hander Jimmy Haynes and a minor leaguer to be named later. In his debut with Baltimore, Berroa went 0-for-5 with three strikeouts in a 3-2 loss to the Toronto Blue Jays, and he stranded six runners.

▶ **July 10:** While the Orioles await word on whether Eric Davis will undergo chemotherapy for colon cancer, they're encouraged by the progress of catcher Chris Hoiles, who is out with a slightly torn knee ligament. Hoiles was expected to miss up to eight weeks after the June 17 injury, but he took batting practice on July 4.

▶ **July 16:** Through July 13, the Orioles were 15-17 in games started by pitchers other than Mike Mussina, Jimmy Key and Scott Erickson. Ideally, they want to make Scott Kamieniecki (6-4 through July 13) their No. 5 starter instead of their fourth.

▶ **July 23:** By July 20, the Orioles' 9½-game lead from June 4 had shrunk to three. The team's sense of futility was vividly expressed by Cal Ripken. He was ejected, for only the third time in his career, after arguing over a called strike and later said he had inappropriately vented on umpire Al Clark.

▶ **July 30:** Davey Johnson said he would not be optimistic about his chances of returning if the Orioles did not make the World Series. He has a higher winning percentage than any other active manager in the majors, and he is working on his third consecutive postseason appearance, but owner Peter Angelos reportedly was displeased with him in October 1996, after the Orioles lost the AL Championship Series. "Basically, I've got a three-year contract, but I feel we've gotta do it in two," said Johnson.

▶ **Aug. 6:** The Orioles made two trades before the July 31 deadline, reacquiring DH Harold Baines from the White Sox and sending right-hander Mike Johnson to Montreal for a player to be named later. Roberto Alomar went on the 15-day disabled list with a strained right groin the night Baines was acquired, underscoring the need for another offensive player. Jeffrey Hammonds, one of the Orioles' hottest hitters, did not start the first three games after Baines' arrival due to a sore Achilles tendon.

▶ **Aug. 13:** Eric Davis rejoined the club in Anaheim on Aug. 8. Davis said he expects to begin light work off the batting tee in mid-August and increase his workout load after the first six-week segment of his chemotherapy for colon cancer is over.

▶ **Aug. 27:** Manager Davey Johnson ran-

kled ace Mike Mussina with an early hook, pulling the right-hander with a 3-2 lead against Minnesota on Aug. 23. Mussina had struck out 11 in five innings while allowing two runs on seven hits. He had thrown 99 pitches, and the bullpen blew his lead before the Orioles rallied for a 5-4 victory.

▶ **Sept. 10:** The Orioles won three out of four in New York to all but wrap up their first division title since 1983, but neither Davey Johnson nor his players would say the race is over. This season the Orioles have dominated the Yankees rivalry, winning seven of eight games, including five of six at Yankee Stadium. Johnson said Cal Ripken's consecutive-game streak would continue even if the Orioles clinch the AL East before the season ends. "Whatever he wants to do, I'll accommodate it," Johnson said.

▶ **Sept. 17:** Roberto Alomar has returned to the starting lineup with gimpy legs but a potent bat. Alomar hiked his average to .312 through the first game of Sept. 15's day-night doubleheader, going 10-for-17 since coming back from a lingering groin injury. But he has not shown his usual range in the field and has run the bases at half speed.

▶ **Sept. 24:** Eric Davis went 2-for-3 with three RBI in a 12-8 victory against Detroit on Sept. 20 and is expected to be included on the postseason roster. Returning from colon-cancer surgery, Davis was hitless in his first 10 at-bats before his breakout game. He's playing while undergoing chemotherapy to prevent the cancer from recurring.

▶ **Oct. 1:** With Randy Johnson pitching Game 1 for Seattle, Davey Johnson could decide to open the Division Series with three of his best hitters on the bench. Roberto Alomar, Rafael Palmeiro and B.J. Surhoff did not start the three times the Orioles faced the left-hander in the regular season, and Johnson wants to stack his lineup with right-handed hitters.

QUOTE OF THE YEAR

"You run the risk of being a little rusty."
—Third baseman Cal Ripken, in late September, on why he doesn't take a day off

BALTIMORE ORIOLES 1997 final stats

BATTERS	BA	SLG	OBA	G	AB	R	H	TB	2B	3B	HR	RBI	BB	SO	SB	CS	E
Ledesma	.352	.500	.437	43	88	24	31	44	5	1	2	11	13	9	1	0	3
Alomar	.333	.500	.390	112	412	64	137	206	23	2	14	60	40	43	9	3	6
Davis	.304	.525	.358	42	158	29	48	83	11	0	8	25	14	47	6	0	1
Baines	.301	.458	.375	137	452	55	136	207	23	0	16	67	55	62	0	1	0
Walton	.294	.441	.333	26	68	8	20	30	1	0	3	9	4	10	0	0	0
Anderson	.288	.469	.393	151	590	97	170	277	39	7	18	73	84	105	18	12	3
Surhoff	.284	.458	.345	147	528	80	150	242	30	4	18	88	49	60	1	1	2
Berroa	.283	.467	.369	156	561	88	159	262	25	0	26	90	76	120	4	4	4
Ripken	.270	.402	.331	162	615	79	166	247	30	0	17	84	56	73	1	0	22
Hammonds	.264	.486	.323	118	397	71	105	193	19	3	21	55	32	73	15	1	5
Hoiles	.259	.419	.375	99	320	45	83	134	15	0	12	49	51	86	1	0	0
Webster	.255	.375	.317	98	259	29	66	97	8	1	7	37	22	46	0	1	3
Palmeiro	.254	.485	.329	158	614	95	156	298	24	2	38	110	67	109	5	2	10
Reboulet	.237	.329	.307	99	228	26	54	75	9	0	4	27	23	44	3	0	7
Bordick	.236	.318	.283	153	509	55	120	162	19	1	7	46	33	66	0	2	13
Dellucci	.222	.370	.344	17	27	3	6	10	1	0	1	3	4	7	0	0	0
Tarasco	.205	.392	.313	100	166	26	34	65	8	1	7	26	25	33	2	2	1
Clyburn	.000	.000	.000	2	3	0	0	0	0	0	0	0	0	2	0	0	0
Greene	.000	.000	.000	5	2	0	0	0	0	0	0	0	1	0	1	0	0	0
Laker	.000	.000	.118	7	14	0	0	0	0	0	0	1	2	9	0	0	1
Rosario	.000	.000	.000	4	3	0	0	0	0	0	0	0	0	1	0	0	1

PITCHERS	W-L	ERA	BA	G	GS	CG	GF	Sho	SV	IP	H	R	ER	HR	BB	SO
Myers	2-3	1.51	.217	61	0	0	57	0	45	59.2	47	12	10	2	22	56
Orosco	6-3	2.32	.169	71	0	0	12	0	0	50.1	29	13	13	6	30	46
Benitez	4-5	2.45	.191	71	0	0	26	0	9	73.1	49	22	20	7	43	106
Williams	0-0	3.00	.220	13	0	0	8	0	0	24.0	20	8	8	0	18	14
Rhodes	10-3	3.02	.218	53	0	0	6	0	1	95.1	75	32	32	9	26	102
Mussina	15-8	3.20	.234	33	33	4	0	1	0	224.2	197	87	80	27	54	218
Key	16-10	3.43	.261	34	34	1	0	1	0	212.1	210	90	81	24	82	141
Erickson	16-7	3.69	.257	34	33	3	0	2	0	221.2	218	100	91	16	61	131
Kamieniecki	10-6	4.01	.261	30	30	0	0	0	0	179.1	179	83	80	20	67	109
Mathews	4-4	4.41	.267	57	0	0	19	0	1	63.1	63	35	31	8	36	39
Mills	2-3	4.89	.270	39	0	0	11	0	0	38.2	41	23	21	5	33	32
Rodriguez	2-1	4.91	.250	6	2	0	1	0	0	22.0	21	15	12	2	8	11
Coppinger	1-1	6.30	.273	5	4	0	1	0	0	20.0	21	14	14	2	16	22
Krivda	4-2	6.30	.328	10	10	0	0	0	0	50.0	67	36	35	7	18	29
Boskie	6-6	6.43	.304	28	9	0	8	0	1	77.0	95	57	55	14	26	50
Johnson	0-1	7.94	.317	14	5	0	5	0	2	39.2	52	36	35	12	16	29
Yan	0-1	15.83	.417	3	2	0	0	0	0	9.2	20	18	17	3	7	4

1998 preliminary roster

PITCHERS (20)
Armando Benitez
Rocky Coppinger
Doug Drabek
Scott Erickson
Chris Fussell
Scott Kamieniecki
Jimmy Key
Rick Krivda
Terry Mathews
Alan Mills
Steve Montgomery
Julio Moreno

Mike Mussina
Jesse Orosco
Billy Percibal
Sidney Ponson
Hector Ramirez
Arthur Rhodes
Nerio Rodriguez
Everett Stull

CATCHERS (4)
Charlie Greene
Chris Hoiles

Melvin Rosario
Lenny Webster

INFIELDERS (6)
Roberto Alomar
Mike Bordick
Carlos Casimiro
Rafael Palmeiro
Jeff Reboulet
Cal Ripken

OUTFIELDERS (10)
Wady Almonte
Brady Anderson
Harold Baines
Joe Carter
Danny Clyburn
Eric Davis
Jeffrey Hammonds
Eugene Kingsale
B.J. Surhoff
Tony Tarasco

Games played by position

PLAYER	G	C	1B	2B	3B	SS	OF	DH
Alomar	112	0	0	109	0	0	0	2
Anderson	151	0	0	0	0	0	124	25
Baines	137	0	0	0	0	0	1	121
Berroa	156	0	0	0	0	0	83	69
Bordick	153	0	0	0	0	153	0	0
Clyburn	2	0	0	0	0	0	1	0
Davis	42	0	0	0	0	0	30	12
Dellucci	17	0	0	0	0	0	9	5
Greene	5	4	0	0	0	0	0	0
Hammonds	118	0	0	0	0	0	114	4
Hoiles	99	87	4	0	1	0	0	8
Laker	7	7	0	0	0	0	0	0
Ledesma	43	0	5	22	11	4	0	0
Palmeiro	158	0	155	0	0	0	0	3
Reboulet	99	0	0	63	12	22	1	1
Ripken	162	0	0	0	162	3	0	0
Rosario	4	4	0	0	0	0	0	0
Surhoff	147	0	3	0	3	0	133	9
Tarasco	100	0	0	0	0	0	81	2
Walton	26	0	5	0	0	0	19	2
Webster	98	97	0	0	0	0	0	1

Sick call: 1997 DL report

PLAYER	Days on the DL
Roberto Alomar	27
Shawn Boskie	16
Rocky Coppinger	157
Eric Davis	112
Chris Hoiles	31
Pete Incaviglia	6
Alan Mills	66
Jerome Walton	129

Minor Leagues

Tops in the organization

BATTER	CLUB	AVG.	G	AB	R	H	HR	RBI
Dellucci, David	Bow	.327	107	385	71	126	20	55
Ledesma, Aaron	Roc	.325	85	326	40	106	3	43
Matos, F.	Roc	.324	101	389	51	126	4	51
Short, Rick	Fre	.319	126	480	73	153	10	72
Foster, Jim	Bow	.317	127	420	88	133	23	110

HOME RUNS

Pickering, Calvin	Del	25
Minor, Ryan	Del	24
Foster, Jim	Bow	23
Several Players Tied at		20

WINS

Krivda, Rick	Roc	14
Yan, Esteban	Roc	11
Rodriguez, Nerio	Roc	11
Peguero, A.	Del	11
Several Players Tied at		10

RBI

Foster, Jim	Bow	110
Minor, Ryan	Del	97
Isom, Johnny	Bow	91
Pickering, Calvin	Del	79
Lamb, David	Bow	77

SAVES

Kohlmeier, Ryan	Del	25
Hernandez, F.	Bow	24
Snyder, Matt	Bow	19
Steph, Rod	Roc	14
Mastrolonardo, D.	Blu	12

STOLEN BASES

Dent, Darrell	Del	60
Frazier, Lou	Roc	37
Fowler, Maleke	Del	36
Matos, Luis	Blu	34
Garavito, Eddy	Blu	26

STRIKEOUTS

Rodriguez, Nerio	Roc	160
Bennett, Joel	Bow	146
Peguero, A.	Del	133
Yan, Esteban	Roc	131
Montgomery, S.	Roc	129

PITCHER	CLUB	W-L	ERA	IP	H	BB	SO
Eibey, Scott	Del	10- 4	1.83	93	65	33	82
Heredia, Maximo	Del	10- 5	2.13	114	97	20	73
Yan, Esteban	Roc	11- 5	3.10	119	107	37	131
Bennett, Joel	Bow	6- 8	3.18	113	89	40	146
Krivda, Rick	Roc	14- 2	3.39	146	122	34	128

1997 salaries

	Bonuses	Total earned salary
Cal Ripken, 3b	50,000	6,850,000
Mike Mussina, p		6,825,000
Roberto Alomar, 2b	75,000	6,354,379
Rafael Palmeiro, 1b	25,000	5,337,021
Brady Anderson, of	50,000	4,050,000
Randy Myers, p	250,000	3,950,000
Chris Hoiles, c		3,600,000
Geronimo Berroa, of		3,300,000
Scott Erickson, p	100,000	3,300,000
Mike Bordick, ss		2,333,333
Jimmy Key, p	50,000	2,340,000
Eric Davis, of		2,200,000
Harold Baines, of	775,000	1,925,000
B.J. Surhoff, of	350,000	1,616,666
Arthur Rhodes, p	900,000	1,600,000
Scott Kamieniecki, p	775,000	1,535,000
Jesse Orosco, p	300,000	1,100,000
Alan Mills, p	100,000	850,000
Terry Matthews, p	45,000	685,000
Shawn Boskie, p		660,000
Jeffrey Hammonds, of	90,000	490,000
Lenny Webster, c	125,000	425,000
Jerome Walton, of	135,000	385,000
Tony Tarasco, of	25,000	270,000
Armando Benitez, p	35,000	275,000
Jeff Reboulet, 2b		200,000
Rocky Coppinger, p		185,000
Rick Krivda, p		175,000
Aaron Ledesma, ss		150,000

Average 1997 salary: $2,171,255
Total 1997 payroll: $62,966,399

Baltimore (1954-1997), includes St. Louis (1902-1953)

Runs: Most, career
1445	CAL RIPKEN, 1981-1997	
1232	Brooks Robinson, 1955-1977	
1091	George Sisler, 1915-1927	
1084	EDDIE MURRAY, 1977-1996	
1013	Harlond Clift, 1934-1943	

Hits: Most, career
2848	Brooks Robinson, 1955-1977
2715	CAL RIPKEN, 1981-1997
2295	George Sisler, 1915-1927
2080	EDDIE MURRAY, 1977-1996
1574	Boog Powell, 1961-1974

2B: Most, career
517	CAL RIPKEN, 1981-1997
482	Brooks Robinson, 1955-1977
363	EDDIE MURRAY, 1977-1996
343	George Sisler, 1915-1927
294	Harlond Clift, 1934-1943

3B: Most, career
145	George Sisler, 1915-1927
88	Baby Doll Jacobson,1915-1926
72	Del Pratt, 1912-1917
72	Jack Tobin, 1916-1925
70	Ken Williams, 1918-1927
68	Brooks Robinson,1955-1977(6)

HR: Most, career
370	CAL RIPKEN, 1981-1997
343	EDDIE MURRAY, 1977-1996
303	Boog Powell, 1961-1974
268	Brooks Robinson, 1955-1977
185	Ken Williams, 1918-1927

RBI: Most, career
1453	CAL RIPKEN, 1981-1997
1357	Brooks Robinson, 1955-1977
1224	EDDIE MURRAY, 1977-1996
1063	Boog Powell, 1961-1974
959	George Sisler, 1915-1927

SB: Most, career
351	George Sisler, 1915-1927
252	Al Bumbry, 1972-1984
247	Burt Shotton, 1909-1917
222	BRADY ANDERSON, 1988-1997
192	Jimmy Austin, 1911-1929

BB: Most, career
1016	CAL RIPKEN, 1981-1997
986	Harlond Clift, 1934-1943
889	Boog Powell, 1961-1974
886	Ken Singleton, 1975-1984
884	EDDIE MURRAY, 1977-1996

BA: Highest, career
.344	George Sisler, 1915-1927
.326	Ken Williams, 1918-1927
.318	Jack Tobin, 1916-1925
.317	Baby Doll Jacobson, 1915-1926
.309	Bob Dillinger, 1946-1949
.301	Bob Boyd, 1956-1960 (8)

On-base avg: Highest, career
.403	Ken Williams, 1918-1927
.401	Frank Robinson, 1966-1971
.394	Harlond Clift, 1934-1943
.388	Ken Singleton, 1975-1984
.388	Randy Milligan, 1989-1992

Slug avg: Highest, career
.558	Ken Williams, 1918-1927
.543	Frank Robinson, 1966-1971
.539	RAFAEL PALMEIRO,1994-1997
.512	Jim Gentile, 1960-1963
.498	EDDIE MURRAY, 1977-1996

Games started: Most, career
521	Jim Palmer, 1965-1984
384	Dave McNally, 1962-1974
328	Mike Flanagan, 1975-1992
309	Scott McGregor, 1976-1988
283	Mike Cuellar, 1969-1976

Complete games: Most, career
211	Jim Palmer, 1965-1984
210	Jack Powell, 1902-1912
174	Barney Pelty, 1903-1912
150	Harry Howell, 1904-1910
143	Urban Shocker, 1918-1924

Saves: Most, career
160	GREGG OLSON, 1988-1993
105	Tippy Martinez, 1976-1986
100	Stu Miller, 1963-1967
76	RANDY MYERS, 1996-1997
74	Eddie Watt, 1966-1973

Shutouts: Most, career
53	Jim Palmer, 1965-1984
33	Dave McNally, 1962-1974
30	Mike Cuellar, 1969-1976
27	Jack Powell, 1902-1912
26	Milt Pappas, 1957-1965

Wins: Most, career
268	Jim Palmer, 1965-1984
181	Dave McNally, 1962-1974
143	Mike Cuellar, 1969-1976
141	Mike Flanagan, 1975-1992
138	Scott McGregor, 1976-1988

K: Most, career
2212	Jim Palmer, 1965-1984
1476	Dave McNally, 1962-1974
1297	Mike Flanagan, 1975-1992
1011	Mike Cuellar, 1969-1976
978	MIKE MUSSINA, 1991-1997

Win pct: Highest, career
.682	MIKE MUSSINA, 1991-1997
.638	Jim Palmer, 1965-1984
.620	Wally Bunker, 1963-1968
.619	Dick Hall, 1961-1971
.619	Mike Cuellar, 1969-1976

ERA: Lowest, career
2.06	Harry Howell, 1904-1910
2.52	Fred Glade, 1904-1907
2.62	Barney Pelty, 1903-1912
2.63	Jack Powell, 1902-1912
2.67	Carl Weilman, 1912-1920
2.86	Jim Palmer, 1965-1984 (6)

Runs: Most, season
145	Harlond Clift, 1936
137	George Sisler, 1920
134	George Sisler, 1922
132	ROBERTO ALOMAR, 1996
132	Jack Tobin, 1921

Hits: Most, season
257	George Sisler, 1920
246	George Sisler, 1922
241	Heinie Manush, 1928
236	Jack Tobin, 1921
224	George Sisler, 1925
211	CAL RIPKEN, 1983 (10)

2B: Most, season
51	Beau Bell, 1937
49	George Sisler, 1920
47	Heinie Manush, 1928
47	CAL RIPKEN, 1983
47	Joe Vosmik, 1937

3B: Most, season
20	Heinie Manush, 1928
20	George Stone, 1906
18	George Sisler, 1920
18	George Sisler, 1921
18	George Sisler, 1922
18	Jack Tobin, 1921
12	Paul Blair, 1967 (24)

HR: Most, season

50	BRADY ANDERSON, 1996	
49	Frank Robinson, 1966	
46	Jim Gentile, 1961	
39	RAFAEL PALMEIRO, 1995	
39	RAFAEL PALMEIRO, 1996	
39	Boog Powell, 1964	
39	Ken Williams, 1922	

RBI: Most, season

155	Ken Williams, 1922
142	RAFAEL PALMEIRO, 1996
141	Jim Gentile, 1961
134	Moose Solters, 1936
124	EDDIE MURRAY, 1985

SB: Most, season

57	Luis Aparicio, 1964
53	BRADY ANDERSON, 1992
51	George Sisler, 1922
46	Armando Marsans, 1916
45	George Sisler, 1918

BB: Most, season

126	Lu Blue, 1929
121	Roy Cullenbine, 1941
118	Harlond Clift, 1938
118	Burt Shotton, 1915
118	Ken Singleton, 1975

BA: Highest, season

.420	George Sisler, 1922
.407	George Sisler, 1920
.378	Heinie Manush, 1928
.371	George Sisler, 1921
.358	George Stone, 1906
.328	Ken Singleton, 1977 (*)
.328	ROBERTO ALOMAR, 1996 (*)

On-base avg: Highest, season

.467	George Sisler, 1922
.452	Roy Cullenbine, 1941
.449	George Sisler, 1920
.442	Bob Nieman, 1956
.439	Ken Williams, 1923

Slug avg: Highest, season

.646	Jim Gentile, 1961
.637	BRADY ANDERSON, 1996
.637	Frank Robinson, 1966
.632	George Sisler, 1920
.627	Ken Williams, 1922

Games started: Most, season

40	Mike Cuellar, 1970
40	Mike Flanagan, 1978
40	Dave McNally, 1969
40	Dave McNally, 1970
40	Bobo Newsom, 1938
40	Jim Palmer, 1976

Complete games: Most, season

36	Jack Powell, 1902
35	Harry Howell, 1905
33	Red Donahue, 1902
33	Jack Powell, 1903
32	Harry Howell, 1904
25	Jim Palmer, 1975 (20)

Saves: Most, season

45	RANDY MYERS, 1997
37	GREGG OLSON, 1990
36	GREGG OLSON, 1992
34	Don Aase, 1986
33	LEE SMITH, 1994

Shutouts: Most, season

10	Jim Palmer, 1975
8	Steve Barber, 1961
7	Milt Pappas, 1964
6	Fred Glade, 1904
6	Harry Howell, 1906
6	Dave McNally, 1972
6	Jim Palmer, 1969
6	Jim Palmer, 1973
6	Jim Palmer, 1976
6	Jim Palmer, 1978

Wins: Most, season

27	Urban Shocker, 1921
25	Steve Stone, 1980
24	Mike Cuellar, 1970
24	Dave McNally, 1970
24	Urban Shocker, 1922

K: Most, season

232	Rube Waddell, 1908
226	Bobo Newsom, 1938
218	MIKE MUSSINA, 1997
204	MIKE MUSSINA, 1996
202	Dave McNally, 1968

Win pct: Highest, season

.808	Alvin Crowder, 1928
.808	Dave McNally, 1971
.800	Jim Palmer, 1969
.792	Wally Bunker, 1964
.783	MIKE MUSSINA, 1992

ERA: Lowest, season

1.59	Barney Pelty, 1906
1.77	Jack Powell, 1906
1.89	Harry Howell, 1908
1.89	Rube Waddell, 1908
1.93	Harry Howell, 1907
1.95	Dave McNally, 1968 (7)

Most pinch-hit homers, season

3	Sam Bowens, 1967
3	Jim Dwyer, 1986
3	Whitey Herzog, 1962
3	Sam Horn, 1991
3	Pat Kelly, 1979

Most pinch-hit homers, career

9	Jim Dwyer, 1980-1988
7	Benny Ayala, 1979-1984

Longest hitting streak

41	George Sisler, 1922
34	George McQuinn, 1938
34	George Sisler, 1925
29	Mel Almada, 1938
28	Ken Williams, 1922
24	RAFAEL PALMEIRO, 1994

Most consecutive scoreless innings

41	GREGG OLSON, 1989-1990
36	Hal Brown, 1961

No-hit games

Earl Hamilton, StL at Det AL, 5-1; Aug. 30, 1912.

Ernie Koob, StL vs Chi AL, 1-0; May 5, 1917.

Bob Groom, StL vs Chi AL, 3-0; May 6, 1917 (2nd game).

Bobo Newsom, StL vs Bos AL, 1-2; Sept. 18, 1934 (lost on 1 hit in the tenth).

Bobo Holloman, StL vs Phi AL, 6-0; May 6, 1953 (first start in the major leagues).

Hoyt Wilhelm, Bal vs NY AL, 1-0; Sept. 20, 1958.

Steve D. Barber (8 ⅔ innings) and Stu Miller (⅓ inning) Bal vs Det AL, 1-2; April 30, 1967 (1st game, lost the game).

Tom Phoebus, Bal vs Bos AL, 6-0; April 27, 1968.

Jim Palmer, Bal vs Oak AL, 8-0; Aug. 13, 1969.

Bob Milacki (6 innings), Mike Flanagan (1 inning), Mark Williamson, (1 inning) and GREGG OLSON (1 inning), Bal at Oak AL, 2-0; July 13, 1991.

John Whitehead, six innings, rain, StL vs Det AL, 4-0; Aug. 5, 1940 (2nd game).

ACTIVE PLAYERS in caps.

Players' years of service are listed by the first and last years with this team and are not necessarily consecutive; all statistics record performances for this team only.

Leader from the franchise's current location is included. If not in the top five, leader's rank is listed in paren-thesis; asterisk (*) indicates player is not in top 25.

New York Yankees

Tino Martinez led the Yankees in home runs, RBI, slugging average and extra-base hits last season.

By Tom DiPace

1997 Yankees: New York couldn't repeat

Second place is never good enough for George Steinbrenner, especially when the New York Yankees' bombastic owner shelled out $65 million to defend his club's World Series crown. But the wild-card format enabled the Yankees to qualify for the playoffs although the Baltimore Orioles led the East from Opening Day to the finish. The Yankees were bounced from the playoffs in five games in the first round by the Cleveland Indians.

It was business as usual in the Bronx, with police reports almost as common as scouting reports. Dwight Gooden and Mark Whiten both had run-ins with the legal system, though neither was charged with a crime. Manager Joe Torre kept the clubhouse on an even keel, balancing a volatile third base situation between Wade Boggs and Charlie Hayes and doing his best to accommodate the tumultuous arrival of Japanese pitcher Hideki Irabu. The unproven Irabu came from Japan through a trade with San Diego and was given a $12.5 million contract, then was bounced from the starting rotation and finished with a 7.09 ERA and no spot on the postseason roster.

Tino Martinez had a career-high 141 RBI, the most for the Yankees since Don Mattingly's 145 in 1985. Martinez also had 44 home runs. Paul O'Neill and Bernie Williams had nearly identical numbers playing alongside each other in right and center field. Williams batted .328, four points better than O'Neill; both had 21 home runs; and O'Neill had the RBI edge, 117 to 100.

Andy Pettitte again was the most reliable starter, winning 18 games with a 2.88 ERA, almost a full run lower than his 1996 mark. David Cone's ERA was even better, 2.82, but he missed many starts with a shoulder injury. Mariano Rivera helped the Yankees forget John Wetteland as he matched the departed closer's save total of the previous year, with 43.

Chad Curtis rescued the Yankees when Williams missed five weeks because of a hamstring injury. Curtis, acquired in a

June trade with the Indians, hit .291 with 12 home runs and 50 RBI in 93 games for the Yankees. The logjam of outfielder–first baseman–DH types led to Cecil Fielder's demanding a trade before the season. He rescinded the demand minutes before the March 15 deadline but then hit only 10 home runs before he went on the DL on July 16 with a fractured thumb.

Steinbrenner loves to shake things up with his Yankees, but 1998 could be a relatively quiet year by Bronx standards. Torre signed an extension that will keep him at the helm through the 1999 season. The team of general manager Bob Watson and Torre has been responsible for two consecutive trips to the postseason, and Steinbrenner has holstered his itchy trigger finger. On the field, the Yankees have a major question to answer. Williams is headed into the final season of his contract, and those negotiations could become stormy with superagent Scott Boras seeking something in the $10 million-a-year range.

The Yankees further stripped their minor league system in mid-season trades, but the organization held on to a few young gems. Catcher Jorge Posada and right-hander Ramiro Mendoza played important roles in New York last season, and some top minor leaguers— second baseman Homer Bush (acquired in the Irabu deal), outfielder Ricky Ledee, left-hander Eric Milton and right-hander Danny Rios—could do so next year.

1997 Yankees: Week-by-week notes

These notes were excerpted from the following issues of Baseball Weekly.

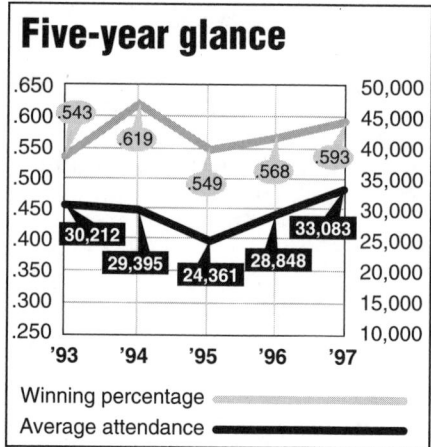

Five-year glance

Winning percentage
Average attendance

▶**April 9:** The first unpromising answer was provided last week of how the Yankees will endure life without the Mariano Rivera–John Wetteland marriage. David Weathers surrendered a two-run homer and Jeff Nelson served up a run-scoring single in the eighth inning of a game against the A's, which turned a 2-1 lead into a 4-2 loss. Last season, the Yanks were 79-2 when they carried a lead into the eighth.

▶**April 23:** After watching another brutal bullpen bashing in a loss to the Brewers that dropped the Yankees' record to 5-10, owner George Steinbrenner reached his boiling point. That wasn't a popular action in the Yankees' clubhouse. "It's way too early to panic," second baseman Mariano Duncan said. "Come on, it's still April. It's too early to think about changes."

▶**April 30:** After four months of courtrooms, boardrooms and backroom negotiations, the Yankees last week finally secured the rights to Japanese pitcher Hideki Irabu from the Padres. In return, the Yankees sent promising yet injured outfielder Ruben Rivera, minor league pitcher Rafael Medina and $3 million to San Diego. The Yankees also received three prospects. On the field, DH Cecil Fielder ended the longest homerless streak of his career, 98 at-bats, on April 26 while driving in five runs in a 10-2 win over the White Sox.

▶**May 7:** First baseman Tino Martinez broke the major league record for RBI in April when he knocked in 34 in the first 27 games. Martinez snapped the mark set last season by Barry Bonds.

▶**May 21:** Charlie Hayes started four of five games last week and nine in a row against left-handers, prompting some to question whether Torre had turned third base into a platoon. Wade Boggs' average had fallen to a season-low .268.

▶**May 28:** Right-hander Dwight Gooden dropped himself in the middle of a controversy and onto George Steinbrenner's hit list last week when he was involved in

a fracas with a Dallas taxi driver. Gooden allegedly slugged Ziauddin Hakim, 44, after the cab driver followed Gooden to the fourth floor of the Yankees' hotel in the early-morning hours after a May 23 victory over the Texas Rangers.

▶**June 4:** After two-plus months of sometimes bitter negotiations, Hideki Irabu and the Yankees agreed last week to a four-year contract worth a guaranteed $12.8 million. The deal could net Irabu, 28, another $3.7 million in 2001 if he lives up to his billing.

▶**June 11:** Two days after George Steinbrenner claimed that Mariano Duncan no longer was a second baseman, Duncan declared his desire to no longer be a Yankee. Feeling he has been unfairly branded a scapegoat for all the problems besetting the defending champions, an angry Duncan demanded a trade. He has lost his starting job to Luis Sojo.

▶**June 18:** The Yankees last week acquired outfielder Chad Curtis from the Indians for reliever David Weathers. Curtis, 30, batted .207 in 29 at-bats in Cleveland.

▶**June 25:** The Yankees took two of three games from the Mets last week in the inaugural regular season subway series. The winners were New York baseball fans as well as the Yankees, who drew 168,719 for the series. It was the best-attended three-game series at Yankee Stadium since a mid-September set against the Red Sox in 1978.

▶July 10: The Yankees were to have sent left-hander Kenny Rogers, Mariano Duncan and minor league pitcher Kevin Henthorne to the Padres for outfielder Greg Vaughn and minor league pitchers Chris Clark and Kerry Taylor. However, Vaughn failed his physical on July 5, and the Yankees canceled the trade. Padres president Larry Lucchino offered to send Vaughn to a second doctor for another opinion, but George Steinbrenner refused. Vaughn, 32, has undergone three right shoulder operations in the past six years.

▶July 16: With an electric atmosphere filling a sold-out Yankee Stadium and the city, Hideki Irabu ignored the circus environment and enjoyed a sterling debut for the Yankees. In 10-3 victory against the Tigers, Irabu's fastball—which topped out at 94 mph—took a backseat to a vicious splitter in the 90s that helped account for six of his nine strikeouts over 6⅔ innings.

▶July 23: The Yankees have been desperate to upgrade their lineup with a big-name slugger, especially when Cecil Fielder broke a thumb and center fielder Bernie Williams strained a hamstring. But trade attempts proved fruitless last week. After all but conceding the AL East to the Orioles, the Yankees closed the gap to three games by July 20.

▶July 30: Hideki Irabu was embroiled in a spitting controversy, banished to the bullpen and then sent to the minors. On July 20 he appeared to spit in the direction of fans as he walked off Milwaukee's County Stadium field to a chorus of boos. By week's end, Irabu was slated to go to the bullpen to correct flaws that resulted in a two-inning, six-run shellacking at the hands of the Mariners in his fourth start. But then an announcement came on July 28 that he was headed to the minors.

▶Aug. 13: Outfielder Mark Whiten expects to hear from the Milwaukee district attorney's office this week as to whether he'll be charged with second-degree sexual assault stemming from a July 21 incident at the team hotel. Whiten, whose wife gave birth to their second child the day before the purported incident, has claimed that the sex was consensual.

▶Aug. 20: Two days after Luis Sojo was lost for the rest of the regular season with a broken ulna in his left forearm, the Yankees acquired middle infielder Rey Sanchez from the Cubs. Sanchez, 29, hit .249 with one homer and 12 RBI in 97 games with Chicago.

▶Aug. 27: Wade Boggs made his first appearance as a pitcher since high school in Tampa 20 years ago when he mopped up in the final inning of a loss last week to the Angels. Thanks to a knuckleball he learned from his father, Boggs, after a leadoff walk to Luis Alicea, retired Tim Salmon on a grounder and Garret Anderson on a slow roller to second, then struck out Todd Greene.

▶Sept. 3: The defensively sound Rey Sanchez, who was batting .450 with a 10-game hitting streak since he was traded from the Cubs on Aug. 16, made a throwing error in the ninth that helped give the Expos a 4-3 victory on Aug. 29.

▶Sept. 10: Joe Girardi was lost for five days because of a fractured left middle finger, injured in a 5-2 loss to the Orioles on Sept. 4, when he got crossed up on a pitch from left-hander David Wells. Wells was hammered during the showdown with his former club.

▶Sept. 17: Wade Boggs has been on fire lately. Heading into last weekend, he was on a 14-for-25 streak and raised his batting average up to .292 following a 3-for-4 performance against the Orioles on Sept. 12.

▶Sept. 24: Right-hander David Cone's five-inning start on Sept. 20 was his first since Aug. 17, and it was good enough to make him a go for the playoffs. Cone, who had suffered from shoulder tendinitis, was expected to start again on Sept. 25 in Cleveland.

▶Oct. 1: Manager Joe Torre plans to keep David Cone on a strict 100-pitch count for the playoffs, though his No. 1 starter wants no strings attached. "I don't have a quota or limit in my mind," Cone said on Sept. 28.

QUOTE OF THE YEAR

"When you're stinking up the joint, you should sit."
—Third baseman Wade Boggs, on being benched during a slump in May

NEW YORK YANKEES 1997 final stats

BATTERS	BA	SLG	OBA	G	AB	R	H	TB	2B	3B	HR	RBI	BB	SO	SB	CS	E
Bush	.364	.364	.364	10	11	2	4	4	0	0	0	3	0	0	0	0	2
Williams	.328	.544	.408	129	509	107	167	277	35	6	21	100	73	80	15	8	2
O'Neill	.324	.514	.399	149	553	89	179	284	42	0	21	117	75	92	10	7	5
Raines	.321	.454	.403	74	271	56	87	123	20	2	4	38	41	34	8	5	1
Sanchez	.312	.420	.338	38	138	21	43	58	12	0	1	15	5	21	0	4	4
Sojo	.307	.372	.355	77	215	27	66	80	6	1	2	25	16	14	3	1	5
Stanley	.297	.507	.393	125	347	61	103	176	25	0	16	65	54	72	0	1	2
T. Martinez	.296	.577	.371	158	594	96	176	343	31	2	44	141	75	75	3	1	8
Boggs	.292	.397	.373	104	353	55	103	140	23	1	4	28	48	38	0	1	4
Jeter	.291	.405	.370	159	654	116	190	265	31	7	10	70	74	125	23	12	18
Curtis	.284	.481	.362	115	349	59	99	168	22	1	15	55	43	59	12	6	4
Whiten	.265	.386	.360	69	215	34	57	83	11	0	5	24	30	47	4	2	5
Girardi	.264	.334	.311	112	398	38	105	133	23	1	1	50	26	53	2	3	5
Fielder	.260	.410	.358	98	361	40	94	148	15	0	13	61	51	87	0	0	0
Hayes	.258	.397	.332	100	353	39	91	140	16	0	11	53	40	66	3	2	13
Cruz	.250	.300	.318	11	20	0	5	6	1	0	0	3	2	4	0	0	0
Posada	.250	.410	.359	60	188	29	47	77	12	0	6	25	30	33	1	2	3
Incaviglia	.247	.370	.308	53	154	19	38	57	4	0	5	12	11	46	0	0	1
Kelly	.242	.358	.324	67	120	25	29	43	6	1	2	10	14	37	8	1	3
Fox	.226	.258	.368	22	31	13	7	8	1	0	0	1	7	9	2	1	1
Pose	.218	.264	.292	54	87	19	19	23	2	1	0	5	9	11	3	1	0
Strawberry	.103	.138	.188	11	29	1	3	4	1	0	0	2	3	9	0	0	0
Figga	.000	.000	.000	2	4	0	0	0	0	0	0	0	0	3	0	0	0

PITCHERS	W-L	ERA	BA	G	GS	CG	GF	Sho	SV	IP	H	R	ER	HR	BB	SO
Boggs	0-0	0.00	.000	1	0	0	1	0	0	1.0	0	0	0	0	1	1
Rivera	6-4	1.88	.237	66	0	0	56	0	43	71.2	65	17	15	5	20	68
Banks	3-0	1.93	.188	5	1	0	1	0	0	14.0	9	3	3	0	6	8
Stanton	6-1	2.57	.205	64	0	0	15	0	3	66.2	50	19	19	3	34	70
Boehringer	3-2	2.63	.225	34	0	0	11	0	0	48.0	39	16	14	4	32	53
Cone	12-6	2.82	.218	29	29	1	0	0	0	195.0	155	67	61	17	86	222
Nelson	3-7	2.86	.191	77	0	0	22	0	2	78.2	53	32	25	7	37	81
Pettitte	18-7	2.88	.256	35	35	4	0	1	0	240.1	233	86	77	7	65	166
Lloyd	1-1	3.31	.293	46	0	0	17	0	1	49.0	55	24	18	6	20	26
Wells	16-10	4.21	.278	32	32	5	0	2	0	218.0	239	109	102	24	45	156
Mendoza	8-6	4.24	.292	39	15	0	9	0	2	133.2	157	67	63	15	28	82
Gooden	9-5	4.91	.283	20	19	0	0	0	0	106.1	116	61	58	14	53	66
Rogers	6-7	5.65	.280	31	22	1	4	0	0	145.0	161	100	91	18	62	78
Mecir	0-4	5.88	.279	25	0	0	11	0	0	33.2	36	23	22	5	10	25
Irabu	5-4	7.09	.311	13	9	0	0	0	0	53.1	69	47	42	15	20	56
Borowski	0-1	9.00	.250	1	0	0	1	0	0	2.0	2	2	2	0	4	2
Rios	0-0	19.29	.563	2	0	0	0	0	0	2.1	9	5	5	3	2	1

1998 preliminary roster

PITCHERS (17)
Jose Alberro
Willie Banks
Joe Borowski
Mike Buddie
David Cone
Darrell Einerston
Darren Holmes
Hideki Irabu
Mike Jerzembeck
Graeme Lloyd
Ramiro Mendoza

Jeff Nelson
Andy Pettitte
Danny Rios
Mariano Rivera
Mike Stanton
David Wells

CATCHERS (3)
Mike Figga
Joe Girardi
Jorge Posada

INFIELDERS (10)
Scott Brosius
Homer Bush
Ivan Cruz
Andy Fox
Derek Jeter
Mike Lowell
Gabby Martinez
Tino Martinez
Luis Sojo
Dale Sveum

OUTFIELDERS (10)
Brian Buchanan
Chad Curtis
Chili Davis
Ricky Ledee
Donzell McDonald
Paul O'Neill
Tim Raines
Chris Singleton
Shane Spencer
Bernie Williams

Games played by position

PLAYER	G	C	1B	2B	3B	SS	OF	DH
Boggs	104	0	0	0	76	0	0	19
Bush	10	0	0	8	0	0	0	1
Cruz	11	0	3	0	0	0	1	4
Curtis	115	0	0	0	0	0	111	0
Fielder	98	0	8	0	0	0	0	89
Figga	2	1	0	0	0	0	0	1
Fox	22	0	0	5	11	2	2	2
Girardi	112	111	0	0	0	0	0	1
Hayes	100	0	0	5	98	0	0	0
Incaviglia	53	0	0	0	0	0	18	31
Jeter	159	0	0	0	0	159	0	0
Kelly	67	0	0	48	0	0	0	16
T. Martinez	158	0	150	0	0	0	0	7
O'Neill	149	0	2	0	0	0	146	2
Posada	60	60	0	0	0	0	0	0
Pose	54	0	0	0	0	0	45	5
Raines	74	0	0	0	0	0	57	13
Sanchez	38	0	0	37	0	6	0	0
Sojo	77	0	2	72	3	4	0	0
Stanley	125	15	43	0	0	0	0	69
Strawberry	11	0	0	0	0	0	4	4
Whiten	69	0	0	0	0	0	57	7
Williams	129	0	0	0	0	0	128	0

Minor Leagues
Tops in the organization

BATTER	CLUB	AVG.	G	AB	R	H	HR	RBI
Martinez, Gabby	Nrw	.322	79	317	52	102	7	56
Lowell, Mike	Col	.315	135	495	96	156	30	92
Howard, Matt	Col	.312	122	478	90	149	6	67
Buchanan, Brian	Nrw	.305	134	531	83	162	14	76
Gomez, Rudy	Nrw	.300	102	393	65	118	5	52

HOME RUNS

Lowell, Mike	Col	30		
Spencer, Shane	Col	30		
Ashby, Chris	Nrw	24		
Cruz, Ivan	Col	24		
Wilson, Tom	Nrw	21		

WINS

Milton, Eric	Nrw	14	
Banks, Willie	Col	14	
Rangel, Julio	GBo	12	
Several Players Tied at	11		

RBI

Cruz, Ivan	Col	95
Lowell, Mike	Col	92
Spencer, Shane	Col	86
Ashby, Chris	Nrw	82
Wilson, Tom	Nrw	80

SAVES

Dingman, Craig	GBo	25
Ford, Ben	Nrw	19
Mota, Daniel	One	18
Tessmer, Jay	Nrw	17
Rose, Scott	Nrw	15

STOLEN BASES

Brown, Vick	Tam	55
Smith, Rod	GBo	54
McDonald, D.	Tam	39
Fox, Andy	Col	28
Darjean, John	One	27

STRIKEOUTS

Milton, Eric	Nrw	162
Jerzembeck, M.	Col	160
Lomon, Kevin	Nrw	131
Banks, Willie	Col	130
Several Players Tied at	122	

PITCHER	CLUB	W-L	ERA	IP	H	BB	SO
De Los Santos, L.	Nrw	11- 7	2.73	175	163	28	116
Lankford, Frank	Col	11- 6	2.78	162	142	37	79
Spence, Cam	GBo	3- 4	2.87	97	85	20	66
Milton, Eric	Nrw	14- 6	3.11	171	137	50	162
Jerzembeck, M.	Col	9- 6	3.13	172	146	53	160
Mitchell, Larry	Nrw	9- 9	3.49	95	98	37	99
Lomon, Kevin	Nrw	10- 8	3.55	129	125	57	131
Rangel, Julio	GBo	12- 9	3.57	164	147	49	122
Randolph, S.	Tam	4- 7	3.87	95	74	63	108
Olivier, Rich	GBo	8- 5	4.13	107	111	51	79

Sick call: 1997 DL report

PLAYER	Days on the DL
Brian Boehringer	87
David Cone	33
Cecil Fielder	62
Dwight Gooden	70
Pat Kelly	39*
Gabby Martinez	20
Tim Raines	81*
Luis Sojo	45
Darryl Strawberry	130
Bernie Williams	35*

* Indicates two separate terms on Disabled List.

1997 salaries

	Bonuses	Total earned salary
Cecil Fielder, dh		9,237,500
David Cone, p		6,666,667
Paul O'Neill, of	50,000	5,500,000
Bernie Williams, of	50,000	5,300,000
Kenny Rogers, p		5,000,000
Tino Martinez, 1b	100,000	4,400,000
David Wells, p	600,000	3,766,666
Tim Raines, of		2,353,644
Hideki Irabu, p		2,325,000
Joe Girardi, c		2,250,000
Mike Stanley, dh		2,100,000
Wade Boggs, 3b		2,000,000
Dwight Gooden, p		2,000,000
Charlie Hayes, 3b	200,000	1,700,000
Mike Stanton, p		1,616,000
Rey Sanchez, ss		1,287,500
Pat Kelly, 2b		1,100,000
Jeff Nelson, p	100,000	1,090,000
Chad Curtis, of	150,000	900,000
Graeme Lloyd, p	5,000	770,000
Darryl Strawberry, of		750,000
Andy Pettitte, p		700,000
Mariano Rivera, p		550,000
Derek Jeter, ss	10,000	550,000
Luis Sojo, 2b	25,000	425,000
Andy Fox, 3b		175,000
Brian Boehringer, p		161,100
Jorge Posada, c		158,500
Ramiro Mendoza, p		157,000

Average 1997 salary: $2,241,020
Total 1997 payroll: $64,989,577

New York (1903-1997)

Runs: Most, career

1959	Babe Ruth, 1920-1934
1888	Lou Gehrig, 1923-1939
1677	Mickey Mantle, 1951-1968
1390	Joe DiMaggio, 1936-1951
1186	Earle Combs, 1924-1935

Hits: Most, career

2721	Lou Gehrig, 1923-1939
2518	Babe Ruth, 1920-1934
2415	Mickey Mantle, 1951-1968
2214	Joe DiMaggio, 1936-1951
2153	Don Mattingly, 1982-1995

2B: Most, career

534	Lou Gehrig, 1923-1939
442	Don Mattingly, 1982-1995
424	Babe Ruth, 1920-1934
389	Joe DiMaggio, 1936-1951
344	Mickey Mantle, 1951-1968

3B: Most, career

163	Lou Gehrig, 1923-1939
154	Earle Combs, 1924-1935
131	Joe DiMaggio, 1936-1951
121	Wally Pipp, 1915-1925
115	Tony Lazzeri, 1926-1937

HR: Most, career

659	Babe Ruth, 1920-1934
536	Mickey Mantle, 1951-1968
493	Lou Gehrig, 1923-1939
361	Joe DiMaggio, 1936-1951
358	Yogi Berra, 1946-1963

RBI: Most, career

1995	Lou Gehrig, 1923-1939
1971	Babe Ruth, 1920-1934
1537	Joe DiMaggio, 1936-1951
1509	Mickey Mantle, 1951-1968
1430	Yogi Berra, 1946-1963

SB: Most, career

326	RICKEY HENDERSON, 1985-1989
251	Willie Randolph, 1976-1988
248	Hal Chase, 1905-1913
233	Roy White, 1965-1979
184	Ben Chapman, 1930-1936
184	Wid Conroy, 1903-1908

BB: Most, career

1847	Babe Ruth, 1920-1934
1733	Mickey Mantle, 1951-1968
1508	Lou Gehrig, 1923-1939
1005	Willie Randolph, 1976-1988
934	Roy White, 1965-1979

BA: Highest, career

.349	Babe Ruth, 1920-1934
.340	Lou Gehrig, 1923-1939
.325	Earle Combs, 1924-1935
.325	Joe DiMaggio, 1936-1951
.317	PAUL O'NEILL, 1993-1997

On-base avg: Highest, career

.484	Babe Ruth, 1920-1934
.447	Lou Gehrig, 1923-1939
.421	Mickey Mantle, 1951-1968
.410	Charlie Keller, 1939-1952
.403	PAUL O'NEILL, 1993-1997

Slug avg: Highest, career

.711	Babe Ruth, 1920-1934
.632	Lou Gehrig, 1923-1939
.579	Joe DiMaggio, 1936-1951
.557	Mickey Mantle, 1951-1968
.526	Reggie Jackson, 1977-1981

Games started: Most, career

438	Whitey Ford, 1950-1967
391	Red Ruffing, 1930-1946
356	Mel Stottlemyre, 1964-1974
323	Ron Guidry, 1975-1988
319	Lefty Gomez, 1930-1942

Complete games: Most, career

261	Red Ruffing, 1930-1946
173	Lefty Gomez, 1930-1942
168	Jack Chesbro, 1903-1909
164	Herb Pennock, 1923-1933
164	Bob Shawkey, 1915-1927

Saves: Most, career

224	Dave Righetti, 1979-1990
151	Rich Gossage, 1978-1989
141	Sparky Lyle, 1972-1978
104	Johnny Murphy, 1932-1946
78	Steve Farr, 1991-1993

Shutouts: Most, career

45	Whitey Ford, 1950-1967
40	Red Ruffing, 1930-1946
40	Mel Stottlemyre, 1964-1974
28	Lefty Gomez, 1930-1942
27	Allie Reynolds, 1947-1954

Wins: Most, career

236	Whitey Ford, 1950-1967
231	Red Ruffing, 1930-1946
189	Lefty Gomez, 1930-1942
170	Ron Guidry, 1975-1988
168	Bob Shawkey, 1915-1927

K: Most, career

1956	Whitey Ford, 1950-1967
1778	Ron Guidry, 1975-1988
1526	Red Ruffing, 1930-1946
1468	Lefty Gomez, 1930-1942
1257	Mel Stottlemyre, 1964-1974

Win pct: Highest, career

.725	Johnny Allen, 1932-1935
.717	Spud Chandler, 1937-1947
.706	Vic Raschi, 1946-1953
.700	Monte Pearson, 1936-1940
.690	Whitey Ford, 1950-1967

ERA: Lowest, career

2.54	Russ Ford, 1909-1913
2.58	Jack Chesbro, 1903-1909
2.72	Al Orth, 1904-1909
2.73	Tiny Bonham, 1940-1946
2.73	George Mogridge, 1915-1920

Runs: Most, season

177	Babe Ruth, 1921
167	Lou Gehrig, 1936
163	Lou Gehrig, 1931
163	Babe Ruth, 1928
158	Babe Ruth, 1920
158	Babe Ruth, 1927

Hits: Most, season

238	Don Mattingly, 1986
231	Earle Combs, 1927
220	Lou Gehrig, 1930
218	Lou Gehrig, 1927
215	Joe DiMaggio, 1937

2B: Most, season

53	Don Mattingly, 1986
52	Lou Gehrig, 1927
48	Don Mattingly, 1985
47	Lou Gehrig, 1926
47	Lou Gehrig, 1928
47	Bob Meusel, 1927

3B: Most, season

23	Earle Combs, 1927
22	Earle Combs, 1930
22	Birdie Cree, 1911
22	Snuffy Stirnweiss, 1945
21	Earle Combs, 1928

HR: Most, season

61	Roger Maris, 1961
60	Babe Ruth, 1927
59	Babe Ruth, 1921
54	Mickey Mantle, 1961
54	Babe Ruth, 1920
54	Babe Ruth, 1928

RBI: Most, season

184	Lou Gehrig, 1931
175	Lou Gehrig, 1927
174	Lou Gehrig, 1930
171	Babe Ruth, 1921
167	Joe DiMaggio, 1937

SB: Most, season

93	RICKEY HENDERSON, 1988
87	RICKEY HENDERSON, 1986
80	RICKEY HENDERSON, 1985
74	Fritz Maisel, 1914
61	Ben Chapman, 1931

BB: Most, season

170	Babe Ruth, 1923
148	Babe Ruth, 1920
146	Mickey Mantle, 1957
144	Babe Ruth, 1921
144	Babe Ruth, 1926

BA: Highest, season

.393	Babe Ruth, 1923
.381	Joe DiMaggio, 1939
.379	Lou Gehrig, 1930
.378	Babe Ruth, 1924
.378	Babe Ruth, 1921

On-base avg: Highest, season

.545	Babe Ruth, 1923
.530	Babe Ruth, 1920
.516	Babe Ruth, 1926
.513	Babe Ruth, 1924
.512	Mickey Mantle, 1957

Slug avg: Highest, season

.847	Babe Ruth, 1920
.846	Babe Ruth, 1921
.772	Babe Ruth, 1927
.765	Lou Gehrig, 1927
.764	Babe Ruth, 1923

Games started: Most, season

51	Jack Chesbro, 1904
45	Jack Powell, 1904
42	Jack Chesbro, 1906
39	Pat Dobson, 1974
39	Whitey Ford, 1961
39	Catfish Hunter, 1975
39	Al Orth, 1906
39	Mel Stottlemyre, 1969
39	Ralph Terry, 1962

Complete games: Most, season

48	Jack Chesbro, 1904
38	Jack Powell, 1904
36	Al Orth, 1906
33	Jack Chesbro, 1903
31	Ray Caldwell, 1915

Saves: Most, season

46	Dave Righetti, 1986
43	MARIANO RIVERA, 1997
43	JOHN WETTELAND, 1996
36	Dave Righetti, 1990
35	Sparky Lyle, 1972

Shutouts: Most, season

9	Ron Guidry, 1978
8	Whitey Ford, 1964
8	Russ Ford, 1910
7	Whitey Ford, 1958
7	Catfish Hunter, 1975
7	Allie Reynolds, 1951
7	Mel Stottlemyre, 1971
7	Mel Stottlemyre, 1972

Wins: Most, season

41	Jack Chesbro, 1904
27	Carl Mays, 1921
27	Al Orth, 1906
26	Joe Bush, 1922
26	Russ Ford, 1910
26	Lefty Gomez, 1934
26	Carl Mays, 1920

K: Most, season

248	Ron Guidry, 1978
239	Jack Chesbro, 1904
222	DAVID CONE, 1997
218	Melido Perez, 1992
217	Al Downing, 1964

Win pct: Highest, season

.893	Ron Guidry, 1978
.862	Whitey Ford, 1961
.842	Ralph Terry, 1961
.839	Lefty Gomez, 1934
.833	Spud Chandler, 1943

ERA: Lowest, season

1.64	Spud Chandler, 1943
1.65	Russ Ford, 1910
1.74	Ron Guidry, 1978
1.82	Jack Chesbro, 1904
1.83	Hippo Vaughn, 1910

Most pinch-hit homers, season

| 4 | Johnny Blanchard, 1961 |

Most pinch-hit homers, career

| 9 | Yogi Berra, 1946-1963 |
| 8 | Bob Cerv, 1951-1962 |

Longest hitting streak

56	Joe DiMaggio, 1941
33	Hal Chase, 1907
29	Roger Peckinpaugh, 1919
29	Earle Combs, 1931
29	Joe Gordon, 1942

Most consecutive scoreless innings

| 33 | Jack Aker, 1969 |

No-hit games

Tom L. Hughes, NY vs Cle AL, 0-5; Aug. 30, 1910 (2nd game; lost on 7 hits in 11 innings after allowing the first hit in the 10th)

George Mogridge, NY at Bos AL, 2-1; April 24, 1917.

Sam Jones, NY at Phi AL, 2-0; Sept. 4, 1923.

Monte Pearson, NY vs Cle AL, 13-0; Aug. 27, 1938 (2nd game).

Allie Reynolds, NY at Cle AL, 1-0; July 12, 1951.

Allie Reynolds, NY vs Bos AL, 8-0; Sept. 28, 1951 (1st game).

Don Larsen, NY at Bro NL, 2-0; Oct. 8, 1956 (World Series, perfect game).

Dave Righetti, NY vs Bos AL, 4-0; July 4, 1983.

Andy Hawkins, NY at Chi AL, 0-4; July 1, 1990 (8 innings, lost the game; bottom of 9th not played).

Jim Abbott, NY vs Cle AL, 4-0; Sept. 4, 1993.

DWIGHT GOODEN, NY vs Sea AL, 2-0; May 14, 1996.

ACTIVE PLAYERS in caps.

Players' years of service are listed by the first and last years with this team and are not necessarily consecutive; all statistics record performances for this team only.

Detroit Tigers

By Russell Becker, Baseball Weekly

In only his first full year in the majors, Tony Clark was the top Tiger last season in homers and RBI.

1997 Tigers: A big change in only a year

It was a season in which a lot went right and very little wrong. After finishing 56 games below .500 in 1996, the Detroit Tigers finished just four games under in 1997. In first baseman Tony Clark, third baseman Travis Fryman and outfielder Bobby Higginson, the Tigers had three players surpass the 100-RBI mark for the first time since 1950. In Willie Blair, Justin Thompson and Brian Moehler, Detroit had three pitchers with 10 or more victories for the first time since 1993. The 79-83 record tied for the team's third best during the 1990s, equaling the 1990 squad's. Detroit's team ERA dropped from an all-time AL-worst 6.38 in 1996 to a respectable 4.56 in 1997.

In 1996, the Tigers ranked 10th in the league with 87 steals. In 1997, they led the AL with 161, thanks to center fielder Brian Hunter, who with 74 by himself became the first Detroit player since Ty Cobb in 1917 to lead the major leagues in stolen bases. The Tigers topped the AL in fielding after placing last in 1996. With a player payroll of just $17 million, Detroit managed to finish third in the East, ahead of big spenders Toronto and Boston.

General Manager Randy Smith says there is still a lot of room for improvement. "We need to be more consistent offensively," he said. The Tigers were shut out more than any club in the league in 1997. The club's two best hitters were Clark and Higginson. Clark led the club with 32 home runs and 117 RBI, while Higginson hit .299 and added 27 homers and 101 RBI.

Rookie shortstop Deivi Cruz, second baseman Damion Easley and Hunter gave Detroit excellent strength up the middle defensively. Easley, considered a dark horse for the job in spring training, finished with 22 home runs and 28 steals. Smith says Cruz was the biggest single factor in the club's improvement this season. Cruz was an offseason acquisition from the Dodgers and showed such outstanding defense in spring training that manager Buddy Bell was willing to not

Team MVP

Tony Clark: When Tony Clark hit 27 home runs in 100 games during 1996, the Tigers knew their big first baseman could be ready to break loose. He did it in 1997, bringing his batting average up 26 points, to .276, and increasing his homers to 32. The former No. 2 draft pick also led the Detroit Tigers with 117 runs batted in.

worry about Cruz's offense. The 22-year-old Cruz batted .241.

Cruz wasn't the only youngster to come through for the Tigers this season. Rookie right-hander Moehler quietly won 11 games as the third man in the rotation. Rookie Raul Casanova ended the season as the No. 1 catcher and showed flashes of brilliance on offense and defense. Bell admits it will be difficult to keep the team's top prospect, right fielder Juan Encarnacion, out of the major leagues next season. "He's even better than I thought he was, and I thought he was very good," said Bell in September, even though Encarnacion hit just .212 in 11 games.

The anchor of the pitching staff appears to be left-hander Thompson, who made it to the All-Star Game in his second season in the big leagues. Not bad considering he won just once and had injury problems as a rookie. Thompson went 15-11 with a 3.02 ERA in 1997. Blair, a 31-year-old right-hander, had a breakout season, going 16-8 with a 4.17 ERA despite missing a month with a fractured jaw. Blair was 25-41 lifetime coming into 1997.

One thing is certain for 1998: Detroit's player payroll will go up from its paltry $17 million. "It has to," said Smith.

1997 Tigers : Week-by-week notes

These notes were excerpted from the following issues of Baseball Weekly.

▶**April 9:** A slow starter throughout his minor league career, first baseman Tony Clark is enjoying his first April in the majors. He had two RBI in four of his first five games while hitting three home runs and batting .500.

▶**April 16:** Detroit won its second and third series, against Chicago on the road and against Minnesota at home, after getting off to an 0-3 start in Minnesota.

▶**April 23:** Manager Buddy Bell and pitching coach Rick Adair held a 30-minute pitchers-only meeting following Detroit's 9-5 loss to Oakland on April 18. In that game, Detroit pitchers issued nine walks, and they are on pace to shatter the major league season record—827 by the 1915 Philadelphia Athletics, whose record was 43-109.

▶**April 30:** The Tigers bullpen is so bad that Opening Day starter Doug Brocail is now the closer. Todd Jones, acquired from Houston in the offseason to be the closer, has struggled with his control and mechanics. Dan Miceli, who had 21 saves for Pittsburgh in 1995, has been hit hard nearly every time he's been under pressure.

▶**May 7:** Despite 1-for-26 and 3-for-29 slumps in April, Tony Clark completed the month with a .288 batting average, with eight home runs and 27 RBI. In his other 49 at-bats, he had 30 hits.

▶**May 14:** The starters have been Detroit's greatest strength. Including a three-hit, 6-0 shutout by right-hander Omar Olivares on May 10, starters had a 2.85 ERA over a 26-game span through May 11. Olivares (2.93), Brian Moehler (3.20) and Justin Thompson (3.83) all had ERAs below 4.00. The three-hitter was the second time in a week that Detroit had shut out the Indians, who beat the Tigers 12 consecutive times in 1996.

▶**May 28:** Willie Blair is progressing well as he recovers from a fractured jaw suffered on May 4, when he was hit with a Julio Franco line drive during a game in

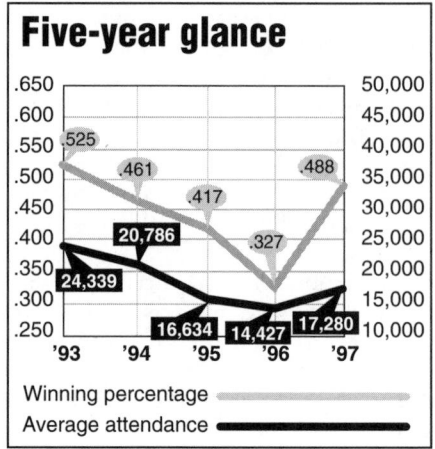

Five-year glance

Winning percentage
Average attendance

Cleveland. Just 20 days after the injury, Blair threw five innings of shutout, one-hit ball on a rehab start for Class A West Michigan, at Fort Wayne.

▶**June 4:** Omar Olivares got the better of another good team on May 31. The same pitcher who shut out Cleveland and Anaheim in the last three weeks beat the Seattle Mariners 4-2. The victory was the ninth in the Tigers' last 12 as they continue to be the most-improved team in the majors. A year ago, they were 13-39 after 52 games. This year, they're 25-27.

▶**June 11:** The Tigers have begun negotiations with first-round pick Matt Anderson, the first overall selection in the draft. Most scouts and GMs who've seen him say he is the best amateur pitcher in 10 years or more. Anderson, 20, throws a 96-98 mph fastball and could step in quickly as a closer. He was 10-1 with a 1.82 ERA, 94 strikeouts and 25 walks in 69 innings at Rice this year.

▶**June 18:** Left-hander Justin Thompson is maintaining his patience despite going just 4-3 during an eight-game stretch in which his ERA was a sparkling 1.71. His overall ERA of 2.81 ranks sixth in the AL.

▶**July 2:** Bobby Higginson leads the AL in outfield assists with 12 despite spending two weeks on the DL with a strained trunk muscle. Higginson's bat is valuable, too. When he was out of the lineup, Detroit had a 4-9 record.

▶**July 10:** Tony Clark was snubbed not once, but three times, in his bid for a spot on the AL All-Star squad. He was originally bypassed when AL manager Joe Torre selected the reserves; again when Chicago first baseman Frank Thomas bowed out because of injury; and once more when Cleveland outfielder David Justice opted out with an injury. Clark is on a 40-homer, 140-RBI pace in his first full season.

▶**July 16:** Jason Thompson brought back the news following his appearance in the All-Star Game that he felt a twinge in his left elbow. An elbow injury forced him to miss the entire 1994 season. Since being drafted by Detroit in 1991, Thompson has yet to go through an entire season without an arm ailment.

▶**July 23:** General manager Randy Smith knows his club might have taken a step backward by trading two-fifths of its rotation to Seattle on July 18, but the deal was made with the future in mind. Omar Olivares and Felipe Lira were traded for right-hander Scott Sanders and two minor leaguers, right-handed reliever Dean Crow and third baseman Carlos Villalobos.

▶**July 30:** Right-hander Todd Jones has pitched well enough that he may fit into the club's long-range plans. After getting off to a slow start, Jones, 29, converted 16 of 17 save opportunities, including 10 in a row.

▶**Aug. 13:** The Tigers passed their victory total for the entire 1996 season with their 54th win, a 3-2 decision at Toronto on Aug. 9. Used exclusively as a starter for the first time in his career, Willie Blair has responded with 11 wins despite missing a month with a fractured jaw. A 31-year old right-hander, Blair entered this year with just 25 wins in seven seasons with his previous five teams.

▶**Aug. 27:** Bobby Higginson, arbitration-eligible for the first time after this season, is seeking a multiyear contract from Randy Smith. He has hiked his average up near .300 and twice has had streaks of seven hits in a row.

▶**Sept. 3:** Through Aug. 31, Detroit was 58-34 in games in which it scored three or more runs. In games in which they scored two or fewer runs, the Tigers were 5-38.

The team ERA was 4.62, way down from last year's AL-record-setting 6.38.

▶**Sept. 10:** Justin Thompson raised his record to 13-10 and lowered his ERA to 2.78—third best in the AL—with a five-hit, 5-1 victory against Anaheim on Sept 6. It was Thompson's fourth complete game, and he has pitched 197 innings.

▶**Sept. 17:** When club president John McHale Jr. went to owner Mike Ilitch to ask for a contract extension for Randy Smith, Ilitch's reply was short and to the point. "He asked me what took so long," McHale said. Smith's contract was extended through 2001. Only seven players from the 40-man major league roster that Smith inherited remain. He's acquired such key players as Todd Jones, center fielder Brian Hunter, shortstop Deivi Cruz, Willie Blair, Doug Brocail, catcher Raul Casanova and second baseman Damion Easley.

▶**Sept. 24:** After finishing 56 games below .500 last year, the Tigers have a shot at finishing .500 or better. The biggest reason for the club's recent success has been the improved work of the bullpen. Bullpen depth helped Detroit win back-to-back extra-inning games against the Yankees and the Orioles on Sept. 18 and 19. Todd Jones got both victories.

▶**Oct. 1:** Tony Clark, Bobby Higginson and third baseman Travis Fryman all topped the 100-RBI mark, a first for a Detroit club since 1950 when Vic Wertz, Hoot Evers and George Kell turned the trick. Starting pitcher Willie Blair is the only Detroit player eligible for free agency this winter. After going 16-8, Blair figures to get offers from elsewhere. He will listen but wants to remain with the Tigers, the first team to give him a shot as a full-time starter for an entire season.

QUOTE OF THE YEAR

"We're still growing, and the goal is not to be a .500 club now as much as it is to be a championship team in the future."
—General manager Randy Smith, after trading starters Omar Olivares and Felipe Lira

DETROIT TIGERS 1997 final stats

BATTERS	BA	SLG	OBA	G	AB	R	H	TB	2B	3B	HR	RBI	BB	SO	SB	CS	E
Hall	.500	.750	.500	2	4	1	2	3	1	0	0	3	0	0	0	0	0
Catalanotto	.308	.385	.379	13	26	2	8	10	2	0	0	3	3	7	0	0	0
Higginson	.299	.520	.379	146	546	94	163	284	30	5	27	101	70	85	12	7	9
Walbeck	.277	.365	.331	47	137	18	38	50	3	0	3	10	12	19	3	3	3
Clark	.276	.500	.376	159	580	105	160	290	28	3	32	117	93	144	1	3	10
Fryman	.274	.440	.326	154	595	90	163	262	27	3	22	102	46	113	16	3	10
Hamelin	.270	.487	.366	110	318	47	86	155	15	0	18	52	48	72	2	1	0
Hunter	.269	.353	.334	162	658	112	177	232	29	7	4	45	66	121	74	18	4
Easley	.264	.471	.362	151	527	97	139	248	37	3	22	72	68	102	28	13	12
Casanova	.243	.332	.308	101	304	27	74	101	10	1	5	24	26	48	1	1	9
Cruz	.241	.314	.263	147	436	35	105	137	26	0	2	40	14	55	3	6	13
Johnson	.237	.338	.262	45	139	13	33	47	6	1	2	18	5	19	1	0	3
Nevin	.235	.414	.306	93	251	32	59	104	16	1	9	35	25	68	0	1	2
Miller	.234	.369	.289	50	111	13	26	41	7	1	2	10	5	24	1	0	3
Nieves	.228	.451	.311	116	359	46	82	162	18	1	20	64	39	157	1	7	4
Trammell	.228	.366	.307	44	123	14	28	45	5	0	4	13	15	35	3	1	0
Encarnacion	.212	.394	.316	11	33	3	7	13	1	1	1	5	3	12	3	1	0
Bartee	.200	.200	.500	12	5	4	1	1	0	0	0	0	2	2	3	1	0
Reed	.196	.214	.278	52	112	6	22	24	2	0	0	8	10	15	3	2	2
Jensen	.182	.182	.250	8	11	1	2	2	0	0	0	1	1	5	0	0	1
Hurst	.176	.412	.263	13	17	1	3	7	1	0	1	1	2	6	0	0	0
Coleman	.071	.071	.133	6	14	0	1	1	0	0	0	0	1	3	0	0	0

PITCHERS	W-L	ERA	BA	G	GS	CG	GF	Sho	SV	IP	H	R	ER	HR	BB	SO
Thompson	15-11	3.02	.233	32	32	4	0	0	0	223.1	188	82	75	20	66	151
Jones	5-4	3.09	.231	68	0	0	51	0	31	70.0	60	29	24	3	35	70
Brocail	3-4	3.23	.256	61	4	0	20	0	2	78.0	74	31	28	10	36	60
Blair	16-8	4.17	.273	29	27	2	0	0	0	175.0	186	85	81	18	46	90
Sager	3-4	4.18	.258	38	1	0	8	0	3	84.0	81	43	39	10	24	53
Moehler	11-12	4.67	.285	31	31	2	0	1	0	175.1	198	97	91	22	61	97
Pugh	1-1	5.00	.188	2	2	0	0	0	0	9.0	6	5	5	0	5	4
Miceli	3-2	5.01	.248	71	0	0	24	0	3	82.2	77	49	46	13	38	79
Dishman	1-2	5.28	.268	7	4	0	1	0	0	29.0	30	18	17	4	8	20
Gaillard	1-0	5.31	.211	16	0	0	5	0	1	20.1	16	12	12	2	10	12
Cummings	2-0	5.47	.311	19	0	0	2	0	0	24.2	22	15	15	3	14	8
Myers	0-4	5.70	.274	88	0	0	23	0	2	53.2	58	36	34	12	25	50
Sanders	6-14	5.86	.278	47	20	1	15	1	2	139.2	152	92	91	30	62	120
Keagle	3-5	6.55	.309	11	10	0	0	0	0	45.1	58	33	33	9	18	33
Bautista	2-2	6.69	.324	21	0	0	4	0	0	40.1	55	32	30	6	12	19
Jarvis	0-3	7.08	.332	23	5	0	10	0	0	54.2	78	46	43	13	22	36
Duran	0-0	7.59	.189	13	0	0	1	0	0	10.2	7	9	9	0	15	11
Hernandez	0-0	40.50	.556	2	0	0	0	0	0	1.1	5	6	6	0	3	2

1998 preliminary roster

PITCHERS (21)
Doug Brocail
Frank Castillo
Francisco Cordero
Dean Crow
Matt Drews
Mike Drumright
Roberto Duran
Bryce Florie
Eddie Gailliard
Apostol Garcia
Todd Jones
Greg Keagle
Brian Moehler
Brian Powell
Willis Roberts
John Rosengren
Sean Runyan
A.J. Sager
Scott Sanders
Justin Thompson
Tim Worrell

CATCHERS (3)
Paul Bako
Raul Casanova
Marcus Jensen

INFIELDERS (9)
Richard Almanzar
Gabe Alvarez
Frank Catalanotto
Tony Clark
Deivi Cruz
Damion Easley
Luis Garcia
Joe Randa
Bip Roberts

OUTFIELDERS (7)
Kimera Bartee
Trey Beamon
Juan Encarnacion
Luis Gonzalez
Bobby Higginson
Gabe Kapler
Brian Hunter

Games played by position

PLAYER	G	C	1B	2B	3B	SS	OF	DH
Bartee	12	0	0	0	0	0	6	3
Casanova	101	92	0	0	0	0	0	1
Catalanotto	13	0	0	6	0	0	0	3
Clark	159	0	158	0	0	0	0	1
Coleman	6	0	0	0	0	0	3	1
Cruz	147	0	0	0	0	147	0	0
Easley	151	0	0	137	0	21	0	4
Encarnacion	11	0	0	0	0	0	10	0
Fryman	154	0	0	0	153	0	0	0
Hall	2	0	0	0	0	0	1	0
Hamelin	110	0	7	0	0	0	0	95
Higginson	146	0	0	0	0	0	143	1
Hunter	162	0	0	0	0	0	162	0
Hurst	13	0	0	0	0	0	12	1
Jensen	8	8	0	0	0	0	0	0
Johnson	45	43	0	0	0	0	0	2
Miller	50	0	3	0	4	31	0	11
Nevin	93	1	7	0	17	0	40	30
Nieves	116	0	0	0	0	0	99	12
Reed	52	0	0	41	0	0	0	5
Trammell	44	0	0	0	0	0	28	14
Walbeck	47	44	0	0	0	0	0	0

Minor Leagues

Tops in the organization

BATTER	CLUB	AVG.	G	AB	R	H	HR	RBI
Mateo, Ruben	Chl	.314	99	385	63	121	12	67
Fick, Robert	WMi	.341	122	463	100	158	16	90
Freire, Alejandro	Lak	.323	130	477	85	154	24	92
Encarnacion, J.	Jax	.323	131	493	91	159	26	90
Sollmann, Scott	WMi	.313	121	460	89	144	0	33
Catalanotto, F.	Tol	.300	134	500	75	150	16	68

HOME RUNS

			WINS		
Trammell, Bubba	Tol	28	Bruner, Clayton	WMi	15
Encarnacion, J.	Jax	26	Borkowski, D.	WMi	15
Ibarra, Jesse	Jax	25	Melendez, Dave	Jax	14
Freire, Alejandro	Lak	24	Powell, Brian	Lak	13
Hurst, Jimmy	Tol	20	Romo, Greg	WMi	12

RBI

			SAVES		
Freire, Alejandro	Lak	92	Cordero, F	WMi	35
Ibarra, Jesse	Jax	91	Gaillard, Eddie	Tol	28
Fick, Robert	WMi	90	Duran, Roberto	Jax	16
Encarnacion, J.	Jax	90	Durkovic, Peter	Lak	10
Kapler, Gabe	Lak	87	Several Players Tied at		9

STOLEN BASES

			STRIKEOUTS		
Johnson, Earl	Jax	42	Keagle, Greg	Tol	140
Sollmann, Scott	WMi	40	Drumright, Mike	Tol	139
Bartee, Kimera	Tol	33	Bruner, Clayton	WMi	135
Barker, Glen	Jax	30	Melendez, Dave	Jax	134
Hernaiz, Juan	Lak	29	Romo, Greg	WMi	124

PITCHER	CLUB	W-L	ERA	IP	H	BB	SO
Quintal, Craig	WMi	11- 6	1.96	156	133	31	88
Darwin, David	Lak	11- 1	1.98	123	93	38	72
Bruner, Clayton	WMi	15- 3	2.38	166	134	48	135
Powell, Brian	Lak	13- 9	2.50	183	153	35	122
Spear, Russell	WMi	11- 6	2.96	140	126	61	112

Sick call: 1997 DL report

PLAYER	Days on the DL
Willie Blair	29
Bobby Higginson	15
Kevin Jarvis	19
Orlando Miller	70
Brian Moehler	15
Phil Nevin	15
Melvin Nieves	15
Justin Thompson	15
Matt Walbeck	81

1997 salaries

	Bonuses	Total earned salary
Travis Fryman, 3b		6,400,000
Scott Sanders, p		1,300,000
Todd Jones, p		975,000
Willie Blair, p		800,000
Jody Reed, 2b	75,000	675,000
Damion Easley, 2b	265,000	675,000
Matt Walbeck, c		550,000
Bob Hamelin, 1b		500,000
Dan Miceli, p	50,000	475,000
Doug Brocail, p		425,000
Bobby Higginson, of		375,000
Melvin Nieves, of		342,500
Orlando Miller, ss		337,500
Brian Hunter, of		310,000
Tony Clark, 1b		260,000
Mike Myers, p		235,000
A.J. Sager, p		200,000
Justin Thompson, p	25,000	198,000
Kevin Jarvis, p		197,000
Phil Nevin, 3b		178,000
Greg Keagle, p		170,000
Raul Casanova, c		157,500
Deivi Cruz, ss		150,000
Brian Moehler, p		150,000
Bubba Trammell, of		150,000

Average 1997 salary: $647,420
Total 1997 payroll: $16,185,500

Detroit (1901-1997)

Runs: Most, career

2088	Ty Cobb, 1905-1926	
1774	Charlie Gehringer, 1924-1942	
1622	Al Kaline, 1953-1974	
1386	Lou Whitaker, 1977-1995	
1242	Donie Bush, 1908-1921	

Hits: Most, career

3900	Ty Cobb, 1905-1926
3007	Al Kaline, 1953-1974
2839	Charlie Gehringer, 1924-1942
2499	Harry Heilmann, 1914-1929
2466	Sam Crawford, 1903-1917

2B: Most, career

665	Ty Cobb, 1905-1926
574	Charlie Gehringer, 1924-1942
498	Al Kaline, 1953-1974
497	Harry Heilmann, 1914-1929
420	Lou Whitaker, 1977-1995

3B: Most, career

284	Ty Cobb, 1905-1926
249	Sam Crawford, 1903-1917
146	Charlie Gehringer, 1924-1942
145	Harry Heilmann, 1914-1929
136	Bobby Veach, 1912-1923

HR: Most, career

399	Al Kaline, 1953-1974
373	Norm Cash, 1960-1974
306	Hank Greenberg, 1930-1946
262	Willie Horton, 1963-1977
245	CECIL FIELDER, 1990-1996

RBI: Most, career

1804	Ty Cobb, 1905-1926
1583	Al Kaline, 1953-1974
1442	Harry Heilmann, 1914-1929
1427	Charlie Gehringer, 1924-1942
1264	Sam Crawford, 1903-1917

SB: Most, career

865	Ty Cobb, 1905-1926
400	Donie Bush, 1908-1921
317	Sam Crawford, 1903-1917
294	Ron LeFlore, 1974-1979
236	Alan Trammell, 1977-1996

BB: Most, career

1277	Al Kaline, 1953-1974
1197	Lou Whitaker, 1977-1995
1186	Charlie Gehringer, 1924-1942
1148	Ty Cobb, 1905-1926
1125	Donie Bush, 1908-1921

BA: Highest, career

.368	Ty Cobb, 1905-1926
.342	Harry Heilmann, 1914-1929
.337	Bob Fothergill, 1922-1930
.325	George Kell, 1946-1952
.321	Heinie Manush, 1923-1927

On-base avg: Highest, career

.434	Ty Cobb, 1905-1926
.420	Johnny Bassler, 1921-1927
.412	Hank Greenberg, 1930-1946
.412	Roy Cullenbine, 1938-1947
.410	Harry Heilmann, 1914-1929

Slug avg: Highest, career

.616	Hank Greenberg, 1930-1946
.518	Harry Heilmann, 1914-1929
.516	Ty Cobb, 1905-1926
.503	Rudy York, 1934-1945
.501	Rocky Colavito, 1960-1963

Games started: Most, career

459	Mickey Lolich, 1963-1975
408	Jack Morris, 1977-1990
395	George Mullin, 1902-1913
388	Hooks Dauss, 1912-1926
373	Hal Newhouser, 1939-1953

Complete games: Most, career

336	George Mullin, 1902-1913
245	Hooks Dauss, 1912-1926
213	Bill Donovan, 1903-1918
212	Hal Newhouser, 1939-1953
200	Tommy Bridges, 1930-1946

Saves: Most, career

154	Mike Henneman, 1987-1995
125	John Hiller, 1965-1980
120	Willie Hernandez, 1984-1989
85	Aurelio Lopez, 1979-1985
55	Terry Fox, 1961-1966

Shutouts: Most, career

39	Mickey Lolich, 1963-1975
34	George Mullin, 1902-1913
33	Tommy Bridges, 1930-1946
33	Hal Newhouser, 1939-1953
29	Bill Donovan, 1903-1918

Wins: Most, career

223	Hooks Dauss, 1912-1926
209	George Mullin, 1902-1913
207	Mickey Lolich, 1963-1975
200	Hal Newhouser, 1939-1953
198	Jack Morris, 1977-1990

K: Most, career

2679	Mickey Lolich, 1963-1975
1980	Jack Morris, 1977-1990
1770	Hal Newhouser, 1939-1953
1674	Tommy Bridges, 1930-1946
1406	Jim Bunning, 1955-1963

Win pct: Highest, career

.654	Denny McLain, 1963-1970
.639	Aurelio Lopez, 1979-1985
.629	Schoolboy Rowe, 1933-1942
.626	Mike Henneman, 1987-1995
.616	Harry Coveleski, 1914-1918

ERA: Lowest, career

2.34	Harry Coveleski, 1914-1918
2.38	Ed Killian, 1904-1910
2.42	Ed Summers, 1908-1912
2.49	Bill Donovan, 1903-1918
2.61	Ed Siever, 1901-1908

Runs: Most, season

147	Ty Cobb, 1911
144	Ty Cobb, 1915
144	Charlie Gehringer, 1930
144	Charlie Gehringer, 1936
144	Hank Greenberg, 1938

Hits: Most, season

248	Ty Cobb, 1911
237	Harry Heilmann, 1921
227	Charlie Gehringer, 1936
226	Ty Cobb, 1912
225	Ty Cobb, 1917
225	Harry Heilmann, 1925

2B: Most, season

63	Hank Greenberg, 1934
60	Charlie Gehringer, 1936
56	George Kell, 1950
55	Gee Walker, 1936
50	Charlie Gehringer, 1934
50	Hank Greenberg, 1940
50	Harry Heilmann, 1927

3B: Most, season

26	Sam Crawford, 1914
25	Sam Crawford, 1903
24	Ty Cobb, 1911
24	Ty Cobb, 1917
23	Ty Cobb, 1912
23	Sam Crawford, 1913

HR: Most, season

58	Hank Greenberg, 1938
51	CECIL FIELDER, 1990
45	Rocky Colavito, 1961
44	CECIL FIELDER, 1991
44	Hank Greenberg, 1946

RBI: Most, season

183	Hank Greenberg, 1937
170	Hank Greenberg, 1935
150	Hank Greenberg, 1940
146	Hank Greenberg, 1938
140	Rocky Colavito, 1961

SB: Most, season

96	Ty Cobb, 1915
83	Ty Cobb, 1911
78	Ron LeFlore, 1979
76	Ty Cobb, 1909
74	BRIAN HUNTER, 1997

BB: Most, season

137	Roy Cullenbine, 1947
135	Eddie Yost, 1959
132	TONY PHILLIPS, 1993
125	Eddie Yost, 1960
124	Norm Cash, 1961

BA: Highest, season

.420	Ty Cobb, 1911
.409	Ty Cobb, 1912
.403	Harry Heilmann, 1923
.401	Ty Cobb, 1922
.398	Harry Heilmann, 1927

On-base avg:Highest, season

.487	Norm Cash, 1961
.486	Ty Cobb, 1915
.481	Harry Heilmann, 1923
.475	Harry Heilmann, 1927
.468	Ty Cobb, 1925

Slug avg: Highest, season

.683	Hank Greenberg, 1938
.670	Hank Greenberg, 1940
.668	Hank Greenberg, 1937
.662	Norm Cash, 1961
.632	Harry Heilmann, 1923

Games started: Most, season

45	Mickey Lolich, 1971
44	George Mullin, 1904
42	Mickey Lolich, 1973
42	George Mullin, 1907
41	Joe Coleman, 1974
41	Mickey Lolich, 1972
41	Mickey Lolich, 1974
41	Denny McLain, 1968
41	Denny McLain, 1969
41	George Mullin, 1905

Complete games: Most, season

42	George Mullin, 1904
35	Roscoe Miller, 1901
35	George Mullin, 1905
35	George Mullin, 1906
35	George Mullin, 1907

Saves: Most, season

38	John Hiller, 1973
32	Willie Hernandez, 1984
31	Willie Hernandez, 1985
31	TODD JONES, 1997
27	Tom Timmermann, 1970

Shutouts: Most, season

9	Denny McLain, 1969
8	Ed Killian, 1905
8	Hal Newhouser, 1945
7	Billy Hoeft, 1955
7	George Mullin, 1904
7	Dizzy Trout, 1944

Wins: Most, season

31	Denny McLain, 1968
29	George Mullin, 1909
29	Hal Newhouser, 1944
27	Dizzy Trout, 1944
26	Hal Newhouser, 1946

K: Most, season

308	Mickey Lolich, 1971
280	Denny McLain, 1968
275	Hal Newhouser, 1946
271	Mickey Lolich, 1969
250	Mickey Lolich, 1972

Win pct: Highest, season

.862	Bill Donovan, 1907
.842	Schoolboy Rowe, 1940
.838	Denny McLain, 1968
.808	Bobo Newsom, 1940
.784	George Mullin, 1909

ERA: Lowest, season

1.64	Ed Summers, 1908
1.71	Ed Killian, 1909
1.78	Ed Killian, 1907
1.81	Hal Newhouser, 1945
1.91	Ed Siever, 1902

Most pinch-hit homers, season

3	Gates Brown, 1968
3	Norm Cash, 1960
3	John Grubb, 1984
3	Larry Herndon, 1986
3	Frank Howard, 1963
3	Charlie Maxwell, 1961
3	Ben Oglivie, 1976
3	Dick Wakefield, 1948
3	Vic Wertz, 1962
3	Gus Zernial, 1958

Most pinch-hit homers, career

16	Gates Brown, 1963-1975
8	Norm Cash, 1960-1974

Longest hitting streak

40	Ty Cobb, 1911
35	Ty Cobb, 1917
30	Goose Goslin, 1934
30	Ron LeFlore, 1976
29	Dale Alexander, 1930
29	Pete Fox, 1935

Most consecutive scoreless innings

33	Harry Coveleskie, 1914

No-hit games

George Mullin, Det vs StL AL, 7-0; July 4, 1912 (2nd game).

Virgil Trucks, Det vs Was AL, 1-0; May 15, 1952.

Virgil Trucks, Det at NY AL, 1-0; Aug. 25, 1952.

Jim Bunning, Det at Bos AL, 3-0; July 20, 1958 (1st game).

Jack Morris, Det at Chi AL, 4-0; April 7, 1984.

ACTIVE PLAYERS in caps.

Players' years of service are listed by the first and last years with this team and are not necessarily consecutive; all statistics record performances for this team only.

DETROIT TIGERS / AL EAST

Boston Red Sox

By Tom DiPace

Rookie shortstop Nomar Garciaparra was a unanimous choice for the AL's Jackie Robinson Award.

1997 Red Sox: Good hit, no pitch—again

Most preseason predictions had the Boston Red Sox finishing fourth and winning 78-80 games. That's just how things turned out for manager Jimy Williams' team, but the Sox were all but out of contention by the end of May. Pitching was the main problem. No starter picked up the slack after Roger Clemens' departure, and only three teams blew more saves than Boston's 25. Although the Red Sox led the league in hitting (.291), they also led in errors (135).

Jackie Robinson Award–winning shortstop Nomar Garciaparra made the season worth watching. He sparkled in the field and showed surprising consistency and power at the plate. He batted .306 and showed speed with 22 stolen bases and 11 triples. His 209 hits were a Red Sox rookie record and the most by an AL rookie in 10 years. He was second to Ken Griffey Jr. in total bases and runs. "He's been our MVP all season," said Mo Vaughn, who put together another solid year (.315, 35 HR, 96 RBI) despite missing three weeks due to knee surgery.

Another rookie, catcher Scott Hatteberg, appeared in 114 games and batted .277. DH Reggie Jefferson was in contention for the batting title for much of the season but slipped to .319 at season's end. John Valentin, ousted by Garciaparra at shortstop, played second and third while hitting .306 with 18 homers and a league-leading 47 doubles. After starting at six different positions in the first half, Jeff Frye settled in at second and finished the season batting .312 with 36 doubles, 51 RBI and 19 steals in 404 at-bats.

Wilfredo Cordero was hitting .300 when domestic and legal problems knocked him for a loop—and ultimately off the team. Shane Mack, whom General Manager Dan Duquette said could be the team's center fielder, hit .315 but played in just 60 games because he couldn't throw or hit for power. Darren Bragg played center and ended up tying Garciaparra for the most games played on the club, but Bragg hit only .257 with

nine home runs. Right fielder Troy O'Leary was a quiet success, batting a solid .309 and driving in 80 runs.

Tom Gordon was the Opening Day starter and the team's closer at the end. He adapted well to his new role, converting 11 of 13 save chances. Butch Henry, who missed all of 1996 while recovering from elbow surgery, made a strong bid for next year's starting rotation, going 2-1 with a 1.48 ERA in five starts after spending most of the year in the bullpen.

There's plenty of room for starters. Aaron Sele bounced back from injury to lead the staff with 13 victories, edging knuckleballer Tim Wakefield, who was 12-15. Jeff Suppan went 7-3 despite a 5.69 ERA. Bret Saberhagen came back from shoulder surgery and was 0-1 (6.58 ERA) in six starts, but he threw five shutout innings in his last game. Steve Avery was 6-7 with a horrendous 6.42 ERA. Right-hander Robinson Checo, imported from Japan, wasn't brought up until September.

The Red Sox caused a stir by failing to call up right-handers Brian Rose and Carl Pavano in September. Rose was the International League Pitcher of the Year, going 17-5 with a 3.02 ERA in 190⅔ innings. Pavano finished 11-6 (3.12 ERA) in 161⅔ innings. Pavano was traded to Montreal in the deal for NL Cy Young winner Pedro Martinez, but Rose has a chance to crack the Sox rotation in '98.

1997 Red Sox: Week-by-week notes

These notes were excerpted from the following issues of Baseball Weekly.

▶**April 9:** Rookie shortstop Nomar Garciaparra had a memorable series in Seattle. He went 4-for-5 in a 10-5 win on April 4 and had four RBI, including a game-winning, three-run homer in the ninth, on April 5 as Boston prevailed 8-6.

▶**April 16:** After 10 games, first baseman Mo Vaughn was still looking for his first home run and first RBI. The Red Sox pitching staff had one victory from a starter. The bullpen's ERA was 5.63. Opponents were 10-for-12 in steal attempts. Boston was 0-3 in extra innings and 0-4 in day games.

▶**April 23:** Mo Vaughn was 0-for-13 with runners in scoring position until April 16, when he connected for three-run homers on consecutive at-bats.

▶**April 30:** It's too early to be talking about the Jackie Robinson Award for best rookie, but Nomar Garciaparra is stating his case. He broke a 1-1 extra-inning tie in Baltimore on April 24 with his fourth homer of the season. Two nights earlier, he homered on his way to a 4-for-4 night.

▶**May 7:** Second baseman John Valentin, in the midst of a 5-for-54 slump and batting .160, was removed from the lineup for two days. Then, in Texas on May 2, Valentin had two hits, including the game-winning single off John Wetteland in the ninth inning. It was his first RBI since April 14.

▶**May 14:** The bullpen has been awful. On May 10, relievers failed to preserve a 5-2 lead in an 11-5 loss to the Rangers. Closer Heathcliff Slocumb took over in the ninth of a 5-5 game and failed to get an out, botching a bases-loaded come-backer and then giving up a grand slam to Ivan Rodriguez. It was Boston's seventh loss in eight games.

▶**May 21:** It took starter Tom Gordon's first victory since April 13, and Boston's first complete game of the season, to end the team's seven-game losing streak on May 17. Boston had lost 11 of 12 games.

▶**May 28:** Through May 25, Heathcliff

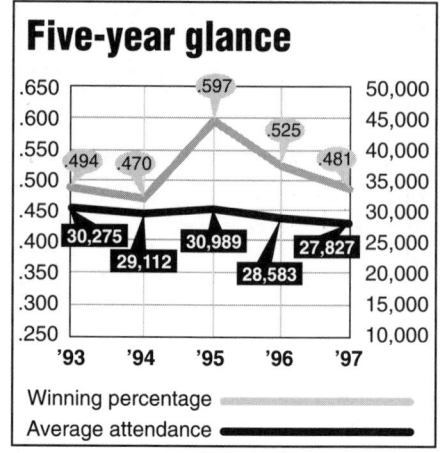

Five-year glance

	'93	'94	'95	'96	'97
Winning percentage	.494	.470	.597	.525	.481
Average attendance	30,275	29,112	30,989	28,583	27,827

Slocumb hadn't had a save opportunity since May 2. He has made seven appearances since then, giving up runs in five of them, as his ERA ballooned to 7.85.

▶**June 4:** Will Mo Vaughn stay or will he go? Vaughn met with general manager Dan Duquette, primarily to discuss trade rumors. On the field, Vaughn broke out in a big way. On May 29 he stroked a two-out, ninth-inning homer off Roberto Hernandez to beat Chicago 2-1. The next night, Vaughn homered against three Yankees pitchers to become the first Red Sox player to have two three-homer games at Fenway.

▶**June 11:** Leads have meant nothing to the bullpen. In the span of four days, it blew a 4-2, ninth-inning lead against the Yankees, a 4-1 lead in Milwaukee and a 7-0, third-inning lead against the Brewers, who scored 13 unanswered runs in two innings on June 4 for Boston's fifth straight loss.

▶**June 18:** Outfielder Wilfredo Cordero's status remained in limbo, on and off the field. After being charged on June 11 with assaulting his wife, Cordero issued an apologetic statement the next night and traveled to New York with the team, but was not seen at Shea Stadium for a series against the Mets. Ana Cordero has refused to testify against her husband.

▶**June 25:** Things deteriorated so badly against Detroit on June 21 that manager

Jimy Williams used utility man Mike Benjamin to pitch the eighth inning. Benjamin responded by retiring all three batters he faced, on nine pitches—the first 1-2-3 inning by a Boston pitcher in 16 innings.

▶July 10: Left-hander Steve Avery made his return to the mound on July 5 after missing more than two months with a groin strain. Avery pitched five innings and was tagged with eight runs.

▶July 23: Beginning their trip to Baltimore and Cleveland 12 games under .500, the Sox won five of six games against the division leaders. The Red Sox finished their season series 7-5 against the Orioles and are 6-5 versus Cleveland.

▶July 30: Right-hander Bret Saberhagen made his first competitive appearance since the 1995 season, a rehab assignment for Class A Lowell. He struck out two and allowed just two of 10 hitters he faced to hit the ball out of the infield.

▶Aug. 6: The deadline-beating trade of Heathcliff Slocumb to the Mariners raises the question, Who will be Boston's closer? One of Boston's future options is to switch Tom Gordon to closer. In exchange for Slocumb, Boston acquired former first-round draft pick Jason Varitek, a catcher, and Derek Lowe, a right-hander who was 2-4 in 12 games for Seattle.

▶Aug. 13: Left-handed DH Reggie Jefferson, who was hitting .359 and had a 22-game hitting streak halted on Aug. 10, should be happy, but he isn't. Jefferson's problem is that he is running some 15-18 plate appearances shy of qualifying for the batting title, and Jimy Williams refuses to bat him against most lefties.

▶Aug. 20: Everybody seemed happy with the Aug. 13 trade that sent right-handed DH Mike Stanley to the Yankees. Stanley returned to New York, where he has enjoyed some of his finest hours, and to a contender. Reggie Jefferson was guaranteed more at-bats and a shot at the batting title. And Dan Duquette shed some salary and picked up a pitching prospect in right-hander Tony Armas, 19.

▶Aug. 27: Tom Gordon moved to the bullpen in anticipation of Bret Saberhagen's addition to the rotation. Gordon registered his first save since 1993, retiring

the side in order in the 13th inning of the nightcap in an Aug. 20 doubleheader in Oakland.

▶Sept. 3: The longest rookie hitting streak in AL history, 30 games, came to an end on Aug. 30 when Nomar Garciaparra went 0-for-3 with a sacrifice fly. Steve Avery, who needed one more start to trigger a $3.9 million option with Boston next season, was sent to the bullpen after giving up 26 runs in 12⅔ innings over his last four games. He is 6-6 with a 6.57 ERA in 17 starts.

▶Sept. 17: The Sox like what they've seen of Tom Gordon in the closer's role, so much so that they're planning to go with him in '98. Gordon is 7-for-7 in save chances. After his third two-homer game of the season, on Sept. 12, Nomar Garciaparra had 28 homers and 90 RBI, the latter a major league record for a leadoff hitter.

▶Sept. 24: Butch Henry has placed himself prominently in Boston's plans for 1998 by going 2-0 with an 0.73 ERA in his first four starts since 1995. Henry missed last season because of elbow surgery. For the season, he's 7-2, with a 3.43 ERA in 35 games. Another veteran on the comeback trail, Bret Saberhagen, enjoyed his most successful start on Sept. 20, pitching five shutout innings against Chicago.

▶Oct. 1: Jimy Williams asserted his on-field control and defied management by giving lefty Steve Avery his 18th start of the season, triggering Avery's $3.9 million option for 1998. Williams defended the decision to start Avery by citing a need for fairness in contracts. "You've got to have good credibility," he said, noting the furor surrounding no-trade-to-Boston clauses in the contracts of Cleveland's Marquis Grissom and David Justice. Reggie Jefferson, hitting .360 when Mike Stanley was traded, finished the season at .319. He batted only .231 after becoming the full-time DH.

QUOTE OF THE YEAR

"This should be a happy time, but I feel like it's just making me sick."

—Designated hitter Reggie Jefferson, on being platooned until the trade of Mike Stanley

BOSTON RED SOX 1997 final stats

BATTERS	BA	SLG	OBA	G	AB	R	H	TB	2B	3B	HR	RBI	BB	SO	SB	CS	E
Varitek	1.000	1.000	1.000	1	1	0	1	1	0	0	0	0	0	0	0	0	0
Jefferson	.319	.470	.358	136	489	74	156	230	33	1	13	67	24	93	1	2	2
Mack	.315	.438	.368	60	130	13	41	57	7	0	3	17	9	24	2	1	0
Vaughn	.315	.560	.420	141	527	91	166	295	24	0	35	96	86	154	2	2	14
Frye	.312	.433	.352	127	404	56	126	175	36	2	3	51	27	44	19	8	12
O'Leary	.309	.479	.358	146	499	65	154	239	32	4	15	80	39	70	0	5	6
Valentin	.306	.499	.372	143	575	95	176	287	47	5	18	77	58	66	7	4	22
Garciaparra	.306	.534	.342	153	684	122	209	365	44	11	30	98	35	92	22	9	21
Naehring	.286	.467	.375	70	259	38	74	121	18	1	9	40	38	40	1	1	3
Cordero	.281	.432	.320	140	570	82	160	246	26	3	18	72	31	122	1	3	2
Hatteberg	.277	.434	.354	114	350	46	97	152	23	1	10	44	40	70	0	1	11
Pozo	.267	.333	.250	4	15	0	4	5	1	0	0	3	0	5	0	0	1
Bragg	.257	.386	.337	153	513	65	132	198	35	2	9	57	61	102	10	6	5
Pemberton	.238	.365	.314	27	63	8	15	23	2	0	2	10	4	13	0	0	2
Haselman	.236	.392	.290	67	212	22	50	83	15	0	6	26	15	44	0	2	7
Benjamin	.233	.328	.262	49	116	12	27	38	9	1	0	7	4	27	2	3	6
Pride	.213	.341	.316	81	164	22	35	56	4	4	3	20	24	46	6	4	1
Tavarez	.174	.246	.216	42	69	12	12	17	3	1	0	9	4	9	0	0	1
Coleman	.167	.208	.167	8	24	2	4	5	1	0	0	2	0	11	1	0	1
Malave	.000	.000	.000	4	4	0	0	0	0	0	0	0	0	2	0	0	0
McKeel	.000	.000	.000	5	3	0	0	0	0	0	0	0	0	1	0	0	0

PITCHERS	W-L	ERA	BA	G	GS	CG	GF	Sho	SV	IP	H	R	ER	HR	BB	SO
Benjamin	0-0	0.00	.000	1	0	0	1	0	0	1.0	0	0	0	0	0	0
Mahay	3-0	2.52	.204	28	0	0	7	0	0	25.0	19	7	7	3	11	22
Checo	1-1	3.38	.235	5	2	0	1	0	0	13.1	12	5	5	0	3	14
Corsi	5-3	3.43	.255	52	0	0	14	0	2	57.2	56	26	22	1	21	40
Henry	7-3	3.52	.277	36	5	0	13	0	6	84.1	89	36	33	6	19	51
Hudson	3-1	3.53	.289	26	0	0	9	0	0	35.2	39	16	14	1	14	14
Gordon	6-10	3.74	.226	42	25	2	16	1	11	182.2	155	85	76	10	78	159
Wakefield	12-15	4.25	.256	35	29	4	2	2	0	201.1	193	109	95	24	87	151
Wasdin	4-6	4.40	.251	53	7	0	10	0	0	124.2	121	68	61	18	38	84
Garces	0-1	4.61	.255	12	0	0	4	0	0	13.2	14	9	7	2	9	12
Trlicek	3-4	4.63	.289	18	0	0	8	0	0	23.1	26	14	12	2	18	10
Sele	13-12	5.38	.279	33	33	1	0	0	0	177.1	196	115	106	25	80	122
Brandenburg	0-2	5.49	.299	31	0	0	5	0	0	41.0	49	25	25	3	16	34
Suppan	7-3	5.69	.305	23	22	0	1	0	0	112.1	140	75	71	12	36	67
Hammond	3-4	5.92	.310	29	8	0	6	0	1	65.1	81	45	43	5	27	48
Lacy	1-1	6.11	.314	33	0	0	12	0	3	45.2	60	34	31	7	22	18
Lowe	2-6	6.13	.279	20	9	0	1	0	0	69.0	74	49	47	11	23	52
Eshelman	3-3	6.33	.330	21	6	0	6	0	0	42.2	58	32	30	3	17	18
Avery	6-7	6.42	.320	22	18	0	1	0	0	96.2	127	76	69	15	49	51
Saberhagen	0-1	6.58	.288	6	6	0	0	0	0	26.0	30	20	19	5	10	14
Mahomes	1-0	8.10	.366	10	0	0	2	0	0	10.0	15	10	9	2	10	5
Grundt	0-0	9.00	.357	2	0	0	0	0	0	3.0	5	3	3	0	0	0
Rose	0-0	12.00	.357	1	1	0	0	0	0	3.0	5	4	4	0	2	3
Borland	0-0	13.50	.400	3	0	0	0	0	0	3.1	6	5	5	1	7	1

1998 preliminary roster

PITCHERS (20)
Steve Avery
Brian Barkley
Rafael Betancourt
Robinson Checo
Jim Corsi
Dennis Eckersley
Rich Garces
Tom Gordon
Butch Henry
Joe Hudson
Kerry Lacy

Derek Lowe
Ron Mahay
Pedro Martinez
Peter Munro
Brian Rose
Bret Saberhagen
Brian Shouse
Tim Wakefield
John Wasdin

CATCHERS (5)
Scott Hatteberg

Jim Leyritz
Walt McKeel
Jason Varitek
B.J. Waszgis

INFIELDERS (9)
Jim Chamblee
Jeff Frye
Nomar Garciaparra
Reggie Jefferson
Tim Naehring
Arquimedez Pozo

Donnie Sadler
John Valentin
Mo Vaughn

OUTFIELDERS (6)
Darren Bragg
Damon Buford
Michael Coleman
Jimmy Hurst
Trot Nixon
Troy O'Leary

Games played by position

PLAYER	G	C	1B	2B	3B	SS	OF	DH
Benjamin	49	0	4	5	19	16	0	1
Bragg	153	0	0	0	1	0	150	0
Coleman	8	0	0	0	0	0	7	0
Cordero	140	0	0	1	0	0	137	2
Frye	127	0	1	80	18	3	13	11
Garciaparra	153	0	0	0	0	153	0	0
Haselman	67	66	0	0	0	0	0	0
Hatteberg	114	106	0	0	0	0	0	1
Jefferson	136	0	12	0	0	0	0	119
Mack	60	0	0	0	0	0	45	5
Malave	4	0	0	0	0	0	4	0
McKeel	5	4	1	0	0	0	0	0
Naehring	70	0	0	0	68	0	0	1
O'Leary	146	0	0	0	0	0	142	1
Pemberton	27	0	0	0	0	0	23	0
Pozo	4	0	0	0	4	0	0	0
Pride	81	0	0	0	0	0	35	23
Tavarez	42	0	0	0	0	0	35	2
Valentin	143	0	0	79	64	0	0	0
Varitek	1	1	0	0	0	0	0	0
Vaughn	141	0	131	0	0	0	0	9

Sick call: 1997 DL report

PLAYER	Days on the DL
Steve Avery	62
Mark Brandenburg	62
Robinson Checo	42
Jim Corsi	29
Rich Garces	46*
Chris Hammond	93
Bill Haselman	39
Butch Henry	49
Shane Mack	25
Tim Naehring	97
Bret Saberhagen	143
Mo Vaughn	23
Tim Wakefield	21

Indicates two separate terms on Disabled List.

1997 salaries

	Bonuses	Total earned salary
Mo Vaughn, 1b		6,350,000
Steve Avery, p		4,850,000
John Valentin, 2b	50,000	3,800,000
Wil Cordero, of	100,000	3,100,000
Tom Gordon, p	150,000	3,050,000
Tim Naehring, 3b		2,700,000
Tim Wakefield, p		2,500,000
Reggie Jefferson, 1b	125,000	2,025,000
Shane Mack, of		1,850,000
Aaron Sele, p		1,126,000
Troy O'Leary, of		1,100,000
Jeff Frye, 2b	150,000	1,050,000
Butch Henry, p	350,000	750,000
Chris Hammond, p		700,000
Bret Saberhagen, p	200,000	700,000
Bill Hasselman, c		650,000
Jim Corsi, p	120,000	470,000
Darren Bragg, of		240,000
Mike Benjamin, ss		200,000
Mark Brandenburg, p		187,500
John Wasdin, p		185,000
Jesus Tavarez, of		175,000
Jeff Suppan, p		151,000
Nomar Garciaparra, ss		150,000
Scott Hatteberg, c		150,000
Joe Hudson, p		150,000
Ron Mahay, p		150,000
Jose Malave, of		150,000

Average 1997 salary: $1,380,696
Total 1997 payroll: $38,659,500

107

Minor Leagues

Tops in the organization

BATTER	CLUB	AVG.	G	AB	R	H	HR	RBI
Liniak, Cole	Tre	.309	117	417	52	129	8	60
Coleman, M.	Paw	.305	130	498	83	152	21	77
Merloni, Lou	Paw	.305	118	420	73	128	10	61
Barnes, John	Mch	.304	130	490	80	149	6	73
Chamblee, J.	Mch	.300	133	487	112	146	22	73

HOME RUNS

Hyzdu, Adam	Paw	23
Pozo, A.	Paw	22
Chamblee, J.	Mch	22
Coleman, M.	Paw	21
Nixon, Trot	Paw	20

WINS

Rose, Brian	Paw	17
Welch, Robb	Mch	13
Farrell, Jim	Paw	12
Barkley, Brian	Tre	12
Pavano, Carl	Paw	11

RBI

Gibralter, David	Tre	86
Hyzdu, Adam	Paw	84
Bryant, Pat	Paw	81
Stenson, Dernell	Mch	80
Coleman, M.	Paw	77

SAVES

Beale, Chuck	Mch	12
Betancourt, R.	Mch	11
Lacy, Kerry	Paw	8
Several Players Tied at		7

STOLEN BASES

Fuller, Aaron	Tre	40
Johnson, R.	Mch	29
Faggett, Ethan	Tre	25
Coleman, M	Paw	24
Padilla, Roy.	Sar	24

STRIKEOUTS

Pena, Juan	Tre	167
Welch, Robb	Mch	158
Cressend, Jack	Sar	149
Pavano, Carl	Paw	147
Sekany, Jason	Sar	135

PITCHER	CLUB	W-L	ERA	IP	H	BB	SO
Rose, Brian	Paw	17- 5	3.02	191	188	46	116
Pavano, Carl	Paw	11- 6	3.12	162	148	34	147
Kinney, Matt	Mch	8- 5	3.53	117	93	78	123
Cressend, Jack	Sar	8-11	3.80	166	163	56	149
Pena, Juan	Tre	9-12	3.87	188	165	54	167

Boston (1901-1997)

Runs: Most, career

1816	Carl Yastrzemski, 1961-1983
1798	Ted Williams, 1939-1960
1435	Dwight Evans, 1972-1990
1249	Jim Rice, 1974-1989
1094	Bobby Doerr, 1937-1951

Hits: Most, career

3419	Carl Yastrzemski, 1961-1983
2654	Ted Williams, 1939-1960
2452	Jim Rice, 1974-1989
2373	Dwight Evans, 1972-1990
2098	WADE BOGGS, 1982-1992

2B: Most, career

646	Carl Yastrzemski, 1961-1983
525	Ted Williams, 1939-1960
474	Dwight Evans, 1972-1990
422	WADE BOGGS, 1982-1992
381	Bobby Doerr, 1937-1951

3B: Most, career

130	Harry Hooper, 1909-1920
106	Tris Speaker, 1907-1915
90	Buck Freeman, 1901-1907
89	Bobby Doerr, 1937-1951
87	Larry Gardner, 1908-1917

HR: Most, career

521	Ted Williams, 1939-1960
452	Carl Yastrzemski, 1961-1983
382	Jim Rice, 1974-1989
379	Dwight Evans, 1972-1990
223	Bobby Doerr, 1937-1951

RBI: Most, career

1844	Carl Yastrzemski, 1961-1983
1839	Ted Williams, 1939-1960
1451	Jim Rice, 1974-1989
1346	Dwight Evans, 1972-1990
1247	Bobby Doerr, 1937-1951

SB: Most, career

300	Harry Hooper, 1909-1920
267	Tris Speaker, 1907-1915
168	Carl Yastrzemski, 1961-1983
141	Heinie Wagner, 1906-1918
134	Larry Gardner, 1908-1917

BB: Most, career

2019	Ted Williams, 1939-1960
1845	Carl Yastrzemski, 1961-1983
1337	Dwight Evans, 1972-1990
1004	WADE BOGGS, 1982-1992
826	Harry Hooper, 1909-1920

BA: Highest, career

.344	Ted Williams, 1939-1960
.338	WADE BOGGS, 1982-1992
.337	Tris Speaker, 1907-1915
.320	Pete Runnels, 1958-1962
.320	Jimmie Foxx, 1936-1942

On-base avg: Highest, career

.482	Ted Williams, 1939-1960
.429	Jimmie Foxx, 1936-1942
.428	WADE BOGGS, 1982-1992
.414	Tris Speaker, 1907-1915
.408	Pete Runnels, 1958-1962

Slug avg: Highest, career

.634	Ted Williams, 1939-1960
.605	Jimmie Foxx, 1936-1942
.532	MO VAUGHN, 1991-1997
.520	Fred Lynn, 1974-1980
.502	Jim Rice, 1974-1989

Games started: Most, career

382	ROGER CLEMENS, 1984-1996
297	Cy Young, 1901-1908
238	Luis Tiant, 1971-1978
232	Mel Parnell, 1947-1956
228	Bill Monbouquette, 1958-1965

Complete games: Most, career

275	Cy Young, 1901-1908
156	Bill Dinneen, 1902-1907
141	George Winter, 1901-1908
121	Joe Wood, 1908-1915
119	Lefty Grove, 1934-1941

Saves: Most, career

132	Bob Stanley, 1977-1989
104	Dick Radatz, 1962-1966
91	Ellis Kinder, 1948-1955
88	Jeff Reardon, 1990-1992
69	Sparky Lyle, 1967-1971

Shutouts: Most, career

38	ROGER CLEMENS, 1984-1996
38	Cy Young, 1901-1908
28	Joe Wood, 1908-1915
26	Luis Tiant, 1971-1978
25	Dutch Leonard, 1913-1918

Wins: Most, career

192	ROGER CLEMENS, 1984-1996
192	Cy Young, 1901-1908
123	Mel Parnell, 1947-1956
122	Luis Tiant, 1971-1978
117	Joe Wood, 1908-1915

K: Most, career

2590	ROGER CLEMENS, 1984-1996
1341	Cy Young, 1901-1908
1075	Luis Tiant, 1971-1978
1043	Bruce Hurst, 1980-1988
986	Joe Wood, 1908-1915

Win pct: Highest, career

.695	Roger Moret, 1970-1975
.684	Dave Ferriss, 1945-1950
.676	Joe Wood, 1908-1915
.659	Babe Ruth, 1914-1919
.640	Tex Hughson, 1941-1949

ERA: Lowest, career

1.99	Joe Wood, 1908-1915
2.00	Cy Young, 1901-1908
2.12	Ernie Shore, 1914-1917
2.13	Dutch Leonard, 1913-1918
2.19	Babe Ruth, 1914-1919

Runs: Most, season

150	Ted Williams, 1949
142	Ted Williams, 1946
141	Ted Williams, 1942
139	Jimmie Foxx, 1938
136	Tris Speaker, 1912

Hits: Most, season

240	WADE BOGGS, 1985
222	Tris Speaker, 1912
214	WADE BOGGS, 1988
213	Jim Rice, 1978
210	WADE BOGGS, 1983

2B: Most, season

67	Earl Webb, 1931
53	Tris Speaker, 1912
51	WADE BOGGS, 1989
51	Joe Cronin, 1938
47	WADE BOGGS, 1986
47	George Burns, 1923
47	Fred Lynn, 1975
47	JOHN VALENTIN, 1997

3B: Most, season

22	Tris Speaker, 1913
20	Buck Freeman, 1903
19	Buck Freeman, 1902
19	Buck Freeman, 1904
19	Larry Gardner, 1914
19	Chick Stahl, 1904

HR: Most, season

50	Jimmie Foxx, 1938
46	Jim Rice, 1978
44	MO VAUGHN, 1996
44	Carl Yastrzemski, 1967
43	Tony Armas, 1984
43	Ted Williams, 1949

RBI: Most, season

175	Jimmie Foxx, 1938
159	Vern Stephens, 1949
159	Ted Williams, 1949
145	Ted Williams, 1939
144	Walt Dropo, 1950
144	Vern Stephens, 1950

SB: Most, season

54	Tommy Harper, 1973
52	Tris Speaker, 1912
46	Tris Speaker, 1913
42	OTIS NIXON, 1994
42	Tris Speaker, 1914

BB: Most, season

162	Ted Williams, 1947
162	Ted Williams, 1949
156	Ted Williams, 1946
145	Ted Williams, 1941
145	Ted Williams, 1942

BA: Highest, season

.406	Ted Williams, 1941
.388	Ted Williams, 1957
.383	Tris Speaker, 1912
.369	Ted Williams, 1948
.368	WADE BOGGS, 1985

On-base avg: Highest, season

.551	Ted Williams, 1941
.526	Ted Williams, 1957
.513	Ted Williams, 1954
.499	Ted Williams, 1942
.499	Ted Williams, 1947

Slug avg: Highest, season

.735	Ted Williams, 1941
.731	Ted Williams, 1957
.704	Jimmie Foxx, 1938
.694	Jimmie Foxx, 1939
.667	Ted Williams, 1946

Games started: Most, season

43	Cy Young, 1902
42	Bill Dinneen, 1902
41	Babe Ruth, 1916
41	Cy Young, 1901
41	Cy Young, 1904

Complete games: Most, season

41	Cy Young, 1902
40	Cy Young, 1904
39	Bill Dinneen, 1902
38	Cy Young, 1901
37	Bill Dinneen, 1904

Saves: Most, season

40	Jeff Reardon, 1991
33	Jeff Russell, 1993
33	Bob Stanley, 1983
31	Bill Campbell, 1977
31	HEATHCLIFF SLOCUMB, 1996

Shutouts: Most, season

10	Joe Wood, 1912
10	Cy Young, 1904
9	Babe Ruth, 1916
8	ROGER CLEMENS, 1988
8	Carl Mays, 1918

Wins: Most, season

34	Joe Wood, 1912
33	Cy Young, 1901
32	Cy Young, 1902
28	Cy Young, 1903
26	Cy Young, 1904

K: Most, season

291	ROGER CLEMENS, 1988
258	Joe Wood, 1912
257	ROGER CLEMENS, 1996
256	ROGER CLEMENS, 1987
246	Jim Lonborg, 1967

Win pct: Highest, season

.882	Bob Stanley, 1978
.872	Joe Wood, 1912
.857	ROGER CLEMENS, 1986
.806	Dave Ferriss, 1946
.793	Ellis Kinder, 1949

ERA: Lowest, season

0.96	Dutch Leonard, 1914
1.26	Cy Young, 1908
1.49	Joe Wood, 1915
1.62	Ray Collins, 1910
1.62	Cy Young, 1901

Most pinch-hit homers, season

5	Joe Cronin, 1943
4	Del Wilber, 1953

Most pinch-hit homers, career

7	Ted Williams, 1939-1960
5	Joe Cronin, 1935-1945

Longest hitting streak

34	Dom DiMaggio, 1949
30	NOMAR GARCIAPARRA, 1997
30	Tris Speaker, 1912
28	WADE BOGGS, 1985
27	Dom DiMaggio, 1952

Most consecutive scoreless innings

45	Cy Young, 1904
42	Rube Foster, 1914
40	Luis Tiant, 1972
39	Ray Culp, 1968
37	Cy Young, 1903

No-hit games

Cy Young, Bos vs Phi AL, 3-0;
  May 5, 1904 (perfect game).
Jesse Tannehill, Bos at Chi AL, 6-0;
  Aug. 17, 1904.
Bill Dinneen, Bos vs Chi AL, 2-0;
  Sept. 27, 1905 (1st game).
Cy Young, Bos at NY AL, 8-0;
  June 30, 1908.
Joe Wood, Bos vs StL AL, 5-0;
  July 29, 1911 (1st game).
Rube Foster, Bos vs NY AL, 2-0;
  June 21, 1916.
Hubert (Dutch) Leonard, Bos vs StL
  AL, 4-0; Aug. 30, 1916.
Ernie Shore, Bos vs Was AL, 4-0;
  June 23, 1917. 1st game, perfect
  game. Shore relieved Babe Ruth
  in the first inning after Ruth had
  been thrown out of the game for
  protesting a walk to the first bat-
  ter. The runner was caught steal-
  ing, and Shore retired the remain-
  ing 26 batters in order.
Hubert (Dutch) Leonard, Bos at Det
  AL, 5-0; June 3, 1918.
Howard Ehmke, Bos at Phi AL, 4-0;
  Sept. 7, 1923.
Mel Parnell, Bos vs Chi AL, 4-0;
  July 14, 1956.
Earl Wilson, Bos vs LA AL, 2-0;
  June 26, 1962.
Bill Monbouquette, Bos at Chi AL,
  1-0; Aug. 1, 1962.
Dave Morehead, Bos vs Cle AL, 2-0;
  Sept. 16, 1965.
Matt Young, Bos at Cle AL, 1-2;
  April 12, 1992 (1st game); 8
  innings, lost the game, bottom of
  9th not played.

ACTIVE PLAYERS in caps.

*Players' years of service are listed by
the first and last years with this team
and are not necessarily consecutive;
all statistics record performances for
this team only.*

Toronto Blue Jays

By H. Darr Beiser, USA TODAY

Roger Clemens' first year with the Blue Jays included a career-high 292 strikeouts as well as 21 wins.

1997 Blue Jays: Clemens couldn't hit, too

The spring began in Dunedin with optimisim. And why not? The 1996 Toronto Blue Jays had holes, and it was thought that general manager Gord Ash had plugged the weak spots: Carlos Garcia would be the every-day second baseman. Orlando Merced would play right field, bat third and replace John Olerud's numbers in the lineup. Catcher Benito Santiago would supply much-needed power.

The most serious question mark was right-hander Roger Clemens. Could he win coming off a four-year record of 40-39? Well, Clemens was awesome, but not much else went right for the team, as Garcia lost his job, Merced played 98 games, Santiago slipped to 13 homers and the Jays had the second-lowest batting average in franchise history. They were last in the league in hitting and last in runs. Their average of .244 for the season was eight points below that of Cincinnati, the worst in the NL, where pitchers take their hacks, and 26 points under the AL average. Manager Cito Gaston paid for the team's last-place finish with his job.

Clemens signed a then-record free-agent deal for a pitcher and showed he wasn't in the twilight of his career, as Boston GM Dan Duquette had said. Clemens was 21-7 with a 2.05 ERA and 292 strikeouts to win pitching's Triple Crown, the first AL pitcher to do so since Detroit's Hal Newhouser in 1945. Clemens' strikeout total was a career high as he led the league for the fourth time. He tied teammate Pat Hentgen for the AL lead in complete games (nine) and won his fifth ERA title, tying him for second-most with Hall of Famers Grover Cleveland Alexander, Walter Johnson and Sandy Koufax. Clemens tied the Jays record for wins in a season and set team records for strikeouts in a season, strikeouts in a game (16) and consecutive wins by a starter (11).

Some young players did make progress. First baseman Carlos Delgado had career highs in homers and RBI. Reliever Paul Quantrill added a forkball, and it made him the most improved player on the

Team MVP

Roger Clemens: The reports of Roger Clemens' demise were exaggerated—grossly exaggerated. In his first year in Toronto after leaving Boston, the league hit .213 against him. His pitching Triple Crown was the first in the majors since Dwight Gooden's in 1985, and his 21 victories tied Jack Morris' team record. His 2.05 ERA was the AL's third lowest in the DH era.

team. He beat even Clemens in ERA, with a 1.94, compared with 5.43 a year earlier. Outfielder Shawn Green sat when Ruben Sierra was brought in, then led the team in batting (.287) when he got his chance. Rookie Kelvim Escobar took over as closer shortly after his promotion from AA Knoxville and had a 2.90 ERA with 14 saves.

But the disappointments were numerous. Garcia, an All-Star with Pittsburgh, hit poorly, but it was his lack of range that finally cost him his job. Santiago was coming off a 30-homer season, but he hit only three homers in the first half of 1997 and complained about playing time. Third baseman Ed Sprague played hurt until mid-September and slipped from 36 homers and 101 RBI in 1996, to 14 homers and 48 RBI before undergoing shoulder surgery.

The Jays' outfield is the team's future. Jose Cruz Jr., obtained from Seattle on July 31 for Mike Timlin and Paul Spoljaric, immediately showed he belonged, hitting the winning homer in his first game with the Jays. Green, in right, hit 16 homers and has a strong arm. Center fielder Shannon Stewart hit seven triples in his first 42 games, while also stealing 10 bases. He's a disciplined leadoff man who knows the importance of drawing a walk.

1997 Blue Jays: Week-by-week notes

These notes were excerpted from the following issues of Baseball Weekly.

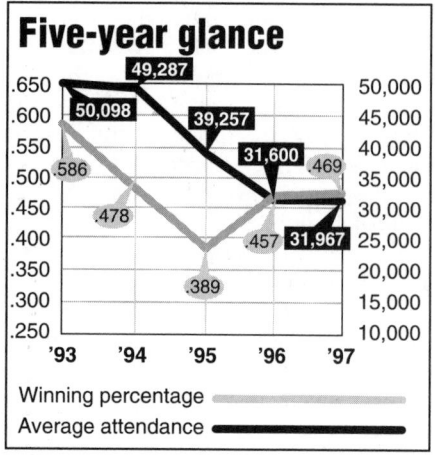

Five-year glance

Winning percentage ———
Average attendance ———

▶**April 9:** Benito Santiago's first two days as a Blue Jay struck both ends of the spectrum. On Opening Day, Santiago struck out four times, tying a club record shared by 22 others. In his second game, Santiago caught Roger Clemens' complete-game masterpiece and hit a two-run homer to break a tie.

▶**April 23:** A group led by Toronto Realtor Murray Frum is hoping to buy the Blue Jays. If they are successful in purchasing 70% of the team from Interbrew S.A., what happens to president and original employee Paul Beeston? Beeston could stay put, perhaps being given a percentage of the team, or he could head to New York as CEO of baseball to work under interim commissioner Bud Selig.

▶**April 30:** In the bullpen, right-hander Mike Timlin blew a save in Anaheim and is 2-for-4 in save opportunities. Righty Tim Crabtree is 1-for-3, and opposing hitters are batting .345 against him. Paul Quantrill, though, has 10⅔ scoreless innings in his last six games.

▶**May 7:** The Jays are last in runs scored, and too many players are pressing. Manager Cito Gaston has dropped second baseman Carlos Garcia from the No. 2 spot in the order to ninth and replaced him with shortstop Alex Gonzalez.

▶**May 14:** Toronto is close to Baltimore as owner of the lowest ERA in the AL, but its offense has a .239 team batting average, more than 10 points lower than the next-worst-hitting club, the Tigers.

▶**May 21:** Pitching injuries continue to plague the Jays. Starters Erik Hanson and Robert Person have shoulder and arm injuries, respectively, and last year's ERA champ, Juan Guzman, threw only 12 warm-up pitches on May 14 before being scratched from his May 18 start against the Indians.

▶**May 28:** Toronto seems to play with enthusiasm only when Roger Clemens or Pat Hentgen starts. Champagne flowed after Clemens' 200th career win, on May 21 against New York. The Rocket, now 8-0, allowed the Yanks four hits and one run in eight innings.

▶**June 4:** Juan Guzman will be lost for a minimum of four weeks after breaking his thumb last week on a comebacker. His spot in the rotation will be taken by Luis Andujar. Erik Hanson is gone until mid-August after shoulder surgery, so the Jays are down two starters. But Roger Clemens became the majors' first 10-game winner with eight strong innings on May 31 against Oakland. His ERA was 1.85. It's still early, but people are already asking him about winning a fourth Cy Young.

▶**June 18:** Murray Frum and his consortium were basically given temporary approval to purchase the Jays on June 11 in Philadelphia at the owners' meetings. The Frum group is attempting to purchase controlling interest from Interbrew S.A., which wants to reduce its interest in the team to 35% from 90%. The change of ownership most likely means that Paul Beeston will move on.

▶**June 25:** Given his first chance to start since June 1, outfielder Shawn Green homered twice on June 16 against the Braves. The release of veteran Ruben Sierra opened the door for Green.

▶**July 2:** Kelvim Escobar registered his first major league win. The 21-year-old came on in relief of Juan Guzman in the fourth inning on June 29 against the Orioles and worked 4⅓ innings, allowing one run and two hits, walking three and striking out five for the victory.

▶July 10: The Blue Jays met the Expos in the first all-Canadian series, with the middle game played before a sellout crowd of more than 50,000 on Canada Day, Canada's 130th anniversary. Montreal edged Toronto 2-1 behind Jeff Juden's 8⅓ innings of two-hit ball.

▶July 16: Roger Clemens was greeted by an equal number of boos and cheers when he returned to Boston's Fenway Park on July 12. But by the eighth inning, the fans were cheering Clemens. He racked up a club-record 16 strikeouts in a 3-1 win over the Red Sox.

▶July 23: Now that Shawn Green is in the lineup, he's producing: three game-winning hits against the Red Sox, then a 3-for-5 game in Texas. Green's average is .302, making him the lone Blue Jay above .300. He's hitting .350 over his last 27 games.

▶July 30: The Jays reeled off a season-high five-game winning streak before losing to Kansas City on July 27. The Jays scored 13 runs on eight hits in their first two wins, against Milwaukee. Kelvim Escobar had back-to-back saves, against the Brewers and the Royals.

▶Aug. 6: Three days after receiving a two-year contract extension, general manager Gord Ash looked like he had earned it. Ash pulled off his best trade by sending former closer Mike Timlin, who had 31 saves last year, and lefty reliever Paul Spoljaric to Seattle for rookie outfielder Jose Cruz Jr., who has hit 13 home runs for the Mariners in only 196 at-bats.

▶Aug. 13: In Jose Cruz Jr.'s first game at SkyDome he hit a solo homer to break a 3-3 tie against the Indians, and in the eighth he threw out the potential tying run at the plate. Cruz made his debut in a Jays uniform on Aug. 1 in Detroit, and his two-run homer provided the win.

▶Aug. 20: With the trade of Otis Nixon to the Dodgers, speedy Shannon Stewart arrived in Toronto as an every-day player. The Jays will use the final six weeks of the season to decide whether Jose Cruz Jr. or Stewart (.346 at AAA Syracuse) will play center.

▶Aug. 27: Roger Clemens worked 7⅓ innings and allowed two earned runs in a 5-3 win against the Royals. He went to 20-4 (his fourth 20-win season) with a 1.80 ERA, eight complete games and two shutouts.

▶Sept. 3: Three names have surfaced as possible successors to Cito Gaston, who's almost certainly out next year: Montreal manager Felipe Alou, Milwaukee manager Phil Garner and Yankees scouting director Gene Michael.

▶Sept. 10: After playing 224 consecutive games, third baseman Ed Sprague shut down his season on Sept. 4. He was to go under the knife on Sept. 9 to repair a torn labrum in his right shoulder. Sprague refused to blame his struggles at the plate on the injury , but he hit .228 with 14 homers and 48 RBI this season, compared with .247, 36 and 101 a year ago.

▶Sept. 17: Chris Carpenter picked up his first major league shutout last week, blanking the Angels 2-0 while facing only one batter over the minimum. In his six starts previous to Sept. 14, Carpenter lowered his ERA each time. Of course, it would have been difficult for the former No. 1 pick to raise it: He's gone from 10.13 to 5.45.

▶Oct. 1: Roger Clemens won the AL Triple Crown of pitching in the ninth inning of the Jays' final game. He did it by striking out Bill Haselman of the Red Sox. His eight strikeouts in 8⅓ innings gave him one more than Seattle's Randy Johnson, and Clemens immediately came out of the game. He led the AL in victories (21), ERA (2.05) and strikeouts (a career-high 292), the first to lead that league in all three categories since Detroit's Hal Newhouser in 1945.

QUOTE OF THE YEAR

"We'll have really fast games, because we'll only have one anthem."
—Reliever Paul Quantrill, on the first Toronto-Montreal series

TORONTO BLUE JAYS 1997 final stats

BATTERS	BA	SLG	OBA	G	AB	R	H	TB	2B	3B	HR	RBI	BB	SO	SB	CS	E
Evans	.289	.421	.341	12	38	7	11	16	2	0	1	2	2	10	0	1	3
Green	.287	.469	.340	135	429	57	123	201	22	4	16	53	36	99	14	3	3
Butler	.286	.357	.375	7	14	3	4	5	1	0	0	2	2	3	0	1	0
Crespo	.286	.464	.333	12	28	3	8	13	0	1	1	5	2	4	0	0	1
Stewart	.286	.446	.368	44	168	25	48	75	13	7	0	22	19	24	10	3	2
Samuel	.284	.516	.364	45	95	13	27	49	5	4	3	15	10	28	5	3	0
Merced	.266	.413	.352	98	368	45	98	152	23	2	9	40	47	62	7	3	3
Delgado	.262	.528	.350	153	519	79	136	274	42	3	30	91	64	133	0	3	12
Nixon	.262	.304	.343	103	401	54	105	122	12	1	1	26	52	54	47	10	1
Mosquera	.250	.375	.250	3	8	0	2	3	1	0	0	0	0	2	0	0	0
Cruz	.248	.499	.315	104	395	59	98	197	19	1	26	68	41	117	7	2	5
Santiago	.243	.387	.279	97	341	31	83	132	10	0	13	42	17	80	1	0	2
Gonzalez	.239	.387	.302	126	426	46	102	165	23	2	12	35	34	94	15	6	8
Duncan	.236	.286	.268	89	339	36	80	97	14	0	1	25	12	78	6	3	8
Carter	.234	.399	.284	157	612	76	143	244	30	4	21	102	40	105	8	2	4
Sprague	.228	.385	.306	138	504	63	115	194	29	4	14	48	51	102	0	1	18
Garcia	.220	.309	.253	103	350	29	77	108	18	2	3	23	15	60	11	3	10
O'Brien	.218	.347	.311	69	225	22	49	78	15	1	4	27	22	45	0	2	3
Sierra	.208	.354	.250	14	48	4	10	17	0	2	1	5	3	13	0	0	1
Brumfield	.207	.282	.268	58	174	22	36	49	5	1	2	20	14	31	4	4	0
T. Perez	.195	.252	.267	40	123	9	24	31	3	2	0	9	11	28	1	1	3
R. Perez	.192	.346	.192	37	78	4	15	27	4	1	2	6	0	16	0	0	0
Martinez	.000	.000	.333	3	2	1	0	0	0	0	0	0	1	1	0	0	1

PITCHERS	W-L	ERA	BA	G	GS	CG	GF	Sho	SV	IP	H	R	ER	HR	BB	SO
Quantrill	6-7	1.94	.297	77	0	0	29	0	5	88.0	103	25	19	5	17	56
Clemens	21-7	2.05	.213	34	34	9	0	3	0	264.0	204	65	60	9	68	292
Almanzar	0-1	2.70	.091	4	0	0	2	0	0	3.1	1	1	1	1	1	4
Robinson	0-0	2.70	.100	3	0	0	2	0	0	3.1	1	1	1	1	1	4
Escobar	3-2	2.90	.237	27	0	0	23	0	14	31.0	28	12	10	1	19	36
Plesac	2-4	3.58	.244	73	0	0	18	0	1	50.1	47	22	20	8	19	61
Janzen	2-1	3.60	.250	12	0	0	6	0	0	25.0	23	11	10	4	13	17
Hentgen	15-10	3.68	.254	35	35	9	0	3	0	264.0	253	116	108	31	71	160
Daal	1-1	4.00	.304	9	3	0	0	0	0	27.0	34	13	12	3	6	28
Williams	9-14	4.35	.269	31	31	0	0	0	0	194.2	201	98	94	31	66	124
Guzman	3-6	4.95	.213	13	13	0	0	0	0	60.0	48	42	33	14	31	52
Carpenter	3-7	5.09	.325	14	13	1	1	1	0	81.1	108	55	46	7	37	55
Person	5-10	5.61	.255	23	22	0	0	0	0	128.1	125	86	80	19	60	99
Andujar	0-6	6.48	.352	17	8	0	5	0	0	50.0	76	45	36	9	21	28
Crabtree	3-3	7.08	.374	37	0	0	16	0	2	40.2	65	32	32	7	17	26
Hanson	0-0	7.80	.254	3	2	0	1	0	0	15.0	15	13	13	3	6	18
Risley	0-1	8.31	.188	3	0	0	1	0	0	4.1	3	4	4	2	2	2
Flener	0-1	9.87	.444	8	1	0	3	0	0	17.1	40	19	19	3	6	9

1998 preliminary roster

PITCHERS (19)
Carlos Almanzar
Chris Carpenter
Roger Clemens
Tim Crabtree
Tom Davey
Kelvim Escobar
Gary Glover
Juan Guzman
Erik Hanson
Pat Hentgen
Randy Myers

Robert Person
Dan Plesac
Paul Quantrill
Bill Risley
Ken Robinson
Steve Sinclair
Woody Williams
Joe Young

CATCHERS (4)
Darrin Fletcher
Julio Mosquera

Benito Santiago
Mike Stanley

INFIELDERS (11)
Felipe Crespo
Carlos Delgado
Tom Evans
Tony Fernandez
Ryan Freel
Alex Gonzalez
Ryan Jones
Michael Peeples

Tomas Perez
Ed Sprague
Kevin Witt

OUTFIELDERS (6)
Jose Cruz
Shawn Green
Robert Perez
Anthony Sanders
Luis Saturria
Shannon Stewart

Games played by position

PLAYER	G	C	1B	2B	3B	SS	OF	DH
Brumfield	58	0	0	0	0	0	47	4
Butler	7	0	0	0	0	0	3	1
Carter	157	0	42	0	0	0	51	64
Crespo	12	0	0	1	7	0	0	2
Cruz	104	0	0	0	0	0	104	0
Delgado	153	0	119	0	0	0	0	33
Duncan	89	0	0	80	0	0	6	2
Evans	12	0	0	0	12	0	0	0
Garcia	103	0	0	96	4	5	0	0
Gonzalez	126	0	0	0	0	125	0	0
Green	135	0	0	0	0	0	91	35
Martinez	3	3	0	0	0	0	0	0
Merced	98	0	1	0	0	0	96	1
Mosquera	3	3	0	0	0	0	0	0
Nixon	103	0	0	0	0	0	102	1
O'Brien	69	69	0	0	0	0	0	0
R. Perez	37	0	0	0	0	0	25	7
T. Perez	40	0	0	8	0	32	0	0
Samuel	45	0	7	4	9	0	2	15
Santiago	97	95	0	0	0	0	0	1
Sierra	14	0	0	0	0	0	7	6
Sprague	138	0	0	0	129	0	0	8
Stewart	44	0	0	0	0	0	41	1

Sick call: 1997 DL report

PLAYER	Days on the DL
Luis Andujar	15
Jacob Brumfield	15
Tim Crabtree	61
Alex Gonzalez	31
Juan Guzman	104*
Erik Hanson	160*
Orlando Merced	61
Tomas Perez	28
Robert Person	19
Bill Risley	164
Benito Santiago	15
Mark Sievert	95
Paul Spoljaric	17
Ed Sprague	25

Indicates two separate terms on Disabled List.

Minor Leagues

Tops in the organization

BATTER	CLUB	AVG.	G	AB	R	H	HR	RBI
Lopez, Luis	Hag	.358	136	503	96	180	11	99
Giles, Tim	Hag	.334	112	380	54	127	12	56
Johnson, Damon	Hag	.325	84	302	44	98	10	55
Abernathy, Brent	Hag	.309	99	379	69	117	1	26
Ramirez, Angel	Knx	.301	92	392	59	118	5	37

HOME RUNS
Witt, Kevin	Knx	30
Sanders, A.	Knx	26
Butler, Rich	Syr	24
Morrison, Greg	Mht	23
Skett, Will	Knx	22

WINS
Lawrence, Clint	Hag	13	
Stevenson, J.	Knx	12	
Harris, D.J.	Knx	9	
Halladay, Roy	Syr	9	
Meiners, Doug	Knx	9	

RBI
Lopez, Luis	Hag	99
Witt, Kevin	Knx	91
Morrison, Greg	Mht	88
Butler, Rich	Syr	87
Skett, Will	Knx	86

SAVES
Robinson, Ken	Syr	17	
Huggins, David	Stc	11	
McClellan, Sean	Hag	11	
Almanzar, Carlos	Syr	11	
Davenport, Joe	Hag	10	

STOLEN BASES
French, Anton	Dun	35
Freel, Ryan	Dun	29
Peeples, Michael	Dun	26
Rivers, Jonathan	Dun	24
Langaigne, S.	Stc	23

STRIKEOUTS
Bale, John	Hag	155	
Glover, Gary	Hag	155	
Lawrence, Clint	Hag	149	
Brandow, Derek	Syr	120	
LaChapelle, Yan	Hag	115	

PITCHER	CLUB	W-L	ERA	IP	H	BB	SO
LaChapelle, Yan	Hag	7- 7	3.26	119	73	74	115
Lawrence, Clint	Hag	13-10	3.54	170	179	40	149
Glover, Gary	Hag	6-17	3.73	174	165	58	155
Graterol, Beiker	Knx	7- 8	3.98	109	117	38	77
Doman, Roger	Knx	8- 5	4.05	111	110	35	79

1997 salaries

	Bonuses	Total earned salary
Roger Clemens, p	150,000	8,400,000
Joe Carter, of		6,500,000
Juan Guzman, p		4,000,000
Erik Hanson, p		3,533,333
Pat Hentgen, p	50,000	3,300,000
Orlando Merced, of		2,700,000
Benito Santiago, c		2,500,000
Carlos Garcia, 2b	150,000	2,550,000
Ed Sprague, 3b		1,900,000
Jacob Brumfield, of	200,000	1,050,000
Dan Plesac, p		800,000
Mariano Duncan, 2b	120,000	870,000
Paul Quantrill, p		700,000
Charlie O'Brien, c		625,000
Carlos Delgado, 1b		500,000
Alex Gonzalez, ss		500,000
Shawn Green, of		500,000
Woody Williams, p		387,500
Bill Risley, p		380,000
Juan Samuel, 2b		375,000
Tim Crabtree, p		245,000
Robert Person, p		185,000
Tomas Perez, ss		185,000
Robert Perez, of		185,000
Luis Andujar, p		170,000
Marty Janzen, p		170,000
Shannon Stewart, of		154,000
Kelvim Escobar, p		150,000
Chris Carpenter, p		150,000
Jose Cruz, of		150,000

Average 1997 salary: $1,460,494
Total 1997 payroll: $43,814,833

Toronto (1977-1997)

116

Runs: Most, career
768	Lloyd Moseby, 1980-1989
641	George Bell, 1981-1990
578	JOE CARTER, 1991-1997
555	TONY FERNANDEZ, 1983-1993
538	Willie Upshaw, 1978-1987

Hits: Most, career
1319	Lloyd Moseby, 1980-1989
1294	George Bell, 1981-1990
1250	TONY FERNANDEZ, 1983-1993
1051	JOE CARTER, 1991-1997
1028	Damaso Garcia, 1980-1986

2B: Most, career
242	Lloyd Moseby, 1980-1989
237	George Bell, 1981-1990
218	JOE CARTER, 1991-1997
213	JOHN OLERUD, 1989-1996
210	TONY FERNANDEZ, 1983-1993

3B: Most, career
70	TONY FERNANDEZ, 1983-1993
60	Lloyd Moseby, 1980-1989
50	Alfredo Griffin, 1979-1993
42	Willie Upshaw, 1978-1987
36	ROBERTO ALOMAR, 1991-1995

HR: Most, career
203	JOE CARTER, 1991-1997
202	George Bell, 1981-1990
179	Jesse Barfield, 1981-1989
149	Lloyd Moseby, 1980-1989
131	Ernie Whitt, 1977-1989

RBI: Most, career
740	George Bell, 1981-1990
736	JOE CARTER, 1991-1997
651	Lloyd Moseby, 1980-1989
527	Jesse Barfield, 1981-1989
518	Ernie Whitt, 1977-1989

SB: Most, career
255	Lloyd Moseby, 1980-1989
206	ROBERTO ALOMAR, 1991-1995
194	Damaso Garcia, 1980-1986
153	TONY FERNANDEZ, 1983-1993
126	DEVON WHITE, 1991-1995

BB: Most, career
547	Lloyd Moseby, 1980-1989
514	JOHN OLERUD, 1989-1996
416	Rance Mulliniks, 1982-1992
403	Ernie Whitt, 1977-1989
390	Willie Upshaw, 1978-1987

BA: Highest, career
.307	ROBERTO ALOMAR, 1991-1995
.293	JOHN OLERUD, 1989-1996
.290	TONY FERNANDEZ, 1983-1993
.288	Damaso Garcia, 1980-1986
.286	George Bell, 1981-1990

On-base avg: Highest, career
.395	JOHN OLERUD, 1989-1996
.389	FRED McGRIFF, 1986-1990
.382	ROBERTO ALOMAR, 1991-1995
.372	Otto Velez, 1977-1982
.365	Rance Mulliniks, 1982-1992

Slug avg: Highest, career
.530	FRED McGRIFF, 1986-1990
.486	George Bell, 1981-1990
.483	Jesse Barfield, 1981-1989
.473	JOE CARTER, 1991-1997
.471	JOHN OLERUD, 1989-1996

Games started: Most, career
405	Dave Stieb, 1979-1992
345	Jim Clancy, 1977-1988
250	JIMMY KEY, 1984-1992
175	TODD STOTTLEMYRE, 1988-1994
173	JUAN GUZMAN, 1991-1997

Complete games: Most, career
103	Dave Stieb, 1979-1992
73	Jim Clancy, 1977-1988
30	PAT HENTGEN, 1991-1997
28	JIMMY KEY, 1984-1992
27	Luis Leal, 1980-1985

Saves: Most, career
217	Tom Henke, 1985-1992
121	Duane Ward, 1986-1995
52	MIKE TIMLIN, 1991-1997
31	Joey McLaughlin, 1980-1984
30	Roy Lee Jackson, 1981-1984

Shutouts: Most, career
30	Dave Stieb, 1979-1992
11	Jim Clancy, 1977-1988
10	JIMMY KEY, 1984-1992
9	PAT HENTGEN, 1991-1997
4	Jesse Jefferson, 1977-1980
4	TODD STOTTLEMYRE, 1988-1994

Wins: Most, career
174	Dave Stieb, 1979-1992
128	Jim Clancy, 1977-1988
116	JIMMY KEY, 1984-1992
82	PAT HENTGEN, 1991-1997
70	JUAN GUZMAN, 1991-1997

K: Most, career
1631	Dave Stieb, 1979-1992
1237	Jim Clancy, 1977-1988
944	JIMMY KEY, 1984-1992
917	JUAN GUZMAN, 1991-1997
783	PAT HENTGEN, 1991-1997

Win pct: Highest, career
.639	Doyle Alexander, 1983-1986
.607	PAT HENTGEN, 1991-1997
.589	JIMMY KEY, 1984-1992
.583	JUAN GUZMAN, 1991-1997
.569	Dave Stieb, 1979-1992

ERA: Lowest, career
3.39	Dave Stieb, 1979-1992
3.42	JIMMY KEY, 1984-1992
3.56	Doyle Alexander, 1983-1986
3.87	John Cerutti, 1985-1990
3.88	PAT HENTGEN, 1991-1997

Runs: Most, season
121	PAUL MOLITOR, 1993
116	DEVON WHITE, 1993
111	George Bell, 1987
110	DEVON WHITE, 1991
109	ROBERTO ALOMAR, 1993
109	JOHN OLERUD, 1993

Hits: Most, season
213	TONY FERNANDEZ, 1986
211	PAUL MOLITOR, 1993
200	JOHN OLERUD, 1993
198	George Bell, 1986
192	ROBERTO ALOMAR, 1993

2B: Most, season

54	JOHN OLERUD, 1993
42	JOE CARTER, 1991
42	CARLOS DELGADO, 1997
42	DEVON WHITE, 1993
41	ROBERTO ALOMAR, 1991
41	George Bell, 1989
41	TONY FERNANDEZ, 1988

3B: Most, season

17	TONY FERNANDEZ, 1990
15	Dave Collins, 1984
15	Alfredo Griffin, 1980
15	Lloyd Moseby, 1984
11	ROBERTO ALOMAR, 1991

HR: Most, season

47	George Bell, 1987
40	Jesse Barfield, 1986
36	FRED McGRIFF, 1989
36	ED SPRAGUE, 1996
35	FRED McGRIFF, 1990

RBI: Most, season

134	George Bell, 1987
121	JOE CARTER, 1993
119	JOE CARTER, 1992
118	Kelly Gruber, 1990
111	PAUL MOLITOR, 1993

SB: Most, season

60	Dave Collins, 1984
55	ROBERTO ALOMAR, 1993
54	Damaso Garcia, 1982
54	OTIS NIXON, 1996
53	ROBERTO ALOMAR, 1991

BB: Most, season

119	FRED McGRIFF, 1989
114	JOHN OLERUD, 1993
94	FRED McGRIFF, 1990
87	ROBERTO ALOMAR, 1992
84	JOHN OLERUD, 1995

BA: Highest, season

.363	JOHN OLERUD, 1993
.341	PAUL MOLITOR, 1994
.332	PAUL MOLITOR, 1993
.326	ROBERTO ALOMAR, 1993
.322	TONY FERNANDEZ, 1987

On-base avg: Highest, season

.473	JOHN OLERUD, 1993
.410	PAUL MOLITOR, 1994
.408	ROBERTO ALOMAR, 1993
.405	ROBERTO ALOMAR, 1992
.402	PAUL MOLITOR, 1993

Slug avg: Highest, season

.605	George Bell, 1987
.599	JOHN OLERUD, 1993
.559	Jesse Barfield, 1986
.552	FRED McGRIFF, 1988
.536	Jesse Barfield, 1985

Games started: Most, season

40	Jim Clancy, 1982
38	Luis Leal, 1982
38	Dave Stieb, 1982
37	Jim Clancy, 1987
36	Doyle Alexander, 1985
36	Jim Clancy, 1984
36	JIMMY KEY, 1987
36	Dave Stieb, 1983
36	Dave Stieb, 1985

Complete games: Most, season

19	Dave Stieb, 1982
15	Jim Clancy, 1980
14	Dave Stieb, 1980
14	Dave Stieb, 1983
12	Jerry Garvin, 1977
12	Tom Underwood, 1979

Saves: Most, season

45	Duane Ward, 1993
34	Tom Henke, 1987
34	Tom Henke, 1992
32	Tom Henke, 1990
32	Tom Henke, 1991

Shutouts: Most, season

5	Dave Stieb, 1982
4	Dave Stieb, 1980
4	Dave Stieb, 1983
4	Dave Stieb, 1988
3	Jim Clancy, 1982
3	Jim Clancy, 1986
3	ROGER CLEMENS, 1997
3	PAT HENTGEN, 1994
3	PAT HENTGEN, 1996
3	PAT HENTGEN, 1997
3	Dave Lemanczyk, 1979

Wins: Most, season

21	ROGER CLEMENS, 1997
21	Jack Morris, 1992
20	PAT HENTGEN, 1996
19	PAT HENTGEN, 1993
18	Dave Stieb, 1990

K: Most, season

292	ROGER CLEMENS, 1997
198	Dave Stieb, 1984
194	JUAN GUZMAN, 1993
187	Dave Stieb, 1983
180	Jim Clancy, 1987

Win pct: Highest, season

.778	Jack Morris, 1992
.762	JUAN GUZMAN, 1992
.750	ROGER CLEMENS, 1997
.750	Dave Stieb, 1990
.739	Doyle Alexander, 1984

ERA: Lowest, season

2.05	ROGER CLEMENS, 1997
2.48	Dave Stieb, 1985
2.64	JUAN GUZMAN, 1992
2.76	JIMMY KEY, 1987
2.83	Dave Stieb, 1984

Most pinch-hit homers, season

2	Jeff Burroughs, 1985
2	Rico Carty, 1979
2	Otto Velez, 1979
2	Ernie Whitt, 1982
2	Al Woods, 1977

Most pinch-hit homers, career

4	Jesse Barfield, 1981-1989
4	Ernie Whitt, 1977-1989

Longest hitting streak

26	JOHN OLERUD, 1993
22	George Bell, 1989
21	Damaso Garcia, 1983
21	Lloyd Moseby, 1983
20	Damaso Garcia, 1980

Most consecutive scoreless innings

31	Dave Stieb, 1988

No-hit game

Dave Stieb, Tor at Cle AL, 3-0;
Sept. 2, 1990.

ACTIVE PLAYERS in caps.

Players' years of service are listed by the first and last years with this team and are not necessarily consecutive; all statistics record performances for this team only.

Cleveland Indians

By Robert Deutsch, USA TODAY

Indians fans took their hats off to newcomer David Justice, who hit .329 in his AL debut.

1997 Indians: 49-year drought continued

The Indians remain the only full-season champion the AL Central has ever known. When October began, that was at least something to hang on to, because Cleveland's third straight division championship had been won with a subpar 86 victories. Yet near the end of the month the Indians were just two outs from winning the World Series after playoff triumphs against the AL's top two teams during the regular season, the Orioles and the Yankees. Of course the Marlins then made a sudden nightmare out of the Tribe's dream month.

Set aside the World Series loss, and the Indians have to feel that their fortunes are on the upswing. They were one of the league's better teams late in the season. Almost to a man, from general manager John Hart to manager Mike Hargrove to the players, the sense in the clubhouse was that a team that had turned over by more than 50% since the previous year's playoffs had taken more than half a season to jell.

Hart's decisions in 1997 were tough ones. Hargrove, rumored to be in trouble for not controlling the clubhouse in previous years and for the club's slow start, got a three-year contract extension in May. One of Hart's most controversial moves was trading free-agent-to-be Kenny Lofton to Atlanta on March 25. A mere 56 days later, he signed the two players he got from Atlanta, Marquis Grissom (now with Milwaukee) and David Justice, to contract extensions through 2002. Hart did the same thing for first baseman Jim Thome. Catcher Sandy Alomar and right fielder Manny Ramirez are signed through 1999, and shortstop Omar Vizquel and third baseman Travis Fryman through 2001 and 2002, respectively. The club holds an option year on all six remaining players.

Some of the Indians had outstanding years. Alomar had a 30-game hitting streak wrapped around the All-Star Game, in which he hit the game-winning home run and became the first player to

be named All-Star MVP in his home stadium. He reached career highs in batting average (.324), homers (21) and RBI (83). Justice, playing with injuries, adjusted quickly to the AL and stabilized the middle of the lineup following the free-agent loss of Albert Belle. Justice hit .329 with 33 homers and 101 RBI. First baseman Jim Thome led the team with 40 homers and 102 RBI.

Pitching was uneven, with starters Jack McDowell, John Smiley, Orel Hershiser, Chad Ogea and Brian Anderson all on the DL at times during the season. Rookie Jaret Wright went from AA to going 8-3 in the big leagues and starting Game 7 of the World Series. Bartolo Colon, another hard-throwing rookie, made a good impression despite a 5.65 ERA in 19 games. Wright and Colon are both 21. Mike Jackson stepped into the closer's role when Jose Mesa was bothered by on- and off-field control problems. Jackson converted 14 of 16 save situations before Mesa won his job back in early August.

Tony Fernandez emerged as the team's best second baseman, though versatile Bip Roberts made more postseason starts. Fernandez had a great year offensively considering he missed all of the 1996 season with a broken right elbow. He hit .286 with 21 doubles and tied a career high with 11 homers in 120 games. He also hit the ALCS-winning home run against Baltimore but made the key error that set up Florida's Series-winning run.

1997 Indians: Week-by-week notes

These notes were excerpted from the following issues of Baseball Weekly.

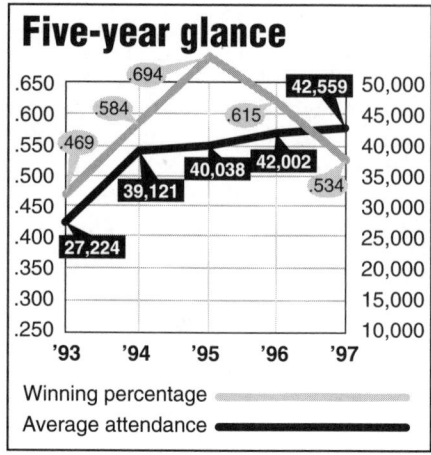

Five-year glance

Winning percentage
Average attendance

▶**April 9:** On April 4, a few hours after the Indians announced that reliever Paul Shuey's contract had been extended through 2000, with a club option for 2001, he was walking to the mound to start the 11th inning in Anaheim with the Indians ahead, 6-4. Shuey loaded the bases and give up a game-winning grand slam to Tim Salmon. Shuey is the closer while Jose Mesa stands trial in Cleveland.

▶**April 16:** Last week was a big one for Jose Mesa. On April 9 he was found not guilty of rape, gross sexual imposition and theft charges in Cuyahoga County Common Pleas Court. On April 10, a judge said police had used improper tactics to search Mesa's car, where they found a concealed weapon. Prosecutors appealed the ruling, but Mesa was free to rejoin the Indians. The Indians activated Mesa and let him pitch the ninth inning of the Tribe's 15-3 victory over Anaheim on April 11.

▶**April 23:** Three starts into his season, Jack McDowell has been sent to the bullpen. Milwaukee pounded McDowell for six earned runs on seven hits in four innings on April 18 in a 10-2 victory. In three starts, McDowell is 0-2 with a 12.51 ERA—19 earned runs, 28 hits and a .438 batting average against in 13⅔ innings.

▶**April 30:** Jose Mesa is still showing rustiness. The Brewers rallied for three runs in the ninth off Mesa on April 26 to win 9-8—Mesa's second blown save in five appearances this season. Milwaukee's rally spoiled a powerful performance by third baseman Matt Williams, who homered twice to make it five in two games, tying the major league record.

▶**May 7:** Left fielder David Justice was leading the American League in batting (.396) and was in the top 10 in home runs (nine) and RBI (22). He reached base safely in all 25 of his starts for Cleveland until being blanked on May 4.

▶**May 14:** So far the Indians haven't missed Albert Belle's power. Through their first 33 games, they lead the majors with 62 homers, including 33 in their last 14 games.

▶**May 28:** Owner Dick Jacobs made a long-term commitment to the Indians last week when he extended the contracts of Jim Thome, David Justice and Marquis Grissom. The guaranteed money is worth $71.5 million and could climb to $93 million with incentives and options.

▶**June 4:** The first reunion with former teammate Albert Belle was split down the middle. The Indians divided a two-game series with Chicago, trading blowouts—the Tribe winning 10-4 on May 26, the Sox winning 8-2 on May 27. Belle went 2-for-8 but hit a grand slam on May 26.

▶**June 11:** Manager Mike Hargrove dropped slumping center fielder Marquis Grissom and Matt Williams in the batting order last week. Grissom went from leadoff to No. 9 and Williams went from cleanup to No. 7.

▶**June 18:** On June 6 against Boston, catcher Sandy Alomar Jr. became the 38th player in history to hit four doubles in a game. Counting his last at-bat from the previous game, Alomar hit five consecutive doubles. Through 49 games, Alomar was hitting .371 (66-for-178) with 18 doubles, 10 homers and 33 RBI.

▶**June 25:** Sandy Alomar Jr. has thrown

out 35% (17-for-49) of the potential base stealers he's faced this year. He also extended his hitting streak to 21 games on June 22.

▶**July 2:** With starters Jack McDowell and Chad Ogea (sore right elbow) on the DL, the Indians have had to go to their farm system. Brian Anderson is 2-1 in four starts, and last week rookie right-hander Jaret Wright won his big league debut with a 10-5 victory against Minnesota.

▶**July 10:** Manny Ramirez can drive Tribe fans crazy. In an 8-6 win over Houston on July 1, Tim Bogar bounced a double down the first base line. The ball rolled under the bench in the Houston bullpen. Ramirez came over from his right field position, waving to the umpire that the ball was out of play. First base umpire Charlie Reliford waved that the ball was in play. By that time, Bogar had circled the bases for an inside-the-park homer.

▶**July 16:** Sandy Alomar Jr.'s 30-game hitting streak ended on July 10 in the Metrodome, two days after he won the All-Star Game for the AL with a two-run homer at Jacobs Field. The streak was the second longest in team history and the second longest by a catcher in big league history.

▶**July 23:** Jose Mesa, in line to be one of the biggest flops of the year when he lost his closer's job and began the season on trial for rape and gun charges, has allowed one earned run in his last 12 games—24 innings, 18 hits and 21 strikeouts. Mike Hargrove foresees the day when Mesa could get his old job back, but not yet. Mike Jackson has 12 saves in that role and has allowed three earned runs in his last 20 games.

▶**July 30:** Marquis Grissom is hitting .321 (44-for-137) with 11 doubles, four homers and 18 RBI in 33 games since being moved back to the leadoff spot on June 17.

▶**Aug. 6:** The Indians had a 4-10 home stand in which they were outscored 68-43, outhomered 15-6, and were held to three or fewer runs in nine games, all of which they lost.

▶**Aug. 13:** Jose Mesa is a closer again. Mike Jackson, 14-for-16 in save situations after replacing Mesa at the end of April, is 0-3 with two blown saves and a 21.00 ERA in his last five appearances. Mesa saved his first game since April 24 on Aug. 9 as he retired the last five hitters in a 4-2 victory against Texas.

▶**Aug. 20:** Jack McDowell's short and disappointing stay with the Indians ended on Aug. 15. McDowell, who underwent surgery on his right elbow on May 20, said he would no longer try to pitch this season because of a bone bruise and nerve damage in the elbow. He is in the final season of a two-year deal worth $10.15 million.

▶**Aug. 27:** Marquis Grissom, battling a 24-for-120 slump, is expected to stay in the No. 9 position for the rest of the regular season. Mike Hargrove appears to be willing to stay with left fielder Brian Giles and shortstop Omar Vizquel in the leadoff spot unless the Indians are able to obtain a veteran leadoff hitter before the Aug. 31 deadline to set playoff rosters.

▶**Sept. 3:** In preparation for the stretch run, the Indians acquired versatile leadoff man Bip Roberts from Kansas City hours before the postseason-roster deadline.

▶**Sept. 10:** Bip Roberts has started three games as leadoff hitter/second baseman and has made three errors. Roberts has played second base before, but not this year. In his home debut with the Tribe, though, Roberts homered to lead off the Sept. 5 game against Chicago.

▶**Oct. 1:** Mike Hargrove shook up his postseason roster by naming rookie Jaret Wright to start Game 2 of the Division Series in Yankee Stadium. The original rotation had Orel Hershiser, Charles Nagy and Wright pitching the first three games. But after Nagy allowed seven runs, six earned, on nine hits in five innings on Sept. 22 against the Yankees, the Indians made the change. Nagy is 0-3 with an 18.00 ERA against New York this year.

QUOTE OF THE YEAR

"Albert and Art—All greedy and all gone!"
—Airplane-pulled banner referring to Albert Belle and former Cleveland Browns owner Art Modell, during Albert Belle's first return to Cleveland

CLEVELAND INDIANS 1997 final stats

BATTERS	BA	SLG	OBA	G	AB	R	H	TB	2B	3B	HR	RBI	BB	SO	SB	CS	E
Wilson	.333	.333	.333	5	15	2	5	5	0	0	0	1	0	2	0	0	1
Justice	.329	.596	.418	139	495	84	163	295	31	1	33	101	80	79	3	5	2
Ramirez	.328	.538	.415	150	561	99	184	302	40	0	26	88	79	115	2	3	7
Alomar	.324	.545	.354	125	451	63	146	246	37	0	21	83	19	48	0	2	12
Candaele	.308	.346	.333	14	26	5	8	9	1	0	0	4	1	1	1	0	0
Roberts	.302	.385	.345	120	431	63	130	166	20	2	4	44	28	67	18	3	7
Borders	.296	.428	.341	55	159	17	47	68	7	1	4	15	9	27	0	2	0
Thome	.286	.579	.423	147	496	104	142	287	25	0	40	102	120	146	1	1	10
Fernandez	.286	.423	.323	120	409	55	117	173	21	1	11	44	22	47	6	6	11
Vizquel	.280	.368	.347	153	565	89	158	208	23	6	5	49	57	58	43	12	10
Sexson	.273	.273	.273	5	11	1	3	3	0	0	0	0	0	2	0	0	0
Giles	.268	.459	.368	130	377	62	101	173	15	3	17	61	63	50	13	3	6
Seitzer	.268	.369	.326	64	198	27	53	73	14	0	2	24	18	25	0	0	3
Manto	.267	.567	.290	16	30	3	8	17	3	0	2	7	1	10	0	0	0
Branson	.264	.403	.329	29	72	5	19	29	4	0	2	7	7	17	0	2	1
Williams	.263	.488	.307	151	596	86	157	291	32	3	32	105	34	108	12	4	12
Grissom	.262	.396	.317	144	558	74	146	221	27	6	12	66	43	89	22	13	3
Hubbard	.250	.333	.308	7	12	3	3	4	1	0	0	0	1	3	2	0	0
Aven	.211	.263	.250	13	19	4	4	5	1	0	0	2	1	5	0	1	0
Casey	.200	.200	.333	6	10	1	2	2	0	0	0	1	1	2	0	0	0
Mitchell	.153	.373	.275	20	59	7	9	22	1	0	4	11	9	11	1	0	1
Diaz	.143	.286	.143	5	7	1	1	2	1	0	0	1	0	2	0	0	1
D. Jackson	.111	.111	.200	8	9	2	1	1	0	0	0	0	0	1	1	0	0

PITCHERS	W-L	ERA	BA	G	GS	CG	GF	Sho	SV	IP	H	R	ER	HR	BB	SO
Mesa	4-4	2.40	.259	66	0	0	38	0	16	82.1	83	28	22	7	28	69
Assenmacher	5-0	2.94	.231	75	0	0	20	0	4	49.0	43	17	16	5	15	53
M. Jackson	2-5	3.24	.215	71	0	0	38	0	15	75.0	59	33	27	3	29	74
Nagy	15-11	4.28	.283	34	34	1	0	1	0	227.0	253	115	108	27	77	149
Wright	8-3	4.38	.238	16	16	0	0	0	0	90.1	81	45	44	9	35	63
Hershiser	14-6	4.47	.272	32	32	1	0	0	0	195.1	199	105	97	26	69	107
Plunk	4-5	4.66	.245	55	0	0	22	0	0	65.2	62	37	34	12	36	66
Anderson	4-2	4.69	.301	8	8	0	0	0	0	48.0	55	28	25	7	11	22
Graves	0-0	4.76	.326	5	0	0	2	0	0	11.1	15	8	6	2	9	4
Ogea	8-9	4.99	.283	21	21	1	0	0	0	126.1	139	79	70	13	47	80
McDowell	3-3	5.09	.282	8	6	0	0	0	0	40.2	44	25	23	6	18	38
Juden	0-1	5.46	.264	8	5	0	0	0	0	31.1	32	21	19	6	15	29
Smiley	2-4	5.54	.304	6	6	0	0	0	0	37.1	45	23	23	9	10	26
Colon	4-7	5.65	.286	19	17	1	0	0	0	94.0	107	66	59	12	45	66
Kline	3-1	5.81	.365	20	1	0	0	0	0	26.1	42	19	17	6	13	17
Jacome	2-0	5.84	.296	28	4	0	2	0	0	49.1	58	33	32	10	20	27
Morman	0-0	5.89	.268	34	0	0	7	0	2	18.1	19	13	12	2	14	13
Shuey	4-2	6.20	.294	40	0	0	16	0	2	45.0	52	31	31	5	28	46
Lopez	3-7	6.93	.322	37	6	0	10	0	0	76.2	101	61	59	11	40	63
Weathers	1-3	8.42	.355	19	1	0	5	0	0	25.2	38	24	24	3	15	18

1998 preliminary roster

PITCHERS (22)
Paul Assenmacher
Rich Batchelor
Bartolo Colon
Maximo De La Rosa
Travis Driskill
Dwight Gooden
Mike Jackson
Jason Jacome
Steve Karsay
Tom Martin
Mike Matthews

Ben McDonald
Jose Mesa
Alvin Morman
Charles Nagy
Chad Ogea
Eric Plunk
Jason Rakers
Paul Shuey
John Smiley
Ron Villone
Jaret Wright

CATCHERS (2)
Sandy Alomar
Einar Diaz

INFIELDERS (9)
Jeff Branson
Russell Branyan
Sean Casey
Chad Fonville
Travis Fryman
Richie Sexson
Jim Thome

Omar Vizquel
Enrique Wilson

OUTFIELDERS (7)
Bruce Aven
Brian Giles
David Justice
Kenny Lofton
Scott Morgan
Alex Ramirez
Manny Ramirez

Games played by position

PLAYER	G	C	1B	2B	3B	SS	OF	DH
Alomar	125	119	0	0	0	0	0	1
Aven	13	0	0	0	0	0	13	0
Borders	55	53	0	0	0	0	0	0
Branson	29	0	0	19	6	2	0	1
Candaele	14	0	0	9	1	0	0	1
Casey	6	0	1	0	0	0	0	3
Diaz	5	5	0	0	0	0	0	0
Fernandez	120	0	0	109	0	10	0	1
Giles	130	0	0	0	0	0	115	9
Grissom	144	0	0	0	0	0	144	0
Hubbard	7	0	0	0	0	0	6	0
D. Jackson	8	0	0	1	0	5	0	0
Justice	139	0	0	0	0	0	78	61
Manto	16	0	6	0	7	0	1	0
Mitchell	20	0	0	0	0	0	1	16
M. Ramirez	150	0	0	0	0	0	146	4
Roberts	120	0	0	13	10	0	94	0
Seitzer	64	0	19	0	13	0	0	24
Sexson	5	0	2	0	0	0	0	1
Thome	147	0	145	0	0	0	0	0
Vizquel	153	0	0	0	0	152	0	0
Williams	151	0	0	0	151	0	0	0
Wilson	5	0	0	1	0	4	0	0

Minor Leagues

Tops in the organization

BATTER	CLUB	AVG.	G	AB	R	H	HR	RBI
Casey, Sean	Buf	.380	82	313	50	119	15	84
Perry, Chan	Akr	.315	119	476	74	150	20	96
Hubbard, T.	Buf	.312	103	375	71	117	16	60
Wilson, Enrique	Buf	.306	118	451	78	138	11	39
Konrady, Dennis	Clm	.301	107	365	60	110	2	43

HOME RUNS

Branyan, Russell	Akr	39
Peoples, Daniel	Kin	34
Sexson, Richie	Buf	31
Glavine, Michael	Clm	28
Morgan, Scott	Akr	25

WINS

Sanders, F.	Kin	11
Brown, Jamie	Wtn	10
Crowell, Jim	Akr	10
Rakers, Jason	Akr	10
Several Players Tied at		9

RBI

Branyan, Russell	Akr	105
Perry, Chan	Akr	96
Sexson, Richie	Buf	88
Casey, Sean	Buf	84
Peoples, Daniel	Kin	84

SAVES

Winchester, S.	Akr	30
Deschenes, M.	Kin	29
Scott, Darryl	Buf	12
Wagner, Ken	Clm	11
Dougherty, A.	Buf	10

STOLEN BASES

Kilburg, Joe	Kin	30
Hubbard, T.	Buf	26
Hamilton, J.	Brl	25
Benefield, Brian	Wtn	23
Scutaro, Marcos	Kin	23

STRIKEOUTS

Rakers, Jason	Akr	139
Hamilton, Jimmy	Clm	137
Moore, Marcus	Buf	135
Sanders, F.	Kin	127
Martinez, W.	Kin	120

PITCHER	CLUB	W-L	ERA	IP	H	BB	SO
Crowell, Jim	Akr	10- 4	2.66	132	109	37	101
Wright, Jaret	Buf	7- 4	2.82	99	73	42	106
Clark, Terry	Buf	7- 3	2.85	95	86	30	63
De La Maza, R.	Buf	9- 4	2.90	115	104	43	73
Martinez, William	Kin	8- 2	3.09	137	125	42	120

Sick call: 1997 DL report

PLAYER	Days on the DL
Brian Anderson	38
Chad Curtis	26
Marquis Grissom	15
Orel Hershiser	15
Dave Justice	17
Albie Lopez	45*
Jack McDowell	139
Alvin Morman	34
Chad Ogea	69
Herb Perry	181
Paul Shuey	59**
John Smiley	9

Indicates two separate terms on Disabled List.
**Indicates three separate terms on Disabled List.*

1997 salaries

	Bonuses	Total earned salary
Matt Williams, 3b	100,000	7,150,000
David Justice, of	100,000	6,300,000
Marquis Grissom, of	50,000	4,850,000
Jack McDowell, p		4,800,000
John Smiley, p		3,750,000
Charles Nagy, p	100,000	3,437,000
Orel Hershiser, p	100,000	3,100,000
Omar Vizquel, ss	50,000	3,050,000
Jim Thome, 1b		2,625,000
Sandy Alomar, c	25,000	2,600,000
Manny Ramirez, of		2,100,000
Mike Jackson, p		2,000,000
Bip Roberts, of	800,000	1,950,000
Jose Mesa, p	100,000	1,947,223
Eric Plunk, p	50,000	1,850,000
Tony Fernandez, ss	200,000	1,550,000
Kevin Seitzer, 3b		1,220,000
Paul Assenmacher, p	50,000	875,000
Jeff Branson, 3b		550,000
Chad Ogea, p		533,333
Pat Borders, c		400,000
Jeff Manto, 3b		240,000
Jason Jacome, p		220,000
Paul Shuey, p		197,000
Jeff Juden, p		185,000
Albie Lopez, p		176,000
Brian Giles, of		175,000
Herbert Perry, 1b		169,000
Alvin Morman, p		165,000
Alexander Ramirez, of		150,000
Jaret Wright, p		150,000

Average 1997 salary: $1,885,970
Total 1997 payroll: $58,465,056

Cleveland (1901-1997)

124

Runs: Most, career

1154	Earl Averill, 1929-1939	
1079	Tris Speaker, 1916-1926	
942	Charlie Jamieson, 1919-1932	
865	Nap Lajoie, 1902-1914	
857	Joe Sewell, 1920-1930	

Hits: Most, career

2046	Nap Lajoie, 1902-1914
1965	Tris Speaker, 1916-1926
1903	Earl Averill, 1929-1939
1800	Joe Sewell, 1920-1930
1753	Charlie Jamieson, 1919-1932

2B: Most, career

486	Tris Speaker, 1916-1926
424	Nap Lajoie, 1902-1914
377	Earl Averill, 1929-1939
375	Joe Sewell, 1920-1930
367	Lou Boudreau, 1938-1950

3B: Most, career

121	Earl Averill, 1929-1939
108	Tris Speaker, 1916-1926
106	Elmer Flick, 1902-1910
89	Joe Jackson, 1910-1915
83	Jeff Heath, 1936-1945

HR: Most, career

242	ALBERT BELLE, 1989-1996
226	Earl Averill, 1929-1939
216	Hal Trosky, 1933-1941
215	Larry Doby, 1947-1958
214	Andre Thornton, 1977-1987

RBI: Most, career

1084	Earl Averill, 1929-1939
919	Nap Lajoie, 1902-1914
911	Hal Trosky, 1933-1941
884	Tris Speaker, 1916-1926
869	Joe Sewell, 1920-1930

SB: Most, career

325	KENNY LOFTON, 1992-1996
254	Terry Turner, 1904-1918
240	Nap Lajoie, 1902-1914
233	Ray Chapman, 1912-1920
207	Elmer Flick, 1902-1910

BB: Most, career

857	Tris Speaker, 1916-1926
766	Lou Boudreau, 1938-1950
725	Earl Averill, 1929-1939
712	Jack Graney, 1908-1922
703	Larry Doby, 1947-1958

BA: Highest, career

.375	Joe Jackson, 1910-1915
.354	Tris Speaker, 1916-1926
.339	Nap Lajoie, 1902-1914
.327	George Burns, 1920-1928
.323	Ed Morgan, 1928-1933

On-base avg: Highest, career

.444	Tris Speaker, 1916-1926
.441	Joe Jackson, 1910-1915
.408	JIM THOME, 1991-1997
.405	Ed Morgan, 1928-1933
.399	Earl Averill, 1929-1939

Slug avg: Highest, career

.580	ALBERT BELLE, 1989-1996
.551	Hal Trosky, 1933-1941
.546	MANNY RAMIREZ, 1993-1997
.542	Joe Jackson, 1910-1915
.542	Earl Averill, 1929-1939

Games started: Most, career

484	Bob Feller, 1936-1956
433	Mel Harder, 1928-1947
350	Bob Lemon, 1941-1958
320	Willis Hudlin, 1926-1940
305	Stan Coveleski, 1916-1924

Complete games: Most, career

279	Bob Feller, 1936-1956
234	Addie Joss, 1902-1910
194	Stan Coveleski, 1916-1924
188	Bob Lemon, 1941-1958
181	Mel Harder, 1928-1947

Saves: Most, career

128	DOUG JONES, 1986-1991
103	JOSE MESA, 1992-1997
53	Ray Narleski, 1954-1958
48	Steve Olin, 1989-1992
46	Jim Kern, 1974-1986
46	Sid Monge, 1977-1981

Shutouts: Most, career

45	Addie Joss, 1902-1910
44	Bob Feller, 1936-1956
31	Stan Coveleski, 1916-1924
31	Bob Lemon, 1941-1958
27	Mike Garcia, 1948-1959

Wins: Most, career

266	Bob Feller, 1936-1956
223	Mel Harder, 1928-1947
207	Bob Lemon, 1941-1958
172	Stan Coveleski, 1916-1924
164	Early Wynn, 1949-1963

K: Most, career

2581	Bob Feller, 1936-1956
2159	Sam McDowell, 1961-1971
1277	Bob Lemon, 1941-1958
1277	Early Wynn, 1949-1963
1161	Mel Harder, 1928-1947

Win pct: Highest, career

.682	OREL HERSHISER, 1995-1997
.667	Vean Gregg, 1911-1914
.663	Johnny Allen, 1936-1940
.630	Cal McLish, 1956-1959
.623	Addie Joss, 1902-1910

ERA: Lowest, career

1.89	Addie Joss, 1902-1910
2.31	Vean Gregg, 1911-1914
2.39	Bob Rhoads, 1903-1909
2.45	Bill Bernhard, 1902-1907
2.50	Otto Hess, 1902-1908

Runs: Most, season

140	Earl Averill, 1931
137	Tris Speaker, 1920
136	Earl Averill, 1936
133	Tris Speaker, 1923
132	KENNY LOFTON, 1996

Hits: Most, season

233	Joe Jackson, 1911
232	Earl Averill, 1936
227	Nap Lajoie, 1910
226	Joe Jackson, 1912
225	Johnny Hodapp, 1930

2B: Most, season

64	George Burns, 1926
59	Tris Speaker, 1923
52	ALBERT BELLE, 1995
52	Tris Speaker, 1921
52	Tris Speaker, 1926

3B: Most, season

26	Joe Jackson, 1912
23	Dale Mitchell, 1949
22	Bill Bradley, 1903
22	Elmer Flick, 1906
20	Jeff Heath, 1941
20	Joe Vosmik, 1935

HR: Most, season

50	ALBERT BELLE, 1995
48	ALBERT BELLE, 1996
43	Al Rosen, 1953
42	Rocky Colavito, 1959
42	Hal Trosky, 1936

RBI: Most, season

162	Hal Trosky, 1936
148	ALBERT BELLE, 1996
145	Al Rosen, 1953
143	Earl Averill, 1931
142	Hal Trosky, 1934

SB: Most, season

75	KENNY LOFTON, 1996
70	KENNY LOFTON, 1993
66	KENNY LOFTON, 1992
61	Miguel Dilone, 1980
60	KENNY LOFTON, 1994

BB: Most, season

123	JIM THOME, 1996
120	JIM THOME, 1997
111	Mike Hargrove, 1980
109	Andre Thornton, 1982
106	Les Fleming, 1942

BA: Highest, season

.408	Joe Jackson, 1911
.395	Joe Jackson, 1912
.389	Tris Speaker, 1925
.388	Tris Speaker, 1920
.386	Tris Speaker, 1916

On-base avg: Highest, season

.483	Tris Speaker, 1920
.479	Tris Speaker, 1925
.474	Tris Speaker, 1922
.470	Tris Speaker, 1916
.469	Tris Speaker, 1923

Slug avg: Highest, season

.714	ALBERT BELLE, 1994
.690	ALBERT BELLE, 1995
.644	Hal Trosky, 1936
.627	Earl Averill, 1936
.623	ALBERT BELLE, 1996

Games started: Most, season

44	George Uhle, 1923
42	Bob Feller, 1946
41	Gaylord Perry, 1973
40	Stan Coveleski, 1921
40	Bob Feller, 1941
40	Gaylord Perry, 1972
40	Dick Tidrow, 1973
40	George Uhle, 1922

Complete games: Most, season

36	Bob Feller, 1946
35	Bill Bernhard, 1904
34	Addie Joss, 1907
33	Otto Hess, 1906
32	George Uhle, 1926

Saves: Most, season

46	JOSE MESA, 1995
43	DOUG JONES, 1990
39	JOSE MESA, 1996
37	DOUG JONES, 1988
32	DOUG JONES, 1989

Shutouts: Most, season

10	Bob Feller, 1946
10	Bob Lemon, 1948
9	Stan Coveleski, 1917
9	Addie Joss, 1906
9	Addie Joss, 1908
9	Luis Tiant, 1968

Wins: Most, season

31	Jim Bagby, 1920
27	Bob Feller, 1940
27	Addie Joss, 1907
27	George Uhle, 1926
26	Bob Feller, 1946
26	George Uhle, 1923

K: Most, season

348	Bob Feller, 1946
325	Sam McDowell, 1965
304	Sam McDowell, 1970
283	Sam McDowell, 1968
279	Sam McDowell, 1969

Win pct: Highest, season

.938	Johnny Allen, 1937
.773	Bill Bernhard, 1902
.773	CHARLES NAGY, 1996
.767	Vean Gregg, 1911
.767	Bob Lemon, 1954

ERA: Lowest, season

1.16	Addie Joss, 1908
1.59	Addie Joss, 1904
1.60	Luis Tiant, 1968
1.71	Addie Joss, 1909
1.72	Addie Joss, 1906

Most pinch-hit homers, season

3	Gene Green, 1962
3	Ron Kittle, 1988
3	Ted Uhlaender, 1970
3	Fred Whitfield, 1965

Most pinch-hit homers, career

8	Fred Whitfield, 1963-1967
5	Chuck Hinton, 1965-1971

Longest hitting streak

31	Nap Lajoie, 1906
30	SANDY ALOMAR, 1997
29	Bill Bradley, 1902
28	Joe Jackson, 1911
28	Hal Trosky, 1936

Most consecutive scoreless innings

41	Luis Tiant, 1968
38	Jim Bagby, 1917

No-hit games

Earl Moore, Cle vs Chi AL, 2-4; May 9, 1901 (lost on two hits in the tenth).

Dusty Rhoades, Cle vs Bos AL, 2-1; Sept. 18, 1908.

Addie Joss, Cle vs Chi AL, 1-0; Oct. 2, 1908 (perfect game).

Addie Joss, Cle at Chi AL, 1-0; April 20, 1910.

Ray Caldwell, Cle at NY AL, 3-0; Sept. 10, 1919 (1st game).

Wes Ferrell, Cle vs StL AL, 9-0; April 29, 1931.

Bob Feller, Cle at Chi AL, 1-0; April 16, 1940 (opening day).

Bob Feller, Cle at NY AL, 1-0; April 30, 1946.

Don Black, Cle vs Phi AL, 3-0; July 10, 1947 (1st game).

Bob Lemon, Cle at Det AL, 2-0; June 30, 1948.

Bob Feller, Cle vs Det AL, 2-1; July 1, 1951 (1st game).

Sonny Siebert, Cle vs Was AL, 2-0; June 10, 1966.

Dick Bosman, Cle vs Oak AL, 4-0; July 19, 1974.

DENNIS ECKERSLEY, Cle vs Cal AL, 1-0; May 30, 1977.

Len Barker, Cle vs Tor AL, 3-0; May 15, 1981 (perfect game).

ACTIVE PLAYERS in caps.

Players' years of service are listed by the first and last years with this team and are not necessarily consecutive; all statistics record performances for this team only.

125

Chicago White Sox

By Russell Becker, *Baseball Weekly*

Rock-steady Frank Thomas both scored and drove in more than 100 runs for the seventh straight season.

1997 White Sox: Reinsdorf gave up in July

There is no category for Most Underachieving Team, but if there was, the Chicago White Sox would have won it in 1997. Their decision to "go for it" in the offseason rang hollow during the season when they traded seven veterans to begin a youth movement while still in Central Division contention. Chairman Jerry Reinsdorf, who had made the November decision to add free-agent Albert Belle, forever will be remembered for this quote in July '97: "Anyone who thinks this White Sox team can catch Cleveland is crazy."

They came close to the Indians before and after the July 31 trade of Wilson Alvarez, Danny Darwin and Roberto Hernandez to the Giants, but never caught them. The White Sox also traded outfielders Tony Phillips and Darren Lewis, catchers Chad Kreuter and Tony Pena, and DH Harold Baines. In all, they got rid of eight players with 92 years of major league experience. The youth movement continued as the White Sox bid goodbye to veteran shortstop Ozzie Guillen, whose option for 1998 was not exercised, and long-time catcher Ron Karkovice, who'd been relegated to the bench.

The Sox staggered manager Terry Bevington by firing him two days after the last game. By the end, there was no cohesion with half the lineup made up of young players. First baseman Frank Thomas was the one player whose performance remained unaffected by what went on around him. He hit .347 and became the first White Sox batting champion since Luke Appling hit .328 in 1943. The Sox reworked and extended Thomas' contract through 2006, for a potential total of $85 million. They also picked up the option on third baseman Robin Ventura. He broke his ankle in spring training, and his absence behind Belle and Thomas in the batting order contributed to the team's 8-17 record in April.

The trade with the Giants and other

late-season shuffling allowed the White Sox to get a better feel for some of their younger players. Reliever Matt Karchner kept the team in the division race by converting all 15 save opportunities as Hernandez's replacement. Catcher Jorge Fabregas came from the Angels in a deal for Tony Phillips and took over the catching job. Despite hitting .280 for the Sox, Fabregas was left unprotected in the expansion draft, and Arizona picked him.

The Sox will rebuild around the kids who gained valuable late-season experience. Rookie center fielder Mike Cameron, who hit 14 homers, heads the list. He hopes to cut down on strikeouts (104) while improving on defense. Room will be made in right field for Magglio Ordonez, who hit .319 with four home runs in just 21 games after being named American Association MVP at AAA Nashville. Scott Eyre fit nicely into Alvarez's left-handed rotation spot with a 4-4 record after leading the AA Southern League in strikeouts with 127.

1997 White Sox: Week-by-week notes

These notes were excerpted from the following issues of Baseball Weekly.

▶**April 9:** Chris Snopek got off to a slow start as the third base replacement for Robin Ventura, who's out at least four months with a broken ankle. Snopek had three errors in the first four games (Ventura had just 11 all of last season) and was 1-for-10 before getting three hits on April 5 in a 15-12 loss to Detroit.

▶**April 23:** First baseman Frank Thomas and left fielder Albert Belle haven't done much for the team's offense with a combined .220 batting average after three weeks, with two home runs (both by Belle) and 15 RBI. The White Sox held a 40-minute meeting when their record fell to 3-9, then lost three of their next four games.

▶**May 7:** The 10-18 White Sox are in their longest and perhaps most important homestand of the season, because manager Terry Bevington's job could be on the line. Sox management dropped the controversial 4-Pack Plan of requiring fans who want tickets to the Cubs series on June 16-18 to also buy tickets to three other games. The Sox instituted the plan because they didn't want the park filled with Cubs fans.

▶**May 14:** The Sox won three games in a row for the first time this season over the weekend. But it's never easy. On May 11, right fielder Lyle Mouton broke his cheek in a collision with center fielder Dave Martinez and will be out three to six weeks. To take Mouton's place, the Sox recalled outfielder Mike Cameron from AAA Nashville.

▶**May 21:** The White Sox trade of Tony Phillips to Anaheim meant that second baseman Ray Durham moved up to leadoff. Durham has a .383 on-base average, compared with Phillips' .441.

▶**May 28:** Frank Thomas reached base 15 consecutive times, one short of Ted Williams' major league record, before flying out against Boston's Rich Garces on May 20. The streak included a home run, three doubles, six singles and five walks.

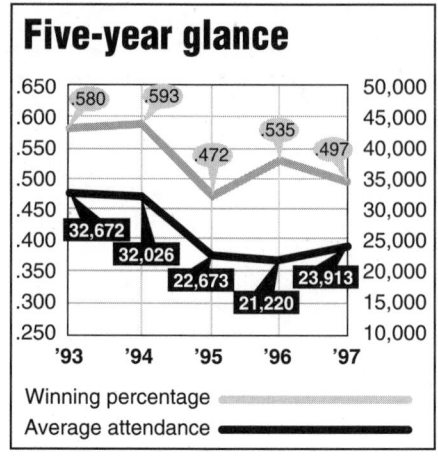

Five-year glance

Winning percentage ▬▬▬
Average attendance ▬▬▬

▶**June 4:** The White Sox have used five third basemen while waiting for Robin Ventura to recover. The result: 10 errors through May, compared with 11 for Ventura all of last season, and a collective average under .250.

▶**June 11:** Albert Belle's best—and worst—moments with the Sox came on June 3 in his first game back in Cleveland. He hit a three-run home run and two doubles to start the first of two Sox victories after being taunted and showered with debris. However, he was fined $5,000 by the league for making an obscene gesture toward the left-field stands.

▶**June 18:** Frank Thomas was put on the disabled list on June 15 for the strained oblique muscles on his left side that had recently sidelined him. The Sox were 2-5 without him, scoring just 14 runs and hitting only .200.

▶**June 25:** Wilson Alvarez has pitched well enough to be 9-2 instead of 5-6 going into June's last week, having received only 14 runs in his losses. Cutting down on walks is a major reason that Alvarez is 3-0 in his last four starts, with an 0.36 ERA.

▶**July 2:** Pitchers were due as much credit as the hitters for a seven-game winning streak that put the White Sox on the heels of Cleveland. Jaime Navarro and James Baldwin each won two games after being a combined 7-14. Matt Karchner headed a bullpen turnaround with 13 scoreless innings to drop his ERA from 6.75 in mid-May to under 3.00.

▶**July 16:** The Sox have only six home runs from their No. 5 hitters, compared with 21 in the third spot, mostly from Frank Thomas, and 18 at cleanup with Albert Belle. Robin Ventura will resume in the fifth spot when he returns from ankle surgery. Thomas started the second half 9-for-17 with three homers and 12 RBI.

▶**July 23:** The anticipated comebacks of Robin Ventura and starter Jason Bere have taken on new urgency. Chris Snopek can't break .230 and has 14 errors at third. Doug Drabek and Jaime Navarro have ERAs over 6.00 and 5.00, respectively. Ventura and Bere are both rehabbing in the minors.

▶**Aug. 6:** The White Sox started tearing down and building up when they traded potential free-agent pitchers Wilson Alvarez and Roberto Hernandez, plus DH Harold Baines and starter Danny Darwin. The moves cleared the way not only for a handful of Giants prospects in the future, but also for White Sox farmhands Mario Valdez, Chris Clemons, Scott Eyre and Nelson Cruz to play now. Getting Frank Thomas off first base was the reason for Baines' going to Baltimore for a player to be named later.

▶**Aug. 13:** In Matt Karchner, the White Sox might have the closer to replace Roberto Hernandez. Karchner saved three games after Hernandez went to the Giants and has a staff-best 2.70 ERA. He also has the attitude for closing. "It's either smoke or be smoked," he said. Scott Eyre and Chris Clemons were a combined 0-4 with an 8.10 ERA in their first four starts.

▶**Aug. 20:** Owner Jerry Reinsdorf is in a show-me mood from White Sox players who remain displeased with his trades. "I'm convinced that the talent we have left can still win," said Reinsdorf, who said before the Giants trade that "anybody who thinks this team can catch Cleveland is crazy."

▶**Aug. 27:** The White Sox finally have a 10-game winner. It's Doug Drabek, whose 5.51 ERA is second worst in the rotation to Jamie Navarro's 5.85.

▶**Sept. 3:** Robin Ventura issued T-shirts that read "Chicago Leftovers" on one side and "We Might Just Be Dumb Enough To Win This" on the other. Jason Bere is one reason the Sox are still in the hunt. He's gone 3-0 with a 2.50 ERA since his return from last September's traumatic elbow surgery.

▶**Sept. 10:** Outfielder Magglio Ordonez will be protected in the Nov. 18 expansion draft. He followed his American Association batting title and MVP award with three home runs in his first five White Sox games.

▶**Sept. 17:** Carlton Fisk's No. 72 was retired with twinges of bitterness from his release in 1993 and his not being allowed into the team's locker room during the playoffs that year. Fisk requested that Jerry Reinsdorf and general manager Ron Schueler not be present.

▶**Sept. 24:** Terry Bevington's two-year stay appears to be over after an underachieving record and two unfortunate incidents. He signaled to the bullpen on Sept. 14 for a reliever when no one was warming up, and had loud words with a coach and then a player on a team flight last week. Frank Thomas, closing in on the club's first batting title since Luke Appling's .328 in 1943, will be the first major leaguer to hit over .300 with 20 home runs, 100 RBI, 100 runs scored and 100 walks for seven seasons in a row, topping Ted Williams' mark of six straight.

▶**Oct. 1:** There was emotion in the dugout and on the field when shortstop Ozzie Guillen and catcher Ron Karkovice played their last Sox games after 13 and nine years, respectively. The players gave Guillen a teary sendoff on Sept. 28 when they held back from running onto the field while he went to shortstop alone, then came out one by one for a handshake and hug. Karkovice homered in his last game, bringing half the team out of the dugout for more hugs.

QUOTE OF THE YEAR

"We didn't realize August 1 was the end of the season."

—Third baseman Robin Ventura, on the late-July trades of Harold Baines, Wilson Alvarez, Roberto Hernandez and Danny Darwin

CHICAGO WHITE SOX 1997 final stats

BATTERS	BA	SLG	OBA	G	AB	R	H	TB	2B	3B	HR	RBI	BB	SO	SB	CS	E
F. Thomas	.347	.611	.456	146	530	110	184	324	35	0	35	125	109	69	1	1	11
Ordonez	.319	.580	.338	21	69	12	22	40	6	0	4	11	2	8	1	2	0
Martin	.300	.371	.320	71	213	24	64	79	7	1	2	27	6	31	1	4	5
Martinez	.286	.413	.356	145	504	78	144	208	16	6	12	55	55	69	12	6	7
Belle	.274	.491	.332	161	634	90	174	311	45	1	30	116	53	105	4	4	10
Durham	.271	.382	.337	155	634	106	172	242	27	5	11	53	61	96	33	16	18
Mouton	.269	.368	.308	88	242	26	65	89	9	0	5	23	14	66	4	4	4
Norton	.265	.441	.306	18	34	5	9	15	2	2	0	1	2	8	0	0	3
Abbott	.263	.368	.263	19	38	8	10	14	1	0	1	2	0	6	0	0	0
Ventura	.262	.426	.373	54	183	27	48	78	10	1	6	26	34	21	0	0	7
Cameron	.259	.433	.356	116	379	63	98	164	18	3	14	55	55	105	23	2	5
Fabregas	.258	.353	.285	121	360	33	93	127	11	1	7	51	14	46	1	1	8
Guillen	.245	.337	.275	142	490	59	120	165	21	6	4	52	22	24	5	3	15
Valdez	.243	.330	.350	54	115	11	28	38	7	0	1	13	17	39	1	0	0
Lewis	.234	.247	.330	81	77	15	18	19	1	0	0	5	11	14	11	4	0
Snopek	.218	.319	.263	86	298	27	65	95	15	0	5	35	18	51	3	2	16
Machado	.200	.333	.250	10	15	1	3	5	0	1	0	2	1	6	0	0	0
Karkovice	.181	.333	.248	51	138	10	25	46	3	0	6	18	11	32	0	0	1
Pena	.164	.179	.250	31	67	4	11	12	1	0	0	8	8	13	0	0	0
Fonville	.111	.111	.200	9	9	1	1	1	0	0	0	1	1	1	2	0	1

PITCHERS	W-L	ERA	BA	G	GS	CG	GF	Sho	SV	IP	H	R	ER	HR	BB	SO
Sirotka	3-0	2.25	.290	7	4	0	1	0	0	32.0	36	9	8	4	5	24
Hernandez	5-1	2.44	.216	46	0	0	43	0	27	48.0	38	15	13	5	24	47
Karchner	3-1	2.91	.258	52	0	0	25	0	15	52.2	50	18	17	4	26	30
Alvarez	9-8	3.03	.232	22	22	2	0	1	0	145.2	126	61	49	9	55	110
Foulke	3-0	3.45	.255	16	0	0	5	0	3	28.2	28	11	11	4	5	21
McElroy	1-3	3.84	.252	61	0	0	16	0	1	75.0	73	36	32	5	22	62
D. Darwin	4-8	4.13	.286	21	17	1	0	0	0	113.1	130	60	52	21	31	62
Simas	3-1	4.14	.279	40	0	0	11	0	1	41.1	46	23	19	6	24	38
C. Castillo	2-1	4.48	.265	37	2	0	14	0	1	66.1	68	35	33	9	33	43
Bere	4-2	4.71	.198	6	6	0	0	0	0	28.2	20	15	15	4	17	21
T. Castillo	4-4	4.91	.296	64	0	0	20	0	4	62.1	74	48	34	6	23	42
Eyre	4-4	5.04	.267	11	11	0	0	0	0	60.2	62	36	34	11	31	36
Baldwin	12-15	5.27	.262	32	32	1	0	0	0	200.0	205	128	117	19	83	140
J. Darwin	0-1	5.27	.298	14	0	0	6	0	0	13.2	17	8	8	1	7	9
Drabek	12-11	5.74	.261	31	31	0	0	0	0	169.1	170	109	108	30	69	85
Navarro	9-14	5.79	.309	33	33	2	0	0	0	209.2	267	155	135	22	73	142
Fordham	0-1	6.23	.266	7	1	0	1	0	0	17.1	17	13	12	2	10	10
Cruz	0-2	6.49	.274	19	0	0	5	0	0	26.1	29	19	19	6	9	23
Levine	2-2	6.91	.313	25	0	0	6	0	0	27.1	35	22	21	4	16	22
Bertotti	0-0	7.36	.450	9	0	0	2	0	0	3.2	9	3	3	0	2	4
L. Thomas	0-0	8.10	.250	5	0	0	0	0	0	3.1	3	3	3	1	2	3
Clemons	0-2	8.53	.345	5	2	0	3	0	0	12.2	19	13	12	4	11	8

1998 preliminary roster

PITCHERS (21)
John Ambrose
James Baldwin
Lorenzo Barcelo
Jason Bere
Mike Bertotti
Carlos Castillo
Tony Castillo
Nelson Cruz
Scott Eyre
Tom Fordham
Keith Foulke
Derek Hasselhoff

Bobby Howry
Matt Karchner
Jaime Navarro
Jason Olsen
Todd Rizzo
Bill Simas
Mike Sirotka
John Snyder
Bryan Ward

CATCHERS (4)
Mark Johnson
Chad Kreuter
Robert Machado
Charlie O'Brien

INFIELDERS (10)
Juan Bautista
Ray Durham
Benji Gil
Carlos Lee
Greg Norton
Sergio Nunez

Chris Snopek
Frank Thomas
Mario Valdez
Robin Ventura

OUTFIELDERS (5)
Jeff Abbott
Albert Belle
Mike Cameron
Magglio Ordonez
Brian Simmons

Games played by position

PLAYER	G	C	1B	2B	3B	SS	OF	DH
Abbott	19	0	0	0	0	0	10	3
Belle	161	0	0	0	0	0	154	7
Cameron	116	0	0	0	0	0	112	4
Durham	155	0	0	153	0	0	0	1
Fabregas	121	113	1	0	0	0	0	0
Fonville	9	0	0	2	0	2	3	1
Guillen	142	0	0	0	0	139	0	0
Karkovice	51	51	0	0	0	0	0	0
Lewis	81	0	0	0	0	0	64	6
Machado	10	10	0	0	0	0	0	0
Martin	71	0	0	9	17	28	0	6
Martinez	145	0	52	0	0	0	105	1
Mouton	88	0	0	0	0	0	67	11
Norton	18	0	0	0	11	0	0	2
Ordonez	21	0	0	0	0	0	19	0
Pena	31	30	0	0	1	0	0	0
Snopek	86	0	0	0	82	4	0	0
F. Thomas	146	0	97	0	0	0	0	49
Valdez	54	0	47	0	1	0	0	2
Ventura	54	0	0	0	54	0	0	0

Minor Leagues

Tops in the organization

BATTER	CLUB	AVG.	G	AB	R	H	HR	RBI
Raven, Luis	Bir	.336	117	456	88	153	30	112
Inglin, Jeff	Hck	.334	135	536	100	179	16	102
Ordonez, M.	Nvl	.329	135	523	65	172	14	90
Abbott, Jeff	Nvl	.327	118	465	88	152	11	63
Lee, Carlos	W-S	.317	139	546	81	173	17	82

HOME RUNS				WINS			
Raven, Luis	Bir	30		Farley, Joe	Hck	14	
Norton, Greg	Nvl	26		Eyre, Scott	Bir	13	
Thomas, Juan	Bir	23		Herbert, Russ	Bir	13	
Berger, Matt	Brs	18		Nichols, James	Hck	12	
Cotton, John	Nvl	18		Cruz, Nelson	Nvl	11	

RBI				SAVES			
Raven, Luis	Bir	112		Darwin, Jeff	Nvl	22	
Inglin, Jeff	Hck	102		Bradford, Chad	W-S	15	
Ordonez, M.	Nvl	90		Newman, Alan	Bir	10	
Thomas, Juan	Bir	83		Iglesias, Mario	Hck	10	
Lee, Carlos	W-S	82		Woods, Brian	Nvl	10	

STOLEN BASES				STRIKEOUTS			
Gomez, Ramon	W-S	53		Lakman, Jason	Hck	168	
Gonzalez, M.	Hck	31		Chantres, Carlos	W-S	158	
Inglin, Jeff	Hck	31		Ambrose, John	W-S	137	
Christensen, M.	Hck	28		Eyre, Scott	Bir	127	
Hollins, D.	Brs	24		Herbert, Russ	Bir	126	

PITCHER	CLUB	W-L	ERA	IP	H	BB	SO
Keyser, Brian	Nvl	7- 5	2.87	119	114	45	68
Sirotka, Mike	Nvl	7- 5	3.28	112	115	22	92
Herbert, Russ	Bir	13- 5	3.63	159	136	80	126
Eyre, Scott	Bir	13- 5	3.84	127	110	55	127
Lakman, Jason	Hck	10- 9	3.90	155	139	70	168

Sick call: 1997 DL report

PLAYER	Days on the DL
Jason Bere	140
Tony Castillo	15
Paco Martin	36*
Lyle Mouton	16
Tony Pena	17
Bill Simas	61*
Frank Thomas	15
Robin Ventura	114

Indicates two separate terms on Disabled List.

1997 salaries

	Bonuses	Total earned salary
Albert Belle, of		10,000,000
Frank Thomas, 1b		7,150,000
Robin Ventura, 3b		6,000,000
Jaime Navarro, p		5,000,000
Ozzie Guillen, ss		4,500,000
Ron Karkovice, c		1,500,000
Doug Drabek, p		1,300,000
Tony Castillo, p	150,000	1,200,000
Chuck McElroy, p		817,000
Dave Martinez, of	225,000	950,000
Jason Bere, p		420,000
Norberto Martin, ss		350,000
Ray Durham, 2b	25,000	310,000
Jorge Fabregas, c	5,000	275,000
James Baldwin, p	10,000	250,000
Lyle Mouton, of		225,000
Matt Karchner, p		200,000
Bill Simas, p		200,000
Jeff Darwin, p		172,500
Mike Sirotka, p		165,000
Mike Cameron, of		160,000
Greg Norton, 3b		155,000
Magglio Ordonez, of		150,000
Scott Eyre, p		150,000
Mario Valdez, 1b		150,000
Keith Foulke, p		150,000

Average 1997 salary: $1,611,519
Total 1997 payroll: $41,899,500

Chicago (1901-1997)

Runs: Most, career

1319	Luke Appling, 1930-1950
1187	Nellie Fox, 1950-1963
1065	Eddie Collins, 1915-1926
893	Minnie Minoso, 1951-1980
791	Luis Aparicio, 1956-1970

Hits: Most, career

2749	Luke Appling, 1930-1950
2470	Nellie Fox, 1950-1963
2007	Eddie Collins, 1915-1926
1749	HAROLD BAINES, 1980-1997
1608	OZZIE GUILLEN, 1985-1997

2B: Most, career

440	Luke Appling, 1930-1950
335	Nellie Fox, 1950-1963
314	HAROLD BAINES, 1980-1997
266	Eddie Collins, 1915-1926
260	Minnie Minoso, 1951-1980

3B: Most, career

104	Shano Collins, 1910-1920
104	Nellie Fox, 1950-1963
102	Luke Appling, 1930-1950
102	Eddie Collins, 1915-1926
82	Johnny Mostil, 1918-1929

HR: Most, career

257	FRANK THOMAS, 1990-1997
220	HAROLD BAINES, 1980-1997
214	Carlton Fisk, 1981-1993
154	Bill Melton, 1968-1975
150	ROBIN VENTURA, 1989-1997

RBI: Most, career

1116	Luke Appling, 1930-1950
966	HAROLD BAINES, 1980-1997
854	FRANK THOMAS, 1990-1997
808	Minnie Minoso, 1951-1980
804	Eddie Collins, 1915-1926

SB: Most, career

368	Eddie Collins, 1915-1926
318	Luis Aparicio, 1956-1970
250	Frank Isbell, 1901-1909
226	LANCE JOHNSON,1988-1995
206	Fielder Jones, 1901-1908

BB: Most, career

1302	Luke Appling, 1930-1950
965	Eddie Collins, 1915-1926
879	FRANK THOMAS, 1990-1997
658	Nellie Fox, 1950-1963
658	Minnie Minoso, 1951-1980

BA: Highest, career

.340	Joe Jackson, 1915-1920
.331	Eddie Collins, 1915-1926
.330	FRANK THOMAS, 1990-1997
.317	Zeke Bonura, 1934-1937
.315	Bibb Falk, 1920-1928

On-base avg: Highest career

.452	FRANK THOMAS, 1990-1997
.426	Eddie Collins, 1915-1926
.407	Joe Jackson, 1915-1920
.399	Luke Appling, 1930-1950
.397	Minnie Minoso, 1951-1980

Slug avg: Highest, career

.600	FRANK THOMAS, 1990-1997
.518	Zeke Bonura, 1934-1937
.499	Joe Jackson, 1915-1920
.470	Ron Kittle, 1982-1991
.468	HAROLD BAINES, 1980-1997

Games started: Most, career

484	Ted Lyons, 1923-1946
483	Red Faber, 1914-1933
390	Billy Pierce, 1949-1961
312	Ed Walsh, 1904-1916
301	Doc White, 1903-1913

Complete games: Most, career

356	Ted Lyons, 1923-1946
273	Red Faber, 1914-1933
249	Ed Walsh, 1904-1916
206	Doc White, 1903-1913
183	Eddie Cicotte, 1912-1920
183	Billy Pierce, 1949-1961

Saves: Most, career

201	Bobby Thigpen, 1986-1993
161	ROBERTO HERNANDEZ, 1991-1997
98	Hoyt Wilhelm, 1963-1968
75	Terry Forster, 1971-1976
57	Wilbur Wood, 1967-1978

Shutouts: Most, career

57	Ed Walsh, 1904-1916
42	Doc White, 1903-1913
35	Billy Pierce, 1949-1961
29	Red Faber, 1914-1933
28	Eddie Cicotte, 1912-1920

Wins: Most, career

260	Ted Lyons, 1923-1946
254	Red Faber, 1914-1933
195	Ed Walsh, 1904-1916
186	Billy Pierce, 1949-1961
163	Wilbur Wood, 1967-1978

K: Most, career

1796	Billy Pierce, 1949-1961
1732	Ed Walsh, 1904-1916
1471	Red Faber, 1914-1933
1332	Wilbur Wood, 1967-1978
1098	Gary Peters, 1959-1969

Win pct: Highest, career

.648	Lefty Williams, 1916-1920
.644	Virgil Trucks, 1953-1955
.616	Jim Kaat, 1973-1975
.615	Juan Pizarro, 1961-1966
.611	JACK McDOWELL, 1987-1994

ERA: Lowest, career

1.81	Ed Walsh, 1904-1916
2.18	Frank Smith, 1904-1910
2.25	Eddie Cicotte, 1912-1920
2.30	Jim Scott, 1909-1917
2.30	Doc White, 1903-1913

Runs: Most, season

135	Johnny Mostil, 1925
120	Zeke Bonura, 1936
120	Fielder Jones, 1901
120	Johnny Mostil, 1926
120	Rip Radcliff, 1936

Hits: Most, season

224	Eddie Collins, 1920
218	Joe Jackson, 1920
208	Buck Weaver, 1920
207	Rip Radcliff, 1936
204	Luke Appling, 1936

2B: Most, season

46	FRANK THOMAS, 1992
45	ALBERT BELLE, 1997
45	Floyd Robinson, 1962
44	Ivan Calderon, 1990
44	Chet Lemon, 1979

3B: Most, season

21	Joe Jackson, 1916
20	Joe Jackson, 1920
18	Jack Fournier, 1915
18	Harry Lord, 1911
18	Minnie Minoso, 1954
18	Carl Reynolds, 1930

HR: Most, season

41	FRANK THOMAS, 1993
40	FRANK THOMAS, 1995
40	FRANK THOMAS, 1996

38	FRANK THOMAS, 1994
37	Dick Allen, 1972
37	Carlton Fisk, 1985

RBI: Most, season

138	Zeke Bonura, 1936
134	FRANK THOMAS, 1996
128	Luke Appling, 1936
128	FRANK THOMAS, 1993
125	FRANK THOMAS, 1997

SB: Most, season

77	Rudy Law, 1983
56	Luis Aparicio, 1959
56	Wally Moses, 1943
53	Luis Aparicio, 1961
53	Eddie Collins, 1917

BB: Most, season

138	FRANK THOMAS, 1991
136	FRANK THOMAS, 1995
127	Lu Blue, 1931
125	TONY PHILLIPS, 1996
122	Luke Appling, 1935
122	FRANK THOMAS, 1992

BA: Highest, season

.388	Luke Appling, 1936
.382	Joe Jackson, 1920
.372	Eddie Collins, 1920
.360	Eddie Collins, 1923
.359	Carl Reynolds, 1930

On-base avg: Highest, season

.487	FRANK THOMAS, 1994
.474	Luke Appling, 1936
.461	Eddie Collins, 1925
.460	Eddie Collins, 1915
.459	FRANK THOMAS, 1996

Slug avg: Highest, season

.729	FRANK THOMAS, 1994
.626	FRANK THOMAS, 1996
.611	FRANK THOMAS, 1997
.607	FRANK THOMAS, 1993
.607	FRANK THOMAS, 1995

Games started: Most, season

49	Ed Walsh, 1908
49	Wilbur Wood, 1972
48	Wilbur Wood, 1973
46	Ed Walsh, 1907
43	Wilbur Wood, 1975

Complete games: Most, season

42	Ed Walsh, 1908
37	Frank Smith, 1909
37	Ed Walsh, 1907
34	Frank Owen, 1904
33	Ed Walsh, 1910
33	Ed Walsh, 1911

Saves: Most, season

57	Bobby Thigpen, 1990
38	ROBERTO HERNANDEZ, 1993
38	ROBERTO HERNANDEZ, 1996
34	Bobby Thigpen, 1988
34	Bobby Thigpen, 1989

Shutouts: Most, season

11	Ed Walsh, 1908
10	Ed Walsh, 1906
8	Reb Russell, 1913
8	Ed Walsh, 1909
8	Wilbur Wood, 1972

Wins: Most, season

40	Ed Walsh, 1908
29	Eddie Cicotte, 1919
28	Eddie Cicotte, 1917
27	Ed Walsh, 1911
27	Ed Walsh, 1912
27	Doc White, 1907

K: Most, season

269	Ed Walsh, 1908
258	Ed Walsh, 1910
255	Ed Walsh, 1911
254	Ed Walsh, 1912
215	Gary Peters, 1967

Win pct: Highest, season

.842	Sandy Consuegra, 1954
.806	Eddie Cicotte, 1919
.774	Clark Griffith, 1901
.759	Richard Dotson, 1983
.750	Reb Russell, 1917
.750	Bob Shaw, 1959
.750	Monty Stratton, 1937
.750	Doc White, 1906

ERA: Lowest, season

1.27	Ed Walsh, 1910
1.41	Ed Walsh, 1909
1.42	Ed Walsh, 1908
1.52	Doc White, 1906
1.53	Eddie Cicotte, 1917

Most pinch-hit homers, season

3	Oscar Gamble, 1977
3	Ron Northey, 1956
3	John Romano, 1959

Most pinch-hit homers, career

| 7 | Jerry Hairston, 1973-1989 |
| 5 | Smoky Burgess, 1964-1967 |

Longest hitting streak

| 27 | Luke Appling, 1936 |
| 27 | ALBERT BELLE, 1997 |

26	Guy Curtwright, 1943
25	LANCE JOHNSON, 1992
23	Minnie Minoso, 1955

Most consecutive scoreless innings

45	Doc White, 1904
39	Billy Pierce, 1953
39	Ed Walsh, 1906
38	Ray Herbert, 1963
37	Joel Horlen, 1968
37	Ed Walsh, 1910

No-hit games

Nixey Callahan, Chi vs Det AL, 3-0; Sept. 20, 1902 (1st game).

Frank Smith, Chi at Det AL, 15-0; Sept. 6, 1905 (2nd game).

Frank Smith, Chi vs Phi AL, 1-0; Sept. 20, 1908.

Ed Walsh, Chi vs Bos AL, 5-0; Aug. 27, 1911.

Jim Scott, Chi at Was AL, 0-1; May 14, 1914 (lost on 2 hits in the tenth).

Joe Benz, Chi vs Cle AL, 6-1; May 31, 1914.

Eddie Cicotte, Chi at StL AL, 11-0; April 14, 1917.

Charlie Robertson, Chi at Det AL, 2-0; April 30, 1922 (perfect game).

Ted Lyons, Chi at Bos AL, 6-0; Aug. 21, 1926.

Vern Kennedy, Chi vs Cle AL, 5-0; Aug. 31, 1935.

Bill Dietrich, Chi vs StL AL, 8-0; June 1, 1937.

Bob Keegan, Chi vs Was AL, 6-0; Aug. 20, 1957 (2nd game).

Joe Horlen, Chi vs Det AL, 6-0; Sept. 10, 1967 (1st game).

Blue Moon Odom (5 innings) and Francisco Barrios (4 innings), Chi at Oak AL, 2-1; July 28, 1976.

Joe Cowley, Chi at Cal AL, 7-1; Sept. 19, 1986.

WILSON ALVAREZ, Chi at Bal AL, 7-0; Aug. 11, 1991.

Ed Walsh, five innings, rain, Chi vs NY AL, 8-1; May 26, 1907.

Melido Perez, six innings, rain, Chi at NY AL, 8-0; July 12, 1990.

ACTIVE PLAYERS in caps.

Players' years of service are listed by the first and last years with this team and are not necessarily consecutive; all statistics record performances for this team only.

By Russell Becker, *Baseball Weekly*

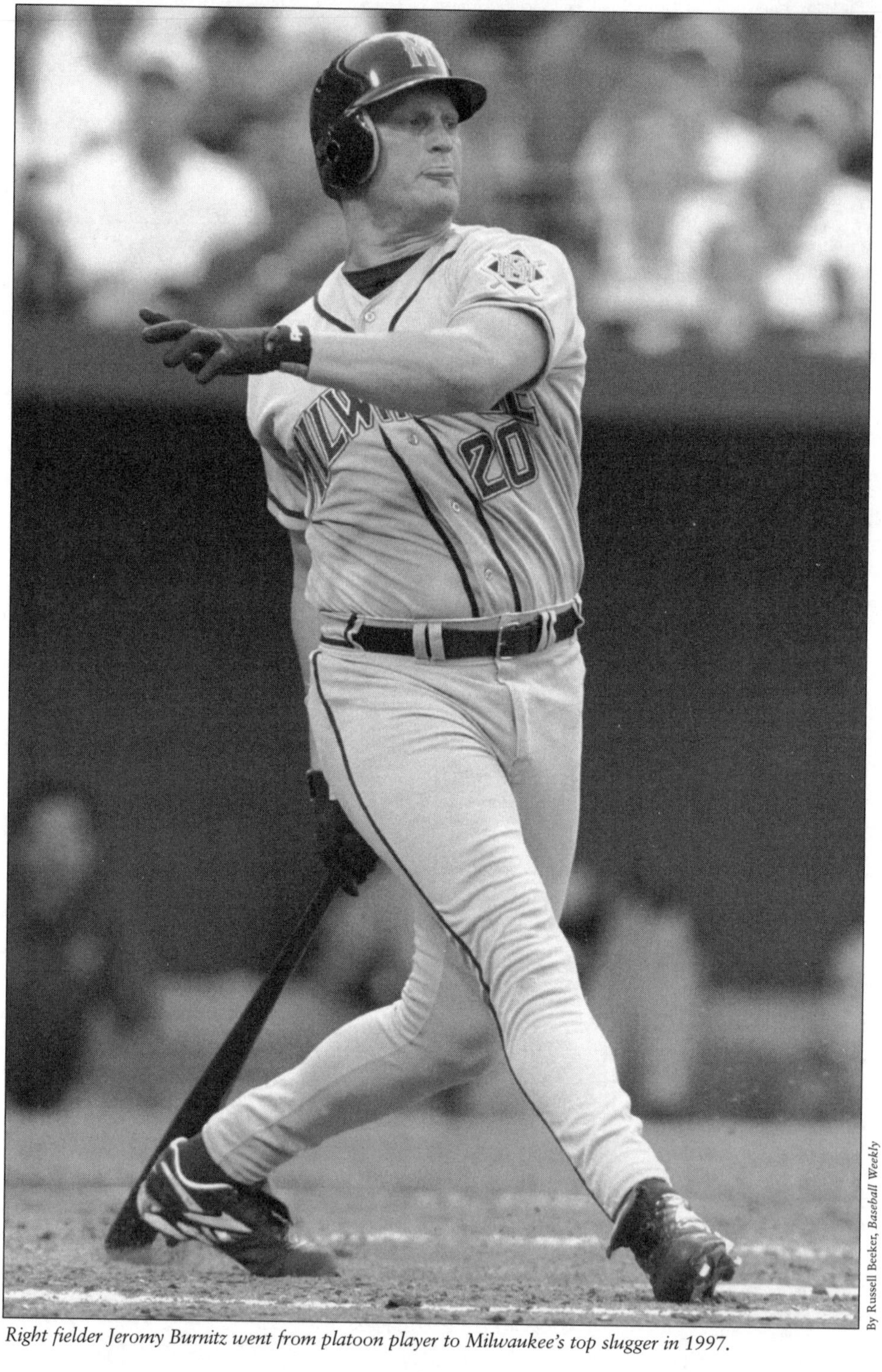

Right fielder Jeromy Burnitz went from platoon player to Milwaukee's top slugger in 1997.

1997 Brewers: Low-priced contenders

The Milwaukee Brewers hung in in the AL Central race on the strength of their pitching, but their hitting just couldn't sustain them, especially in September. Jeff Cirillo, Dave Nilsson, Jose Valentin and others slumped during the key portion of the race. general manager Sal Bando tried to add some veteran help in Julio Franco and Darrin Jackson, but they were not enough. The loss of John Jaha, Marc Newfield and Ben McDonald to injuries also hurt.

Manager Phil Garner managed to keep the Brewers competitive by juggling his lineup most of the season. He also got solid starting pitching from the likes of Jose Mercedes, Bryce Florie and Joel Adamson in various parts of the season. The bullpen combination of Mike Fetters and Bob Wickman as setup men and Doug Jones as the closer was also a big factor in Milwaukee's staying in contention.

The shoulder injuries to Jaha, Newfield and McDonald were the biggest disappointments. Jaha, who hit 32 homers in 1996, was expected to provide a good deal of the Brewers' power, but he struggled early in the season. He eventually had surgery. Newfield, who was acquired in the 1996 trade for Greg Vaughn, was projected as the starting left fielder, but he was dogged by shoulder problems and also had surgery. The Brewers were looking to trade McDonald for some hitting help when he, too, had to have surgery. After the season he was traded to Cleveland for center fielder Marquis Grissom.

The veteran Jones has to top the list of Milwaukee heroes. The 40-year-old reliever set a Brewers save record with 36. Wickman also was effective, pitching in middle and short relief. He appeared in 74 games and led the league with 28 holds. Opponents averaged only .164 against him with runners in scoring position.

Right fielder Jeromy Burnitz was the offensive star. He became the third Brewer in team history to get more than 20 home runs and 20 steals, and his 27 homers and 85 RBI were team highs. Burnitz started the season as a platoon

Team MVP

Jeromy Burnitz: Jeromy Burnitz came to Milwaukee late in the 1996 season when the Indians traded him for Kevin Seitzer. The left-handed Burnitz quickly went from marginal major leaguer to every-day offensive force, leading Milwaukee this year in homers and RBI while showing good speed as well. The former Mets first-round pick batted .281 and hit the first grand slam ever off Baltimore's Jimmy Key.

player, but showed he could hit lefties to earn an every-day job. Infielder Mark Loretta was the unsung hero. He played all the infield spots and hit a respectable .287, second highest on the team to Cirillo's .288. He filled in when second baseman Fernando Vina went down to injury, and hit .421 in June.

The Brewers, now in the NL Central, are looking to build for 2000, when Miller Park is scheduled to be ready. They have signed a core of younger players that they hope will add up to a winner. Third baseman Cirillo, Milwaukee's sole All-Star representative, signed a four-year, $12 million contract. Nilsson, who played first base and the outfield, is signed through 1999. Shortstop Valentin, Vina and pitcher Cal Eldred are others who have signed long-term contracts and are seen as part of the core. The Brewers would like to add righthander Jeff D'Amico to that group. He already is signed for 1998, and the Brewers are convinced he is a star for the future. Left-handed pitcher Scott Karl could be added to the list after he rebounded from a 2-10 start to pitch well in the second half. Garner is signed through 1999 and is well-liked in the Brewers organization. There were rumors about his being a prime candidate for jobs in Chicago, Toronto and elsewhere, but he has denied that he is interested.

MILWAUKEE BREWERS / AL CENTRAL

1997 Brewers: Week-by-week notes

These notes were excerpted from the following issues of Baseball Weekly.

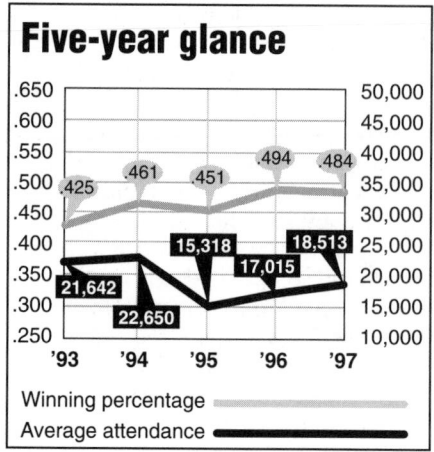

Five-year glance

Winning percentage
Average attendance

▶**April 9:** Manager Phil Garner had to juggle his pitching staff in the first week. Right-hander Cal Eldred threw 44 pitches before an April 3 game at Texas was rained out. Because Garner does not want Eldred to get out of rotation and suffer a setback in his recovery from surgery similar to the one Tommy John once had, he moved Eldred to the home opener on April 7. That pushed right-hander Jeff D'Amico to April 9 for his season debut.

▶**April 16:** After 42,893 fans braved 35-degree weather for the Brewers' home opener, three of the next four games were canceled because of cold and snow. Only about 1,000 people attended the one game that was played, on April 10.

▶**April 23:** Second baseman Fernando Vina is expected to miss two months after breaking his left ankle on April 19 while sliding into second in Cleveland. Vina was the Brewers' hottest hitter. His injury came the game after he hit a grand slam and drove in five runs in a 10-2 win against the Indians, and he was hitting .321.

▶**April 30:** The bullpen has been overworked, partly because the staff gave up 35 earned runs in a week. The team ERA jumped from 3.39 to 4.50, and right-hander Sean Maloney had to be called up from AAA Tucson on April 27 to help out.

▶**May 7:** Left-hander Scott Karl continued to struggle and was winless through May 4. He lost his fifth in a row on April 30, and Phil Garner doesn't have any good options to replace him. Lefty relievers Angel Miranda and Ron Villone have been inconsistent.

▶**May 14:** Mike Fetters joined Doug Jones in a productive bullpen combination. Fetters came off the DL on May 5 and earned a win a couple of days later, with Jones getting the save. Then on May 10, Fetters set up a win for Jones with 1⅔ scoreless innings of relief.

▶**May 21:** The Brewers' offense has missed the run production of first baseman John Jaha and outfielder Marc Newfield, who have had nagging leg problems. As of May 18, the Brewers' were next to last in the AL in runs scored, with 188 in 39 games.

▶**June 4:** Outfielder Jeromy Burnitz was moved to the third spot in the lineup and responded with two home runs in a May 31 win against the White Sox. Burnitz is hitting .308 and slugging .577.

▶**June 11:** Despite their lack of power, the Brewers tied the franchise record for their biggest rally when they came back from a 7-0 deficit on June 4 to beat the Red Sox 13-11.

▶**June 18:** Scott Karl dropped to 2-8 after a 9-5 loss to the Cubs on June 14. Karl gave up six runs on 10 hits in 4⅓ innings. His ERA ballooned to 5.02, but Phil Garner said that Karl's spot in the rotation is still secure.

▶**June 25:** Jeromy Burnitz showed plenty to fans from the Show Me State of Missouri. After starring in a three-game sweep of the Cardinals, Burnitz homered and hit two doubles in a 7-5 win against the Royals on June 20. The Brewers upped their home record to 24-9, the best record at home in the majors, through June 22.

▶**July 16:** The Brewers averaged 4.48 runs per game in the season's first half, compared with 5.87 in the first half of last season. They had 66 home runs compared with 98. Last season, Greg Vaughn, who later was traded to the Padres, and John Jaha, who is on the DL with a shoulder problem, were the Brewers' big guns in the first half.

▶**July 23:** Ben McDonald had been the subject of trade rumors, but he will not come off the DL until Aug. 2, after the trading deadline. McDonald went on the DL on July 19 after complaining of shoulder stiffness. The Brewers reportedly were looking to trade the right-hander because he is eligible for free agency after this season, but his injury makes him tough to trade.

▶**July 30:** The Brewers' medical problems reached epidemic proportions when Doug Jones and Jeff D'Amico suffered injuries. The Brewers already have John Jaha and Marc Newfield on the DL. One player the Brewers need to snap out of a slump is third baseman Jeff Cirillo. He was hitting over .300 at the All-Star break but had fallen to .277 by July 27.

▶**Aug. 6:** The Brewers' nine-game winning streak came to a halt with a 14-4 thumping by Seattle on Aug. 2, but many still wondered if Phil Garner had done it with mirrors. Despite many pitching injuries, starters had an 0.93 ERA during the streak. For the Aug. 2 game, the Brewers drew 43,215 fans, the largest crowd at Milwaukee County Stadium since 1994.

▶**Aug. 13:** First baseman Dave Nilsson and Jeromy Burnitz went on power surges. Nilsson hit two homers on Aug. 5 against Anaheim, his third two-homer game this season. He increased his homer total to 20 through Aug. 10. Burnitz set a club record with homers in five consecutive games and now has 21 overall.

▶**Aug. 20:** After clearing waivers, DH Julio Franco was picked up from the Indians to provide run production and leadership for the Brewers. The Brewers also picked up veteran pitcher Mark Davis for a player to be named later. Davis, the 1989 Cy Young Award winner, was the first player dealt by the Arizona Diamondbacks. He had been pitching for Tucson, the Brewers' AAA affiliate, on loan.

▶**Aug. 27:** Phil Garner became the winningest manager in Brewers history, passing Tom Trebelhorn's 422 total. Scott Karl won his seventh in a row on Aug. 23 with a 5-2 win against the Tigers. On July 4, Karl was 2-10; now he's 9-10. In 54⅔ innings during the streak, Karl had a 2.65 ERA.

▶**Sept. 3:** Right-hander Pete Harnisch, 30, disgruntled because the Mets had moved him to the bullpen, was obtained by the Brewers for minor league outfielder Donny Moore. General manager Sal Bando also went after some help in the outfield when he acquired veteran Darrin Jackson from the Twins on Aug. 30 for a player to be named later. Jackson, 34, has a lifetime .257 average with 70 homers and 266 RBI.

▶**Sept. 17:** The Brewers just couldn't get clutch hits as they dropped out of contention with a losing streak that had reached five games through Sept. 14. Jeromy Burnitz became just the third Brewer in history to have 20 or more home runs and 20 or more steals in a single season, with 24 homers and 20 stolen bases.

▶**Sept. 24:** Doug Jones set a Brewers' save record when he earned his 34th in a 7-4 win against the Twins on Sept. 19. Jones eclipsed the season record established by Dan Plesac in 1989. The 34 saves are not a personal high for Jones, 40, who had 43 for Cleveland in 1990.

▶**Oct. 1:** Pete Harnisch put himself into the Brewers' thinking with a 4-2 win over the Orioles on Sept. 26. Harnisch, who is trying to come back from clinical depression, will be one of several late-season acquisitions on the bubble for next season. One player who very likely will be asked back is Darrin Jackson.

QUOTE OF THE YEAR

"That ain't Chuckie's game. Chuckie hacks on 2-and-0."
—Outfielder Chuck Carr, on why he ignored manager Phil Garner's take sign; Carr was immediately sent down to the minors

MILWAUKEE BREWERS 1997 final stats

BATTERS	BA	SLG	OBA	G	AB	R	H	TB	2B	3B	HR	RBI	BB	SO	SB	CS	E
Cirillo	.288	.426	.367	154	580	74	167	247	46	2	10	82	60	74	4	3	17
Loretta	.287	.388	.354	132	418	56	120	162	17	5	5	47	47	60	5	5	15
Levis	.285	.335	.361	99	200	19	57	67	7	0	1	19	24	17	1	0	2
Burnitz	.281	.553	.382	153	494	85	139	273	37	8	27	85	75	111	20	13	7
Nilsson	.278	.446	.352	156	554	71	154	247	33	0	20	81	65	88	2	3	6
Vina	.275	.361	.312	79	324	37	89	117	12	2	4	28	12	23	8	7	7
Franco	.270	.360	.369	120	430	68	116	155	16	1	7	44	69	116	15	6	4
Jackson	.261	.384	.279	75	211	26	55	81	9	1	5	36	6	31	4	1	1
Valentin	.253	.407	.310	136	494	58	125	201	23	1	17	58	39	109	19	8	20
Williams	.253	.369	.282	155	566	73	143	209	32	2	10	41	19	90	23	9	3
Stinnett	.250	.361	.308	30	36	2	9	13	4	0	0	3	3	9	0	0	1
Unroe	.250	.688	.333	32	16	3	4	11	1	0	2	5	2	9	2	0	2
Mieske	.249	.391	.300	84	253	39	63	99	15	3	5	21	19	50	1	0	5
Jaha	.247	.494	.354	46	162	25	40	80	7	0	11	26	25	40	1	0	2
Voigt	.245	.490	.331	72	151	20	37	74	9	2	8	22	19	36	1	2	1
Matheny	.244	.338	.294	123	320	29	78	108	16	1	4	32	17	68	0	1	5
Newfield	.229	.299	.295	50	157	14	36	47	8	0	1	18	14	27	0	0	1
Dunn	.229	.347	.242	44	118	17	27	41	5	0	3	9	2	39	3	0	4
Diaz	.220	.300	.235	16	50	4	11	15	2	1	0	7	1	5	0	0	0
Banks	.206	.265	.267	28	68	9	14	18	1	0	1	8	6	17	0	1	2
Williamson	.204	.259	.254	24	54	2	11	14	3	0	0	6	4	8	0	1	2
Huson	.203	.224	.238	84	143	12	29	32	3	0	0	11	5	15	3	0	1
Carr	.130	.196	.184	26	46	3	6	9	3	0	0	0	2	11	1	0	0

PITCHERS	W-L	ERA	BA	G	GS	CG	GF	Sho	SV	IP	H	R	ER	HR	BB	SO
Jones	6-6	2.02	.215	75	0	0	73	0	36	80.1	62	20	18	4	9	82
Wickman	7-6	2.73	.252	74	0	0	20	0	1	95.2	89	32	29	8	41	78
Villone	1-0	3.42	.271	50	0	0	15	0	0	52.2	54	23	20	4	36	40
Fetters	1-5	3.45	.244	51	0	0	20	0	6	70.1	62	30	27	4	33	62
Adamson	5-3	3.54	.265	30	6	0	3	0	0	76.1	78	36	30	13	19	56
Mercedes	7-10	3.79	.248	29	23	2	1	1	0	159.0	146	76	67	24	53	80
Miranda	0-0	3.86	.309	10	0	0	1	0	0	14.0	17	6	6	1	9	8
McDonald	8-7	4.06	.237	21	21	1	0	0	0	133.0	120	68	60	13	36	110
Florie	4-4	4.32	.262	32	8	0	6	0	0	75.0	74	43	36	4	42	53
Karl	10-13	4.47	.279	32	32	1	0	0	0	193.1	212	103	96	23	67	119
D'Amico	9-7	4.71	.264	23	23	1	0	1	0	135.2	139	81	71	25	43	94
Eldred	13-15	4.99	.266	34	34	1	0	1	0	202.0	207	118	112	31	89	122
Harnisch	1-1	5.14	.245	4	3	0	0	0	0	14.0	13	9	8	1	12	10
Maloney	0-0	5.14	.304	3	0	0	2	0	0	7.0	7	4	4	1	2	5
Woodard	3-3	5.15	.269	7	7	0	0	0	0	36.2	39	25	21	5	6	32
Reyes	1-2	5.46	.274	19	0	0	7	0	1	29.2	32	19	18	4	9	28
Davis	0-0	5.51	.323	19	0	0	3	0	0	16.1	21	10	10	4	5	14
McAndrew	1-1	8.38	.304	5	4	0	0	0	0	19.1	24	19	18	1	23	8
Wagner	1-0	9.00	.375	2	0	0	1	0	0	2.0	3	2	2	1	0	0
Hansell	0-0	9.64	.263	3	0	0	1	0	0	4.2	5	5	5	1	1	5
Misuraca	0-0	11.32	.333	5	0	0	2	0	0	10.1	15	13	13	5	7	10

1998 preliminary roster

PITCHERS (16)
Jeff D'Amico
Valerio De Los Santos
Cal Eldred
Horacio Estrada
Chad Fox
Doug Jones
Jeff Juden
Scott Karl
Sean Maloney
Jose Mercedes
Mike Myers
Mike Pasqualicchio
Al Reyes
Paul Wagner
Bob Wickman
Steve Woodard

CATCHERS (3)
Bobby Hughes
Jesse Levis
Mike Matheny

INFIELDERS (10)
Ronnie Belliard
Jeff Cirillo
John Jaha
Mike Kinkade
Mark Loretta
Dave Nilsson
Santiago Perez
Jose Valentin
Fernando Vina
Antone Williamson

OUTFIELDERS (7)
Brian Banks
Jeromy Burnitz
Todd Dunn
Marquis Grissom
Geoff Jenkins
Scott Krause
Marc Newfield

Games played by position

PLAYER	G	C	1B	2B	3B	SS	OF	DH
Banks	28	0	5	0	1	0	15	1
Burnitz	153	0	0	0	0	0	149	0
Carr	26	0	0	0	0	0	23	1
Cirillo	154	0	0	0	150	0	0	2
Diaz	16	0	0	14	1	1	0	0
Dunn	44	0	0	0	0	0	27	14
Franco	120	0	14	35	0	0	0	70
Huson	84	0	21	32	2	0	9	4
Jackson	75	0	0	0	0	0	70	0
Jaha	46	0	27	0	0	0	0	20
Levis	99	78	0	0	0	0	0	8
Loretta	132	0	19	63	15	44	0	1
Matheny	123	121	2	0	0	0	0	0
Mieske	84	0	0	0	0	0	74	5
Newfield	50	0	0	0	0	0	28	18
Nilsson	156	0	74	0	0	0	22	59
Stinnett	30	25	0	0	0	0	0	1
Unroe	32	0	23	1	2	0	2	0
Valentin	136	0	0	0	0	134	0	1
Vina	79	0	0	77	0	0	0	1
Voigt	72	0	19	0	6	0	40	1
Williams	155	0	0	0	0	0	154	1
Williamson	24	0	14	0	0	0	0	4

Minor Leagues

Tops in the organization

BATTER	CLUB	AVG.	G	AB	R	H	HR	RBI
Kinkade, Mike	EIP	.385	125	468	112	180	12	109
Krause, Scott	EIP	.361	125	474	97	171	16	88
Lopiccolo, J.	Blt	.332	112	410	72	136	17	80
Klassen, Danny	EIP	.331	135	519	112	172	14	81
Diaz, Eddy	Tcn	.329	94	356	65	117	9	70

HOME RUNS
Barker, Kevin	EIP	23
Dunn, Todd	Tcn	18
Bunkley, Antuan	Hel	17
Lopiccolo, Jamie	Blt	17
Krause, Scott	EIP	16

WINS
Smith, Travis	EIP	16
Woodard, Steve	Tcn	15
Fieldbinder, Mick	EIP	13
Passini, Brian	Stk	10
Several Players Tied at		9

RBI
Kinkade, Mike	EIP	109
Barker, Kevin	EIP	108
Krause, Scott	EIP	88
Klassen, Danny	EIP	81
Lopiccolo, J.	Blt	80

SAVES
Mullins, Greg	EIP	32
Paredes, R.	Blt	15
Hommel, Brian	Stk	14
Reyes, Alberto	Tcn	7
Several Players Tied at		6

STOLEN BASES
Martinez, Greg	Tcn	39
Green, Chad	Stk	37
Iapoce, Anthony	Stk	22
Kominek, Toby	Stk	22
Several Players Tied at		21

STRIKEOUTS
Passini, Brian	Stk	150
Estrada, H.	EIP	127
Garcia, Jose	Blt	126
Levrault, Allen	Blt	112
Smith, Travis	EIP	107

PITCHER	CLUB	W-L	ERA	IP	H	BB	SO
Rossiter, Mike	EIP	9- 1	2.70	107	105	35	90
Woodard, Steve	Tcn	15- 3	3.01	143	139	26	103
Fieldbinder, M.	EIP	13- 9	3.43	181	196	50	88
Wunsch, Kelly	Stk	7- 9	3.46	143	141	62	98
Passini, Brian	Stk	10-10	3.64	168	154	56	150

Sick call: 1997 DL report

PLAYER	Days on the DL
Jeff D'Amico	45
Mike Fetters	31
Bryce Florie	18
John Jaha	120
Doug Jones	17
Ben McDonald	74
Matt Mieske	25
Angel Miranda	19
Marc Newfield	105*
Steve Sparks	181
Kelly Stinnett	37
Jose Valentin	21
Fernando Vina	89
Steve Woodard	32

Indicates two separate terms on Disabled List.

1997 salaries

	Bonuses	Total earned salary
Ben McDonald, p		5,000,000
John Jaha, 1b		3,387,500
Pete Harnisch, p		3,213,400
Dave Nilsson, 1b	400,000	2,700,000
Mike Fetters, p	100,000	1,725,000
Jose Valentin, ss		1,445,666
Bob Wickman, p	216,000	1,216,000
Matt Mieske, of		950,000
Fernando Vina, 2b		810,000
Cal Eldred, p		766,666
Gerald Williams, of	250,000	700,000
Doug Jones, p	300,004	600,004
Jeff Cirillo, 3b		350,000
Darrin Jackson, of	75,000	275,000
Scott Karl, p		250,000
Jeff Huson, 2b	15,000	240,000
Marc Newfield, of		225,000
Jeromy Burnitz, of		225,000
Bryce Florie, p		215,000
Mike Matheny, c		210,000
Jesse Levis, c		207,500
Ron Villone, p		205,000
Mark Davis, p		200,000
Steve Sparks, p		175,000
Jeff D'Amico, p		172,500
Mark Loretta, ss		167,500
Al Reyes, p		153,000
Jose Mercedes, p		153,000
Joel Adamson, p		151,000
Julio Franco, 1b		150,000
Jack Voigt, of		150,000
Brian Banks, of		150,000
Steve Woodard, p		150,000

Average 1997 salary: $808,750
Total 1997 payroll: $26,688,736

Milwaukee (1970-1997), includes Seattle (1969)

Runs: Most, career

1632	Robin Yount, 1974-1993
1275	PAUL MOLITOR, 1978-1992
821	Cecil Cooper, 1977-1987
726	Jim Gantner, 1976-1992
596	Don Money, 1973-1983

Hits: Most, career

3142	Robin Yount, 1974-1993
2281	PAUL MOLITOR, 1978-1992
1815	Cecil Cooper, 1977-1987
1696	Jim Gantner, 1976-1992
1168	Don Money, 1973-1983

2B: Most, career

583	Robin Yount, 1974-1993
405	PAUL MOLITOR, 1978-1992
345	Cecil Cooper, 1977-1987
262	Jim Gantner, 1976-1992
215	Don Money, 1973-1983

3B: Most, career

126	Robin Yount, 1974-1993
86	PAUL MOLITOR, 1978-1992
42	Charlie Moore, 1973-1986
38	Jim Gantner, 1976-1992
33	Cecil Cooper, 1977-1987

HR: Most, career

251	Robin Yount, 1974-1993
208	Gorman Thomas, 1973-1986
201	Cecil Cooper, 1977-1987
176	Ben Oglivie, 1978-1986
169	GREG VAUGHN, 1989-1996

RBI: Most, career

1406	Robin Yount, 1974-1993
944	Cecil Cooper, 1977-1987
790	PAUL MOLITOR, 1978-1992
685	Ben Oglivie, 1978-1986
605	Gorman Thomas, 1973-1986

SB: Most, career

412	PAUL MOLITOR, 1978-1992
271	Robin Yount, 1974-1993
137	Jim Gantner, 1976-1992
136	Tommy Harper, 1969-1971
112	PAT LISTACH, 1992-1996

BB: Most, career

966	Robin Yount, 1974-1993
755	PAUL MOLITOR, 1978-1992
501	Gorman Thomas, 1973-1986
440	Don Money, 1973-1983
432	Ben Oglivie, 1978-1986

BA: Highest, career

.303	PAUL MOLITOR, 1978-1992
.302	Cecil Cooper, 1977-1987
.300	KEVIN SEITZER, 1992-1996
.290	DARRYL HAMILTON, 1988-1995
.285	Robin Yount, 1974-1993

On-base avg: Highest, career

.376	KEVIN SEITZER, 1992-1996
.367	PAUL MOLITOR, 1978-1992
.360	JOHN JAHA, 1992-1997
.358	Johnny Briggs, 1971-1975
.355	Mike Hegan, 1969-1977

Slug avg: Highest, career

.476	JOHN JAHA, 1992-1997
.470	Cecil Cooper, 1977-1987
.461	Gorman Thomas, 1973-1986
.461	Ben Oglivie, 1978-1986
.459	GREG VAUGHN, 1989-1996

Games started: Most, career

268	Jim Slaton, 1971-1983
231	Moose Haas, 1976-1985
217	Mike Caldwell, 1977-1984
216	Bill Wegman, 1985-1995
205	Teddy Higuera, 1985-1994

Complete games: Most, career

81	Mike Caldwell, 1977-1984
69	Jim Slaton, 1971-1983
55	Moose Haas, 1976-1985
51	Jim Colborn, 1972-1976
50	Teddy Higuera, 1985-1994
50	Lary Sorensen, 1977-1980

Saves: Most, career

133	DAN PLESAC, 1986-1992
97	Rollie Fingers, 1981-1985
79	MIKE FETTERS, 1992-1997
61	DOUG HENRY, 1991-1994
61	Ken Sanders, 1970-1972

Shutouts: Most, career

19	Jim Slaton, 1971-1983
18	Mike Caldwell, 1977-1984
12	Teddy Higuera, 1985-1994
10	Bill Travers, 1974-1980
8	Chris Bosio, 1986-1992
8	Moose Haas, 1976-1985

Wins: Most, career

117	Jim Slaton, 1971-1983
102	Mike Caldwell, 1977-1984
94	Teddy Higuera, 1985-1994
91	Moose Haas, 1976-1985
81	Bill Wegman, 1985-1995

K: Most, career

1081	Teddy Higuera, 1985-1994
929	Jim Slaton, 1971-1983
800	Moose Haas, 1976-1985
749	Chris Bosio, 1986-1992
696	Bill Wegman, 1985-1995

Win pct: Highest, career

.606	Pete Vuckovich, 1981-1986
.595	Teddy Higuera, 1985-1994
.560	Mike Caldwell, 1977-1984
.542	CAL ELDRED, 1991-1997
.535	Moose Haas, 1976-1985

ERA: Lowest, career

3.61	Teddy Higuera, 1985-1994
3.65	Jim Colborn, 1972-1976
3.72	Lary Sorensen, 1977-1980
3.74	Mike Caldwell, 1977-1984
3.76	Chris Bosio, 1986-1992

Runs: Most, season

136	PAUL MOLITOR, 1982
133	PAUL MOLITOR, 1991
129	Robin Yount, 1982
121	Robin Yount, 1980
115	PAUL MOLITOR, 1988

Hits: Most, season

219	Cecil Cooper, 1980
216	PAUL MOLITOR, 1991
210	Robin Yount, 1982
205	Cecil Cooper, 1982
203	Cecil Cooper, 1983

2B: Most, season

49	Robin Yount, 1980
46	JEFF CIRILLO, 1996
46	JEFF CIRILLO, 1997
46	Robin Yount, 1982
44	Cecil Cooper, 1979

3B: Most, season

16	PAUL MOLITOR, 1979
13	PAUL MOLITOR, 1991
12	Robin Yount, 1982
11	Robin Yount, 1988
10	FERNANDO VINA, 1996
10	Robin Yount, 1980
10	Robin Yount, 1983

HR: Most, season

45	Gorman Thomas, 1979
41	Ben Oglivie, 1980
39	Gorman Thomas, 1982
38	Gorman Thomas, 1980
36	George Scott, 1975

RBI: Most, season

126	Cecil Cooper, 1983
123	Gorman Thomas, 1979
122	Cecil Cooper, 1980
121	Cecil Cooper, 1982
118	JOHN JAHA, 1996
118	Ben Oglivie, 1980

SB: Most, season

73	Tommy Harper, 1969
54	PAT LISTACH, 1992
45	PAUL MOLITOR, 1987
41	DARRYL HAMILTON, 1992
41	PAUL MOLITOR, 1982
41	PAUL MOLITOR, 1983
41	PAUL MOLITOR, 1988

BB: Most, season

98	Gorman Thomas, 1979
95	Tommy Harper, 1969
89	Darrell Porter, 1975
89	GREG VAUGHN, 1993
87	Johnny Briggs, 1973

BA: Highest, season

.353	PAUL MOLITOR, 1987
.352	Cecil Cooper, 1980
.331	DAVE NILSSON, 1996
.331	Robin Yount, 1982
.327	Willie Randolph, 1991

On-base avg: Highest, season

.438	PAUL MOLITOR, 1987
.424	Willie Randolph, 1991
.414	Sixto Lezcano, 1979
.407	DAVE NILSSON, 1996
.406	KEVIN SEITZER, 1996

Slug avg: Highest, season

.578	Robin Yount, 1982
.573	Sixto Lezcano, 1979
.566	PAUL MOLITOR, 1987
.563	Ben Oglivie, 1980
.553	JEROMY BURNITZ, 1997

Games started: Most, season

38	Jim Slaton, 1973
38	Jim Slaton, 1976
36	Jim Colborn, 1973
36	CAL ELDRED, 1993
36	Marty Pattin, 1971
36	Lary Sorensen, 1978

Complete games: Most, season

23	Mike Caldwell, 1978
22	Jim Colborn, 1973
17	Lary Sorensen, 1978
16	Mike Caldwell, 1979
16	Lary Sorensen, 1979

Saves: Most, season

36	DOUG JONES, 1997
33	DAN PLESAC, 1989
32	MIKE FETTERS, 1996
31	Ken Sanders, 1971
30	DAN PLESAC, 1988

Shutouts: Most, season

6	Mike Caldwell, 1978
5	Marty Pattin, 1971
4	Mike Caldwell, 1979
4	Jim Colborn, 1973
4	Teddy Higuera, 1986
4	Bill Parsons, 1971
4	Jim Slaton, 1971

Wins: Most, season

22	Mike Caldwell, 1978
20	Jim Colborn, 1973
20	Teddy Higuera, 1986
18	Teddy Higuera, 1987
18	Lary Sorensen, 1978
18	Pete Vuckovich, 1982

K: Most, season

240	Teddy Higuera, 1987
207	Teddy Higuera, 1986
192	Teddy Higuera, 1988
180	CAL ELDRED, 1993
173	Chris Bosio, 1989

Win pct: Highest, season

.750	Pete Vuckovich, 1982
.727	Mike Caldwell, 1979
.727	Chris Bosio, 1992
.710	Mike Caldwell, 1978
.682	Bill Wegman, 1991

ERA: Lowest, season

2.36	Mike Caldwell, 1978
2.45	Teddy Higuera, 1988
2.79	Teddy Higuera, 1986
2.81	Bill Travers, 1976
2.83	Jim Lonborg, 1972

Most pinch-hit homers, season

2	Max Alvis, 1970
2	JEROMY BURNITZ, 1997
2	Bobby Darwin, 1975
2	Bob Hansen, 1974
2	Andy Kosco, 1971
2	Ken McMullen, 1977
2	MATT MIESKE, 1995

Most pinch-hit homers, career

3	MATT MIESKE, 1993-1997
2	Max Alvis, 1970
2	JEROMY BURNITZ, 1996-1997
2	Bobby Darwin, 1975-1976
2	Bob Hansen, 1974-1976
2	Mike Hegan, 1969-1977
2	Andy Kosco, 1971
2	Ken McMullen, 1977

Longest hitting streak

39	PAUL MOLITOR, 1987
24	Dave May, 1973
22	Cecil Cooper, 1980
19	DARRYL HAMILTON, 1991
19	PAUL MOLITOR, 1989
19	PAUL MOLITOR, 1990
19	Robin Yount, 1989

Most consecutive scoreless innings

32	Ted Higuera, 1987

No-hit game

Juan Nieves, Mil at Bal AL, 7-0; April 15, 1987.

ACTIVE PLAYERS in caps.

Players' years of service are listed by the first and last years with this team and are not necessarily consecutive; all statistics record performances for this team only.

Minnesota Twins

By Paul Battaglia, AP/Wide World Photos

Brad Radke won 12 more games than any other Twin and was tied for second in AL victories.

1997 Twins: No pitching, no power

The Minnesota Twins finished their worst full season since 1982 with questions about the franchise's future home, the retirement plans of their future Hall of Famer and a trade request by their best player. Paul Molitor, 41, brought his family to the park for the last series of the season in case it proved to be the 3,000-hit man's last. All-Star Chuck Knoblauch posed for a picture with friend and soon-to-be-former teammate Pat Meares.

It was a season to forget. The Twins carried high hopes into April but finished 68-94, renewing complaints about two old problems—a dearth of starting pitching and power that left the Twins ranked next-to-last in ERA and last in home runs. Also, owner Carl Pohlad was making noises about moving to Charlotte.

The long season wasn't without some highlights. Brad Radke became the Twins' first 20-game winner since Scott Erickson in 1991. He became the first pitcher since 1951 to win 20 for a team that didn't win 70 games. Molitor hit .300 and led the team in average, doubles, and RBI while displaying his usual leadership qualities. Knoblauch had a good season, with a .291 average and 62 stolen bases, but it didn't measure up to his three previous years. Greg Swindell jump-started his career by moving to the bullpen and leading the league in relief innings.

The season began with rookie third baseman Todd Walker looking like a Jackie Robinson Award candidate and Ron Coomer looking like a career-long backup. But Walker got demoted and Coomer became one of the Twins' few solid every-day players, hitting .299 and finishing second on the team in RBI. Alas, the Walkers on the team were more numerous. Where to start?

At the beginning of the season, Frank Rodriguez was the No. 2 starter, Dan Serafini was on the verge of making the Twins' rotation, Scott Stahoviak and Rich Becker were supposedly emerging into quality every-day players, Matt Lawton was a promising outfielder, Marty Cordova was poised on the brink of stardom and Terry Steinbach was prepared to have a Molitor-like homecoming. None of it happened. Rodriguez wound up in long relief, Serafini didn't make it to the bigs until September, Stahoviak and Becker struggled, Lawton was inconsistent, Cordova suffered a heel injury that spurred a season-long slump and Steinbach was disappointing.

The Twins' record since Terry Ryan became general manager is 202-266 (.432). Their record over the last five years under manager Tom Kelly is 326-417 (.439). The Twins have finished 12th, 13th or last in the American League in pitching in each of the last five years. The Twins will enter 1998 depending on the expected growth of a large group of young players to improve what has been a dreadful on-field product.

Walker hit .194 in his first stint in early 1997. When he returned, he hit better and got to play at second base, his natural position, because Knoblauch requested a trade. Serafini looked promising in September. He's been one of the organization's top prospects for five years. Shortstop Denny Hocking is a valuable switch-hitting utility player with speed, a strong arm and the ability to play seven positions. Right-handed pitcher Shane Bowers could contribute in '98. Catcher Damian Miller has won a job as Terry Steinbach's backup. Left-handed pitcher Travis Miller began to display some promise at the end of the '97 season and will be considered for the '98 rotation.

Team MVP

Brad Radke: Brad Radke's 20-10 season was all the more remarkable considering the Twins' poor record. The highlight for the right-hander, who posted a 3.87 earned run average, was a 12-game winning streak in the middle of the season. Radke threw four complete games and struck out 174 while walking only 48.

143

1997 Twins: Week-by-week notes

These notes were excerpted from the following issues of Baseball Weekly.

▶**April 16:** The Twins placed left fielder Marty Cordova on the 15-day DL on April 11. They called up Chris Latham from AAA Salt Lake City to replace him, because Latham plays all three outfield positions. Center fielder Rich Becker is sick, and right fielder Brent Brede is recovering from a bruised foot.

▶**April 23:** The Twins are missing their potential 3-4-5 hitters in DH Paul Molitor, Marty Cordova and first baseman Scott Stahoviak, yet they won four consecutive games last week before losing 10-6 to Seattle on April 20.

▶**April 30:** The Twins were about to finish what would have been their biggest comeback in history, but closer Rick Aguilera allowed bottom-of-the-ninth homers to the A's Brent Mayne and Matt Stairs to blow a three-run lead, and the Twins lost 12-11 in the 11th. Minnesota had overcome an 8-1 Oakland lead.

▶**May 7:** Here's the state of the pitching staff: Gregg Olson has a 20.86 ERA, and he walked the only two batters he faced on May 3 to force in the winning run in a 6-5 loss to Toronto. But his job is safe, at least temporarily. The bullpen had an overall ERA of 8.38 during the eight-game losing streak that ended on May 2.

▶**May 14:** Through May 11, the Twins had trailed in 18 consecutive games and in 31 of 37 games this season. They had lost 14 of their last 17. The Twins' best pitcher has been Bob Tewksbury. And he's 1-5, but with a 3.27 ERA.

▶**May 21:** The Twins called up outfielder Darrin Jackson from AAA Salt Lake City, and in his first big-league game since 1994, he hit a grand slam and drove in a career-high six runs to pace an 11-5 win over the Red Sox. But rookie third baseman Todd Walker, expected to contend for the Jackie Robinson Award, was hitting .204 with one homer and six RBI.

▶**May 28:** On May 18 the Red Sox lost

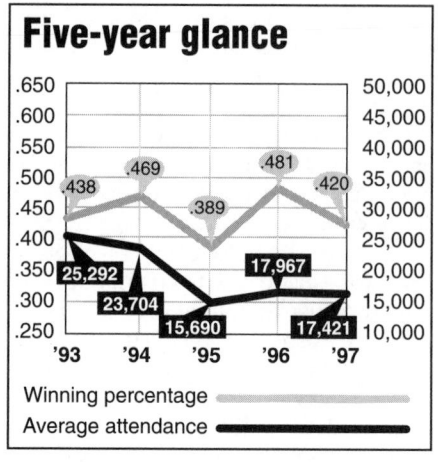

Five-year glance

	'93	'94	'95	'96	'97
Winning percentage	.438	.469	.389	.481	.420
Average attendance	25,292	23,704	15,690	17,967	17,421

two balls in the roof, creating the rallies that gave the Twins a victory. Red Sox manager Jimy Williams called the Metrodome "the world's largest indoor handball court." The Twins retired Kirby Puckett's No. 34 on May 25, culminating a weekend spent honoring him. They also "retired" the seat where his game-winning homer in Game 6 of the '91 World Series landed, by painting it gold.

▶**June 4:** Owner Carl Pohlad said last week that unless there's a special legislative session this year that approves construction of a new ballpark, the team will be put up for sale or the Pohlads will seek to move the team on their own. Pohlad said he would ask major league baseball's nine-man executive council, of which he is a member, for permission to begin pursuing the Twins' sale or relocation options.

▶**June 11:** After Todd Walker's demotion to Salt Lake City in late May, third baseman Ron Coomer is getting his first opportunity to play every day in the majors, at the age of 30. In his first two weeks as a starter, Coomer hit .370.

▶**June 25:** Through June 22, the Twins had won 15 of 26. Their three-game winning streak of June 17-20 was their first of that length since mid-April. The bullpen has a 3.28 ERA for the last month.

▶**July 2:** The Twins are receiving solid contributions from two unsung performers on the left side of their infield. Shortstop Pat Meares deserves some votes for team MVP, and Ron Coomer, a role player the last two years, has taken the team lead in homers. Meares is hitting .282, while Coomer is tied with Paul Molitor for the team lead at .317.

▶July 10: General manager Terry Ryan, asked to assess the first half of what was supposed to be the breakthrough year for the Twins, refused to concede the division title. "This has been a very disappointing start," Ryan said. "But I believe we're still capable of making a run at this thing."

▶July 16: The six pitchers who have filled the last two slots in the Twins' rotation—Scott Aldred, Frank Rodriguez, LaTroy Hawkins, Dave Stevens, Greg Swindell and Kevin Jarvis—are a combined 5-20 with a 7.52 ERA.

▶July 23: Second baseman Chuck Knoblauch has returned to his old, aggressive approach at the plate. The results: He hit over .400 on the Twins' West Coast road trip and is batting .346 over the last month. Last year he used a compact stroke and hit .341, but now he's swinging more from the heels to generate power.

▶July 30: On July 25, right-hander Brad Radke became the first Twin ever to win 10 consecutive starts, beating Baltimore 5-2. The next target for him is the team record for consecutive victories—12, held by Scott Erickson.

▶Aug. 6: Right-hander Frank Rodriguez has been waiting to get back into the rotation most of the season. Now he may have another long wait. Rodriguez started on July 28, and he allowed 11 hits and eight runs in four innings as the Twins lost 10-3 to the Royals.

▶Aug. 13: Brad Radke's 12-game winning streak ended on Aug. 9, when the Yankees beat him 4-1 at the Metrodome. Radke's streak, along with the reunion weekend honoring the 1987 world champs, drew a crowd of 42,151, the second largest of the season.

▶Aug. 27: The Twins went 1-10 on a recent road trip—and also lost to their AA team in New Britain, Conn. They finally won at Detroit to end a franchise-record-tying

10-game losing streak. The team traded first baseman Greg Colbrunn to Atlanta and outfielder Roberto Kelly to Seattle.

▶Sept. 3: Bob Tewksbury finally earned career victory No. 100 on Aug. 27, in his seventh try. After the game, he toasted manager Tom Kelly with a paper cup of champagne, one of the few times this season any Twin has felt like celebrating. Tewksbury's win gave the Twins their first two-game winning streak in August.

▶Sept. 10: Carl Pohlad denied that he has a standing offer from NationsBank—one of the country's largest banking companies—to move the team to Charlotte after the 1998 season.

▶Sept. 17: St. Paul native Paul Molitor says he will consider playing for a different team in 1998 if he's not content with the Twins' direction this fall, but Tom Kelly said he plans to return next season, as long as Pohlad retains ownership of the team and Terry Ryan is retained. Kelly is baseball's longest-tenured manager, having been hired during the 1986 season. His record is 844-876, but with two World Series wins, in 1987 and '91.

▶Sept. 24: It took 10 innings on Sept. 21 as Brad Radke became the first Twins pitcher to win 20 games since Scott Erickson in 1991. He is the first Minnesota pitcher to go 10 innings since Jack Morris in Game 7 of the 1991 World Series against Atlanta.

▶Oct. 1: Chuck Knoblauch, the Twins' highest-paid player, has requested a trade. He wants to be dealt to a contender and has given the Twins a list of about six teams he would like to play for. Knoblauch signed a five-year, $30 million contract extension in August 1996, which started this year. Brad Radke finished 20-10, becoming the first AL pitcher since the St. Louis Browns' Ned Garver, in 1951, to win 20 games with a team that didn't win 70.

QUOTE OF THE YEAR

"I think we've played as good as we can play."
—Manager Tom Kelly, assessing the last-place Twins at the All-Star break

MINNESOTA TWINS 1997 final stats

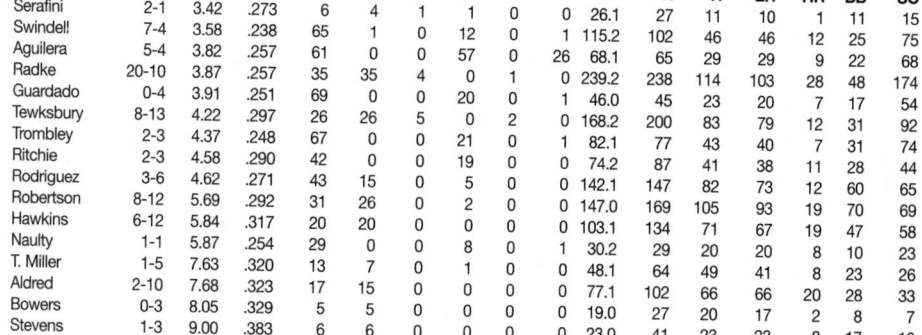

BATTERS	BA	SLG	OBA	G	AB	R	H	TB	2B	3B	HR	RBI	BB	SO	SB	CS	E
Ortiz	.327	.449	.353	15	49	10	16	22	3	0	1	6	2	19	0	0	1
Molitor	.305	.435	.351	135	538	63	164	234	32	4	10	89	45	73	11	4	1
Coomer	.298	.438	.324	140	523	63	156	229	30	2	13	85	22	91	4	3	11
Knoblauch	.291	.411	.390	156	611	117	178	251	26	10	9	58	84	84	62	10	12
Valentin	.286	.286	.286	4	7	1	2	2	0	0	0	0	0	3	0	0	0
Colbrunn	.281	.415	.307	70	217	24	61	90	14	0	5	26	8	38	1	2	6
Meares	.276	.410	.323	134	439	63	121	180	23	3	10	60	18	86	7	7	20
Brede	.274	.389	.347	61	190	25	52	74	11	1	3	21	21	38	7	2	4
D. Miller	.273	.379	.282	25	66	5	18	25	1	0	2	13	2	12	0	0	0
Myers	.267	.436	.328	62	165	24	44	72	11	1	5	28	16	29	0	0	3
Becker	.264	.395	.354	132	443	61	117	175	22	3	10	45	62	130	17	5	5
Hocking	.257	.360	.308	115	253	28	65	91	12	4	2	25	18	51	3	5	4
Steinbach	.248	.394	.302	122	447	60	111	176	27	1	12	54	35	106	6	1	6
Lawton	.248	.415	.366	142	460	74	114	191	29	3	14	60	76	81	7	4	7
Cordova	.246	.434	.305	103	378	44	93	164	18	4	15	51	30	92	5	3	2
Walker	.237	.353	.288	52	156	15	37	55	7	1	3	16	11	30	7	0	4
Stahoviak	.229	.400	.301	91	275	33	63	110	17	0	10	33	24	73	5	2	7
Latham	.182	.227	.182	15	22	4	4	5	1	0	0	1	0	8	0	0	1
Hunter	—	—	—	1	0	0	0	0	0	0	0	0	0	0	0	0	0

PITCHERS	W-L	ERA	BA	G	GS	CG	GF	Sho	SV	IP	H	R	ER	HR	BB	SO
Serafini	2-1	3.42	.273	6	4	1	1	0	0	26.1	27	11	10	1	11	15
Swindell	7-4	3.58	.238	65	1	0	12	0	1	115.2	102	46	46	12	25	75
Aguilera	5-4	3.82	.257	61	0	0	57	0	26	68.1	65	29	29	9	22	68
Radke	20-10	3.87	.257	35	35	4	0	1	0	239.2	238	114	103	28	48	174
Guardado	0-4	3.91	.251	69	0	0	20	0	1	46.0	45	23	20	7	17	54
Tewksbury	8-13	4.22	.297	26	26	5	0	2	0	168.2	200	83	79	12	31	92
Trombley	2-3	4.37	.248	67	0	0	21	0	1	82.1	77	43	40	7	31	74
Ritchie	2-3	4.58	.290	42	0	0	19	0	0	74.2	87	41	38	11	28	44
Rodriguez	3-6	4.62	.271	43	15	0	5	0	0	142.1	147	82	73	12	60	65
Robertson	8-12	5.69	.292	31	26	0	2	0	0	147.0	169	105	93	19	70	69
Hawkins	6-12	5.84	.317	20	20	0	0	0	0	103.1	134	71	67	19	47	58
Naulty	1-1	5.87	.254	29	0	0	8	0	1	30.2	29	20	20	8	10	23
T. Miller	1-5	7.63	.320	13	7	0	1	0	0	48.1	64	49	41	8	23	26
Aldred	2-10	7.68	.323	17	15	0	0	0	0	77.1	102	66	66	20	28	33
Bowers	0-3	8.05	.329	5	5	0	0	0	0	19.0	27	20	17	2	8	7
Stevens	1-3	9.00	.383	6	6	0	0	0	0	23.0	41	23	23	8	17	16

1998 preliminary roster

PITCHERS (19)
Rick Aguilera
Chris Cumberland
Eddie Guardado
Jeff Harris
Latroy Hawkins
Travis Miller
Mike Morgan
Dan Naulty
Dan Perkins
Brad Radke
Fred Rath

Mark Redman
Todd Ritchie
Frankie Rodriguez
Benj Sampson
Dan Serafini
Greg Swindell
Bob Tewksbury
Mike Trombley

CATCHERS (3)
A.J. Pierzynski
Terry Steinbach
Javier Valentin

INFIELDERS (10)
Ron Coomer
Cleatus Davidson
Denny Hocking
Chuck Knoblauch
Corey Koskie
Pat Meares
Doug Mientkiewicz
Paul Molitor
David Ortiz
Todd Walker

OUTFIELDERS (8)
Marty Cordova
Torii Hunter
Chris Latham
Matt Lawton
Marc Lewis
Otis Nixon
Alex Ochoa
Ryan Radmanovich

Games played by position

PLAYER	G	C	1B	2B	3B	SS	OF	DH
Becker	132	0	0	0	0	0	128	0
Brede	61	0	15	0	0	0	42	1
Colbrunn	70	0	64	0	0	0	0	2
Coomer	140	0	9	0	119	0	7	7
Cordova	103	0	0	0	0	0	101	2
Hocking	115	0	1	15	39	44	20	1
Hunter	1	0	0	0	0	0	0	0
Knoblauch	156	0	0	153	0	1	0	1
Latham	15	0	0	0	0	0	10	0
Lawton	142	0	0	0	0	0	138	0
Meares	134	0	0	0	0	134	0	0
D. Miller	25	20	0	0	0	0	0	3
Molitor	135	0	12	0	0	0	0	122
Myers	62	38	0	0	0	0	0	10
Ortiz	15	0	11	0	0	0	0	1
Stahoviak	91	0	81	0	0	0	0	5
Steinbach	122	116	2	0	0	0	0	1
Valentin	4	4	0	0	0	0	0	0
Walker	52	0	0	8	40	0	0	2

Sick call: 1997 DL report

PLAYER	Days on the DL
Marty Cordova	46
Roberto Kelly	15
Pat Meares	15
Paul Molitor	18
Greg Myers	15
Dan Naulty	98
Kirby Puckett	181
Scott Stahoviak	44
Bob Tewksbury	50*

Indicates two separate terms on Disabled List.

Minor Leagues

Tops in the organization

BATTER	CLUB	AVG.	G	AB	R	H	HR	RBI
Brede, Brent	SLk	.354	84	328	82	116	9	76
Walker, Todd	SLk	.345	83	322	69	111	11	53
Miller, Damian	SLk	.338	85	314	48	106	11	82
Shave, Jon	SLk	.329	103	395	75	130	7	60
Ortiz, David	SLk	.317	140	539	90	171	31	124

HOME RUNS
Rupp, Chad	SLk	32
Ortiz, David	SLk	31
Radmanovich, R.	SLk	28
Koskie, Corey	Nbr	23
Patterson, Jacob	FtW	20

WINS
Lincoln, Mike	FtM	13
Bowers, Shane	SLk	13
Cobb, Trevor	Nbr	13
Cumberland, C.	Nbr	12
Several Players Tied at		11

RBI
Ortiz, David	SLk	124
Rupp, Chad	SLk	94
Miller, Damian	SLk	82
Jones, Jacque	FtM	82
Patterson, Jacob	FtW	80

SAVES
Rath, Fred	SLk	17
Niedermaier, B.	SLk	17
Stentz, Brent	FtM	17
Garza, Chris	FtW	15
Gourdin, Tom	Nbr	15

STOLEN BASES
Felston, Anthony	FtW	45
Davidson, C.	FtW	39
Allen, Chad	Nbr	29
Rivas, Luis	FtW	28
Several Players Tied at		26

STRIKEOUTS
Bell, Jason	Nbr	142
Hooten, David	FtW	138
Redman, Mark	SLk	125
LaRosa, Tom	FtM	118
Serafini, Dan	SLk	118

PITCHER	CLUB	W-L	ERA	IP	H	BB	SO
Garza, Chris	FtW	5- 2	1.99	95	67	38	90
Lincoln, Mike	FtM	13- 4	2.28	134	130	25	75
Radlosky, Rob	FtM	9- 5	2.59	128	87	37	109
Hooten, David	FtW	11- 8	2.61	166	134	54	138
Baptist, Travis	SLk	9- 7	2.83	108	96	35	78

1997 salaries

	Bonuses	Total earned salary
Kirby Puckett, of		7,200,000
Chuck Knoblauch, 2b	150,000	6,150,000
Paul Molitor, dh		3,500,000
Rick Aguilera, p	75,000	3,075,000
Terry Steinbach, c		2,850,000
Bob Tewksbury, p		2,000,000
Pat Meares, ss		1,425,000
Marty Cordova, of		800,000
Greg Swindell, p	250,000	750,000
Greg Myers, c		575,000
Brad Radke, p	50,000	450,000
Mike Trombley, p		375,000
Eddie Guardado, p		300,000
Scott Stahoviak, 1b		275,000
Rich Becker, of		260,000
Francisco Rodriguez, p		220,000
Rich Robertson, p		205,000
Ron Coomer, 3b		170,000
Dan Naulty, p		165,000
Dennis Hocking, 3b		152,500
Brent Brede, of		150,000
Todd Ritchie, p		150,000
LaTroy Hawkins, p		150,000
Matt Lawton, of		150,000
Travis Miller, p		150,000
Damian Miller, c		150,000

Average 1997 salary: $1,222,981
Total 1997 payroll: $31,797,500

Minnesota (1961-1997), includes Washington (1901-1960)

Runs: Most, career

1466	Sam Rice,	1915-1933
1258	Harmon Killebrew,	1954-1974
1154	Joe Judge,	1915-1932
1071	Kirby Puckett,	1984-1995
1037	Buddy Myer,	1925-1941

Hits: Most, career

2889	Sam Rice,	1915-1933
2304	Kirby Puckett,	1984-1995
2291	Joe Judge,	1915-1932
2100	Clyde Milan,	1907-1922
2085	Rod Carew,	1967-1978

2B: Most, career

479	Sam Rice,	1915-1933
421	Joe Judge,	1915-1932
414	Kirby Puckett,	1984-1995
391	Mickey Vernon,	1939-1955
329	Tony Oliva,	1962-1976

3B: Most, career

183	Sam Rice,	1915-1933
157	Joe Judge,	1915-1932
125	Goose Goslin,	1921-1938
113	Buddy Myer,	1925-1941
108	Mickey Vernon,	1939-1955
90	Rod Carew,	1967-1978 (8)

HR: Most, career

559	Harmon Killebrew,	1954-1974
293	Kent Hrbek,	1981-1994
256	Bob Allison,	1958-1970
220	Tony Oliva,	1962-1976
207	Kirby Puckett,	1984-1995

RBI: Most, career

1540	Harmon Killebrew,	1954-1974
1086	Kent Hrbek,	1981-1994
1085	Kirby Puckett,	1984-1995
1045	Sam Rice,	1915-1933
1026	Mickey Vernon,	1939-1955

SB: Most, career

495	Clyde Milan,	1907-1922
346	Sam Rice,	1915-1933
321	George Case,	1937-1947
276	CHUCK KNOBLAUCH,	1991-1997
271	Rod Carew,	1967-1978

BB: Most, career

1505	Harmon Killebrew,	1954-1974
1274	Eddie Yost,	1944-1958
943	Joe Judge,	1915-1932
864	Buddy Myer,	1925-1941
838	Kent Hrbek,	1981-1994

BA: Highest, career

.334	Rod Carew,	1967-1978
.328	Heinie Manush,	1930-1935
.323	Sam Rice,	1915-1933
.323	Goose Goslin,	1921-1938
.318	Kirby Puckett,	1984-1995

On-base avg: Highest, career

.393	Rod Carew,	1967-1978
.393	Buddy Myer,	1925-1941
.392	John Stone,	1934-1938
.391	CHUCK KNOBLAUCH,	1991-1997
.389	Eddie Yost,	1944-1958

Slug avg: Highest, career

.514	Harmon Killebrew,	1954-1974
.502	Goose Goslin,	1921-1938
.500	Roy Sievers,	1954-1959
.481	Jimmie Hall,	1963-1966
.481	Kent Hrbek,	1981-1994

Games started: Most, career

666	Walter Johnson,	1907-1927
433	Jim Kaat,	1959-1973
345	Bert Blyleven,	1970-1988
331	Camilo Pascual,	1954-1966
259	Frank Viola,	1982-1989

Complete games: Most, career

531	Walter Johnson,	1907-1927
206	Case Patten,	1901-1908
141	Bert Blyleven,	1970-1988
139	Tom Hughes,	1904-1913
133	Jim Kaat,	1959-1973

Saves: Most, career

210	RICK AGUILERA,	1989-1997
108	Ron Davis,	1982-1986
104	Jeff Reardon,	1987-1989
96	Firpo Marberry,	1923-1936
88	Al Worthington,	1964-1969

Shutouts: Most, career

110	Walter Johnson,	1907-1927
31	Camilo Pascual,	1954-1966
29	Bert Blyleven,	1970-1988
23	Jim Kaat,	1959-1973
23	Dutch Leonard,	1938-1946

Wins: Most, career

417	Walter Johnson,	1907-1927
190	Jim Kaat,	1959-1973
149	Bert Blyleven,	1970-1988
145	Camilo Pascual,	1954-1966
128	Jim Perry,	1963-1972

K: Most, career

3509	Walter Johnson,	1907-1927
2035	Bert Blyleven,	1970-1988
1885	Camilo Pascual,	1954-1966
1851	Jim Kaat,	1959-1973
1214	Frank Viola,	1982-1989

Win pct: Highest, career

.622	Firpo Marberry,	1923-1936
.602	Sam Jones,	1928-1931
.599	Walter Johnson,	1907-1927
.598	Earl Whitehill,	1933-1936
.588	Mudcat Grant,	1964-1967

ERA: Lowest, career

2.17	Walter Johnson,	1907-1927
2.64	Doc Ayers,	1913-1919
2.75	Harry Harper,	1913-1919
2.77	Charlie Smith,	1906-1909
2.83	Bert Gallia,	1912-1917
3.15	Jim Perry,	1963-1972 (10)

Runs: Most, season

140	CHUCK KNOBLAUCH,	1996
128	Rod Carew,	1977
127	Joe Cronin,	1930
126	Zoilo Versalles,	1965
122	Buddy Lewis,	1938

Hits: Most, season

239	Rod Carew,	1977
234	Kirby Puckett,	1988
227	Sam Rice,	1925
225	PAUL MOLITOR,	1996
223	Kirby Puckett,	1986

2B: Most, season

51	Mickey Vernon, 1946
50	Stan Spence, 1946
46	MARTY CORDOVA, 1996
45	Joe Cronin, 1933
45	CHUCK KNOBLAUCH, 1994
45	Kirby Puckett, 1989
45	Zoilo Versalles, 1965

3B: Most, season

20	Goose Goslin, 1925
19	Joe Cassidy, 1904
19	Cecil Travis, 1941
18	Joe Cronin, 1932
18	Goose Goslin, 1923
18	Sam Rice, 1923
18	Howie Shanks, 1921
18	John Stone, 1935
16	Rod Carew, 1977 (11)

HR: Most, season

49	Harmon Killebrew, 1964
49	Harmon Killebrew, 1969
48	Harmon Killebrew, 1962
46	Harmon Killebrew, 1961
45	Harmon Killebrew, 1963

RBI: Most, season

140	Harmon Killebrew, 1969
129	Goose Goslin, 1924
126	Joe Cronin, 1930
126	Joe Cronin, 1931
126	Harmon Killebrew, 1962

SB: Most, season

88	Clyde Milan, 1912
75	Clyde Milan, 1913
63	Sam Rice, 1920
62	CHUCK KNOBLAUCH, 1997
62	Danny Moeller, 1913

BB: Most, season

151	Eddie Yost, 1956
145	Harmon Killebrew, 1969
141	Eddie Yost, 1950
131	Harmon Killebrew, 1967
131	Eddie Yost, 1954

BA: Highest, season

.388	Rod Carew, 1977
.379	Goose Goslin, 1928
.376	Ed Delahanty, 1902
.364	Rod Carew, 1974
.359	Rod Carew, 1975

On-base avg: Highest, season

.454	Buddy Myer, 1938
.453	Ed Delahanty, 1902
.449	Rod Carew, 1977
.448	CHUCK KNOBLAUCH, 1996
.442	Goose Goslin, 1928

Slug avg: Highest, season

.614	Goose Goslin, 1928
.606	Harmon Killebrew, 1961
.590	Ed Delahanty, 1902
.584	Harmon Killebrew, 1969
.579	Roy Sievers, 1957

Games started: Most, season

42	Walter Johnson, 1910
42	Jim Kaat, 1965
41	Jim Kaat, 1966
40	Bert Blyleven, 1973
40	Bob Groom, 1912
40	Walter Johnson, 1914
40	Jim Perry, 1970

Complete games: Most, season

38	Walter Johnson, 1910
37	Case Patten, 1904
36	Walter Johnson, 1911
36	Walter Johnson, 1916
36	Al Orth, 1902
25	Bert Blyleven, 1973 (*)

Saves: Most, season

42	RICK AGUILERA, 1991
42	Jeff Reardon, 1988
41	RICK AGUILERA, 1992
34	RICK AGUILERA, 1993
34	Ron Perranoski, 1970

Shutouts: Most, season

11	Walter Johnson, 1913
9	Bert Blyleven, 1973
9	Walter Johnson, 1914
9	Bob Porterfield, 1953
8	Walter Johnson, 1910
8	Walter Johnson, 1917
8	Walter Johnson, 1918
8	Camilo Pascual, 1961

Wins: Most, season

36	Walter Johnson, 1913
33	Walter Johnson, 1912
28	Walter Johnson, 1914
27	Walter Johnson, 1915
26	Alvin Crowder, 1932
25	Jim Kaat, 1966 (6)

K: Most, season

313	Walter Johnson, 1910
303	Walter Johnson, 1912
258	Bert Blyleven, 1973
249	Bert Blyleven, 1974
243	Walter Johnson, 1913

Win pct: Highest, season

.837	Walter Johnson, 1913
.800	Stan Coveleski, 1925
.800	Firpo Marberry, 1931
.774	Frank Viola, 1988
.773	Bill Campbell, 1976

ERA: Lowest, season

1.14	Walter Johnson, 1913
1.27	Walter Johnson, 1918
1.36	Walter Johnson, 1910
1.39	Walter Johnson, 1912
1.49	Walter Johnson, 1919
2.49	Dave Goltz, 1978 (*)

Most pinch-hit homers, season

4	Don Mincher, 1964

Most pinch-hit homers, career

8	Bob Allison, 1958-1970
7	Don Mincher, 1961-1966

Longest hitting streak

33	Heine Manush, 1933
31	Ken Landreaux, 1980
31	Sam Rice, 1924
29	Sam Rice, 1920
28	Sam Rice, 1930

Most consecutive scoreless innings

55	Walter Johnson, 1913
40	Walter Johnson, 1918
37	Walter Johnson, 1913

No-hit games

Walter Johnson, Was at Bos AL, 1-0; July 1, 1920.

Bobby Burke, Was vs Bos AL, 5-0; Aug. 8, 1931.

Jack Kralick, Min vs KC AL, 1-0; Aug. 26, 1962.

Dean Chance, Min at Cle AL, 2-1; Aug. 25, 1967 (2nd game).

SCOTT ERICKSON, Min vs Mil AL, 6-0; April 27, 1994.

Jay Cashion, six innings, called so Cleveland could catch train, Was vs Cle AL, 2-0; Aug. 20, 1912 (2nd game).

Walter Johnson, seven innings, rain, Was vs StL AL, 2-0; Aug. 25, 1924.

Dean Chance, five perfect innings, rain, Min vs Bos AL, 2-0; Aug. 6, 1967.

ACTIVE PLAYERS in caps.

Players' years of service are listed by the first and last years with this team and are not necessarily consecutive; all statistics record performances for this team only.

Leader from the franchise's current location is included. If not in the top five, leader's rank is listed in paren- thesis; asterisk (*) indicates player is not in top 25.

Kansas City Royals

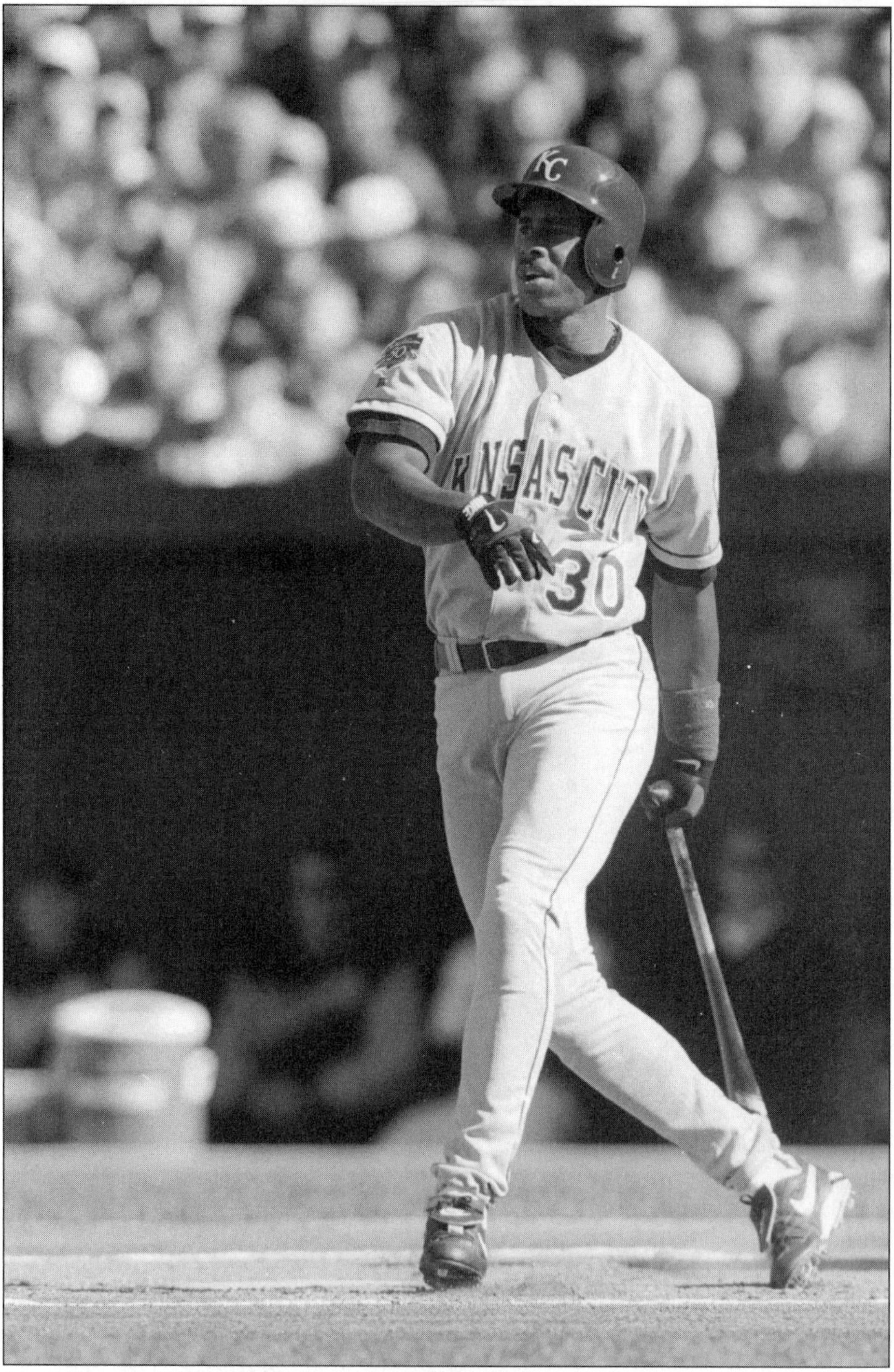

By Russell Becker, Baseball Weekly

Jose Offerman settled in at second base in 1997, hitting .297 while committing only nine errors.

1997 Royals: Down at the bottom again

The Kansas City Royals concluded 1997 as they did 1996, and that's not exactly where they wanted to be. For the only two times in franchise history, the Royals finished last. A loss on the final day to the Chicago White Sox, coupled with a Minnesota victory at Cleveland, dropped the Royals into the AL Central's basement. Only Oakland had a worse record in the major leagues. The Royals' 33-47 home record was the worst. And they were 10-25 against Cleveland, Chicago and Milwaukee.

When the Royals broke camp, they thought they had put together a contending club, one that would finish at .500 at worst. They added $10 million to their payroll by signing veterans Jeff King, Jay Bell and Chili Davis. But with the team 36-46 at the All-Star break, manager Bob Boone was fired. Under Tony Muser, the Royal's fifth manager since 1991, Kansas City went 31-48. The turmoil mounted as the board of directors put the franchise on the market, triggering the auction process as set out by the estate of former owner Ewing Kauffman.

Despite batting .238, King drove in a career-high 112 runs, which tied him for third place on the Royals' all-time single-season list. He hit 27 home runs and led the club with 30 doubles. Bell hit .291, set career highs with 21 homers and 92 RBI, and topped the club in total bases (264), hits (167) and runs (89). Davis, at age 37, drove in 90 runs and slugged a career-high 30 home runs. Because of the newcomers, the Royals had three players with 20 or more homers for the first time since 1988 and at least 90 RBI for the first time since 1979.

The pitching, however, failed, as the Royals looked at 25 arms during the season. The biggest disappointment was left-hander Chris Haney. He broke his ankle in April and suffered an elbow strain in June. After winning 10 games and pitching 228 innings in 1996, Haney was 1-2 and restricted to 24⅔ innings in 1997. Longtime ace Kevin Appier, who

Team MVP

Jay Bell: The Kansas City Royals took a gamble when they traded for Jay Bell. After all, his batting average had declined for three consecutive years in Pittsburgh, to a career-low .250. But he became arguably the best all-around shortstop the Royals have ever had, combining strong defense with a .291 average and career highs in home runs and RBI.

ranked among the American League leaders with 196 strikeouts and a 3.40 ERA, won only nine games because of lack of run support.

The other somewhat bright spots on the pitching staff were at opposite ends of the experience spectrum. Jose Rosado, who had less than a season of major league experience, made the All-Star Game but faded in the stretch, finishing 9-12. Veteran closer Jeff Montgomery, who had shoulder surgery in September 1996, finished strong. He led the club with 14 saves although he didn't pick up his first until June 14. The bullpen had allowed better than six runs per nine innings during the first half of the season.

Jose Offerman solidified second base with good defense and a .297 batting average. Catcher Mike Sweeney and outfielder Johnny Damon also displayed promise at times. But outfielder Jermaine Dye went on the DL twice and then was sent to the minors. Dye wound up hitting .236 with seven homers and 22 RBI in 75 games. Outfielder Roderick Myers missed the first half of last season with a broken wrist and hit .256 in 31 games. He could crack the starting outfield in 1998. Jeremy Giambi, the younger brother of Oakland's Jason Giambi, could come on quickly. He hit .321 last year with AA Wichita.

151

1997 Royals: Week-by-week notes

These notes were excerpted from the following issues of Baseball Weekly.

▶**April 9:** Right fielder Jermaine Dye was hitless in his first four games, going 0-for-14. Bip Roberts' home run on April 5 at the Metrodome was his first since May 20 of last year and his first in the AL.

▶**April 16:** The Royals hit home runs in six consecutive games, through April 13. In the last two seasons, the Royals were outhomered 318-242.

▶**April 23:** Seven Royals have gone on the DL, with left-hander Chris Haney, Jermaine Dye and closer Jeff Montgomery joining second baseman Jose Offerman, reliever Jaime Bluma, right-hander Rick Huisman and outfielder Rod Myers.

▶**April 30:** The bullpen has been in shambles. On the recent West Coast trip, it went 0-2 with three blown saves and nearly blew a six-run lead in Seattle, with the Royals holding on to a 12-10 victory.

▶**May 7:** DH Chili Davis became the 75th player to reach 300 career home runs, on April 29. He is the third to hit 300 without having a 30-homer season, after Al Kaline and Harold Baines.

▶**May 14:** Center fielder Tom Goodwin is on a 16-for-39 (.410) tear with an 11-game hitting streak, after collecting just 11 hits in his first 81 at-bats. He's raised his average from .136 to .225 and scored 11 runs in the 11 games. Goodwin drove in runs in back-to-back games last week after 113 at-bats without an RBI, dating back to Sept. 8.

▶**May 21:** Jermaine Dye, obtained in a trade for Michael Tucker, who's now hitting .343 for Atlanta, was optioned on May 18 to AAA Omaha. Dye is hitting .188 with one home run and two RBI.

▶**May 28:** The Royals snapped a seven-game losing streak, their longest since 1992, with an 11-5 win on May 24 against Seattle.

▶**June 4:** Right-hander Kevin Appier is still waiting to pick up his 100th career victory, after five failures. In his past three

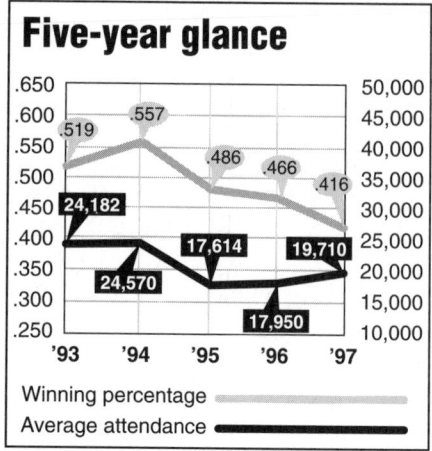

Five-year glance

Winning percentage

Average attendance

starts, Appier has allowed four earned runs but is 0-2 with a no-decision. The offense has backed him with only two runs in those three starts.

▶**June 11:** Tony and Marie Rosado have seen their son, left-hander Jose Rosado, 22, pitch twice in the big leagues. He is 2-0, allowing one run in 16⅔ innings when his parents are spectators. Rosado's record is 5-3, and his ERA is 3.06, the seventh best in the AL. On June 7 against Texas, Chili Davis homered from both sides of the plate for the 10th time in his career, one short of the record held by Eddie Murray.

▶**June 18:** On June 14, Jeff Montgomery logged his first save since Aug. 31, 1996. He had shoulder surgery in September '96. Montgomery is the Royals' all-time saves leader, with 243.

▶**June 25:** First baseman Jeff King had a 14-game hitting streak snapped on June 22. It was the longest by a Royal this season and one shy of King's career high. During the streak, King had five doubles, seven home runs, 15 runs scored, 16 RBI and 11 walks.

▶**July 2:** Shortstop Jay Bell hit his fourth career grand slam and drove in a career-high five runs in a 16-3 rout of Milwaukee on June 27. He leads the club in RBI with 55.

▶**July 10:** The Royals limped to the All-Star break sagging in the standings. They dropped eight consecutive games through July 6. One bright spot: Jeff King was selected the AL player of the month for June. King hit .355 for the month and led the league with 29 RBI, 72 total bases and 24 runs scored.

▶**July 16:** In addition to replacing manager Bob Boone with Tony Muser, the Royals fired hitting instructor Greg Luzinski and first base coach Mitchell Page. They were replaced by two former Royals—Tom Poquette, who had been the club's roving minor league hitting coach, and Frank White, a member of the club's Hall of Fame. The Royals dropped their first four games under Muser through July 13, and their 12-game losing streak is the longest in the 29-year history of the franchise and the longest in the AL this year.

▶**July 23:** In an effort to shore up a struggling bullpen, the Royals acquired Hector Carrasco, who has a fastball clocked in the mid-90s, in a four-player trade with the Reds. The Royals sent outfielders Jon Nunnally and Chris Stynes to Cincinnati for right-handers Carrasco and Scott Service, who was dispatched to AAA Omaha.

▶**July 30:** The search for a power-hitting third baseman ended when the Royals acquired Dean Palmer from the Rangers for Tom Goodwin. Palmer, who has 155 career home runs, was hitting .245 with 14 home runs and 55 RBI in 94 games for Texas.

▶**Aug. 6:** The Royals hit five home runs, one shy of their club record, in drubbing Boston 10-3 on Aug. 2. Dean Palmer hit two, including a 445-foot blast, and Chili Davis, outfielder Yamil Benitez and catcher Mike Macfarlane hit one each. Since joining the Royals on July 26, Palmer has hit .378 (14-for-37) with eight RBI in his first 10 games

▶**Aug. 20:** Kevin Appier snapped a personal five-game losing streak, matching the longest of his career, when he beat Detroit 2-1 on Aug. 16. Appier is 7-10 overall, which does not do justice to his 3.10 ERA.

▶**Aug. 27:** It's the little things that are costing the Royals, who lost four consecutive games from Aug. 20-23 by one or two runs. Things such as missing cutoff men, failing to advance runners or turn double plays and making errors have proved costly. The Royals are 16-29 since Tony Muser replaced Bob Boone.

▶**Sept. 3:** Chili Davis hit 12 home runs in August to tie John Mayberry's club record for most home runs in a month. Jeff King loves interleague games. He is 16-for-42 with seven home runs, 11 runs scored and 19 RBI in 12 games against NL clubs through Aug. 31.

▶**Sept. 10:** The Royals have assured themselves of finishing below .500 for the third consecutive year and for the 12th time in the club's 29-year history. It is the first time they have had a losing record for three consecutive seasons.

▶**Sept. 17:** The Royals would like to have Chili Davis back next year. But they're at the mercy of the realignment committee, which will determine whether they will have a need for him. Davis has been strictly a DH for the Royals and has seldom played in the field the past few years. If the Royals switch to the NL, a possibility in some realignment plans, they will not need a DH.

▶**Sept. 24:** Team of the 90s: The Royals have lost 90 games for only the fourth time in franchise history. They lost 90 in 1992, 97 in 1970 and 93 in 1969. Despite that, the club has three players with 90 or more RBI—Jeff King (98), Chili Davis (90) and Jay Bell (90)—for the first time since 1979.

▶**Oct. 1:** Left-hander Chris Haney, who missed most of the year with a broken ankle and a strained elbow, will have surgery on his foot on Oct. 3 to remove a bone spur and repair the fracture that never healed properly. Haney, a 10-game winner in '96, was limited to eight appearances, including three starts, and 24⅔ innings because of the injuries.

QUOTE OF THE YEAR

"It was like I had eight at-bats and never hit the ball out of the infield."
—Tony Muser, on his eight previous managerial job interviews before the Royals hired him

KANSAS CITY ROYALS 1997 final stats

BATTERS	BA	SLG	OBA	G	AB	R	H	TB	2B	3B	HR	RBI	BB	SO	SB	CS	E
Hansen	.309	.426	.394	34	94	11	29	40	6	1	1	14	13	29	3	2	1
Offerman	.297	.394	.359	106	424	59	126	167	23	6	2	39	41	64	9	10	9
Bell	.291	.461	.368	153	573	89	167	264	28	3	21	92	71	101	10	6	10
Sutton	.290	.406	.338	27	69	9	20	28	2	0	2	8	5	12	0	0	0
Davis	.279	.509	.386	140	477	71	133	243	20	0	30	90	85	96	6	3	0
Halter	.276	.382	.341	74	123	16	34	47	5	1	2	10	10	28	4	3	1
Damon	.275	.386	.338	146	472	70	130	182	12	8	8	48	42	70	16	10	4
Benitez	.267	.440	.307	53	191	22	51	84	7	1	8	21	10	49	2	2	4
Myers	.257	.386	.370	31	101	14	26	39	7	0	2	9	17	22	4	0	1
Palmer	.256	.445	.310	143	542	70	139	241	31	1	23	86	41	134	2	2	19
Stewart	.250	.375	.250	5	8	1	2	3	1	0	0	0	0	0	0	0	0
Sweeney	.242	.363	.306	84	240	30	58	87	8	0	7	31	17	33	3	2	3
Nunnally	.241	.414	.353	13	29	8	7	12	0	1	1	4	5	7	0	0	0
Howard	.241	.321	.287	80	162	24	39	52	8	1	1	13	10	31	2	2	7
Vitiello	.238	.400	.322	51	130	11	31	52	6	0	5	18	14	37	0	0	1
King	.238	.451	.341	155	543	84	129	245	30	1	28	112	89	96	16	5	5
Macfarlane	.237	.401	.316	82	257	34	61	103	14	2	8	35	24	47	0	2	4
Dye	.236	.369	.284	75	263	26	62	97	14	0	7	22	17	51	2	1	6
Paquette	.230	.393	.263	77	252	26	58	99	15	1	8	33	10	57	2	2	12
Martinez	.226	.323	.351	16	31	3	7	10	1	1	0	3	6	8	0	0	1
Long	.222	.222	.300	6	9	2	2	2	0	0	0	2	0	3	0	0	0
Fasano	.211	.342	.231	13	38	4	8	13	2	0	1	1	1	12	0	0	1
Cooper	.201	.308	.283	75	159	12	32	49	6	1	3	15	17	32	1	1	0
Spehr	.171	.257	.237	17	35	3	6	9	0	0	1	2	2	12	0	0	0

PITCHERS	W-L	ERA	BA	G	GS	CG	GF	Sho	SV	IP	H	R	ER	HR	BB	SO
Santiago	0-0	1.93	.333	4	0	0	3	0	0	4.2	7	2	1	0	2	1
Whisenant	1-0	2.84	.211	24	0	0	3	0	0	19.0	15	7	6	0	12	16
Veres	4-0	3.31	.273	24	0	0	7	0	1	35.1	36	17	13	4	7	28
Appier	9-13	3.40	.243	34	34	4	0	1	0	235.2	215	96	89	24	74	196
Montgomery	1-4	3.49	.240	55	0	0	37	0	14	59.1	53	24	23	9	18	48
Perez	2-0	3.54	.214	16	0	0	4	0	0	20.1	15	8	8	2	8	17
Converse	0-0	3.60	.222	3	0	0	1	0	0	5.0	4	2	2	2	5	3
Pichardo	3-5	4.22	.273	47	0	0	26	0	11	49.0	51	24	23	7	24	34
Haney	1-2	4.38	.290	8	3	0	1	0	0	24.2	29	16	12	1	5	16
De La Maza	0-0	4.50	.125	1	0	0	0	0	0	2.0	1	1	1	1	1	1
Rosado	9-12	4.69	.264	33	33	2	0	0	0	203.1	208	117	106	26	73	129
Service	0-3	4.76	.274	12	0	0	1	0	0	17.0	17	9	9	1	5	19
Belcher	13-12	5.02	.288	32	32	3	0	1	0	213.1	242	128	119	31	70	113
Casian	0-2	5.06	.299	32	0	0	6	0	0	26.2	32	15	15	5	6	16
Walker	3-3	5.44	.271	50	0	0	15	0	0	43.0	46	28	26	6	20	24
Carrasco	1-6	5.45	.227	28	0	0	11	0	0	34.2	29	21	21	4	16	30
Pittsley	5-8	5.46	.277	21	21	0	0	0	0	112.0	120	72	68	15	54	52
Rusch	6-9	5.50	.301	30	27	1	0	0	0	170.1	206	111	104	28	52	116
Olson	4-3	5.58	.299	45	0	0	18	0	1	50.0	58	35	31	3	28	34
Bones	4-7	5.97	.325	21	11	1	2	0	0	78.1	102	59	52	10	25	36
Mik. Williams	0-2	6.43	.333	10	0	0	4	0	1	14.0	20	11	10	1	8	10
Bevil	1-2	6.61	.267	18	0	0	11	0	1	16.1	16	13	12	1	9	13
Mit. Williams	0-1	10.80	.367	7	0	0	4	0	0	6.2	11	8	8	2	7	10
McDill	0-0	13.50	.214	3	0	0	1	0	0	4.0	3	6	6	1	8	2

1998 preliminary roster

PITCHERS (19)
Kevin Appier
Tim Belcher
Brian Bevil
Jaime Bluma
Tim Byrdak
Roland De La Maza
Bart Evans
Pat Flury
Chris Haney
Jeff Montgomery
Hipolito Pichardo

Jim Pittsley
Ken Ray
Jose Rosado
Glendon Rusch
Jose Santiago
Scott Service
Jamie Walker
Matt Whisenant

CATCHERS (3)
Sal Fasano
Mike Macfarlane

Mike Sweeney

INFIELDERS (12)
Jeff Conine
Carlos Febles
Shane Halter
Jed Hansen
Jeff King
Mendy Lopez
Felix Martinez
Hall Morris
Jose Offerman

Dean Palmer
Larry Sutton
Joe Vitiello

OUTFIELDERS (5)
Johnny Damon
Jermaine Dye
Ryan Long
Roderick Myers
Mark Quinn

Games played by position

PLAYER	G	C	1B	2B	3B	SS	OF	DH
Bell	153	0	0	0	4	149	0	0
Benitez	53	0	0	0	0	0	52	0
Cooper	75	0	8	0	39	0	0	5
Damon	146	0	0	0	0	0	136	5
Davis	140	0	0	0	0	0	0	133
Dye	75	0	0	0	0	0	75	0
Fasano	13	12	0	0	0	0	0	1
Halter	74	0	0	18	12	5	32	4
Hansen	34	0	0	31	0	0	0	0
Howard	80	0	0	34	7	9	23	5
King	155	0	150	0	0	0	0	2
Long	6	0	0	0	0	0	5	1
Macfarlane	82	81	0	0	0	0	0	0
Martinez	16	0	0	0	0	12	0	2
Myers	31	0	0	0	0	0	26	0
Nunnally	13	0	0	0	0	0	9	0
Offerman	106	0	0	101	0	0	0	1
Palmer	143	0	0	0	141	0	0	1
Paquette	77	0	0	0	72	0	4	0
Spehr	17	17	0	0	0	0	0	0
Stewart	5	4	0	0	0	0	0	1
Sutton	27	0	12	0	0	0	1	3
Sweeney	84	76	0	0	0	0	0	3
Vitiello	51	0	1	0	0	0	28	12

Minor Leagues

Tops in the organization

BATTER	CLUB	AVG.	G	AB	R	H	HR	RBI
Miranda, Tony	Lan	.341	104	387	85	132	5	72
Giambi, Jeremy	Wch	.326	105	384	83	125	16	73
Brown, Dermal	Spo	.326	73	298	67	97	13	73
Mendez, Carlos	Wch	.325	129	507	72	165	12	90
Quinn, Mark	Wch	.324	113	395	77	128	18	90

HOME RUNS
Pough, P. C.	Oma	22	
Pellow, Kit	Wch	21	
Benitez, Yamil	Oma	21	
Long, Ryan	Oma	19	
Sutton, Larry	Oma	19	

WINS
Sanders, Allen	Lan	12
Calero, Enrique	Wch	11
Baird, Brandon	Lan	10
Harrison, Brian	Oma	10
Several Players Tied at		9

RBI
Pellow, Kit	Wch	93
Quinn, Mark	Wch	90
Mendez, Carlos	Wch	90
Gonzalez, Raul	Wch	74
Several Players Tied at		73

SAVES
Service, Scott	Oma	24
Rodriguez, C.	Lan	12
Prihoda, S.	Wch	10
Several Players Tied at		8

STOLEN BASES
Carr, Jeremy	Oma	51
Febles, Carlos	Wil	49
Moore, K.	Lan	43
Hallmark, Patrick	Wil	30
Williams, Micah	Lan	22

STRIKEOUTS
Moreno, Orber	Lan	128
Chapman, Jake	Wil	122
Mullen, Scott	Wil	121
Grundy, Phillip	Wch	117
Durbin, Chad	Lan	116

PITCHER	CLUB	W-L	ERA	IP	H	BB	SO
Brewer, Ryan	Wil	5- 4	3.34	105	100	29	93
Sanders, Allen	Lan	12- 7	3.78	140	143	32	79
Chapman, Jake	Wil	8- 9	3.85	154	163	59	122
Saier, Matt	Wch	9- 7	3.95	144	143	63	100
Mullen, Scott	Wil	9- 6	4.04	152	154	57	121

Sick call: 1997 DL report

PLAYER	Days on the DL
Jaime Bluma	181
Scott Cooper	40
Chili Davis	13
Jermaine Dye	57*
Chris Haney	131*
David Howard	18
Rick Huisman	66
Mike Macfarlane	33*
Jeff Montgomery	15
Rod Myers	100
Jose Offerman	61**
Hipolito Pichardo	52
Bip Roberts	25
Glendon Rusch	15
Jose Santiago	21
Randy Veres	97
Joe Vitiello	92*
Jamie Walker	19

Indicates two separate terms on Disabled List.
**Indicates three separate terms on Disabled List.*

1997 salaries

	Bonuses	Total earned salary
Jay Bell, ss		5,000,000
Dean Palmer, 3b		4,800,000
Kevin Appier, p		4,800,000
Chili Davis, of		3,800,000
Jeff King, 1b		2,500,000
Jeff Montgomery, p		2,300,000
Tim Belcher, p	300,000	2,300,000
Chris Haney, p		1,700,000
Jose Offerman, 2b	200,000	1,600,000
Mike Macfarlane, c	7,500	887,500
Hipolito Pichardo, p	80,000	780,000
David Howard, 2b	37,500	762,500
Hector Carrasco, p	30,000	560,000
Rickey Bones, p	240,000	390,000
Scott Cooper, 3b	25,000	375,000
Johnny Damon, of		240,000
Scott Service, p		225,000
Joe Vitiello, of		210,000
Gregg Olson, p	60,000	210,000
Jose Rosado, p	30,000	200,000
Jermaine Dye, of		175,000
Mike Sweeney, c	10,000	175,000
Jamie Bluma, p		165,000
Yamil Benitez, of		150,000
Shane Halter, 2b		150,000
Larry Sutton, 1b		150,000
Jamie Walker, p		150,000
Glendon Rusch, p		150,000
Jed Hansen, 2b		150,000
Matt Whisenant, p		150,000

Average 1997 salary: $1,173,500
Total 1997 team payroll $35,205,000

Kansas City (1969-1997)

156

Runs: Most, career

1583	George Brett, 1973-1993
1074	Amos Otis, 1970-1983
1060	Willie Wilson, 1976-1990
912	Frank White, 1973-1990
873	Hal McRae, 1973-1987

Hits: Most, career

3154	George Brett, 1973-1993
2006	Frank White, 1973-1990
1977	Amos Otis, 1970-1983
1968	Willie Wilson, 1976-1990
1924	Hal McRae, 1973-1987

2B: Most, career

665	George Brett, 1973-1993
449	Hal McRae, 1973-1987
407	Frank White, 1973-1990
365	Amos Otis, 1970-1983
241	Willie Wilson, 1976-1990

3B: Most, career

137	George Brett, 1973-1993
133	Willie Wilson, 1976-1990
65	Amos Otis, 1970-1983
63	Hal McRae, 1973-1987
58	Frank White, 1973-1990

HR: Most, career

317	George Brett, 1973-1993
193	Amos Otis, 1970-1983
169	Hal McRae, 1973-1987
160	Frank White, 1973-1990
143	John Mayberry, 1972-1977

RBI: Most, career

1595	George Brett, 1973-1993
1012	Hal McRae, 1973-1987
992	Amos Otis, 1970-1983
886	Frank White, 1973-1990
552	John Mayberry, 1972-1977

SB: Most, career

612	Willie Wilson, 1976-1990
340	Amos Otis, 1970-1983
336	Freddie Patek, 1971-1979
201	George Brett, 1973-1993
178	Frank White, 1973-1990

BB: Most, career

1096	George Brett, 1973-1993
739	Amos Otis, 1970-1983
616	Hal McRae, 1973-1987
561	John Mayberry, 1972-1977
413	Freddie Patek, 1971-1979

BA: Highest, career

.305	George Brett, 1973-1993
.294	KEVIN SEITZER, 1986-1991
.293	WALLY JOYNER, 1992-1995
.293	Hal McRae, 1973-1987
.290	DANNY TARTABULL, 1987-1991

On-base avg: Highest, career

.380	KEVIN SEITZER, 1986-1991
.376	DANNY TARTABULL, 1987-1991
.375	Darrell Porter, 1977-1980
.374	John Mayberry, 1972-1977
.371	WALLY JOYNER, 1992-1995

Slug avg: Highest, career

.518	DANNY TARTABULL, 1987-1991
.487	George Brett, 1973-1993
.480	Bo Jackson, 1986-1990
.469	Willie Aikens, 1980-1983
.459	Steve Balboni, 1984-1988

Games started: Most, career

392	Paul Splittorff, 1970-1984
327	MARK GUBICZA, 1984-1996
302	Dennis Leonard, 1974-1986
244	KEVIN APPIER, 1989-1997
226	BRET SABERHAGEN, 1984-1991

Complete games: Most, career

103	Dennis Leonard, 1974-1986
88	Paul Splittorff, 1970-1984
64	BRET SABERHAGEN, 1984-1991
61	Larry Gura, 1976-1985
53	Steve Busby, 1972-1980
53	Dick Drago, 1969-1973

Saves: Most, career

256	JEFF MONTGOMERY, 1988-1997
238	Dan Quisenberry, 1979-1988
58	Doug Bird, 1973-1978
49	Steve Farr, 1985-1990
40	Ted Abernathy, 1970-1972

Shutouts: Most, career

23	Dennis Leonard, 1974-1986
17	Paul Splittorff, 1970-1984
16	MARK GUBICZA, 1984-1996
14	Larry Gura, 1976-1985
14	BRET SABERHAGEN, 1984-1991

Wins: Most, career

166	Paul Splittorff, 1970-1984
144	Dennis Leonard, 1974-1986
132	MARK GUBICZA, 1984-1996
111	Larry Gura, 1976-1985
110	BRET SABERHAGEN, 1984-1991

K: Most, career

1366	MARK GUBICZA, 1984-1996
1364	KEVIN APPIER, 1989-1997
1323	Dennis Leonard, 1974-1986
1093	BRET SABERHAGEN, 1984-1991
1057	Paul Splittorff, 1970-1984

Win pct: Highest, career

.593	Al Fitzmorris, 1969-1976
.587	Larry Gura, 1976-1985
.585	BRET SABERHAGEN, 1984-1991
.576	Doug Bird, 1973-1978
.576	Dennis Leonard, 1974-1986

ERA: Lowest, career

2.55	Dan Quisenberry, 1979-1988
3.21	BRET SABERHAGEN, 1984-1991
3.30	KEVIN APPIER, 1989-1997
3.46	Al Fitzmorris, 1969-1976
3.48	Marty Pattin, 1974-1980

Runs: Most, season

133	Willie Wilson, 1980
119	George Brett, 1979
113	Willie Wilson, 1979
108	George Brett, 1985
105	George Brett, 1977
105	KEVIN SEITZER, 1987

Hits: Most, season

230	Willie Wilson, 1980
215	George Brett, 1976
212	George Brett, 1979
207	KEVIN SEITZER, 1987
195	George Brett, 1975

2B: Most, season

54	Hal McRae, 1977
46	Hal McRae, 1982
45	George Brett, 1978
45	George Brett, 1990
45	Frank White, 1982

3B: Most, season

21	Willie Wilson, 1985	
20	George Brett, 1979	
15	Willie Wilson, 1980	
15	Willie Wilson, 1982	
15	Willie Wilson, 1987	

HR: Most, season

36	Steve Balboni, 1985
35	GARY GAETTI, 1995
34	John Mayberry, 1975
34	DANNY TARTABULL, 1987
32	Bo Jackson, 1989

RBI: Most, season

133	Hal McRae, 1982
118	George Brett, 1980
112	George Brett, 1985
112	Al Cowens, 1977
112	JEFF KING, 1997
112	Darrell Porter, 1979

SB: Most, season

83	Willie Wilson, 1979
79	Willie Wilson, 1980
66	TOM GOODWIN, 1996
59	Willie Wilson, 1983
59	Willie Wilson, 1987

BB: Most, season

122	John Mayberry, 1973
121	Darrell Porter, 1979
119	John Mayberry, 1975
103	George Brett, 1985
103	Paul Schaal, 1971

BA: Highest, season

.390	George Brett, 1980
.335	George Brett, 1985
.333	George Brett, 1976
.332	Hal McRae, 1976
.332	Willie Wilson, 1982

On-base avg: Highest, season

.454	George Brett, 1980
.436	George Brett, 1985
.421	Darrell Porter, 1979
.417	John Mayberry, 1973
.416	John Mayberry, 1975

Slug avg: Highest, season

.664	George Brett, 1980
.599	BOB HAMELIN, 1994
.593	DANNY TARTABULL, 1991
.585	George Brett, 1985
.563	George Brett, 1979

Games started: Most, season

40	Dennis Leonard, 1978
38	Steve Busby, 1974
38	Dennis Leonard, 1980
38	Paul Splittorff, 1973
38	Paul Splittorff, 1978

Complete games: Most, season

21	Dennis Leonard, 1977
20	Steve Busby, 1974
20	Dennis Leonard, 1978
18	Steve Busby, 1975
16	Larry Gura, 1980
16	Dennis Leonard, 1976

Saves: Most, season

45	JEFF MONTGOMERY, 1993
45	Dan Quisenberry, 1983
44	Dan Quisenberry, 1984
39	JEFF MONTGOMERY, 1992
37	Dan Quisenberry, 1985

Shutouts: Most, season

6	Roger Nelson, 1972
5	Dennis Leonard, 1977
5	Dennis Leonard, 1979
4	Bill Butler, 1969
4	Dick Drago, 1971
4	Al Fitzmorris, 1974
4	MARK GUBICZA, 1988
4	Larry Gura, 1980
4	Dennis Leonard, 1978
4	BRET SABERHAGEN, 1987
4	BRET SABERHAGEN, 1989

Wins: Most, season

23	BRET SABERHAGEN, 1989
22	Steve Busby, 1974
21	Dennis Leonard, 1978
20	MARK GUBICZA, 1988
20	Dennis Leonard, 1977
20	Dennis Leonard, 1980
20	BRET SABERHAGEN, 1985
20	Paul Splittorff, 1973

K: Most, season

244	Dennis Leonard, 1977
207	KEVIN APPIER, 1996
206	Bob Johnson, 1970
198	Steve Busby, 1974
196	KEVIN APPIER, 1997

Win pct: Highest, season

.800	Larry Gura, 1978
.793	BRET SABERHAGEN, 1989
.769	BRET SABERHAGEN, 1985
.762	DAVID CONE, 1994
.727	Paul Splittorff, 1977

ERA: Lowest, season

2.08	Roger Nelson, 1972
2.16	BRET SABERHAGEN, 1989
2.46	KEVIN APPIER, 1992
2.56	KEVIN APPIER, 1993
2.69	Charlie Leibrandt, 1985

Most pinch-hit homers, season

2	Carmelo Martinez, 1991
2	Hal McRae, 1986

Most pinch-hit homers, career

2	Steve Balboni, 1984-1988
2	JIM EISENREICH, 1987-1991
2	BOB HAMELIN, 1993-1996
2	Chuck Harrison, 1969-1971
2	Carmelo Martinez, 1991
2	Hal McRae, 1973-1987
2	Bob Oliver, 1969-1972
2	Amos Otis, 1970-1983

Longest hitting streak

30	George Brett, 1980
22	BRIAN McRAE, 1991
19	Amos Otis, 1974
18	GREGG JEFFERIES, 1992
18	Ed Kirkpatrick, 1973
18	Lou Piniella, 1971
18	Willie Wilson, 1984

Most consecutive scoreless innings

31	BRET SABERHAGEN, 1989

No-hit games

Steve Busby, KC at Det AL, 3-0; April 16, 1973.

Steve Busby, KC at Mil AL, 2-0; June 19, 1974.

Jim Colborn, KC vs Tex AL, 6-0; May 14, 1977.

BRET SABERHAGEN, KC vs Chi AL, 7-0; Aug. 26, 1991.

ACTIVE PLAYERS in caps.

Players' years of service are listed by the first and last years with this team and are not necessarily consecutive; all statistics record performances for this team only.

Seattle Mariners

By Russell Becker, Baseball Weekly

Ken Griffey was a unanimous MVP pick as he led the American League in home runs and total bases.

1997 Mariners: Griffey led the juggernaut

Coming out of spring training as a consensus American League favorite, the Seattle Mariners sputtered through bullpen problems to finish May with a .500 record and in third place in the AL West. But a 20-7 June—the best month in franchise history—vaulted Seattle back to the top, and a strong finish in September earned them their second division title in three years.

Ken Griffey Jr. slugged 56 home runs, tied for the seventh-highest total in history, and won his first MVP award. Jay Buhner became the 10th player in history to reach 40 homers in three straight seasons, and first baseman Paul Sorrento hit a career-high 31 homers as Seattle broke the major league record for homers with 264. Randy Johnson (20-4, 2.28 ERA) successfully returned from back surgery to his old dominant form, and despite missing four starts down the stretch because of tendinitis in a finger, he won 20 in a season for the first time.

But Seattle's success went beyond the obvious big-numbers, big-money guys. Second baseman Joey Cora hit .300 and earned his first All-Star selection. After starting the season as a platoon player, Cora's club-record 24-game hitting streak earned him the every-day starting job. Rob Ducey, a 32-year-old journeyman outfielder, signed as a minor league free agent in the offseason and provided the team's best defense in left field, as well as a consistent left-handed bat off the bench. Ducey became even more important when outfielder Jose Cruz Jr. was traded in what may become a key to the Mariners' future.

The Seattle bullpen blew 27 saves in 1997. The lack of consistency was driving manager Lou Piniella to distraction and threatened the team's lead in the West. So general manager Woody Woodward sent the highly regarded Cruz to the Toronto Blue Jays for relievers Mike Timlin and Paul Spoljaric. Another prospect, Jason Varitek, went to Boston for closer Heathcliff Solcumb. Yes, the Mariners

Team MVP

Ken Griffey Jr.: Somehow Ken Griffey Jr. missed Boston and Cleveland. Amazingly he didn't hit home runs there in 1997 in a 56-homer season that led the AL. His major-league-leading 147 RBI was the majors' fifth-highest total in the last 48 years, and he became one of six major leaguers to hit 100 or more homers over a two-year period.

won the division before being eliminated in the first round of the playoffs by Baltimore. But they still racked up 12 blown saves in the final two months after the trades.

Seattle's offense reigned supreme as usual. The team's 264 home runs set a major league record, and its .485 slugging percentage was the third highest in major league history. Griffey led the majors with 147 RBI, and with Buhner's 109 and Edgar Martinez's 108, Seattle had three 100-RBI men for the third consecutive season. Griffey and Buhner's combined 96 home runs was the third-highest teammate total in history.

There could be even more help on the way. The Mariners have two rookies and a near rookie who could make an impact next season. Both rookies are outfielders, including Raul Ibanez, a former catcher who hit his first major league homer this September. The other outfielder is 23-year-old lefty hitter Shane Monahan, the club's top minor league prospect, who hit .300 with 14 homers and 88 RBI in 128 games in AA and AAA. The near rookie, Ken Cloude, a pitcher, is expected to fill the biggest role for next year's Mariners. After making the jump from AA, Cloude, 22, had an Aug. 9 debut against the White Sox in which he took a perfect game into the sixth and a no-hitter into the seventh. He finished 4-2 with a 5.12 ERA and was Seattle's fourth starter on its playoff roster.

1997 Mariners: Week-by-week notes

These notes were excerpted from the following issues of Baseball Weekly.

▶**April 16:** Ace left-hander Randy Johnson earned his first victory since May 12, 1996, when he beat the Red Sox on April 11. He threw 97 pitches, with 60 strikes. Center fielder Ken Griffey Jr. was AL Player of the Week for the sixth time in his career. Through eight games he led the league in homers (six), total bases (35) and runs scored (14).

▶**April 23:** Manager Lou Piniella moved right-hander Scott Sanders to the bullpen on April 20 so that he can work on his delivery and correct his long-ball problems. Sanders (0-4) has given up eight home runs in only 19⅔ innings. Sanders was 9-5 with a 3.38 ERA for San Diego last year.

▶**April 30:** Ken Griffey Jr. hit three home runs on April 25, giving him a record 13 for April. When Russ Davis delivered a pinch-hit homer on April 24 in the eighth inning, it gave third baseman Davis hits in five consecutive at-bats. Davis, who didn't have even a three-hit game to his credit before this season, had a 4-for-4 night with a career-high four RBI against the Royals.

▶**May 7:** Randy Johnson's back-to-back eight-inning, one-run performance improved his record to 4-0 and convinced him that his surgically repaired back is strong again.

▶**May 14:** Until May 8 against Baltimore, Randy Johnson hadn't lost since Aug. 1, 1995, a string of 16 straight victories. Johnson had to go back to the mound trailing 2-1 after an hour-long rain delay. Then consecutive singles by Cal Ripken and Pete Incaviglia and a three-run home run by Chris Hoiles, all with two outs in the sixth, ended Johnson's chance to continue the streak, which was one short of the AL record.

▶**May 21:** As of May 18, Seattle had lost six of eight games, including their last four in a row, as Texas took over first in the AL West. Unearned runs cost the Mariners

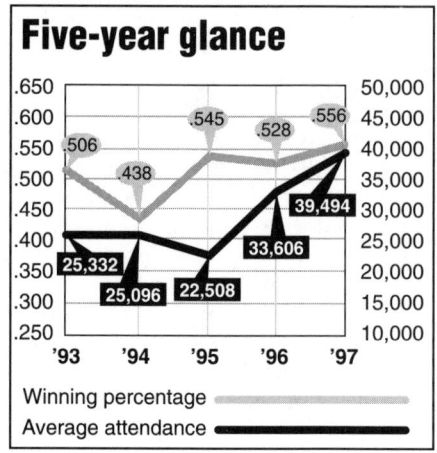

Five-year glance

Winning percentage
Average attendance

dearly in two one-run losses. Seattle gave up three unearned runs on May 12 at Milwaukee and one on May 15 at home against Chicago.

▶**May 28:** Second baseman Joey Cora finished play on May 25 as the AL's third-leading hitter, with a .372 average. He raised it 125 points in 20 games—the length of his career-high hitting streak. His streak was the longest in the majors this season and only one short of the club record.

▶**June 4:** After being sent down in March, rookie Jose Cruz Jr. was called up from AAA Tacoma to make his big league debut. Considered a Jackie Robinson Award favorite when he hit .339 with four homers in spring training, Cruz was in the starting lineup against the Tigers on May 31. Batting second and playing left field, he went 0-for-4 but missed getting two hits by just inches.

▶**June 11:** It took Jose Cruz Jr. until his eighth at-bat to get his first hit, a double. In his ninth he hit another double, and in his 13th he ripped his first home run. After Cruz had played one week, he was batting .320 with three homers and six RBI.

▶**June 25:** A few weeks ago, they looked more like the three-headed monster of a horror-picture bullpen, but after two strong weeks of mix-and-matched roles, the trio of Bobby Ayala, Scott Sanders and Norm Charlton has become the team's three-headed closer. Ayala (six saves) has replaced lefty Charlton (10 saves, seven blown saves) as the primary closer, but Piniella said he plans to use any of the three to set up or close as needed. Sanders finished off a 5-4 win against the Rangers on June 20 for his second save.

▶July 2: Shortstop Alex Rodriguez (bruised chest wall) was activated from the 15-day DL on June 27 and hit a two-run homer that night off the third pitch he saw from Anaheim's Chuck Finley. He had two of the three hits off Allen Watson the next night.

▶July 10: When Alex Rodriguez and designated hitter Edgar Martinez were voted to the All-Star Game as starters, they became just the second and third Mariners ever so honored. In the club's previous 20 years, only Ken Griffey Jr. had been voted to the starting lineup.

▶July 23: The Mariners say their July 18 two-for-one trade of pitchers with the Tigers is just the first step in their search for pitching help for the stretch run. They acquired veteran pitchers Omar Olivares and Felipe Lira for Scott Sanders (and two minor leaguers). Through July 19 the staff had converted only 21 of its 35 save chances.

▶July 30: Left-hander Jamie Moyer, now 11-3, improved his record to 24-6 over the past year and a half after beating the Yankees on July 25. Since joining the Mariners in a trade from the Red Sox a year ago, Moyer is 17-5 with a 4.05 ERA in 29 starts.

▶Aug. 6: They got the bullpen help they needed, but the Mariners weren't happy about the July 31 late-night trade flurry. After declaring rising star Jose Cruz Jr. off limits, the Mariners relented, trading him to Toronto for relievers Mike Timlin and Paul Spoljaric. Cruz hit .268 with 12 homers in 48 games for Seattle. General manager Woody Woodward also pulled off a last-minute deal with Boston to get Heathcliff Slocumb for minor leaguers Derek Lowe and Jason Varitek.

▶Aug. 13: On Aug. 8, Randy Johnson became the first pitcher in history to strike out 19 or more batters twice in the same season, and his best efforts came against the heart of the White Sox order.

Mike Cameron, Frank Thomas, Albert Belle and Robin Ventura went 0-for-15 against Johnson with 14 strikeouts.

▶Aug. 20: Despite an Aug. 15 loss to the Orioles, Randy Johnson's 13 strikeouts allowed him to tie a major league record for most strikeouts in consecutive appearances, with 32.

▶Aug. 27: Last week's trade for outfielder Roberto Kelly reaped immediate rewards for Seattle as Kelly went 2-for-5 in each of two wins, then hit a game-tying home run in the ninth inning of an eventual loss to the Yankees on Aug. 23.

▶Sept. 3: The Mariners' bullpen had a baseball-worst 6.20 ERA with 16 blown saves in 40 chances before the July 31 trades. Since then, the relievers have a 5.12 ERA with six blown saves in 12 tries.

▶Sept. 10: Playing without Randy Johnson, Russ Davis and Alex Rodriguez for most of the week, the Mariners expanded a one-game lead over Anaheim in the AL West into five in the first six days of September. Ken Griffey Jr. hit his 50th home run on Sept. 7.

▶Sept. 17: Randy Johnson returned to the mound after missing four starts because of a finger injury, and he looked like he had never left. On Sept. 13 he went six innings, allowing one hit, one walk and one unearned run, striking out eight.

▶Oct. 1: Four days after Randy Johnson beat Anaheim and clinched the AL West title, he pitched two innings of relief against the A's to become the first 20-game winner in Mariners history. In relief of Omar Olivares, Johnson pitched the fifth and sixth innings of a 9-3 win against Oakland on Sept. 27. The Mariners finished the season with 264 homers, breaking Baltimore's year-old major league record of 257.

QUOTE OF THE YEAR

"You'll notice only one of them is a pitcher."
—Manager Lou Piniella, explaining why the Mariners, with seven 1996-97 All-Stars, weren't dominating their division

SEATTLE MARINERS 1997 final stats

BATTERS	BA	SLG	OBA	G	AB	R	H	TB	2B	3B	HR	RBI	BB	SO	SB	CS	E
Rohrmeier	.333	.333	.455	7	9	4	3	3	0	0	0	2	2	4	0	0	0
E. Martinez	.330	.554	.456	155	542	104	179	300	35	1	28	108	119	86	2	4	1
Griffey	.304	.646	.382	157	608	125	185	393	34	3	56	147	76	121	15	4	6
Rodriguez	.300	.496	.350	141	587	100	176	291	40	3	23	84	41	99	29	6	24
Cora	.300	.441	.359	149	574	105	172	253	40	4	11	54	53	49	6	7	17
Blowers	.293	.427	.376	68	150	22	44	64	5	0	5	20	21	33	0	0	4
Kelly	.291	.470	.333	105	368	58	107	173	26	2	12	59	22	67	9	5	0
Marzano	.287	.356	.340	39	87	7	25	31	3	0	1	10	7	15	0	0	5
Ducey	.287	.524	.311	76	143	25	41	75	15	2	5	10	6	31	3	3	1
Amaral	.284	.326	.327	89	190	34	54	62	5	0	1	21	10	34	12	8	3
R. Davis	.271	.488	.317	119	420	57	114	205	29	1	20	63	27	100	6	2	18
Wilson	.270	.423	.326	146	508	66	137	215	31	1	15	74	39	72	7	2	6
Sorrento	.269	.514	.345	146	457	68	123	235	19	0	31	80	51	112	0	2	4
Wilkins	.250	.583	.286	5	12	2	3	7	1	0	1	4	1	2	0	0	0
Sheets	.247	.416	.299	32	89	18	22	37	3	0	4	9	7	34	2	0	8
Buhner	.243	.506	.383	157	540	104	131	273	18	2	40	109	119	175	0	0	1
Gates	.238	.351	.298	65	151	18	36	53	8	0	3	20	14	21	0	0	5
Tinsley	.197	.279	.263	49	122	12	24	34	6	2	0	6	11	34	2	0	0
Espinoza	.181	.194	.213	33	72	3	13	14	1	0	0	7	2	12	1	1	3
Ibanez	.154	.346	.154	11	26	3	4	9	0	1	1	4	0	6	0	0	0
Guevara	.000	.000	.000	5	4	0	0	0	0	0	0	0	0	2	1	0	1
Raabe	.000	.000	.250	2	3	0	0	0	0	0	0	0	1	2	0	0	0

PITCHERS	W-L	ERA	BA	G	GS	CG	GF	Sho	SV	IP	H	R	ER	HR	BB	SO
Johnson	20-4	2.28	.194	30	29	5	0	2	0	213.0	147	60	54	20	77	291
Carmona	0-0	3.18	.150	4	0	0	1	0	0	5.2	3	3	2	1	2	6
Timlin	6-4	3.22	.257	64	0	0	31	0	10	72.2	69	30	26	8	20	45
Fassero	16-9	3.61	.249	35	35	2	0	1	0	234.1	226	108	94	21	84	189
Spoljaric	0-3	3.69	.236	57	0	0	10	0	3	70.2	61	30	29	4	36	70
Ayala	10-5	3.82	.260	71	0	0	33	0	8	96.2	91	45	41	14	41	92
Moyer	17-5	3.86	.256	30	30	2	0	0	0	188.2	187	82	81	21	43	113
Olivares	6-10	4.97	.276	32	31	3	0	2	0	177.1	191	109	98	18	81	103
Cloude	4-2	5.12	.218	10	9	0	0	0	0	51.0	41	32	29	8	26	46
Slocumb	0-9	5.16	.286	76	0	0	61	0	27	75.0	84	45	43	6	49	64
Manzanillo	0-1	5.40	.275	16	0	0	4	0	0	18.1	19	13	11	3	17	18
McCarthy	1-1	5.46	.230	37	0	0	4	0	0	29.2	26	21	18	4	16	34
Wells	2-0	5.75	.314	46	1	0	19	0	2	67.1	88	49	43	11	18	51
Holzemer	0-0	6.00	.250	14	0	0	2	0	1	9.0	9	6	6	0	8	7
Wolcott	5-6	6.03	.314	19	18	0	0	0	0	100.0	129	71	67	22	29	58
Lira	5-11	6.34	.295	28	18	1	3	1	0	110.2	132	82	78	18	55	73
T. Davis	0-0	6.75	.231	2	0	0	1	0	0	6.2	6	5	5	1	4	10
Charlton	3-8	7.27	.312	71	0	0	38	0	14	69.1	89	59	56	7	47	55
D. Martinez	1-5	7.71	.327	9	9	0	0	0	0	49.0	65	46	42	8	29	17
Hurtado	1-2	9.00	.329	13	1	0	2	0	0	19.0	25	19	19	5	15	10
Maddux	1-0	10.13	.400	6	0	0	1	0	0	10.2	20	12	12	1	8	7
Torres	0-0	27.00	.412	2	0	0	1	0	0	3.1	7	10	10	0	3	0

162

1998 preliminary roster

PITCHERS (21)
Bobby Ayala
Rafael Carmona
Ken Cloude
Tim Davis
Jeff Fassero
Tony Fossas
Brett Hinchcliffe
Edwin Hurtado
Randy Johnson
Felipe Lira
Damaso Marte
Greg McCarthy

Ivan Montane
Jamie Moyer
Heathcliff Slocumb
Cam Smith
Paul Spoljaric
Mac Suzuki
Mike Timlin
Bob Wells
Jordan Zimmerman

CATCHERS (2)
Rick Wilkins
Dan Wilson

INFIELDERS (10)
Joey Cora
Russ Davis
Giomar Guevara
Aaron Holbert
Jeff Huson
Pat Listach
Edgar Martinez
Alex Rodriguez
Dan Rohrmeier
David Segui

OUTFIELDERS (7)
Rich Amaral
Jay Buhner
Rob Ducey
Charles Gipson
Ken Griffey
Raul Ibanez
Shane Monahan

Games played by position

PLAYER	G	C	1B	2B	3B	SS	OF	DH
Amaral	89	0	14	11	1	1	52	3
Blowers	68	0	49	0	10	0	6	1
Buhner	157	0	0	0	0	0	154	2
Cora	149	0	0	142	0	0	0	0
R. Davis	119	0	0	0	117	0	0	1
Ducey	76	0	0	0	0	0	69	0
Espinoza	33	0	0	14	1	17	0	0
Gates	65	0	1	21	32	5	1	1
Griffey	157	0	0	0	0	0	153	4
Guevara	5	0	0	2	0	1	0	2
Ibanez	11	0	0	0	0	0	8	1
Kelly	105	0	0	0	0	0	88	13
E. Martinez	155	0	7	0	1	0	0	144
Marzano	39	37	0	0	0	0	0	1
Raabe	2	0	0	1	2	0	0	0
Rodriguez	141	0	0	0	0	140	0	1
Rohrmeier	7	0	3	0	0	0	0	4
Sheets	32	0	0	2	21	9	0	0
Sorrento	146	0	139	0	0	0	0	1
Tinsley	49	0	0	0	0	0	41	5
Wilkins	5	3	0	0	0	0	0	2
Wilson	146	144	0	0	0	0	0	0

Sick call: 1997 DL report

PLAYER	Days on the DL
Russ Davis	32
Tim Davis	158
Rob Ducey	18
Alvaro Espinoza	15
Greg Hibbard	181
Mike Maddux	21
Josias Manzanillo	64*
Jamie Moyer	28
Alex Rodriguez	15
Tim Scott	87
Lee Tinsley	107*
Rick Wilkins	19

Indicates two separate terms on Disabled List.

Minor Leagues

Tops in the organization

BATTER	CLUB	AVG.	G	AB	R	H	HR	RBI
Raabe, Brian	Tac	.352	135	543	101	191	14	80
Villalobos, Carlos	Lnc	.341	86	296	71	101	11	53
Christian, Eddie	Tac	.330	103	373	66	123	5	48
Torres, Paul	Tac	.323	121	427	64	138	11	77
Harrison, Adonis	Wsc	.318	125	412	61	131	7	62

HOME RUNS

Rohrmeier, Dan	Tac	33
Regan, Jason	Lnc	31
Clifford, Jim	Lnc	25
Correa, Miguel	Mem	21
Zinter, Alan	Tac	20

RBI

Rohrmeier, Dan	Tac	120
Monahan, Shane	Tac	88
Ibanez, Raul	Tac	84
Clifford, Jim	Lnc	82
Mathis, Joe	Lnc	82

STOLEN BASES

Brock, Tarrik	Lnc	40
Moreno, Jose	Mrn	31
Gipson, Charles	Mem	31

WINS

Mays, Joe	Lnc	16
Luce, Robert	Mem	15

SAVES

Spencer, Sean	Lnc	18
Holdridge, David	Tac	18
Holzemer, Mark	Tac	13
Fitzgerald, Brian	Wsc	10
Palki, Jeromy	Wsc	8

STRIKEOUTS

Mays, Joe	Lnc	161
Fuentes, Brian	Wsc	153
Abbott, Paul	Tac	130
Marte, Damaso	Lnc	127
Cloude, Ken	Mem	124

PITCHER	CLUB	W-L	ERA	IP	H	BB	SO
Stark, Dennis	Lnc	7- 4	2.17	108	65	43	122
Luce, Robert	Mem	15- 3	3.33	162	190	38	98
Fuentes, Brian	Wsc	6- 7	3.56	119	84	59	153
Mays, Joe	Lnc	16- 7	3.59	178	170	57	161
Ayala, Julio	Wsc	11- 3	3.67	103	114	30	81

163

1997 salaries

	Bonuses	Total earned salary
Ken Griffey, of	375,000	7,885,532
Randy Johnson, p	50,000	6,325,000
Jay Buhner, of		4,827,962
Jeff Fassero, p		3,466,666
Edgar Martinez, dh	50,000	3,050,000
Norm Charlton, p		2,950,000
Heathcliff Slocumb, p	25,000	2,300,000
Jamie Moyer, p		1,700,000
Paul Sorrento, 1b		1,500,000
Mike Timlin, p		1,300,000
Omar Olivares, p	25,000	1,125,000
Dan Wilson, c	100,000	1,125,000
Alex Rodriguez, ss	50,000	1,062,500
Joey Cora, 2b	275,000	1,025,000
Roberto Kelly, of		750,000
Bobby Ayala, p	300,000	900,000
Rich Amaral, of		550,000
Mike Blowers, 1b		400,000
Lee Tinsley, of		400,000
Bob Wells, p		280,000
John Marzano, c		250,000
Tim Davis, p		217,500
Rob Ducey, of		200,000
Paul Spoljaric, p		185,000
Russ Davis, 3b	10,000	185,000
Brian Raabe, 2b		160,000
Andy Sheets, ss		152,500
Greg Hibbard, p		152,000
Tim Scott, p		150,000
Rick Wilkins, c		150,000
Raul Ibanez, of		150,000

Average 1997 salary: $1,470,150
Total 1997 payroll: $45,574,660

Seattle (1977-1997)

Runs: Most, career

820	KEN GRIFEY, 1989-1997	
708	EDGAR MARTINEZ, 1987-1997	
666	JAY BUHNER, 1988-1997	
563	Alvin Davis, 1984-1991	
543	Harold Reynolds, 1983-1992	

Hits: Most, career

1389	KEN GRIFFEY, 1989-1997
1210	EDGAR MARTINEZ, 1987-1997
1163	Alvin Davis, 1984-1991
1063	Harold Reynolds, 1983-1992
1035	JAY BUHNER, 1988-1997

2B: Most, career

291	EDGAR MARTINEZ, 1987-1997
261	KEN GRIFFEY, 1989-1997
212	Alvin Davis, 1984-1991
200	Harold Reynolds, 1983-1992
191	JAY BUHNER, 1988-1997

3B: Most, career

48	Harold Reynolds, 1983-1992
26	Phil Bradley, 1983-1987
24	KEN GRIFFEY, 1989-1997
23	Spike Owen, 1983-1986
20	Ruppert Jones, 1977-1979

HR: Most, career

294	KEN GRIFFEY, 1989-1997
250	JAY BUHNER, 1988-1997
160	Alvin Davis, 1984-1991
145	EDGAR MARTINEZ, 1987-1997
115	Jim Presley, 1984-1989

RBI: Most, career

872	KEN GRIFFEY, 1989-1997
781	JAY BUHNER, 1988-1997
667	Alvin Davis, 1984-1991
592	EDGAR MARTINEZ, 1987-1997
418	Jim Presley, 1984-1989

SB: Most, career

290	Julio Cruz, 1977-1983
228	Harold Reynolds, 1983-1992
123	KEN GRIFFEY, 1989-1997
107	Phil Bradley, 1983-1987
102	Henry Cotto, 1988-1993

BB: Most, career

674	EDGAR MARTINEZ, 1987-1997
672	Alvin Davis, 1984-1991
614	JAY BUHNER, 1988-1997
580	KEN GRIFFEY, 1989-1997
391	Harold Reynolds, 1983-1992

BA: Highest, career

.317	EDGAR MARTINEZ, 1987-1997
.302	KEN GRIFFEY, 1989-1997
.301	Phil Bradley, 1983-1987
.290	Bruce Bochte, 1978-1982
.281	Alvin Davis, 1984-1991

On-base avg: Highest, career

.423	EDGAR MARTINEZ, 1987-1997
.392	Ken Phelps, 1983-1988
.382	Phil Bradley, 1983-1987
.381	Alvin Davis, 1984-1991
.381	KEN GRIFFEY, 1989-1997

Slug avg: Highest, career

.562	KEN GRIFFEY, 1989-1997
.521	Ken Phelps, 1983-1988
.513	EDGAR MARTINEZ, 1987-1997
.503	JAY BUHNER, 1988-1997
.466	TINO MARTINEZ, 1990-1995

Games started: Most, career

243	RANDY JOHNSON, 1989-1997
217	Mike Moore, 1982-1988
173	MARK LANGSTON, 1984-1989
147	Jim Beattie, 1980-1986
146	Glenn Abbott, 1977-1983

Complete games: Most, career

56	Mike Moore, 1982-1988
45	RANDY JOHNSON, 1989-1997
41	MARK LANGSTON, 1984-1989
30	Jim Beattie, 1980-1986
28	Glenn Abbott, 1977-1983

Saves: Most, career

98	Mike Schooler, 1988-1992
66	NORM CHARLTON, 1993-1997
52	Bill Caudill, 1982-1983
48	BOBBY AYALA, 1994-1997
36	Shane Rawley, 1978-1981

Shutouts: Most, career

17	RANDY JOHNSON, 1989-1997
9	MARK LANGSTON, 1984-1989
9	Mike Moore, 1982-1988
7	Floyd Bannister, 1979-1982
6	Jim Beattie, 1980-1986

Wins: Most, career

121	RANDY JOHNSON, 1989-1997
74	MARK LANGSTON, 1984-1989
66	Mike Moore, 1982-1988
56	ERIK HANSON, 1988-1993
45	Matt Young, 1983-1990

K: Most, career

1949	RANDY JOHNSON, 1989-1997
1078	MARK LANGSTON, 1984-1989
937	Mike Moore, 1982-1988
740	ERIK HANSON, 1988-1993
597	Matt Young, 1983-1990

Win pct: Highest, career

.654	RANDY JOHNSON, 1989-1997
.525	MARK LANGSTON, 1984-1989
.509	ERIK HANSON, 1988-1993
.444	Floyd Bannister, 1979-1982
.415	Glenn Abbott, 1977-1983

ERA: Lowest, career

3.33	RANDY JOHNSON, 1989-1997
3.69	ERIK HANSON, 1988-1993
3.75	Floyd Bannister, 1979-1982
4.01	MARK LANGSTON, 1984-1989
4.04	BILL SWIFT, 1985-1991

Runs: Most, season

141	ALEX RODRIGUEZ, 1996
125	KEN GRIFFEY, 1996
125	KEN GRIFFEY, 1997
121	EDGAR MARTINEZ, 1995
121	EDGAR MARTINEZ, 1996

Hits: Most, season

215	ALEX RODRIGUEZ, 1996
192	Phil Bradley, 1985
185	KEN GRIFFEY, 1997
184	Harold Reynolds, 1989
182	EDGAR MARTINEZ, 1995

2B: Most, season

54	ALEX RODRIGUEZ, 1996
52	EDGAR MARTINEZ, 1995
52	EDGAR MARTINEZ, 1996
46	EDGAR MARTINEZ, 1992
42	KEN GRIFFEY, 1991

3B: Most, season

11	Harold Reynolds, 1988
10	Phil Bradley, 1987
9	Ruppert Jones, 1979
9	Harold Reynolds, 1989
8	Phil Bradley, 1985
8	Al Cowens, 1982
8	Ruppert Jones, 1977
8	Spike Owen, 1984
8	Harold Reynolds, 1987

HR: Most, season

56	KEN GRIFFEY, 1997
49	KEN GRIFFEY, 1996
45	KEN GRIFFEY, 1993
44	JAY BUHNER, 1996
40	JAY BUHNER, 1995
40	JAY BUHNER, 1997
40	KEN GRIFFEY, 1994

RBI: Most, season

147	KEN GRIFFEY, 1997
140	KEN GRIFFEY, 1996
138	JAY BUHNER, 1996
123	ALEX RODRIGUEZ, 1996
121	JAY BUHNER, 1995

SB: Most, season

60	Harold Reynolds, 1987
59	Julio Cruz, 1978
49	Julio Cruz, 1979
46	Julio Cruz, 1982
45	Julio Cruz, 1980

BB: Most, season

123	EDGAR MARTINEZ, 1996
119	JAY BUHNER, 1997
119	EDGAR MARTINEZ, 1997
116	EDGAR MARTINEZ, 1995
101	Alvin Davis, 1989

BA: Highest, season

.358	ALEX RODRIGUEZ, 1996
.356	EDGAR MARTINEZ, 1995
.343	EDGAR MARTINEZ, 1992
.330	EDGAR MARTINEZ, 1997
.327	EDGAR MARTINEZ, 1996

On-base avg: Highest, season

.479	EDGAR MARTINEZ, 1995
.464	EDGAR MARTINEZ, 1996
.456	EDGAR MARTINEZ, 1997
.424	Alvin Davis, 1989
.414	ALEX RODRIGUEZ, 1996

Slug avg: Highest, season

.674	KEN GRIFFEY, 1994
.646	KEN GRIFFEY, 1997
.631	ALEX RODRIGUEZ, 1996
.628	EDGAR MARTINEZ, 1995
.628	KEN GRIFFEY, 1996

Games started: Most, season

37	Mike Moore, 1986
36	MARK LANGSTON, 1986
35	Floyd Bannister, 1982
35	JEFF FASSERO, 1997
35	STERLING HITCHCOCK, 1996
35	MARK LANGSTON, 1987
35	MARK LANGSTON, 1988
35	Matt Young, 1985

Complete games: Most, season

14	MARK LANGSTON, 1987
14	Mike Moore, 1985
13	Mike Parrott, 1979
12	Jim Beattie, 1984
12	Mike Moore, 1987

Saves: Most, season

33	Mike Schooler, 1989
30	Mike Schooler, 1990
26	Bill Caudill, 1982
26	Bill Caudill, 1983
20	NORM CHARLTON, 1996

Shutouts: Most, season

4	Dave Fleming, 1992
4	RANDY JOHNSON, 1994
3	Floyd Bannister, 1982
3	Brian Holman, 1991
3	RANDY JOHNSON, 1993
3	RANDY JOHNSON, 1995
3	MARK LANGSTON, 1987
3	MARK LANGSTON, 1988
3	Mike Moore, 1988

Wins: Most, season

20	RANDY JOHNSON, 1997
19	RANDY JOHNSON, 1993
19	MARK LANGSTON, 1987
18	ERIK HANSON, 1990
18	RANDY JOHNSON, 1995

K: Most, season

308	RANDY JOHNSON, 1993
294	RANDY JOHNSON, 1995
291	RANDY JOHNSON, 1997
262	MARK LANGSTON, 1987
245	MARK LANGSTON, 1986

Win pct: Highest, season

.900	RANDY JOHNSON, 1995
.833	RANDY JOHNSON, 1997
.773	JAMIE MOYER, 1997
.704	RANDY JOHNSON, 1993
.667	ERIK HANSON, 1990

ERA: Lowest, season

2.28	RANDY JOHNSON, 1997
2.48	RANDY JOHNSON, 1995
3.19	RANDY JOHNSON, 1994
3.24	ERIK HANSON, 1990
3.24	RANDY JOHNSON, 1993

Most pinch-hit homers, season

2	Greg Briley, 1992
2	Gary Gray, 1981
2	Ken Phelps, 1986
2	Leon Roberts, 1978
2	PAUL SORRENTO, 1997

Most pinch-hit homers, career

4	Ken Phelps, 1983-1988

Longest hitting streak

24	JOEY CORA, 1997
21	Dan Meyer, 1979
21	Richie Zisk, 1982
20	ALEX RODRIGUEZ, 1996
19	Phil Bradley, 1986

Most consecutive scoreless innings

34	MARK LANGSTON, 1988

No-hit games

RANDY JOHNSON, Sea vs Det AL, 2-0; June 2, 1990.

Chris Bosio, Sea vs Bos AL, 7-0; April 22, 1993.

ACTIVE PLAYERS in caps.

Players' years of service are listed by the first and last years with this team and are not necessarily consecutive; all statistics record performances for this team only.

Anaheim Angels

Tim Salmon finished in the AL's top 10 in homers, RBI, walks, sacrifice flies and game-winning RBI.

By Russell Becker, *Baseball Weekly*

1997 Angels: Tony, Terry and Disney

It was a season like most others for the Angels, one that ended in September instead of October, but this one was a bit different. This one, and new manager Terry Collins, provided optimism, perhaps even confidence, that 1998 could indeed be Anaheim's season to cherish.

But no AL team endured the trauma that the Angels did in '97. Their season began to unravel on Aug. 10 when lead-off hitter Tony Phillips was arrested on felony possession of cocaine charges, and it went spiraling downhill when left-hander Chuck Finley fell and broke a bone in his left wrist and catcher Todd Greene broke his right wrist the next night. The Angels were in first place in the AL West with a 66-50 record when Phillips was arrested. They were never the same. The Angels lost eight of their next 11 games, fell one half game behind the Mariners, and then found themselves in a tug of war between baseball and the Walt Disney Co. over baseball's drug policy. The Angels wound up losing 21 of 30 and fell out of the race. "As much as you try to forget it, it was the story," Collins said.

Phillips admits he hurt the team. "I left myself open for that," he said. "I'll take responsibility for the situation I put these other guys into." Rickey Henderson, who was acquired because of Phillips' arrest, batted only .183 after joining the Angels.

On the field, right fielder Tim Salmon is still the best player nobody knows. Salmon had a great year, hitting .296 with 33 homers and 129 RBI, and batting .346 with runners in scoring position. Left fielder Garret Anderson hit .303 with 36 doubles and 92 RBI. Darrin Erstad, in his first full season at first base, hit .299 with 16 homers, 77 RBI and 99 runs scored. Infielder Dave Hollins hit .288 with 16 homers, 85 RBI and 101 runs scored despite having an injured knee that required surgery. No Angel played with more determination and more fire.

Finley went 13-6 with a 4.23 ERA, tying the franchise record with 10 consecutive

wins, when he broke his wrist. The rest of the expected starters were a huge disappointment. Collins went into spring training believing he had a rotation of Finley, Mark Langston, Allen Watson, Mark Gubicza and Jim Abbott. Abbott was released before the season began, and injuries to Langston (elbow) and Gubicza (shoulder) limited them to a combined 11 starts. Right-hander Jason Dickson went into spring training competing for the No. 5 spot in the rotation and wound up as No. 2, going 13-9 with a 4.29 ERA.

The Angels are concerned about several players who had injuries to rehabilitate in the offseason. Hollins (knee), shortstop Gary DiSarcina (elbow) and center fielder Jim Edmonds (both knees) had offseason surgeries. Also, Finley, Greene, second baseman Randy Velarde, and Langston and Gubicza are rehabilitating from their in-season surgeries. If everyone shows up healthy, the Angels believe that they can win the AL West in 1998. Their nucleus is made up of veteran players. The stadium will be refurbished. Their attitudes have been adjusted. And the Angels could get a much-needed boost from their farm system in 1998. They are hoping that AA pitchers Jarrod Washburn and, perhaps, Scott Schoeneweis could be ready.

1997 Angels: Week-by-week notes

These notes were excerpted from the following issues of Baseball Weekly.

▶**April 9:** The Angels knocked out half the seats in the stadium and still couldn't sell out Opening Day. With capacity reduced from 64,593 to about 34,000 because of the renovation of Anaheim Stadium, the Angels drew 30,874 to their opener against Boston.

▶**April 16:** The Angels' ERA stood at 7.12 through nine games, with three of the five starters in double digits: Mark Gubicza (20.25), Allen Watson (13.50) and Shigetoshi Hasegawa (11.57). Knuckleballer Dennis Springer might move into the starting rotation.

▶**April 23:** Allen Watson was charged with misdemeanor assault following an argument during which a man was punched in the face at a Missouri riverboat casino. Watson could face up to $1,000 in fines and a year in jail. Rookie Jason Dickson started four games through April 20, pitching two complete games and seven innings in another start, making him an early Jackie Robinson Award candidate. No other Angels starter has pitched seven innings in a game this season.

▶**April 30:** Right fielder Tim Salmon was in a 3-for-36 slump when Collins moved him from the cleanup spot to the No. 5 hole on April 20 in Kansas City. In his next five games Salmon went 12-for-27 with two homers and eight RBI.

▶**May 7:** Left-hander Chuck Finley has a new nickname—Hard Luck Chuck. On May 1, Finley was making his fourth start and looking for his first win, and had a 2-0 lead against the Red Sox in the middle of the fifth inning when a torrential downpour hit Fenway Park. The game was called after a one-hour, 55-minute delay, three outs short of what would have been an official victory.

▶**May 14:** In 23 games through May 10, the Angels pitching staff had a 3.83 ERA, but the club was 11-12 in that span. The offense ranks 12th in the league in home runs, last in extra-base hits, last in walks

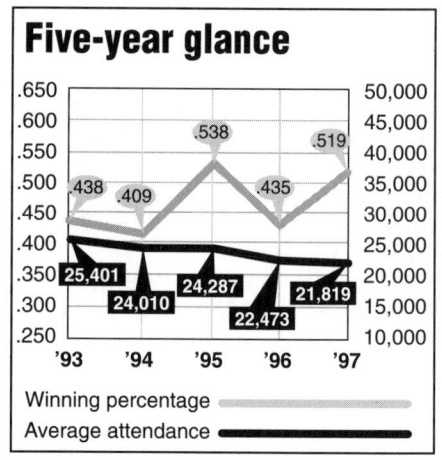

Five-year glance

Winning percentage
Average attendance

and 11th in runs. It averaged 3.2 runs in 11 games on its last road trip.

▶**May 21:** Tony Phillips, a spark of the 1995 Angels before leaving as a free agent, was back in the Anaheim lineup on May 18, hitting leadoff and playing left field. He went 0-for-2 but scored a run in his debut, a 5-4 Angels win over Milwaukee. Phillips, hitting .310, was part of a four-player trade with the Chicago White Sox that also brought catcher Chad Kreuter to Anaheim for left-handed reliever Chuck McElroy and catcher Jorge Fabregas.

▶**May 28:** Take one look at Dennis Springer's slightly frumpy, 5-10, 190-pound physique and one thing comes to mind: slow-pitch softball player. But this unorthodox pitcher has an unorthodox pitch, a knuckleball that he has used to record three consecutive victories, including a May 23 complete-game seven-hitter for a 12-2 road win against Toronto.

▶**June 4:** Catcher Todd Greene has been on a tear since being demoted to AAA Vancouver on April 14, batting .395 with 19 homers and 54 RBI in his first 36 games there. It's a performance that may force the Angels to recall the catcher soon and find a place for him in their lineup three or four times a week.

▶**June 18:** Center fielder Jim Edmonds made the best catch of his life in a 6-2 victory at Kansas City on June 10, sprinting straight back to the warning track in the bottom of the fifth inning to make a full-extension, over-the-shoulder diving grab of David Howard's drive with two on, two out and the game tied 1-1. The ball was nestled in the tip of Edmonds' glove as he landed face first in front of the wall.

▶July 2: Chuck Finley, an All-Star in the past two seasons, concluded a winless June in which he posted a 7.12 ERA and allowed nine home runs in 30 innings. His record is now 3-6.

▶July 16: The Angels clinched their first series victory from Oakland since 1986, their last division championship season. The series is a landslide as of July 13: Angels 10, A's 0, by a combined score of 75-39.

▶July 23: The Angels backed away from pursuing Mark McGwire, for now, and set their sights on acquiring a starting pitcher before the July 31 trading deadline. Todd Greene hit safely in the first seven games since his recall from Vancouver, including the first two-homer game of his career.

▶July 30: The Angels abandoned their four-man rotation, with the sore elbow of Jason Dickson compelling Terry Collins to halt the experiment. "I've got to find a starter," Collins said. Mark Langston, who made his first rehab start on July 26, is scheduled to rejoin the rotation on Aug. 9. The Angels would prefer to trade for a starter before then.

▶Aug. 6: The Angels finally got their starter when they acquired Ken Hill from Texas for catcher Jim Leyritz and a player to be named later. Hill, 31, won 16 games last season for the third time in five years, but he hasn't dominated many games this season, with a 6-8 record and 5.06 ERA.

▶Aug. 13: Tony Phillips was arrested on Aug. 10 after he allegedly bought a small quantity of freebase cocaine at a motel in Anaheim. Phillips initially was penciled in at his usual leadoff spot for the Aug. 10 game against Baltimore, but after talking with Angels team officials, he left for Scottsdale, Ariz., to spend time with his family.

▶Aug. 20: The Angels suspended troubled Tony Phillips indefinitely on Aug. 18.

Uncertain of Phillips' availability, the team acquired left fielder and future Hall of Famer Rickey Henderson from the Padres for third baseman George Arias of Vancouver and two minor league pitchers.

▶Aug. 27: An arbitration panel ordered the Angels to reinstate Tony Phillips and chided the parent Walt Disney Co. for suspending him in violation of baseball rules. In accordance with baseball's drug policy, Phillips had visited doctors representing the players' union and the owners' player relations committee. Those doctors cleared Phillips to return after he agreed to random drug testing and outpatient counseling.

▶Sept. 3: Less than a week after losing Todd Greene to a broken right wrist, Anaheim lost Chuck Finley to a broken left wrist. Both are expected to miss the rest of the season. Finley, 13-6 with a 4.23 ERA, tied a club record by winning his last 10 decisions.

▶Sept. 10: Mark Langston declared his season over after elbow pain prevented him from pitching even a simulated game. Langston, 37, went 2-4 with a 5.85 ERA in nine games this season. His $14 million, three-year contract expires this season, and he has indicated he would accept a severe pay cut to return.

▶Sept. 17: Anaheim had a 1-5 trip through Detroit and Toronto that sent the Angels spiraling out of contention. They lost seven of their first eight games in September and fell from one game behind Seattle to five back with 17 to play.

▶Oct. 1: The Angels' top priority this off-season is to improve their pitching. They are expected to pursue free-agent starter Darryl Kile and will attempt to sign Ken Hill to a long-term contract extension. Hill (9-12) seemed to cement his status with strong outings in his last six appearances, in which he went 3-1. The Angels can pick up his '98 salary at $4.6 million.

QUOTE OF THE YEAR

"Many other people have put themselves in the same situation that I was in, and they've come out in body bags."
—Tony Phillips, commenting on his drug use

ANAHEIM ANGELS 1997 final stats

BATTERS	BA	SLG	OBA	G	AB	R	H	TB	2B	3B	HR	RBI	BB	SO	SB	CS	E
Encarnacion	.412	.647	.412	11	17	2	7	11	1	0	1	4	0	1	2	0	3
Eenhoorn	.350	.550	.333	11	20	2	7	11	1	0	1	6	0	2	0	0	3
Arias	.333	.333	.333	3	6	1	2	2	0	0	0	1	0	0	0	0	0
Anderson	.303	.409	.334	154	624	76	189	255	36	3	8	92	30	70	10	4	3
Erstad	.299	.466	.360	139	539	99	161	251	34	4	16	77	51	86	23	8	11
Salmon	.296	.517	.394	157	582	95	172	301	28	1	33	129	95	142	9	12	11
Edmonds	.291	.500	.368	133	502	82	146	251	27	0	26	80	60	80	5	7	5
Greene	.290	.556	.328	34	124	24	36	69	6	0	9	24	7	25	2	0	0
Hollins	.288	.430	.363	149	572	101	165	246	29	2	16	85	62	124	16	6	29
Phillips	.275	.391	.392	141	534	96	147	209	34	2	8	57	102	118	13	10	11
Grebeck	.270	.365	.359	63	126	12	34	46	9	0	1	6	18	11	0	1	2
Turner	.261	.522	.393	13	23	4	6	12	1	1	1	2	5	8	0	0	0
Howell	.259	.540	.305	77	174	25	45	94	7	0	14	34	13	36	1	0	3
Alicea	.253	.369	.375	128	388	59	98	143	16	7	5	37	69	65	22	8	12
DiSarcina	.246	.326	.271	154	549	52	135	179	28	2	4	47	17	29	7	8	15
Kreuter	.231	.341	.310	89	255	25	59	87	9	2	5	21	29	66	0	3	5
Murray	.219	.319	.273	46	160	13	35	51	7	0	3	15	13	24	1	0	0
Palmeiro	.216	.261	.307	74	134	19	29	35	2	2	0	8	17	11	2	2	2
Henderson	.183	.261	.343	32	115	21	21	30	3	0	2	7	26	23	16	4	0
Velarde	—	—	—	1	0	0	0	0	0	0	0	0	0	0	0	0	0

PITCHERS	W-L	ERA	BA	G	GS	CG	GF	Sho	SV	IP	H	R	ER	HR	BB	SO
Williams	0-0	0.00	.250	1	0	0	1	0	0	1.0	1	0	0	0	1	0
Chavez	0-0	0.93	.206	7	0	0	2	0	0	9.2	7	1	1	1	5	10
Cadaret	0-0	3.29	.220	15	0	0	6	0	0	13.2	11	5	5	1	8	11
Holtz	3-4	3.32	.228	66	0	0	11	0	2	43.1	38	21	16	7	15	40
Percival	5-5	3.46	.205	55	0	0	46	0	27	52.0	40	20	20	6	22	72
DeLucia	6-4	3.61	.204	33	0	0	13	0	3	42.1	29	18	17	5	27	42
Harris	5-4	3.62	.274	61	0	0	17	0	0	79.2	82	33	32	7	38	56
Hasegawa	3-7	3.93	.269	50	7	0	17	0	0	116.2	118	60	51	14	46	83
Finley	13-6	4.23	.248	25	25	3	0	1	0	164.0	152	79	77	20	65	155
Dickson	13-9	4.29	.289	33	32	2	1	1	0	203.2	236	111	97	32	56	115
James	5-5	4.31	.283	58	0	0	22	0	7	62.2	69	32	30	3	28	57
Hill	9-12	4.55	.268	31	31	1	0	0	0	190.0	194	103	96	19	95	106
Watson	12-12	4.93	.279	35	34	0	0	0	0	199.0	220	121	109	37	73	141
Springer	9-9	5.18	.267	32	28	3	0	1	0	194.2	199	118	112	32	73	75
May	2-1	5.23	.277	29	2	0	7	0	0	51.2	56	31	30	6	25	42
Bovee	0-0	5.40	.231	3	0	0	3	0	0	3.1	3	2	2	1	1	5
Langston	2-4	5.85	.316	9	9	0	0	0	0	47.2	61	34	31	8	29	30
Perisho	0-2	6.00	.324	11	8	0	2	0	0	45.0	59	34	30	6	28	35
Gross	2-1	6.75	.313	12	3	0	2	0	0	25.1	30	20	19	4	20	20
Gubicza	0-1	25.07	.481	2	2	0	0	0	0	4.2	13	13	13	2	3	5

1998 preliminary roster

PITCHERS (19)
Mike Bovee
Tony Chavez
Brian Cooper
Rich DeLucia
Jason Dickson
Geoff Edsell
Chuck Finley
Mike Freehill
Mike Gubicza
Pep Harris

Shigetoshi Hasegawa
Ken Hill
Mike Holtz
Mike James
Darrell May
Omar Olivares
Troy Percival
Jarrod Washburn
Allen Watson

CATCHERS (3)
Angelo Encarnacion
Todd Greene
Matt Walbeck

INFIELDERS (8)
Justin Baughman
Nelson Castro
Gary DiSarcina
Robert Eenhoorn
Dave Hollins

Phil Nevin
Chris Pritchett
Randy Velarde

OUTFIELDERS (6)
Garret Anderson
Jim Edmonds
Darin Erstad
Norm Hutchins
Orlando Palmeiro
Tim Salmon

Games played by position

PLAYER	G	C	1B	2B	3B	SS	OF	DH
Alicea	128	0	0	105	12	0	0	6
Anderson	154	0	0	0	0	0	148	4
Arias	3	0	0	0	1	0	0	1
DiSarcina	154	0	0	0	0	153	0	0
Edmonds	133	0	11	0	0	0	115	8
Eenhoorn	11	0	0	3	5	2	0	0
Encarnacion	11	11	0	0	0	0	0	0
Erstad	139	0	126	0	0	0	1	9
Grebeck	63	0	0	26	15	20	3	2
Greene	34	26	0	0	0	0	0	8
Henderson	32	0	0	0	0	0	13	19
Hollins	149	0	14	0	135	0	0	0
Howell	77	0	12	0	24	0	0	22
Kreuter	89	80	2	0	0	0	0	2
Murray	46	0	0	0	0	0	0	45
Palmeiro	74	0	0	0	0	0	52	11
Phillips	141	0	0	43	10	0	63	26
Salmon	157	0	0	0	0	0	153	4
Turner	13	8	2	0	0	0	1	1
Velarde	1	0	0	0	0	0	0	0

Sick call: 1997 DL report

PLAYER	Days on the DL
Jim Edmonds	16
Chuck Finley	54*
Todd Greene	39
Mark Gubicza	170
Mike James	24
Mark Langston	128*
Eddie Murray	53
Steve Ontiveros	181
Orlando Palmeiro	15
Troy Percival	39
Jeff Schmidt	12
Chris Turner	100
Randy Velarde	175*

Indicates two separate terms on Disabled List.

Minor Leagues

Tops in the organization

BATTER	CLUB	AVG.	G	AB	R	H	HR	RBI
Stewart, Paxton	Boi	.333	72	282	59	94	7	45
Guiel, Aaron	Mdl	.329	116	419	91	138	22	85
Burke, Jamie	Van	.327	124	455	81	149	6	75
White, Derrick	Van	.313	126	451	66	141	11	68
Bolick, Frank	Van	.309	130	459	87	142	24	93

HOME RUNS

Norton, Chris	Van	28
Greene, Todd	Van	25
Bolick, Frank	Van	24
Guiel, Aaron	Mdl	22
Several Players Tied at		19

WINS

Washburn, J.	Van	15
Edsell, Geoff	Van	14
Bovee, Mike	Van	12
Darrell, Tommy	CR	12
Several Players Tied at		11

RBI

Bolick, Frank	Van	93
Guiel, Aaron	Mdl	85
Norton, Chris	Van	83
Sasser, Rob	CR	77
Several Players Tied at		75

SAVES

Chavez, Anthony	Van	21
Freehill, Mike	LkE	18
Skuse, Nick	Van	16
Donaldson, Bo	Boi	15
Hill, Jason	LkE	15

STOLEN BASES

Baughman, J.	LkE	68
Durrington, Trent	LkE	52
Hutchins, Norm	LkE	39
Sasser, Rob	CR	37
Abbott, Chuck	CR	31

STRIKEOUTS

Ortiz, Ramon	CR	225
Washburn, Jarrod	Van	152
Bovee, Mike	Van	132
Buckley, Travis	Van	119
Stockstill, Jason	CR	116

PITCHER	CLUB	W-L	ERA	IP	H	BB	SO
Rojas, Renney	But	8-4	3.51	110	113	19	65
Cooper, Brian	LkE	7-3	3.54	117	111	27	104
Ortiz, Ramon	CR	11-10	3.58	181	156	53	225
Williams, Shad	Van	6-2	3.82	99	98	41	52
Bovee, Mike	Van	12-5	3.86	191	209	48	132

1997 salaries

	Bonuses	Total earned salary
Ken Hill, p	100,000	4,850,000
Mark Langston, p		4,000,000
Chuck Finley, p		4,000,000
Tim Salmon, of		3,500,000
Rickey Henderson, of	1,045,000	3,045,000
Gary DiSarcina, ss	100,000	2,700,000
Jim Edmonds, of	175,000	2,275,000
Tony Phillips, if	400,000	2,200,000
Dave Hollins, 3b	150,000	2,050,000
Mark Gubicza, p		1,600,000
Allen Watson, p	100,000	1,300,000
Randy Velarde, 2b		800,000
Luis Alicea, 2b	300,000	650,000
Troy Percival, p	100,000	650,000
Chad Kreuter, c	222,500	647,500
Rich Delucia, p		625,000
Garret Anderson, of	100,000	600,000
Shigetoshi Hasegawa, p	275,000	575,000
Craig Grebeck, 2b		400,000
Jack Howell, 3b		400,000
Mike James, p	30,000	330,000
Greg Cadaret, p		250,000
Dennis Springer, p	15,000	195,000
Angel Encarnacion, c		175,000
Darin Erstad, 1b		175,000
Michael Holtz, p		165,000
Orlando Palmeiro, of		163,000
Jason Dickson, p	5,000	162,000
Pep Harris, p	2,500	157,500
Christopher Turner, c		155,000
Steve Ontiveros, p		154,000
Todd Greene, c		153,000
Darrell May, p		152,000

Average 1997 salary: $1,189,515
Total 1997 payroll: $39,254,000

Anaheim (1997), includes California (1965-1996) and Los Angeles (1961-1964)

Runs: Most, career

889	Brian Downing, 1978-1990
691	Jim Fregosi, 1961-1971
601	Bobby Grich, 1977-1986
520	CHILI DAVIS, 1988-1996
481	Don Baylor, 1977-1982

Hits: Most, career

1588	Brian Downing, 1978-1990
1408	Jim Fregosi, 1961-1971
1103	Bobby Grich, 1977-1986
973	CHILI DAVIS, 1988-1996
968	Rod Carew, 1979-1985

2B: Most, career

282	Brian Downing, 1978-1990
219	Jim Fregosi, 1961-1971
183	Bobby Grich, 1977-1986
170	WALLY JOYNER, 1986-1991
167	CHILI DAVIS, 1988-1996

3B: Most, career

70	Jim Fregosi, 1961-1971
32	Mickey Rivers, 1970-1975
27	Luis Polonia, 1990-1993
27	Dick Schofield, 1983-1996
25	Bobby Knoop, 1964-1969

HR: Most, career

222	Brian Downing, 1978-1990
156	CHILI DAVIS, 1988-1996
154	Bobby Grich, 1977-1986
153	TIM SALMON, 1992-1997
141	Don Baylor, 1977-1982

RBI: Most, career

846	Brian Downing, 1978-1990
618	CHILI DAVIS, 1988-1996
557	Bobby Grich, 1977-1986
546	Jim Fregosi, 1961-1971
523	Don Baylor, 1977-1982

SB: Most, career

186	Gary Pettis, 1982-1987
174	Luis Polonia, 1990-1993
139	Sandy Alomar, 1969-1974
126	Mickey Rivers, 1970-1975
123	DEVON WHITE, 1985-1990

BB: Most, career

866	Brian Downing, 1978-1990
630	Bobby Grich, 1977-1986
558	Jim Fregosi, 1961-1971
493	CHILI DAVIS, 1988-1996
426	TIM SALMON, 1992-1997

BA: Highest, career

.314	Rod Carew, 1979-1985
.294	Luis Polonia, 1990-1993
.293	TIM SALMON, 1992-1997
.293	Juan Beniquez, 1981-1985
.290	JIM EDMONDS, 1993-1997

On-base avg: Highest, career

.393	Rod Carew, 1979-1985
.392	TIM SALMON, 1992-1997
.379	Albie Pearson, 1961-1966
.372	Brian Downing, 1978-1990
.370	Bobby Grich, 1977-1986

Slug avg: Highest, career

.527	TIM SALMON, 1992-1997
.503	JIM EDMONDS, 1993-1997
.464	CHILI DAVIS, 1988-1996
.463	Doug DeCinces, 1982-1987
.455	WALLY JOYNER, 1986-1991

Games started: Most, career

312	CHUCK FINLEY, 1986-1997
288	Nolan Ryan, 1972-1979
272	Mike Witt, 1981-1990
218	Frank Tanana, 1973-1980
210	MARK LANGSTON, 1990-1997

Complete games: Most, career

156	Nolan Ryan, 1972-1979
92	Frank Tanana, 1973-1980
70	Mike Witt, 1981-1990
55	CHUCK FINLEY, 1986-1997
51	Clyde Wright, 1966-1973

Saves: Most, career

126	Bryan Harvey, 1987-1992
66	TROY PERCIVAL, 1995-1997
65	Dave LaRoche, 1970-1980
61	Donnie Moore, 1985-1988
58	Bob Lee, 1964-1966

Shutouts: Most, career

40	Nolan Ryan, 1972-1979
24	Frank Tanana, 1973-1980
21	Dean Chance, 1961-1966
14	George Brunet, 1964-1969
13	CHUCK FINLEY, 1986-1997
13	Geoff Zahn, 1981-1985

Wins: Most, career

142	CHUCK FINLEY, 1986-1997
138	Nolan Ryan, 1972-1979
109	Mike Witt, 1981-1990
102	Frank Tanana, 1973-1980
88	MARK LANGSTON, 1990-1997

K: Most, career

2416	Nolan Ryan, 1972-1979
1739	CHUCK FINLEY, 1986-1997
1283	Mike Witt, 1981-1990
1233	Frank Tanana, 1973-1980
1112	MARK LANGSTON, 1990-1997

Win pct: Highest, career

.567	Frank Tanana, 1973-1980
.557	Andy Messersmith, 1968-1972
.553	Geoff Zahn, 1981-1985
.543	MARK LANGSTON, 1990-1997
.542	CHUCK FINLEY, 1986-1997

ERA: Lowest, career

2.78	Andy Messersmith, 1968-1972
2.83	Dean Chance, 1961-1966
3.07	Nolan Ryan, 1972-1979
3.08	Frank Tanana, 1973-1980
3.13	George Brunet, 1964-1969

Runs: Most, season

120	Don Baylor, 1979
120	JIM EDMONDS, 1995
119	TONY PHILLIPS, 1995
115	Albie Pearson, 1962
114	Carney Lansford, 1979

Hits: Most, season

202	Alex Johnson, 1970
189	GARRET ANDERSON, 1997
188	Carney Lansford, 1979
186	Don Baylor, 1979
186	Billy Moran, 1962

2B: Most, season

42	Doug DeCinces, 1982
42	Johnny Ray, 1988
38	Fred Lynn, 1982
37	Brian Downing, 1982
36	GARRET ANDERSON, 1997

3B: Most, season

13	Jim Fregosi, 1968
13	Mickey Rivers, 1975
13	DEVON WHITE, 1989
12	Jim Fregosi, 1963
11	Bobby Knoop, 1966
11	Mickey Rivers, 1974

HR: Most, season

39	Reggie Jackson, 1982
37	Bobby Bonds, 1977
37	Leon Wagner, 1962
36	Don Baylor, 1979
34	Don Baylor, 1978
34	WALLY JOYNER, 1987
34	TIM SALMON, 1995

RBI: Most, season

139	Don Baylor, 1979
129	TIM SALMON, 1997
117	WALLY JOYNER, 1987
115	Bobby Bonds, 1977
112	CHILI DAVIS, 1993

SB: Most, season

70	Mickey Rivers, 1975
56	Gary Pettis, 1985
55	Luis Polonia, 1993
51	Luis Polonia, 1992
50	Gary Pettis, 1986

BB: Most, season

113	TONY PHILLIPS, 1995
106	Brian Downing, 1987
96	Albie Pearson, 1961
95	Albie Pearson, 1962
95	TIM SALMON, 1997

BA: Highest, season

.339	Rod Carew, 1983
.331	Rod Carew, 1980
.330	TIM SALMON, 1995
.329	Alex Johnson, 1970
.326	Brian Downing, 1979

On-base avg: Highest, season

.429	TIM SALMON, 1995
.429	CHILI DAVIS, 1995
.420	Albie Pearson, 1961
.418	Brian Downing, 1979
.410	CHILI DAVIS, 1994

Slug avg: Highest, season

.594	TIM SALMON, 1995
.561	CHILI DAVIS, 1994
.548	Doug DeCinces, 1982
.543	Bobby Grich, 1981
.537	Bobby Grich, 1979

Games started: Most, season

41	Nolan Ryan, 1974
40	Bill Singer, 1973
39	Nolan Ryan, 1972
39	Nolan Ryan, 1973
39	Nolan Ryan, 1976
39	Clyde Wright, 1970

Complete games: Most, season

26	Nolan Ryan, 1973
26	Nolan Ryan, 1974
23	Frank Tanana, 1976
22	Nolan Ryan, 1977
21	Nolan Ryan, 1976

Saves: Most, season

46	Bryan Harvey, 1991
37	LEE SMITH, 1995
36	TROY PERCIVAL, 1996
31	Donnie Moore, 1985
27	TROY PERCIVAL, 1997
27	Minnie Rojas, 1967

Shutouts: Most, season

11	Dean Chance, 1964
9	Nolan Ryan, 1972
7	Nolan Ryan, 1976
7	Frank Tanana, 1977
6	Jim McGlothlin, 1967

Wins: Most, season

22	Nolan Ryan, 1974
22	Clyde Wright, 1970
21	Nolan Ryan, 1973
20	Dean Chance, 1964
20	Andy Messersmith, 1971
20	Bill Singer, 1973

K: Most, season

383	Nolan Ryan, 1973
367	Nolan Ryan, 1974
341	Nolan Ryan, 1977
329	Nolan Ryan, 1972
327	Nolan Ryan, 1976

Win pct: Highest, season

.773	Bert Blyleven, 1989
.704	MARK LANGSTON, 1991
.692	Geoff Zahn, 1982
.690	Dean Chance, 1964
.682	MARK LANGSTON, 1995

ERA: Lowest, season

1.65	Dean Chance, 1964
2.28	Nolan Ryan, 1972
2.40	CHUCK FINLEY, 1990
2.43	Frank Tanana, 1976
2.52	Andy Messersmith, 1969

Most pinch-hit homers, season

4	JACK HOWELL, 1996
3	Joe Adcock, 1966
3	George Hendrick, 1987

Most pinch-hit homers, career

7	JACK HOWELL, 1985-1997
4	George Hendrick, 1985-1988
4	Ruppert Jones, 1985-1987

Longest hitting streak

25	Rod Carew, 1982
23	JIM EDMONDS, 1995
22	Sandy Alomar, 1970
21	Bobby Grich, 1981
20	Bobby Grich, 1979

Most consecutive scoreless innings

36	Jim McGlothlin, 1967

No-hit games

Bo Belinsky, LA vs Bal AL, 2-0; May 5, 1962.

Clyde Wright, Cal vs Oak AL, 4-0; July 3, 1970.

Nolan Ryan, Cal at KC AL, 3-0; May 15, 1973.

Nolan Ryan, Cal at Det AL, 6-0; July 15, 1973.

Nolan Ryan, Cal vs Min AL, 4-0; Sept. 28, 1974.

Nolan Ryan, Cal vs Bal AL, 1-0; June 1, 1975.

Mike Witt, Cal at Tex AL, 1-0; Sept. 30, 1984 (perfect game).

MARK LANGSTON (7 innings) and Mike Witt (2 innings), Cal vs Sea AL, 1-0; April 11, 1990.

ACTIVE PLAYERS in caps.

Players' years of service are listed by the first and last years with this team and are not necessarily consecutive; all statistics record performances for this team only.

173

Texas Rangers

By Russell Becker, *Baseball Weekly*

Gold Glove catcher Ivan Rodriguez had a great offensive season, finishing fifth in the AL in hits.

1997 Rangers: Wetteland had little to close

Conventional wisdom held that the lack of a top-notch closer was the key reason Texas was knocked out by the Yankees in the first round of the 1996 playoffs, and by getting the one from the team that beat them, World Series MVP John Wetteland, the Rangers were automatic World Series contenders. So much for conventional wisdom. The Rangers were in contention through the All-Star break but slumped badly in the second half. They finished 77-85, 13 games out of first place.

Blame can be affixed to the usual suspects of injuries and bad play. Juan Gonzalez, league MVP in 1996, missed the first month of the season, and Will Clark and Mark McLemore the last. Also missing huge chunks of time were pitchers Roger Pavlik, John Burkett, Danny Patterson and Xavier Hernandez. DH Mickey Tettleton, bothered by a knee injury, retired. When the club fell off the pace, third baseman Dean Palmer, staff ace Ken Hill and left-handed setup man Ed Vosberg were traded.

Young players counted on to contribute failed. Benji Gil was handed the regular shortstop job, but didn't keep it. He finished with a .224 batting average and 19 errors. Damon Buford was the every-day center fielder for most of the season and played dazzling defense at times, but he hit .224 and the club traded for Tom Goodwin. Rookie pitcher Julio Santana's results (4-6, 6.75 ERA) didn't match his potential.

The rotation at times included the likes of Terry Clark, Tanyon Sturtze, Jose Alberro and Eric Moody, so it was no surprise that the rotation that won 75 games in 1996 fell to fewer than 50 victories in 1997. The typical September lineup included Domingo Cedeno and Alex Diaz as regulars. Untested third baseman Fernando Tatis was summoned from AA to replace Palmer. It wasn't the team the Rangers envisioned when they broke camp.

There were the usual standouts: Gonzalez hit .296 with 42 home runs and

Team MVP

Ivan Rodriguez: "Pudge" Rodriguez's arm strikes fear into opposing base runners. Rangers management was equally frightened at mid-season when they thought they'd have to trade him or lose him to free agency. But in the midst of his best offensive year (.313, 20 homers, 77 RBI), baseball's best defensive catcher signed a five-year, $42 million deal.

131 RBI despite playing only 133 games. Ivan Rodriguez, who signed a five-year deal when he was on the verge of being traded, played his usual Gold Glove defense and hit .313 with a career-high 20 homers. Rusty Greer also had a career high in homers, with 26, and he batted .321 and probably led the league in diving catches.

Darren Oliver emerged as the top winner on the pitching staff, winning 13 games and turning in a career-high 201⅓ innings. Wetteland had 31 saves, and his 1.94 ERA was almost a full run lower than when he led the league in 1996 with 43 saves. Danny Patterson emerged as a more-than-competent setup man.

The most pleasant surprise was Lee Stevens, who ended up playing regularly at first base, at DH and in the outfield because of injuries to Tettleton, Clark and Jim Leyritz. He responded with a .300 batting average and 21 homers. Looking to the future, it appears that the Rangers have their third baseman in Tatis. He finished with eight homers in 223 at-bats. However, Tatis' .256 average isn't enough to assure him of a job when the club goes to spring training next season. "I can't say any of the young guys will be on the ballclub next year," manager Johnny Oates said. The 22-year-old Tatis won't be at the forefront of a youth movement, because the talent in the farm system is at least another year away.

1997 Rangers: Week-by-week notes

These notes were excerpted from the following issues of Baseball Weekly.

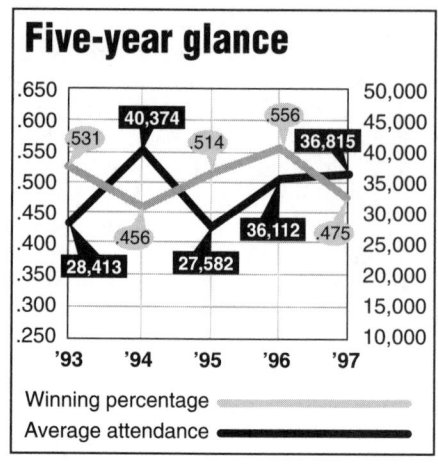

Five-year glance

Winning percentage
Average attendance

▶**April 16:** The Rangers miss outfielder Juan Gonzalez and first baseman Will Clark, their No. 4 and No. 5 hitters, who are out with hand injuries, not to mention departed free agents Darryl Hamilton and Kevin Elster. The club had seven or fewer hits in six of the first seven games. The team that hit .283 and averaged 5.69 runs per game in '96 hit .218 and scored 4.86 runs in the early going.

▶**April 23:** Roger Pavlik etched his name in the record books, but not in a way he'll want to remember. The right-hander became the first AL pitcher ever to walk the first four batters in a game when he did it in a 6-5 loss to the Blue Jays on April 18. Before that, Ken Hill, John Burkett, Bobby Witt and Darren Oliver had combined to allow just four runs in 30⅓ innings as Texas put together a four-game winning streak.

▶**May 7:** The Rangers were 14-10 in April even though Juan Gonzalez didn't play, Will Clark didn't make his first appearance until April 18, DH Mickey Tettleton went on the DL on April 18, leadoff batter Mark McLemore batted .167 and No. 3 hitter Rusty Greer drove in just seven runs. As a team they hit .249, second lowest in the league. They held their own because of the pitching, which had an ERA of 3.80 for the month, second best in the AL, behind the Blue Jays' 3.73.

▶**May 14:** Even though Juan Gonzalez doesn't quite have his timing back, he drove in 12 runs in his first eight games, exploding for a grand slam and six RBI in the Rangers' 11-5 win on May 10 against the Red Sox.

▶**May 28:** The pitching staff that kept the Rangers in the upper echelons of the division in the early going took two major hits last week. Roger Pavlik had surgery on May 23 to remove bone chips from the back of his right elbow and is expected to be out at least 12 weeks, and reliever

Danny Patterson, 4-3 with a 1.54 ERA, went on the DL with a partial tear of his right rotator cuff.

▶**June 4:** Will Clark hit .394 in May, the best-ever mark for a Ranger in the month.

▶**June 11:** Closer John Wetteland worked 3⅔ innings in a 6-3 victory against the Twins on June 5, his longest outing since 1990. Wetteland, who was 3-0 with a 1.09 ERA after the game, got through the stint with an economical 33 pitches.

▶**June 18:** Rangers leadoff hitters are last in the AL in batting average, on-base percentage, runs and stolen bases. Until June 14, third baseman Dean Palmer had gone 27 games without a homer, the longest drought of his career.

▶**June 25:** Second baseman Mark McLemore is back atop the lineup, after tearing a ligament in his right thumb in the first game of the season and finally going on the DL on May 15. In his first eight games back at leadoff, he hit .316 and scored six runs.

▶**July 2:** Pitching and defense are the big reasons why Texas is watching the Mariners disappear over the horizon. After their fifth three-error game, a 7-4 loss to the A's on June 27, the Rangers were on pace to commit 132 miscues, compared with 87 last year. Rangers starters were 75-47 in 1996, but were 25-32 through June 29.

▶**July 10:** Veteran slugger Mickey Tettleton announced his retirement on July 6. Tettleton finished his 14-year career with 245 home runs and 732 RBI. He ranks eighth in major league history in home runs by a switch-hitter and was 11th among active players with 949 walks.

▶**July 16:** Bobby Witt is among the four biggest winners in the majors since last year's All-Star break. The right-hander was 19-8 in that period, and he's up there with Roger Clemens (20-8), Pat Hentgen (20-10) and Denny Neagle (19-7).

▶**July 23:** The Rangers' chances of repeating as division champs continue to fade. They dropped to a season-worst three under .500 with a 6-5 loss to the Tigers on July 19 and are seven games behind the Mariners in the AL West. Texas is 9-21 in one-run games.

▶**July 30:** The Rangers appeared to acknowledge that defending the division title is a lost cause when they traded Dean Palmer to the Royals for center fielder Tom Goodwin. The deal came on July 25, with the club 9½ games out of first. Palmer, 28, was making $4.8 million and can be a free agent at the end of season.

▶**Aug. 6:** On July 31, All-Star catcher Ivan Rodriguez agreed to a five-year, $42 million deal that takes effect next season. The Rodriguez signing gives the Rangers the best catching tandem in baseball. Two days earlier, as a hedge against losing Rodriguez, they traded Ken Hill to the Angels for Jim Leyritz.

▶**Aug. 13:** The Rangers broke camp in April with a rotation of Ken Hill, John Burkett, Darren Oliver, Bobby Witt and Roger Pavlik. Flash forward to August. Only Oliver and Witt remain in the rotation. Hill was traded to the Angels. Pavlik went on the disabled list on May 7 and isn't close to returning. Burkett left his Aug. 4 start before the sixth inning because of fatigue in his right shoulder and went on the DL for the first time in his career.

▶**Aug. 20:** On Aug. 16 in Yankee Stadium, where he helped win the World Series last year, John Wetteland pitched two perfect innings, was the winning pitcher in an 8-5 victory in 10 innings, and doubled in a run and scored in the 10th. The Rangers lost their DH when Ivan Rodriguez moved behind the plate to replace Jim Leyritz after the eighth inning.

▶**Aug. 27:** Left fielder Rusty Greer had the biggest night of his career on Aug. 22, hitting two homers and driving in six runs, his most for a single game. To prove it wasn't a fluke, Greer did it again the next day—two more homers and six more RBI.

▶**Sept. 3:** Left-hander Darren Oliver was 9-4 with 3.68 ERA from June 1 through the end of August; the team's other starting pitchers were 11-32 with an ERA just under 6.00.

▶**Sept. 10:** The Rangers rallied from a five-run deficit in the ninth inning to defeat the Dodgers 13-12 on Sept. 2, as Rusty Greer hit a two-out single to drive in the game-winner. It was the fourth time this season that Greer drove in the deciding run in the team's final at-bat.

▶**Sept. 17:** Rookie third baseman Fernando Tatis was reunited with his father last week. Tatis lost track of his father when he was 4 years old, and Fernando Sr. left the Dominican Republic. The two were reunited by phone when a friend of Fernando Sr. saw a story about the younger Tatis' search for his father, who had played for the Astros' minor league system in the early '70s. They met in person when Fernando Sr. traveled to Arlington with his family.

▶**Oct. 1:** The news in September wasn't all bad. Juan Gonzalez set a club record with 10 homers in the final month and tied another team record with 26 RBI, and Ivan Rodriguez hit his 20th homer on Sept. 27, a club record for a catcher.

QUOTE OF THE YEAR

"Make the last-place manager pick the All-Star team as punishment for finishing last."
—Manager Johnny Oates, on the thankless task of picking All-Star reserves

TEXAS RANGERS 1997 final stats

BATTERS	BA	SLG	OBA	G	AB	R	H	TB	2B	3B	HR	RBI	BB	SO	SB	CS	E
Brown	.400	1.000	.400	4	5	1	2	5	0	0	1	1	0	0	0	0	1
W. Clark	.326	.496	.400	110	393	56	128	195	29	1	12	51	49	62	0	0	4
Greer	.321	.531	.405	157	601	112	193	319	42	3	26	87	83	87	9	5	12
Rodriguez	.313	.484	.360	150	597	98	187	289	34	4	20	77	38	89	7	3	7
Stevens	.300	.514	.336	137	426	58	128	219	24	2	21	74	23	83	1	3	3
Gonzalez	.296	.589	.335	133	533	87	158	314	24	3	42	131	33	107	0	0	4
Cedeno	.282	.400	.334	113	365	49	103	146	19	6	4	36	27	77	3	3	17
Leyritz	.277	.393	.379	121	379	58	105	149	11	0	11	64	60	78	2	1	3
Ripken	.276	.374	.300	71	203	18	56	76	9	1	3	24	9	32	0	1	5
McLemore	.261	.330	.338	89	349	47	91	115	17	2	1	25	40	54	7	5	8
Goodwin	.260	.336	.314	150	574	90	149	193	26	6	2	39	44	88	50	16	3
Tatis	.256	.404	.297	60	223	29	57	90	9	0	8	29	14	42	3	0	7
Simms	.252	.459	.298	59	111	13	28	51	8	0	5	22	8	27	0	1	2
Buford	.224	.339	.287	122	366	49	82	124	18	0	8	39	30	83	18	7	3
Gil	.224	.325	.263	110	317	35	71	103	13	2	5	31	17	96	1	2	19
Diaz	.222	.333	.268	28	90	8	20	30	4	0	2	12	5	13	1	1	1
Newson	.213	.462	.333	81	169	23	36	78	10	1	10	23	31	53	3	0	5
Mercedes	.213	.298	.302	23	47	4	10	14	4	0	0	4	6	25	0	0	1
Devereaux	.208	.250	.275	29	72	8	15	18	3	0	0	7	7	10	1	0	0
Frias	.192	.231	.222	14	26	4	5	6	1	0	0	1	1	4	0	0	0
Sagmoen	.140	.256	.174	21	43	2	6	11	2	0	1	4	2	13	0	0	0
Tettleton	.091	.318	.167	17	44	5	4	14	1	0	3	4	3	12	0	0	0
Silvestri	.000	.000	.000	2	4	0	0	0	0	0	0	0	0	1	0	0	0

PITCHERS	W-L	ERA	BA	G	GS	CG	GF	Sho	SV	IP	H	R	ER	HR	BB	SO
Wetteland	7-2	1.94	.182	61	0	0	58	0	31	65.0	43	18	14	5	21	63
Bailes	1-0	2.86	.231	24	0	0	7	0	0	22.0	18	9	7	2	10	14
Heredia	1-0	3.20	.197	10	0	0	3	0	0	19.2	14	9	7	2	16	8
Gunderson	2-1	3.26	.241	60	0	0	11	0	1	49.2	45	19	18	5	15	31
Patterson	10-6	3.42	.263	54	0	0	17	0	1	71.0	70	29	27	3	23	69
Oliver	13-12	4.20	.271	32	32	3	0	1	0	201.1	213	111	94	29	82	104
Moody	0-1	4.26	.329	10	1	0	3	0	0	19.0	26	10	9	4	2	12
Pavlik	3-5	4.37	.267	11	11	0	0	0	0	57.2	59	29	28	7	31	35
Hernandez	0-4	4.56	.262	44	0	0	20	0	0	49.1	51	27	25	7	22	36
Burkett	9-12	4.56	.307	30	30	2	0	0	0	189.1	240	106	96	20	30	139
Helling	3-3	4.58	.235	10	8	0	1	0	0	55.0	47	29	28	5	21	46
Vosberg	1-2	4.61	.277	42	0	0	16	0	0	41.0	44	23	21	3	15	29
Witt	12-12	4.82	.294	34	32	3	1	0	0	209.0	245	118	112	33	74	121
Whiteside	4-1	5.08	.296	42	1	0	8	0	0	72.2	85	45	41	4	26	44
T. Clark	1-7	6.00	.307	13	9	0	2	0	0	57.0	70	41	38	6	23	24
Santana	4-6	6.75	.323	30	14	0	3	0	0	104.0	141	86	78	16	49	64
Alberro	0-3	7.94	.303	10	4	0	2	0	0	28.1	37	33	25	4	17	11
Sturtze	1-1	8.27	.338	9	5	0	1	0	0	32.2	45	30	30	6	18	18
Eversgerd	0-2	20.25	.556	3	0	0	1	0	0	1.1	5	3	3	0	3	2

1998 preliminary roster

PITCHERS (23)
Scott Bailes
Mark Brandenburg
John Burkett
Ryan Glynn
Eric Gunderson
Rick Helling
Xavier Hernandez
Jonathan Johnson
Brandon Knight
Danny Lee Kolb
Alan Levine

Eric Moody
Darren Oliver
Danny Patterson
Matt Perisho
Julio Santana
Aaron Sele
Dan Smith
Tanyon Sturtze
Larry Thomas
John Wetteland
Matt Whiteside
Bobby Witt

CATCHERS (3)
Kevin Brown
Bill Haselman
Ivan Rodriguez

INFIELDERS (8)
Luis Alicea
Domingo Cedeno
Will Clark
Kevin Elster
Mark McLemore
Rob Sasser

Lee Stevens
Fernando Tatis

OUTFIELDERS (5)
Juan Gonzalez
Tom Goodwin
Rusty Greer
Roberto Kelly
Mark Little

Games played by position

PLAYER	G	C	1B	2B	3B	SS	OF	DH
Brown	4	4	0	0	0	0	0	0
Buford	122	0	0	0	0	0	117	3
Cedeno	113	0	0	65	3	43	0	2
W. Clark	110	0	100	0	0	0	0	7
Devereaux	29	0	0	0	0	0	28	0
Diaz	28	0	1	1	0	0	23	0
Frias	14	0	0	1	0	12	0	0
Gil	110	0	0	0	0	106	0	4
Gonzalez	133	0	0	0	0	0	64	69
Goodwin	150	0	0	0	0	0	147	0
Greer	157	0	0	0	0	0	153	2
Leyritz	121	69	24	0	0	0	0	22
McLemore	89	0	0	89	0	0	1	0
Mercedes	23	23	0	0	0	0	0	0
Newson	81	0	0	0	0	0	58	9
Ripken	71	0	9	25	13	31	0	0
Rodriguez	150	143	0	0	0	0	0	5
Sagmoen	21	0	1	0	0	0	17	1
Silvestri	2	0	0	0	1	1	0	0
Simms	59	0	2	0	0	0	19	28
Stevens	137	0	62	0	0	0	22	38
Tatis	60	0	0	0	60	0	0	0
Tettleton	17	0	0	0	0	0	0	13

Minor Leagues

Tops in the organization

BATTER	CLUB	AVG.	G	AB	R	H	HR	RBI
Mateo, Ruben	Chl	.314	99	385	63	121	12	67
Tatis, Fernando	Tul	.314	102	382	73	120	24	61
King, Cesar	Tul	.304	105	352	57	107	7	45
Murphy, Mike	OkC	.301	119	399	67	120	9	44
Morris, Warren	OkC	.300	136	526	81	158	13	78
Barkett, Andy	Tul	.299	130	471	82	141	8	65
Diaz, Alex	OkC	.286	105	426	65	122	12	49
Gorecki, Ryan	Chl	.273	101	388	52	106	0	24
O'Neill, Doug	Tul	.271	129	443	71	120	20	65
Frias, Hanley	OkC	.264	132	484	64	128	5	46

HOME RUNS
Smith, Bubba	OkC	27
Collier, Dan	Tul	26
Tatis, Fernando	Tul	24
O'Neill, Doug	Tul	20
Brown, Kevin	OkC	19

WINS
Lee, Corey	Chl	15
Silva, Ted	Tul	13
Knight, Brandon	Tul	13
Glynn, Ryan	Tul	9
Several Players Tied at		8

RBI
Smith, Bubba	OkC	94
Collier, Dan	Tul	79
Morris, Warren	OkC	78
Vessel, Andrew	Tul	75
Brumbaugh, Cliff	Chl	70

SAVES
Bailey, Cory	OkC	15
Venafro, Michael	Tul	11
Elder, David	Pul	6
Warren, Brian	OkC	6
Several Players Tied at		5

STOLEN BASES
Frias, Hanley	OkC	35
Nunez, Juan	Pul	26
Diaz, Alex	OkC	26
Sergio, Thomas	Pul	25
Dransfeldt, Kelly	Chl	25

STRIKEOUTS
Knight, Brandon	Tul	175
Lee, Corey	Chl	147
Silva, Ted	Tul	121
Glynn, Ryan	Tul	114
Several Players Tied at		113

PITCHER	CLUB	W-L	ERA	IP	H	BB	SO
Cook, Derrick	Chl	7- 4	2.84	92	86	27	67
Knight, Brandon	Tul	13- 8	3.35	183	165	57	175
Moody, Eric	OkC	5- 6	3.46	112	114	21	72
Lee, Corey	Chl	15- 5	3.47	161	132	60	147
Silva, Ted	Tul	13-10	4.09	172	178	42	121

Sick call: 1997 DL report

PLAYER	Days on the DL
John Burkett	26
Domingo Cedeno	37
Will Clark	52*
Juan Gonzalez	31
Eric Gunderson	20
Xavier Hernandez	58
Ken Hill	23
Mark McLemore	70*
Warren Newson	50*
Danny Patterson	28
Roger Pavlik	118
Billy Ripken	34*
Julio Santana	26
Mickey Tettleton	68

Indicates two separate terms on Disabled List.

1997 salaries

	Bonuses	Total earned salary
Juan Gonzalez, of	100,000	7,500,000
Ivan Rodriguez, c	175,000	6,825,000
Will Clark, 1b		5,657,365
John Wetteland, p	75,000	4,575,000
John Burkett, p		3,550,000
Roger Pavlik, p		2,850,000
Bobby Witt, p		2,000,000
Mark McLemore, 2b		1,800,000
Jim Leyritz, c	200,000	1,916,972
Tom Goodwin, of		1,050,000
Darren Oliver, p	75,000	1,075,000
Xavier Hernandez, p		600,000
Warren Newson, of	25,000	375,000
Matt Whiteside, p	75,000	375,000
Rusty Greer, of		358,333
Lee Stevens, 1b	70,000	300,000
Domingo Cedeno, ss	10,000	285,000
Billy Ripken, 2b		275,000
Alex Diaz, of		250,000
Damon Buford, of		225,000
Benji Gil, ss		200,000
Terry Clark, p		200,000
Mike Simms, of		200,000
Rick Helling, p		165,000
Eric Gunderson, p		160,000
Wilson Heredia, p		150,000
Julio Santana, p		150,000
Bryan Eversgerd, p		150,000
Scott Bailes, p		150,000
Fernando Tatis, 3b		150,000

Average 1997 salary: $1,384,304
Total 1997 payroll: $42,913,425

179

Texas (1972-1997), includes Washington (1961-1971)

Runs: Most, career

631	Toby Harrah, 1969-1986	
571	RUBEN SIERRA, 1986-1992	
567	JUAN GONZALEZ, 1989-1997	
544	Frank Howard, 1965-1972	
482	Jim Sundberg, 1974-1989	

Hits: Most, career

1180	Jim Sundberg, 1974-1989
1174	Toby Harrah, 1969-1986
1141	Frank Howard, 1965-1972
1132	RUBEN SIERRA, 1986-1992
1060	Buddy Bell, 1979-1989

2B: Most, career

226	RUBEN SIERRA, 1986-1992
200	Jim Sundberg, 1974-1989
197	Buddy Bell, 1979-1989
196	JUAN GONZALEZ, 1989-1997
192	IVAN RODRIGUEZ, 1991-1997

3B: Most, career

43	RUBEN SIERRA, 1986-1992
30	Chuck Hinton, 1961-1964
27	Ed Brinkman, 1961-1975
27	Jim Sundberg, 1974-1989
24	Ed Stroud, 1967-1970

HR: Most, career

256	JUAN GONZALEZ, 1989-1997
246	Frank Howard, 1965-1972
154	DEAN PALMER, 1989-1997
153	RUBEN SIERRA, 1986-1992
149	Larry Parrish, 1982-1988

RBI: Most, career

790	JUAN GONZALEZ, 1989-1997
701	Frank Howard, 1965-1972
656	RUBEN SIERRA, 1986-1992
568	Toby Harrah, 1969-1986
522	Larry Parrish, 1982-1988

SB: Most, career

161	Bump Wills, 1977-1981
153	Toby Harrah, 1969-1986
144	Dave Nelson, 1970-1975
129	Oddibe McDowell, 1985-1994
98	JULIO FRANCO, 1989-1993

BB: Most, career

708	Toby Harrah, 1969-1986
575	Frank Howard, 1965-1972
544	Jim Sundberg, 1974-1989
435	Mike Hargrove, 1974-1978
404	Pete O'Brien, 1982-1988

BA: Highest, career

.319	Al Oliver, 1978-1981
.312	RUSTY GREER, 1994-1997
.307	JULIO FRANCO, 1989-1993
.303	Mickey Rivers, 1979-1984
.296	RAFAEL PALMEIRO, 1989-1993

On-base avg: Highest, career

.399	Mike Hargrove, 1974-1978
.392	RUSTY GREER, 1994-1997
.382	JULIO FRANCO, 1989-1993
.367	Frank Howard, 1965-1972
.366	RAFAEL PALMEIRO, 1989-1993

Slug avg: Highest, career

.557	JUAN GONZALEZ, 1989-1997
.503	Frank Howard, 1965-1972
.500	RUSTY GREER, 1994-1997
.474	RAFAEL PALMEIRO, 1989-1993
.471	RUBEN SIERRA, 1986-1992

Games started: Most, career

313	Charlie Hough, 1980-1990
256	BOBBY WITT, 1986-1997
190	Fergie Jenkins, 1974-1981
186	KEVIN BROWN, 1986-1994
155	Dick Bosman, 1966-1973

Complete games: Most, career

98	Charlie Hough, 1980-1990
90	Fergie Jenkins, 1974-1981
55	Gaylord Perry, 1975-1980
40	KEVIN BROWN, 1986-1994
36	Joe Coleman, 1965-1970

Saves: Most, career

134	Jeff Russell, 1985-1996
83	Ron Kline, 1963-1966
64	Darold Knowles, 1967-1977
58	Tom Henke, 1982-1994
37	Jim Kern, 1979-1981

Shutouts: Most, career

17	Fergie Jenkins, 1974-1981
12	Gaylord Perry, 1975-1980
11	Charlie Hough, 1980-1990
9	Dick Bosman, 1966-1973
8	Jim Bibby, 1973-1984

Wins: Most, career

139	Charlie Hough, 1980-1990
99	BOBBY WITT, 1986-1997
93	Fergie Jenkins, 1974-1981
78	KEVIN BROWN, 1986-1994
70	KENNY ROGERS, 1989-1995

K: Most, career

1452	Charlie Hough, 1980-1990
1375	BOBBY WITT, 1986-1997
939	Nolan Ryan, 1989-1993
895	Fergie Jenkins, 1974-1981
742	KEVIN BROWN, 1986-1994

Win pct: Highest, career

.578	KENNY ROGERS, 1989-1995
.567	Nolan Ryan, 1989-1993
.564	Fergie Jenkins, 1974-1981
.549	KEVIN BROWN, 1986-1994
.548	ROGER PAVLIK, 1992-1997

ERA: Lowest, career

3.26	Gaylord Perry, 1975-1980
3.35	Dick Bosman, 1966-1973
3.41	Jon Matlack, 1978-1983
3.43	Nolan Ryan, 1989-1993
3.51	Joe Coleman, 1965-1970

Runs: Most, season

124	RAFAEL PALMEIRO, 1993
116	IVAN RODRIGUEZ, 1996
115	RAFAEL PALMEIRO, 1991
112	RUSTY GREER, 1997
111	Frank Howard, 1969

Hits: Most, season

210	Mickey Rivers, 1980
209	Al Oliver, 1980
203	RAFAEL PALMEIRO, 1991
203	RUBEN SIERRA, 1991
201	JULIO FRANCO, 1991

2B: Most, season

49	RAFAEL PALMEIRO, 1991	
47	IVAN RODRIGUEZ, 1996	
44	RUBEN SIERRA, 1991	
43	Al Oliver, 1980	
42	Buddy Bell, 1979	
42	RUSTY GREER, 1997	
42	Larry Parrish, 1984	

3B: Most, season

14	RUBEN SIERRA, 1989
12	Chuck Hinton, 1963
10	David Hulse, 1993
10	RUBEN SIERRA, 1986
10	Ed Stroud, 1968

HR: Most, season

48	Frank Howard, 1969
47	JUAN GONZALEZ, 1996
46	JUAN GONZALEZ, 1993
44	Frank Howard, 1968
44	Frank Howard, 1970

RBI: Most, season

144	JUAN GONZALEZ, 1996
131	JUAN GONZALEZ, 1997
126	Frank Howard, 1970
119	RUBEN SIERRA, 1989
118	Jeff Burroughs, 1974
118	JUAN GONZALEZ, 1993

SB: Most, season

52	Bump Wills, 1978
51	Dave Nelson, 1972
50	OTIS NIXON, 1995
45	Cecil Espy, 1989
44	Billy Sample, 1983

BB: Most, season

132	Frank Howard, 1970
113	Toby Harrah, 1985
109	Toby Harrah, 1977
107	Mike Hargrove, 1978
107	MICKEY TETTLETON, 1995

BA: Highest, season

.341	JULIO FRANCO, 1991
.333	Mickey Rivers, 1980
.332	RUSTY GREER, 1996
.329	WILL CLARK, 1994
.329	Buddy Bell, 1980

On-base avg: Highest, season

.432	Toby Harrah, 1985
.431	WILL CLARK, 1994
.420	Mike Hargrove, 1977
.416	Frank Howard, 1970
.408	JULIO FRANCO, 1991

Slug avg: Highest, season

.643	JUAN GONZALEZ, 1996
.632	JUAN GONZALEZ, 1993
.589	JUAN GONZALEZ, 1997
.574	Frank Howard, 1969
.554	RAFAEL PALMEIRO, 1993

Games started: Most, season

41	Jim Bibby, 1974
41	Fergie Jenkins, 1974
40	Charlie Hough, 1987
37	Fergie Jenkins, 1975
37	Fergie Jenkins, 1979

Complete games: Most, season

29	Fergie Jenkins, 1974
22	Fergie Jenkins, 1975
21	Gaylord Perry, 1976
18	Jon Matlack, 1978
17	Charlie Hough, 1984

Saves: Most, season

40	Tom Henke, 1993
38	Jeff Russell, 1989
31	Mike Henneman, 1996
31	JOHN WETTELAND, 1997
30	Jeff Russell, 1991

Shutouts: Most, season

6	Bert Blyleven, 1976
6	Fergie Jenkins, 1974
5	Jim Bibby, 1974
5	Bert Blyleven, 1977
4	Tom Cheney, 1963
4	Joe Coleman, 1969
4	Fergie Jenkins, 1975
4	Fergie Jenkins, 1978
4	Doc Medich, 1981
4	Camilo Pascual, 1968
4	Gaylord Perry, 1975
4	Gaylord Perry, 1977

Wins: Most, season

25	Fergie Jenkins, 1974
21	KEVIN BROWN, 1992
19	Jim Bibby, 1974
18	Charlie Hough, 1987
18	Fergie Jenkins, 1978

K: Most, season

301	Nolan Ryan, 1989
232	Nolan Ryan, 1990
225	Fergie Jenkins, 1974
223	Charlie Hough, 1987
221	BOBBY WITT, 1990

Win pct: Highest, season

.708	KENNY ROGERS, 1995
.692	Fergie Jenkins, 1978
.676	Fergie Jenkins, 1974
.656	KEVIN BROWN, 1992
.652	ROGER PAVLIK, 1996

ERA: Lowest, season

2.19	Dick Bosman, 1969
2.27	Jon Matlack, 1978
2.40	Dick Donovan, 1961
2.42	RICK HONEYCUTT, 1983
2.60	Pete Richert, 1965

Most pinch-hit homers, season

3	Brant Alyea, 1969
3	Don Lock, 1966
3	Tom McCraw, 1971
3	Darrell Porter, 1987
3	Rick Reichardt, 1970
3	Rusty Staub, 1980

Most pinch-hit homers, career

6	Brant Alyea, 1965-1969
6	Geno Petralli, 1985-1993

Longest hitting streak

24	Mickey Rivers, 1980
22	Jim Sundberg, 1978
21	Buddy Bell, 1980
21	JUAN GONZALEZ, 1996
21	Johnny Grubb, 1979
21	Al Oliver, 1980

Most consecutive scoreless innings

36	Charlie Hough, 1983

No-hit games

Jim Bibby, Tex at Oak AL, 6-0; July 30, 1973.

Bert Blyleven, Tex at Cal AL, 6-0; Sept. 22, 1977.

Nolan Ryan, Tex at Oak AL, 5-0; June 11, 1990.

Nolan Ryan, Tex vs Tor AL, 3-0; May 1, 1991.

KENNY ROGERS, Tex vs Cal AL, 4-0; July 28, 1994 (perfect game).

ACTIVE PLAYERS in caps.

Players' years of service are listed by the first and last years with this team and are not necessarily consecutive; all statistics record performances for this team only.

Oakland Athletics

By Andy Kuno, AP/Wide World Photos

Despite starting the season as a reserve, Matt Stairs slugged .582 and ended the year as the team's big bat.

1997 Athletics: No longer a Marked team

The Oakland Athletics lost free agents Terry Steinbach and Mike Bordick before the 1997 season and tried to compensate by adding former Bash Brother Jose Canseco. The change didn't click, mostly because it didn't address the team's primary need, pitching. The A's worsened a club record, as their 5.20 ERA in 1996 rose to 5.48. The A's set the all-time record for fewest complete games (two), tied the one for fewest shutouts (one) and allowed opponents a .300 batting average, the first time that had been done in the AL in half a century.

"Probably the expectations were too high," former General Manager Sandy Alderson said. The A's expected to put a heavy-hitting team on the field, even without Steinbach's 35 homers, by putting Canseco in a lineup with Geronimo Berroa and Mark McGwire. That combination didn't last. First to go was Berroa, who was traded to Baltimore on June 27 for pitcher Jimmy Haynes. Five weeks later, with the A's certain they wouldn't be able to re-sign McGwire, he was traded to St. Louis for pitchers T.J. Mathews, Eric Ludwick and Blake Stein. The day McGwire left was just about the end for Canseco, too. He was a non-factor the final two months of the season.

The A's liked some of what they saw from new pitchers, including rookie Brad Rigby and newcomer Haynes, and were pleased with the healthy return of Steve Karsay, who had missed the previous 2½ seasons with injuries. In the second half of the season, though, they lost starter after starter to injuries, including Karsay.

Offensively, left fielder Matt Stairs (.298, 27 homers) and first baseman Jason Giambi (.295, 41 doubles, 20 homers) had big years. Rookie Scott Spiezio not only became a terrific second baseman after being converted from third base halfway through the spring, but he also hit 14 homers. Right fielder Ben Grieve played only the final month of the season, but he hit .312 and had 24 RBI in as many games. Dave Magadan (.303)

Team MVP

Matt Stairs: Matt Stairs began the 1997 season with 11 major league homers. He had shown up in the majors four separate times for a total of 100 games. He finally got his chance and the result was 27 home runs, the most among those who finished the season in Oakland, and a .298 batting average in just 352 at-bats.

was a pinch-hitter until Canseco's injury forced Magadan into the lineup as the DH. He never stopped hitting.

A huge disappointment was third baseman Scott Brosius, who saw his average (.203) drop off 101 points from 1996 and his homers cut in half, from 22 to 11. Shortstop Tony Batista, coming off a .298 rookie year, suffered a 96-point tumble and took himself out of the A's plans for the future. Right-hander Ariel Prieto (6-8, 5.04) has yet to find his promise, and right-hander Willie Adams (3-5, 8.18) began the season as the A's No. 2 starter, but by the end of the year he was in the minors.

Manager Art Howe and all of his coaches will return for a third season. But it's clear to all that there will not be a fourth season if the A's don't improve in 1998. The recent past was bleak and the immediate road ahead is rough, but the A's do have hope on the horizon. Grieve moved like a rocket through the A's minor league system and seems ready to handle right field for the foreseeable future. Not too far behind him is shortstop Miguel Tejada. He is likely to start the season in AAA Edmonton, but could be the A's regular shortstop by mid-1998.

1997 Athletics: Week-by-week notes

These notes were excerpted from the following issues of Baseball Weekly.

▶**April 16:** Despite leading the AL West for the first time since 1994, the 7-4 A's batting average was only 10th in the league, and four of the 10 semiregulars were hitting under .200: shortstop Tony Batista, third baseman Scott Brosius, center fielder Ernie Young and catcher Izzy Molina. Outfielders Jose Canseco and Jason Giambi and catcher George Williams were only in the .250 range.

▶**April 30:** April has long been a pox on Jose Canseco's bat, and this time around (.242, three homers) is no exception. Normally the No. 3 hitter this year, Canseco got a rare chance to bat cleanup on April 26, and the third hitter, first baseman Mark McGwire, was walked five times, the last three intentionally.

▶**May 7:** Mark McGwire is going where no man has gone before. His home run in the third inning on April 30 dented the scoreboard at Cleveland's Jacobs Field. That blast was measured at 485 feet, the longest ever hit at the park. Since baseball began keeping track of distances, in 1992, McGwire has recorded the longest homers in six AL parks—in Cleveland, Detroit, Minnesota, Chicago, Toronto and Seattle.

▶**May 14:** Oakland lost nine of the first 12 games of their season-longest 13-game road trip. In seven of the 12 games, Oakland hitters struck out 10 or more times. The A's have won just eight of 26 games through May 11.

▶**May 21:** Mark McGwire isn't happy to read that he's as good as gone from the A's. The first baseman will be a free agent at the end of the season and has said he wants to play for a team that is a contender. With the A's buried in the cellar in the AL West, the belief in the Bay Area is that his days are numbered.

▶**May 28:** Willie Adams has been removed from the rotation and put into the bullpen. Mike Oquist was slated to start in Adams' spot on May 27 in

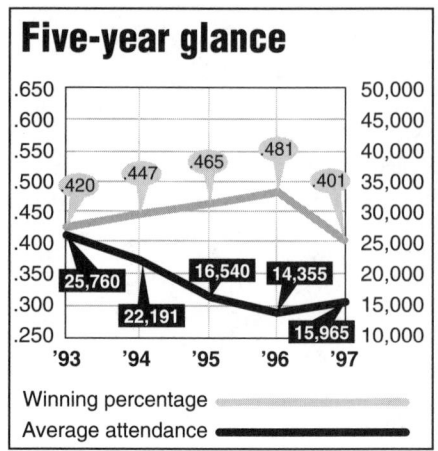

Five-year glance

Winning percentage
Average attendance

Kansas City. Manager Art Howe pulled Adams after 10 starts in which the right-hander went 2-5 with a 9.00 ERA.

▶**June 4:** The error committed by second baseman Scott Spiezio in the third inning on May 31 was his first after 21 errorless games. He leads AL second basemen in assists (173) and double plays (46).

▶**June 11:** With 23 homers in the club's first 62 games, Mark McGwire is on pace to hit 60 homers. On the other hand, the A's gave up 81 homers in the first 62 games, tied with Cleveland for the most yielded in the AL.

▶**June 18:** Mark McGwire played in his 67th game on June 15, all but two of the A's contests and quite an about-face for him. McGwire missed 32 games last year, 40 in 1995 and more than three-quarters of the team's games in 1993 and 1994 with heel problems.

▶**June 25:** Assistant general manager Billy Beane said the club isn't close to a deal to trade either outfielder Geronimo Berroa or, possibly, Mark McGwire. But with outfielder Matt Stairs hitting .350, Beane admits that Oakland has to find a way to get Stairs in the lineup more often, so Berroa may go.

▶**July 2:** The A's will have to wait a few weeks to see how good the trade was that sent Geronimo Berroa to Baltimore in exchange for pitcher Jimmy Haynes and a player to be named later. Haynes will get his first three or four starts at AAA Edmonton before Oakland makes a decision on bringing him up. Matt Stairs and promising Patrick Lennon are expected to platoon in right, and Jose Canseco will DH full-time.

▶July 10: Art Howe said he will start the second half of the season with four pitchers in place in the rotation: Steve Karsay (2-8), Ariel Prieto (6-5), Brad Rigby (0-2) and, if healthy, Mike Oquist (2-2). The fifth spot, Howe says, "is a question mark."

▶July 16: The first three games after the All-Star break saw starting pitchers hammered mercilessly by the Angels. After a 14-4 loss to Anaheim on July 11, Art Howe said he came close to snapping at the players. Howe didn't call a team meeting, but he did address the pitchers as a group.

▶July 23: Jose Canseco became the new Oakland Coliseum home run distance record holder with a 460-foot shot on July 19 off Frankie Rodriguez of Minnesota.

▶Aug. 6: A green-and-gold sign hung in the left field bleachers for home games this year. It contained a single word: "Optimism." Since the July 31 trade of Mark McGwire to St. Louis, the sign hasn't made an appearance. Of the three pitchers picked up in the McGwire trade, only T.J. Mathews came directly to Oakland. Eric Ludwick was moved to Edmonton and Blake Stein to AA Huntsville.

▶Aug. 13: The A's started the season with a core of power players. But Geronimo Berroa and Mark McGwire were traded. Jose Canseco and Scott Brosius went on the DL, and now Oakland's lineup reflects a young team with limited power. In 20 games through Aug. 10, the A's had been shut out five times and had not scored more than five runs in a game. Since McGwire's farewell, the A's have hit three homers.

▶Aug. 20: The A's seem to have finally broken through offensively. Oakland scored 28 runs on 37 hits, 10 of them home runs, in three games, Aug. 14-16. Before that, it needed nine games to score 28 runs.

▶Aug. 27: Art Howe has been so displeased by what he's seen from starter Ariel Prieto in two starts back from the DL that Howe considered sending him back to Edmonton. Prieto, 6-8 with a 5.04 ERA, has allowed 230 hits, walks and hit batters in 125 innings. Despite his troubles, Prieto leads A's starters in wins.

▶Sept. 3: Pinch-hitter and third baseman Dave Magadan made a small adjustment in his stance, and it has made all the difference in the world. Through Aug. 30 he had hits in eight consecutive at-bats, tying Brent Gates' 1994 club record. In the process, Magadan has pumped his average from .294 to .321. The 34-year-old veteran was hitting .270 at the All-Star break.

▶Sept. 10: The A's had been waiting since the June 1994 draft for the arrival of Ben Grieve. He made his A's debut last week, and the right fielder disappointed no one. The son of former Rangers general manager Tom Grieve broke in with three doubles and five RBI on Sept. 3. In the minors, Grieve hit 31 homers and drove in 136 runs in 127 games before his promotion.

▶Sept. 17: Given the chance to work as closer, newcomer T.J. Mathews pitched three times between Aug. 29 and Sept. 4, giving up seven runs in 2⅓ innings. Pitching coach Bob Cluck then worked with Mathews for two days, trying to get him to use a higher release point. Mathews then allowed one run in four innings in four appearances, picking up two wins and a save.

▶Oct. 1: Sandy Alderson is mulling turning over GM duties to Billy Beane. Alderson would concentrate more on the big picture as club president. On Sept. 28, he announced that the whole coaching staff would be retained despite a season in which the A's led the majors in losses.

QUOTE OF THE YEAR

"Once it hit the overhang, I thought,
That ball's radioactive."
—Outfielder Jose Canseco, on a 485-foot
Mark McGwire home run in Cleveland

OAKLAND ATHLETICS 1997 final stats

BATTERS	BA	SLG	OBA	G	AB	R	H	TB	2B	3B	HR	RBI	BB	SO	SB	CS	E
Grieve	.312	.473	.402	24	93	12	29	44	6	0	3	24	13	25	0	0	0
Magadan	.303	.391	.414	128	271	38	82	106	10	1	4	30	50	40	1	0	5
Stairs	.298	.582	.386	133	352	62	105	205	19	0	27	73	50	60	3	2	4
Lennon	.293	.388	.374	56	116	14	34	45	6	1	1	14	15	35	0	1	3
Giambi	.293	.495	.362	142	519	66	152	257	41	2	20	81	55	89	0	1	7
Mayne	.289	.406	.343	85	256	29	74	104	12	0	6	22	18	33	1	0	2
Williams	.289	.388	.397	76	201	30	58	78	9	1	3	22	35	46	0	1	6
McGwire	.284	.628	.383	105	366	48	104	230	24	0	34	81	58	98	1	0	6
Bournigal	.279	.333	.339	79	222	29	62	74	9	0	1	20	16	19	2	1	6
McDonald	.263	.394	.361	78	236	47	62	93	11	4	4	14	36	49	13	8	5
Sheldon	.250	.375	.308	13	24	2	6	9	0	0	1	2	1	6	0	0	2
Mashore	.247	.330	.370	92	279	55	69	92	10	2	3	18	50	82	5	4	2
Spiezio	.243	.388	.300	147	538	58	131	209	28	4	14	65	44	75	9	3	7
Brito	.238	.314	.285	66	172	17	41	54	5	1	2	14	10	38	1	0	5
Canseco	.235	.461	.325	108	388	56	91	179	19	0	23	74	51	122	8	2	5
Lesher	.229	.366	.275	46	131	17	30	48	4	1	4	16	9	30	4	1	3
Bellhorn	.228	.357	.324	68	224	33	51	80	9	1	6	19	32	70	7	1	9
Young	.223	.349	.303	71	175	22	39	61	7	0	5	15	19	57	1	3	4
Brosius	.203	.317	.259	129	479	59	97	152	20	1	11	41	34	102	9	4	10
Batista	.202	.330	.265	68	188	22	38	62	10	1	4	18	14	31	2	2	8
Tejada	.202	.333	.240	26	99	10	20	33	3	2	2	10	2	22	2	0	4
Molina	.198	.324	.219	48	111	6	22	36	3	1	3	7	3	17	0	0	2

PITCHERS	W-L	ERA	BA	G	GS	CG	GF	Sho	SV	IP	H	R	ER	HR	BB	SO
Johnstone	0-0	2.84	.292	5	0	0	1	0	0	6.1	7	2	2	0	7	4
Taylor	3-4	3.82	.254	72	0	0	45	0	23	73.0	70	32	31	3	36	66
Small	9-5	4.28	.294	71	0	0	22	0	4	96.2	109	50	46	6	40	57
Mathews	6-2	4.40	.293	24	0	0	14	0	3	28.2	34	18	14	5	12	24
Haynes	3-6	4.42	.262	13	13	0	0	0	0	73.1	74	38	36	7	40	65
Johnson	4-1	4.53	.272	38	0	0	12	0	2	45.2	49	28	23	4	31	43
Rigby	1-7	4.87	.302	14	14	0	0	0	0	77.2	92	44	42	14	22	34
Oquist	4-6	5.02	.266	19	17	1	0	0	0	107.2	111	62	60	15	43	72
Prieto	6-8	5.04	.306	22	22	0	0	0	0	125.0	155	84	70	16	70	90
Mohler	1-10	5.13	.301	62	10	0	16	0	1	101.2	116	65	58	11	54	66
Groom	2-2	5.15	.292	78	0	0	7	0	3	64.2	75	38	37	9	24	45
Kubinski	0-0	5.68	.255	11	0	0	3	0	0	12.2	12	9	8	2	6	10
Witasick	0-0	5.73	.304	8	0	0	1	0	0	11.0	14	7	7	2	6	8
Acre	2-0	5.74	.318	15	0	0	5	0	0	15.2	21	10	10	1	8	12
Karsay	3-12	5.77	.304	24	24	0	0	0	0	132.2	166	92	85	20	47	92
Reyes	3-4	5.82	.316	37	6	0	9	0	0	77.1	101	52	50	13	25	43
Wengert	5-11	6.04	.321	49	12	1	16	0	2	134.0	177	96	90	21	41	68
Telgheder	4-6	6.06	.324	20	19	0	0	0	0	101.0	134	71	68	15	35	55
Lorraine	3-1	6.37	.354	12	6	0	1	0	0	29.2	45	22	21	2	15	18
Haught	0-0	7.15	.279	6	0	0	2	0	0	11.1	12	9	9	3	6	11
Wojciechowski	0-2	7.84	.386	2	2	0	0	0	0	10.1	17	9	9	2	1	5
Adams	3-5	8.18	.307	13	12	0	0	0	0	58.1	73	53	53	9	32	37
Ludwick	1-4	8.25	.330	6	5	0	0	0	0	24.0	32	24	22	7	16	14
Lewis	2-0	9.64	.316	14	0	0	5	0	0	18.2	24	21	20	7	15	12
Montgomery	0-1	9.95	.385	4	0	0	0	0	0	6.1	10	7	7	2	8	1
Brewer	0-0	13.50	.444	3	0	0	1	0	0	2.0	4	3	3	1	2	1

1998 preliminary roster

PITCHERS (21)
Willie Adams
Tom Bennett
Doug Bochtler
Tom Candiotti
Carl Dale
Jeff D'Amico
Mike Fetters
Buddy Groom
Jimmy Haynes
Bill King
Tim Kubinski
T.J. Mathews
Mike Mohler
Mike Oquist
Ariel Prieto
Brad Rigby
Kenny Rogers
Aaron Small
Blake Stein
Billy Taylor
Jay Witasick

CATCHERS (2)
Ramon Hernandez
George Williams

INFIELDERS (9)
Kurt Abbott
Mike Blowers
Mark Bellhorn
Rafael Bournigal
Jason Giambi
Dave Magadan
Scott Spiezio
Miguel Tejada
Jorge Velandra

OUTFIELDERS (7)
Ryan Christenson
Ben Grieve
Brian Lesher
Shane Mack
Jason McDonald
Matt Stairs
Ernie Young

Games played by position

PLAYER	G	C	1B	2B	3B	SS	OF	DH
Batista	68	0	0	1	4	61	0	1
Bellhorn	68	0	0	17	40	1	0	3
Bournigal	79	0	0	7	0	74	0	0
Brito	66	0	0	27	27	14	0	0
Brosius	129	0	0	0	107	30	22	0
Canseco	108	0	0	0	0	0	44	60
Giambi	142	0	51	0	0	0	68	25
Grieve	24	0	0	0	0	0	24	0
Lennon	56	0	0	0	0	0	36	17
Lesher	46	0	3	0	0	0	32	3
Magadan	128	0	30	0	49	0	0	25
Mashore	92	0	0	0	0	0	89	0
Mayne	85	83	0	0	0	0	0	0
McDonald	78	0	0	0	0	0	74	0
McGwire	105	0	101	0	0	0	0	0
Molina	48	48	0	0	0	0	0	0
Sheldon	13	0	0	1	1	12	0	0
Spiezio	147	0	0	146	1	0	0	0
Stairs	133	0	7	0	0	0	89	17
Tejada	26	0	0	0	0	26	0	0
Williams	76	67	0	0	0	0	0	1
Young	71	0	0	0	0	0	66	1

Sick call: 1997 DL report

PLAYER	Days on the DL
Tony Batista	16
Rafael Bournigal	30
Billy Brewer	22
Tilson Brito	22
Scott Brosius	22
Jose Canseco	52*
Steve Karsay	54
Patrick Lennon	23
Damon Mashore	64
Mike Oquist	37
Ariel Prieto	72*
Carlos Reyes	22
Brad Rigby	15
Scott Spiezio	17
Dave Telgheder	76
George Williams	53*
Jay Witasick	74
Steve Wojciechowski	72

* Indicates two separate terms on Disabled List.

Minor Leagues

Tops in the organization

BATTER	CLUB	AVG.	G	AB	R	H	HR	RBI
Grieve, Ben	Edm	.350	127	480	127	168	31	136
Neill, Mike	Hvl	.333	129	507	132	169	14	83
Hinch, A.J.	Edm	.328	134	458	93	150	24	97
Bowles, Justin	Mod	.327	107	394	66	129	7	51
Cromer, D.T.	Hvl	.323	134	545	100	176	15	121

HOME RUNS

Grieve, Ben	Edm	31
Coolbaugh, Mike	Hvl	30
Hinch, A.J.	Edm	24
Marcinczyk, T.R.	Mod	23
Tejada, Miguel	Hvl	22

WINS

Rivette, Scott	Hvl	12
Nelson, Chris	Hvl	12
Laxton, Brett	Vis	11
Price, Jamey	Edm	11
Abbott, Todd	Vis	11

RBI

Grieve, Ben	Edm	136
Coolbaugh, Mike	Hvl	132
Cromer, D.T.	Hvl	121
Hernandez, R.	Hvl	109
Chavez, Eric	Vis	100

SAVES

Weinberg, Todd	Hvl	23
Gunther, Kevin	Mod	17
Bussa, Todd	Hvl	15
Haught, Gary	Edm	11
Acre, Mark	Edm	11

STOLEN BASES

Espada, Josue	Vis	46
Smith, Demond	Hvl	41
Rosario, Omar	Ath	40
McDonald, J.	Edm	31
Soriano, Jose	Mod	28

STRIKEOUTS

Gregg, Kevin	Vis	136
Rivette, Scott	Hvl	129
Nelson, Chris	Hvl	124
Laxton, Brett	Vis	121
Noriega, Ray	Mod	119

PITCHER	CLUB	W-L	ERA	IP	H	BB	SO
Laxton, Brett	Vis	11- 5	2.99	139	141	50	121
Wallace, Flint	Mod	10- 4	3.73	99	105	34	59
Noriega, Ray	Mod	5- 8	4.04	156	161	69	119
King, Bill	Hvl	9- 7	4.19	176	216	28	103
Rivette, Scott	Hvl	12-10	4.31	165	199	50	129
O'Dell, Jacob	Vis	8- 5	4.54	151	159	47	117
Nelson, Chris	Hvl	12- 6	4.60	147	171	32	124
Lorraine, Andrew	Edm	8- 6	4.74	118	143	34	75
D'Amico, Jeffrey	Edm	8- 5	4.86	128	157	40	108
Leyva, Julian	Mod	4- 9	4.92	139	148	38	90

1997 salaries

	Bonuses	Total earned salary
Jose Canseco, of	225,000	4,725,000
Scott Brosius, 3b		2,550,000
Billy Taylor, p		575,000
Buddy Groom, p	25,000	390,000
Dave Magadan, inf	50,000	255,000
Mike Mohler, p		250,000
T.J. Mathews, p		240,000
Brent Mayne, c		225,000
Jason Giambi, of		205,000
Carlos Reyes, p		200,000
Ernie Young, of		195,000
Mike Oquist, p	20,000	195,000
Ariel Prieto, p		194,000
Rafael Bournigal, ss		182,500
Don Wengert, p		172,500
Dane Johnson, p		172,500
Dave Telgheder, p		165,000
Jimmy Haynes, p		165,000
George Williams, c		165,000
Matt Stairs, of		165,000
Tony Batista, ss		162,500
Tilson Brito, ss		160,000
Steve Karsay, p		160,000
Aaron Small, p		155,000
Steve Wojciechowski, p		154,000
Damon Mashore, of		154,000
Andrew Lorraine, p		154,000
Brian Lesher, of		152,000
Scott Spiezio, 2b		151,000
Patrick Lennon, of		150,000
Tim Kubinski, p		150,000
Jason McDonald, ss		150,000
Miguel Tejada, ss		150,000
Brad Rigby, p		150,000
Mark Bellhorn, 2b		150,000

Average 1997 salary: $388,400
Total 1997 payroll: $13,594,000

Oakland(1968-1997), includes Philadelphia (1901-1954) and Kansas City (1955-1967)

Runs: Most, career

1169	RICKEY HENDERSON, 1979-1995
997	Bob Johnson, 1933-1942
983	Bert Campaneris, 1964-1976
975	Jimmie Foxx, 1925-1935
969	Al Simmons, 1924-1944

Hits: Most, career

1882	Bert Campaneris, 1964-1976
1827	Al Simmons, 1924-1944
1705	Jimmy Dykes, 1918-1932
1640	RICKEY HENDERSON, 1979-1995
1617	Bob Johnson, 1933-1942

2B: Most, career

365	Jimmy Dykes, 1918-1932
348	Al Simmons, 1924-1944
319	Harry Davis, 1901-1917
307	Bob Johnson, 1933-1942
292	Bing Miller, 1922-1934
273	RICKEY HENDERSON, 1979-1995 (8)

3B: Most, career

102	Danny Murphy, 1902-1913
98	Al Simmons, 1924-1944
88	Frank Baker, 1908-1914
85	Eddie Collins, 1906-1930
82	Harry Davis, 1901-1917
70	Bert Campaneris, 1964-1976 (12)

HR: Most, career

363	MARK McGWIRE, 1986-1997
302	Jimmie Foxx, 1925-1935
269	Reggie Jackson, 1967-1987
254	JOSE CANSECO, 1985-1997
252	Bob Johnson, 1933-1942

RBI: Most, career

1178	Al Simmons, 1924-1944
1075	Jimmie Foxx, 1925-1935
1040	Bob Johnson, 1933-1942
941	MARK McGWIRE, 1986-1997
796	Sal Bando, 1966-1976

SB: Most, career

801	RICKEY HENDERSON, 1979-1995
566	Bert Campaneris, 1964-1976
376	Eddie Collins, 1906-1930
232	Bill North, 1973-1978
223	Harry Davis, 1901-1917

BB: Most, career

1109	RICKEY HENDERSON, 1979-1995
1043	Max Bishop, 1924-1933
853	Bob Johnson, 1933-1942
847	MARK McGWIRE, 1986-1997
820	Elmer Valo, 1940-1956

BA: Highest, career

.356	Al Simmons, 1924-1944
.339	Jimmie Foxx, 1925-1935
.337	Eddie Collins, 1906-1930
.321	Mickey Cochrane, 1925-1933
.321	Frank Baker, 1908-1914
.293	RICKEY HENDERSON, 1979-1995 (17)

On-base avg: Highest, career

.440	Jimmie Foxx, 1925-1935
.426	Ferris Fain, 1947-1952
.423	Eddie Collins, 1906-1930
.423	Max Bishop, 1924-1933
.412	RICKEY HENDERSON, 1979-1995

Slug avg: Highest, career

.640	Jimmie Foxx, 1925-1935
.584	Al Simmons, 1924-1944
.551	MARK McGWIRE, 1986-1997
.520	Bob Johnson, 1933-1942
.507	JOSE CANSECO, 1985-1997

Games started: Most, career

458	Eddie Plank, 1901-1914
340	Catfish Hunter, 1965-1974
288	Chief Bender, 1903-1914
267	Lefty Grove, 1925-1933
267	Rube Walberg, 1923-1933

Complete games: Most, career

362	Eddie Plank, 1901-1914
228	Chief Bender, 1903-1914
179	Lefty Grove, 1925-1933
168	Rube Waddell, 1902-1907
116	Catfish Hunter, 1965-1974 (8)

Saves: Most, career

320	DENNIS ECKERSLEY, 1987-1995
136	Rollie Fingers, 1968-1976
73	John Wyatt, 1961-1969
61	Jay Howell, 1985-1987
58	Jack Aker, 1964-1968

Shutouts: Most, career

59	Eddie Plank, 1901-1914
37	Rube Waddell, 1902-1907
36	Chief Bender, 1903-1914
31	Catfish Hunter, 1965-1974
28	Vida Blue, 1969-1977
28	Jack Coombs, 1906-1914

Wins: Most, career

284	Eddie Plank, 1901-1914
195	Lefty Grove, 1925-1933
193	Chief Bender, 1903-1914
171	Eddie Rommel, 1920-1932
161	Catfish Hunter, 1965-1974

K: Most, career

1985	Eddie Plank, 1901-1914
1576	Rube Waddell, 1902-1907
1536	Chief Bender, 1903-1914
1523	Lefty Grove, 1925-1933
1520	Catfish Hunter, 1965-1974

Win pct: Highest, career

.712	Lefty Grove, 1925-1933
.654	Chief Bender, 1903-1914
.637	Eddie Plank, 1901-1914
.632	Jack Coombs, 1906-1914
.615	Bob Welch, 1988-1994 (6)

ERA: Lowest, career

1.97	Rube Waddell, 1902-1907
2.15	Cy Morgan, 1909-1912
2.32	Chief Bender, 1903-1914
2.39	Eddie Plank, 1901-1914
2.60	Jack Coombs, 1906-1914
2.91	Rollie Fingers, 1968-1976 (8)

Runs: Most, season

152	Al Simmons, 1930
151	Jimmie Foxx, 1932
145	Nap Lajoie, 1901
144	Al Simmons, 1932
137	Eddie Collins, 1912
123	Reggie Jackson, 1969 (10)

Hits: Most, season

253	Al Simmons, 1925
232	Nap Lajoie, 1901
216	Al Simmons, 1932
214	Doc Cramer, 1935
213	Jimmie Foxx, 1932
187	JOSE CANSECO, 1988 (*)

2B: Most, season

53	Al Simmons, 1926
48	Nap Lajoie, 1901
48	Wally Moses, 1937
47	Harry Davis, 1905
47	Eric McNair, 1932
41	JASON GIAMBI, 1997 (15)

3B: Most, season

21	Frank Baker, 1912
19	Frank Baker, 1909
18	Danny Murphy, 1910
17	Danny Murphy, 1904

| 12 | Bert Campaneris, 1965 (*) |
| 12 | Phil Garner, 1976 (*) |

HR: Most, season

58	Jimmie Foxx, 1932
52	MARK McGWIRE, 1996
49	MARK McGWIRE, 1987
48	Jimmie Foxx, 1933
47	Reggie Jackson, 1969

RBI: Most, season

169	Jimmie Foxx, 1932
165	Al Simmons, 1930
163	Jimmie Foxx, 1933
157	Al Simmons, 1929
156	Jimmie Foxx, 1930
124	JOSE CANSECO, 1988 (13)

SB: Most, season

130	RICKEY HENDERSON, 1982
108	RICKEY HENDERSON, 1983
100	RICKEY HENDERSON, 1980
81	Eddie Collins, 1910
75	Bill North, 1976

BB: Most, season

149	Eddie Joost, 1949
136	Ferris Fain, 1949
133	Ferris Fain, 1950
128	Max Bishop, 1929
128	Max Bishop, 1930
118	Sal Bando, 1970 (10)

BA: Highest, season

.426	Nap Lajoie, 1901
.390	Al Simmons, 1931
.387	Al Simmons, 1925
.381	Al Simmons, 1930
.365	Eddie Collins, 1911
.325	RICKEY HENDERSON, 1990 (*)

On-base avg: Highest, season

.469	Jimmie Foxx, 1932
.467	MARK McGWIRE, 1996
.463	Jimmie Foxx, 1929
.463	Nap Lajoie, 1901
.461	Jimmie Foxx, 1935

Slug avg: Highest, season

.749	Jimmie Foxx, 1932
.730	MARK McGWIRE, 1996
.708	Al Simmons, 1930
.703	Jimmie Foxx, 1933
.653	Jimmie Foxx, 1934

Games started: Most, season

46	Rube Waddell, 1904
43	Eddie Plank, 1904
41	Catfish Hunter, 1974
41	Eddie Plank, 1905

Complete games: Most, season

| 39 | Rube Waddell, 1904 |

37	Eddie Plank, 1904
35	Jack Coombs, 1910
35	Chick Fraser, 1901
35	Eddie Plank, 1905
28	Rick Langford, 1980 (14)

Saves: Most, season

51 ·	DENNIS ECKERSLEY, 1992
48	DENNIS ECKERSLEY, 1990
45	DENNIS ECKERSLEY, 1988
43	DENNIS ECKERSLEY, 1991
36	Bill Caudill, 1984
36	DENNIS ECKERSLEY, 1993

Shutouts: Most, season

13	Jack Coombs, 1910
8	Vida Blue, 1971
8	Joe Bush, 1916
8	Eddie Plank, 1907
8	Rube Waddell, 1904
8	Rube Waddell, 1906

Wins: Most, season

31	Jack Coombs, 1910
31	Lefty Grove, 1931
28	Jack Coombs, 1911
28	Lefty Grove, 1930
27	Eddie Rommel, 1922
27	Rube Waddell, 1905
27	Bob Welch, 1990

K: Most, season

349	Rube Waddell, 1904
302	Rube Waddell, 1903
301	Vida Blue, 1971
287	Rube Waddell, 1905
232	Rube Waddell, 1907

Win pct: Highest, season

.886	Lefty Grove, 1931
.850	Chief Bender, 1914
.849	Lefty Grove, 1930
.821	Chief Bender, 1910
.818	Bob Welch, 1990

ERA: Lowest, season

1.30	Jack Coombs, 1910
1.39	Harry Krause, 1909
1.48	Rube Waddell, 1905
1.55	Cy Morgan, 1910
1.58	Chief Bender, 1910
1.82	Vida Blue, 1971 (10)

Most pinch-hit homers, season

4	Jeff Burroughs, 1982
3	Bob Cerv, 1957
3	Allie Clark, 1952
3	Frank Fernandez, 1970
3	Rich McKinney, 1977
3	Kite Thomas, 1952

Most pinch-hit homers, career

| 5 | Mike Aldrete, 1993-1995 |
| 5 | Jeff Burroughs, 1982-1984 |

| 5 | Gus Zernial, 1951-1957 |

Longest hitting streak

29	Billy Lamar, 1925
28	Bing Miller, 1929
27	Socks Seybold, 1901
27	Al Simmons, 1931
26	Bob Johnson, 1938
24	Carney Lansford, 1984

Most consecutive scoreless innings

53	Jack Coombs, 1910
43	Rube Waddell, 1905
37	Mike Torrez, 1976

No-hit games

Weldon Henley, Phi at StL AL, 6-0; July 22, 1905 (1st game).

Chief Bender, Phi vs Cle AL, 4-0; May 12, 1910.

Joe Bush, Phi vs Cle AL, 5-0; Aug. 26, 1916.

Dick Fowler, Phi vs StL AL, 1-0; Sept. 9, 1945 (2nd game).

Bill McCahan, Phi vs Was AL, 3-0; Sept. 3, 1947.

Catfish Hunter, Oak vs Min AL, 4-0; May 8, 1968 (perfect game).

Vida Blue, Oak vs Min AL, 6-0; Sept. 21, 1970.

Vida Blue (5 innings), Glenn Abbott (1 inning), Paul Lindblad (1 inning) and Rollie Fingers (2 innings), Oak vs Cal AL, 5-0; Sept. 28,1975.

Mike Warren, Oak vs Chi AL, 3-0; Sept. 29, 1983.

Dave Stewart, Oak at Tor AL, 5-0; June 29, 1990.

Rube Waddell, five innings, rain, Phi vs StL AL, 2-0; Aug. 15, 1905.

Jimmy Dygert (3 innings) and Rube Waddell (2 innings), five innings, rain, Phi vs Chi AL, 4-3; Aug. 29, 1906. (Waddell allowed hit and two runs in 6th, but rain caused game to revert to 5 innings).

Rube Vickers, five perfect innings, darkness, Phi at Was AL, 4-0; Oct. 5, 1907 (2nd game).

ACTIVE PLAYERS in caps.

Players' years of service are listed by the first and last years with this team and are not necessarily consecutive; all statistics record performances for this team only.

Leader from the franchise's current location is included. If not in the top five, leader's rank is listed in parenthesis; asterisk (*) indicates player is not in top 25.

Tampa Bay Devil Rays

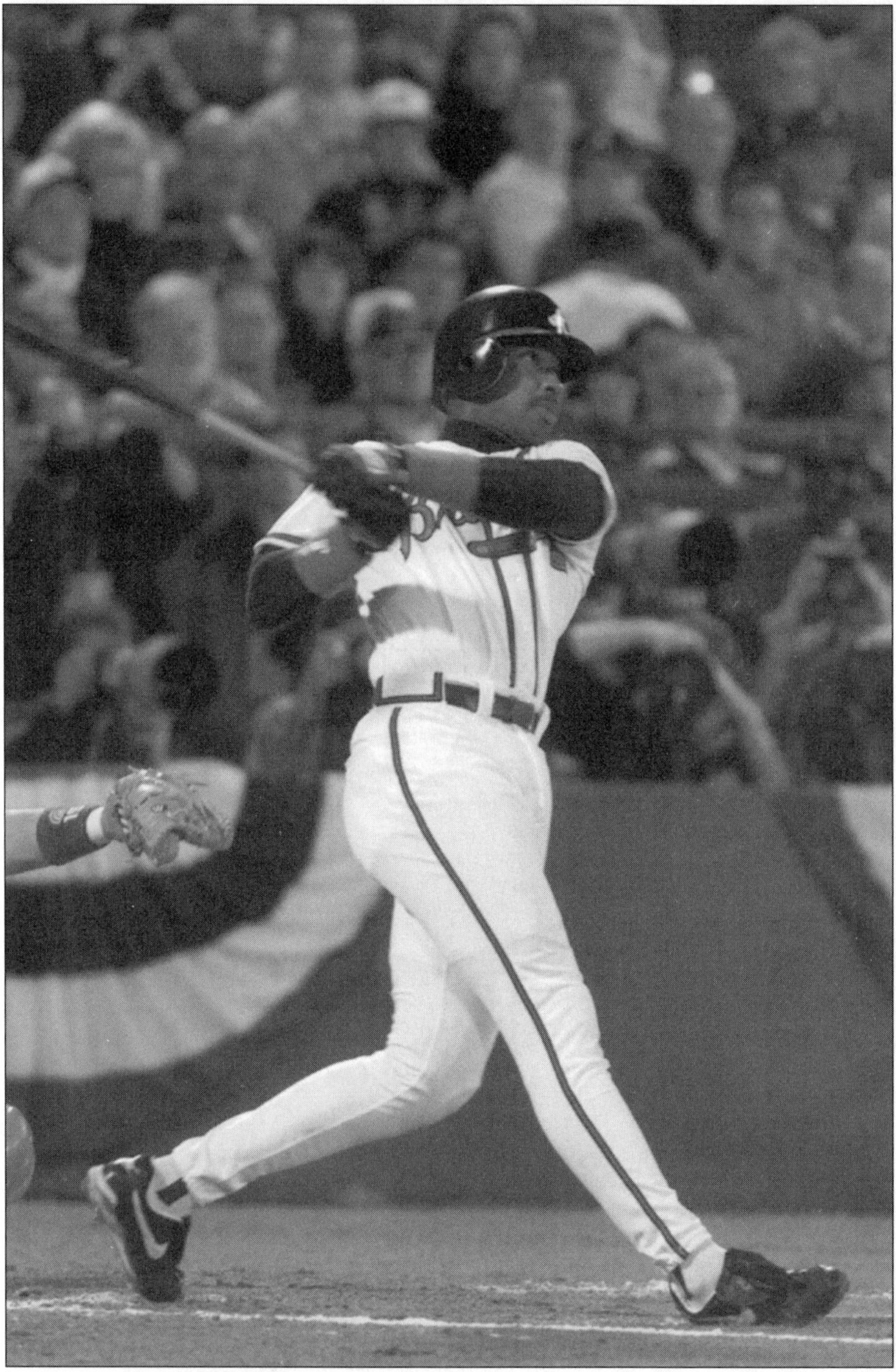

Former Braves first baseman Fred McGriff will most likely be Tampa Bay's main power source in 1998.

1998 Devil Rays will be young and fast

The Tampa Bay Devil Rays spent the better part of the seven-hour expansion draft picking young pitchers and speedy outfielders. Then they swung some blockbuster trades that will bring a little maturity to Tropicana Field next season as well. Within minutes of their final pick, general manager Chuck LaMar announced that the Rays had acquired first baseman and Tampa native Fred McGriff from Atlanta, shortstop Kevin Stocker from Philadelphia and catcher John Flaherty from San Diego. They also signed free-agent closer Roberto Hernandez from San Francisco, and in December they added starter Wilson Alvarez, another Giants free agent, who signed a five-year, $35 million contract. "We couldn't be more pleased with the way the expansion draft went," LaMar said. "We think we have a great combination of young players and experienced players. We're going to try to be as competitive as we can, as quick as we can. McGriff and [Roberto] Hernandez give us that opportunity."

The Devil Rays peddled the following players on draft day:

▶Outfielder Bobby Abreu, their third pick in the draft, to the Phillies for Stocker, who hit .266 last season.

▶Shortstop Andy Sheets, their 12th pick, and pitcher Brian Boehringer, their 15th pick, to the Padres for Flaherty, who hit .273 with 46 RBI.

▶First baseman Dmitri Young, their eighth pick, back to Cincinnati as the player to be named later in the previous week's acquisition of outfielder Mike Kelly from the Reds.

The Devil Rays spent most of the draft stockpiling pitching and speed. They drafted 18 pitchers, eight outfielders, eight infielders and one catcher before the trades were announced. Devil Rays manager Larry Rothschild said, "We drafted a lot of pitching, [including] some young guys who will be in the minor leagues who should come through. So I think in pitching, there's strength in numbers. . . . You need a lot to get a few through." The Devil

Rays also went for some speed, primarily in outfielders Quinton McCracken and Rich Butler, as well as second baseman Miguel Cairo. "We play on turf [at Tropicana Field], so we have to have speed," Rothschild said.

The Devil Rays tabbed Florida Marlins left-handed pitcher Tony Saunders as their first selection. Of course, Saunders is no stranger to Rothschild and Devil Rays pitching coach Rick Williams. Rothschild was Saunders' pitching coach this year with Florida, while Williams was his coach at AAA Charlotte, where he made three starts. The Devil Rays took McCracken from Colorado with their second pick.

McCracken, nicknamed "Q," stole 28 bases last year and will probably be a table setter with the Devil Rays, along with Cairo, who has stolen 127 bases in four minor league seasons. He led the American Association with 40 steals last season and was second in the league with 159 hits. Later on, the Devil Rays got a potential sleeper with their 22nd pick in outfielder Kerry Robinson from St. Louis. He hit .321 at AA Arkansas with 40 stolen bases.

Catchers Flaherty and Mike Difelice will get a look at a lot of pitchers: Tampa Bay took pitchers with 11 of their 14 picks in the second round. The Devil Rays took a flyer on Cleveland right-hander Albie Lopez with their 10th pick of the round. Once a bright prospect for the Indians, Lopez was just 3-7 with a 6.93 ERA in 37 appearances last season. Still, Rothschild loves his stuff. "I saw him pitch in spring training a couple of years ago, and he really pitched well," Rothschild said. "Maybe a fresh situation will invigorate him a little bit and let the ability come out." Lopez agreed a change of scenery will be good: "Cleveland had me going up and down, they had me in a setup role, in a long role, all over the place. I'm hoping I get to a place where I have a solid role." The Rays also took a third-round gamble on Braves lefty Terrell Wade, limited by injuries to 42 innings last season.

1997 Devil Rays: Week-by-week notes

These notes were excerpted from the following issues of Baseball Weekly.

▶**July 10:** The Rays' top executives and scouts are in full gallop preparing for the Nov. 18 expansion draft and upcoming free-agent season. Ten key members of the staff will spend the next three months on the road scouting every player in the major leagues while other staffers will be watching the minors. A $62 million renovation of Tropicana Field is more than halfway done and on target for an early 1998 completion.

▶**July 16:** The master plan calls for the major league manager to be hired at the end of the current season. So don't expect the firing of any current managers to necessarily change that timetable. General manager Chuck LaMar is looking for someone who, in addition to the standard qualifications, has teaching ability, communication skills and an understanding of the scouting and player development system.

▶**July 23:** Devil Rays management has high expectations for 1998 in terms of attendance. Managing general partner Vince Naimoli figures to sell out every game, for a first-season figure of more than 3.66 million. Single-game tickets are expected to go on sale Nov. 15; the Rays have sold about 21,000 season tickets and plan to cap those sales at 27,000. Tropicana Field is expected to hold about 45,200.

▶**July 30:** Right-hander Matt White, who received a $10.2 million bonus, got the first win of his pro career on July 24. Pitching for Hudson Valley in the Class A New York–Penn League, White held New Jersey to three hits over seven innings. Overall, White is 1-5 with a 6.46 ERA.

▶**Aug. 6:** Looking to be freed from their geographically challenged assignment to the AL West, the Devil Rays are hoping a radical realignment plan is approved. Chuck LaMar just returned from the Far East, where he met with Japanese and Korean baseball officials about striking a deal for a working agreement.

▶**Aug. 20:** Outfielder Alex Sanchez, of Charleston (S.C.) in the Class A South Atlantic League, leads all of pro baseball with 74 steals through Aug. 16, and Matt White has improved to 4-5 with a 4.57 ERA.

▶**Sept. 3:** The Devil Rays took another step to increase their worldwide presence last week, signing a working agreement with the Seibu Lions, one of the top clubs in Japanese baseball. The Lions will scout all levels of play in Japan on Tampa Bay's behalf, while the Rays will help Seibu find players for its four foreign-player slots.

▶**Sept. 10:** The Rays signed two promising 16-year-old Dominican shortstops: Nestor Fernandez, who is the nephew of Cleveland's Tony Fernandez, and Ramon Soler. Former Princeton infielder Jared Sandberg, nephew of Ryne, was named the organization's August player of the month after he batted .350 with 27 RBI and five home runs in the Appalachian League. Gulf Coast League left-hander Marquis Roberts' 0.51 ERA was the lowest in the league since Yankees closer Mariano Rivera's 0.17 in 1990.

▶**Sept. 24:** San Francisco's Wilson Alvarez, who will be one of the top left-handers on the free-agent market, said he would like to sign with the Rays because he is building a home in Sarasota.

▶**Oct. 1:** Among the potential Devil Ray managerial candidates, for which interviews could begin as early as this week, are Red Sox coach Grady Little, Dodgers coach Mike Scioscia, Rangers coach Bucky Dent, Padres coach Davey Lopes and Cubs AAA manager Tim Johnson. Other possible candidates are Angels coach Larry Bowa, Tigers coach Larry Parrish, Marlins coaches Jerry Manuel and Larry Rothschild, and Yankees coach Chris Chambliss.

QUOTE OF THE YEAR

"I think he's just trying to do too much."
—Player personnel director Bill Livesey, on right-hander Matt White, who had walked 12, hit eight batters and thrown four wild pitches in 16⅔ innings in Class A

1998 preliminary roster

PITCHERS (19)
Wilson Alvarez
Dan Carlson
Mike Duvall
Vaughn Eshelman
Rick Gorecki
Roberto Hernandez
Santos Hernandez
Jason Johnson
John LeRoy
Albie Lopez
Jim Mecir

Jose Paniagua
Bryan Rekar
Tony Saunders
Dennis Springer
Ramon Tatis
Terrell Wade
Rick White
Esteban Yan

CATCHERS (2)
Mike Difelice
John Flaherty

INFIELDERS (10)
Wade Boggs
Miguel Cairo
Steve Cox
Brooks Kieschnick
Aaron Ledesma
Fred McGriff
Herbert Perry
Bobby Smith
Paul Sorrento
Kevin Stocker

OUTFIELDERS (9)
Rich Butler
Mike Kelly
Dave Martinez
Quinton McCracken
Carlos Mendoza
Kerry Robinson
Bubba Trammell
Luke Wilcox
Randy Winn

Minor Leagues

Tops in the organization

BATTER	CLUB	AVG.	G	AB	R	H	HR	RBI
Berns, Robert	Pri	.327	64	245	53	80	9	61
Blosser, Greg	OkC	.308	106	367	73	113	24	59
Hoover, Paul	Pri	.303	66	251	55	76	4	37
Sandberg, Jared	Pri	.303	69	271	62	82	17	70
Scioneaux, D.	Hdv	.300	70	273	48	82	0	23
Quatraro, Matthew	Csc	.299	78	294	35	88	7	42
Romano, Scott	StP	.298	99	359	54	107	7	67
Fraraccio, Dan	StP	.296	129	463	67	137	1	63
Sanchez, Alex	Csc	.289	131	537	73	155	0	34
Carr, Dustin	Hdv	.288	74	281	46	81	5	47

HOME RUNS

Blosser, Greg	OkC	24
Sandberg, Jared	Pri	17
Several Players Tied at		11

WINS

Manias, James	StP	13
Ortega, Pablo	Csc	12
Callaway, M.	StP	11
Several Players Tied at		9

RBI

Sandberg, Jared	Pri	70
Becker, Brian	Csc	70
Romano, Scott	StP	67
Fraraccio, Dan	StP	63
Berns, Robert	Pri	61

SAVES

Daniels, John	StP	29
Benesh, Edward	Csc	15
Reyes, Eddy	Hdv	14
White, Rick	ORL	12

STOLEN BASES

Sanchez, Alex	Csc	92
Bain, Tyler	Csc	33
McCain, Marcus	Csc	26
Buccheri, Jim	StP	25
Patel, Manny	StP	24

STRIKEOUTS

Bowers, Cedrick	Csc	164
Ortega, Pablo	Csc	142
Kaufman, John	StP	121
Manias, James	StP	119
Several Players Tied at		109

PITCHER	CLUB	W-L	ERA	IP	H	BB	SO
Ortega, Pablo	Csc	12-10	2.86	189	173	30	142
Wheeler, Daniel	Hdv	6-7	3.00	84	75	17	81
Leon, Scott	Csc	6-12	3.17	156	151	41	109
Bowers, Cedrick	Csc	8-10	3.21	157	119	78	164
Callaway, Michael	StP	11-7	3.22	171	162	39	109
Kaufman, John	StP	9-5	3.37	150	138	66	121
Arrojo, Rolando	StP	5-6	3.43	89	73	13	73
Madison, Scott	Hdv	6-5	3.77	91	94	30	58
Manias, James	StP	13-5	3.78	171	163	40	119
White, Matt	Hdv	4-6	4.07	84	78	29	82

Atlanta Braves

By H. Darr Beiser, USA TODAY

A routine season: Greg Maddux was second in the NL in wins and ERA and was runner-up in Cy Young voting.

1997 Braves: Only the postseason mattered

Everything else in baseball seems to change but the Atlanta Braves. They just kept rolling, becoming the first team to win six straight division titles (discounting the 1994 strike season). Yet by their standards, anything short of winning the World Series is viewed as not enough. So the Braves' upset loss to the wild-card Florida Marlins, a team they beat by nine games in the NL East, was even more crushing than the previous year's World Series defeat by the Yankees.

As usual, the team's starting pitching was extraordinary. Denny Neagle led the league with 20 wins, and Greg Maddux was second with 19. John Smoltz and Tom Glavine combined for another 29 wins. Altogether the big four were 68-28 with a 2.79 earned run average. Surprisingly, Neagle at times was the anchor, lowering his ERA more than one-third of a run over the final two months, to 2.97. Maddux was his usual sensational self and just missed finishing with more wins than walks. He walked just 20 batters in 232⅔ innings. Two of the biggest moves of the year were the re-signings of Glavine and Maddux, ensuring that the four-man rotation is in place for at least three more seasons.

The offense was good, as shortstop Jeff Blauser made a strong comeback after two miserable seasons by batting .308 with 17 homers. Mr. Steady, third baseman Chipper Jones, again drove in more than 100 runs and was the only player on the club to score 100 runs. Right fielder Michael Tucker made a big impact, coming over from the Royals in the spring and providing consistent offense and defense.

Despite their gaudy record, the Braves did have some setbacks and deficiencies. They lost setup man Mike Bielecki for the season from an already-thin bullpen because of a rotator-cuff injury. Even closer Mark Wohlers slipped, blowing seven saves and finishing with a 3.50 ERA, compared with last year's 3.03. Also, center fielder Kenny Lofton was

Team MVP

Greg Maddux: Greg Maddux was in control again. In addition to his 19-4 record and 2.20 ERA, he easily led the majors with 0.77 walks per nine innings. He had streaks of 38 and 36 innings without a walk and posted three of the six lowest-pitch-count complete games of the year in the majors: 78, 86 and 90. He now has the lowest ERA over a six-year span since World War II, at 2.14 since 1992.

hobbled by injuries after a hot April and didn't give Atlanta much speed at the leadoff spot. He had 27 steals and led the league by being caught 20 times. No one on the club had more than 24 homers, and first baseman Fred McGriff had just 22, his fewest since 1987. While rookie outfielder Andruw Jones was superb defensively, he hit just .231 and was never given Jackie Robinson Award consideration.

The Braves were thrilled with what they saw from some of their youngsters, especially the way first baseman Randall Simon played after coming up in September. Simon went 6-for-14 and may be the club's first baseman of the future. His defense is sound too. Atlanta is looking at right-hander Kevin Millwood as a possible fifth starter. He was spotty at times but finished 5-3 with a 4.03 ERA. Another 1997 rookie who will help next season is reliever Mike Cather, a right-handed sidewinder who at the end of the season became the main setup man for Wohlers. Cather finished with a 2.39 ERA and even did a good job of getting out lefties.

Whatever the makeup of the 1998 Braves, Smoltz vows a strong return. "This organization is not going to put its head in the sand," he said. "We're going to fight hard. Maybe next year we'll be underdogs."

195

1997 Braves: Week-by-week notes

These notes were excerpted from the following issues of Baseball Weekly.

▶**April 9:** Right-hander Greg Maddux allowed three hits in eight innings on April 6, winning 4-0 in a game that lasted just one hour and 47 minutes, the fastest major league game in five years. He threw 89 pitches before closer Mark Wohlers came on to pitch the ninth.

▶**April 16:** This from Scott Boras, agent for Greg Maddux: "Greg has let the Braves know that the last time he signed with them, he did so for less [$27.5 million, when the Yankees offered $34 million] because he wanted to play there. But he's told them that this time he's going to get what he's worth."

▶**April 23:** How well is the trade for right fielder Michael Tucker working out? He's hitting .386 with one home run and 14 RBI. Jermaine Dye, who was sent to Kansas City for Tucker, is hitting .194 and was just placed on the DL.

▶**April 30:** Mark Wohlers has blown two of his last three save opportunities and admits he is having problems with his release point. He has been doing extra work on the side with pitching coach Leo Mazzone. Wohlers walked 10 in his first 11 appearances. Despite Wohlers' problems, the Braves were 17-5 and off to their best start in franchise history.

▶**May 7:** Left-hander Tom Glavine, who was 4-0 with a 1.64 ERA in April, was the NL pitcher of the month. Even when he lost his first game, on May 3 to the Pirates, he gave up just one earned run and lowered his ERA to 1.56.

▶**May 14:** Catcher Javier Lopez watched his batting average slip 71 points in his last 33 at-bats before homering on his first at-bat on May 10, snapping an 0-for-19 skid.

▶**May 21:** Michael Tucker doubled with two outs in the ninth inning on May 16 to break up the bid for a no-hitter by St. Louis' Alan Benes. The Braves went on to win 1-0 in 13 innings. The next day, center fielder Kenny Lofton went 5-for-5,

and the Braves pounded the Cardinals for 19 hits in an 11-6 win. Even right-hander John Smoltz had two hits, to lift his batting average to .435 (10-for-23).

▶**May 28:** He remains one of the best pitchers in the game, and Tom Glavine was rewarded for it last week as he signed a four-year deal worth $33 million, with a Braves option for a fifth year at $9 million. There is a $1 million buyout for that year, bringing the guaranteed money to $34 million.

▶**June 18:** Kenny Lofton missed the first two games against the Orioles last week because of back spasms. The Braves lost both days. Lofton was back in the lineup on June 15.

▶**June 25:** John Smoltz has gone winless in his last five starts. After going 14-1 in his first 16 starts last season, he is just 6-6 with a 3.19 ERA this year. His biggest problem recently has been the long ball—six homers in his last 19 innings. On June 17, manager Bobby Cox picked up his 900th win. He is second to Tony La Russa (1,439) among active managers.

▶**July 2:** The Braves have stolen 67 bases, though Kenny Lofton has just 19. The biggest surprise on the base paths has been third baseman Chipper Jones, who has stolen 11 bases and hasn't been caught yet. Overall, the Braves' stolen base success rate is 71.3%.

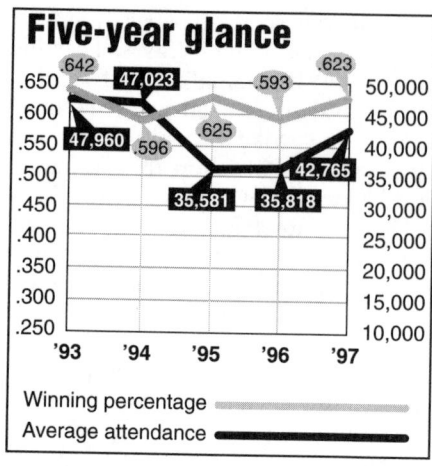

Five-year glance

.642 · 47,023 · .593 · .623
.596 · .625
47,960
35,581 · 35,818 · 42,765

'93 '94 '95 '96 '97

Winning percentage
Average attendance

▶**July 10:** In one of his best starts ever, on July 2, Greg Maddux shut out the Yankees 2-0. He threw just 86 pitches (63 strikes), allowed three singles and pitched to just one batter over the minimum. Maddux has now gone five consecutive starts without a walk.

▶**July 16:** Despite having the best record in baseball, the Braves were upset with the performance of their bullpen and overhauled it on July 12 by sending Brad Clontz, Paul Byrd and Joe Borowski to AAA Richmond. The club then called up starter Kevin Millwood and relievers Chad Fox and Mike Cather.

▶**July 23:** Through July 20, the Braves were 24-25 against teams that had winning records. Also, after a 12-1 start at Turner Field, the Braves are just 18-18 at their new home.

▶**July 30:** Kenny Lofton remains on the DL with a groin injury but might be able to return next week. When he does, Bobby Cox will have a pleasant logjam in the outfield. Rookie Andruw Jones has been sensational, especially defensively as a fill-in for Lofton. Left fielder Ryan Klesko has provided much of the club's power in July, and Michael Tucker has also been productive. Greg Maddux threw just 78 pitches (only 15 balls) in a win against the Cubs on July 22, his lowest pitch count ever for a nine-inning complete game.

▶**Aug. 13:** Greg Maddux now has a five-year, $57.5 million contract to go along with his four Cy Young Awards. Maddux, 31, is the game's highest-paid player, surpassing the Giants' Barry Bonds ($11.45 million a year, starting in 1999) and the White Sox's Albert Belle ($11 million average, current). Maddux has 121 victories since 1991, the most in the majors.

▶**Aug. 20:** Greg Maddux's new $57.5 million deal, which starts next season, means Kenny Lofton most likely will be playing elsewhere in 1998. Also, the club might choose not to bring back either second baseman Mark Lemke or shortstop Jeff Blauser, who, like Lofton, are eligible for free agency. The club has Andruw Jones to replace Lofton and Tony Graffanino to

take over Lemke's spot.

▶**Aug. 27:** The Braves placed Mark Lemke on the 15-day DL and might have lost him for the next month. The Braves replaced Lemke on the roster with utility infielder Keith Lockhart, who had been on the DL.

▶**Sept. 3:** In back-to-back games at Fenway Park over the weekend, the Braves scored 24 runs on 35 hits and bashed five homers. The team had been struggling at the plate.

▶**Sept. 10:** When left-hander Denny Neagle picked up his 20th victory on Sept. 7, it was the seventh 20-win season by a current Braves pitcher this decade. Tom Glavine has three, Greg Maddux two and John Smoltz one.

▶**Sept. 17:** The Braves are the first NL team since the 1951-56 Brooklyn Dodgers to win 90 or more games for six years in a row (excluding the strike-shortened 1994 season).

▶**Sept. 24:** The Braves set a major league record of 12 grand slams in a season, the most recent coming when Ryan Klesko went deep on Sept. 17 against the Mets' Bobby Jones. For the fifth consecutive year (excluding '94), the Braves will most likely finish with the best record in the league, an NL record. The only other club that had five years in a row with the best record in its league was the Yankees, in 1949-53 and 1960-64.

▶**Oct. 1:** Shortstop Rafael Belliard hit his first home run in more than 10 years, on Sept. 26 at Shea Stadium off Brian Bohannon. It was the second round-tripper of his career and his first in 1,869 at-bats. Belliard's other homer came on May 5, 1987, off the late Eric Show of the Padres. The next day, closer Mark Wohlers limped into the postseason, blowing his seventh save, in his last appearance of the regular season in a 2-1 loss to the Mets. Wohlers finished with 33 saves.

QUOTE OF THE YEAR

"They made me a nice deal."
—Pitcher Greg Maddux, on his five-year,
$57.5 million contract

ATLANTA BRAVES 1997 final stats

BATTERS	BA	SLG	OBA	G	AB	R	H	TB	2B	3B	HR	RBI	BB	SO	SB	CS	E
Simon	.429	.500	.467	13	14	2	6	7	1	0	0	1	1	2	0	0	0
Lofton	.333	.428	.409	122	493	90	164	211	20	6	5	48	64	83	27	20	5
Blauser	.308	.482	.405	151	519	90	160	250	31	4	17	70	70	101	5	1	16
C. Jones	.295	.479	.371	157	597	100	176	286	41	3	21	111	76	88	20	5	15
Lopez	.295	.534	.361	123	414	52	122	221	28	1	23	68	40	82	1	1	6
Tucker	.283	.445	.347	138	499	80	141	222	25	7	14	56	44	116	12	7	5
Lockhart	.279	.476	.337	96	147	25	41	70	5	3	6	32	14	17	0	0	3
Colbrunn	.278	.444	.316	28	54	3	15	24	3	0	2	9	2	11	0	0	1
McGriff	.277	.441	.356	152	564	77	156	249	25	1	22	97	68	112	5	0	13
Gregg	.263	.368	.300	13	19	1	5	7	2	0	0	0	1	2	1	1	0
Klesko	.261	.490	.334	143	467	67	122	229	23	6	24	84	48	130	4	4	6
Graffanino	.258	.446	.344	104	186	33	48	83	9	1	8	20	26	46	6	4	5
Giovanola	.250	.250	.400	14	8	0	2	2	0	0	0	0	2	1	0	0	0
Lemke	.245	.316	.306	109	351	33	86	111	17	1	2	26	33	51	2	0	10
Bautista	.243	.398	.282	64	103	14	25	41	3	2	3	9	5	24	2	0	1
A. Jones	.231	.416	.329	153	399	60	92	166	18	1	18	70	56	107	20	11	7
Perez	.215	.335	.259	73	191	20	41	64	5	0	6	18	10	35	0	1	5
Spehr	.214	.500	.214	8	14	2	3	7	1	0	1	4	0	4	1	0	2
Belliard	.211	.296	.219	72	71	9	15	21	3	0	1	3	1	17	0	1	1
Mordecai	.173	.222	.227	61	81	8	14	18	2	1	0	3	6	16	0	1	0
Myers	.111	.111	.200	9	9	0	1	1	0	0	0	1	1	3	0	0	0

PITCHERS	W-L	ERA	BA	G	GS	CG	GF	Sho	SV	IP	H	R	ER	HR	BB	SO
Leroy	1-0	0.00	.143	1	0	0	0	0	0	2.0	1	0	0	0	3	3
Maddux	19-4	2.20	.236	33	33	5	0	2	0	232.2	200	58	57	9	20	177
Cather	2-4	2.39	.174	35	0	0	10	0	0	37.2	23	12	10	1	19	29
Embree	3-1	2.54	.221	66	0	0	15	0	0	46.0	36	13	13	1	20	45
Glavine	14-7	2.96	.226	33	33	5	0	2	0	240.0	197	86	79	20	79	152
Neagle	20-5	2.97	.233	34	34	4	0	4	0	233.1	204	87	77	18	49	172
Ligtenberg	1-0	3.00	.211	15	0	0	9	0	1	15.0	12	5	5	4	4	19
Smoltz	15-12	3.02	.242	35	35	7	0	2	0	256.0	234	97	86	21	63	241
Fox	0-1	3.29	.231	30	0	0	8	0	0	27.1	24	12	10	4	16	28
Wohlers	5-7	3.50	.224	71	0	0	55	0	33	69.1	57	29	27	4	38	92
Borowski	2-2	3.75	.287	20	0	0	8	0	0	24.0	27	11	10	2	16	6
Clontz	5-1	3.75	.286	51	0	0	16	0	1	48.0	52	24	20	3	18	42
Millwood	5-3	4.03	.282	12	8	0	2	0	0	51.1	55	26	23	1	21	42
Bielecki	3-7	4.08	.250	50	0	0	7	0	2	57.1	56	33	26	9	21	60
Byrd	4-4	5.26	.235	31	4	0	9	0	0	53.0	47	34	31	6	28	37
Wade	2-3	5.36	.349	12	9	0	1	0	0	42.0	60	31	25	6	16	35
Brock	0-0	5.58	.288	7	6	0	1	0	0	30.2	34	23	19	2	19	16

1998 preliminary roster

PITCHERS (19)
Pedro Borbon
Micah Bowie
Paul Byrd
Mike Cather
Bruce Chen
Brad Clontz
Derrin Ebert
Brian Edmondson
Alan Embree
Tom Glavine
Dwayne Jacobs

Kerry Ligtenberg
Greg Maddux
Kevin Millwood
Damian Moss
Denny Neagle
John Rocker
John Smoltz
Mark Wohlers

CATCHERS (4)
Fernando Lunar
Javy Lopez

Pascual Matos
Eddie Perez

INFIELDERS (8)
Andres Galarraga
Tony Graffanino
Wes Helms
Chipper Jones
Keith Lockhart
Randall Simon
Walt Weiss
Glenn Williams

OUTFIELDERS (7)
Danny Bautista
Damon Hollins
Andruw Jones
Ryan Klesko
George Lombard
Michael Tucker
Gerald Williams

Games played by position

PLAYER	G	C	1B	2B	3B	SS	OF
Bautista	64	0	0	0	0	0	57
Belliard	72	0	0	7	0	53	0
Blauser	151	0	0	0	0	149	0
Colbrunn	28	0	14	0	0	0	0
Giovanola	14	0	0	1	8	1	0
Graffanino	104	0	1	75	2	2	0
Gregg	13	0	1	0	0	0	6
A. Jones	153	0	0	0	0	0	147
C. Jones	157	0	0	0	152	0	5
Klesko	143	0	22	0	0	0	130
Lemke	109	0	0	104	0	0	0
Lockhart	96	0	0	20	11	0	0
Lofton	122	0	0	0	0	0	122
Lopez	123	117	0	0	0	0	0
McGriff	152	0	149	0	0	0	0
Mordecai	61	0	3	4	19	4	1
Myers	9	2	0	0	0	0	0
Perez	73	64	6	0	0	0	0
Simon	13	0	6	0	0	0	0
Spehr	8	7	0	0	0	0	0
Tucker	138	0	0	0	0	0	129

Sick call: 1997 DL report

PLAYER	Days on the DL
Danny Bautista	22
Mike Bielecki	43
Pedro Borbon	181
Bryan Harvey	96
Mark Lemke	39
Keith Lockhart	16
Kenny Lofton	39*
Javier Lopez	16
Terrell Wade	114

* Indicates two separate terms on Disabled List.

1997 salaries

	Bonuses	Total earned salary
John Smoltz,p		$7,000,000
Greg Maddux,p	275,000	6,775,000
Fred McGriff,1b	250,000	5,500,000
Tom Glavine,p	50,000	5,050,000
Kenny Lofton,of	75,000	4,825,000
Jeff Blauser,ss	520,000	4,020,000
Denny Neagle,p	110,000	3,610,000
Mark Wohlers,p		3,000,000
Ryan Klesko,of		2,450,000
Javier Lopez,c	25,000	2,050,000
Mark Lemke,2b		2,000,000
Chipper Jones,3b	25,000	1,525,000
Greg Colbrunn,1b		750,000
Mike Bielecki,p	10,000	707,500
Keith Lockhart,2b		290,000
Rafael Belliard,ss		250,000
Michael Tucker,of		250,000
Brad Clontz,p		245,000
Alan Embree,p		206,000
Danny Bautista,of		200,000
Pedro Borbon,p		185,000
Terrell Wade,p		180,000
Paul Byrd,p		175,000
Eduardo Perez,c		172,500
Tony Graffanino,2b		152,500
Andruw Jones,of		152,500
Tim Spehr,c		150,000
Chad Fox,p		150,000
Mike Cather,p		150,000

Average 1997 Salary: $1,799,000
Total 1997 Payroll: $52,171,000

Minor Leagues

Tops in the organization

BATTER	CLUB	AVG.	G	AB	R	H	HR	RBI
Gregg, Tommy	Rmd	.332	115	385	52	128	9	54
Hacker, Steve	Mac	.324	117	460	80	149	33	119
Warner, Mike	Grv	.320	91	303	58	97	7	35
Burke, Mark	Eug	.320	71	266	46	85	10	52
Simon, Randall	Rmd	.308	133	519	62	160	14	102

HOME RUNS

Hacker, Steve	Mac	33
Johnson, Adam	Dur	26
Swann, Pedro	Grv	24
Whatley, Gabe	Grv	23
Hessman, M.	Mac	21

WINS

Marquis, Jason	Mac	14
Bell, Rob	Mac	14
Chen, Bruce	Mac	12
King, Raymond	Dur	11
Ebert, Derrin	Grv	11

RBI

Hacker, Steve	Mac	119
Simon, Randall	Rmd	102
Johnson, Adam	Dur	92
Whatley, Gabe	Grv	87
Swann, Pedro	Grv	83

SAVES

Cortes, David	Grv	23
Butler, Adam	Grv	22
Giard, Ken	Grv	18
Brow, Scott	Rmd	18
Ligtenberg, K.	Rmd	17

STOLEN BASES

Pendergrass,T.	Mac	70
Lombard, G.	Dur	35
Trippy, Joe	Dur	34
Thorpe, A.D.	Mac	29
Lewis, Marc	Grv	21

STRIKEOUTS

Chen, Bruce	Mac	182
Bell, Rob	Mac	140
Rocker, John	Grv	135
Marquis, Jason	Mac	121
Woodall, Brad	Rmd	117

PITCHER	CLUB	W-L	ERA	IP	H	BB	SO
Perez, Odalis	Mac	4-5	1.65	87	67	27	100
Shiell, Jason	Mac	10-5	2.86	129	113	32	101
Millwood, Kevin	Rmd	10-5	3.02	122	97	40	107
Brock, Chris	Rmd	10-6	3.34	119	97	51	83
Chen, Bruce	Mac	12-7	3.51	146	120	44	182

Atlanta (1966-1997), includes Boston (1876-1952) and Milwaukee (1953-1965)

Runs: Most, career

2107	Hank Aaron, 1954-1974
1452	Eddie Mathews, 1952-1966
1291	Herman Long, 1890-1902
1134	Fred Tenney, 1894-1911
1103	Dale Murphy, 1976-1990

Hits: Most, career

3600	Hank Aaron, 1954-1974
2201	Eddie Mathews, 1952-1966
1994	Fred Tenney, 1894-1911
1901	Dale Murphy, 1976-1990
1900	Herman Long, 1890-1902

2B: Most, career

600	Hank Aaron, 1954-1974
338	Eddie Mathews, 1952-1966
306	Dale Murphy, 1976-1990
295	Herman Long, 1890-1902
291	Tommy Holmes, 1942-1951

3B: Most, career

103	Rabbit Maranville, 1912-1935
96	Hank Aaron, 1954-1974
91	Herman Long, 1890-1902
80	John Morrill, 1876-1888
79	Bill Bruton, 1953-1960

HR: Most, career

733	Hank Aaron, 1954-1974
493	Eddie Mathews, 1952-1966
371	Dale Murphy, 1976-1990
239	Joe Adcock, 1953-1962
215	Bob Horner, 1978-1986

RBI: Most, career

2202	Hank Aaron, 1954-1974
1388	Eddie Mathews, 1952-1966
1143	Dale Murphy, 1976-1990
964	Herman Long, 1890-1902
927	Hugh Duffy, 1892-1900

SB: Most, career

431	Herman Long, 1890-1902
331	Hugh Duffy, 1892-1900
274	Billy Hamilton, 1896-1901
260	Bobby Lowe, 1890-1901
260	Fred Tenney, 1894-1911
240	Hank Aaron, 1954-1974 (6)

BB: Most, career

1376	Eddie Mathews, 1952-1966
1297	Hank Aaron, 1954-1974
912	Dale Murphy, 1976-1990
750	Fred Tenney, 1894-1911
598	Billy Nash, 1885-1895

BA: Highest, career

.338	Billy Hamilton, 1896-1901
.332	Hugh Duffy, 1892-1900
.327	Chick Stahl, 1897-1900
.317	Rico Carty, 1963-1972
.317	Ralph Garr, 1968-1975

On-base avg: Highest, career

.456	Billy Hamilton, 1896-1901
.398	Bob Elliott, 1947-1951
.394	Hugh Duffy, 1892-1900
.388	Rico Carty, 1963-1972
.387	Chick Stahl, 1897-1900

Slug avg: Highest, career

.567	Hank Aaron, 1954-1974
.538	RYAN KLESKO, 1992-1997
.533	Wally Berger, 1930-1937
.517	Eddie Mathews, 1952-1966
.516	FRED McGRIFF, 1993-1997

Games started: Most, career

635	Warren Spahn, 1942-1964
595	Phil Niekro, 1964-1987
501	Kid Nichols, 1890-1901
331	TOM GLAVINE, 1987-1997
330	Lew Burdette, 1951-1963

Complete games: Most, career

475	Kid Nichols, 1890-1901
374	Warren Spahn, 1942-1964
268	Vic Willis, 1898-1905
242	Jim Whitney, 1881-1885
226	John Clarkson, 1888-1892
226	Phil Niekro, 1964-1987

Saves: Most, career

141	Gene Garber, 1978-1987
104	MARK WOHLERS, 1991-1997
78	Cecil Upshaw, 1966-1973
57	Rick Camp, 1976-1985
55	MIKE STANTON, 1989-1995

Shutouts: Most, career

63	Warren Spahn, 1942-1964
44	Kid Nichols, 1890-1901
43	Phil Niekro, 1964-1987
30	Lew Burdette, 1951-1963
29	Tommy Bond, 1877-1881

Wins: Most, career

356	Warren Spahn, 1942-1964
329	Kid Nichols, 1890-1901
268	Phil Niekro, 1964-1987
179	Lew Burdette, 1951-1963
153	TOM GLAVINE, 1987-1997

K: Most, career

2912	Phil Niekro, 1964-1987
2493	Warren Spahn, 1942-1964
1769	JOHN SMOLTZ, 1988-1997
1672	Kid Nichols, 1890-1901
1364	TOM GLAVINE, 1987-1997

Win pct: Highest, career

.730	GREG MADDUX, 1993-1997
.679	Fred Klobedanz, 1896-1902
.655	Harry Staley, 1891-1894
.645	John Clarkson, 1888-1892
.643	Kid Nichols, 1890-1901

ERA: Lowest, career

2.13	GREG MADDUX, 1993-1997
2.21	Tommy Bond, 1877-1881
2.49	Jim Whitney, 1881-1885
2.52	Art Nehf, 1915-1919
2.62	Dick Rudolph, 1913-1927

Runs: Most, season

160	Hugh Duffy, 1894
158	Bobby Lowe, 1894
152	Billy Hamilton, 1896
152	Billy Hamilton, 1897
149	Herman Long, 1893
131	Dale Murphy, 1983 (9)

Hits: Most, season

237	Hugh Duffy, 1894
224	Tommy Holmes, 1945
223	Hank Aaron, 1959
219	Ralph Garr, 1971
218	Felipe Alou, 1966

2B: Most, season

51	Hugh Duffy, 1894
47	Tommy Holmes, 1945
46	Hank Aaron, 1959
44	Wally Berger, 1931
44	Lee Maye, 1964
41	CHIPPER JONES, 1997 (8)

3B: Most, season

20	Dick Johnston, 1887
20	Harry Stovey, 1891
19	Chick Stahl, 1899
18	Dick Johnston, 1888
18	Ray Powell, 1921
17	Ralph Garr, 1974 (6)

HR: Most, season

47	Hank Aaron, 1971
47	Eddie Mathews, 1953
46	Eddie Mathews, 1959
45	Hank Aaron, 1962
44	Hank Aaron, 1957

44   Hank Aaron, 1963
44   Hank Aaron, 1966
44   Hank Aaron, 1969
44   Dale Murphy, 1987

RBI: Most, season

145	Hugh Duffy, 1894
135	Eddie Mathews, 1953
132	Hank Aaron, 1957
132	Jimmy Collins, 1897
130	Hank Aaron, 1963
130	Wally Berger, 1935
127	Hank Aaron, 1966 (9)

SB: Most, season

84	King Kelly, 1887
83	Billy Hamilton, 1896
72	OTIS NIXON, 1991
68	King Kelly, 1889
66	Billy Hamilton, 1897

BB: Most, season

131	Bob Elliott, 1948
127	Jim Wynn, 1976
126	Darrell Evans, 1974
124	Darrell Evans, 1973
124	Eddie Mathews, 1963

BA: Highest, season

.440	Hugh Duffy, 1894
.387	Rogers Hornsby, 1928
.373	Dan Brouthers, 1889
.369	Billy Hamilton, 1898
.366	Rico Carty, 1970

On-base avg: Highest, season

.502	Hugh Duffy, 1894
.498	Rogers Hornsby, 1928
.480	Billy Hamilton, 1898
.477	Billy Hamilton, 1896
.462	Dan Brouthers, 1889
.454	Rico Carty, 1970 (7)

Slug avg: Highest, season

.694	Hugh Duffy, 1894
.669	Hank Aaron, 1971
.636	Hank Aaron, 1959
.632	Rogers Hornsby, 1928
.627	Eddie Mathews, 1953

Games started: Most, season

72	John Clarkson, 1889
67	Charlie Buffinton, 1884
64	Tommy Bond, 1879
63	Jim Whitney, 1881
44	Phil Niekro, 1979 (22)

Complete games: Most, season

68	John Clarkson, 1889
63	Charlie Buffinton, 1884
59	Tommy Bond, 1879
58	Tommy Bond, 1877
23	Phil Niekro, 1979 (*)

Saves: Most, season

39	MARK WOHLERS, 1996
33	MARK WOHLERS, 1997
30	Gene Garber, 1982
27	MIKE STANTON, 1993
27	Cecil Upshaw, 1969

Shutouts: Most, season

11	Tommy Bond, 1879
9	Tommy Bond, 1878
8	Charlie Buffinton, 1884
8	John Clarkson, 1889
7	Kid Nichols, 1890
7	Togie Pittinger, 1902
7	Warren Spahn, 1947
7	Warren Spahn, 1951
7	Warren Spahn, 1963
7	Irv Young, 1905
6	Phil Niekro, 1974 (11)

Wins: Most, season

49	John Clarkson, 1889
48	Charlie Buffinton, 1884
43	Tommy Bond, 1879
40	Tommy Bond, 1877
40	Tommy Bond, 1878
24	JOHN SMOLTZ, 1996 (*)

K: Most, season

417	Charlie Buffinton, 1884
345	Jim Whitney, 1883
284	John Clarkson, 1889
276	JOHN SMOLTZ, 1996
270	Jim Whitney, 1884

Win pct: Highest, season

.905	GREG MADDUX, 1995
.842	Tom Hughes, 1916
.826	GREG MADDUX, 1997
.810	Phil Niekro, 1982
.800	DENNY NEAGLE, 1997

ERA: Lowest, season

1.56	GREG MADDUX, 1994
1.63	GREG MADDUX, 1995
1.87	Phil Niekro, 1967
1.90	Bill James, 1914
1.96	Tommy Bond, 1879

Most pinch-hit homers, season

5	Butch Nieman, 1945
4	TOMMY GREGG, 1990

Most pinch-hit homers, career

7	Joe Adcock, 1953-1962
6	TOMMY GREGG, 1988-1997
6	Mike Lum, 1967-1981

Longest hitting streak

37	Tommy Holmes, 1945
31	Rico Carty, 1970
29	Rowland Office, 1976
28	MARQUIS GRISSOM, 1996
27	Hugh Duffy, 1893

Most consecutive scoreless innings

41	Art Nehf, 1917
29	Phil Niekro, 1974

No-hit games

Jack Stivetts, Bos vs Bro NL, 11-0;
    Aug. 6, 1892.

Frank (Jeff) Pfeffer, Bos vs Cin NL,
    6-0; May 8, 1907.

George Davis, Bos vs Phi NL, 7-0;
    Sept. 9, 1914 (2nd game).

Tom L. Hughes, Bos vs Pit NL, 2-0;
    June 16, 1916.

Jim Tobin, Bos vs Bro NL, 2-0;
    April 27, 1944.

Vern Bickford, Bos vs Bro NL, 7-0;
    Aug. 11, 1950.

Jim Wilson, Mil vs Phi NL, 2-0;
    June 12, 1954.

Lew Burdette, Mil vs Phi NL, 1-0;
    Aug. 18, 1960.

Warren Spahn, Mil vs Phi NL, 4-0;
    Sept. 16, 1960.

Warren Spahn, Mil vs SF NL, 1-0;
    April 28, 1961.

Phil Niekro, Atl vs SD NL, 9-0;
    Aug. 5, 1973.

KENT MERCKER (six innings),
    MARK WOHLERS (two innings)
    and Alejandro Pena (one inning),
    Atl at SD NL, 1-0; Sept. 11, 1991.

KENT MERCKER, Atl at LA NL, 6-0;
    April 8, 1994.

Jack Stivetts, five innings, called so
    Boston could catch train to
    Cleveland for Temple Cub play-
    offs, Bos at Was NL, 6-0;
    Oct. 15, 1892 (2nd game).

Jim Tobin, five innings, darkness,
    Bos vs Phi NL, 7-0; June 22,
    1944 (2nd game).

ACTIVE PLAYERS in caps.

Players' years of service are listed by the first and last years with this team and are not necessarily consecutive; all statistics record performances for this team only.

Leader from the franchise's current location is included. If not in the top five, leader's rank is listed in parenthesis; asterisk (*) indicates player is not in top 25.

Florida Marlins

By Tom DiPace

Besides winning his third straight Gold Glove, Charles Johnson hit a career-high 19 homers last year.

1997 Marlins: Leyland won it all, at last

One year and some $175 million later, the Marlins ended up just about where owner Wayne Huizenga hoped when he agreed to bankroll a free-agent spree targeted toward getting Florida to the postseason. But not quite, because losing $30 million and putting the team up for sale in June weren't part of the plan. The billionaire admitted he made some bad business moves in committing $89 million to free agents, then adding $17.5 million to closer Robb Nen and $61 million to right fielder Gary Sheffield. But while Huizenga may have miscalculated, GM Dave Dombrowski and manager Jim Leyland did not. They had a good idea what it would take to get the Marlins to the postseason, and after Dombrowski gave him the pieces, Leyland arranged a playoff-puzzle solution. Walking through Pro Player Stadium with the World Series trophy in hand certainly salved some of Huizenga's wounds and may have him reconsidering the sale idea.

The Marlins won the wild card and had the second-best record (92-70) in the league, behind Atlanta's, and three of the biggest contributors to Florida's success were free-agent signees: Moises Alou, Bobby Bonilla and Alex Fernandez. Alou led the team with 23 home runs and 115 RBI, setting career highs in both categories. Bonilla was serviceable at third base and batted .297 with a club-record 39 doubles, 17 home runs and 96 RBI despite playing all season with wrist and Achilles tendon injuries. Fernandez (17-12, 3.59) was a reliable innings-eater until his playoff arm injury, which jeopardizes his future.

Among the organization's holdovers, Charles Johnson became the first NL catcher to play a season of at least 100 games without an error, and he batted .250 with 19 home runs and 63 RBI. Kevin Brown (16-8, 2.69 ERA) threw a no-hitter against San Francisco and has given the Marlins 33 wins in two seaons since signing a three-year, $12.6 million contract, which now looks like a big bar-

gain. Shortstop Edgar Renteria had eight game-winning hits, including the final one of 1997, the 11th-inning single that won the World Series. Cuban rookie Livan Hernandez (9-3, 3.18 ERA) spent most of the first half at AAA Charlotte, but won his initial nine decisions for Florida and capped his year with NLCS and World Series MVP selections.

Sheffield, however, batted .250 with 21 home runs and 71 RBI, hardly what the Marlins were looking for when they gave him a record contract extension in April. He let things get to him, including being pitched around early and not getting what he considered a fair strike zone later. Original Marlin Jeff Conine (.242, 17 home runs, 61 RBI) struggled mightily before the All-Star break, leading Florida to make the July 27 trade for Darren Daulton and platoon the two at first base down the stretch.

The Marlins have greatly reduced their payroll for 1998 by unloading Alou, Nen, Brown, Conine and center fielder Devon White, but the options for the future seem almost endless because Florida has developed one of the game's strongest farm systems. Two of the most promising kids are AA shortstop Alex Gonzalez, not to be confused with Toronto's shortstop, and center fielder Mark Kotsay. At first base, the Marlins may give Cliff Floyd the opportunity to earn a full-time job, but he has to show he can stay healthy.

1997 Marlins: Week-by-week notes

These notes were excerpted from the following issues of Baseball Weekly.

▸**April 9:** On April 2 right fielder Gary Sheffield wore a designer suit, a gold watch smothered in diamonds on one wrist, a diamond-encrusted bracelet on the other, and diamond studs in both ears. He looked like a million bucks. Actually, $61 million, the figure on his six-year contract extension, which runs from 1998 through 2003. There also is an $11 million club option for 2004, plus a long list of award incentives. Opposing pitchers must be impressed: Sheffield walked 13 times in Florida's first six games.

▸**April 16:** Right-hander Alex Fernandez ignored temperatures in the mid-30s and put on a masterly display in Chicago during a 1-0 victory on April 10 against the Cubs in Chicago, his home for seven seasons with the crosstown White Sox. His no-hit bid ended with one out in the ninth inning when Dave Hansen got a pinch-hit single.

▸**April 23:** The Marlins had the fifth-best ERA (3.07) in the NL and had given up just four home runs in 16 games. The 1996 Cy Young runner-up, right-hander Kevin Brown (2-0, 0.96 ERA), has picked up where he left off last year. But the Marlins had scored just 64 runs in 17 games. Third baseman Bobby Bonilla was batting .276 with no home runs and four RBI, and second baseman Luis Castillo and shortstop Edgar Renteria weren't getting on base. Batting leadoff, Castillo was 10-for-50 with three walks in his past 11 games, and No. 2 hitter Renteria was 5-for-41 with 11 strikeouts and two walks in his past 10.

▸**April 30:** The Marlins went 0-5 in San Francisco and Colorado last week and have lost seven in a row on the road. They have a 9-2 record at home and a 3-7 road record. Last season, the Marlins were 52-29 at home and 23-58 on the road, tied with the Rockies for the worst road record in the NL. Outfielder Moises Alou stayed hot even when most players

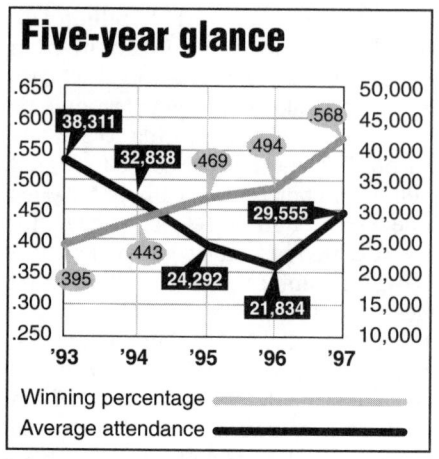

Five-year glance

38,311	.568
32,838	.494
	.469
	29,555
.443	
.395	24,292
	21,834

'93 '94 '95 '96 '97

Winning percentage
Average attendance

cooled off. Alou leads the Marlins in nearly every major hitting category, including home runs (seven) and RBI (23).

▸**May 7:** The Marlins have fallen far short of offensive expectations. They have been especially ineffective in clutch situations, with a league-worst .175 average (7-for-40) with the bases loaded and a second-worst .222 average with runners on base.

▸**May 21:** The Marlins swept two games at Atlanta and won their first two games at Pittsburgh last week to raise their road record to 8-11. They had a 5-0 road trip that included a 5-3 10-inning victory on May 18 at Pittsburgh, where Jim Leyland received a mixture of cheers and boos in his first visit since leaving the Pirates with four years left on his contract.

▸**May 28:** Florida won nine of 11 games to stay within 5½ games of Atlanta, and the Marlins have mostly done it without injured starters Gary Sheffield, center fielder Devon White and Luis Castillo.

▸**June 4:** The Marlins were tied with San Francisco for the third-best record (31-22) in baseball, even after being swept in a weekend homestand against the Rockies. But it's been a frustrating start for their franchise player, Gary Sheffield. He came off a 15-day stint on the DL on May 29 and was batting only .220 with five home runs and 16 RBI in 42 games through June 1. He has drawn 45 walks.

June 11: Florida's defense is what concerns Jim Leyland the most. The Marlins have 49 errors in 58 games, and their .979 fielding percentage is the fourth worst in the NL.

June 18: On June 10 in San Francisco, Kevin Brown pitched his first career no-hitter and came within one base runner of a perfect game in a 9-0 victory against the Giants. Brown struck out seven and walked none; the only man to reach base was Marvin Benard, who was hit by a pitch on the right knee with two outs in the eighth.

June 25: Left-hander Al Leiter has been struggling on the road. He allowed four earned runs in three innings of a June 18 interleague loss at Tiger Stadium, dropping his road record to 2-4 with an 8.37 ERA. He is 3-1 with a 1.48 ERA in five home starts.

July 2: The Marlins barely had time to unpack after a 6-3 road trip when their owner slapped a "For Sale" sign on the franchise on June 26. Wayne Huizenga says he's had enough of bathing in red ink (a projected $30 million loss this year). He's getting out of the baseball business.

July 10: After taking a called third strike on July 5 at Shea Stadium, Gary Sheffield turned and questioned the judgment of home plate umpire Jerry Meals. Within 10 seconds, he was ejected, for the second time this season. Sheffield is convinced his struggles at the plate (.242, nine home runs, 37 RBI) have been caused more by umpires than pitchers.

July 23: Cuban rookie right-hander Livan Hernandez raised his record to 3-0 in four fill-in starts and will remain the No. 4 starter while the Marlins pursue a trade for another arm.

July 30: Catcher Charles Johnson has been one the hottest hitters in the NL. The two-time Gold Glove catcher was batting .475 (19-for-40) since the All-Star break, with six home runs and 13 RBI. Johnson, who was at .217 in early June, has raised his average to .264 with 12 home runs and 38 RBI.

Aug. 6: The Marlins are so impressed with rookies Tony Saunders and Livan Hernandez that they have stopped pursuing a veteran starter before the trade deadline. Left-hander Saunders (3-3, 3.07 ERA) and Hernandez (5-0, 2.25 ERA) have become entrenched at the back of a five-man rotation headed by veterans Kevin Brown, Alex Fernandez and Al Leiter. The team hoped Devon White's return would provide a spark at the top of the lineup, but White was 6-for-33 (.182) in the leadoff role through Aug. 3.

Aug. 27: Bobby Bonilla said former Phillie Darren Daulton has provided a big spark for the Marlins with his aggressiveness and winning attitude. The first baseman went 3-for-3 on Aug. 22 and had a triple and scored all of Florida's runs the next day in a 3-0 win against St. Louis.

Sept. 3: Craig Counsell, a rookie second baseman, has batted .368 with 12 runs scored and 12 RBI in 29 games since he was acquired from Colorado in a trade for pitcher Mark Hutton.

Sept. 10: Through Sept. 7, Florida's record was 26-12 against division leaders Baltimore (3-0), Atlanta (8-4), Houston (7-4) and Los Angeles (6-4).

Sept. 17: The Marlins' division-title hopes were all but extinguished when they lost five of six at Los Angeles and San Diego, dropping them from 2½ to 6½ games behind Atlanta. Florida blew leads in four of the five losses.

Sept. 24: Moises Alou's two-run homer on Sept. 19 was his 23rd, setting a personal record. Alou ranks among league leaders with a career-best 113 RBI and a .331 average with runners in scoring position.

Oct. 1: The Marlins hauled 12 cases of champagne with them to Montreal, champagne that had been on ice when they failed to clinch against the Mets at home. After winning in Montreal on Sept. 23, the Marlins went through 12 cases of champagne, 10 cases of beer and a keg before leaving the stadium at about 1:30 a.m.

QUOTE OF THE YEAR

"I got booed even when I was having the best season of my career last year."
—Right fielder Gary Sheffield, on his hometown fans

FLORIDA MARLINS 1997 final stats

BATTERS	BA	SLG	OBA	G	AB	R	H	TB	2B	3B	HR	RBI	BB	SO	SB	CS	E
Booty	.600	.600	.667	4	5	2	3	3	0	0	0	1	1	1	0	0	1
Natal	.500	1.500	.571	4	4	2	2	6	1	0	1	3	2	0	0	0	0
Zaun	.301	.441	.415	58	143	21	43	63	10	2	2	20	26	18	1	0	8
Counsell	.299	.396	.376	52	164	20	49	65	9	2	1	16	18	17	1	1	3
Bonilla	.297	.468	.378	153	562	77	167	263	39	3	17	96	73	94	6	6	22
Alou	.292	.493	.373	150	538	88	157	265	29	5	23	115	70	85	9	5	3
Morman	.286	.857	.286	4	7	3	2	6	1	0	1	2	0	2	1	0	0
Eisenreich	.280	.372	.345	120	293	36	82	109	19	1	2	34	30	28	0	0	2
Wehner	.278	.333	.333	44	36	8	10	12	2	0	0	2	2	5	1	0	0
Renteria	.277	.340	.327	154	617	90	171	210	21	3	4	52	45	108	32	15	17
Abbott	.274	.433	.315	94	252	35	69	109	18	2	6	30	14	68	3	1	8
Daulton	.263	.463	.378	136	395	68	104	183	21	8	14	63	76	74	6	1	7
Dunwoody	.260	.500	.362	19	50	7	13	25	2	2	2	7	7	21	2	0	2
Johnson	.250	.454	.347	124	416	43	104	189	26	1	19	63	60	109	0	2	0
Sheffield	.250	.446	.424	135	444	86	111	198	22	1	21	71	121	79	11	7	5
Arias	.247	.301	.352	74	93	13	23	28	2	0	1	11	12	12	0	1	2
White	.245	.370	.338	74	265	37	65	98	13	1	6	34	32	65	13	5	2
Cangelosi	.245	.302	.321	103	192	28	47	58	8	0	1	12	19	33	5	1	0
Conine	.242	.405	.337	151	405	46	98	164	13	1	17	61	57	89	2	0	8
Castillo	.240	.270	.310	75	263	27	63	71	8	0	0	8	27	53	16	10	9
Floyd	.234	.445	.354	61	137	23	32	61	9	1	6	19	24	33	6	2	3
Milliard	.200	.200	.314	8	30	2	6	6	0	0	0	2	3	3	1	1	0
Kotsay	.192	.250	.250	14	52	5	10	13	1	1	0	4	4	7	3	0	0

PITCHERS	W-L	ERA	BA	G	GS	CG	GF	Sho	SV	IP	H	R	ER	HR	BB	SO
Cangelosi	0-0	0.00	.000	1	0	0	1	0	0	1.0	0	0	0	0	1	0
Brown	16-8	2.69	.240	33	33	6	0	2	0	237.1	214	77	71	10	66	205
Ojala	1-2	3.14	.252	7	5	0	1	0	0	28.2	28	10	10	4	18	19
Hernandez	9-3	3.18	.229	17	17	0	0	0	0	96.1	81	39	34	5	38	72
Powell	7-2	3.28	.242	74	0	0	23	0	2	79.2	71	35	29	3	30	65
Fernandez	17-12	3.59	.238	32	32	5	0	1	0	220.2	193	93	88	25	69	183
Vosberg	1-1	3.75	.313	17	0	0	6	0	1	12.0	15	7	5	0	6	8
Pall	0-0	3.86	.300	2	0	0	0	0	0	2.1	3	1	1	1	1	0
Nen	9-3	3.89	.250	73	0	0	65	0	35	74.0	72	35	32	7	40	81
Cook	1-2	3.90	.267	59	0	0	12	0	0	62.1	64	28	27	4	28	63
Heredia	5-3	4.29	.243	56	0	0	10	0	0	56.2	53	30	27	3	30	54
Leiter	11-9	4.34	.241	27	27	0	0	0	0	151.1	133	78	73	13	91	132
Helling	2-6	4.38	.232	31	8	0	8	0	0	76.0	61	38	37	12	48	53
Stanifer	1-2	4.60	.261	36	0	0	10	0	1	45.0	43	23	23	9	16	28
Saunders	4-6	4.61	.244	22	21	0	0	0	0	111.1	99	62	57	12	64	102
Alfonseca	1-3	4.91	.324	17	0	0	2	0	0	25.2	36	16	14	3	10	19
Miller	0-1	9.82	.364	7	0	0	1	0	0	7.1	12	8	8	2	7	7
Whisenant	0-0	16.88	.333	4	0	0	2	0	0	2.2	4	6	5	0	6	4

1998 preliminary roster

PITCHERS (17)
Antonio Alfonseca
Manuel Barrios
Victor Darensbourg
Alex Fernandez
Oscar Henriquez
Felix Heredia
Livan Hernandez
Andy Larkin
Al Leiter
Eric Ludwick
Jesus Martinez
Brian Meadows
Rafael Medina
Blaine Mull
Jay Powell
Rob Stanifer
Mike Villano

CATCHERS (2)
Charles Johnson
Gregg Zaun

INFIELDERS (11)
Bobby Bonilla
Josh Booty
Luis Castillo
Craig Counsell
Brandon Cromer
Amaury Garcia
Alex Gonzalez
Ryan Jackson
Derrick Lee
Ralph Milliard
Edgar Renteria

OUTFIELDERS (8)
Fletcher Bates
John Cangelosi
Todd Dunwoody
Jim Eisenreich
Cliff Floyd
Mark Kotsay
Julio Ramirez
Gary Sheffield

Games played by position

PLAYER	G	C	1B	2B	3B	SS	OF
Abbott	94	0	0	54	4	7	10
Alou	150	0	0	0	0	0	150
Arias	74	0	0	0	37	11	0
Bonilla	153	0	2	0	149	0	0
Booty	4	0	0	0	4	0	0
Cangelosi	103	0	0	0	0	0	58
Castillo	75	0	0	70	0	0	0
Conine	151	0	145	0	0	0	1
Counsell	52	0	0	51	0	0	0
Daulton	136	0	42	0	0	0	73
Dunwoody	19	0	0	0	0	0	14
Eisenreich	120	0	29	0	0	0	55
Floyd	61	0	9	0	0	0	38
Johnson	124	123	0	0	0	0	0
Kotsay	14	0	0	0	0	0	14
Milliard	8	0	0	8	0	0	0
Morman	4	0	1	0	0	0	2
Natal	4	4	0	0	0	0	0
Renteria	154	0	0	0	0	153	0
Sheffield	135	0	0	0	0	0	132
Wehner	44	0	0	0	6	0	27
White	74	0	0	0	0	0	71
Zaun	58	50	1	0	0	0	0

Sick call: 1997 DL report

PLAYER	Days on the DL
Alex Arias	18
Luis Castillo	15
Cliff Floyd	87*
Bill Hurst	30
Al Leiter	35*
Matt Mantei	181
Kurt Miller	153
Tony Saunders	52
Gary Sheffield	15
John Wehner	65
Matt Whisenant	94
Devon White	85*

Indicates two separate terms on Disabled List.

Minor Leagues

Tops in the organization

BATTER	CLUB	AVG.	G	AB	R	H	HR	RBI
Franco, Raul	Uti	.352	72	293	41	103	3	38
Hastings, Lionel	Prt	.344	93	279	55	96	10	35
Millar, Kevin	Prt	.342	135	511	94	175	32	131
Funaro, Joe	Bre	.319	125	470	67	150	4	53
Morman, Russ	Chr	.319	117	395	82	126	33	99

HOME RUNS

Morman, Russ	Chr	33
Millar, Kevin	Prt	32
Jackson, Ryan	Prt	26
Roskos, John	Prt	24
Dunwoody, T.	Chr	23

WINS

Cornelius, Reid	Chr	17
Billingsley, Brent	KnC	14
Mercado, Hector	Prt	11
Dempster, Ryan	Bre	10
Several Players Tied At		9

RBI

Millar, Kevin	Prt	131
Morman, Russ	Chr	99
Jackson, Ryan	Prt	98
Daubach, Brian	Chr	93
Horne, Tyrone	KnC	91

SAVES

Duvall, Mike	Prt	24
Sanchez, Martin	KnC	22
Chergey, Dan	Chr	13
Jacobsen, Joe	Prt	11
Mendoza, R.	Chr	9

STOLEN BASES

Winn, Randy	Prt	51
Garcia, Amaury	Bre	45
Ramirez, Julio	KnC	41
Harvey, Aaron	Bre	30
Podsednik, S.	KnC	28

STRIKEOUTS

Billingsley, Brent	KnC	175
Cames, Aaron	KnC	157
Rodgers, Bobby	KnC	138
Dempster, Ryan	Bre	131
Mercado, H.	Prt	126

PITCHER	CLUB	W-L	ERA	IP	H	BB	SO
Billingsley, B.	KnC	14- 7	3.01	171	146	50	175
Getz, Rod	Bre	9-12	3.23	164	166	39	92
Haynes, Heath	Prt	9- 1	3.25	111	105	23	112
Ojala, Kirt	Chr	8- 7	3.50	149	148	55	119
Townsend, D.	Prt	8- 8	3.77	141	140	52	81

1997 salaries

	Bonuses	Total earned salary
Alex Fernandez,p		7,000,000
Gary Sheffield,of		6,100,000
Bobby Bonilla,of		5,600,000
Darren Daulton,1b	25,000	4,825,000
Kevin Brown,p	10,000	4,510,000
Moises Alou,of		4,500,000
Devon White,of		3,400,000
Robb Nen,p	80,000	3,080,000
Al Leiter,p		2,900,000
Jeff Conine,1b		2,800,000
Jim Eisenreich,of		1,400,000
Livan Hernandez,p	75,000	1,050,000
Dennis Cook,p		850,000
Kurt Abbott,2b		650,000
John Cangelosi,of		525,000
Ed Vosberg,p		450,000
Alex Arias,3b		450,000
Cliff Floyd,of		390,000
Charles Johnson,c		290,000
John Wehner,of		235,000
Matt Mantei,p		225,000
Jay Powell,p		208,000
Greg Zaun,c		205,000
Edgar Renteria,ss		180,000
Kurt Miller,p		163,000
Felix Heredia,p		153,000
Bill Hurst,p		151,000
Antonio Alfonseca,p		150,000
Craig Counsell,2b		150,000
Tony Saunders,p		150,000

Average 1997 salary: $1,758,000
Total 1997 payroll: $52,740,000

Florida (1993-1997)

Runs: Most, career

344	GARY SHEFFIELD, 1993-1997
337	JEFF CONINE, 1993-1997
190	CHUCK CARR, 1993-1995
173	KURT ABBOTT, 1994-1997
158	EDGAR RENTERIA, 1996-1997

Hits: Most, career

737	JEFF CONINE, 1993-1997
501	GARY SHEFFIELD, 1993-1997
343	KURT ABBOTT, 1994-1997
339	GREG COLBRUNN, 1994-1996
331	CHUCK CARR, 1993-1995

2B: Most, career

122	JEFF CONINE, 1993-1997
87	GARY SHEFFIELD, 1993-1997
71	KURT ABBOTT, 1994-1997
58	CHUCK CARR, 1993-1995
58	GREG COLBRUNN, 1994-1996

3B: Most, career

19	KURT ABBOTT, 1994-1997
14	JEFF CONINE, 1993-1997
8	BENITO SANTIAGO, 1993-1994
8	QUILVIO VERAS, 1995-1996
7	DEVON WHITE, 1996-1997

HR: Most, career

116	GARY SHEFFIELD, 1993-1997
98	JEFF CONINE, 1993-1997
45	GREG COLBRUNN, 1994-1996
44	CHARLES JOHNSON, 1994-1997
40	KURT ABBOTT, 1994-1997

RBI: Most, career

422	JEFF CONINE, 1993-1997
352	GARY SHEFFIELD, 1993-1997
189	GREG COLBRUNN, 1994-1996
156	KURT ABBOTT, 1994-1997
143	CHARLES JOHNSON, 1994-1997

SB: Most, career

115	CHUCK CARR, 1993-1995
70	GARY SHEFFIELD, 1993-1997
64	QUILVIO VERAS, 1995-1996
48	EDGAR RENTERIA, 1996-1997
35	DEVON WHITE, 1996-1997

BB: Most, career

398	GARY SHEFFIELD, 1993-1997
277	JEFF CONINE, 1993-1997
147	CHARLES JOHNSON, 1994-1997
131	QUILVIO VERAS, 1995-1996
117	CHUCK CARR, 1993-1995

BA: Highest, career

.291	JEFF CONINE, 1993-1997
.290	EDGAR RENTERIA, 1996-1997
.289	Bret Barberie, 1993-1994
.289	GARY SHEFFIELD, 1993-1997
.284	GREG COLBRUNN, 1994-1996

On-base avg: Highest, career

.429	GARY SHEFFIELD, 1993-1997
.360	JEFF CONINE, 1993-1997
.350	Bret Barberie, 1993-1994
.340	EDGAR RENTERIA, 1996-1997
.335	ALEX ARIAS, 1993-1997

Slug avg: Highest, career

.547	GARY SHEFFIELD, 1993-1997
.467	JEFF CONINE, 1993-1997
.451	GREG COLBRUNN, 1994-1996
.428	KURT ABBOTT, 1994-1997
.427	DEVON WHITE, 1996-1997

Games started: Most, career

115	PAT RAPP, 1993-1997
78	CHRIS HAMMOND, 1993-1996
65	KEVIN BROWN, 1996-1997
60	AL LEITER, 1996-1997
55	Charlie Hough, 1993-1994

Complete games: Most, career

11	KEVIN BROWN, 1996-1997
7	PAT RAPP, 1993-1997
5	JOHN BURKETT, 1995-1996
5	ALEX FERNANDEZ, 1997
5	CHRIS HAMMOND, 1993-1996

Saves: Most, career

108	ROBB NEN, 1993-1997
51	Bryan Harvey, 1993-1995
9	Jeremy Hernandez, 1994-1995
7	TERRY MATHEWS, 1994-1996
4	JAY POWELL, 1995-1997

Shutouts: Most, career

5	KEVIN BROWN, 1996-1997
4	PAT RAPP, 1993-1997
3	CHRIS HAMMOND, 1993-1996
1	Ryan Bowen, 1993-1995
1	ALEX FERNANDEZ, 1997
1	MARK GARDNER, 1994-1995
1	Charlie Hough, 1993-1994
1	AL LEITER, 1996-1997

Wins: Most, career

37	PAT RAPP, 1993-1997
33	KEVIN BROWN, 1996-1997
29	CHRIS HAMMOND, 1993-1996
27	AL LEITER, 1996-1997
20	JOHN BURKETT, 1995-1996
20	ROBB NEN, 1993-1997

K: Most, career

384	PAT RAPP, 1993-1997
364	KEVIN BROWN, 1996-1997
332	AL LEITER, 1996-1997
328	ROBB NEN, 1993-1997
324	CHRIS HAMMOND, 1993-1996

Win pct: Highest, career

.635	KEVIN BROWN, 1996-1997
.586	ALEX FERNANDEZ, 1997
.563	AL LEITER, 1996-1997
.556	ROBB NEN, 1993-1997
.492	CHRIS HAMMOND, 1993-1996

ERA: Lowest, career

2.30	KEVIN BROWN, 1996-1997
3.41	ROBB NEN, 1993-1997
3.51	AL LEITER, 1996-1997
3.59	ALEX FERNANDEZ, 1997
4.18	PAT RAPP, 1993-1997

Runs: Most, season

118	GARY SHEFFIELD, 1996
90	EDGAR RENTERIA, 1997
88	MOISES ALOU, 1997
86	GARY SHEFFIELD, 1997
86	QUILVIO VERAS, 1995

Hits: Most, season

175	JEFF CONINE, 1996
174	JEFF CONINE, 1993
171	EDGAR RENTERIA, 1997
167	BOBBY BONILLA, 1997
163	GARY SHEFFIELD, 1996

2B: Most, season

39	BOBBY BONILLA, 1997
37	DEVON WHITE, 1996
33	GARY SHEFFIELD, 1996
32	JEFF CONINE, 1996
32	TERRY PENDLETON, 1995

3B: Most, season

7	KURT ABBOTT, 1995
7	KURT ABBOTT, 1996
7	QUILVIO VERAS, 1995
6	JEFF CONINE, 1994
6	BENITO SANTIAGO, 1993
6	DEVON WHITE, 1996

HR: Most, season

42	GARY SHEFFIELD, 1996
27	GARY SHEFFIELD, 1994
26	JEFF CONINE, 1996
25	JEFF CONINE, 1995
23	MOISES ALOU, 1997
23	GREG COLBRUNN, 1995

RBI: Most, season

120	GARY SHEFFIELD, 1996
115	MOISES ALOU, 1997
105	JEFF CONINE, 1995
96	BOBBY BONILLA, 1997
95	JEFF CONINE, 1996

SB: Most, season

58	CHUCK CARR, 1993
56	QUILVIO VERAS, 1995
32	CHUCK CARR, 1994
32	EDGAR RENTERIA, 1997
25	CHUCK CARR, 1995

BB: Most, season

142	GARY SHEFFIELD, 1996
121	GARY SHEFFIELD, 1997
80	QUILVIO VERAS, 1995
79	WALT WEISS, 1993
73	BOBBY BONILLA, 1997

BA: Highest, season

.319	JEFF CONINE, 1994
.314	GARY SHEFFIELD, 1996
.302	JEFF CONINE, 1995
.301	Bret Barberie, 1994
.297	BOBBY BONILLA, 1997

On-base avg: Highest, season

.465	GARY SHEFFIELD, 1996
.424	GARY SHEFFIELD, 1997
.392	Jerry Browne, 1994
.384	QUILVIO VERAS, 1995
.379	JEFF CONINE, 1995

Slug avg: Highest, season

.624	GARY SHEFFIELD, 1996
.526	JEFF CONINE, 1994
.520	JEFF CONINE, 1995
.493	MOISES ALOU, 1997
.484	JEFF CONINE, 1996

Games started: Most, season

34	Charlie Hough, 1993
33	Jack Armstrong, 1993
33	KEVIN BROWN, 1997
33	AL LEITER, 1996
32	KEVIN BROWN, 1996
32	ALEX FERNANDEZ, 1997
32	CHRIS HAMMOND, 1993

Complete games: Most, season

6	KEVIN BROWN, 1997
5	KEVIN BROWN, 1996
5	ALEX FERNANDEZ, 1997
4	JOHN BURKETT, 1995
3	CHRIS HAMMOND, 1995
3	PAT RAPP, 1995

Saves: Most, season

45	Bryan Harvey, 1993
35	ROBB NEN, 1996
35	ROBB NEN, 1997
23	ROBB NEN, 1995
15	ROBB NEN, 1994

Shutouts: Most, season

3	KEVIN BROWN, 1996
2	KEVIN BROWN, 1997
2	CHRIS HAMMOND, 1995
2	PAT RAPP, 1995
1	Ryan Bowen, 1993
1	ALEX FERNANDEZ, 1997
1	MARK GARDNER, 1995
1	CHRIS HAMMOND, 1994
1	Charlie Hough, 1994
1	AL LEITER, 1996
1	PAT RAPP, 1994
1	PAT RAPP, 1997

Wins: Most, season

17	KEVIN BROWN, 1996
17	ALEX FERNANDEZ, 1997
16	KEVIN BROWN, 1997
16	AL LEITER, 1996
14	JOHN BURKETT, 1995
14	PAT RAPP, 1995

K: Most, season

205	KEVIN BROWN, 1997
200	AL LEITER, 1996
183	ALEX FERNANDEZ, 1997
159	KEVIN BROWN, 1996
132	AL LEITER, 1997

Win pct: Highest, season

.667	KEVIN BROWN, 1997
.667	PAT RAPP, 1995
.607	KEVIN BROWN, 1996
.586	ALEX FERNANDEZ, 1997
.571	AL LEITER, 1996

ERA: Lowest, season

1.89	KEVIN BROWN, 1996
2.69	KEVIN BROWN, 1997
2.93	AL LEITER, 1996
3.44	PAT RAPP, 1995
3.59	ALEX FERNANDEZ, 1997

Most pinch-hit homers, season

2	KURT ABBOTT, 1996
2	Andre Dawson, 1996

Most pinch-hit homers, career

2	KURT ABBOTT, 1994-1997
2	Andre Dawson, 1995-1996

Longest hitting streak

22	EDGAR RENTERIA, 1996
21	GREG COLBRUNN, 1996
17	GREG COLBRUNN, 1995
15	Bret Barbarie, 1993
15	CHUCK CARR, 1993

Most consecutive scoreless innings

26	Luis Aquino, 1994
24	CHRIS HAMMOND, 1994
24	PAT RAPP, 1995

No-hit games

AL LEITER, Fla vs. Col NL, 11-0;
May 11,1996.
KEVIN BROWN, Fla at SF NL, 9-0;
June 10, 1997.

ACTIVE PLAYERS in caps.

Players' years of service are listed by the first and last years with this team and are not necessarily consecutive; all statistics record performances for this team only.

New York Mets

NEW YORK METS / NL EAST

210

1998 BASEBALL WEEKLY ALMANAC

By Tom DiPace

Todd Hundley fought through injuries to lead the Mets with 30 home runs and a .549 slugging average.

1997 Mets: Better than anyone had hoped

They stood there on the last day at Shea Stadium and watched their season play back in front of them, and for some, tears of joy began to fill their eyes. For the New York Mets, a team seemingly stuck in a spiral of misery, 1997 proved to be a most stunning and welcome success. Yes, it was amazin', as they say in New York. A year after managing only 71 wins, they finished 88-74 for their first winning season since 1990.

John Olerud supposedly couldn't play anymore. The lefty first baseman, acquired from the Blue Jays after the '96 season, proved he wasn't washed up at age 29, leading the club with 102 RBI and adding a .294 average and 22 homers. Of all the club's budding stars, Edgardo Alfonzo proved to be the real deal. The third baseman batted .315, and he combined with shortstop Rey Ordonez to form the best defensive left side of an infield in the league. Butch Huskey, a 240-pound outfielder, provided the most pleasant surprise with 24 home runs and a .287 average.

Todd Hundley's season was cut short by reconstructive elbow surgery, and he will likely miss a good chunk of '98. That is not good news for the Mets because there probably isn't a tougher player in baseball than Hundley. The catcher and soul of this club made his second consecutive All-Star appearance and hit .273 with 30 homers and 86 RBI.

Rick Reed was perhaps a bigger surprise than the Mets' final record. The former replacement player became a real big leaguer at the age of 31. He led a rag-tag starting staff with a 2.89 ERA, and was described by manager Bobby Valentine as a keeper. General manager Steve Phillips, who took over for the fired Joe McIlvaine in July, doesn't have to worry about his manager. Valentine, in his first full season after replacing Dallas Green, was awarded a three-year contract extension in August.

The continued improvement of the Mets could depend on Jason Isringhausen, Bill Pulsipher and Paul Wilson. The three

young pitchers combined for two victories and a lot of heartache. Isringhausen was the only one who made it back to Shea, and he showed that he has a long way to go to become the staff ace everyone thought he would be. Pulsipher never beat the control problems that arose after having reconstructive elbow surgery, and Wilson never recovered from his shoulder and elbow surgery.

This meant that the Mets starting pitching load fell to Reed, Mark Clark, Dave Mlicki and Bobby Jones. Jones began the season as the team's stopper at 12-3 but finished 15-9 with a 3.69 ERA, and Clark was traded to the Cubs. Pete Harnisch, the team's Opening Day starter, spent most of the year sidelined due to depression. He struggled upon his return and had an ugly shouting match with Valentine before being traded to Milwaukee. The Mets hope for a contribution next season from right-hander Juan Acevedo, who spent '97 being shuffled between AAA Norfolk and Shea. He is a natural starter who struggled out of the bullpen.

The team's biggest hope is for a rebirth by Isringhause, Pulsipher and Wilson. The Mets' best hitting prospect remains hard-luck outfielder Jay Payton, fresh off two major reconstructive surgeries. Payton, 24, whom some scouts have compared to Kirby Puckett, didn't play at all last season and says he still has elbow pain.

1997 Mets: Week-by-week notes

These notes were excerpted from the following issues of Baseball Weekly.

▶**April 9:** First baseman John Olerud continues to look like a different player. He hit safely in the club's first four games, going 7-for-16. However, the club's other comeback candidate, second baseman Carlos Baerga, still looks lost at the plate as he batted .154 through his first five games.

▶**April 16:** The Mets hope that Opening Day starter Pete Harnisch can return from his bout with depression and anxiety in the next 10 days. Right-hander Bobby Jones has picked up the slack for the depleted rotation, winning his first two starts and allowing only four runs in 16 innings.

▶**April 23:** Right-hander Jason Isringhausen was forced to miss his last start at AAA Norfolk in his minor league rehab with a jammed wrist. How did he do it? By punching a trash can after a shaky first inning against Toledo.

▶**April 30:** Right-hander Rick Reed, a former replacement player for the Reds, pitched a seven-hitter against his former team for his first big league win since 1994, lowering his ERA to 1.32. He has allowed just 17 hits and four walks in 27 innings. Reed, 31, entered this season with a 9-15 career record and a 4.63 ERA.

▶**May 7:** Jason Isringhausen's ailment appears to be tuberculosis and not something life-threatening. The news wasn't as good for Bill Pulsipher. The Mets optioned the left-hander to Class A Port St. Lucie after he went 0-4 with a 6.92 ERA and walked a whopping 32 hitters in 26 innings at Norfolk.

▶**May 14:** Quietly the Mets have become one of the hottest teams in baseball. Through May 11 the club had won 11 of its last 15 games. The winning spree put them at 19-18. Bobby Jones is the staff ace, running his record to 6-2 with a 2.67 ERA after shutting out the Cardinals for eight innings on May 10.

▶**May 21:** Closer John Franco has dazzled,

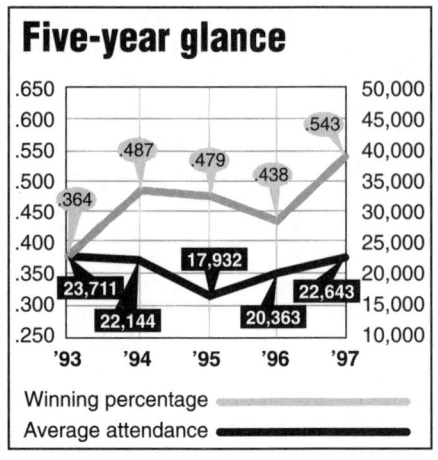

Five-year glance

Winning percentage
Average attendance

with an 0.46 ERA. He recorded his 12th save on May 17, running his scoreless innings streak to 18⅔.

▶**May 28:** Things are looking up for left fielder Bernard Gilkey, who's been mired in a season-long slump. He hit a home run and a double on May 23, then another homer the next day to boost his average to .208.

▶**June 4:** The Mets have 14 wins in their last 19 games and are 30-23 overall. They finished May an astounding 18-9. They even beat their nemesis, Montreal fireballer Pedro Martinez, who hadn't lost to anybody this season and hadn't lost to the Mets in his life.

▶**June 11:** The Mets have lost shortstop Rey Ordonez for four to six weeks with a broken hand. Manny Alexander, who will replace him, has started 23 games this season, 15 at second and eight at short.

▶**June 18:** Right-hander Mark Clark had a no-hitter for seven innings in a 5-2 win on June 14, but Red Sox pinch-hitter Reggie Jefferson singled to open the eighth. Clark also got his first hit in 46 at-bats, dating to last season—a home run.

▶**June 25:** Bobby Jones continues to impress. He matched his career high in victories with his NL-leading 12th win on June 20 in a 1-0 victory against the Pirates. Jones had won eight consecutive starts before lasting only four innings against the Red Sox his previous time out.

▸**July 10:** Todd Hundley has a hyper-extended right elbow. The tough and gritty catcher will try to put off surgery as long as he can, but how long can he last? Hundley, the heart and soul of this team, is batting .300 with 19 homers and 51 RBI in 77 games.

▸**July 16:** Third baseman Edgardo Alfonzo had his 20-game hitting streak snapped on July 11, then injured his right hamstring the next day. It's not serious.

▸**July 23:** With the Mets enjoying their best season this decade, general manager Joe McIlvaine was sacked as general manager. The move was made, according to co-owner Fred Wilpon, because McIlvaine didn't grasp the entire scope of the position. Manager Bobby Valentine tried to counter allegations that he had lobbied for the firing behind closed doors.

▸**July 30:** New GM Steve Phillips reiterated he is looking for a reliever to complement John Franco and setup man Greg McMichael, before the trading deadline.

▸**Aug. 13:** By the ninth inning on Aug. 10, Mel Rojas had been in New York for all of three hours and the boos had already started. Before his nightmare was over, Rojas—the key to a six-player swap with the Cubs—had served up five runs in the ninth inning in an 8-3 loss to the Astros.

▸**Aug. 20:** Right-hander Pete Harnisch was thrust into the rotation as a critical cog after missing four months with clinical depression. After pitching triumphantly in his first start back, Harnisch got buried by the Astros on Aug. 11, allowing eight runs and 10 hits in 4⅔ innings.

▸**Aug. 27:** Bobby Valentine picked a very public fight with Todd Hundley last week following a recent slump, implying to reporters that Hundley is out carousing on a nightly basis, and saying he needs to get more sleep. "I would never put one of my players through that," responded Hundley, whose mother is stricken with cancer. Hundley didn't let Valentine affect him at all over the weekend. With the Mets fading from the wild-card race, Hundley paced them to two desperately needed wins, hitting a game-tying, two-run homer in the bottom of the ninth in a

9-8 victory against the Padres on Aug. 22. He came back the next day with a grand slam in a 9-5 win.

▸**Sept. 3:** It was another strange week for Bobby Valentine. The beleaguered manager received a three-year contract extension, got trashed by Pete Harnisch (who was traded to Milwaukee on Aug. 31) and saw his team fade further from the wild-card race.

▸**Sept. 10:** Butch Huskey, who has 21 homers, is now almost certain to be protected in the November expansion draft. Huskey hit his third home run in as many games at Wrigley Field on Sept. 7 and extended his hitting streak to 15 games.

▸**Sept. 17:** The game epitomized a season. On Sept. 13 at Shea Stadium, the Mets trailed the Expos 6-0 entering the ninth, but they won the game 9-6. Minor league call-up Roberto Petagine hit a two-run single, and outfielder Carl Everett followed with a two-out grand slam on a 3-2 pitch. Bernard Gilkey then won the game with a pinch-hit three-run homer in the 11th.

▸**Sept. 24:** Jason Isringhausen allowed seven runs and 10 hits over three innings to the Braves last week. Since his comeback, he is 2-2 with an 8.03 ERA, having allowed 34 hits in 24⅔ innings. Rey Ordonez went 37 at-bats without a hit before a fifth-inning single on Sept. 19, the most ever by a Mets position player.

▸**Oct. 1:** Some of the glow from the Mets' season dimmed when Todd Hundley underwent reconstructive surgery on his right elbow last week. He will miss at least one-third of next season and maybe more. One of the biggest surprises this year was former replacement player turned ace Rick Reed, who capped his campaign with eight innings of one-run ball in a victory against the Braves on Sept. 27. He finished 13-9 with a 2.89 ERA.

QUOTE OF THE YEAR

"Welcome to New York."
—Manager Bobby Valentine, to reliever
Mel Rojas after he gave up
five runs in his first inning as a Met

NEW YORK METS 1997 final stats

BATTERS	BA	SLG	OBA	G	AB	R	H	TB	2B	3B	HR	RBI	BB	SO	SB	CS	E
Alfonzo	.315	.432	.391	151	518	84	163	224	27	2	10	72	63	56	11	6	12
Olerud	.294	.489	.400	154	524	90	154	256	34	1	22	102	85	67	0	0	7
Huskey	.287	.503	.319	142	471	61	135	237	26	2	24	81	25	84	8	5	15
Tomberlin	.286	.286	.375	6	7	0	2	2	0	0	0	0	1	3	0	0	0
Pratt	.283	.396	.372	39	106	12	30	42	6	0	2	19	13	32	0	1	2
Baerga	.281	.396	.311	133	467	53	131	185	25	1	9	52	20	54	2	6	14
M. Franco	.276	.399	.330	112	163	21	45	65	5	0	5	21	13	23	1	0	4
Hundley	.273	.549	.394	132	417	78	114	229	21	2	30	86	83	116	2	3	10
Lopez	.270	.365	.330	78	178	19	48	65	12	1	1	19	12	42	2	4	9
Hardtke	.268	.411	.323	30	56	9	15	23	2	0	2	8	4	6	1	1	1
Mendoza	.250	.250	.500	15	12	6	3	3	0	0	0	1	4	2	0	0	0
Gilkey	.249	.417	.338	145	518	85	129	216	31	1	18	78	70	111	7	11	3
Everett	.248	.420	.308	142	443	58	110	186	28	3	14	57	32	102	17	9	7
Bieser	.246	.290	.346	47	69	16	17	20	3	0	0	4	7	20	2	3	0
Ochoa	.244	.349	.300	113	238	31	58	83	14	1	3	22	18	32	3	4	2
McRae	.242	.383	.326	153	562	86	136	215	32	7	11	43	65	84	17	10	4
Ordonez	.216	.256	.255	120	356	35	77	91	5	3	1	33	18	36	11	5	9
Castillo	.203	.220	.304	35	59	3	12	13	1	0	0	7	9	16	0	1	2
Thurman	.167	.167	.167	11	6	0	1	1	0	0	0	0	0	0	0	1	0
Gilbert	.136	.273	.174	29	22	3	3	6	0	0	1	1	1	8	1	0	1
Petagine	.067	.067	.222	12	15	2	1	1	0	0	0	2	3	6	0	0	0
Morgan	.000	.000	.000	1	1	0	0	0	0	0	0	0	0	0	0	0	0

PITCHERS	W-L	ERA	BA	G	GS	CG	GF	Sho	SV	IP	H	R	ER	HR	BB	SO
J. Franco	5-3	2.55	.226	59	0	0	53	0	36	60.0	49	18	17	3	20	53
Reed	13-9	2.89	.239	33	31	2	0	0	0	208.1	186	76	67	19	31	113
McMichael	7-10	2.98	.233	73	0	0	23	0	7	87.2	73	34	29	8	27	81
Crawford	4-3	3.30	.216	19	2	0	9	0	0	46.1	36	18	17	7	13	25
Lidle	7-2	3.53	.274	54	2	0	20	0	2	81.2	86	38	32	7	20	54
Acevedo	3-1	3.59	.286	25	2	0	4	0	0	47.2	52	24	19	6	22	33
Jones	15-9	3.63	.242	30	30	2	0	1	0	193.1	177	88	78	24	63	125
Bohanon	6-4	3.82	.258	19	14	0	0	0	0	94.1	95	49	40	9	34	66
Mlicki	8-12	4.00	.259	32	32	1	0	1	0	193.2	194	89	86	21	76	157
Kashiwada	3-1	4.31	.289	35	0	0	11	0	0	31.1	35	15	15	4	18	19
Wendell	3-5	4.36	.240	65	0	0	21	0	5	76.1	68	42	37	7	53	64
Reynoso	6-3	4.53	.275	16	16	1	0	1	0	91.1	95	47	46	7	29	47
Rojas	0-6	4.64	.241	77	0	0	50	0	15	85.1	78	47	44	15	36	93
Manuel	0-1	5.26	.324	19	0	0	6	0	0	25.2	35	18	15	6	13	21
Jordan	1-2	5.33	.304	22	0	0	4	0	0	27.0	31	17	16	1	15	19
Borland	0-1	6.08	.220	13	0	0	5	0	1	13.1	11	9	9	1	14	7
Isringhausen	2-2	7.58	.336	6	6	0	0	0	0	29.2	40	27	25	3	22	25
Trlicek	0-0	8.00	.303	9	0	0	4	0	0	9.0	10	9	8	2	5	4
Harnisch	0-1	8.06	.327	6	5	0	0	0	0	25.2	35	24	23	5	11	12
Perez	0-1	8.31	.375	9	0	0	1	0	0	8.2	15	8	8	2	4	7

1998 preliminary roster

PITCHERS (21)
Juan Acevedo
Brian Bohanon
Dennis Cook
Joe Crawford
Octavio Dotel
John Franco
Arnold Gooch
John Hudek
Jason Isringhausen
Bobby Jones
Greg McMichael
Hector Mercado

Dave Mlicki
Bill Pulsipher
Rick Reed
Armando Reynoso
Mel Rojas
Jesus Sanchez
Derek Wallace
Turk Wendell
Paul Wilson

CATCHERS (4)
Alberto Castillo
Todd Hundley

Todd Pratt
Vance Wilson

INFIELDERS (7)
Edgardo Alfonzo
Carlos Baerga
Matt Franco
Luis Lopez
John Olerud
Rey Ordonez
Roberto Petagine

OUTFIELDERS (8)
Carl Everett
Bernard Gilkey
Scott Hunter
Butch Huskey
Terrence Long
Brian McRae
Jay Payton
Preston Wilson

Games played by position

PLAYER	G	C	1B	2B	3B	SS	OF
Alfonzo	151	0	0	3	143	12	0
Baerga	133	0	0	131	0	0	0
Bieser	47	2	0	0	0	0	21
Castillo	35	34	0	0	0	0	0
Everett	142	0	0	0	0	0	128
M. Franco	112	0	13	0	39	0	1
Gilbert	29	0	0	8	3	6	1
Gilkey	145	0	0	0	0	0	136
Hardtke	30	0	0	21	1	0	0
Hundley	132	122	0	0	0	0	0
Huskey	142	0	22	0	15	0	92
Lopez	78	0	0	20	4	45	0
McRae	153	0	0	0	0	0	148
Mendoza	15	0	0	0	0	0	3
Morgan	1	0	0	0	1	0	0
Ochoa	113	0	0	0	0	0	88
Olerud	154	0	146	0	0	0	0
Ordonez	120	0	0	0	0	118	0
Petagine	12	0	6	0	0	0	1
Pratt	39	36	0	0	0	0	0
Thurman	11	0	0	0	0	0	7
Tomberlin	6	0	0	0	0	0	2

Sick call: 1997 DL report

PLAYER	Days on the DL
Manny Alexander	46*
Shawn Gilbert	18
Pete Harnisch	125
Jason Isringhausen	148
Lance Johnson	45
Rey Ordonez	39
Yorkis Perez	65
Bill Pulsipher	32
Armando Reynoso	88*
Andy Tomberlin	173
Ricky Trlicek	109
Derek Wallace	181
Paul Wilson	151

Indicates two separate terms on Disabled List.

Minor Leagues
Tops in the organization

BATTER	CLUB	AVG.	G	AB	R	H	HR	RBI
Petagine, R.	Nor	.317	129	441	90	140	31	100
Agbayani, B.	Nor	.310	127	468	90	145	11	51
Ramirez, D.	Clb	.305	130	478	82	146	1	42
Seefried, Tate	Nor	.295	129	431	70	127	32	92
Moreno, Juan	Ptf	.289	71	287	35	83	2	41

HOME RUNS

Raleigh, Matt	Bng	37	Sanchez, J.	Bng	13
Seefried, Tate	Nor	32	Murray, Dan	SLu	12
Petagine, R.	Nor	31	Pumphrey, K.	Clb	12
Wilson, Preston	Bng	30	Roberts, Grant	Clb	11
Bates, Fletcher	Bng	23	Kessel, Kyle	Clb	11

WINS (included above)

RBI

			SAVES		
Petagine, R.	Nor	100	Welch, Mike	Mof	20
Wilson, Preston	Bng	95	Lisio, Joseph	SLu	16
Seefried, Tate	Bng	92	Lyons, Mike	Clb	14
Raleigh, Matt	Bng	74	Turrentine, Rich	Bng	13
Haltiwanger, G.	Clb	73	Cammack, Eric	Ptf	8

STOLEN BASES

			STRIKEOUTS		
Ramirez, Daniel	Clb	51	Sanchez, Jesus	Bng	176
Agbayani, B.	Nor	29	Kessel, Kyle	Clb	151
Bruce, Maurice	Ptf	26	Yarnall, Ed	Bng	148
Hunter, Scott	Bng	24	Herbison, Brett	Clb	146
Long, Terrence	SLu	24	Pumphrey, K.	Clb	133

PITCHER	CLUB	W-L	ERA	IP	H	BB	SO
Comer, Scott	PtF	7-1	1.74	93	71	12	98
Roberts, Grant	Clb	11-3	2.36	130	98	44	122
Edmondson, B.	Nor	6-3	2.49	90	79	44	83
Bohanon, Brian	Nor	9-3	2.63	96	88	32	84
Kessel, Kyle	Clb	11-11	2.72	169	131	53	151

1997 salaries

	Bonuses	Total earned salary
John Olerud,1b		6,500,000
Carlos Baerga,2b		4,791,667
Mel Rojas,p		4,583,333
Todd Hundley,c	25,000	4,150,000
Brian McRae,of		3,900,000
Bernard Gilkey,of		3,850,000
John Franco,p	250,000	3,000,000
Bobby Jones,p		1,925,000
Greg McMichael,p		1,100,000
Armando Reynoso,p		1,000,000
Dave Mlicki,p		610,000
Yorkis Perez,p		375,000
Turk Wendell,p		350,000
Luis Lopez,ss		275,000
Edgardo Alfonzo,3b		215,000
Butch Huskey,of		212,000
Rick Reed,p		212,000
Jason Isringhausen,p		212,000
Carl Everett,of		205,000
Brian Bohanon,p		205,000
Todd Pratt,c		200,000
Andy Tomberlin,of		200,000
Rey Ordonez,ss		192,500
Rick Trlicek,p		177,500
Matt Franco,3b		160,000
Ricardo Jordan,p		155,000
Alex Ochoa,of		152,000
Derek Wallace,p		151,500
Cory Lidle,p		150,000

Average 1997 salary: $1,352,052
Total 1997 payroll: $39,209,500

New York (1962-1997)

216

Runs: Most, career

662	DARRYL STRAWBERRY, 1983-1990
627	Howard Johnson, 1985-1993
592	Mookie Wilson, 1980-1989
563	Cleon Jones, 1963-1975
536	Ed Kranepool, 1962-1979

Hits: Most, career

1418	Ed Kranepool, 1962-1979
1188	Cleon Jones, 1963-1975
1112	Mookie Wilson, 1980-1989
1029	Bud Harrelson, 1965-1977
1025	DARRYL STRAWBERRY, 1983-1990

2B: Most, career

225	Ed Kranepool, 1962-1979
214	Howard Johnson, 1985-1993
187	DARRYL STRAWBERRY, 1983-1990
182	Cleon Jones, 1963-1975
170	Mookie Wilson, 1980-1989

3B: Most, career

62	Mookie Wilson, 1980-1989
45	Bud Harrelson, 1965-1977
33	Cleon Jones, 1963-1975
31	Steve Henderson, 1977-1980
30	DARRYL STRAWBERRY, 1983-1990

HR: Most, career

252	DARRYL STRAWBERRY, 1983-1990
192	Howard Johnson, 1985-1993
154	Dave Kingman, 1975-1983
122	Kevin McReynolds, 1987-1994
121	TODD HUNDLEY, 1990-1997

RBI: Most, career

733	DARRYL STRAWBERRY, 1983-1990
629	Howard Johnson, 1985-1993
614	Ed Kranepool, 1962-1979
521	Cleon Jones, 1963-1975
468	Keith Hernandez, 1983-1989

SB: Most, career

281	Mookie Wilson, 1980-1989
202	Howard Johnson, 1985-1993
191	DARRYL STRAWBERRY, 1983-1990
152	Lee Mazzilli, 1976-1989
116	Lenny Dykstra, 1985-1989

BB: Most, career

580	DARRYL STRAWBERRY, 1983-1990
573	Bud Harrelson, 1965-1977
556	Howard Johnson, 1985-1993
482	Wayne Garrett, 1969-1976
471	Keith Hernandez, 1983-1989

BA: Highest, career

.297	Keith Hernandez, 1983-1989
.292	DAVE MAGADAN, 1986-1992
.283	Wally Backman, 1980-1988
.281	Cleon Jones, 1963-1975
.278	Lenny Dykstra, 1985-1989

On-base avg: Highest, career, all-time

.391	DAVE MAGADAN, 1986-1992
.387	Keith Hernandez, 1983-1989
.359	DARRYL STRAWBERRY, 1983-1990
.358	Rusty Staub, 1972-1985
.357	Lee Mazzilli, 1976-1989

Slug avg: Highest, career

.520	DARRYL STRAWBERRY, 1983-1990
.460	Kevin McReynolds, 1987-1994
.459	Howard Johnson, 1985-1993
.453	Dave Kingman, 1975-1983
.447	TODD HUNDLEY, 1990-1997

Games started: Most, career, all-time

395	Tom Seaver, 1967-1983
346	Jerry Koosman, 1967-1978
303	DWIGHT GOODEN, 1984-1994
250	SID FERNANDEZ, 1984-1993
241	Ron Darling, 1983-1991

Complete games: Most, career

171	Tom Seaver, 1967-1983
108	Jerry Koosman, 1967-1978
67	DWIGHT GOODEN, 1984-1994
65	Jon Matlack, 1971-1977
41	Al Jackson, 1962-1969

Saves: Most, career

211	JOHN FRANCO, 1990-1997
107	JESSE OROSCO, 1979-1987
86	Tug McGraw, 1965-1974
84	Roger McDowell, 1985-1989
69	Neil Allen, 1979-1983

Shutouts: Most, career

44	Tom Seaver, 1967-1983
26	Jerry Koosman, 1967-1978
26	Jon Matlack, 1971-1977
23	DWIGHT GOODEN, 1984-1994
15	DAVID CONE, 1987-1992

Wins: Most, career

198	Tom Seaver, 1967-1983
157	DWIGHT GOODEN, 1984-1994
140	Jerry Koosman, 1967-1978
99	Ron Darling, 1983-1991
98	SID FERNANDEZ, 1984-1993

K: Most, career

2541	Tom Seaver, 1967-1983
1875	DWIGHT GOODEN, 1984-1994
1799	Jerry Koosman, 1967-1978
1449	SID FERNANDEZ, 1984-1993
1159	DAVID CONE, 1987-1992

Win pct: Highest, career

.649	DWIGHT GOODEN, 1984-1994
.625	DAVID CONE, 1987-1992
.615	Tom Seaver, 1967-1983
.586	Ron Darling, 1983-1991
.573	BOBBY JONES, 1993-1997

ERA: Lowest, career

2.57	Tom Seaver, 1967-1983
3.03	Jon Matlack, 1971-1977
3.08	DAVID CONE, 1987-1992
3.09	Jerry Koosman, 1967-1978
3.10	DWIGHT GOODEN, 1984-1994

Runs: Most, season

117	LANCE JOHNSON, 1996
108	BERNARD GILKEY, 1996
108	Howard Johnson, 1991
108	DARRYL STRAWBERRY, 1987
107	Tommie Agee, 1970

Hits: Most, season

227	LANCE JOHNSON, 1996
191	Felix Millan, 1975
185	Felix Millan, 1973
183	Keith Hernandez, 1985
182	Tommie Agee, 1970

2B: Most, season

44	BERNARD GILKEY, 1996
41	Howard Johnson, 1989
40	GREGG JEFFERIES, 1990
37	Lenny Dykstra, 1987
37	Howard Johnson, 1990
37	Felix Millan, 1975
37	EDDIE MURRAY, 1992
37	Joel Youngblood, 1979

3B: Most, season

21	LANCE JOHNSON, 1996
10	Mookie Wilson, 1984
9	Steve Henderson, 1978
9	Charlie Neal, 1962
9	Frank Taveras, 1979
9	Mookie Wilson, 1982

HR: Most, season

41	TODD HUNDLEY, 1996
39	DARRYL STRAWBERRY, 1987
39	DARRYL STRAWBERRY, 1988
38	Howard Johnson, 1991
37	Dave Kingman, 1976
37	Dave Kingman, 1982
37	DARRYL STRAWBERRY, 1990

RBI: Most, season

117	BERNARD GILKEY, 1996
117	Howard Johnson, 1991
112	TODD HUNDLEY, 1996
108	DARRYL STRAWBERRY, 1990
105	Gary Carter, 1986
105	Rusty Staub, 1975

SB: Most, season

58	Mookie Wilson, 1982
54	Mookie Wilson, 1983
50	LANCE JOHNSON, 1996
46	Mookie Wilson, 1984
42	Frank Taveras, 1979

BB: Most, season

97	Keith Hernandez, 1984
97	DARRYL STRAWBERRY, 1987
95	Bud Harrelson, 1970
94	Keith Hernandez, 1986
93	Lee Mazzilli, 1979

BA: Highest, season

.340	Cleon Jones, 1969
.333	LANCE JOHNSON, 1996
.328	DAVE MAGADAN, 1990
.319	Cleon Jones, 1971
.317	BERNARD GILKEY, 1996

On-base avg: Highest, season

.422	Cleon Jones, 1969
.417	DAVE MAGADAN, 1990
.413	Keith Hernandez, 1986
.409	Keith Hernandez, 1984
.400	JOHN OLERUD, 1997

Slug avg: Highest, season

.583	DARRYL STRAWBERRY, 1987
.562	BERNARD GILKEY, 1996
.559	Howard Johnson, 1989
.550	TODD HUNDLEY, 1996
.549	TODD HUNDLEY, 1997

Games started: Most, season

36	Jack Fisher, 1965
36	Tom Seaver, 1970
36	Tom Seaver, 1973
36	Tom Seaver, 1975
35	Ron Darling, 1985
35	Gary Gentry, 1969
35	DWIGHT GOODEN, 1985
35	Jerry Koosman, 1973
35	Jerry Koosman, 1974
35	Jon Matlack, 1976
35	Tom Seaver, 1968
35	Tom Seaver, 1969
35	Tom Seaver, 1971
35	Tom Seaver, 1972
35	Craig Swan, 1979
35	Frank Viola, 1990
35	Frank Viola, 1991

Complete games: Most, season

21	Tom Seaver, 1971
19	Tom Seaver, 1970
18	Tom Seaver, 1967
18	Tom Seaver, 1969
18	Tom Seaver, 1973

Saves: Most, season

36	JOHN FRANCO, 1997
33	JOHN FRANCO, 1990
31	JESSE OROSCO, 1984
30	JOHN FRANCO, 1991
30	JOHN FRANCO, 1994

Shutouts: Most, season

8	DWIGHT GOODEN, 1985
7	Jerry Koosman, 1968
7	Jon Matlack, 1974
6	Jerry Koosman, 1969
6	Jon Matlack, 1976

Wins: Most, season

25	Tom Seaver, 1969
24	DWIGHT GOODEN, 1985
22	Tom Seaver, 1975
21	Jerry Koosman, 1976
21	Tom Seaver, 1972

K: Most, season

289	Tom Seaver, 1971
283	Tom Seaver, 1970
276	DWIGHT GOODEN, 1984
268	DWIGHT GOODEN, 1985
251	Tom Seaver, 1973

Win pct: Highest, season

.870	DAVID CONE, 1988
.857	DWIGHT GOODEN, 1985
.783	Bob Ojeda, 1986
.781	Tom Seaver, 1969
.739	DWIGHT GOODEN, 1986

ERA: Lowest, season

1.53	DWIGHT GOODEN, 1985
1.76	Tom Seaver, 1971
2.08	Tom Seaver, 1973
2.08	Jerry Koosman, 1968
2.20	Tom Seaver, 1968

Most pinch-hit homers, season

4	Danny Heep, 1983
4	Mark Carreon, 1989

Most pinch-hit homers, career

8	Mark Carreon, 1987-1991
6	Ed Kranepool, 1962-1979
6	Rusty Staub, 1972-1985

Most consecutive games, batting safely

24	Hubie Brooks, 1984
23	Cleon Jones, 1970
23	Mike Vail, 1975
20	Tommie Agee, 1970
20	BUTCH HUSKEY, 1997

Most consecutive scoreless innings

31	Jerry Koosman, 1973

No-hit games

None

ACTIVE PLAYERS in caps.

Players' years of service are listed by the first and last years with this team and are not necessarily consecutive; all statistics record performances for this team only.

Montreal Expos

By Andrew Vaughan, AP/Wide World Photos

Rookie outfielder Vladimir Guerrero batted .302 in 1997 despite going on the DL three times.

1997 Expos: Alou finally couldn't keep up

Somebody asked Felipe Alou about the meaning of meaningless games in late September, when a team is out of contention, and the Expos manager held up his hands. "It's been September around here since sometime in August," he said. The Expos and their $17 million payroll were simply blown out of the water by the Braves and the Marlins. Injuries to rookie outfielder Vladimir Guerrero and outfielder Henry Rodriguez drove home the reality of the Expos' tenuous financial position, as their replacements struggled. "I look at us as having fallen back into the middle of the league because of injuries," said GM Jim Beattie.

There were positive elements to the season. The Expos put together a franchise-record-tying 10-game winning streak in June and had a 12-3 record in interleague play. They had Cy Young Award winner Pedro Martinez, who became the 14th pitcher this century to record 300-plus strikeouts. Martinez put together his season despite having the second-worst run support in the league among ERA-title qualifiers. Lansing, who had 45 doubles and 70 RBI, established himself as a top second baseman. They had four players hit 20 or more homers: Rondell White (28), Rodriguez (26), David Segui (21) and Mike Lansing (20).

But it wasn't enough, and after a year in which the club drew only 1.5 million fans despite drastically reduced ticket prices, team president Claude Brochu claimed the team lost $13 million. Beattie and Brochu announced that there would be cutbacks in 1998 and that Martinez and Lansing were on the trade block.

Shortstop Mark Grudzielanek had 54 doubles, a major league record for his position. But he made 32 errors, and his batting average dropped 33 points from 1996. First baseman Segui, hitting out of the cleanup spot for 119 games, batted .307. Catcher Darrin Fletcher had a .513 slugging percentage and hit 17 home runs. Third baseman Doug Strange had 12 homers and drove in 47 runs after replacing Shane Andrews, who missed

most of the year with a nerve inflammation in his shoulder.

Left-hander Carlos Perez went 12-13 (3.88 ERA) with a major-league-leading five shutouts, after missing all of 1996 because of shoulder surgery. Right-hander Dustin Hermanson, a reliever throughout his professional career, went 8-8 with a 3.69 ERA as a starter. Closer Ugueth Urbina had 27 saves and a 3.78 ERA.

Beattie couldn't have been any clearer about his intentions for 1998 than he was in his news conference after the season. Expos fans were told to wait until next century. "Everything we do from this point forward will point to fielding a championship club in our new stadium," said Beattie. "We'll point to 2001 rather than 1998." Before 1997 had ended, Martinez, Segui, Lansing, Rodriguez and Fletcher were already gone.

The coming season promises to be a trying one for whatever fans the Expos have left. The club says that it wants to keep core young players like Guerrero, Grudzielanek and Urbina. Guerrero, who missed a total of 52 games, needs to stay healthier. Ryan McGuire, whose sweet lefty swing and versatility made him a valuable contributor off the bench, will become the club's primary utility player. Brad Fullmer and Orlando Cabrera will become key every-day players. Fullmer is a left-handed hitter who crushed 33 homers at three levels in 1997. Cabrera, who hit .285 in the minors with 12 homers, 58 RBI and 47 steals, could become the Expos' leadoff hitter and second baseman.

1997 Expos: Week-by-week notes

These notes were excerpted from the following issues of Baseball Weekly.

▶**April 9:** Left-hander Carlos Perez tossed seven innings of seven-hit ball in his first major league start since Sept. 22, 1995. He got the win in the 9-4 conquest of the Cardinals on April 3. Shoulder surgery shut him down in 1996. On April 6, reliever Lee Smith appeared in his 1,000th major league game, joining Hoyt Wilhelm (1,070), Kent Tekulve (1,050) and Goose Gossage (1,002) as the only pitchers to reach the mark.

▶**April 16:** Shortstop Mark Grudzielanek had a difficult start, going 6-for-34. He also made three errors in a game against the Rockies and later admitted he was taking his offensive woes with him on to the field.

▶**April 30:** Lee Smith has put 1996 behind him and says that pitching in Montreal for manager Felipe Alou "is just like Christmas compared to what went on last year," when he pitched for the Angels and the Reds. Smith has become an integral part of the bullpen and did not allow a run in his first eight games as an Expo.

▶**May 7:** Mark Grudzielanek had a 17-game hitting streak end on May 3. The streak, which was four games away from the Expos' high set by Delino DeShields in 1993, matched Grudzielanek's previous career best. He went 29-for-69 (.420) during the streak.

▶**May 14:** It was one for the record books when the Expos banged out 13 runs on 13 hits in the sixth inning of a 19-3 win against the Giants. The May 7 outburst set a major league record for a sixth inning. The Expos set or tied seven club records, including most batters in an inning (17) and most consecutive hits (eight).

▶**May 21:** The Expos' 14-13 win against the Giants on May 16 was accomplished after Montreal came back from an 11-2 deficit. It was the largest comeback in club history.

▶**May 28:** Catchers Darrin Fletcher and Chris Widger had driven in 42 runs

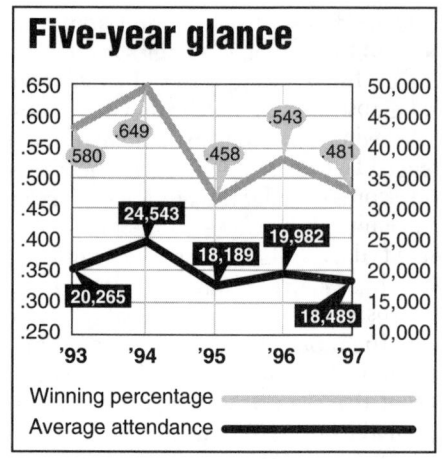

Five-year glance

	'93	'94	'95	'96	'97
Winning percentage	.580	.649	.458	.543	.481
Average attendance	20,265	24,543	18,189	19,982	18,489

between them after 47 games and were hitting .288 with 10 home runs. Opposing teams have been successful on about 89% of their stolen base attempts, but it was a trade-off that manager Felipe Alou was willing to make.

▶**June 4:** Right-hander Pedro Martinez's eight-game winning streak ended on May 28 when the Mets beat him 7-0. Martinez had been 10-0 lifetime against the Mets, who scored five unearned runs in the game.

▶**June 11:** Right fielder Vladimir Guerrero was placed on the 15-day DL on June 5. He aggravated a pulled right hamstring trying to make a throw to the infield in a game against the Braves. The injury came two days after first baseman David Segui underwent arthroscopic surgery on a torn meniscus in his left knee. Meanwhile, center fielder Rondell White is hobbling with a pulled hamstring.

▶**June 18:** Carlos Perez is back. Perez, who made the NL All-Star team in 1995 as a rookie, was named NL pitcher of the week after tossing back-to-back shutouts.

▶**June 25:** The hourglass has been turned over. Montreal's business community has a year to commit to $70-to-$80 million worth of seat licenses and private boxes, or the Expos will leave town before the 1999 season. On the field, the Expos won two of three interleague games at Camden Yards, though the one loss snapped a 10-game winning streak that equaled a franchise record. Carlos Perez pitched his third shutout in four games in the rubber match.

▶**July 10:** Right-hander Jeff Juden finished out his first half with an exclamation point, tossing a complete game in an Expos win against the Braves on July 6. Juden, 11-2, extended his winning streak to six consecutive games. Juden also was the winning pitcher in the Expos' 2-1 win against the Blue Jays on Canada Day, when he beat his boyhood idol, Roger Clemens, at SkyDome.

▶**July 16:** Vladimir Guerrero, the club's best hitter heading into the break, was lost for three to four weeks after he was hit on the left hand by the Reds' Stan Belinda. Guerrero was hitting .329 with six home runs and 26 RBI. It was his third trip to the DL this year.

▶**July 23:** Lee Smith, 39, the major league career save leader with 478, decided to retire while at the team's hotel in Fort Lauderdale before a game against the Marlins. He called general manager Jim Beattie and then talked to Felipe Alou. With Smith gone, Alou said he would use either Dave Veres or Anthony Telford to spell closer Ugueth Urbina.

▶**Aug. 6:** Whatever anger existed in the clubhouse after the Expos' failure to make a major deal at the trading deadline, it did not appear to extend to the trade of Jeff Juden to the Indians. Juden angered a number of his teammates during a recent start in Houston when he hit the Astros' Chuck Carr with a pitch with two out in the fifth inning of a 2-2 game and then served up a two-run home run by Jeff Bagwell. To make matters worse, Juden verbally assaulted Pedro Martinez and utility man F.P. Santangelo during a team charter.

▶**Aug. 20:** After a recent 1-0 loss to the Dodgers, Pedro Martinez led the league in ERA (1.70), complete games (11) and opponents' batting average (.175). He was second in strikeouts (219, to Curt Schilling's 232) and tied with Carlos Perez and Darryl Kile with a league-leading four shutouts.

▶**Aug. 27:** Nowhere have the Expos been hurt more by a reluctance to spend money than in their starting pitching. When right-hander Mike Johnson beat St. Louis on Aug. 21 it was the first win out of the No. 4 and No. 5 spots in the rotation since righty Jim Bullinger beat the Reds on July 11.

▶**Sept. 3:** Pedro Martinez broke the team record for strikeouts on Aug. 30 in a win over the Yankees when he struck out 10, giving him 255. Bill Stoneman, currently the Expos' vice president of baseball operations, held the club record of 251, set in 1971. Mark Grudzielanek tied the Expos' record for doubles on Aug. 29 when he hit his 46th, equaling Warren Cromartie's total in 1979.

▶**Sept. 10:** Brad Fullmer, who was called up from AAA Ottawa on Sept. 2, has played first base this year but will likely be in left field next year. He slugged a two-run, pinch-hit home run off the Boston's Bret Saberhagen in his first major league at-bat, becoming the 73rd first-time hitter to do so.

▶**Sept. 17:** F.P. Santangelo left the Expos three games into their 12-game road trip, returning to Montreal to have his hand examined. Santangelo broke his right thumb sliding into second base. He has been mired in a .169 hitting funk since the All-Star break.

▶**Oct. 1:** The team that perfected winning cheap is going to downsize even more in 1998, as the Expos try to cope with what president Claude Brochu said was a $13 million loss. Brochu told manager Felipe Alou and his coaches that the club would not re-sign veterans such as David Segui and Darrin Fletcher. The status of Mike Lansing and Pedro Martinez was not discussed, but that was taken to mean neither player would be back. Mark Grudzielanek finished with 54 doubles, tying Alex Rodriguez's major league mark for shortstops, set last year.

QUOTE OF THE YEAR

"It fills an emptiness I've had in my life a long time. I consider myself a whole person now."
—Catcher Darrin Fletcher, after stealing his first base, in his 659th game

MONTREAL EXPOS 1997 final stats

BATTERS	BA	SLG	OBA	G	AB	R	H	TB	2B	3B	HR	RBI	BB	SO	SB	CS	E
Segui	.307	.505	.380	125	459	75	141	232	22	3	21	68	57	66	1	0	6
Guerrero	.302	.483	.350	90	325	44	98	157	22	2	11	40	19	39	3	4	12
Fullmer	.300	.575	.349	19	40	4	12	23	2	0	3	8	2	7	0	0	2
Meulens	.292	.583	.379	16	24	6	7	14	1	0	2	6	4	10	0	1	0
Lansing	.281	.472	.338	144	572	86	161	270	45	2	20	70	45	92	11	5	9
Fletcher	.277	.513	.323	96	310	39	86	159	20	1	17	55	17	35	1	1	4
Grudzielanek	.273	.384	.307	156	649	76	177	249	54	3	4	51	23	76	25	9	32
White	.270	.478	.316	151	592	84	160	283	29	5	28	82	31	111	16	8	3
Chavez	.269	.269	.259	13	26	0	7	7	0	0	0	2	0	5	1	0	0
Strange	.257	.428	.332	118	327	40	84	140	16	2	12	47	36	76	0	2	13
McGuire	.256	.397	.320	84	199	22	51	79	15	2	3	17	19	34	1	4	3
Santangelo	.249	.374	.379	130	350	56	87	131	19	5	5	31	50	73	8	5	3
Vidro	.249	.367	.297	67	169	19	42	62	12	1	2	17	11	20	1	0	4
Rodriguez	.244	.479	.306	132	476	55	116	228	28	3	26	83	42	149	3	3	3
Widger	.234	.403	.290	91	278	30	65	112	20	3	7	37	22	59	2	0	11
Orsulak	.227	.340	.310	106	150	13	34	51	12	1	1	7	18	17	0	1	1
Stankiewicz	.224	.336	.250	76	107	11	24	36	9	0	1	5	4	22	1	1	3
Cabrera	.222	.222	.263	16	18	4	4	4	0	0	0	2	1	3	1	2	1
Andrews	.203	.438	.232	18	64	10	13	28	3	0	4	9	3	20	0	0	6
Obando	.128	.277	.241	41	47	3	6	13	1	0	2	9	6	14	0	0	0

PITCHERS	W-L	ERA	BA	G	GS	CG	GF	Sho	SV	IP	H	R	ER	HR	BB	SO
Martinez	17-8	1.90	.184	31	31	13	0	4	0	241.1	158	65	51	16	67	305
Valdes	4-4	3.13	.240	48	7	0	9	0	2	95.0	84	36	33	2	39	54
Bennett	0-1	3.18	.247	16	0	0	3	0	0	22.2	21	9	8	2	9	8
Telford	4-6	3.24	.236	65	0	0	17	0	1	89.0	77	34	32	11	33	61
Falteisek	0-0	3.38	.286	5	0	0	2	0	0	8.0	8	4	3	0	3	2
Veres	2-3	3.48	.278	53	0	0	11	0	1	62.0	68	28	24	5	27	47
Hermanson	8-8	3.69	.234	32	28	1	0	1	0	158.1	134	68	65	15	66	136
Urbina	5-8	3.78	.215	63	0	0	50	0	27	64.1	52	29	27	9	29	84
Perez	12-13	3.88	.260	33	32	8	0	5	0	206.2	206	109	89	21	48	110
Juden	11-5	4.22	.255	22	22	3	0	0	0	130.0	125	64	61	17	57	107
Thurman	1-0	5.40	.186	5	2	0	1	0	0	11.2	8	9	7	3	4	8
DeHart	2-1	5.52	.292	23	0	0	7	0	0	29.1	33	21	18	7	14	29
Bullinger	7-12	5.56	.276	36	25	2	4	2	0	155.1	165	106	96	17	74	87
Smith	0-1	5.82	.308	25	0	0	14	0	5	21.2	28	16	14	2	8	15
Johnson	2-5	5.94	.277	11	11	0	0	0	0	50.0	54	34	33	8	21	28
Kline	1-3	6.15	.307	26	0	0	7	0	0	26.1	31	18	18	4	10	20
Torres	0-0	7.25	.284	12	0	0	3	0	0	22.1	25	19	18	2	12	11
Daal	1-2	9.79	.378	33	0	0	6	0	1	30.1	48	35	33	4	15	16
Paniagua	1-2	12.00	.372	9	3	0	0	0	0	18.0	29	24	24	2	16	8
Stull	0-1	16.20	.438	3	0	0	1	0	0	3.1	7	7	6	1	4	2
Cormier	0-1	33.75	.500	1	1	0	0	0	0	1.1	4	5	5	1	1	0

1998 preliminary roster

PITCHERS (18)
Jason Baker
Miguel Batista
Shayne Bennett
Rick DeHart
Steve Falteisek
Dustin Hermanson
Mike Johnson
Steve Kline
Trey Moore
Carl Pavano
Carlos Perez

Jeremy Powell
Anthony Telford
Mike Thurman
Ugueth Urbina
Marc Valdes
Javier Vazquez
Matt Wagner

CATCHERS (3)
Raul Chavez
Bob Henley
Chris Widger

INFIELDERS (10)
Shane Andrews
Hiram Bocachica
Orlando Cabrera
Trace Coquilette
Jose Fernandez
Brad Fullmer
Mark Grudzielanek
Ryan McGuire
Andy Stankiewicz
Jose Vidro

OUTFIELDERS (6)
Vladimir Guerrero
Terry Jones
F.P. Santangelo
Fernando Segiugnol
Darond Stovall
Rondell White

Games played by position

PLAYER	G	C	1B	2B	3B	SS	OF
Andrews	18	0	0	0	18	0	0
Cabrera	16	0	0	4	0	6	0
Chavez	13	13	0	0	0	0	0
Fletcher	96	83	0	0	0	0	0
Fullmer	19	0	8	0	0	0	2
Grudzielanek	156	0	0	0	0	156	0
Guerrero	90	0	0	0	0	0	85
Lansing	144	0	0	144	0	0	0
McGuire	84	0	30	0	0	0	44
Meulens	16	0	3	0	0	0	8
Obando	41	0	0	0	0	0	15
Orsulak	106	0	15	0	0	0	63
Rodriguez	132	0	3	0	0	0	126
Santangelo	130	0	0	7	32	1	99
Segui	125	0	125	0	0	0	0
Stankiewicz	76	0	0	25	3	14	0
Strange	118	0	1	3	105	0	2
Vidro	67	0	0	5	36	0	0
White	151	0	0	0	0	0	151
Widger	91	85	0	0	0	0	0

Sick call: 1997 DL report

PLAYER	Days on the DL
Shane Andrews	151
Rheal Cormier	176
Darrin Fletcher	15
Vladimir Guerrero	61**
Sherman Obando	64
David Segui	17
Doug Strange	15
Dave Veres	30
Mark Wagner	181

** Indicates three separate terms on Disabled List.

1997 salaries

	Bonuses	Total earned salary
Pedro Martinez,p	115,000	3,615,000
Mike Lansing,2b		2,700,000
Henry Rodriguez,of		2,300,000
David Segui,1b		1,550,000
Darrin Fletcher,c		1,350,000
Rheal Cormier,p		1,050,000
Dave Veres,p		725,000
Joe Orsulak,of		650,000
Jim Bullinger,p	25,000	525,000
Rondell White,of		500,000
Shane Andrews,3b		225,000
Mark Grudzielanek,ss		220,000
Andy Stankiewicz,ss		220,000
Doug Strange,3b	20,000	220,000
F.P. Santangelo,of		212,500
Carlos Perez,p	45,000	210,000
Sherman Obando,of		185,000
Ugueth Urbina,p		175,000
Dustin Hermanson,p		163,000
Jose Paniagua,p		155,000
Matt Wagner,p		155,000
Chris Widger,c		152,500
Marc Valdes,p		152,500
Anthony Telford,p		150,000
Jose Vidro,3b		150,000
Vladimir Guerrero,of		150,000
Michael Johnson,p		150,000
Shayne Bennett,p		150,000
Ryan McGuire,1b		150,000
Steven Kline,p		150,000

Average 1997 salary: $615,350
Total 1997 payroll: $18,460,500

Minor Leagues

Tops in the organization

BATTER	CLUB	AVG.	G	AB	R	H	HR	RBI
Fullmer, Brad	Ott	.308	118	448	73	138	22	79
Samuels, Scott	Hrb	.306	84	278	38	85	6	39
Henley, Bob	Hrb	.304	79	280	41	85	12	49
Fernandez, Jose	Hrb	.291	126	446	59	130	13	69
Blandford, Paul	Cpf	.289	113	398	63	115	5	40

HOME RUNS

Alcantara, Israel	Hrb	27
Meulens, H.	Ott	24
Fullmer, Brad	Ott	22
Schwab, Chris	Wpb	20
Lukachyk, Rob	Ott	19

WINS

Evans, Keith	Wpb	14
Parker, Christian	Wpb	11
Smart, J.D.	Hrb	11
Moore, Trey	Hrb	11
Several Players Tied at		10

RBI

Stovall, Darond	Ott	87
Coquillette, T.	Hrb	84
Seguignol,F.	Wpb	83
Fullmer, Brad	Ott	79
Ware, Jeremy	Cpf	77

SAVES

Fleetham, Ben	Hrb	31
Young, Tim	Hrb	23
Bennett, Shayne	Ott	16
Bullinger, Kirk	Ott	11
Several Players Tied at		8

STOLEN BASES

Cabrera, O.	Ott	47
James, K.	Vmt	37
Denning, Wes	Cpf	34
Ware, Jeremy	Cpf	32
Bocachica, H.	Hrb	29

STRIKEOUTS

Weber, Neil	Hrb	148
Vazquez, Javier	Hrb	147
Moore, Trey	Hrb	137
Stull, Everett	Ott	130
Evans, Keith	Wpb	122

PITCHER	CLUB	W-L	ERA	IP	H	BB	SO
Blank, Matt	Vmt	6- 4	1.69	96	74	14	84
Vazquez, Javier	Hrb	10- 3	1.86	155	113	40	147
Powell, Jeremy	Wpb	9-10	3.02	155	162	62	121
Evans, Keith	Wpb	14-11	3.02	182	155	29	122
Parker, Christian	Wpb	11-11	3.14	172	168	54	116

Montreal (1969-1997)

Runs: Most, career

934	TIM RAINES, 1979-1990	
828	Andre Dawson, 1976-1986	
737	Tim Wallach, 1980-1992	
707	Gary Carter, 1974-1992	
446	Warren Cromartie, 1974-1983	

Hits: Most, career

1694	Tim Wallach, 1980-1992
1598	TIM RAINES, 1979-1990
1575	Andre Dawson, 1976-1986
1427	Gary Carter, 1974-1992
1063	Warren Cromartie, 1974-1983

2B: Most, career

360	Tim Wallach, 1980-1992
295	Andre Dawson, 1976-1986
274	Gary Carter, 1974-1992
273	TIM RAINES, 1979-1990
222	Warren Cromartie, 1974-1983

3B: Most, career

81	TIM RAINES, 1979-1990
67	Andre Dawson, 1976-1986
31	Tim Wallach, 1980-1992
30	Warren Cromartie, 1974-1983
25	DELINO DeSHIELDS, 1990-1993
25	Mitch Webster, 1985-1988

HR: Most, career

225	Andre Dawson, 1976-1986
220	Gary Carter, 1974-1992
204	Tim Wallach, 1980-1992
118	Bob Bailey, 1969-1975
106	ANDRES GALARRAGA, 1985-1991

RBI: Most, career

905	Tim Wallach, 1980-1992
838	Andre Dawson, 1976-1986
823	Gary Carter, 1974-1992
552	TIM RAINES, 1979-1990
466	Bob Bailey, 1969-1975

SB: Most, career

634	TIM RAINES, 1979-1990
266	MARQUIS GRISSOM, 1989-1994
253	Andre Dawson, 1976-1986
187	DELINO DeSHIELDS, 1990-1993
139	Rodney Scott, 1976-1982

BB: Most, career

775	TIM RAINES, 1979-1990
582	Gary Carter, 1974-1992
514	Tim Wallach, 1980-1992
502	Bob Bailey, 1969-1975
370	Ron Fairly, 1969-1974

BA: Highest, career

.301	TIM RAINES, 1979-1990
.294	Rusty Staub, 1969-1979
.292	MOISES ALOU, 1990-1996
.288	Ellis Valentine, 1975-1981
.282	LARRY WALKER, 1989-1994

On-base avg: Highest, career

.402	Rusty Staub, 1969-1979
.390	TIM RAINES, 1979-1990
.390	Ron Hunt, 1971-1974
.381	Ron Fairly, 1969-1974
.368	Bob Bailey, 1969-1975

Slug avg: Highest, career

.497	Rusty Staub, 1969-1979
.489	MOISES ALOU, 1990-1996
.483	LARRY WALKER, 1989-1994
.476	Andre Dawson, 1976-1986
.476	Ellis Valentine, 1975-1981

Games started: Most, career

393	Steve Rogers, 1973-1985
233	DENNIS MARTINEZ, 1986-1993
193	Bryn Smith, 1981-1989
192	Steve Renko, 1969-1976
170	Bill Gullickson, 1979-1985

Complete games: Most, career

129	Steve Rogers, 1973-1985
46	Bill Stoneman, 1969-1973
41	DENNIS MARTINEZ, 1986-1993
40	Steve Renko, 1969-1976
31	Bill Gullickson, 1979-1985

Saves: Most, career

152	Jeff Reardon, 1981-1986
109	MEL ROJAS, 1990-1996
105	JOHN WETTELAND, 1992-1994
101	Tim Burke, 1985-1991
75	Mike Marshall, 1970-1973

Shutouts: Most, career

37	Steve Rogers, 1973-1985
15	Bill Stoneman, 1969-1973
13	DENNIS MARTINEZ, 1986-1993
8	Woodie Fryman, 1975-1983
8	Charlie Lea, 1980-1987
8	PEDRO MARTINEZ, 1994-1997
8	Scott Sanderson, 1978-1983
8	Bryn Smith, 1981-1989

Wins: Most, career

158	Steve Rogers, 1973-1985
100	DENNIS MARTINEZ, 1986-1993
81	Bryn Smith, 1981-1989
72	Bill Gullickson, 1979-1985
68	Steve Renko, 1969-1976

K: Most, career

1621	Steve Rogers, 1973-1985
973	DENNIS MARTINEZ, 1986-1993
843	PEDRO MARTINEZ, 1994-1997
838	Bryn Smith, 1981-1989
831	Bill Stoneman, 1969-1973

Win pct: Highest, career

.661	KEN HILL, 1992-1994
.625	PEDRO MARTINEZ, 1994-1997
.623	Tim Burke, 1985-1991
.581	DENNIS MARTINEZ, 1986-1993
.573	Charlie Lea, 1980-1987

ERA: Lowest, career

3.06	PEDRO MARTINEZ, 1994-1997
3.06	DENNIS MARTINEZ, 1986-1993
3.17	Steve Rogers, 1973-1985
3.20	JEFF FASSERO, 1991-1996
3.28	Bryn Smith, 1981-1989

Runs: Most, season

133	TIM RAINES, 1983
123	TIM RAINES, 1987
115	TIM RAINES, 1985
107	Andre Dawson, 1982
106	TIM RAINES, 1984

Hits: Most, season

204	Al Oliver, 1982
201	MARK GRUDZIELANEK, 1996
194	TIM RAINES, 1986
192	TIM RAINES, 1984
189	Andre Dawson, 1983

2B: Most, season

54	MARK GRUDZIELANEK, 1997
46	Warren Cromartie, 1979
45	MIKE LANSING, 1997
44	LARRY WALKER, 1994
43	Al Oliver, 1982

3B: Most, season

13	TIM RAINES, 1985	
13	Rodney Scott, 1980	
13	Mitch Webster, 1986	
12	Andre Dawson, 1979	
11	Ron LeFlore, 1980	

HR: Most, season

36	HENRY RODRIGUEZ, 1996
32	Andre Dawson, 1983
31	Gary Carter, 1977
30	Larry Parrish, 1979
30	Rusty Staub, 1970

RBI: Most, season

123	Tim Wallach, 1987
113	Andre Dawson, 1983
109	Al Oliver, 1982
106	Gary Carter, 1984
103	HENRY RODRIGUEZ, 1996
103	Ken Singleton, 1973

SB: Most, season

97	Ron LeFlore, 1980
90	TIM RAINES, 1983
78	MARQUIS GRISSOM, 1992
78	TIM RAINES, 1982
76	MARQUIS GRISSOM, 1991

BB: Most, season

123	Ken Singleton, 1973
112	Rusty Staub, 1970
110	Rusty Staub, 1969
100	Bob Bailey, 1974
97	Bob Bailey, 1971
97	TIM RAINES, 1983

BA: Highest, season

.339	MOISES ALOU, 1994
.334	TIM RAINES, 1986
.331	Al Oliver, 1982
.330	TIM RAINES, 1987
.322	LARRY WALKER, 1994

On-base avg: Highest, season

.429	TIM RAINES, 1987
.426	Rusty Staub, 1969
.425	Ken Singleton, 1973
.422	Ron Fairly, 1973
.413	TIM RAINES, 1986

Slug avg: Highest, season

.592	MOISES ALOU, 1994
.587	LARRY WALKER, 1994
.562	HENRY RODRIGUEZ, 1996
.553	Andre Dawson, 1981
.551	Larry Parrish, 1979

Games started: Most, season

40	Steve Rogers, 1977
39	Bill Stoneman, 1971
38	Steve Rogers, 1974
37	Carl Morton, 1970
37	Steve Renko, 1971
37	Steve Rogers, 1979
37	Steve Rogers, 1980

Complete games: Most, season

20	Bill Stoneman, 1971
19	Ross Grimsley, 1978
17	Steve Rogers, 1977
14	Steve Rogers, 1980
14	Steve Rogers, 1982

Saves: Most, season

43	JOHN WETTELAND, 1993
41	Jeff Reardon, 1985
37	JOHN WETTELAND, 1992
36	MEL ROJAS, 1996
35	Jeff Reardon, 1986

Shutouts: Most, season

5	DENNIS MARTINEZ, 1991
5	CARLOS PEREZ, 1997
5	Steve Rogers, 1979
5	Steve Rogers, 1983
5	Bill Stoneman, 1969

Wins: Most, season

20	Ross Grimsley, 1978
19	Steve Rogers, 1982
18	Carl Morton, 1970
18	Bryn Smith, 1985
17	Bill Gullickson, 1983
17	PEDRO MARTINEZ, 1997
17	Steve Rogers, 1977
17	Steve Rogers, 1983
17	Bill Stoneman, 1971

K: Most, season

305	PEDRO MARTINEZ, 1997
251	Bill Stoneman, 1971
222	JEFF FASSERO, 1996
222	PEDRO MARTINEZ, 1996
206	Steve Rogers, 1977

Win pct: Highest, season

.783	Bryn Smith, 1985
.762	KEN HILL, 1994
.704	Steve Rogers, 1982
.696	DENNIS MARTINEZ, 1989
.680	PEDRO MARTINEZ, 1997

ERA: Lowest, season

1.90	PEDRO MARTINEZ, 1997
2.39	DENNIS MARTINEZ, 1991
2.39	MARK LANGSTON, 1989
2.40	Steve Rogers, 1982
2.44	Pascual Perez, 1988

Most pinch-hit homers, season

4	Hal Breeden, 1973
3	CLIFF FLOYD, 1996

Most pinch-hit homers, career

5	Jose Morales, 1973-1977
4	Hal Breeden, 1972-1975
4	Jerry White, 1974-1983

Longest hitting streak

21	DELINO DeSHIELDS, 1993
19	Warren Cromartie, 1979
19	Andre Dawson, 1980
18	Warren Cromartie, 1980
18	Pepe Mangual, 1975
18	F. P. SANTANGELO, 1997
18	DAVID SEGUI, 1995

Most consecutive scoreless innings

32	Woodie Fryman, 1975

No-hit games

Bill Stoneman, Mon at Phi NL, 7-0; April 17, 1969.

Bill Stoneman, Mon vs NY NL, 7-0; Oct. 2, 1972 (1st game).

Charlie Lea, Mon vs SF NL, 4-0; May 10, 1981 (2nd game).

MARK GARDNER, Mon at LA NL, 0-1; July 26, 1991 (9 innings, lost on two hits in 10th, relieved by JEFF FASSERO, who allowed one more hit).

DENNIS MARTINEZ, Mon at LA NL, 2-0; July 28, 1991 (perfect game).

PEDRO MARTINEZ (9 innings) and MEL ROJAS (1 inning), Mon at SD NL, 1-0; June 3,1995 (Martinez pitched nine perfect innings, but allowed a hit in the 10th; Rojas relieved and finished the game).

David Palmer, five perfect innings, rain, Mon at StL NL, 4-0; April 21, 1984 (2nd game).

Pascual Perez, five innings, rain, Mon at Phi NL, 1-0; Sept. 24, 1988.

ACTIVE PLAYERS in caps.

Players' years of service are listed by the first and last years with this team and are not necessarily consecutive; all statistics record performances for this team only.

Philadelphia Phillies

Right-hander Curt Schilling was in the NL's top 10 in almost every pitching category last season.

1997 Phillies: There's hope for next year

Charles Dickens could have been a beat writer for the 1997 Philadelphia Phillies. He would have called their year *A Tale of Two Seasons*. In their first 81 games, the Phillies won 23 times. Of the next 81, they won 45. There was one constant. Curt Schilling made management look smart for signing him to a three-year contract extension, worth an average of $5.15 million per season, that takes effect in 1998. All he did was strike out 319 batters, the 10th-highest total in this century. He won a career-high 17 games even though the bullpen blew five saves behind him.

As high as the expectations for Scott Rolen were, he exceeded them. He became the first Phillies rookie to win the Jackie Robinson Award since Richie Allen in 1964. Rolen batted .283 with 21 homers and 92 runs batted in. All easily exceeded the totals (.196, 18, 52) that Mike Schmidt had as a rookie in 1973. Beyond the numbers, Rolen was an outstanding base runner, had a shortstop's range and demonstrated precocious leadership skills.

There were other less obvious bright spots. At the All-Star break, the Phillies were still wondering whether Mike Lieberthal had the right stuff to be their catcher of the future. By the end of the season, he had taken charge behind the plate and produced 20 home runs and 77 RBI. Those 20 home runs were matched by first baseman Rico Brogna. Brogna's .252 average and 81 RBI were not good for a first baseman, but a Phillies team that emphasized taut infield defense couldn't have turned its season around without Brogna's glove work. Shortstop Kevin Stocker made just 11 errors all year.

Still, for a team to tie the Cubs for the worst record in the league, there had to be problems: Left fielder Gregg Jefferies was a career .296 hitter coming into the season. Healthy for the first time since he signed a four-year, $20 million contract before the 1995 season, he hit .256. Right hander Mark Leiter lost 17 games, the

---

---

most in the majors. Danny Tartabull was guaranteed $2.3 million to be the right fielder and cleanup hitter. He fouled a pitch off his foot on Opening Day and was lost for the season. Wendell Magee Jr. was the center fielder when the season opened. He was demoted to AAA Scranton/Wilkes-Barre in May and never returned.

Don't look for the Phillies to make headlines in baseball's financial pages. The players they will rely on for 1998 are under contract or ineligible for free agency. And new club president Dave Montgomery has made it plain that there is no money in the budget for major acquisitions. If the Phillies are to improve, they'll need help from their current youngsters. Left-hander Matt Beech was 4-9 with a 5.07 ERA, and at one point, he made 22 starts without a win. Righty Garrett Stephenson had a 5.90 ERA for AAA Scranton/Wilkes-Barre, but he ended up 8-6 with a 3.15 ERA for the Phillies. With Lieberthal already in place, catcher Bobby Estalella gives the organization a chance to contemplate being in the same position the Padres were with Benito Santiago and Sandy Alomar Jr. in the late '80s. Two young outfielders who got their starts in other organizations, Midre Cummings and Billy McMillon, are also in the mix, but upgrading the outfield is still a priority.

1997 Phillies: Week-by-week notes

These notes were excerpted from the following issues of Baseball Weekly.

▶**April 9:** On April 3 the Phillies gave Curt Schilling everything he asked for: a three-year, $15.45 million extension; the $6.5 million option year for 2001 (that will become fully guaranteed if he pitches the easily attained total of 450 innings the previous three years); and a blanket no-trade clause and plenty of award bonuses.

▶**April 16:** Darren Daulton in right field? The previously unthinkable became the Phillies' best solution when Danny Tartabull and Rex Hudler went on the DL following the April 11 home opener.

▶**April 23:** It took manager Terry Francona only 10 games to shake up his lineup—after the Phillies were averaging less than two runs per game. He moved left fielder Gregg Jefferies from the third spot to leadoff. Second baseman Mickey Morandini went from leadoff to second. Also moved up: first baseman Rico Brogna (fifth to third), catcher Mike Lieberthal (seventh to fifth) and center fielder Wendell Magee Jr. (eighth to seventh). Shortstop Kevin Stocker was dropped from second to eighth.

▶**April 30:** Mike Lieberthal hit five home runs in the Phillies' first 18 games. Lieberthal has never hit more than seven homers in any of his seven previous professional seasons.

▶**May 7:** Terry Francona moved heralded rookie third baseman Scott Rolen into the third spot in the batting order on May 2. "We think Scotty is going to be our No. 3 hitter for about the next 15 years," Francona said.

▶**May 21:** Right-hander Bobby Munoz cleared irrevocable waivers on May 16. That completed a long, hard fall from June 1994, when he was the NL's pitcher of the month and seemed to be on the verge of establishing himself as a part of the Phillies' future. When he got off to a 1-5 start with an 8.91 ERA this year, the Phillies finally ran out of patience.

Five-year glance

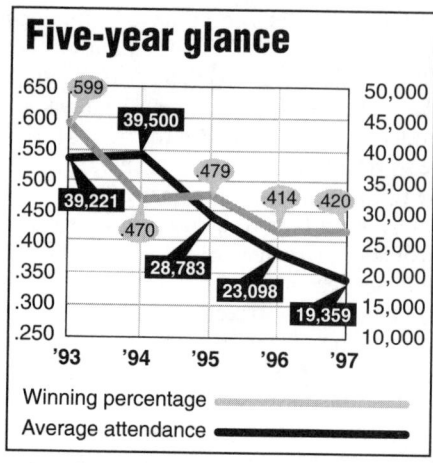

Winning percentage
Average attendance

▶**May 28:** Right-hander Garrett Stephenson, 25, was a desperation call-up when lefty Matt Beech tripped over third base and sprained his ankle; he was promoted despite a 5.90 ERA at AAA Scranton/Wilkes-Barre. Then he went 2-0 with a 1.35 ERA in his first three starts for the Phillies. Curt Schilling's ERA dropped from 4.13 to 3.18 on May 23, and it wasn't even his day to pitch. On May 22, official scorer Bob Kenney awarded Met Bernard Gilkey an infield hit on a grounder to third. The Mets went on to score eight runs. The next day, Kenney switched his call and charged Scott Rolen with an error, making all the runs unearned.

▶**June 4:** The Phillies used nine starting pitchers in the first two months, and more changes are brewing. Waiting in the wings as June arrived were right-handers Mike Grace and Tyler Green. Both have been recovering from injuries.

▶**June 18:** General manager Lee Thomas said that while he is pleased with the progress former No. 1 draft choice Wayne Gomes is making, there was no plan to rush the right-handed reliever to the majors. So, naturally, Gomes made his major league debut two days later on June 13, pitching a scoreless seventh inning against the Blue Jays.

▶**June 25:** The announcement that president Bill Giles was stepping aside from day-to-day operation of the team dropped a bombshell on a franchise in the midst of its most unsuccessful season in decades. It is suspected that Giles took himself away from the firing line because he had grown weary of being blamed for the team's shortcomings.

▶**July 2:** The frustrations of losing more frequently than any team in baseball may be starting to show on the Phillies. Reliever Reggie Harris was suspended for five games and fined $1,000 by NL president Leonard Coleman on June 25 after admitting he had thrown at Braves center fielder Andruw Jones three days earlier. Then Darren Daulton was ejected by home plate umpire Terry Tata on June 27 for arguing after he was called out on strikes.

▶**July 10:** The Phillies went 1-12 during the part of the schedule that ended on July 2 and had them playing the Braves, the Marlins and the Orioles. In their first 84 games, the Phillies were held to one or no runs an amazing 19 times, including six shutouts.

▶**July 16:** At the All-Star break, Lee Thomas said his first goal for the second half of the season was for pitchers to throw more strikes. The Phillies then walked 12 in their first game back and lost to the Marlins by one run.

▶**July 23:** As if things weren't bad enough for the team with baseball's worst record, their first trip after the All-Star break started with a terrifying, storm-tossed flight to Florida. The trip ended with a plane crash—sort of. The second of two buses that picked the team up at Philadelphia International Airport after a flight from Atlanta in the early morning hours of July 16 ran into the wing of the chartered plane as it pulled away. Several players were shaken up, but nobody was seriously injured. On the field, when the Phillies beat the Expos on July 16, it was their first two-game winning streak since May 17-18 against Houston.

▶**July 30:** An era ended on July 21 when Darren Daulton agreed to accept a trade to the Marlins for minor league outfielder Billy McMillon. Drafted in 1980, he had longer continuous service with one organization than any player in the NL. After getting off to a 3-1, 2.81 start,

Mark Leiter was 2-10 with an 8.04 ERA in his next 15 starts.

▶**Aug. 6:** When Tyler Green beat the Padres on July 29, he had gone 799 days between big-league victories. Green spent most of that time recovering from shoulder surgery.

▶**Aug. 13:** Through Aug. 10, Phillies pitchers had turned in 11 quality starts (at least six innings, three or fewer earned runs) in 12 games. The Phillies won nine of those starts despite an offense that continued to rank at the bottom of the league. The Phillies, 24-61 at the All-Star break, are 16-14 since the break.

▶**Aug. 27:** Billy McMillon went 3-for-5 with a grand slam in his Phillies debut, on Aug. 18. McMillon's slam gave him four RBI after just two Phillies at-bats. The player he replaced on the roster, Ricky Otero, had three RBI in 151 at-bats this season.

▶**Sept. 10:** Yankee killers: Curt Schilling struck out a career-high 16 batters in a 5-1 win in front of a roaring crowd of 50,869, the largest of the season at Veterans Stadium, on Labor Day. Mike Grace took another giant step forward in his remarkable comeback on Sept. 2, using just 84 pitches to earn a complete-game victory. The Phillies then completed a sweep of the defending world champion Yankees the next day, rallying from a three-run deficit to win in the bottom of the ninth.

▶**Sept. 24:** With eight strikeouts on Sept. 21 in an 11-3 loss to Chicago, Curt Schilling matched Houston's J.R. Richard for most strikeouts by an NL right-hander (313), with one start remaining. The Phillies end the season with a pretty good idea of what their rotation will be in 1998. Barring injuries, it will be Schilling, Mike Grace, Matt Beech, Tyler Green and Garrett Stephenson.

▶**Oct. 1:** After falling to a 30-72 record on July 27, the Phillies went 38-22 the rest of the way.

QUOTE OF THE YEAR

"It was God's way of saying he's tired of watching us play bad baseball."
—Hitting coach Hal McRae, on a terrifying, storm-tossed Phillies charter flight

PHILADELPHIA PHILLIES / NL EAST

229

PHILADELPHIA PHILLIES 1997 final stats

BATTERS	BA	SLG	OBA	G	AB	R	H	TB	2B	3B	HR	RBI	BB	SO	SB	CS	E
Estalella	.345	.793	.472	13	29	9	10	23	1	0	4	9	7	7	0	0	0
Morandini	.295	.380	.371	150	553	83	163	210	40	2	1	39	62	91	16	13	6
Butler	.292	.416	.326	43	89	10	26	37	9	1	0	13	5	8	1	0	0
Barron	.286	.423	.330	57	189	22	54	80	12	1	4	24	12	38	0	1	2
Rolen	.283	.469	.377	156	561	93	159	263	35	3	21	92	76	138	16	6	24
Sefcik	.269	.345	.298	61	119	11	32	41	3	0	2	6	4	9	1	2	4
Stocker	.266	.355	.335	149	504	51	134	179	23	5	4	40	51	91	11	6	11
Jordan	.266	.412	.273	84	177	19	47	73	8	0	6	30	3	26	0	1	6
Cummings	.264	.411	.330	115	314	35	83	129	22	6	4	31	31	56	2	3	1
Jefferies	.256	.391	.333	130	476	68	122	186	25	3	11	48	53	27	12	6	3
McMillon	.256	.400	.293	37	90	10	23	36	5	1	2	14	6	24	2	1	2
Brogna	.252	.433	.293	148	543	68	137	235	36	1	20	81	33	116	12	3	7
Otero	.252	.318	.339	50	151	20	38	48	6	2	0	3	19	15	0	3	0
Lieberthal	.246	.442	.314	134	455	59	112	201	27	1	20	77	44	76	3	4	12
Amaro	.234	.314	.320	117	175	18	41	55	6	1	2	21	21	24	1	1	1
May	.228	.295	.266	83	149	8	34	44	5	1	1	13	8	26	4	1	3
Hudler	.221	.377	.264	50	122	17	27	46	4	0	5	10	6	28	1	0	3
Robertson	.211	.316	.268	22	38	3	8	12	2	1	0	4	0	6	1	0	0
Magee	.200	.261	.254	38	115	7	23	30	4	0	1	9	9	20	1	4	4
Relaford	.184	.316	.279	15	38	3	7	12	1	2	0	6	5	6	3	0	1
Parent	.150	.177	.198	39	113	4	17	20	3	0	0	8	7	39	0	1	1
Tartabull	.000	.000	.364	3	7	2	0	0	0	0	0	0	4	4	0	0	0

PITCHERS	W-L	ERA	BA	G	GS	CG	GF	Sho	SV	IP	H	R	ER	HR	BB	SO
Schilling	17-11	2.97	.224	35	35	7	0	2	0	254.1	208	96	84	25	58	319
Stephenson	8-6	3.15	.244	20	18	2	0	0	0	117.0	104	45	41	11	38	81
Brewer	1-2	3.27	.188	25	0	0	4	0	0	22.0	15	8	8	2	11	16
Grace	3-2	3.46	.230	6	6	1	0	1	0	39.0	32	16	15	3	10	26
Bottalico	2-5	3.65	.245	69	0	0	61	0	34	74.0	68	31	30	7	42	89
Portugal	0-2	4.61	.321	3	3	0	0	0	0	13.2	17	8	7	0	5	2
Spradlin	4-8	4.74	.274	76	0	0	23	0	1	81.2	86	45	43	9	27	67
Plantenberg	0-0	4.91	.255	35	0	0	9	0	0	25.2	25	14	14	1	12	12
Green	4-4	4.93	.247	14	14	0	0	0	0	76.2	72	50	42	8	45	58
Blazier	1-1	5.03	.290	36	0	0	7	0	0	53.2	62	31	30	8	21	42
Beech	4-9	5.07	.279	24	24	0	0	0	0	136.2	147	81	77	25	57	120
Ramos	0-2	5.14	.288	4	2	0	0	0	0	14.0	15	9	8	3	6	4
Winston	2-0	5.25	.178	7	1	0	1	0	0	12.0	8	8	7	4	3	8
Gomes	5-1	5.27	.274	37	0	0	13	0	0	42.2	45	26	25	4	24	24
Harris	1-3	5.30	.263	50	0	0	13	0	0	54.1	55	33	32	1	43	45
Karp	1-1	5.40	.218	15	1	0	1	0	0	15.0	12	12	9	2	9	18
Leiter	10-17	5.67	.292	31	31	3	0	0	0	182.2	216	132	115	25	64	148
Maduro	3-7	7.23	.294	15	13	0	0	0	0	71.0	83	59	57	12	41	31
Mimbs	0-3	7.53	.272	17	1	0	2	0	0	28.2	31	27	24	6	27	29
Ruffcorn	0-3	7.71	.275	18	4	0	3	0	0	39.2	42	40	34	4	36	33
Nye	0-2	8.25	.392	4	2	0	1	0	0	12.0	20	11	11	2	9	7
Munoz	1-5	8.91	.338	8	7	0	1	0	0	33.1	47	35	33	4	15	20
Ryan	1-0	9.58	.344	22	0	0	10	0	0	20.2	31	23	22	5	13	10

1998 preliminary roster

PITCHERS (17)
Matt Beech
Rob Blazier
Ricky Bottalico
Rob Burger
Tony Fiore
Wayne Gomes
Mike Grace
Tyler Green
Mark Leiter
Carlton Loewer
Calvin Maduro
Mark Portugal
Curt Schilling
Jerry Spradlin
Garrett Stephenson
Mike Welch
Greg Whiteman

CATCHERS (3)
Bobby Estalella
Mike Lieberthal
Mark Parent

INFIELDERS (12)
Marlon Anderson
Alex Arias
Rico Brogna
Steve Carver
David Doster
Dan Held
Rex Hudler
Kevin Jordan
Mickey Morandini
Desi Relaford
Scott Rolen
Kevin Sefcik

OUTFIELDERS (7)
Bob Abreu
Tony Barron
Midre Cummings
Lenny Dykstra
Gregg Jefferies
Wendell Magee
Billy McMillon

Games played by position

PLAYER	G	C	1B	2B	3B	SS	OF
Amaro	117	0	1	0	0	0	72
Barron	57	0	0	0	0	0	53
Brogna	148	0	145	0	0	0	0
Butler	43	0	0	0	0	0	25
Cummings	115	0	0	0	0	0	79
Estalella	13	11	0	0	0	0	0
Hudler	50	0	0	6	0	0	35
Jefferies	130	0	0	0	0	0	124
Jordan	84	0	25	6	12	0	0
Lieberthal	134	129	0	0	0	0	0
Magee	38	0	0	0	0	0	38
May	83	0	0	0	0	0	56
McMillon	37	0	0	0	0	0	23
Morandini	150	0	0	146	0	1	0
Otero	50	0	0	0	0	0	42
Parent	39	38	0	0	0	0	0
Relaford	15	0	0	0	0	12	0
Robertson	22	0	5	0	0	0	5
Rolen	156	0	0	0	155	0	0
Sefcik	61	0	0	22	4	10	0
Stocker	149	0	0	0	0	147	0
Tartabull	3	0	0	0	0	0	3

Sick call: 1997 DL report

PLAYER	Days on the DL
Matt Beech	16
Billy Brewer	42
Rob Butler	22
Lenny Dykstra	181
Mike Grace	85
Tyler Green	62
Rex Hudler	84*
Gregg Jefferies	15
Mark Leiter	24
Ryan Nye	25
Mark Portugal	167*
Edgar Ramos	45
Scott Ruffcorn	42
Ken Ryan	123*
Garrett Stephenson	32*
Danny Tartabull	174

* Indicates two separate terms on Disabled List.

Minor Leagues

Tops in the organization

BATTER	CLUB	AVG.	G	AB	R	H	HR	RBI
Barron, Tony	SWB	.328	92	329	51	108	18	78
Burnham, Gary	Bat	.325	73	289	44	94	5	45
Zuber, Jon	SWB	.315	126	435	85	137	6	64
Doster, David	SWB	.315	108	410	70	129	16	79
McNamara, R.	Bat	.312	72	295	55	92	6	54

HOME RUNS

Held, Dan	Rea	26
Barron, Tony	SWB	18
Key, Jeff	Clw	17
Several Players Tied at		16

RBI

Key, Jeff	Clw	87
Held, Dan	Rea	86
Doster, David	SWB	79
Barron, Tony	SWB	78
Francia, David	Clw	75

STOLEN BASES

Rollins, Jimmy	Pdt	46
Francia, David	Clw	44
Taylor, Reggie	Clw	40
Relaford, Desi	SWB	29
Anderson, M.	Rea	27

WINS

Stevens, Kris	Clw	12
Coggin, David	Clw	11
Burger, Rob	Clw	11
Fiore, Tony	SWB	11
Allen, Brandon	Pdt	11

SAVES

Brannan, Ryan	Rea	30
Kawabata, Kyle	Pdt	16
Black, Brett	Bat	15
Heflin, Bronson	SWB	13
Tober, Dave	Pdt	10

STRIKEOUTS

Thomas, Evan	Rea	172
Burger, Rob	Clw	154
Loewer, Carlton	SWB	152
Stevens, Kris	Clw	125
Fiore, Tony	SWB	120

PITCHER	CLUB	W-L	ERA	IP	H	BB	SO
Cotton, Joseph	Bat	7- 4	2.99	96	90	29	74
Stevens, Kris	Clw	12- 7	3.26	160	146	61	125
Thomas, Evan	Rea	8-11	3.27	168	166	55	172
Fiore, Tony	SWB	11- 8	3.33	165	149	66	120
Allen, Brandon	Pdt	11- 8	3.54	153	153	38	91

1997 salaries

	Bonuses	Total earned salary
Lenny Dykstra, of		6,000,000
Gregg Jefferies, of		5,500,000
Curt Schilling, p		3,500,000
Mark Portugal, p		2,350,000
Danny Tartabull, of		2,000,000
Mark Leiter, p		1,900,000
Mickey Morandini, 2b		1,850,000
Rex Hudler, inf		1,150,000
Ken Ryan, p		900,000
Kevin Stocker, ss	65,000	890,000
Ricky Bottalico, p		425,000
Mark Parent, c		400,000
Rico Brogna, 1b	60,000	450,000
Ruben Amaro, of		235,000
Mike Lieberthal, c		215,000
Billy Brewer, p	25,000	200,000
Mike Grace, p		185,000
Midre Cummings, of		180,000
Tyler Green, p	25,000	180,000
Reggie Harris, p		175,000
Kevin Jordan, 2b	5,000	175,000
Scott Ruffcorn, p		158,500
Billy McMillon, of		153,000
Tony Barron, of		150,000
Ron Blazier, p		150,000
Jerry Spradlin, p		150,000
Mike Robertson, 1b		150,000
Ryan Karp, p		150,000
Garrett Stephenson, p		150,000
Kevin Sefcik, ss		150,000
Wayne Gomes, p		150,000
Scott Rolen, 3b		150,000
Matt Beech, p		150,000

Average 1997 salary: $929,439
Total 1997 payroll: $30,671,500

Philadelphia (1883-1997)

Runs: Most, career

1506	Mike Schmidt, 1972-1989
1367	Ed Delahanty, 1888-1901
1114	Richie Ashburn, 1948-1959
963	Chuck Klein, 1928-1944
924	Sam Thompson, 1889-1898

Hits: Most, career

2234	Mike Schmidt, 1972-1989
2217	Richie Ashburn, 1948-1959
2213	Ed Delahanty, 1888-1901
1812	Del Ennis, 1946-1956
1798	Larry Bowa, 1970-1981

2B: Most, career

442	Ed Delahanty, 1888-1901
408	Mike Schmidt, 1972-1989
337	Sherry Magee, 1904-1914
336	Chuck Klein, 1928-1944
310	Del Ennis, 1946-1956

3B: Most, career

157	Ed Delahanty, 1888-1901
127	Sherry Magee, 1904-1914
106	Sam Thompson, 1889-1898
97	Richie Ashburn, 1948-1959
84	Johnny Callison, 1960-1969

HR: Most, career

548	Mike Schmidt, 1972-1989
259	Del Ennis, 1946-1956
243	Chuck Klein, 1928-1944
223	Greg Luzinski, 1970-1980
217	Cy Williams, 1918-1930

RBI: Most, career

1595	Mike Schmidt, 1972-1989
1286	Ed Delahanty, 1888-1901
1124	Del Ennis, 1946-1956
983	Chuck Klein, 1928-1944
957	Sam Thompson, 1889-1898

SB: Most, career

508	Billy Hamilton, 1890-1895
411	Ed Delahanty, 1888-1901
387	Sherry Magee, 1904-1914
289	Jim Fogarty, 1884-1889
288	Larry Bowa, 1970-1981

BB: Most, career

1507	Mike Schmidt, 1972-1989
946	Richie Ashburn, 1948-1959
946	Roy Thomas, 1899-1911
693	Willie Jones, 1947-1959
643	Ed Delahanty, 1888-1901

BA: Highest, career

.361	Billy Hamilton, 1890-1895
.348	Ed Delahanty, 1888-1901
.338	Elmer Flick, 1898-1901
.333	Sam Thompson, 1889-1898
.326	Chuck Klein, 1928-1944

On-base avg: Highest, career

.468	Billy Hamilton, 1890-1895
.421	Roy Thomas, 1899-1911
.419	Elmer Flick, 1898-1901
.415	Ed Delahanty, 1888-1901
.400	John Kruk, 1989-1994

Slug avg: Highest, career

.553	Chuck Klein, 1928-1944
.530	Dick Allen, 1963-1976
.527	Mike Schmidt, 1972-1989
.510	Dolph Camilli, 1934-1937
.508	Ed Delahanty, 1888-1901

Games started: Most, career

499	Steve Carlton, 1972-1986
472	Robin Roberts, 1948-1961
301	Chris Short, 1959-1972
280	Pete Alexander, 1911-1930
262	Curt Simmons, 1947-1960

Complete games: Most, career

272	Robin Roberts, 1948-1961
219	Pete Alexander, 1911-1930
185	Steve Carlton, 1972-1986
165	Charlie Ferguson, 1884-1887
156	Bill Duggleby, 1898-1907

Saves: Most, career

103	Steve Bedrosian, 1986-1989
102	MITCH WILLIAMS, 1991-1993
94	Tug McGraw, 1975-1984
90	Ron Reed, 1976-1983
69	RICKY BOTTALICO, 1994-1997

Shutouts: Most, career

61	Pete Alexander, 1911-1930
39	Steve Carlton, 1972-1986
35	Robin Roberts, 1948-1961
24	Chris Short, 1959-1972
23	Jim Bunning, 1964-1971

Wins: Most, career

241	Steve Carlton, 1972-1986
234	Robin Roberts, 1948-1961
190	Pete Alexander, 1911-1930
132	Chris Short, 1959-1972
115	Curt Simmons, 1947-1960

K: Most, career

3031	Steve Carlton, 1972-1986
1871	Robin Roberts, 1948-1961
1585	Chris Short, 1959-1972
1409	Pete Alexander, 1911-1930
1197	Jim Bunning, 1964-1971

Win pct: Highest, career

.676	Pete Alexander, 1911-1930
.642	Tom Seaton, 1912-1913
.607	Charlie Ferguson, 1884-1887
.606	Charlie Buffinton, 1887-1889
.600	Red Donahue, 1898-1901
.600	Ron Reed, 1976-1983

ERA: Lowest, career

1.79	George McQuillan, 1907-1916
2.18	Pete Alexander, 1911-1930
2.48	Tully Sparks, 1897-1910
2.61	Frank Corridon, 1904-1909
2.63	Earl Moore, 1908-1913

Runs: Most, season

192	Billy Hamilton, 1894
166	Billy Hamilton, 1895
158	Chuck Klein, 1930
152	Chuck Klein, 1932
152	Lefty O'Doul, 1929

Hits: Most, season

254	Lefty O'Doul, 1929
250	Chuck Klein, 1930
238	Ed Delahanty, 1899
226	Chuck Klein, 1932
223	Chuck Klein, 1933

2B: Most, season

59	Chuck Klein, 1930
55	Ed Delahanty, 1899
50	Chuck Klein, 1932
49	Ed Delahanty, 1895
48	Dick Bartell, 1932

3B: Most, season

27	Sam Thompson, 1894
23	Nap Lajoie, 1897
21	Ed Delahanty, 1892
21	Sam Thompson, 1895
19	JUAN SAMUEL, 1984
19	George Wood, 1887

HR: Most, season

48	Mike Schmidt, 1980
45	Mike Schmidt, 1979
43	Chuck Klein, 1929
41	Cy Williams, 1923
40	Dick Allen, 1966
40	Chuck Klein, 1930
40	Mike Schmidt, 1983

RBI: Most, season

170	Chuck Klein, 1930
165	Sam Thompson, 1895
146	Ed Delahanty, 1893
145	Chuck Klein, 1929
143	Don Hurst, 1932

SB: Most, season

111	Billy Hamilton, 1891
102	Jim Fogarty, 1887
102	Billy Hamilton, 1890
99	Jim Fogarty, 1889
98	Billy Hamilton, 1894

BB: Most, season

129	Lenny Dykstra, 1993
128	Mike Schmidt, 1983
126	Billy Hamilton, 1894
125	Richie Ashburn, 1954
121	Von Hayes, 1987

BA: Highest, season

.410	Ed Delahanty, 1899
.407	Ed Delahanty, 1894
.404	Billy Hamilton, 1894
.404	Ed Delahanty, 1895
.398	Lefty O'Doul, 1929

On-base avg: Highest, season

.523	Billy Hamilton, 1894
.500	Ed Delahanty, 1895
.490	Billy Hamilton, 1895
.478	Ed Delahanty, 1894
.472	Ed Delahanty, 1896

Slug avg: Highest, season

.687	Chuck Klein, 1930
.657	Chuck Klein, 1929
.654	Sam Thompson, 1895
.646	Chuck Klein, 1932
.644	Mike Schmidt, 1981

Games started: Most, season

61	John Coleman, 1883
55	Kid Gleason, 1890
50	Ed Daily, 1885
49	Gus Weyhing, 1892
47	Charlie Ferguson, 1884

Complete games: Most, season

59	John Coleman, 1883
54	Kid Gleason, 1890
49	Ed Daily, 1885
46	Charlie Ferguson, 1884
46	Gus Weyhing, 1892

Saves: Most, season

43	MITCH WILLIAMS, 1993
40	Steve Bedrosian, 1987
34	RICKY BOTTALICO, 1996
34	RICKY BOTTALICO, 1997
32	HEATHCLIFF SLOCUMB, 1995

Shutouts: Most, season

16	Pete Alexander, 1916
12	Pete Alexander, 1915
9	Pete Alexander, 1913
8	Pete Alexander, 1917
8	Steve Carlton, 1972
8	Ben Sanders, 1888

Wins: Most, season

38	Kid Gleason, 1890
33	Pete Alexander, 1916
32	Gus Weyhing, 1892
31	Pete Alexander, 1915
30	Pete Alexander, 1917
30	Charlie Ferguson, 1886

K: Most, season

319	CURT SCHILLING, 1997
310	Steve Carlton, 1972
286	Steve Carlton, 1980
286	Steve Carlton, 1982
275	Steve Carlton, 1983

Win pct: Highest, season

.800	TOMMY GREENE, 1993
.800	Robin Roberts, 1952
.769	Charlie Ferguson, 1886
.760	Larry Christenson, 1977
.760	John Denny, 1983

ERA: Lowest, season

1.22	Pete Alexander, 1915
1.53	George McQuillan, 1908
1.55	Pete Alexander, 1916
1.83	Lew Richie, 1908
1.83	Pete Alexander, 1917

Most pinch-hit homers, season

5	Gene Freese, 1959
4	Rip Repulski, 1958
4	Del Unser, 1979

Most pinch-hit homers, career

9	Cy Williams, 1918-1930
6	Gavvy Cravath, 1912-1920
6	Rick Joseph, 1967-1970
6	Del Unser, 1973-1982

Longest hitting streak

36	Billy Hamilton, 1894
31	Ed Delahanty, 1899
26	Chuck Klein, 1930
26	Chuck Klein, 1930 (2nd streak)
24	Willie Montanez, 1974

Most consecutive scoreless innings

41	Grover Cleveland Alexander, 1911

No-hit games

Joe Borden, Phi vs Chi NA, 4-0; July 28, 1875.
Charlie Ferguson, Phi vs Pro NL, 1-0; Aug. 29, 1885.
Red Donahue, Phi vs Bos NL, 5-0; July 8, 1898.
Chick Fraser, Phi at Chi NL, 10-0; Sept. 18, 1903 (2nd game).
Johnny Lush, Phi at Bro NL, 6-0; May 1, 1906.
Jim Bunning, Phi at NY NL, 6-0; June 21, 1964 (1st game, perfect game).
Rick Wise, Phi at Cin NL, 4-0; June 23, 1971.
TERRY MULHOLLAND, Phi vs SF NL, 6-0; Aug.15, 1990.
Tommy Greene, Phi at Mon NL, 2-0; May 23, 1991.

ACTIVE PLAYERS in caps.

Players' years of service are listed by the first and last years with this team and are not necessarily consecutive; all statistics record performances for this team only.

233

Houston Astros

By Mitchell Layton

Jeff Bagwell slugged .592 and finished third in the National League's MVP voting last year.

1997 Astros: Mediocrity won the division

Though they never had a lead in the entire three-game playoff sweep by the Braves, the Astros were still pleased to make the playoffs for the first time in 11 years. Houston, which took over first place for good on July 18, had much to be thankful for in 1997. They won the NL Central despite winning only 84 game and getting a major-league-worst 11 home runs from their cleanup hitters. First baseman Jeff Bagwell hit only .246 after the All-Star break, there were injuries to several key players and the bullpen foundered the final two months of the season. But second baseman Craig Biggio set a franchise record for runs scored (146). By producing a .309 batting average with 191 hits, 22 home runs, 81 RBI and 47 stolen bases, he was a constant in a Houston offense that roller-coastered between anemic and prolific, with more long spells of the former than the latter.

Darryl Kile (19-7) won more games than any other Houston pitcher has in this decade while establishing career highs for starts (34), complete games (six), shutouts (four) and innings pitched (255⅔). He also struck out 205 batters. With Shane Reynolds hurting, Mike Hampton starting slowly and Sid Fernandez bowing out early to injury, the Astros desperately needed Kile. He won 10 in a row between June 20 and Aug. 22 and was the biggest reason Houston was able to stay near the top all year. Fernandez made only one start, went on the disabled list and then retired. But Chris Holt (8-12) gave the Astros more than 200 innings and a 3.52 ERA, and Rule 5 acquisition Ramon Garcia (9-8, 3.69 ERA) picked up the slack. Billy Wagner started fast but finished poorly as the closer, and the club will be looking to shore up a bullpen that was a glaring weakness during much of 1997.

When Derek Bell was a bust in center field, the Astros had to find a center fielder fast, and Chuck Carr answered

Team MVP

Jeff Bagwell: As Jeff Bagwell goes, so go the Houston Astros. In a position in which he can often be pitched around, the first baseman still managed to hit .286, whack 43 home runs and drive in 135 runs. He also stole 31 bases in 41 attempts and hit 40 doubles while playing in every game.

the call by hitting .276 and playing excellent defense in 63 games. The Astros were counting on third baseman Sean Berry to have an encore performance in 1997 after he hit .282 with 17 homers and 95 RBI despite having an injured shoulder during 1996. Berry never really got going, but Bill Spiers stepped in and hit a team-high .320. Spiers also played spectacular defense and was the team's best pinch-hitter.

Pat Listach, the starter at shortstop and the No. 2 hitter between Biggio and Bagwell coming out of spring training, was paid $750,000 and hit .182 in 52 games before he was released.

The Astros got a good look at the future as Richard Hidalgo and Russ Johnson each spent time in Houston this season. Hidalgo made the biggest impression. The 22-year-old Venezuelan hit .306 in 19 games and played solid defense in center field and showed he had the strongest outfield arm on the club. He hit .279 with 11 homers and 78 RBI at AAA New Orleans. "I was very impressed with what I saw of him," manager Larry Dierker said. Johnson quickly made his presence felt with his scrappy play and a bat that has some sting (.300 in 21 games). A line-drive hitter with some power, the Astros feel he will also give the team a solid defender at third.

1997 Astros: Week-by-week notes

These notes were excerpted from the following issues of Baseball Weekly.

▶**April 9:** Manager Larry Dierker's wish for a fast start was granted as the Astros capped a 5-1 homestand with a three-game sweep of the Cardinals. The Astros were 2-11 against St. Louis last year. The sweep followed two victories in three games with Atlanta, including wins against Cy Young winners John Smoltz and Greg Maddux.

▶**April 23:** Left-hander Sid Fernandez underwent a battery of examinations, including blood tests, an MRI and nerve tests to see if there was any damage to his left biceps, where he has tendinitis.

▶**April 30:** Larry Dierker has waited for center fielder Derek Bell (.207, no homers) and left fielder Luis Gonzalez (.203) to get going offensively, but outfielder Thomas Howard's continued steady hitting (.444) may force the manager to play him more.

▶**May 7:** Since his first two starts, left-hander Mike Hampton has struggled. Hampton is 0-3 in his last five starts, and in 21⅓ innings has allowed 19 earned runs, 11 walks, and 31 hits.

▶**May 14:** Talk of the Astros' possibly leaving Houston resurfaced again on May 8 after the Texas House amended the stadium-funding proposal that had previously been approved by Harris County voters and county commissioners. The bill was amended to take away cities' rights to impose higher hotel taxes, a source of funding the Astros deemed essential to getting the new stadium financed, and also stripped the provision exempting Houston from holding another referendum on building the downtown ballpark.

▶**May 21:** Derek Bell underwent surgery on May 16 to have a hematoma on his left calf muscle drained. The center fielder is expected to miss three to four weeks. Bell was hitting .333 (14-for-42) with two homers and six RBI since moving to the No. 2 spot in the order on May 2.

▶**May 28:** Hard-throwing right-hander

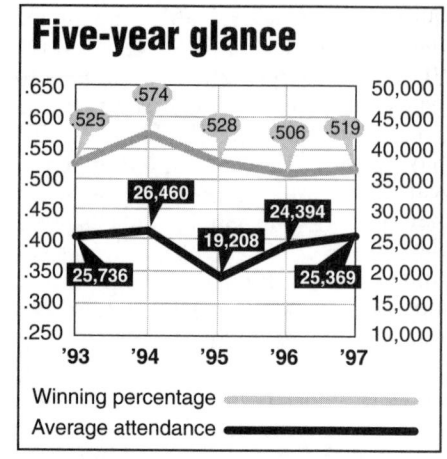

Five-year glance

	'93	'94	'95	'96	'97
Winning percentage	.525	.574	.528	.506	.519
Average attendance	25,736	26,460	19,208	24,394	25,369

Winning percentage
Average attendance

Darryl Kile is putting together an All-Star year. Kile, 5-2, leads the league in innings with 81⅓ and is among the leaders in ERA (5th, at 1.88) and strikeouts (11th, with 54). The Astros nearly gave up on him two years ago.

▶**June 4:** The Astros' slide continues, but general manager Gerry Hunsicker isn't planning on wholesale changes soon. The Astros are 12-22 since April 25 and fell three games under .500 on June 1 for the first time this season. The Astros do not have a home run from the cleanup spot this season. Their three outfielders have a combined seven home runs and a .252 average. In their last 17 games the Astros gave up six runs or more nine times.

▶**June 11:** John Hudek's roller-coaster career took a turn for the worse on June 2 when the Astros' former All-Star closer was optioned to AAA New Orleans. Hudek had given up 10 earned runs in his last 7⅓ innings. Hudek missed more than a year after season-ending surgery to remove part of a rib in July 1995.

▶**June 18:** Seeing 20-20: Luis Gonzalez's sixth-inning homer against the Royals on June 16 extended his hitting streak to 20 games. First baseman Jeff Bagwell hit his 20th homer of the season on June 13. He is only the second player in franchise history (along with Glenn Davis) to hit 20 or more homers in five consecutive seasons.

▶June 25: Luis Gonzalez tied a club record with his 23-game hitting streak, which was snapped on June 21 by four Cubs pitchers. Gonzalez's streak tied the mark set by Art Howe in 1981.

▶July 2: The Astros hope to have solved their center field problems with the addition of Chuck Carr, who became the fifth player to start in center for the Astros this year. He had two hits in five trips, stole a base and made a pair of fine defensive plays during his first two games.

▶July 10: Pat Listach, the man who was supposed to be the regular shortstop this year, was placed on waivers for the purpose of giving him his unconditional release last week after hitting .182 in 52 games.

▶July 16: Right-hander Tommy Greene will undergo surgery on July 16 to repair a torn right rotator cuff. Greene is out for the season after making just two starts.

▶July 23: In somewhat of a surprise move, the Astros sent rookie Bob Abreu to New Orleans on July 16. Abreu, touted as a Jackie Robinson Award candidate after winning the starting right field job during spring training, was hitting .240 and had made only six plate appearances since coming off the DL on July 1. Abreu became expendable when Chuck Carr was acquired to play center, which enabled Derek Bell to move back to right.

▶July 30: Third baseman Sean Berry and first baseman J.R. Phillips homered in a comeback 9-8 win on July 26 against the Montreal Expos, as Houston bolted to the top of the NL Central with its 15th win in 18 games.

▶Aug. 6: The Astros had the best July in franchise history, going 19-7. Among the biggest July stars were Darryl Kile, who continued his quest for the Cy Young Award with a 6-0 record and a 1.59 ERA, running his season mark to 15-3; Mike Hampton, who went 5-0 with a 2.25 ERA; and second baseman Craig Biggio, who hit .356 and scored 30 runs. The Astros' team ERA for the month was 2.95.

▶Aug. 13: Jeff Bagwell surpassed the 30-home-run and 100-RBI plateaus on Aug. 9. He has achieved those levels in the same season three times (1994, '96,

and '97), an Astros record. Craig Biggio became the first Houston player to score 100 or more runs in three consecutive seasons.

▶Aug. 20: The Astros are puzzled by Billy Wagner's abrupt reversal. The left-hander has been ineffective since posting his last save, on July 29. Wagner was 3-0 with an 0.69 ERA in July, but 0-2 with a 10.13 ERA in August.

▶Aug. 27: Sean Berry's disappointing season took yet another turn for the worse on Aug. 23, when he strained a left calf muscle and was placed on the 15-day DL. Berry is hitting .243 with eight homers and 32 RBI. This time last year, he was hitting .275 with 13 homers and 73 RBI despite playing the entire season with a torn rotator cuff in his right shoulder, which required off-season surgery.

▶Sept. 17: The Astros have waited all season for right-hander Shane Reynolds to find the form that enabled him to win a team-high 16 games last year. That patience might soon pay dividends. In his last three starts, Reynolds, 6-9 for the year, has a 3.15 ERA, and he has walked only one batter in his last $17\frac{2}{3}$ innings.

▶Sept. 24: Jeff Bagwell set a career high and a club season record with his 40th homer, on Sept. 16. He added two more later in the week. Craig Biggio set the major league record for most games without grounding into a double play in a season, 155.

▶Oct. 1: The Astros clinched the NL Central with a 9-1 Mike Hampton victory over the Cubs on Sept. 25. The Astros drew more than two million fans for the fourth time in franchise history. They took over first place on July 18 and never relinquished the lead.

QUOTE OF THE YEAR

"This is a terrible day for the people of Houston."
—Club president Tal Smith, after the Texas legislature rescinded Houston's right to impose a hotel tax, which was to be used to build a new stadium

HOUSTON ASTROS 1997 final stats

238

BATTERS	BA	SLG	OBA	G	AB	R	H	TB	2B	3B	HR	RBI	BB	SO	SB	CS	E
Knorr	.375	.750	.375	4	8	1	3	6	0	0	1	1	0	2	0	0	0
Spiers	.320	.481	.438	132	291	51	93	140	27	4	4	48	61	42	10	5	18
Biggio	.309	.501	.415	162	619	146	191	310	37	8	22	81	84	107	47	10	18
Hidalgo	.306	.484	.358	19	62	8	19	30	5	0	2	6	4	18	1	0	0
Johnson	.300	.417	.364	21	60	7	18	25	1	0	2	9	6	14	1	1	1
Bagwell	.286	.592	.425	162	566	109	162	335	40	2	43	135	127	122	31	10	11
Carr	.276	.417	.333	63	192	34	53	80	11	2	4	17	15	37	11	5	4
Bell	.276	.438	.344	129	493	67	136	216	29	3	15	71	40	94	15	7	8
Eusebio	.274	.305	.364	60	164	12	45	50	2	0	1	18	19	27	0	1	4
Ausmus	.266	.358	.326	130	425	45	113	152	25	1	4	44	38	78	14	6	7
Gutierrez	.261	.363	.315	102	303	33	79	110	14	4	3	34	21	50	5	2	8
Gonzalez	.258	.376	.345	152	550	78	142	207	31	2	10	68	71	67	10	7	5
Berry	.256	.422	.318	96	301	37	77	127	24	1	8	43	25	53	1	5	16
Abreu	.250	.372	.329	59	188	22	47	70	10	2	3	26	21	48	7	2	2
Bogar	.249	.390	.320	97	241	30	60	94	14	4	4	30	24	42	4	1	6
Howard	.247	.353	.323	107	255	24	63	90	16	1	3	22	26	48	1	2	0
Montgomery	.235	.324	.276	29	68	8	16	22	4	1	0	4	5	18	0	0	0
Rivera	.231	.385	.286	7	13	2	3	5	0	1	0	3	1	6	0	0	2
Mouton	.211	.322	.287	86	180	24	38	58	9	1	3	23	18	30	9	7	0
Pena	.211	.368	.273	9	19	2	4	7	3	0	0	2	2	3	0	0	0
Listach	.182	.227	.247	52	132	13	24	30	2	2	0	6	11	24	4	2	6
Phillips	.133	.333	.125	13	15	2	2	5	0	0	1	4	0	7	0	0	0
Ramos	.000	.000	.133	14	12	0	0	0	0	0	0	0	1	2	0	0	0

PITCHERS	W-L	ERA	BA	G	GS	CG	GF	Sho	SV	IP	H	R	ER	HR	BB	SO
Cabrera	0-0	1.17	.125	12	0	0	6	0	0	15.1	6	2	2	1	6	18
Martin	5-3	2.09	.254	55	0	0	18	0	2	56.0	52	13	13	2	23	36
Magnante	3-1	2.27	.223	40	0	0	14	0	1	47.2	39	16	12	2	11	43
Kile	19-7	2.57	.225	34	34	6	0	4	0	255.2	208	87	73	19	94	205
Wagner	7-8	2.85	.204	62	0	0	49	0	23	66.1	49	23	21	5	30	106
Holt	8-12	3.52	.263	33	32	0	0	0	0	209.2	211	98	82	17	61	95
Fernandez	1-0	3.60	.211	1	1	0	0	0	0	5.0	4	2	2	1	2	3
Garcia	9-8	3.69	.262	42	20	1	5	1	1	158.2	155	71	65	20	52	120
Hampton	15-10	3.83	.257	34	34	7	0	2	0	223.0	217	105	95	16	77	139
Reynolds	9-10	4.23	.267	30	30	2	0	0	0	181.0	189	92	85	19	47	152
Springer	3-3	4.23	.232	54	0	0	13	0	3	55.1	48	28	26	4	27	74
Henriquez	0-1	4.50	.167	4	0	0	1	0	0	4.0	2	2	2	0	3	3
Minor	1-0	4.50	.277	11	0	0	5	0	1	12.0	13	7	6	1	5	6
Lima	1-6	5.28	.271	52	1	0	15	0	2	75.0	79	45	44	9	16	63
Hudek	1-3	5.98	.252	40	0	0	20	0	4	40.2	38	27	27	8	33	36
Wall	2-5	6.26	.317	8	8	0	0	0	0	41.2	53	31	29	8	16	25
Greene	0-1	7.00	.286	2	2	0	0	0	0	9.0	10	7	7	2	5	11
Barrios	0-0	12.00	.400	2	0	0	0	0	0	3.0	6	4	4	0	3	3

1998 preliminary roster

PITCHERS (16)
Jose Cabrera
Scott Elarton
Freddy Garcia
Ramon Garcia
Mike Grzanich
John Halama
Mike Hampton
Chris Holt
Jose Lima
Mike Magnante
Trever Miller

C.J. Nitkowski
Shane Reynolds
Brian Sikorski
Billy Wagner
Mike Walter

CATCHERS (4)
Brad Ausmus
Ramon Castro
Tony Eusebio
Mitch Meluskey

INFIELDERS (9)
Jeff Bagwell
Craig Biggio
Tim Bogar
Carlos Guillen
Ricky Gutierrez
Carlos Hernandez
Russ Johnson
Bill Spiers
Daryle Ward

OUTFIELDERS (7)
Moises Alou
Derek Bell
Dave Clark
Carl Everett
Richard Hidalgo
Ray Montgomery
James Mouton

Games played by position

PLAYER	G	C	1B	2B	3B	SS	OF
Abreu	59	0	0	0	0	0	53
Ausmus	130	129	0	0	0	0	0
Bagwell	162	0	159	0	0	0	0
Bell	129	0	0	0	0	0	125
Berry	96	0	0	0	85	0	0
Biggio	162	0	0	160	0	0	0
Bogar	97	0	1	0	14	80	0
Carr	63	0	0	0	0	0	59
Eusebio	60	43	0	0	0	0	0
Gonzalez	152	0	1	0	0	0	146
Gutierrez	102	0	0	9	22	64	0
Hidalgo	19	0	0	0	0	0	19
Howard	107	0	0	0	0	0	62
Johnson	21	0	0	3	14	0	0
Knorr	4	3	2	0	0	0	0
Listach	52	0	0	0	0	31	6
Montgomery	29	0	0	0	0	0	18
Mouton	86	0	0	0	0	0	61
Pena	9	8	0	0	0	0	0
Phillips	13	0	3	0	0	0	3
Ramos	14	0	0	0	0	0	2
Rivera	7	0	0	1	0	6	0
Spiers	132	0	8	4	84	28	0

Sick call: 1997 DL report

PLAYER	Days on the DL
Bob Abreu	37
Derek Bell	30
Sean Berry	30*
Sid Fernandez	109
Tommy Greene	81
Ricky Gutierrez	35
Randy Knorr	15
Tom Martin	16
Ray Montgomery	103
Shane Reynolds	34
Mark Small	27
Russell Springer	23

* Indicates two separate terms on Disabled List.

Minor Leagues

Tops in the organization

BATTER	CLUB	AVG.	G	AB	R	H	HR	RBI
Ward, Daryle	NO	.334	128	470	76	157	21	98
Meluskey, Mitch	NO	.303	124	413	71	125	17	67
Cutshall, Patrick	Aub	.297	76	273	54	81	8	34
Rodriguez, Noel	Kis	.294	98	313	38	92	8	53
Hernandez, C.	Jck	.292	92	363	62	106	4	33

HOME RUNS

Ward, Daryle	NO	21
Phillips, J.R.	NO	21
Burns, Kevin	QC	20
Meluskey, M.	NO	17
Gonzalez, J.	Jck	16

WINS

Miller, Wade	Kis	15
Sikorski, Brian	Jck	13
Halama, John	NO	13
Robertson, J.	QC	11
Elarton, Scott	NO	11

RBI

Ward, Daryle	NO	98
Burns, Kevin	NO	86
Hidalgo, Richard	NO	78
Truby, Chris	Kis	75
Phillips, J.R.	NO	71

SAVES

Diorio, Mike	Kis	20
Hecht, Brian	QC	12
Henriquez, O.	NO	12
Grzanich, Mike	Jck	12
Several Players Tied at		9

STOLEN BASES

Lugo, Julio	Kis	35
Dallimore, Brian	Kis	24
Mitchell, D.	Jck	22
Truby, Chris	Kis	21
Johnson, Ric	Kis	21

STRIKEOUTS

Elarton, Scott	NO	191
Nitkowski, C.J.	NO	141
Robertson, J.	QC	135
Garcia, Freddy	Kis	131
Johnson, Mark	Kis	127

PITCHER	CLUB	W-L	ERA	IP	H	BB	SO
Miller, Wade	Kis	15- 5	2.38	159	124	24	126
Garcia, Freddy	Kis	10- 8	2.56	179	165	49	131
Halama, John	NO	13- 3	2.58	171	150	32	126
Blanco, Alberto	Kis	8- 4	2.71	126	89	49	110
Gutierrez, Jim	Jck	4- 5	2.97	100	107	25	59

1997 salaries

	Bonuses	Total earned salary
Jeff Bagwell,1b	25,000	8,040,000
Craig Biggio,2b	100,000	6,280,000
Derek Bell,of		3,250,000
Sean Berry,3b	50,000	2,250,000
Shane Reynolds,p	50,000	2,050,000
Darryl Kile,p		1,700,000
Mike Hampton,p	120,000	1,420,000
Luis Gonzalez,of	400,000	1,400,000
Brad Ausmus,c		1,075,000
Thomas Howard,of		750,000
Tony Eusebio,c		650,000
Bill Spiers,3b		600,000
Tony Pena,c	50,000	425,000
Ricky Gutierrez,ss		420,000
John Hudek,p	37,500	412,500
Russ Springer,p	75,000	400,000
Sid Fernandez,p		375,000
Tommy Greene,p		300,000
Randy Knorr,c		300,000
Mike Magnante,p		290,000
Tim Bogar,ss		275,000
Chuck Carr,of	100,000	250,000
Billy Wagner,p		185,000
Jose Lima,p		170,000
Ramon Garcia,p		160,000
Ray Montgomery,of		155,000
Tom Martin,p		150,000
Bob Abreu,of		150,000
Richard Hidalgo,of		150,000
Chris Holt,p		150,000

Average 1997 Salary: $1,139,417
Total 1997 Payroll: $34,182,500

Houston (1962-1997)

Runs: Most, career

890	Cesar Cedeno, 1970-1981
874	CRAIG BIGGIO, 1988-1997
871	Jose Cruz, 1975-1987
829	Jim Wynn, 1963-1973
676	Terry Puhl, 1977-1990

Hits: Most, career

1937	Jose Cruz, 1975-1987
1659	Cesar Cedeno, 1970-1981
1470	CRAIG BIGGIO, 1988-1997
1448	Bob Watson, 1966-1979
1357	Terry Puhl, 1977-1990

2B: Most, career

343	Cesar Cedeno, 1970-1981
335	Jose Cruz, 1975-1987
282	CRAIG BIGGIO, 1988-1997
246	JEFF BAGWELL, 1991-1997
241	Bob Watson, 1966-1979

3B: Most, career

80	Jose Cruz, 1975-1987
63	Joe Morgan, 1963-1980
62	Roger Metzger, 1971-1978
56	Terry Puhl, 1977-1990
55	Cesar Cedeno, 1970-1981
55	Craig Reynolds, 1979-1989

HR: Most, career

223	Jim Wynn, 1963-1973
187	JEFF BAGWELL, 1991-1997
166	Glenn Davis, 1984-1990
163	Cesar Cedeno, 1970-1981
139	Bob Watson, 1966-1979

RBI: Most, career

942	Jose Cruz, 1975-1987
782	Bob Watson, 1966-1979
778	Cesar Cedeno, 1970-1981
724	JEFF BAGWELL, 1991-1997
719	Jim Wynn, 1963-1973

SB: Most, career

487	Cesar Cedeno, 1970-1981
288	Jose Cruz, 1975-1987
268	CRAIG BIGGIO, 1988-1997
219	Joe Morgan, 1963-1980
217	Terry Puhl, 1977-1990

BB: Most, career

847	Jim Wynn, 1963-1973
730	Jose Cruz, 1975-1987
678	Joe Morgan, 1963-1980
634	CRAIG BIGGIO, 1988-1997
627	JEFF BAGWELL, 1991-1997

BA: Highest, career

.304	JEFF BAGWELL, 1991-1997
.297	Bob Watson, 1966-1979
.292	Jose Cruz, 1975-1987
.289	Cesar Cedeno, 1970-1981
.288	CRAIG BIGGIO, 1988-1997

On-base avg: Highest, career

.409	JEFF BAGWELL, 1991-1997
.377	CRAIG BIGGIO, 1988-1997
.374	Joe Morgan, 1963-1980
.364	Bob Watson, 1966-1979
.362	Jim Wynn, 1963-1973

Slug avg: Highest, career

.536	JEFF BAGWELL, 1991-1997
.483	Glenn Davis, 1984-1990
.454	Cesar Cedeno, 1970-1981
.445	Jim Wynn, 1963-1973
.444	Bob Watson, 1966-1979

Games started: Most, career

320	Larry Dierker, 1964-1976
301	Joe Niekro, 1975-1985
282	Nolan Ryan, 1980-1988
267	Bob Knepper, 1981-1989
259	Mike Scott, 1983-1991

Complete games: Most, career

106	Larry Dierker, 1964-1976
82	Joe Niekro, 1975-1985
78	Don Wilson, 1966-1974
76	J.R. Richard, 1971-1980
42	Mike Scott, 1983-1991

Saves: Most, career

199	Dave Smith, 1980-1990
76	Fred Gladding, 1968-1973
72	Joe Sambito, 1976-1984
62	DOUG JONES, 1992-1993
50	Ken Forsch, 1970-1980

Shutouts: Most, career

25	Larry Dierker, 1964-1976
21	Joe Niekro, 1975-1985
21	Mike Scott, 1983-1991
20	Don Wilson, 1966-1974
19	J.R. Richard, 1971-1980

Wins: Most, career

144	Joe Niekro, 1975-1985
137	Larry Dierker, 1964-1976
110	Mike Scott, 1983-1991
107	J.R. Richard, 1971-1980
106	Nolan Ryan, 1980-1988

K: Most, career

1866	Nolan Ryan, 1980-1988
1493	J.R. Richard, 1971-1980
1487	Larry Dierker, 1964-1976
1318	Mike Scott, 1983-1991
1283	Don Wilson, 1966-1974

Win pct: Highest, career

.634	MARK PORTUGAL, 1989-1993
.609	Jim Ray, 1965-1973
.601	J.R. Richard, 1971-1980
.577	PETE HARNISCH, 1991-1994
.576	Mike Scott, 1983-1991

ERA: Lowest, career

2.53	Dave Smith, 1980-1990
3.13	Nolan Ryan, 1980-1988
3.15	Don Wilson, 1966-1974
3.15	J.R. Richard, 1971-1980
3.18	Ken Forsch, 1970-1980

Runs: Most, season

146	CRAIG BIGGIO, 1997
123	CRAIG BIGGIO, 1995
117	Jim Wynn, 1972
113	CRAIG BIGGIO, 1996
113	Jim Wynn, 1969

Hits: Most, season

195	Enos Cabell, 1978
191	CRAIG BIGGIO, 1997
189	Jose Cruz, 1983
187	Jose Cruz, 1984
185	Jose Cruz, 1980
185	Greg Gross, 1974

2B: Most, season

48	JEFF BAGWELL, 1996
44	CRAIG BIGGIO, 1994
44	Rusty Staub, 1967
41	CRAIG BIGGIO, 1993
40	JEFF BAGWELL, 1997
40	DEREK BELL, 1996
40	Cesar Cedeno, 1971

3B: Most, season

14	Roger Metzger, 1973
13	Jose Cruz, 1984
13	STEVE FINLEY, 1992
13	STEVE FINLEY, 1993
12	Joe Morgan, 1965
12	Craig Reynolds, 1981

HR: Most, season

43	JEFF BAGWELL, 1997
39	JEFF BAGWELL, 1994
37	Jim Wynn, 1967
34	Glenn Davis, 1989
33	Jim Wynn, 1969

RBI: Most, season

135	JEFF BAGWELL, 1997
120	JEFF BAGWELL, 1996
116	JEFF BAGWELL, 1994
113	DEREK BELL, 1996
110	Bob Watson, 1977

SB: Most, season

65	Gerald Young, 1988
64	Eric Yelding, 1990
61	Cesar Cedeno, 1977
58	Cesar Cedeno, 1976
57	Cesar Cedeno, 1974

BB: Most, season

148	Jim Wynn, 1969
135	JEFF BAGWELL, 1996
127	JEFF BAGWELL, 1997
110	Joe Morgan, 1969
106	Jim Wynn, 1970

BA: Highest, season

.368	JEFF BAGWELL, 1994
.334	DEREK BELL, 1995
.333	Rusty Staub, 1967
.324	Bob Watson, 1975
.320	Cesar Cedeno, 1972

On-base avg: Highest, season

.451	JEFF BAGWELL, 1994
.451	JEFF BAGWELL, 1996
.436	Jim Wynn, 1969
.425	JEFF BAGWELL, 1997
.415	CRAIG BIGGIO, 1997

Slug avg: Highest, season

.750	JEFF BAGWELL, 1994
.592	JEFF BAGWELL, 1997
.570	JEFF BAGWELL, 1996
.537	Cesar Cedeno, 1973
.537	Cesar Cedeno, 1972

Games started: Most, season

40	Jerry Reuss, 1973
39	J.R. Richard, 1976
38	Bob Knepper, 1986
38	Joe Niekro, 1979
38	Joe Niekro, 1983
38	Joe Niekro, 1984
38	J.R. Richard, 1979

Complete games: Most, season

20	Larry Dierker, 1969
19	J.R. Richard, 1979
18	Don Wilson, 1971
17	Larry Dierker, 1970
16	Mike Cuellar, 1967
16	Joe Niekro, 1982
16	J.R. Richard, 1978

Saves: Most, season

36	DOUG JONES, 1992
33	Dave Smith, 1986
29	Fred Gladding, 1969
27	Dave Smith, 1985
27	Dave Smith, 1988

Shutouts: Most, season

6	Dave Roberts, 1973
5	Larry Dierker, 1972
5	Bob Knepper, 1981
5	Bob Knepper, 1986
5	Joe Niekro, 1979
5	Joe Niekro, 1982
5	Mike Scott, 1986
5	Mike Scott, 1988

Wins: Most, season

21	Joe Niekro, 1979
20	Larry Dierker, 1969
20	Joe Niekro, 1980
20	J.R. Richard, 1976
20	Mike Scott, 1989

K: Most, season

313	J.R. Richard, 1979
306	Mike Scott, 1986
303	J.R. Richard, 1978
270	Nolan Ryan, 1987
245	Nolan Ryan, 1982

Win pct: Highest, season

.818	MARK PORTUGAL, 1993
.731	DARRYL KILE, 1997
.692	Mike Scott, 1985
.667	Mike Scott, 1989
.656	Joe Niekro, 1979

ERA: Lowest, season

2.18	Bob Knepper, 1981
2.21	DANNY DARWIN, 1990
2.22	Mike Cuellar, 1966
2.22	Mike Scott, 1986
2.33	Larry Dierker, 1969

Most pinch-hit homers, season

5	Cliff Johnson, 1974
3	Joe Gaines, 1965

Most pinch-hit homers, career

8	Cliff Johnson, 1972-1977
6	Denny Walling, 1977-1992

Longest hitting streak

23	LUIS GONZALEZ, 1997
23	Art Howe, 1981
22	Cesar Cedeno, 1977
21	Lee May, 1973
21	Dickie Thon, 1982

Most consecutive scoreless innings

31	J.R. Richard, 1980

No-hit games

Don Nottebart, Hou vs Phi NL, 4-1;
  May 17, 1963.

Ken T. Johnson, Hou vs Cin NL, 0-1;
  April 23, 1964 (lost the game).

Don Wilson, Hou vs Atl NL, 2-0;
  June 18, 1967.

Don Wilson, Hou at Cin NL, 4-0;
  May 1, 1969.

Larry Dierker, Hou vs Mon NL, 6-0;
  July 9, 1976.

Ken Forsch, Hou vs Atl NL, 6-0;
  April 7, 1979.

Nolan Ryan, Hou vs LA NL, 5-0;
  Sept. 26, 1981.

Mike Scott, Hou vs SF NL, 2-0;
  Sept. 25, 1986.

DARRYL KILE, Hou vs NY NL, 7-1;
  Sept. 8, 1993.

ACTIVE PLAYERS in caps.

Players' years of service are listed by the first and last years with this team and are not necessarily consecutive; all statistics record performances for this team only.

Pittsburgh Pirates

By Susan Sterner, AP/Wide World Photos

Second baseman Tony Womack scored 85 runs and sparked the Pirates with a league-leading 60 stolen bases.

1997 Pirates: A stunning runner-up finish

The Pirates' surprising second-place finish in the NL Central made them one of baseball's most compelling stories this season. This inexperienced team, which began spring training with 70 players in camp and started the season with a major-league-low $9.1 million payroll, stumped the experts and won 79 games, nine more than GM Cam Bonifay envisioned it winning in a best-case scenario.

"It was the most fun I've had in a season except for when I played," said manager Gene Lamont, a former catcher. The Pirates might have won a division championship this season were it not for injuries to John Ericks, Kevin Elster, Jermaine Allensworth, Joe Randa, Kevin Young and Al Martin. If just Randa and Young had remained healthy, the Pirates might have won half a dozen more games and the division.

Of course, one could also suggest that those who filled in for the injured players did well enough and that the Pirates finished right where they should have. "I think the most impressive part of the season was when [Elster, Allensworth and Martin] got hurt," owner Kevin McClatchy said. "At that point, I think people thought we'd start to fade, but somehow we were still able to compete." It was pretty much that way the entire season. The Pirates would lose three straight games and appear headed into the tank. Then they would win two in a row and jump back into contention.

The performances of Young, second baseman Tony Womack and closer Rich Loiselle were big reasons why they hung in. Had Young not been injured, he might have hit 25 home runs, driven in 100 runs and been an outside candidate for Most Valuable Player. Womack became a solid leadoff batter and led the league in stolen bases with 60, the first Pirate to lead the league in steals since 1979. Loiselle, inheriting the closer role from Ericks in early May, had 29 saves, the second-highest total for a rookie in baseball history.

The recap of the Pirates' season

MAJOR LEAGUE REPORT

PITTSBURGH PIRATES / NL CENTRAL

Team MVP

Rich Loiselle: Of all the unlikely stories produced by the Pittsburgh Pirates in 1997, Rich Loiselle might have been the least expected. He was acquired from Houston during the 1996 season, when the Astros wanted veteran pitcher Danny Darwin. As a rookie in 1997, Loiselle took over the closer role, saving 29 games and making a team-high 72 appearances.

wouldn't be complete without mentioning shortstop Kevin Polcovich, who almost quit baseball when he wasn't invited to the major league spring training camp in 1997. Polcovich became the regular at shortstop after Elster was hurt and did a solid job until he too went down with an injury. On Aug. 29, he severely sprained his left ankle in Milwaukee and didn't play again.

Expectations will be higher in 1998. "It's not going to be fun and games anymore. Not after this year," veteran infielder Dale Sveum said. "We've accidentally put ourselves in the position where the fans and the press are going to look at us differently." But they probably shouldn't, because the team is very young and inexperienced.

Jose Guillen, 21, led what's expected to be a charge of youthful talent for the Pirates during the next few years. He hit 14 homers, drove in 70 runs and showed marked improvement defensively in the second half of his rookie season. The Pirates also got a look at outfielder Adrian Brown and pitcher Jose Silva, both rookies. Silva could land a spot in the starting rotation or the bullpen next season. Shortstops Abraham Nunez and Lou Collier, and pitcher Jeff Wallace, all of whom played some for the Pirates in 1997, could contribute more in 1998.

1997 Pirates: Week-by-week notes

These notes were excerpted from the following issues of Baseball Weekly.

▶**April 9:** The Pirates are an extremely young team. For example, closer John Ericks is the elder statesman in the bullpen—with one year and 26 days in the major leagues.

▶**April 16:** Steve Cooke, who missed most of the last two seasons with shoulder problems, got his first win as a starter since June 21, 1994, when he combined on a one-hitter in San Diego on April 8. The Pirates finished their season-opening West Coast trip 4-4. The starters compiled an ERA of 1.84, and John Ericks saved all four victories without allowing a run.

▶**April 23:** The Pirates finished last weekend at a surprising 8-8 for the season—especially since they were averaging just over three runs per game going into the weekend. "We've been putting it together since day one," said second baseman Tony Womack. "We're not as bad as people think, and we can only get better."

▶**April 30:** First baseman Kevin Young, who batted .089 (4-for-45) against right-handers with Kansas City last year, had four hits in his first eight at-bats against righties this season.

▶**May 7:** Starting pitching was better than expected throughout the first month. At the end of April, the starters' ERA (3.15) ranked fifth in the league.

▶**May 14:** The Pirates, in first place in the NL Central for a few days last week, stood inside the stadium gates on May 9 to shake hands and pose for pictures—and then went on to beat Atlanta 9-0. Tony Womack said it was no publicity stunt, but a sincere effort to win back support in the majors' second-smallest market. The Pirates hit five home runs in a game for the first time in almost 10 years in a 14-3 win at Colorado on May 7, with outfielders Al Martin and Jose Guillen, catcher Jason Kendall, shortstop Kevin Elster, and third baseman Joe Randa delivering the blows.

▶**May 21:** On May 14, the Pirates poured

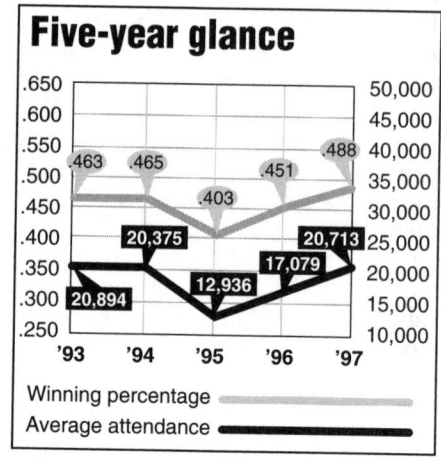

Five-year glance

Winning percentage
Average attendance

across nine runs in the eighth inning to beat Colorado 15-10. Al Martin's first grand slam capped the comeback. But the Pirates' season took a huge downward turn on May 16, when they lost Kevin Elster for at least eight weeks because of a broken left wrist he sustained during a 3-1 loss to Florida.

▶**May 28:** From May 15 to May 22, the Pirates lost center fielder Jermaine Allensworth, Kevin Elster and Al Martin to the DL. Martin was the most recent casualty, going on the DL on May 22 with a sprained right hand.

▶**June 4:** Manager Gene Lamont thinks the Pirates can become like the Expos. "I'd like to think our players can become like theirs," he said. "I think they've done the same thing we're trying to do. They gave guys chances—guys who basically were from their own system. They gave them an extended look to see if they could play, same as we're doing. And the players show you if they can or can't."

▶**June 18:** Entering the weekend, the Pirates were 25-17 when their starter pitched at least six innings. The bullpen has survived John Ericks' injury because rookies Rich Loiselle and Ricardo Rincon have stepped up to save games.

▶**June 25:** Right-hander Jason Schmidt has had a remarkably inconsistent season. He's made 13 starts but only once—

April 27 and May 2—has he been able to pitch more than six innings back-to-back. He's had starts as short as one, two and 3⅓ innings. Another starter, Esteban Loaiza, was 4-0 with a 2.44 ERA through seven starts. In his last seven, he's 1-4 with a 5.32 ERA.

▶**July 2:** Jermaine Allensworth, who missed 34 games with a broken left hand, returned to the lineup on June 23 with two hits, including a bases-loaded triple, in a 6-0 win in Houston that ended a six-game losing streak.

▶**July 10:** Tony Womack broke a club record on July 4 in the first inning against St. Louis when he stole his 32nd consecutive base without being caught. Hall of Famer Max Carey set the club record of 31 in 1922. Five innings later, the streak ended. Mike Difelice threw out Womack while he was trying to steal second on a pitchout.

▶**July 16:** The unbelievable Pirates had a seven-game winning streak, stood at .500 (43-43) and owned first place in the NL Central division at the All-Star break. One reason for success: Rookie Jose Guillen, who began the season 1-for-20, has a .261 batting average, seven homers and 35 RBI.

▶**July 23:** The Mets' Juan Acevedo hit Jason Kendall with a pitch in the eighth inning on July 15. That marked the 56th time a Pirate was hit by a pitch this season, breaking the club record of 55 set in 1993. The Pirates are on a pace to get hit by pitches 99 times this season. The major league record is 84, set last year by Houston.

▶**Aug. 6:** The baseball gods handed the Pirates another setback on Aug. 3. The Bucs learned they'll be without Kevin Young, their top run producer, for at least four weeks because of a ligament injury to his right thumb. The Pirates left home on July 18 tied with Houston for first place in the NL Central division. By the time they played their next home game, on July 31, they were 6½ games behind the Astros.

▶**Aug. 13:** Rich Loiselle converted his 18th save in 20 opportunities on Aug. 5 against Atlanta. And he did it impressively, striking out the side in the ninth and

getting the last two strikeouts with the tying run on third.

▶**Aug. 20:** The Pirates had another improbable victory on Aug. 12, stunning closer Mark Wohlers and the Braves with a four-run ninth inning that gave them a 5-2 win.

▶**Aug. 27:** Jose Guillen continued his second-half surge. On Aug. 16 in Miami, he drove in five runs to help beat Florida 10-5. In 37 games through Aug. 21, Guillen hit .312 (39-for-125) with six home runs and 24 RBI. He was at Class A Lynchburg a year ago.

▶**Sept. 3:** The Pirates picked up shortstop Shawon Dunston from the Chicago Cubs on Aug. 31 for a player to be named later. Dunston, 34, is hitting .284 in 114 games and led the Cubs with 29 stolen bases. The Pirates' regular shortstop, Kevin Polcovich, injured his ankle on Aug. 29 against Milwaukee and was placed on the 15-day DL.

▶**Sept. 10:** Shawon Dunston made a spectacular debut in front of 43,380 on Sept. 2, hitting two home runs and driving in four to lead the Pirates to a 6-4 win against Cleveland.

▶**Sept. 17:** The Pirates limped home from a rough 1-5 trip to Cincinnati and Montreal 3½ games behind first-place Houston and only 2½ ahead of third-place St. Louis. General manager Cam Bonifay said that "there's been more concern about winning and losing than playing good baseball."

▶**Oct. 1:** The Pirates stayed in the Central Division race until Sept. 25, when Houston eliminated them with a 9-1 victory against the Cubs. Only one rookie has saved more games than Rich Loiselle did this season. The right-hander, who didn't get his first save until May 2, finished with 29 saves. Todd Worrell of St. Louis had 36 saves in 1986.

QUOTE OF THE YEAR

"I'm waiting for Mark Grace to call me and tease me about waiting to get to Pittsburgh to be a home run hitter."

—Shortstop Shawon Dunston, after homering twice in his Pirates debut

PITTSBURGH PIRATES 1997 final stats

BATTERS	BA	SLG	OBA	G	AB	R	H	TB	2B	3B	HR	RBI	BB	SO	SB	CS	E
Ward	.353	.587	.420	71	167	33	59	98	16	1	7	33	18	17	4	1	0
Randa	.302	.451	.366	126	443	58	134	200	27	9	7	60	41	64	4	2	21
Young	.300	.535	.332	97	333	59	100	178	18	3	18	74	16	89	11	2	5
Dunston	.300	.451	.312	132	490	71	147	221	22	5	14	57	8	75	32	8	15
Kendall	.294	.434	.391	144	486	71	143	211	36	4	8	49	49	53	18	6	11
Martin	.291	.473	.359	113	423	64	123	200	24	7	13	59	45	83	23	7	6
Smith	.285	.503	.374	71	193	29	55	97	13	1	9	35	28	36	3	1	0
Womack	.278	.374	.326	155	641	85	178	240	26	9	6	50	43	109	60	7	20
Polcovich	.273	.396	.350	84	245	37	67	97	16	1	4	21	21	45	2	2	12
Guillen	.267	.412	.300	143	498	58	133	205	20	5	14	70	17	88	1	2	9
Sveum	.261	.451	.319	126	306	30	80	138	20	1	12	47	27	81	0	3	8
Osik	.257	.362	.322	49	105	10	27	38	9	1	0	7	9	21	0	1	2
Allensworth	.255	.339	.340	108	369	55	94	125	18	2	3	43	44	79	14	7	4
Williams	.240	.385	.327	38	96	12	23	37	5	0	3	12	11	25	1	0	2
Nunez	.225	.375	.289	19	40	3	9	15	2	2	0	6	3	10	1	0	0
Elster	.225	.449	.327	39	138	14	31	62	6	2	7	25	21	39	0	2	1
M. Johnson	.215	.315	.345	78	219	30	47	69	10	0	4	29	43	78	1	1	5
A. Brown	.190	.252	.273	48	147	17	28	37	6	0	1	10	13	18	8	4	1
E. Brown	.179	.284	.304	66	95	16	17	27	2	1	2	6	10	32	5	1	3
Garcia	.150	.400	.190	20	40	4	6	16	1	0	3	5	2	17	0	0	3
Collier	.135	.135	.158	18	37	3	5	5	0	0	0	0	3	11	1	0	0

PITCHERS	W-L	ERA	BA	G	GS	CG	GF	Sho	SV	IP	H	R	ER	HR	BB	SO
Dessens	0-0	0.00	.167	3	0	0	1	0	0	3.1	2	0	0	0	0	2
Wallace	0-0	0.75	.200	11	0	0	1	0	0	12.0	8	2	1	0	8	14
Ericks	1-0	1.93	.200	10	0	0	10	0	6	9.1	7	3	2	1	4	6
Christiansen	3-0	2.94	.274	39	0	0	9	0	0	33.2	37	11	11	2	17	37
Loiselle	1-5	3.10	.269	72	0	0	58	0	29	72.2	76	29	25	7	24	66
Rincon	4-8	3.45	.230	62	0	0	23	0	4	60.0	51	26	23	5	24	71
Cordova	11-8	3.63	.259	29	29	2	0	2	0	178.2	175	80	72	14	49	121
Sodowsky	2-2	3.63	.249	45	0	0	8	0	0	52.0	49	22	21	6	34	51
Wilkins	9-5	3.69	.242	70	0	0	21	0	2	75.2	65	33	31	7	33	47
Wagner	0-0	3.94	.279	14	0	0	2	0	0	16.0	17	7	7	3	13	9
Loaiza	11-11	4.13	.279	33	32	1	0	0	0	196.1	214	99	90	17	56	122
Cooke	9-15	4.30	.285	32	32	0	0	0	0	167.1	184	95	80	15	77	109
Lieber	11-14	4.49	.263	33	32	1	0	0	0	188.1	193	102	94	23	51	160
Peters	2-2	4.58	.277	31	1	0	5	0	0	37.1	38	23	19	6	21	17
Schmidt	10-9	4.60	.265	32	32	2	0	0	0	187.2	193	106	96	16	76	136
Silva	2-1	5.94	.347	11	4	0	0	0	0	36.1	52	26	24	4	16	30
J. Johnson	0-0	6.00	.400	3	0	0	0	0	0	6.0	10	4	4	2	1	3
Ruebel	3-2	6.32	.302	44	0	0	9	0	0	62.2	77	50	44	8	27	50
Wainhouse	0-1	8.04	.301	25	0	0	6	0	0	28.0	34	28	25	2	17	21
Granger	0-0	18.00	.417	9	0	0	1	0	0	5.0	10	10	10	3	8	4

1998 preliminary roster

PITCHERS (21)
Jimmy Anderson
Martin Brazoban
Jason Christiansen
Francisco Cordova
Kane Davis
Elmer Dessens
Elvin Hernandez
Sean Lawrence
Jon Lieber
Esteban Loiaza
Rich Loiselle
Javier Martinez

Chris Peters
Jose Pett
Jason Philips
Ricardo Rincon
Jason Schmidt
Jose Silva
Jeff Tabaka
Jeff Wallace
Marc Wilkens

CATCHERS (2)
Jason Kendall
Keith Osik

INFIELDERS (8)
Lou Collier
Brandon Cromer
Freddy Garcia
Abraham Nunez
Kevin Polcovich
Doug Strange
Tony Womack
Ron Wright
Kevin Young

OUTFIELDERS (10)
Jermaine Allensworth
Adrian Brown
Emil Brown
Jose Guillen
Al Martin
Manny Martinez
Mark Smith
T.J. Staton
Turner Ward

Games played by position

PLAYER	G	C	1B	2B	3B	SS	OF
Allensworth	108	0	0	0	0	0	104
A. Brown	48	0	0	0	0	0	38
E. Brown	66	0	0	0	0	0	42
Collier	18	0	0	0	0	18	0
Dunston	132	0	0	0	0	126	7
Elster	39	0	0	0	0	39	0
Garcia	20	0	2	0	10	0	0
Guillen	143	0	0	0	0	0	136
M. Johnson	78	0	63	0	0	0	0
Kendall	144	142	0	0	0	0	0
Martin	113	0	0	0	0	0	110
Nunez	19	0	0	9	0	12	0
Osik	49	32	1	4	1	0	0
Polcovich	84	0	0	2	1	80	0
Randa	126	0	0	13	120	0	0
Smith	71	0	9	0	0	0	42
Sveum	126	0	21	2	47	28	0
Ward	71	0	0	0	0	0	54
Williams	38	0	26	0	0	0	0
Womack	155	0	0	152	0	4	0
Young	97	0	77	0	12	0	11

Sick call: 1997 DL report

PLAYER	Days on the DL
Jermaine Allensworth	38
Jason Christiansen	88
Francisco Cordova	15
Kane Davis	73
Kevin Elster	135
John Ericks	153
Al Martin	33
Kevin Polcovich	16
Joe Randa	29
Ricardo Rincon	15
Matt Ruebel	16
Mark Smith	23
Clint Sodowsky	15
Paul Wagner	108
Kevin Young	40

1997 salaries

	Bonuses	Total earned salary
Shawon Dunston,ss	325,000	2,325,000
Al Martin,of		2,266,666
Kevin Elster,ss		1,650,000
Kevin Young,1b	50,000	400,000
Dale Sveum,3b	75,000	400,000
Jon Lieber,p		335,000
Turner Ward,of		300,000
Eddie Williams,1b		250,000
Jason Kendall,c		235,000
Joe Randa,3b		220,000
Jason Schmidt,p		210,000
Francisco Cordova,p		210,000
Esteban Loaiza,p		200,000
John Ericks,p		200,000
Jason Christiansen,p		195,000
Keith Osik,c		175,000
Steve Cooke,p	125,000	300,000
Marc Wilkins,p		162,500
Tony Womack,2b		160,000
Matt Ruebel,p		160,000
Jermaine Allensworth,of		160,000
Clint Sodowsky,p		155,000
Rich Loiselle,p		155,000
Mark Smith,of		150,000
Kevin Polcovich,ss		150,000
Jason Johnson,p		150,000
Jose Guillen,of		150,000
Kane Davis,p		150,000
Abraham Nunez,ss		150,000
Emil Brown,of		150,000
Jeffrey Wallace,p		150,000
Ricardo Rincon,p		150,000

Average 1997 salary: $380,443
Total 1997 payroll: $12,174,166

Minor Leagues

Tops in the organization

BATTER	CLUB	AVG.	G	AB	R	H	HR	RBI
Martinez, Manny	Cgy	.331	109	420	78	139	16	66
Collier, Lou	Cgy	.330	112	397	65	131	1	48
Bridges, Kary	Cgy	.317	99	378	52	120	3	35
Brown, Adrian	Cgy	.313	99	393	82	123	3	34
Tolentino, Jose	Cgy	.308	88	305	52	94	16	69

HOME RUNS

Ramirez, Aramis	Lyn	29
Garcia, Freddy	Car	24
Sanders, Tracy	Car	21
Hermansen, C	Car	20
Wilson, Craig	Lyn	19

WINS

McDade, Neal	Lyn	12
Arroyo, Bronson	Lyn	12
Phillips, Jason	Car	12
Lambert, K.	Eri	11
Johnson, Jason	Car	11

RBI

Ramirez, Aramis	Lyn	114
Sanford, Chance	Cgy	96
Sanders, Tracy	Car	78
Garcia, Freddy	Car	74
Several Players Tied at		72

SAVES

Daniels, David	Lyn	22
Maskivish, Joe	Car	17
Ryan, Matt	Car	14
Paugh, Rick	Aug	13
Cook, O.J.	Eri	10

STOLEN BASES

Freeman, T.	Eri	47
Schreiber, Stan	Aug	40
Nunez, Abraham	Car	39
Asche, Mike	Lyn	33
Several Players Tied at		29

STRIKEOUTS

Phillips, Jason	Car	162
Ah Yat, Paul	Lyn	157
Johnson, Jason	Car	155
Haynie, Jason	Lyn	150
Benson, Kris	Car	138

PITCHER	CLUB	W-L	ERA	IP	H	BB	SO
Ah Yat, Paul	Lyn	10- 2	2.35	138	119	20	157
McDade, Neal	Lyn	12- 4	2.82	131	121	30	119
Bacci, Anthony	Eri	9- 6	3.12	113	99	50	74
Alvarado, Carlos	Aug	6- 5	3.27	113	114	45	109
Mathews, Del	Car	7- 7	3.27	99	101	33	99

247

PITTSBURGH PIRATES / NL CENTRAL

Pittsburgh (1887-1997)

Runs: Most, career

1521	Honus Wagner, 1900-1917
1493	Paul Waner, 1926-1940
1416	Roberto Clemente, 1955-1972
1414	Max Carey, 1910-1926
1195	Willie Stargell, 1962-1982

Hits: Most, career

3000	Roberto Clemente, 1955-1972
2967	Honus Wagner, 1900-1917
2868	Paul Waner, 1926-1940
2416	Max Carey, 1910-1926
2416	Pie Traynor, 1920-1937

2B: Most, career

558	Paul Waner, 1926-1940
551	Honus Wagner, 1900-1917
440	Roberto Clemente, 1955-1972
423	Willie Stargell, 1962-1982
375	Max Carey, 1910-1926

3B: Most, career

232	Honus Wagner, 1900-1917
187	Paul Waner, 1926-1940
166	Roberto Clemente, 1955-1972
164	Pie Traynor, 1920-1937
156	Fred Clarke, 1900-1915

HR: Most, career

475	Willie Stargell, 1962-1982
301	Ralph Kiner, 1946-1953
240	Roberto Clemente, 1955-1972
176	BARRY BONDS, 1986-1992
166	Dave Parker, 1973-1983

RBI: Most, career

1540	Willie Stargell, 1962-1982
1475	Honus Wagner, 1900-1917
1305	Roberto Clemente, 1955-1972
1273	Pie Traynor, 1920-1937
1177	Paul Waner, 1926-1940

SB: Most, career

688	Max Carey, 1910-1926
639	Honus Wagner, 1900-1917
412	Omar Moreno, 1975-1982
312	Patsy Donovan, 1892-1899
271	Tommy Leach, 1900-1918

BB: Most, career

937	Willie Stargell, 1962-1982
918	Max Carey, 1910-1926
909	Paul Waner, 1926-1940
877	Honus Wagner, 1900-1917
795	Ralph Kiner, 1946-1953

BA: Highest, career

.340	Paul Waner, 1926-1940
.336	Kiki Cuyler, 1921-1927
.328	Honus Wagner, 1900-1917
.327	Matty Alou, 1966-1970
.324	Arky Vaughan, 1932-1941
.324	Elmer Smith, 1892-1901

On-base avg: Highest, career

.415	Arky Vaughan, 1932-1941
.415	Elmer Smith, 1892-1901
.410	George Grantham, 1925-1931
.407	Paul Waner, 1926-1940
.405	Ralph Kiner, 1946-1953

Slug avg: Highest, career

.567	Ralph Kiner, 1946-1953
.529	Willie Stargell, 1962-1982
.513	Kiki Cuyler, 1921-1927
.512	Dick Stuart, 1958-1962
.503	BARRY BONDS, 1986-1992

Games started: Most, career

477	Bob Friend, 1951-1965
369	Wilbur Cooper, 1912-1924
364	Vern Law, 1950-1967
353	Babe Adams, 1907-1926
299	Sam Leever, 1898-1910

Complete games: Most, career

263	Wilbur Cooper, 1912-1924
241	Sam Leever, 1898-1910
209	Deacon Phillippe, 1900-1911
206	Babe Adams, 1907-1926
167	Pud Galvin, 1887-1892

Saves: Most, career

188	Roy Face, 1953-1968
158	Kent Tekulve, 1974-1985
133	Dave Giusti, 1970-1976
61	STAN BELINDA, 1989-1993
59	Al McBean, 1961-1970

Shutouts: Most, career

44	Babe Adams, 1907-1926
39	Sam Leever, 1898-1910
35	Bob Friend, 1951-1965
33	Wilbur Cooper, 1912-1924
28	Vern Law, 1950-1967
28	Lefty Leifield, 1905-1912

Wins: Most, career

202	Wilbur Cooper, 1912-1924
194	Babe Adams, 1907-1926
194	Sam Leever, 1898-1910
191	Bob Friend, 1951-1965
168	Deacon Phillippe, 1900-1911

K: Most, career

1682	Bob Friend, 1951-1965
1652	Bob Veale, 1962-1972
1191	Wilbur Cooper, 1912-1924
1159	John Candelaria, 1975-1993
1092	Vern Law, 1950-1967

Win pct: Highest, career

.683	Nick Maddox, 1907-1910
.667	Jesse Tannehill, 1897-1902
.660	Sam Leever, 1898-1910
.659	Vic Willis, 1906-1909
.656	Emil Yde, 1924-1927

ERA: Lowest, career

2.08	Vic Willis, 1906-1909
2.38	Lefty Leifield, 1905-1912
2.47	Sam Leever, 1898-1910
2.50	Deacon Phillippe, 1900-1911
2.60	Bob Harmon, 1914-1918

Runs: Most, season

148	Jake Stenzel, 1894
145	Patsy Donovan, 1894
144	Kiki Cuyler, 1925
142	Paul Waner, 1928
140	Max Carey, 1922

Hits: Most, season

237	Paul Waner, 1927
234	Lloyd Waner, 1929
231	Matty Alou, 1969
223	Lloyd Waner, 1927
223	Paul Waner, 1928

2B: Most, season

62	Paul Waner, 1932
53	Paul Waner, 1936
50	Paul Waner, 1928
47	Adam Comorosky, 1930
45	Dave Parker, 1979
45	Andy Van Slyke, 1992
45	Honus Wagner, 1900

3B: Most, season

36	Chief Wilson, 1912
28	Harry Davis, 1897
27	Jimmy Williams, 1899
26	Kiki Cuyler, 1925
23	Adam Comorosky, 1930
23	Elmer Smith, 1893

HR: Most, season

54	Ralph Kiner, 1949
51	Ralph Kiner, 1947
48	Willie Stargell, 1971
47	Ralph Kiner, 1950
44	Willie Stargell, 1973

RBI: Most, season

131	Paul Waner, 1927
127	Ralph Kiner, 1947
127	Ralph Kiner, 1949
126	Honus Wagner, 1901
125	Willie Stargell, 1971

SB: Most, season

96	Omar Moreno, 1980
77	Omar Moreno, 1979
71	Omar Moreno, 1978
71	Billy Sunday, 1888
70	Frank Taveras, 1977

BB: Most, season

137	Ralph Kiner, 1951
127	BARRY BONDS, 1992
122	Ralph Kiner, 1950
119	Elbie Fletcher, 1940
118	Elbie Fletcher, 1941
118	Arky Vaughan, 1936

BA: Highest, season

.385	Arky Vaughan, 1935
.381	Honus Wagner, 1900
.380	Paul Waner, 1927
.374	Jake Stenzel, 1895
.373	Paul Waner, 1936

On-base avg: Highest, season

.491	Arky Vaughan, 1935
.456	BARRY BONDS, 1992
.454	Elmer Smith, 1896
.453	Arky Vaughan, 1936
.452	Ralph Kiner, 1951

Slug avg: Highest, season

.658	Ralph Kiner, 1949
.646	Willie Stargell, 1973
.639	Ralph Kiner, 1947
.628	Willie Stargell, 1971
.627	Ralph Kiner, 1951

Games started: Most, season

55	Ed Morris, 1888
53	Mark Baldwin, 1892
51	Mark Baldwin, 1891
50	Pud Galvin, 1888
50	Pink Hawley, 1895
50	Frank Killen, 1896

Complete games: Most, season

54	Ed Morris, 1888
49	Pud Galvin, 1888
48	Mark Baldwin, 1891
47	Pud Galvin, 1887
46	Harry Staley, 1889

Saves: Most, season

34	Jim Gott, 1988
31	Kent Tekulve, 1978
31	Kent Tekulve, 1979
30	Dave Giusti, 1971
29	RICH LOISELLE, 1997

Shutouts: Most, season

8	Babe Adams, 1920
8	Jack Chesbro, 1902
8	Lefty Leifield, 1906
8	Al Mamaux, 1915
7	Steve Blass, 1968
7	Wilbur Cooper, 1917
7	Sam Leever, 1903
7	Bob Veale, 1965
7	Vic Willis, 1908

Wins: Most, season

36	Frank Killen, 1893
31	Pink Hawley, 1895
30	Frank Killen, 1896
29	Ed Morris, 1888
28	Jack Chesbro, 1902
28	Pud Galvin, 1887

K: Most, season

276	Bob Veale, 1965
250	Bob Veale, 1964
229	Bob Veale, 1966
213	Bob Veale, 1969
199	Larry McWilliams, 1983

Win pct: Highest, season

.947	Roy Face, 1959
.842	Emil Yde, 1924
.824	Jack Chesbro, 1902
.806	Howie Camnitz, 1909
.800	John Candelaria, 1977
.800	Ed Doheny, 1902
.800	Sam Leever, 1905

ERA: Lowest, season

1.56	Howie Camnitz, 1908
1.62	Howie Camnitz, 1909
1.66	Sam Leever, 1907
1.73	Vic Willis, 1906
1.87	Lefty Leifield, 1906

Most pinch-hit homers, season

4	MARK JOHNSON, 1996
3	Gene Freese, 1964
3	Ham Hyatt, 1913
3	Jose Pagan, 1969
3	Al Rubeling, 1944
3	Bob Skinner, 1956
3	Willie Stargell, 1982
3	Ed Stevens, 1948
3	Dick Stuart, 1959

Most pinch-hit homers, career

8	Willie Stargell 1962-1982
6	John Milner, 1978-1982
6	Dick Stuart, 1958-1962

Longest hitting streak

27	Jimmy Williams, 1899
26	Danny O'Connell, 1953
25	Clyde Barnhart, 1925
25	Charlie Grimm, 1923
25	Fred Lindstrom, 1933

Most consecutive scoreless innings

41	Jack Chesbro, 1902
36	Ed Morris, 1888

No-hit games

Nick Maddox, Pit vs Bro NL, 2-1; Sept. 20, 1907.

Cliff Chambers, Pit at Bos NL, 3-0; May 6, 1951 (2nd game).

Harvey Haddix, Pit at Mil NL, 0-1; May 26, 1959 (lost on one hit in 13 innings after pitching 12 perfect innings).

Bob Moose, Pit at NY NL, 4-0; Sept. 20, 1969.

Dock Ellis, Pit at SD NL, 2-0; June 12, 1970 (1st game).

John Candelaria, Pit vs LA NL, 2-0; Aug. 9, 1976.

FRANCISCO CORDOVA (nine innings) and RICARDO RINCON (one inning), Pit vs Hou NL, 3-0; July 12, 1997.

Lefty Leifield, six innings, darkness, Pit at Phi NL, 8-0; Sept. 26, 1906 (2nd game).

Howie Camnitz, five innings, agreement, Pit at NY NL, 1-0; Aug. 23, 1907 (2nd game).

ACTIVE PLAYERS in caps.

Players' years of service are listed by the first and last years with this team and are not necessarily consecutive; all statistics record performances for this team only.

Cincinnati Reds

By Russell Becker, Baseball Weekly

Versatile Willie Greene played infield and outfield while leading the Reds with 26 homers and 91 RBI.

1997 Reds: Lights out for Knight

The gate never opened for the Cincinnati Reds in 1997. Before spring training finished, closer Jeff Brantley's shoulder was shot, shortstop Barry Larkin's left heel was beginning a season-long ache, and rightfielder Reggie Sanders had an sore lower back. Before the Reds could make the proper adjustments to compensate for the loss of the Fireman of the Year and their two main offensive operatives, they stumbled through a 7-18 April, burying themselves for good. The Reds were 13 games under .500 and locked in fourth place when manager Ray Knight was fired. He was replaced on July 25 by Jack McKeon, who guided the team to a 33-30 record and pulled them into third place.

A replacement was found for Brantley. His 1996 setup man, Jeff Shaw, stepped in to win the National League saves title, with 42, two short of the club record established a year earlier by Brantley. The Reds are the first NL team to have different pitchers win back-to-back top reliever titles. Help was not found for Larkin, who played only 73 games but batted .317 before season-ending surgery in early September, or for Sanders, who played 86 games and hit 19 homers with 56 RBI. The slack was taken up somewhat by third baseman Willie Greene, who hit only .252 but led the team in homers (26) and RBI (91).

The double-entry of Jon Nunnally and Chris Stynes arrived from the Royals on July 15 in a trade that sent pitchers Hector Carrasco and Scott Service to the Royals. Nunnally and Stynes became the two best offensive weapons on the team during the last half of the season. Nunnally hit .318 with 13 homers and 35 RBI in 64 games. Stynes started the last 49 games of the season and hit .348 with six homers and 27 RBI.

Catcher Joe Oliver tore a ligament in his left thumb the last week of spring training making a sweep tag and missed the month of April. The team ERA was above 6.00. When Oliver returned, the

pitching stabilized, and Cincinnati pitchers posted a 3.99 ERA in his 93 starts. He was hitting .299 at the All-Star break but wore down offensively in the last month.

Outfielder Ruben Sierra was acquired in the offseason to play left field and bat cleanup. But he played poorly and was released in May. Terry Pendleton was brought in as a utility infielder and tutor for Greene. Pendleton was injured early in the year and was released shortly after the All-Star break.

The 66-year-old McKeon, hired on an interim basis, did so well reviving stability in the clubhouse and urging the best out of young players that he was named to manage the club in 1998. His team will be much different—younger and cheaper, as the Reds start a rebuilding process. Rookie right-hander Brett Tomko was called up from AAA Indianapolis a month into the season and slipped into the rotation, where he won 11 games. Right-hander Dave Burba, who won five straight starts in September, is expected to anchor the starters. Felix Rodriguez, dubbed "The Intimidator" by McKeon because of his 98-mph fastball, most likely will work out of the bullpen. Pokey Reese stepped in at shortstop for the injured Larkin and played flashy defense, but tired down the stretch and hit only .219. McKeon says that Larkin, if healthy, is his shortstop, but he'll find some place for Reese, maybe second base.

1997 Reds: Week-by-week notes

These notes were excerpted from the following issues of Baseball Weekly.

▶**April 9:** Closer Jeff Brantley was placed on the DL on April 2. He has rotator cuff tendinitis. Brantley set a club record with 44 saves last season. Jeff Shaw recorded a save in his first opportunity, but blew a save on April 5.

▶**April 16:** During a five-game losing streak, the Reds hit .193 (33-for-171) and Cincinnati pitchers posted an 8.37 ERA.

▶**April 23:** Center fielder Deion Sanders continued to be the only offensive light. While the Reds were losing six of seven road games in Atlanta and Pittsburgh, Sanders went 13-for-29 with nine stolen bases. Through 18 games, Sanders was batting .403 with 15 steals. Despite being on base 39 times in 82 plate appearances, he had scored only nine runs.

▶**April 30:** Shortstop Barry Larkin's sore left heel is reducing one of the best players in the major leagues to a weak hitter and limited fielder. Larkin is batting only .227 with one homer and five steals. The best news of the season came on April 26, when lefty Pete Schourek won his first game in nearly a year, beating the Phillies 10-2.

▶**May 7:** The second base situation continues to plague the club. Regular Bret Boone was hitting .128 with only four hits in his last 40 at-bats. Backup second baseman Jeff Branson was even worse. During the same period as Boone's skid, Branson was 0-for-25. The Reds set a club record for defeats in April, going 7-18.

▶**May 14:** The Reds gave up on four-time All-Star outfielder Ruben Sierra, designating him for assignment for the purpose of giving him his release. After 31 games, Sierra was hitting .244 with only two homers, seven RBI and 28 strikeouts in 95 at-bats.

▶**May 21:** Barry Larkin is hitting .096 with runners in scoring position (3-31), .133 with runners on third (2-15) and .000 with runners on third and less than two outs (0-6). His numbers mirror the team's: .182, .156, and .175, respectively, for those situations.

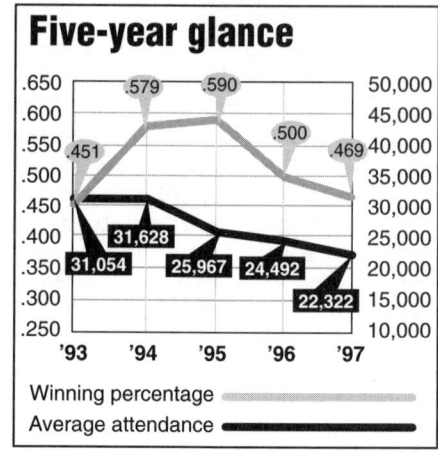

Five-year glance

| | '93 | '94 | '95 | '96 | '97 |

Winning percentage: .451, .579, .590, .500, .469
Average attendance: 31,054, 31,628, 25,967, 24,492, 22,322

Winning percentage ▬▬
Average attendance ▬▬

▶**May 28:** Things were getting considerably better for Reds pitchers in May than they had been in April, when the staff had a 6.36 ERA. In their first 21 games in May, the staff ERA was 3.38, dropping the overall figure to 4.86.

▶**June 4:** Barry Larkin had a 10-game hitting streak, tying since-released outfielder Ruben Sierra for longest on the team this year. The streak (18-for-32) lifted Larkin's average to .314. During his tear, he fell one short of tying the NL record for most times reaching base consecutively, 14, by Pedro Guerrero. After 13 straight, Larkin and Philadelphia's Curt Schilling put on a nine-pitch battle before Larkin flied to deep right.

▶**June 11:** Reliever Hector Carrasco is asking to be traded. Despite leading NL relievers with 41⅓ innings and having a 2.18 ERA, on June 7 Carrasco was sent back to the minors. He was recalled the next day because starter Mike Morgan went on the DL.

▶**June 18:** Lefty Kent Mercker came within one inning of pitching the Reds' first complete game on June 14. Jeff Shaw came in to finish, even though the Reds led 5-0 and Mercker had given up only four hits.

▶**June 25:** Barry Larkin worried all year about his sore left heel and the possibility of blowing out his Achilles tendon. It hasn't happened, but Larkin landed on the

DL when he strained his left calf muscle running out a double in Cleveland on June 16. He is expected to miss two to six weeks.

▶**July 2:** After a 2-for-29 slide dropped his average below .300 (.296) for the first time this season, Deion Sanders had a long, closed-door session with manager Ray Knight and asked for a day off on June 29. Sanders hit .252 in May and is batting .247 in June, and his on-base percentage is now an ordinary .346.

▶**July 10:** During Reggie Sanders' absence, third baseman Willie Greene moved to right field for the first time in his career and played well. He leads the team with 13 homers and 42 RBI, and during his 22 starts in right he hit .344 with six home runs and 13 RBI.

▶**July 16:** Mike Morgan and Ray Knight made peace during the All-Star break after a war of words that erupted on July 4 in Houston. Morgan had said he did not respect Knight and that others on the club felt the same way. Witnesses heard Knight berating Morgan, and Morgan later said the manager brought up the fact that Morgan had 160 major league losses.

▶**July 23:** An unconventional six-man rotation hatched by Ray Knight lasted only two days before pitching coach Don Gullett persuaded him to make a revision. With off days and possible rainouts, Knight realized the errors of his way.

▶**July 30:** Jack McKeon, 66, became the oldest man to manage the Reds when he replaced the fired Ray Knight on July 25. McKeon is in his fifth year with the Reds, mostly as a senior adviser for player personnel. He last managed with San Diego in 1990. General manager Jim Bowden had backed Knight publicly, even though several players expressed dissatisfaction with Knight's "in your face" style.

▶**Aug. 6:** Jim Bowden unloaded nearly $8 million in a trade that sent left-hander John Smiley and utility man Jeff Branson to the Cleveland Indians for four minor-league prospects. Smiley has two more years in his contract at $3.75 million per year, plus incentives. Branson is making $500,000.

▶**Aug. 13:** Outfielder Curtis Goodwin was sent to Indianapolis after storming out of the clubhouse and threatening to quit prior to a game on Aug. 7. Taking Goodwin's roster spot was Chris Stynes, 23, who had a 19-game hitting streak and a .360 average at Indianapolis. Stynes made his Cincinnati debut on Aug. 9 and slapped three consecutive singles, stole a base and scored a run.

▶**Aug. 20:** First he had hits in his first seven at-bats. Then he put together a seven-game hitting streak. It didn't matter where he played—second base, left field or third base. Chris Stynes, 24, is seizing the opportunity by the throat. Stynes was a throw-in on the July 15 trade that sent righties Hector Carrasco and Scott Service to Kansas City for outfielder Jon Nunnally.

▶**Sept. 3:** Before family and friends, and a crowd of 31,920, Pete Rose Jr. got a hit in his major league debut—a single in the fourth inning. Pete Rose, baseball's all-time hit leader with 4,256, held up his index finger to celebrate his son's hit No. 1.

▶**Sept. 10:** Deion Sanders is officially finished with baseball for 1997. The Reds gave him permission to leave the club and join the NFL Dallas Cowboys for the rest of the season. Barry Larkin underwent heel and Achilles tendon surgery on Sept. 3 and is done for the season.

▶**Sept. 24:** The "interim" was removed from Jack McKeon's title last week as he and the Reds agreed to a one-year deal to manage in 1998. The incredible run of closer Jeff Shaw continued. He had saves in 15 consecutive appearances, a club record, en route to taking over the Rolaids Fireman of the Year lead with 40 saves.

▶**Oct. 1:** Right-hander Dave Burba came off the DL (back spasms) in late August and went 5-0 with a 2.63 ERA in his five September starts.

QUOTE OF THE YEAR

"It's either him or me. If he's back, I'll be somewhere else."
—Manager Ray Knight, after an argument with pitcher Mike Morgan, three weeks before Knight was fired

CINCINNATI REDS 1997 final stats

BATTERS	BA	SLG	OBA	G	AB	R	H	TB	2B	3B	HR	RBI	BB	SO	SB	CS	E
Stynes	.348	.485	.394	49	198	31	69	96	7	1	6	28	11	13	11	2	2
Timmons	.333	.444	.333	6	9	1	3	4	1	0	0	0	0	1	0	0	1
Nunnally	.318	.602	.400	65	201	38	64	121	12	3	13	35	26	51	7	3	2
Larkin	.317	.473	.440	73	224	34	71	106	17	3	4	20	47	24	14	3	5
Kelly	.293	.543	.338	73	140	27	41	76	13	2	6	19	10	30	6	1	2
Morris	.276	.351	.328	96	333	42	92	117	20	1	1	33	23	43	3	1	7
D. Sanders	.273	.363	.329	115	465	53	127	169	13	7	5	23	34	67	56	13	4
Harris	.273	.374	.327	120	238	32	65	89	13	1	3	28	18	18	4	3	3
Taubensee	.268	.457	.323	108	254	26	68	116	18	0	10	34	22	66	0	1	5
Owens	.263	.263	.311	27	57	8	15	15	0	0	0	3	4	11	3	2	1
Oliver	.258	.415	.313	111	349	28	90	145	13	0	14	43	25	58	1	3	7
R. Sanders	.253	.510	.347	86	312	52	79	159	19	2	19	56	42	93	13	7	5
Goodwin	.253	.306	.316	85	265	27	67	81	11	0	1	12	24	53	22	13	0
Greene	.253	.459	.354	151	495	62	125	227	22	1	26	91	78	111	6	0	17
Perez	.253	.475	.321	106	297	44	75	141	18	0	16	52	29	76	5	1	2
Pendleton	.248	.354	.320	50	113	11	28	40	9	0	1	17	12	14	2	1	3
A. Boone	.245	.265	.275	16	49	5	12	13	1	0	0	5	2	5	1	0	3
Sierra	.244	.389	.292	25	90	6	22	35	5	1	2	7	6	21	0	0	0
B. Boone	.223	.332	.298	139	443	40	99	147	25	1	7	46	45	101	5	5	2
Jackson	.222	.481	.323	12	27	6	6	13	2	1	1	2	4	7	1	1	1
Reese	.219	.287	.284	128	397	48	87	114	15	0	4	26	31	82	25	7	15
Fordyce	.208	.292	.267	47	96	7	20	28	5	0	1	8	8	15	2	0	3
Watkins	.207	.276	.207	17	29	2	6	8	2	0	0	0	0	5	1	0	0
Branson	.153	.235	.210	65	98	9	15	23	3	1	1	5	7	23	1	0	4
Rose	.143	.143	.250	11	14	2	2	2	0	0	0	0	2	9	0	0	2

PITCHERS	W-L	ERA	BA	G	GS	CG	GF	Sho	SV	IP	H	R	ER	HR	BB	SO
Shaw	4-2	2.38	.227	78	0	0	62	0	42	94.2	79	26	25	7	12	74
Sullivan	5-3	3.24	.220	59	0	0	15	0	1	97.1	79	36	35	12	30	96
Tomko	11-7	3.43	.234	22	19	0	1	0	0	126.0	106	50	48	14	47	95
Carrasco	1-2	3.68	.250	38	0	0	11	0	0	51.1	51	25	21	3	25	46
Belinda	1-5	3.71	.229	84	0	0	18	0	1	99.1	84	42	41	11	33	114
Brantley	1-1	3.86	.205	13	0	0	9	0	1	11.2	9	5	5	2	7	16
Mercker	8-11	3.92	.250	28	25	0	0	0	0	144.2	135	65	63	16	62	75
Remlinger	8-8	4.14	.223	69	12	2	10	0	2	124.0	100	61	57	11	60	145
Rodriguez	0-0	4.30	.271	26	1	0	13	0	0	46.0	48	23	22	2	28	34
White	2-2	4.39	.253	12	6	0	2	0	1	41.0	39	20	20	6	8	25
Tabaka	0-0	4.50	.143	3	0	0	1	0	0	2.0	1	1	1	1	1	1
Burba	11-10	4.73	.255	30	27	2	1	0	0	160.0	157	88	84	22	73	131
Morgan	9-12	4.78	.266	31	30	1	0	0	0	162.0	165	91	86	13	49	103
Smiley	9-10	5.23	.296	20	20	0	0	0	0	117.0	139	76	68	17	31	94
Schourek	5-8	5.42	.241	18	17	0	0	0	0	84.2	78	59	51	18	38	59
Winchester	0-0	6.00	.360	5	0	0	4	0	0	6.0	9	5	4	1	2	3
Graves	0-0	6.14	.413	10	0	0	1	0	0	14.2	26	14	10	0	11	7
Lewis	0-0	6.35	.200	4	0	0	0	0	0	5.2	4	5	4	3	3	4
Eischen	0-0	6.75	.333	1	0	0	0	0	0	1.1	2	2	1	0	1	2
Carrara	0-1	7.84	.333	2	2	0	0	0	0	10.1	14	9	9	4	6	5
Martinez	1-1	9.45	.286	8	0	0	1	0	0	6.2	8	9	7	1	7	4
Crowell	0-1	9.95	.414	2	1	0	1	0	0	6.1	12	7	7	2	5	3
Jarvis	0-1	10.13	.344	9	0	0	3	0	1	13.1	21	16	15	4	7	12
Bones	0-1	10.19	.378	9	2	0	2	0	0	17.2	31	22	20	2	11	8
Service	0-0	11.81	.458	4	0	0	2	0	0	5.1	11	7	7	1	1	3

1998 preliminary roster

PITCHERS (18)
Justin Atchley
Stan Belinda
Dave Burba
Steve Cooke
Jim Crowell
Keith Glauber
Danny Graves
Mark Hutton
Curt Lyons
Eddie Priest
Mike Remlinger

Jeff Shaw
Scott Sullivan
Brett Tomko
David Weathers
Gabe White
Todd Williams
Scott Winchester

CATCHERS (4)
Brook Fordyce
Jason LaRue
Eddie Taubensee

Justin Towle

INFIELDERS (12)
Aaron Boone
Bret Boone
Willie Greene
Lenny Harris
Damian Jackson
Mark Johnson
Barry Larkin
Eric Owens
Eduardo Perez

Pokey Reese
Chris Stynes
Dmitri Young

OUTFIELDERS (6)
Darron Ingram
Melvin Nieves
Jon Nunnally
Reggie Sanders
Ozzie Timmons
Pat Watkins

Games played by position

PLAYER	G	C	1B	2B	3B	SS	OF
A. Boone	16	0	0	1	13	0	0
B. Boone	139	0	0	136	0	0	0
Branson	65	0	0	14	27	11	0
Fordyce	47	30	0	0	0	0	0
Goodwin	85	0	0	0	0	0	71
Greene	151	0	7	0	103	3	39
Harris	120	0	11	20	13	0	42
Jackson	12	0	0	3	0	6	0
Kelly	73	0	0	0	0	0	59
Larkin	73	0	0	0	0	63	0
Morris	96	0	89	0	0	0	0
Nunnally	65	0	0	0	0	0	60
Oliver	111	106	4	0	0	0	0
Owens	27	0	0	2	0	0	18
Pendleton	50	0	0	0	32	0	0
Perez	106	0	67	0	8	0	12
Reese	128	0	0	8	8	110	0
Rose	11	0	1	0	2	0	0
D. Sanders	115	0	0	0	0	0	113
R. Sanders	86	0	0	0	0	0	85
Sierra	25	0	0	0	0	0	24
Stynes	49	0	0	8	3	0	38
Taubensee	108	64	7	0	0	0	11
Timmons	6	0	0	0	0	0	1
Watkins	17	0	0	0	0	0	15

Minor Leagues

Tops in the organization

BATTER	CLUB	AVG.	G	AB	R	H	HR	RBI
Clark, Brady	Bur	.325	126	459	108	149	11	63
Williams, Jason	Cng	.317	137	527	87	167	12	69
Mottola, Chad	Ind	.317	129	458	68	145	12	77
LaRue, Jason	CWV	.315	132	473	78	149	8	81
Parsons, Jason	CWV	.311	131	460	87	143	20	102

HOME RUNS			WINS		
Ingram, Darron	Bur	29	Carlyle, Buddy	CWV	14
Murray, Glenn	Cng	26	Peterson, Jay	Bur	14
Rose, Pete	Cng	25	LeBlanc, Eric	Cng	12
Boone, Aaron	Ind	22	Carrara, G.	Ind	12
Hunter, Brian	Ind	21	Klingenbeck, S.	Ind	12

RBI			SAVES		
Parsons, Jason	CWV	102	Williams, Todd	Ind	33
Rose, Pete	Cng	99	Cushman, D.	Bur	19
Ingram, Darron	Bur	97	Gower, Tim	Cng	13
Hunter, Brian	Ind	85	Lewis, Richie	Ind	9
LaRue, Jason	CWV	81	Several Players Tied at		7

STOLEN BASES			STRIKEOUTS		
Campbell, Wylie	CWV	34	Priest, Eddie	Cng	133
Clark, Brady	Bur	31	Rose, Ted	CWV	132
Larkin, Stephen	CWV	28	Klingenbeck, S.	Ind	119
Jackson, Damian	Ind	24	Peterson, Jay	Bur	112
Owens, Eric	Ind	23	Carlyle, Buddy	CWV	111

PITCHER	CLUB	W-L	ERA	IP	H	BB	SO
Rose, Ted	CWV	11- 6	2.51	129	108	27	132
Carlyle, Buddy	CWV	14- 5	2.77	143	130	27	111
White, Gabe	Ind	7- 4	2.82	118	119	18	62
Walker, Mike	Ind	9- 6	2.98	103	80	46	80
Carrara, G.	Ind	12- 5	3.51	121	111	51	105

Sick call: 1997 DL report

PLAYER	Days on the DL
Jeff Brantley	146*
Dave Burba	20
Joey Eischen	178*
Brook Fordyce	20
Steve Gibralter	181
Barry Larkin	74*
Kent Mercker	15
Mike Morgan	16
Hal Morris	44*
Terry Pendleton	44*
Jose Rijo	181
Reggie Sanders	76*
Pete Schourek	67*
John Smiley	15

* Indicates two separate terms on Disabled List.

1997 salaries

	Bonuses	Total earned salary
Jose Rijo,p		6,150,000
Barry Larkin,ss		5,300,000
Reggie Sanders,of		3,700,000
Hal Morris,1b		3,100,000
Jeff Brantley,p		2,800,000
Pete Schourek,p		2,640,000
Dave Burba,p		2,100,000
Bret Boone,2b		1,700,000
Deion Sanders,of		1,200,000
Kent Mercker,p	600,000	1,700,000
Stan Belinda,p	500,000	950,000
Eddie Taubensee,c	25,000	900,000
Jeff Shaw,p		650,000
Lenny Harris,3b	50,000	650,000
Mike Morgan,p		500,000
Joe Oliver,c	75,000	375,000
Willie Greene,3b		300,000
Pedro Martinez,p		216,000
Jon Nunnally,of		190,000
Eduardo Perez,1b		180,000
Mike Kelly,of		175,000
Felix Rodriguez,p		175,000
Chris Stynes,2b		165,000
Daniel Graves,p		160,000
Mike Remlinger,p		155,000
Gabe White,p		150,000
Pokey Reese,ss		150,000
Brook Fordyce,c		150,000
Scott Sullivan,p		150,000
Brett Tomko,p		150,000

Average 1997 salary: $1,229,367
Total 1997 payroll: $36,881,000

Cincinnati (1890-1997)

Runs: Most, career

1741	Pete Rose, 1963-1986
1091	Johnny Bench, 1967-1983
1043	Frank Robinson, 1956-1965
993	Dave Concepcion, 1970-1988
978	Vada Pinson, 1958-1968

Hits: Most, career

3358	Pete Rose, 1963-1986
2326	Dave Concepcion, 1970-1988
2048	Johnny Bench, 1967-1983
1934	Tony Perez, 1964-1986
1881	Vada Pinson, 1958-1968

2B: Most, career

601	Pete Rose, 1963-1986
389	Dave Concepcion, 1970-1988
381	Johnny Bench, 1967-1983
342	Vada Pinson, 1958-1968
339	Tony Perez, 1964-1986

3B: Most, career

152	Edd Roush, 1916-1931
115	Pete Rose, 1963-1986
112	Bid McPhee, 1890-1899
96	Vada Pinson, 1958-1968
94	Curt Walker, 1924-1930

HR: Most, career

389	Johnny Bench, 1967-1983
324	Frank Robinson, 1956-1965
287	Tony Perez, 1964-1986
251	Ted Kluszewski, 1947-1957
244	George Foster, 1971-1981

RBI: Most, career

1376	Johnny Bench, 1967-1983
1192	Tony Perez, 1964-1986
1036	Pete Rose, 1963-1986
1009	Frank Robinson, 1956-1965
950	Dave Concepcion, 1970-1988

SB: Most, career

406	Joe Morgan, 1972-1979
337	Arlie Latham, 1890-1895
321	Dave Concepcion, 1970-1988
320	Bob Bescher, 1908-1913
316	Bid McPhee, 1890-1899

BB: Most, career

1210	Pete Rose, 1963-1986
891	Johnny Bench, 1967-1983
881	Joe Morgan, 1972-1979
736	Dave Concepcion, 1970-1988
698	Frank Robinson, 1956-1965

BA: Highest, career

.332	Cy Seymour, 1902-1906
.331	Edd Roush, 1916-1931
.325	Jake Beckley, 1897-1903
.314	Bubbles Hargrave, 1921-1928
.311	Rube Bressler, 1917-1927

On-base avg: Highest, career

.415	Joe Morgan, 1972-1979
.390	Dummy Hoy, 1894-1902
.389	Frank Robinson, 1956-1965
.379	Pete Rose, 1963-1986
.379	Rube Bressler, 1917-1927

Slug avg: Highest, career

.554	Frank Robinson, 1956-1965
.514	George Foster, 1971-1981
.512	Ted Kluszewski, 1947-1957
.510	ERIC DAVIS, 1984-1996
.498	Wally Post, 1949-1963

Games started: Most, career

356	Eppa Rixey, 1921-1933
322	Paul Derringer, 1933-1942
320	Dolf Luque, 1918-1929
298	Tom Browning, 1984-1994
296	Bucky Walters, 1938-1948

Complete games: Most, career

209	Noodles Hahn, 1899-1905
195	Bucky Walters, 1938-1948
189	Paul Derringer, 1933-1942
188	Frank Dwyer, 1892-1899
184	Bob Ewing, 1902-1909

Saves: Most, career

148	JOHN FRANCO, 1984-1989
119	Clay Carroll, 1968-1975
88	JEFF BRANTLEY, 1994-1997
88	Rob Dibble, 1988-1993
88	Tom Hume, 1977-1987

Shutouts: Most, career

32	Bucky Walters, 1938-1948
30	Jim Maloney, 1960-1970
29	Johnny Vander Meer, 1937-1949
25	Ken Raffensberger, 1947-1954
24	Paul Derringer, 1933-1942
24	Noodles Hahn, 1899-1905
24	Dolf Luque, 1918-1929

Wins: Most, career

179	Eppa Rixey, 1921-1933
161	Paul Derringer, 1933-1942
160	Bucky Walters, 1938-1948
154	Dolf Luque, 1918-1929
134	Jim Maloney, 1960-1970

K: Most, career

1592	Jim Maloney, 1960-1970
1449	Mario Soto, 1977-1988
1289	Joe Nuxhall, 1944-1966
1251	Johnny Vander Meer, 1937-1949
1201	Jose Rijo, 1988-1995

Win pct: Highest, career

.674	Don Gullett, 1970-1976
.653	Pedro Borbon, 1970-1979
.623	Jim Maloney, 1960-1970
.623	Clay Carroll, 1968-1975
.621	Gary Nolan, 1967-1977

ERA: Lowest, career

2.18	Fred Toney, 1915-1918
2.37	Bob Ewing, 1902-1909
2.52	Noodles Hahn, 1899-1905
2.62	Hod Eller, 1917-1921
2.65	Pete Schneider, 1914-1918

Runs: Most, season

134	Frank Robinson, 1962
131	Vada Pinson, 1959
130	Pete Rose, 1976
129	Arlie Latham, 1894
126	Tommy Harper, 1965

Hits: Most, season

230	Pete Rose, 1973
219	Cy Seymour, 1905
218	Pete Rose, 1969
215	Pete Rose, 1976
210	Pete Rose, 1968
210	Pete Rose, 1975

2B: Most, season

51	Frank Robinson, 1962
51	Pete Rose, 1978
47	Vada Pinson, 1959
47	Pete Rose, 1975
45	George Kelly, 1929
45	Pete Rose, 1974

3B: Most, season

26	John Reilly, 1890
22	Sam Crawford, 1902
22	Jake Daubert, 1922
22	Bid McPhee, 1890
22	Mike Mitchell, 1911

HR: Most, season

52	George Foster, 1977
49	Ted Kluszewski, 1954
47	Ted Kluszewski, 1955
45	Johnny Bench, 1970
40	Johnny Bench, 1972
40	George Foster, 1978
40	Ted Kluszewski, 1953
40	Tony Perez, 1970
40	Wally Post, 1955

RBI: Most, season

149	George Foster, 1977	
148	Johnny Bench, 1970	
141	Ted Kluszewski, 1954	
136	Frank Robinson, 1962	
130	Deron Johnson, 1965	

SB: Most, season

87	Arlie Latham, 1891
81	Bob Bescher, 1911
80	ERIC DAVIS, 1986
79	Dave Collins, 1980
76	Dusty Miller, 1896

BB: Most, season

132	Joe Morgan, 1975
120	Joe Morgan, 1974
117	Joe Morgan, 1977
115	Joe Morgan, 1972
114	Joe Morgan, 1976

BA: Highest, season

.377	Cy Seymour, 1905
.372	Bug Holliday, 1894
.351	Edd Roush, 1923
.351	Mike Donlin, 1903
.348	Edd Roush, 1924

On-base avg: Highest, season

.466	Joe Morgan, 1975
.449	Augie Galan, 1947
.444	Joe Morgan, 1976
.429	Cy Seymour, 1905
.428	Pete Rose, 1969

Slug avg: Highest, season

.642	Ted Kluszewski, 1954
.631	George Foster, 1977
.624	Frank Robinson, 1962
.611	Frank Robinson, 1961
.595	Frank Robinson, 1960

Games started: Most, season

49	Elton Chamberlain, 1892
47	Tony Mullane, 1891
45	Billy Rhines, 1890
45	Billy Rhines, 1891
42	Noodles Hahn, 1901
42	Pete Schneider, 1917
42	Fred Toney, 1917

Complete games: Most, season

45	Billy Rhines, 1890
43	Elton Chamberlain, 1892
42	Tony Mullane, 1891
41	Noodles Hahn, 1901
40	Billy Rhines, 1891

Saves: Most, season

44	JEFF BRANTLEY, 1996
42	JEFF SHAW, 1997
39	JOHN FRANCO, 1988
37	Clay Carroll, 1972
35	Wayne Granger, 1970

Shutouts: Most, season

7	Jack Billingham, 1973
7	Hod Eller, 1919
7	Fred Toney, 1917
6	Ewell Blackwell, 1947
6	Noodles Hahn, 1902
6	Jack Harper, 1904
6	DANNY JACKSON, 1988
6	Dolf Luque, 1923
6	Jim Maloney, 1963
6	Ken Raffensberger, 1952
6	Billy Rhines, 1890
6	Fred Toney, 1915
6	Johnny Vander Meer, 1941
6	Bucky Walters, 1944
6	Jake Weimer, 1906

Wins: Most, season

28	Billy Rhines, 1890
27	Pink Hawley, 1898
27	Dolf Luque, 1923
27	Bucky Walters, 1939
25	Paul Derringer, 1939
25	Eppa Rixey, 1922

K: Most, season

274	Mario Soto, 1982
265	Jim Maloney, 1963
244	Jim Maloney, 1965
242	Mario Soto, 1983
239	Noodles Hahn, 1901

Win pct: Highest, season

.826	Elmer Riddle, 1941
.821	Bob Purkey, 1962
.789	Don Gullett, 1975
.783	Tom Browning, 1988
.781	Paul Derringer, 1939

ERA: Lowest, season

1.58	Fred Toney, 1915
1.73	Bob Ewing, 1907
1.77	Noodles Hahn, 1902
1.82	Dutch Ruether, 1919
1.86	Andy Coakley, 1908

Most pinch-hit homers, season

5	Jerry Lynch, 1961
4	Bob Thurman, 1957

Most pinch-hit homers, career

13	Jerry Lynch, 1957-1963
7	Tony Perez, 1964-1986

Longest hitting streak

44	Pete Rose, 1978
30	Elmer Smith, 1898
29	HAL MORRIS, 1996
27	Vada Pinson, 1965
27	Edd Roush, 1920
27	Edd Roush, 1924

Most consecutive scoreless innings

32	Jim Maloney, 1968-69
27	Tom Seaver, 1977

No-hit games

Bumpus Jones, Cin vs Pit NL, 7-1; Oct. 15, 1892 (first game in the major leagues).

Ted Breitenstein, Cin vs Pit NL, 11-0; April 22, 1898.

Noodles Hahn, Cin vs Phi NL, 4-0; July 12, 1900.

Fred Toney, Cin at Chi NL, 1-0; May 2, 1917 (10 innings).

Hod Eller, Cin vs StL NL, 6-0; May 11, 1919.

Johnny Vander Meer, Cin vs Bos NL, 3-0; June 11, 1938.

Johnny Vander Meer, Cin at Bro NL, 6-0; June 15, 1938 (next start after June 11).

Clyde Shoun, Cin vs Bos NL, 1-0; May 15, 1944.

Ewell Blackwell, Cin vs Bos NL, 6-0; June 18, 1947.

Johnny Klippstein (seven innings), Hershell Freeman (one inning) and Joe Black (three innings), Cin at Mil NL, 1-2; May 26, 1956 (lost on 3 hits in 11 innings after allowing the first hit in the 10th).

Jim Maloney, Cin vs NY NL, 0-1; June 14, 1965 (lost on two hits in 11 innings after pitching 10 hitless innings).

Jim Maloney, Cin at Chi NL, 1-0; Aug. 19, 1965 (1st game, 10 innings).

George Culver, Cin at Phi NL, 6-1; July 29, 1968 (2nd game).

Jim Maloney, Cin vs Hou NL, 10-0; April 30, 1969.

Tom Seaver, Cin vs StL NL, 4-0; June 16, 1978.

Tom Browning, Cin vs LA NL, 1-0; Sept. 16, 1988 (perfect game).

Elton Chamberlain, seven innings, darkness, Cin vs Bos NL, 6-0; Sept. 23, 1893 (2nd game).

Jake Weimer, seven innings, agreement, Cin vs Bro NL, 1-0; Aug. 24, 1906 (2nd game).

ACTIVE PLAYERS in caps.

Players' years of service are listed by the first and last years with this team and are not necessarily consecutive; all statistics record performances for this team only.

St. Louis Cardinals

Ray Lankford led the Cardinals with 31 homers and 98 RBI despite missing almost a month with injuries.

1997 Cardinals: The offense shut down

Cardinals manager Tony La Russa, when asked what the most disappointing aspect of the 1997 season was, said, "The most disappointing thing is the record. Your record shows you how well or how poorly you competed." Why did St. Louis go 73-89?

If there was a major reason for the Cardinals' fallout besides injuries, it would be strikeouts—1,191 of them. That was a Cardinals record and just 12 off the NL mark set by the 1968 Mets. It meant that runners weren't being advanced and that potential two- or three-run innings became one-run innings. The Cardinals had 225 one-run innings compared with 171 multiple-run innings, a low figure considering that they had a team-record 143 home runs. They were 11th in runs scored, with 689.

Not for one day were the Cardinals over .500, and they reached that level only on July 2. They lost the next four to Pittsburgh, and the bottom dropped out. The Cards did not play strong fundamental ball, and La Russa said, "I blame myself most, for not having the foresight to see where the problems were coming from."

There were strengths: First baseman Mark McGwire kept fan interest alive with his prodigious home run pace, which netted him 58, tied for fourth best of all time; center fielder Ray Lankford had 31 homers and 98 RBI and was batting over .300 until the last week of the season; rookie Matt Morris won 12 games and pitched a staff-high 217 innings; second baseman Delino DeShields had career highs in almost every offensive category, including a league-leading 14 triples; and Willie McGee, nearly 39, quietly put together his second straight .300 season in 300 at-bats, far more than he expected to get.

But there were too many holes, especially the offensive one created when right fielder Brian Jordan, out much of the year with a bad back, went from 104 RBI to 10. In addition, left fielder Ron Gant dipped to .229, catcher Tom Pagnozzi

had a torn hip flexor and batted just 50 times, and left-hander Donovan Osborne won just three games because of a hernia and a groin injury.

McGwire came from Oakland too late to provide much help in '97 except the added gate as he pursued Roger Maris' record. The Cardinals were only 22-33 when he was with the team. But when he signed on to return, the team's optimism for next year grew.

The silver lining in the cloud of injuries last season was that St. Louis got to look at a slew of rookies. The most impressive was catcher Eli Marrero, who had 20 home runs at AAA Louisville and two homers and four stolen bases for the Cardinals in the last three weeks of the season. Marrero threw out six of 10 runners who tried to steal against him and gained the confidence of the pitching staff and pitching coach Dave Duncan. Right-hander Manny Aybar showed a lot in his last two starts, in which he gave up just two earned runs in 12 innings. Aybar could be a fourth or fifth starter in 1998, a middle reliever or even a setup man. His fastball and slider are above average but he doesn't have the good changeup yet to be a quality starter. Right-hander Curtis King, a hard thrower, made his mark as the club's primary setup man and could be the club's closer in the near future.

1997 Cardinals: Week-by-week notes

These notes were excerpted from the following issues of Baseball Weekly.

▶**April 9:** For the first time in 106 seasons, the Cardinals lost their first six games.

▶**April 16:** While the 2-7 Cardinals' pitching staff was holding opposing hitters to a .245 batting average, the Cardinals were hitting .201, and only .172 with men in scoring position. First baseman Dmitri Young had the highest average of any regular, at .280.

▶**April 23:** The Cards made the most of a little when they scored three runs in a doubleheader in Hawaii against the Padres—and won both games. After Mark Petkovsek had reeled off six scoreless innings of relief in the first game, a 1-0 win, right-hander Alan Benes fired a complete-game 2-1 win.

▶**April 30:** The Cardinals are in an offensive malaise, but help is on the way. Center fielder Ray Lankford made an auspicious return from rotator cuff surgery. He had two hits in each of his first three games, including a home run.

▶**May 7:** There was good and bad news for the rotation on back-to-back days in the first week of May. On May 1 rookie Matt Morris, who's just 22, retired the first 17 men he faced in a 3-2 win against Florida. It was Morris' first major league triumph. But the next day, left-hander Donovan Osborne aggravated a groin injury, putting him on the 15-day DL.

▶**May 14:** Outfielder Brian Jordan was told to rest his back for 10 to 14 days. Surgery will not be necessary to repair what team surgeon Stan London called a "minor disk problem" between the fourth and fifth lumbar vertebrae. Jordan is hitting .278 but has no homers in 79 at-bats.

▶**May 21:** After throwing 8⅔ hitless innings at Atlanta on May 16, Alan Benes had given up just three earned runs and 12 hits in his last 24⅓ innings over three games—and had an 0-2 record to show for it. Michael Tucker broke up Benes' no-hitter with a two-out double in the

Five-year glance

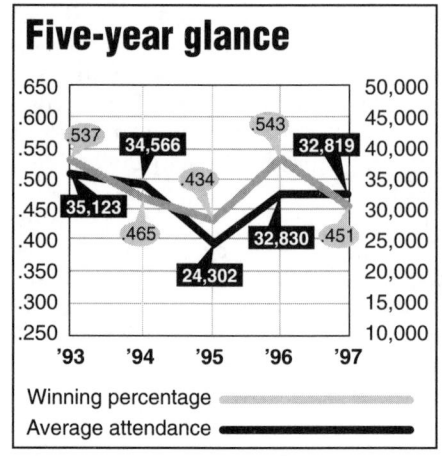

Winning percentage
Average attendance

ninth, and the Braves won the game 1-0 in 13 innings.

▶**May 28:** Left fielder Ron Gant was going through a strange slump. He had five hits in 42 at-bats, but four of them were home runs. Matt Morris pitched his first complete game, but, emblematic of the Cards' season, it was a 2-0 loss to San Francisco's Shawn Estes.

▶**June 4:** Matt Morris gained his second victory in a brilliant 2-1 win against Los Angeles on May 29. Morris (2-3, 2.64 ERA) was in AA at this time last year. Right-hander Todd Stottlemyre made baseball history on May 25 when he gained his 100th career pitching win. His father, Mel Stottlemyre, won 164 games for the Yankees, and the Stottlemyres, who already hold the record for most victories by a father-son combo, are now the first to each win 100 games.

▶**June 11:** Infielder-outfielder John Mabry extended his hitting streak to 18 games. On May 18, Mabry was hitting .240. Now he's at .307.

▶**June 18:** Right-hander Andy Benes, a former Padre, pitched for the first time at Qualcomm Stadium since he was traded away in 1995. He beat the Padres 9-1 on June 9 and has won 22 of his last 27 decisions. He is 5-2 this year and owes much of his success to the changeup he has developed.

▶**June 25:** The Cardinals dropped five of

their first six interleague games, tying four other teams for the worst interleague mark. The Cardinals have dropped to eight games under .500.

▶**July 2:** Closer Dennis Eckersley moved into second place on the all-time save list with No. 368 on June 26 in Cincinnati.

▶**July 10:** The Cardinals allowed themselves little margin for error in their interleague sweep of the Minnesota Twins, winning 2-1, 2-0 and 2-1. Matt Morris, who won the first of those games, has held teams to two earned runs or fewer in nine starts.

▶**July 16:** Ray Lankford, frustrated with his team's spinning its wheels offensively, said, "I think we need another strong hitter in the lineup.... We need somebody who can play every day and give us some runs."

▶**July 23:** The Cardinals gave left-hander Fernando Valenzuela the option of going on the DL rather than being waived. Valenzuela wouldn't have it, saying it would be dishonest. He was 0-4 with a 5.56 ERA with the Cardinals and 2-12, 4.96 overall this year. Valenzuela walked six hitters and plunked one in 2⅔ innings in his final outing, at Cincinnati on July 14.

▶**July 30:** Gary Gaetti, hitting nearly .350 with six homers since the All-Star break, wants to come back next year at age 39. But the Cardinals have made no secret they are seeking another third baseman for the future—which may be now.

▶**Aug. 6:** The acquisition of Mark McGwire from Oakland should add substance to an offense that has scored two runs or fewer on 43 occasions. Tony La Russa applauded the move but said, "We've got to get on base in front of McGwire." The Cardinals were 3-9 against first-place Houston after beating the Astros 11 out of 13 last year.

▶**Aug. 13:** Mark McGwire, after going 2-for-25 on the road, ripped a mammoth homer in his second at-bat at home and drew a number of standing ovations at Busch Stadium before and after the 441-foot blast. McGwire had gone 71 at-bats between homers, his longest stretch since 1991.

▶**Aug. 27:** John Mabry was lost for the year in a freak accident. He suffered a broken jaw when hit by a liner off the bat of Montreal's Mark Grudzielanek during batting practice on Aug. 19.

▶**Sept. 3:** Brian Jordan, still having trouble with a bulging disk in his lower back, decided to call it quits for the season on Aug. 25. Through Sept. 1, when Mark McGwire drives in a run, the Cardinals are 7-1. When he plays and doesn't drive in a run, they are 4-14.

▶**Sept. 10:** It took 112 appearances and an untimely home run by Colorado's Ellis Burks, but Dennis Eckersley finally gained his first victory as a Cardinals reliever, on Sept. 6. Eckersley, 0-10 in two years with St. Louis, would have preferred his 34th save, but Burks homered to tie the game in the 12th before the Cardinals won in the 13th.

▶**Sept. 17:** Mark McGwire joined extremely select company on Sept. 10 when he hit his 50th homer (his 16th as a Cardinal). The homer made him just the second man in history—Babe Ruth is the other—to have back-to-back 50-homer seasons. After going homerless in his first 26 at-bats as a Cardinal, McGwire hit 16 in his next 81.

▶**Sept. 24:** Ray Lankford hit his 30th home run on Sept. 16, the most ever by a St. Louis center fielder. The Cardinals will have rookie pitchers start their last 19 games because of injuries to the team's veterans.

▶**Oct. 1:** Second baseman Delino DeShields will most likely have his $3 million option picked up after enjoying his best season. He hit .295 with 14 triples, 11 homers, 58 RBI and 55 steals. Mark McGwire, who has signed for three more years, hit his 58th home run on the last day of the season, tying him with Jimmie Foxx and Hank Greenberg for the most ever by a right-handed batter.

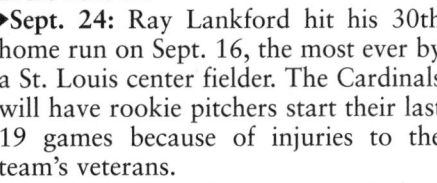

QUOTE OF THE YEAR

"They're playing a team with a losing record, too."
—Manager Tony La Russa, upon being told the Cards were to play 26 straight games against teams then under .500

ST. LOUIS CARDINALS 1997 final stats

BATTERS	BA	SLG	OBA	G	AB	R	H	TB	2B	3B	HR	RBI	BB	SO	SB	CS	E
Franklin	.324	.500	.378	17	34	6	11	17	0	0	2	2	3	10	0	0	0
McGee	.300	.420	.347	122	300	29	90	126	19	4	3	38	22	59	8	2	2
DeShields	.295	.448	.357	150	572	92	169	256	26	14	11	58	55	72	55	14	19
Lankford	.295	.585	.411	133	465	94	137	272	36	3	31	98	95	125	21	11	9
Mabry	.284	.371	.352	116	388	40	110	144	19	0	5	36	39	77	0	1	1
Ordaz	.273	.318	.304	12	22	3	6	7	1	0	0	1	1	2	3	0	1
Clayton	.266	.398	.306	154	576	75	153	229	39	5	9	61	33	109	30	10	19
Young	.258	.363	.335	110	333	38	86	121	14	3	5	34	38	63	6	5	13
McGwire	.253	.684	.411	51	174	38	44	119	3	0	24	42	43	61	2	0	1
Gaetti	.251	.404	.305	148	502	63	126	203	24	1	17	69	36	88	7	3	7
Sheaffer	.250	.288	.296	76	132	10	33	38	5	0	0	11	8	17	1	0	2
Plantier	.248	.438	.331	52	121	13	30	53	8	0	5	18	13	30	0	3	1
Lampkin	.245	.380	.335	108	229	28	56	87	8	1	7	22	28	30	2	1	5
Marrero	.244	.422	.271	17	45	4	11	19	2	0	2	7	2	13	4	0	3
Difelice	.238	.331	.297	93	260	16	62	86	10	1	4	30	19	61	1	1	6
Jordan	.234	.269	.311	47	145	17	34	39	5	0	0	10	10	21	6	1	0
Gant	.229	.388	.310	139	502	68	115	195	21	4	17	62	58	162	14	6	6
Pagnozzi	.220	.340	.235	25	50	4	11	17	3	0	1	8	1	7	0	0	0
Bell	.211	.310	.261	66	142	9	30	44	7	2	1	12	10	28	1	0	8
Livingstone	.164	.194	.194	65	67	4	11	13	2	0	0	6	3	11	1	0	2
Gallego	.163	.209	.178	27	43	6	7	9	2	0	0	1	1	6	0	0	1
Scarsone	.100	.100	.250	5	10	0	1	1	0	0	0	0	2	5	1	0	0
Green	.097	.097	.152	20	31	5	3	3	0	0	0	1	2	5	0	0	1
R. Mejia	.071	.143	.067	7	14	0	1	2	1	0	0	2	0	5	0	0	1
Berblinger	.000	.000	.000	7	5	1	0	0	0	0	0	0	0	1	0	0	0
Gulan	.000	.000	.100	5	9	2	0	0	0	0	0	1	1	5	0	0	0

PITCHERS	W-L	ERA	BA	G	GS	CG	GF	Sho	SV	IP	H	R	ER	HR	BB	SO
Gaetti	0-0	0.00	.500	1	0	0	1	0	0	0.1	1	0	0	0	0	0
McGraw	0-0	0.00	.333	2	0	0	2	0	0	1.2	2	0	0	0	1	0
Mathews	4-4	2.15	.238	40	0	0	12	0	0	46.0	41	14	11	4	18	46
Frascatore	5-2	2.48	.247	59	0	0	17	0	0	80.0	74	25	22	5	33	58
King	4-2	2.76	.325	30	0	0	8	0	0	29.1	38	14	9	0	11	13
Al. Benes	9-9	2.89	.219	23	23	2	0	0	0	161.2	128	60	52	13	68	160
An. Benes	10-7	3.10	.230	26	26	0	0	0	0	177.0	149	64	61	9	61	175
Morris	12-9	3.19	.258	33	33	3	0	0	0	217.0	208	88	77	12	69	149
Beltran	1-2	3.48	.237	35	4	0	16	0	1	54.1	47	25	21	3	17	50
Fossas	2-7	3.83	.298	71	0	0	14	0	0	51.2	62	32	22	7	26	41
Stottlemyre	12-9	3.88	.231	28	28	0	0	0	0	181.0	155	86	78	16	65	160
Eckersley	1-5	3.91	.238	57	0	0	47	0	36	53.0	49	24	23	9	8	45
Aybar	2-4	4.24	.263	12	12	0	0	0	0	68.0	66	33	32	8	29	41
Painter	1-1	4.76	.213	14	0	0	4	0	0	17.0	13	9	9	1	8	11
Osborne	3-7	4.93	.274	14	14	0	0	0	0	80.1	84	46	44	10	23	51
Valenzuela	2-12	4.96	.295	18	18	1	0	0	0	89.0	106	61	49	12	46	61
Petkovsek	4-7	5.06	.292	55	2	0	19	0	2	96.0	109	61	54	14	31	51
Bautista	0-0	6.57	.300	11	0	0	3	0	0	12.1	15	10	9	2	2	4
Raggio	1-2	6.89	.336	15	4	0	5	0	0	31.1	44	24	24	1	16	21
Busby	0-2	8.79	.393	3	3	0	0	0	0	14.1	24	14	14	2	4	6
Lowe	0-2	9.35	.365	6	4	0	1	0	0	17.1	27	21	18	2	10	8
Ludwick	0-1	9.45	.400	5	0	0	3	0	0	6.2	12	7	7	1	6	7
Honeycutt	0-0	13.50	.500	2	0	0	2	0	0	2.0	5	3	3	0	1	2

1998 preliminary roster

PITCHERS (18)
Armando Almanza
Manny Aybar
Rigo Beltran
Alan Benes
Jeff Brantley
Mike Busby
Rick Croushore
John Frascatore
Rick Heiserman
Curtis King
Sean Lowe
Kent Merker
Matt Morris
Donovan Osborne
Lance Painter
Mark Petkovsek
Brady Raggio
Todd Stottlemyre

CATCHERS (4)
Tom Lampkin

Eli Marrero
Tom Pagnozzi
Danny Sheaffer

INFIELDERS (10)
David Bell
Royce Clayton
Delino DeShields
Gary Gaetti
David Howard
John Mabry

Mark McGwire
Luis Ordaz
Placido Polanco
Chris Richard

OUTFIELDERS (6)
Ron Gant
Scarborough Green
Brian Jordan
Ray Lankford
Willie McGee
Juan Munoz

Games played by position

PLAYER	G	C	1B	2B	3B	SS	OF
Bell	66	0	0	23	35	13	0
Berblinger	7	0	0	4	0	0	0
Clayton	154	0	0	0	0	153	0
DeShields	150	0	0	147	0	0	0
Difelice	93	91	1	0	0	0	0
Franklin	17	0	0	0	0	0	13
Gaetti	148	0	20	0	132	0	0
Gallego	27	0	0	11	7	10	0
Gant	139	0	0	0	0	0	128
Green	20	0	0	0	0	0	19
Gulan	5	0	0	0	3	0	0
Jordan	47	0	0	0	0	0	44
Lampkin	108	86	0	0	0	0	0
Lankford	133	0	0	0	0	0	131
Livingstone	65	0	2	1	5	0	1
Mabry	116	0	49	0	1	0	78
Marrero	17	17	0	0	0	0	0
McGee	122	0	0	0	0	0	81
McGwire	51	0	50	0	0	0	0
Mejia	7	0	0	3	0	0	1
Ordaz	12	0	0	0	0	11	0
Pagnozzi	25	13	2	0	1	0	0
Plantier	52	0	0	0	0	0	35
Scarsone	5	0	0	2	1	0	2
Sheaffer	76	9	0	3	30	0	22
Young	110	0	74	0	0	0	17

Minor Leagues

Tops in the organization

BATTER	CLUB	AVG.	G	AB	R	H	HR	RBI
Clapp, Stubby	PrW	.318	78	267	51	85	4	46
Robinson, Kerry	Lou	.318	137	532	80	169	2	62
Butler, Brent	Peo	.306	129	480	81	147	15	71
Kleiner, Stacy	Ark	.304	107	365	44	111	5	42
Costo, Tim	Lou	.303	121	400	52	121	14	54

HOME RUNS			WINS		
Freitas, Joe	Peo	33	Politte, Cliff	Ark	15
Dishington, N.	PrW	28	Weibl, Clint	PrW	12
Leon, Jose	Peo	20	DeLeon, Jose	Peo	11
Marrero, Eli	Lou	20	Logan, Marcus	Ark	11
Haas, Chris	PrW	19	Several Players Tied at		9

RBI			SAVES		
Dishington, Nate	PrW	106	Almanza, A.	PrW	36
Freitas, Joe	Peo	86	Crafton, Kevin	Peo	29
Munoz, Juan	Ark	79	King, Curt	Lou	19
Haas, Chris	PrW	76	Franks, Lance	PrW	12
Butler, Brent	Peo	71	Several Players Tied at		9

STOLEN BASES			STRIKEOUTS		
Robinson, Kerry	Lou	40	Politte, Cliff	Ark	144
Hogan, Todd	Peo	28	Avrard, Corey	PrW	144
Woolf, Jason	PrW	26	Weibl, Clint	PrW	135
Bradshaw, Terry	Lou	26	Nussbeck, Mark	Peo	132
Farley, Cordell	PrW	25	Dewitt, Matt	Peo	121

PITCHER	CLUB	W-L	ERA	IP	H	BB	SO
Politte, Cliff	Ark	15- 2	2.22	158	124	40	144
Jimenez, Jose	PrW	9- 7	3.09	146	128	42	81
Aybar, Manny	Lou	5- 8	3.48	137	131	45	114
Croushore, Rick	Lou	8- 7	3.64	136	148	50	108
Reames, Jay	Peo	6- 9	3.98	133	132	86	83

Sick call: 1997 DL report

PLAYER	Days on the DL
Brian Barber	63
David Bell	62
Andy Benes	27
Alan Benes	60
Rick Honeycutt	147*
Danny Jackson	49
Brian Jordan	117**
Ray Lankford	21
Scott Livingstone	21
John Mabry	35
Willie McGee	17
Roberto Mejia	170
Donovan Osborne	87
Tom Pagnozzi	128*
Lance Painter	145*
Phil Plantier	21
Dmitri Young	18

* Indicates two separate terms on Disabled List.
** Indicates three separate terms on Disabled List.

1997 salaries

	Bonuses	Total earned salary
Mark McGwire,1b	50,000	7,150,000
Andy Benes,p		4,850,000
Ron Gant,of		4,500,000
Ray Lankford,of	50,000	4,466,667
Todd Stottlemyre,p		4,100,000
Brian Jordan,of		3,300,000
Donovan Osborne,p		2,750,000
Royce Clayton,ss	50,000	2,650,000
Gary Gaetti,3b		2,100,000
Tom Pagnozzi,c		1,900,000
Dennis Eckersley,p		1,750,000
Delino DeShields,2b		1,600,000
Willie McGee,of	300,000	1,300,000
Tony Fossas,p		750,000
Scott Livingstone,3b		600,000
Rick Honeycutt,p		500,000
Tom Lampkin,c	100,000	500,000
Danny Sheaffer,c		425,000
John Mabry,of		390,000
Lance Painter,p		375,000
Phil Plantier,of		340,000
Mark Petkovsek,p		325,000
Alan Benes,p		240,000
Roberto Mejia,2b		185,000
David Bell,3b		170,000
John Frascatore,p		155,000
Mike Difelice,c		152,500
Rigo Beltran,p		150,000
Jose Bautista,p		150,000
Scarborough Green,of		150,000
Curtis King,p		150,000
Matt Morris,p		150,000

Average 1997 salary: $1,508,568
Total 1997 payroll: $48,274,167

St. Louis (1892-1997)

Runs: Most, career

1949	Stan Musial, 1941-1963	
1427	Lou Brock, 1964-1979	
1089	Rogers Hornsby, 1915-1933	
1071	Enos Slaughter, 1938-1953	
1025	Red Schoendienst, 1945-1963	

Hits: Most, career

3630	Stan Musial, 1941-1963
2713	Lou Brock, 1964-1979
2110	Rogers Hornsby, 1915-1933
2064	Enos Slaughter, 1938-1953
1980	Red Schoendienst, 1945-1963

2B: Most, career

725	Stan Musial, 1941-1963
434	Lou Brock, 1964-1979
377	Joe Medwick, 1932-1948
367	Rogers Hornsby, 1915-1933
366	Enos Slaughter, 1938-1953

3B: Most, career

177	Stan Musial, 1941-1963
143	Rogers Hornsby, 1915-1933
135	Enos Slaughter, 1938-1953
121	Lou Brock, 1964-1979
119	Jim Bottomley, 1922-1932

HR: Most, career

475	Stan Musial, 1941-1963
255	Ken Boyer, 1955-1965
193	Rogers Hornsby, 1915-1933
181	Jim Bottomley, 1922-1932
172	Ted Simmons, 1968-1980

RBI: Most, career

1951	Stan Musial, 1941-1963
1148	Enos Slaughter, 1938-1953
1105	Jim Bottomley, 1922-1932
1072	Rogers Hornsby, 1915-1933
1001	Ken Boyer, 1955-1965

SB: Most, career

888	Lou Brock, 1964-1979
549	VINCE COLEMAN, 1985-1990
433	Ozzie Smith, 1982-1996
287	WILLIE McGEE, 1982-1997
203	Jack Smith, 1915-1926

BB: Most, career

1599	Stan Musial, 1941-1963
876	Ozzie Smith, 1982-1996
838	Enos Slaughter, 1938-1953
681	Lou Brock, 1964-1979
660	Rogers Hornsby, 1915-1933

BA: Highest, career

.359	Rogers Hornsby, 1915-1933
.336	Johnny Mize, 1936-1941
.335	Joe Medwick, 1932-1948
.331	Stan Musial, 1941-1963
.326	Chick Hafey, 1924-1931

On-base avg: Highest, career

.427	Rogers Hornsby, 1915-1933
.419	Johnny Mize, 1936-1941
.417	Stan Musial, 1941-1963
.413	Joe Cunningham, 1954-1961
.402	Miller Huggins, 1910-1916

Slug avg: Highest, career

.600	Johnny Mize, 1936-1941
.568	Rogers Hornsby, 1915-1933
.568	Chick Hafey, 1924-1931
.559	Stan Musial, 1941-1963
.545	Joe Medwick, 1932-1948

Games started: Most, career

482	Bob Gibson, 1959-1975
401	Bob Forsch, 1974-1988
388	Jesse Haines, 1920-1937
320	Bill Doak, 1913-1929
243	Bill Sherdel, 1918-1932

Complete games: Most, career

255	Bob Gibson, 1959-1975
208	Jesse Haines, 1920-1937
196	Ted Breitenstein, 1892-1901
144	Bill Doak, 1913-1929
144	Bill Sherdel, 1918-1932

Saves: Most, career

160	LEE SMITH, 1990-1993
129	TODD WORRELL, 1985-1992
127	Bruce Sutter, 1981-1984
66	DENNIS ECKERSLEY, 1996-1997
64	Lindy McDaniel, 1955-1962

Shutouts: Most, career

56	Bob Gibson, 1959-1975
30	Bill Doak, 1913-1929
28	Mort Cooper, 1938-1945
25	Harry Brecheen, 1940-1952
24	Jesse Haines, 1920-1937

Wins: Most, career

251	Bob Gibson, 1959-1975
210	Jesse Haines, 1920-1937
163	Bob Forsch, 1974-1988
153	Bill Sherdel, 1918-1932
144	Bill Doak, 1913-1929

K: Most, career

3117	Bob Gibson, 1959-1975
1095	Dizzy Dean, 1930-1937
1079	Bob Forsch, 1974-1988
979	Jesse Haines, 1920-1937
951	Steve Carlton, 1965-1971

Win pct: Highest, career

.718	Ted Wilks, 1944-1951
.705	John Tudor, 1985-1990
.677	Mort Cooper, 1938-1945
.667	Al Hrabosky, 1970-1977
.641	Dizzy Dean, 1930-1937

ERA: Lowest, career

2.52	John Tudor, 1985-1990
2.67	Slim Sallee, 1908-1916
2.67	Jack Taylor, 1904-1906
2.74	Johnny Lush, 1907-1910
2.74	Red Ames, 1915-1919

Runs: Most, season

142	Jesse Burkett, 1901
141	Rogers Hornsby, 1922
135	Stan Musial, 1948
133	Rogers Hornsby, 1925
132	Joe Medwick, 1935

Hits: Most, season

250	Rogers Hornsby, 1922
237	Joe Medwick, 1937
235	Rogers Hornsby, 1921
230	Stan Musial, 1948
230	Joe Torre, 1971

2B: Most, season

64	Joe Medwick, 1936
56	Joe Medwick, 1937
53	Stan Musial, 1953
52	Enos Slaughter, 1939
51	Stan Musial, 1944

3B: Most, season

29	Perry Werden, 1893
25	Roger Connor, 1894
25	Tom Long, 1915
20	Jim Bottomley, 1928
20	Duff Cooley, 1895
20	Rogers Hornsby, 1920
20	Stan Musial, 1943
20	Stan Musial, 1946

HR: Most, season

43	Johnny Mize, 1940	
42	Rogers Hornsby, 1922	
39	Rogers Hornsby, 1925	
39	Stan Musial, 1948	
36	Stan Musial, 1949	

RBI: Most, season

154	Joe Medwick, 1937
152	Rogers Hornsby, 1922
143	Rogers Hornsby, 1925
138	Joe Medwick, 1936
137	Jim Bottomley, 1929
137	Johnny Mize, 1940
137	Joe Torre, 1971

SB: Most, season

118	Lou Brock, 1974
110	VINCE COLEMAN, 1985
109	VINCE COLEMAN, 1987
107	VINCE COLEMAN, 1986
81	VINCE COLEMAN, 1988

BB: Most, season

136	Jack Clark, 1987
136	Jack Crooks, 1892
121	Jack Crooks, 1893
116	Miller Huggins, 1910
107	Stan Musial, 1949

BA: Highest, season

.424	Rogers Hornsby, 1924
.403	Rogers Hornsby, 1925
.401	Rogers Hornsby, 1922
.397	Rogers Hornsby, 1921
.396	Jesse Burkett, 1899

On-base avg: Highest, season

.507	Rogers Hornsby, 1924
.489	Rogers Hornsby, 1925
.463	Jesse Burkett, 1899
.459	Jack Clark, 1987
.459	Rogers Hornsby, 1922

Slug avg: Highest, season

.756	Rogers Hornsby, 1925
.722	Rogers Hornsby, 1922
.702	Stan Musial, 1948
.696	Rogers Hornsby, 1924
.652	Chick Hafey, 1930

Games started: Most, season

50	Ted Breitenstein, 1894
50	Ted Breitenstein, 1895
47	Jack Taylor, 1898
45	Kid Gleason, 1892
45	Kid Gleason, 1893

Complete games: Most, season

46	Ted Breitenstein, 1894
46	Ted Breitenstein, 1895
43	Kid Gleason, 1892
42	Jack Taylor, 1898
40	Jack Powell, 1899
40	Cy Young, 1899

Saves: Most, season

47	LEE SMITH, 1991
45	Bruce Sutter, 1984
43	LEE SMITH, 1992
43	LEE SMITH, 1993
36	DENNIS ECKERSLEY, 1997
36	Tom Henke, 1995
36	Bruce Sutter, 1982
36	TODD WORRELL, 1986

Shutouts: Most, season

13	Bob Gibson, 1968
10	Mort Cooper, 1942
10	John Tudor, 1985
7	Harry Brecheen, 1948
7	Mort Cooper, 1944
7	Dizzy Dean, 1934
7	Bill Doak, 1914

Wins: Most, season

30	Dizzy Dean, 1934
28	Dizzy Dean, 1935
27	Ted Breitenstein, 1894
26	Cy Young, 1899
24	Dizzy Dean, 1936
24	Jesse Haines, 1927

K: Most, season

274	Bob Gibson, 1970
270	Bob Gibson, 1965
269	Bob Gibson, 1969
268	Bob Gibson, 1968
245	Bob Gibson, 1964

Win pct: Highest, season

.811	Dizzy Dean, 1934
.810	Ted Wilks, 1944
.789	Harry Brecheen, 1945
.778	Johnny Beazley, 1942
.767	Bob Gibson, 1970

ERA: Lowest, season

1.12	Bob Gibson, 1968
1.72	Bill Doak, 1914
1.78	Mort Cooper, 1942
1.90	Max Lanier, 1943
1.93	John Tudor, 1985

Most pinch-hit homers, season

4	George Crowe, 1959
4	George Crowe, 1960
4	Carl Sawatski, 1961

Most pinch-hit homers, career

8	George Crowe, 1959-1961
6	Gerald Perry, 1991-1995
6	Carl Sawatski, 1960-1963

Longest hitting streak

33	Rogers Hornsby, 1922
30	Stan Musial, 1950
29	Ken Boyer, 1959
29	Harry Walker, 1943
28	Joe Medwick, 1935
28	Red Schoendienst, 1954

Most consecutive scoreless innings

47	Bob Gibson, 1968
37	George Bradley, 1876

No-hit games

George Bradley, StL vs Har NL, 2-0; July 15, 1876.

Jesse Haines, StL vs Bos NL, 5-0; July 17, 1924.

Paul Dean, StL at Bro NL, 3-0; Sept. 21, 1934 (2nd game).

Lon Warneke, StL at Cin NL, 2-0; Aug. 30, 1941.

Ray Washburn, StL at SF NL, 2-0; Sept. 18, 1968.

Bob Gibson, StL at Pit NL, 11-0; Aug. 14, 1971.

Bob Forsch, StL vs Phi NL, 5-0; April 16, 1978.

Bob Forsch, StL vs Mon NL, 3-0; Sept. 26, 1983.

Stoney McGlynn, seven innings, agreement, StL at Bro NL, 1-1; Sept. 24, 1906 (2nd game).

Ed Karger, seven perfect innings, agreement, StL vs Bos NL, 4-0; Aug. 11, 1907 (2nd game).

Johnny Lush, six innings, rain, StL at Bro NL, 2-0; Aug. 6, 1908.

ACTIVE PLAYERS in caps.

Players' years of service are listed by the first and last years with this team and are not necessarily consecutive; all statistics record performances for this team only.

Chicago Cubs

First baseman Mark Grace's .409 on-base average led the Cubs and was in the NL's top 10.

1997 Cubs: Doomed in April, dismal all year

For the Cubs, it was a season that went downhill starting on Opening Day. Not only did they lose an NL-record 14 straight games to start the season, but they also lost a major-league-high 55 games on the road and tied Philadelphia for the league's worst record. The good news is that the Cubs could have the nation's first draft pick next June. A coin flip with the Phillies will decide the issue, making one of those losers a winner.

Almost every phase of the game created problems for the Cubs. They were last in fielding for the first half of the season, and their offense was so anemic that they had an 0-75 record when trailing after eight innings. Power? Right fielder Sammy Sosa acounted for more than 28% of the team's 127 homers. And pitching? The staff set a franchise record by allowing 185 home runs. The starters had only six complete games, which is a franchise low for a nonstrike season. Manager Jim Riggleman and Sosa had a dugout argument when Sosa tried to steal a base despite being flashed a hold sign. Riggleman is fully aware of the consequences if things don't improve in his fourth season for a team with a $40 million payroll.

A few things went right. Although neither was around until after the All-Star break, Kevin Tapani and Mark Clark produced veteran leadership for the starting staff. Tapani finished with a 9-3 record and 3.39 ERA, proving that his surgically repaired right hand was healthy enough to enable the pitcher to win. Clark finished 6-1 with a 2.86 ERA after his trade from the Mets, 14-8 overall. Mark Grace continued his run of excellent performances at first base and ended with his typical .319 batting average. Overlooked most of the season, rookie Kevin Orie battled injuries to hit .275 with eight homers and 44 RBI. Also, former No. 1 draft choice Doug Glanville hit .300 in his first full season, taking over left field after a handful of minor league candidates,

most notably Brooks Kieschnick and Brant Brown, fizzled.

The Cubs have all their major players either signed or committed for 1998, which may not be good considering the season they just had. Along the way, the Cubs traded potential free-agent shortstop Shawon Dunston and avoided another problem when second baseman Ryne Sandberg announced his retirement. That leaves holes to fill in the middle infield, with Manny Alexander the front-runner for one of the two spots. Starter Kerry Wood, the No. 1 draft choice two years ago, struck out more than one batter per inning at AAA Iowa in 1997 and is ready to come to the major leagues.

General manager Ed Lynch badly wants a better performance than he got from the disappointing bullpen, after failing the last two seasons with closers Doug Jones and Mel Rojas. Young Terry Adams filled the role after Rojas was traded, but finished with a 2-9 record, a 4.62 ERA and four blown saves in 22 chances.

Sadly for the Cubs, most of the other top talent in their farm system won't be ready for next season.

1997 Cubs: Week-by-week notes

These notes were excerpted from the following issues of Baseball Weekly.

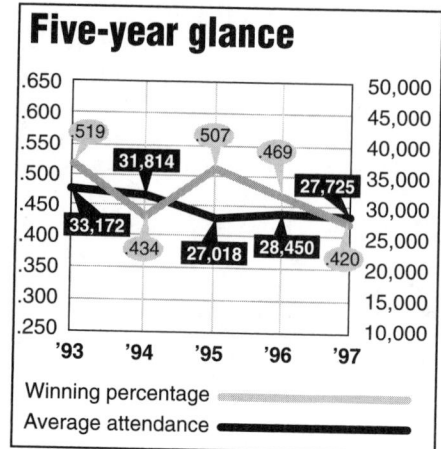

Five-year glance

Winning percentage
Average attendance

▶**April 9:** As they were swept in the opening series by the Marlins, the Cubs also lost leading hitter Mark Grace to the DL with a badly strained right hamstring. At the time, Grace had one-third of the team's hits, half of its RBI and its only homer. Plagued by light hitting, so-so pitching and porous fielding, the Cubs lost their first six games.

▶**April 16:** After having the worst start in club history with their eighth consecutive loss, the players held a team meeting. It didn't help, as their 0-10 start tied the modern-day NL record set by the 1988 Atlanta Braves. Left-hander Terry Mulholland had a 1.93 ERA after his first three starts, but no victories. His teammates have hit .118 and scored three runs in his starts.

▶**April 23:** Despite the embarrassing 1-14 start, manager Jim Riggleman's job was not in jeopardy, according to general manager Ed Lynch. The Cubs went 0-14 on April 20 by losing the first game of a doubleheader to the New York Mets 8-2. But the club then ended the second-worst streak to start a season—behind Baltimore's 0-21 opening in 1988—and the most consecutive losses in Cubs history by beating the Mets 4-3.

▶**April 30:** When the Cubs won back-to-back games in New York for their first victories, it was the first time they had taken two in a row since Sept. 8-10 of last season.

▶**May 7:** The problem-plagued Cubs now have to worry about $4.5 million closer Mel Rojas. He blew a save and walked four batters in one inning against the Dodgers on May 2 and was also unable to close out a victory the next night. Young setup man Terry Adams had to do that, which made him unscored upon in 16⅓ innings.

▶**May 14:** The Cubs' record was 10-9 following their 0-14 start. The slow turnaround was helped by their leadoff man, center fielder Brian McRae, who had

been the worst of the worst, with a .119 average as late as April 21. He put together an 11-game hitting streak that ended on May 10.

▶**May 28:** Jim Riggleman is demoting veterans Mel Rojas and Ryne Sandberg. Rojas, with a 5.32 ERA, and Sandberg, hitting .198, earned their demotions. Terry Adams takes over as closer, and Rey Sanchez is at second, at least when he isn't at shortstop for Shawon Dunston. Sammy Sosa continued on a tear, hitting his ninth homer in 18 games on May 24.

▶**June 4:** The Cubs rose in the weak NL Central even though they had not won three games in a row all season. Much of the offensive turnaround has come from Shawon Dunston. After 13 games, Dunston was hitting .106. He then went on a .360 tear for the next 36.

▶**June 11:** Rookie Jeremi Gonzalez won his first two major league starts, then lost in Montreal despite allowing just two runs in six innings. "He's probably got as good stuff as anyone on the staff," pitching coach Phil Regan said.

▶**June 25:** Frank Castillo's demotion from the rotation never happened. He kept his spot—and apparently will keep it—despite allowing seven hits and five runs in only 1⅓ innings on June 21 in Houston. The starters' situation was complicated when starter Steve Trachsel allowed six runs in 2⅓ innings on June 20.

July 2: To get his team out of its offensive doldrums, Jim Riggleman juggled his lineup. The most significant move was batting Sammy Sosa third and Mark Grace fourth. It paid dividends on June 28, as Sosa started paying back for a new $42 million contract and Grace gave himself a 33rd-birthday present. In a 5-2 win over Houston, both of them homered.

July 10: The Cubs put together a season-high five consecutive wins before letting the lowly Phillies beat them with a 9-7 come-from-behind victory on July 6. Ryne Sandberg went nearly two months without a home run, then hit two of them on back-to-back days in Philadelphia.

July 23: The team's doubleheader sweep of Colorado on July 19 was their first since June 8, 1992, at Busch Stadium. It also was only their third sweep in 36 double headers since 1985. During that time, they split 20 and were swept in 13.

July 30: The Cubs are the second-worst team in the NL for good reason. They are last in on-base percentage, next to last in walks and are being outhomered by nearly 50. The team recently went 310 batters without a home run.

Aug. 6: If Ryne Sandberg continues to play as well as he did on Aug. 2, the day he announced his retirement, he might have to stick around. He hit two home runs to help the Cubs beat the Dodgers and break a nine-game losing streak.

Aug. 13: The six-player trade with the Mets was considered only the first step in a massive rebuilding before next season starts. Not only did Ed Lynch free up money to acquire new players by dumping Brian McRae and Mel Rojas, but he also gained a starting shortstop for next season (Manny Alexander) and a center fielder (Lance Johnson) who could be used in another trade. The Cubs also acquired Mark Clark to gain much-needed veteran starting help. They traded Turk Wendell, who was buried in middle relief.

Aug. 20: The arrival of Manny Alexander meant the departure of Rey Sanchez, who went to the Yankees for minor league pitcher Frisco Parotte, 21.

Sept. 3: After returning from surgery on his right hand, Kevin Tapani's first four victories came against the Indians, the Braves, the Marlins and the Dodgers, all of whom could make the playoffs. The Cubs traded Shawon Dunston, who will be a free agent at the end of the year, to Pittsburgh for a player to be named later.

Sept. 10: When Ryne Sandberg homered on Sept. 6, it only continued his hot hitting since announcing his retirement on Aug. 2. That gave him six homers, six doubles, 18 RBI and a .359 average since then.

Sept. 17: The starting staff is taking shape for next season, thanks to pitchers Mark Clark and Kevin Tapani. Clark became the first Cub to throw back-to-back complete games since Greg Maddux in October 1991, and Tapani won four games in a row as the season dwindled down to its final two weeks. The rotation next season probably will contain Clark, Tapani, Steve Trachsel, Jeremi Gonzalez and most likely Kerry Wood, who was not called up from AAA Iowa this season because he would have to have been protected in the expansion draft.

Sept. 24: Cubs fans packed Wrigley Field on Sept. 20 to say goodbye to second baseman Ryne Sandberg, who is retiring after the season. Sandberg retires as the all-time home run hitter and fielding leader among second basemen, a 10-time All-Star, a nine-time Gold Glove winner and the 1984 MVP. Fittingly, the Cubs lost the game to Sandberg's original team, the Phillies, 3-2, by giving up three ninth-inning runs.

Oct. 1: With the Cubs fashioning one of the worst records in baseball, Ed Lynch knows the fourth season of his regime will have to get better, or else. With Terry Adams developing as a closer, the highest priority is obtaining some power to go with Sammy Sosa.

QUOTE OF THE YEAR

"I don't think you can characterize our first half as anything other than, you know, awful."

—General manager Ed Lynch, on the team's 37-50 record at the All-Star break

CHICAGO CUBS 1997 final stats

BATTERS	BA	SLG	OBA	G	AB	R	H	TB	2B	3B	HR	RBI	BB	SO	SB	CS	E
Grace	.319	.465	.409	151	555	87	177	258	32	5	13	78	88	45	2	4	6
Hansen	.311	.450	.429	90	151	19	47	68	8	2	3	21	31	32	1	2	7
Johnson	.307	.422	.370	111	410	60	126	173	16	8	5	39	42	31	20	12	7
D. Clark	.301	.462	.386	102	143	19	43	66	8	0	5	32	19	34	1	0	2
Glanville	.300	.392	.333	146	474	79	142	186	22	5	4	35	24	46	19	11	3
Lowery	.286	.286	.412	9	14	2	4	4	0	0	0	0	3	3	1	0	0
Orie	.275	.431	.350	114	364	40	100	157	23	5	8	44	39	57	2	2	9
Hernandez	.273	.486	.323	121	183	33	50	89	8	5	7	26	14	42	2	5	8
Alexander	.266	.383	.320	87	248	37	66	95	12	4	3	22	17	54	13	1	11
Sandberg	.264	.403	.308	135	447	54	118	180	26	0	12	64	28	94	7	4	8
Houston	.260	.342	.290	72	196	15	51	67	10	0	2	28	9	35	1	0	5
Servais	.260	.361	.311	122	385	34	100	139	21	0	6	45	24	56	0	1	8
Sosa	.251	.480	.300	162	642	90	161	308	31	4	36	119	45	174	22	12	8
Sanchez	.249	.307	.287	97	205	14	51	63	9	0	1	12	11	26	4	2	6
Cairo	.241	.276	.313	16	29	7	7	8	1	0	0	1	2	3	0	0	0
Brown	.234	.409	.286	46	137	15	32	56	7	1	5	15	7	28	2	1	2
Hubbard	.203	.250	.227	29	64	4	13	16	0	0	1	2	2	21	0	0	1
Kieschnick	.200	.356	.294	39	90	9	18	32	2	0	4	12	12	21	1	0	2
Jennings	.167	.222	.158	9	18	1	3	4	1	0	0	2	0	2	0	0	0

PITCHERS	W-L	ERA	BA	G	GS	CG	GF	Sho	SV	IP	H	R	ER	HR	BB	SO
Pisciotta	3-1	3.18	.200	24	0	0	7	0	0	28.1	20	10	10	1	16	21
Patterson	1-6	3.34	.222	76	0	0	12	0	0	59.1	47	23	22	9	10	58
Tapani	9-3	3.39	.242	13	13	1	0	1	0	85.0	77	33	32	7	23	55
M. Clark	14-8	3.82	.270	32	31	3	0	0	0	205.0	213	96	87	24	59	123
Bottenfield	2-3	3.86	.259	64	0	0	20	0	2	84.0	82	39	36	13	35	74
Gonzalez	11-9	4.25	.236	23	23	1	0	1	0	144.0	126	73	68	16	69	93
Trachsel	8-12	4.51	.287	34	34	0	0	0	0	201.1	225	110	101	32	69	160
Foster	10-7	4.61	.255	26	25	1	0	0	0	146.1	141	79	75	27	66	118
Adams	2-9	4.62	.306	74	0	0	39	0	18	74.0	91	43	38	3	40	64
Morel	0-0	4.76	.304	8	0	0	5	0	0	11.1	14	6	6	3	7	7
Tatis	1-1	5.34	.308	56	0	0	12	0	0	55.2	66	36	33	13	29	33
Batista	0-5	5.70	.267	11	6	0	2	0	0	36.1	36	24	23	4	24	27
Myers	0-0	6.00	.333	5	1	0	2	0	0	9.0	12	6	6	1	7	6
Telemaco	0-3	6.16	.303	10	5	0	2	0	0	38.0	47	26	26	4	11	29
Casian	0-1	7.45	.364	12	0	0	1	0	0	9.2	16	9	8	3	2	7
Swartzbaugh	0-1	9.00	.364	2	2	0	0	0	0	8.0	12	8	8	1	7	4
Stevens	0-2	9.64	.333	10	0	0	0	0	0	9.1	13	11	10	0	9	13

1998 preliminary roster

PITCHERS (18)
Terry Adams
Mark Clark
Jose Espinal
Kevin Foster
Jeremi Gonzalez
Alan Mahaffey
Kurt Miller
Rodney Myers
Bob Patterson
Marc Pisciotta
Steve Rain
Jason Ryan
Justin Speier
Dave Stevens
David Swartzbaugh
Kevin Tapani
Amaury Telemaco
Steve Trachsel

CATCHERS (5)
Pat Cline
Tyler Houston
Mike Hubbard
Sandy Martinez
Scott Servais

INFIELDERS (9)
Manny Alexander
Jeff Blauser
Mark Grace
Jason Hardtke
Jose Hernandez
Jason Maxwell
Rod McCall
Jose Nieves

Kevin Orie

OUTFIELDERS (8)
Brant Brown
Doug Glanville
Robin Jennings
Lance Johnson
Terrell Lowery
Henry Rodriguez
Sammy Sosa
Pedro Valdes

Games played by position

PLAYER	G	C	1B	2B	3B	SS	OF
Alexander	87	0	0	35	1	54	0
Brown	46	0	12	0	0	0	27
Cairo	16	0	0	9	0	2	0
D. Clark	102	0	0	0	0	0	25
Glanville	146	0	0	0	0	0	138
Grace	151	0	148	0	0	0	0
Hansen	90	0	4	1	51	0	0
Hernandez	121	0	1	20	47	21	6
Houston	72	41	2	1	12	1	0
Hubbard	29	20	0	0	1	0	0
Jennings	9	0	0	0	0	0	5
Johnson	111	0	0	0	0	0	105
Kieschnick	39	0	0	0	0	0	27
Lowery	9	0	0	0	0	0	6
Orie	114	0	0	0	112	3	0
Sanchez	97	0	0	32	1	63	0
Sandberg	135	0	0	126	0	0	0
Servais	122	118	1	0	0	0	0
Sosa	162	0	0	0	0	0	161

Sick call: 1997 DL report

PLAYER	Days on the DL
Larry Casian	15
Shawon Dunston	15
Kevin Foster	15
Mark Grace	15
Tyler Houston	46*
Kevin Orie	30
Kevin Tapani	112

Indicates two separate terms on Disabled List.

Minor Leagues

Tops in the organization

BATTER	CLUB	AVG.	G	AB	R	H	HR	RBI
Jasco, Elinton	Day	.335	84	281	50	94	1	22
Valette, Ramon	Day	.332	106	371	54	123	6	50
Gazarek, Marty	Orl	.331	76	290	55	96	10	52
Abreu, Dennis	Rkf	.321	126	483	71	155	1	37
Porter, Bo	Orl	.304	130	471	91	143	18	68

HOME RUNS

McCall, Rod	Orl	26
Kieschnick, B.	Iwa	21
Jennings, R.	Iwa	20
Porter, Bo	Orl	18
Vieira, Scott	Day	18

WINS

Norton, Phillip	Orl	13
Several Players Tied at		10

RBI

Vieira, Scott	Day	80
Hall, Ronnie	Day	78
Freeman, Ricky	Orl	77
Zuleta, Julio	Rkf	77
McCall, Rod	Orl	75

SAVES

Pisciotta, Marc	Iwa	22
Schaffer, Trevor	Rkf	21
Kelley, Jason	Wpt	12
Ricketts, Chad	Orl	11
Several Players Tied at		9

STOLEN BASES

Meyers, Chad	Rkf	54
Cairo, Miguel	Iwa	40
Abreu, Dennis	Rkf	36
Jasco, Elinton	Day	32
Hall, Doug	Rkf	26

STRIKEOUTS

Wood, Kerry	Iwa	186
Duncan, C.	Orl	165
Norton, Phillip	Orl	165
Cannon, Jon	Day	143
Ryan, Jay	Day	140

PITCHER	CLUB	W-L	ERA	IP	H	BB	SO
Duncan, C.	Orl	10- 6	2.11	167	127	64	165
Swartzbaugh, D.	Iwa	8- 7	2.82	134	129	48	97
Norton, Phillip	Orl	13- 5	2.96	158	140	58	165
Cannon, Jon	Day	10- 6	2.96	143	117	60	143
Steenstra, K.	Iwa	5-10	3.92	161	161	41	111

1997 salaries

	Bonuses	Total earned salary
Sammy Sosa,of		5,500,000
Mark Grace,1b		4,525,000
Kevin Tapani,p		3,750,000
Ryne Sandberg,2b		3,700,000
Lance Johnson,of	50,000	3,050,000
Mark Clark,p	150,000	2,200,000
Steve Trachsel,p		2,100,000
Scott Servais,c	70,000	1,370,000
Bob Patterson,p	150,000	1,050,000
Jose Hernandez,3b		450,000
Dave Clark,of	150,000	450,000
Dave Hansen,3b	75,000	325,000
Kevin Foster,p		275,000
Terry Adams,p		215,000
Dave Stevens,p		210,000
Manny Alexander,ss		205,000
Kent Bottenfield,p		195,000
Tyler Houston,c		185,000
Doug Glanville,of		155,000
Miguel Batista,p		153,000
Mike Hubbard,c		153,000
Ramon Tatis,p		150,000
Marc Pisciotta,p		150,000
Kevin Orie,3b		150,000
Jeremi Gonzalez,p		150,000

Average 1997 Salary: $1,232,640
Total 1997 Payroll: $30,816,000

Chicago (1876-1997)

Runs: Most, career

1719	Cap Anson, 1876-1897
1409	Jimmy Ryan, 1885-1900
1316	RYNE SANDBERG, 1982-1997
1306	Billy Williams, 1959-1974
1305	Ernie Banks, 1953-1971

Hits: Most, career

2995	Cap Anson, 1876-1897
2583	Ernie Banks, 1953-1971
2510	Billy Williams, 1959-1974
2385	RYNE SANDBERG, 1982-1997
2193	Stan Hack, 1932-1947

2B: Most, career

528	Cap Anson, 1876-1897
407	Ernie Banks, 1953-1971
403	RYNE SANDBERG, 1982-1997
402	Billy Williams, 1959-1974
391	Gabby Hartnett, 1922-1940

3B: Most, career

142	Jimmy Ryan, 1885-1900
124	Cap Anson, 1876-1897
117	Frank Schulte, 1904-1916
106	Bill Dahlen, 1891-1898
99	Phil Cavarretta, 1934-1953

HR: Most, career

512	Ernie Banks, 1953-1971
392	Billy Williams, 1959-1974
337	Ron Santo, 1960-1973
282	RYNE SANDBERG, 1982-1997
231	Gabby Hartnett, 1922-1940

RBI: Most, career

1879	Cap Anson, 1876-1897
1636	Ernie Banks, 1953-1971
1353	Billy Williams, 1959-1974
1290	Ron Santo, 1960-1973
1153	Gabby Hartnett, 1922-1940

SB: Most, career

400	Frank Chance, 1898-1912
399	Bill Lange, 1893-1899
369	Jimmy Ryan, 1885-1900
344	RYNE SANDBERG, 1982-1997
304	Joe Tinker, 1902-1916

BB: Most, career

1092	Stan Hack, 1932-1947
1071	Ron Santo, 1960-1973
952	Cap Anson, 1876-1897
911	Billy Williams, 1959-1974
794	Phil Cavarretta, 1934-1953

BA: Highest, career

.336	Riggs Stephenson, 1926-1934
.330	Bill Lange, 1893-1899
.329	Cap Anson, 1876-1897
.325	Kiki Cuyler, 1928-1935
.323	Bill Everitt, 1895-1900

On-base avg: Highest, career

.412	Hack Wilson, 1926-1931
.408	Riggs Stephenson, 1926-1934
.401	Bill Lange, 1893-1899
.395	Cap Anson, 1876-1897
.394	Stan Hack, 1932-1947

Slug avg: Highest, career

.590	Hack Wilson, 1926-1931
.512	Hank Sauer, 1949-1955
.507	Andre Dawson, 1987-1992
.503	Billy Williams, 1959-1974
.500	SAMMY SOSA, 1992-1997

Games started: Most, career

347	Fergie Jenkins, 1966-1983
343	Rick Reuschel, 1972-1984
339	Bill Hutchison, 1889-1895
339	Charlie Root, 1926-1941
297	Bill Lee, 1934-1947

Complete games: Most, career

317	Bill Hutchison, 1889-1895
252	Larry Corcoran, 1880-1885
240	Clark Griffith, 1893-1900
206	Mordecai Brown, 1904-1916
188	Jack Taylor, 1898-1907

Saves: Most, career

180	LEE SMITH, 1980-1987
133	Bruce Sutter, 1976-1980
112	RANDY MYERS, 1993-1995
63	Don Elston, 1953-1964
60	Phil Regan, 1968-1972

Shutouts: Most, career

48	Mordecai Brown, 1904-1916
35	Hippo Vaughn, 1913-1921
31	Ed Reulbach, 1905-1913
29	Fergie Jenkins, 1966-1983
28	Orval Overall, 1906-1913

Wins: Most, career

201	Charlie Root, 1926-1941
188	Mordecai Brown, 1904-1916
181	Bill Hutchison, 1889-1895
175	Larry Corcoran, 1880-1885
167	Fergie Jenkins, 1966-1983

K: Most, career

2038	Fergie Jenkins, 1966-1983
1432	Charlie Root, 1926-1941
1367	Rick Reuschel, 1972-1984
1224	Bill Hutchison, 1889-1895
1138	Hippo Vaughn, 1913-1921

Win pct: Highest, career

.800	Al Spalding, 1876-1878
.773	Jim McCormick, 1885-1886
.706	John Clarkson, 1884-1887
.686	Mordecai Brown, 1904-1916
.677	Ed Reulbach, 1905-1913

ERA: Lowest, career

1.80	Mordecai Brown, 1904-1916
1.85	Jack Pfiester, 1906-1911
1.91	Orval Overall, 1906-1913
2.14	Jake Weimer, 1903-1905
2.24	Ed Reulbach, 1905-1913

Runs: Most, season

156	Rogers Hornsby, 1929
155	Kiki Cuyler, 1930
155	King Kelly, 1886
152	Woody English, 1930
150	George Gore, 1886

Hits: Most, season

229	Rogers Hornsby, 1929
228	Kiki Cuyler, 1930
227	Billy Herman, 1935
214	Woody English, 1930
212	Frank Demaree, 1936

2B: Most, season

57	Billy Herman, 1935
57	Billy Herman, 1936
51	MARK GRACE, 1995
50	Kiki Cuyler, 1930
49	Riggs Stephenson, 1932
49	Ned Williamson, 1883

3B: Most, season

21	Vic Saier, 1913
21	Frank Schulte, 1911
19	Bill Dahlen, 1892
19	Bill Dahlen, 1896
19	RYNE SANDBERG, 1984

HR: Most, season

56	Hack Wilson, 1930
49	Andre Dawson, 1987
48	Dave Kingman, 1979
47	Ernie Banks, 1958
45	Ernie Banks, 1959

RBI: Most, season

190	Hack Wilson, 1930
159	Hack Wilson, 1929
149	Rogers Hornsby, 1929
147	Cap Anson, 1886
143	Ernie Banks, 1959

SB: Most, season

84	Bill Lange, 1896
76	Walt Wilmot, 1890
74	Walt Wilmot, 1894
73	Bill Lange, 1897
67	Frank Chance, 1903
67	Bill Lange, 1895

BB: Most, season

147	Jimmy Sheckard, 1911
122	Jimmy Sheckard, 1912
116	Richie Ashburn, 1960
113	Cap Anson, 1890
108	Johnny Evers, 1910

BA: Highest, season

.389	Bill Lange, 1895
.388	King Kelly, 1886
.380	Rogers Hornsby, 1929
.372	Heinie Zimmerman, 1912
.371	Cap Anson, 1886

On-base avg: Highest, season

.483	King Kelly, 1886
.459	Rogers Hornsby, 1929
.456	Bill Lange, 1895
.454	Hack Wilson, 1930
.450	Frank Chance, 1905

Slug avg: Highest, season

.723	Hack Wilson, 1930
.679	Rogers Hornsby, 1929
.630	Gabby Hartnett, 1930
.618	Hack Wilson, 1929
.614	Ernie Banks, 1958

Games started: Most, season

70	John Clarkson, 1885
70	Bill Hutchison, 1892
66	Bill Hutchison, 1890
60	Larry Corcoran, 1880
60	Al Spalding, 1876

Complete games: Most, season

68	John Clarkson, 1885
67	Bill Hutchison, 1892
65	Bill Hutchison, 1890
57	Larry Corcoran, 1880
57	Larry Corcoran, 1884
57	Terry Larkin, 1879

Saves: Most, season

53	RANDY MYERS, 1993
38	RANDY MYERS, 1995
37	Bruce Sutter, 1979
36	LEE SMITH, 1987
36	MITCH WILLIAMS, 1989

Shutouts: Most, season

10	John Clarkson, 1885
9	Pete Alexander, 1919
9	Mordecai Brown, 1906
9	Mordecai Brown, 1908
9	Bill Lee, 1938
9	Orval Overall, 1909

Wins: Most, season

53	John Clarkson, 1885
47	Al Spalding, 1876
44	Bill Hutchison, 1891
43	Larry Corcoran, 1880
42	Bill Hutchison, 1890

K: Most, season

314	Bill Hutchison, 1892
313	John Clarkson, 1886
308	John Clarkson, 1885
289	Bill Hutchison, 1890
274	Fergie Jenkins, 1970

Win pct: Highest, season

.941	Rick Sutcliffe, 1984
.875	Fred Goldsmith, 1880
.833	King Cole, 1910
.833	Jim McCormick, 1885
.826	Ed Reulbach, 1906

ERA: Lowest, season

1.04	Mordecai Brown, 1906
1.15	Jack Pfiester, 1907
1.17	Carl Lundgren, 1907
1.31	Mordecai Brown, 1909
1.33	Jack Taylor, 1902

Most pinch-hit homers, season

3	Thad Bosley, 1985
3	DAVE CLARK, 1997
3	Kevin Roberson, 1994
3	Willie Smith, 1969
3	Chuck Tanner, 1958

Most pinch-hit homers, career

6	Thad Bosley, 1983-1986
6	Kevin Roberson, 1993-1995

Longest hitting streak

42	Bill Dahlen, 1894
30	Cal McVey, 1876
30	JEROME WALTON, 1989
28	Bill Dahlen, 1894 (2nd streak)
28	Ron Santo, 1966

Most consecutive scoreless innings

50	Ed Reulbach, 1908-1909
39	Mordecai Brown, 1908
38	John Clarkson, 1885
38	Bill Lee, 1938

No-hit games

Larry Corcoran, Chi vs Bos NL, 6-0; Aug. 19, 1880.

Larry Corcoran, Chi vs Wor NL, 5-0; Sept. 20, 1882.

Larry Corcoran, Chi vs Pro NL, 6-0; June 27, 1884.

John Clarkson, Chi at Pro NL, 4-0; July 27, 1885.

Walter Thornton, Chi vs Bro NL, 2-0; Aug. 21, 1898 (2nd game).

Bob Wicker, Chi at NY NL, 1-0; June 11, 1904 (won in 12 innings after allowing one hit in the 10th).

Jimmy Lavender, Chi at NY NL, 2-0; Aug. 31, 1915 (1st game).

Hippo Vaughn, Chi vs Cin NL, 0-1; May 2, 1917 (lost on two hits in the 10th; Fred Toney pitched a no-hitter in this game).

Sam Jones, Chi vs Pit NL, 4-0; May 12, 1955.

Don Cardwell, Chi vs StL NL, 4-0; May 15, 1960 (2nd game).

Ken Holtzman, Chi vs Atl NL, 3-0; Aug. 19, 1969.

Ken Holtzman, Chi at Cin NL, 1-0; June 3, 1971.

Burt Hooton, Chi vs Phi NL, 4-0; April 16, 1972.

Milt Pappas, Chi vs SD NL, 8-0; Sept. 2, 1972.

George Van Haltren, six innings, rain, Chi vs Pit NL, 1-0, June 21,1888.

King Cole, seven innings, called so Chicago could catch train, Chi at StL NL, 4-0; July 31, 1910 (2nd game).

ACTIVE PLAYERS in caps.

Players' years of service are listed by the first and last years with this team and are not necessarily consecutive; all statistics record performances for this team only.

San Francisco Giants

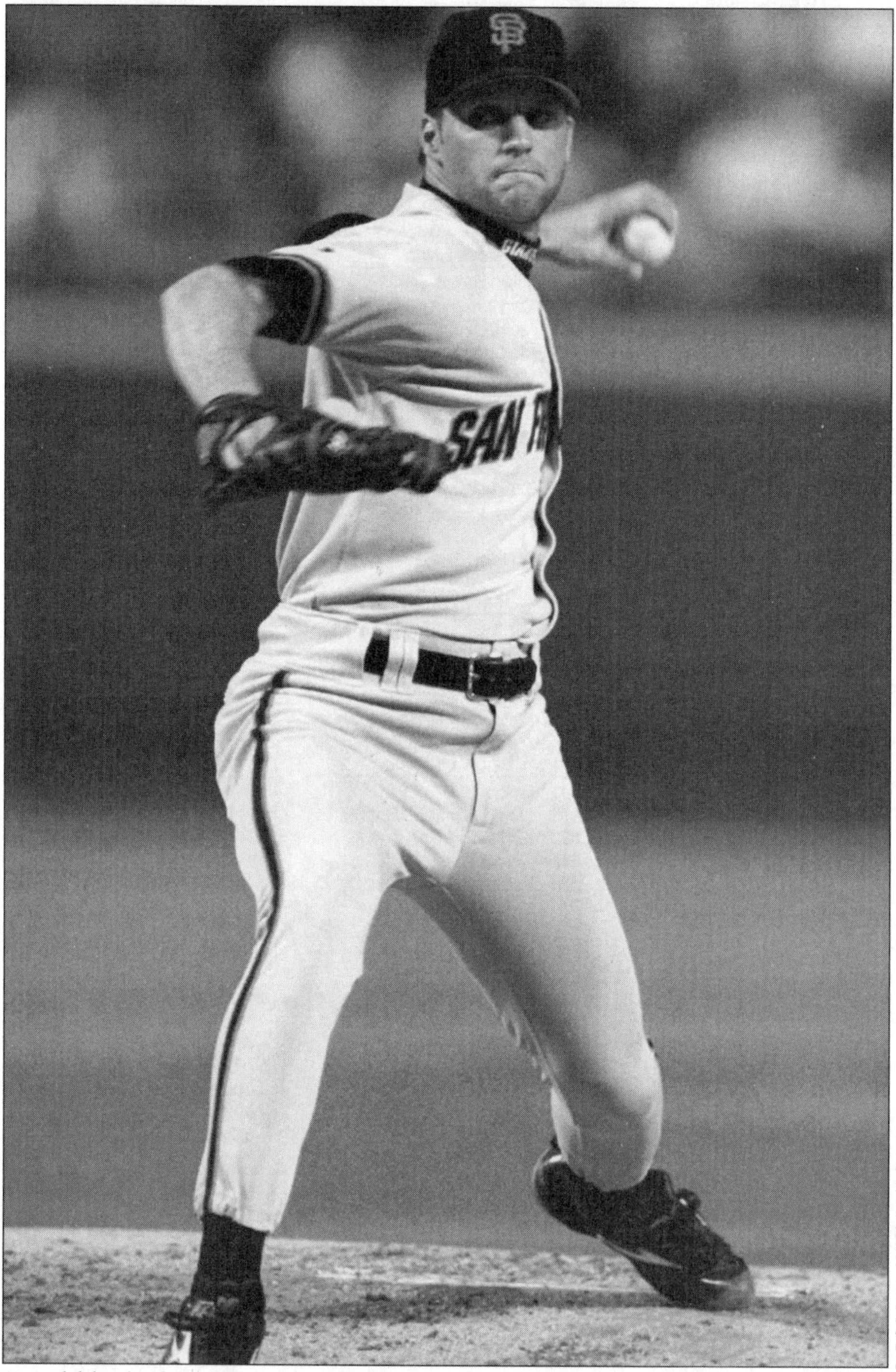

Young left-hander Shawn Estes stabilized the Giants' rotation and led the team with 19 wins and a 3.18 ERA.

1997 Giants: Daring trades paid off big

For the San Francisco Giants who experienced the pain of 1993, with the 103 victories and second place, making the playoffs in 1997 was a nice cure. Only two Giants, left fielder Barry Bonds and closer Rod Beck, remained from the '93 season. But the '97 NL West championship was felt among their former teammates. Maybe that's why manager Dusty Baker received so many congratulatory messages from his '93 team, all of whom offered best wishes as the Giants embarked on the playoffs, which turned out to be a short run—three difficult losses to the eventual World Series champs, the Marlins.

The Giants were probably the most surprising team in baseball, winning the NL West after consecutive last-place finishes. GM Brian Sabean reshaped the roster, replacing injury-prone veterans with cheaper, younger talent that jelled in a hurry. The Giants trailed the rival Dodgers by two games entering a late-Sepember two-game series in San Francisco. They swept the series and never looked back, clinching the division in the next-to-last game.

Perhaps the season's defining moment was when Beck ran charging off the field, yelling and pumping his fists after escaping a bases-loaded, no-out situation against the Dodgers. The Giants celebrated wildly during their two-game sweep, and the Dodgers said they would remember it. "This team is defined by emotion, and emotion is spontaneous," Sabean said. "I've got all the respect in the world for [the Dodgers'] organization and the talent on their team, but this isn't a fluke."

There were no doubters among the NL West champs. "I knew this team had the heart and desire," said second baseman Jeff Kent, the team leader in RBI with 121. Kent, first baseman J.T. Snow and Bonds became the Giants' first threesome since 1947 to collect 100 RBI apiece. Pitcher Shawn Estes became the first Giants lefty with as many as 19 victories since Ron Bryant's 24-win season in 1973. Kirk Rueter established career

Team MVP

Shawn Estes: Shawn Estes made the Giants' Opening Day roster for the first time in his career and responded with a 19-victory season, tied with Greg Maddux for second in the National League. The 24-year-old left-hander was the club leader in most pitching categories, posting a 3.18 ERA, striking out 181 in 201 innings and allowing opposition batters just a .223 average.

highs for wins (13) and starts (32).

"This was just a magical year, not just for me, but for everyone in the clubhouse," said Beck, who had 37 saves. Beck was helped (if also threatened) by the acquisition of Roberto Hernandez, in the same July 31 deal that brought in starter Wilson Alvarez, who won the division clincher. That was the last of a string of deals by Sabean that led to a 22-game improvement over 1996. Sabean's first deal was his most controversial. He sent popular third baseman Matt Williams to Cleveland for Kent, shortstop Jose Vizcaino and reliever Julian Tavarez. Kent hit 29 home runs and carried the team early in the season when Bonds started slowly. Vizcaino hit .266, and Tavarez led the majors in appearances with 89 as part of a much deeper bullpen that reduced Beck's workload.

Mark Gardner joined Estes and Rueter to give the Giants a solid rotation through most of the season, though second-year man Osvaldo Fernandez was shut down after 11 starts and had season-ending elbow surgery.

J.T. Snow came to San Francisco in a pre-season trade with Anaheim and won a Gold Glove. Darryl Hamilton, who hit leadoff and played center field, was signed as a free agent, and catcher Brian Johnson was acquired from Detroit in mid-July and hit 11 home runs. Two were September game-winners, including one in extra innings during that crucial series with Los Angeles.

1997 Giants: Week-by-week notes

These notes were excerpted from the following issues of Baseball Weekly.

▶**April 16:** The Giants were satisfied after going 5-3 in their first homestand. The team had a 2.50 ERA, and the Giants' staff was the first to throw two shutouts. After failing on Opening Day, the bullpen went 2-0 with five saves and a 1.89 ERA over seven games. Most surprising was that the pitchers allowed only one home run, a grand slam by Pittsburgh's Mark Johnson.

▶**April 23:** Through 16 games the Giants were 13-3, including a nine-game winning streak, their quickest start since 1971. Their eighth consecutive victory was the stunner. Playing on a cloudy day in San Francisco, the Giants caught an incredible break when the sun broke through for just a moment—when Florida's Gary Sheffield looked up for right fielder Glenallen Hill's lazy fly ball to right in the eighth inning. Sheffield was blinded by the sun, Hill's ball fell for a two-run double, and the Giants beat the Marlins 3-2.

▶**April 30:** Despite opening the season on the DL, left-hander Shawn Estes became the first NL pitcher to pick up four victories. The latest was his finest. He threw a 2-0, two-hit shutout in Houston for his first complete game. First baseman J.T. Snow, a switch-hitter, opened the season 1-for-18 (.056) batting right-handed. Snow also struggled right-handed last season, batting .199 from the right side and .285 from the left.

▶**May 7:** At 17-7, the Giants enjoyed their third-winningest April in club history. The pitching staff posted a 2.90 ERA in April, second best in the NL to Atlanta. The defense committed only 13 errors, fewest in the league. The offense produced steady clutch hitting despite a .240 team average.

▶**May 21:** Despite building an 11-2 advantage through three innings against Montreal on May 16, the Giants lost 14-13—their biggest blown lead since June 15, 1952, when the New York Giants wasted an 11-0 cushion at the Polo Grounds.

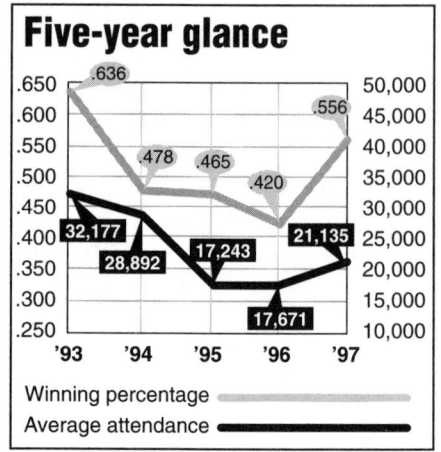

Five-year glance

.636
.556
.478
.465
.420

32,177
28,892
17,243
21,135
17,671

'93 '94 '95 '96 '97

Winning percentage
Average attendance

▶**June 4:** The Giants finished 14-14 in May, marking the first time since 1993 that the Giants have gone two consecutive months without a losing record. Center fielder Darryl Hamilton, hobbled by a strained hamstring, didn't go on the DL, but he has missed 11 starts through June 1.

▶**June 11:** Shawn Estes hit his first home run as a big leaguer off Florida's Alex Fernandez. It was his first homer since high school. The homer was Estes' first hit of the season. He was 0-for-18 before going deep. In his career, he's 4-for-44.

▶**June 18:** Angels pitcher Allen Watson and shortstop Rich Aurilia first crossed paths on the prep diamonds in New York. Last season, they were teammates on the Giants. On June 14, they met again when Watson faced the Giants in Anaheim. Aurilia greeted his old pal with his first career grand slam.

▶**June 25:** The Giants went 5-1 in their first peek at interleague play, including two-game sweeps of the Angels and the Mariners. Outfielder Stan Javier did his best work against the AL, hitting his first three homers of the season.

▶**July 2:** The Giants have used their bullpen more than any team in the majors—239 times through June 29. Julian Tavarez was tied for most appearances among NL pitchers, with 46. Rich Rodriguez (42) was tied for third, Doug Henry (41) tied for fifth, and closer Rod

Beck and Jim Poole (38) tied for eighth.

▶**July 16:** Right-hander Mark Gardner has nine wins despite having all kinds of first-inning troubles. His opening-inning ERA is 9.00. In 19 starts, he's allowed 30 hits and walked nine in that inning.

▶**July 23:** One day after sending rookie catcher Marcus Jensen to Detroit for catcher Brian Johnson, general manager Brian Sabean acquired starter Pat Rapp from Florida for two prospects.

▶**July 30:** The Giants were actively pursuing a starter before the July 31 trade deadline. Other than Mark Gardner, Shawn Estes and left-hander Kirk Rueter, it's trouble. The main problem is Pat Rapp, who went on the DL with a muscle strain in his left side. Acquired in a trade from the Marlins, Rapp was hurt in his first start. With the pitching staff struggling, the Giants lost 11 of 17 following the All-Star break, with a staff ERA of 5.59.

▶**Aug. 6:** Brian Sabean, criticized all winter for trading Matt Williams, received nothing but praise for acquiring pitchers Wilson Alvarez, Roberto Hernandez and Danny Darwin for six minor leaguers from the White Sox on July 31. The Giants, who led the NL West by six games at the All-Star break, struggled the rest of July and lost 13 of 21 before the trade.

▶**Aug. 13:** Last week the Giants acquired left-hander Terry Mulholland on a waiver claim from the Cubs. It's Mulholland's third stint with the Giants. He was 6-12 with a 4.07 ERA for Chicago, and he was set to join the Giants' bullpen.

▶**Aug. 20:** Shawn Estes is 7-0 with a 1.80 ERA in games following Giants losses. Mark Gardner is 7-1 with a 2.31 ERA after such games. One day last week after a bitter one-run loss, Estes struck out 10 batters in a 7-3 victory against the Cubs. He's now 15-4, the most victories by a Giants left-hander since Vida Blue won 18 in 1978.

▶**Aug. 27:** When second baseman Jeff Kent notches his 100th RBI, he'll become only the fifth San Francisco infielder and the only middle infielder to reach the century mark. He had a run-scoring double on Aug. 24, increasing his total to a career-high 99.

▶**Sept. 3:** The Giants have yielded the most unearned runs (76) in the league and committed the most errors (107), but solid defense allowed them to keep close to Los Angeles through the games of this weekend. Shawn Estes won his 18th game as he was bailed out by a couple of superb defensive plays by Jeff Kent and Darryl Hamilton.

▶**Sept. 10:** For the first time this season, Rod Beck was pulled from a save situation. The Astros had runners at first and third and Jeff Bagwell coming up, and manager Dusty Baker summoned Roberto Hernandez to replace Beck, who had allowed singles to Bob Abreu, Craig Biggio and Bill Spiers. Hernandez struck out Bagwell and Derek Bell to save the Giants' 5-3 victory.

▶**Sept. 17:** When the NL chose Sept. 10 as the makeup date for an Aug. 21 rainout at Veterans Stadium, the Giants were furious. It was supposed to be their off-day before a pivotal road trip through Miami and Atlanta. Well, it worked out for the Giants. They flew into town at 3 a.m, but before flying out, they overcame seven strong innings by Curt Schilling and beat the Phillies 5-3 on Jeff Kent's ninth-inning home run.

▶**Sept. 24:** In an emotional series that won't soon be forgotten, the Giants defeated the Dodgers in two straight games to move into a first-place tie in the NL West. Brian Johnson's homer leading off the 12th gave the Giants a 6-5 victory and a series sweep. Left fielder Barry Bonds homered in three consecutive games, including both against the Dodgers.

▶**Oct. 1:** The Giants' 6-1 victory against San Diego on Sept. 27 gave them the NL West title. In the clincher, Wilson Alvarez pitched seven shutout innings and Rod Beck tossed a perfect ninth inning. It was the Giants' eighth win in 10 games and their 90th of the season.

QUOTE OF THE YEAR

"Everyone who watched the Ken Griffey–Barry Bonds show forgot to change the channel to Stan Javier."
—Left fielder Barry Bonds, on the star of the Giants-Mariners interleague series

SAN FRANCISCO GIANTS 1997 final stats

BATTERS	BA	SLG	OBA	G	AB	R	H	TB	2B	3B	HR	RBI	BB	SO	SB	CS	E
Powell	.308	.410	.372	27	39	8	12	16	1	0	1	3	4	11	1	1	0
Mueller	.292	.428	.369	128	390	51	114	167	26	3	7	44	48	71	4	3	14
Bonds	.291	.585	.446	159	532	123	155	311	26	5	40	101	145	87	37	8	5
Javier	.286	.395	.368	142	440	69	126	174	16	4	8	50	56	70	25	3	7
Snow	.281	.510	.387	157	531	81	149	271	36	1	28	104	96	104	6	4	7
Johnson	.279	.525	.333	56	179	19	50	94	7	2	11	27	14	26	0	1	2
Aurilia	.275	.500	.321	46	102	16	28	51	8	0	5	19	8	15	1	1	3
Hamilton	.270	.365	.354	125	460	78	124	168	23	3	5	43	61	61	15	10	5
Lewis	.267	.431	.318	118	341	50	91	147	14	6	10	42	23	62	3	2	14
Vizcaino	.266	.350	.323	151	568	77	151	199	19	7	5	50	48	87	8	8	16
Hill	.261	.435	.297	128	398	47	104	173	28	4	11	64	19	87	7	4	9
Berryhill	.257	.359	.335	73	167	17	43	60	8	0	3	23	20	29	0	0	3
Kent	.250	.472	.316	155	580	90	145	274	38	2	29	121	48	133	11	3	16
Benard	.228	.289	.315	84	114	13	26	33	4	0	1	13	13	29	3	1	1
Wilkins	.195	.316	.257	66	190	18	37	60	5	0	6	23	17	65	0	0	5
Cruz	.160	.200	.241	16	25	3	4	5	1	0	0	3	3	4	0	0	1
Jensen	.149	.216	.222	30	74	5	11	16	2	0	1	3	7	23	0	0	2
Delgado	.143	.286	.143	8	7	1	1	2	1	0	0	0	0	0	0	0	0
Mirabelli	.143	.143	.250	6	7	0	1	1	0	0	0	0	1	3	0	0	0

PITCHERS	W-L	ERA	BA	G	GS	CG	GF	Sho	SV	IP	H	R	ER	HR	BB	SO
Hernandez	5-2	2.48	.238	28	0	0	7	0	4	32.2	29	9	9	2	14	35
Rodriguez	4-3	3.17	.264	71	0	0	15	0	1	65.1	65	24	23	7	21	32
Estes	19-5	3.18	.223	32	32	3	0	2	0	201.0	162	80	71	12	100	181
Johnstone	0-0	3.38	.234	13	0	0	2	0	0	18.2	15	7	7	1	7	15
Rueter	13-6	3.45	.264	32	32	0	0	0	0	190.2	194	83	73	17	51	115
Beck	7-4	3.47	.249	73	0	0	66	0	37	70.0	67	31	27	7	8	53
Tavarez	6-4	3.87	.277	89	0	0	13	0	0	88.1	91	43	38	6	34	38
Mulholland	6-13	4.24	.267	40	27	1	5	0	0	186.2	190	100	88	24	51	99
Gardner	12-9	4.29	.272	30	30	2	0	1	0	180.1	188	92	86	28	57	136
Alvarez	4-3	4.48	.224	11	11	0	0	0	0	66.1	54	36	33	9	36	69
Henry	4-5	4.71	.261	75	0	0	25	0	3	70.2	70	45	37	5	41	69
Rapp	5-8	4.83	.288	27	25	1	0	1	0	141.2	158	83	76	16	72	92
Darwin	1-3	4.91	.288	10	7	0	0	0	0	44.0	51	26	24	5	14	30
Fernandez	3-4	4.95	.314	11	11	0	0	0	0	56.1	74	39	31	9	15	31
VanLandingham	4-7	4.96	.237	18	17	0	1	0	0	89.0	80	56	49	11	59	52
Roa	2-5	5.21	.333	28	3	0	4	0	0	65.2	86	40	38	8	20	34
Creek	1-2	6.75	.240	3	3	0	0	0	0	13.1	12	12	10	1	14	14
Poole	3-1	7.11	.353	63	0	0	11	0	0	49.1	73	44	39	6	25	26
Carlson	0-0	7.63	.317	6	0	0	2	0	0	15.1	20	14	13	5	8	14
Foulke	1-5	8.26	.324	11	8	0	0	0	0	44.2	60	41	41	9	18	33
Bailey	0-1	8.38	.375	7	0	0	4	0	0	9.2	15	9	9	1	4	5
DeLucia	0-0	10.80	.500	3	0	0	0	0	0	1.2	6	3	2	0	0	2
Arocha	0-0	11.32	.370	6	0	0	2	0	0	10.1	17	14	13	2	5	7

1998 preliminary roster

PITCHERS (20)
Cory Bailey
Darin Blood
Troy Brohawn
Danny Darwin
Shawn Estes
Osvaldo Fernandez
Mark Gardner
Orel Hershiser
John Johnstone
Joe Nathan
Robb Nen
Russ Ortiz
Ricky Pickett
Jim Poole
Steve Reed
Joe Roa
Rich Rodriguez
Kirk Rueter
Steve Soderstrom
Julian Tavarez

CATCHERS (3)
Brian Johnson
Brent Mayne
Doug Mirabelli

INFIELDERS (8)
Rich Aurilia
Wilson Delgado
Pedro Felix
Charlie Hayes
Jeff Kent
Ramon Martinez
Bill Mueller
J.T. Snow

OUTFIELDERS (8)
Marvin Benard
Barry Bonds
Jacob Cruz
Darryl Hamilton
Stan Javier
Calvin Murray
Dante Powell
Armando Rios

Games played by position

PLAYER	G	C	1B	2B	3B	SS	OF
Aurilia	46	0	0	0	0	36	0
Benard	84	0	0	0	0	0	36
Berryhill	73	51	1	0	0	0	0
Bonds	159	0	0	0	0	0	159
Cruz	16	0	0	0	0	0	11
Delgado	8	0	0	3	0	1	0
Hamilton	125	0	0	0	0	0	118
Hill	128	0	0	0	0	0	97
Javier	142	0	3	0	0	0	130
Jensen	30	28	0	0	0	0	0
Johnson	56	55	2	0	0	0	0
Kent	155	0	13	148	0	0	0
Lewis	118	0	0	29	69	0	0
Mirabelli	6	6	0	0	0	0	0
Mueller	128	0	0	0	122	0	0
Powell	27	0	0	0	0	0	22
Snow	157	0	156	0	0	0	0
Vizcaino	151	0	0	5	0	147	0
Wilkins	66	57	0	0	0	0	0

Sick call: 1997 DL report

PLAYER	Days on the DL
Damon Berryhill	38*
Dan Carlson	10
Shawn Estes	6
Osvaldo Fernandez	126*
Darryl Hamilton	22
Mark Lewis	12
Bill Mueller	17
Pat Rapp	17
Desi Wilson	5

Indicates two separate terms on Disabled List.

1997 salaries

	Bonuses	Total earned salary
Barry Bonds,of		8,666,667
Wilson Alvarez,p		4,662,500
Roberto Hernandez,p		4,620,000
Rod Beck,p	250,000	3,183,380
Jose Vizcaino,ss		2,800,000
Jeff Kent,2b	75,000	2,625,000
Terry Mulholland,p	100,000	2,400,000
J.T. Snow,1b	25,000	1,825,000
Darryl Hamilton,of		1,750,000
Glenallen Hill,of		1,700,000
Mark Lewis,3b	64,000	1,664,000
Stan Javier,of	250,000	1,350,000
Osvaldo Fernandez,p	25,000	958,333
Mark Gardner,p	350,000	900,000
Jim Poole,p	50,000	850,000
Julian Tavarez,p		683,333
Brian Johnson,c	50,000	600,000
Doug Henry,p	50,000	550,000
Danny Darwin,p	200,000	475,000
Damon Berryhill,c	166,665	466,665
Rich Rodriguez,p	100,000	300,000
Kirk Rueter,p	10,000	260,000
Marvin Benard,of		185,000
Rich Aurilia,ss		175,000
Shawn Estes,p		162,500
Bill Mueller,3b		160,000
Dante Powell,of		150,000

Average 1997 salary: $1,634,162
Total 1997 payroll: $44,122,378

Minor Leagues

Tops in the organization

BATTER	CLUB	AVG.	G	AB	R	H	HR	RBI
Cruz, Jacob	Phx	.361	127	493	97	178	12	95
McCarty, Dave	Phx	.353	121	434	85	153	22	92
Wilson, Todd	SJ	.345	130	502	66	173	5	88
Wilson, Desi	Phx	.344	121	451	76	155	7	53
Young, Travis	S-K	.334	76	320	80	107	1	34

HOME RUNS

Glendenning, M.	Bak	33
Minor, Damon	Bak	31
McCarty, Dave	Phx	22
Williams, Keith	Shr	22
Simonton, Benji	Shr	20

WINS

Carlson, Dan	Phx	13
Brohawn, Troy	Shr	13
Grote, Jason	Bak	12
Several Players Tied at		10

RBI

Williams, Keith	Shr	106
Ball, Jeff	Phx	103
Glendenning, M.	Bak	100
Minor, Damon	Bak	99
Cruz, Jacob	Phx	95

SAVES

Pageler, Mick	Bak	29
Johnstone, J.	Phx	24
Howry, Bob	Shr	22
Hernandez,S.	Shr	21
Travis, Jesse	S-K	16

STOLEN BASES

Garland, Tim	SJ	65
Murray, Calvin	Shr	52
Byas, Michael	S-K	51
Young, Travis	S-K	40
Powell, Dante	Phx	34

STRIKEOUTS

Brester, Jason	SJ	172
Vining, Kenneth	SJ	142
Creek, Doug	Phx	137
Malloy, William	Bak	124
Ortiz, Russ	Phx	120

PITCHER	CLUB	W-L	ERA	IP	H	BB	SO
Brohawn, Troy	Shr	13- 5	2.56	169	148	64	98
Leese, Brandon	SJ	7- 5	3.05	112	99	46	99
Grote, Jason	Bak	12- 8	3.45	156	156	59	116
Carlson, Dan	Phx	13- 3	3.68	115	105	37	115
Oropesa, Eddie	Shr	7- 7	3.92	124	122	64	65

San Francisco (1958-1997), includes New York (1883-1957)

Runs: Most, career

2011	Willie Mays, 1951-1972
1859	Mel Ott, 1926-1947
1313	Mike Tiernan, 1887-1899
1120	Bill Terry, 1923-1936
1113	Willie McCovey, 1959-1980

Hits: Most, career

3187	Willie Mays, 1951-1972
2876	Mel Ott, 1926-1947
2193	Bill Terry, 1923-1936
1974	Willie McCovey, 1959-1980
1834	Mike Tiernan, 1887-1899

2B: Most, career

504	Willie Mays, 1951-1972
488	Mel Ott, 1926-1947
373	Bill Terry, 1923-1936
308	Willie McCovey, 1959-1980
291	Travis Jackson, 1922-1936

3B: Most, career

162	Mike Tiernan, 1887-1899
139	Willie Mays, 1951-1972
131	Roger Connor, 1883-1894
117	Larry Doyle, 1907-1920
112	Bill Terry, 1923-1936

HR: Most, career

646	Willie Mays, 1951-1972
511	Mel Ott, 1926-1947
469	Willie McCovey, 1959-1980
247	MATT WILLIAMS, 1987-1996
226	Orlando Cepeda, 1958-1966

RBI: Most, career

1860	Mel Ott, 1926-1947
1859	Willie Mays, 1951-1972
1388	Willie McCovey, 1959-1980
1078	Bill Terry, 1923-1936
929	Travis Jackson, 1922-1936

SB: Most, career

428	Mike Tiernan, 1887-1899
354	George Davis, 1893-1903
336	Willie Mays, 1951-1972
334	George Burns, 1911-1921
332	John Ward, 1883-1894

BB: Most, career

1708	Mel Ott, 1926-1947
1394	Willie Mays, 1951-1972
1168	Willie McCovey, 1959-1980
747	Mike Tiernan, 1887-1899
631	George Burns, 1911-1921

BA: Highest, career

.341	Bill Terry, 1923-1936
.332	George Davis, 1893-1903
.322	Ross Youngs, 1917-1926
.322	Frankie Frisch, 1919-1926
.308	Barry Bonds, 1993-1997 (12)

On-base avg: Highest, career

.446	BARRY BONDS, 1993-1997
.414	Mel Ott, 1926-1947
.403	Roger Bresnahan, 1902-1908
.402	Roger Connor, 1883-1894
.399	Ross Youngs, 1917-1926

Slug avg: Highest, career

.619	BARRY BONDS, 1993-1997
.564	Willie Mays, 1951-1972
.549	Johnny Mize, 1942-1949
.536	KEVIN MITCHELL, 1987-1991
.535	Orlando Cepeda, 1958-1966

Games started: Most, career

550	C. Mathewson, 1900-1916
446	Juan Marichal, 1960-1973
431	Carl Hubbell, 1928-1943
412	Mickey Welch, 1883-1892
403	Amos Rusie, 1890-1898

Complete games: Most, career

433	C. Mathewson, 1900-1916
391	Mickey Welch, 1883-1892
372	Amos Rusie, 1890-1898
260	Carl Hubbell, 1928-1943
244	Juan Marichal, 1960-1973 (6)

Saves: Most, career

199	ROD BECK, 1991-1997
127	Gary Lavelle, 1974-1984
125	Greg Minton, 1975-1987
83	Randy Moffitt, 1972-1981
78	Frank Linzy, 1963-1970

Shutouts: Most, career

79	C. Mathewson, 1900-1916
52	Juan Marichal, 1960-1973
36	Carl Hubbell, 1928-1943
29	Amos Rusie, 1890-1898
28	Mickey Welch, 1883-1892

Wins: Most, career

372	C. Mathewson, 1900-1916
253	Carl Hubbell, 1928-1943
238	Juan Marichal, 1960-1973
238	Mickey Welch, 1883-1892
234	Amos Rusie, 1890-1898

K: Most, career

2499	C. Mathewson, 1900-1916
2281	Juan Marichal, 1960-1973
1835	Amos Rusie, 1890-1898
1677	Carl Hubbell, 1928-1943
1606	Gaylord Perry, 1962-1971

Win pct: Highest, career

.693	Sal Maglie, 1945-1955
.680	Tim Keefe, 1885-1891
.664	C. Mathewson, 1900-1916
.656	Jesse Barnes, 1918-1923
.630	Juan Marichal, 1960-1973 (11)

ERA: Lowest, career

2.12	C. Mathewson, 1900-1916
2.38	Joe McGinnity, 1902-1908
2.43	Jeff Tesreau, 1912-1918
2.45	Red Ames, 1903-1913
2.82	Gary Lavelle 1974-1984 (12)

Runs: Most, season

147	Mike Tiernan, 1889
139	Bill Terry, 1930
138	Mel Ott, 1929
137	Johnny Mize, 1947
136	George Van Haltren, 1896
134	Bobby Bonds, 1970 (6)

Hits: Most, season

254	Bill Terry, 1930
231	Freddy Lindstrom, 1928
231	Freddy Lindstrom, 1930
226	Bill Terry, 1929
208	Willie Mays, 1958 (13)

2B: Most, season

46	Jack Clark, 1978
43	Willie Mays, 1959
43	Bill Terry, 1931
42	George Kelly, 1921
42	Bill Terry, 1932

3B: Most, season

27	George Davis, 1893
25	Larry Doyle, 1911
22	Roger Connor, 1887
21	Mike Tiernan, 1890
21	Mike Tiernan, 1895
21	George Van Haltren, 1896
12	Willie Mays, 1960 (*)

HR: Most, season

52	Willie Mays, 1965
51	Willie Mays, 1955

51   Johnny Mize, 1947
49   Willie Mays, 1962
47   Willie Mays, 1964
47   KEVIN MITCHELL, 1989

RBI: Most, season

151   Mel Ott, 1929
142   Orlando Cepeda, 1961
141   Willie Mays, 1962
138   Johnny Mize, 1947

SB: Most, season

111   John Ward, 1887
65   George Davis, 1897
62   George Burns, 1914
62   John Ward, 1889
61   Josh Devore, 1911
58   Bill North, 1979 (7)

BB: Most, season

151   BARRY BONDS, 1996
145   BARRY BONDS, 1997
144   Eddie Stanky, 1950
137   Willie McCovey, 1970
127   Eddie Stanky, 1951

BA: Highest, season

.401   Bill Terry, 1930
.379   Freddy Lindstrom, 1930
.372   Bill Terry, 1929
.371   Roger Connor, 1885
.347   Willie Mays, 1958 (23)

On-base avg: Highest, season

.461   BARRY BONDS, 1996
.460   Eddie Stanky, 1950
.458   BARRY BONDS, 1993
.458   Mel Ott, 1930
.453   Willie McCovey, 1969

Slug avg: Highest, season

.677   BARRY BONDS, 1993
.667   Willie Mays, 1954
.659   Willie Mays, 1955
.656   Willie McCovey, 1969
.647   BARRY BONDS, 1994

Games started: Most, season

65   Mickey Welch, 1884
64   Tim Keefe, 1886
62   Amos Rusie, 1890
62   Amos Rusie, 1892
41   Gaylord Perry, 1970 (*)

Complete games: Most, season

62   Tim Keefe, 1886
62   Mickey Welch, 1884
59   Amos Rusie, 1892
56   Amos Rusie, 1890
56   Mickey Welch, 1886
30   Juan Marichal, 1968 (*)

Saves: Most, season

48   ROD BECK, 1993
37   ROD BECK, 1997
35   ROD BECK, 1996
33   ROD BECK, 1995
30   Greg Minton, 1982

Shutouts: Most, season

11   C. Mathewson, 1908
10   Carl Hubbell, 1933
10   Juan Marichal, 1965
9   Joe McGinnity, 1904

Wins: Most, season

44   Mickey Welch, 1885
42   Tim Keefe, 1886
39   Mickey Welch, 1884
37   C. Mathewson, 1908
26   Juan Marichal, 1968 (25)

K: Most, season

345   Mickey Welch, 1884
341   Amos Rusie, 1890
337   Amos Rusie, 1891
335   Tim Keefe, 1888
248   Juan Marichal, 1963 (11)

Win pct: Highest, season

.833   Hoyt Wilhelm, 1952
.818   Sal Maglie, 1950
.814   Joe McGinnity, 1904
.813   Carl Hubbell, 1936
.806   Juan Marichal, 1966 (7)

ERA: Lowest, season

1.14   C. Mathewson, 1909
1.28   C. Mathewson, 1905
1.43   C. Mathewson, 1908
1.44   Fred Anderson, 1917
1.99   Bobby Bolin, 1968 (16)

Most pinch-hit homers, season

4   Mike Ivie, 1978
4   Ernie Lombardi, 1946
4   Candy Maldonado, 1986
4   Ernie Riles, 1990
4   Bill Taylor, 1955

Most pinch-hit homers, career

13   Willie McCovey, 1959-1980
9   Bobby Hofman, 1949-1957

Longest hitting streak

33   George Davis, 1893
27   Charlie Hickman, 1900
26   Jack Clark, 1978
24   Mike Donlin, 1908
24   Fred Lindstrom, 1930
24   Willie McCovey, 1963

Most consecutive scoreless innings

45   Carl Hubbell, 1933
45   Sal Maglie, 1950
40   Gaylord Perry, 1967
39   C. Mathewson, 1901
39   Gaylord Perry, 1970

No-hit games

Amos Rusie, NY vs Bro NL, 6-0; July 31, 1891.

C. Mathewson, NY at StL NL, 5-0; July 15, 1901.

C. Mathewson, NY at Chi NL, 1-0; June 13, 1905.

Hooks Wiltse, NY vs Phi NL, 1-0; July 4, 1908 (1st game, 10 innings).

Red Ames, NY vs Bro NL. 0-3; April 15, 1909 (lost on 7 hits in 13 innings after allowing the first hit in the 10th).

Jeff Tesreau, NY at Phi NL, 3-0; Sept. 6, 1912 (1st game).

Rube Marquard, NY vs Bro NL, 2-0; April 15, 1915.

Jesse Barnes, NY vs Phi NL, 6-0; May 7, 1922.

Carl Hubbell, NY vs Pit NL, 11-0; May 8, 1929.

Juan Marichal, SF vs Hou NL, 1-0; June 15, 1963.

Gaylord Perry, SF vs StL NL, 1-0; Sept. 17, 1968.

Ed Halicki, SF vs NY NL, 6-0; Aug. 24, 1975 (2nd game).

John Montefusco, SF at Atl NL, 9-0; Sept. 29, 1976.

Ed Crane, seven innings, darkness, NY vs Was NL, 3-0; Sept. 27, 1888.

Red Ames, five innings, darkness, NY at StL NL, 5-0; Sept. 14, 1903 (2nd game, first game in the major leagues).

Mike McCormick, five innings, rain, SF at Phi NL, 3-0; June 12, 1959 (allowed hit in sixth, but rain caused game to revert to five innings).

Sam Jones, seven innings, rain, SF at StL NL, 4-0; Sept. 26, 1959.

ACTIVE PLAYERS in caps.

Players' years of service are listed by the first and last years with this team and are not necessarily consecutive; all statistics record performances for this team only.

Leader from the franchise's current location is included. If not in the top five, leader's rank is listed in parenthesis; asterisk (*) indicates player is not in top 25.

Los Angeles Dodgers

Mike Piazza had perhaps the greatest offensive season ever by a catcher, hitting .362 with 40 homers.

By Tom DiPace

1997 Dodgers: The pieces didn't add up

The Dodgers started the season as favorites to win the NL West because they seemed to have all of the pieces in place: standout pitching, a high-powered offense, improved defense and experience. But six months later, all they had to show for it was a disappointing second-place finish. "This is a team we thought could get to the World Series," manager Bill Russell said.

The Dodgers (88-74) failed to win the big games down the stretch. Their two biggest losses came on Sept. 17 and 18 to the Giants, eventual winners of the NL West. The Dodgers entered the two-game series with a two-game lead. Particularly painful for the Dodgers, who lost 13 of 19 during one stretch in the final month, was their 6-5 loss in 12 innings to San Francisco in the finale of the series, a game they could have won earlier. "That was our season right there," first baseman Eric Karros said. "Bases loaded. Nobody out. And we couldn't score. We were never the same."

Still, much did go right after a weak start. The Dodgers were stuck at 39-42 at the end of June and trailed the Giants by eight games. Then they went 39-18 to enter September with a 2½-game lead. Catcher Mike Piazza was runner-up to Colorado's Larry Walker for the MVP Award and set career highs in average (.362), hits (201), homers (40), RBI (124), runs scored (104) and games (152). He became the first Dodger to hit 40 homers since Brooklyn's Duke Snider, in 1957.

Karros topped 30 homers and 100 RBI for the third consecutive season. Right fielder Raul Mondesi won a Gold Glove and became the first 30-30 player (homers and stolen bases) in franchise history. Third baseman Todd Zeile was the fourth Dodger to reach 30 home runs. Tom Candiotti, who started the season in the bullpen but was inserted into the starting rotation when Ramon Martinez was injured, responded by posting a 7-5 record in 18 starts.

The team's pitching looks solid for the

future. Left-hander Dennis Reyes, 20, who pitched well as a fill-in when Ismael Valdes was injured, could be a starter next season. Reyes went 2-3 with a 3.83 ERA in 14 games. The rotation is anchored by Hideo Nomo (14-12, 4.25 ERA), Valdes (10-11, 2.65 ERA) and Chan Ho Park, who had a breakout season at 14-8, 3.38. Though closer Todd Worrell faltered late in the season, Los Angeles has two highly regarded young bullpen arms in Darren Dreifort and Antonio Osuna.

Overall, once again the Dodgers appear to have very few holes. "We've got good talent and an excellent level of control as far as player contracts are concerned," said Fred Claire, the team's executive vice president. Paul Konerko, MVP of the Pacific Coast League, appears ready for the majors. The 21-year-old third baseman–first baseman batted .323 with 37 homers and 127 RBI at AAA Albuquerque. He has the best chance the Dodgers have to retake the NL Jackie Robinson Award, which they won from 1992 to '96. Second baseman Wilton Guerrero was the team's likely 1997 candidate, but he lost his starting job to Eric Young, acquired from Colorado. Nearly as disappointing was left fielder Todd Hollandsworth, the 1996 Jackie Robinson winner, who batted just .247 with four homers and 31 RBI.

1997 Dodgers: Week-by-week notes

These notes were excerpted from the following issues of Baseball Weekly.

▶**April 9:** During a moving pregame salute on April 5 at Dodger Stadium, Jackie Robinson was hailed as a hero who had the courage to push for social change in an era of racism. Rachel Robinson urged fans to continue her husband's legacy. "The greatest tribute we can pay to Jackie is for each of us to commit ourselves to social change in the future and today," she said.

▶**April 16:** Catcher Mike Piazza was hit by a pitch thrown by Francisco Cordova of the Pirates on April 11 and was not expected to return to the lineup until April 15. Piazza is leading the team with a .344 average.

▶**April 23:** The Dodgers have a major-league-leading 2.22 ERA. The team, however, was hitting .250. Third baseman Todd Zeile was the main offender, at .164.

▶**April 30:** The Dodgers ranked 26th among baseball's 28 teams in runs, with 69, and had scored two or fewer runs in eight of their first 20 games.

▶**May 7:** The Dodgers extended their major league record to 600 consecutive games without a left-handed starter on May 5 when Hideo Nomo faced Cincinnati. The streak began after Bob Ojeda's start against the Reds on Sept. 24, 1992.

▶**May 14:** First baseman Eric Karros prefers not to talk about it, but his slow start—.236 with three homers and 13 RBI through May 11—is probably the result of tendinitis in his left shoulder.

▶**May 28:** Executive vice president Fred Claire had some simple advice for his struggling club, which had lost six straight games as of May 24: Relax. The Dodgers then snapped their longest losing streak in nearly two years with a 10-3 victory against the Braves, piling up 14 hits—three of them homers—against Tom Glavine and two relievers. Los Angeles was tied with Toronto for the fewest runs (160) in baseball after 45 games.

▶**June 4:** Second baseman Wilton

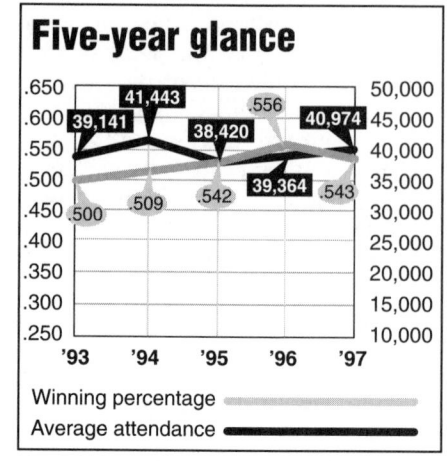

Five-year glance

Winning percentage
Average attendance

Guerrero was ejected from the June 1 game against St. Louis for using an illegal bat and was suspended for eight games by National League president Leonard Coleman. Guerrero, who admitted that he knew his bat was corked, is eligible to return on June 10.

▶**June 18:** In a surprise move on June 12, the Dodgers demoted left fielder Todd Hollandsworth, the 1996 NL Jackie Robinson Award winner for top rookie, to AAA Albuquerque and called up power-hitting outfielder Karim Garcia. In 64 games, Hollandsworth was batting just .232 with two homers and 18 RBI.

▶**June 25:** On June 21, a day after saying that Ramon Martinez was being given an extra day of rest because he was tired, the Dodgers acknowledged that their No. 1 starter has pain in his throwing shoulder. Martinez missed his scheduled start that day and was replaced by knuckleballer Tom Candiotti, who pitched seven scoreless innings in an 11-0 victory against the Giants.

▶**July 2:** After Hideo Nomo fell to 7-7 with a loss on June 28, only one of the team's original five starters has a winning record, and that pitcher, Ramon Martinez, is on the DL. The Dodgers had lost 10 consecutive games to the Padres before their 10-4 victory on June 29.

▶**July 10:** Todd Hollandsworth is back in the big leagues. He was demoted to Albuquerque on June 12, but he batted

.429 and was recalled 17 days later. To make room for Hollandsworth, the Dodgers demoted Karim Garcia, who appeared overmatched in his first extended look at major league pitching. Garcia hit just .128 (5-for-39) with one homer and eight RBI in 15 games.

▶July 16: Switch-hitter Wilton Guerrero's left shoulder has improved enough to let him bat right-handed, but he's still on the bench because Tripp Cromer is playing well. Cromer was batting .414 (12-for-29) with seven RBI in eight games as Guerrero's replacement. Jerry Doggett, who broadcast Dodgers games for 32 years before retiring in 1987, died on July 7 at his home in northern California.

▶July 23: The Dodgers' offense was one of the big reasons they won 11 of 12 from July 1 to July 15. During that stretch, which allowed them to move back into contention in the NL West, they outscored their opponents 87-46.

▶July 30: The Dodgers got a scare on July 26 when starter Hideo Nomo was hit above his right elbow by a line drive hit by the Phillies' Scott Rolen. Nomo, who was working on a no-hitter when he was hit with two outs in the fourth inning, left the game with what was termed a contusion. He is expected to make his next start.

▶Aug. 6: For the first time since 1979, the Dodgers have four players with at least 20 homers: Eric Karros (24), right fielder Raul Mondesi (23), Todd Zeile (22) and Mike Piazza (22).

▶Aug. 20: In a move that Fred Claire believes will propel his team to a division title, the Dodgers acquired center fielder Otis Nixon on Aug. 12 from Toronto for minor league catcher Bobby Cripps. Claire followed that six days later by trading pitcher Pedro Astacio to the Rockies for second baseman Eric Young.

▶Aug. 27: Rookie Wilton Guerrero, once a Jackie Robinson Award candidate, now finds himself back in the minor leagues. He was sent to Albuquerque on Aug. 22, four days after the team acquired Eric Young. Guerrero was demoted partly because he was caught in a numbers crunch. With two doubleheaders in a span of five days, the Dodgers needed pitching help. But he was also demoted because of frequent mental lapses and difficulty in turning the double play.

▶Sept. 3: Infielder Tripp Cromer, whose surprising offensive punch helped propel the Dodgers back into the pennant race, is scheduled to have season-ending elbow surgery next week. Cromer, who batted .291 with four homers and 20 RBI in 28 games, will have a torn ligament replaced.

▶Sept. 10: Todd Worrell is still the team's closer, but manager Bill Russell said bringing in the slumping reliever in a save situation is no longer automatic. Worrell's role became tenuous after he went 1-4 with four blown saves and an 8.74 ERA from Aug. 3 to Sept. 2. Russell said Worrell has not lost any velocity on his fastball nor the bite on his curve, but has struggled because of poor location.

▶Sept. 17: Mike Piazza, batting .359 with 33 homers and 103 RBI, has shown a tendency to fade down the stretch. His career average of .288 in September is his lowest for any month. But he is off to a fast start this month, batting .500 (11-for-22) with a homer and six RBI in his first five games.

▶Sept. 24: Hall of Fame broadcaster Vin Scully said he will stay with the team after the ownership changes. The Dodgers are expected to be sold to Rupert Murdoch and his Fox Corp.

▶Oct. 1: Will Fred Claire break up the Dodgers? While the Dodgers have the nucleus of their team under contract for next season, the club will have a new closer next season—Todd Worrell had 35 saves but blew nine—and Otis Nixon, shortstop Greg Gagne and Eric Young may not return.

QUOTE OF THE YEAR

"Any mention of any owner, manager, coach, player or scout under contract to another organization is not appropriate."
—Executive vice president Fred Claire, after Tom Lasorda said he would hire Mets manager Bobby Valentine to manage the Dodgers if Lasorda became GM under new ownership

LOS ANGELES DODGERS 1997 final stats

BATTERS	BA	SLG	OBA	G	AB	R	H	TB	2B	3B	HR	RBI	BB	SO	SB	CS	E
Ingram	.444	.444	.500	12	9	2	4	4	0	0	0	1	1	3	1	0	0
Blanco	.400	1.000	.400	3	5	1	2	5	0	0	1	1	0	1	0	0	0
Piazza	.362	.638	.431	152	556	104	201	355	32	1	40	124	69	77	5	1	16
Mondesi	.310	.541	.360	159	616	95	191	333	42	5	30	87	44	105	32	15	4
Lewis	.299	.403	.349	26	77	7	23	31	3	1	1	10	6	17	3	2	1
Guerrero	.291	.403	.305	111	357	39	104	144	10	9	4	32	8	52	6	5	4
Cromer	.291	.465	.333	28	86	8	25	40	3	0	4	20	6	16	0	1	3
Murray	.286	.286	.444	9	7	0	2	2	0	0	0	3	2	2	0	0	0
Butler	.283	.324	.363	105	343	52	97	111	8	3	0	18	42	40	15	10	1
Young	.280	.397	.359	155	622	106	174	247	33	8	8	61	71	54	45	14	18
Nixon	.274	.349	.323	42	175	30	48	61	6	2	1	18	13	24	12	2	1
Cedeno	.273	.392	.362	80	194	31	53	76	10	2	3	17	25	44	9	1	2
Zeile	.268	.459	.365	160	575	89	154	264	17	0	31	90	85	112	8	7	26
Karros	.266	.459	.329	162	628	86	167	288	28	0	31	104	61	116	15	7	11
Gagne	.251	.354	.298	144	514	49	129	182	20	3	9	57	31	120	2	5	16
Hollandsworth	.247	.368	.286	106	296	39	73	109	20	2	4	31	17	60	5	5	3
Ashley	.244	.435	.293	71	131	12	32	57	7	0	6	19	8	46	0	0	4
Anthony	.243	.419	.349	47	74	8	18	31	3	2	2	5	12	18	2	0	1
Liriano	.227	.330	.274	76	88	10	20	29	6	0	1	11	6	12	0	0	2
Prince	.220	.360	.275	47	100	17	22	36	5	0	3	14	5	15	0	0	1
Riggs	.200	.250	.333	9	20	3	4	5	1	0	0	1	4	3	1	0	0
Kirby	.169	.200	.280	46	65	6	11	13	2	0	0	4	10	12	0	0	0
Castro	.147	.213	.220	40	75	3	11	16	3	1	0	4	7	20	0	0	1
Fonville	.143	.143	.250	9	14	1	2	2	0	0	0	1	2	3	0	1	1
Konerko	.143	.143	.250	6	7	0	1	1	0	0	0	0	1	2	0	0	0
Garcia	.128	.205	.239	15	39	5	5	8	0	0	1	8	6	14	0	0	0
Hale	.083	.083	.214	14	12	0	1	1	0	0	0	0	2	4	0	0	0

PITCHERS	W-L	ERA	BA	G	GS	CG	GF	Sho	SV	IP	H	R	ER	HR	BB	SO
Judd	0-0	0.00	.364	1	0	0	0	0	0	2.2	4	0	0	0	0	4
Osuna	3-4	2.19	.209	48	0	0	18	0	0	61.2	46	15	15	6	19	68
Hall	3-2	2.30	.283	63	0	0	20	0	2	54.2	58	15	14	3	26	39
Valdes	10-11	2.65	.234	30	30	0	0	0	0	196.2	171	68	58	16	47	140
Dreifort	5-2	2.86	.202	48	0	0	15	0	4	63.0	45	21	20	3	34	63
Radinsky	5-1	2.89	.236	75	0	0	14	0	3	62.1	54	22	20	4	21	44
Park	14-8	3.38	.213	32	29	2	1	0	0	192.0	149	80	72	24	70	166
Candiotti	10-7	3.60	.248	41	18	0	6	0	0	135.0	128	60	54	21	40	89
Martinez	10-5	3.64	.243	22	22	1	0	0	0	133.2	123	64	54	14	68	120
Reyes	2-3	3.83	.280	14	5	0	0	0	0	47.0	51	21	20	4	18	36
Nomo	14-12	4.25	.243	33	33	1	0	0	0	207.1	193	104	98	23	92	233
Harkey	1-0	4.30	.211	10	0	0	5	0	0	14.2	12	8	7	3	5	6
Worrell	2-6	5.28	.250	65	0	0	55	0	35	59.2	60	38	35	12	23	61
Guthrie	1-4	5.32	.272	62	0	0	18	0	1	69.1	71	44	41	12	30	42
Gorecki	1-0	15.00	.346	4	1	0	2	0	0	6.0	9	10	10	3	6	6

1998 preliminary roster

PITCHERS (17)
Will Brunson
Jim Bruske
Marc Deschenes
Darren Dreifort
Ignacio Flores
Mark Guthrie
Darren Hall
Mike Judd
Frank Lankford
Ramon Martinez
Hideo Nomo

Antonio Osuna
Chan Ho Park
Scott Radinsky
Gary Rath
Dennis Reyes
Ismael Valdes

CATCHERS (5)
Henry Blanco
Paul LoDuca
Angel Pena
Mike Piazza

Tom Prince

INFIELDERS (12)
Juan Castro
Tripp Cromer
Wilton Guerrero
Garey Ingram
Eric Karros
Paul Konerko
Mike Metcalfe
Brian Richardson
Adam Riggs

Jose Vizcaino
Eric Young
Todd Zeile

OUTFIELDERS (6)
Billy Ashley
Roger Cedeno
Kevin Gibbs
Todd Hollandsworth
Matt Luke
Raul Mondesi

Games played by position

PLAYER	G	C	1B	2B	3B	SS	OF
Anthony	47	0	0	0	0	0	21
Ashley	71	0	0	0	0	0	35
Blanco	3	0	1	0	1	0	0
Butler	105	0	0	0	0	0	91
Castro	40	0	0	14	3	22	0
Cedeno	80	0	0	0	0	0	71
Cromer	28	0	0	17	1	10	0
Fonville	9	0	0	3	0	0	0
Gagne	144	0	0	0	0	143	0
Garcia	15	0	0	0	0	0	12
Guerrero	111	0	0	90	0	5	0
Hale	14	0	0	0	2	0	0
Hollandsworth	106	0	0	0	0	0	99
Ingram	12	0	0	0	0	0	7
Karros	162	0	162	0	0	0	0
Kirby	46	0	0	0	0	0	26
Konerko	6	0	1	0	1	0	0
Lewis	26	0	0	0	0	0	25
Liriano	76	0	2	17	1	1	0
Mondesi	159	0	0	0	0	0	159
Murray	9	0	0	0	0	0	0
Nixon	42	0	0	0	0	0	42
Piazza	152	139	0	0	0	0	0
Prince	47	45	0	0	0	0	0
Riggs	9	0	0	8	0	0	0
Young	155	0	0	154	0	0	0
Zeile	160	0	0	0	160	0	0

Sick call: 1997 DL report

PLAYER	Days on the DL
Brett Butler	27
Juan Castro	58
Roger Cedeno	54*
Tripp Cromer	62
Darren Dreifort	36
Karim Garcia	10
Todd Hollandsworth	35*
Nelson Liriano	11
Ramon Martinez	66
Ismael Valdes	22

* Indicates two separate terms on Disabled List.

1997 salaries

	Bonuses	Total earned salary
Mike Piazza,c		7,000,000
Ramon Martinez,p		4,800,000
Eric Karros,1b		4,500,000
Todd Worrell,p		3,750,000
Eric Young,2b		3,200,000
Todd Zeile,3b		3,100,000
Greg Gagne,ss		3,000,000
Tom Candiotti,p		3,000,000
Raul Mondesi,of		2,700,000
Otis Nixon,of		2,500,000
Brett Butler,of	1,233,304	1,733,304
Mark Guthrie,p		1,600,000
Darren Lewis,of	25,000	1,325,000
Scott Radinsky,p		900,000
Hideo Nomo,p		900,000
Ismael Valdes,p		900,000
Todd Hollandsworth,of		550,000
Nelson Liriano,2b		375,000
Darren Hall,p	90,000	365,000
Tom Prince,c		350,000
Antonio Osuna,p		300,000
Billy Ashley,of		275,000
Chan Ho Park,p		270,000
Darren Dreifort,p		220,000
Juan Castro,ss		215,000
Roger Cedeno,of		200,000
Tripp Cromer,2b		181,000
Garey Ingram,2b		176,000

Average 1997 salary: $1,728,047
Total 1997 payroll: $48,385,304

Minor Leagues
Tops in the organization

BATTER	CLUB	AVG.	G	AB	R	H	HR	RBI
Gibbs, Kevin	San	.335	101	358	89	120	2	34
LoDuca, Paul	San	.327	105	385	63	126	7	69
Konerko, Paul	Abq	.323	130	483	97	156	37	127
Roberge, J.P.	San	.322	134	516	94	166	17	105
Beltre, Adrian	VB	.317	123	435	95	138	26	104

HOME RUNS			WINS		
Konerko, Paul	Abq	37	Pearsall, J.J.	SBr	14
Williams, Eddie	Abq	29	Reyes, Dennis	Abq	14
Diaz, Juan	VB	26	Williams, Jeff	SBr	12
Beltre, Adrian	VB	26	Pyc, Dave	Abq	12
Anderson, Cliff	SBr	21	Mitchell, Dean	SBr	11

RBI			SAVES		
Konerko, Paul	Abq	127	Ricabal, Dan	VB	28
Roberge, J.P.	San	105	Kubenka, Jeff	San	25
Beltre, Adrian	VB	104	LaGarde, Joe	San	17
Richardson, B.	San	90	Mitchell, Dean	SBr	16
Diaz, Juan	VB	86	Harkey, Mike	Abq	15

STOLEN BASES			STRIKEOUTS		
Metcalfe, Mike	SBr	67	Judd, Mike	San	169
Nelson, Charles	VB	53	Lilly, Ted	SBr	158
Avila, Rolo	SBr	52	O'Shaughnessy, J.	Sav	150
Gibbs, Kevin	San	49	Masaoka, Onan	VB	132
Pimentel, Jose	VB	41	Pincavitch, Kevin	SBr	130

PITCHER	CLUB	W-L	ERA	IP	H	BB	SO
Feliciano, Pedro	VB	3- 7	2.67	108	93	39	95
Lilly, Ted	SBr	7- 8	2.81	135	116	32	158
Mitchell, Dean	SBr	11- 5	2.85	123	110	26	119
Judd, Mike	San	10- 7	3.15	166	136	72	169
Flores, Ignacio	San	10- 7	3.25	133	125	39	102

Los Angeles (1958-1997), includes Brooklyn (1890-1957)

Runs: Most, career

1338	Pee Wee Reese, 1940-1958
1255	Zack Wheat, 1909-1926
1199	Duke Snider, 1947-1962
1163	Jim Gilliam, 1953-1966
1088	Gil Hodges, 1943-1961

Hits: Most, career

2804	Zack Wheat, 1909-1926
2170	Pee Wee Reese, 1940-1958
2091	Willie Davis, 1960-1973
1995	Duke Snider, 1947-1962
1968	Steve Garvey, 1969-1982

2B: Most, career

464	Zack Wheat, 1909-1926
343	Duke Snider, 1947-1962
333	Steve Garvey, 1969-1982
330	Pee Wee Reese, 1940-1958
324	Carl Furillo, 1946-1960

3B: Most, career

171	Zack Wheat, 1909-1926
110	Willie Davis, 1960-1973
97	Hy Myers, 1909-1922
87	Jake Daubert, 1910-1918
82	John Hummel, 1905-1915
82	Duke Snider, 1947-1962

HR: Most, career

389	Duke Snider, 1947-1962
361	Gil Hodges, 1943-1961
242	Roy Campanella, 1948-1957
228	Ron Cey, 1971-1982
211	Steve Garvey, 1969-1982

RBI: Most, career

1271	Duke Snider, 1947-1962
1254	Gil Hodges, 1943-1961
1210	Zack Wheat, 1909-1926
1058	Carl Furillo, 1946-1960
992	Steve Garvey, 1969-1982

SB: Most, career

490	Maury Wills, 1959-1972
418	Davey Lopes, 1972-1981
335	Willie Davis, 1960-1973
298	Tom Daly, 1890-1901
290	Steve Sax, 1981-1988

BB: Most, career

1210	Pee Wee Reese, 1940-1958
1036	Jim Gilliam, 1953-1966
925	Gil Hodges, 1943-1961
893	Duke Snider, 1947-1962
765	Ron Cey, 1971-1982

BA: Highest, career

.352	Willie Keeler, 1893-1902
.339	Babe Herman, 1926-1945
.337	Jack Fournier, 1923-1926
.334	MIKE PIAZZA, 1992-1997
.317	Zack Wheat, 1909-1926

On-base avg: Highest, career

.421	Jack Fournier, 1923-1926
.416	Augie Galan, 1941-1946
.409	Jackie Robinson, 1947-1956
.405	Eddie Stanky, 1944-1947
.398	MIKE PIAZZA, 1992-1997 (6)

Slug avg: Highest, career

.576	MIKE PIAZZA, 1992-1997
.557	Babe Herman, 1926-1945
.553	Duke Snider, 1947-1962
.552	Jack Fournier, 1923-1926
.528	Reggie Smith, 1976-1981

Games started: Most, career

533	Don Sutton, 1966-1988
465	Don Drysdale, 1956-1969
335	Claude Osteen, 1965-1973
332	Brickyard Kennedy, 1892-1901
327	Dazzy Vance, 1922-1935

Complete games: Most, career

279	Brickyard Kennedy, 1892-1901
212	Dazzy Vance, 1922-1935
205	Burleigh Grimes, 1918-1926
186	Nap Rucker, 1907-1916
167	Don Drysdale, 1956-1969

Saves: Most, career

127	TODD WORRELL, 1993-1997
125	Jim Brewer, 1964-1975
101	Ron Perranoski, 1961-1972
85	Jay Howell, 1988-1992
83	Clem Labine, 1950-1960

Shutouts: Most, career

52	Don Sutton, 1966-1988
49	Don Drysdale, 1956-1969
40	Sandy Koufax, 1955-1966
38	Nap Rucker, 1907-1916
34	Claude Osteen, 1965-1973

Wins: Most, career

233	Don Sutton, 1966-1988
209	Don Drysdale, 1956-1969
190	Dazzy Vance, 1922-1935
177	Brickyard Kennedy, 1892-1901
165	Sandy Koufax, 1955-1966

K: Most, career

2696	Don Sutton, 1966-1988
2486	Don Drysdale, 1956-1969
2396	Sandy Koufax, 1955-1966
1918	Dazzy Vance, 1922-1935
1759	FERNANDO VALENZUELA, 1980-1990

Win pct: Highest, career

.715	Preacher Roe, 1948-1954
.682	Jay Hughes, 1899-1902
.674	Tommy John, 1972-1978
.658	Billy Loes, 1950-1956
.655	Sandy Koufax, 1955-1966

ERA: Lowest, career

2.31	Jeff Pfeffer, 1913-1921
2.42	Nap Rucker, 1907-1916
2.56	Ron Perranoski, 1961-1972
2.58	Rube Marquard, 1915-1920
2.62	Jim Brewer, 1964-1975

Runs: Most, season

148	Hub Collins, 1890
143	Babe Herman, 1930
140	Mike Griffin, 1895
140	Willie Keeler, 1899
130	Maury Wills, 1962 (10)

Hits: Most, season

241	Babe Herman, 1930
230	Tommy Davis, 1962
221	Zack Wheat, 1925
219	Lefty O'Doul, 1932
217	Babe Herman, 1929

2B: Most, season

52	Johnny Frederick, 1929
48	Babe Herman, 1930
47	Wes Parker, 1970
44	Johnny Frederick, 1930
43	Augie Galan, 1944
43	Babe Herman, 1931
43	Steve Sax, 1986

3B: Most, season

26	George Treadway, 1894
22	Hy Myers, 1920
20	Dan Brouthers, 1892
20	Tommy Corcoran, 1894
19	Jimmy Sheckard, 1901
16	Willie Davis, 1970 (12)

HR: Most, season

43	Duke Snider, 1956
42	Gil Hodges, 1954
42	Duke Snider, 1953
42	Duke Snider, 1955
41	Roy Campanella, 1953
40	MIKE PIAZZA, 1997 (6)

RBI: Most, season

153	Tommy Davis, 1962
142	Roy Campanella, 1953

136	Duke Snider, 1955
130	Jack Fournier, 1925
130	Babe Herman, 1930
130	Gil Hodges, 1954
130	Duke Snider, 1954

SB: Most, season

104	Maury Wills, 1962
94	Maury Wills, 1965
88	John Ward, 1892
85	Hub Collins, 1890
77	Davey Lopes, 1975

BB: Most, season

148	Eddie Stanky, 1945
137	Eddie Stanky, 1946
119	Dolph Camilli, 1938
116	Pee Wee Reese, 1949
110	Jim Wynn, 1975 (6)

BA: Highest, season

.393	Babe Herman, 1930
.381	Babe Herman, 1929
.379	Willie Keeler, 1899
.375	Zack Wheat, 1924
.368	Lefty O'Doul, 1932
.362	MIKE PIAZZA, 1997 (7)

On-base avg: Highest, season

.467	Mike Griffin, 1894
.455	Babe Herman, 1930
.446	Jack Fournier, 1925
.444	Mike Griffin, 1895
.440	Jackie Robinson, 1952
.434	Wally Moon, 1961 (9)

Slug avg: Highest, season

.678	Babe Herman, 1930
.647	Duke Snider, 1954
.638	MIKE PIAZZA, 1997
.628	Duke Snider, 1955
.627	Duke Snider, 1953

Games started: Most, season

44	George Haddock, 1892
44	Brickyard Kennedy, 1893
44	Adonis Terry, 1890
43	Tom Lovett, 1891
42	Don Drysdale, 1963
42	Don Drysdale, 1965
42	Ed Stein, 1892

Complete games: Most, season

40	Brickyard Kennedy, 1893
39	George Haddock, 1892
39	Tom Lovett, 1890
39	Tom Lovett, 1891
27	Sandy Koufax, 1965 (*)
27	Sandy Koufax, 1966 (*)

Saves: Most, season

44	TODD WORRELL, 1996
35	TODD WORRELL, 1997
32	TODD WORRELL, 1995
28	Jay Howell, 1989
25	Jim Gott, 1993

Shutouts: Most, season

11	Sandy Koufax, 1963
9	Don Sutton, 1972
8	TIM BELCHER, 1989
8	Don Drysdale, 1968
8	OREL HERSHISER, 1988
8	Sandy Koufax, 1965
8	FERNANDO VALENZUELA, 1981

Wins: Most, season

30	Tom Lovett, 1890
29	George Haddock, 1892
28	Jay Hughes, 1899
28	Joe McGinnity, 1900
28	Dazzy Vance, 1924
27	Sandy Koufax, 1966 (6)

K: Most, season

382	Sandy Koufax, 1965
317	Sandy Koufax, 1966
306	Sandy Koufax, 1963
269	Sandy Koufax, 1961
262	Dazzy Vance, 1924

Win pct: Highest, season

.889	Freddie Fitzsimmons, 1940
.880	Preacher Roe, 1951
.864	OREL HERSHISER, 1985
.842	Ron Perranoski, 1963
.833	Sandy Koufax, 1963

ERA: Lowest, season

1.58	Rube Marquard, 1916
1.68	Ned Garvin, 1904
1.73	Sandy Koufax, 1966
1.74	Sandy Koufax, 1964
1.87	Kaiser Wilhelm, 1908

Most pinch-hit homers, season

6	Johnny Frederick, 1932
5	Lee Lacy, 1978
5	BILLY ASHLEY, 1996

Most pinch-hit homers, career

8	Johnny Frederick, 1929-1934
8	Lee Lacy, 1972-1978
7	BILLY ASHLEY, 1992-1997
7	Duke Snider, 1947-1962

Longest hitting streak

31	Willie Davis, 1969
29	Zack Wheat, 1916
27	Joe Medwick, 1942
27	Duke Snider, 1953
26	Willie Keeler, 1902
26	Zack Wheat, 1918

Most consecutive scoreless innings

59	OREL HERSHISER, 1988
58	Don Drysdale, 1968
39	Don Newcombe, 1956

No-hit games

Tom Lovett, Bro vs NY NL, 4-0; June 22, 1891.

Mal Eason, Bro at StL NL, 2-0; July 20, 1906.

Harry McIntyre, Bro vs Pit NL, 0-1; Aug. 1, 1906 (lost on four hits in 13 innings after allowing the first hit in the 11th).

Nap Rucker, Bro vs Bos NL, 6-0; Sept. 5, 1908 (2nd game).

Dazzy Vance, Bro vs Phi NL, 10-1; Sept. 13, 1925 (1st game).

Tex Carleton, Bro at Cin NL, 3-0; April 30, 1940.

Ed Head, Bro vs Bos NL, 5-0; April 23, 1946.

Rex Barney, Bro at NY NL, 2-0; Sept. 9, 1948.

Carl Erskine, Bro vs Chi NL, 5-0; June 19, 1952.

Carl Erskine, Bro vs NY NL, 3-0; May 12, 1956.

Sal Maglie, Bro vs Phi NL, 5-0; Sept. 25, 1956.

Sandy Koufax, LA vs NY NL, 5-0; June 30, 1962.

Sandy Koufax, LA vs SF NL, 8-0; May 11, 1963.

Sandy Koufax, LA at Phi NL, 3-0; June 4, 1964.

Sandy Koufax, LA vs Chi NL, 1-0; Sept. 9, 1965 (perfect game).

Bill Singer, LA vs Phi NL, 5-0; July 20, 1970.

Jerry Reuss, LA at SF NL, 8-0; June 27, 1980.

FERNANDO VALENZUELA, LA vs StL NL, 6-0; June 29, 1990.

KEVIN GROSS, LA vs SF NL, 2-0; Aug. 17, 1992.

RAMON MARTINEZ, LA vs Fla NL, 7-0; July 14, 1995.

HIDEO NOMO, LA at Col, 9-0; Sept. 17, 1996.

Ed Stein, six innings, rain, Bro vs Chi NL, 6-0; June 2, 1894.

Fred Frankhouse, seven and two-thirds innings, rain, Bro vs Cin NL, 5-0; Aug. 27, 1937.

ACTIVE PLAYERS in caps.

Players' years of service are listed by the first and last years with this team and are not necessarily consecutive; all statistics record performances for this team only.

Leader from the franchise's current location is included. If not in the top five, leader's rank is listed in paren-thesis; asterisk (*) indicates player is not in top 25.

Colorado Rockies

Larry Walker's .366 average and league-leading 49 homers helped him to win Colorado's first MVP trophy.

1997 Rockies: Thin air, thinner pitching

The Colorado Rockies finished 83-79 and third in the National League West for the second straight season. The outlook was bright when the Rockies got off to a 21-9 start. But Kevin Ritz, Mark Thompson, Bill Swift, Jamey Wright and Roger Bailey—the five starters in the team's Opening Day rotation—were all on the disabled list at one point. A lack of pitching depth eventually caught up with manager Don Baylor's club. The Rockies seemingly fell out of the race when they lost 15 of 16 games in July. They climbed back above .500 by winning 20 of 25 games in August and September, but they were never able to pull closer than 4½ games of first place.

The standard perception is that Colorado hitters put up big numbers at Coors Field and struggle on the road. That wasn't the case with Larry Walker in 1997. Walker finished with 49 homers, 130 RBI and a .366 average, making a serious run at becomng the first Triple Crown winner since 1967. Walker hit .346 with 29 homers, 62 RBI and a .733 slugging percentage away from Coors Field. First baseman Andres Galarraga led the league in RBI for the second straight year, and third baseman Vinny Castilla hit 40 homers for the second straight season.

Colorado led the NL in hitting at .288 and set an NL record with 239 homers. The Rockies had four 30-homer players for the fourth consecutive year and a trio with 40 for the second straight season. Despite a persistent hamstring injury, center fielder Ellis Burks hit .290 with 32 homers and 82 RBI. Left fielder Dante Bichette, gimpy all season following reconstructive knee surgery in October 1996, batted .308 with 26 homers and 118 RBI. Even backup catcher Jeff Reed hit .297 with a career-high 17 homers. He took significant time away from Kirt Manwaring, who threw out only 24 of 101 runners attempting to steal while hitting .226 with no power.

The Rockies' pitching staff should be better in 1998, as Wright and Bailey will benefit from having had a full year under their belts. The Rockies finished with a 5.25 ERA, but the situation stabilized in August thanks to the acquisition of Dodger Pedro Astacio, who went 5-1 for the Rockies, and Frank Castillo, who went 6-3. Rookie right-hander John Thomson pitched well late in the year. Veteran Jerry DiPoto settled nicely into the closer role, getting 16 saves in 21 chances.

Neifi Perez and Todd Helton also figure prominently in the Rockies' plans for 1998. The Rockies traded Eric Young to Los Angeles to make room for Perez. He impressed the Rockies with his play at second base, but his range and arm are better suited for shortstop. Perez closed out the season with a five-hit game against Los Angeles and set a club record for triples (10) in a season. The Rockies see Helton as a line-drive hitter in the Keith Hernandez–Don Mattingly mold. Helton spent October in the instructional league to learn the outfield but may get a chance at first base, his best position, with the departure of Galarraga, who signed with Atlanta as a free agent.

Stephen Shoemaker, a hard thrower in AA last year, may win a job in the Rockies bullpen. Outfielders Derrick Gibson and Edgard Velazquez are top prospects in the organization, but look for both of them to begin the 1998 season with AAA Colorado Springs.

Team MVP

Larry Walker: Larry Walker didn't win the Triple Crown. But that's about the only negative thing you could find to say about the Rockies right fielder in 1997. He won a Gold Glove in addition to his home run title and was second in batting (.366) and third in RBI (130). Topping it off was his winning the league MVP Award.

1997 Rockies: Week-by-week notes

These notes were excerpted from the following issues of Baseball Weekly.

▶**April 9:** Right fielder Larry Walker hit .476 (10-for-21) with six homers in the first five games of the season-opening road trip to Cincinnati and Montreal. Those numbers were a significant departure from last season, when he batted .142 with six homers in 127 road at-bats.

▶**April 16:** After losing their first two games in Cincinnati, the Rockies reeled off seven consecutive victories against the Expos and the Reds. The rotation of Kevin Ritz, Bill Swift, Mark Thompson, Jamey Wright and Roger Bailey went 7-0 with a 3.00 ERA in that span.

▶**April 23:** Two days after right-hander Roger Bailey beat Chicago 4-0 at Wrigley Field for the first complete-game road shutout in franchise history, the pitching staff had a few setbacks. Manager Don Baylor learned on April 18 that right-handers Swift and Thompson would each miss a start because of injuries.

▶**April 30:** Colorado pitchers allowed a league-high 624 walks last year. Through the first three weeks of this season, they had allowed 54 walks, the fewest in the league. The Rockies also made only 11 errors in the first 20 games, tied with San Francisco for best in the NL.

▶**May 7:** Catcher Kirt Manwaring will never win a Silver Slugger award to put alongside his 1993 Gold Glove, but he's doing his share for the offense. He batted .333 in the team's first 27 games.

▶**May 14:** On April 15, Mark Thompson was 3-0 and apparently on his way to a big year. Then he went 0-3 with a 12.71 ERA in his next three starts. His fastball, clocked at 90-94 mph on the radar gun last season, was suddenly registering 84-87 mph. The Rockies sent him for an MRI test, and it revealed a rotator cuff strain, so Thompson is on the 15-day DL.

▶**May 28:** While the Rockies lost 10 of 13 games on their longest road trip of the season, their closer also lost his ability to throw strikes. Closer Bruce Ruffin

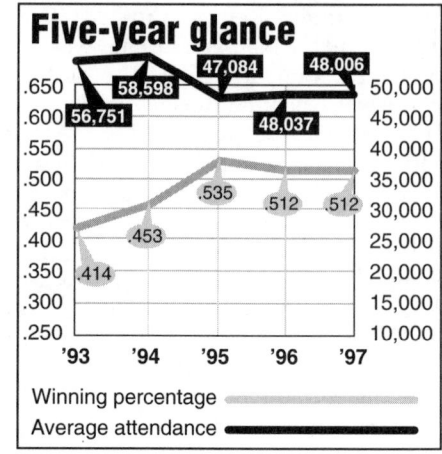

Five-year glance

Winning percentage
Average attendance

walked three consecutive batters in a 10-4 loss to New York. and didn't pitch again on the trip. After four discouraging bullpen sessions, he went on the DL on May 25. After batting .360 with nine homers and 25 RBI in April, third baseman Vinny Castilla hit .151 (11-for-73) with six RBI in Colorado's first 23 games in May.

▶**June 4:** Things turned ugly when a pitch from Florida's Dennis Cook hit first baseman Andres Galarraga in the left elbow on May 31. Galarraga, who suffered a broken left hand when he was hit by Chicago's Kevin Foster in April, charged the mound in anger. Both benches emptied before umpires restored order, and Galarraga was ejected. It's understandable that the Marlins might have wanted to keep Galarraga honest. In addition to a 529-foot blast off Kevin Brown earlier that day, Galarraga also pounded shots that traveled 445 and 451 feet during the series.

▶**June 11:** Kirt Manwaring has yet to live up to his reputation as one of baseball's better throwers. Through the first 59 games, he threw out 18% (9-for-51) of runners attempting to steal. Last season, he checked in at 45% (37-for-83) with San Francisco and Houston.

▶**June 18:** Larry Walker homered in a 7-1 victory against Oakland on June 14 and again in a 5-2 loss the next day to raise his average to .417. Don Baylor said he doesn't think a .400 season is out of the question. Walker, true to form, cringed at the mere mention of .400. "I'd say I have about a 'zero percent' chance of doing it," he said.

▶**July 2:** Left fielder Dante Bichette hit two home runs off Mark Gardner and drove in six runs in Colorado's 9-2 victory against San Francisco on June 28. It marked the 15th time in 16 games that Bichette had hit safely. Bichette has been tentative in the outfield and has had difficulty driving the ball. He hit only 10 homers in Colorado's first 79 games. But he's made some adjustments with his hands and continues to see improvement with his reconstructed knee.

▶**July 10:** Reliever Jerry DiPoto broke Bruce Ruffin's franchise record for consecutive shutout innings when he extended his streak to 17 in a 4-0 loss to San Francisco on July 4. During his roll, DiPoto has pared his ERA from 7.49 to 4.97.

▶**July 16:** When the Rockies signed right-hander Kevin Ritz to a three-year, $9 million contract over the winter, they were looking for 200 innings, 15 or so victories and stability at the top of their rotation. But Ritz spent the better part of April, May and June getting pummeled, and now he's lost for the season with an injury. Colorado's Opening Day rotation consisted of Ritz, Bill Swift, Mark Thompson, Jamey Wright and Roger Bailey. All five have been on the DL.

▶**July 23:** The Rockies dropped a doubleheader on July 19 at Wrigley Field before scoring a 9-5 victory the next day. They have 15 losses in 17 games. After topping out at 21-9 on May 6, the Rockies have gone 24-45.

▶**July 30:** Amid speculation that general manager Bob Gebhard or Don Baylor might be in trouble, owner Jerry McMorris threw his support behind both men. After winning only two of their first 18 games in July, the Rockies won five consecutive games through July 27.

▶**Aug. 6:** The Rockies took a major step toward the future when they summoned first baseman–outfielder Todd Helton from Colorado Springs. Helton was hit-

ting .352 with 16 homers and 88 RBI at Colorado Springs. In his first game, he hit a home run and a single in a 6-5 loss to Pittsburgh.

▶**Aug. 13:** Neifi Perez isn't just another slap-hitting middle infielder from the Dominican Republic. In his first 142 at-bats with Colorado this season, Perez batted .303 with 16 extra-base hits—seven doubles, four triples and five home runs.

▶**Aug. 20:** Jerry DiPoto is settling in as Colorado's closer. He converted his sixth consecutive save on Aug. 17 in a 6-4 victory against the Mets.

▶**Sept. 10:** Roger Bailey, Colorado's most effective pitcher in April and May, has been stuck on nine victories since July 26. He has failed to win in eight consecutive starts and is now 9-9 with a 4.42 ERA.

▶**Sept. 17:** The Rockies traded away their only bona fide leadoff hitter when they sent second baseman Eric Young to Los Angeles for pitcher Pedro Astacio in August. But veteran shortstop Walt Weiss, who is most comfortable batting second or eighth, has done a creditable job of filling the void.

▶**Sept. 24:** Larry Walker made history twice with one swing in Colorado's 2-1 victory against Los Angeles on Sept. 20. With his 45th double, he tied the team record shared by Ellis Burks and Charlie Hayes. More important, he became the first NL player to reach the 400-total-base mark since the Braves' Hank Aaron in 1959. Jim Rice did it for Boston in 1978. Walker also broke Andres Galarraga's club record when he hit his 48th home run last week in San Diego.

▶**Oct. 1:** Andres Galarraga became the first player to lead the NL in RBI in back-to-back seasons since Atlanta's Dale Murphy in 1982 and '83. He finished with 140 for a two-year total of 290 RBI.

QUOTE OF THE YEAR

"You can't just say, 'We need a leadoff hitter.' We might have a player at that position."

—General manager Bob Gebhard, responding to criticism after trading leadoff man Eric Young

COLORADO ROCKIES 1997 final stats

BATTERS	BA	SLG	OBA	G	AB	R	H	TB	2B	3B	HR	RBI	BB	SO	SB	CS	E
Gonzales	.500	.500	.500	2	2	0	1	1	0	0	0	1	0	0	0	0	0
Walker	.366	.720	.452	153	568	143	208	409	46	4	49	130	78	90	33	8	2
Raabe	.333	.333	.333	2	3	0	1	1	0	0	0	0	0	1	0	0	0
Galarraga	.318	.585	.389	154	600	120	191	351	31	3	41	140	54	141	15	8	15
Bichette	.308	.510	.343	151	561	81	173	286	31	2	26	118	30	90	6	5	3
Castilla	.304	.547	.356	159	612	94	186	335	25	2	40	113	44	108	2	4	21
J. Reed	.297	.535	.386	90	256	43	76	137	10	0	17	47	35	55	2	1	6
McCracken	.292	.360	.374	147	325	69	95	117	11	1	3	36	42	62	28	11	4
Perez	.291	.444	.333	83	313	46	91	139	13	10	5	31	21	43	4	3	9
Burks	.290	.571	.363	119	424	91	123	242	19	2	32	82	47	75	7	2	4
Pulliam	.284	.463	.333	59	67	15	19	31	3	0	3	9	5	15	0	1	1
Helton	.280	.484	.337	35	93	13	26	45	2	1	5	11	8	11	0	1	0
Weiss	.270	.384	.377	121	393	52	106	151	23	5	4	38	66	56	5	2	10
Echevarria	.250	.350	.318	15	20	4	5	7	2	0	0	0	2	5	0	0	0
Bates	.240	.397	.338	62	121	17	29	48	10	0	3	11	15	27	0	1	3
Manwaring	.226	.276	.291	104	337	22	76	93	6	4	1	27	30	78	1	5	3
Vander Wal	.174	.228	.255	76	92	7	16	21	2	0	1	11	10	33	1	1	1

PITCHERS	W-L	ERA	BA	G	GS	CG	GF	Sho	SV	IP	H	R	ER	HR	BB	SO
DeJean	5-0	3.99	.280	55	0	0	15	0	2	67.2	74	34	30	4	24	38
S. Reed	4-6	4.04	.219	63	0	0	23	0	6	62.1	49	28	28	10	27	43
Astacio	12-11	4.14	.258	33	31	2	2	1	0	202.1	200	98	93	24	61	166
Bailey	9-10	4.29	.283	29	29	5	0	2	0	91.0	210	103	91	27	70	84
McCurry	1-4	4.43	.277	33	0	0	14	0	0	40.2	43	22	20	7	20	19
Hutton	3-2	4.48	.314	40	1	0	9	0	0	60.1	72	34	30	10	26	39
Munoz	3-3	4.53	.294	64	0	0	16	0	2	45.2	52	25	23	4	13	26
DiPoto	5-3	4.70	.288	74	0	0	33	0	16	95.2	108	56	50	6	33	74
Thomson	7-9	4.71	.296	27	27	2	0	1	0	166.1	193	94	87	15	51	106
Ruffin	0-2	5.32	.220	23	0	0	15	0	7	22.0	18	15	13	3	18	31
Holmes	9-2	5.34	.314	42	0	0	10	0	3	89.1	113	58	53	12	36	70
Beckett	0-0	5.40	.167	2	0	0	2	0	0	1.2	1	1	1	0	1	2
Castillo	12-12	5.42	.300	34	33	0	0	0	0	184.1	220	121	111	25	69	126
Leskanic	4-0	5.55	.271	55	0	0	23	0	2	58.1	59	36	36	8	24	53
Rekar	1-0	5.79	.282	2	2	0	0	0	0	9.1	11	7	6	3	6	4
Ritz	6-8	5.87	.330	18	18	1	0	0		0	107.1	142	72	70	16	46	56
Wright	8-12	6.25	.327	26	26	1	0	0	0	149.2	198	113	104	19	71	59
Swift	4-6	6.34	.318	14	13	0	1	0	0	65.1	85	57	46	11	26	29
Burke	2-5	6.56	.329	17	9	0	1	0	0	59.0	83	46	43	13	26	39
Thompson	3-3	7.89	.323	6	6	0	0	0	0	29.2	40	27	26	8	13	9
Scott	1-1	8.14	.337	17	0	0	2	0	0	21.0	30	20	19	2	7	16
Jones	1-1	8.38	.380	4	4	0	0	0	0	19.1	30	18	18	2	12	5
Minchey	0-0	13.50	.556	2	0	0	0	0	0	2.0	5	3	3	0	1	1

294

1998 preliminary roster

PITCHERS (23)
Pedro Astacio
Roger Bailey
Robbie Beckett
Mark Brownson
John Burke
Mike DeJean
Jerry DiPoto
Lariel Gonzalez
Luther Hackman
Mark Hutton
Bobby Jones

Darryl Kile
Curtis Leskanic
Jeff McCurry
Chuck McElroy
Scott Randall
Kevin Ritz
Mike Saipe
Steve Shoemaker
Mark Thompson
John Thomson
Mike Vavrek
Jamey Wright

CATCHERS (2)
Kirt Manwaring
Jeff Reed

INFIELDERS (7)
Jason Bates
Vinny Castilla
Mike Coolbaugh
Todd Helton
Mike Lansing
Neifi Perez
Chris Sexton

OUTFIELDERS (8)
Dante Bichette
Ellis Burks
Angel Echevarria
Derrick Gibson
Curtis Goodwin
John Vander Wal
Edgard Velazquez
Larry Walker

Games played by position

PLAYER	G	C	1B	2B	3B	SS	OF
Bates	62	0	0	22	6	16	0
Bichette	151	0	0	0	0	0	139
Burks	119	0	0	0	0	0	112
Castilla	159	0	0	0	157	0	0
Coles	21	0	0	0	3	0	2
Echevarria	15	0	0	0	0	0	7
Galarraga	154	0	154	0	0	0	0
Gonzales	2	0	0	0	1	0	0
Helton	35	0	8	0	0	0	15
Manwaring	104	100	0	0	0	0	0
McCracken	147	0	0	0	0	0	132
Perez	83	0	0	41	2	45	0
Pulliam	59	0	0	0	0	0	33
Raabe	2	0	0	1	0	0	0
J. Reed	90	78	0	0	0	0	0
Vander Wal	76	0	5	0	0	0	9
Walker	153	0	3	0	0	0	151
Weiss	121	0	0	0	0	119	0

Minor Leagues

Tops in the organization

BATTER	CLUB	AVG.	G	AB	R	H	HR	RBI
Perez, Neifi	CSp	.363	68	303	68	110	8	46
Helton, Todd	CSp	.352	99	392	87	138	16	88
Counsell, Craig	CSp	.335	96	376	77	126	5	63
Howitt, Dann	CSp	.332	102	316	57	105	14	62
Gibson, Derrick	CSp	.332	140	539	105	179	26	87

HOME RUNS

Gibson, Derrick	CSp	26
Quinlan, Tom	CSp	23
Light, Tal	Sal	20
Several Players Tied at		18

WINS

Minchey, Nate	CSp	15
Westbrook, Jake	Ash	14
Vavrek, Mike	NHv	14
Saipe, Mike	CSp	12
Several Players Tied at		11

RBI

Quinlan, Tom	CSp	113
Helton, Todd	CSp	88
Gibson, Derrick	CSp	87
Barry, Jeff	CSp	82
Curtis, Kevin	NHv	82

SAVES

Bost, Heath	NHv	23
Lee, David	Ash	22
Petrosian, Ara	Por	13
Kramer, Tom	CSp	11
Macca, Chris	NHv	9

STOLEN BASES

Hutchison, B.	Ash	81
Neubart, G.	Sal	50
Jones, Terry	CSp	36
Figgins, D.	Rck	30
Petrick, Ben	Sal	30

STRIKEOUTS

Shoemaker,S.	CSp	214
Brownson, Mark	NHv	170
Saipe, Mike	CSp	163
Chacon, Shawn	Ash	149
Vavrek, Mike	NHv	149

PITCHER	CLUB	W-L	ERA	IP	H	BB	SO
Vavrek, Mike	NHv	14- 5	2.43	185	149	52	149
Kusiewicz, M.	Sal	10-10	3.27	146	140	42	118
Shoemaker, S.	CSp	10- 8	3.60	168	118	95	214
Nicholson, J.	Ash	8- 9	3.78	136	128	36	115
Randall, Scott	Sal	9-10	3.84	176	167	66	128
Saipe, Mike	CSp	12- 8	3.84	197	201	53	163

Sick call: 1997 DL report

PLAYER	Days on the DL
Garvin Alston	181
Roger Bailey	15
Ellis Burks	31
Mike DeJean	21
Darren Holmes	15
Curt Leskanic	11
Kevin Ritz	80
Bruce Ruffin	123*
Bill Swift	59
Mark Thompson	144
Walt Weiss	17
Jamey Wright	24

Indicates two separate terms on Disabled List.

1997 salaries

	Bonuses	Total earned salary
Larry Walker,of	575,000	6,325,000
Dante Bichette,of	500,000	5,166,667
Andres Galarraga,1b	250,000	4,950,000
Ellis Burks,of		4,000,000
Pedro Astacio,p		2,900,000
Walt Weiss,ss	100,000	2,700,000
Kevin Ritz,p		2,500,000
Vinny Castilla,3b	225,000	2,225,000
Frank Castillo,p	340,000	1,740,000
Kirt Manwaring,c	25,000	1,675,000
Steve Reed,p	100,000	1,200,000
Bruce Ruffin,p		1,000,000
Darren Holmes,p		997,500
Jeff Reed,c	100,000	650,000
Jerry DiPoto,p	25,000	550,000
Curt Leskanic,p	16,667	516,667
Mike Munoz,p	20,000	350,000
Mark Thompson,p		252,000
Mark Hutton,p		205,000
Roger Bailey,p		200,000
Quinton McCracken,of		198,000
Jason Bates,ss		195,000
Jamey Wright,p		169,500
Garvin Alston,p		152,000
Harvey Pulliam,of		150,000
Mike De Jean,p		150,000
Neifi Perez,ss		150,000
John Thomson,p		150,000
Todd Helton,1b		150,000

Average 1997 salary: $1,423,356
Total 1997 payroll: $41,567,334

Colorado (1993-1997)

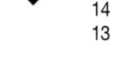

Runs: Most, career

476	ANDRES GALARRAGA, 1993-1997
464	DANTE BICHETTE, 1993-1997
378	ERIC YOUNG, 1993-1997
325	VINNY CASTILLA, 1993-1997
307	ELLIS BURKS, 1994-1997

Hits: Most, career

882	DANTE BICHETTE, 1993-1997
843	ANDRES GALARRAGA, 1993-1997
669	VINNY CASTILLA, 1993-1997
626	ERIC YOUNG, 1993-1997
469	WALT WEISS, 1994-1997

2B: Most, career

184	DANTE BICHETTE, 1993-1997
155	ANDRES GALARRAGA, 1993-1997
113	VINNY CASTILLA, 1993-1997
102	ERIC YOUNG, 1993-1997
95	LARRY WALKER, 1995-1997

3B: Most, career

28	ERIC YOUNG, 1993-1997
19	ELLIS BURKS, 1994-1997
14	DANTE BICHETTE, 1993-1997
14	WALT WEISS, 1994-1997
13	ANDRES GALARRAGA, 1993-1997
13	LARRY WALKER, 1995-1997

HR: Most, career

172	ANDRES GALARRAGA, 1993-1997
145	DANTE BICHETTE, 1993-1997
124	VINNY CASTILLA, 1993-1997
103	LARRY WALKER, 1995-1997
99	ELLIS BURKS, 1994-1997

RBI: Most, career

579	ANDRES GALARRAGA, 1993-1997
571	DANTE BICHETTE, 1993-1997
364	VINNY CASTILLA, 1993-1997
289	LARRY WALKER, 1995-1997
283	ELLIS BURKS, 1994-1997

SB: Most, career

180	ERIC YOUNG, 1993-1997
85	DANTE BICHETTE, 1993-1997
67	LARRY WALKER, 1995-1997
55	ANDRES GALARRAGA, 1993-1997
49	ELLIS BURKS, 1994-1997

BB: Most, career

300	WALT WEISS, 1994-1997
254	ERIC YOUNG, 1993-1997
169	ANDRES GALARRAGA, 1993-1997
163	ELLIS BURKS, 1994-1997
147	LARRY WALKER, 1995-1997

BA: Highest, career

.325	LARRY WALKER, 1995-1997
.316	ANDRES GALARRAGA, 1993-1997
.316	DANTE BICHETTE, 1993-1997
.311	ELLIS BURKS, 1994-1997
.306	Mike Kingery, 1994-1995

On-base avg: Highest, career

.404	LARRY WALKER, 1995-1997
.383	ELLIS BURKS, 1994-1997
.378	ERIC YOUNG, 1993-1997
.375	WALT WEISS, 1994-1997
.375	Mike Kingery, 1994-1995

Slug avg: Highest, career

.648	LARRY WALKER, 1995-1997
.596	ELLIS BURKS, 1994-1997
.577	ANDRES GALARRAGA, 1993-1997
.547	DANTE BICHETTE, 1993-1997
.527	VINNY CASTILLA, 1993-1997

Games started: Most, career

96	KEVIN RITZ, 1994-1997
87	ARMANDO REYNOSO, 1993-1996
59	Marvin Freeman, 1994-1996
46	ROGER BAILEY, 1995-1997
41	MARK THOMPSON, 1994-1997
41	JAMEY WRIGHT, 1996-1997

Complete games: Most, career

5	ROGER BAILEY, 1995-1997
5	ARMANDO REYNOSO, 1993-1996
3	David Nied, 1993-1996
3	KEVIN RITZ, 1994-1997
3	MARK THOMPSON, 1994-1997

Saves: Most, career

60	BRUCE RUFFIN, 1993-1997
46	DARREN HOLMES, 1993-1997
18	CURT LESKANIC, 1993-1997
16	JERRY DiPOTO, 1997-1997
15	STEVE REED, 1993-1997

Shutouts: Most, career

2	ROGER BAILEY, 1995-1997
1	David Nied, 1993-1996
1	MARK THOMPSON, 1994-1997
1	JOHN THOMSON, 1997

Wins: Most, career

39	KEVIN RITZ, 1994-1997
30	ARMANDO REYNOSO, 1993-1996
25	STEVE REED, 1993-1997
23	DARREN HOLMES, 1993-1997
20	Marvin Freeman, 1994-1996

K: Most, career

334	KEVIN RITZ, 1994-1997
319	BRUCE RUFFIN, 1993-1997
297	DARREN HOLMES, 1993-1997
283	CURT LESKANIC, 1993-1997
275	STEVE REED, 1993-1997

Win pct: Highest, career

.639	DARREN HOLMES, 1993-1997
.581	STEVE REED, 1993-1997
.576	CURT LESKANIC, 1993-1997
.526	Marvin Freeman, 1994-1996
.520	KEVIN RITZ, 1994-1997

ERA: Lowest, career

3.68	STEVE REED, 1993-1997
3.84	BRUCE RUFFIN, 1993-1997
4.42	DARREN HOLMES, 1993-1997
4.65	ARMANDO REYNOSO, 1993-1996
4.90	ROGER BAILEY, 1995-1997

Runs: Most, season

143	LARRY WALKER, 1997
142	ELLIS BURKS, 1996
120	ANDRES GALARRAGA, 1997
119	ANDRES GALARRAGA, 1996
114	DANTE BICHETTE, 1996

Hits: Most, season

211	ELLIS BURKS, 1996
208	LARRY WALKER, 1997
198	DANTE BICHETTE, 1996
197	DANTE BICHETTE, 1995
191	VINNY CASTILLA, 1996
191	ANDRES GALARRAGA, 1997

2B: Most, season

46	LARRY WALKER, 1997
45	ELLIS BURKS, 1996
45	CHARLIE HAYES, 1993
43	DANTE BICHETTE, 1993
39	DANTE BICHETTE, 1996
39	ANDRES GALARRAGA, 1996

3B: Most, season

10	NEIFI PEREZ, 1997	
9	ERIC YOUNG, 1995	
8	ELLIS BURKS, 1996	
8	Mike Kingery, 1994	
8	ERIC YOUNG, 1993	

HR: Most, season

49	LARRY WALKER, 1997
47	ANDRES GALARRAGA, 1996
41	ANDRES GALARRAGA, 1997
40	DANTE BICHETTE, 1995
40	ELLIS BURKS, 1996
40	VINNY CASTILLA, 1996
40	VINNY CASTILLA, 1997

RBI: Most, season

150	ANDRES GALARRAGA, 1996
141	DANTE BICHETTE, 1996
140	ANDRES GALARRAGA, 1997
130	LARRY WALKER, 1997
128	DANTE BICHETTE, 1995
128	ELLIS BURKS, 1996

SB: Most, season

53	ERIC YOUNG, 1996
42	ERIC YOUNG, 1993
35	ERIC YOUNG, 1995
33	LARRY WALKER, 1997
32	ELLIS BURKS, 1996
32	ERIC YOUNG, 1997

BB: Most, season

98	WALT WEISS, 1995
80	WALT WEISS, 1996
78	LARRY WALKER, 1997
66	WALT WEISS, 1997
63	ERIC YOUNG, 1993

BA: Highest, season

.370	ANDRES GALARRAGA, 1993
.366	LARRY WALKER, 1997
.344	ELLIS BURKS, 1996
.340	DANTE BICHETTE, 1995
.324	ERIC YOUNG, 1996

On-base avg: Highest, season

.452	LARRY WALKER, 1997
.408	ELLIS BURKS, 1996
.403	ANDRES GALARRAGA, 1993
.403	WALT WEISS, 1995
.393	ERIC YOUNG, 1996

Slug avg: Highest, season

.720	LARRY WALKER, 1997
.639	ELLIS BURKS, 1996
.620	DANTE BICHETTE, 1995
.607	LARRY WALKER, 1995
.602	ANDRES GALARRAGA, 1993

Games started: Most, season

35	KEVIN RITZ, 1996
30	ARMANDO REYNOSO, 1993
30	ARMANDO REYNOSO, 1996
29	ROGER BAILEY, 1997
28	KEVIN RITZ, 1995
28	MARK THOMPSON, 1996

Complete games: Most, season

5	ROGER BAILEY, 1997
4	ARMANDO REYNOSO, 1993
3	MARK THOMPSON, 1996
2	David Nied, 1994
2	KEVIN RITZ, 1996
2	JOHN THOMSON, 1997

Saves: Most, season

25	DARREN HOLMES, 1993
24	BRUCE RUFFIN, 1996
16	JERRY DiPOTO, 1997
16	BRUCE RUFFIN, 1994
14	DARREN HOLMES, 1995

Shutouts: Most, season

2	ROGER BAILEY, 1997
1	David Nied, 1994
1	MARK THOMPSON, 1996
1	JOHN THOMSON, 1997

Wins: Most, season

17	KEVIN RITZ, 1996
12	ARMANDO REYNOSO, 1993
11	KEVIN RITZ, 1995
10	Marvin Freeman, 1994
9	ROGER BAILEY, 1997
9	DARREN HOLMES, 1997
9	David Nied, 1994
9	STEVE REED, 1993
9	BILL SWIFT, 1995
9	MARK THOMPSON, 1996

K: Most, season

126	BRUCE RUFFIN, 1993
120	KEVIN RITZ, 1995
117	ARMANDO REYNOSO, 1993
107	CURT LESKANIC, 1995
106	JOHN THOMSON, 1997

Win pct: Highest, season

.833	Marvin Freeman, 1994
.607	KEVIN RITZ, 1996
.522	ARMANDO REYNOSO, 1993

ERA: Lowest, season

4.00	ARMANDO REYNOSO, 1993
4.21	KEVIN RITZ, 1995
4.29	ROGER BAILEY, 1997
4.71	JOHN THOMSON, 1997
4.96	ARMANDO REYNOSO, 1996

Most pinch-hit homers, season

4	Howard Johnson, 1994
4	JOHN VANDER WAL, 1995

Most pinch-hit homers, career

9	JOHN VANDER WAL, 1994-1997
4	Howard Johnson, 1994

Longest hitting streak

23	DANTE BICHETTE, 1995
22	VINNY CASTILLA, 1997
19	DANTE BICHETTE, 1995 (2nd streak)
19	ERIC YOUNG, 1995
16	DANTE BICHETTE, 1994
16	LARRY WALKER, 1997
16	ERIC YOUNG, 1996

Most consecutive scoreless innings

16	BRUCE RUFFIN, 1993
14	KEVIN RITZ, 1996

No-hit games

ACTIVE PLAYERS in caps.

Players' years of service are listed by the first and last years with this team and are not necessarily consecutive; all statistics record performances for this team only.

San Diego Padres

By David Zalubowski, AP/Wide World Photos

Tony Gwynn's career-high 17 homers and 119 RBI complemented his league-leading .372 batting average.

1997 Padres: The first shall be last

The Padres became the first National League West club to slide from first to worst in a single season, falling from 91 victories to 76. But they can take solace in the fact that San Francisco went from worst to first, and the Padres believe they can repeat the feat. The Padres were second in the league in runs (795) but ranked 13th in ERA (4.98) and committed the most errors (132). Catcher John Flaherty said, "If you're not a fundamentally sound ball club, you're going to be exposed. And we were."

Right fielder Tony Gwynn was very sound at age 37. Not only did he bat .372—his second-highest average—to win his eighth NL batting crown, but he also posted career highs in hits (220), doubles (49), total bases (324), home runs (17) and RBI (119). With the 220 hits, Gwynn put himself exactly that number shy of 3,000 in his career. Left fielder Greg Vaughn, though, hit only .216 with 18 homers and 57 RBI after signing a three-year, $15 million contract. He started wearing contact lenses in August. Third baseman Ken Caminiti, the 1996 league MVP, was hurt all year and slipped to .290 with 26 homers.

Closer Trevor Hoffman was a rock in an ocean of trouble in the bullpen. Hoffman won or saved 43 of the club's 76 victories and converted 37 of 43 save opportunities. Veteran right-hander Pete Smith, free from the chronic shoulder tendinitis that sidetracked his career, had 10 quality starts out of 15. The Padres hoped for 35 wins from Joey Hamilton (12-7, 4.25 ERA) and Andy Ashby (9-11, 4.13 ERA), but both spent time on the DL, and their mediocrity was a big reason why GM Kevin Towers fired pitching coach Dan Warthen.

If the Padres are to revert to their championship form of 1996, they pretty much must do it from within. The Padres say they've lost $41 million since the John Moores–Larry Lucchino ownership took control in December 1994. Moores is convinced the Padres need a new ballpark

to thrive in their market. A public vote on a new baseball-only park is likely to come in 1998. Despite the money problems, the Padres picked up the $3.75 million option on first baseman Wally Joyner's contract. Joyner, 35, batted a career-high .327 with 13 homers and 83 RBI.

The Padres' eight starting position players average 31.4 years old, so a youth movement isn't far away. It won't happen this year, as all eight regulars are signed with the club at least through the 1998 season, but 1997 saw the first influx of the club's next generation. First baseman Derrek Lee got his first taste of the big leagues, batting .259 with 24 strikeouts in 54 at-bats. Outfielder Ruben Rivera, acquired from the Yankees in the Hideki Irabu trade, was injured most of the year but got 20 September at-bats. A strong showing in winter ball might have him pushing Vaughn.

Right-hander Will Cunnane's numbers (6-3, 5.81 ERA) weren't impressive, but he pitched in every role except closer, and manager Bruce Bochy raved about his resiliency. He will compete for a spot in the rotation in spring training. Left-hander Heath Murray (1-2, 6.75 ERA) was disappointing in his 17-game big-league stint and suffered from shoulder problems, but he will be in the mix for a starting spot.

1997 Padres: Week by week notes

These notes were excerpted from the following issues of Baseball Weekly.

▶**April 9**: After being shut out by the Mets' Pete Harnisch for five innings on Opening Day, the Padres scored 11 runs in the sixth en route to a 12-5 victory. The explosion, which started with consecutive homers by shortstop Chris Gomez, pinch-hitter Rickey Henderson and second baseman Quilvio Veras, established a modern-day NL record for runs in an inning on Opening Day.

▶**April 16**: Before breaking out at Philadelphia in an 8-3 victory to open the road trip, the Padres batted .198 in the final five games of their opening home-stand and scored just five runs in dropping two of three to Pittsburgh. The pitchers certainly did their jobs. They combined for a 2.39 ERA in the last seven games, but the Padres went 3-4. Right fielder Tony Gwynn's homer off Pirates lefty Matt Ruebel on April 9 was Gwynn's first in 277 at-bats.

▶**April 30**: With the trade of Hideki Irabu's rights contingent on the Yankees' signing the pitcher, Padres officials were happy about landing outfielder Ruben Rivera and right-hander Rafael Medina. "We got the two players from their organization that we wanted," said president Larry Lucchino. Right-hander Andy Ashby lasted at least seven innings in each of his first five starts while posting a 2.11 ERA.

▶**May 7**: Five Padres went on the DL in an eight-day span—pitcher Dario Veras, center fielder Steve Finley, first baseman Wally Joyner, pitcher Joey Hamilton and infielder Scott Livingstone. The injury list didn't end there. Left fielder Greg Vaughn had an MRI on his sore right knee, though no damage was found. And out-fielder Rickey Henderson, who had been subbing for Finley, missed four games because of a strained calf.

▶**May 14**: Manager Bruce Bochy decided to yank Greg Vaughn from the lineup for a few days to give him time to clear his head. The rest ended up being for only

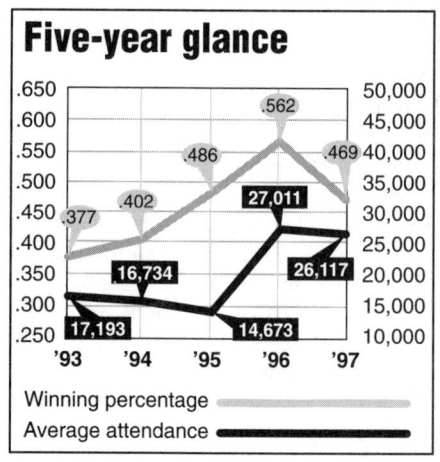

Five-year glance

Winning percentage
Average attendance

one day because Rickey Henderson went on the DL. Batting .179 overall and .071 with runners in scoring position, Vaughn didn't last long in his return to action. He was ejected for the first time in his career for arguing strike calls by umpire Steve Rippley.

▶**May 21**: In his 1996 MVP season, third baseman Ken Caminiti played through a torn left rotator cuff, a painful lower abdominal strain, a bad back, a pulled hamstring and sore knees. He missed only 16 games. So it was no surprise he lobbied hard against going on the DL after reinjuring a strained hamstring on May 11. This time he was overruled by general manager Kevin Towers and was put on the 15-day DL.

▶**May 28**: The Padres finally fashioned their first winning streak. They won five in a row from May 19 to 23, including a three-game sweep of the Dodgers at San Diego's renamed Qualcomm Stadium.

▶**June 4**: After they switched places in the lineup, on May 27, Steve Finley went 8-for-19 with six RBI, and Tony Gwynn, his average up to .408, was 8-for-12 with four runs scored. Gwynn went back to hitting second, and Finley now hits third.

▶**June 11**: When Rickey Henderson returned from a calf injury, he played so well that Bruce Bochy couldn't take him out of the lineup. Henderson started three consecutive games in left field, going 8-

for-13 with a pair of walks.

▶**June 25:** From June 11 to 19, Padres opponents scored at least seven runs in eight consecutive games.

▶**July 2:** Closer Trevor Hoffman's save at San Francisco on June 23 was his 109th as a Padre, breaking the team record established by Rollie Fingers. Steve Finley had a three-homer game at San Francisco and a two-homer game at Los Angeles last week.

▶**July 10:** The Yankees called off the Greg Vaughn trade when he failed their physical. The Yankees said Vaughn's right rotator cuff, which has had three surgeries, is damaged, and they voided the July 5 deal, which would have sent left-hander Kenny Rogers and infielder Mariano Duncan to San Diego.

▶**July 16:** Tony Gwynn continues to have his best season ever. He homered twice against Colorado on July 11, giving him 15 and topping his previous career best, in 1986. It was only the second two-homer game of Gwynn's career.

▶**July 30:** Since the Padres were pounded by San Francisco for 13 runs in the seventh inning on July 13, they have gone 9-2 with a 2.52 ERA. At 13-4 since the All-Star break, the Padres had sliced seven games off their deficit in the NL West.

▶**Aug. 6:** Kevin Towers has all but decided to pick up the option on the contract of Wally Joyner. The 35-year-old is due to make $3.75 million in 1998. Joyner was batting .344—fourth in the NL—with eight home runs and 61 RBI. His career-high .311 came in 1994.

▶**Aug. 13:** The failure to acquire a starting pitcher before the trade deadline has been magnified by a collapse of the rotation. Joey Hamilton has won six consecutive decisions and hasn't lost in nine starts, but no other starter has won since July 26, when left-hander Sterling Hitchcock stopped the Mets.

▶**Aug. 20:** The trade of Rickey Henderson to the Angels gives Quilvio Veras a second chance at the leadoff job he lost to Henderson in May. Veras actually is thankful he ceded the role for a few months because it gave him the chance to watch Henderson. Veras reached base five times in five plate appearances on Aug. 15 against the Cubs.

▶**Aug. 27:** On Aug. 20, Tony Gwynn got his 100th RBI of the season. At 37, he became the oldest player to reach the century mark for the first time.

▶**Sept. 3:** At the club's prompting, Greg Vaughn submitted to an eye exam on Aug. 29 and it was determined that he is nearsighted. He was fitted with contact lenses for the first time. Vaughn was in an 0-for-27 skid when he went to the eye-wear, dropping his batting average to .206.

▶**Sept. 10:** By winning the season series against Seattle 3-1, the Padres established their only all-time winning record against any opponent. Their best record against any NL team is 170-173 versus the Mets.

▶**Sept. 17:** Kevin Towers has refused to give pitching coach Dan Warthen a vote of confidence. The Padres, third in the league in ERA last season—Warthen's first as pitching coach—now rank ahead of only Colorado, with a 4.88 ERA. Towers said he will wait until consulting with Bruce Bochy after the season before making a decision, but several pitchers are already lobbying for Warthen's return.

▶**Sept. 24:** Tony Gwynn said he probably will have surgery after the season to clear debris from his left knee. He had offseason surgery on the knee three consecutive years, 1991-93. Gwynn also divulged that he has been playing with a blood clot in his right leg since late August.

▶**Oct. 1:** Another year, another notch in Tony Gwynn's bat as he took his eighth batting title with a .372 average, six points ahead of Colorado's Larry Walker. Gwynn, whose club-record 220 hits led the majors, had his best overall season in 15 years in the big leagues, with career highs of 17 home runs and 119 RBI. He is now tied with Honus Wagner for the most NL batting titles.

QUOTE OF THE YEAR

"It would be a shallow, cowardly way to finish the season if you want to point the finger at him."
—Closer Trevor Hoffman, on others' blaming pitching coach Dan Warthen for the Padres' poor pitching

SAN DIEGO PADRES 1997 final stats

BATTERS	BA	SLG	OBA	G	AB	R	H	TB	2B	3B	HR	RBI	BB	SO	SB	CS	E
Gwynn	.372	.547	.409	149	592	97	220	324	49	2	17	119	43	28	12	5	4
Joyner	.327	.486	.390	135	455	59	149	221	29	2	13	83	51	51	3	5	4
Hernandez	.313	.448	.328	50	134	15	42	60	7	1	3	14	3	27	0	2	3
Caminiti	.290	.508	.389	137	486	92	141	247	28	0	26	90	80	118	11	2	24
Sweeney	.280	.360	.358	115	164	16	46	59	7	0	2	23	20	32	2	3	2
Beamon	.277	.323	.309	43	65	5	18	21	3	0	0	7	2	17	1	2	2
Henderson	.274	.375	.422	88	288	63	79	108	11	0	6	27	71	62	29	4	7
Shipley	.273	.446	.306	63	139	22	38	62	9	0	5	19	7	20	1	1	6
Flaherty	.273	.387	.323	129	439	38	120	170	21	1	9	46	33	62	4	4	11
Shumpert	.273	.455	.324	13	33	4	9	15	3	0	1	6	3	4	0	0	2
Q. Veras	.265	.328	.357	145	539	74	143	177	23	1	3	45	72	84	33	12	11
Finley	.261	.475	.313	143	560	101	146	266	26	5	28	92	43	92	15	3	4
Lee	.259	.370	.365	22	54	9	14	20	3	0	1	4	9	24	0	0	0
Gomez	.253	.326	.326	150	522	62	132	170	19	2	5	54	53	114	5	8	15
Rivera	.250	.300	.318	17	20	2	5	6	1	0	0	1	2	9	2	1	0
Cianfrocco	.245	.355	.328	89	220	25	54	78	12	0	4	26	25	80	7	1	7
Jones	.243	.441	.322	92	152	24	37	67	9	0	7	25	16	45	7	2	4
Arias	.227	.273	.227	11	22	2	5	6	1	0	0	2	0	1	0	0	1
Vaughn	.216	.393	.322	120	361	60	78	142	10	0	18	57	56	110	7	4	1
Romero	.208	.333	.240	21	48	7	10	16	0	0	2	4	2	18	1	0	0
Velandia	.103	.172	.133	14	29	0	3	5	2	0	0	0	1	7	0	0	3
Slaught	.000	.000	.200	20	20	2	0	0	0	0	0	0	5	4	0	0	0

PITCHERS	W-L	ERA	BA	G	GS	CG	GF	Sho	SV	IP	H	R	ER	HR	BB	SO
Hoffman	6-4	2.66	.200	70	0	0	59	0	37	81.1	59	25	24	9	24	111
Bruske	4-1	3.63	.228	28	0	0	6	0	0	44.2	37	22	18	4	25	32
Ashby	9-11	4.13	.266	30	30	2	0	0	0	200.2	207	108	92	17	49	144
Hamilton	12-7	4.25	.271	31	29	1	1	0	0	192.2	199	100	91	22	69	124
Menhart	2-3	4.70	.256	9	8	0	0	0	0	44.0	42	23	23	6	13	22
Bochtler	3-6	4.77	.229	54	0	0	13	0	2	60.1	51	35	32	3	50	46
Smith	7-6	4.81	.267	37	15	0	7	0	1	118.0	120	66	63	16	52	68
D. Veras	2-1	5.11	.280	23	0	0	7	0	0	24.2	28	18	14	5	12	21
Worrell	4-8	5.16	.280	60	10	0	14	0	3	106.1	116	67	61	14	50	81
Hitchcock	10-11	5.20	.276	32	28	1	1	0	0	161.0	172	102	93	24	55	106
Erdos	2-0	5.27	.293	11	0	0	2	0	0	13.2	17	9	8	1	4	13
Cunnane	6-3	5.81	.305	54	8	0	16	0	0	91.1	114	69	59	11	49	79
Batchelor	3-1	5.97	.339	23	0	0	8	0	0	28.2	40	23	19	2	14	18
Bergman	2-4	6.09	.316	44	9	0	13	0	0	99.0	126	72	67	11	38	74
Murray	1-2	6.75	.376	17	3	0	1	0	0	33.1	50	25	25	3	21	16
Kroon	0-1	7.15	.280	12	0	0	2	0	0	11.1	14	9	9	2	5	12
Jackson	2-9	7.58	.351	17	13	0	0	0	0	67.2	98	64	57	11	28	32
Long	0-0	8.18	.340	10	0	0	4	0	0	11.0	17	11	10	1	8	8
Burrows	0-2	10.45	.286	13	0	0	4	0	0	10.1	12	13	12	1	8	8

1998 preliminary roster

PITCHERS (20)
Andy Ashby
Sean Bergman
Brian Boehringer
Kevin Brown
Matt Clement
Will Cunnane
Domingo Guzman
Joey Hamilton
Sterling Hitchcock
Trevor Hoffman
Marc Kroon
Rafael Medina

Paul Menhart
Dan Miceli
Heath Murray
Jim Sak
Pete Smith
Dario Veras
Ed Vosberg
Donne Wall
Don Wengert

CATCHERS (3)
Carlos Hernandez
Greg Myers

Mandy Romero

INFIELDERS (10)
George Arias
Ken Caminiti
Cesarin Carmona
Archi Cianfrocco
Ed Giovanola
Chris Gomez
Wally Joyner
Juan Melo
Andy Sheets
Quilvio Veras

OUTFIELDERS (7)
Mike Darr
Steve Finley
Tony Gwynn
Gary Matthews
Ruben Rivera
Mark Sweeney
Greg Vaughn

Games played by position

PLAYER	G	C	1B	2B	3B	SS	OF
Arias	11	0	0	0	8	0	0
Beamon	43	0	0	0	0	0	20
Caminiti	137	0	0	0	133	0	0
Cianfrocco	89	0	39	12	38	5	2
Finley	143	0	0	0	0	0	140
Flaherty	129	124	0	0	0	0	0
Gomez	150	0	0	0	0	149	0
Gwynn	149	0	0	0	0	0	143
Henderson	88	0	0	0	0	0	78
Hernandez	50	44	4	0	0	0	0
Jones	92	0	0	0	0	0	61
Joyner	135	0	131	0	0	0	0
Lee	22	0	21	0	0	0	0
Rivera	17	0	0	0	0	0	7
Romero	21	19	0	0	0	0	0
Shipley	63	0	4	16	2	21	0
Shumpert	13	0	0	7	2	0	3
Slaught	20	6	0	0	0	0	0
Sweeney	115	0	11	0	0	0	45
Vaughn	120	0	0	0	0	0	94
Velandia	14	0	0	5	3	6	0
Q. Veras	145	0	0	142	0	0	0

Sick call: 1997 DL report

PLAYER	Days on the DL
Andy Ashby	26
Doug Bochtler	15
Jim Bruske	19
Ken Caminiti	15
Steve Finley	16
Joey Hamilton	23
Rickey Henderson	15
Carlos Hernandez	33
Sterling Hitchcock	27
Chris Jones	19
Wally Joyner	15
Scott Livingstone	27
Heath Murray	20
Phil Plantier	66
Ruben Rivera	134
Craig Shipley	66*
Dario Veras	91*

Indicates two separate terms on Disabled List.

Minor Leagues

Tops in the organization

BATTER	CLUB	AVG.	G	AB	R	H	HR	RBI
Mitchell, Michael	RC	.350	109	440	78	154	17	106
Darr, Mike	RC	.344	134	521	104	179	15	94
Shockey, Greg	RC	.339	103	401	60	136	14	78
Beamon, Trey	LVg	.328	90	329	64	108	5	49
Lee, Derrek	LVg	.324	125	472	86	153	13	64

HOME RUNS

Allen, Dustin	Mob	17
Davis, Ben	RC	17
Mitchell, M.	RC	17
Romero, Mandy	LVg	16
Darr, Mike	RC	15

WINS

Newman, Eric	RC	13
Clement, Matt	Mob	12
Hoff, Steve	RC	11
Walters, Brett	Mob	10
Zancanaro, Dave	Mob	10

RBI

Mitchell, M.	RC	106
Darr, Mike	RC	94
Alvarez, Gabe	Mob	78
Shockey, Greg	RC	78
Davis, Ben	RC	76

SAVES

Sak, James	RC	27
Erdos, Todd	Mob	27
Kroon, Marc	LVg	15
Camp, Shawn	Idf	12
Lopez, Rodrigo	Cln	9

STOLEN BASES

Lindsey, Rodney	Cln	70
Prieto, Chris	Mob	30
Darr, Mike	RC	23
Guerrero, Joel	Pdr	22
Briggs, Stoney	LVg	18

STRIKEOUTS

Clement, Matt	Mob	201
Newman, Eric	RC	141
Hoff, Steve	RC	137
Taylor, Kerry	LVg	133
Guzman, D.	Orc	130

PITCHER	CLUB	W-L	ERA	IP	H	BB	SO
Clement, Matt	Mob	12- 8	2.05	189	157	63	201
Lopez, Rodrigo	Cln	6- 8	3.18	122	103	42	123
Tollberg, Brian	Mob	6- 3	3.72	123	123	24	108
Anderson, Bill	RC	8- 4	3.82	111	86	57	124
Szymborski, T.	Cln	5- 7	3.88	135	141	46	74

1997 salaries

	Bonuses	Total earned salary
Tony Gwynn,of	575,000	4,575,000
Greg Vaughn,of		4,000,000
Wally Joyner,1b	50,000	3,800,000
Andy Ashby,p	200,000	3,400,000
Ken Caminiti,3b	100,000	3,150,000
Steve Finley,of	50,000	2,986,672
Trevor Hoffman,p		1,500,000
Sterling Hitchcock,p		1,200,000
John Flaherty,c		900,000
Chris Gomez,ss	50,000	850,000
Tim Worrell,p	75,000	835,000
Joey Hamilton,p		675,000
Craig Shipley,ss		500,000
Carlos Hernandez,c		425,000
Archi Cianfrocco,3b		400,000
Chris Jones,of		380,000
Pete Smith,p	155,000	435,000
Sean Bergman,p		275,000
Quilvio Veras,2b	50,000	310,000
Doug Bochtler,p		250,000
Jim Bruske,p		185,000
Mark Sweeney,of		185,000
Paul Menhart,p		175,000
Dario Veras,p		172,000
Will Cunnane,p		150,000

Average 1997 salary: $1,268,547
Total 1997 payroll: $31,713,672

San Diego (1969-1997)

Runs: Most, career

1237	TONY GWYNN, 1982-1997
599	Dave Winfield, 1973-1980
484	Gene Richards, 1977-1983
442	Nate Colbert, 1969-1974
430	Garry Templeton, 1982-1991

Hits: Most, career

2780	TONY GWYNN, 1982-1997
1135	Garry Templeton, 1982-1991
1134	Dave Winfield, 1973-1980
994	Gene Richards, 1977-1983
817	Terry Kennedy, 1981-1986

2B: Most, career

460	TONY GWYNN, 1982-1997
195	Garry Templeton, 1982-1991
179	Dave Winfield, 1973-1980
158	Terry Kennedy, 1981-1986
130	Nate Colbert, 1969-1974

3B: Most, career

84	TONY GWYNN, 1982-1997
63	Gene Richards, 1977-1983
39	Dave Winfield, 1973-1980
36	Garry Templeton, 1982-1991
29	Cito Gaston, 1969-1974

HR: Most, career

163	Nate Colbert, 1969-1974
154	Dave Winfield, 1973-1980
107	TONY GWYNN, 1982-1997
92	KEN CAMINITI, 1995-1997
85	BENITO SANTIAGO, 1986-1992

RBI: Most, career

973	TONY GWYNN, 1982-1997
626	Dave Winfield, 1973-1980
481	Nate Colbert, 1969-1974
427	Garry Templeton, 1982-1991
424	Terry Kennedy, 1981-1986

SB: Most, career

308	TONY GWYNN, 1982-1997
242	Gene Richards, 1977-1983
171	Alan Wiggins, 1981-1985
148	BIP ROBERTS, 1986-1995
147	Ozzie Smith, 1978-1981

BB: Most, career

707	TONY GWYNN, 1982-1997
463	Dave Winfield, 1973-1980
423	Gene Tenace, 1977-1980
350	Nate Colbert, 1969-1974
338	Gene Richards, 1977-1983

BA: Highest, career

.340	TONY GWYNN, 1982-1997
.298	BIP ROBERTS, 1986-1995
.291	Gene Richards, 1977-1983
.286	Johnny Grubb, 1972-1976
.284	Dave Winfield, 1973-1980

On-base avg: Highest, career

.403	Gene Tenace, 1977-1980
.390	TONY GWYNN, 1982-1997
.363	Johnny Grubb, 1972-1976
.361	BIP ROBERTS, 1986-1995
.357	Dave Winfield, 1973-1980

Slug avg: Highest, career

.468	Nate Colbert, 1969-1974
.464	Dave Winfield, 1973-1980
.455	TONY GWYNN, 1982-1997
.422	Gene Tenace, 1977-1980
.409	Steve Garvey, 1983-1987

Games started: Most, career

253	Randy Jones, 1973-1980
230	Eric Show, 1981-1990
208	Ed Whitson, 1983-1991
186	ANDY BENES, 1989-1995
172	Andy Hawkins, 1982-1988

Complete games: Most, career

71	Randy Jones, 1973-1980
35	Eric Show, 1981-1990
34	Clay Kirby, 1969-1973
31	Steve Arlin, 1969-1974
29	Bruce Hurst, 1989-1993

Saves: Most, career

133	TREVOR HOFFMAN, 1993-1997
108	Rollie Fingers, 1977-1980
83	Rich Gossage, 1984-1987
78	MARK DAVIS, 1987-1994
64	Craig Lefferts, 1984-1992

Shutouts: Most, career

18	Randy Jones, 1973-1980
11	Steve Arlin, 1969-1974
11	Eric Show, 1981-1990
10	Bruce Hurst, 1989-1993
8	ANDY BENES, 1989-1995

Wins: Most, career

100	Eric Show, 1981-1990
92	Randy Jones, 1973-1980
77	Ed Whitson, 1983-1991
69	ANDY BENES, 1989-1995
60	Andy Hawkins, 1982-1988

K: Most, career

1036	ANDY BENES, 1989-1995
951	Eric Show, 1981-1990
802	Clay Kirby, 1969-1973
767	Ed Whitson, 1983-1991
677	Randy Jones, 1973-1980

Win pct: Highest, career

.591	Bruce Hurst, 1989-1993
.575	JOEY HAMILTON, 1994-1997
.535	Eric Show, 1981-1990
.517	Ed Whitson, 1983-1991
.515	Dave Dravecky, 1982-1987

ERA: Lowest, career

3.12	Dave Dravecky, 1982-1987
3.27	Bruce Hurst, 1989-1993
3.30	Randy Jones, 1973-1980
3.57	ANDY BENES, 1989-1995
3.59	Eric Show, 1981-1990

Runs: Most, season

126	STEVE FINLEY, 1996
119	TONY GWYNN, 1987
110	RICKEY HENDERSON, 1996
109	KEN CAMINITI, 1996
107	TONY GWYNN, 1986

Hits: Most, season

220	TONY GWYNN, 1997
218	TONY GWYNN, 1987
213	TONY GWYNN, 1984
211	TONY GWYNN, 1986
203	TONY GWYNN, 1989

2B: Most, season

49	TONY GWYNN, 1997
45	STEVE FINLEY, 1996
42	Terry Kennedy, 1982
41	TONY GWYNN, 1993
37	KEN CAMINITI, 1996

3B: Most, season

13	TONY GWYNN, 1987
12	Gene Richards, 1978
12	Gene Richards, 1981
11	Bill Almon, 1977
11	TONY GWYNN, 1991
11	Gene Richards, 1977

HR: Most, season

40	KEN CAMINITI, 1996
38	Nate Colbert, 1970
38	Nate Colbert, 1972
35	FRED McGRIFF, 1992
34	PHIL PLANTIER, 1993
34	Dave Winfield, 1979

RBI: Most, season

130	KEN CAMINITI, 1996
119	TONY GWYNN, 1997
118	Dave Winfield, 1979
115	JOE CARTER, 1990
111	Nate Colbert, 1972

SB: Most, season

70	Alan Wiggins, 1984
66	Alan Wiggins, 1983
61	Gene Richards, 1980
57	Ozzie Smith, 1980
56	TONY GWYNN, 1987
56	Gene Richards, 1977

BB: Most, season

132	Jack Clark, 1989
125	RICKEY HENDERSON, 1996
125	Gene Tenace, 1977
105	FRED McGRIFF, 1991
105	Gene Tenace, 1979

BA: Highest, season

.394	TONY GWYNN, 1994
.372	TONY GWYNN, 1997
.370	TONY GWYNN, 1987
.368	TONY GWYNN, 1995
.358	TONY GWYNN, 1993

On-base avg: Highest, season

.454	TONY GWYNN, 1994
.447	TONY GWYNN, 1987
.415	Gene Tenace, 1977
.410	RICKEY HENDERSON, 1996
.410	Jack Clark, 1989

Slug avg: Highest, season

.621	KEN CAMINITI, 1996
.580	GARY SHEFFIELD, 1992
.568	TONY GWYNN, 1994
.558	Dave Winfield, 1979
.556	FRED McGRIFF, 1992

Games started: Most, season

40	Randy Jones, 1976
39	Randy Jones, 1979
37	Steve Arlin, 1972
37	Gaylord Perry, 1978
36	Randy Jones, 1975
36	Randy Jones, 1978
36	Clay Kirby, 1971

Complete games: Most, season

25	Randy Jones, 1976
18	Randy Jones, 1975
14	Dave Roberts, 1971
13	Clay Kirby, 1971
13	Eric Show, 1988

Saves: Most, season

44	MARK DAVIS, 1989
42	TREVOR HOFFMAN, 1996
38	RANDY MYERS, 1992
37	Rollie Fingers, 1978
37	TREVOR HOFFMAN, 1997

Shutouts: Most, season

6	Randy Jones, 1975
6	Fred Norman, 1972
5	Randy Jones, 1976
4	Steve Arlin, 1971
4	Bruce Hurst, 1990
4	Bruce Hurst, 1992

Wins: Most, season

22	Randy Jones, 1976
21	Gaylord Perry, 1978
20	Randy Jones, 1975
18	Andy Hawkins, 1985
16	La Marr Hoyt, 1985
16	Tim Lollar, 1982
16	Eric Show, 1988
16	Ed Whitson, 1989

K: Most, season

231	Clay Kirby, 1971
189	ANDY BENES, 1994
185	Pat Dobson, 1970
184	JOEY HAMILTON, 1996
179	ANDY BENES, 1993
179	Bruce Hurst, 1989

Win pct: Highest, season

.778	Gaylord Perry, 1978
.692	Andy Hawkins, 1985
.667	La Marr Hoyt, 1985
.652	Bruce Hurst, 1991
.640	Tim Lollar, 1982

ERA: Lowest, season

2.10	Dave Roberts, 1971
2.24	Randy Jones, 1975
2.60	Ed Whitson, 1990
2.66	Ed Whitson, 1989
2.69	Bruce Hurst, 1989

Most pinch-hit homers, season

5	Jerry Turner, 1978
3	ARCHI CIANFROCCO, 1995
3	Luis Salazar, 1989

Most pinch-hit homers, career

9	Jerry Turner, 1974-1983

Longest hitting streak

34	BENITO SANTIAGO, 1987
27	JOHN FLAHERTY, 1996
25	TONY GWYNN, 1983
23	BIP ROBERTS, 1994
21	Bobby Brown, 1983
21	STEVE FINLEY, 1996

Most consecutive scoreless innings

30	Randy Jones, 1980

No-hit games

ACTIVE PLAYERS in caps.

Players' years of service are listed by the first and last years with this team and are not necessarily consecutive; all statistics record performances for this team only.

Arizona Diamondbacks

By H. Darr Beiser, USA TODAY

The Diamondbacks got a big bopper in Matt Williams, who slugged 33 homers in 1997 for Cleveland.

1998 Diamondbacks are ready to compete

With their state-of-the-art ballpark and money-making business plan, the Arizona Diamondbacks might soon become the model for a 21st-century baseball team. But in conducting their expansion draft, they followed one the game's oldest adages: You can never have enough pitching. The Diamondbacks used 21 of their 35 selections on pitchers. After several trades, the Diamondbacks still had 18 pitchers remaining from draft day. "The strategy was to get good arms," said Mel Didier, the Diamondbacks' director of player development. "It takes a lot of good arms to make a few good pitchers." The Diamondbacks used seven of their first-round picks on pitchers: postseason standout Brian Anderson of Cleveland, Boston right-hander Jeff Suppan, Cory Lidle of the Mets, Milwaukee left-hander Joel Adamson, the Yankees' Ben Ford, Montreal's Neil Weber and Jason Boyd of Philadelphia.

The Diamondbacks made a big splash after the draft when they announced the acquisitions of center fielder Devon White from the Marlins and third baseman Travis Fryman from the Tigers. Then, on Dec. 1, Fryman was traded with reliever Tom Martin to Cleveland for All-Star third baseman Matt Williams, who signed a five-year, $45 million contract extension as part of the negotiations. The Indians also demanded $3 million in cash to complete the deal, so in a highly unusual move, Williams agreed to reduce his 1998 salary from $7 million to $4.5 million to free up the cash. Williams' three children live with their mother in a Phoenix suburb, and he was determined to be near them. The Diamondbacks committed $10.3 million for 1998 to White and free-agent shortstop Jay Bell. White, a cornerstone of the Blue Jays' World Series winners of 1992 and 1993, has seen his skills decline in recent years. With the Marlins in the midst of a fire sale before the ownership transfer of the team, White and his $3.5 million salary had to go.

Arizona general manager Joe Garagiola Jr. said the Diamondbacks had rated Tony Saunders (the Devil Rays' top selection), Anderson and Suppan as the top three players available, in no particular order. Ford has starred in the Arizona Fall League and is a favorite of Arizona manager Buck Showalter, whose staff has a significant Yankees pedigree, but the team's most highly regarded pick was Anderson. The club's selection of White Sox catcher Jorge Fabregas with their fourth pick was a mild surprise, but Fabregas, 27, made just $275,000 in a breakthrough '97 season, batting .280 for the Sox in 100 games with seven home runs and 48 RBI.

Didier's prior employment by the Dodgers had an impact on Arizona's picks. The team selected L.A. outfielder Karim Garcia in the first round and took one-time Dodger Omar Daal from Toronto in the second. Garcia, 22, struggled to find playing time and has undergone arm and shoulder operations. The Diamondbacks drafted just four outfielders: Garcia, Kansas City's Yamil Benitez, Brent Brede of Minnesota and Baltimore's David Delluci.

The Diamondbacks' projected infield will include rookie Travis Lee at first base, Bell at shortstop and Williams at third base. The club also drafted second baseman Edwin Diaz from Texas and Oakland second baseman–shortstop Tony Batista, as well as Brewers shortstop prospect Danny Klassen, who batted .331 with 81 RBI at AA El Paso last season.

The Diamondbacks could rank as high as second in revenues during their inaugural season. The club's new Bank One Ballpark and lucrative broadcasting and marketing contracts could enable it to foot a payroll of $40-$45 million in its inaugural season, but the club could opt to keep payroll at a more modest $30-$35 million, thereby recouping more of the $300 million in start-up costs, including the $130 million franchise fee and $100 million in ballpark cost overruns. "We don't have a [payroll] number," said owner Jerry Colangelo. "What we do feel we have the capability of doing is pulling the trigger when we believe it's appropriate." They've already shown it.

1997 Diamondbacks: Week-by-week notes

These notes were excerpted from the following issues of Baseball Weekly.

▶July 10: High-priced youngsters Travis Lee ($10 million) and John Patterson ($6.1 million) have gone in different directions. First baseman Lee, 22, last year's Golden Spikes Award winner for college player of the year from San Diego State and an Olympian, began the season with the High Desert affiliate and tore up the Class A California League, then was loaned to the Milwaukee Brewers' AAA affiliate in Tucson. He did not skip a beat and entered play on July 6 with a .323 average, nine home runs and 22 RBI. Right-hander Patterson, 19, began the season in extended spring training and joined South Bend of the Class A Midwest League around May 1, where he was 0-4 with a 4.67 ERA in eight starts. He hurt his shoulder in early June and only now is working his way back into shape.

▶July 16: The Diamondbacks announced on July 11 that they have signed their No. 1 pick in this year's draft, Jack Cust, 18, of Immaculata High School in Flemington, N.J. Terms were not announced for Cust, the 30th overall selection, although his bonus most likely is in the $800,000 range. He was to report to Peoria in the Arizona Rookie League. The 6-foot-2, 195-pound Cust has been a first baseman, but the Diamondbacks envision him as an outfielder or a third baseman. Jerry Colangelo, Arizona's managing general partner, is firm about remaining in the NL West and not switching leagues.

▶July 30: Progress on Arizona's new home, Bank One Ballpark, continued with the installation of the facility's first seats. The team has sold 33,000 season tickets and hopes to have a final count of about 37,000, leaving about 12,000 for single-game sales.

▶Aug. 6: High Desert outfielder Mike Stoner led the California League through July 30 in RBI (103), hits (155), slugging percentage (.604) and runs (89), and was second in hitting (.350).

▶Aug. 13: The Diamondbacks will be the host team for the Nov. 18 expansion draft. The likely site will be the Phoenix Civic Plaza, near the Diamondbacks' downtown Phoenix stadium. The draft will be held in conjunction with the annual general managers' meetings on Nov. 13-16 in Scottsdale.

▶Aug. 20: The team made its first major league trade when it sent left-handed reliever Mark Davis to the Brewers for future considerations. Davis was the 1989 NL Cy Young winner with San Diego.

▶Aug. 27: On Aug. 28, the torch officially will be passed from the AAA Phoenix Firebirds (a Giants affiliate) to the Diamondbacks in a ceremony before the Firebirds' regular-season home finale against Tucson.

▶Sept. 10: Arizona is sending about 50 players to various winter leagues. Mel Didier, director of player development, said the Dodgers and the Expos had success with a similar strategy when he was with them. Most of the organization's best young prospects—such as first-round picks Nick Bierbrodt (1996, left-handed pitcher) and Jack Cust—will be in the Arizona Fall League.

▶Sept. 17: High Desert gave the Arizona organization its first championship. The Mavericks defeated San Bernardino three games to none for the California League title. High Desert was 6-0 in the playoffs after finishing 83-57 in the regular season.

▶Sept. 24: Former Braves infielder Andres Thomas has joined the organization. He will oversee the Diamondbacks' baseball academy in his native Dominican Republic.

▶Oct. 1: Bank One Ballpark, the team's 48,500-seat, retractable-roof, natural-turf home, continued to take shape. The cost is now at $354 million, $253 million of which is provided through a quarter-cent sales tax in Maricopa County. The remainder is provided by the team's investors.

QUOTE OF THE YEAR

"It's an American League problem—they created it."

—Managing general partner Jerry Colangelo, on the attempt to get Arizona to switch leagues

1998 preliminary roster

PITCHERS (23)
Joel Adamson
Brian Anderson
Willie Blair
Jason Boyd
Hector Carrasco
Chris Clemons
Bryan Corey
Omar Daal
Ynocencio De La Cruz
Todd Erdos
Ben Ford

Russ Jacobs
Marty Janzen
Cory Lidle
Kirk Ojala
Steven Randolph
Felix Rodriguez
Martin Sanchez
Clint Sodowsky
Russ Springer
Jeff Suppan
Neil Weber
Bob Wolcott

CATCHERS (3)
Jorge Fabregas
Damian Miller
Kelly Stinnett

INFIELDERS (7)
Tony Batista
Jay Bell
Mike Bell
Edwin Diaz
Hanley Frias

Danny Klassen
Matt Williams

OUTFIELDERS (6)
Yamil Benitez
Brent Brede
David Dellucci
Karim Garcia
Chris Jones
Devon White

Minor Leagues

Tops in the organization

BATTER	CLUB	AVG.	G	AB	R	H	HR	RBI
Stoner, Mike	HD	.358	136	567	115	203	33	142
Lee, Travis	Tcn	.331	120	453	105	150	32	109
Conti, Jason	HD	.315	131	517	93	163	5	51
Ryan, Rob	SB	.314	121	421	71	132	8	73
Maddox, Garry	HD	.306	101	409	89	125	7	44

HOME RUNS

Cameron, Stanton	HD	33
Stoner, Mike	HD	33
Lee, Travis	Tcn	32
Hartman, Ron	HD	17
Adams, John	SB	10

WINS

Sobkoviak, Jeff	HD	14
Sabel, Erik	HD	11
Penny, Brad	SB	10
Robbins, Jason	HD	9
Several Players Tied at		8

RBI

Stoner, Mike	HD	142
Cameron, Stanton	HD	113
Lee, Travis	Tcn	109
Hartman, Ron	HD	102
Ryan, Rob	SB	73

SAVES

Tuttle, Dave	HD	19
Harvell, Pete	SB	13
Bloomer, Chris	Lth	9
Crews, Jason	SB	9
Frias, Miguel	Lth	8

STOLEN BASES

Conti, Jason	HD	31
Maddox, Garry	HD	25
Rexrode, Jackie	Lth	22
Goligoski, Jason	HD	15
Spivey, Ernest	HD	14

STRIKEOUTS

Robbins, Jason	HD	153
Nunez, Vladimir	HD	142
Penny, Brad	SB	116
Sobkoviak, Jeff	HD	101
Patterson, John	SB	95

PITCHER	CLUB	W-L	ERA	IP	H	BB	SO
Michalak, Chris	HD	3- 7	2.65	85	76	31	74
Penny, Brad	SB	10- 5	2.73	119	91	43	116
Crews, Jason	SB	4- 6	3.18	82	78	27	74
McCutcheon, M.	SB	7- 5	3.41	106	104	49	67
Rodriguez, Larry	SB	4-11	3.62	104	102	37	72

Final American League team statistics

BATTING	BA	SLG	OBA	AB	R	H	TB	2B	3B	HR	RBI	LOB	BB	SO	SB	CS	E
Anaheim	.272	.416	.346	5628	829	1531	2343	279	25	161	775	1203	617	953	126	72	123
Baltimore	.268	.429	.341	5584	812	1498	2394	264	22	196	780	1198	586	952	63	26	97
Boston	.291	.463	.352	5781	851	1684	2676	373	32	185	810	1221	514	1044	68	48	135
Chicago	.273	.417	.341	5491	779	1498	2288	260	28	158	740	1148	569	901	106	52	127
Cleveland	.286	.467	.358	5556	868	1589	2594	301	22	220	810	1181	617	955	118	59	106
Detroit	.258	.415	.332	5481	784	1415	2275	268	32	176	743	1071	578	1164	161	72	92
Kansas City	.264	.407	.333	5599	747	1478	2278	256	35	158	711	1176	561	1061	130	66	91
Milwaukee	.260	.398	.325	5444	681	1415	2168	294	27	135	643	1118	494	967	103	55	121
Minnesota	.270	.409	.333	5634	772	1522	2303	305	40	132	730	1156	495	1121	151	52	101
New York	.287	.436	.362	5710	891	1636	2490	325	23	161	846	1276	676	954	99	58	104
Oakland	.260	.423	.339	5589	764	1451	2362	274	23	197	714	1221	642	1181	71	36	122
Seattle	.280	.485	.355	5614	925	1574	2720	312	21	264	890	1149	626	1110	89	40	126
Texas	.274	.438	.334	5651	807	1547	2473	311	27	187	773	1149	500	1116	72	37	121
Toronto	.244	.389	.310	5473	654	1333	2131	275	41	147	627	1113	487	1138	134	50	94
Totals	.271	.428	.340	78235	11164	21171	33495	4097	398	2477	10592	16380	7962	14617	1491	723	1560

	Starters							Relievers						Total
PITCHING	W-L	ERA	IP	CG	SHO	BB	SO	W-L	ERA	IP	SV	BB	SO	ERA
Anaheim	53-51	5.01	965.1	9	3	377	618	31-27	3.55	489.1	39	228	432	4.52
Baltimore	65-40	4.19	983.1	8	4	335	701	33-24	3.33	477.2	59	228	438	3.91
Boston	50-53	4.95	909.1	7	3	365	619	28-31	4.70	542.1	40	246	368	4.85
Chicago	57-64	4.97	965.1	6	1	370	628	23-17	4.25	457.0	52	205	333	4.73
Cleveland	60-53	4.90	955.0	4	1	364	607	26-22	4.38	470.2	39	211	429	4.73
Detroit	58-63	4.46	958.0	13	5	336	602	21-20	4.76	487.2	42	216	380	4.56
Kansas City	47-61	4.81	1002.0	11	2	344	645	20-33	4.47	441.0	29	187	316	4.70
Milwaukee	57-62	4.47	950.0	6	3	346	617	21-21	3.75	477.1	44	196	399	4.22
Minnesota	50-76	5.42	906.0	10	3	318	515	18-18	4.33	528.0	30	177	393	5.00
New York	72-42	4.12	1017.1	11	3	341	775	24-24	3.22	450.1	51	191	390	3.84
Oakland	29-73	5.94	858.2	2	0	366	545	36-24	4.82	586.2	38	276	408	5.48
Seattle	66-46	4.47	985.2	9	3	362	698	24-26	5.47	462.0	38	236	399	4.78
Texas	49-66	5.11	959.0	8	1	355	586	28-19	3.88	470.2	33	186	339	4.69
Toronto	57-62	3.99	1054.0	19	7	356	837	19-24	3.77	388.2	34	141	313	3.92
Totals	770-812	4.75	13469.0	123	39	4935	9103	352-336	4.21	6729.1	568	2924	5337	4.56

Final National League team statistics

BATTING	BA	SLG	OBA	AB	R	H	TB	2B	3B	HR	RBI	LOB	BB	SO	SB	CS	E
Atlanta	.270	.426	.343	5528	791	1490	2354	268	37	174	755	1177	597	1160	108	58	114
Chicago	.263	.396	.321	5489	687	1444	2172	269	39	127	642	1093	451	1003	116	60	112
Cincinnati	.253	.389	.321	5484	651	1386	2135	269	27	142	612	1144	518	1113	190	67	106
Colorado	.288	.478	.357	5603	923	1611	2677	269	40	239	869	1124	562	1060	137	65	111
Florida	.259	.395	.346	5439	740	1410	2146	272	28	136	703	1248	686	1074	115	58	116
Houston	.259	.403	.344	5502	777	1427	2220	314	40	133	720	1221	633	1085	171	74	131
Los Angeles	.268	.418	.330	5544	742	1488	2318	242	33	174	706	1120	498	1079	131	64	116
Montreal	.258	.425	.316	5526	691	1423	2346	339	34	172	659	1091	420	1084	75	46	132
New York	.262	.405	.332	5524	777	1448	2237	274	28	153	741	1111	550	1029	97	74	120
Philadelphia	.255	.385	.322	5443	668	1390	2098	290	35	116	622	1152	519	1032	92	56	108
Pittsburgh	.262	.404	.329	5503	725	1440	2222	291	52	129	686	1168	481	1161	160	50	131
St. Louis	.255	.396	.324	5524	689	1409	2188	269	39	144	654	1140	543	1191	164	60	123
San Diego	.271	.407	.342	5609	795	1519	2282	275	16	152	761	1207	604	1129	140	60	132
San Francisco	.258	.414	.337	5485	784	1415	2271	266	37	172	746	1199	642	1120	121	49	125
Total	.263	.410	.333	77203	10440	20300	31666	3907	485	2163	9876	16195	7704	15320	1817	841	1677

	Starters							Relievers						Total
PITCHING	W-L	ERA	IP	CG	SHO	BB	SO	W-L	ERA	IP	SV	BB	SO	ERA
Atlanta	75-37	3.05	1096.2	21	10	270	843	26-24	3.56	369.0	37	180	353	3.18
Chicago	56-61	4.43	958.2	6	2	367	668	12-33	4.46	470.1	37	223	404	4.44
Cincinnati	60-66	4.67	914.1	5	0	347	657	16-20	3.99	534.2	49	211	502	4.41
Colorado	54-59	5.48	954.1	9	3	363	526	29-20	4.80	478.1	38	203	344	5.25
Florida	64-49	3.76	988.1	12	4	423	801	28-21	3.97	458.1	39	216	387	3.83
Houston	62-50	3.61	1043.0	16	7	344	722	22-28	3.83	416.0	37	167	416	3.66
Los Angeles	63-52	3.73	1014.1	6	1	373	863	25-22	3.40	445.0	45	173	369	3.62
Montreal	57-57	3.93	965.2	27	12	346	773	21-27	4.54	481.1	37	211	365	4.14
New York	61-48	3.90	993.2	7	3	317	621	27-26	4.06	465.2	49	187	361	3.95
Philadelphia	51-71	4.63	971.2	13	3	367	835	17-23	5.38	448.2	35	249	374	4.85
Pittsburgh	53-57	4.25	943.0	6	2	317	659	26-26	4.34	493.0	41	243	421	4.28
St. Louis	50-58	3.92	1001.0	5	0	371	802	23-31	3.80	454.2	39	165	328	3.88
San Diego	47-62	4.98	933.2	5	0	348	613	29-24	4.99	516.1	43	248	446	4.98
San Francisco	60-48	4.25	920.2	5	0	379	685	30-24	4.75	525.1	45	199	359	4.39
Totals	813-775	4.16	13699.0	143	50	4932	10068	331-349	4.30	6556.2	571	2875	5429	4.20

League forecasts

▶ **1998 overview**
▶ **1998 American League division forecasts**

▶ **1998 National League division forecasts**

USA SNAPSHOTS®

A look at statistics that shape the sports world

Champagne six-pack

By clinching the National League East, the Braves became the first major league team to win six consecutive division or league championships. Title streaks:

Team Streak(s)	Braves (1991-97)[1]	Athletics (1971-75)	Yankees (1949-53) (1960-64)	N.Y. Giants (1921-24)	Yankees (1936-39) (1955-58)
	6	5	5 twice	4	4 twice

1 – excludes the 1994 strike season

Source: Elias Sports Bureau

By Scott Boeck and Dave Merrill, USA TODAY

An expansion-driven offensive explosion?

The most popular example is 1961. Not only did Roger Maris have 162 games in which to break Babe Ruth's home run record (set over 154 games), but Maris was hitting in a league watered down by expansion. So the argument goes. There's no denying that the American League's expansion from eight to 10 teams created opportunities for pitchers who would otherwise have been in the minors, but research says Maris did not exploit them in clouting his 61 homers. Elias Sports Bureau research showed that Maris had 166 at-bats against pitchers who made 25 starts or saved 10 games in the previous, pre-expansion season. He hit 23 homers against them, one for every 7.2 at-bats. Against other pitchers, Maris knocked 38 dingers, one for every 11.2 at-bats. Had he hit home runs against all pitchers at the same rate he did against established pitchers, Maris would have hit 82 homers for the season.

Whenever there's expansion, the thought is that offenses will benefit because there isn't enough pitching for the established teams, not to mention the new ones. With expansion, might Mark McGwire or Ken Griffey topple Maris' record this year? Rick Cerone, a Yankees broadcaster, was the Opening Day catcher for the expansion Toronto Blue Jays in 1977. Home runs per game rose 50% (from 1.15 to 1.73) in the major leagues from '76 to '77. To Cerone, an overall jump isn't important for the top sluggers to threaten Maris' record again. "If Griffey or McGwire would've had an average July, they would've broken the record," he says.

National League 1997 MVP Larry Walker says that contrary to popular belief, hitters are not salivating at the idea of facing two dozen additional pitchers. "If a guy's pitching in the big leagues, you approach him no different than anyone else," Walker says. "If you get too confident, before you know it, you're in the clubhouse breaking things."

There hasn't been much of that lately for Walker, Griffey, McGwire, Tony Gwynn or other hitting stars. And while Maris' record could fall and the magical .400 batting average could be eclipsed, thinner pitching staffs won't be the sole reason. Smaller ballparks, tiny strike zones, stronger hitters and thinner bats are as responsible for the offensive upswing as is mediocre pitching. You can argue that the last wave of expansion, in 1993, helped speed the process.

We've seen remarkable increases in power since then. When the Orioles hit 257 homers in 1996 to break the '61 Yankees record of 240, two other teams also surpassed the old mark. Seattle broke the record again last season, with 264. Expanding by two teams may be akin to throwing another log on an already roaring fire. "I don't think anyone's going to be surprised when Griffey or Walker or anybody of that caliber hits 50 home runs," ESPN commentator Harold Reynolds says. "The surprise is when a guy like Damion Easley hits 22 home runs and his previous career high is eight."

In addition to McGwire, Griffey and Walker, others, including Mike Piazza, Albert Belle and Frank Thomas, could challenge Maris' record. Batting .400 is going to be more difficult. Gwynn, the eight-time batting champion, is considered the player with the most realistic shot, although Walker gave it a run in 1997. Making Walker's accomplishment—ending at .366—more surprising is the .285 career average he entered the season with.

"The major difference [in pitching] is going to be in middle and long relief," Giants manager Dusty Baker says. "Starters and closers are basically going to be pretty good. Where expansion's really going to take its toll is in finding quality left-handers. There aren't enough left-handers available to get left-handed hitters out."

While there's no guarantee that records will be broken next year, there's more than enough evidence to suggest another season of staggering offensive numbers, with or without expansion.

AL East: New kid in high-stakes game

The new Tampa Bay Devil Rays have a stadium, a roster, a manager, a front office . . . uh, do they have a printing press for the money they'll need to print to keep up with the big boys? This is the American League East, where the race to lock up the top talent can be as intense as the race for a division title. This is a win-at-all-costs division, and if you think that philosophy is limited to George Steinbrenner's Yankees and Peter Angelos' Orioles, guess again.

For a second consecutive season, the Blue Jays have raided a division foe to step up in the race. Taking Roger Clemens from Boston paid off with a Cy Young Award season in 1997, but Toronto still stumbled home last in the division. This time the prime target was closer Randy Myers, who led Baltimore into the ALCS with 45 saves in 46 opportunities. Now the Blue Jays have the last two Cy Young winners in Clemens and Pat Hentgen, plus a dominant closer to go with them. But new manager Tim Johnson has 22 games to make up on the Orioles, not to mention the Yankees and the Red Sox to climb over. That climb will have to include more big numbers from youngsters Jose Cruz, Carlos Delgado and Shawn Green.

Boston, another 1997 disappointment, now has that year's other Cy Young Award winner. Red Sox general manager Dan Duquette tried to quiet critical fans and media and make a significant statement to his players when he traded pitching prospects to Montreal for Pedro Martinez. Duquette then persuaded Martinez to stay, giving him a six-year, $75 million contract, and the GM hopes that other Red Sox players will believe that management is serious about becoming a contender. That message was especially pointed at first baseman Mo Vaughn, but the future of this club now also revolves around last year's sensational rookie, Nomar Garciaparra. The 1997 Jackie Robinson Award winner put up numbers (30 home runs, 98 RBI) unheard of by a rookie shortstop or a leadoff man. But depth on offense and on the mound will probably still separate Boston from Baltimore and New York.

The Orioles were the division's dominant team in 1997, but the season wasn't without turmoil. Plus, this is a club that has willingly fallen into the free-agent cycle, signing more big names to replace the ones that leave. It's worked well so far, with back-to-back playoff seasons for a team whose only homegrown regulars are third baseman Cal Ripken and starter Mike Mussina. But outfielder Jeffrey Hammonds, another farm-system product, is moving into a more prominent role in the offense, and Mussina was easily the best pitcher in baseball in 1997's postseason. The Orioles won despite having second baseman Roberto Alomar struggle all season with injuries and having first baseman Rafael Palmeiro hit more than 40 points below his career average. Mussina, Scott Erickson and Jimmy Key combine for the best or second-best big three starters in the division. The Yankees, however, may match them.

With left-hander Andy Pettitte, New York has a potent 1-2 as long as David Cone can remain healthy. And Myers' departure from Baltimore clearly gives the Yankees a head-to-head edge with closer Mariano Rivera. The New York offense broke loose in 1997 as first baseman Tino Martinez had a career year with 44 home runs and Paul O'Neill hit .324 with 117 RBI.

All of which has to seem quite daunting to the Devil Rays. That could be a blessing in disguise, however, as expectations can't be overly high in Tampa Bay, giving general manager Chuck LaMar more room to be patient and build an expansion team the right way, with young players and a strong farm system. Local favorite Fred McGriff comes home to play first base and help keep the fans happy while the Devil Rays build a speed-oriented turf team. Lefty Wilson Alvarez will anchor the rotation.

AL Central: Indians are still on top

When the losing team cleans out its lockers the day after the World Series, the general manager often looks over the scene and wonders, "Now what?" Cleveland general manager John Hart pretty much knew the answer to that question. Set aside the stinging defeat in Game 7 of the World Series, and the Indians have to feel their fortunes are on the upswing. They were one of the league's better teams in the latter stages of the season and knocked off the AL's top two, Baltimore and New York, in the playoffs. More important, Hart heads into 1998 with six offensive starters under contract through 1999 or beyond—David Justice, Jim Thome, Sandy Alomar, Manny Ramirez, Travis Fryman and Omar Vizquel. That's in keeping with Hart's philosophy of putting most of his long-term investments in offense. The one place in the Indians organization where a balance exists between pitching and hitting is in the farm system. While Cleveland continues to produce some promising offensive talent, the best of the pitching crop will have a more immediate impact in 1998. Jaret Wright burst into the rotation in August 1997, and next in line is Bartolo Colon.

The only other team besides Cleveland with prospects looking up is the Detroit Tigers, who caught a break by moving out of the tough AL East and into a division where a playoff berth is more obtainable. The Tigers' 79 victories last year would have put them just one win behind second-place Chicago in the AL Central. Detroit hopes the best of its prospects, outfielder Juan Encarnacion, can join left fielder Bobby Higginson and first baseman Tony Clark as offensive forces. Center fielder Brian Hunter, who had 74 stolen bases, and defensive whiz shortstop Deivi Cruz will be joined by third baseman Joe Randa, who was Pittsburgh's regular last season and replaces longtime Tiger Travis Fryman. Development of the pitching staff lags a bit behind the offense, but Detroit GM Randy Smith is constantly tweaking and tinkering to support young left-hander Justin Thompson, who won 15 games last year in his first full season.

If the White Sox are to maintain their best-threat-to-Cleveland status in the division, the supporting cast around the big three of Frank Thomas, Albert Belle and Robin Ventura will have to change. Center fielder Mike Cameron was the first to make an impact last season, getting into 116 games. But the cameo appearances of right fielder Magglio Ordonez and first baseman Mario Valdez could expand into significant roles this year. The White Sox are on the verge of having a much deeper offensive lineup, but the major question is whether it will emerge this season.

The question marks in Kansas City are far more significant. The Royals continue to grope for the right mix of young and veteran players. Youngsters such as outfielder Johnny Damon and catcher Mike Sweeney may be joined by outfielder Roderick Myers this year. Veterans Jeff King and Jose Offerman are coming off solid seasons on the right side of the infield, but shortstop Jay Bell opted to sign with expansion team Arizona and DH Chili Davis went to the Yankees. Jose Rosado is the best hope for a young pitching star to move into a supporting role behind Kevin Appier. Rosado is especially important because 13-game winner Tim Belcher is getting old.

In Minnesota, the Twins have been fighting for the very life of the franchise, with the stadium issue and the possible move to North Carolina overshadowing everything else. Lost in the shuffle are some exciting young players, especially right-handed starter Brad Radke, who accounted for 20 of Minnesota's 68 victories last year. The Twins must hope that first baseman David Ortiz finds better rookie success than highly touted third baseman Todd Walker did last year, though Walker will get another shot. Soft seasons from outfielders Marty Cordova and Matt Lawton created doubt about their long-term potential.

AL West: Who's got some pitching?

It wouldn't be the Texas Rangers' turn now, would it? The Seattle Mariners and the Rangers have taken turns winning the American League West title the past three years despite the best intentions of the Anaheim Angels. And in the game's last four-team division, at least until some further expansion causes a yet-to-be-imagined structure, the aforementioned three-quarters of the division again will vie for the trip to the postseason.

The obvious difference between Texas' 1996 run to the playoffs and its disappointing 1997 season was that the bottom fell out of the Rangers' thin pitching staff. The division's winner usually produces enough consistent offense to overcome its pitching deficiencies, and the Mariners did exactly that in 1997, blotting out the frustration caused by an inconsistent bullpen. There's no reason to expect anything different in 1998. Ken Griffey is the league's No. 1 threat to Roger Maris' home run record. Edgar Martinez remains one of the game's most consistent elite hitters, regularly grinding out a .330 average and adding 100 RBI and 30 or so homers. Right fielder Jay Buhner and shortstop Alex Rodriguez had offensive drop-offs in 1997, so if they rebound, it's not unreasonable to expect even more from the team that set a major league record for home runs in 1997. What's left? Pitching. Pitching that's very left. When Jeff Fassero and Jamie Moyer, both lefties, combined for 33 victories in 1997, the Mariners had done their best job yet of finding someone other than left-hander Randy Johnson to win big games.

The Rangers got through 1996 with a five-man rotation intact, but they weren't so fortunate in 1997. Darren Oliver emerged as the big winner with 13, and he and John Burkett will have to chew up significant innings this season. Aaron Sele, acquired from Boston, and Rick Helling, reacquired from Florida late last season, will also contribute. The bullpen is good, with closer John Wetteland in

place and Danny Patterson emerging as one of the game's better setup men.

The Rangers began patching up offensive problems that even Juan Gonzalez's 42 home runs and 131 RBI couldn't overcome, bringing over Tom Goodwin from Kansas City late last season to fill a center field–leadoff void. Lee Stevens got to play every day when Will Clark was hurt late in the season, and Stevens will see regular duty at first base or DH. Left fielder Rusty Greer has quietly emerged as one of the league's better No. 3 hitters, and Ivan Rodriguez is the game's premier offense-defense combination at catcher.

The Angels have to find ways to overcome patchwork pitching. Right fielder Tim Salmon is the undisputed offensive star of this team, coming off a 33-homer, 129-RBI season, though third baseman Dave Hollins is its heart and soul. His 85 RBI contributed to a potent batting order that also features Darin Erstad, Jim Edmonds and Garret Anderson. Jason Dickson pitched his way to the All-Star Game as a rookie, but this team will win only if veterans Chuck Finley and Ken Hill can anchor the staff and help get the ball to overpowering closer Troy Percival and a deep setup corps led by right-hander Mike James and lefty Mike Holtz.

The AL West is a four-team division, but the Athletics will be able to move out of the basement only with a collapse by one of the other teams. The trading of Mark McGwire to St. Louis and Geronimo Berroa to Baltimore last season erased any doubt about whether the Athletics were taking the bottoming-out route to rebuilding. The road back up is not without its golden bricks to build on. The most sparkling one this year will be Ben Grieve, the rookie right fielder who begins the season with the burden of being the Jackie Robinson Award favorite. Other than flashy shortstop Miguel Tejada, the other youngsters aren't quite such sure things, so manager Art Howe and new general manager Billy Beane have a daunting task in front of them.

NL East: Atlanta wants it all

The balance of power in the National League East took an abrupt shift in October. Or was that just a mirage? The Florida Marlins' World Series trophy was no mirage, but the Braves enter 1998 as the defending division champ and the favorite to repeat. Of course, in Atlanta the regular-season successes are expected. The mixed results of recent Octobers are what drive this decade's most successful NL franchise.

Since the Marlins stalled Atlanta a couple of games short of another World Series appearance, the Braves have moved forward and the Marlins have tried not to slip too far backward. Atlanta general manager John Schuerholz went into his usual aggressive offseason mode. He sent Fred McGriff to expansion Tampa Bay and replaced him at first base with Colorado slugger Andres Galarraga. Longtime shortstop Jeff Blauser was allowed to leave as a free agent, and another ex-Rookie, Walt Weiss, came on board. Yet for all the high-level tinkering, the Braves never let go of their dominant starting pitching—Greg Maddux, John Smoltz, Tom Glavine and Denny Neagle.

That was something the Marlins strived to match in 1997, but when Tony Saunders was lost in the expansion draft, that was merely a secondary setback in a process that began in the playoffs when Alex Fernandez suffered a rotator cuff injury that most likely will keep him out of the 1998 season. Keeping up with Atlanta over the 162-game long haul seems unlikely again, but don't feel too sorry for Florida. It has developed one of baseball's more fertile farm systems. Pitcher Livan Hernandez, catcher Charles Johnson and shortstop Edgar Renteria are already key components on the team. Look for more in 1998, including outfielders Todd Dunwoody and Mark Kotsay.

The Marlins may have their hands full maintaining their runner-up status. The New York Mets hung right on the Marlins' tail all season, finishing only four games out of Florida's wild-card playoff spot and tying for the fourth-best record in the National League. New York seemed to have the fewest personnel concerns through the winter because first baseman John Olerud, the only free agent from the 1997 club, re-signed in November, but their once highly regarded young pitchers, Paul Wilson, Jason Isringhausen and Bill Pulsipher, have had a baffling string of injuries and illnesses. The Mets' surprising rise in 1997 was done with a rotation that had only two 10-game winners, and one of those was journeyman Rick Reed. An elbow injury to catcher Todd Hundley required reconstructive surgery, and his availability for any of this season is questionable.

The Montreal Expos finally ran out of the magic that kept them in several recent races, and now GM Jim Beattie admits he is building a young club he hopes will contend early in the next century, coinciding with a hoped-for new stadium. To that end, Beattie sent away Cy Young Award winner Pedro Martinez and second baseman Mike Lansing in payroll-driven trades the night of the expansion draft. He stockpiled blue-chip prospects in those deals, but the payoff isn't likely to show up in 1998. Offensively, super talent Vladimir Guerrero hit well despite repeated trips to the disabled list in '97, and center fielder Rondell White is becoming a force. Two more young players could take over the right side of the infield, Brad Fullmer at first base and Orlando Cabrera at second.

The Philadelphia Phillies made the biggest gains in the second half of 1997, climbing from a 24-61 record at the All-Star break to 68-94. Sure, that was still 33 games behind the Braves, but Atlanta was only one game better than Philadelphia over the second half. The Phils' rebuilding will be done around an offensive nucleus that includes Jackie Robinson Award–winning third baseman Scott Rolen, catcher Mike Lieberthal, shortstop prospect Desi Relaford and a couple of young outfielders acquired in trades, Bobby Abreu and Billy McMillon.

NL Central: Someone will finish sixth

The National League Central got plenty of attention in 1997, but it wasn't terribly positive. The Houston Astros were champions with an 84-78 record. The Pittsburgh Pirates were one of baseball's feel-good stories despite a 79-83 year, good enough for second place in the division that often was derided as Comedy Central. This division will be worth noticing in 1998, if only because of the most notable result of realignment: Someone in the National League Central gets to be the only sixth-place team in baseball in 1998. That's because Milwaukee is back in the National League. Coming off a 78-83 season, the Brewers look like they'll fit right in with this group.

But the relative newcomer who could have the biggest effect on the NL Central is Mark McGwire. The slugging first baseman joined the St. Louis Cardinals too late to help make up any ground in the race last year, but he should have an impact this year. If the Cardinals can get full, healthy years out of outfielders Ray Lankford and Brian Jordan in front of McGwire, their offense will be as good as any in the division. St. Louis' pitching staff is headed by youngsters Alan Benes and Matt Morris.

Houston did nothing to hurt itself by taking the first run at the dismantling of the Marlins. The Astros grabbed outfielder Moises Alou, most significant because he helps balance an offense too dependent on perennial All-Stars Jeff Bagwell and Craig Biggio. That extra offensive support, plus the emergence of outfielder Richard Hidalgo, could help Houston put together its best offense in years.

Pittsburgh indeed was the Cinderella story of 1997, and the Pirates have top-flight youngsters at virtually every position. Outfielder Jose Guillen jumped all the way from Class A in 1996 to major league regular in 1997, joining catcher Jason Kendall, second baseman Tony Womack and center fielder Jermaine Allensworth. Expect Allensworth to be pushed by Adrian Brown. Outfielder Emil Brown and powerful first baseman Ron Wright also could snare roster spots, and Pittsburgh feels so good about third baseman Freddy Garcia that incumbent Joe Randa was let go in the expansion draft. Pitching is equally promising, with closer Rich Loiselle coming off a 29-save rookie year to back up a rotation of Jon Lieber, Esteban Loaiza, Jason Schmidt, Steve Cooke and Francisco Cordova.

Cincinnati continues along its usual path, with general manager Jim Bowden employing his bargain-basement strategy to plug holes and create depth. A mid-season trade with Kansas City was a prime example as acquisitions Jon Nunnally and Chris Stynes both hit over .300. Bowden, who says he can't compete for free agents at any level, went after powerful but inconsistent Melvin Nieves in a deal with Detroit. Plus, if third baseman Willie Greene's 26 home runs and first baseman Eduardo Perez's 16 mean they finally are reaching their predicted stardom, the Reds could regain some offensive punch.

The Cubs have reason to believe they can avoid that sixth-place label. A late-season trade with the Mets for center fielder Lance Johnson and pitcher Mark Clark was a huge help. Clark bolsters a pitching staff that will be helped by a full season from Kevin Tapani, who went 9-3 after returning from injury. Young Jeremi Gonzalez and Kevin Foster showed signs of progress, and phenom Kerry Wood most likely will get his shot at the rotation.

Milwaukee is the mystery team, but manager Phil Garner's hustling group is made for National League baseball. The biggest challenge will be fitting the bats into the lineup. Dave Nilsson will probably become the left fielder after he and John Jaha split time at first base and DH in the American League. Recently acquired center fielder Marquis Grissom, All-Star third baseman Jeff Cirillo and middle infielders Jose Valentin and Fernando Vina form a solid nucleus. The Brewers need to deepen the pitching staff led by Cal Eldred and Scott Karl.

NL West: Anything could happen

Last to first. First to last. A playoff taste for everybody in the division. And now a new team. The National League West remains the least predictable of baseball's six divisions. Over the past three seasons, all four teams have made at least one playoff appearance, with a different division winner each year. The 1997 champ, San Francisco, jumped from last the previous season, swapping places with 1996 leader San Diego. This year the Arizona Diamondbacks are part of the mix.

The expansion Diamondbacks shouldn't be expected to dive right into the annual jumble in the standings, but then again, why not? Arizona proved it will be willing to spend money to win, going after free-agent shortstop Jay Bell and making a draft-day trade for third baseman Travis Fryman, whom they then traded to Cleveland for even pricier Matt Williams. But no expansion team has played .500 baseball in its first season, and the Diamondbacks probably won't be an exception.

San Francisco was the unlikely 1997 winner, jumping out quickly and refusing to fold against the pressure of the favored Dodgers. In fact, it was L.A. that crumbled in key games down the stretch. The Giants pulled off the title with baseball's biggest collection of free-agents-to-be, especially on the pitching staff, a fact not lost as they reworked the roster in the off-season. Closer Robb Nen was the first and most significant acquisition, as a free agent from Florida, because San Francisco had both Rod Beck and Roberto Hernandez on the free-agent list. But the offense is less of a worry, with Barry Bonds, Jeff Kent and J.T. Snow returning in the middle of the order. They will need to stay healthy, however, because the organization's depth has been severely depleted by trades in the past six months.

Los Angeles still must overcome its underchiever label. The Dodgers survived the expansion draft with all of its veteran players, despite persistent rumors that infielders Eric Karros, Todd Zeile and Eric Young might be taken. Their most significant new face is Paul Konerko, converted from catcher because Mike Piazza was in his way, who can play first or third base. The Dodgers remain the division's deepest team in pitching, despite an off-year from Hideo Nomo (14-12, 4.25 ERA). Chan Ho Park picked up much of that slack, and young talents Dennis Reyes and Darren Dreifort will have more of an impact this year.

San Diego paid offseason attention to replenishing its pitching staff, which now features ex-Marlin Kevin Brown along with closer deluxe Trevor Hoffman. The offense certainly figures to be better, considering that third baseman Ken Caminiti had a sub-par first half in 1997 as he came back from shoulder problems; center fielder Steve Finley fought through some first-half injury problems; and second baseman Quilvio Veras didn't regain his running form until after the All-Star Game. The potent bat of Tony Gwynn is a sure thing, but the big question is in left field, where Greg Vaughn hasn't rediscovered the power stroke he had in the American League.

The Colorado Rockies will give us a good look at the newest Blake Street Bomber, first baseman–outfielder Todd Helton, as first baseman Andres Galarraga opted for Atlanta's free-agent offer. Second baseman Mike Lansing came over from Montreal in a trade, filling the gap left by the late-season trade of Eric Young to Los Angeles. And shortstop Walt Weiss also left for Atlanta and will be replaced by exciting young Neifi Perez. The Young trade addressed the perennial Colorado question—pitching. Pedro Astacio came in the Young deal and immediately became the top arm on the staff. Add in Daryl Kyle, acquired as a free agent, and the Rockies finally can boast some veteran help to take the heat off promising youngsters Jamey Wright, Roger Bailey and John Thomson. If the Rockies can put a more balanced team on the field, then there is another reason to believe this division could be turned topsy-turvy one more time.

Final player statistics

1998 Baseball Weekly Almanac

Stats key for pitchers:

T–Throws right or left; **W**–Wins; **L**–Losses; **ERA**–Earned run average; **G**–Games; **GS**–Games started; **CG**–Complete games; **SHO**–Shutouts; **GF**–Games finished in relief; **SV**–Saves; **IP**–Innings pitched; **H**–Hits; **R**–Runs; **ER**–Earned runs; **HR**–Home runs; **BB**–Bases on balls; **SO**–Strikeouts; **WP**–Wild pitches; **BA**–Batting average against; **RV**–Rotisserie value.

Rotisserie values are provided by John Hunt. Dollar values are based on each player occupying a roster spot on a standard Rotisserie league team for an entire season. Players with no value (NV) had no effect or a negative effect on a Rotisserie team in 1997. In a standard 12-team league only 276 players can be active at one time.

Stats key for batters:

B–Bats right, left, or both; **BA**–Batting average; **G**–Games; **AB**–At-bats; **R**–Runs; **H**–Hits; **TB**–Total Bases; **2B**–Doubles; **3B**–Triples; **HR**–Home runs; **RBI**–Runs batted in; **SH**–Sacrifice hits; **SF**–Sacrifice flies; **BB**–Bases on balls; **SO**–Strikeouts; **SB**–Stolen bases; **CS**–Caught stealing; **SLG**–Slugging average; **OBA**–On-base average; **RV**–Rotisserie value.

Players are listed alphabetically by position within each league. Each player is listed at the position where he played the most games in 1997; statistics are for all games played in 1997.

Statistics are provided by the Elias Sports Bureau.

American League designated hitters

Name/Team	B	BA	G	AB	R	H	TB	2B	3B	HR	RBI	SH	SF	BB	SO	SB	CS	SLG	OBA	RV
Baines, Harold, ChiA-Bal.	L	.301	137	452	55	136	207	23	0	16	67	0	3	55	62	0	1	.458	.375	14
Canseco, Jose, Oak.	R	.235	108	388	56	91	179	19	0	23	74	0	4	51	122	8	2	.461	.325	12
Carter, Joe, Tor.	R	.234	157	612	76	143	244	30	4	21	102	0	9	40	105	8	2	.399	.284	11
Casey, Sean, Cle.	L	.200	6	10	1	2	2	0	0	0	1	0	0	1	2	0	0	.200	.333	NV
Cruz, Ivan, NYA	L	.250	11	20	0	5	6	1	0	0	3	0	0	2	4	0	0	.300	.318	NV
Davis, Chili, K.C.	B	.279	140	477	71	133	243	20	0	30	90	0	4	85	96	6	3	.509	.386	21
Fielder, Cecil, NYA	R	.260	98	361	40	94	148	15	0	13	61	0	6	51	87	0	0	.410	.358	6
Franco, Julio, Cle.-Mil.	R	.270	120	430	68	116	155	16	1	7	44	1	4	69	116	15	6	.360	.369	12
Gonzalez, Juan, Tex.	R	.296	133	533	87	158	314	24	3	42	131	0	10	33	107	0	0	.589	.335	29
Hamelin, Bob, Det.	L	.270	110	318	47	86	155	15	0	18	52	0	2	48	72	2	1	.487	.366	10
Henderson, Rickey, Ana.	R	.183	32	115	21	21	30	3	0	2	7	1	0	26	23	16	4	.261	.343	3
Incaviglia, Pete, Bal.-NYA	R	.247	53	154	19	38	57	4	0	5	12	0	1	11	46	0	0	.370	.308	NV
Jefferson, Reggie, Bos.	L	.319	136	489	74	156	230	33	1	13	67	1	3	24	93	1	2	.470	.358	17
Martinez, Edgar, Sea.	R	.330	155	542	104	179	300	35	1	28	108	0	6	119	86	2	4	.554	.456	30
Mitchell, Kevin, Cle.	R	.153	20	59	7	9	22	1	0	4	11	0	0	9	11	1	0	.373	.275	NV
Molitor, Paul, Min.	R	.305	135	538	63	164	234	32	4	10	89	2	12	45	73	11	4	.435	.351	21
Murray, Eddie, Ana.	B	.219	46	160	13	35	51	7	0	3	15	0	3	13	24	1	0	.319	.273	NV
Rohrmeier, Dan, Sea.	R	.333	7	9	4	3	3	0	0	0	2	0	0	2	4	0	0	.333	.455	NV
Samuel, Juan, Tor.	R	.284	45	95	13	27	49	5	4	3	15	1	0	10	28	5	3	.516	.364	3
Seitzer, Kevin, Cle.	R	.268	64	198	27	53	73	14	0	2	24	2	2	18	25	0	0	.369	.326	NV
Simms, Mike, Tex.	R	.252	59	111	13	28	51	8	0	5	22	0	2	8	27	0	1	.459	.298	NV
Stanley, Mike, Bos.-NYA	R	.297	125	347	61	103	176	25	0	16	65	0	8	54	72	0	0	.507	.393	12
Tettleton, Mickey, Tex.	B	.091	17	44	5	4	14	1	0	3	4	0	0	3	12	0	0	.318	.167	NV

American League catchers

Name/Team	B	BA	G	AB	R	H	TB	2B	3B	HR	RBI	SH	SF	BB	SO	SB	CS	SLG	OBA	RV
Alomar, Sandy, Cle.	R	.324	125	451	63	146	246	37	0	21	83	6	1	19	48	0	2	.545	.354	21
Borders, Pat, Cle.	R	.296	55	159	17	47	68	7	1	4	15	0	0	9	27	0	2	.428	.341	1
Brown, Kevin L., Tex.	R	.400	4	5	1	2	5	0	0	1	1	0	0	0	0	0	0	1.000	.400	NV
Casanova, Raul, Det.	B	.243	101	304	27	74	101	10	1	5	24	0	1	26	48	1	1	.332	.308	NV
Diaz, Einar, Cle.	R	.143	5	7	1	1	2	1	0	0	1	0	0	0	2	0	0	.286	.143	NV
Encarnacion, Angelo, Ana.	R	.412	11	17	2	7	11	1	0	1	4	0	0	0	1	2	0	.647	.412	NV
Fabregas, J., Ana.-ChiA	L	.258	121	360	33	93	127	11	1	7	51	6	4	14	46	1	1	.353	.285	3
Fasano, Sal, K.C.	R	.211	13	38	4	8	13	2	0	1	1	0	0	1	12	0	0	.342	.231	NV
Figga, Mike, NYA	R	.000	2	4	0	0	0	0	0	0	0	0	0	0	3	0	0	.000	.000	NV
Girardi, Joe, NYA	R	.264	112	398	38	105	133	23	1	1	50	5	2	26	53	2	3	.334	.311	2
Greene, Charlie, Bal.	R	.000	5	2	0	0	0	0	0	0	1	0	0	1	0	0	0	.000	.000	NV
Greene, Todd, Ana.	R	.290	34	124	24	36	69	6	0	9	24	0	0	7	25	2	0	.556	.328	4
Haselman, Bill, Bos.	R	.236	67	212	22	50	83	15	0	6	26	1	2	15	44	1	2	.392	.290	NV
Hatteberg, Scott, Bos.	L	.277	114	359	46	97	152	23	1	10	44	2	1	40	70	0	1	.434	.354	6
Hoiles, Chris, Bal.	R	.259	99	320	45	83	134	15	0	12	49	0	3	51	86	1	0	.419	.375	5
Jensen, Marcus, Det.	B	.182	8	11	1	2	2	0	0	0	1	0	0	1	5	0	0	.182	.250	NV
Johnson, Brian, Det.	R	.237	45	139	13	33	47	6	1	2	18	2	1	5	19	1	0	.338	.262	NV
Karkovice, Ron, ChiA	R	.181	51	138	10	25	46	3	0	6	18	4	5	11	32	0	0	.333	.248	NV
Kreuter, Chad, ChiA-Ana.	B	.231	89	255	25	59	87	9	2	5	21	1	0	29	66	0	3	.341	.310	NV
Laker, Tim, Bal.	R	.000	7	14	0	0	0	0	0	0	1	1	1	2	9	0	0	.000	.118	NV
Levis, Jesse, Mil.	L	.285	99	200	19	57	67	7	0	1	19	5	2	24	17	1	0	.335	.361	1
Leyritz, Jim, Ana.-Tex.	R	.277	121	379	58	105	149	11	0	11	64	4	6	60	78	2	1	.393	.379	9
Macfarlane, Mike, K.C.	R	.237	82	257	34	61	103	14	2	8	35	3	1	24	47	0	2	.401	.316	NV
Machado, Robert, ChiA	R	.200	10	15	1	3	5	0	1	0	2	1	0	1	6	0	0	.333	.250	NV
Martinez, Sandy, Tor.	L	.000	3	2	1	0	0	0	0	0	0	0	0	1	1	0	0	.000	.333	NV
Marzano, John, Sea.	R	.287	39	87	7	25	31	3	0	1	10	2	0	7	15	0	0	.356	.340	NV
Matheny, Mike, Mil.	R	.244	123	320	29	78	108	16	1	4	32	9	3	17	68	0	1	.338	.294	NV
Mayne, Brent, Oak.	L	.289	85	256	29	74	104	12	0	6	22	2	2	18	33	1	0	.406	.343	4
McKeel, Walt, Bos.	R	.000	5	3	0	0	0	0	0	0	0	0	0	0	1	0	0	.000	.000	NV
Mercedes, Henry, Tex.	R	.213	23	47	4	10	14	4	0	0	4	3	0	6	25	0	0	.298	.302	NV
Miller, Damian, Min.	R	.273	25	66	5	18	25	1	0	2	13	0	3	2	12	0	0	.379	.282	NV
Molina, Izzy, Oak.	R	.198	48	111	6	22	36	3	1	3	7	1	0	3	17	0	0	.324	.219	NV
Mosquera, Julio, Tor.	R	.250	3	8	0	2	3	1	0	0	0	0	0	0	2	0	0	.375	.250	NV
Myers, Greg, Min.	L	.267	62	165	24	44	72	11	1	5	28	0	2	16	29	0	0	.436	.328	1
O'Brien, Charlie, Tor.	R	.218	69	225	22	49	78	15	1	4	27	3	6	22	45	0	2	.347	.311	NV
Pena, Tony, ChiA	R	.164	31	67	4	11	12	1	0	0	8	0	1	8	13	0	0	.179	.250	NV
Posada, Jorge, NYA	B	.250	60	188	29	47	77	12	0	6	25	1	2	30	33	1	2	.410	.359	1
Rodriguez, Ivan, Tex.	R	.313	150	597	98	187	289	34	4	20	77	1	4	38	89	7	3	.484	.360	24
Rosario, Mel, Bal.	B	.000	4	3	0	0	0	0	0	0	0	0	0	0	1	0	0	.000	.000	NV
Santiago, Benito, Tor.	R	.243	97	341	31	83	132	10	0	13	42	1	5	17	80	1	0	.387	.279	3
Spehr, Tim, K.C.	R	.171	17	35	3	6	9	0	0	1	2	0	0	2	12	0	0	.257	.237	NV
Steinbach, Terry, Min.	R	.248	122	447	60	111	176	27	1	12	54	0	4	35	106	6	1	.394	.302	6

American League catchers

Name/Team	B	BA	G	AB	R	H	TB	2B	3B	HR	RBI	SH	SF	BB	SO	SB	CS	SLG	OBA	RV
Stewart, Andy, K.C.	R	.250	5	8	1	2	3	1	0	0	0	0	0	0	0	0	0	.375	.250	NV
Stinnett, Kelly, Mil.	R	.250	30	36	2	9	13	4	0	0	3	0	0	3	9	0	0	.361	.308	NV
Sweeney, Mike, K.C.	R	.242	84	240	30	58	87	8	0	7	31	1	2	17	33	3	2	.363	.306	2
Turner, Chris, Ana.	R	.261	13	23	4	6	12	1	1	1	2	1	0	5	8	0	0	.522	.393	NV
Valentin, Javier, Min.	B	.286	4	7	1	2	2	0	0	0	0	0	0	0	3	0	0	.286	.286	NV
Varitek, Jason, Bos.	B	1.000	1	1	0	1	1	0	0	0	0	0	0	0	0	0	0	1.000	1.000	NV
Walbeck, Matt, Det.	B	.277	47	137	18	38	50	3	0	3	10	0	2	12	19	3	3	.365	.331	1
Webster, Lenny, Bal.	R	.255	98	259	29	66	97	8	1	7	37	3	1	22	46	0	1	.375	.317	2
Wilkins, Rick, Sea.	L	.250	5	12	2	3	7	1	0	1	4	0	1	1	2	0	0	.583	.286	NV
Williams, George, Oak.	B	.289	76	201	30	58	78	9	1	3	22	2	1	35	46	0	1	.388	.397	1
Wilson, Dan, Sea.	R	.270	146	508	66	137	215	31	1	15	74	8	3	39	72	7	2	.423	.326	13

American League first basemen

Name/Team	B	BA	G	AB	R	H	TB	2B	3B	HR	RBI	SH	SF	BB	SO	SB	CS	SLG	OBA	RV
Blowers, Mike, Sea.	R	.293	68	150	22	44	64	5	0	5	20	4	2	21	33	0	0	.427	.376	2
Clark, Tony, Det.	B	.276	159	580	105	160	290	28	3	32	117	0	5	93	144	1	3	.500	.376	21
Clark, Will, Tex.	L	.326	110	393	56	128	195	29	1	12	51	0	5	49	62	0	0	.496	.400	14
Colbrunn, Greg, Min.	R	.281	70	217	24	61	90	14	0	5	26	0	2	8	38	1	2	.415	.307	3
Delgado, Carlos, Tor.	L	.262	153	519	79	136	274	42	3	30	91	0	4	64	133	0	3	.528	.350	15
Erstad, Darin, Ana.	L	.299	139	539	99	161	251	34	4	16	77	5	6	51	86	23	8	.466	.360	27
Jaha, John, Mil.	R	.247	46	162	25	40	80	7	0	11	26	0	2	25	40	1	0	.494	.354	3
King, Jeff, K.C.	R	.238	155	543	84	129	245	30	1	28	112	1	12	89	96	16	5	.451	.341	20
Martinez, Tino, NYA	L	.296	158	594	96	176	343	31	2	44	141	0	13	75	75	3	1	.577	.371	33
McGwire, Mark, Oak.	R	.284	105	366	48	104	230	24	0	34	81	0	5	58	98	1	0	.628	.383	20
Nilsson, Dave, Mil.	L	.278	156	554	71	154	247	33	0	20	81	1	7	65	88	2	3	.446	.352	15
Ortiz, David, Min.	L	.327	15	49	10	16	22	3	0	1	6	0	0	2	19	0	0	.449	.353	NV
Palmeiro, Rafael, Bal.	L	.254	158	614	95	156	298	24	2	38	110	0	6	67	109	5	2	.485	.329	21
Sexson, Richie, Cle.	R	.273	5	11	1	3	3	0	0	0	0	0	0	2	0	0	0	.273	.273	NV
Sorrento, Paul, Sea.	L	.269	146	457	68	123	235	19	0	31	80	0	2	51	112	0	2	.514	.345	16
Stahoviak, Scott, Min.	L	.229	91	275	33	63	110	17	0	10	33	0	4	24	73	5	4	.400	.301	3
Stevens, Lee, Tex.	L	.300	137	426	58	128	219	24	2	21	74	1	3	23	83	1	3	.514	.336	17
Sutton, Larry, K.C.	L	.290	27	69	9	20	28	2	0	2	8	1	0	5	12	0	0	.406	.338	NV
Thomas, Frank, ChiA	R	.347	146	530	110	184	324	35	0	35	125	0	7	109	69	1	1	.611	.456	36
Thome, Jim, Cle.	L	.286	147	496	104	142	287	25	0	40	102	0	8	120	146	1	1	.579	.423	25
Unroe, Tim, Mil.	R	.250	32	16	3	4	11	1	0	2	5	0	0	2	9	2	0	.688	.333	NV
Valdez, Mario, ChiA	L	.243	54	115	11	28	38	7	0	1	13	0	2	17	39	1	0	.330	.350	NV
Vaughn, Mo, Bos.	L	.315	141	527	91	166	295	24	0	35	96	0	3	86	154	2	2	.560	.420	28
Williamson, Antone, Mil.	L	.204	24	54	2	11	14	3	0	0	6	1	1	4	8	0	1	.259	.254	NV

American League second basemen

Name/Team	B	BA	G	AB	R	H	TB	2B	3B	HR	RBI	SH	SF	BB	SO	SB	CS	SLG	OBA	RV
Alicea, Luis, Ana.	B	.253	128	388	59	98	143	16	7	5	37	4	2	69	65	22	8	.369	.375	12
Alomar, Roberto, Bal.	B	.333	112	412	64	137	206	23	2	14	60	7	7	40	43	9	3	.500	.390	21
Branson, Jeff, Cle.	L	.264	29	72	5	19	29	4	0	2	7	0	2	7	17	0	2	.403	.329	NV
Brito, Tilson, Tor.-Oak.	R	.238	66	172	17	41	54	5	1	2	14	2	2	10	38	1	0	.314	.285	NV
Bush, Homer, NYA	R	.364	10	11	2	4	4	0	0	0	3	0	0	0	0	0	0	.364	.364	NV
Candaele, Casey, Cle.	B	.308	14	26	5	8	9	1	0	0	4	0	0	1	1	1	0	.346	.333	NV
Catalanotto, Frank, Det.	L	.308	13	26	2	8	10	2	0	0	3	0	0	3	7	0	0	.385	.379	NV
Cedeno, Domingo, Tex.	B	.282	113	365	49	103	146	19	6	4	36	2	1	27	77	3	3	.400	.334	5
Cora, Joey, Sea.	B	.300	149	574	105	172	253	40	4	11	54	8	9	53	49	6	7	.441	.359	15
Diaz, Eddy, Min.	R	.220	16	50	4	11	15	2	1	0	7	0	0	1	5	0	0	.300	.235	NV
Duncan, Mrn., NYA-Tor.	R	.236	89	339	36	80	97	14	0	1	25	1	0	12	78	6	3	.286	.268	NV
Durham, Ray, ChiA	B	.271	155	634	106	172	242	27	5	11	53	2	8	61	96	33	16	.382	.337	24
Easley, Damion, Det.	R	.264	151	527	97	139	248	37	3	22	72	4	5	68	102	28	13	.471	.362	25
Fernandez, Tony, Cle.	B	.286	120	409	55	117	173	21	1	11	44	6	3	22	47	6	6	.423	.323	11
Frye, Jeff, Bos.	R	.312	127	404	56	126	175	36	2	3	51	2	7	27	44	19	8	.433	.352	18
Garcia, Carlos, Tor.	R	.220	103	350	29	77	108	18	2	3	23	10	4	15	60	11	3	.309	.253	NV
Grebeck, Craig, Ana.	R	.270	63	126	12	34	46	9	0	1	6	5	1	18	11	0	1	.365	.359	NV
Guevara, Giomar, Sea.	R	.000	5	4	0	0	0	0	0	0	0	0	0	0	2	1	0	.000	.000	NV
Halter, Shane, K.C.	R	.276	74	123	16	34	47	5	1	2	10	4	0	10	28	4	3	.382	.341	1
Hansen, Jed, K.C.	R	.309	34	94	11	29	40	6	1	1	14	2	1	13	29	3	2	.426	.394	1
Howard, David, K.C.	B	.241	80	162	24	39	52	8	1	1	13	3	1	10	31	2	2	.321	.287	NV
Huson, Jeff, Mil.	L	.203	84	143	12	29	32	3	0	0	11	2	1	5	15	3	0	.224	.238	NV
Kelly, Pat, NYA	R	.242	67	120	25	29	43	6	1	2	10	2	1	14	37	8	1	.358	.324	1
Knoblauch, Chuck, Min.	R	.291	156	611	117	178	251	26	10	9	58	0	4	84	84	62	10	.411	.390	43
Ledesma, Aaron, Bal.	R	.352	43	88	24	31	44	5	1	2	11	1	1	13	9	1	0	.500	.437	2

American League second basemen

Name/Team	B	BA	G	AB	R	H	TB	2B	3B	HR	RBI	SH	SF	BB	SO	SB	CS	SLG	OBA	RV
Loretta, Mark, Mil.	R	.287	132	418	56	120	162	17	5	5	47	5	10	47	60	5	5	.388	.354	8
McLemore, Mark, Tex.	B	.261	89	349	47	91	115	17	2	1	25	6	2	40	54	7	5	.330	.338	2
Offerman, Jose, K.C.	B	.297	106	424	59	126	167	23	6	2	39	6	0	41	64	9	10	.394	.359	10
Phillips, Tony, ChiA-Ana.	B	.275	141	534	96	147	209	34	2	8	57	5	4	102	118	13	10	.391	.392	13
Reboulet, Jeff, Bal.	R	.237	99	228	26	54	75	9	0	4	27	11	2	23	44	3	0	.329	.307	NV
Reed, Jody, Det.	R	.196	52	112	6	22	24	2	0	0	8	3	1	10	15	3	2	.214	.278	NV
Sanchez, Rey, NYA	R	.312	38	138	21	43	58	12	0	1	15	5	1	5	21	0	4	.420	.338	1
Sojo, Luis, NYA	R	.307	77	215	27	66	80	6	1	2	25	5	2	16	14	3	1	.372	.355	4
Spiezio, Scott, Oak.	B	.243	147	538	58	131	209	28	4	14	65	3	4	44	75	9	3	.388	.300	8
Valentin, John, Bos.	R	.306	143	575	95	176	287	47	5	18	77	1	5	58	66	7	4	.499	.372	22
Vina, Fernando, Mil.	L	.275	79	324	37	89	117	12	2	4	28	2	3	12	23	8	7	.361	.312	6

American League third basemen

Name/Team	B	BA	G	AB	R	H	TB	2B	3B	HR	RBI	SH	SF	BB	SO	SB	CS	SLG	OBA	RV
Arias, George, Ana.	R	.333	3	6	1	2	2	0	0	0	1	0	0	0	0	0	0	.333	.333	NV
Bellhorn, Mark, Oak.	B	.228	68	224	33	51	80	9	1	6	19	5	0	32	70	7	1	.357	.324	2
Benjamin, Mike, Bos.	R	.233	49	116	12	27	38	9	1	0	7	1	1	4	27	2	3	.328	.262	NV
Boggs, Wade, NYA	L	.292	104	353	55	103	140	23	1	4	28	2	4	48	38	0	1	.397	.373	4
Brosius, Scott, Oak.	R	.203	129	479	59	97	152	20	1	11	41	5	4	34	102	9	4	.317	.259	NV
Cirillo, Jeff, Mil.	R	.288	154	580	74	167	247	46	2	10	82	4	3	60	74	4	3	.426	.367	14
Coomer, Ron, Min.	R	.298	140	523	63	156	229	30	2	13	85	0	5	22	91	4	3	.438	.324	17
Cooper, Scott, K.C.	L	.201	75	159	12	32	49	6	1	3	15	2	2	17	32	1	1	.308	.283	NV
Crespo, Felipe, Tor.	B	.286	12	28	3	8	13	0	1	1	5	1	0	2	4	0	0	.464	.333	NV
Davis, Russ, Sea.	R	.271	119	420	57	114	205	29	1	20	63	3	2	27	100	6	2	.488	.317	14
Eenhoorn, Robert, Ana.	R	.350	11	20	2	7	11	1	0	1	6	0	1	0	2	0	0	.550	.333	NV
Evans, Tom, Tor.	R	.289	12	38	7	11	16	2	0	1	2	0	0	2	10	0	1	.421	.341	NV
Fox, Andy, NYA	L	.226	22	31	13	7	8	1	0	0	1	2	0	7	9	2	1	.258	.368	NV
Fryman, Travis, Det.	R	.274	154	595	90	163	262	27	3	22	102	0	11	46	113	16	3	.440	.326	24
Gates, Brent, Sea.	B	.238	65	151	18	36	53	8	0	3	20	2	3	14	21	0	0	.351	.298	NV
Hayes, Charlie, NYA	R	.258	100	353	39	91	140	16	0	11	53	0	4	40	66	3	2	.397	.332	6
Hollins, Dave, Ana.	R	.288	149	572	101	165	246	29	2	16	85	1	5	62	124	16	6	.430	.363	23
Howell, Jack, Ana.	L	.259	77	174	25	45	94	7	0	14	34	1	3	13	36	1	0	.540	.305	5
Magadan, Dave, Oak.	L	.303	128	271	38	82	106	10	1	4	30	4	1	50	40	1	0	.391	.414	5
Manto, Jeff, Cle.	R	.267	16	30	3	8	17	3	0	2	7	0	0	1	10	0	0	.567	.290	NV
Naehring, Tim, Bos.	R	.286	70	259	38	74	121	18	1	9	40	0	3	38	40	1	1	.467	.375	6
Norton, Greg, ChiA	R	.265	18	34	5	9	15	2	2	0	1	1	0	2	8	0	0	.441	.306	NV
Palmer, Dean, Tex.-K.C.	R	.256	143	542	70	139	241	31	1	23	86	1	5	41	134	2	2	.445	.310	12
Paquette, Craig, K.C.	R	.230	77	252	26	58	99	15	1	8	33	1	2	10	57	2	2	.393	.263	1
Pozo, Arquimedez, Bos.	R	.267	4	15	0	4	5	1	0	0	3	1	1	0	5	0	0	.333	.250	NV
Raabe, Brian, Sea.	R	.000	2	3	0	0	0	0	0	0	0	0	0	1	2	0	0	.000	.250	NV
Ripken, Cal, Bal.	R	.270	162	615	79	166	247	30	0	17	84	0	10	56	73	1	0	.402	.331	12
Sheets, Andy, Sea.	R	.247	32	89	18	22	37	3	0	4	9	5	1	7	34	2	0	.416	.299	NV
Silvestri, Dave, Tex.	R	.000	2	4	0	0	0	0	0	0	0	0	0	0	1	0	0	.000	.000	NV
Snopek, Chris, ChiA	R	.218	86	298	27	65	95	15	0	5	35	4	2	18	51	3	2	.319	.263	NV
Sprague, Ed, Tor.	R	.228	138	504	63	115	194	29	4	14	48	0	1	51	102	0	1	.385	.306	NV
Tatis, Fernando, Tex.	R	.256	60	223	29	57	90	9	0	8	29	2	2	14	42	3	0	.404	.297	3
Ventura, Robin, ChiA	L	.262	54	183	27	48	78	10	1	6	26	0	3	34	21	0	0	.426	.373	1
Walker, Todd, Min.	L	.237	52	156	15	37	55	7	1	3	16	1	2	11	30	7	0	.353	.288	2
Williams, Matt, Cle.	R	.263	151	596	86	157	291	32	3	20	105	0	2	34	108	12	4	.488	.307	23

American League shortstops

Name/Team	B	BA	G	AB	R	H	TB	2B	3B	HR	RBI	SH	SF	BB	SO	SB	CS	SLG	OBA	RV
Batista, Tony, Oak.	R	.202	68	188	22	38	62	10	1	4	18	3	0	14	31	2	2	.330	.265	NV
Bell, Jay, K.C.	R	.291	153	573	89	167	264	28	3	21	92	3	9	71	101	10	6	.461	.368	23
Bordick, Mike, Bal.	R	.236	153	509	55	120	162	19	1	7	46	12	4	33	66	0	2	.318	.283	NV
Bournigal, Rafael, Oak.	R	.279	79	222	29	62	74	9	0	1	20	7	0	16	19	2	1	.333	.339	1
Cruz, Deivi, Det.	R	.241	147	436	35	105	137	26	0	2	40	14	3	14	55	3	6	.314	.263	NV
DiSarcina, Gary, Ana.	R	.246	154	549	52	135	179	28	2	4	47	8	5	17	29	7	8	.326	.271	2
Espinoza, Alvaro, Sea.	R	.181	33	72	3	13	14	1	0	0	7	3	0	2	12	1	1	.194	.213	NV
Frias, Hanley, Tex.	B	.192	14	26	4	5	6	1	0	0	1	0	0	1	4	0	0	.231	.222	NV
Garciaparra, Nomar, Bos.	R	.306	153	684	122	209	365	44	11	30	98	2	7	35	92	22	9	.534	.342	37
Gil, Benji, Tex.	R	.224	110	317	35	71	103	13	2	5	31	6	4	17	96	1	2	.325	.263	NV
Gonzalez, Alex, Tor.	R	.239	126	426	46	102	165	23	2	12	35	11	2	34	94	15	6	.387	.302	8
Guillen, Ozzie, ChiA	L	.245	142	490	59	120	165	21	6	4	52	11	4	22	24	5	3	.337	.275	2
Hocking, Denny, Min.	B	.257	115	253	28	65	91	12	4	2	25	5	1	18	51	3	5	.360	.308	1
Jackson, Damian, Cle.	R	.111	8	9	2	1	1	0	0	0	0	0	0	0	1	1	0	.111	.200	NV

American League shortstops

Name/Team	B	BA	G	AB	R	H	TB	2B	3B	HR	RBI	SH	SF	BB	SO	SB	CS	SLG	OBA	RV
Jeter, Derek, NYA	R	.291	159	654	116	190	265	31	7	10	70	8	2	74	125	23	12	.405	.370	24
Martin, Norberto, ChiA	R	.300	71	213	24	64	79	7	1	2	27	0	0	6	31	1	4	.371	.320	3
Martinez, Mata, K.C.	B	.226	16	31	3	7	10	1	1	0	3	1	0	6	8	0	0	.323	.351	NV
Meares, Pat, Min.	R	.276	134	439	63	121	180	23	3	10	60	3	7	18	86	7	7	.410	.323	11
Miller, Orlando, Det.	R	.234	50	111	13	26	41	7	1	2	10	1	1	5	24	1	0	.369	.289	NV
Perez, Tomas, Tor.	B	.195	40	123	9	24	31	3	2	0	9	3	0	11	28	1	1	.252	.267	NV
Ripken, Billy, Tex.	R	.276	71	203	18	56	76	9	1	3	24	1	5	9	32	0	1	.374	.300	1
Rodriguez, Alex, Sea.	R	.300	141	587	100	176	291	40	3	23	84	4	1	41	99	29	6	.496	.350	35
Sheldon, Scott, Oak.	R	.250	13	24	2	6	9	0	0	1	2	1	0	1	6	0	0	.375	.308	NV
Tejada, Miguel, Oak.	R	.202	26	99	10	20	33	3	2	2	10	0	0	2	22	2	0	.333	.240	NV
Valentin, Jose, Mil.	B	.253	136	494	58	125	201	23	1	17	58	4	5	39	109	19	8	.407	.310	16
Vizquel, Omar, Cle.	B	.280	153	565	89	158	208	23	6	5	49	16	2	57	58	43	12	.368	.347	28
Wilson, Enrique, Cle.	B	.333	5	15	2	5	5	0	0	0	1	0	0	0	2	0	0	.333	.333	NV

American League outfielders

Name/Team	B	BA	G	AB	R	H	TB	2B	3B	HR	RBI	SH	SF	BB	SO	SB	CS	SLG	OBA	RV
Abbott, Jeff, ChiA	R	.263	19	38	8	10	14	1	0	1	2	0	0	0	6	0	0	.368	.263	NV
Amaral, Rich, Sea.	R	.284	89	190	34	54	62	5	0	1	21	5	2	10	34	12	8	.326	.327	6
Anderson, Brady, Bal.	L	.288	151	590	97	170	277	39	7	18	73	2	1	84	105	18	12	.469	.393	24
Anderson, Garret, Ana.	L	.303	154	624	76	189	255	36	3	8	92	1	5	30	70	10	4	.409	.334	21
Aven, Bruce, Cle.	R	.211	13	19	4	4	5	1	0	0	2	0	0	1	5	0	1	.263	.250	NV
Banks, Brian, Mil.	B	.206	28	68	9	14	18	1	0	1	8	0	1	6	17	0	1	.265	.267	NV
Bartee, Kimera, Det.	B	.200	12	5	4	1	1	0	0	0	0	0	0	2	2	3	1	.200	.500	NV
Becker, Rich, Min.	L	.264	132	443	61	117	175	22	3	10	45	2	2	62	130	17	5	.395	.354	13
Belle, Albert, ChiA	R	.274	161	634	90	174	311	45	1	30	116	0	8	53	105	4	4	.491	.332	22
Benitez, Yamil, K.C.	R	.267	53	191	22	51	84	7	1	8	21	2	0	10	49	2	2	.440	.307	3
Berroa, G., Oak.-Bal.	R	.283	156	561	88	159	262	25	0	26	90	0	7	76	120	4	4	.467	.369	20
Bragg, Darren, Bos.	L	.257	153	513	65	132	198	35	2	9	57	5	4	61	102	10	6	.386	.337	9
Brede, Brent, Min.	L	.274	61	190	25	52	74	11	1	3	21	1	1	21	38	7	2	.389	.347	4
Brumfield, Jacob, Tor.	R	.207	58	174	22	36	49	5	1	2	20	1	1	14	31	4	4	.282	.268	NV
Buford, Damon, Tex.	R	.224	122	366	49	82	124	18	0	8	39	3	2	30	83	18	7	.339	.287	7
Buhner, Jay, Sea.	R	.243	157	540	104	131	273	18	2	40	109	0	1	119	175	0	0	.506	.383	17
Burnitz, Jeromy, Mil.	L	.281	153	494	85	139	273	37	8	27	85	3	0	75	111	20	13	.553	.382	27
Butler, Rich, Tor.	L	.286	7	14	3	4	5	1	0	0	2	0	0	2	3	0	1	.357	.375	NV
Cameron, Mike, ChiA	R	.259	116	379	63	98	164	18	3	14	55	2	5	55	105	23	2	.433	.356	18
Carr, Chuck, Mil.	B	.130	26	46	3	6	9	3	0	0	1	0	2	2	11	1	0	.196	.184	NV
Clyburn, Danny, Bal.	R	.000	2	3	0	0	0	0	0	0	0	0	0	0	2	0	0	.000	.000	NV
Coleman, Michael, Bos.	R	.167	8	24	2	4	5	1	0	0	2	1	0	0	11	1	0	.208	.167	NV
Coleman, Vince, Det.	B	.071	6	14	0	1	1	0	0	0	0	0	0	1	3	0	0	.071	.133	NV
Cordero, Wilfredo, Bos.	R	.281	140	570	82	160	246	26	3	18	72	0	4	31	122	1	3	.432	.320	13
Cordova, Marty, Min.	R	.246	103	378	44	93	164	18	4	15	51	0	2	30	92	5	3	.434	.305	7
Cruz, Jose., Sea.-Tor.	B	.248	104	395	59	98	197	19	1	26	68	1	5	41	117	7	2	.499	.315	14
Curtis, Chad, Cle.-NYA	R	.284	115	349	59	99	168	22	1	15	55	2	9	43	59	12	6	.481	.362	16
Damon, Johnny, K.C.	L	.275	146	472	70	130	182	12	8	8	48	6	1	42	70	16	10	.386	.338	14
Davis, Eric, Bal.	R	.304	42	158	29	48	83	11	0	8	25	0	3	14	47	6	0	.525	.358	7
Dellucci, Dave, Bal.	L	.222	17	27	3	6	10	1	0	1	3	0	0	4	7	0	0	.370	.344	NV
Devereaux, Mike, Tex.	R	.208	29	72	8	15	18	3	0	0	7	0	1	7	10	1	0	.250	.275	NV
Diaz, Alex, Tex.	R	.222	28	90	8	20	30	4	0	2	12	0	1	5	13	1	1	.333	.268	NV
Ducey, Rob, Sea.	L	.287	76	143	25	41	75	15	2	5	10	0	2	6	31	3	3	.524	.311	2
Dunn, Todd, Mil.	R	.229	44	118	17	27	41	5	0	3	9	0	0	2	39	3	0	.347	.242	NV
Dye, Jermaine, K.C.	R	.236	75	263	26	62	97	14	0	7	22	1	1	17	51	2	1	.369	.284	NV
Edmonds, Jim, Ana.	L	.291	133	502	82	146	251	27	0	26	80	0	5	60	80	5	7	.500	.368	20
Encarnacion, Juan, Det.	R	.212	11	33	3	7	13	1	1	1	5	0	0	3	12	3	1	.394	.316	NV
Fonville, Chad, ChiA	B	.111	9	9	1	1	1	0	0	0	1	1	0	1	1	2	0	.111	.200	NV
Giambi, Jason, Oak.	L	.293	142	519	66	152	257	41	2	20	81	0	8	55	89	0	1	.495	.362	16
Giles, Brian, Cle.	L	.268	130	377	62	101	173	15	3	17	61	3	7	63	50	13	3	.459	.368	16
Goodwin, Tom, K.C.-Tex.	L	.260	150	574	90	149	193	26	6	2	39	11	3	44	88	50	16	.336	.314	26
Green, Shawn, Tor.	L	.287	135	429	57	123	201	22	4	16	53	1	4	36	99	14	3	.469	.340	18
Greer, Rusty, Tex.	L	.321	157	601	112	193	319	42	3	26	87	1	2	83	87	9	5	.531	.405	30
Grieve, Ben, Oak.	L	.312	24	93	12	29	44	6	0	3	24	1	0	13	25	0	0	.473	.402	2
Griffey, Ken, Sea.	L	.304	157	608	125	185	393	34	3	56	147	0	12	76	121	15	4	.646	.382	46
Grissom, Marquis, Cle.	R	.262	144	558	74	146	221	27	6	12	66	6	9	43	89	22	13	.396	.317	18
Hall, Joe, Det.	R	.500	2	4	1	2	3	1	0	0	3	0	0	0	0	0	0	.750	.500	NV
Hammonds, Jeffrey, Bal.	R	.264	118	397	71	105	193	19	3	21	55	0	2	32	73	15	1	.486	.323	17
Higginson, Bobby, Det.	L	.299	146	546	94	163	284	30	5	27	101	0	4	70	85	12	7	.520	.379	28
Hubbard, Trinidad, Cle.	R	.250	7	12	3	3	4	1	0	0	0	0	0	1	3	2	0	.333	.308	NV
Hunter, Brian, Det.	R	.269	162	658	112	177	232	29	7	4	45	8	5	66	121	74	18	.353	.334	41
Hurst, Jimmy, Det.	R	.176	13	17	1	3	7	1	0	1	1	0	0	2	6	0	0	.412	.263	NV

American League outfielders

Name/Team	B	BA	G	AB	R	H	TB	2B	3B	HR	RBI	SH	SF	BB	SO	SB	CS	SLG	OBA	RV
Ibanez, Raul, Sea.	L	.154	11	26	3	4	9	0	1	1	4	0	0	0	6	0	0	.346	.154	NV
Jackson, Darrin, Min.-Mil.	R	.261	75	211	26	55	81	9	1	5	36	5	2	6	31	4	1	.384	.279	4
Justice, David, Cle.	L	.329	139	495	84	163	295	31	1	33	101	0	7	80	79	3	5	.596	.418	30
Kelly, Roberto, Min.-Sea.	R	.291	105	368	58	107	173	26	2	12	59	2	3	22	67	9	5	.470	.333	14
Latham, Chris, Min.	B	.182	15	22	4	4	5	1	0	0	1	0	0	0	8	0	0	.227	.182	NV
Lawton, Matt, Min.	L	.248	142	460	74	114	191	29	3	14	60	1	1	76	81	7	4	.415	.366	8
Lennon, Patrick, Oak.	R	.293	56	116	14	34	45	6	1	1	14	0	0	15	35	0	1	.388	.374	NV
Lesher, Brian, Oak.	R	.229	46	131	17	30	48	4	1	4	16	0	2	9	30	4	1	.366	.275	NV
Lewis, Darren, ChiA	R	.234	81	77	15	18	19	1	0	0	5	5	0	11	14	11	4	.247	.330	2
Long, Ryan, K.C.	R	.222	6	9	2	2	2	0	0	0	2	0	0	0	3	0	0	.222	.300	NV
Mack, Shane, Bos.	R	.315	60	130	13	41	57	7	0	3	17	2	2	9	24	2	1	.438	.368	3
Malave, Jose, Bos.	R	.000	4	4	0	0	0	0	0	0	0	0	0	0	2	0	0	.000	.000	NV
Martinez, Dave, ChiA	L	.286	145	504	78	144	208	16	6	12	55	5	6	55	69	12	6	.413	.356	16
Mashore, Damon, Oak.	R	.247	92	279	55	69	92	10	2	3	18	7	1	50	82	5	4	.330	.370	NV
McDonald, Jason, Oak.	B	.263	78	236	47	62	93	11	4	4	14	2	1	36	49	13	8	.394	.361	6
Merced, Orlando, Tor.	L	.266	98	368	45	98	152	23	2	9	40	0	2	47	62	7	3	.413	.352	7
Mieske, Matt, Mil.	R	.249	84	253	39	63	99	15	3	5	21	0	1	19	50	1	0	.391	.300	NV
Mouton, Lyle, ChiA	R	.269	88	242	26	65	89	9	0	5	23	0	3	14	66	4	4	.368	.308	3
Myers, Rod, K.C.	L	.257	31	101	14	26	39	7	0	2	9	2	0	17	22	4	0	.386	.370	NV
Nevin, Phil, Det.	R	.235	93	251	32	59	104	16	1	9	35	0	1	25	68	0	1	.414	.306	1
Newfield, Marc, Mil.	R	.229	50	157	14	36	47	8	0	1	18	0	3	14	27	0	0	.299	.295	NV
Newson, Warren, Tex.	L	.213	81	169	23	36	78	10	1	10	23	0	1	31	53	3	0	.462	.333	1
Nieves, Melvin, Det.	B	.228	116	359	46	82	162	18	1	20	64	0	2	39	157	1	7	.451	.311	6
Nixon, Otis, Tor.	B	.262	103	401	54	105	122	9	1	1	26	6	5	52	54	47	10	.304	.343	23
Nunnally, Jon, K.C.	L	.241	13	29	8	7	12	0	1	1	4	0	0	5	7	0	0	.414	.353	NV
O'Leary, Troy, Bos.	L	.309	146	499	65	154	239	32	4	15	80	1	4	39	70	0	5	.479	.358	17
O'Neill, Paul, NYA	L	.324	149	553	89	179	284	42	0	21	117	0	9	75	92	10	7	.514	.399	31
Ordonez, Magglio, ChiA	R	.319	21	69	12	22	40	6	0	4	11	1	0	2	8	1	2	.580	.338	1
Palmeiro, Orlando, Ana.	L	.216	74	134	19	29	35	2	2	0	8	3	1	17	11	2	2	.261	.307	NV
Pemberton, Rudy, Bos.	R	.238	27	63	8	15	23	2	0	2	10	0	0	4	13	0	0	.365	.314	NV
Perez, Robert, Tor.	R	.192	37	78	4	15	27	4	1	2	6	0	0	0	16	0	0	.346	.192	NV
Pose, Scott, NYA	L	.218	54	87	19	19	23	2	1	0	5	0	0	9	11	3	1	.264	.292	NV
Pride, Curtis, Det.-Bos.	L	.213	81	164	22	35	56	4	4	3	20	2	1	24	46	6	4	.341	.316	NV
Raines, Tim, NYA	B	.321	74	271	56	87	123	20	2	4	38	0	6	41	34	8	5	.454	.403	11
Ramirez, Manny, Cle.	R	.328	150	561	99	184	302	40	0	26	88	0	4	79	115	2	3	.538	.415	27
Roberts, Bip, K.C.-Cle.	B	.302	120	431	63	130	166	20	2	4	44	1	5	28	67	18	3	.385	.345	17
Sagmoen, Marc, Tex.	L	.140	21	43	2	6	11	2	0	1	4	0	1	2	13	0	0	.256	.174	NV
Salmon, Tim, Ana.	R	.296	157	582	95	172	301	28	1	33	129	0	11	95	142	9	12	.517	.394	31
Sierra, Ruben, Tor.	B	.208	14	48	4	10	17	0	2	1	5	0	1	3	13	0	0	.354	.250	NV
Stairs, Matt, Oak.	L	.298	133	352	62	105	205	19	0	27	73	1	4	50	60	3	2	.582	.386	19
Stewart, Shannon, Tor.	R	.286	44	168	25	48	75	13	7	0	22	0	2	19	24	10	3	.446	.368	5
Strawberry, Darryl, NYA	L	.103	11	29	1	3	4	1	0	0	2	0	0	3	9	0	0	.138	.188	NV
Surhoff, B.J., Bal.	L	.284	147	528	80	150	242	30	4	18	88	3	10	49	60	1	1	.458	.345	15
Tarasco, Tony, Bal.	L	.205	100	166	26	34	65	8	1	7	26	1	0	25	33	2	2	.392	.313	NV
Tavarez, Jesus, Bos.	B	.174	42	69	12	12	17	3	1	0	9	0	1	4	9	0	0	.246	.216	NV
Tinsley, Lee, Sea.	B	.197	49	122	12	24	34	6	2	0	6	0	0	11	34	2	0	.279	.263	NV
Trammell, Bubba, Det.	R	.228	44	123	14	28	45	5	0	4	13	0	2	15	35	3	1	.366	.307	NV
Vitiello, Joe, K.C.	R	.238	51	130	11	31	52	6	0	5	18	0	0	14	37	0	0	.400	.322	NV
Voigt, Jack, Mil.	R	.245	72	151	20	37	74	9	2	8	22	2	1	19	36	1	2	.490	.331	1
Walton, Jerome, Bal.	R	.294	26	68	8	20	30	1	0	3	9	2	0	4	10	0	0	.441	.333	NV
Whiten, Mark, NYA	B	.265	69	215	34	57	83	11	0	5	24	1	0	30	47	4	2	.386	.360	3
Williams, Bernie, NYA	B	.328	129	509	107	167	277	35	6	21	100	0	8	73	80	15	8	.544	.408	32
Williams, Gerald, Mil.	R	.253	155	566	73	143	209	32	2	10	41	5	5	19	90	23	9	.369	.282	13
Young, Ernie, Oak.	R	.223	71	175	22	39	61	7	0	5	15	2	2	19	57	1	3	.349	.303	NV

American League relief pitchers (batting)

Name/Team	B	BA	G	AB	R	H	TB	2B	3B	HR	RBI	SH	SF	BB	SO	SB	CS	SLG	OBA
Adamson, Joel, Mil.	L	.000	30	3	0	0	0	0	0	0	0	0	0	0	0	0	0	.000	.000
Castillo, Tony J., ChiA	L	.000	64	1	0	0	0	0	0	0	0	0	0	0	0	0	0	.000	.000
Castillo, Carlos, ChiA	R	1.000	37	1	0	1	1	0	0	0	0	0	0	0	0	0	0	1.000	1.000
Eshelman, Vaughn, Bos.	L	.250	21	4	1	1	1	0	0	0	0	0	0	0	1	0	0	.250	.250
Gross, Kevin, Ana.	R	.000	12	1	0	0	0	0	0	0	0	0	0	0	1	0	0	.000	.000
Henry, Butch, Bos.	L	---	36	0	0	0	0	0	0	0	0	1	0	0	0	0	0	---	---
Holtz, Mike, Ana.	L	.000	66	1	0	0	0	0	0	0	0	0	0	0	1	0	0	.000	.000
Jones, Doug, Mil.	R	---	75	0	0	0	0	0	0	0	0	0	0	1	0	0	0	---	1.000
Lopez, Albie, Cle.	R	.000	37	1	0	0	0	0	0	0	0	0	0	0	1	0	0	.000	.000
Lowe, Derek, Sea.-Bos.	R	.000	20	3	0	0	0	0	0	0	0	0	0	0	2	0	0	.000	.000
Manzanillo, Josias, Sea.	R	.000	16	1	0	0	0	0	0	0	0	0	0	0	0	0	0	.000	.000

American League relief pitchers (batting)

Name/Team	B	BA	G	AB	R	H	TB	2B	3B	HR	RBI	SH	SF	BB	SO	SB	CS	SLG	OBA
May, Darrell, Ana.	L	.000	29	2	0	0	0	0	0	0	0	0	0	0	2	0	0	.000	.000
Morman, Alvin, Cle.	R	.000	34	1	0	0	0	0	0	0	0	0	0	0	0	0	0	.000	.000
Orosco, Jesse, Bal.	R	---	71	0	0	0	0	0	0	0	0	0	0	1	0	0	0	---	1.000
Plunk, Eric, Cle.	R	.000	56	1	0	0	0	0	0	0	0	0	0	0	1	0	0	.000	.000
Quantrill, Paul, Tor.	L	.000	77	1	0	0	0	0	0	0	0	0	0	0	1	0	0	.000	.000
Rhodes, Arthur, Bal.	L	.000	54	1	0	0	0	0	0	0	0	0	0	0	1	0	0	.000	.000
Ritchie, Todd, Min.	R	.000	42	2	0	0	0	0	0	0	0	0	0	0	0	0	0	.000	.000
Rodriguez, Frankie, Min.	R	.000	43	1	0	0	0	0	0	0	0	0	0	0	0	0	0	.000	.000
Santana, Julio, Tex.	R	.500	30	2	0	1	1	0	0	0	0	0	0	0	0	0	0	.500	.500
Shuey, Paul, Cle.	R	.000	40	1	0	0	0	0	0	0	0	0	0	0	1	0	0	.000	.000
Small, Aaron, Oak.	R	.000	71	1	0	0	0	0	0	0	0	0	0	0	0	0	0	.000	.000
Spoljaric, Paul, Tor.-Sea.	R	.000	57	1	0	0	0	0	0	0	0	0	0	0	0	0	0	.000	.000
Trombley, Mike, Min.	R	.000	67	1	0	0	0	0	0	0	0	0	0	0	1	0	0	.000	.000
Villone, Ron, Mil.	L	.000	50	1	0	0	0	0	0	0	0	0	0	0	1	0	0	.000	.000
Wells, Bob, Sea.	R	---	46	0	1	0	0	0	0	0	0	0	0	1	0	0	0	---	1.000
Wetteland, John, Tex.	R	1.000	61	1	1	1	2	1	0	0	1	0	0	0	0	0	0	2.000	1.000

American League starting pitchers (batting)

Name/Team	B	BA	G	AB	R	H	TB	2B	3B	HR	RBI	SH	SF	BB	SO	SB	CS	SLG	OBA
Alvarez, Wilson, ChiA	L	.000	22	3	0	0	0	0	0	0	0	0	0	0	2	0	0	.000	.000
Appier, Kevin, K.C.	R	.000	34	6	0	0	0	0	0	0	0	0	0	0	5	0	0	.000	.000
Avery, Steve, Bos.	L	.000	24	1	0	0	0	0	0	0	0	0	0	0	0	0	0	.000	.000
Baldwin, James, ChiA	R	.000	32	3	0	0	0	0	0	0	1	0	0	0	2	0	0	.000	.000
Belcher, Tim, K.C.	R	.000	32	6	0	0	0	0	0	0	0	0	0	0	1	0	0	.000	.000
Blair, Willie, Det.	R	.000	29	4	0	0	0	0	0	0	0	0	0	0	3	0	0	.000	.000
Burkett, John, Tex.	R	.200	30	5	1	1	1	0	0	0	0	0	0	0	1	0	0	.200	.200
Clark, Terry, Cle.-Tex.	R	1.000	13	1	0	1	1	0	0	0	0	0	0	0	0	0	0	1.000	1.000
Clemens, Roger, Tor.	R	.500	34	2	1	1	2	1	0	0	0	0	0	1	0	0	0	1.000	.667
Cloude, Ken, Sea.	R	.000	10	2	0	0	0	0	0	0	0	0	0	0	0	0	0	.000	.000
Colon, Bartolo, Cle.	R	.000	19	1	0	0	0	0	0	0	0	0	0	0	1	0	0	.000	.000
Cone, David, NYA	L	.000	29	3	0	0	0	0	0	0	0	0	0	0	2	0	0	.000	.000
D'Amico, Jeff, Mil.	R	.000	23	4	0	0	0	0	0	0	1	0	0	0	3	0	0	.000	.000
Darwin, Danny, ChiA	R	.000	21	3	0	0	0	0	0	0	1	0	0	0	3	0	0	.000	.000
Dickson, Jason, Ana.	L	.000	33	2	0	0	0	0	0	0	0	0	0	0	0	0	0	.000	.000
Drabek, Doug, ChiA	R	.000	32	1	1	0	0	0	0	0	0	1	0	0	1	0	0	.000	.000
Eldred, Cal, Mil.	R	.000	34	3	0	0	0	0	0	0	1	0	0	0	0	0	0	.000	.000
Erickson, Scott, Bal.	R	.000	34	2	0	0	0	0	0	0	0	2	0	1	2	0	0	.000	.333
Eyre, Scott, ChiA	L	.500	11	2	0	1	1	0	0	0	0	0	0	0	0	0	0	.500	.500
Fassero, Jeff, Sea.	L	.200	35	5	0	1	1	0	0	0	0	0	0	0	2	0	0	.200	.200
Finley, Chuck, Ana.	L	.000	25	6	1	0	0	0	0	0	0	0	0	0	2	0	0	.000	.000
Gooden, Dwight, NYA	R	.000	20	4	0	0	0	0	0	0	0	0	0	0	1	0	0	.000	.000
Hawkins, LaTroy, Min.	R	.000	20	1	0	0	0	0	0	0	0	0	0	0	1	0	0	.000	.000
Haynes, Jimmy, Oak.	R	.000	13	2	0	0	0	0	0	0	0	0	0	0	1	0	0	.000	.000
Helling, Rick, Tex.	R	.000	10	3	0	0	0	0	0	0	0	0	0	0	0	0	0	.000	.000
Hentgen, Pat, Tor.	R	.000	35	7	0	0	0	0	0	0	0	0	0	0	2	0	0	.000	.000
Hershiser, Orel, Cle.	R	.000	32	3	0	0	0	0	0	0	0	1	0	0	1	0	0	.000	.250
Hill, Ken, Tex.-Ana.	R	.500	31	2	0	1	2	1	0	0	2	1	0	0	1	0	0	1.000	.500
Irabu, Hideki, NYA	R	.000	13	1	0	0	0	0	0	0	0	0	0	0	0	0	0	.000	.000
Kamieniecki, Scott, Bal.	R	.000	30	2	0	0	0	0	0	0	0	0	0	0	2	0	0	.000	.000
Karl, Scott, Mil.	L	.000	32	4	0	0	0	0	0	0	0	0	0	0	3	0	0	.000	.000
Keagle, Greg, Det.	R	.000	11	1	0	0	0	0	0	0	0	0	0	0	1	0	0	.000	.000
Key, Jimmy, Bal.	R	.000	34	2	0	0	0	0	0	0	1	0	0	0	2	0	0	.000	.000
Ludwick, Eric, Oak.	R	.000	6	2	0	0	0	0	0	0	0	0	0	0	1	0	0	.000	.000
McDonald, Ben, Mil.	R	.000	21	1	0	0	0	0	0	0	0	0	0	0	1	0	0	.000	.000
Mercedes, Jose, Mil.	R	.000	29	2	0	0	0	0	0	0	0	0	0	0	2	0	0	.000	.000
Moehler, Brian, Det.	R	.000	31	3	0	0	0	0	0	0	0	0	0	0	2	0	0	.000	.000
Moyer, Jamie, Sea.	L	.333	30	3	0	1	1	0	0	0	0	0	0	0	0	0	0	.333	.333
Mussina, Mike, Bal.	L	.250	33	4	0	1	1	0	0	0	0	0	0	0	1	0	0	.250	.250
Nagy, Charles, Cle.	L	.200	34	5	1	1	1	0	0	0	0	0	0	0	1	0	0	.200	.200
Navarro, Jaime, ChiA	R	.000	33	1	0	0	0	0	0	0	0	1	0	0	0	0	0	.000	.000
Ogea, Chad, Cle.	R	.000	21	2	0	0	0	0	0	0	0	2	0	0	1	0	0	.000	.000
Olivares, Omar, Det.-Sea.	R	.600	35	5	2	3	5	0	1	0	2	0	0	0	1	0	0	1.000	.600
Oliver, Darren, Tex.	R	.500	32	2	1	1	1	0	0	0	2	0	0	1	0	0	0	.500	.667
Oquist, Mike, Oak.	R	.250	21	4	0	1	1	0	0	0	0	0	0	1	0	0	0	.250	.250
Perisho, Matt, Ana.	L	.000	11	1	0	0	0	0	0	0	0	0	0	0	1	0	0	.000	.000
Person, Robert, Tor.	R	.000	23	4	0	0	0	0	0	0	0	0	0	1	1	0	0	.000	.200
Pittsley, Jim, K.C.	R	.500	21	2	0	1	2	1	0	0	0	0	0	0	1	0	0	1.000	.500
Radke, Brad, Min.	R	.000	35	3	0	0	0	0	0	0	1	0	0	0	0	0	0	.000	.000

American League starting pitchers (batting)

Name/Team	B	BA	G	AB	R	H	TB	2B	3B	HR	RBI	SH	SF	BB	SO	SB	CS	SLG	OBA
Rigby, Brad, Oak.	R	.000	14	3	0	0	0	0	0	0	0	0	0	0	2	0	0	.000	.000
Robertson, Rich, Min.	L	.200	31	5	0	1	1	0	0	0	0	0	0	0	2	0	0	.200	.200
Rogers, Kenny, NYA	L	.000	31	3	0	0	0	0	0	0	0	0	0	0	0	0	0	.000	.000
Rosado, Jose, K.C.	L	.000	34	2	0	0	0	0	0	0	0	0	0	1	0	0	0	.000	.000
Rusch, Glendon, K.C.	L	.000	30	3	0	0	0	0	0	0	0	0	0	0	2	0	0	.000	.000
Saberhagen, Bret, Bos.	R	.000	6	1	0	0	0	0	0	0	0	0	0	0	0	0	0	.000	.000
Sele, Aaron, Bos.	R	.000	33	2	0	0	0	0	0	0	0	0	0	0	1	0	0	.000	.000
Sirotka, Mike, ChiA	L	.000	7	1	0	0	0	0	0	0	0	0	0	0	1	0	0	.000	.000
Springer, Dennis, Ana.	R	.000	32	3	0	0	0	0	0	0	0	0	0	0	3	0	0	.000	.000
Suppan, Jeff, Bos.	R	.000	23	2	0	0	0	0	0	0	0	0	0	0	1	0	0	.000	.000
Telgheder, Dave, Oak.	R	.000	20	2	0	0	0	0	0	0	0	0	0	0	0	0	0	.000	.000
Tewksbury, Bob, Min.	R	.200	26	5	0	1	1	0	0	0	1	0	0	0	0	0	0	.200	.200
Thompson, Justin, Det.	L	.000	32	2	0	0	0	0	0	0	0	0	0	1	0	0	0	.000	.000
Wakefield, Tim, Bos.	R	.000	35	1	0	0	0	0	0	0	0	0	0	0	0	0	0	.000	.000
Williams, Woody, Tor.	R	.500	31	2	0	1	1	0	0	0	0	0	0	0	1	0	0	.500	.500
Witt, Bobby, Tex.	R	.333	35	6	1	2	6	1	0	1	2	0	0	0	1	0	0	1.000	.333
Wolcott, Bob, Sea.	R	.000	19	1	0	0	0	0	0	0	0	0	0	0	0	0	0	.000	.000
Wright, Jaret, Cle.	R	.000	16	3	0	0	0	0	0	0	0	2	0	0	1	0	0	.000	.000

National League catchers

Name/Team	B	BA	G	AB	R	H	TB	2B	3B	HR	RBI	SH	SF	BB	SO	SB	CS	SLG	OBA	RV
Ausmus, Brad, Hou.	R	.266	130	425	45	113	152	25	1	4	44	6	6	38	78	14	6	.358	.326	9
Berryhill, Damon, S.F.	B	.257	73	167	17	43	60	8	0	3	23	0	1	20	29	0	0	.359	.335	1
Castillo, Alberto, NYN	R	.203	35	59	3	12	13	1	0	0	7	2	1	9	16	0	1	.220	.304	NV
Chavez, Raul, Mon.	R	.269	13	26	0	7	7	0	0	0	2	0	1	0	5	1	0	.269	.259	NV
Difelice, Mike, St.L	R	.238	93	260	16	62	86	10	1	4	30	6	1	19	61	1	1	.331	.297	NV
Estalella, Bobby, Phi.	R	.345	13	29	9	10	23	1	0	4	9	0	0	7	7	0	0	.793	.472	1
Eusebio, Tony, Hou.	R	.274	60	164	12	45	50	2	0	1	18	0	0	19	27	0	1	.305	.364	1
Flaherty, John, S.D.	R	.273	129	439	38	120	170	21	1	9	46	2	2	33	62	4	4	.387	.323	8
Fletcher, Darrin, Mon.	L	.277	96	310	39	86	159	20	1	17	55	0	2	17	35	1	1	.513	.323	11
Fordyce, Brook, Cin.	R	.208	47	96	7	20	28	5	0	1	8	0	1	8	15	2	0	.292	.267	NV
Hernandez, Carlos, S.D.	R	.313	50	134	15	42	60	7	1	3	14	1	0	3	27	0	2	.448	.328	3
Houston, Tyler, ChiN	L	.260	72	196	15	51	67	10	0	2	28	0	2	9	35	1	0	.342	.290	2
Hubbard, Mike, ChiN	R	.203	29	64	4	13	16	0	0	1	2	0	0	2	21	0	0	.250	.227	NV
Hundley, Todd, NYN	B	.273	132	417	78	114	229	21	2	30	86	0	5	83	116	2	3	.549	.394	19
Jensen, Marcus, S.F.	B	.149	30	54	5	11	16	2	0	1	3	0	0	7	23	0	0	.216	.222	NV
Johnson, Brian, S.F.	R	.279	56	179	19	50	94	7	2	11	27	3	3	14	26	0	1	.525	.333	6
Johnson, Charles, Fla.	R	.250	124	416	43	104	189	26	1	19	63	3	2	60	109	0	2	.454	.347	9
Kendall, Jason, Pit.	R	.294	144	486	71	143	211	36	4	8	49	1	5	49	53	18	6	.434	.391	17
Knorr, Randy, Hou.	R	.375	8	8	1	3	6	0	0	1	1	0	0	0	2	0	0	.750	.375	NV
Lampkin, Tom, St.L	L	.245	108	229	28	56	87	8	1	7	22	4	2	28	30	2	1	.380	.335	2
Lieberthal, Mike, Phi.	R	.246	134	455	59	112	201	27	1	20	77	0	7	44	76	3	4	.442	.314	10
Lopez, Javier, Atl.	R	.295	123	414	52	122	221	28	1	23	68	1	4	40	82	1	1	.534	.361	18
Manwaring, Kirt, Col.	R	.226	104	337	22	76	93	6	4	1	27	4	2	30	78	1	5	.276	.291	NV
Marrero, Eli, St.L	R	.244	17	45	4	11	19	2	0	2	7	0	1	2	13	4	0	.422	.271	1
Mirabelli, Doug, S.F.	R	.143	6	7	0	1	1	0	0	0	0	0	0	1	3	0	0	.143	.250	NV
Myers, Greg, Atl.	L	.111	9	9	0	1	1	0	0	0	1	0	0	1	3	0	0	.111	.200	NV
Natal, Bob, Fla.	R	.500	4	4	2	2	6	1	0	1	3	0	1	2	0	0	0	1.500	.571	NV
Oliver, Joe, Cin.	R	.258	111	349	28	90	145	13	0	14	43	2	5	25	58	1	3	.415	.313	7
Osik, Keith, Pit.	R	.257	49	105	10	27	38	9	1	0	7	2	0	9	21	0	1	.362	.322	NV
Pagnozzi, Tom, St.L	R	.220	25	50	4	11	17	3	0	1	8	0	0	1	7	0	0	.340	.235	NV
Parent, Mark, Phi.	R	.150	39	113	4	17	20	3	0	0	8	0	1	7	39	0	1	.177	.198	NV
Pena, Tony, Hou.	R	.211	9	19	2	4	7	3	0	0	2	0	1	2	3	0	0	.368	.273	NV
Perez, Eddie, Atl.	R	.215	73	191	20	41	64	5	0	6	18	1	2	10	35	0	1	.335	.259	NV
Piazza, Mike, L.A.	R	.362	152	556	104	201	355	32	1	40	124	0	5	69	77	5	1	.638	.431	46
Pratt, Todd, NYN	R	.283	39	106	12	30	42	6	0	2	19	0	0	13	32	0	1	.396	.372	1
Prince, Tom, L.A.	R	.220	47	100	17	22	36	5	0	3	14	4	1	5	15	0	0	.360	.275	NV
Reed, Jeff, Col.	L	.297	90	256	43	76	137	10	0	17	47	5	0	35	55	2	1	.535	.386	12
Romero, Mandy, S.D.	B	.208	21	48	7	10	16	0	0	2	4	0	0	2	18	1	0	.333	.240	NV
Servais, Scott, ChiN	R	.260	122	385	36	100	139	21	0	6	45	7	3	24	56	0	1	.361	.311	4
Slaught, Don, S.D.	R	.000	20	20	2	0	0	0	0	0	0	1	0	5	4	0	0	.000	.200	NV
Spehr, Tim, Atl.	R	.214	8	14	2	3	7	1	0	1	4	0	0	0	4	1	0	.500	.214	NV
Taubensee, Eddie, Cin.	L	.268	108	254	26	68	116	18	0	10	34	1	5	22	66	0	1	.457	.323	5
Widger, Chris, Mon.	R	.234	91	278	30	65	112	20	3	7	37	2	2	22	59	2	0	.403	.290	2
Wilkins, Rick, S.F.	L	.195	66	190	18	37	60	5	0	6	23	0	3	17	65	0	0	.316	.257	NV
Zaun, Gregg, Fla.	B	.301	58	143	21	43	63	10	2	2	20	1	0	26	18	1	0	.441	.415	3

National League first basemen

Name/Team	B	BA	G	AB	R	H	TB	2B	3B	HR	RBI	SH	SF	BB	SO	SB	CS	SLG	OBA	RV
Bagwell, Jeff, Hou.	R	.286	162	566	109	162	335	40	2	43	135	0	8	127	122	31	10	.592	.425	42
Blanco, Henry, L.A.	R	.400	3	5	1	2	5	0	0	1	1	0	0	0	1	0	0	1.000	.400	NV
Brogna, Rico, Phi.	L	.252	148	543	68	137	235	36	1	20	81	0	4	33	116	12	3	.433	.293	15
Cianfrocco, Archi, S.D.	R	.245	89	220	25	54	78	12	0	4	26	1	2	25	80	7	1	.355	.328	3
Colbrunn, Greg, Atl.	R	.278	28	54	3	15	24	3	0	2	9	1	0	2	11	0	0	.444	.316	NV
Conine, Jeff, Fla.	R	.242	151	405	46	98	164	13	1	17	61	0	2	57	89	2	0	.405	.337	7
Fullmer, Brad, Mon.	L	.300	19	40	4	12	23	2	0	3	8	0	0	2	7	0	0	.575	.349	1
Galarraga, Andres, Col.	R	.318	154	600	120	191	351	31	3	41	140	0	3	54	141	15	8	.585	.389	43
Grace, Mark, ChiN	L	.319	151	555	87	177	258	32	5	13	78	1	8	88	45	2	4	.465	.409	22
Johnson, Mark, Pit.	L	.215	78	219	30	47	69	10	0	4	29	0	3	43	78	1	1	.315	.345	NV
Jordan, Kevin, Phi.	R	.266	84	177	19	47	73	8	0	6	30	0	3	3	26	0	1	.412	.273	3
Joyner, Wally, S.D.	L	.327	135	455	59	149	221	29	2	13	83	0	10	51	51	3	5	.486	.390	22
Karros, Eric, L.A.	R	.266	162	628	86	167	288	28	0	31	104	0	9	61	116	15	7	.459	.329	25
Konerko, Paul, L.A.	R	.143	6	7	0	1	1	0	0	0	0	0	0	1	2	0	0	.143	.250	NV
Lee, Derrek, S.D.	R	.259	22	54	9	14	20	3	0	1	4	0	0	9	24	0	0	.370	.365	NV
McGriff, Fred, Atl.	L	.277	152	564	77	156	249	25	1	22	97	0	5	68	112	5	0	.441	.356	19
McGuire, Ryan, Mon.	L	.256	84	199	22	51	79	15	2	3	17	3	1	19	34	1	4	.397	.320	1
McGwire, Mark, St.L	R	.253	51	174	38	44	119	3	0	24	42	0	2	43	61	2	0	.684	.411	11
Morris, Hal, Cin.	L	.276	96	333	42	92	117	20	1	1	33	4	1	23	43	3	0	.351	.328	4
Murray, Eddie, L.A.	B	.286	9	7	0	2	2	0	0	0	3	0	0	2	2	0	0	.286	.444	NV
Olerud, John, NYN	L	.294	154	524	90	154	256	34	1	22	102	0	8	85	67	0	0	.489	.400	21
Perez, Eduardo, Cin.	R	.253	106	297	44	75	141	18	0	16	52	0	2	29	76	5	1	.475	.321	9
Petagine, Roberto, NYN	L	.067	12	15	2	1	1	0	0	0	2	0	0	3	6	0	0	.067	.222	NV
Phillips, J.R., Hou.	L	.133	13	15	2	2	5	0	0	1	4	0	1	0	7	0	0	.333	.125	NV
Robertson, Mike, Phi.	L	.211	22	38	3	8	12	2	1	0	4	0	0	0	6	1	0	.316	.268	NV
Segui, David, Mon.	B	.307	125	459	75	141	232	22	3	21	68	0	6	57	66	1	0	.505	.380	19
Simon, Randall, Atl.	L	.429	13	14	2	6	7	1	0	0	1	0	0	1	2	0	0	.500	.467	NV
Snow, J.T., S.F.	B	.281	157	531	81	149	271	36	1	28	104	2	7	96	124	6	4	.510	.387	23
Williams, Eddie, L.A.-Pit.	R	.240	38	96	12	23	37	5	0	3	12	1	1	11	25	1	0	.385	.327	NV
Young, Dmitri, St.L	B	.258	110	333	38	86	121	14	3	5	34	1	3	38	63	6	5	.363	.335	4
Young, Kevin, Pit.	R	.300	97	333	59	100	178	18	3	18	74	1	8	16	89	11	2	.535	.332	20

National League second basemen

Name/Team	B	BA	G	AB	R	H	TB	2B	3B	HR	RBI	SH	SF	BB	SO	SB	CS	SLG	OBA	RV
Abbott, Kurt, Fla.	R	.274	94	252	35	69	109	18	2	6	30	6	0	14	68	3	1	.433	.315	5
Baerga, Carlos, NYN	B	.281	133	467	53	131	185	25	1	9	52	3	5	20	54	2	6	.396	.311	10
Bates, Jason, Col.	B	.240	62	121	17	29	48	10	0	3	11	0	0	15	27	0	1	.397	.338	NV
Berblinger, Jeff, St.L	R	.000	7	5	1	0	0	0	0	0	0	0	1	0	1	0	0	.000	.000	NV
Biggio, Craig, Hou.	R	.309	162	619	146	191	310	37	8	22	81	0	7	84	107	47	10	.501	.415	41
Boone, Bret, Cin.	R	.223	139	443	40	99	147	25	1	7	46	4	5	45	101	5	5	.332	.298	NV
Cairo, Miguel, ChiN	R	.241	16	29	7	7	8	1	0	0	1	0	0	2	3	0	0	.276	.313	NV
Castillo, Luis, Fla.	B	.240	75	263	27	63	71	8	0	0	8	1	0	27	53	16	10	.270	.310	3
Counsell, Craig, Col.-Fla.	L	.299	52	164	20	49	65	9	2	1	16	3	1	18	17	1	1	.396	.376	2
Cromer, Tripp, L.A.	R	.291	28	86	8	25	40	3	0	4	20	2	1	6	16	0	1	.465	.333	2
Delgado, Wilson, S.F.	B	.143	8	7	1	1	2	1	0	0	0	1	0	0	2	0	0	.286	.143	NV
DeShields, Delino, St.L	L	.295	150	572	92	169	256	26	14	11	58	7	6	55	72	55	14	.448	.357	34
Fonville, Chad, L.A.	B	.143	9	14	1	2	2	0	0	0	1	0	0	2	3	0	1	.143	.250	NV
Gallego, Mike, St.L	R	.163	27	43	6	7	9	2	0	0	1	1	1	1	6	0	0	.209	.178	NV
Gilbert, Shawn, NYN	R	.136	29	22	3	3	6	0	0	1	1	0	0	1	8	1	0	.273	.174	NV
Graffanino, Tony, Atl.	R	.258	104	186	33	48	83	9	1	8	20	3	5	26	46	6	4	.446	.344	5
Guerrero, Wilton, L.A.	B	.291	111	357	39	104	144	10	9	4	32	13	2	8	52	6	5	.403	.305	8
Hardtke, Jason, NYN	R	.268	30	56	9	15	23	2	0	2	8	0	1	4	6	1	1	.411	.323	NV
Kent, Jeff, S.F.	R	.250	155	580	90	145	274	38	2	29	121	0	10	48	133	11	3	.472	.316	21
Lansing, Mike, Mon.	R	.281	144	572	86	161	270	45	2	20	70	6	3	45	92	11	5	.472	.338	19
Lemke, Mark, Atl.	B	.245	109	351	33	86	111	17	1	2	26	8	5	33	51	2	0	.316	.306	NV
Liriano, Nelson, L.A.	B	.227	76	88	10	20	29	6	0	1	11	2	1	6	12	0	0	.330	.274	4
Lockhart, Keith, Atl.	L	.279	96	147	25	41	70	5	3	6	32	3	4	14	17	0	0	.476	.337	4
Mejia, Roberto, St.L	R	.071	7	14	0	1	2	0	0	0	2	1	0	0	5	0	0	.143	.067	NV
Milliard, Ralph, Fla.	R	.200	8	30	2	6	6	0	0	0	2	1	0	3	3	1	1	.200	.314	NV
Morandini, Mickey, Phi.	L	.295	150	553	83	163	210	40	2	1	39	12	5	62	91	16	13	.380	.371	14
Raabe, Brian, Col.	R	.333	2	3	0	1	1	0	0	0	0	0	0	0	1	0	0	.333	.333	NV
Riggs, Adam, L.A.	R	.200	9	20	3	4	5	1	0	0	1	0	0	4	3	1	0	.250	.333	NV
Sandberg, Ryne, ChiN	R	.264	135	447	54	118	180	26	0	12	64	0	3	28	94	7	4	.403	.308	11
Scarsone, Steve, St.L	R	.100	5	10	0	1	1	0	0	0	0	0	0	2	5	1	0	.100	.250	NV
Sefcik, Kevin, Phi.	R	.269	61	119	11	32	41	3	0	2	6	7	0	4	9	1	2	.345	.298	NV
Shumpert, Terry, S.D.	R	.273	13	33	4	9	15	3	0	1	6	0	1	3	4	0	0	.455	.324	NV
Stankiewicz, Andy, Mon.	R	.224	76	107	11	24	36	9	0	1	5	7	1	4	22	1	1	.336	.250	NV
Veras, Quilvio, S.D.	B	.265	145	539	74	143	177	23	1	3	45	9	4	72	84	33	12	.328	.357	16

National League second basemen

Name/Team	B	BA	G	AB	R	H	TB	2B	3B	HR	RBI	SH	SF	BB	SO	SB	CS	SLG	OBA	RV
Womack, Tony, Pit.	L	.278	155	641	85	178	240	26	9	6	50	2	0	43	109	60	7	.374	.326	30
Young, Eric, Col.-L.A.	R	.280	155	622	106	174	247	33	8	8	61	10	6	71	54	45	14	.397	.359	27

National League third basemen

Name/Team	B	BA	G	AB	R	H	TB	2B	3B	HR	RBI	SH	SF	BB	SO	SB	CS	SLG	OBA	RV
Alfonzo, Edgardo, NYN	R	.315	151	518	84	163	224	27	2	10	72	8	5	63	56	11	6	.432	.391	22
Andrews, Shane, Mon.	R	.203	18	64	10	13	28	3	0	4	9	0	2	3	20	0	0	.438	.232	NV
Arias, Alex, Fla.	R	.247	74	93	13	23	28	2	0	1	11	4	0	12	12	0	1	.301	.352	NV
Arias, George, S.D.	R	.227	11	22	2	5	6	1	0	0	2	0	0	0	1	0	0	.273	.227	NV
Bell, David, St.L	R	.211	66	142	9	30	44	7	2	1	12	2	1	10	28	1	0	.310	.261	NV
Berry, Sean, Hou.	R	.256	96	301	37	77	127	24	1	8	43	1	6	25	53	1	5	.422	.318	4
Bonilla, Bobby, Fla.	B	.297	153	562	77	167	263	39	3	17	96	0	8	73	94	6	6	.468	.378	22
Boone, Aaron, Cin.	R	.245	16	49	5	12	13	1	0	0	5	1	0	2	5	1	0	.265	.275	NV
Booty, Josh, Fla.	R	.600	4	5	2	3	3	0	0	0	1	0	0	1	1	0	0	.600	.667	NV
Branson, Jeff, Cin.	L	.153	65	98	9	15	23	3	1	1	5	1	0	7	23	1	0	.235	.210	NV
Caminiti, Ken, S.D.	B	.290	137	486	92	141	247	28	0	26	90	0	7	80	118	11	2	.508	.389	24
Castilla, Vinny, Col.	R	.304	159	612	94	186	335	25	2	40	113	0	4	44	108	2	4	.547	.356	32
Coles, Darnell, Col.	R	.318	21	22	1	7	11	1	0	1	2	0	0	0	6	0	0	.500	.348	NV
Franco, Matt, NYN	L	.276	112	163	21	45	65	5	0	5	21	0	0	13	23	1	0	.399	.330	3
Gaetti, Gary, St.L	R	.251	148	502	63	126	203	24	1	17	69	4	6	36	88	7	3	.404	.305	11
Garcia, Freddy, Pit.	R	.150	20	40	4	6	16	1	0	3	5	0	0	2	17	0	0	.400	.190	NV
Giovanola, Ed, Atl.	L	.250	14	8	0	2	2	0	0	0	0	0	0	2	1	0	0	.250	.400	NV
Gonzales, Rene, Col.	R	.500	2	2	0	1	1	0	0	0	1	0	0	0	0	0	0	.500	.500	NV
Greene, Willie, Cin.	L	.253	151	495	62	125	227	22	1	26	91	1	3	78	111	6	0	.459	.354	16
Gulan, Mike, St.L	R	.000	5	9	2	0	0	0	0	0	1	0	0	1	5	0	0	.000	.100	NV
Hale, Chip, L.A.	L	.083	14	12	0	1	1	0	0	0	0	0	0	2	4	0	0	.083	.214	NV
Hansen, Dave, ChiN	L	.311	90	151	19	47	68	8	2	3	21	2	1	31	32	1	2	.450	.429	4
Hernandez, Jose, ChiN	R	.273	121	183	33	50	89	8	5	7	26	1	1	14	42	2	5	.486	.323	4
Johnson, Russ, Hou.	R	.300	21	60	7	18	25	1	0	2	9	1	0	6	14	1	1	.417	.364	1
Jones, Chipper, Atl.	B	.295	157	597	100	176	286	41	3	21	111	0	6	76	88	20	5	.479	.371	30
Lewis, Mark, S.F.	R	.267	118	341	50	91	147	14	6	10	42	1	3	23	62	3	2	.431	.318	7
Livingstone, S., S.D.-St.L	L	.164	65	67	4	11	13	2	0	0	6	0	2	3	11	1	0	.194	.194	NV
Mordecai, Mike, Atl.	R	.173	61	81	8	14	18	2	1	0	3	1	1	6	16	0	1	.222	.227	NV
Morgan, Kevin, NYN	R	.000	1	1	0	0	0	0	0	0	0	0	0	0	0	0	0	.000	.000	NV
Mueller, Bill, S.F.	B	.292	128	390	51	114	167	26	3	7	44	6	6	48	71	4	3	.428	.369	10
Orie, Kevin, ChiN	R	.275	114	364	40	100	157	23	5	8	44	3	4	39	57	2	2	.431	.350	7
Pendleton, Terry, Cin.	B	.248	50	113	11	28	40	9	0	1	17	0	0	12	14	2	1	.354	.320	NV
Randa, Joe, Pit.	R	.302	126	443	58	134	200	27	9	7	60	4	5	41	64	4	2	.451	.366	14
Rolen, Scott, Phi.	L	.283	156	561	93	159	263	35	3	21	92	0	7	76	138	16	6	.469	.377	24
Rose, Pete Jr., Cin.	L	.143	11	14	2	2	2	0	0	0	0	0	0	2	5	0	0	.143	.250	NV
Sheaffer, Danny, St.L	R	.250	76	132	10	33	38	5	0	0	11	4	1	8	17	1	0	.288	.296	NV
Spiers, Bill, Hou.	L	.320	132	291	51	93	140	27	4	4	48	1	1	61	42	10	5	.481	.438	14
Strange, Doug, Mon.	B	.257	118	327	40	84	140	16	2	12	47	5	2	36	76	0	2	.428	.332	6
Sveum, Dale, Pit.	B	.261	126	306	30	80	138	20	1	12	47	4	2	27	81	0	3	.451	.319	6
Vidro, Jose, Mon.	B	.249	67	169	19	42	62	12	1	2	17	0	3	11	20	1	0	.367	.297	NV
Zeile, Todd, L.A.	R	.268	160	575	89	154	264	17	0	31	90	0	6	85	112	8	7	.459	.365	21

National League shortstops

Name/Team	B	BA	G	AB	R	H	TB	2B	3B	HR	RBI	SH	SF	BB	SO	SB	CS	SLG	OBA	RV
Alexander, M., NYN-ChiN	R	.266	87	248	37	66	95	12	4	3	22	3	1	17	54	13	1	.383	.320	6
Aurilia, Rich, S.F.	R	.275	46	102	16	28	51	8	0	5	19	1	2	8	15	1	1	.500	.321	3
Belliard, Rafael, Atl.	R	.211	72	71	9	15	21	3	0	1	3	4	1	1	17	0	1	.296	.219	NV
Blauser, Jeff, Atl.	R	.308	151	519	90	160	250	31	4	17	70	5	9	70	101	5	1	.482	.405	21
Bogar, Tim, Hou.	R	.249	97	241	30	60	94	14	4	4	30	3	4	24	42	4	1	.390	.320	2
Cabrera, Orlando, Mon.	R	.222	16	18	4	4	4	0	0	0	2	1	0	1	3	1	2	.222	.263	NV
Castro, Juan, L.A.	R	.147	40	75	3	11	16	3	1	0	4	2	0	7	20	0	0	.213	.220	NV
Clayton, Royce, St.L	R	.266	154	576	75	153	229	39	5	9	61	2	5	33	109	30	10	.398	.306	18
Collier, Lou, Pit.	R	.135	18	37	3	5	5	0	0	0	3	0	0	1	11	1	0	.135	.158	NV
Dunston, S., ChiN-Pit.	R	.300	132	490	71	147	221	22	5	14	57	5	5	8	75	32	8	.451	.312	27
Elster, Kevin, Pit.	R	.225	39	138	14	31	62	6	2	7	25	2	2	21	39	0	2	.449	.327	1
Gagne, Greg, L.A.	R	.251	144	514	49	129	182	20	3	9	57	3	1	31	120	2	5	.354	.298	5
Gomez, Chris, S.D.	R	.253	150	522	62	132	170	19	2	5	54	3	3	53	114	5	8	.326	.326	4
Grudzielanek, Mark, Mon.	R	.273	156	649	76	177	249	54	3	4	51	3	3	23	76	25	9	.384	.307	15
Gutierrez, Ricky, Hou.	R	.261	102	303	33	79	110	14	4	3	34	0	0	21	50	5	2	.363	.315	4
Jackson, Damian, Cin.	R	.222	12	27	6	6	13	2	1	1	2	1	0	4	7	1	1	.481	.323	NV
Larkin, Barry, Cin.	R	.317	73	224	34	71	106	17	3	4	20	1	1	47	24	14	3	.473	.440	11

National League shortstops

Name/Team	B	BA	G	AB	R	H	TB	2B	3B	HR	RBI	SH	SF	BB	SO	SB	CS	SLG	OBA	RV
Listach, Pat, Hou.	B	.182	52	132	13	24	30	2	2	0	6	5	2	11	24	4	2	.227	.247	NV
Lopez, Luis M., NYN	B	.270	78	178	19	48	65	12	1	1	19	2	0	12	42	2	4	.365	.330	1
Nunez, Abraham, Pit.	B	.225	19	40	3	9	15	2	2	0	6	0	1	3	10	1	0	.375	.289	NV
Ordaz, Luis, St.L	R	.273	12	22	3	6	7	1	0	0	1	0	0	1	2	3	0	.318	.304	NV
Ordonez, Rey, NYN	R	.216	120	356	35	77	91	5	3	1	33	14	2	18	36	11	5	.256	.255	NV
Perez, Neifi, Col.	B	.291	83	313	46	91	139	13	10	5	31	5	4	21	43	4	3	.444	.333	7
Polcovich, Kevin, Pit.	R	.273	84	245	37	67	97	16	1	4	21	2	2	21	45	2	2	.396	.350	3
Reese, Pokey, Cin.	B	.219	128	397	48	87	114	15	0	4	26	4	0	31	82	25	7	.287	.284	5
Relaford, Desi, Phi.	B	.184	15	38	3	7	12	1	2	0	6	1	0	5	6	3	0	.316	.279	NV
Renteria, Edgar, Fla.	R	.277	154	617	90	171	210	21	3	4	52	19	6	45	108	32	15	.340	.327	19
Rivera, Luis, Hou.	R	.231	7	13	2	3	5	0	1	0	3	1	0	1	6	0	0	.385	.286	NV
Sanchez, Rey, ChiN	L	.249	97	205	14	51	63	9	0	1	12	4	0	11	26	4	2	.307	.287	NV
Shipley, Craig, S.D.	R	.273	63	139	22	38	62	9	0	5	19	1	1	7	20	1	1	.446	.306	3
Stocker, Kevin, Phi.	B	.266	149	504	51	134	179	23	5	4	40	2	1	51	91	11	6	.355	.335	8
Velandia, Jorge, S.D.	R	.103	14	29	0	3	5	2	0	0	0	0	0	1	7	0	0	.172	.133	NV
Vizcaino, Jose, S.F.	B	.266	151	568	77	151	199	19	7	5	50	13	1	48	87	8	8	.350	.323	8
Weiss, Walt, Col.	B	.270	121	393	52	106	151	23	5	4	38	7	1	66	56	5	2	.384	.377	6

National League outfielders

Name/Team	B	BA	G	AB	R	H	TB	2B	3B	HR	RBI	SH	SF	BB	SO	SB	CS	SLG	OBA	RV
Abreu, Bob, Hou.	L	.250	59	188	22	47	70	10	2	3	26	0	0	21	48	7	2	.372	.329	3
Allensworth, Jermaine, Pit.	R	.255	108	369	55	94	125	18	2	3	43	9	6	44	79	14	7	.339	.340	7
Alou, Moises, Fla.	R	.292	150	538	88	157	265	29	5	23	115	0	7	70	85	9	5	.493	.373	26
Amaro, Ruben, Phi.	B	.234	117	175	18	41	55	6	1	2	21	0	2	21	24	1	1	.314	.320	NV
Anthony, Eric, L.A.	L	.243	47	74	8	18	31	3	2	2	5	0	0	12	18	2	0	.419	.349	NV
Ashley, Billy, L.A.	R	.244	71	131	12	32	57	7	0	6	19	0	0	8	46	0	0	.435	.293	1
Barron, Tony, Phi.	R	.286	57	189	22	54	80	12	1	4	24	2	3	12	38	0	1	.423	.330	3
Bautista, Danny, Atl.	R	.243	64	103	14	25	41	3	2	3	9	2	1	5	24	2	0	.398	.282	NV
Beamon, Trey, S.D.	L	.277	43	65	5	18	21	3	0	0	7	0	0	2	17	1	2	.323	.309	NV
Bell, Derek, Hou.	R	.276	129	493	67	136	216	29	3	15	71	0	2	40	94	15	7	.438	.344	18
Benard, Marvin, S.F.	L	.228	84	114	13	26	33	4	0	1	13	0	1	13	29	3	1	.289	.315	NV
Bichette, Dante, Col.	R	.308	151	561	81	173	286	31	2	26	118	0	7	30	90	6	5	.510	.343	29
Bieser, Steve, NYN	L	.246	47	69	16	17	20	3	0	0	4	0	1	7	20	2	3	.290	.346	NV
Bonds, Barry, S.F.	L	.291	159	532	123	155	311	26	5	40	101	0	5	145	87	37	8	.585	.446	41
Brown, Adrian, Pit.	B	.190	48	147	17	28	37	6	0	1	10	2	1	13	18	8	4	.252	.273	NV
Brown, Brant, ChiN	L	.234	46	137	15	32	56	7	1	5	15	1	0	7	28	2	1	.409	.286	1
Brown, Emil, Pit.	R	.179	66	95	16	17	27	2	1	2	6	0	0	10	32	5	1	.284	.304	NV
Burks, Ellis, Col.	R	.290	119	424	91	123	242	19	2	32	82	1	2	47	75	7	2	.571	.363	24
Butler, Brett, L.A.	L	.283	105	343	52	97	111	8	3	0	18	15	0	42	40	15	10	.324	.363	8
Butler, Rob, Phi.	L	.292	43	89	10	26	37	9	1	0	13	0	1	5	8	1	0	.416	.326	1
Cangelosi, John, Fla.	B	.245	103	192	28	47	58	8	0	1	12	1	1	19	33	5	1	.302	.321	NV
Carr, Chuck, Hou.	B	.276	63	192	34	53	80	11	2	4	17	6	1	15	37	11	5	.417	.333	6
Cedeno, Roger, L.A.	B	.273	80	194	31	53	76	10	2	3	17	3	2	25	44	9	1	.392	.362	5
Clark, Dave, ChiN	L	.301	102	143	19	43	66	8	0	5	32	0	2	19	34	1	0	.462	.386	5
Cruz, Jacob, S.F.	L	.160	16	25	3	4	5	1	0	0	3	0	1	3	4	0	0	.200	.241	NV
Cummings, Midre, Pit.-Phi.	L	.264	115	314	35	83	129	22	6	4	31	2	2	31	56	2	3	.411	.330	3
Daulton, Darren, Phi.-Fla.	L	.263	136	395	68	104	183	21	8	14	63	0	9	76	74	6	1	.463	.378	11
Dunwoody, Todd, Fla.	L	.260	19	50	7	13	25	2	2	2	7	0	0	7	21	2	0	.500	.362	NV
Echevarria, Angel, Col.	R	.250	15	20	4	5	7	2	0	0	0	0	0	2	5	0	0	.350	.318	NV
Eisenreich, Jim, Fla.	L	.280	120	293	36	82	109	19	1	2	34	3	4	30	28	0	0	.372	.345	4
Everett, Carl, NYN	B	.248	142	443	58	110	186	28	3	14	57	3	2	32	102	17	9	.420	.308	12
Finley, Steve, S.D.	L	.261	143	560	101	146	266	26	5	28	92	2	7	43	92	15	3	.475	.313	21
Floyd, Cliff, Fla.	L	.234	61	137	23	32	61	9	1	6	19	1	1	24	33	6	2	.445	.354	3
Franklin, Micah, St.L	B	.324	17	34	6	11	17	0	0	2	2	0	0	3	10	0	0	.500	.378	NV
Gant, Ron, St.L	R	.229	139	502	68	115	195	21	4	17	62	0	1	58	162	14	6	.388	.310	9
Garcia, Karim, L.A.	L	.128	15	39	5	5	8	0	0	1	8	0	1	6	14	0	0	.205	.239	NV
Gilkey, Bernard, NYN	R	.249	145	518	85	129	216	31	1	18	78	0	12	70	111	7	11	.417	.338	11
Glanville, Doug, ChiN	R	.300	146	474	79	142	186	22	5	4	35	9	2	24	46	19	11	.392	.333	16
Gonzalez, Luis, Hou.	L	.258	152	550	78	142	207	31	2	10	68	0	5	71	67	10	7	.376	.345	10
Goodwin, Curtis, Cin.	L	.253	85	265	27	67	81	11	0	1	12	6	1	24	53	22	13	.306	.316	7
Green, Scarborough, St.L	R	.097	20	31	5	3	3	0	0	0	1	0	0	2	5	0	0	.097	.152	NV
Gregg, Tommy, Atl.	L	.263	13	19	1	5	7	2	0	0	0	0	0	1	2	1	1	.368	.300	NV
Guerrero, Vladimir, Mon.	R	.302	90	325	44	98	157	22	2	11	40	0	3	19	39	3	4	.483	.350	11
Guillen, Jose, Pit.	R	.267	143	498	58	133	205	20	5	14	70	0	3	17	88	1	2	.412	.300	10
Gwynn, Tony, S.D.	L	.372	149	592	97	220	324	49	2	17	119	1	12	43	28	12	5	.547	.409	43
Hamilton, Darryl, S.F.	L	.270	125	460	78	124	168	23	3	5	43	6	2	61	61	15	10	.365	.354	10
Harris, Lenny, Cin.	L	.273	120	238	32	65	89	13	1	3	28	3	2	18	18	4	3	.374	.327	4
Helton, Todd, Col.	L	.280	35	93	13	26	45	2	1	5	11	0	0	8	11	0	1	.484	.337	2

National League outfielders

Name/Team	B	BA	G	AB	R	H	TB	2B	3B	HR	RBI	SH	SF	BB	SO	SB	CS	SLG	OBA	RV
Henderson, Rickey, S.D.	R	.274	88	288	63	79	108	11	0	6	27	0	2	71	62	29	4	.375	.422	15
Hidalgo, Rich, Hou.	R	.306	19	62	8	19	30	5	0	2	6	0	0	4	18	1	0	.484	.358	1
Hill, Glenallen, S.F.	R	.261	128	398	47	104	173	28	4	11	64	0	7	19	87	7	4	.435	.297	10
Hollandsworth, Todd, L.A.	L	.247	106	296	39	73	109	20	2	4	31	2	2	17	60	5	5	.368	.286	2
Howard, Thomas, Hou.	L	.247	107	255	24	63	90	16	1	3	22	1	1	26	48	1	2	.353	.323	NV
Hudler, Rex, Phi.	R	.221	50	122	17	27	46	4	0	5	10	1	0	6	28	1	0	.377	.264	NV
Huskey, Butch, NYN	R	.287	142	471	61	135	237	26	2	24	81	0	8	25	84	8	5	.503	.319	21
Ingram, Garey, L.A.	R	.444	12	9	2	4	4	0	0	0	1	0	0	1	3	1	0	.444	.500	NV
Javier, Stan, S.F.	B	.286	142	440	69	126	174	16	4	8	50	2	7	56	70	25	3	.395	.368	18
Jefferies, Gregg, Phi.	B	.256	130	476	68	122	186	25	3	11	48	0	0	53	27	12	6	.391	.333	9
Jennings, Robin, ChiN	L	.167	9	18	1	3	4	1	0	0	2	0	1	0	2	0	0	.222	.158	NV
Johnson, L., NYN-ChiN	L	.307	111	410	60	126	173	16	8	5	39	0	2	42	31	20	12	.422	.370	17
Jones, Andruw, Atl.	R	.231	153	399	60	92	166	18	1	18	70	5	3	56	107	20	11	.416	.329	14
Jones, Chris C., S.D.	R	.243	92	152	24	37	67	9	0	7	25	1	1	16	45	7	2	.441	.322	4
Jordan, Brian, St.L	R	.234	47	145	17	34	39	5	0	0	10	0	0	10	21	6	1	.269	.311	NV
Kelly, Mike, Cin.	R	.293	73	140	27	41	76	13	2	6	19	0	1	10	30	6	1	.543	.338	6
Kieschnick, Brooks, ChiN	L	.200	39	90	9	18	32	2	0	4	12	0	0	12	21	1	0	.356	.294	NV
Kirby, Wayne, L.A.	R	.169	46	65	6	11	13	2	0	0	4	0	0	10	12	0	0	.200	.280	NV
Klesko, Ryan, Atl.	L	.261	143	467	67	122	229	23	6	24	84	1	2	48	130	4	4	.490	.334	15
Kotsay, Mark, Fla.	L	.192	14	52	5	10	13	1	1	0	4	1	0	4	7	3	0	.250	.250	NV
Lankford, Ray, St.L	L	.295	133	465	94	137	272	36	3	31	98	0	5	95	125	21	11	.585	.411	31
Lewis, Darren, L.A.	R	.299	26	77	7	23	31	3	1	1	10	2	0	6	17	3	2	.403	.349	2
Lofton, Kenny, Atl.	L	.333	122	493	90	164	211	20	6	5	48	2	3	64	83	27	20	.428	.409	27
Lowery, Terrell, ChiN	R	.286	9	14	2	4	4	0	0	0	0	0	0	3	3	1	0	.286	.412	NV
Mabry, John, St.L	L	.284	116	388	40	110	144	19	0	5	36	2	2	39	77	0	1	.371	.352	6
Magee, Wendell, Phi.	R	.200	38	115	7	23	30	4	0	1	9	0	2	9	20	1	4	.261	.254	NV
Martin, Al, Pit.	L	.291	113	423	64	123	200	24	7	13	59	1	5	45	83	23	7	.473	.359	21
May, Derrick, Phi.	L	.228	83	149	8	34	44	5	1	1	13	0	1	8	26	4	1	.295	.266	NV
McCracken, Quinton, Col.	B	.292	147	325	69	95	117	11	1	3	36	6	1	42	62	28	11	.360	.374	16
McGee, Willie, St.L	B	.300	122	300	29	90	126	19	4	3	38	0	1	22	59	8	2	.420	.347	9
McMillon, Billy, Fla.-Phi.	L	.256	37	90	10	23	36	5	1	2	14	0	3	6	24	2	1	.400	.293	1
McRae, Brian, ChiN-NYN	B	.242	153	562	86	136	215	32	7	11	43	4	2	65	84	17	10	.383	.326	8
Mendoza, Carlos, NYN	L	.250	15	12	6	3	3	0	0	0	1	0	0	4	2	0	0	.250	.500	NV
Meulens, Hensley, Mon.	R	.292	16	24	6	7	14	1	0	2	6	0	1	4	10	0	1	.583	.379	NV
Mondesi, Raul, L.A.	R	.310	159	616	95	191	333	42	5	30	87	1	3	44	105	32	15	.541	.360	39
Montgomery, Ray, Hou.	R	.235	29	68	8	16	22	4	1	0	4	0	3	5	18	0	0	.324	.276	NV
Morman, Russ, Fla.	R	.286	4	7	3	2	6	1	0	1	2	0	0	0	2	1	0	.857	.286	NV
Mouton, James, Hou.	R	.211	86	180	24	38	58	9	1	3	23	2	2	18	30	9	7	.322	.287	1
Nixon, Otis, L.A.	B	.274	42	175	30	48	61	6	2	1	18	2	1	13	24	12	2	.349	.323	1
Nunnally, Jon, Cin.	L	.318	65	201	38	64	121	12	3	13	35	1	1	26	51	7	3	.602	.400	13
Obando, Sherman, Mon.	R	.128	41	47	3	6	13	1	0	2	9	0	0	6	14	0	0	.277	.241	NV
Ochoa, Alex, NYN	R	.244	113	238	31	58	83	14	1	3	22	2	2	18	32	3	4	.349	.300	1
Orsulak, Joe, Mon.	L	.227	106	150	13	34	51	12	1	1	7	2	0	18	17	0	1	.340	.310	NV
Otero, Ricky, Phi.	B	.252	50	151	20	38	48	6	2	0	3	3	0	19	15	0	3	.318	.339	NV
Owens, Eric, Cin.	R	.263	27	57	8	15	15	0	0	0	3	0	0	4	11	3	2	.263	.311	NV
Plantier, Phil, S.D.-St.L	R	.248	52	121	13	30	53	8	0	5	18	0	2	13	30	0	3	.438	.331	1
Powell, Dante, S.F.	R	.308	27	39	8	12	16	1	0	1	3	1	0	4	11	1	1	.410	.372	NV
Pulliam, Harvey, Col.	R	.284	59	67	15	19	31	3	0	3	9	0	0	5	15	0	1	.463	.333	1
Ramos, Ken, Hou.	L	.000	14	12	0	0	0	0	0	0	1	0	1	2	0	0	0	.000	.133	NV
Rivera, Ruben, S.D.	R	.250	17	20	2	5	6	1	0	0	1	0	0	2	9	2	1	.300	.318	NV
Rodriguez, Henry, Mon.	L	.244	132	476	55	116	228	28	3	26	83	0	3	42	149	3	3	.479	.306	13
Sanders, Deion, Cin.	B	.273	115	465	53	127	169	13	7	5	23	2	2	34	67	56	13	.363	.329	24
Sanders, Reggie, Cin.	R	.253	86	312	52	79	159	19	2	19	56	1	0	42	93	13	7	.510	.347	14
Santangelo, F.P., Mon.	B	.249	130	350	56	87	131	19	5	5	31	12	3	50	73	8	5	.374	.379	4
Sheffield, Gary, Fla.	R	.250	135	444	86	111	198	22	1	21	71	0	2	121	79	11	7	.446	.424	14
Sierra, Ruben, Cin.	B	.244	25	90	6	22	35	5	1	2	7	0	0	6	21	0	0	.389	.292	NV
Smith, Mark, Pit.	R	.285	71	193	29	55	97	13	1	9	35	0	1	28	36	3	1	.503	.374	7
Sosa, Sammy, ChiN	R	.251	162	642	90	161	308	31	4	36	119	0	5	45	174	22	12	.480	.300	27
Stynes, Chris, Cin.	R	.348	49	198	31	69	96	7	1	6	28	2	0	11	13	11	2	.485	.394	13
Sweeney, Mark, St.L-S.D.	L	.280	115	164	16	46	59	7	0	2	23	1	2	20	32	2	3	.360	.358	3
Tartabull, Danny, Phi.	R	.000	3	7	2	0	0	0	0	0	0	0	0	4	4	0	0	.000	.364	NV
Thurman, Gary, NYN	R	.167	11	6	0	1	1	0	0	0	0	0	0	0	0	0	1	.167	.167	NV
Timmons, Ozzie, Cin.	R	.333	6	9	1	3	4	1	0	0	0	0	0	0	1	0	0	.444	.333	NV
Tomberlin, Andy, NY-N	R	.286	6	7	0	2	2	0	0	0	0	0	0	1	3	0	0	.286	.375	NV
Tucker, Michael, Atl.	L	.283	138	499	80	141	222	25	7	14	56	4	1	44	116	12	6	.445	.347	16
Vander Wal, John, Col.	L	.174	76	92	7	16	21	2	0	1	11	0	0	10	33	1	1	.228	.255	NV
Vaughn, Greg, S.D.	R	.216	120	361	60	78	142	10	0	18	57	0	3	56	110	7	4	.393	.322	6
Walker, Larry, Col.	L	.366	153	568	143	208	409	46	4	49	130	0	4	78	90	33	8	.720	.452	61
Ward, Turner, Pit.	B	.353	71	167	33	59	98	16	1	7	33	3	1	18	17	4	1	.587	.420	11
Watkins, Pat, Cin.	R	.207	17	29	2	6	8	2	0	0	0	1	0	0	5	1	0	.276	.207	NV

National League outfielders

Name/Team	B	BA	G	AB	R	H	TB	2B	3B	HR	RBI	SH	SF	BB	SO	SB	CS	SLG	OBA	RV
Wehner, John, Fla.	R	.278	44	36	8	10	12	2	0	0	2	1	0	2	5	1	0	.333	.333	NV
White, Devon, Fla.	B	.245	74	265	37	65	98	13	1	6	34	0	4	32	65	13	5	.370	.338	6
White, Rondell, Mon.	R	.270	151	592	84	160	283	29	5	28	82	1	4	31	111	16	8	.478	.316	23

National League relief pitchers (batting)

Name/Team	B	BA	G	AB	R	H	TB	2B	3B	HR	RBI	SH	SF	BB	SO	SB	CS	SLG	OBA
Acevedo, Juan, NYN	R	.000	25	6	0	0	0	0	0	0	0	1	0	0	5	0	0	.000	.000
Adams, Terry, ChiN	R	.000	74	2	0	0	0	0	0	0	0	0	0	0	1	0	0	.000	.000
Alfonseca, Antonio, Fla.	R	.000	17	3	0	0	0	0	0	0	0	0	0	0	3	0	0	.000	.000
Arocha, Rene, S.F.	R	.000	6	1	0	0	0	0	0	0	0	0	0	0	1	0	0	.000	.000
Bailey, Cory, S.F.	R	1.000	7	1	0	1	1	0	0	0	0	0	0	0	0	0	0	1.000	1.000
Belinda, Stan, Cin.	R	.333	84	3	0	1	1	0	0	0	0	0	0	0	1	0	0	.333	.333
Beltran, Rigo, St.L	L	.143	35	7	1	1	2	1	0	0	0	0	0	0	1	0	0	.286	.143
Bennett, Shayne, Mon.	R	.000	16	1	0	0	0	0	0	0	0	0	0	1	0	0	0	.000	.000
Bergman, Sean, S.D.	R	.231	44	13	2	3	4	1	0	0	0	3	0	0	7	0	0	.308	.231
Bielecki, Mike, Atl.	R	.000	50	2	0	0	0	0	0	0	0	0	0	1	1	0	0	.000	.333
Blazier, Ron, Phi.	R	.400	36	5	0	2	2	0	0	0	0	1	0	0	1	0	0	.400	.400
Bones, Ricky, Cin.	R	.000	9	2	0	0	0	0	0	0	0	0	0	0	0	0	0	.000	.000
Borland, Toby, NYN	R	---	13	0	0	0	0	0	0	0	0	1	0	0	0	0	0	---	---
Bottalico, Ricky, Phi.	L	.000	69	1	0	0	0	0	0	0	0	0	0	0	1	0	0	.000	.000
Bottenfield, Kent, ChiN	R	.000	64	4	0	0	0	0	0	0	0	4	0	0	3	0	0	.000	.000
Brewer, Billy, Phi.	L	.000	25	1	0	0	0	0	0	0	0	0	0	0	1	0	0	.000	.000
Bruske, Jim, S.D.	R	.167	29	6	0	1	2	1	0	0	0	0	0	0	1	0	0	.333	.167
Byrd, Paul, Atl.	R	.143	31	7	0	1	1	0	0	0	1	2	0	0	2	0	0	.143	.143
Cabrera, Jose, Hou.	R	.000	12	2	0	0	0	0	0	0	0	0	0	0	0	0	0	.000	.000
Candiotti, Tom, L.A.	R	.094	42	32	0	3	3	0	0	0	2	9	0	1	10	0	0	.094	.121
Carlson, Dan, S.F.	R	.000	6	3	0	0	0	0	0	0	0	0	0	0	0	0	0	.000	.000
Casian, Larry, ChiN	R	.000	12	1	0	0	0	0	0	0	0	0	0	0	1	0	0	.000	.000
Cather, Mike, Atl.	R	.000	35	1	0	0	0	0	0	0	0	0	0	0	0	0	0	.000	.000
Clontz, Brad, Atl.	R	.000	51	1	0	0	0	0	0	0	0	0	0	0	1	0	0	.000	.000
Cook, Dennis, Fla.	L	.556	61	9	2	5	8	0	0	1	2	0	0	0	0	0	0	.889	.556
Crawford, Joe, NYN	L	.000	19	11	0	0	0	0	0	0	0	0	0	0	5	0	0	.000	.000
Crowell, James, Cin.	R	.000	2	2	0	0	0	0	0	0	0	0	0	0	0	0	0	.000	.000
Cunnane, Will, S.D.	R	.357	55	14	4	5	7	0	1	0	4	1	0	2	4	0	0	.500	.438
Daal, Omar, Mon.	L	.200	33	5	0	1	1	0	0	0	1	0	0	0	0	0	0	.200	.200
DeHart, Rick, Mon.	L	.000	23	2	0	0	0	0	0	0	0	0	0	2	0	0	0	.000	.000
DeJean, Mike, Col.	R	.333	56	3	0	1	2	1	0	0	0	1	0	0	1	0	0	.667	.333
DiPoto, Jerry, Col.	R	.111	74	9	0	1	1	0	0	0	0	0	0	0	5	0	0	.111	.111
Dreifort, Darren, L.A.	R	.143	48	7	0	1	1	0	0	0	0	0	0	0	5	0	0	.143	.143
Eischen, Joey, Cin.	L	.000	1	1	0	0	0	0	0	0	0	0	0	0	0	0	0	.000	.000
Erdos, Todd, S.D.	R	.000	11	1	0	0	0	0	0	0	0	0	0	0	1	0	0	.000	.000
Falteisek, Steve, Mon.	R	.000	5	2	0	0	0	0	0	0	0	1	0	0	2	0	0	.000	.000
Frascatore, John, St.L	R	.000	59	3	0	0	0	0	0	0	0	0	0	0	2	0	0	.000	.000
Garcia, Ramon, Hou.	R	.111	42	36	2	4	6	2	0	0	5	7	1	0	13	0	0	.167	.132
Gomes, Wayne, Phi.	R	.000	37	2	0	0	0	0	0	0	0	0	0	1	1	0	0	.000	.333
Gorecki, Rick, L.A.	R	---	4	0	1	0	0	0	0	0	0	1	0	0	0	0	0	---	---
Graves, Danny, Cin.	R	.000	10	1	0	0	0	0	0	0	0	0	0	0	1	0	0	.000	.000
Guthrie, Mark, L.A.	B	.250	62	4	0	1	1	0	0	0	0	1	0	0	0	0	0	.250	.250
Harkey, Mike, L.A.	R	.000	10	1	0	0	0	0	0	0	0	2	0	0	1	0	0	.000	.000
Helling, Rick, Fla.	R	.091	31	11	0	1	1	0	0	0	0	1	0	0	5	0	0	.091	.091
Henry, Doug, S.F.	R	.000	75	4	0	0	0	0	0	0	0	0	0	0	2	0	0	.000	.000
Heredia, Felix, Fla.	L	.500	56	2	0	1	1	0	0	0	0	1	0	0	1	0	0	.500	.500
Hernandez, Roberto, S.F.	R	.500	28	2	0	1	1	0	0	0	0	0	0	0	1	0	0	.500	.500
Hoffman, Trevor, S.D.	R	.333	70	3	0	1	1	0	0	0	1	0	0	0	1	0	0	.333	.333
Holmes, Darren, Col.	R	.158	42	19	2	3	6	0	0	1	2	3	1	0	9	0	0	.316	.150
Hutton, Mark, Fla.-Col.	R	.000	40	3	0	0	0	0	0	0	0	0	0	0	0	0	0	.000	.000
Jarvis, Kevin, Cin.	L	.000	9	1	0	0	0	0	0	0	0	0	0	0	0	0	0	.000	.000
Johnson, Jason, Pit.	R	.000	3	1	0	0	0	0	0	0	0	0	0	0	1	0	0	.000	.000
Johnstone, John, S.F.	R	.000	13	2	0	0	0	0	0	0	0	0	0	0	1	0	0	.000	.000
Jordan, Ricardo, NYN	L	.000	22	1	0	0	0	0	0	0	0	0	0	0	1	0	0	.000	.000
Judd, Michael, L.A.	R	.000	1	1	0	0	0	0	0	0	0	0	0	0	1	0	0	.000	.000
Kashiwada, Takashi, NYN	L	.000	35	1	0	0	0	0	0	0	0	0	0	0	1	0	0	.000	.000
King, Curtis, St.L	R	.000	30	1	0	0	0	0	0	0	0	0	0	0	0	0	0	.000	.000
Kline, Steve, Mon.	B	.000	26	1	0	0	0	0	0	0	0	0	0	0	1	0	0	.000	.000
Leskanic, Curtis, Col.	R	.000	55	1	0	0	0	0	0	0	0	0	0	0	1	0	0	.000	.000
Lewis, Richie, Cin.	R	1.000	4	1	0	1	1	0	0	0	0	0	0	0	0	0	0	1.000	1.000
Lidle, Cory, NYN	R	.000	54	5	1	0	0	0	0	0	0	0	0	1	4	0	0	.000	.167
Lima, Jose, Hou.	R	.000	52	3	0	0	0	0	0	0	0	2	0	0	3	0	0	.000	.000

National League relief pitchers (batting)

Name/Team	B	BA	G	AB	R	H	TB	2B	3B	HR	RBI	SH	SF	BB	SO	SB	CS	SLG	OBA
Loiselle, Rich, Pit.	R	.000	72	1	0	0	0	0	0	0	0	0	0	0	1	0	0	.000	.000
Magnante, Mike, Hou.	L	.000	40	3	0	0	0	0	0	0	0	0	0	0	2	0	0	.000	.000
Manuel, Barry, NYN	R	.000	19	2	0	0	0	0	0	0	0	0	0	0	1	0	0	.000	.000
Martin, Tom, Hou.	L	.000	55	3	0	0	0	0	0	0	0	0	0	0	1	0	0	.000	.000
Mathews, T.J., St.L	R	.000	40	1	0	0	0	0	0	0	0	0	0	0	0	0	0	.000	.000
McCurry, Jeff, Col.	R	.000	33	1	0	0	0	0	0	0	0	0	0	0	1	0	0	.000	.000
McMichael, Greg, NYN	R	.667	73	3	0	2	2	0	0	0	0	0	0	0	1	0	0	.667	.667
Mimbs, Michael, Phi.	L	.000	17	2	1	0	0	0	0	0	0	0	0	0	0	0	0	.000	.000
Munoz, Mike, Col.	L	.000	64	1	0	0	0	0	0	0	0	0	0	1	1	0	0	.000	.500
Murray, Heath, S.D.	L	.000	17	6	0	0	0	0	0	0	0	0	0	0	1	0	0	.000	.000
Nye, Ryan, Phi.	R	.000	4	2	0	0	0	0	0	0	0	1	0	0	1	0	0	.000	.000
Osuna, Antonio, L.A.	R	.500	48	2	0	1	1	0	0	0	0	0	0	0	0	0	0	.500	.500
Painter, Lance, St.L	L	.000	14	1	0	0	0	0	0	0	0	0	0	0	1	0	0	.000	.000
Pall, Donn, Fla.	R	.000	2	1	0	0	0	0	0	0	0	0	0	0	1	0	0	.000	.000
Paniagua, Jose, Mon.	R	.000	9	5	0	0	0	0	0	0	0	0	0	0	3	0	0	.000	.000
Patterson, Bob, ChiN	R	.000	76	1	0	0	0	0	0	0	0	0	0	0	0	0	0	.000	.000
Perez, Yorkis, NYN	R	.000	9	1	0	0	0	0	0	0	0	0	0	0	0	0	0	.000	.000
Peters, Chris, Pit.	L	.250	31	4	0	1	1	0	0	0	2	0	0	0	2	0	0	.250	.250
Petkovsek, Mark, St.L	R	.091	55	11	0	1	1	0	0	0	0	1	0	1	2	0	0	.091	.167
Pisciotta, Marc, ChiN	R	.000	24	1	0	0	0	0	0	0	0	0	0	0	1	0	0	.000	.000
Poole, Jim, S.F.	L	---	63	0	0	0	0	0	0	0	0	1	0	0	0	0	0	---	---
Powell, Jay, Fla.	R	.500	74	4	0	2	2	0	0	0	1	0	0	0	1	0	0	.500	.500
Radinsky, Scott, L.A.	L	.000	75	4	0	0	0	0	0	0	0	0	0	0	4	0	0	.000	.000
Raggio, Brady, St.L	R	.000	15	3	0	0	0	0	0	0	0	1	1	0	0	0	0	.000	.000
Ramos, Edgar, Phi.	R	.000	4	3	0	0	0	0	0	0	0	0	1	0	2	0	0	.000	.000
Reed, Steve, Col.	R	.000	63	1	0	0	0	0	0	0	0	0	0	0	0	0	0	.000	.000
Remlinger, Mike, Cin.	L	.095	71	21	1	2	4	2	0	0	6	3	0	2	11	0	0	.190	.174
Reyes, Dennis, L.A.	R	.000	14	9	1	0	0	0	0	0	0	1	0	1	5	1	0	.000	.100
Rincon, Ricardo, Pit.	L	.000	62	1	0	0	0	0	0	0	0	1	0	0	1	0	0	.000	.000
Roa, Joe, S.F.	R	.133	28	15	0	2	2	0	0	0	0	0	0	1	5	0	0	.133	.188
Rodriguez, Felix, Cin.	R	.000	26	3	0	0	0	0	0	0	0	0	0	0	0	0	0	.000	.000
Rodriguez, Rich, S.F.	L	.333	71	3	1	1	1	0	0	0	0	0	0	1	1	0	0	.333	.500
Rojas, Mel, ChiN-NYN	R	.000	77	1	0	0	0	0	0	0	0	0	0	0	0	0	0	.000	.000
Ruebel, Matt, Pit.	L	.000	44	7	0	0	0	0	0	0	0	1	0	0	7	0	0	.000	.000
Ruffcorn, Scott, Phi.	R	.000	18	6	0	0	0	0	0	0	0	1	0	1	6	0	0	.000	.143
Shaw, Jeff, Cin.	R	.000	78	3	0	0	0	0	0	0	0	1	0	0	3	0	0	.000	.000
Silva, Jose, Pit.	R	.143	11	7	1	1	1	0	0	0	0	3	0	0	4	0	0	.143	.143
Smith, Pete J., S.D.	R	.167	38	30	2	5	8	1	1	0	3	6	0	1	16	0	0	.267	.194
Sodowsky, Clint, Pit.	L	.500	45	2	0	1	1	0	0	0	0	0	0	0	0	0	0	.500	.500
Spradlin, Jerry, Phi.	B	.000	76	1	0	0	0	0	0	0	0	0	0	0	1	0	0	.000	.000
Springer, Russ, Hou.	R	.000	54	1	0	0	0	0	0	0	0	0	0	0	0	0	0	.000	.000
Stanifer, Rob, Fla.	R	.667	36	3	1	2	3	1	0	0	1	0	0	0	0	0	0	1.000	.750
Stevens, Dave, ChiN	R	.000	10	1	0	0	0	0	0	0	0	0	0	0	0	0	0	.000	.000
Stull, Everett, Mon.	R	---	3	0	0	0	0	0	0	0	0	1	0	0	0	0	0	---	---
Sullivan, Scott, Cin.	R	.000	59	7	0	0	0	0	0	0	0	2	0	0	4	0	0	.000	.000
Tatis, Ramon, ChiN	L	.000	56	3	0	0	0	0	0	0	0	0	0	1	3	0	0	.000	.250
Tavarez, Julian, S.F.	R	.000	89	1	0	0	0	0	0	0	0	0	0	0	1	0	0	.000	.000
Telemaco, Amaury, ChiN	R	.222	10	9	0	2	2	0	0	0	0	0	0	1	6	0	0	.222	.300
Telford, Anthony, Mon.	R	.200	65	15	0	3	4	1	0	0	1	1	0	0	3	0	0	.267	.200
Thurman, Mike, Mon.	R	.500	5	2	1	1	1	0	0	0	0	1	0	0	1	0	0	.500	.500
Torres, Salomon, Mon.	R	.000	12	6	0	0	0	0	0	0	0	0	0	0	4	0	0	.000	.000
Urbina, Ugueth, Mon.	R	.000	63	5	0	0	0	0	0	0	0	0	0	0	4	0	0	.000	.000
Valdes, Marc, Mon.	R	.105	48	19	0	2	2	0	0	0	0	1	0	1	9	0	0	.105	.150
Veres, Dave, Mon.	R	1.000	53	1	0	1	1	0	0	0	0	0	0	0	0	0	0	1.000	1.000
Wagner, Paul, Pit.	R	.000	14	1	0	0	0	0	0	0	0	0	0	0	1	0	0	.000	.000
Wagner, Billy, Hou.	L	.000	62	1	0	0	0	0	0	0	0	0	0	0	0	0	0	.000	.000
Wainhouse, Dave, Pit.	L	.000	25	2	0	0	0	0	0	0	0	0	0	0	0	0	0	.000	.000
Wendell, Turk, ChiN-NYN	L	.000	65	5	1	0	0	0	0	0	0	0	0	1	3	0	0	.000	.167
White, Gabe, Cin.	L	.111	12	9	0	1	1	0	0	0	1	2	0	0	7	0	0	.111	.111
Wilkins, Marc, Pit.	R	.000	70	4	0	0	0	0	0	0	0	1	1	0	1	3	0	0	.000	.200
Winston, Darrin, Phi.	R	.500	7	2	0	1	1	0	0	0	0	1	0	0	1	0	0	.500	.667
Wohlers, Mark, Atl.	R	.000	71	2	0	0	0	0	0	0	0	0	0	0	2	0	0	.000	.000
Worrell, Tim, S.D.	R	.200	60	15	3	3	3	0	0	0	1	0	0	2	8	0	0	.200	.294

National League starting pitchers (batting)

Name/Team	B	BA	G	AB	R	H	TB	2B	3B	HR	RBI	SH	SF	BB	SO	SB	CS	SLG	OBA
Alvarez, Wilson, S.F.	L	.130	11	23	1	3	3	0	0	0	1	1	0	2	5	0	0	.130	.200
Ashby, Andy, S.D.	R	.067	31	60	1	4	5	1	0	0	1	7	0	2	24	0	0	.083	.097

National League starting pitchers (batting)

Name/Team	B	BA	G	AB	R	H	TB	2B	3B	HR	RBI	SH	SF	BB	SO	SB	CS	SLG	OBA
Astacio, Pedro, L.A.-Col.	R	.130	33	54	2	7	8	1	0	0	1	11	0	0	24	0	0	.148	.130
Aybar, Manny, St.L	R	.143	12	21	0	3	3	0	0	0	1	0	0	0	9	0	0	.143	.143
Bailey, Roger, Col.	R	.210	30	62	9	13	14	1	0	0	2	5	0	2	15	0	0	.226	.234
Batista, Miguel, ChiN	R	.000	11	8	0	0	0	0	0	0	0	0	0	0	5	0	0	.000	.000
Beech, Matt, Phi.	L	.167	24	30	1	5	6	1	0	0	1	11	0	0	14	0	0	.200	.167
Benes, Alan, St.L	R	.173	23	52	1	9	11	2	0	0	3	2	0	0	16	0	0	.212	.173
Benes, Andy, St.L	R	.218	26	55	4	12	14	2	0	0	5	8	0	1	14	0	0	.255	.246
Bohanon, Brian, NYN	L	.182	21	33	0	6	6	0	0	0	4	1	1	0	15	0	0	.182	.176
Brock, Chris, Atl.	R	.100	7	10	0	1	1	0	0	0	1	0	0	0	2	0	0	.100	.100
Brown, Kevin, Fla.	R	.125	33	72	4	9	10	1	0	0	4	6	0	5	25	0	0	.139	.182
Bullinger, Jim, Mon.	R	.209	36	43	2	9	13	1	0	1	2	3	0	0	15	0	0	.302	.209
Burba, Dave, Cin.	R	.196	30	46	2	9	9	0	0	0	2	4	0	1	18	0	0	.196	.245
Burke, John, Col.	L	.158	18	19	1	3	3	0	0	0	0	2	0	0	6	0	0	.158	.158
Busby, Mike, St.L	R	.500	3	4	0	2	2	0	0	0	0	0	0	0	2	0	0	.500	.500
Carrara, Giovanni, Cin.	R	.000	2	2	0	0	0	0	0	0	0	2	0	0	2	0	0	.000	.000
Castillo, Frank, ChiN-Col.	R	.121	34	58	1	7	7	0	0	0	5	10	1	1	19	0	0	.121	.133
Clark, Mark, NYN-ChiN	R	.030	32	66	3	2	5	0	0	1	3	6	0	4	31	0	0	.076	.086
Cooke, Steve, Pit.	R	.058	32	52	2	3	4	1	0	0	1	7	0	0	18	0	0	.077	.058
Cordova, Francisco, Pit.	R	.089	29	56	2	5	5	0	0	0	0	8	0	4	26	0	0	.089	.150
Creek, Doug, S.F.	L	.333	3	3	1	1	1	0	0	0	0	2	0	0	1	0	0	.333	.333
Darwin, Danny, S.F.	R	.133	10	15	0	2	3	1	0	0	2	0	0	0	8	0	0	.200	.133
Estes, Shawn, S.F.	R	.147	36	68	8	10	13	0	0	1	3	7	0	1	24	0	0	.191	.183
Fernandez, Alex, Fla.	R	.152	33	66	3	10	16	6	0	0	4	7	1	6	20	0	0	.242	.219
Fernandez, Sid, Hou.	L	.000	1	1	0	0	0	0	0	0	0	0	0	0	1	0	0	.000	.000
Fernandez, Osvaldo, S.F.	R	.000	12	17	0	0	0	0	0	0	0	0	0	2	13	0	0	.000	.105
Foster, Kevin, ChiN	R	.128	30	47	3	6	7	1	0	0	4	11	0	1	20	0	0	.149	.146
Foulke, Keith, S.F.	R	.154	11	13	0	2	2	0	0	0	0	2	0	0	4	0	0	.154	.154
Gardner, Mark, S.F.	R	.115	32	61	0	7	7	0	0	0	2	3	0	1	30	0	0	.115	.143
Glavine, Tom, Atl.	L	.222	33	63	6	14	14	0	0	0	7	17	0	7	13	0	0	.222	.310
Gonzalez, Jeremi, ChiN	R	.100	23	40	1	4	4	0	0	0	1	8	0	3	12	0	0	.100	.163
Grace, Mike, Phi.	R	.083	6	12	0	1	1	0	0	0	0	0	0	0	9	0	0	.083	.083
Green, Tyler, Phi.	R	.308	14	26	2	8	11	3	0	0	2	1	0	0	5	0	0	.423	.308
Greene, Tommy, Hou.	R	.333	3	3	1	1	2	1	0	0	1	1	0	0	1	0	0	.667	.333
Hamilton, Joey, S.D.	R	.130	31	54	4	7	13	0	0	2	6	9	2	1	26	0	0	.241	.140
Hampton, Mike, Hou.	R	.137	34	73	6	10	13	1	1	0	8	10	1	5	21	0	1	.178	.190
Harnisch, Pete, NYN	R	.000	6	8	0	0	0	0	0	0	0	1	0	0	3	0	0	.000	.000
Hermanson, Dustin, Mon.	R	.104	32	48	1	5	9	1	0	1	1	5	0	2	24	0	0	.188	.140
Hernandez, Livan, Fla.	R	.172	17	29	2	5	7	2	0	0	2	3	0	1	6	0	0	.241	.200
Hitchcock, Sterling, S.D.	L	.100	32	50	4	5	5	0	0	0	1	8	0	3	30	0	1	.100	.151
Holt, Chris, Hou.	R	.090	33	67	6	6	6	0	0	0	1	9	0	1	33	0	0	.090	.103
Isringhausen, Jason, NYN	R	.143	6	7	1	1	1	0	0	0	1	1	1	0	4	0	0	.143	.125
Jackson, Danny, St.L-S.D.	R	.100	17	20	1	2	2	0	0	0	0	1	0	1	8	0	1	.100	.143
Johnson, Mike, Mon.	L	.077	11	13	1	1	1	0	0	0	1	2	0	0	5	0	0	.077	.077
Jones, Bobby, NYN	R	.129	30	62	4	8	10	2	0	0	4	4	0	3	18	0	0	.161	.169
Jones, Bobby M., Col.	R	.200	4	5	1	1	1	0	0	0	0	1	0	0	0	0	0	.200	.333
Juden, Jeff, Mon.	R	.140	22	43	1	6	8	2	0	0	4	2	0	1	24	0	0	.186	.178
Kile, Darryl, Hou.	R	.124	34	89	4	11	14	3	0	0	7	10	0	3	38	0	0	.157	.179
Leiter, Al, Fla.	L	.104	27	48	2	5	5	0	0	0	1	2	0	3	25	0	0	.104	.157
Leiter, Mark, Phi.	R	.118	31	51	2	6	6	0	0	0	4	10	0	2	28	0	0	.118	.151
Lieber, Jon, Pit.	L	.121	33	58	1	7	9	2	0	0	8	2	0	4	23	0	0	.155	.177
Loaiza, Esteban, Pit.	R	.167	33	60	4	10	11	1	0	0	5	8	0	1	17	0	0	.183	.180
Lowe, Sean, St.L	R	.333	6	3	0	1	1	0	0	0	0	0	0	0	1	0	0	.333	.333
Maddux, Greg, Atl.	R	.104	33	67	3	7	9	2	0	0	4	6	0	5	21	1	0	.134	.167
Maduro, Calvin, Phi.	R	.050	16	20	1	1	1	0	0	0	0	1	0	0	12	0	0	.050	.050
Martinez, Pedro J., Mon.	R	.116	31	69	5	8	12	2	1	0	0	9	0	3	28	0	0	.174	.153
Martinez, Ramon, L.A.	L	.190	22	42	5	8	9	1	0	0	1	5	0	0	11	0	0	.214	.190
Menhart, Paul, S.D.	R	.000	9	12	0	0	0	0	0	0	0	2	0	0	4	0	0	.000	.000
Mercker, Kent, Cin.	R	.156	31	45	3	7	10	1	1	0	1	4	0	4	23	0	0	.222	.224
Millwood, Kevin, Atl.	R	.000	12	12	0	0	0	0	0	0	0	1	0	1	8	0	0	.000	.077
Mlicki, Dave, NYN	R	.188	33	48	3	9	12	3	0	0	3	3	1	3	22	0	0	.250	.231
Morgan, Mike, Cin.	R	.091	31	44	1	4	6	0	1	0	2	9	0	0	14	0	0	.136	.111
Morris, Matt, St.L	R	.205	34	73	4	15	17	2	0	0	6	2	0	5	36	0	1	.233	.256
Mulholland, T., ChiN-S.F.	R	.164	40	55	1	9	12	3	0	0	2	4	0	0	27	0	0	.218	.164
Munoz, Bobby, Phi.	R	.300	8	10	2	3	4	1	0	0	1	1	0	0	1	0	0	.400	.300
Neagle, Denny, Atl.	L	.153	34	72	6	11	15	1	0	1	7	9	0	4	35	0	0	.208	.197
Nomo, Hideo, L.A.	R	.159	33	69	3	11	16	5	0	0	2	5	0	1	32	0	0	.232	.171
Ojala, Kirt, Fla.	L	.000	7	7	0	0	0	0	0	0	0	1	0	0	2	0	0	.000	.000
Osborne, Donovan, St.L	L	.208	14	24	2	5	6	1	0	0	2	1	0	0	6	1	0	.250	.208
Park, Chan Ho, L.A.	R	.176	32	51	5	9	13	4	0	0	2	11	0	4	21	0	0	.255	.236
Perez, Carlos, Mon.	L	.172	33	64	3	11	16	2	0	1	2	5	0	2	31	0	0	.250	.197

National League starting pitchers (batting)

Name/Team	B	BA	G	AB	R	H	TB	2B	3B	HR	RBI	SH	SF	BB	SO	SB	CS	SLG	OBA
Portugal, Mark, Phi.	R	.000	3	4	0	0	0	0	0	0	0	0	0	0	2	0	0	.000	.000
Rapp, Pat, Fla.-S.F.	R	.106	27	47	3	5	8	0	0	1	2	4	0	0	16	0	0	.170	.106
Reed, Rick, NYN	R	.175	33	57	6	10	18	5	0	1	5	6	0	3	18	0	0	.316	.217
Rekar, Bryan, Col.	R	.250	2	4	1	1	1	0	0	0	0	0	0	0	1	0	0	.250	.250
Reynolds, Shane, Hou.	R	.113	30	53	3	6	9	3	0	0	2	7	0	2	31	0	0	.170	.145
Reynoso, Armando, NYN	R	.241	16	29	3	7	10	0	0	1	3	0	1	2	15	0	0	.345	.281
Ritz, Kevin, Col.	R	.057	18	35	4	2	2	0	0	0	0	2	0	4	15	1	0	.057	.154
Rueter, Kirk, S.F.	L	.138	32	65	5	9	9	0	0	0	5	7	0	3	14	0	0	.138	.176
Saunders, Tony, Fla.	L	.081	22	37	2	3	6	0	0	1	1	1	0	2	19	0	0	.162	.128
Schilling, Curt, Phi.	R	.173	35	81	4	14	15	1	0	0	1	12	1	1	32	1	0	.185	.181
Schmidt, Jason, Pit.	R	.107	32	56	2	6	8	2	0	0	2	9	0	2	26	0	0	.143	.138
Schourek, Pete, Cin.	L	.167	19	24	1	4	7	0	0	1	2	6	0	0	8	1	0	.292	.167
Smiley, John, Cin.	L	.100	20	40	0	4	5	1	0	0	2	2	0	0	10	0	0	.125	.100
Smoltz, John, Atl.	R	.228	36	79	10	18	21	3	0	0	4	6	0	9	22	1	1	.266	.307
Stephenson, Garrett, Phi.	R	.094	20	32	0	3	4	1	0	0	1	5	0	1	16	0	0	.125	.121
Stottlemyre, Todd, St.L	R	.236	29	55	6	13	19	4	1	0	4	5	0	8	13	0	0	.345	.333
Swartzbaugh, Dave, ChiN	R	.000	2	4	0	0	0	0	0	0	0	0	0	0	1	0	0	.000	.000
Swift, Bill, Col.	R	.211	16	19	2	4	5	1	0	0	2	4	0	4	4	0	0	.263	.375
Tapani, Kevin, ChiN	R	.136	13	22	2	3	3	0	0	0	0	4	0	2	12	1	0	.136	.208
Thompson, Mark, Col.	R	.182	6	11	1	2	6	1	0	1	1	2	0	0	5	0	0	.545	.182
Thomson, John, Col.	R	.213	27	47	2	10	10	0	0	0	5	6	0	2	23	0	0	.213	.245
Tomko, Brett, Cin.	R	.139	24	36	2	5	6	1	0	0	3	3	0	1	14	0	0	.167	.162
Trachsel, Steve, ChiN	R	.117	34	60	5	7	10	3	0	0	4	11	0	5	19	0	0	.167	.185
Valdes, Ismael, L.A.	R	.088	30	57	0	5	6	1	0	0	1	7	0	3	17	1	0	.105	.133
Valenzuela, F., S.D.-St.L	L	.182	19	22	1	4	4	0	0	0	2	6	0	0	3	0	0	.182	.182
VanLandingham,Wm.,S.F.	R	.115	18	26	1	3	4	1	0	0	0	2	0	1	13	0	0	.154	.148
Wade, Terrell, Atl.	L	.250	12	12	0	3	3	0	0	0	1	1	0	2	5	0	0	.250	.357
Wall, Donne, Hou.	R	.100	8	10	0	1	1	0	0	0	0	1	0	1	4	0	0	.100	.182
Wright, Jamey, Col.	R	.125	26	48	4	6	7	1	0	0	3	3	0	3	22	0	0	.146	.176

American League relief pitchers

Name/Team	T	W	L	ERA	G	GS	CG	SHO	GF	SV	IP	H	R	ER	HR	BB	SO	WP	BA	RV
Acre, Mark, Oak.	R	2	0	5.74	15	0	0	0	5	0	15.2	21	10	10	1	8	12	0	.318	NV
Adamson, Joel, Mil.	L	5	3	3.54	30	6	0	0	3	0	76.1	78	36	30	13	19	56	0	.265	6
Aguilera, Rick, Min.	R	5	4	3.82	61	0	0	0	57	26	68.1	65	29	29	9	22	68	3	.257	19
Alberro, Jose, Tex.	R	0	3	7.94	10	4	0	0	2	0	28.1	37	33	25	4	17	11	3	.303	NV
Almanzar, Carlos, Tor.	R	0	1	2.70	4	0	0	0	2	0	3.1	1	1	1	1	1	4	0	.091	NV
Andujar, Luis, Tor.	R	0	6	6.48	17	8	0	0	5	0	50.0	76	45	36	9	21	28	2	.352	NV
Assenmacher, Paul, Cle.	L	5	0	2.94	75	0	0	0	20	4	49.0	43	17	16	5	15	53	4	.231	8
Ayala, Bobby, Sea.	R	10	5	3.82	71	0	0	0	33	8	96.2	91	45	41	14	41	92	6	.260	11
Bailes, Scott, Tex.	R	1	0	2.86	24	0	0	0	7	0	22.0	18	9	7	2	10	14	0	.231	1
Banks, Willie, NYA	R	3	0	1.93	5	1	0	0	1	0	14.0	9	3	3	0	6	8	0	.188	2
Bautista, Jose, Det.	R	2	2	6.69	21	0	0	0	4	0	40.1	55	32	30	6	12	19	1	.324	NV
Benitez, Armando, Bal.	R	4	5	2.45	71	0	0	0	26	0	73.1	49	22	20	7	43	106	1	.191	12
Benjamin, Mike, Bos.	R	0	0	0.00	1	0	0	0	1	0	1.0	0	0	0	0	0	0	0	.000	NV
Bertotti, Mike, ChiA	L	0	0	7.36	9	0	0	0	2	0	3.2	9	3	3	0	2	4	0	.450	NV
Bevil, Brian, K.C.	R	1	2	6.61	18	0	0	0	11	1	16.1	16	13	12	1	9	13	2	.267	NV
Boehringer, Brian, NYA	R	3	2	2.63	34	0	0	0	11	0	48.0	39	16	14	4	32	53	2	.225	2
Boggs, Wade, NYA	R	0	0	0.00	1	0	0	0	1	0	1.0	1	0	0	0	1	1	0	.000	NV
Borland, Toby, Bos.	R	0	0	13.50	3	0	0	0	1	0	3.1	6	5	5	1	7	1	0	.400	NV
Borowski, Joe, NYA	R	0	1	9.00	1	0	0	0	1	0	2.0	2	2	2	0	4	2	0	.250	NV
Boskie, Shawn, Bal.	R	6	6	6.43	28	9	0	0	8	1	77.0	95	57	55	14	26	50	1	.304	NV
Bovee, Mike, Ana.	R	0	0	5.40	3	0	0	0	3	0	3.1	3	2	2	1	1	5	0	.231	NV
Brandenburg, Mark, Bos.	R	0	2	5.49	31	0	0	0	5	0	41.0	49	25	25	3	16	34	0	.299	NV
Brewer, Billy, Oak.	L	0	0	13.50	3	0	0	0	1	0	2.0	4	3	3	1	2	1	0	.444	NV
Brocail, Doug, Det.	R	3	4	3.23	61	4	0	0	20	2	78.0	74	31	28	10	36	60	6	.256	4
Cadaret, Greg, Ana.	L	0	0	3.29	15	0	0	0	6	0	13.2	11	5	5	1	8	11	3	.220	NV
Carmona, Rafael, Sea.	R	0	0	3.18	4	0	0	0	1	0	5.2	3	3	2	1	2	6	1	.150	NV
Carrasco, Hector, K.C.	R	1	6	5.45	28	0	0	0	11	0	34.2	29	21	21	4	16	30	8	.227	NV
Casian, Larry, K.C.	L	0	2	5.06	32	0	0	0	6	0	26.2	32	15	15	5	6	16	1	.299	NV
Castillo, Tony J., ChiA	L	4	4	4.91	64	0	0	0	20	4	62.1	74	48	34	6	23	42	0	.296	NV
Castillo, Carlos, ChiA	R	2	1	4.48	37	2	0	0	14	1	66.1	68	35	33	9	33	43	3	.265	NV
Charlton, Norm, Sea.	L	3	8	7.27	71	0	0	0	38	14	69.1	89	59	56	7	47	55	7	.312	NV
Chavez, Anthony, Ana.	R	0	0	0.93	7	0	0	0	2	0	9.2	7	1	1	1	5	10	0	.206	NV
Checo, Robinson, Bos.	R	1	1	3.38	5	2	0	0	1	0	13.1	12	5	5	0	3	14	0	.235	1
Clemons, Chris, ChiA	R	0	2	8.53	5	2	0	0	3	0	12.2	19	13	12	4	11	8	1	.345	NV
Converse, Jim, K.C.	R	0	0	3.60	3	0	0	0	1	0	5.0	4	2	2	2	5	3	0	.222	NV
Corsi, Jim, Bos.	R	5	3	3.43	52	0	0	0	14	2	57.2	56	26	22	1	21	40	2	.255	5

American League relief pitchers

Name/Team	T	W	L	ERA	G	GS	CG	SHO	GF	SV	IP	H	R	ER	HR	BB	SO	WP	BA	RV
Crabtree, Tim, Tor.	R	3	3	7.08	37	0	0	0	16	2	40.2	65	32	32	7	17	26	4	.374	NV
Cruz, Nelson, ChiA	R	0	2	6.49	19	0	0	0	5	0	26.1	29	19	19	6	9	23	3	.274	NV
Cummings, John, Det.	L	2	0	5.47	19	0	0	0	2	0	24.2	32	22	15	3	14	8	3	.311	NV
Daal, Omar, Tor.	L	1	1	4.00	9	3	0	0	0	0	27.0	34	13	12	3	6	28	1	.304	NV
Darwin, Jeff, ChiA	R	0	1	5.27	14	0	0	0	6	0	13.2	17	8	8	1	7	9	3	.298	NV
Davis, Mark W., Mil.	L	0	0	5.51	19	0	0	0	3	0	16.1	21	10	10	4	5	14	0	.323	NV
Davis, Tim, Sea.	L	0	0	6.75	2	0	0	0	1	0	6.2	6	5	5	1	4	10	0	.231	NV
De La Maza, Roland, K.C.	R	0	0	4.50	1	0	0	0	0	0	2.0	1	1	1	1	1	1	1	.125	NV
DeLucia, Rich, Ana.	R	6	4	3.61	33	0	0	0	13	3	42.1	29	18	17	5	27	42	1	.204	5
Duran, Roberto, Det.	L	0	0	7.59	13	0	0	0	1	0	10.2	7	9	9	0	15	11	1	.189	NV
Escobar, Kelvim, Tor.	R	3	2	2.90	27	0	0	0	23	14	31.0	28	12	10	1	19	36	0	.237	8
Eshelman, Vaughn, Bos.	L	3	3	6.83	21	6	0	0	6	0	42.2	58	32	30	3	17	18	2	.330	NV
Eversgerd, Bryan, Tex.	L	0	2	20.25	3	0	0	0	1	0	1.1	5	3	3	0	3	2	0	.556	NV
Fetters, Mike, Mil.	R	1	5	3.45	51	0	0	0	20	6	70.1	62	30	27	4	33	62	2	.244	5
Flener, Huck, Tor.	L	0	1	9.87	8	1	0	0	3	0	17.1	40	19	19	3	6	9	2	.444	NV
Florie, Bryce, Mil.	R	4	4	4.32	32	8	0	0	6	0	75.0	74	43	36	4	42	53	4	.262	NV
Fordham, Tom, ChiA	L	0	1	6.23	7	1	0	0	1	0	17.1	17	13	12	2	10	10	0	.266	NV
Foulke, Keith, ChiA	R	3	0	3.45	16	0	0	0	5	3	28.2	28	11	11	4	5	21	0	.255	4
Gaillard, Eddie, Det.	R	1	0	5.31	16	0	0	0	5	1	20.1	16	12	12	2	10	12	0	.211	NV
Garces, Rich, Bos.	R	0	1	4.61	12	0	0	0	4	0	13.2	14	9	7	2	9	12	0	.255	NV
Graves, Danny, Cle.	R	0	0	4.76	5	0	0	0	2	0	11.1	15	8	6	2	9	4	0	.326	NV
Groom, Buddy, Oak.	L	2	2	5.15	78	0	0	0	7	3	64.2	75	38	37	9	24	45	3	.292	NV
Gross, Kevin, Ana.	R	2	1	6.75	12	3	0	0	2	0	25.1	30	20	19	4	20	20	2	.313	NV
Grundt, Ken, Bos.	L	0	0	9.00	2	0	0	0	0	0	3.0	5	3	3	0	0	0	0	.357	NV
Guardado, Eddie, Min.	L	0	4	3.91	69	0	0	0	20	1	46.0	45	23	20	7	17	54	2	.251	1
Gunderson, Eric, Tex.	L	2	1	3.26	60	0	0	0	11	0	49.2	45	19	18	5	15	31	2	.241	4
Hammond, Chris, Bos.	L	3	4	5.92	29	8	0	0	6	1	65.1	81	45	43	5	27	48	2	.310	NV
Haney, Chris, K.C.	L	1	2	4.38	8	3	0	0	1	0	24.2	29	16	12	1	5	16	1	.290	NV
Hansell, Greg, Mil.	R	0	0	9.64	3	0	0	0	1	0	4.2	5	5	5	1	1	5	0	.263	NV
Harris, Pep, Ana.	R	5	4	3.62	61	0	0	0	17	0	79.2	82	33	32	7	38	56	3	.274	1
Hasegawa, S., Ana.	R	3	7	3.93	50	7	0	0	17	0	116.2	118	60	51	14	46	83	2	.269	2
Haught, Gary, Oak.	R	0	0	7.15	6	0	0	0	2	0	11.1	12	9	9	3	6	11	1	.279	NV
Henry, Butch, Bos.	L	7	3	3.52	36	5	0	0	13	6	84.1	89	36	33	6	19	51	0	.277	11
Heredia, Wilson, Tex.	R	1	0	3.20	10	0	0	0	3	0	19.2	14	9	7	2	16	8	0	.197	NV
Hernandez, Fernando, Det.	R	0	0	40.50	2	0	0	0	0	0	1.1	5	6	6	0	3	2	0	.556	NV
Hernandez, Xavier, Tex.	R	0	4	4.56	44	0	0	0	20	0	49.1	51	27	25	7	22	36	5	.262	NV
Hernandez, Roberto, ChiA	R	5	1	2.44	46	0	0	0	43	27	48.0	38	15	13	5	24	47	2	.216	20
Holtz, Mike, Ana.	L	3	4	3.32	66	0	0	0	11	2	43.1	38	21	16	7	15	40	1	.228	5
Holzemer, Mark, Sea.	L	0	0	6.00	14	0	0	0	2	1	9.0	9	6	6	0	8	7	0	.250	NV
Hudson, Joe, Bos.	R	3	1	3.53	26	0	0	0	9	0	35.2	39	16	14	1	14	14	1	.289	1
Hurtado, Edwin, Sea.	R	1	2	9.00	13	1	0	0	2	0	19.0	25	19	19	5	15	10	2	.329	NV
Jackson, Mike R., Cle.	R	2	5	3.24	71	0	0	0	38	15	75.0	59	33	27	3	29	74	2	.215	14
Jacome, Jason, K.C.-Cle.	L	2	0	5.84	28	4	0	0	2	0	49.1	58	33	32	10	20	27	2	.296	NV
James, Mike, Ana.	R	5	5	4.31	58	0	0	0	22	7	62.2	69	32	30	3	28	57	1	.283	3
Janzen, Marty, Tor.	R	2	1	3.60	12	0	0	0	6	0	25.0	23	11	10	4	13	17	0	.250	1
Jarvis, Kevin, Min.-Det.	R	0	3	7.08	23	5	0	0	10	0	54.2	78	46	43	13	22	36	2	.332	NV
Johnson, Dane, Oak.	R	4	1	4.53	38	0	0	0	12	2	45.2	49	28	23	4	31	43	4	.272	NV
Johnson, Mike, Bal.	R	0	1	7.94	14	5	0	0	5	2	39.2	52	36	35	12	16	29	1	.317	NV
Johnstone, John, Oak.	R	0	0	2.84	5	0	0	0	1	0	6.1	7	2	2	0	7	4	0	.292	NV
Jones, Doug, Mil.	R	6	6	2.02	75	0	0	0	73	36	80.1	62	20	18	4	9	82	2	.215	37
Jones, Todd, Det.	R	5	4	3.09	68	0	0	0	51	31	70.0	60	29	24	3	35	70	7	.231	21
Karchner, Matt, ChiA	R	3	1	2.91	52	0	0	0	25	15	52.2	50	18	17	4	26	30	6	.258	10
Kline, Steve, Cle.	L	3	1	5.81	20	1	0	0	0	0	26.1	42	19	17	6	13	17	3	.365	NV
Kubinski, Tim, Oak.	L	0	0	5.68	11	0	0	0	3	0	12.2	12	9	8	2	6	10	0	.255	NV
Lacy, Kerry, Bos.	R	1	1	6.11	33	0	0	0	12	3	45.2	60	34	31	7	22	18	0	.314	NV
Levine, Al, ChiA	R	2	2	6.91	25	0	0	0	6	0	27.1	35	22	21	4	16	22	2	.313	NV
Lewis, Richie, Oak.	R	2	0	9.64	14	0	0	0	5	0	18.2	24	21	20	7	15	12	2	.316	NV
Lloyd, Graeme, NYA	L	1	1	3.31	46	0	0	0	17	1	49.0	55	24	18	6	20	26	3	.293	NV
Lopez, Albie, Cle.	R	3	7	6.93	37	6	0	0	10	0	76.2	101	61	59	11	40	63	5	.322	NV
Lorraine, Andrew, Oak.	L	3	1	6.37	12	6	0	0	1	0	29.2	45	22	21	2	15	18	0	.354	NV
Lowe, Derek, Sea.-Bos.	R	2	6	6.13	20	9	0	0	1	0	69.0	74	49	47	11	23	52	2	.279	NV
Maddux, Mike, Sea.	R	1	0	10.13	6	0	0	0	1	0	10.2	20	12	12	1	8	7	1	.400	NV
Mahay, Ron, Bos.	L	0	0	2.52	28	0	0	0	7	0	25.0	19	7	7	3	11	22	3	.204	3
Mahomes, Pat, Bos.	R	1	1	8.10	10	0	0	0	2	0	10.0	15	10	9	2	10	5	1	.366	NV
Maloney, Sean, Mil.	R	0	0	5.14	3	0	0	0	2	0	7.0	7	4	4	1	2	5	2	.304	NV
Manzanillo, Josias, Sea.	R	0	1	5.40	16	0	0	0	4	0	18.1	19	13	11	3	17	18	2	.275	NV
Mathews, Terry, Bal.	R	4	4	4.41	57	0	0	0	19	1	63.1	63	35	31	8	36	39	3	.267	NV
Mathews, T.J., Oak.	R	6	2	4.40	24	0	0	0	14	3	28.2	34	18	14	5	12	24	0	.293	2
May, Darrell, Ana.	L	2	1	5.23	29	2	0	0	7	0	51.2	56	31	30	6	25	42	2	.277	NV
McCarthy, Greg, Sea.	L	1	1	5.46	37	0	0	0	4	0	29.2	26	21	18	4	16	34	4	.230	NV

American League relief pitchers

Name/Team	T	W	L	ERA	G	GS	CG	SHO	GF	SV	IP	H	R	ER	HR	BB	SO	WP	BA	RV
McDill, Allen, K.C.	L	0	0	13.50	3	0	0	0	1	0	4.0	3	6	6	1	8	2	0	.214	NV
McElroy, C., Ana.-ChiA	L	1	3	3.84	61	0	0	0	16	1	75.0	73	36	32	5	22	62	1	.252	3
Mecir, Jim, NYA	R	0	4	5.88	25	0	0	0	11	0	33.2	36	23	22	5	10	25	1	.279	NV
Mendoza, Ramiro, NYA	R	8	6	4.24	39	15	0	0	9	2	133.2	157	67	63	15	28	82	2	.292	6
Mesa, Jose, Cle.	R	4	4	2.40	66	0	0	0	38	16	82.1	83	28	22	7	28	69	1	.259	15
Miceli, Dan, Det.	R	3	2	5.01	71	0	0	0	24	3	82.2	77	49	46	13	38	79	3	.248	1
Mills, Alan, Bal.	R	2	3	4.89	39	0	0	0	11	0	38.2	41	23	21	5	33	32	2	.270	NV
Miranda, Angel, Mil.	L	0	0	3.86	10	0	0	0	1	0	14.0	17	6	6	1	9	8	2	.309	NV
Misuraca, Mike, Mil.	R	0	0	11.32	5	0	0	0	2	0	10.1	15	13	13	5	7	10	1	.333	NV
Mohler, Mike, Oak.	L	1	10	5.13	62	10	0	0	16	1	101.2	116	65	58	11	54	66	4	.301	NV
Montgomery, Jeff, K.C.	R	1	4	3.49	55	0	0	0	37	14	59.1	53	24	23	9	18	48	5	.240	11
Montgomery, Steve, Oak.	R	0	1	9.95	4	0	0	0	0	0	6.1	10	7	7	2	8	1	0	.385	NV
Moody, Eric, Tex.	R	0	1	4.26	10	1	0	0	3	0	19.0	26	10	9	4	2	12	0	.329	NV
Morman, Alvin, Cle.	L	0	0	5.89	34	0	0	0	7	2	18.1	19	13	12	2	14	13	1	.268	NV
Myers, Mike, Det.	L	0	4	5.70	88	0	0	0	23	2	53.2	58	36	34	12	25	50	0	.274	NV
Myers, Randy, Bal.	L	2	3	1.51	61	0	0	0	57	45	59.2	47	12	10	2	22	56	3	.217	32
Naulty, Dan, Min.	R	1	1	5.87	29	0	0	0	8	1	30.2	29	20	20	8	10	23	3	.254	NV
Nelson, Jeff, NYA	R	3	7	2.86	77	0	0	0	22	2	78.2	53	32	25	7	37	81	4	.191	10
Olson, Gregg, Min.-K.C.	R	4	3	5.58	45	0	0	0	18	1	50.0	58	35	31	3	28	34	1	.299	NV
Orosco, Jesse, Bal.	L	6	3	2.32	71	0	0	0	12	0	50.1	29	13	13	6	30	46	1	.169	8
Patterson, Danny, Tex.	R	10	6	3.42	54	0	0	0	17	1	71.0	70	29	27	3	23	69	7	.263	9
Percival, Troy, Ana.	R	5	5	3.46	55	0	0	0	46	27	52.0	40	20	20	6	22	72	5	.205	20
Perez, Mike, K.C.	R	2	0	3.54	16	0	0	0	4	0	20.1	15	8	8	2	8	17	1	.214	1
Pichardo, Hipolito, K.C.	R	3	5	4.22	47	0	0	0	26	11	49.0	51	24	23	7	24	34	2	.273	5
Plesac, Dan, Tor.	L	2	4	3.58	73	0	0	0	18	1	50.1	47	22	20	8	19	61	2	.244	2
Plunk, Eric, Cle.	R	4	5	4.66	55	0	0	0	22	0	65.2	62	37	34	12	36	66	4	.245	NV
Quantrill, Paul, Tor.	R	6	7	1.94	77	0	0	0	29	5	88.0	103	25	19	5	17	56	1	.297	12
Reyes, Carlos, Oak.	R	3	4	5.82	37	6	0	0	9	0	77.1	101	52	50	13	25	43	2	.316	NV
Reyes, Al, Mil.	R	1	2	5.46	19	0	0	0	7	1	29.2	32	19	18	4	9	28	1	.274	NV
Rhodes, Arthur, Bal.	L	10	3	3.02	53	0	0	0	6	1	95.1	75	32	32	9	26	102	2	.218	17
Rios, Danny, NYA	R	0	0	19.29	2	0	0	0	1	0	2.1	9	5	5	3	2	1	0	.563	NV
Risley, Bill, Tor.	R	0	1	8.31	3	0	0	0	1	0	4.1	3	4	4	2	2	2	0	.188	NV
Ritchie, Todd, Min.	R	2	3	4.58	42	0	0	0	19	0	74.2	87	41	38	11	28	44	11	.290	NV
Rivera, Mariano, NYA	R	6	4	1.88	66	0	0	0	56	43	71.2	65	17	15	5	20	68	2	.237	34
Robinson, Ken, Tor.	R	0	0	2.70	3	0	0	0	2	0	3.1	1	1	1	1	1	4	0	.100	NV
Rodriguez, Frankie, Min.	R	3	6	4.62	43	15	0	0	5	0	142.1	147	82	73	12	60	65	6	.271	NV
Rodriguez, Nerio, Bal.	R	2	1	4.91	6	2	0	0	1	0	22.0	21	15	12	2	8	11	1	.250	NV
Sager, A.J., Det.	R	3	4	4.18	38	1	0	0	8	3	84.0	81	43	39	10	24	53	0	.258	6
Sanders, Scott, Sea.-Det.	R	6	14	5.86	47	20	1	1	15	2	139.2	152	92	91	30	62	120	8	.278	NV
Santana, Julio, Tex.	R	4	6	6.75	30	14	0	0	3	0	104.0	141	86	78	16	49	64	8	.323	NV
Santiago, Jose, K.C.	R	0	0	1.93	4	0	0	0	3	0	4.2	7	2	1	0	2	1	0	.333	NV
Service, Scott, K.C.	R	0	3	4.76	12	0	0	0	1	0	17.0	17	9	9	1	5	19	0	.274	NV
Shuey, Paul, Cle.	R	4	2	6.20	40	0	0	0	16	0	45.0	52	31	31	5	28	46	2	.294	NV
Simas, Bill, ChiA	R	3	1	4.14	40	0	0	0	11	1	41.1	46	23	19	6	24	38	2	.279	NV
Slocumb, H., Bos.-Sea.	R	0	9	5.16	76	0	0	0	61	27	75.0	84	45	43	6	49	64	10	.286	4
Small, Aaron, Oak.	R	9	5	4.28	71	0	0	0	22	4	96.2	109	50	46	6	40	57	4	.294	3
Spoljaric, Paul, Tor.-Sea.	L	0	3	3.69	57	0	0	0	10	3	70.2	61	30	29	4	36	70	6	.236	2
Stanton, Mike, NYA	L	6	1	2.57	64	0	0	0	15	6	66.2	50	19	19	3	34	70	3	.205	9
Swindell, Greg, Min.	L	7	4	3.58	65	1	0	0	12	1	115.2	102	46	46	12	25	75	0	.238	15
Taylor, Bill, Oak.	R	3	4	3.82	72	0	0	0	45	23	73.0	70	32	31	3	36	66	0	.254	13
Thomas, Larry, ChiA	L	0	0	8.10	5	0	0	0	0	0	3.1	3	3	3	1	2	0	0	.250	NV
Timlin, Mike, Tor.-Sea.	R	6	4	3.22	64	0	0	0	31	10	72.2	69	30	26	8	20	45	1	.257	13
Torres, Salomon, Sea.	R	0	0	27.00	2	0	0	0	2	0	3.1	7	10	10	0	3	0	0	.412	NV
Trlicek, Rick, Bos.	R	4	4	4.63	18	0	0	0	8	0	23.1	26	14	12	2	18	10	2	.289	NV
Trombley, Mike, Min.	R	2	3	4.37	67	0	0	0	21	1	82.1	77	43	40	7	31	74	5	.248	2
Veres, Randy, K.C.	R	4	0	3.31	24	0	0	0	7	1	35.1	36	17	13	4	7	28	4	.273	4
Villone, Ron, Mil.	L	1	0	3.42	50	0	0	0	15	0	52.2	54	23	20	4	36	40	3	.271	NV
Vosberg, Ed, Tex.	L	1	2	4.61	42	0	0	0	16	0	41.0	44	23	21	3	15	29	1	.277	NV
Wagner, Paul, Mil.	R	1	0	9.00	2	0	0	0	1	0	2.0	3	2	2	1	0	0	0	.375	NV
Walker, Jamie, K.C.	L	3	3	5.44	50	0	0	0	15	0	43.0	46	28	26	6	20	24	2	.271	NV
Wasdin, John, Bos.	R	4	6	4.40	53	7	0	0	10	0	124.2	121	68	61	18	38	84	4	.251	5
Weathers, David, NYA-Cle.	R	1	3	8.42	19	1	0	0	5	0	25.2	38	24	24	3	15	18	3	.355	NV
Wells, Bob, Sea.	R	2	0	5.75	46	1	0	0	19	2	67.1	88	49	43	11	18	51	1	.314	NV
Wengert, Don, Oak.	R	5	11	6.04	49	12	1	0	16	0	134.0	177	96	90	21	41	68	2	.321	NV
Wetteland, John, Tex.	R	7	2	1.94	61	0	0	0	58	31	65.0	43	18	14	5	21	63	1	.182	30
Whisenant, Matt, K.C.	L	1	0	2.84	24	0	0	0	3	0	19.0	15	7	6	0	12	16	3	.211	NV
Whiteside, Matt, Tex.	R	4	1	5.08	42	1	0	0	8	0	72.2	85	45	41	4	26	44	3	.296	NV
Wickman, Bob, Mil.	R	7	6	2.73	74	0	0	0	20	1	95.2	89	32	29	8	41	78	8	.252	9
Williams, Brian, Bal.	R	0	0	3.00	13	0	0	0	8	0	24.0	20	8	8	0	18	14	1	.220	NV
Williams, Mike, K.C.	R	0	2	6.43	10	0	0	0	4	1	14.0	20	11	10	1	8	10	0	.333	NV

American League relief pitchers

Name/Team	T	W	L	ERA	G	GS	CG	SHO	GF	SV	IP	H	R	ER	HR	BB	SO	WP	BA	RV
Williams, Mitch, K.C.	L	0	1	10.80	7	0	0	0	4	0	6.2	11	8	8	2	7	10	2	.367	NV
Williams, Shad, Ana.	R	0	0	0.00	1	0	0	0	1	0	1.0	1	0	0	0	1	0	0	.250	NV
Witasick, Jay, Oak.	R	0	0	5.73	8	0	0	0	1	0	11.0	14	7	7	2	6	8	0	.304	NV

American League starting pitchers

Name/Team	T	W	L	ERA	G	GS	CG	SHO	GF	SV	IP	H	R	ER	HR	BB	SO	WP	BA	RV
Adams, Willie, Oak.	R	3	5	8.18	13	12	0	0	0	0	58.1	73	53	53	9	32	37	2	.307	NV
Aldred, Scott, Min.	L	2	10	7.68	17	15	0	0	0	0	77.1	102	66	66	20	28	33	7	.323	NV
Alvarez, Wilson, ChiA	L	9	8	3.03	22	22	2	1	0	0	145.2	126	61	49	9	55	110	4	.232	16
Anderson, Brian, Cle.	L	4	2	4.69	8	8	0	0	0	0	48.0	55	28	25	7	11	22	1	.301	1
Appier, Kevin, K.C.	R	9	13	3.40	34	34	4	1	0	0	235.2	215	96	89	24	74	196	14	.243	21
Avery, Steve, Bos.	L	6	7	6.42	22	18	0	0	1	0	96.2	127	76	69	15	49	51	4	.320	NV
Baldwin, James, ChiA	R	12	15	5.27	32	32	1	0	0	0	200.0	205	128	117	19	83	140	14	.262	1
Belcher, Tim, K.C.	R	13	12	5.02	32	32	3	1	0	0	213.1	242	128	119	31	70	113	7	.288	1
Bere, Jason, ChiA	R	4	2	4.71	6	6	0	0	0	0	28.2	20	15	15	4	17	21	1	.198	1
Blair, Willie, Det.	R	16	8	4.17	29	27	2	0	0	0	175.0	186	85	81	18	46	90	6	.273	13
Bones, Ricky, K.C.	R	4	7	5.97	21	11	1	0	2	0	78.1	102	59	52	10	25	36	1	.325	NV
Bowers, Shane, Min.	R	0	3	8.05	5	5	0	0	0	0	19.0	27	20	17	2	8	7	1	.329	NV
Burkett, John, Tex.	R	9	12	4.56	30	30	2	0	0	0	189.1	240	106	96	20	30	139	1	.307	2
Carpenter, Chris, Tor.	R	3	7	5.09	14	13	1	1	1	0	81.1	108	55	46	7	37	55	7	.325	NV
Clark, Terry, Cle.-Tex.	R	1	7	6.00	13	9	0	0	2	0	57.0	70	41	38	6	23	24	1	.307	NV
Clemens, Roger, Tor.	R	21	7	2.05	34	34	9	3	0	0	264.0	204	65	60	9	68	292	4	.213	54
Cloude, Ken, Sea.	R	4	2	5.12	10	9	0	0	0	0	51.0	41	32	29	8	26	46	2	.218	1
Colon, Bartolo, Cle.	R	4	7	5.65	19	17	1	0	0	0	94.0	107	66	59	12	45	66	5	.286	NV
Cone, David, NYA	R	12	6	2.82	29	29	1	0	0	0	195.0	155	67	61	17	86	222	14	.218	23
Coppinger, Rocky, Bal.	R	1	1	6.30	5	4	0	0	1	0	20.0	21	14	14	2	16	22	1	.273	NV
D'Amico, Jeff, Mil.	R	9	7	4.71	23	23	1	1	0	0	135.2	139	81	71	25	43	94	3	.264	5
Darwin, Danny, ChiA	R	4	8	4.13	21	17	1	0	0	0	113.1	130	60	52	21	31	62	1	.286	2
Dickson, Jason, Ana.	R	13	9	4.29	33	32	2	1	1	0	203.2	236	111	97	32	56	115	4	.289	6
Dishman, Glenn, Det.	L	1	2	5.28	7	4	0	0	1	0	29.0	30	18	17	4	8	20	0	.268	NV
Drabek, Doug, ChiA	R	12	11	5.74	31	31	0	0	0	0	169.1	170	109	108	30	69	85	12	.261	NV
Eldred, Cal, Mil.	R	13	15	4.99	34	34	1	1	0	0	202.0	207	118	112	31	89	122	5	.266	1
Erickson, Scott, Bal.	R	16	7	3.69	34	33	3	2	0	0	221.2	218	100	91	16	61	131	11	.257	21
Eyre, Scott, ChiA	L	4	4	5.04	11	11	0	0	0	0	60.2	62	36	34	11	31	36	2	.267	NV
Fassero, Jeff, Sea.	L	16	9	3.61	35	35	2	1	0	0	234.1	226	108	94	21	84	189	13	.249	19
Finley, Chuck, Ana.	L	13	6	4.23	25	25	3	1	0	0	164.0	152	79	77	20	65	155	10	.248	11
Gooden, Dwight, NYA	R	9	5	4.91	20	19	0	0	0	0	106.1	116	61	58	14	53	66	8	.283	NV
Gordon, Tom, Bos.	R	6	10	3.74	42	25	2	1	16	11	182.2	155	85	76	10	78	159	5	.226	17
Gubicza, Mark, Ana.	R	0	1	25.07	2	2	0	0	0	0	4.2	13	13	13	2	3	5	0	.481	NV
Guzman, Juan, Tor.	R	3	6	4.95	13	13	0	0	0	0	60.0	48	42	33	14	31	52	4	.213	1
Hanson, Erik, Tor.	R	0	0	7.80	3	2	0	0	1	0	15.0	15	13	13	3	6	18	1	.254	NV
Harnisch, Pete, Mil.	R	1	1	5.14	4	3	0	0	0	0	14.0	13	9	8	1	12	10	1	.245	NV
Hawkins, LaTroy, Min.	R	6	12	5.84	20	20	0	0	0	0	103.1	134	71	67	19	47	58	6	.317	NV
Haynes, Jimmy, Oak.	R	3	6	4.42	13	13	0	0	0	0	73.1	74	38	36	7	40	66	4	.262	NV
Helling, Rick, Tex.	R	3	3	4.58	10	8	0	0	1	0	55.0	47	29	28	5	21	46	3	.235	2
Hentgen, Pat, Tor.	R	15	10	3.68	35	35	9	3	0	0	264.0	253	116	108	31	71	160	6	.254	25
Hershiser, Orel, Cle.	R	14	6	4.47	32	32	1	0	0	0	195.1	199	105	97	26	69	107	11	.272	9
Hill, Ken, Tex.-Ana.	R	9	12	4.55	31	31	1	0	0	0	190.0	194	103	96	19	95	106	7	.268	NV
Irabu, Hideki, NYA	R	5	4	7.09	13	9	0	0	0	0	53.1	69	47	42	15	20	56	4	.311	NV
Johnson, Randy, Sea.	L	20	4	2.28	30	29	5	2	0	0	213.0	147	60	54	20	77	291	4	.194	43
Juden, Jeff, Cle.	R	0	1	5.46	8	5	0	0	0	0	31.1	32	21	19	6	15	29	1	.264	NV
Kamienecki, Scott, Bal.	R	10	6	4.01	30	30	0	0	0	0	179.1	179	83	80	20	67	109	5	.261	9
Karl, Scott, Mil.	L	10	13	4.47	32	32	1	0	0	0	193.1	212	103	96	23	67	119	6	.279	3
Karsay, Steve, Oak.	R	3	12	5.77	24	24	0	0	0	0	132.2	166	92	85	20	47	92	7	.304	NV
Keagle, Greg, Det.	R	3	5	6.55	11	10	0	0	0	0	45.1	58	33	33	9	18	33	1	.309	NV
Key, Jimmy, Bal.	L	16	10	3.43	34	34	1	1	0	0	212.1	210	90	81	24	82	141	4	.261	16
Krivda, Rick, Bal.	L	4	2	6.30	10	10	0	0	0	0	50.0	67	36	35	7	18	29	0	.328	NV
Langston, Mark, Ana.	L	2	4	5.85	9	9	0	0	0	0	47.2	61	34	31	8	29	30	1	.316	NV
Lira, Felipe, Det.-Sea.	R	5	11	6.34	28	18	1	1	3	0	110.2	132	82	78	18	55	73	7	.295	NV
Ludwick, Eric, Oak.	R	1	4	8.25	6	5	0	0	0	0	24.0	32	24	22	7	16	14	0	.330	NV
Martinez, Dennis, Sea.	R	1	5	7.71	9	9	0	0	0	0	49.0	65	46	42	8	29	17	0	.327	NV
McAndrew, Jamie, Mil.	R	1	1	8.38	5	4	0	0	0	0	19.1	24	19	18	1	23	8	2	.304	NV
McDonald, Ben, Mil.	R	8	7	4.06	21	21	1	0	0	0	133.0	120	68	60	13	36	110	3	.237	13
McDowell, Jack, Cle.	R	3	3	5.09	8	6	0	0	0	0	40.2	44	25	23	6	18	38	1	.282	NV
Mercedes, Jose, Mil.	R	7	10	3.79	29	23	2	1	1	0	159.0	146	76	67	24	53	80	1	.248	12
Miller, Travis, Min.	L	1	5	7.63	13	7	0	0	0	1	48.1	64	49	41	8	23	26	5	.320	NV
Moehler, Brian, Det.	R	11	12	4.67	31	31	2	1	0	0	175.1	198	97	91	22	61	97	3	.285	1
Moyer, Jamie, Sea.	L	17	5	3.86	30	30	2	0	0	0	188.2	187	82	81	21	43	113	3	.256	21

American League starting pitchers

Name/Team	T	W	L	ERA	G	GS	CG	SHO	GF	SV	IP	H	R	ER	HR	BB	SO	WP	BA	RV
Mussina, Mike, Bal.	R	15	8	3.20	33	33	4	1	0	0	224.2	197	87	80	27	54	218	5	.234	32
Nagy, Charles, Cle.	R	15	11	4.28	34	34	1	1	0	0	227.0	253	115	108	27	77	149	5	.283	7
Navarro, Jaime, ChiA	R	9	14	5.79	33	33	2	0	0	0	209.2	267	155	135	22	73	142	14	.309	NV
Ogea, Chad, Cle.	R	8	9	4.99	21	21	1	0	0	0	126.1	139	79	70	13	47	80	4	.283	NV
Olivares, Omar, Det.-Sea.	R	6	10	4.97	32	31	3	2	0	0	177.1	191	109	98	18	81	103	5	.276	NV
Oliver, Darren, Tex.	L	13	12	4.20	32	32	3	1	0	0	201.1	213	111	94	29	82	104	7	.271	5
Oquist, Mike, Oak.	R	4	6	5.02	19	17	1	0	0	0	107.2	111	62	60	15	43	72	2	.266	NV
Pavlik, Roger, Tex.	R	3	5	4.37	11	11	0	0	0	0	57.2	59	29	28	7	31	35	0	.267	NV
Perisho, Matt, Ana.	L	0	2	6.00	11	8	0	0	2	0	45.0	59	34	30	6	28	35	5	.324	NV
Person, Robert, Tor.	R	5	10	5.61	23	22	0	0	0	0	128.1	125	86	80	19	60	99	7	.255	NV
Pettitte, Andy, NYA	L	18	7	2.88	35	35	4	1	0	0	240.1	233	86	77	7	65	166	7	.256	30
Pittsley, Jim, K.C.	R	5	8	5.46	21	21	0	0	0	0	112.0	120	72	68	15	54	52	3	.277	NV
Prieto, Ariel, Oak.	R	6	8	5.04	22	22	0	0	0	0	125.0	155	84	70	16	70	90	7	.306	NV
Pugh, Tim, Det.	R	1	1	5.00	2	2	0	0	0	0	9.0	6	5	5	0	5	4	0	.188	NV
Radke, Brad, Min.	R	20	10	3.87	35	35	4	1	0	0	239.2	238	114	103	28	48	174	1	.257	28
Rigby, Brad, Oak.	R	1	7	4.87	14	14	0	0	0	0	77.2	92	44	42	14	22	34	3	.302	NV
Robertson, Rich, Min.	L	8	12	5.69	31	26	0	0	2	0	147.0	169	105	93	19	70	69	10	.292	NV
Rogers, Kenny, NYA	L	6	7	5.65	31	22	1	0	4	0	145.0	161	100	91	18	62	78	2	.280	NV
Rosado, Jose, K.C.	L	9	12	4.69	33	33	2	0	0	0	203.1	208	117	106	26	73	129	4	.264	4
Rose, Brian, Bos.	R	0	0	12.00	1	1	0	0	0	0	3.0	5	4	4	0	2	3	0	.357	NV
Rusch, Glendon, K.C.	L	6	9	5.50	30	27	1	0	0	0	170.1	206	111	104	28	52	116	0	.301	NV
Saberhagen, Bret, Bos.	R	0	1	6.58	6	6	0	0	0	0	26.0	30	20	19	5	10	14	1	.288	NV
Sele, Aaron, Bos.	R	13	12	5.38	33	33	1	0	0	0	177.1	196	115	106	25	80	122	7	.279	NV
Serafini, Dan, Min.	L	2	1	3.42	6	4	1	0	1	0	26.1	27	11	10	1	11	15	1	.273	1
Sirotka, Mike, ChiA	L	3	0	2.25	7	4	0	0	1	0	32.0	36	9	8	4	5	24	0	.290	3
Smiley, John, Cle.	L	2	4	5.54	6	6	0	0	0	0	37.1	45	23	23	9	10	26	3	.304	NV
Springer, Dennis, Ana.	R	9	9	5.18	32	28	3	1	0	0	194.2	199	118	112	32	73	75	7	.267	1
Stevens, Dave, Min.	R	1	3	9.00	6	6	0	0	0	0	23.0	41	23	23	8	17	16	1	.383	NV
Sturtze, Tanyon, Tex.	R	1	1	8.27	9	5	0	0	1	0	32.2	45	30	30	6	18	18	1	.338	NV
Suppan, Jeff, Bos.	R	7	3	5.69	23	22	0	0	1	0	112.1	140	75	71	12	36	67	5	.305	NV
Telgheder, Dave, Oak.	R	4	6	6.06	20	19	0	0	0	0	101.0	134	71	68	15	35	55	4	.324	NV
Tewksbury, Bob, Min.	R	8	13	4.22	26	26	5	2	0	0	168.2	200	83	79	12	31	92	2	.297	6
Thompson, Justin, Det.	L	15	11	3.02	32	32	4	0	0	0	223.1	188	82	75	20	66	151	4	.233	32
Wakefield, Tim, Bos.	R	12	15	4.25	35	29	4	2	6	0	201.1	193	109	95	24	87	151	6	.256	8
Watson, Allen, Ana.	L	12	12	4.93	35	34	0	0	0	0	199.0	220	121	109	37	73	141	8	.279	1
Wells, David, NYA	L	16	10	4.21	32	32	5	2	0	0	218.0	239	109	102	24	45	156	8	.278	16
Williams, Woody, Tor.	R	9	14	4.35	31	31	0	0	0	0	194.2	201	98	94	31	66	124	7	.269	6
Witt, Bobby, Tex.	R	12	12	4.82	34	32	3	0	1	0	209.0	245	118	112	33	74	121	7	.294	NV
Wojciechowski, S., Oak.	L	0	2	7.84	2	2	0	0	0	0	10.1	17	9	9	2	1	5	0	.386	NV
Wolcott, Bob, Sea.	R	5	6	6.03	19	18	0	0	0	0	100.0	129	71	67	22	29	58	0	.314	NV
Woodard, Steve, Mil.	R	3	3	5.15	7	7	0	0	0	0	36.2	39	25	21	5	6	32	0	.269	1
Wright, Jaret, Cle.	R	8	3	4.38	16	16	0	0	0	0	90.1	81	45	44	9	35	63	1	.238	6
Yan, Esteban, Bal.	R	0	1	15.83	3	2	0	0	0	0	9.2	20	18	17	3	7	4	1	.417	NV

National League relief pitchers

Name/Team	T	W	L	ERA	G	GS	CG	SHO	GF	SV	IP	H	R	ER	HR	BB	SO	WP	BA	RV
Acevedo, Juan, NYN	R	3	1	3.59	25	2	0	0	4	0	47.2	52	24	19	6	22	33	0	.286	NV
Adams, Terry, ChiN	R	2	9	4.62	74	0	0	0	39	18	74.0	91	43	38	3	40	64	6	.306	7
Alfonseca, Antonio, Fla.	R	1	3	4.91	17	0	0	0	2	0	25.2	36	16	14	3	10	19	1	.324	NV
Arocha, Rene, S.F.	R	0	0	11.32	6	0	0	0	0	0	10.1	17	14	13	2	5	7	0	.370	NV
Bailey, Cory, S.F.	R	0	1	8.38	7	0	0	0	4	0	9.2	15	9	9	1	4	5	0	.375	NV
Barrios, Manuel, Hou.	R	0	0	12.00	2	0	0	0	0	0	3.0	6	4	4	0	3	3	0	.400	NV
Batchelor, Rich, St.L-S.D.	R	3	1	5.97	23	0	0	0	8	0	28.2	40	23	19	2	14	18	1	.339	NV
Bautista, Jose, St.L	R	0	0	6.57	11	0	0	0	3	0	12.1	15	10	9	2	2	4	1	.300	NV
Beck, Rod, S.F.	R	7	4	3.47	73	0	0	0	66	37	70.0	67	31	27	7	8	53	1	.249	33
Beckett, Robbie, Col.	L	0	0	5.40	2	0	0	0	2	0	1.2	1	1	1	0	1	2	0	.167	NV
Belinda, Stan, Cin.	R	1	5	3.71	84	0	0	0	18	1	99.1	84	42	41	11	33	114	5	.229	3
Beltran, Rigo, St.L	L	1	2	3.48	35	4	0	0	16	1	54.1	47	25	21	3	17	50	1	.237	1
Bennett, Shayne, Mon.	R	0	1	3.18	16	0	0	0	3	0	22.2	21	9	8	2	9	8	0	.247	NV
Bergman, Sean, S.D.	R	2	4	6.09	44	9	0	0	13	0	99.0	126	72	67	11	38	74	6	.316	NV
Bielecki, Mike, Atl.	R	3	7	4.08	50	0	0	0	7	2	57.1	56	33	26	9	21	60	1	.250	1
Blazier, Ron, Phi.	R	1	1	5.03	36	0	0	0	7	0	53.2	62	31	30	8	21	42	2	.290	NV
Bochtler, Doug, S.D.	R	3	6	4.77	54	0	0	0	13	2	60.1	51	35	32	3	50	46	5	.229	NV
Bones, Ricky, Cin.	R	0	1	10.19	9	2	0	0	2	0	17.2	31	22	20	2	11	8	0	.378	NV
Borland, Toby, NYN	R	0	1	6.08	13	0	0	0	5	1	13.1	11	9	9	1	14	7	3	.220	NV
Borowski, Joe, Atl.	R	2	2	3.75	20	0	0	0	8	0	24.0	27	11	10	2	16	6	0	.287	NV
Bottalico, Ricky, Phi.	R	2	5	3.65	69	0	0	0	61	34	74.0	68	31	30	7	42	89	3	.245	24
Bottenfield, Kent, ChiN	R	2	3	3.86	64	0	0	0	20	2	84.0	82	39	36	13	35	74	2	.259	1

National League relief pitchers

Name/Team	T	W	L	ERA	G	GS	CG	SHO	GF	SV	IP	H	R	ER	HR	BB	SO	WP	BA	RV
Brantley, Jeff, Cin.	R	1	1	3.86	13	0	0	0	9	1	11.2	9	5	5	2	7	16	2	.205	NV
Brewer, Billy, Phi.	L	1	2	3.27	25	0	0	0	4	0	22.0	15	8	8	2	11	16	1	.188	NV
Bruske, Jim, S.D.	R	4	1	3.63	28	0	0	0	6	0	44.2	37	22	18	4	25	32	4	.228	1
Burrows, Terry, S.D.	L	0	2	10.45	13	0	0	0	4	0	10.1	12	13	12	1	8	8	0	.286	NV
Byrd, Paul, Atl.	R	4	4	5.26	31	4	0	0	9	0	53.0	47	34	31	6	28	37	3	.235	NV
Cabrera, Jose, Hou.	R	0	0	1.17	12	0	0	0	6	0	15.1	6	2	2	1	6	18	0	.125	NV
Candiotti, Tom, L.A.	R	10	7	3.60	41	18	0	0	6	0	135.0	128	60	54	21	40	89	4	.248	8
Cangelosi, John, Fla.	L	0	0	0.00	1	0	0	0	1	0	1.0	0	0	0	0	1	0	0	.000	
Carlson, Dan, S.F.	R	0	0	7.63	6	0	0	0	2	0	15.1	20	14	13	5	8	14	0	.317	NV
Carrasco, Hector, Cin.	R	1	2	3.68	38	0	0	0	11	0	51.1	51	25	21	3	25	46	3	.250	NV
Casian, Larry, ChiN	L	0	1	7.45	12	0	0	0	1	0	9.2	16	9	8	3	2	7	0	.364	NV
Cather, Mike, Atl.	R	2	4	2.39	35	0	0	0	10	0	37.2	23	12	10	1	19	29	0	.174	2
Christiansen, Jason, Pit.	L	3	0	2.94	39	0	0	0	9	0	33.2	37	11	11	2	17	37	4	.274	NV
Clontz, Brad, Atl.	R	5	1	3.75	51	0	0	0	16	1	48.0	52	24	20	3	18	42	1	.286	1
Cook, Dennis, Fla.	L	1	2	3.90	59	0	0	0	12	0	62.1	64	28	27	4	28	63	0	.267	NV
Crawford, Joe, NYN	L	4	3	3.30	19	2	0	0	9	0	46.1	36	18	17	7	13	25	0	.216	3
Crowell, James, Cin.	L	0	1	9.95	2	1	0	0	1	0	6.1	12	7	7	2	5	3	0	.414	NV
Cunnane, Will, S.D.	R	6	3	5.81	54	8	0	0	16	0	91.1	114	69	59	11	49	79	3	.305	NV
Daal, Omar, Mon.	L	1	2	9.79	33	0	0	0	6	1	30.1	48	35	33	4	15	16	1	.378	NV
DeHart, Rick, Mon.	L	2	1	5.52	23	0	0	0	7	0	29.1	33	21	18	7	14	29	2	.292	NV
DeJean, Mike, Col.	R	5	0	3.99	55	0	0	0	15	2	67.2	74	34	30	4	24	38	2	.280	NV
DeLucia, Rich, S.F.	R	0	0	10.80	3	0	0	0	0	0	1.2	6	3	2	0	0	2	1	.500	NV
Dessens, Elmer, Pit.	R	0	0	0.00	3	0	0	0	1	0	3.1	2	0	0	0	0	2	0	.167	NV
DiPoto, Jerry, Col.	R	5	3	4.70	74	0	0	0	33	16	95.2	108	56	50	6	33	74	4	.288	10
Dreifort, Darren, L.A.	R	5	2	2.86	48	0	0	0	16	4	63.0	45	21	20	3	34	63	3	.202	7
Eckersley, Dennis, St.L	R	1	5	3.91	57	0	0	0	47	36	53.0	49	24	23	9	8	45	2	.238	28
Eischen, Joey, Cin.	L	0	0	6.75	1	0	0	0	0	0	1.1	2	2	1	0	1	2	1	.333	NV
Embree, Alan, Atl.	L	3	1	2.54	66	0	0	0	15	0	46.0	36	13	13	1	20	45	3	.221	2
Erdos, Todd, S.D.	R	2	0	5.27	11	0	0	0	2	0	13.2	17	9	8	1	4	13	3	.293	NV
Ericks, John, Pit.	R	1	0	1.93	10	0	0	0	10	6	9.1	7	3	2	1	4	6	0	.200	3
Falteisek, Steve, Mon.	R	0	0	3.38	5	0	0	0	2	0	8.0	8	4	3	0	2	2	0	.286	NV
Fossas, Tony, St.L	L	2	7	3.83	71	0	0	0	14	0	51.2	62	32	22	7	26	41	0	.298	NV
Fox, Chad, Atl.	R	1	3	3.29	30	0	0	0	8	0	27.1	24	12	10	4	16	28	4	.231	NV
Franco, John, NYN	L	5	3	2.55	59	0	0	0	53	36	60.0	49	18	17	3	20	53	6	.226	32
Frascatore, John, St.L	R	5	2	2.48	59	0	0	0	17	0	80.0	74	25	22	5	33	58	4	.247	5
Gaetti, Gary, St.L	R	0	0	0.00	1	0	0	0	1	0	0.1	1	0	0	0	0	0	0	.500	
Garcia, Ramon, Hou.	R	9	8	3.69	42	20	1	1	5	1	158.2	155	71	65	20	52	120	3	.262	8
Gomes, Wayne, Phi.	R	5	1	5.27	37	0	0	0	13	0	42.2	45	26	25	4	24	24	2	.274	NV
Gorecki, Rick, L.A.	R	1	0	15.00	4	1	0	0	2	0	6.0	9	10	10	3	6	0	0	.346	NV
Granger, Jeff, Pit.	L	0	0	18.00	9	0	0	0	1	0	5.0	10	10	10	3	8	4	2	.417	NV
Graves, Danny, Cin.	R	0	0	6.14	10	0	0	0	1	0	14.2	26	14	10	0	11	7	1	.413	NV
Guthrie, Mark, L.A.	L	1	4	5.32	62	0	0	0	18	1	69.1	71	44	41	12	30	42	2	.272	NV
Hall, Darren, L.A.	R	3	2	2.30	63	0	0	0	20	2	54.2	58	15	14	3	26	39	0	.283	2
Harkey, Mike, L.A.	R	1	0	4.30	10	0	0	0	5	0	14.2	12	8	7	3	5	6	0	.211	NV
Harris, Reggie, Phi.	R	1	3	5.30	50	0	0	0	13	0	54.1	55	33	32	1	43	45	5	.263	NV
Helling, Rick, Fla.	R	2	6	4.38	31	8	0	0	8	0	76.0	61	38	37	12	48	53	0	.232	NV
Henriquez, Oscar, Hou.	R	0	1	4.50	4	0	0	0	1	0	4.0	2	2	2	0	3	3	0	.167	NV
Henry, Doug, S.F.	R	4	5	4.71	75	0	0	0	25	3	70.2	70	45	37	5	41	69	3	.261	NV
Heredia, Felix, Fla.	L	5	3	4.29	56	0	0	0	10	0	56.2	53	30	27	3	30	54	2	.243	NV
Hernandez, Roberto, S.F.	R	5	2	2.48	28	0	0	0	7	4	32.2	29	9	9	2	14	35	1	.238	5
Hoffman, Trevor, S.D.	R	6	4	2.66	70	0	0	0	59	37	81.1	59	25	24	9	24	111	7	.200	36
Holmes, Darren, Col.	R	9	2	5.34	42	6	0	0	10	3	89.1	113	58	53	12	36	70	4	.314	NV
Honeycutt, Rick, St.L	L	0	0	13.50	2	0	0	0	2	0	2.0	5	3	3	0	1	2	1	.500	NV
Hudek, John, Hou.	R	1	3	5.98	40	0	0	0	20	4	40.2	38	27	27	8	33	36	4	.252	NV
Hutton, Mark, Fla.-Col.	R	3	2	4.48	40	1	0	0	9	0	60.1	72	34	30	10	26	39	3	.314	NV
Jarvis, Kevin, Cin.	R	0	1	10.13	9	0	0	0	3	1	13.1	21	16	15	4	7	12	2	.344	NV
Johnson, Jason, Pit.	R	0	0	6.00	3	0	0	0	0	0	6.0	10	4	4	2	1	3	0	.400	NV
Johnstone, John, S.F.	R	0	0	3.38	13	0	0	0	2	0	18.2	15	7	7	1	7	15	0	.234	NV
Jordan, Ricardo, NYN	L	1	2	5.33	22	0	0	0	4	0	27.0	31	17	16	1	15	19	0	.304	NV
Judd, Michael, L.A.	R	0	0	0.00	1	0	0	0	0	0	2.2	4	0	0	0	0	4	0	.364	NV
Karp, Ryan, Phi.	L	1	1	5.40	15	1	0	0	1	0	15.0	12	12	9	2	9	18	1	.218	NV
Kashiwada, Takashi, NYN	L	3	1	4.31	35	0	0	0	11	0	31.1	35	15	15	4	18	19	4	.289	NV
King, Curtis, St.L	R	4	2	2.76	30	0	0	0	8	0	29.1	38	14	9	0	11	13	2	.325	NV
Kline, Steve, Mon.	L	1	3	6.15	26	0	0	0	7	0	26.1	31	18	18	4	10	20	1	.307	NV
Kroon, Marc, S.D.	R	0	1	6.35	12	0	0	0	2	0	11.1	14	9	8	2	5	12	1	.280	NV
Leroy, John, Atl.	R	1	0	0.00	1	0	0	0	0	0	2.0	1	0	0	0	3	3	0	.143	NV
Leskanic, Curtis, Col.	R	4	0	5.55	55	0	0	0	23	2	58.1	59	36	36	8	24	53	4	.271	NV
Lewis, Richie, Cin.	R	0	0	6.35	4	0	0	0	0	0	5.2	4	5	4	3	3	4	0	.200	NV
Lidle, Cory, NYN	R	7	2	3.53	54	2	0	0	20	2	81.2	86	38	32	7	20	54	2	.274	5
Ligtenberg, Kerry, Atl.	R	1	0	3.00	15	0	0	0	9	1	15.0	12	5	5	4	4	19	0	.211	NV

National League relief pitchers

Name/Team	T	W	L	ERA	G	GS	CG	SHO	GF	SV	IP	H	R	ER	HR	BB	SO	WP	BA	RV
Lima, Jose, Hou.	R	1	6	5.28	52	1	0	0	15	2	75.0	79	45	44	9	16	63	2	.271	NV
Loiselle, Rich, Pit.	R	1	5	3.10	72	0	0	0	58	29	72.2	76	29	25	7	24	66	4	.269	22
Long, Joey, S.D.	L	0	0	8.18	10	0	0	0	4	0	11.0	17	11	10	1	8	8	1	.340	NV
Ludwick, Eric, St.L	R	0	1	9.45	5	0	0	0	3	0	6.2	12	7	7	1	6	7	0	.400	NV
Magnante, Mike, Hou.	L	3	1	2.27	40	0	0	0	14	1	47.2	39	16	12	2	11	43	2	.223	5
Manuel, Barry, NYN	R	0	1	5.26	19	0	0	0	6	0	25.2	35	18	15	6	13	21	0	.324	NV
Martin, Tom, Hou.	L	5	3	2.09	55	0	0	0	18	2	56.0	52	13	13	2	23	36	3	.254	5
Martinez, Pedro A., Cin.	L	1	1	9.45	8	0	0	0	1	0	6.2	8	9	7	1	7	4	0	.286	NV
Mathews, T.J., St.L	R	4	4	2.15	40	0	0	0	12	0	46.0	41	14	11	4	18	46	1	.238	3
McCurry, Jeff, Col.	R	1	4	4.43	33	0	0	0	14	0	40.2	43	22	20	7	20	19	2	.277	NV
McGraw, Tom, St.L	L	0	0	0.00	2	0	0	0	2	0	1.2	2	0	0	0	1	0	0	.333	NV
McMichael, Greg, NYN	R	7	10	2.98	73	0	0	0	23	7	87.2	73	34	29	8	27	81	5	.233	13
Miller, Kurt, Fla.	R	0	1	9.82	7	0	0	0	1	0	7.1	12	8	8	2	7	7	0	.364	NV
Mimbs, Michael, Phi.	L	0	3	7.53	17	1	0	0	2	0	28.2	31	27	24	6	27	29	4	.272	NV
Minchey, Nate, Col.	R	0	0	13.50	2	0	0	0	0	0	2.0	5	3	3	0	1	1	0	.556	NV
Minor, Blas, Hou.	R	1	0	4.50	11	0	0	0	5	1	12.0	13	7	6	1	5	6	4	.277	NV
Morel, Ramon, Pit.-ChiN	R	0	0	4.76	8	0	0	0	5	0	11.1	14	6	6	3	7	7	0	.304	NV
Munoz, Mike, Col.	L	3	3	4.53	64	0	0	0	16	2	45.2	52	25	23	4	13	26	3	.294	NV
Murray, Heath, S.D.	L	1	2	6.75	17	3	0	0	1	0	33.1	50	25	25	3	21	16	1	.376	NV
Myers, Rodney, ChiN	R	0	0	6.00	5	1	0	0	2	0	9.0	12	6	6	1	7	6	0	.333	NV
Nen, Robb, Fla.	R	9	3	3.89	73	0	0	0	65	35	74.0	72	35	32	7	40	81	5	.250	28
Nye, Ryan, Phi.	R	0	2	8.25	4	2	0	0	1	0	12.0	20	11	11	2	9	7	0	.392	NV
Osuna, Antonio, L.A.	R	3	4	2.19	48	0	0	0	18	0	61.2	46	15	15	6	19	68	2	.209	6
Painter, Lance, St.L	L	1	1	4.76	14	0	0	0	4	0	17.0	13	9	9	1	8	11	0	.213	NV
Pall, Donn, Fla.	R	0	0	3.86	2	0	0	0	0	0	2.1	3	1	1	1	1	0	0	.300	NV
Paniagua, Jose, Mon.	R	1	2	12.00	9	3	0	0	0	0	18.0	29	24	24	2	16	8	1	.372	NV
Patterson, Bob, ChiN	L	1	6	3.34	76	0	0	0	12	0	59.1	47	23	22	9	10	58	1	.222	3
Perez, Yorkis, NYN	L	0	1	8.31	9	0	0	0	1	0	8.2	15	8	8	2	4	7	1	.375	NV
Peters, Chris, Pit.	L	2	2	4.58	31	1	0	0	5	0	37.1	38	23	19	6	21	17	4	.277	NV
Petkovsek, Mark, St.L	R	4	7	5.06	55	2	0	0	19	2	96.0	109	61	54	14	31	51	2	.292	NV
Pisciotta, Marc, ChiN	R	3	1	3.18	24	0	0	0	7	0	28.1	20	10	10	1	16	21	2	.200	1
Plantenberg, Erik, Phi.	L	0	0	4.91	35	0	0	0	9	0	25.2	25	14	14	1	12	12	2	.255	NV
Poole, Jim Ri., S.F.	L	3	1	7.11	63	0	0	0	11	0	49.1	73	44	39	6	25	26	5	.353	NV
Powell, Jay, Fla.	R	7	2	3.28	74	0	0	0	23	2	79.2	71	35	29	3	30	65	3	.242	6
Radinsky, Scott, L.A.	L	5	1	2.89	75	0	0	0	14	3	62.1	54	22	20	4	21	44	0	.236	6
Raggio, Brady, St.L	R	1	2	6.89	15	4	0	0	5	0	31.1	44	24	24	1	16	21	3	.336	NV
Ramos, Edgar, Phi.	R	0	2	5.14	4	2	0	0	0	0	14.0	15	9	8	3	6	4	1	.288	NV
Reed, Steve, Col.	R	4	6	4.04	63	0	0	0	23	6	62.1	49	28	28	10	27	43	0	.219	6
Remlinger, Mike, Cin.	L	8	8	4.14	69	12	2	0	10	2	124.0	100	61	57	11	60	145	12	.223	5
Reyes, Dennis, L.A.	L	2	3	3.83	14	5	0	0	0	0	47.0	51	21	20	4	18	36	2	.280	NV
Rincon, Ricardo, Pit.	L	4	8	3.45	62	0	0	0	23	4	60.0	51	26	23	5	24	71	2	.230	5
Roa, Joe, S.F.	R	2	5	5.21	28	3	0	0	4	0	65.2	86	40	38	8	20	34	0	.333	NV
Rodriguez, Felix, Cin.	R	0	0	4.30	26	1	0	0	13	0	46.0	48	23	22	2	28	34	4	.271	NV
Rodriguez, Rich, S.F.	L	4	3	3.17	71	0	0	0	15	1	65.1	65	24	23	7	21	32	0	.264	3
Rojas, Mel, ChiN-NYN	R	6	4	4.64	77	0	0	0	50	15	85.1	78	47	44	15	36	93	3	.241	8
Ruebel, Matt, Pit.	L	3	2	6.32	44	0	0	0	9	0	62.2	77	50	44	8	27	50	4	.302	NV
Ruffcorn, Scott, Phi.	R	0	3	7.71	18	4	0	0	3	0	39.2	42	40	34	4	36	33	6	.275	NV
Ruffin, Bruce, Col.	L	0	2	5.32	23	0	0	0	15	7	22.0	18	15	13	3	18	31	2	.220	1
Ryan, Ken, Phi.	R	1	0	9.58	22	0	0	0	10	0	20.2	31	23	22	5	13	10	0	.344	NV
Scott, Tim, S.D.-Col.	R	1	1	8.14	17	0	0	0	2	0	21.0	30	20	19	2	7	16	0	.337	NV
Service, Scott, Cin.	R	0	0	11.81	4	0	0	0	2	0	5.1	11	7	7	1	1	3	2	.458	NV
Shaw, Jeff, Cin.	R	4	2	2.38	78	0	0	0	62	42	94.2	79	26	25	7	12	74	1	.227	42
Silva, Jose, Pit.	R	2	1	5.94	11	4	0	0	0	0	36.1	52	26	24	4	16	30	0	.347	NV
Smith, Lee, Mon.	R	0	1	5.82	25	0	0	0	14	5	21.2	28	16	14	2	8	15	0	.308	NV
Smith, Pete J., S.D.	R	7	6	4.81	37	15	0	0	7	1	118.0	120	66	63	16	52	68	0	.267	NV
Sodowsky, Clint, Pit.	R	2	2	3.63	45	0	0	0	8	0	52.0	49	22	21	6	34	51	6	.249	NV
Spradlin, Jerry, Phi.	R	4	8	4.74	76	0	0	0	23	1	81.2	86	45	43	9	27	67	5	.274	NV
Springer, Russ, Hou.	R	3	3	4.23	54	0	0	0	13	3	55.1	48	28	26	4	27	74	4	.232	1
Stanifer, Rob, Fla.	R	1	2	4.60	36	0	0	0	10	1	45.0	43	23	23	9	16	28	1	.261	NV
Stevens, Dave, ChiN	R	0	2	9.64	10	0	0	0	0	0	9.1	13	11	10	0	9	13	0	.333	NV
Stull, Everett, Mon.	R	0	1	16.20	3	0	0	0	1	0	3.1	7	7	6	1	4	2	0	.438	NV
Sullivan, Scott, Cin.	R	5	3	3.24	59	0	0	0	15	1	97.1	79	36	35	12	30	96	7	.220	7
Tabaka, Jeff, Cin.	L	0	0	4.50	3	0	0	0	1	0	2.0	1	1	1	1	1	1	0	.143	NV
Tatis, Ramon, ChiN	L	1	1	5.34	56	0	0	0	12	0	55.2	66	36	33	13	29	33	4	.308	NV
Tavarez, Julian, S.F.	R	6	4	3.87	89	0	0	0	13	0	88.1	91	43	38	6	34	38	4	.277	1
Telemaco, Amaury, ChiN	R	0	3	6.16	10	5	0	0	2	0	38.0	47	26	26	4	11	29	1	.303	NV
Telford, Anthony, Mon.	R	4	6	3.24	65	0	0	0	17	1	89.0	77	34	32	11	33	61	6	.236	5
Thurman, Mike, Mon.	R	1	0	5.40	5	2	0	0	1	0	11.2	8	9	7	3	4	8	0	.186	NV
Torres, Salomon, Mon.	R	0	0	7.25	12	0	0	0	3	0	22.1	25	19	18	2	12	11	3	.284	NV
Trlicek, Rick, NYN	R	0	0	8.00	9	0	0	0	4	0	9.0	10	9	8	2	5	4	2	.303	NV

340

National League relief pitchers

Name/Team	T	W	L	ERA	G	GS	CG	SHO	GF	SV	IP	H	R	ER	HR	BB	SO	WP	BA	RV
Urbina, Ugueth, Mon.	R	5	8	3.78	63	0	0	0	50	27	64.1	52	29	27	9	29	84	2	.215	23
Valdes, Marc, Mon.	R	4	4	3.13	48	7	0	0	9	2	95.0	84	36	33	2	39	54	2	.240	5
Veras, Dario, S.D.	R	2	1	5.11	23	0	0	0	7	0	24.2	28	18	14	5	12	21	0	.280	NV
Veres, Dave, Mon.	R	2	3	3.48	53	0	0	0	11	1	62.0	68	28	24	5	27	47	7	.278	NV
Vosberg, Ed, Fla.	L	1	1	3.75	17	0	0	0	6	1	12.0	15	7	5	0	6	8	1	.313	NV
Wagner, Paul, Pit.	R	0	0	3.94	14	0	0	0	2	0	16.0	17	7	7	3	13	9	3	.279	NV
Wagner, Billy, Hou.	L	7	8	2.85	62	0	0	0	49	23	66.1	49	23	21	5	30	106	3	.204	23
Wainhouse, Dave, Pit.	R	0	1	8.04	25	0	0	0	6	0	28.0	34	28	25	2	17	21	1	.301	NV
Wallace, Jeff, Pit.	L	0	0	0.75	11	0	0	0	1	0	12.0	8	2	1	0	8	14	1	.200	NV
Wendell, Turk, ChiN-NYN	R	3	5	4.36	65	0	0	0	21	5	76.1	68	42	37	7	53	64	4	.240	NV
Whisenant, Matt, Fla.	L	0	0	16.88	4	0	0	0	2	0	2.2	4	6	5	0	6	4	0	.333	NV
White, Gabe, Cin.	L	2	2	4.39	12	6	0	0	2	1	41.0	39	20	20	6	8	25	0	.253	1
Wilkins, Marc, Pit.	R	9	5	3.69	70	0	0	0	21	2	75.2	65	33	31	7	33	47	5	.242	6
Winchester, Scott, Cin.	R	0	0	6.00	5	0	0	0	4	0	6.0	9	5	4	1	2	3	0	.360	NV
Winston, Darrin, Phi.	L	2	0	5.25	7	1	0	0	1	0	12.0	8	8	7	4	3	8	0	.178	NV
Wohlers, Mark, Atl.	R	5	7	3.50	71	0	0	0	55	33	69.1	57	29	27	4	38	92	4	.224	27
Worrell, Tim, S.D.	R	4	8	5.16	60	10	0	0	14	3	106.1	116	67	61	14	50	81	2	.280	NV
Worrell, Todd, L.A.	R	2	6	5.28	65	0	0	0	55	35	59.2	60	38	35	12	23	61	1	.250	23

National League starting pitchers

Name/Team	T	W	L	ERA	G	GS	CG	SHO	GF	SV	IP	H	R	ER	HR	BB	SO	WP	BA	RV
Alvarez, Wilson, S.F.	L	4	3	4.48	11	11	0	0	0	0	66.1	54	36	33	9	36	69	1	.224	NV
Ashby, Andy, S.D.	R	9	11	4.13	30	30	2	0	0	0	200.2	207	108	92	17	49	144	3	.266	6
Astacio, Pedro, L.A.-Col.	R	12	10	4.14	33	31	2	1	2	0	202.1	200	98	93	24	61	166	6	.258	8
Aybar, Manny, St.L	R	2	4	4.24	12	12	0	0	0	0	68.0	66	33	32	8	29	41	1	.263	NV
Bailey, Roger, Col.	R	9	10	4.29	29	29	5	2	0	0	191.0	210	103	91	27	70	84	4	.283	1
Batista, Miguel, ChiN	R	0	5	5.70	11	6	0	0	2	0	36.1	36	24	23	4	24	27	2	.267	NV
Beech, Matt, Phi.	L	4	9	5.07	24	24	0	0	0	0	136.2	147	81	77	25	57	120	6	.279	NV
Benes, Alan, St.L	R	9	9	2.89	23	23	2	0	0	0	161.2	128	60	52	13	68	160	9	.219	13
Benes, Andy, St.L	R	10	7	3.10	26	26	0	0	0	0	177.0	149	64	61	9	61	175	7	.230	14
Bohanon, Brian, NYN	L	6	4	3.82	19	14	0	0	0	0	94.1	95	49	40	9	34	66	3	.258	2
Brock, Chris, Atl.	R	0	0	5.58	7	6	0	0	1	0	30.2	34	23	19	2	19	16	2	.288	NV
Brown, Kevin, Fla.	R	16	8	2.69	33	33	6	2	0	0	237.1	214	77	71	10	66	205	7	.240	25
Bullinger, Jim, Mon.	R	7	12	5.56	36	25	2	2	4	0	155.1	165	106	96	17	74	87	7	.276	NV
Burba, Dave, Cin.	R	11	10	4.73	30	27	2	0	1	0	160.0	157	88	84	22	73	131	6	.255	1
Burke, John, Col.	R	2	5	6.56	17	9	0	0	1	0	59.0	83	46	43	13	26	39	4	.329	NV
Busby, Mike, St.L	R	0	2	8.79	3	3	0	0	0	0	14.1	24	14	14	2	4	6	0	.393	NV
Carrara, Giovanni, Cin.	R	0	1	7.84	2	2	0	0	0	0	10.1	14	9	9	4	6	5	0	.333	NV
Castillo, Frank, ChiN-Col.	R	12	12	5.42	34	33	0	0	0	0	184.1	220	121	111	25	69	126	3	.300	NV
Clark, Mark, NYN-ChiN	R	14	8	3.82	32	31	3	0	0	0	205.0	213	96	87	24	59	123	4	.270	10
Cooke, Steve, Pit.	L	9	15	4.30	32	32	0	0	0	0	167.1	184	95	80	15	77	109	8	.285	NV
Cordova, Francisco, Pit.	R	11	8	3.63	29	29	2	2	0	0	178.2	175	80	72	14	49	121	4	.259	10
Cormier, Rheal, Mon.	L	0	1	33.75	1	1	0	0	0	0	1.1	4	5	5	1	1	0	0	.500	NV
Creek, Doug, S.F.	L	1	2	6.75	3	3	0	0	0	0	13.1	12	12	10	1	14	14	0	.240	NV
Darwin, Danny, S.F.	R	1	3	4.91	10	7	0	0	0	0	44.0	51	26	24	5	14	30	0	.288	NV
Estes, Shawn, S.F.	L	19	5	3.18	32	32	3	2	0	0	201.0	162	80	71	12	100	181	10	.223	18
Fernandez, Alex, Fla.	R	17	12	3.59	32	32	5	1	0	0	220.2	193	93	88	25	69	183	9	.238	18
Fernandez, Sid, Hou.	L	1	0	3.60	1	1	0	0	0	0	5.0	4	2	2	1	2	3	0	.211	NV
Fernandez, Osvaldo, S.F.	R	3	4	4.95	11	11	0	0	0	0	56.1	74	39	31	9	15	31	2	.314	NV
Foster, Kevin, ChiN	R	10	7	4.61	26	25	1	0	0	0	146.1	141	79	75	27	66	118	3	.255	1
Foulke, Keith, S.F.	R	1	5	8.26	11	8	0	0	0	0	44.2	60	41	41	9	18	33	1	.324	NV
Gardner, Mark, S.F.	R	12	9	4.29	30	30	2	1	0	0	180.1	188	92	86	28	57	136	3	.272	4
Glavine, Tom, Atl.	L	14	7	2.96	33	33	5	2	0	0	240.0	197	86	79	20	79	152	3	.226	23
Gonzalez, Jeremi, ChiN	R	11	9	4.25	23	23	1	1	0	0	144.0	126	73	68	16	69	93	1	.236	4
Grace, Mike, Phi.	R	3	2	3.46	6	6	1	1	0	0	39.0	32	16	15	3	10	26	2	.230	1
Green, Tyler, Phi.	R	4	4	4.93	14	14	0	0	0	0	76.2	72	50	42	8	45	58	7	.247	NV
Greene, Tommy, Hou.	R	0	1	7.00	2	2	0	0	0	0	9.0	10	7	7	2	5	11	0	.286	NV
Hamilton, Joey, S.D.	R	12	7	4.25	31	29	1	0	1	0	192.2	199	100	91	22	69	124	7	.271	4
Hampton, Mike, Hou.	L	15	10	3.83	34	34	7	2	0	0	223.0	217	105	95	16	77	139	6	.257	11
Harnisch, Pete, NYN	R	0	1	8.06	6	5	0	0	0	0	25.2	35	24	23	5	11	12	1	.327	NV
Hermanson, Dustin, Mon.	R	8	8	3.69	32	28	1	1	0	0	158.1	134	68	65	15	66	136	4	.234	7
Hernandez, Livan, Fla.	R	9	3	3.18	17	17	0	0	0	0	96.1	81	39	34	6	38	72	0	.229	7
Hitchcock, Sterling, S.D.	L	10	11	5.20	32	28	1	0	1	0	161.0	172	102	93	24	55	106	6	.276	NV
Holt, Chris, Hou.	R	8	12	3.52	33	32	0	0	0	0	209.2	211	98	82	17	61	95	1	.263	9
Isringhausen, Jason, NYN	R	2	2	7.58	6	6	0	0	0	0	29.2	40	27	25	3	22	25	3	.336	NV
Jackson, Danny, St.L-S.D.	L	2	2	7.58	17	13	0	0	0	0	67.2	98	64	57	11	28	32	2	.351	NV
Johnson, Mike, Mon.	R	2	5	5.94	11	11	0	0	0	0	50.0	54	34	33	8	21	28	4	.277	NV
Jones, Bobby, NYN	R	15	9	3.63	30	30	2	1	0	0	193.1	177	88	78	24	63	125	3	.242	14

National League starting pitchers

Name/Team	T	W	L	ERA	G	GS	CG	SHO	GF	SV	IP	H	R	ER	HR	BB	SO	WP	BA	RV
Jones, Bobby M., Col.	L	1	1	8.38	4	4	0	0	0	0	19.1	30	18	18	2	12	5	0	.380	NV
Juden, Jeff, Mon.	R	11	5	4.22	22	22	3	0	0	0	130.0	125	64	61	17	57	107	7	.255	3
Kile, Darryl, Hou.	R	19	7	2.57	34	34	6	4	0	0	255.2	208	87	73	19	94	205	7	.225	28
Leiter, Al, Fla.	L	11	9	4.34	27	27	0	0	0	0	151.1	133	78	73	13	91	132	2	.241	1
Leiter, Mark, Phi.	R	10	17	5.67	31	31	3	0	0	0	182.2	216	132	115	25	64	148	11	.292	NV
Lieber, Jon, Pit.	R	11	14	4.49	33	32	1	0	0	0	188.1	193	102	94	23	51	160	3	.263	4
Loaiza, Esteban, Pit.	R	11	11	4.13	33	32	1	0	0	0	196.1	214	99	90	17	56	122	2	.279	4
Lowe, Sean, St.L	R	0	2	9.35	6	4	0	0	1	0	17.1	27	21	18	2	10	8	0	.365	NV
Maddux, Greg, Atl.	R	19	4	2.20	33	33	5	2	0	0	232.2	200	58	57	9	20	177	0	.236	37
Maduro, Calvin, Phi.	R	3	7	7.23	15	13	0	0	0	0	71.0	83	59	57	12	41	31	6	.294	NV
Martinez, Pedro J., Mon.	R	17	8	1.90	31	31	13	4	0	0	241.1	158	65	51	16	67	305	3	.184	40
Martinez, Ramon, L.A.	R	10	5	3.64	22	22	1	0	0	0	133.2	123	64	54	14	68	120	1	.243	5
Menhart, Paul, S.D.	R	2	3	4.70	9	8	0	0	0	0	44.0	42	23	23	6	13	22	4	.256	NV
Mercker, Kent, Cin.	L	8	11	3.92	28	25	0	0	0	0	144.2	135	65	63	16	62	75	2	.250	4
Millwood, Kevin, Atl.	R	5	3	4.03	12	8	0	0	2	0	51.1	55	26	23	1	21	42	1	.282	NV
Mlicki, Dave, NYN	R	8	12	4.00	32	32	1	1	0	0	193.2	194	89	86	21	76	157	5	.259	3
Morgan, Mike, Cin.	R	9	12	4.78	31	30	1	0	0	0	162.0	165	91	86	13	49	103	7	.266	1
Morris, Matt, St.L	R	12	9	3.19	33	33	3	0	0	0	217.0	208	88	77	12	69	149	5	.258	15
Mulholland, T., ChiN-S.F.	L	6	13	4.24	40	27	1	0	5	0	186.2	190	100	88	24	51	99	3	.267	3
Munoz, Bobby, Phi.	R	1	5	8.91	8	7	0	0	1	0	33.1	47	35	33	4	15	20	3	.338	NV
Neagle, Denny, Atl.	L	20	5	2.97	34	34	4	4	0	0	233.1	204	87	77	18	49	172	3	.233	28
Nomo, Hideo, L.A.	R	14	12	4.25	33	33	1	0	0	0	207.1	193	104	98	23	92	233	10	.243	6
Ojala, Kirt, Fla.	L	1	2	3.14	7	5	0	0	1	0	28.2	28	10	10	4	18	19	0	.252	NV
Osborne, Donovan, St.L	L	3	7	4.93	14	14	0	0	0	0	80.1	84	46	44	10	23	51	1	.274	NV
Park, Chan Ho, L.A.	R	14	8	3.38	32	29	2	0	1	0	192.0	149	80	72	24	70	166	4	.213	17
Perez, Carlos, Mon.	L	12	13	3.88	33	32	8	5	0	0	206.2	206	109	89	21	48	110	2	.260	11
Portugal, Mark, Phi.	R	0	2	4.61	3	3	0	0	0	0	13.2	17	8	7	0	5	2	0	.321	NV
Rapp, Pat, Fla.-S.F.	R	5	8	4.83	27	25	1	1	0	0	141.2	158	83	76	16	72	92	8	.288	NV
Reed, Rick, NYN	R	13	9	2.89	33	31	2	0	0	0	208.1	186	76	67	19	31	113	0	.239	24
Rekar, Bryan, Col.	R	1	0	5.79	2	2	0	0	0	0	9.1	11	7	6	3	6	4	0	.282	NV
Reynolds, Shane, Hou.	R	9	10	4.23	30	30	2	0	0	0	181.0	189	92	85	19	47	152	5	.267	5
Reynoso, Armando, NYN	R	6	3	4.53	16	16	1	1	0	0	91.1	95	47	46	7	29	47	4	.275	1
Ritz, Kevin, Col.	R	6	8	5.87	18	18	1	0	0	0	107.1	142	72	70	16	46	56	7	.330	NV
Rueter, Kirk, S.F.	L	13	6	3.45	32	32	0	0	0	0	190.2	194	83	73	17	51	115	3	.264	12
Saunders, Tony, Fla.	L	4	6	4.61	22	21	0	0	0	0	111.1	99	62	57	12	64	102	2	.244	NV
Schilling, Curt, Phi.	R	17	11	2.97	35	35	7	2	0	0	254.1	208	96	84	25	58	319	5	.224	29
Schmidt, Jason, Pit.	R	10	9	4.60	32	32	2	0	0	0	187.2	193	106	96	16	76	136	8	.265	1
Schourek, Pete, Cin.	L	5	8	5.42	18	17	0	0	0	0	84.2	78	59	51	18	38	59	2	.241	NV
Smiley, John, Cin.	L	9	10	5.23	20	20	0	0	0	0	117.0	139	76	68	17	31	94	2	.296	NV
Smoltz, John, Atl.	R	15	12	3.02	35	35	7	2	0	0	256.0	234	97	86	21	63	241	10	.242	24
Stephenson, Garrett, Phi.	R	8	6	3.15	20	18	2	0	0	0	117.0	104	45	41	11	38	81	1	.244	9
Stottlemyre, Todd, St.L	R	12	9	3.88	28	28	0	0	0	0	181.0	155	86	78	16	65	160	6	.231	11
Swartzbaugh, Dave, ChiN	R	0	1	9.00	2	2	0	0	0	0	8.0	12	8	8	1	7	4	0	.364	NV
Swift, Bill, Col.	R	4	6	6.34	14	13	0	0	1	0	65.1	85	57	46	11	26	29	2	.318	NV
Tapani, Kevin, ChiN	R	9	3	3.39	13	13	1	1	0	0	85.0	77	33	32	7	23	55	0	.242	7
Thompson, Mark, Col.	R	3	3	7.89	6	6	0	0	0	0	29.2	40	27	26	8	13	9	0	.323	NV
Thomson, John, Col.	R	7	9	4.71	27	27	2	1	0	0	166.1	193	94	87	15	51	106	2	.296	NV
Tomko, Brett, Cin.	R	11	7	3.43	22	19	0	0	1	0	126.0	106	50	48	14	47	95	5	.234	10
Trachsel, Steve, ChiN	R	8	12	4.51	34	34	0	0	0	0	201.1	225	110	101	32	69	160	4	.287	NV
Valdes, Ismael, L.A.	R	10	11	2.65	30	30	0	0	0	0	196.2	171	68	58	16	47	140	3	.234	21
Valenzuela, F., S.D.-St.L	L	2	12	4.96	18	18	1	0	0	0	89.0	106	61	49	12	46	61	4	.295	NV
VanLandingham, Wm., S.F.R	R	4	7	4.96	18	17	0	0	1	0	89.0	80	56	49	11	59	52	9	.237	NV
Wade, Terrell, Atl.	L	2	3	5.36	12	9	0	0	1	0	42.0	60	31	25	6	16	35	1	.349	NV
Wall, Donne, Hou.	R	2	5	6.26	8	8	0	0	0	0	41.2	53	31	29	8	16	25	2	.317	NV
Wright, Jamey, Col.	R	8	12	6.25	26	26	1	0	0	0	149.2	198	113	104	19	71	59	6	.327	NV

Minor league report

▶Player of the Year
▶All-Star Team
▶Overall leaders and
 season highlights

▶1997 league
 wrap-ups
▶Final AAA and AA
 player stats

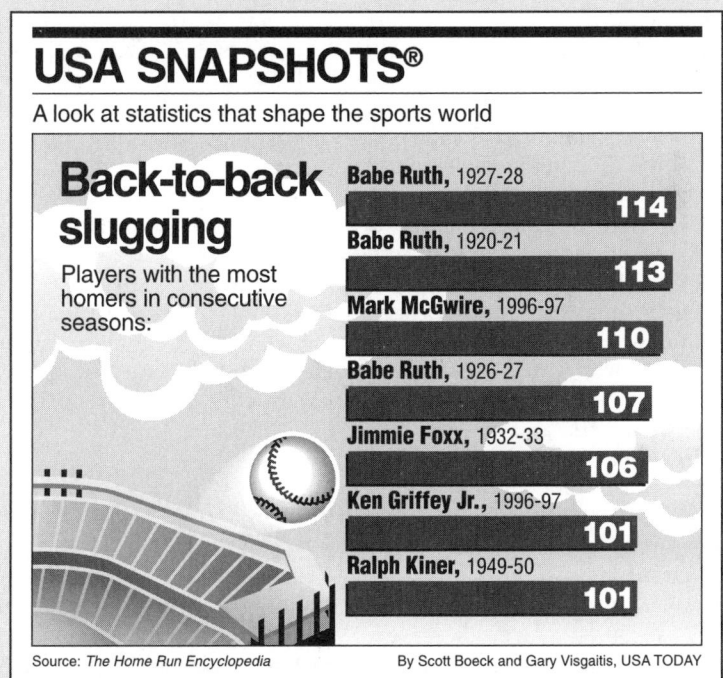

USA SNAPSHOTS®

A look at statistics that shape the sports world

Back-to-back slugging

Players with the most homers in consecutive seasons:

Babe Ruth, 1927-28 — **114**
Babe Ruth, 1920-21 — **113**
Mark McGwire, 1996-97 — **110**
Babe Ruth, 1926-27 — **107**
Jimmie Foxx, 1932-33 — **106**
Ken Griffey Jr., 1996-97 — **101**
Ralph Kiner, 1949-50 — **101**

Source: *The Home Run Encyclopedia*   By Scott Boeck and Gary Visgaitis, USA TODAY

1997 wrap-up: A major shake-up for AAA

In the world of minor league baseball, in which secrets are as hard to keep intact as 40-game hitting streaks and rumors are as frequent as Thirsty Thursday promotions, the July 9 announcement that AAA would undergo a massive realignment for the 1998 season was a true bombshell. The decision to go from three leagues to two was made public just a few minutes before the first pitch of the AAA All-Star Game in Des Moines. The eight-team American Association, which had been operating with few interruptions since 1902, was dissolved, with its clubs dispersed into the International and Pacific Coast leagues.

The newly reformed International League will consist of 14 teams: the incumbent 10 (Charlotte, Columbus, Norfolk, Ottawa, Pawtucket, Richmond, Rochester, Scranton/Wilkes-Barre, Syracuse and Toledo), expansion Durham and the American Association's Buffalo, Indianapolis and Louisville.

The Pacific Coast League will add six teams, to make a 16-team circuit: the incumbents (Albuquerque, Calgary, Colorado Springs, Edmonton, Las Vegas, Salt Lake City, Tacoma, Tucson and Vancouver); Fresno, the new home for incumbent Phoenix (displaced due to the arrival of the Diamondbacks); expansion Memphis; and Iowa, Nashville, New Orleans, Oklahoma City and Omaha from the American Association. The PCL also inherits from the American Association its well-respected president, W. Branch Rickey III, as longtime PCL president Bill Cutler retired after more than 50 years in pro baseball.

While it's not on the schedule for 1998, hopes are high that the champions of the two AAA leagues will soon meet in the postseason in a Little World Series. In the American Association's farewell season, the Buffalo Bisons, the Cleveland Indians' top farm team, swept the Iowa Cubs in three games to win the league's final championship.

Player of the Year

Playing his third position in four pro seasons, Los Angeles Dodgers third base prospect Paul Konerko was named *Baseball Weekly*'s 1997 Minor League Player of the Year. Konerko hit .323 with 37 homers, second best in the minors, and 127 RBI for the AAA Albuquerque Dukes while making rapid progress in his first season at the hot corner.

Konerko, just 21, was the Dodgers' first-round draft pick in 1994 out of high school in Paradise Valley, Ariz., where he was selected as a promising catcher. After leading the short-season Northwest League that summer with 58 RBI in 67 games, he moved to first base the next summer at Class A San Bernardino. Hitting .277 with 19 homers and 77 RBI, he helped lead that club to the California League title. In 1996, Konerko moved up to AA San Antonio, where, as the youngest player in the minors at that level, he hit .300 with 29 homers.

"He's a very special young hitter, and you don't see them come along like that too often," said Glenn Hoffman, Konerko's manager with the Dukes. "His makeup is so superior to anybody else's, and to me that's why he's going to be not just a good major league player but a great one."

Konerko made his major league debut with the Dodgers in September after earning PCL Most Valuable Player honors. He got one hit in seven at-bats with the parent club, playing a game each at first and third.

Baseball Weekly Minor League All-Star Team

Joining Konerko on the debut *Baseball Weekly* team are the following players:
▶**Travis Lee**, High Desert (A)/Tucson (AAA), 1B: In his debut season as a pro, the future star of the Arizona Diamondbacks hit a combined .333 with 32 homers and 109 RBI.

▶**Warren Morris**, Charlotte (A), 2B: Nicknamed "ESPY" when he won that award for his bottom-of-the-ninth heroics, which won the College World Series in 1996 for LSU, this Olympian hit .302 with 12 homers, 76 RBI and 16 steals in his first full season for the Texas Rangers farm team.

▶**Brent Butler**, Peoria (Ill., A), SS: The 19-year-old Cardinals prospect, in his first full season after winning Appalachian League MVP honors in '96, had a .309 average for the Chiefs, with 15 homers and 71 RBI.

▶**Jim Foster**, Frederick (A)/Bowie (AA), C: The Baltimore system's up-and-comer achieved the rare feat for a catcher of hitting for the cycle; overall he combined to bat .315 with 23 homers and 106 RBI.

▶**Brian Raabe**, Tacoma (AAA), UT: The popular veteran played 1997 with the Mariners' PCL team after spending most of his career in the Twins system, hitting .352 with 14 homers and 80 RBI prior to a late-season trade to the Colorado Rockies.

▶**Mike Stoner**, High Desert (A), OF: Stoner had the single best season statistically of any minor leaguer. The Diamondbacks farmhand became the first minor leaguer this decade to collect at least 200 hits (203) as well as the first in the '90s to drive in more than 140 runs (142). He tied for the California League lead with 33 homers but fell three points shy of the batting title, at .358.

▶**Jacob Cruz**, Phoenix (AAA), OF: The former second-round pick by the Giants out of ASU lit it up close to home, hitting .361 with 12 homers, 93 RBI and 18 steals in the Firebirds' final season.

▶**Ben Grieve**, Huntsville (AA)/Edmonton (AAA), OF: The son of former Texas GM Tom Grieve showed why the A's made him the second selection in the nation in 1994, as he achieved career highs in nearly every category, hitting .350 with 31 homers and 136 RBI at his two stops.

▶**Kevin Millar**, Portland (Maine, AA), DH: The non-drafted free agent from Lamar University, signed out of an independent league, continued to torture opposing pitching as he has since the

Marlins brought him into the fold in 1994. He cruised to Eastern League MVP honors, hitting .342 with 32 homers and 131 RBI.

▶**Clayton Bruner**, West Michigan (A), SP: The Tigers farmhand led the top starting staff in the minors with a 15-3 record and a 2.38 ERA.

▶**Matt Clement**, Rancho Cucamonga (A)/Mobile (AA), SP: A third-round pick by San Diego in 1993, Clement was among the tops in the minors in ERA and strikeouts, combining to go 12-8 with a 2.05 ERA and 201 strikeouts in 189 innings.

▶**Courtney Duncan**, Daytona (A)/Orlando (AA), SP: After finishing 1996 by winning 11 in a row for short-season Williamsport, the Cubs' 20th-round draftee out of Grambling picked up where he'd left off and combined to go 10-6 with a 2.11 ERA in his first full campaign.

▶**Cliff Politte**, Prince William (A)/Arkansas (AA), SP: Selected in the 54th round of the 1995 draft, the Cardinals farmhand, himself the son of a former Cardinals minor leaguer, was 15-2 with a 2.22 ERA in two stops last season.

▶**Brian Rose**, Pawtucket (AAA), SP: The poised Red Sox prospect became the first hurler to win International League pitcher of the week honors three times in one season and, not surprisingly, was the league's Pitcher of the Year.

▶**Francisco Cordero**, West Michigan (A), Closer: Cordero, who didn't turn 20 until the end of the season, set a franchise record with 35 saves, and he limited opposing hitters to an average under .200 while posting an 0.99 ERA.

▶**Marv Foley**, Rochester (AAA), Manager of the Year: When his Red Wings, the top Orioles farm team, won the International League title, the 44-year-old Foley became the first manager to win championships in all three AAA leagues—he'd already won with Vancouver of the PCL in 1989 and Iowa of the American Association in '93. With the demise of the American Association, the former catcher (.224 average in five AL seasons) will probably remain the only one, too.

Overall leaders

Perhaps the single most impressive full-season campaign in 1997 was the one posted by High Desert outfielder **Mike Stoner**, a converted first baseman who wasn't even drafted after his junior year at the University of North Carolina. As a fifth-year senior, however, he was eligible to sign prior to the 1996 draft, and the Arizona Diamondbacks had done their homework. They inked the Atlantic Coast Conference all-star to a pro contract, and he repaid them a year later by leading the minor leagues in RBI (142) and hits (203). The California League MVP just missed winning the triple crown, as his 33 homers tied for tops in the league but his .358 average was edged out by the Visalia catcher **Ramon Hernandez's** .361.

Leading the minors in homers was Cleveland third base prospect **Russell Branyan**, who went yard 39 times for Class A Kinston and AA Akron. Branyan hit 40 homers for Class A Columbus in 1996, becoming just the fourth minor leaguer in the past 10 years to hit that plateau.

Milwaukee's AA El Paso club boasted the top two batters in the minors in third baseman **Mike Kinkade**, who hit .385, and outfielder **Scott Krause**, who batted .361 to barely edge AAA Phoenix outfielder **Jacob Cruz** and Hernandez, who each also hit .361.

Charleston (S.C.) RiverDogs outfielder **Alex Sanchez**, just a few years removed from escaping Cuba on a raft, became the first minor leaguer this decade to top the 90-steal mark, with 92.

A trio of minor leaguers hit 50 doubles apiece, all from Class A—Winston-Salem third baseman **Carlos Lee**, West Michigan first baseman **Robert Fick** and Charleston (W.Va.) catcher **Jason LaRue**—while 29-year-old outfielder **Jovino Carvajal** of AAA Vancouver led the minors in triples with 20.

Oakland's top outfield prospect, Ben Grieve, led the minors in both on-base average (.461) and slugging average (.640), spending most of his summer at AA Huntsville prior to a late-season promotion to AAA Edmonton.

Among pitchers, three minor league starters had ERAs below 2.00. Montreal farmhand **Javier Vazquez**, who posted a 1.86 between Class A West Palm Beach and AA Harrisburg, and the Detroit organization's pair of **Craig Quintal** of Class A West Michigan (1.96) and **David Darwin**, who split his season between West Michigan and Class A Lakeland (1.98).

Boston prospect **Brian Rose** and Florida farmhand **Reid Cornelius** each notched 17 wins, with all of Rose's coming for AAA Pawtucket and Cornelius sharing the wealth between AA Portland (Maine) and AAA Charlotte.

Armando Almanza of Class A Prince William edged out **Francisco Cordero** of West Michigan by one in the save category with 36, as both young relievers set franchise records.

Three minor league hurlers topped the 200-strikeout mark this season, led by Anaheim prospect **Ramon Ortiz**, who fanned 225 at Class A Cedar Rapids, the most by a minor leaguer since Steve Gasser in 1986 (225 for Kenosha of the Midwest League). Colorado prospect **Steve Shoemaker** struck out 214 in three stops, while Padres farmhand **Matt Clement** fanned 201 between Class A Rancho Cucamonga and AA Mobile.

Great performances

It wasn't just the major leagues that saw balls flying out of the ballparks. Two minor leaguers posted four-homer games in 1997. Veteran first baseman **J.R. Phillips** of AAA New Orleans did it in a seven-inning game on May 21 against the Omaha Royals, while AAA Toledo outfielder **Bubba Trammell** needed 13 innings to hit four out on Aug. 9 against the Richmond Braves. Tulsa outfielder **Dan Collier**, meanwhile, set a Texas League record by homering in seven consecutive games from June 12 to 19. That broke a record of six games in a row that had just been tied two months earlier by first baseman **Daryle Ward** of Jackson (Miss.).

While just three players had six-hit games in 1996 (and Colorado Springs shortstop Neifi Perez had a rare seven-hit game), 11 collected six hits in a game in 1997. On Aug. 11, Athletics second base prospect **Monty Davis** may have had the best single game of any minor leaguer, when he not only became the only player to score six runs in a game this year, but also added nine RBI, which tied Lake Elsinore's **Chris Norton** for best of the year. Eleven players had eight-RBI games, and **Brad Tyler** of Richmond had a six-RBI inning on May 21 against Charlotte.

Jacksonville first baseman **Jesse Ibarra** became only the second minor leaguer ever to switch-hit grand slams in one game when he did so on July 25 against Memphis, and Toledo outfielder **Kimera Bartee** had a six-steal game on June 7 against Columbus.

Robert Fick of West Michigan and **Lance Downing** of the Diamondbacks' Arizona League club tied for the longest hitting streak in the minors this season, as each posted 32-game streaks. Phoenix Firebirds outfielder **Jacob Cruz** had a 54-game streak, ending on July 31, in which he reached base safely by either hit or walk, while a fellow Giants farmhand, **Travis Young** of short-season Salem-Keizer, had a 54-game streak intact at season's end. In addition, Portland (Maine) first baseman **Kevin Millar** had a 46-game streak that was still alive.

Two pitchers fanned 16 in a game, and each did it in just seven innings—Salem's **Steve Shoemaker** on May 24 against Prince William, and Hickory's **Jason Lakman** on July 31 against Augusta. Lakman's outing included a five-strikeout inning. Charleston (W.Va.) hurler **Ted Rose** fanned eight in a row on Aug. 15 against Hagerstown.

Cliff Politte of Prince William and **Mike Vavrek** of New Haven shared the honors for the longest winning streak among pitchers, as each reeled off 12 in a row. Elizabethton ace **Pablo Perez** had a 10-game streak intact at season's end.

Salem's **Mike Kusiewicz** had a 32⅓-inning scoreless streak snapped on Aug. 14, while Birmingham's **Alan Newman** went 35 innings without allowing an earned run. **Ryan Franklin** of Memphis posted a 14-inning hitless streak, which included a complete-game no-hitter on April 21, one of 18 no-hitters thrown in 1997. Six of those no-nos were nine-inning, complete-game efforts: **David Borkowski** of West Michigan, on April 20 against Kane County; **Ted Lilly** of San Bernardino, on May 10 against Lake Elsinore; **Bartolo Colon** of Buffalo, on June 20 against New Orleans; **Alberto Blanco** of Kissimmee, on June 25 against Daytona; **Ramon Ortiz** of Cedar Rapids, on Aug. 7 against Quad City; and **Aaron Cames** of Kane County, on Aug. 24 against Peoria.

The Indianapolis Indians of the AAA American Association and the rookie-level Arizona Cubs both had 14-game winning streaks to top all teams. The Bluefield Orioles scored a season-high 29 runs in a victory against Danville in Appalachian League action on July 13, including a 13-run sixth inning (aided by six wild pitches in that frame from Danville pitcher Tim Lyons).

Attendance

Minor league attendance in 1997 rose by more than a million fans over the previous year, as 28 teams set single-season attendance records. According to the National Association, the governing body of the minor leagues, attendance soared to 34,691,716, a 4.2% increase over the '96 figure of 33,293,383. The total attendance was the fourth highest of all time and the best since 1949, when there were 448 teams in 59 leagues.

Six of the 15 leagues that charge admission set attendance records: Eastern (AA); California (A); Florida State (A); South Atlantic (A); New York–Penn (short-season A); and Northwest (short-season A). The Carolina League (A) missed its record by a mere 10,000 fans.

—by Lisa Winston

Class AAA WRAP-UPS

American Association

The Buffalo Bisons took home the title, sweeping the Iowa Cubs in three games to win the last American Association championship in the circuit's history—its teams are being dispersed into the International and Pacific Coast leagues in a massive realignment. Buffalo rallied from a 2-1 deficit in a five-game series to beat Indianapolis in the semifinals and then got off to a quick start at home in the finals, led by pitchers Ben Blomdahl and Brian Anderson. In the 5-4 10-inning clincher, DH Sean Casey wrote himself into the Buffalo history books with a game-winning home run. League MVP honors went to Nashville outfielder Magglio Ordonez, who was also the league's batting champion.

League leaders: BA: **Magglio Ordonez**, Nashville, .329. HR: **Richie Sexson**, Buffalo 31. RBI: **Bubba Smith**, Oklahoma City, 94. SB: **Miguel Cairo**, Iowa, 40. ERA: **John Halama**, New Orleans, 2.58. W: **Halama**, 13. K: **C.J. Nitkowski**, New Orleans, 141. SV: **Scott Service**, Omaha, 24.

AMERICAN ASSOCIATION (AAA)

Eastern Division

	W	L	Pct.	GB
Buffalo	87	57	.604	—
Indianapolis	85	59	.590	2
Nashville	74	69	.517	12.5
Louisville	58	85	.406	28.5

Western Division

	W	L	Pct.	GB
Iowa	74	69	.517	—
New Orleans	74	70	.514	.5
Oklahoma City	61	82	.427	13
Omaha	61	83	.424	13.5

Semifinals: Buffalo 3, Indianapolis 2; Iowa 3, New Orleans 0.
Finals: Buffalo 3, Iowa 0.

\# Switch-hitter
* Left-handed

Final AAA and AA Player Stats

American Association

Buffalo Bisons (Indians) AAA

BATTING	AVG	AB	R	H	2B	3B	HR	RBI	BB	SO	SB
Aven, Bruce, OF	.287	432	69	124	27	3	17	77	50	99	10
*Brewer, Rod, DH	.161	31	3	5	1	0	2	5	8	9	0
Busch, Mike, DH	.181	166	24	30	4	0	12	29	22	68	0
#Candaele, Casey, 2B	.228	311	39	71	21	0	7	38	31	43	1
*Casey, Sean, DH	.361	72	12	26	7	0	5	18	9	11	0
*Curtis, Randy, OF	.270	111	14	30	7	0	5	15	14	22	1
Diaz, Einar, C	.256	336	40	86	18	2	3	31	18	34	2
Hubbard, Trenidad, OF	.312	375	71	117	22	1	16	60	57	52	26
#Listach, Pat, SS	.260	73	3	19	1	1	0	2	12	10	6
#Lovullo, Torey, 3B	.227	321	40	73	18	0	12	40	51	64	0
Manto, Jeff, 3B	.321	187	37	60	11	0	20	54	31	43	0
Norman, Les, OF	.259	428	71	111	20	1	17	56	43	80	7
Ramirez, Alex, OF	.286	416	59	119	19	8	11	44	24	95	10
Scutaro, Marcos, 2B	.263	57	8	15	3	0	1	6	6	8	0
Sexson, Richie, 1B	.260	434	57	113	20	2	31	88	27	87	5
Soliz, Steve, C	.192	151	12	29	5	0	1	13	10	40	0
*Thomas, Greg, DH	.077	13	1	1	1	0	0	2	3	6	0
Thompson, Ryan, OF	.242	66	10	16	0	0	1	6	5	16	2
#Wilson, Enrique, SS	.306	451	78	138	20	3	11	39	42	41	9

PITCHING	W	L	ERA	G	SV	IP	H	R	ER	BB	SO
*Anderson, Brian	7	1	3.05	15	0	85.2	78	33	29	15	60
*Barfield, John	0	1	27.00	1	0	1.0	3	3	3	0	1
Blomdahl, Ben	7	8	4.76	29	0	104.0	110	64	55	31	60
*Cadaret, Greg	2	2	4.86	29	4	50.0	46	31	27	35	49
Clark, Terry	7	3	2.85	25	3	94.2	86	34	30	30	63
Colon, Bartolo	7	1	2.22	10	0	56.2	45	15	14	23	54
DeLaMaza, Roland	9	4	2.90	34	2	115.0	104	42	37	43	73
DeLaRosa, Maximo	2	2	6.49	15	0	43.0	43	34	31	33	31
Dougherty, Anthony	2	0	3.77	18	2	28.2	31	17	12	18	21
Driskill, Travis	8	7	4.65	29	0	147.0	159	86	76	60	102
*Ilsley, Blaise	0	0	2.19	9	0	12.1	12	3	3	1	7
*Jacome, Jason	3	1	3.16	7	0	37.0	41	14	13	10	23
Kirkreit, Daron	1	0	0.00	1	0	7.0	3	0	0	1	2
*Kline, Steven	3	3	4.03	20	1	51.1	53	26	23	13	41
Lopez, Albie	1	0	0.00	7	1	11.1	6	0	0	2	13
*Matthews, Mike	0	2	7.71	5	0	21.0	32	19	18	10	17
Montgomery, Steve	1	2	5.63	7	1	8.0	12	6	5	3	5
Moore, Marcus	5	3	2.54	10	0	71.0	54	26	20	31	72
*Morman, Alvin	0	1	3.38	11	0	13.1	15	5	5	2	17
Ogea, Chad	1	1	4.29	4	0	21.0	24	10	10	6	11
Rakers, Jason	1	0	0.00	1	0	7.0	5	0	0	1	3
Scott, Darryl	5	6	2.88	48	12	65.2	52	24	21	28	29
Sexton, Jeff	2	1	5.32	15	0	23.2	17	14	14	12	15
Shuey, Paul	0	0	3.60	2	0	5.0	4	2	2	4	6
Weathers, David	4	3	3.15	11	0	68.2	71	37	24	17	51
*Whitten, Casey	0	0	0.00	2	0	1.0	1	0	0	0	0
Wright, Jaret	4	1	1.80	7	0	45.0	30	16	9	19	47

Indianapolis Indians (Reds) AAA

BATTING	AVG	AB	R	H	2B	3B	HR	RBI	BB	SO	SB
*Bako, Paul, C	.243	321	34	78	14	1	8	43	34	81	0
Belk, Tim, 1B	.290	255	37	74	18	1	8	38	26	45	5
Boone, Aaron, 3B	.290	476	79	138	30	4	22	75	40	81	12
Boone, Bret, 2B	.286	7	1	2	1	0	0	1	2	2	1
*Branson, Jeff, SS	.211	57	7	12	3	0	1	4	6	10	0
Fordyce, Brook, C	.234	47	7	11	2	0	2	6	5	6	1
Garcia, Guillermo, C	.238	151	16	36	2	0	10	20	9	46	0
*Goodwin, Curtis, OF	.276	116	14	32	4	1	1	7	15	20	11
#Hall, Billy, 2B	.200	20	3	4	0	0	0	3	1	6	0
Hunter, Brian, 1B	.281	506	74	142	36	4	21	85	42	76	9
Jackson, Damian, SS	.288	337	63	97	18	1	4	20	47	62	24
*Johnson, Mark, 1B	.000	4	0	0	0	0	0	0	2	2	0
Kelly, Mike, OF	.348	92	28	32	8	0	7	18	23	23	7
Kmak, Joe, C	.158	38	6	6	0	0	1	2	5	6	0

BATTING	AVG	AB	R	H	2B	3B	HR	RBI	BB	SO	SB
Magdaleno, Ricky, SS	.206	155	20	32	11	0	4	14	16	48	0
Mitchell, Keith, OF	.265	407	72	108	24	1	15	60	72	65	10
Mottola, Chad, OF	.289	284	33	82	10	6	7	45	16	43	12
Murray, Glenn, OF	.167	12	1	2	1	0	0	0	2	3	0
Oliver, Joe, C	.333	9	1	3	0	0	1	1	0	1	0
Owens, Eric, 2B	.286	391	56	112	15	4	11	44	42	55	23
#Pendleton, Terry, 3B	.167	12	2	2	0	0	0	2	4	1	0
Reese, Pokey, SS	.236	72	12	17	2	0	4	11	9	12	4
*Rose, Pete, 3B	.225	40	2	9	2	0	0	1	2	11	0
Sanders, Reggie, OF	.211	19	1	4	0	0	0	1	1	6	0
Stynes, Chris, 2B	.285	418	67	119	26	1	9	61	21	30	7
Timmons, Ozzie, OF	.253	407	46	103	14	1	14	55	60	100	1
Watkins, Pat, OF	.280	325	46	91	14	7	9	35	24	55	13

PITCHING	W	L	ERA	G	SV	IP	H	R	ER	BB	SO
Bolton, Rodney	9	8	4.30	28	0	169.2	185	96	81	47	108
Carrara, Giovanni	12	5	3.51	19	0	120.2	111	50	47	51	105
Carrasco, Hector	0	0	6.23	3	1	4.1	5	3	3	3	4
*Crowell, Jim	1	1	2.75	3	0	19.2	19	7	6	8	6
*Eischen, Joey	1	0	1.27	26	2	42.2	41	7	6	13	26
Graves, Danny	3	3	3.95	30	7	54.2	52	25	24	16	26
Klingenbeck, Scott	12	8	3.96	27	0	170.2	180	85	75	41	119
Lewis, Richie	0	1	1.52	27	9	29.2	22	7	5	7	33
*Martinez, Pedro	4	3	3.47	28	0	80.1	70	37	31	35	36
Nix, James	3	0	8.82	12	0	16.1	18	16	16	16	13
Parris, Steve	2	3	3.57	5	0	35.1	26	15	14	11	27
Reed, Chris	0	1	5.79	3	0	14.0	19	11	9	9	4
Rodriguez, Felix	3	3	1.01	23	1	26.2	22	10	3	16	26
Salkeld, Roger	4	8	6.75	36	1	88.0	91	75	66	60	88
Sullivan, Scott	3	1	1.30	19	2	27.2	16	4	4	4	23
*Tabaka, Jeff	3	2	2.65	58	3	57.2	44	19	17	19	68
Tomko, Brett	6	3	2.95	10	0	61.0	53	21	20	9	60
Walker, Mike	9	6	2.98	55	7	102.2	80	35	34	46	80
*White, Gabe	7	4	2.82	20	0	118.0	119	46	37	18	62
Williams, Todd	2	0	2.13	12	2	12.2	11	4	3	6	11
Winchester, Scott	0	0	0.00	4	0	5.2	2	0	0	2	2

Iowa Cubs (Cubs) AAA

BATTING	AVG	AB	R	H	2B	3B	HR	RBI	BB	SO	SB
*Brown, Brant, OF	.301	256	51	77	19	3	16	51	31	44	6
Cairo, Miguel, 2B	.279	569	82	159	35	4	5	46	24	54	40
#Caraballo, Ramon, 2B	.211	133	16	28	8	0	4	21	18	25	5
Cholowsky, Dan, C	.185	65	12	12	2	0	1	4	9	17	2
Cline, Pat, C	.221	95	6	21	2	0	3	10	10	24	0
Dalesandro, Mark, C	.262	405	48	106	14	0	8	48	33	51	0
Dowler, Dee, OF	.230	100	14	23	2	0	2	12	10	16	6
Freeman, Ricky, 1B	.169	77	7	13	0	0	1	4	8	20	1
*Houston, Tyler, 3B	.217	23	0	5	2	0	0	4	0	2	0
Hubbard, Mike, C	.280	186	24	52	15	1	6	26	11	23	2
*Jennings, Robin, OF	.276	464	67	128	25	5	20	71	56	73	5
*Kieschnick, B., OF	.258	360	57	93	21	0	21	66	36	89	0
Lisanti, Bob, C	.364	11	2	4	0	0	0	1	2	5	0
Lowery, Terrell, OF	.301	386	69	116	28	3	17	71	65	97	9
*McCall, Rod, 1B	.263	255	38	67	10	0	20	55	31	90	0
McIntosh, Tim, C	.259	54	9	14	3	0	2	8	3	14	0
Molina, Jose, C	.333	3	0	1	0	0	0	0	1	1	0
Nava, Lipso, 3B	.266	319	37	85	17	1	9	36	22	53	2
Orie, Kevin, 3B	.375	32	7	12	4	0	1	8	5	5	0
Pegues, Steve, OF	.375	24	3	9	2	0	0	1	0	3	0
Petersen, Chris, SS	.240	391	49	94	16	2	3	33	32	89	1
*Valdes, Pedro, OF	.284	464	65	132	30	1	14	60	48	67	9
*Williams, Harold, DH	.179	28	2	5	2	0	1	2	2	8	0
Wilson, Brandon, SS	.236	242	28	57	5	4	1	17	20	48	8

PITCHING	W	L	ERA	G	SV	IP	H	R	ER	BB	SO
Batista, Miguel	9	4	4.20	31	0	122.0	117	60	57	38	95
Fletcher, Paul	10	6	3.56	54	0	78.1	63	32	31	39	67
Gonzalez, Jeremi	2	2	3.48	10	0	62.0	47	27	24	21	58
Hart, Jason	0	1	18.00	1	0	1.0	1	2	2	2	3
Heredia, Gil	4	2	3.86	31	1	46.2	54	22	20	9	30
Lyons, Curt	0	2	6.37	8	0	29.2	35	23	21	21	26
Myers, Rodney	7	8	4.09	24	0	140.2	140	76	64	38	79
Pisciotta, Marc	6	2	2.36	42	22	45.2	29	12	12	23	48
Rain, Steve	7	1	5.89	40	1	44.1	51	30	29	34	50
Ratliff, Jon	1	3	5.57	9	1	32.1	30	20	20	7	25
Russell, Lagrande	0	3	12.54	7	0	18.2	36	26	26	8	3
*Sauveur, Rich	1	3	3.38	39	2	45.1	46	19	17	21	37

Class AAA WRAP-UPS

International League

With Rochester's five-game victory over Columbus, Red Wings manager Marv Foley became the first manager in minor league history to win championships in all three AAA leagues—he won with Vancouver (Pacific Coast League) in 1989 and Iowa (American Association) in '93. Columbus swept the Wings in three games last year for the coveted Governors' Cup, but this year Rochester's Julio Moreno allowed one earned run in five innings in Game 5, and the bullpen hung on for the deciding 4-3 win. A veteran won the league's MVP award as Norfolk first baseman Roberto Petagine took home the honors, while rookie hurler Brian Rose of Pawtucket was the loop's Pitcher of the Year as well as its top rookie.

League leaders: BA: **Tommy Gregg**, Richmond, .332. HR: **Russ Morman**, Charlotte, 33. RBI: **Randall Simon**, Richmond, 102. SB: **Kimera Simon**, Toledo, 33. ERA: **Brian Rose**, Pawtucket, 3.02. W: **Rose**, 17. K: **Nerio Rodriguez**, Rochester, 160. SV: **Eddie Gaillard**, Toledo, 28.

INTERNATIONAL LEAGUE (AAA)

Eastern Division

	W	L	Pct.	GB
Rochester	83	58	.589	—
Pawtucket	81	60	.574	2
Scranton/W.B.	66	76	.465	17.5
Syracuse	55	87	.387	28.5
Ottawa	54	86	.386	28.5

Western Division

	W	L	Pct.	GB
Columbus	79	63	.556	—
Charlotte	76	65	.539	2.5
Norfolk	75	67	.528	4
Richmond	70	72	.493	9
Toledo	68	73	.482	10.5

Semifinals: Rochester 3, Pawtucket 1; Columbus 3, Charlotte 1.
Finals: Rochester 3, Columbus 2.

Switch-hitter
* Left-handed

Class AAA WRAP-UPS

Pacific Coast League

The Edmonton Trappers successfully defended their Pacific Coast League title, beating the Phoenix Firebirds three games to one. A paid crowd of just over 2,000 passed through the gates of Scottsdale Stadium for the final Phoenix Firebirds game. The club moves to Fresno next year, to make room for the expansion Arizona Diamondbacks. The Trappers were led in the finals by Jeff D'Amico, who pitched 5⅓ innings of one-hit ball in the last game and had a postseason ERA of 0.00. League MVP honors went to Albuquerque third baseman Paul Konerko, who was also *Baseball Weekly*'s Minor League Player of the Year. Konerko led the loop in homers and RBI while batting .323.

League leaders: BA: Jacob Cruz, Phoenix, .361. HR: Paul Konerko, Albuquerque, 37. RBI: Konerko, 127. SB: Terry Jones, Colorado Springs, 36. ERA: Edwin Hurtado, Tacoma, 3.88. W: Nate Minchey, Colorado Springs, 15. K: Doug Creek, Phoenix, 137. SV: John Johnstone, Phoenix, 24.

PACIFIC COAST LEAGUE (AAA)

Northern Division

	W	L	Pct.	GB
Edmonton	80	64	.556	—
Tacoma	75	66	.532	3.5
Vancouver	75	68	.524	4.5
Salt Lake	72	71	.503	7.5
Calgary	60	78	.435	17

Southern Division

	W	L	Pct.	GB
Phoenix	88	55	.615	—
Colo. Springs	76	64	10	.5
Tucson	64	78	.451	23.5
Albuquerque	62	79	.440	25
Las Vegas	56	85	.397	31

Semifinals: Phoenix 3, Colorado Springs 0; Edmonton 3, Vancouver 0.
Finals: Edmonton 3, Phoenix 1

Switch-hitter
* Left-handed

PITCHING	W	L	ERA	G	SV	IP	H	R	ER	BB	SO
Speier, Justin	2	0	0.00	8	1	12.1	5	0	0	1	9
Steenstra, Kennie	5	10	3.92	25	0	160.2	161	85	70	41	111
Stevens, Dave	1	1	4.70	6	1	7.2	8	4	4	5	8
Swartzbaugh, Dave	8	7	2.82	24	1	134.0	129	55	42	48	97
Tapani, Kevin	0	1	4.00	1	0	9.0	5	4	4	1	4
Telemaco, Amaury	5	9	4.51	18	0	113.2	121	70	57	38	75
*VanRyn, Ben	2	2	4.59	51	3	80.1	88	43	41	25	64
Wood, Kerry	4	2	4.68	10	0	57.2	35	35	30	52	80

Louisville Redbirds (Cardinals) AAA

BATTING	AVG	AB	R	H	2B	3B	HR	RBI	BB	SO	SB
Bell, David, 2B	.227	22	3	5	0	0	1	4	0	6	0
Berblinger, Jeff, 2B	.263	513	63	135	19	7	11	58	55	98	24
*Bradshaw, Terry, OF	.249	453	79	113	17	6	8	43	61	79	26
Costo, Tim, 1B	.303	400	52	121	26	2	14	54	41	72	4
*Coughlin, Kevin, OF	.257	35	2	9	1	0	0	2	1	7	0
Difelice, Mike, C	.250	4	1	1	0	0	1	1	0	1	0
#Franklin, Micah, OF	.221	326	49	72	14	1	12	48	51	74	2
Gallego, Mike, SS	.278	18	0	5	1	0	0	1	3	5	1
*Giannelli, Ray, OF	.221	95	12	21	4	0	3	12	17	18	0
#Green, Scrbrgh., OF	.254	209	26	53	11	2	3	13	22	55	10
Gulan, Mike, 3B	.267	412	50	110	20	6	14	61	28	121	5
Holbert, Aaron, SS	.255	314	32	80	14	3	4	32	15	56	9
Jordan, Brian, OF	.150	20	1	3	0	0	0	2	1	2	0
*Koslofski, Kevin, OF	.211	285	37	60	14	3	9	27	43	78	1
*Livingstone, Scott, 1B	.360	25	4	9	1	0	0	2	2	3	0
Marrero, Eli, C	.273	395	60	108	21	7	20	68	25	53	4
Mejia, Roberto, 2B	.333	21	3	7	1	0	1	2	0	4	0
Nevers, Tom, SS	.233	227	22	53	9	0	8	27	12	48	1
Pagnozzi, Tom, C	.000	5	0	0	0	0	0	0	0	1	0
*Plantier, Phil, OF	.258	31	6	8	3	0	1	10	6	3	0
*Robinson, Kerry, OF	.111	9	0	1	0	0	0	0	0	1	0
Rupp, Brian, 1B	.275	189	17	52	7	2	0	16	19	36	1
Scarsone, Steve, 2B	.154	26	5	4	0	0	1	3	7	10	0
Stefanski, Mike, C	.305	197	26	60	10	0	6	22	12	20	0
Warner, Ron, OF	.232	276	43	64	16	0	7	30	42	45	4
Wimmer, Chris, 2B	.167	12	0	2	0	0	0	1	0	1	0
#Young, Dmitri, OF	.274	84	10	23	7	0	4	14	13	15	1

PITCHING	W	L	ERA	G	SV	IP	H	R	ER	BB	SO
Arrandale, Matt	2	6	3.67	56	1	83.1	84	38	34	38	32
Aybar, Manny	5	8	3.48	22	0	137.0	131	60	53	45	114
Badorek, Mike	0	0	18.00	1	0	2.0	4	4	4	2	3
Barber, Brian	4	8	6.90	18	0	92.2	111	80	71	44	74
Batchelor, Rich	0	2	4.50	12	5	14.0	18	9	7	6	10
Bautista, Jose	2	0	0.00	11	0	17.1	3	0	0	2	11
*Beltran, Rigo	5	2	2.32	9	0	54.1	45	17	14	21	46
Benes, Andy	0	0	1.80	1	0	5.0	3	1	1	1	5
Busby, Mike	4	8	4.61	15	0	93.2	95	49	48	30	65
Carpenter, Brian	0	0	4.32	4	1	8.1	11	4	4	5	9
Croushore, Rich	1	2	2.47	14	1	43.2	37	14	12	13	41
*Detmers, Kris	3	3	7.20	10	0	35.0	43	28	28	17	22
Glauber, Keith	1	3	5.17	15	5	15.2	18	14	9	4	14
Heiserman, Rick	0	0	4.50	1	0	2.0	2	1	1	1	0
*Jackson, Danny	1	0	1.80	4	0	25.0	20	6	5	8	14
King, Curt	2	1	2.05	16	3	22.0	19	5	5	6	9
Lowe, Sean	6	10	4.37	26	1	131.2	142	74	64	53	117
Ludwick, Eric	6	8	2.93	24	4	80.0	67	31	26	26	85
Matranga, Jeff	3	3	5.57	37	0	53.1	75	34	33	13	30
Maxcy, Brian	2	2	3.76	30	9	38.1	36	18	16	24	22
*McGraw, Tom	1	4	5.33	45	0	49.0	55	34	29	26	39
*Osborne, Donovan	0	1	4.73	3	0	13.1	13	7	7	5	13
*Painter, Lance	1	0	5.23	18	0	20.2	18	14	12	4	22
Raggio, Brady	8	11	4.17	22	0	138.0	145	68	64	32	91
*Wiegandt, Scott	1	3	4.45	40	0	64.2	57	34	32	36	55

Nashville Sounds (White Sox) AAA

BATTING	AVG	AB	R	H	2B	3B	HR	RBI	BB	SO	SB
Abbott, Jeff, OF	.327	465	88	152	35	3	11	63	41	52	12
Battle, Allen, OF	.222	27	6	6	1	0	2	5	5	7	0
#Brady, Doug, 2B	.238	370	43	88	12	3	7	36	18	47	13
Cameron, Mike, OF	.275	120	21	33	7	3	6	17	18	31	4
*Cappuccio, Carm., OF	.220	177	22	39	11	0	4	21	16	24	1
*Cotton, John, OF	.269	323	45	87	14	3	11	50	24	94	8
Downs, Brian, C	.222	18	1	4	0	0	0	1	0	5	0
#Evans, Jason, OF	.284	194	38	55	10	1	1	27	49	45	6

BATTING	AVG	AB	R	H	2B	3B	HR	RBI	BB	SO	SB
Leius, Scott, 3B	.240	104	15	25	2	0	7	17	11	6	0
Machado, Robert, C	.269	308	43	83	18	0	8	30	12	61	5
Menechino, Frankie, 2B	.230	113	20	26	4	0	4	11	26	31	3
#Norton, Greg, 3B	.275	414	82	114	27	1	26	76	57	101	3
Ordonez, Magglio, OF	.329	523	65	172	29	3	14	90	32	61	14
#Pearson, Eddie, 1B	.223	148	17	33	4	0	4	16	6	23	1
#Polidor, Wil, 2B	.097	31	2	3	0	0	0	2	0	4	0
Schall, Gene, DH	.196	112	11	22	0	1	5	17	11	32	1
Snopek, Chris, SS	.233	73	8	17	4	0	3	8	7	13	0
*Valdez, Mario, 1B	.280	282	44	79	20	1	15	61	43	77	1
*Ventura, Robin, 3B	.400	15	3	6	1	0	2	5	2	1	0
Vinas, Julio, DH	.232	314	39	73	12	2	11	41	25	72	4
Wilson, Craig, SS	.272	453	71	123	20	2	6	42	48	31	4
Wrona, Rick, C	.246	211	22	52	15	0	6	22	3	41	1

PITCHING	W	L	ERA	G	SV	IP	H	R	ER	BB	SO
Bere, Jason	1	1	5.59	4	0	19.1	23	13	12	7	13
*Bertotti, Mike	5	9	5.35	21	0	107.2	91	70	64	105	87
Castillo, Carlos	0	0	1.50	4	3	6.0	4	1	1	0	4
Clemons, Chris	5	5	4.55	22	0	124.2	115	73	63	65	70
Cruz, Nelson	11	7	5.11	21	0	123.1	139	75	70	31	93
Darwin, Jeff	4	3	4.53	47	22	53.2	60	32	27	24	44
*Fordham, Tom	6	7	4.74	21	0	114.0	113	64	60	53	90
Foulke, Keith	0	0	5.79	1	0	4.2	8	3	3	0	4
Hasselhoff, Derek	1	1	9.82	6	0	7.1	9	8	8	7	2
Heathcott, Mike	2	3	7.33	17	0	27.0	39	23	22	12	23
Johnson, Barry	4	1	3.55	14	2	25.1	24	10	10	11	10
Jones, Stacy	0	0	54.00	1	0	0.1	4	3	2	0	0
Karchner, Matt	2	1	1.93	13	3	18.2	12	5	4	6	11
Keyser, Brian	7	5	2.87	44	1	119.0	114	44	38	45	68
Levine, Alan	1	1	7.13	26	2	35.1	58	32	28	11	29
*Parque, Jim	1	0	4.22	2	0	10.2	9	5	5	9	5
Pratt, Rich	9	8	4.58	29	0	149.1	165	89	76	50	71
*Rizzo, Todd	4	5	3.57	54	6	70.2	63	39	28	33	60
Sirotka, Mike	7	5	3.28	19	0	112.1	115	49	41	22	92
Smith, Chuck	0	3	8.81	20	0	31.2	39	33	31	23	29
*Thomas, Larry	3	2	3.94	44	2	48.0	47	21	21	18	53
Woods, Brian	1	2	7.71	14	0	23.1	34	24	20	20	22

New Orleans Zephyrs (Astros) AAA

BATTING	AVG	AB	R	H	2B	3B	HR	RBI	BB	SO	SB
*Abreu, Bob, OF	.268	194	25	52	9	4	2	22	21	49	7
Bell, Derek, OF	.154	13	0	2	0	0	0	1	1	1	1
Berry, Sean, 3B	.333	9	1	3	0	0	0	0	3	3	0
*Bridges, Kary, 2B	.172	64	6	11	1	2	0	3	5	9	1
#Carr, Chuck, OF	.246	65	8	16	1	0	0	3	8	14	5
Christopherson, Eric, C	.190	21	3	4	0	0	0	0	4	7	0
*Colon, Dennis, 1B	.270	400	49	108	23	1	6	64	42	48	2
Flora, Kevin, OF	.257	109	14	28	1	3	2	14	16	25	8
Grebeck, Brian, SS	.126	103	15	13	1	0	0	8	21	17	1
#Guillen, Carlos, SS	.308	13	3	4	1	0	0	0	0	4	0
Gutierrez, Ricky, SS	.185	27	2	5	1	0	0	4	2	4	0
Haney, Todd, 2B	.282	454	63	128	25	0	2	63	43	50	5
Hidalgo, Richard, OF	.279	526	74	147	37	5	11	78	35	57	6
Johnson, Russ, 3B	.276	445	72	123	16	6	4	49	66	78	7
Knorr, Randy, C	.238	244	22	58	10	0	5	27	22	38	0
*Maas, Kevin, DH	.219	260	38	57	23	1	7	34	48	56	0
*McNabb, Buck, OF	.158	19	2	3	0	1	0	0	1	6	0
#Meluskey, Mitch, C	.250	172	22	43	7	0	3	21	25	38	0
Montgomery, Ray, OF	.288	73	17	21	5	0	6	13	11	15	1
Mora, Melvin, OF	.257	370	55	95	15	3	2	38	47	52	7
*Phillips, J.R., OF	.290	411	59	119	28	0	21	71	39	112	0
Probst, Alan, C	.223	112	8	25	6	0	2	10	9	27	0
*Ramos, Ken, OF	.289	253	32	73	9	1	0	22	45	15	2
Rivera, Luis, SS	.238	382	46	91	23	4	3	45	34	51	5
*Robles, Oscar, 2B	.333	3	0	1	0	0	0	0	1	1	0
*Ward, Daryle, 1B	.375	48	4	18	1	0	2	8	7	7	0

PITCHING	W	L	ERA	G	SV	IP	H	R	ER	BB	SO
Barrios, Manuel	4	8	3.27	57	0	82.2	70	32	30	34	77
Cabrera, Jose	5	2	2.21	36	0	61.0	39	15	15	20	59
Elarton, Scott	4	4	5.33	9	0	54.0	51	36	32	17	50
*Fernandez, Sid	0	1	4.32	2	0	8.1	7	4	4	3	7
Gardiner, Mike	2	1	8.13	11	0	31.0	43	32	28	14	24
Greene, Tommy	5	3	3.38	13	0	74.2	59	30	28	25	75
Gutierrez, Jim	0	1	3.27	7	0	11.0	11	4	4	2	8
*Halama, John	13	3	2.58	26	0	171.0	150	57	49	32	126

Class AA WRAP-UPS

Eastern League

The Harrisburg Senators successfully defended their Eastern League title against the same club they had edged the previous year, the Portland (Maine) Sea Dogs. Right fielder Scott Samuels went 3-for-3 with a home run and a double to lead Harrisburg to a 4-3 win in the deciding fourth game of the playoff finals. Left fielder Chris Stowers also homered in the clincher. It was Portland, though, that took home the bulk of the postseason honors, as Sea Dogs first baseman Kevin Millar easily won MVP honors, just missing the Triple Crown by five home runs. In addition, Portland outfielder Mark Kotsay was named the league's Rookie of the Year.

League leaders: BA: **Kevin Millar**, Portland .342. HR: **Matt Raleigh**, Binghamton, 37. RBI: **Millar**, 131. SB: **Aaron Fuller**, Trenton, 40. ERA: **Mike Vavrek**, New Haven, 2.57. W: **Jesus Sanchez**, Binghamton, 13. K: **Sanchez**, 176. SV: **Ben Fleetham**, Harrisburg, 30.

EASTERN LEAGUE (AA)
Northern Division

	W	L	Pct.	GB
Portland	79	63	.556	—
Norwich	73	69	.514	6
New Britain	70	72	.493	9
Binghamton	66	76	.465	13
New Haven	64	78	.451	15

Southern Division

	W	L	Pct.	GB
Harrisburg	86	56	.606	—
Bowie	75	67	.528	11
Reading	74	68	.521	12
Trenton	71	70	.504	14.5
Akron	51	90	.362	34.5

Semifinals: Harrisburg 3, Bowie 2; Portland 3, Norwich 2.
Finals: Harrisburg 3, Portland 1.

Switch-hitter
* Left-handed

Class AA WRAP-UPS

Southern League

The finals featured two teams, the Greenville Braves and the Huntsville Stars, that didn't clinch their spots in the postseason until the final few days of the regular season. While the first-half winners, the Knoxville Smokies and the Mobile BayBears, knew long ago where they'd be spending the first week of September, it took late-season heroics for Greenville to knock off pesky Orlando and Huntsville to finish off Birmingham. The hottest bat in the playoffs belonged to Huntsville catcher Ramon Hernandez, who hit .531 with seven homers, including a two-homer, six-RBI game in the finals. League MVP honors went to another Huntsville player, outfielder Ben Grieve, who was also *USA TODAY*'s Minor League Player of the Year.

League leaders: BA: **Mike Neill,** Huntsville, .340. HR: **Luis Raven,** Birmingham, **Mike Coolbaugh,** Huntsville, **Kevin Witt,** Knoxville, 30. RBI: **Coolbaugh,** 132. SB: **Earl Johnson,** Jacksonville, 42. ERA: **Russell Herbert,** Birmingham, 3.63. W: **Herbert, Scott Eyre,** Birmingham, 13. K: **Earl Byrne,** Orlando, 128. SV: **Todd Williams,** Chattanooga, 31.

SOUTHERN LEAGUE (AA)
Eastern Division

	W	L	Pct.	GB
Knoxville	75	63	.543	—
Greenville	74	66	.529	2
Jacksonville	66	73	.475	9.5
Orlando	63	75	.457	12
Carolina	55	82	.401	19.5

Western Division

	W	L	Pct.	GB
Huntsville	77	62	.554	—
Birmingham	76	62	.551	.5
Mobile	69	68	.504	7
Chattanooga	70	69	.504	7
Memphis	67	72	.482	10

Semifinals: Greenville 3, Knoxville 1; Huntsville 3, Mobile 2.
Finals: Greenville 3, Huntsville 2.

Switch-hitter
* Left-handed

PITCHING	W	L	ERA	G	SV	IP	H	R	ER	BB	SO
Henriquez, Oscar	4	5	2.80	60	12	74.0	65	28	23	27	80
Hudek, John	0	0	0.44	19	7	20.2	3	1	1	3	26
*Magnante, Mike	2	3	4.50	17	1	24.0	31	14	12	5	23
Manzanillo, Josias	0	0	4.40	11	0	14.1	17	7	7	6	11
*Miller, Trever	6	7	3.30	29	0	163.2	177	71	60	54	99
*Mimbs, Mark	1	2	4.36	22	1	33.0	36	19	16	9	26
Minor, Blas	3	3	2.27	23	6	31.2	20	8	8	9	27
Mlicki, Doug	4	3	3.60	14	0	30.0	27	12	12	10	18
*Mounce, Tony	0	0	1.93	1	0	4.2	2	1	1	6	6
*Nitkowski, C.J.	8	10	3.98	28	0	174.1	183	82	77	56	141
Patrick, Bronswell	6	5	3.22	30	0	100.2	108	45	36	30	88
Reynolds, Shane	1	0	0.00	1	0	5.0	3	0	0	1	6
Small, Mark	1	1	5.79	7	0	9.1	11	9	6	3	7
Wall, Donne	8	7	3.85	17	0	110.0	109	49	47	24	84

Oklahoma City 89ers (Rangers) AAA

BATTING	AVG	AB	R	H	2B	3B	HR	RBI	BB	SO	SB
*Anthony, Eric, OF	.444	36	3	16	2	0	2	9	2	7	0
Bell, Mike, 2B	.235	328	35	77	18	2	5	38	29	78	4
*Blosser, Greg, OF	.303	178	33	54	11	1	12	27	27	46	6
Brown, Kevin, C	.241	403	56	97	18	2	19	50	38	111	2
*Castleberry, Kevin, OF	.270	111	14	30	6	1	1	9	9	21	1
#Cedeno, Domingo, 2B	.357	28	0	10	2	0	0	2	0	6	0
#Diaz, Alex, OF	.286	426	65	122	25	2	12	49	33	53	26
Diaz, Edwin, 2B	.110	73	6	8	3	1	1	4	2	27	1
Estrada, Osmani, 2B	.226	288	22	65	9	0	1	20	20	37	7
#Frias, Hanley, SS	.264	484	64	128	17	4	5	46	56	72	35
Little, Mark, OF	.263	415	72	109	23	4	15	45	39	100	21
#McLemore, Mark, 2B	.100	10	0	1	0	0	0	1	1	1	1
Mercedes, Henry, C	.246	57	6	14	3	0	1	4	9	12	0
*Morris, Warren, 2B	.219	32	3	7	1	0	1	3	3	5	0
Murphy, Mike, OF	.329	243	37	80	13	5	5	25	38	66	14
O'Neill, Doug, OF	.194	31	2	6	3	0	0	1	3	10	1
Ortiz, Luis, 1B	.305	82	9	25	5	0	1	11	5	7	1
*Sagmoen, Marc, OF	.263	418	47	110	32	6	5	44	26	95	4
Silvestri, Dave, 3B	.240	467	54	112	25	3	17	68	55	104	4
Simms, Mike, OF	.385	39	7	15	4	0	3	8	6	8	0
Smith, Bubba, 1B	.255	514	60	131	30	1	27	94	53	139	2
Tackett, Jeff, C	.273	209	23	57	15	0	5	19	26	49	4
#Tettleton, Mickey, DH	.444	9	4	4	1	0	0	0	6	1	0

PITCHING	W	L	ERA	G	SV	IP	H	R	ER	BB	SO
Alberro, Jose	5	6	4.22	16	0	91.2	90	48	43	29	59
*Bailes, Scott	2	3	3.98	44	4	43.0	46	22	19	13	37
Bailey, Cory	3	4	3.40	42	15	50.1	49	20	19	23	38
Brower, Jim	2	1	7.23	4	0	18.2	30	17	15	8	7
Buckles, Bucky	0	0	0.77	5	0	11.2	12	3	1	4	5
*Burgos, John	2	0	2.57	7	0	28.0	27	8	8	8	15
Burkett, John	1	0	3.60	1	0	5.0	6	2	2	2	3
Davis, Clint	6	1	3.20	40	0	70.1	55	28	25	46	53
Dedrick, Jim	0	0	5.91	8	3	10.2	16	7	7	10	2
*Eversgerd, Bryan	1	3	4.24	26	0	76.1	91	48	36	24	43
Gross, Kevin	2	3	4.83	6	0	31.2	35	18	17	6	26
*Hartvigson, Chad	2	2	6.66	14	2	25.2	35	21	19	9	22
Heredia, Wilson	7	12	4.97	27	0	168.1	167	106	93	70	113
Johnson, Jonathan	1	8	7.29	13	1	58.0	83	54	47	29	33
*Kell, Rob	1	0	8.86	11	0	21.1	30	24	21	16	20
Manning, David	1	3	4.40	5	0	28.2	33	17	14	9	15
*Miranda, Angel	0	3	11.30	11	0	14.1	24	19	18	6	14
Moody, Eric	5	6	3.46	35	1	112.0	114	49	43	21	72
Pavlik, Roger	0	0	0.00	1	0	6.0	2	0	0	0	4
Powell, John	0	0	4.50	1	0	4.0	5	2	2	1	2
Santana, Julio	0	0	15.00	1	0	3.0	9	6	5	2	1
*Smith, Dan	3	14	5.64	23	0	129.1	154	88	81	42	67
Sturtze, Tanyon	8	6	5.10	25	0	114.2	133	76	65	47	79
*Urbani, Tom	3	2	4.19	21	1	43.0	53	21	20	13	21
Warren, Brian	5	5	3.62	41	6	69.2	73	30	28	22	39
Whiteside, Matt	1	1	3.54	10	1	28.0	30	14	11	13	11
York, Mike	0	1	8.10	4	0	10.0	12	9	9	12	1

Omaha Royals (Royals) AAA

BATTING	AVG	AB	R	H	2B	3B	HR	RBI	BB	SO	SB
Benitez, Yamil, OF	.295	329	61	97	14	1	21	71	24	82	12
Brooks, Rayme, DH	.000	9	0	0	0	0	0	0	0	4	0
Carr, Jeremy, OF	.267	120	17	32	3	2	2	9	15	17	12
Dye, Jermaine, OF	.306	144	21	44	6	0	10	25	9	25	0

BATTING	AVG	AB	R	H	2B	3B	HR	RBI	BB	SO	SB
Fasano, Sal, C	.164	152	17	25	7	0	4	14	12	53	0
Halter, Shane, 3B	.265	49	10	13	1	1	2	9	6	10	0
Hansen, Jed, 2B	.268	380	43	102	20	2	11	44	32	78	8
Hatcher, Chris, OF	.230	222	34	51	9	0	11	24	17	68	0
Long, Ryan, OF	.265	411	48	109	26	0	19	56	18	98	2
Lopez, Mendy, 3B	.231	52	6	12	2	0	1	6	8	21	0
#Martinez, Felix, SS	.254	410	55	104	19	4	2	36	29	86	21
Medrano, Tony, 2B	.203	59	10	12	0	0	4	9	4	5	0
#Merchant, Mark, OF	.000	5	0	0	0	0	0	0	0	4	0
*Myers, Rod, OF	.254	142	21	36	10	0	2	10	15	37	6
*Nunnally, Jon, OF	.278	230	35	64	11	1	15	33	39	67	8
Ortiz, Hector, C	.190	63	7	12	3	0	0	3	13	15	0
Paquette, Craig, 3B	.308	91	9	28	6	0	3	20	6	26	0
Pough, Pork Chop, 3B	.252	433	63	109	20	1	22	59	53	113	0
Seitzer, Brad, 3B	.190	63	4	12	3	0	0	4	5	10	0
Sisco, Steve, 2B	.261	188	23	49	8	0	3	12	8	34	2
Stewart, Andy, C	.274	288	38	79	10	1	6	24	18	43	1
*Sutton, Larry, 1B	.300	380	61	114	27	1	19	72	61	57	0
Sweeney, Mike, C	.236	144	22	34	8	1	10	29	18	20	0
Vitiello, Joe, DH	.214	42	5	9	1	0	3	9	5	16	0

PITCHING	W	L	ERA	G	SV	IP	H	R	ER	BB	SO
Bevil, Brian	2	1	4.38	26	1	39.0	34	22	19	22	47
Brewington, Jamie	2	2	8.31	7	0	21.2	21	21	20	13	20
Converse, Jim	2	1	6.75	6	0	17.1	18	13	13	9	13
Flury, Pat	1	0	6.07	18	0	26.2	29	18	18	16	24
Grimsley, Jason	1	5	6.68	7	0	31.0	36	26	23	29	22
*Haney, Chris	1	0	3.79	4	0	19.0	16	12	8	6	7
Harrison, Brian	10	12	5.05	30	0	178.1	208	114	100	55	83
Huisman, Rick	1	5	3.62	37	2	59.2	59	29	24	35	57
*Johns, Doug	1	5	7.56	9	0	41.2	58	36	35	11	24
*McDill, Allen	5	2	5.88	23	2	64.1	80	42	42	26	51
Montgomery, Jeff	0	0	0.00	2	0	2.0	1	0	0	1	2
Olsen, Steve	4	5	5.76	22	0	84.1	96	67	54	48	43
Olson, Gregg	3	1	3.31	9	0	35.1	30	13	13	10	20
*Patterson, Ken	2	2	4.11	22	4	30.2	34	17	14	10	28
*Pennington, Brad	2	1	4.32	35	0	50.0	41	28	24	41	48
Perez, Mike	4	1	4.71	34	8	36.1	38	22	19	18	29
Pichardo, Hipolito	0	0	5.79	5	1	4.2	5	3	3	3	3
Pittsley, Jim	1	2	4.42	7	0	38.2	36	21	19	20	30
Ray, Ken	5	12	6.37	25	0	113.0	131	86	80	63	96
*Rusch, Glendon	0	1	4.50	1	0	6.0	7	3	3	1	2
Seanez, Rudy	2	5	6.51	28	0	47.0	53	42	34	25	46
Service, Scott	3	2	2.59	49	24	48.2	39	15	14	16	69
Smith, Toby	1	3	7.84	17	3	20.2	24	19	18	15	11
Toth, Robert	5	2	2.75	15	0	52.1	50	18	16	19	30
VanPoppel, Todd	1	5	8.03	11	0	37.0	50	36	33	24	27
Veres, Randy	1	1	6.60	11	0	15.0	15	11	11	5	19
*Watkins, Scott	0	0	6.46	9	0	15.1	19	13	11	6	15
Williams, Mike	3	6	4.22	20	5	79.0	71	41	37	38	68
*Williams, Mitch	0	0	2.08	3	0	8.2	6	2	2	5	8
Zimmerman, Mike	1	3	10.59	7	0	26.1	41	32	31	20	17

International League

Charlotte Knights (Marlins) AAA

BATTING	AVG	AB	R	H	2B	3B	HR	RBI	BB	SO	SB
Berg, David, SS	.295	424	76	125	26	6	9	47	55	71	16
#Castillo, Luis, 2B	.354	130	25	46	5	0	0	5	16	22	8
#Clapinski, Chris, 2B	.262	340	62	89	24	2	12	52	48	64	14
*Cole, Alex, OF	.210	105	20	22	5	0	2	7	18	20	4
*Daubach, Brian, 1B	.278	461	66	128	40	2	21	93	65	126	1
Delgado, Alex, C	.211	38	1	8	1	0	0	6	3	7	0
*Dunwoody, Todd, OF	.262	401	74	105	16	7	23	62	39	129	25
*Floyd, Cliff, OF	.366	131	27	48	10	0	9	33	10	29	7
Kmak, Joe, C	.237	93	7	22	6	1	0	12	11	28	1
Kuilan, Hector, C	.103	39	3	4	0	0	0	3	2	8	0
Lucca, Lou, 3B	.284	292	40	83	22	1	18	51	22	56	5
Milliard, Ralph, 2B	.265	132	19	35	5	1	4	18	9	21	5
Morman, Russ, 1B	.319	395	86	126	17	2	33	99	58	89	3
Natal, Rob, C	.267	251	34	67	17	2	11	49	19	37	2
#Olmeda, Jose, OF	.207	242	24	50	11	1	1	29	21	41	3
Redmond, Mike, C	.213	61	8	13	5	1	1	2	1	10	0
Rodriguez, Maximo, C	.048	21	2	1	0	0	0	1	0	7	0
Sheff, Chris, OF	.255	322	54	82	23	1	11	43	43	76	16

Class AA WRAP-UPS

Texas League

In Game 7 of the playoffs, the San Antonio Missions rode a two-run fourth inning to a 2-0 victory at Shreveport to take the title. The Missions won the first three games of the series at home, but the Captains then took full advantage of their home field, winning the next three, two by shutouts. Both teams dominated their divisions all season, winning both halves of the split-season schedule to eliminate a semifinal round. Shreveport, which has now been in the playoffs 12 of the last 13 years, finished the season 76-62. League MVP honors went to El Paso's slugging third baseman, Mike Kinkade, who led the minors in both batting average and errors.

League leaders: BA: **Mike Kinkade**, El Paso, .385. HR: **Dan Collier**, Tulsa, 26. RBI: **Kinkade**, 109. SB: **Calvin Murray**, Shreveport, 52. ERA: **Troy Brohawn**, Shreveport, 2.56. W: **Travis Smith**, El Paso, 16. K: **Jarrod Washburn**, Midland, 146. SV: **Bobby Howry**, Shreveport, 22.

TEXAS LEAGUE (AA)
Eastern Division

	W	L	Pct.	GB
Shreveport	76	62	.551	—
Arkansas	68	72	.486	9
Jackson	66	73	.475	10.5
Tulsa	61	78	.439	15.5

Western Division

	W	L	Pct.	GB
San Antonio	84	55	.604	—
El Paso	74	66	.529	10.5
Midland	64	75	.460	20
Wichita	64	76	.457	20.5

Finals: San Antonio 4, Shreveport 3.

Switch-hitter
* Left-handed

Class A WRAP-UPS

California League

The High Desert Mavericks swept the San Bernardino Stampede in three straight to capture the league title to cap a perfect postseason. The Mavericks' one-two punch of league MVP Mike Stoner and veteran Stanton Cameron continued to drive the club as they had all season. Stoner became the first minor leaguer this decade to collect 200 hits as well as the first to top 140 RBI. Cameron hit .524 in the six post-season games, including all three High Desert RBI in the final game's 3-2 win. On the mound, Cuban emigrant Vladimir Nunez picked up the win in the clincher, striking out 11 of the Stampede.

League leaders: BA: **Ramon Hernandez**, Visalia, .361. HR: **Mike Stoner**, High Desert, **Stanton Cameron**, High Desert, **Michael Glendenning**, Bakersfield, 33. RBI: **Stoner**, 142. SB: **Justin Baughman**, Lake Elsinore, 68. ERA: **Ted Lilly**, San Bernardino, 2.81. W: **Jeff Sobkoviak**, High Desert, **J.J. Pearsall**, San Bernardino, 14. K: **Jason Brester**, San Jose, 172. SV: **Mike Pageler**, Bakersfield, 29.

CALIFORNIA LEAGUE (A)
Valley Division

	W	L	Pct.	GB
High Desert	83	57	.593	—
Lancaster	75	66	.532	8.5
Modesto	74	67	.525	9.5
Stockton	70	70	.500	13
San Jose	60	80	.429	23

Freeway Division

	W	L	Pct.	GB
Rancho Cuca.	77	63	.550	—
Visalia	71	69	.507	6
S. Bernardino	68	72	.486	9
Bakersfield	62	78	.443	15
Lake Elsinore	61	79	.436	16

Quarterfinals: San Bernardino 2, Visalia 0; Lancaster 2, Stockton 1. **Semifinals:** San Bernardino 3, Rancho Cucamonga 2; High Desert 3, Lancaster 0. **Finals:** High Desert 3, San Bernardino 0.

BATTING	AVG	AB	R	H	2B	3B	HR	RBI	BB	SO	SB
Torres, Tony, 2B	.279	68	9	19	3	0	1	8	7	26	3
Wehner, John, 3B	.280	93	16	26	5	0	3	11	6	18	3
*Wilson, Pookie, OF	.253	146	27	37	6	1	2	13	17	26	1

PITCHING	W	L	ERA	G	SV	IP	H	R	ER	BB	SO
Alfonseca, Antonio	7	2	4.32	46	7	58.1	58	34	28	20	45
Castro, Tony	0	0	4.91	2	0	3.2	2	2	2	2	1
Chergey, Dan	3	1	3.14	27	6	43.0	37	18	15	9	40
Cornelius, Reid	12	5	5.10	22	0	130.2	134	82	74	43	80
*Darensbourg, Vic	4	2	4.38	27	2	24.2	22	12	12	15	21
*Gonzalez, Gabe	2	2	2.74	37	3	42.2	38	15	13	14	24
Harvey, Bryan	0	0	0.00	2	0	1.1	0	0	0	0	0
Hernandez, Livan	5	3	3.98	14	0	81.1	76	39	36	38	58
Hurst, William	1	2	7.76	27	3	29.0	39	27	25	22	15
Juelsgaard, Jarod	1	3	6.04	21	0	50.2	65	41	34	39	31
Larkin, Andy	6	11	6.05	28	0	144.1	166	109	97	76	103
Mendoza, Reynol	7	8	5.49	46	9	114.2	134	79	70	57	93
*Mercado, Hector	0	1	9.00	1	0	5.0	5	5	5	5	1
Miller, Kurt	2	1	3.58	21	0	27.2	25	12	11	22	31
Norris, Joe	0	0	11.81	9	0	16.0	23	22	21	13	10
*Ojala, Kirt	8	7	3.50	25	0	149.0	148	74	58	55	119
Pall, Donn	4	7	3.39	59	8	79.2	82	40	30	11	70
Press, Gregg	0	0	4.50	1	0	6.0	5	3	3	4	2
*Saunders, Tony	1	0	2.77	3	0	13.0	9	4	4	6	9
Seelbach, Chris	5	0	6.26	16	0	50.1	58	36	35	34	50
Stanifer, Robby	4	0	4.88	22	5	27.2	34	16	15	7	25
*Ward, Bryan	2	9	6.93	15	0	75.1	102	62	58	30	48
*Whisenant, Matt	2	1	7.20	16	0	15.0	16	12	12	12	19

Columbus Clippers (Yankees) AAA

BATTING	AVG	AB	R	H	2B	3B	HR	RBI	BB	SO	SB
Barker, Tim, 2B	.279	208	36	58	10	2	5	30	32	41	14
Bellinger, Clay, 3B	.274	416	55	114	31	3	12	59	34	74	10
Brown, Ron, OF	.182	33	4	6	0	1	0	1	2	3	1
Buchanan, Brian, OF	.279	61	8	17	1	0	4	7	4	11	2
Bush, Homer, 2B	.247	275	36	68	10	3	2	26	25	56	12
*Carpenter, Bubba, OF	.280	271	47	76	12	4	6	39	48	46	4
*Cruz, Ivan, 1B	.300	417	69	125	35	1	24	95	65	78	4
*Delvecchio, Nick, DH	.179	95	16	17	1	1	4	10	17	39	1
Figga, Mike, C	.244	390	48	95	14	4	12	54	18	104	3
*Fox, Andy, 3B	.274	318	66	87	11	4	6	33	54	64	28
Howard, Matt, SS	.312	478	90	149	28	7	6	67	54	33	22
Incaviglia, Pete, OF	.308	13	1	4	1	0	0	2	0	4	0
#Jimenez, D'Angelo, SS	.143	7	1	1	0	0	0	1	0	1	0
Kelly, Pat, 2B	.341	44	8	15	4	0	2	6	4	6	1
*Ledee, Ricky, OF	.306	170	38	52	12	1	10	39	21	49	4
#Long, R.D., 3B	.184	49	6	9	2	0	2	6	2	18	2
Lowell, Mike, 3B	.276	210	36	58	13	1	15	45	23	34	2
*Luke, Matt, OF	.228	337	42	77	19	3	8	45	29	64	0
*Pose, Scott, OF	.308	227	50	70	10	7	2	32	32	29	13
#Raines, Tim, OF	.154	13	1	2	0	0	0	0	3	2	0
*Ronan, Marc, C	.276	156	16	43	12	0	1	19	27	24	1
Russo, Paul, DH	.136	22	3	3	0	0	2	4	5	6	0
Spencer, Shane, OF	.241	452	78	109	34	4	30	86	71	105	0
*Strawberry, Darryl, DH	.289	38	8	11	3	0	6	19	8	10	0
Troilo, Jason, C	.136	22	1	3	2	0	0	1	4	9	0
Wilson, Tom, C	.000	3	0	0	0	0	0	0	1	0	0

PITCHING	W	L	ERA	G	SV	IP	H	R	ER	BB	SO
Alberro, Jose	0	1	3.38	1	0	8.0	5	4	3	1	6
Arocha, Rene	1	0	1.86	4	0	9.2	7	2	2	2	10
Banks, Willie	14	5	4.27	33	3	154.0	164	87	73	45	130
Bowen, Ryan	0	1	9.00	2	0	10.0	15	10	10	5	7
Buddie, Mike	6	6	2.64	53	2	75.0	85	24	22	25	67
Converse, Jim	0	2	3.32	10	1	19.0	22	8	7	11	13
Edenfield, Ken	1	0	6.92	9	0	13.0	23	19	10	8	11
Eiland, Dave	4	2	6.64	13	0	62.1	80	47	46	14	43
Gardiner, Mike	5	4	3.92	14	0	85.0	83	40	37	24	65
Gooden, Dwight	1	1	3.75	2	0	12.0	7	5	5	4	10
Irabu, Hideki	2	0	1.67	4	0	27.0	19	7	5	5	28
Jerzembeck, Mike	7	5	3.59	20	0	130.1	125	55	52	37	118
Lankford, Frank	7	4	2.69	15	0	93.2	84	33	28	22	40
Lomon, Kevin	1	1	6.28	3	0	14.1	21	12	10	7	14
Mecir, Jim	1	1	1.00	24	11	27.0	14	4	3	6	34
Mendoza, Ramiro	0	0	5.68	1	0	6.1	7	6	4	1	4
Pavlas, Dave	1	3	4.62	26	12	25.1	33	14	13	4	34

PITCHING	W	L	ERA	G	SV	IP	H	R	ER	BB	SO
*Polley, Dale	2	2	3.75	62	2	48.0	47	20	20	20	49
Reyes, Carlos	0	0	18.00	1	0	2.0	5	4	4	0	2
Ricken, Ray	11	7	5.54	26	0	152.2	172	104	94	81	99
Rios, Dan	7	4	3.08	58	3	84.2	73	37	29	31	53
Rose, Scott	2	2	3.70	26	11	24.1	24	11	10	6	13
*Rumer, Tim	4	7	6.16	17	0	68.2	79	54	47	41	46
*Urso, Sal	0	3	4.73	24	0	45.2	59	29	24	19	44
Weathers, David	2	2	3.19	5	0	36.2	35	18	13	7	35

Norfolk Tides (Mets) AAA

BATTING	AVG	AB	R	H	2B	3B	HR	RBI	BB	SO	SB
Agbayani, Benny, OF	.310	468	90	145	24	2	11	51	67	106	29
Azuaje, Jesus, 2B	.306	49	11	15	3	0	1	6	7	8	1
*Bieser, Steve, OF	.164	122	6	20	5	0	0	4	9	20	4
Castillo, Alberto, C	.217	83	4	18	1	0	1	8	17	16	1
Chamberlain, Wes, OF	.274	336	33	92	16	2	7	50	24	58	7
#Diaz, Alex, OF	.077	26	0	2	1	0	0	1	2	3	0
Espinosa, Ramon, OF	.338	77	7	26	3	1	0	8	2	10	2
*Franco, Matt, OF	.269	26	5	7	2	0	0	0	2	2	0
*Geisler, Phil, OF	.256	336	28	86	24	0	9	57	24	90	2
Gilbert, Shawn, SS	.264	288	53	76	13	1	8	33	43	64	16
Greene, Charlie, C	.206	238	27	49	7	0	8	28	9	54	1
#Hardtke, Jason, 2B	.276	388	46	107	23	3	11	45	40	54	3
Jaime, Angel, OF	.192	26	3	5	1	0	0	5	0	7	0
Lopez, Jose, 3B	.333	6	1	2	0	0	0	0	0	2	0
#Lopez, Luis, SS	.330	203	32	67	12	1	4	19	9	29	2
*Martin, Jim, OF	.250	104	10	26	4	2	3	18	8	44	5
McClain, Scott, 3B	.280	429	71	120	29	2	21	64	64	93	1
*Mendoza, Carlos, OF	.143	35	3	5	0	1	0	0	3	4	1
Moore, Mike, OF	.241	83	10	20	4	0	2	6	9	33	1
Morgan, Kevin, SS	.273	256	34	70	11	1	2	20	27	26	6
*Petagine, Roberto, 1B	.317	441	90	140	32	1	31	100	85	92	0
Pratt, Todd, C	.301	206	42	62	8	3	9	34	26	48	1
Pye, Eddie, 2B	.083	12	3	1	0	0	0	0	4	2	0
Saunders, Chris, 3B	.249	173	24	43	9	0	0	24	37	37	2
*Seefried, Tate, 1B	.229	96	11	22	6	1	3	13	13	31	2

PITCHING	W	L	ERA	G	SV	IP	H	R	ER	BB	SO
Acevedo, Juan	6	6	3.86	18	0	116.2	111	55	50	34	99
*Bohanon, Brian	9	3	2.63	15	0	96.0	88	37	28	32	84
*Crawford, Joe	8	2	3.52	16	0	99.2	109	45	39	31	72
Dougherty, Jim	10	1	1.45	49	4	62.0	45	11	10	43	59
Edmondson, Brian	4	3	2.90	31	1	68.1	62	27	22	37	65
Harnisch, Pete	1	1	5.40	3	0	16.2	16	12	10	10	16
Isringhausen, Jason	0	2	4.05	3	0	20.0	20	10	9	8	17
*Jordan, Ricardo	0	1	2.79	34	1	29.0	20	11	9	24	34
*Kashiwada, Takashi	0	1	4.73	14	0	13.1	11	9	7	5	12
Lidle, Cory	4	2	3.64	7	0	42.0	46	20	17	10	34
Manuel, Barry	2	5	4.87	19	0	61.0	60	36	33	21	52
Myers, Jimmy	2	4	1.83	45	2	69.0	57	23	14	33	31
*Perez, Yorkis	1	0	3.48	17	3	20.2	22	9	8	7	24
*Pulsipher, Bill	0	5	7.81	8	0	27.2	23	29	24	38	18
*Roberts, Chris	0	4	2.89	7	0	37.1	38	17	12	17	21
*Sauerbeck, Scott	1	0	3.60	1	0	5.0	3	2	2	4	4
Seanez, Rudy	1	0	4.05	9	0	13.1	12	8	6	11	17
Shepherd, Keith	8	8	4.37	19	0	107.0	119	61	52	55	78
Tam, Jeff	7	5	4.67	40	6	111.2	137	72	58	14	67
Wallace, Derek	0	1	9.00	1	0	1.0	2	2	1	1	0
Welch, Mike	2	2	3.66	46	20	51.2	53	21	21	16	35
Withem, Shannon	9	10	4.34	29	0	155.2	167	85	75	48	109
*Yarnall, Ed	0	1	14.40	1	0	5.0	11	8	8	7	2

Ottawa Lynx (Expos) AAA

BATTING	AVG	AB	R	H	2B	3B	HR	RBI	BB	SO	SB
Andrews, Shane, 3B	.250	12	3	3	0	0	1	1	1	0	0
#Blum, Geoffrey, 2B	.248	407	59	101	21	2	3	35	52	73	14
Cabrera, Jolbert, 3B	.283	191	28	54	10	4	0	12	11	31	15
Cabrera, Orlando, SS	.262	122	17	32	5	2	2	14	7	16	8
Chavez, Raul, C	.245	310	31	76	17	0	4	46	18	42	1
*Fullmer, Brad, 1B	.297	91	13	27	7	0	3	17	3	10	1
Lott, Billy, OF	.222	108	12	24	5	0	2	18	8	22	1
#Lovullo, Torey, 2B	.141	64	6	9	3	0	0	6	6	13	0
*Lukachyk, Rob, OF	.248	286	39	71	16	1	12	39	32	69	18
*McGuire, Ryan, 1B	.299	184	37	55	11	1	3	15	36	29	5
Meulens, Hensley, 3B	.274	423	81	116	20	2	24	75	62	119	19
Morales, Francisco, C	.111	18	2	2	0	1	1	4	1	6	0

Class A WRAP-UPS

Carolina League

In a series that saw no game decided by more than two runs, the Lynchburg (Va.) Hillcats upset the favored Kinston Indians, three games to one, to take home the Mills Cup, awarded annually to the league champion. The Hillcats won the second-half championship in the league's Northern Division and went on to sweep first-half champ Frederick in a best-of-three series to advance. Kinston, a Cleveland affiliate, had won both halves of the Southern Division with an 87-53 record, earning a bye to the finals. Lynchburg was paced all season by league MVP Aramis Ramirez, a slugging third baseman.

League leaders: BA: **Rick Short**, Frederick, .319. HR: **Danny Peoples**, Kinston, 34. RBI: **Aramis Ramirez**, Lynchburg, 114. SB: **Ramon Gomez**, Winston-Salem, 53. ERA: **Cliff Politte**, Prince William, 2.24. W: **Bronson Arroyo**, Lynchburg, **Clint Weibl**, Prince William, 12. K: **Carlos Chantres**, Winston-Salem, 158. SV: **Armando Almanza**, Prince William, 36.

CAROLINA LEAGUE (A)
Northern Division

	W	L	Pct.	GB
Lynchburg	82	58	.586	—
Prince William	69	70	.496	12.5
Frederick	69	71	.493	13
Wilmington	62	78	.443	20

Southern Division

	W	L	Pct.	GB
Kinston	87	53	.621	—
Salem	63	75	.457	23
Durham	63	76	.453	23.5
Win.-Salem	63	77	.450	24

Semifinals: Lynchburg 2, Frederick 0.
Finals: Lynchburg 3, Kinston 1.

Switch-hitter
* Left-handed

Class A WRAP-UPS

Florida State League

No matter what the expansion Tampa Bay Devil Rays do in their first major league seasons, they'll have a long way to go to top the full-season debut of their top Class A farm club. The St. Petersburg Devil Rays edged out a Los Angeles farm club, the Vero Beach Dodgers, three games to two to win the league championship. It was the Tampa Bay organization's first championship, and the third title for manager Bill Evers, who won Texas League championships with Shreveport in 1990 and '91. Though Vero fell in the finals, the club did boast the league MVP in third baseman Adrian Beltre, a five-tool prospect.

League leaders: BA: Ramon Valette, Daytona, .332. HR: Adrian Beltre, Vero Beach, 26. RBI: Beltre, 104. SB: Vick Brown, Tampa, 55. ERA: Courtney Duncan, Daytona, 1.63. W: Corey Lee, Charlotte, 15. K: Rob Burger, Clearwater, 154. SV: John Daniels, St. Petersburg, 29.

FLORIDA STATE LEAGUE (A)

Eastern Division

	W	L	Pct.	GB
Kissimmee	71	66	.518	—
W. Palm Beach	69	66	.511	1
Vero Beach	70	67	.511	1
Daytona	65	73	.471	6.5
Brevard Co.	62	76	.449	9.5
St. Lucie	54	81	.400	16

Western Division

	W	L	Pct.	GB
St. Petersburg	81	56	.591	—
Lakeland	81	57	.587	.5
Fort Myers	81	58	.583	1
Tampa	70	66	.515	10.5
Clearwater	70	68	.507	11.5
Charlotte	68	71	.489	14
Sarasota	63	75	.457	18.5
Dunedin	57	82	.410	25

Semifinals: Vero Beach 2, Kissimmee 1; St. Petersburg 2, Lakeland 0.
Finals: St. Petersburg 3, Vero Beach 2.

Switch-hitter
* Left-handed

356

BATTING	AVG	AB	R	H	2B	3B	HR	RBI	BB	SO	SB
Obando, Sherman, OF	.238	21	5	5	0	0	3	8	5	7	0
Pegues, Steve, OF	.300	190	19	57	12	1	3	28	9	29	4
Rossy, Rico, SS	.251	375	56	94	23	0	10	52	37	64	5
*Saffer, Jon, OF	.267	483	81	129	20	9	15	60	76	74	13
*Samuels, Scott, OF	.345	55	6	19	3	0	1	7	7	12	2
Schu, Rick, 3B	.190	21	3	4	1	0	1	3	0	4	0
Seitzer, Brad, 1B	.250	56	4	14	1	0	1	7	8	11	1
Siddall, Joe, C	.274	164	18	45	12	1	1	16	21	42	1
#Stovall, Darond, OF	.243	342	40	83	23	2	4	48	31	114	10
#Strange, Doug, 3B	.429	7	3	3	1	0	0	0	1	1	0
Thurman, Gary, OF	.228	184	23	42	8	1	0	17	29	44	12
Valrie, Kerry, OF	.221	113	12	25	6	3	3	20	4	22	3
#Vidro, Jose, 3B	.323	279	40	90	17	0	13	47	22	40	2

PITCHING	W	L	ERA	G	SV	IP	H	R	ER	BB	SO
Alvarez, Tavo	4	8	4.82	37	0	106.1	123	61	57	42	86
Aucoin, Derek	0	1	22.74	8	0	6.1	5	16	16	21	5
*Baxter, Bob	0	0	12.79	4	0	6.1	11	10	9	3	4
Bennett, Shayne	1	2	1.57	25	14	34.1	23	8	6	21	29
Bullinger, Kirk	3	4	1.71	22	5	31.2	17	7	6	10	15
Bunch, Mel	4	4	6.35	16	0	78.0	102	63	55	45	58
*DeHart, Rick	0	4	4.00	43	2	63.0	60	33	28	22	57
Dedrick, Jim	0	1	7.07	8	0	14.0	15	12	11	13	14
*Dixon, Tim	1	1	9.64	5	0	9.1	12	10	10	5	8
Falteisek, Steve	6	9	3.96	22	0	125.0	135	67	55	54	56
Fleetham, Ben	1	2	2.00	9	1	9.0	2	3	2	10	14
Henderson, Rod	5	9	4.95	26	1	123.2	136	72	68	49	103
Heredia, Gil	0	4	4.70	28	0	44.0	50	29	23	9	41
Paniagua, Jose	8	10	4.64	22	0	137.2	164	79	71	44	87
*Pulido, Carlos	5	2	5.42	44	0	76.1	84	47	46	25	44
Ricci, Chuck	2	2	4.67	22	0	27.0	22	16	14	25	27
Schmidt, Curt	0	3	6.61	31	5	31.1	44	24	23	22	18
Stull, Everett	8	10	5.82	27	0	159.1	166	110	103	86	130
Thurman, Mike	1	3	5.49	4	0	19.2	17	13	12	9	15
Torres, Salomon	0	0	5.40	2	0	5.0	7	5	3	2	2
*Urbani, Thomas	3	1	2.61	30	0	41.1	37	13	12	12	25
*Weber, Neil	2	5	7.94	9	0	39.2	46	46	35	40	27

Pawtucket Red Sox (Red Sox) AAA

BATTING	AVG	AB	R	H	2B	3B	HR	RBI	BB	SO	SB
*Abad, Andy, OF	.273	227	28	62	7	0	9	32	36	47	3
Allison, Chris, 2B	.280	25	2	7	2	0	0	1	1	0	0
Benjamin, Mike, SS	.248	105	12	26	4	1	4	12	8	20	4
Bennett, Gary, C	.214	224	16	48	7	1	4	22	18	39	1
Borrero, Richie, C	.255	51	4	13	1	0	2	6	1	17	0
Bryant, Pat, OF	.294	34	3	10	2	1	0	4	1	11	2
*Carey, Todd, 1B	.216	380	35	82	16	0	12	58	34	114	1
Coleman, Michael, OF	.319	113	27	36	9	2	7	19	12	27	4
Correia, Rod, SS	.195	128	17	25	4	1	1	15	5	14	3
*Dodson, Bo, 1B	.295	61	8	18	6	0	0	6	5	11	0
Hyzdu, Adam, OF	.276	413	77	114	21	1	23	84	72	113	10
Malave, Jose, OF	.297	427	87	127	24	2	17	70	55	78	12
McKeel, Walt, C	.253	237	34	60	15	0	6	30	34	39	0
Merloni, Lou, 2B	.297	165	24	49	10	0	5	24	15	20	0
*Nixon, Trot, OF	.244	475	80	116	18	3	20	61	63	86	11
Pozo, Arquimedez, 3B	.284	377	61	107	18	1	22	70	37	55	4
*Pride, Curtis, OF	.000	3	0	0	0	0	0	0	0	2	0
Rodriguez, Tony, SS	.249	285	27	71	12	0	2	19	9	47	5
Sadler, Donnie, 2B	.212	481	74	102	18	2	11	36	57	121	20
#Tavarez, Jesus, OF	.266	229	43	61	6	3	3	20	27	31	22
#Varitek, Jason, C	.197	66	6	13	5	0	1	5	8	12	0
*Williams, Juan, OF	.198	81	11	16	4	0	3	10	20	35	2
Woods, Tyrone, DH	.352	105	16	37	3	1	9	28	11	35	1

PITCHING	W	L	ERA	G	SV	IP	H	R	ER	BB	SO
*Avery, Steve	1	0	0.00	1	0	5.0	1	0	0	3	1
Blais, Mike	1	4	8.31	10	0	13.0	10	15	12	10	10
Borland, Toby	2	0	3.99	28	2	47.1	50	22	21	25	46
Brandenburg, Mark	2	1	2.41	9	0	18.2	13	6	5	3	23
Checo, Robinson	4	2	3.42	9	0	55.1	41	22	21	16	56
Corsi, Jim	0	0	0.00	2	1	2.1	2	0	0	1	3
*Eshelman, Vaughn	3	4	4.86	14	1	66.2	63	38	36	22	57
Farrell, Jim	0	0	0.00	1	0	5.0	4	0	0	2	6
Fernandez, Jared	0	3	5.79	11	0	60.2	76	45	39	28	33
Garces, Rich	2	1	1.45	26	5	31.0	24	5	5	13	42
*Grundt, Ken	4	2	5.32	49	3	47.1	59	30	28	22	28
Hudson, Joe	2	1	2.25	29	7	32.0	25	22	8	23	14

1998 BASEBALL WEEKLY ALMANAC

PITCHING	W	L	ERA	G	SV	IP	H	R	ER	BB	SO
Lacy, Kerry	5	3	4.73	23	8	32.1	36	18	17	11	21
Lowe, Derek	4	0	2.37	6	0	30.1	23	8	8	11	21
*Mahay, Ron	1	0	0.00	2	0	4.2	3	0	0	1	6
Mahomes, Pat	5	1	2.84	18	7	31.2	22	11	10	17	40
Meacham, Rusty	3	3	4.78	28	1	43.1	54	23	23	15	42
*Mimbs, Mark	3	8	5.06	15	0	83.2	97	58	47	35	81
*Orellano, Rafael	3	5	7.14	16	0	69.1	65	58	55	55	46
Pavano, Carl	11	6	3.12	23	0	161.2	148	62	56	34	147
Peterson, Dean	0	1	3.00	2	0	3.0	2	1	1	1	2
Rose, Brian	17	5	3.02	27	0	190.2	188	74	64	46	116
Ruffin, Johnny	0	1	4.50	6	0	14.0	5	7	7	16	16
Saberhagen, Bret	0	1	3.27	2	0	11.0	11	4	4	1	9
Suppan, Jeff	5	1	3.71	9	0	60.2	51	26	25	15	40
Valdez, Carlos	0	4	4.69	35	1	78.2	73	49	41	46	64
Walker, Pete	0	0	5.40	7	0	11.2	14	8	7	7	8

Richmond Braves (Braves) AAA

BATTING	AVG	AB	R	H	2B	3B	HR	RBI	BB	SO	SB
Ayrault, Joe, C	.286	56	11	16	2	0	3	5	4	17	0
Bautista, Danny, OF	.282	170	28	48	10	3	2	28	19	30	1
*Giovanola, Ed, 3B	.291	395	65	115	23	5	2	46	64	56	2
*Gregg, Tommy, OF	.332	385	52	128	36	1	9	54	46	64	3
Helms, Wes, 3B	.191	110	11	21	4	0	3	15	10	34	1
Hollins, Damon, OF	.265	498	73	132	31	3	20	63	45	84	7
Lewis, T.R., OF	.295	363	65	107	20	5	7	58	37	71	8
*Malloy, Marty, 2B	.285	414	66	118	19	5	2	25	41	61	17
#Martinez, Pablo, 2B	.257	296	32	76	14	1	4	20	26	77	9
Mordecai, Mike, 2B	.311	122	23	38	10	0	3	15	9	17	0
Rodarte, Raul, OF	.242	95	13	23	4	0	0	10	10	22	2
*Simon, Randall, 1B	.308	519	62	160	45	1	14	102	17	76	1
Smith, Bobby, SS	.246	357	47	88	10	2	12	47	44	109	6
Spehr, Tim, C	.192	120	13	23	5	0	3	14	12	37	0
Tejero, Fausto, C	.231	225	31	52	11	0	6	28	23	41	0
Toth, Dave, C	.196	46	6	9	3	0	0	5	4	8	0
*Tyler, Brad, OF	.264	383	69	101	15	10	18	77	55	110	13
Valle, Dave, C	.211	38	2	8	0	0	0	2	1	7	0

PITCHING	W	L	ERA	G	SV	IP	H	R	ER	BB	SO
Borowski, Joe	1	2	3.58	21	2	37.2	32	16	15	19	34
Brock, Chris	10	6	3.34	20	0	118.2	97	50	44	51	83
Brow, Scott	5	9	4.45	61	18	83.0	89	48	41	35	62
Byrd, Paul	2	1	3.18	3	0	17.0	14	6	6	1	14
Carlyle, Ken	4	1	2.84	16	0	69.2	69	26	22	19	48
Cather, Mike	0	0	1.73	13	3	26.0	17	6	5	9	22
Clontz, Brad	0	0	0.00	16	6	22.0	10	1	0	2	24
Dyer, Mike	2	1	4.87	29	1	40.2	42	25	22	24	23
Fox, Chad	1	0	3.70	13	0	24.1	24	10	10	14	25
Harrison, Tommy	9	7	4.20	22	0	122.0	118	64	57	40	92
*Hartgraves, Dean	7	4	4.48	50	3	72.1	76	38	36	39	56
Hostetler, Mike	1	2	9.43	5	0	21.0	33	23	22	9	14
Ligtenberg, Kerry	0	3	4.32	14	1	25.0	21	13	12	2	35
Luebbers, Larry	3	14	5.38	27	0	144.0	180	101	86	44	91
Millwood, Kevin	7	0	1.93	9	0	60.2	38	13	13	16	46
Rogers, Bryan	1	1	5.17	21	0	38.1	45	26	22	16	25
*Rogers, Kevin	0	2	7.36	10	0	11.0	15	11	9	5	9
Schutz, Carl	4	6	5.33	27	0	79.1	83	56	47	51	66
*Thobe, Tom	5	2	4.14	19	0	71.2	70	37	33	22	36

Rochester Red Wings (Orioles) AAA

BATTING	AVG	AB	R	H	2B	3B	HR	RBI	BB	SO	SB
Berry, Mike, 3B	.299	177	23	53	11	3	1	19	13	31	1
*Bullett, Scott, OF	.250	512	73	128	24	8	9	58	45	112	19
#Carney, Bartt, OF	.000	6	1	0	0	0	0	0	3	2	0
Clyburn, Danny, OF	.300	520	91	156	33	5	20	76	53	107	14
Davis, Tommy, 1B	.304	438	74	133	22	2	15	62	43	90	6
Forbes, P.J., 2B	.272	434	67	118	22	2	8	54	35	42	15
Foster, Jim, DH	.556	9	4	5	2	0	0	4	3	0	0
#Frazier, Lou, OF	.248	302	40	75	12	4	2	39	36	68	24
Gresham, Kris, C	.107	28	1	3	1	0	0	0	2	8	0
Gruber, Kelly, 2B	.250	144	26	36	9	2	2	23	15	14	1
Johns, Keith, SS	.000	1	0	0	0	0	0	0	0	0	0
Laker, Tim, DH	.259	290	45	75	11	1	11	37	34	49	1
Lawrence, Chip, SS	.233	43	9	10	0	1	0	7	3	8	1
Ledesma, Aaron, SS	.325	326	40	106	26	1	3	43	35	48	12
Luzinski, Ryan, C	.208	125	12	26	7	1	2	16	19	49	0
Martinez, Eddy, SS	.074	27	0	2	1	0	0	3	1	8	0

Class A WRAP-UPS
Midwest League

The biggest playoff surprise came in the first round, when Fort Wayne knocked off West Michigan in two games. The Lansing Lugnuts won the championship in five games over the Kane County Cougars by winning the final game 9-7. Though West Michigan did not win the title, it did have the loop's MVP in first baseman Robert Fick, whose early-season 32-game hitting streak tied him for tops in the minors, as did his 50 doubles. He was edged out for the batting title by Lansing's Tony Miranda.

League leaders: BA: **Tony Miranda**, Lansing, .341. HR: **Joe Freitas**, Peoria, 33. RBI: **Darron Ingram**, Burlington, 97. SB: **Rodney Lindsey**, Clinton, 70. ERA: **Craig Quintal**, West Michigan, 1.96. W: **Clayton Bruner**, West Michigan, **David Borkowski**, West Michigan, 15. K: **Ramon Ortiz**, Cedar Rapids, 225. SV: **Francisco Cordero**, West Michigan, 35.

MIDWEST LEAGUE (A)
Eastern Division

	W	L	Pct.	GB
West Michigan	92	39	.702	—
Michigan	70	67	.511	25
Lansing	69	68	.504	26
Fort Wayne	68	67	.504	26
South Bend	54	83	.394	41

Central Division

	W	L	Pct.	GB
Wisconsin	76	63	.547	—
Kane County	70	68	.507	5.5
Peoria	70	69	.504	6
Rockford	66	66	.500	6.5
Beloit	60	73	.451	13

Western Division

	W	L	Pct.	GB
Burlington	72	68	.514	—
Clinton	65	71	.478	5
Cedar Rapids	62	76	.449	9
Quad City	59	75	.440	10

Quarterfinals: Cedar Rapids 2, Burlington 0; Kane County 2, Wisconsin 0; Fort Wayne 2, West Michigan 0; Lansing 2, Michigan 1. *Semifinals:* Kane County 2, Cedar Rapids 0; Lansing 2, Fort Wayne 0. *Finals:* Lansing 3, Kane County 2.

Class A
WRAP-UPS

South Atlantic League

After two days of rain delays, the Delmarva Shorebirds swept the Greensboro Bats to win the South Atlantic title in two games. The club was paced by third baseman Ryan Minor and first baseman Calvin Pickering, who hit four homers in the playoffs. League MVP honors, however, went to batting champion Luis Lopez of the Hagerstown Suns.

League leaders: BA: Luis Lopez, Hagerstown, .358. HR: Steve Hacker, Macon, 33. RBI: Hacker, 119. SB: Alex Sanchez, Charleston (SC), 92. ERA: Maximo Heredia, Delmarva, 2.13. W: Jake Westbrook, Asheville, Buddy Carlyle, Charleston (WV), Joe Farley, Hickory, Rob Bell, Macon, Jason Marquis, Macon, 14. K: Bruce Chen, Macon, 182. SV: Ryan Kohlmeier, Delmarva, 24.

SOUTH ATLANTIC LEAGUE (A)
Northern Division

	W	L	Pct.	GB
Charleston (WV)	76	62	.551	—
Delmarva	77	65	.542	1
Cape Fear	66	74	.471	11
Hagerstown	65	73	.471	11

Central Division

	W	L	Pct.	GB
Columbia	77	63	.550	—
Hickory	76	64	.543	1
Greensboro	75	65	.536	2
Piedmont	70	72	.493	8
Asheville	62	76	.449	14
Charleston (SC)	60	82	.423	18

Southern Division

	W	L	Pct.	GB
Macon	80	60	.571	—
Augusta	71	71	.500	10
Savannah	63	77	.450	17
Columbus	62	76	.449	17

Quarterfinals: Greensboro 2, Columbia 0; Delmarva 2, Hickory 0; Macon 2, Augusta 1; Charleston (WV) 2, Cape Fear 0.
Semifinals: Delmarva 2, Charleston (WV) 1; Greensboro 2, Macon 0.
Finals: Delmarva 2, Greensboro 0.

BATTING	AVG	AB	R	H	2B	3B	HR	RBI	BB	SO	SB
Matos, Francisco, 2B	.324	389	51	126	17	4	4	51	9	42	8
#Ojeda, Augie, SS	.234	47	5	11	3	1	0	6	8	4	1
Otanez, Willis, 3B	.208	168	20	35	9	0	5	25	15	35	0
*Tarasco, Tony, OF	.200	35	4	7	0	0	2	6	7	7	0
*Tolentino, Jose, 1B	.211	57	6	12	2	0	1	9	14	11	0
Waszgis, B.J., C	.260	315	61	82	15	1	13	48	56	78	1
*Wawruck, Jim, OF	.271	339	47	92	20	3	5	35	34	64	12

PITCHING	W	L	ERA	G	SV	IP	H	R	ER	BB	SO
Bennett, Chris	4	2	3.54	25	1	40.2	40	17	16	7	28
Carrara, Giovanni	4	2	4.44	8	0	46.2	45	23	23	16	48
Coppinger, Rocky	1	2	5.52	3	0	14.2	16	10	9	11	9
Corbin, Archie	4	3	4.00	43	5	69.2	47	32	31	62	66
Greer, Ken	0	2	5.79	15	1	23.1	30	15	15	5	14
Haynes, Jimmy	5	4	3.44	16	0	102.0	89	49	39	55	113
*Johns, Doug	3	1	3.74	9	0	55.1	57	25	23	13	42
*Krivda, Rick	14	2	3.39	22	0	146.0	122	61	55	34	128
Montgomery, Steve	0	2	12.15	2	0	6.2	15	12	9	3	2
Ramirez, Hector	8	7	4.91	39	3	102.2	114	65	56	38	50
Rodriguez, Nerio	11	10	3.90	27	0	168.1	124	82	73	62	160
Sackinsky, Brian	1	0	5.11	2	0	12.1	12	7	7	3	6
Schrenk, Steve	4	7	4.66	25	0	125.2	127	73	65	36	99
*Shouse, Brian	6	2	2.27	54	9	71.1	48	21	18	21	81
Steph, Rod	3	3	4.25	41	14	48.2	49	24	23	12	51
Swift, Billy	0	1	4.91	2	0	3.2	2	2	2	3	2
Williams, Brian	4	3	3.89	22	8	69.1	68	33	30	23	78
Yan, Esteban	11	5	3.10	34	2	119.0	107	54	41	37	131

Scranton/WB Red Barons (Phillies) AAA

BATTING	AVG	AB	R	H	2B	3B	HR	RBI	BB	SO	SB
#Amador, Manuel, 3B	.343	70	12	24	5	0	1	9	6	11	0
Angeli, Doug, 3B	.224	241	24	54	11	2	2	19	27	53	0
Barron, Tony, OF	.328	329	51	108	21	4	18	78	27	64	3
*Bowers, Brent, OF	.255	110	15	28	2	0	3	7	8	28	1
#Burton, Darren, OF	.249	253	34	63	16	3	8	39	19	40	3
*Butler, Rob, OF	.282	71	8	20	4	0	0	9	1	9	0
Doster, David, 2B	.315	410	70	129	32	2	16	79	30	60	5
Estalella, Bobby, C	.233	433	63	101	32	0	16	65	56	109	3
Flores, Jose, 2B	.250	204	32	51	14	1	1	18	28	51	3
#Fox, Eric, OF	.280	264	41	74	17	3	3	26	21	50	2
Hudler, Rex, DH	.333	9	0	3	0	0	0	0	0	0	0
Jordan, Kevin, 3B	.300	30	5	9	2	2	0	2	2	6	2
Magee, Wendell, OF	.245	294	39	72	20	1	10	39	30	56	4
*McMillon, Billy, OF	.284	296	52	84	26	1	12	47	44	75	10
Millan, Adan, C	.500	2	0	1	0	0	0	1	1	0	0
Northeimer, Jamie, C	.154	13	1	2	0	0	0	1	1	6	0
#Otero, Ricky, OF	.331	160	24	53	10	5	1	15	13	13	5
#Relaford, Desi, SS	.267	517	82	138	34	4	9	53	43	77	29
Robertson, Mike, 1B	.298	416	61	124	17	3	12	72	58	67	0
Sefcik, Kevin, 2B	.333	123	19	41	11	2	1	7	9	11	5
Wedge, Eric, C	.256	129	25	33	8	1	7	36	22	40	0
*Zuber, Jon, OF	.315	435	85	137	37	2	6	64	79	53	3

PITCHING	W	L	ERA	G	SV	IP	H	R	ER	BB	SO
*Beech, Matt	3	1	5.70	5	0	30.0	24	20	19	10	38
Blazier, Ron	0	3	3.68	11	1	14.2	17	9	6	3	10
*Brewer, Billy	2	1	3.00	11	1	9.0	10	7	3	5	9
Fiore, Tony	3	5	3.86	9	0	60.2	60	34	26	26	56
*Fortugno, Tim	0	1	6.62	19	3	17.2	21	13	13	8	15
Gomes, Wayne	3	1	2.37	26	7	38.0	31	11	10	24	36
Grace, Mike	5	6	4.56	12	0	75.0	84	43	38	27	55
Green, Tyler	4	8	6.10	12	0	72.1	80	54	49	29	40
Hawblitzel, Ryan	6	9	4.99	34	2	115.1	132	65	64	33	80
Heflin, Bronson	1	1	2.28	35	13	43.1	29	17	11	25	36
Holman, Craig	3	1	4.64	48	3	75.2	100	44	39	27	75
*Karp, Ryan	4	3	4.19	32	1	73.0	72	35	34	42	55
Loewer, Carlton	5	13	4.60	29	0	184.0	198	120	94	50	152
Maduro, Calvin	6	4	4.99	13	0	79.1	71	48	44	57	53
*Mimbs, Mike	4	2	5.98	11	0	43.2	52	33	29	20	41
Nye, Ryan	4	10	5.52	17	0	109.1	117	70	67	32	85
*Plantenberg, Erik	0	2	7.53	18	0	14.1	22	12	12	9	12
Ruffcorn, Scott	2	0	1.16	5	0	31.0	22	6	4	10	20
Ryan, Ken	4	0	4.50	3	1	4.0	5	2	2	3	3
Stephenson, Garrett	3	1	5.90	7	0	29.0	27	19	19	12	27
*Winston, Darrin	7	4	3.43	39	0	89.1	74	38	34	36	66

Syracuse Chiefs (Blue Jays) AAA

BATTING	AVG	AB	R	H	2B	3B	HR	RBI	BB	SO	SB
*Aldrete, Mike, 1B	.297	74	8	22	5	0	0	8	17	15	0
Aude, Rich, 1B	.283	350	48	99	23	2	15	59	26	88	3
Brito, Jorge, C	.233	30	3	7	3	0	2	4	3	10	1
*Butler, Rich, OF	.300	537	93	161	30	9	24	87	60	107	20
Cradle, Rickey, OF	.120	25	4	3	0	0	1	3	2	9	0
#Crespo, Felipe, OF	.259	290	53	75	12	0	12	26	46	38	7
DeLaCruz, Lorenzo, DH	.219	128	11	28	4	0	5	13	6	35	1
Evans, Tom, 3B	.263	376	60	99	17	1	15	65	53	104	1
*Giannelli, Ray, DH	.175	80	9	14	4	0	0	8	18	20	1
Henry, Santiago, SS	.241	116	15	28	5	1	2	16	2	21	5
Jones, Ryan, 1B	.138	123	8	17	5	1	3	16	15	28	0
Manto, Jeff, DH	.205	132	18	27	5	1	3	11	22	30	1
*Martinez, Sandy, C	.224	322	28	72	12	1	4	29	27	76	7
#Melhuse, Adam, C	.237	118	7	28	5	1	2	9	12	18	1
Mosquera, Julio, C	.229	35	5	8	1	0	0	1	2	5	0
Mummau, Rob, 2B	.255	333	47	85	17	2	8	40	35	60	2
#Patzke, Jeff, 2B	.285	316	38	90	25	2	2	29	51	66	0
#Perez, Tomas, SS	.224	303	32	68	13	0	1	20	37	67	3
Ramirez, Angel, OF	.174	23	4	4	1	0	0	0	0	7	0
#Roberts, Lonell, OF	.156	173	17	27	4	0	3	10	19	50	6
Rodriguez, Luis, C	.000	2	0	0	0	0	0	0	0	2	0
#Sierra, Ruben, OF	.219	32	5	7	2	0	1	5	2	6	0
#Soriano, Fred, SS	.114	44	3	5	1	1	0	4	1	7	2
Stewart, Shannon, OF	.346	208	41	72	13	1	5	24	36	26	9
Thompson, Ryan, OF	.288	330	37	95	23	1	16	58	21	59	4
*Whitmore, Darrell, OF	.256	195	23	50	15	0	4	21	24	54	7

PITCHING	W	L	ERA	G	SV	IP	H	R	ER	BB	SO
Almanzar, Carlos	5	1	1.41	32	3	51.0	30	9	8	8	47
Andujar, Luis	1	6	5.54	13	1	39.0	37	25	24	14	29
*Bogott, Kurt	1	3	7.89	16	0	21.2	23	20	19	15	16
Brandow, Derek	7	11	5.41	31	0	143.0	161	103	86	91	120
*Brown, Chad	0	3	6.34	22	0	38.1	41	32	27	26	26
Cain, Tim	3	5	5.68	30	2	52.1	60	35	33	26	27
Carpenter, Chris	4	9	4.50	19	0	120.0	113	64	60	53	97
Crabtree, Tim	0	0	9.82	3	1	3.2	7	4	4	1	3
Czajkowski, Jim	0	2	3.18	16	0	22.2	21	11	8	14	13
*Daal, Omar	3	1	1.51	7	0	41.2	28	8	7	11	38
Doman, Roger	1	2	7.59	8	0	10.2	11	9	9	6	8
*Flener, Huck	6	6	4.14	20	0	124.0	126	71	57	43	58
Freeman, Marvin	0	0	9.00	1	0	1.0	1	1	1	1	0
Halladay, Roy	7	10	4.58	22	0	125.2	132	74	64	53	64
Janzen, Marty	0	5	7.20	22	1	65.0	76	58	52	36	56
*Lukasiewicz, Mark	2	3	5.17	30	0	31.1	37	22	18	13	31
Person, Robert	1	0	0.00	1	0	7.0	4	1	0	2	5
Rhine, Kendall	0	0	9.00	1	0	2.0	2	2	2	3	0
Risley, Bill	1	2	8.22	11	0	15.1	19	15	14	10	20
Robinson, Ken	7	7	2.56	56	17	81.0	44	24	23	36	96
Romano, Michael	2	4	4.25	40	0	108.0	100	56	51	74	83
Sievert, Mark	0	0	3.38	1	0	5.1	5	3	2	2	5
Sinclair, Steve	0	0	6.00	6	0	9.0	11	6	6	3	9
Smith, Brian	7	11	5.37	31	0	137.1	169	89	82	51	73

Toledo Mud Hens (Tigers) AAA

BATTING	AVG	AB	R	H	2B	3B	HR	RBI	BB	SO	SB
Barker, Glen, OF	.191	47	9	9	1	0	1	3	5	15	6
#Bartee, Kimera, OF	.218	501	67	109	13	7	3	33	52	154	33
#Bream, Scott, 2B	.231	91	11	21	1	0	0	0	13	31	0
Casanova, Raul, C	.195	41	1	8	0	0	1	3	3	8	0
*Catalanotto, Frank, 2B	.300	500	75	150	32	3	16	68	47	80	12
Hajek, Dave, 3B	.217	253	27	55	14	2	4	32	21	18	0
Hall, Joe, OF	.251	271	35	68	18	2	6	30	22	48	2
*Hamelin, Bob, 1B	.242	91	14	22	7	0	6	24	27	24	0
Holbert, Ray, SS	.242	372	43	90	18	7	7	37	32	109	16
Hurst, Jimmy, OF	.271	377	51	102	11	3	18	58	47	115	14
*Hyers, Tim, 1B	.274	424	61	116	22	3	12	55	41	65	1
#Jensen, Marcus, C	.175	80	5	14	5	0	0	9	9	25	0
Johnson, Brian, C	.143	21	0	3	2	0	0	1	0	2	0
Komminsk, Brad, DH	.667	3	0	2	1	0	0	0	0	0	0
Makarewicz, Scott, C	.235	340	34	80	15	1	7	38	14	68	0
Miller, Orlando, SS	.267	30	3	8	1	0	1	5	2	5	2
#Mitchell, Tony, OF	.186	70	7	13	2	0	2	9	16	19	1
Nevin, Phil, 1B	.158	19	1	3	0	0	1	3	2	9	0
Rodriguez, Adam, C	.200	70	4	14	2	0	1	3	3	17	0

New York–Penn League (SS)

The two division champions with the best records in the league, Oneonta and Erie, were upset in the opening round, before Pittsfield edged wild-card entry Batavia two games to one in the finals. The winning run in Game 3 was driven in by pinch-hitter Kevin McCarthy in the bottom of the ninth. The title gave the parent Mets two short-season championships in just three "baby" clubs. MVP honors went to Erie shortstop Kevin Haverbusch, who edged out several promising young pitchers for the honor.

League leaders: BA: **Raul Franco**, Utica, .352. HR: **Andrew Dominique**, Batavia, **Alexander Steele**, Jamestown, 14. RBI: **Kevin Haverbusch**, Erie, **Derrick Lankford**, Erie, 55. SB: **Terrence Freeman**, Erie, 46. ERA: **Matt Blank**, Vermont, 1.69. W: **Kris Lambert**, Erie, 11. K: **Scott Comer**, Pittsfield, 98. SV: **Daniel Mota**, Oneonta, 17.

NEW YORK–PENN LEAGUE (SS-A)
McNamara Division

	W	L	Pct.	GB
Pittsfield	42	32	.568	—
Lowell	38	38	.500	5
New Jersey	35	39	.473	7
Hudson Valley	35	40	.467	7.5
Vermont	35	41	.461	8

Pinckney Division

	W	L	Pct.	GB
Oneonta	49	25	.662	—
Watertown	39	36	.520	10.5
Utica	36	38	.486	13
Williamsport	29	46	.387	20.5
Auburn	29	47	.382	21

Stedler Division

	W	L	Pct.	GB
Erie	50	26	.658	—
Batavia	47	27	.635	2
St. Catharines	35	40	.467	14.5
Jamestown	25	49	.338	24

Semifinals: Pittsfield 2, Erie 0; Batavia 2, Oneonta 0.
Finals: Pittsfield 2, Batavia 1.

Class A WRAP-UPS

Northwest League (SS)

When the Boise Hawks took a quick 2-0 lead in the best-of-five series over the Portland (Ore.) Rockies, it appeared that the Northwest League championship would be short and sweet. Short it wasn't. Sweet it was—if you're a Rockies fan. The Rockies made the most of their home-field advantage, winning the last three games to take the league title. Once the series moved to Portland, so did the momentum. The Rockies squeaked out a 2-1 victory in Game 3 and continued its fine pitching the next night with a 6-0 shutout from Josh Kalinowski. Portland scored all of its runs in the first three innings of the 4-2 clincher, as Michael Johns hit a home run and Efrain Alamo had two RBI.

League leaders: BA: Geoffrey Tomlinson, Spokane, .338. HR: Mike Marchiano, Everett, 15. RBI: Dermal Brown, Spokane, 73. SB: Mike Byas, Salem-Keizer, 51. ERA: Justin Miller, Portland, 2.14. W: Matt Wise, Boise, Mike Riley, Salem-Keizer, 9. K: Riley, 96. SV: Jesse Travis, Salem-Keizer, 16.

NORTHWEST LEAGUE (SS-A)

Northern Division

	W	L	Pct.	GB
Boise	51	25	.671	—
Spokane	45	31	.592	6
Everett	29	47	.382	22
Yakima	23	53	.303	28

Southern Division

	W	L	Pct.	GB
Portland	44	32	.579	—
S. Oregon	41	35	.539	3
Salem-Keizer	40	36	.526	4
Eugene	31	45	.408	13

Finals: Portland 3, Boise 2.

switch-hitter
* Left-handed

BATTING	AVG	AB	R	H	2B	3B	HR	RBI	BB	SO	SB
Rodriguez, Steve, 3B	.233	425	57	99	30	1	4	38	26	58	18
Smith, Ira, DH	.243	148	19	36	8	0	1	13	11	29	0
Trammell, Bubba, OF	.251	319	56	80	15	1	28	75	38	91	2
#Walbeck, Matt, C	.305	59	6	18	2	1	1	8	4	15	0

PITCHING	W	L	ERA	G	SV	IP	H	R	ER	BB	SO
*Barnes, Brian	7	10	6.71	32	0	115.1	143	100	86	57	86
Blair, Willie	0	0	0.00	1	0	7.0	1	1	0	2	4
Crow, Dean	3	0	7.85	18	2	18.1	26	16	16	10	10
*Cummings, John	2	1	2.76	19	0	16.1	13	6	5	6	7
*Dace, Derek	0	0	3.60	5	0	10.0	13	8	4	6	6
*Dishman, Glenn	7	6	3.87	21	1	114.0	112	53	49	32	77
Drews, Matt	0	2	6.60	3	0	15.0	14	11	11	14	7
Drumright, Mike	5	10	5.06	23	0	133.1	134	78	75	91	115
Fermin, Ramon	4	2	4.93	41	0	80.1	103	53	44	33	46
Gaillard, Eddie	1	4	4.25	55	28	53.0	52	27	25	24	54
Gallaher, Kevin	1	1	4.74	9	0	19.0	16	12	10	17	13
Goldsmith, Gary	0	0	4.50	1	0	2.0	2	1	1	0	1
Greene, Rick	6	8	2.83	57	1	70.0	49	29	22	32	51
Harriger, Denny	11	8	3.99	27	0	167.0	159	87	74	63	109
Hernandez, Fernando	6	5	4.11	55	4	76.2	71	44	35	51	98
Jarvis, Kevin	0	1	6.75	2	0	8.0	7	6	6	4	5
Keagle, Greg	11	7	3.81	23	0	151.1	136	68	64	61	140
Pugh, Tim	3	5	4.29	19	0	109.0	115	60	52	28	97
*Rosengren, John	1	3	3.99	54	2	56.1	44	29	25	49	53

Pacific Coast League

Albuquerque Dukes (Dodgers) AAA

BATTING	AVG	AB	R	H	2B	3B	HR	RBI	BB	SO	SB
*Anthony, Eric, OF	.343	105	18	36	6	1	7	27	11	28	2
Battle, Howard, 3B	.237	139	14	33	3	2	3	16	6	23	1
Blanco, Henry, C	.313	294	38	92	20	1	6	47	37	63	7
Castro, Juan, SS	.307	101	11	31	5	2	2	11	4	20	1
#Cedeno, Roger, OF	.354	113	21	40	4	4	2	9	22	16	5
Cromer, Tripp, SS	.321	140	25	45	8	6	5	24	14	34	4
*Demetral, Chris, 2B	.250	24	1	6	2	0	1	1	6	3	0
#Fonville, Chad, OF	.218	371	49	81	5	2	0	22	30	39	23
*Garcia, Karim, OF	.305	262	53	80	17	6	20	66	23	70	11
#Guerrero, Wilton, SS	.400	45	9	18	0	1	0	5	2	3	3
*Hale, Chip, 1B	.267	247	43	66	16	0	2	30	58	26	3
*Hollandsworth, T., OF	.429	56	13	24	4	3	1	14	4	4	2
Huckaby, Ken, C	.199	201	14	40	5	1	0	18	9	36	1
*Kirby, Wayne, OF	.335	269	57	90	16	5	10	43	26	33	18
Konerko, Paul, 3B	.323	483	97	156	31	1	37	127	64	61	2
*Marrero, Oreste, OF	.262	263	38	69	20	0	9	42	24	70	1
Maurer, Ron, SS	.275	349	61	96	21	4	8	50	39	59	3
#Murray, Eddie, 1B	.308	26	4	8	1	0	2	9	3	3	0
Parker, Rick, OF	.272	151	33	41	7	3	6	21	10	26	6
Pennyfeather, Wm., OF	.254	402	59	102	21	4	17	54	26	73	11
Riggs, Adam, 2B	.304	227	59	69	8	3	13	28	29	39	12
*Spearman, Vernon, OF	.217	92	13	20	3	1	0	8	14	11	5
Steed, Dave, C	.213	47	8	10	4	0	1	4	4	19	0
Williams, Eddie, DH	.366	279	73	102	17	0	29	76	37	45	0

PITCHING	W	L	ERA	G	SV	IP	H	R	ER	BB	SO
Ahearne, Pat	2	4	4.90	20	0	60.2	82	43	33	20	44
Anderson, Mike	0	0	10.80	6	1	10.0	18	12	12	1	9
Brown, Alvin	4	6	6.13	12	0	61.2	74	50	42	35	43
*Brunson, William	1	1	6.49	27	0	26.1	39	19	19	10	25
Dreifort, Darren	0	0	1.59	2	0	5.2	2	1	1	3	4
Dressendorfer, Kirk	0	2	4.50	7	0	30.0	43	18	15	10	14
*Elvira, Narciso	0	0	16.88	4	0	2.2	5	6	5	3	4
Garcia, Jose	3	3	5.12	33	0	45.2	57	27	26	14	44
Harkey, Mike	2	2	2.10	47	15	55.2	50	14	13	11	57
Herges, Matt	0	8	8.89	31	0	85.0	120	92	84	46	61
Hubbs, Dan	6	4	3.90	62	3	94.2	103	45	41	38	87
*Kubenka, Jeffrey	0	2	8.59	8	2	7.1	11	9	7	2	10
*Martinez, Jesus	7	1	6.21	26	0	84.0	112	64	58	52	80
Munoz, Bobby	0	5	6.71	35	0	53.2	73	43	40	26	33
Osuna, Antonio	1	1	1.93	13	6	14.0	9	3	3	4	26
*Pyc, Dave	12	12	5.33	31	1	152.0	181	104	90	50	106
*Rath, Gary	7	11	6.05	24	0	132.1	177	107	89	49	100
*Reyes, Dennis	6	3	5.65	10	0	57.1	70	40	36	33	45
*Roach, Petie	0	5	5.29	31	1	49.1	56	31	29	27	33
Treadwell, Jody	10	5	5.12	27	1	128.1	143	80	73	54	108
Weaver, Eric	0	3	6.42	21	0	68.2	101	53	49	38	54

Calgary Cannons (Pirates) AAA

BATTING	AVG	AB	R	H	2B	3B	HR	RBI	BB	SO	SB
Allensworth, J., OF	.400	20	5	8	3	1	0	1	2	4	1
Beasley, Tony, 2B	.273	220	36	60	7	5	1	28	25	23	11
*Bridges, Kary, 2B	.263	95	9	25	4	0	0	6	7	6	1
#Brown, Adrian, OF	.319	248	53	79	10	1	1	19	27	38	20
Chamberlain, Wes, OF	.317	60	7	19	4	0	2	9	0	14	1
Collier, Lou, SS	.330	397	65	131	31	5	1	48	37	47	12
*Cromer, Brandon, SS	.232	228	30	53	15	2	8	36	19	46	3
Edge, Tim, C	.235	187	23	44	13	2	3	22	13	50	0
Garcia, Freddy, 3B	.240	121	21	29	6	0	5	17	9	20	0
Hazlett, Steve, OF	.298	94	18	28	12	2	3	15	12	19	1
*Johnson, Mark, 1B	.339	115	28	39	11	1	6	16	22	28	4
Lott, Billy, OF	.314	239	45	75	18	0	15	55	35	56	6
Martinez, Manny, OF	.331	420	78	139	34	1	16	66	33	80	17
Marx, Tim, C	.250	300	42	75	18	2	3	40	23	42	9
Polcovich, Kevin, SS	.306	62	7	19	4	0	1	9	1	7	0
Randa, Joe, 3B	.364	11	4	4	1	0	1	4	3	4	0
*Sanford, Chance, 3B	.292	325	58	95	27	9	6	60	39	82	9
*Secrist, Reed, 3B	.264	121	19	32	7	3	5	18	14	32	0
Smith, Mark, OF	.372	137	37	51	14	1	14	42	21	15	2
*Staton, T.J., OF	.236	199	30	47	14	0	2	22	22	51	3
Thobe, Steve, 3B	.255	102	16	26	8	0	5	14	15	25	2
*Tolentino, Jose, 1B	.308	305	52	94	24	0	16	69	31	49	2
#Ward, Turner, OF	.340	209	44	71	18	3	9	44	24	26	7
Wright, Ron, 1B	.304	336	50	102	31	0	16	63	24	81	0

PITCHING	W	L	ERA	G	SV	IP	H	R	ER	BB	SO
*Anderson, Jimmy	7	6	5.68	21	0	103.0	124	78	65	64	71
*Beatty, Blaine	1	2	23.63	3	0	5.1	18	14	14	3	2
Briscoe, John	0	1	12.27	4	0	7.1	18	11	10	2	7
Carter, John	1	2	14.57	15	0	25.1	45	41	41	27	18
Crawford, Carlos	1	5	5.94	9	0	50.0	60	43	33	19	26
Ericks, John	0	0	12.86	6	0	7.0	14	11	10	1	10
*Gonzales, Frank	1	0	7.26	25	1	31.0	43	25	25	9	24
*Granger, Jeff	1	7	5.55	30	1	82.2	111	63	51	33	68
Greer, Ken	0	3	8.46	15	0	22.1	33	22	21	7	16
*Halperin, Mike	1	0	6.43	15	0	28.0	44	24	20	24	18
Johnson, Barry	5	2	4.13	34	1	56.2	55	30	26	23	51
*Lawrence, Sean	8	9	4.21	26	0	143.1	154	83	67	57	116
Morel, Ramon	6	7	5.75	27	0	101.2	131	71	65	42	72
*Peters, Chris	2	4	4.38	14	1	51.1	52	32	25	30	55
Pett, Jose	0	3	9.64	3	0	14.0	25	15	15	8	8
Schmidt, Curt	2	3	4.26	25	7	31.2	43	19	15	14	30
*Shaw, Curtis	0	3	5.23	21	0	31.0	31	26	18	18	23
Shepherd, Keith	0	1	7.64	10	0	17.2	23	16	15	14	16
Silva, Jose	5	1	3.41	17	0	66.0	74	27	25	22	54
Sodowsky, Clint	0	1	6.59	8	1	13.2	19	10	10	6	9
Taylor, Scott	5	4	2.59	42	4	76.1	69	29	22	19	53
Wainhouse, David	2	0	5.92	25	1	38.0	46	25	25	13	24
Wilson, Gary	6	3	5.87	21	0	84.1	115	59	55	22	54

Colo. Springs Sky Sox (Rockies) AAA

BATTING	AVG	AB	R	H	2B	3B	HR	RBI	BB	SO	SB
#Barry, Jeff, OF	.300	273	46	82	13	3	13	70	30	45	5
#Bates, Jason, SS	.237	135	21	32	6	1	3	18	13	36	1
*Boston, D.J., 1B	.333	6	1	2	0	0	0	0	0	3	0
Cholowsky, Dan, C	.333	84	17	28	6	0	5	19	15	21	1
*Counsell, Craig, 2B	.335	376	77	126	31	6	5	63	45	38	12
Echevarria, Angel, OF	.322	295	59	95	24	0	13	80	28	47	6
Gibson, Derrick, OF	.423	78	14	33	7	0	3	12	5	9	0
Gonzales, Rene, 2B	.283	339	50	96	21	1	3	42	43	49	2
Gubanich, Creighton, C	.310	277	40	86	19	0	15	57	19	79	1
#Hall, Billy, OF	.255	51	6	13	0	2	0	6	3	11	3
*Helton, Todd, 1B	.352	392	87	138	31	2	16	88	61	68	3
*Howitt, Dann, DH	.332	316	57	105	29	0	14	62	32	71	2
*Huson, Jeff, 3B	.350	20	3	7	3	0	1	5	2	2	0
Jones, Terry, OF	.270	363	70	98	14	4	1	25	25	49	36
Owens, Jayhawk, C	.260	289	57	75	17	0	10	34	55	98	4
#Perez, Neifi, SS	.363	303	68	110	24	3	8	46	17	27	8
Pulliam, Harvey, OF	.401	137	44	55	10	2	12	43	21	19	1
Quinlan, Tom, 3B	.285	509	85	145	36	2	23	113	50	117	1
Sexton, Chris, SS	.268	112	18	30	3	1	1	8	16	21	1
Shumpert, Terry, 3B	.288	146	26	42	11	1	2	18	11	27	3
Strittmatter, Mark, C	.246	114	16	28	8	0	2	12	11	21	0
*Vanderwal, John, 1B	.408	103	29	42	12	1	3	19	11	28	1
Velazquez, Edgard, OF	.281	438	70	123	24	10	17	73	34	119	6

Rookie League WRAP-UPS

Appalachian League

Break up Bluefield! The Orioles defended their Appalachian League championship with a two-game sweep of the Pulaski Rangers, marking their third consecutive trip to the postseason. But perhaps the real drama came in the one-game playoff forced by a tie atop the standings between Bluefield and the upstart Princeton Devil Rays. Bluefield needed 10 innings to get past their neighbor from 10 miles away, 5-4, before routing Pulaski, 8-0 and 4-2. Aided all season in the late innings by its only all-star, closer David Mastrolonardo, Bluefield got tremendous late-season help in its rotation by teenage Australian phenom John Stephens, who struck out 11 in six innings in the playoff versus Princeton.

League leaders: BA: David Orndorff, Elizabethton, .368. HR: Matt Berger, Bristol, 18. RBI: Jared Sandberg, Princeton, 68. SB: Joe Kilburg, Burlington, 29. ERA: Dan DeYoung, Pulaski, 1.91. W: Pablo Perez, Elizabethon, 10. K: Trey Poland, Pulaski, 106. SV: David Mastrolonardo, Bluefield, Lance Franks, Johnson City, 12.

APPALACHIAN LEAGUE
(Rookie)
North Division

	W	L	Pct.	GB
Bluefield	39	29	.580	—
Princeton	39	29	.580	—
Burlington	32	36	.471	7
Danville	30	38	.441	9
Martinsville	29	39	.426	10

South Division

	W	L	Pct.	GB
Pulaski	43	25	.632	—
Elizabethton	38	30	.559	5
Kingsport	37	31	.544	6
Bristol	30	38	.441	13
Johnson City	23	45	.338	20

Finals: Bluefield 2, Pulaski 0.

\# Switch-hitter
* Left-handed

Rookie League WRAP-UPS

Pioneer League

The Billings Mustangs took full advantage of their not having to share the Cincinnati Reds' young prospects. They swept two games from Great Falls en route to the Pioneer League championship. In previous years, when Cincinnati had a second short-season team at Princeton, the pickings were slimmer for Billings. But this year the Reds cut that second club, and that decision meant a Billings bonanza. In the finals' opener, Josh Harris pitched a three-hit shutout, and the Mustangs clinched it with a 4-3 win as DH Andy Burress, who hit .533 in the postseason, homered and had two RBI.

League leaders: BA: **Greg Morrison**, Medicine Hat, .448. HR: **Morrison**, 23. RBI: Morrison, 88. SB: **Ramon Moreta**, Great Falls, 29. ERA: **John Sneed**, Medicine Hat, 1.29. W: **Scott Williamson**, Billings, Renney Rojas, Butte, 8. K: **Williamson**, 101. SV: **Shawn Camp**, Idaho Falls, 12.

PIONEER LEAGUE (Rookie)

Northern Division

	W	L	Pct.	GB
Great Falls	40	32	.556	—
Lethbridge	39	33	.542	1
Helena	37	34	.521	2.5
Medicine Hat	26	46	.361	14

Southern Division

	W	L	Pct.	GB
Billings	39	32	.549	—
Idaho Falls	39	33	.542	.5
Ogden	37	35	.514	2.5
Butte	30	42	.417	9.5

Semifinals: Billings 2, Idaho Falls 0; Great Falls 2, Lethbridge 0. **Finals:** Billings 2, Great Falls 0.

Switch-hitter
* Left-handed

PITCHING	W	L	ERA	G	SV	IP	H	R	ER	BB	SO
Ausanio, Joe	0	0	29.45	3	0	3.2	14	13	12	3	3
*Beckett, Robbie	1	3	6.79	45	1	54.1	61	49	41	47	67
Bost, Heath	0	1	21.00	2	0	3.0	10	8	7	1	3
Bourgeois, Steve	9	7	5.99	33	0	121.2	154	96	81	66	86
Burke, John	1	2	5.82	3	0	17.0	23	14	11	14	15
Dejean, Mike	0	1	5.40	10	4	10.0	17	6	6	7	9
*Farmer, Michael	5	5	6.75	18	0	54.2	70	42	41	18	29
Henderson, Ryan	2	4	8.90	19	0	30.1	40	32	30	23	29
Hope, John	4	3	7.22	43	0	99.2	115	85	80	65	67
*Jones, Bobby	7	11	5.14	25	0	133.0	135	89	76	71	104
Kramer, Tom	3	2	5.23	51	11	62.0	57	42	36	40	56
*Lee, Mark	1	2	6.28	48	3	67.1	93	49	47	21	63
Leskanic, Curt	0	0	3.79	10	2	19.0	11	9	8	18	20
McCurry, Jeff	1	1	5.09	16	3	17.2	17	12	10	6	13
Minchey, Nate	15	6	4.51	27	0	157.2	172	87	79	53	107
Moore, Joel	3	1	7.76	5	0	26.2	47	26	23	12	20
Rekar, Bryan	10	9	5.46	28	0	145.0	169	96	88	39	116
*Ruffin, Bruce	0	0	3.38	2	0	2.2	1	1	1	0	2
Saipe, Mike	4	3	5.52	10	0	60.1	74	42	37	24	40
Scott, Tim	0	0	1.23	12	3	14.2	7	2	2	3	18
Shoemaker, Stephen	1	1	8.41	5	0	20.1	23	19	19	17	27
Stidham, Phil	5	2	9.91	26	0	36.1	55	43	40	26	20
Swift, Billy	0	1	12.00	1	0	3.0	4	4	4	3	4
Thompson, Mark	0	0	12.00	1	0	3.0	6	4	4	1	1
Thomson, John	4	2	3.43	7	0	42.0	36	18	16	14	49
Wright, Jamey	1	0	1.64	2	0	11.0	9	3	2	5	11

Edmonton Trappers (Athletics) AAA

BATTING	AVG	AB	R	H	2B	3B	HR	RBI	BB	SO	SB
Batista, Tony, SS	.315	124	25	39	10	1	3	21	17	18	2
#Bellhorn, Mark, 2B	.328	241	54	79	18	3	11	46	64	59	6
#Castro, Jose, 2B	.167	6	0	1	0	0	0	0	1	2	0
Christenson, Ryan, OF	.286	49	12	14	2	2	2	5	11	11	2
*Cox, Steve, 1B	.274	467	84	128	34	1	15	93	88	90	1
Garrison, Webster, 2B	.289	429	70	124	24	2	15	80	57	91	5
*Grieve, Ben, OF	.426	108	27	46	11	1	7	28	12	16	0
*Herrera, Jose, OF	.297	421	64	125	21	2	4	41	42	64	7
Hinch, A.J., C	.376	125	23	47	7	0	4	24	20	13	2
Lennon, Patrick, DH	.343	134	28	46	7	0	9	35	22	34	0
Lesher, Brian, OF	.323	415	85	134	27	5	21	78	64	86	14
Martins, Eric, 2B	.280	82	17	23	7	1	1	8	11	19	0
*Mayne, Brent, C	.000	3	0	0	0	0	0	0	0	1	0
#McDonald, Jason, OF	.264	276	74	73	14	6	4	30	74	58	31
Molina, Izzy, C	.261	218	33	57	11	3	6	34	12	27	2
Morales, Willie, C	.291	179	23	52	12	0	5	35	11	27	0
*Neill, Mike, OF	.190	21	3	4	0	0	0	3	7	7	1
Sheldon, Scott, SS	.315	422	89	133	39	6	19	77	59	104	5
#Smith, Demond, OF	.219	151	22	33	3	4	5	22	23	31	10
#Williams, George, C	.000	7	0	0	0	0	0	0	1	1	0
Wood, Jason, 3B	.321	505	83	162	35	7	19	87	45	74	2
Young, Ernie, OF	.323	195	39	63	10	0	9	45	37	46	5

PITCHING	W	L	ERA	G	SV	IP	H	R	ER	BB	SO
Acre, Mark	3	4	4.15	43	11	47.2	48	27	22	20	46
Adams, Willie	5	4	6.45	13	0	75.1	105	57	54	19	58
Boever, Joe	10	8	4.99	53	9	92.0	112	54	51	23	81
*Brewer, Billy	0	0	5.63	7	1	8.0	8	5	5	6	11
*Burrows, Terry	3	7	6.08	44	2	60.2	79	42	41	34	50
Chouinard, Bobby	6	6	6.03	25	0	100.0	129	80	67	26	58
D'Amico, Jeffrey	1	2	8.22	10	1	30.2	42	29	28	6	19
Daspit, Jamie	0	2	6.83	13	0	27.2	31	22	21	9	14
Haught, Gary	1	1	3.59	30	11	42.2	37	20	17	13	31
Haynes, Jimmy	0	2	4.85	5	0	29.2	36	22	16	11	24
Hollins, Stacy	0	0	10.13	1	0	2.2	5	4	3	3	2
Jimenez, Miguel	0	2	11.15	7	1	15.1	29	19	19	11	11
Johnson, Dane	1	1	5.63	14	6	16.0	17	11	10	8	13
Kjos, Ryan	0	1	36.00	1	0	2.0	6	8	8	3	2
*Kubinski, Tim	4	4	4.50	47	7	76.0	64	39	38	34	53
Lewis, Richie	1	1	5.85	11	1	20.0	24	13	13	14	25
*Lorraine, Andrew	8	6	4.74	23	0	117.2	143	72	62	34	75
Ludwick, Eric	1	1	3.32	6	0	19.0	22	7	7	4	20
Montgomery, Steve	2	1	5.79	30	3	46.2	61	30	30	17	38
Nichting, Chris	7	13	7.76	33	1	131.0	170	120	113	46	90
Oquist, Mike	6	1	3.25	9	0	52.2	57	23	19	16	37
Phillips, Tony	4	2	5.44	40	0	81.0	95	56	49	27	46
Price, Jamey	2	0	1.64	2	0	11.0	9	3	2	1	10
Prieto, Ariel	0	0	1.50	2	0	6.0	4	1	1	1	7

PITCHING	W	L	ERA	G	SV	IP	H	R	ER	BB	SO
Reyes, Carlos	2	0	3.48	5	0	31.0	30	14	12	3	23
Ricci, Chuck	0	0	16.88	4	0	5.1	10	10	10	6	5
Rigby, Brad	8	4	4.37	15	0	82.1	95	49	40	26	49
Small, Aaron	1	0	0.00	1	0	5.0	1	0	0	0	4
Witasick, Jay	3	2	4.28	13	0	27.1	25	13	13	15	17
*Wojciechowski, Steve	8	2	3.84	26	1	65.2	68	33	28	23	49

Las Vegas Stars (Padres) AAA

BATTING	AVG	AB	R	H	2B	3B	HR	RBI	BB	SO	SB
Arias, George, 3B	.283	431	75	122	32	4	12	65	42	59	3
*Beamon, Trey, OF	.328	329	64	108	19	4	5	49	48	58	14
Briggs, Stoney, OF	.269	435	58	117	21	5	11	57	28	122	18
*Brown, Ray, OF	.257	140	12	36	13	0	2	15	11	28	1
Bush, Homer, 2B	.277	155	25	43	10	1	3	14	7	40	5
Colbert, Craig,	1.000	2	0	2	1	0	0	0	0	0	0
#Dascenzo, Doug, OF	.277	433	61	120	23	4	9	45	45	42	16
Encarnacion, Angelo, C	.245	253	27	62	12	1	3	23	15	32	1
Hajek, Dave, 2B	.340	156	25	53	14	1	0	25	14	6	7
*Helfand, Eric, C	.315	238	31	75	21	1	6	33	28	47	1
Hernandez, Carlos, C	.400	10	1	4	0	0	1	5	1	3	0
*Joyner, Wally, 1B	.250	8	1	2	0	0	0	1	0	1	0
Keefe, Jamie, OF	.190	58	10	11	2	2	1	6	10	24	0
*Lee, Derek, OF	.294	231	22	68	16	1	5	35	32	35	4
Lee, Derrek, 1B	.324	472	86	153	29	2	13	64	60	116	17
#Melo, Juan, SS	.271	48	6	13	4	0	1	6	1	10	0
*Plantier, Phil, OF	.429	56	13	24	6	0	5	9	4	8	1
Poe, Charles, OF	.261	180	28	47	9	3	8	34	22	32	1
Rivera, Ruben, DH	.250	48	6	12	5	1	1	6	1	20	1
#Romero, Mandy, C	.308	91	19	28	4	1	3	13	11	19	0
Scarsone, Steve, 2B	.231	251	37	58	13	1	11	35	38	78	2
Shipley, Craig, SS	.316	19	0	6	3	0	0	1	0	5	0
Tatum, Jim, OF	.317	161	21	51	12	1	9	25	8	39	1
#Tredaway, Chad, 3B	.257	409	58	105	23	1	7	50	34	63	6
Velandia, Jorge, SS	.272	405	46	110	15	2	3	35	29	62	13

PITCHING	W	L	ERA	G	SV	IP	H	R	ER	BB	SO
*Baron, Jim	0	0	11.25	4	0	4.0	8	5	5	3	3
Batchelor, Rich	3	0	6.43	15	0	21.0	23	15	15	8	19
Boze, Marshall	0	7	7.62	14	0	52.0	68	51	44	29	44
Bruske, Jim	5	4	4.90	16	0	68.0	73	41	37	22	67
Castillo, Marino	6	5	5.14	30	0	126.0	146	88	72	43	102
Drahman, Brian	2	1	6.33	33	1	42.2	51	32	30	28	39
Hancock, Ryan	3	3	4.20	43	2	79.1	81	44	37	40	63
Hook, Chris	0	7	8.79	19	0	56.1	80	64	55	49	35
Kaufman, Brad	0	5	8.07	6	0	32.1	40	37	29	15	19
Kroon, Marc	1	3	4.54	46	15	41.2	34	22	21	22	53
*Long, Joey	0	0	4.82	16	0	18.2	17	10	10	12	13
Maddux, Mike	0	2	4.29	4	0	21.0	24	11	10	11	18
Medina, Rafael	4	5	7.56	13	0	66.2	90	60	56	39	50
Menhart, Paul	4	14	6.06	26	1	127.2	154	92	86	55	95
Mintz, Steve	5	2	8.05	27	5	34.2	50	31	31	17	28
*Murray, Heath	6	8	5.45	19	0	109.0	142	72	66	41	99
Scanlan, Bob	3	1	3.53	36	1	51.0	51	24	20	17	20
Schmitt, Todd	5	2	5.03	48	4	53.2	55	34	30	38	59
Smith, Pete	3	2	4.28	6	0	33.2	38	16	16	6	24
Spencer, Stan	3	2	3.75	8	0	48.0	48	23	20	18	47
Taylor, Kerry	7	9	4.31	22	0	144.0	150	84	69	55	103
Veras, Dario	0	2	5.02	12	2	14.1	14	8	8	6	13
*Zancanaro, Dave	0	3	15.53	3	0	13.1	27	24	23	8	9

Phoenix Firebirds (Giants) AAA

BATTING	AVG	AB	R	H	2B	3B	HR	RBI	BB	SO	SB
Aurilia, Rich, SS	.294	34	9	10	2	0	1	5	5	4	2
Ball, Jeff, 3B	.321	470	90	151	38	3	18	103	58	84	10
*Benard, Marvin, OF	.333	60	14	20	5	0	0	5	11	9	4
#Berryhill, Damon, C	.385	13	0	5	0	0	0	1	2	1	0
Bonds, Bobby, OF	.000	1	0	0	0	0	0	0	0	0	0
Canizaro, Jay, 2B	.198	81	12	16	7	0	2	12	9	24	2
*Cruz, Jacob, OF	.361	493	97	178	45	3	12	95	64	64	18
#Delgado, Wilson, SS	.288	416	47	120	22	4	9	56	24	70	9
Florez, Tim, 2B	.301	402	57	121	24	4	7	61	32	68	6
*Hamilton, Darryl, OF	.286	14	1	4	1	0	1	2	0	2	0
Jones, Dax, OF	.255	271	48	69	7	5	3	28	39	39	9
Kennedy, Darryl, C	.173	98	10	17	4	0	0	8	6	13	1
Martinez, Ramon, 2B	.281	57	6	16	2	0	1	7	5	9	1
*Mayes, Craig, C	.095	21	2	2	1	0	0	0	1	5	0

Rookie League WRAP-UPS

Arizona League

In the only league that doesn't feature playoffs, the Cubs won the title by a comfortable 4½-game margin over their nearest rival, the Mariners. Todd Noel, the teenager drafted by Chicago in the first round of 1996, was named the top right-hander in the league, and he was joined by three teammates, third baseman Todd Fereday, catcher Brad Ramsey and reliever Shane Sullivan, on the league all-star team. Padres outfielder Kevin Burford was the league's MVP.

League leaders: BA: Kevin Burford, Padres, .389. HR: Jesus Basabe, Athletics, 11. RBI: Burford, 50. SB: Omar Rosario, Athletics, 40. ERA: Todd Noel, Cubs, 1.98. W: Juan Pena, Athletics, Shane Heams, Mariners, Wascar Serrano, Padres, 6. K: Ryan Price, Rockies, 98. SV: Shane Sullivan, Cubs, 9.

ARIZONA LEAGUE (Rookie)

	W	L	Pct.	GB
Cubs	34	21	.618	—
Mariners	30	26	.536	4.5
Athletics	29	27	.518	5.5
Diamondbacks	27	29	.482	7.5
Padres	25	30	.455	9
Rockies	22	34	.393	12.5

Switch-hitter
* Left-handed

Rookie League WRAP-UPS

Gulf Coast League

The Mets swept to the league title by knocking off the Yankees in the semifinals and then taking two from the Rangers, 2-0 and 8-3, in the finals. Right-hander Geoff Goetz, the Mets' first-round pick in the June draft, got the victory in the clincher. The team was skippered by two men, Mickey Brantley for the first half and ex-Mets infielder Doug Flynn for the second.

League leaders: BA: **Willy Ruiz**, Royals, .360. HR: **Michael Rivera**, Tigers, 10. RBI: **Jose Taveras**, Royals, 39. SB: **Tottie Myers**, Expos, 24. ERA: **Marquis Roberts**, Devil Rays, 0.51. W: **Wilfredo Rodriguez**, Astros, **Francisco Vanderhorst**, Royals, **Geraldo Padua**, Yankees, 8. K: **Mark Martinez**, Red Sox, 78. SV: **Jake Jacobs**, Twins, 10.

GULF COAST LEAGUE (Rookie)
Eastern Division

	W	L	Pct.	GB
Mets	42	18	.700	—
Marlins	31	28	.525	10.5
Expos	25	35	.417	17
Braves	21	38	.356	20.5

Northern Division

	W	L	Pct.	GB
Yankees	40	20	.667	—
Tigers	31	29	.517	9
Devil Rays	25	35	.417	15
Astros	24	36	.400	16

Western Division

	W	L	Pct.	GB
Royals	36	24	.600	—
Rangers	34	26	.567	2
Red Sox	31	28	.525	4.5
Twins	28	32	.467	8
Pirates	27	32	.458	8.5
Orioles	27	33	.450	9
White Sox	26	34	.433	10

Semifinals: Rangers 1, Royals 0; Mets 1, Yankees 0.
Finals: Mets 2, Rangers 0.
Switch-hitter
* Left-handed

BATTING	AVG	AB	R	H	2B	3B	HR	RBI	BB	SO	SB
McCarty, Dave, 1B	.353	434	85	153	27	5	22	92	49	75	9
Mirabelli, Doug, C	.265	332	49	88	23	2	8	48	58	69	1
Powell, Dante, OF	.241	452	91	109	24	4	11	42	52	105	34
#Roberson, Kevin, OF	.287	349	60	100	19	5	14	67	37	98	9
Rowland, Rich, C	.237	59	10	14	5	0	2	13	7	13	0
*Unrat, Chris, C	.500	2	0	1	0	0	0	0	1	0	0
Williams, Keith, OF	.200	5	0	1	0	0	0	0	0	2	0
*Wilson, Desi, 1B	.344	451	76	155	27	6	7	53	44	73	16
Woods, Ken, 3B	1.000	1	0	1	0	0	0	1	0	0	0
Zosky, Eddie, 3B	.278	241	38	67	10	4	9	45	16	38	3

PITCHING	W	L	ERA	G	SV	IP	H	R	ER	BB	SO
Arocha, Rene	7	3	4.76	18	0	111.2	121	59	59	27	68
Bailey, Cory	4	0	1.56	13	3	17.1	16	4	3	6	14
Carlson, Dan	13	3	3.88	29	3	109.0	102	53	47	36	108
Corps, Edwin	2	1	5.68	7	0	19.0	26	14	12	8	8
*Creek, Doug	8	6	4.93	25	0	129.2	140	76	71	66	137
Fernandez, Osvaldo	0	0	3.00	2	0	12.0	10	5	4	3	4
Foulke, Keith	5	4	4.50	12	0	76.0	79	38	38	15	54
Frontera, Chad	2	0	6.20	5	0	24.2	32	19	17	9	13
*Hancock, Lee	0	1	6.10	7	0	10.1	23	7	7	4	9
*Hartvigson, Chad	2	2	5.37	17	0	53.2	63	34	32	17	52
Johnstone, John	0	3	4.03	38	24	38.0	34	17	17	15	30
Ortiz, Russ	4	3	5.51	14	0	85.0	96	57	52	34	70
*Peterson, Mark	0	0	7.36	3	0	3.2	6	4	3	1	2
Phillips, Randy	5	4	3.04	21	0	47.1	44	20	16	18	21
*Pickett, Ricky	3	3	3.19	61	12	67.2	52	27	24	49	85
Purdy, Shawn	10	3	4.37	56	2	82.1	103	45	40	33	42
Rapp, Pat	2	0	3.60	3	0	15.0	16	6	6	9	6
Roa, Joe	3	1	4.75	6	0	36.0	43	21	19	11	16
Soderstrom, Steve	4	8	6.47	31	1	105.2	141	81	76	52	78
Taulbee, Andy	2	2	7.52	19	0	40.2	64	41	34	14	20
VanLandingham, Bill	1	1	9.00	4	0	17.0	20	19	17	21	7
Vanderweele, Doug	6	4	4.59	36	1	68.2	99	38	35	18	35
Villano, Mike	5	3	4.16	13	0	71.1	75	36	33	27	41

Salt Lake Buzz (Twins) AAA

BATTING	AVG	AB	R	H	2B	3B	HR	RBI	BB	SO	SB
*Alvarez, Rafael, OF	.271	48	10	13	1	1	0	5	6	9	5
Baez, Kevin, SS	.274	383	38	105	25	3	5	54	29	74	3
*Brede, Brent, OF	.354	328	82	116	27	4	9	76	47	62	4
Castellano, Pedro, 3B	.358	165	29	59	9	1	7	36	20	31	0
Cordova, Marty, OF	.375	24	5	9	4	0	1	4	2	3	1
Durant, Mike, C	.206	223	33	46	13	1	8	36	21	42	4
Horn, Jeff, C	.333	78	16	26	6	0	1	13	11	22	0
Jackson, Darrin, OF	.300	80	14	24	3	3	1	12	5	17	3
Johnson, J.J., OF	.146	82	6	12	1	1	0	5	4	24	2
#Latham, Chris, OF	.309	492	78	152	22	5	8	58	58	110	21
Miller, Damian, C	.338	314	48	106	19	3	11	82	29	62	6
*Ogden, Jamie, OF	.286	367	67	105	18	5	14	53	35	99	14
*Ortiz, David, 1B	.214	42	5	9	1	0	4	10	2	11	0
*Radmanovich, R., OF	.264	485	92	128	25	4	28	78	67	138	11
Rupp, Chad, 1B	.272	426	77	116	19	7	32	94	49	112	2
Shave, Jon, SS	.329	395	75	130	27	3	7	60	39	62	6
Simons, Mitch, 2B	.299	462	87	138	34	10	5	59	47	48	26
*Smith, Jeff, C	.250	12	2	3	2	0	0	2	1	3	0
*Stahoviak, Scott, 1B	.214	28	5	6	0	0	2	10	5	8	0
*Walker, Todd, 3B	.345	322	69	111	20	1	11	53	46	49	5

PITCHING	W	L	ERA	G	SV	IP	H	R	ER	BB	SO
*Aldred, Scott	3	3	7.03	7	0	39.2	56	39	31	16	23
*Baptist, Travis	4	1	2.08	7	0	47.2	47	16	11	9	28
Bowers, Shane	6	2	4.79	9	0	56.1	64	35	30	14	46
Dreyer, Steve	1	0	7.36	27	2	44.0	65	38	36	10	34
Duncan, Calvin	0	0	7.94	5	0	11.1	17	13	10	3	16
Gandarillas, Gus	1	0	3.18	11	2	22.2	22	8	8	6	13
Hawkins, Latroy	9	4	5.45	14	0	76.0	100	53	46	16	53
Klingenbeck, Scott	0	0	1.29	1	0	7.0	6	1	1	0	6
Legault, Kevin	1	3	7.52	16	0	26.1	39	24	22	7	18
Linebarger, Keith	4	6	6.63	41	5	97.2	135	79	72	42	59
*Looney, Brian	0	2	2.19	17	1	24.2	20	7	6	10	21
*Miller, Travis	10	6	4.73	21	0	125.2	140	73	66	57	86
Naulty, Dan	0	1	11.37	6	0	6.1	11	10	8	2	5
Niedermaier, Brad	2	1	5.88	16	0	26.0	29	22	17	13	20
*Ohme, Kevin	2	5	5.62	56	11	73.2	70	49	46	34	43
Parra, Jose	2	8	6.03	50	8	94.0	126	73	63	30	61

PITCHING	W	L	ERA	G	SV	IP	H	R	ER	BB	SO
Rath, Fred	0	1	1.64	10	3	11.0	11	2	2	2	11
*Redman, Mark	8	15	6.31	29	1	158.1	204	123	111	80	125
Roberts, Brett	1	3	6.90	24	1	58.2	89	51	45	33	33
*Serafini, Dan	9	7	4.97	28	0	152.0	166	87	84	55	118
Stevens, Dave	9	3	4.30	16	0	90.0	93	52	43	31	71

Tacoma Rainiers (Mariners) AAA

BATTING	AVG	AB	R	H	2B	3B	HR	RBI	BB	SO	SB
Bonnici, Jim, 1B	.250	4	0	1	0	0	0	1	1	1	0
*Castro, Jose, OF	.000	1	0	0	0	0	0	0	0	0	0
#Christian, Eddie, OF	.319	135	16	43	5	1	1	9	14	24	3
#Cruz, Jose, OF	.268	190	33	51	16	2	6	30	34	44	3
Decker, Steve, C	.297	350	40	104	25	1	10	52	22	37	0
*Ducey, Rob, OF	.324	74	8	24	8	0	0	11	8	15	0
Espinoza, Alvaro, 2B	.333	12	1	4	0	0	0	1	2	1	0
*Gates, Brent, 2B	.455	33	7	15	3	0	0	6	4	2	0
Gipson, Charles, 3B	.314	35	5	11	3	0	0	5	4	3	0
Griffey, Craig, OF	.333	3	1	1	0	1	0	0	0	0	0
Guevara, Giomar, 2B	.244	176	29	43	5	1	2	13	5	39	3
Haney, Todd, 3B	.353	17	3	6	4	0	0	2	2	2	0
*Ibanez, Raul, OF	.304	438	84	133	30	5	15	84	32	75	7
*Leach, Jalal, OF	.308	415	56	128	26	3	9	55	32	74	6
Millette, Joe, 3B	.211	123	12	26	2	1	0	5	8	23	1
*Monahan, Shane, OF	.294	85	15	25	4	0	2	12	5	21	5
Raabe, Brian, 2B	.352	543	101	191	35	4	14	80	38	20	1
*Reimer, Kevin, DH	.345	168	21	58	18	0	3	21	12	22	0
Rohrmeier, Dan, OF	.297	471	86	140	43	4	33	120	45	81	1
Sealy, Scot, 1B	.273	55	8	15	3	0	3	10	5	13	0
Sheets, Andy, SS	.259	401	57	104	23	0	14	53	46	97	7
Silvestre, Juan, OF	.250	28	5	7	3	0	0	0	2	9	0
#Tinsley, Lee, OF	.181	105	15	19	2	1	2	7	12	34	1
Torres, Paul, 3B	.301	209	24	63	19	0	5	22	14	31	1
*Varitek, Jason, C	.254	307	54	78	13	0	15	48	34	71	0
*Wilkins, Rick, C	.338	68	16	23	8	0	1	14	8	12	0
#Zinter, Alan, 1B	.287	404	69	116	19	4	20	70	64	113	3

PITCHING	W	L	ERA	G	SV	IP	H	R	ER	BB	SO
Abbott, Paul	8	4	4.13	17	0	93.2	80	48	43	29	117
Berumen, Andres	9	4	4.91	34	0	113.2	127	71	62	64	114
Carmona, Rafael	2	5	3.79	32	4	59.1	52	31	25	35	56
Crow, Dean	4	2	4.78	33	7	43.1	56	25	23	19	36
*Davis, Tim	1	0	3.60	1	0	5.0	4	2	2	3	5
Franklin, Ryan	5	5	4.18	14	0	90.1	97	48	42	24	59
Gajkowski, Steve	5	3	3.87	44	2	93.0	100	43	40	24	48
Harikkala, Tim	6	8	6.43	21	0	113.1	160	93	81	50	86
Holdridge, David	1	1	2.96	15	1	24.1	21	9	8	13	24
*Holzemer, Mark	1	0	2.20	37	13	41.0	32	10	10	10	38
Hurtado, Edwin	10	6	3.88	20	0	132.1	139	60	57	37	100
Lira, Felipe	2	0	3.43	3	0	21.0	21	8	8	5	17
Lowe, Derek	3	4	3.45	10	0	57.1	53	26	22	20	49
Manzanillo, Josias	0	0	6.43	11	1	14.0	16	10	10	8	15
*Manzanillo, Ravelo	2	1	6.52	18	1	29.0	34	22	21	22	25
*McCarthy, Greg	2	1	3.27	22	3	22.0	21	8	8	16	34
*Moyer, Jamie	1	0	0.00	1	0	5.0	1	0	0	0	6
Pacheco, Alex	0	2	8.78	15	0	27.2	45	27	27	15	21
Smith, Ryan	1	0	0.00	1	0	5.0	4	0	0	1	2
Suzuki, Mac	4	9	5.94	32	0	83.1	79	60	55	64	63
Witte, Trey	5	1	5.29	32	0	66.1	82	49	39	26	52
Wolcott, Bob	1	3	5.11	7	0	37.0	40	23	21	7	29

Tucson Toros (Brewers) AAA

BATTING	AVG	AB	R	H	2B	3B	HR	RBI	BB	SO	SB
*Andreopoulos, Alex, C	.400	15	3	6	1	0	0	1	0	1	0
#Banks, Brian, OF	.296	378	53	112	26	3	10	63	35	83	7
Belliard, Ronnie, 2B	.282	443	80	125	35	4	4	55	61	69	10
Brown, Jarvis, OF	.265	385	65	102	21	3	6	35	52	84	14
Diaz, Eddy, 3B	.329	356	65	117	24	3	9	70	26	25	0
Dunn, Todd, OF	.304	332	66	101	31	4	18	66	39	83	5
Felix, Lauro, 2B	.319	47	7	15	5	0	1	5	5	15	0
Hughes, Bobby, C	.310	290	43	90	29	2	7	51	24	46	0
#Iapoce, Anthony, OF	.333	21	5	7	4	0	0	3	1	4	0
*Jenkins, Geoff, OF	.236	347	44	82	24	3	10	56	33	87	0
Johns, Keith, SS	.264	333	45	88	21	3	5	36	43	61	4
#Kellner, Frank, SS	.287	230	31	66	14	4	0	25	16	38	2
*Lee, Travis, 1B	.300	227	42	68	16	2	14	46	31	46	2
*Martinez, Greg, OF	.417	12	2	5	2	0	0	3	0	1	0

Batting leaders across all leagues

BATTING AVERAGE
(minimum 388 TPA)

Player	Club	Lg.	BA
Kinkade, Mike	EIP	Tex	.385
Krause, Scott	EIP	Tex	.361
*Cruz, Jacob	Phx	PCL	.361
Lopez, Luis	Hag	SAL	.358
Stoner, Mike	HD	Cal	.358
McCarty, Dave	Phx	PCL	.353
Raabe, Brian	Tac	PCL	.352
*Helton, Todd	CSp	PCL	.352
*Mitchell, M.	RC	Cal	.350
T*Grieve, Ben	Edm	PCL	.345
Wilson, Todd	SJ	Cal	.345
*Darr, Mike	RC	Cal	.344
*Wilson, Desi	Phx	PCL	.344
Millar, Kevin	Prt	East	.342

SLUGGING PERCENTAGE

Player	Club	Lg.	SLUG
T*Grieve, Ben	Edm	PCL	.640
T*Lee, Travis	Tcn	PCL	.631
Stoner, Mike	HD	Cal	.628
Morman, Russ	Chr	Int	.623
Konerko, Paul	Abq	PCL	.621
T*Branyan, R.	Akr	East	.620
Hacker, Steve	Mac	SAL	.620
Rohrmeier, Dan	Tac	PCL	.616
Raven, Luis	Bir	Sou	.612
T*Guiel, Aaron	Mob	Sou	.607
T#Curtis, Matt	LkE	Cal	.607
*Petagine, R.	Nor	Int	.605
Millar, Kevin	Prt	East	.605
McCarty, Dave	Phx	PCL	.590
Kinkade, Mike	EIP	Tex	.588

ON-BASE AVERAGE

Player	Club	Lg.	OBA
T*Grieve, Ben	Edm	PCL	.461
Kinkade, Mike	EIP	Tex	.455
#Gibbs, Kevin	SAn	Tex	.451
T Christenson, R.	Edm	PCL	.437
T Foster, Jim	Bow	East	.435
T*Guiel, Aaron	Mob	Sou	.435
T Menechino, F.	Bir	Sou	.434
*Horne, Tyrone	KnC	Mid	.434
*Cruz, Jacob	Phx	PCL	.434
*Helton, Todd	CSp	PCL	.434
T*Giambi, J.	Wch	Tex	.431
*Ryan, Rob	SBn	Mid	.431
T*Lee, Travis	Tcn	PCL	.431

Switch-hitter
* Left-handed
T Player has been with more than one team; listed with last team.
(Players in major leagues are listed with last minor league club.)

Batting leaders across all leagues

(Cont'd from previous page)

HOME RUNS

Player	Club	Lg.	HR
T*Branyan, R.	Akr	East	39
Konerko, Paul	Abq	PCL	37
Raleigh, Matt	Bng	East	37
Peoples, Daniel	Kin	Caro	34
Cameron, S.	HD	Cal	33
Freitas, Joe	Peo	Mid	33
Glendenning, M.	Bak	Cal	33
Hacker, Steve	Mac	SAL	33
Morman, Russ	Chr	Int	33
Rohrmeier, Dan	Tac	PCL	33
Stoner, Mike	HD	Cal	33
T*Lee, Travis	Tcn	PCL	32
Millar, Kevin	Prt	East	32
Rupp, Chad	SLk	PCL	32
T*Seefried, Tate	Nor	Int	32

RUNS BATTED IN

Player	Club	Lg.	RBI
Stoner, Mike	HD	Cal	142
T*Grieve, Ben	Edm	PCL	135
Coolbaugh, Mike	Hvl	Sou	132
Millar, Kevin	Prt	East	131
Konerko, Paul	Abq	PCL	127
T*Ortiz, David	SLk	PCL	124
*Cromer, D.T.	Hvl	Sou	121
Rohrmeier, Dan	Tac	PCL	120
Hacker, Steve	Mac	SAL	119
Ramirez, Aramis	Lyn	Caro	114
Cameron, S.	HD	Cal	113
Quinlan, Tom	CSp	PCL	113
Raven, Luis	Bir	Sou	112
T Foster, Jim	Bow	East	110

BATTING	AVG	AB	R	H	2B	3B	HR	RBI	BB	SO	SB
Newfield, Marc, OF	.323	31	4	10	1	0	1	3	4	6	0
Seitzer, Brad, 3B	.316	234	50	74	13	3	9	42	22	33	0
Stinnett, Kelly, C	.321	209	50	67	15	3	10	43	42	46	1
Unroe, Tim, 3B	.291	234	45	68	17	1	9	46	9	62	3
*Vina, Fernando, 2B	.474	19	3	9	3	0	1	5	3	1	0
Voigt, Jack, OF	.272	235	36	64	20	0	5	40	43	57	4
Wachter, Derek, OF	.289	142	24	41	12	0	2	28	18	28	2
*Williamson, Antone, 1B	.286	304	53	87	20	5	5	41	49	41	3

PITCHING	W	L	ERA	G	SV	IP	H	R	ER	BB	SO
*Adamson, Joel	2	1	4.36	6	0	33.0	38	16	16	8	24
*Bolton, Tom	5	10	6.92	23	0	95.0	142	80	73	32	71
Bones, Ricky	5	0	2.79	8	0	42.0	40	18	13	8	22
Brewington, Jamie	1	3	10.18	6	0	20.1	33	26	23	17	13
Browne, Byron	0	1	5.23	3	0	10.1	13	9	6	8	7
*Davis, Mark	0	2	3.57	17	2	22.2	19	9	9	12	19
Fetters, Mike	0	0	10.80	2	0	1.2	1	2	2	1	0
Gardner, Scott	1	0	3.00	1	0	6.0	6	2	2	3	6
Grimsley, Jason	5	10	5.70	36	4	85.1	96	70	54	43	65
*Grott, Matt	3	1	4.79	55	4	88.1	94	57	47	33	58
Hansell, Greg	2	3	4.64	40	2	87.1	99	52	45	27	76
*Huber, Jeff	3	7	4.74	40	5	62.2	67	36	33	22	37
Maloney, Sean	0	2	4.82	15	5	18.2	24	10	10	3	21
McAndrew, Jamie	7	8	6.79	22	0	108.2	132	87	82	65	63
Minor, Blas	2	2	4.03	12	1	29.0	36	21	13	15	21
Misuraca, Mike	8	7	4.98	33	1	108.1	119	68	60	39	62
*Montoya, Norm	6	10	6.25	27	0	131.0	175	100	91	38	75
*Pace, Scotty	0	0	1.59	2	0	5.2	6	2	1	4	2
Reyes, Alberto	2	4	5.02	38	7	57.1	52	39	32	34	70
*Roberson, Sid	0	2	11.45	10	0	22.0	47	29	28	14	8
Rodriguez, Frankie	3	1	4.40	12	0	47.0	53	25	23	19	41
Sadler, Al	1	0	1.50	1	0	6.0	7	1	1	4	1
Tyler, Josh	0	0	0.00	1	0	1.0	0	0	0	0	0
VanEgmond, Tim	1	0	9.00	1	0	1.0	3	1	1	0	0
Ware, Jeff	5	8	6.71	25	0	106.0	127	98	79	80	69
Woodard, Steve	1	0	0.00	1	0	7.0	3	0	0	1	6

Vancouver Canadians (Angels) AAA

BATTING	AVG	AB	R	H	2B	3B	HR	RBI	BB	SO	SB
#Bass, Kevin, OF	.333	12	4	4	0	0	1	1	3	2	0
Betten, Randy, 2B	.279	61	9	17	4	0	1	12	7	21	1
#Bolick, Frank, DH	.304	362	61	110	27	4	16	66	46	70	4
Burke, Jamie, C	.296	27	4	8	1	0	0	3	3	2	0
#Caceres, Edgar, 2B	.310	258	30	80	13	0	2	37	19	23	6
#Carvajal, Jovino, OF	.285	480	80	137	20	20	2	51	21	85	28
Cruz, Fausto, 2B	.288	413	52	119	28	1	11	67	18	81	5
Eenhoorn, Robert, SS	.308	455	77	140	29	5	12	58	25	59	1
Greene, Todd, C	.354	260	51	92	22	0	25	75	20	31	5
Monzon, Jose, C	.234	47	2	11	2	0	0	6	4	8	1
Norton, Chris, 1B	.200	5	1	1	0	0	1	1	0	2	0
*Pritchett, Chris, 1B	.279	383	60	107	30	3	7	47	42	72	5
#Riley, Marquis, OF	.264	242	33	64	6	0	0	8	36	27	27
*Singleton, Duane, OF	.206	383	56	79	17	3	5	36	37	79	15
Thurston, Jerrey, C	.236	195	17	46	3	1	4	19	8	59	3
Turner, Chris, 1B	.370	135	26	50	10	0	4	22	14	22	0
White, Derrick, OF	.324	414	64	134	35	2	11	65	44	73	11
#Williams, Reggie, OF	.250	40	10	10	3	0	2	5	6	13	3
Wolff, Mike, OF	.282	266	58	75	15	0	21	64	53	75	6

PITCHING	W	L	ERA	G	SV	IP	H	R	ER	BB	SO
Bene, Bill	0	1	7.24	19	0	27.1	28	25	22	26	29
Bovee, Mike	4	3	3.44	12	0	89.0	92	38	34	25	71
Buckley, Travis	7	11	5.11	32	1	176.0	223	116	100	51	119
*Cadaret, Greg	0	1	3.14	9	3	14.1	11	5	5	4	16
Chavez, Anthony	4	1	2.54	28	15	28.1	21	8	8	6	22
*Dunbar, Matt	1	0	6.85	14	0	23.2	32	18	18	14	20
Edsell, Geoff	14	11	5.15	30	0	183.1	196	121	105	96	95
Ellis, Robert	9	10	5.92	29	0	149.0	185	108	98	83	70
*Fortugno, Tim	4	2	5.23	34	0	31.0	29	21	18	17	36
*Frey, Steve	3	3	5.01	31	4	41.1	45	23	23	21	28
Gohr, Greg	5	1	3.80	8	0	47.1	51	23	20	14	27
Gross, Kevin	1	0	1.64	2	0	11.0	7	2	2	0	5
Janicki, Pete	1	4	7.80	42	1	47.1	48	43	41	44	23
Macey, Fausto	1	3	8.10	9	0	40.0	47	39	36	32	23
*May, Darrell	7	5	3.26	13	0	80.0	65	31	29	31	62
*Perisho, Matt	4	4	5.33	9	0	52.1	68	42	31	29	47
Schmidt, Jeff	1	2	5.32	27	10	22.0	22	14	13	20	14

Switch-hitter
* Left-handed
T Player has been with more than one team; listed with last team.
(Players in major leagues are listed with last minor league club.)

PITCHING	W	L	ERA	G	SV	IP	H	R	ER	BB	SO
Skuse, Nick	0	0	0.00	1	0	1.0	0	0	0	0	2
Springer, Dennis	1	1	3.00	2	0	15.0	12	6	5	6	7
*Washburn, Jarrod	0	0	3.60	1	0	5.0	4	2	2	2	6
Williams, Shad	6	2	3.82	40	0	99.0	98	52	42	41	52

Eastern League

Akron Aeros (Indians) AA

BATTING	AVG	AB	R	H	2B	3B	HR	RBI	BB	SO	SB
*Betts, Todd, 3B	.246	439	65	108	25	1	20	69	73	97	1
Betzsold, James, OF	.265	434	76	115	21	5	19	79	60	119	4
*Branyan, Russell, 3B	.234	137	26	32	4	0	12	30	28	56	0
*Casey, Sean, 1B	.386	241	38	93	19	1	10	66	23	34	0
Claudio, Patricio, OF	.212	33	6	7	1	0	0	6	3	14	2
Curtis, Chad, OF	.389	18	5	7	1	0	3	6	0	3	0
*Curtis, Randy, OF	.237	93	19	22	3	0	5	15	22	27	2
*Glass, Chip, OF	.259	394	74	102	17	4	5	37	56	61	16
Gross, Rafael, 2B	.286	49	7	14	4	0	0	2	2	13	3
Harriss, Robin, C	.267	146	24	39	8	0	1	17	20	36	0
*Mercedes, G., SS	.208	288	37	60	7	1	0	27	28	38	2
*Miller, David, OF	.301	509	84	153	27	9	4	61	48	77	22
Morgan, Scott, OF	.174	69	11	12	3	0	2	6	8	20	1
*Morris, Bobby, 2B	.252	119	17	30	9	1	1	15	22	21	1
Moyle, Mike, C	.231	342	56	79	15	0	16	53	53	71	3
Mulligan, Sean, C	.429	7	1	3	1	0	0	1	1	0	0
Neal, Mike, 2B	.282	457	77	129	24	2	17	69	55	103	8
Perry, Chan, 1B	.315	476	74	150	34	2	20	96	28	61	3
*Riggs, Kevin, 2B	.225	178	34	40	9	0	1	20	34	35	3
*Thomas, Greg, 1B	.244	242	27	59	13	2	7	42	29	50	2

PITCHING	W	L	ERA	G	SV	IP	H	R	ER	BB	SO
Badorek, Mike	1	2	6.12	4	0	25.0	40	22	17	6	15
*Baker, Scott	2	1	3.42	4	0	26.1	25	11	10	4	12
Bennett, Erik	2	3	4.81	11	0	24.1	26	13	13	9	20
Briscoe, John	0	1	3.94	33	5	32.0	41	19	14	12	28
Calmus, Lance	1	1	6.10	5	0	10.1	6	7	7	9	10
Camp, Jared	2	8	6.19	12	0	64.0	79	49	44	26	39
Carter, John	1	2	9.00	19	0	39.0	51	45	39	26	24
*Crowell, Jim	1	0	4.50	3	0	18.0	13	12	9	11	7
DeLaRosa, Maximo	4	9	4.44	17	0	97.1	112	63	48	32	70
Dougherty, Anthony	2	2	2.54	28	8	39.0	31	11	11	19	31
Gordon, Mike	1	2	4.15	6	0	30.1	37	28	14	14	16
Granata, Chris	1	0	7.20	4	0	5.0	8	5	4	4	3
*Gray, Dennis	0	2	12.27	10	0	7.1	13	10	10	9	5
Kirkreit, Daron	8	9	5.20	26	0	117.2	131	96	68	69	83
Lopez, Albie	0	0	0.00	1	0	1.0	2	0	0	2	2
Martinez, Johnny	1	8	4.96	32	2	49.0	63	32	27	26	31
*Matthews, Mike	6	8	3.82	19	0	113.0	116	62	48	57	69
Mesa, Rafael	0	1	4.21	14	0	25.2	36	13	12	9	7
Montoya, Wilmer	0	0	11.57	2	0	2.1	4	3	3	2	2
Moore, Marcus	3	5	4.94	13	0	71.0	84	50	39	32	63
*Najera, Noe	4	8	6.06	25	0	84.2	96	63	57	40	50
Perez, Julio	1	0	5.63	9	1	24.0	27	16	15	13	23
Rakers, Jason	1	4	4.39	7	0	41.0	36	21	20	11	31
Sexton, Jeff	2	0	4.75	16	1	47.1	55	27	25	15	38
Shuey, Paul	0	0	3.38	3	0	8.0	10	3	3	0	9
Vaught, Jay	2	3	5.22	29	1	70.2	65	43	41	40	56
Warrecker, Teddy	1	5	11.53	10	0	32.0	44	50	41	40	25
Weber, Lenny	1	0	15.43	6	0	9.1	22	17	16	9	8
Wertz, Bill	1	0	9.61	11	0	19.2	32	24	21	12	7
*Whitten, Casey	1	3	5.87	4	0	15.1	20	12	10	11	14
Winchester, Scott	0	0	3.86	6	1	7.0	8	3	3	2	8
Wright, Jaret	3	3	3.67	8	0	54.0	43	26	22	23	59

Binghamton Mets (Mets) AA

BATTING	AVG	AB	R	H	2B	3B	HR	RBI	BB	SO	SB
Azuaje, Jesus, 2B	.278	331	50	92	15	1	6	37	45	42	11
#Bates, Fletcher, OF	.257	245	44	63	14	2	12	34	26	71	9
Espinosa, Ramon, OF	.271	255	32	69	7	1	11	37	13	39	10
Grifol, Pedro, C	.200	200	15	40	6	0	3	15	9	29	1
#Hardtke, Jason, 2B	.385	26	3	10	2	0	1	4	2	2	0
Hunter, Scott, OF	.256	289	45	74	12	2	10	31	25	52	24
Knowles, Eric, SS	.236	157	16	37	10	0	3	22	16	34	7
Lopez, Jose, 3B	.246	207	31	51	10	1	11	26	13	63	4

Batting leaders across all leagues

(Cont'd from previous page)

STOLEN BASES

Player	Club	Lg.	SB
*Sanchez, Alex	CSC	SAL	92
Hutchison, B.	Ash	SAL	81
#Pendergrass, T.	Mac	SAL	70
Lindsey, Rodney	Cln	Mid	70
Baughman, Justin	LkE	Cal	68
Metcalfe, Mike	SBr	Cal	67
Garland, Tim	SJ	Cal	65
*Dent, Darrell	Del	SAL	60
Brown, Vick	Tam	FSL	55
Meyers, Chad	Rkf	Mid	54
#Smith, Rod	GBo	SAL	54
Gomez, Ramon	W-S	Caro	53
*Nelson, Charles	VB	FSL	53

RUNS

Player	Club	Lg.	R
T*Neill, Mike	Hvl	Sou	132
T*Grieve, Ben	Edm	PCL	127
T Christenson, R.	Edm	PCL	120
Stoner, Mike	HD	Cal	115
Chamblee, James	Mch	Mid	112
Kinkade, Mike	EIP	Tex	112
Klassen, Danny	EIP	Tex	112
#Simmons, Brian	Bir	Sou	108
Clark, Brady	Bur	Mid	108
T Cabrera, O.	Ott	Int	107
Garland, Tim	SJ	Cal	106
T Gibson, Derrick	CSp	PCL	105
Moore, Kenderick	Lan	Mid	105
T*Lee, Travis	Tcn	PCL	105
*Darr, Mike	RC	Cal	104

WALKS

Player	Club	Lg.	BB
*Johnson, Mark	W-S	Caro	106
T Menechino, F.	Bir	Sou	105
T Christenson, R.	Edm	PCL	105
*Horne, Tyrone	KnC	Mid	104
Stcknschndr, E.	VB	FSL	101
*Mientkiewicz, D.	Nbr	East	98
*DeCinces, Tim	Del	SAL	97
*Fuller, Aaron	Tre	East	95
Cameron, S.	HD	Cal	93
T*Grieve, Ben	Edm	PCL	93
*Koskie, Corey	Nbr	East	90
*McClure, Brian	Cln	Mid	90
*Ryan, Rob	SBn	Mid	89

Switch-hitter
* Left-handed
T Player has been with more than one team; listed with last team.
(Players in major leagues are listed with last minor league club.)

Batting leaders across all leagues

(Cont'd from previous page)

TOTAL BASES

Player	Club	Lg.	TB
Stoner, Mike	HD	Cal	356
Millar, Kevin	Prt	East	309
T*Grieve, Ben	Edm	PCL	307
T*Ortiz, David	SLk	PCL	306
Coolbaugh, Mike	Hvl	Sou	303
Konerko, Paul	Abq	PCL	300
Gibson, Derrick	CSp	PCL	292
Cameron, S.	HD	Cal	290
Rohrmeier, Dan	Tac	PCL	290
T*Lee, Travis	Tcn	PCL	286
Hacker, Steve	Mac	SAL	285
*Minor, Damon	Bak	Cal	283
Lee, Carlos	W-S	Caro	282
*Butler, Rich	Syr	Int	281
Raven, Luis	Bir	Sou	279

STRIKEOUTS

Player	Club	Lg.	K
Ingram, Darron	Bur	Mid	195
T*Haas, Chris	PrW	Caro	182
T Light, Tal	Sal	Caro	180
#Abbott, Chuck	CR	Mid	170
Raleigh, Matt	Bng	East	169
Hessman, M.	Mac	SAL	167
Booty, Josh	Prt	East	166
Lindsey, Rodney	Cln	Mid	161
Coffee, Gary	Wil	Caro	157
T Diaz, Juan	VB	FSL	156
#Bartee, Kimera	Tol	Int	154
T Thomas, Juan	Bir	Sou	153
*VanderGriend, J.	LkE	Cal	153
Swinton, J.	Stk	Cal	152
T Schwab, Chris	WPB	FSL	152

HITS

Player	Club	Lg.	H
Stoner, Mike	HD	Cal	203
Raabe, Brian	Tac	PCL	191
Kinkade, Mike	ElP	Tex	180
Lopez, Luis	Hag	SAL	180
*Darr, Mike	RC	Cal	179
T Gibson, Derrick	CSp	PCL	179
Inglin, Jeff	Hck	SAL	179
*Cruz, Jacob	Phx	PCL	179
*Cromer, D.T.	Hvl	Sou	176
Millar, Kevin	Prt	East	175
T#Caruso, M.	W-S	Caro	174
Lee, Carlos	W-S	Caro	173
Wilson, Todd	SJ	Cal	173

\# Switch-hitter
* Left-handed
T Player has been with more than one team; listed with last team.
(Players in major leagues are listed with last minor league club.)

BATTING	AVG	AB	R	H	2B	3B	HR	RBI	BB	SO	SB
Mahalik, John, 2B	.218	188	19	41	12	0	1	18	11	39	2
Maness, Dwight, OF	.189	259	33	49	13	3	5	31	24	73	4
*Martin, Jim, OF	.233	90	17	21	2	0	8	14	16	37	6
*Mendoza, Carlos, OF	.382	228	36	87	12	2	1	13	14	25	14
Moore, Mike, OF	.300	130	19	39	11	1	2	13	18	47	7
Morales, Elvin, C	.250	4	0	1	0	0	0	0	0	1	0
Morgan, Kevin, SS	.194	191	16	37	7	0	1	10	19	25	11
#Parra, Franklin, 2B	.200	15	2	3	1	0	0	1	0	5	0
Polanco, Enohel, SS	.300	263	34	79	13	4	3	32	17	59	7
Raleigh, Matt, 3B	.196	398	71	78	15	0	37	74	79	169	0
Saunders, Chris, 3B	.324	111	16	36	13	0	3	22	12	20	3
*Seefried, Tate, 1B	.313	335	59	105	16	0	29	79	54	99	9
Wilson, Preston, OF	.286	259	37	74	12	1	19	47	21	71	7
Wilson, Vance, C	.276	322	46	89	17	0	15	40	20	46	2
#Zorrilla, Julio, 2B	.125	24	2	3	1	0	0	0	0	5	0

PITCHING	W	L	ERA	G	SV	IP	H	R	ER	BB	SO
*Arroyo, Luis	0	0	3.07	7	0	14.2	14	6	5	6	9
Carpenter, Brian	0	1	9.00	17	0	23.0	37	23	23	12	22
Dotel, Octavio	3	4	5.98	12	0	55.2	66	50	37	38	40
Edmondson, Brian	2	0	1.23	14	3	22.0	17	4	3	7	18
*Fesh, Sean	3	1	3.25	45	4	55.1	60	26	20	24	37
Figueroa, Nelson	5	11	4.34	33	0	143.0	137	76	69	68	116
Gooch, Arnold	10	12	5.09	27	0	161.0	179	106	91	76	98
Guerra, Mark	4	8	3.23	48	7	94.2	96	46	34	30	74
*Howard, Chris	0	0	1.15	13	1	15.2	6	2	2	7	16
*Perez, Yorkis	2	1	0.66	12	0	27.1	15	4	2	12	39
*Pierson, Jason	2	2	7.88	13	0	16.0	33	22	14	7	7
*Pulsipher, Bill	0	0	1.42	10	0	12.2	11	3	2	7	12
*Roberts, Chris	5	8	4.96	19	0	105.1	103	69	58	33	66
*Roque, Rafael	1	1	6.84	16	0	26.1	35	26	20	17	23
*Sanchez, Jesus	13	10	4.30	26	0	165.1	146	87	79	61	176
*Sauerbeck, Scott	8	9	4.93	27	0	131.1	144	89	72	50	88
Short, Barry	2	0	2.61	6	0	10.1	9	3	3	4	6
*Tolar, Kevin	1	1	5.12	22	0	31.2	38	20	18	22	26
Turrentine, Rich	2	4	5.23	61	13	62.0	66	38	36	54	58
*Vasquez, Leoner	0	1	10.13	1	0	5.1	7	6	6	2	2
*Yarnall, Ed	3	2	3.06	5	0	32.1	20	11	11	11	32

Bowie Baysox (Orioles) AA

BATTING	AVG	AB	R	H	2B	3B	HR	RBI	BB	SO	SB
Almonte, Wady, OF	.207	222	25	46	7	2	6	25	27	64	2
Bautista, Juan, SS	.250	68	9	17	1	0	0	3	5	17	1
Berry, Mike, 3B	.230	204	34	47	10	0	8	30	24	53	1
Bogle, Bryan, OF	.255	384	50	98	17	0	13	58	27	92	3
#Carney, Bartt, OF	.269	156	27	42	5	0	0	8	31	31	8
*Clark, Howie, 3B	.287	314	39	90	16	0	9	37	32	38	2
Daedelow, Craig, DH	.000	1	0	0	0	0	0	0	0	1	0
*Dellucci, David, OF	.327	385	71	126	29	3	20	55	58	69	11
Foster, Jim, C	.275	211	36	58	12	0	7	41	36	31	1
#Frazier, Lou, OF	.233	103	20	24	4	2	0	8	21	20	13
Garcia, Jesse, 2B	.236	437	52	103	18	1	5	42	38	71	7
Hoiles, Chris, C	.143	7	1	1	1	0	0	2	3	2	0
Isom, Johnny, OF	.274	518	70	142	28	4	20	91	44	121	1
#Kingsale, Eugene, OF	.413	46	8	19	6	0	0	4	5	4	5
Kirgan, Chris, 1B	.230	504	72	116	25	0	19	71	60	141	0
*Lamb, David, SS	.331	269	46	89	20	2	4	38	34	35	0
Lasater, Chris, C	.250	4	0	1	0	0	0	0	0	1	0
Lawrence, Chip, 3B	.231	13	1	3	0	0	0	0	1	3	0
*LeCronier, Jason, OF	.300	10	0	3	0	0	0	2	0	4	0
Luzinski, Ryan, C	.284	81	12	23	4	0	5	15	10	17	3
#Martin, Lincoln, 2B	.292	24	3	7	2	0	0	3	3	2	0
Martinez, Eddy, SS	.156	45	3	7	3	0	0	1	6	12	2
*Ojeda, Augie, SS	.294	204	33	60	9	1	2	23	31	17	7
Otanez, Willis, DH	.333	78	13	26	9	0	3	13	9	19	0
*Paxton, Chris, C	.136	22	1	3	1	0	0	1	1	7	0
#Rosario, Mel, C	.263	430	68	113	26	1	12	60	27	106	4

PITCHING	W	L	ERA	G	SV	IP	H	R	ER	BB	SO
Bennett, Chris	2	1	2.89	10	0	18.2	15	9	6	11	9
Bennett, Joel	6	8	3.18	44	4	113.1	89	45	40	40	146
Bullard, Jason	7	2	2.62	61	3	92.2	84	39	27	38	77
Cafaro, Rocco	3	3	5.40	13	0	48.1	50	34	29	16	43
Coppinger, Rocky	1	1	4.80	3	0	15.0	15	9	8	3	15
Curtis, Chris	6	1	3.62	36	2	87.0	100	41	35	17	48
*Dykhoff, Radhames	0	0	8.31	7	0	8.2	10	9	8	7	7
Falkenborg, Brian	0	1	16.20	1	0	1.2	3	3	3	3	0

PITCHING	W	L	ERA	G	SV	IP	H	R	ER	BB	SO
Fussell, Chris	1	8	7.11	19	0	82.1	102	71	65	58	71
Gallaher, Kevin	1	5	4.46	26	8	42.1	50	27	21	15	36
Greer, Ken	1	1	4.08	11	0	17.2	17	9	8	3	12
Hernandez, Francis	0	0	1.59	6	0	5.2	7	1	1	4	2
Kohlmeier, Ryan	0	0	0.00	2	1	2.2	0	0	0	2	5
*Lane, Aaron	0	1	7.94	7	0	5.2	6	5	5	7	4
Maine, Dalton	0	0	0.00	9	0	12.2	4	0	0	6	11
Montgomery, Steve	10	5	3.10	24	0	136.1	116	56	47	52	127
Moreno, Julio	9	6	3.83	27	0	138.2	141	76	59	64	106
*Osteen, Gavin	1	1	2.05	18	0	30.2	20	7	7	11	22
*Parrish, John	1	0	1.80	1	0	5.0	3	1	1	2	3
Percibal, Billy	0	1	3.00	1	0	6.0	5	2	2	1	5
Ponson, Sidney	2	7	5.42	13	0	74.2	77	51	45	32	56
Saneaux, Francisco	0	0	8.56	8	0	13.2	8	14	13	32	13
Shepherd, Alvie	10	6	5.33	22	0	106.1	98	68	63	57	80
Smith, Hut	5	4	4.22	14	0	81.0	90	45	38	22	46
Snyder, Matt	7	5	4.16	67	19	80.0	89	48	37	42	68
Steph, Rod	1	0	1.32	7	0	13.2	6	3	2	3	9

Harrisburg Senators (Expos) AA

BATTING	AVG	AB	R	H	2B	3B	HR	RBI	BB	SO	SB
Alcantara, Israel, 3B	.282	301	48	85	9	2	27	68	29	84	4
#Bady, Edward, OF	.210	267	36	56	8	4	1	22	21	62	15
Bocachica, Hiram, SS	.278	443	82	123	19	3	11	35	41	98	29
Brinkley, Josh, 3B	.315	54	8	17	2	0	2	6	1	12	0
Cabrera, Jolbert, 2B	.251	171	28	43	9	0	2	11	28	28	5
Cabrera, Orlando, SS	.308	133	34	41	13	2	5	20	15	18	7
Campos, Jesus, OF	.308	286	33	88	12	1	5	36	8	24	6
Carvajal, Jhonny, 3B	.259	378	36	98	12	1	1	31	27	66	10
Coquillette, Trace, 2B	.259	293	46	76	17	3	10	51	25	40	9
Fernandez, Jose, 3B	.229	96	10	22	3	1	4	11	11	28	2
*Fullmer, Brad, 1B	.311	357	60	111	24	2	19	62	30	25	6
*Haas, Matthew, 3B	.211	19	2	4	1	0	1	4	4	2	1
Henley, Bob, C	.304	280	41	85	19	0	12	49	32	40	5
*Lukachyk, Rob, OF	.275	153	26	42	6	3	7	26	11	26	5
Morales, Francisco, C	.204	49	5	10	1	0	2	4	3	22	0
Ortiz, Bo, OF	.223	188	24	42	2	3	7	21	12	25	5
Pachot, John, C	.279	323	40	90	23	5	7	50	22	42	6
*Peterson, Nate, OF	.243	140	17	34	4	2	4	18	17	27	1
Post, Dave, 2B	.263	156	26	41	10	0	3	18	24	24	5
*Samuels, Scott, OF	.296	223	32	66	19	1	5	32	34	43	13
#Stovall, Darond, OF	.284	169	29	48	4	1	9	39	23	30	4
*Stowers, Chris, OF	.288	59	9	17	4	2	0	4	5	11	3
Valdez, Trovin, OF	.310	42	8	13	2	0	0	4	4	9	2

PITCHING	W	L	ERA	G	SV	IP	H	R	ER	BB	SO
Bennett, Shayne	4	2	4.40	23	2	47.0	47	28	23	20	38
*Benz, Jacob	4	1	2.33	23	2	38.2	39	12	10	20	36
Bullinger, Kirk	3	0	2.67	21	6	27.0	22	9	8	6	21
Bunch, Mel	3	3	4.20	9	0	49.1	45	27	23	22	50
Cole, Jason	2	3	3.57	37	0	58.0	52	31	23	19	31
DaSilva, Fernando	0	3	13.83	12	0	13.2	21	23	21	10	11
Dedrick, Jim	2	1	2.79	15	1	19.1	18	8	6	8	17
*Dixon, Timothy	5	2	3.38	37	0	69.1	66	34	26	24	75
Fleetham, Ben	2	1	3.04	49	30	50.1	28	21	17	33	69
*Forster, Scott	3	6	2.27	17	0	79.1	77	45	20	48	71
*Martinez, Ramiro	4	4	3.69	37	1	75.2	64	36	31	33	69
McCommon, Jason	6	3	5.01	29	0	82.2	81	50	46	39	58
Mitchell, Scott	1	0	3.63	4	0	17.1	11	7	7	3	13
*Moore, Trey	11	6	4.15	27	0	162.2	152	91	75	66	137
*Phelps, Tom	10	6	4.71	18	0	101.1	115	68	53	39	86
Smart, J.D.	6	3	3.69	12	0	70.2	75	34	29	24	43
Stevenson, Rodney	0	0	3.86	4	0	7.0	9	5	3	5	6
Thurman, Mike	9	6	3.81	20	0	115.2	102	54	49	30	85
Vazquez, Javier	4	0	1.07	6	0	42.0	15	5	5	12	47
*Weber, Neil	7	6	3.83	18	0	112.2	93	56	48	51	121
*Young, Tim	0	0	0.00	1	0	2.0	1	0	0	0	3

New Britain Rock Cats (Twins) AA

BATTING	AVG	AB	R	H	2B	3B	HR	RBI	BB	SO	SB
Allen, Chad, OF	.252	115	20	29	9	1	4	18	9	21	2
*Alvarez, Rafael, OF	.255	47	5	12	0	0	2	7	5	9	1
Brown, Armann, OF	.152	46	4	7	3	0	0	1	9	13	1
Ferguson, Jeff, DH	.244	135	19	33	4	0	1	21	12	31	1
Fortin, Troy, C	.234	47	11	11	2	0	0	4	3	7	0
Fraser, Joe, OF	.239	238	33	57	11	1	1	16	29	50	11

Batting leaders across all leagues

(Cont'd from previous page)

DOUBLES

Player	Club	Lg.	2B
*Fick, Robert	WMi	Mid	50
LaRue, Jason	CWV	SAL	50
Lee, Carlos	W-S	Caro	50
Lopez, Luis	Hag	SAL	47
Nicholas, Darrell	ElP	Tex	47
T Burke, Jamie	Van	PCL	45
*Cruz, Jacob	Phx	PCL	45
*Simon, Randall	Rmd	Int	45
Stoner, Mike	HD	Cal	44
Rohrmeier, Dan	Tac	PCL	43
Buxbaum, Danny	Mdl	Tex	42
Minor, Ryan	Del	SAL	42
T#Lamb, David	Bow	East	41
Marcinczyk, T.R.	Mod	Cal	41

TRIPLES

Player	Club	Lg.	3B
#Carvajal, Jovino	Van	PCL	20
*Mathis, Joe	Lnc	Cal	15
#Green, Chad	Stk	Cal	14
Lugo, Julio	Kis	FSL	14
T#Bates, Fletcher	Bng	East	13
T#Caruso, M.	W-S	Caro	13
T Christenson, R.	Edm	PCL	13
#Mota, Tony	SBr	Cal	13
Richardson, Brian	SAn	Tex	13

EXTRA BASE HITS

Player	Club	Lg.	EBH
Stoner, Mike	HD	Cal	82
Rohrmeier, Dan	Tac	PCL	80
T*Grieve, Ben	Edm	PCL	74
T*Branyan, R.	Akr	East	71
T*Ortiz, David	SLk	PCL	71
Lee, Carlos	W-S	Caro	71
T*Barker, Kevin	ElP	Tex	69
T#Bates, Fletcher	Bng	East	69
Coolbaugh, Mike	Hvl	Sou	69
*Fick, Robert	WMi	Mid	69
T*Guiel, Aaron	Mob	Sou	69
Hacker, Steve	Mac	SAL	69
Konerko, Paul	Abq	PCL	69
T*Lee, Travis	Tcn	PCL	69

Switch-hitter
* Left-handed
T Player has been with more than one team; listed with last team.
(Players in major leagues are listed with last minor league club.)

Batting leaders across all leagues

(Cont'd from previous page)

SACRIFICE HITS

Player	Club	Lg.	SH
Garcia, Jesse	Bow	East	24
Moore, Brandon	Bir	Sou	21
#Rodriguez, Juan	CR	Mid	18
Reynoso, B.	RC	Cal	18
#Durrington, Trent	LkE	Cal	17
Hutchison, B.	Ash	SAL	16
T#Zorrilla, Julio	SLu	FSL	16
Livingston, Doug	Ash	SAL	15
Paz, Richard	Del	SAL	15
#Venghaus, Jeff	KnC	Mid	15

SACRIFICE FLIES

Player	Club	Lg.	SF
*Johnson, Adam	Dur	Caro	16
#Seguignol, F.	WPB	FSL	14
Beltre, Adrian	VB	FSL	11
Castro, Ramon	Kis	FSL	11
T Hernandez, R.	Hvl	Sou	11
T Lowell, Mike	Col	Int	11
Stoner, Mike	HD	Cal	11
Kapler, Gabe	Lak	FSL	10
*Tucker, Jon	VB	FSL	10
Barrett, Michael	WPB	FSL	10
*Daubach, Brian	Chr	Int	10
T Hartman, Ron	HD	Cal	10

HIT-BY-PITCH

Player	Club	Lg.	HBP
Kominek, Toby	Stk	Cal	24
*Clifford, Jim	Lnc	Cal	22
*Anderson, Cliff	SBr	Cal	20
T Coquillette, T.	Hrb	East	20
T Dallimore, Brian	Kis	FSL	20
T*Francia, David	Clw	FSL	20
T Skett, Will	Knx	Sou	20
Encarnacion, J.	Jax	Sou	19
T*Guiel, Aaron	Mob	Sou	19
Moore, Kenderick	Lan	Mid	19
*Stenson, Dernell	Mch	Mid	19
*Johnson, Nick	GBo	SAL	18
Hall, Ronnie	Day	FSL	18
Held, Dan	Rea	East	18

Notes

Switch-hitter
* Left-handed
T Player has been with more than one team; listed with last team.
(Players in major leagues are listed with last minor league club.)

BATTING	AVG	AB	R	H	2B	3B	HR	RBI	BB	SO	SB
Gunderson, Shane, OF	.256	117	17	30	7	3	2	10	19	31	7
Horn, Jeff, C	.255	184	17	47	10	0	4	26	19	24	2
Hunter, Torii, OF	.231	471	57	109	22	2	8	56	47	94	8
Johnson, J.J., OF	.236	356	60	84	11	3	3	42	38	94	13
*Koskie, Corey, 3B	.286	437	88	125	26	6	23	79	90	106	9
Lane, Ryan, 2B	.259	444	63	115	26	2	5	56	43	59	18
*Legree, Keith, OF	.242	343	46	83	19	2	9	58	56	70	10
*Mientkiewicz, D., 1B	.255	467	87	119	28	2	15	61	98	67	21
Moriarty, Mike, SS	.221	421	60	93	22	5	6	48	53	68	12
*Ortiz, David, DH	.322	258	40	83	22	2	14	56	21	78	2
Schaeffer, Jon, C	.207	29	1	6	2	0	0	4	2	7	1
*Smith, Jeff, C	.222	18	1	4	1	0	0	3	2	4	0
#Valentin, Javier, C	.243	370	41	90	17	0	8	50	30	61	2

PITCHING	W	L	ERA	G	SV	IP	H	R	ER	BB	SO
*Baptist, Travis	5	6	3.41	36	0	60.2	49	27	23	26	50
Barcelo, Marc	0	1	8.61	7	1	23.0	27	22	22	28	9
Bell, Jason	11	9	3.39	28	0	164.2	163	71	62	64	142
Bowers, Shane	7	2	3.41	14	0	71.1	65	29	27	22	59
*Carrasco, Troy	4	4	4.96	31	1	65.1	69	53	36	44	46
*Cobb, Trevor	6	4	3.43	19	1	94.1	77	41	36	39	68
*Cumberland, Chris	12	10	3.99	26	0	160.1	193	102	71	61	83
Gandarillas, Gus	2	4	4.70	17	0	61.1	67	34	32	15	29
Gourdin, Tom	2	2	5.31	49	15	61.0	62	36	36	29	32
Harris, Jeff	2	1	2.34	28	3	42.1	30	15	11	16	44
Legault, Kevin	5	1	4.50	40	3	70.0	74	37	35	26	40
Linebarger, Keith	0	1	7.20	1	0	5.0	5	4	4	3	1
*Mahaffey, Alan	1	2	3.57	13	1	22.2	19	11	9	10	29
Morse, Paul	3	11	5.98	37	1	111.1	124	91	74	70	75
Mott, Tom	0	0	0.00	1	0	1.1	2	0	0	0	0
Perez, David	0	1	6.75	1	0	4.0	5	3	3	1	3
Perkins, Dan	7	10	4.91	24	0	144.2	158	94	79	53	114
Rath, Fred	3	3	2.68	33	12	50.1	43	17	15	13	33
*Rushing, Will	1	2	3.97	3	0	11.1	14	5	5	3	9
*Sampson, Benj	10	6	4.19	25	0	118.0	112	56	55	49	92
Trinidad, Hector	0	2	6.33	6	0	21.1	26	18	15	8	11

New Haven Ravens (Rockies) AA

BATTING	AVG	AB	R	H	2B	3B	HR	RBI	BB	SO	SB
#Barry, Jeff, OF	.219	146	21	32	4	0	5	12	4	34	3
Barthol, Blake, C	.243	325	42	79	12	2	6	39	31	76	5
Bernhardt, Steve, 2B	.213	315	35	67	14	0	6	38	27	46	2
*Boston, D.J., 1B	.287	293	53	84	14	2	7	49	49	63	1
Curtis, Kevin, OF	.273	429	65	117	30	0	18	82	41	104	1
Feuerstein, Dave, OF	.260	104	8	27	4	3	0	10	7	20	2
Garcia, Vicente, 2B	.155	58	9	9	2	0	2	11	12	19	0
Gibson, Derrick, OF	.317	461	91	146	24	2	23	75	36	100	20
Giudice, John, OF	.250	216	26	54	8	2	5	30	16	49	5
#Grunewald, Keith, 2B	.242	310	41	75	11	1	0	24	25	78	7
#Hall, Billy, 2B	.220	59	8	13	2	1	1	7	7	10	7
Holdren, Nate, 1B	.183	82	9	15	2	0	4	9	3	28	0
#Jarrett, Link, SS	.303	261	19	79	9	1	1	27	18	30	2
*Lewis, Anthony, OF	.228	167	32	38	9	0	12	36	13	39	1
Light, Tal, 3B	.241	83	10	20	6	0	5	11	5	36	0
*Newstrom, Doug, C	.266	244	29	65	10	1	1	43	39	32	9
*Osborne, Mark, DH	.000	5	1	0	0	0	0	0	2	4	0
*Pledger, Kinnis, OF	.254	201	35	51	10	2	10	26	30	53	2
Sexton, Chris, SS	.297	360	65	107	22	4	1	38	62	37	8
Shumpert, Terry, 2B	.235	17	2	4	0	0	1	1	0	2	0
*Taylor, Jamie, 3B	.325	329	43	107	17	1	8	41	35	49	2
*Wells, Forry, OF	.224	98	16	22	4	0	2	7	21	37	1

PITCHING	W	L	ERA	G	SV	IP	H	R	ER	BB	SO
Bost, Heath	2	2	3.56	38	20	43.0	44	18	17	10	45
Brownson, Mark	10	9	4.19	29	0	184.2	172	101	86	55	170
Byrd, Matt	1	3	5.01	10	0	23.1	22	15	13	12	17
Dejean, Mike	0	1	6.00	2	0	3.0	3	2	2	2	2
Hackman, Luther	0	6	7.82	10	0	50.2	58	49	44	34	34
Henderson, Ryan	2	5	4.80	24	0	50.2	54	29	27	27	46
*Kammerer, James	0	0	3.60	1	0	5.0	3	2	2	3	1
*Kusiewicz, Mike	2	4	6.35	10	0	28.1	41	28	20	10	11
Macca, Chris	0	4	7.77	46	9	44.0	47	40	38	55	29
*Million, Doug	0	5	9.23	10	0	40.0	64	46	41	36	19
Moore, Joel	6	4	3.84	19	0	77.1	77	38	33	35	47
Norman, Scott	1	5	6.75	29	1	41.1	58	38	31	15	21
Peever, Lloyd	5	5	5.50	20	0	73.2	70	49	45	24	46
Pool, Matt	3	5	4.28	29	0	48.1	57	36	23	16	23

PITCHING	W	L	ERA	G	SV	IP	H	R	ER	BB	SO
*Price, Tom	1	3	3.16	48	0	57.0	55	25	20	21	48
Saipe, Mike	8	5	3.10	19	0	136.2	127	57	47	29	123
Shoemaker, Stephen	6	4	3.02	14	0	95.1	64	36	32	53	111
Stidham, Phil	0	0	3.72	8	1	9.2	10	4	4	8	7
*Vavrek, Mike	12	3	2.57	17	0	122.2	94	38	35	34	101
*Watkins, Scott	2	0	3.52	13	0	15.1	9	6	6	3	8
Zolecki, Mike	3	5	5.08	16	0	56.2	64	38	32	32	32

Norwich Navigators (Yankees) AA

BATTING	AVG	AB	R	H	2B	3B	HR	RBI	BB	SO	SB
Ashby, Chris, 1B	.249	457	92	114	20	1	24	82	80	95	10
*Bierek, Kurt, OF	.271	473	77	128	32	2	18	78	56	89	4
Brown, Randy, SS	.250	396	61	99	13	4	11	57	47	124	11
Brown, Ron, OF	.287	362	47	104	17	3	5	50	35	59	5
Buchanan, Brian, OF	.309	470	75	145	25	2	10	69	32	85	11
Dennis, Les, SS	.333	30	4	10	1	0	0	2	5	11	1
*Donato, Daniel, 3B	.275	349	44	96	16	1	5	43	26	44	7
*Dukart, Derek, 3B	.344	32	4	11	2	0	0	5	3	4	0
Fithian, Grant, C	.281	253	38	71	16	1	8	51	41	52	1
Gomez, Rudy, 2B	.300	393	65	118	18	7	5	52	61	64	11
Hawkins, Kraig, OF	.261	188	36	49	6	1	0	16	26	37	12
Hinds, Rob, 2B	.244	119	15	29	4	1	0	12	12	31	1
Lobaton, Jose, SS	.193	197	16	38	6	0	1	15	12	60	2
#Long, R.D., SS	.281	89	18	25	5	1	2	17	13	21	5
Lowell, Mike, 3B	.344	285	60	98	17	0	15	47	48	30	2
Martinez, Gabby, SS	.321	312	49	100	12	5	6	54	11	44	21
#Raines, Tim, OF	.286	7	0	2	1	0	0	2	0	2	0
Ramirez, Angel, OF	.000	1	0	0	0	0	0	0	0	1	0
#Smith, Sloan, OF	.200	5	1	1	0	0	0	0	1	2	0
*Strawberry, Darryl, OF	.000	2	0	0	0	0	0	0	0	1	0
*Wilcox, Luke, OF	.277	300	45	83	13	1	6	34	18	36	13
Wilson, Tom, C	.296	419	88	124	21	4	21	80	86	126	1

PITCHING	W	L	ERA	G	SV	IP	H	R	ER	BB	SO
Beverlin, Jason	1	0	7.78	25	0	41.2	50	38	36	24	42
Buddie, Mike	0	0	0.00	1	0	1.0	0	0	0	0	3
Croghan, Andy	2	1	5.72	42	4	67.2	72	48	43	36	85
*Cumberland, Chris	11	10	4.02	25	0	154.2	188	100	69	59	81
DeLaCruz, Francisco	0	1	3.24	2	0	8.1	8	3	3	7	0
Delossantos, Luis	1	1	2.52	4	0	25.0	23	9	7	7	15
Ford, Ben	4	3	4.22	28	1	42.2	35	28	20	19	38
Gooden, Dwight	3	0	3.00	3	0	18.0	13	6	6	5	14
Henthorne, Kevin	2	1	3.31	33	2	73.1	72	32	27	14	64
*Hubbard, Mark	0	0	15.43	2	0	2.1	6	4	4	1	0
Irabu, Hideki	1	1	4.50	2	0	10.0	13	5	5	0	9
Jerzembeck, Mike	2	1	1.71	8	0	42.0	21	10	8	16	42
Lankford, Frank	4	2	2.90	11	0	68.1	58	28	22	15	39
Lomon, Kevin	9	7	3.21	18	0	115.0	104	51	41	50	117
Maeda, Katsuhiro	8	10	4.56	25	0	124.1	117	75	63	62	76
*Milton, Eric	6	3	3.13	14	0	77.2	59	29	27	36	67
Mitchell, Larry	9	9	3.49	57	0	95.1	98	45	37	37	99
Resz, Greg	5	4	4.70	25	0	90.0	94	59	47	43	75
Ricken, Ray	0	2	6.75	2	0	10.2	12	8	8	5	13
Rose, Scott	0	2	2.67	21	4	30.1	34	17	9	8	20
Schlomann, Brett	1	4	7.85	10	0	47.0	66	43	41	17	36
Tessmer, Jay	3	6	5.31	55	17	62.2	78	41	37	24	51
*Urso, Sal	1	1	1.26	7	1	14.1	14	2	2	5	13

Portland Sea Dogs (Marlins) AA

BATTING	AVG	AB	R	H	2B	3B	HR	RBI	BB	SO	SB
Booty, Josh, 3B	.210	448	42	94	19	2	20	69	27	166	2
Cook, Hayward, OF	.295	166	37	49	13	0	5	21	13	44	2
Gonzalez, Alex, SS	.254	449	69	114	16	4	19	65	27	83	4
Hastings, Lionel, 2B	.344	279	55	96	21	0	10	35	39	53	6
*Jackson, Ryan, OF	.312	491	87	153	28	4	26	98	51	85	2
Koeyers, Ramsey, C	.259	286	37	74	14	1	12	50	15	67	0
*Kotsay, Mark, OF	.306	438	103	134	27	2	20	77	75	65	17
Millar, Kevin, 1B	.342	511	94	175	34	2	32	131	66	53	2
Milliard, Ralph, 2B	.275	69	13	19	1	2	0	5	7	8	3
Reeves, Glenn, OF	.351	222	53	78	14	2	6	35	39	43	9
Rodriguez, Victor, 2B	.277	401	63	111	18	4	3	38	30	43	13
Roskos, John, C	.308	451	66	139	31	1	24	84	50	81	4
Torres, Tony, 2B	.260	50	12	13	2	1	2	4	8	15	2
*Wilson, Pookie, OF	.252	115	15	29	6	0	3	14	11	15	2
#Winn, Randy, OF	.292	384	66	112	15	6	8	36	42	92	35

Batting leaders across all leagues

(Cont'd from previous page)

CAUGHT STEALING

Player	Club	Lg.	CS
*Sanchez, Alex	CSC	SAL	40
Metcalfe, Mike	SBr	Cal	32
T Winn, Randy	Prt	East	28
Abreu, Dennis	Rkf	Mid	26
Ramirez, Daniel	Clb	SAL	25
Avila, Rolo	SBr	Cal	24
*Taylor, Reggie	Clw	FSL	23
T*Robinson, Kerry	Lou	AmAs	23
Lindsey, Rodney	Cln	Mid	23
T*Bergeron, Peter	SBr	Cal	21
Gomez, Ramon	W-S	Caro	21
*Christensen, M.	Hck	SAL	20
T*Conti, Jason	HD	Cal	20
#Smith, Rod	GBo	SAL	20
*Trippy, Joe	Dur	Caro	20

TOUGHEST TO STRIKE OUT

Player	Club	Lg.	TPA/SO
*Gorecki, Ryan	Chl	FSL	36.00
Raabe, Brian	Tac	PCL	30.35
Figueroa, Luis	Wsc	Mid	24.95
T#Caruso, M.	W-S	Caro	22.85
T*Bridges, Kary	Cgy	PCL	18.84
T Hajek, Dave	LVg	PCL	18.71
Howard, Matt	Col	Int	16.61
Wilson, Craig	Nvl	AmAs	16.58
LoDuca, Paul	SAn	Tex	16.41
Diaz, Eddy	Tcn	PCL	16.08
T Allison, Chris	Paw	Int	15.68
Torres, Jaime	Tam	FSL	14.97
T Stynes, Chris	Ind	AmAs	14.97
Macias, Jose	Lak	FSL	14.79
T*Fullmer, Brad	Ott	Int	14.26

SWITCH-HITTERS

Player	Club	Lg.	BA
Gibbs, Kevin	SAn	Tex	.335
TChristian, Eddie	Tac	PCL	.330
Tatis, Fernando	Tul	Tex	.314
TBrown, Adrian	Cgy	PCL	.313
TCaruso, M.	W-S	Caro	.311
TBolick, Frank	Van	PCL	.309
Latham, Chris	SLk	PCL	.309
Wilson, Enrique	Buf	AmAs	.306
TCurtis, Matt	LkE	Cal	.305
Proctor, Murph	SBr	Cal	.304
TOjeda, Augie	Roc	Int	.303
TMeluskey, M.	NO	AmAs	.303
Lopez, Mickey	ElP	Tex	.300
TPearson, Eddie	Nvl	AmAs	.298
T Winn, Randy	Prt	East	.298

Switch-hitter
* Left-handed
T Player has been with more than one team; listed with last team.
(Players in major leagues are listed with last minor league club.)

Pitching leaders across all leagues

ERA (MINIMUM 112 IP)

Player	Club	Lg.	ERA
T Vazquez, Javier	Hrb	East	1.86
Quintal, Craig	WMi	Mid	1.96
T*Darwin, David	Lak	FSL	1.98
T Clement, Matt	Mob	Sou	2.05
T Duncan, C.	Orl	Sou	2.11
Heredia, Maximo	Del	SAL	2.13
T Politte, Cliff	Ark	Tex	2.19
Lincoln, Mike	FtM	FSL	2.28
T*Ah Yat, Paul	Lyn	Caro	2.35
Roberts, Grant	Clb	SAL	2.36
Bruner, Clayton	WMi	Mid	2.38

WINS

Player	Club	Lg.	W
T Cornelius, Reid	Chr	Int	17
Rose, Brian	Paw	Int	17
T Carrara, G.	Ind	AmAs	16
T Mays, Joe	Lnc	Cal	16
Smith, Travis	ElP	Tex	16
Borkowski, David	WMi	Mid	15
Bruner, Clayton	WMi	Mid	15
*Lee, Corey	Chl	FSL	15
T Luce, Robert	Mem	Sou	15
T Miller, Wade	Kis	FSL	15
Minchey, Nate	CSp	PCL	15
T Politte, Cliff	Ark	Tex	15
T*Washburn, J.	Van	PCL	15
T Woodard, Steve	Tcn	PCL	15

COMPLETE GAMES

Player	Club	Lg.	CG
Ortiz, Ramon	CR	Mid	8
Powell, Brian	Lak	FSL	8
Edsell, Geoff	Van	PCL	6
*Krivda, Rick	Roc	Int	6
*Lee, Corey	Chl	FSL	6
T Miller, Wade	Kis	FSL	6
T*Norton, Phillip	Orl	Sou	6
T Woodard, Steve	Tcn	PCL	6

Notes

Switch-hitter
* Left-handed
T Player has been with more than one team; listed with last team.
(Players in major leagues are listed with last minor league club.)

PITCHING

	W	L	ERA	G	SV	IP	H	R	ER	BB	SO
*Burgus, Travis	4	3	6.75	16	0	52.0	63	47	39	26	29
Castro, Tony	1	2	4.58	27	0	39.1	47	21	20	17	21
Chavez, Carlos	2	1	5.26	30	1	39.1	35	23	23	16	32
Chergey, Dan	2	0	3.23	32	7	39.0	30	14	14	7	44
Cornelius, Reid	5	0	2.73	6	0	33.0	32	11	10	17	24
*Duvall, Mike	4	6	1.84	45	18	68.1	63	20	14	20	49
*Gonzalez, Gabe	3	2	2.11	29	3	42.2	43	12	10	5	28
Gonzalez, Juan	0	1	6.75	17	0	29.1	32	25	22	10	21
Haynes, Heath	5	1	2.97	47	3	72.2	69	25	24	16	73
Hernandez, Livan	0	0	2.25	1	0	4.0	2	1	1	7	2
Hurst, Bill	0	0	0.00	2	0	2.0	1	0	0	0	2
Jacobsen, Joe	5	5	5.09	47	11	58.1	76	44	33	23	48
Mantei, Matt	1	0	6.75	5	0	4.0	1	3	3	8	7
Meadows, Brian	9	7	4.61	29	0	175.2	204	99	90	48	115
*Mercado, Hector	11	3	3.96	31	0	129.2	129	66	57	44	125
Mix, Greg	7	7	4.73	30	0	102.2	121	70	54	32	74
Norris, Joe	2	0	6.75	9	0	12.0	11	9	9	5	14
Parisi, Mike	1	3	7.08	9	0	40.2	56	36	32	14	27
Press, Gregg	7	11	4.98	28	0	144.2	178	101	80	41	93
Rector, Bobby	2	2	4.81	6	0	33.2	45	20	18	11	23
*Saunders, Tony	0	0	9.00	1	0	2.0	3	2	2	1	3
Townsend, Dave	3	7	4.87	15	0	77.2	86	49	42	36	30
*Ward, Bryan	6	3	3.91	12	0	76.0	71	39	33	19	69

Reading Phillies (Phillies) AA

BATTING

	AVG	AB	R	H	2B	3B	HR	RBI	BB	SO	SB
#Amador, Manuel, 3B	.243	169	17	41	9	1	2	22	20	29	0
*Anderson, Marlon, 2B	.266	553	88	147	18	6	10	62	42	77	27
Angeli, Doug, SS	.223	148	25	33	5	1	5	19	16	28	1
#Burton, Darren, OF	.315	184	23	58	11	3	8	34	9	39	1
*Carver, Steve, OF	.262	282	41	74	11	3	15	43	36	69	2
Costello, Brian, OF	.194	36	6	7	2	1	1	5	2	12	0
Dawkins, Walt, OF	.239	331	48	79	13	1	8	40	35	90	4
Guiliano, Matt, SS	.226	367	38	83	15	3	7	37	34	99	7
Held, Dan, 1B	.272	525	80	143	31	4	26	86	42	116	1
Hudler, Rex, OF	.348	23	5	8	2	0	1	5	1	2	0
Huff, Larry, 3B	.264	425	58	112	21	3	5	41	36	57	24
Millan, Adan, C	.244	266	43	65	10	0	9	43	44	52	0
Northeimer, Jamie, C	.200	100	14	20	6	0	1	16	25	22	0
#Pagano, Scott, OF	.274	468	77	128	16	3	3	44	48	62	17
Royster, Aaron, OF	.257	412	59	106	18	5	15	62	53	104	2
Tremie, Chris, C	.203	295	20	60	11	1	2	31	36	61	0
Wesemann, Jason, 3B	.182	11	4	2	0	0	1		2	2	0

PITCHING

	W	L	ERA	G	SV	IP	H	R	ER	BB	SO
Barbao, Joe	2	3	5.23	52	2	75.2	101	53	44	28	33
Boyd, Jason	10	6	4.82	48	0	115.2	113	65	62	64	98
Brannan, Ryan	4	2	3.10	45	20	52.1	52	18	18	20	39
*Censale, Silvio	9	4	4.36	20	0	107.1	88	58	52	56	102
Costa, Tony	7	12	5.24	28	0	165.0	174	111	96	72	110
*Dodd, Robert	9	4	3.25	63	8	80.1	61	29	29	21	94
Fiore, Tony	8	3	3.01	17	0	104.2	89	47	35	40	64
*Foster, Mark	2	2	6.35	9	1	17.0	20	16	12	8	9
Grace, Mike	1	3	5.75	4	0	20.1	28	17	13	6	10
Hunter, Rich	6	11	4.69	29	0	163.0	191	100	85	60	104
*Manning, Len	3	1	5.34	28	0	62.1	66	40	37	46	41
Ryan, Ken	0	0	0.00	2	0	2.0	1	0	0	1	4
Thomas, Evan	3	6	4.12	15	0	83.0	98	51	38	32	83
Troutman, Keith	6	5	3.77	57	7	107.1	94	48	45	34	103
Westbrook, Destry	0	2	8.20	26	4	45.0	70	49	41	22	38
*Whiteman, Greg	4	4	4.05	9	0	53.1	57	27	24	21	31

Trenton Thunder (Red Sox) AA

BATTING

	AVG	AB	R	H	2B	3B	HR	RBI	BB	SO	SB
*Abad, Andy, 1B	.303	165	37	50	13	0	8	24	33	27	2
Borrero, Richie, C	.251	203	31	51	12	1	3	23	13	46	2
Bryant, Pat, OF	.288	379	73	109	20	3	19	77	60	76	18
Coleman, Michael, OF	.301	385	56	116	17	8	14	58	41	89	20
Correia, Rod, 2B	.293	249	40	73	18	1	7	33	22	32	4
Depastino, Joe, C	.254	276	51	70	14	1	17	55	32	63	1
Derosso, Tony, 3B	.216	357	50	77	18	1	14	40	26	94	13
#Epperson, Chad, 1B	.333	9	2	3	1	0	0	1	0	2	1
*Faggett, Ethan, OF	.286	56	10	16	2	0	2	8	8	17	2
#Fuller, Aaron, OF	.260	481	87	125	17	6	6	46	95	84	40
Gibralter, David, 1B	.274	478	70	131	25	1	14	86	44	103	3
Haselman, Bill, C	.231	26	3	6	1	0	2	3	2	2	0

BATTING	AVG	AB	R	H	2B	3B	HR	RBI	BB	SO	SB
Jackson, Gavin, SS	.272	301	46	82	12	0	1	46	48	36	2
Liniak, Cole, 3B	.280	200	20	56	11	0	2	18	17	29	0
*Madonna, Chris, C	.341	41	7	14	3	0	0	6	6	11	2
McKeel, Walt, DH	.160	25	0	4	2	0	0	4	1	2	0
Merloni, Lou, 3B	.310	255	49	79	17	4	5	37	30	43	3
Ortiz, Nick, 2B	.281	288	47	81	17	2	8	53	27	55	3
#Tebbs, Nate, 2B	.313	16	2	5	0	0	0	0	2	1	0
*Williams, Juan, OF	.200	200	34	40	5	1	12	30	33	63	0

PITCHING	W	L	ERA	G	SV	IP	H	R	ER	BB	SO
*Barkley, Brian	12	9	4.94	29	0	178.2	208	113	98	79	121
*Betti, Rich	2	0	6.35	3	0	39.2	42	29	28	17	30
Blais, Mike	2	0	3.32	18	5	21.2	26	11	8	12	14
*Cannon, Kevan	1	1	2.81	13	1	16.0	7	7	5	12	11
Cederblad, Brett	0	0	8.68	6	0	9.1	12	10	9	2	7
Checo, Robinson	1	0	2.35	1	0	7.2	6	3	2	1	9
Farrell, Jim	12	7	4.37	26	0	162.2	173	93	79	57	110
Fernandez, Jared	4	6	5.41	21	0	121.1	138	90	73	66	73
*Gonzales, Frank	3	1	5.88	14	2	26.0	29	18	17	16	14
*Hale, Chad	0	0	8.31	3	0	4.1	5	5	4	5	2
Hecker, Doug	1	0	2.57	4	0	7.0	5	2	2	9	7
*Mahay, Ron	3	3	3.10	17	5	40.2	29	16	14	13	47
Munro, Peter	7	10	4.95	22	0	116.1	113	76	64	47	109
*Orellano, Rafael	0	1	17.05	2	0	6.1	14	12	12	7	5
Pena, Juan	5	6	4.73	16	0	97.0	98	56	51	31	79
Peterson, Dean	1	3	4.60	33	5	58.2	67	30	30	30	48
*Ramirez, Felix	4	2	5.44	18	2	41.1	43	28	25	20	29
Rose, Brian	2	1	2.84	15	0	25.1	23	8	8	10	18
Saberhagen, Bret	0	0	0.00	2	0	8.0	2	0	0	1	9
*Smetana, Steve	1	2	2.95	18	3	21.1	25	9	7	7	16
Tweedlie, Brad	4	6	5.77	41	5	57.2	62	41	37	44	30
Walker, Pete	0	0	4.05	8	3	13.1	14	6	6	7	13
Yennaco, Jay	5	11	6.33	21	0	122.1	146	89	86	54	73

Southern League

Birmingham Barons (White Sox) AA

BATTING	AVG	AB	R	H	2B	3B	HR	RBI	BB	SO	SB
Alvarez, Clemente, C	.202	242	29	49	10	1	3	23	27	49	0
Bautista, Juan, SS	.239	46	6	11	3	0	0	4	3	15	0
Coolbaugh, Scott, 3B	.289	235	35	68	18	0	11	50	37	60	0
*Cotton, John, 2B	.290	124	23	36	10	2	7	26	9	33	1
#Evans, Jason, OF	.305	223	33	68	16	1	5	25	28	51	2
Fagley, Dan, C	.368	19	1	7	1	0	0	0	0	5	0
Finn, John, 3B	.276	246	49	68	15	0	0	27	39	28	13
*Liefer, Jeff, OF	.238	474	67	113	24	9	15	71	38	115	2
McKinnon, Sandy, OF	.271	332	58	90	20	1	4	31	31	68	13
Menechino, Frankie, 2B	.299	318	78	95	28	4	12	60	79	77	7
Moore, Brandon, SS	.256	414	58	106	15	1	1	47	45	48	4
Mouton, Lyle, OF	.182	11	1	2	0	0	1	1	1	4	0
Paul, Josh, C	.296	115	18	34	5	0	1	16	12	25	6
#Pearson, Eddie, 1B	.327	382	59	125	33	1	5	59	23	50	1
#Polidor, Wil, 2B	.269	93	11	25	2	1	0	13	1	16	0
Raven, Luis, DH	.336	456	88	153	30	3	30	112	46	126	4
#Sawkiw, Warren, C	.286	7	1	2	0	0	1	3	0	1	0
#Simmons, Brian, OF	.262	546	108	143	28	12	15	72	88	124	15
Thomas, Juan, 1B	.302	311	50	94	16	2	10	55	23	92	1
*Topham, Ryan, OF	.213	47	6	10	5	1	0	8	6	15	1
*Ventura, Robin, 3B	.294	17	3	5	1	0	1	2	1	1	0
Wrona, Rick, C	.252	103	11	26	7	1	2	24	3	12	0

PITCHING	W	L	ERA	G	SV	IP	H	R	ER	BB	SO
Barcelo, Lorenzo	2	1	4.86	6	0	33.1	36	20	18	9	29
Beirne, Kevin	6	4	4.92	13	0	75.0	76	51	41	41	49
Bere, Jason	0	1	7.71	2	0	7.0	8	7	6	2	7
Buteaux, Shane	2	2	4.19	44	2	73.0	74	41	34	34	34
*Christman, Scott	2	7	9.05	15	0	63.2	100	74	64	38	39
*Eyre, Scott	13	5	3.84	22	0	126.2	110	61	54	55	127
Hasselhoff, Derek	5	2	2.41	18	3	33.2	35	10	9	11	22
Heathcott, Mike	3	1	1.83	30	7	59.0	50	20	12	25	47
Herbert, Russ	13	5	3.63	27	0	158.2	136	72	64	80	126
Howry, Bob	0	0	2.84	12	2	12.2	16	4	4	3	3
Lundquist, David	0	0	8.78	7	0	13.1	26	20	13	5	15
*Newman, Alan	7	3	2.49	44	10	72.1	55	34	20	40	64
Nunez, Maximo	0	0	7.64	14	0	17.2	19	18	15	13	14
Olsen, Jason	9	14	4.88	28	0	160.1	183	101	87	58	121

Pitching leaders across all leagues

(Cont'd from previous page)

SHUTOUTS

Player	Club	Lg.	SO
Ortiz, Ramon	CR	Mid	4
Cames, Aaron	KnC	Mid	3
T Evans, Keith	WPB	FSL	3
Hurtado, Edwin	Tac	PCL	3
*Krivda, Rick	Roc	Int	3
T Rakers, Jason	Akr	East	3
Stepka, Tom	Sal	Caro	3
T Stevens, Kris	Clw	FSL	3

LOSSES

Player	Club	Lg.	L
T Kaufman, Brad	Mob	Sou	18
Glover, Gary	Hag	SAL	17
T Green, Jason	QC	Mid	15
T Grimsley, Jason	Oma	AmAs	15
*Redman, Mark	SLk	PCL	15
Roberts, Willis	Jax	Sou	15
T*Smith, Dan	OkC	AmAs	15

WALKS

Player	Club	Lg.	BB
T Wood, Kerry	Iwa	AmAs	131
Ambrose, John	W-S	Caro	117
T Saneaux, F.	Fre	Caro	116
T Avrard, Corey	PrW	Caro	113
Pincavitch, Kevin	SBr	Cal	112
*Bertotti, Mike	Nvl	AmAs	105
T Drumright, Mike	Tol	Int	104
Kaye, Justin	Wsc	Mid	104
*Coble, Jason	GBo	SAL	96
Edsell, Geoff	Van	PCL	96
T Shoemaker, S.	CSp	PCL	95
T Fernandez, J.	Tre	East	94
Hall, Yates	PrW	Caro	94
Burger, Rob	Clw	FSL	93
*Pearsall, J.J.	SBr	Cal	93

Switch-hitter
* Left-handed
T Player has been with more than one team; listed with last team.
(Players in major leagues are listed with last minor league club.)

Pitching leaders across all leagues

(Cont'd from previous page)

PITCHING	W	L	ERA	G	SV	IP	H	R	ER	BB	SO
Smith, Chuck	2	2	3.16	25	0	62.2	63	35	22	27	57
Snyder, John	7	8	4.64	20	0	114.1	130	76	59	43	90
Theodile, Robert	2	0	5.49	19	1	57.1	72	43	35	35	41
Woods, Brian	1	5	6.31	35	10	45.2	49	41	32	28	35

WILD PITCHES

Player	Club	Lg.	WP
T Saneaux, F.	Fre	Caro	31
Gregg, Kevin	VIS	Cal	28
Pincavitch, Kevin	SBr	Cal	27
Montgomery, G.	Peo	Mid	27
Coggin, David	Clw	FSL	24
Lakman, Jason	Hck	SAL	24
Garrett, Josh	Mch	Mid	23
T Grimsley, Jason	Oma	AmAs	23
Malloy, William	Bak	Cal	23
Vanwormer, Marc	SBn	Mid	23
T*Rocker, John	Grv	Sou	22
T Bene, Bill	Mdl	Tex	21
Kaye, Justin	Wsc	Mid	21
Sanchez, Mike	Sav	SAL	21
T Warrecker, T.	Kin	Caro	21

BALKS

Player	Club	Lg.	B
Levrault, Allen	BLT	Mid	12
T Bermudez, M.	Bak	Cal	10
T Irabu, Hideki	Col	Int	8
*Brester, Jason	SJ	Cal	7
*Byrne, Earl	Orl	Sou	7
Callaway, Michael	StP	FSL	7
Espinal, Jose	Rkf	Mid	7
Lyons, Jonathan	Sar	FSL	7
T*Milton, Eric	Nrw	East	7
*Pratt, Rich	Nvl	AmAs	7
*Stewart, Scott	SLu	FSL	7

SAVES

Player	Club	Lg.	SV
*Almanza, A.	PrW	Caro	36
Cordero, F.	WMi	Mid	35
T Williams, Todd	Ind	AmAs	33
T Winchester, S.	Ind	AmAs	33
T*Mullins, Greg	EIP	Tex	32
T Fleetham, Ben	Hrb	East	31
T Brannan, Ryan	Rea	East	30
Crafton, Kevin	Peo	Mid	29
Daniels, John	StP	FSL	29
T Deschenes, M.	Kin	Caro	29
Pageler, Mick	Bak	Cal	29
Gaillard, Eddie	Tol	Int	28
Ricabal, Dan	VB	FSL	28
Erdos, Todd	Mob	Sou	27
Sak, James	RC	Cal	27

 # Switch-hitter
* Left-handed
T Player has been with more than one team; listed with last team.
(Players in major leagues are listed with last minor league club.)

Carolina Mudcats (Pirates) AA

BATTING	AVG	AB	R	H	2B	3B	HR	RBI	BB	SO	SB
Asche, Mike, 3B	.214	42	2	9	1	1	0	2	4	6	0
Beasley, Tony, 2B	.274	117	15	32	5	0	0	12	7	16	2
*Bonifay, Ken, 3B	.176	68	11	12	4	1	1	7	17	23	1
*Bridges, Kary, 2B	.336	283	43	95	17	1	3	29	9	10	9
#Brown, Adrian, OF	.303	145	29	44	4	4	2	15	18	12	9
*Conger, Jeff, OF	.196	138	15	27	5	1	3	12	19	53	4
*Cromer, Brandon, SS	.228	193	23	44	12	4	4	14	29	50	1
Espinosa, Ramon, OF	.278	72	10	20	2	1	1	10	3	15	0
Garcia, Freddy, 3B	.291	282	47	82	17	4	19	57	18	56	0
Hanel, Marcus, C	.237	173	15	41	5	0	2	12	9	39	0
Hazlett, Steve, OF	.235	153	22	36	7	3	2	17	14	31	1
Hermansen, Chad, OF	.275	487	87	134	31	4	20	70	69	136	18
*Holifield, Rick, OF	.216	185	27	40	12	5	5	23	14	59	8
Jordan, Ricky, DH	.314	188	25	59	9	2	7	33	8	25	0
*Martin, Al, OF	.111	9	0	1	0	0	0	0	0	0	0
Mendez, Sergio, C	.233	146	17	34	10	1	2	12	6	33	1
#Mitchell, Tony, OF	.091	11	0	1	0	0	0	1	1	4	0
Miyake, Chris, SS	.000	9	1	0	0	0	0	0	0	4	0
#Nunez, Abraham, SS	.328	198	31	65	6	1	1	14	20	28	10
Peterson, Charles, OF	.251	442	59	111	26	4	7	68	40	105	20
Polcovich, Kevin, 3B	.320	50	13	16	5	0	3	7	10	4	4
*Sanders, Tracy, 1B	.271	376	77	102	23	1	21	78	74	88	7
*Sanford, Chance, 2B	.262	149	30	39	10	2	9	36	20	39	3
Smith, Mark, OF	.417	12	5	5	1	0	3	4	0	1	0
*Staton, T.J., OF	.290	207	33	60	11	2	6	33	12	60	8
*Sweet, Jon, C	.245	273	22	67	15	1	1	27	15	20	1
Thobe, Steve, 3B	.293	181	21	53	10	0	7	32	13	52	4
*Whitmore, Darrell, DH	.333	9	1	3	2	0	0	2	0	2	0

PITCHING	W	L	ERA	G	SV	IP	H	R	ER	BB	SO
*Anderson, Jimmy	2	1	1.46	4	0	24.2	16	6	4	9	23
*Beatty, Blaine	0	5	5.38	19	0	82.0	104	61	49	27	41
Benson, Kris	3	5	4.98	14	0	68.2	81	49	38	32	66
*Brown, Michael	0	0	18.00	1	0	2.0	5	5	4	1	2
Carter, John	0	0	54.00	1	0	1.0	4	6	6	2	0
Chaves, Rafael	0	2	8.59	5	0	7.1	12	8	7	4	6
*Christiansen, Jason	0	1	4.20	8	1	15.0	17	7	7	5	25
Cook, O.J.	0	0	20.25	1	0	1.1	5	3	3	1	2
Crawford, Carlos	3	2	4.19	29	4	62.1	62	34	29	25	39
Davis, Kane	0	3	3.77	6	0	28.2	22	17	12	16	23
Dillinger, John	6	4	6.00	23	0	81.0	88	66	54	52	64
Fredrickson, Scott	0	3	6.08	19	1	23.2	22	21	16	19	17
Freitas, John	1	0	13.50	6	1	5.1	8	8	8	4	2
Garrett, Hal	1	2	8.78	6	0	13.1	19	14	13	6	7
*Halperin, Mike	6	7	3.87	17	0	93.0	102	54	40	40	66
Hernandez, Elvin	2	7	5.73	17	0	92.2	104	67	59	26	66
Johnson, Jason	3	3	4.08	9	0	57.1	56	31	26	16	63
*Kelly, Jeff	6	11	4.65	31	0	127.2	134	79	66	85	83
Konuszewski, Dennis	1	0	4.43	15	0	22.1	20	12	11	15	21
Maskivish, Joe	0	1	6.19	15	0	16.0	20	11	11	4	7
*Mathews, Del	5	2	3.04	21	1	50.1	53	25	17	20	51
*Paugh, Rick	0	0	5.63	5	0	8.0	8	5	5	1	3
Pett, Jose	4	4	3.51	14	0	74.1	76	37	29	25	39
Phillips, Jason	1	2	2.32	4	0	31.0	21	8	8	9	22
*Pickford, Kevin	1	2	7.36	21	1	29.1	48	29	24	15	24
Ryan, Matt	4	3	2.22	48	14	52.2	32	18	13	21	43
*Shaw, Curtis	1	1	2.81	27	0	41.2	30	23	13	28	46
Wagner, Paul	0	1	10.13	12	0	16.0	25	20	18	16	20
*Wallace, Jeff	4	8	5.40	38	3	43.1	43	37	26	36	39
Williams, Jeff	0	0	10.80	3	0	3.1	6	5	4	4	3
Wilson, Gary	1	2	5.65	7	1	28.2	34	19	18	5	19

Chattanooga Lookouts (Reds) AA

BATTING	AVG	AB	R	H	2B	3B	HR	RBI	BB	SO	SB
Allen, Marlon, 1B	.255	196	27	50	15	2	4	23	26	39	0
Broach, Donald, OF	.274	402	62	110	15	4	0	31	35	47	12
*Coughlin, Kevin, OF	.292	168	22	49	7	0	3	15	15	20	0
*Dismuke, Jamie, 1B	.286	98	21	28	5	0	4	25	18	10	0
Eddie, Steve, 3B	.287	394	57	113	25	4	8	49	21	64	3

BATTING	AVG	AB	R	H	2B	3B	HR	RBI	BB	SO	SB
Garcia, Guillermo, C	.284	74	11	21	1	1	4	19	8	13	0
Gibralter, Steve, OF	.258	97	20	25	9	0	2	12	13	22	0
Gordon, Keith, OF	.167	12	2	2	0	0	1	2	3	7	1
Grall, Gregory, DH	.250	4	0	1	0	0	0	0	0	2	0
Griffey, Craig, OF	.223	300	48	67	8	2	0	20	37	63	14
#Hall, Billy, 2B	.256	215	31	55	4	2	3	19	24	35	13
Kelly, Mike, OF	.350	60	14	21	7	0	3	12	3	16	3
Koelling, Brian, 2B	.280	279	50	78	9	3	3	22	28	49	18
Ladell, Cleveland, OF	.344	32	3	11	1	0	0	4	0	3	1
Larson, Brandon, SS	.268	41	4	11	5	1	0	6	1	10	0
Magdaleno, Ricky, SS	.262	187	33	49	13	1	8	34	42	51	1
Mottola, Chad, OF	.362	174	35	63	9	3	5	32	16	23	7
Murray, Glenn, OF	.283	329	66	93	16	2	26	73	56	91	7
Presto, Nick, SS	.226	31	2	7	1	0	0	6	2	7	1
#Price, Corey, 2B	.333	3	0	1	0	0	0	0	1	1	0
*Rose, Pete, 3B	.308	445	75	137	31	0	25	98	34	63	0
Rumfield, Toby, 1B	.287	331	35	95	22	1	5	38	18	32	0
Sanders, Reggie, OF	.545	11	3	6	1	1	1	3	1	2	0
Towle, Justin, C	.309	418	62	129	37	5	11	70	55	77	5
Wagner, Mark, 3B	.250	4	0	1	0	0	0	1	0	0	0
Watkins, Pat, OF	.350	177	35	62	15	1	7	30	15	16	9
Williams, Jason, 2B	.310	271	38	84	21	1	5	28	18	35	5

PITCHING	W	L	ERA	G	SV	IP	H	R	ER	BB	SO
*Atchley, Justin	4	2	4.70	13	0	67.0	75	45	35	14	48
Boggs, Robert	1	3	7.59	9	0	40.1	53	36	34	21	35
Bryant, Adam	1	0	7.00	6	0	9.0	15	8	7	1	4
Caruthers, Clay	2	4	9.09	9	0	34.2	63	36	35	17	30
*Courtright, John	5	7	6.82	20	0	92.1	137	79	70	42	42
*Crowell, Jim	2	1	2.84	3	0	19.0	19	6	6	5	14
Cushman, Dwayne	0	0	16.20	1	0	1.2	4	3	3	1	1
Donnelly, Brendan	6	4	3.27	62	6	82.2	71	43	30	37	64
*Doyle, Tom	7	3	3.51	65	0	66.2	62	32	26	38	46
Etler, Todd	0	3	6.57	23	0	37.0	38	29	27	24	29
Gower, Tim	2	0	4.57	24	0	45.1	52	24	23	12	28
Jean, Domingo	1	1	9.75	10	1	12.0	17	20	13	15	9
Koppe, Clint	2	5	7.38	13	0	68.1	82	58	56	44	33
LeBlanc, Eric	2	4	5.58	8	0	50.0	53	35	31	21	25
Lott, Brian	6	7	6.77	25	0	91.2	108	76	69	50	62
McKenzie, Scott	2	0	5.77	30	0	53.0	74	37	34	19	30
Nix, James	6	1	3.13	28	0	37.1	31	15	13	20	32
Parris, Steve	6	2	4.13	14	0	80.2	78	44	37	29	68
*Priest, Eddie	4	6	3.44	14	0	91.2	101	39	35	17	63
Reed, Chris	6	8	5.34	23	0	129.2	140	93	77	68	96
*Tryon, Eric	0	4	8.31	6	0	26.0	35	27	24	16	7
Williams, Todd	3	3	2.10	48	31	55.2	38	16	13	25	45
Winchester, Scott	2	1	1.69	9	3	10.2	9	4	2	3	3

Greenville Braves (Braves) AA

BATTING	AVG	AB	R	H	2B	3B	HR	RBI	BB	SO	SB
Ayrault, Joe, C	.242	33	6	8	2	0	2	4	6	8	0
Benbow, Lou, 1B	.232	315	39	73	14	1	9	34	34	80	4
#Brito, Luis, SS	.289	336	35	97	12	0	1	36	15	25	4
Cordero, Edward, SS	.400	5	1	2	0	0	0	0	0	1	0
Eaglin, Mike, 2B	.288	396	62	114	15	3	5	47	41	66	15
*Grijak, Kevin, 1B	.250	240	35	60	12	1	13	48	18	35	0
Helms, Wes, 3B	.296	314	50	93	14	1	11	44	33	50	3
Hicks, Jamie, 1B	.294	17	3	5	0	0	1	1	2	3	1
Jimenez, Manny, SS	.291	430	59	125	24	2	5	45	22	70	3
Lewis, Marc, OF	.273	512	64	140	17	3	17	67	25	84	21
Magee, Danny, 3B	.273	22	1	6	0	0	1	3	1	6	0
Mahoney, Mike, C	.228	298	46	68	17	0	8	46	28	75	1
McBride, Charles, OF	.244	127	24	31	5	0	5	15	11	20	0
Monds, Wonderful, OF	.315	89	21	28	5	0	8	15	20	23	6
Norris, Dax, C	.333	9	3	3	0	0	1	3	0	1	0
Rodarte, Raul, OF	.221	172	29	38	8	1	7	22	26	30	10
*Swann, Pedro, OF	.286	465	78	133	29	2	24	83	49	75	5
Toth, Dave, C	.245	184	23	45	9	0	7	24	25	35	2
*Warner, Mike, OF	.320	303	58	97	22	3	7	35	61	61	12
*Whatley, Gabe, OF	.303	310	60	94	17	5	15	57	50	42	5

PITCHING	W	L	ERA	G	SV	IP	H	R	ER	BB	SO
Arnold, Jamie	0	1	11.57	1	0	4.2	10	6	6	2	3
*Bowie, Micah	3	2	3.50	8	0	43.2	34	19	17	26	41
Briggs, Anthony	6	3	5.44	19	0	94.1	91	64	57	43	59
*Brooks, Antone	1	0	4.79	14	0	20.2	21	14	11	8	10
*Butler, Adam	5	1	2.57	46	22	49.0	40	16	14	15	56

Pitching leaders across all leagues

(Cont'd from previous page)

GAMES

Player	Club	Lg.	G
Ricabal, Dan	VB	FSL	75
*Prihoda, Stephen	Wch	Tex	70
Snyder, Matt	Bow	East	67
T Brannan, Ryan	Rea	East	66
T*Gonzalez, G.	Chr	Int	66
*Doyle, Tom	Cng	Sou	65
T Glauber, Keith	Lou	AmAs	65
*Dodd, Robert	Rea	East	63
Donnelly, B.	Cng	Sou	62
Hubbs, Dan	Abq	PCL	62
*Polley, Dale	Col	Int	62
*West, Adam	Peo	Mid	62

INNINGS PITCHED

Player	Club	Lg.	IP
T Saipe, Mike	CSp	PCL	197.0
T*Washburn, J.	Van	PCL	194.1
Darrell, Tommy	CR	Mid	191.2
T Bovee, Mike	Van	PCL	191.0
Rose, Brian	Paw	Int	190.2
T Clement, Matt	Mob	Sou	189.0
Ortega, Pablo	CSC	SAL	188.2
T Pena, Juan	Tre	East	188.1
T Elarton, Scott	NO	AmAs	187.1
T*Vavrek, Mike	NHv	East	185.1
Brownson, M.	NHv	East	184.2
Smith, Travis	ElP	Tex	184.1
Loewer, Carlton	SWB	Int	184.0
Edsell, Geoff	Van	PCL	183.1
Powell, Brian	Lak	FSL	183.1

STRIKEOUTS

Player	Club	Lg.	SO
Ortiz, Ramon	CR	Mid	225
T Shoemaker, S.	CSp	PCL	214
T Clement, Matt	Mob	Sou	201
T Elarton, Scott	NO	AmAs	191
T Wood, Kerry	Iwa	AmAs	186
*Chen, Bruce	Mac	SAL	182
T*Vining, Kenneth	W-S	Caro	180
*Sanchez, Jesus	Bng	East	176
*Billingsley, Brent	KnC	Mid	175
T Knight, Brandon	Tul	Tex	175
*Brester, Jason	SJ	Cal	172
T Thomas, Evan	Rea	East	172
Brownson, Mark	NHv	East	170
T Judd, Mike	SAn	Tex	169
Lakman, Jason	Hck	SAL	168

Switch-hitter

* Left-handed

T Player has been with more than one team; listed with last team.

(Players in major leagues are listed with last minor league club.)

Pitching leaders across all leagues

(Cont'd from previous page)

HIT-BY-PITCH

Player	Club	Lg.	HBP
T Clement, Matt	Mob	Sou	21
Pumphrey, Kenny	Clb	SAL	20
Pincavitch, Kevin	SBr	Cal	19
T Townsend, Dave	Prt	East	19
T Warrecker, T.	Kin	Caro	18
Brammer, John	Clb	SAL	18
T De La Cruz, F.	Mdl	Tex	18
Tilton, Ira	Pdt	SAL	17
Welch, Robb	Mch	Mid	17
Stephens, Jason	LkE	Cal	16
T Aucoin, Derek	WPB	FSL	16
Kaye, Justin	Wsc	Mid	16
T Drews, Matt	Tol	Int	16
T Rossiter, Mike	EIP	Tex	16
T Wood, Kerry	Iwa	AmAs	16

HITS ALLOWED

Player	Club	Lg.	HA
Buckley, Travis	Van	PCL	223
King, Bill	Hvl	Sou	216
T*Washburn, J.	Van	PCL	215
T Fernandez, J.	Tre	East	214
Darrell, Tommy	CR	Mid	212
Smith, Travis	EIP	Tex	210
T Bovee, Mike	Van	PCL	209
*Barkley, Brian	Tre	East	208
Harrison, Brian	Oma	AmAs	208
Stepka, Tom	Sal	Caro	205
Meadows, Brian	Prt	East	204
*Redman, Mark	SLk	PCL	204
T Saipe, Mike	CSp	PCL	201

ERA (WORST)

Player	Club	Lg.	ERA
T Macey, Fausto	Mdl	Tex	8.05
Nichting, Chris	Edm	PCL	7.76
Kaye, Justin	Wsc	Mid	7.30
T De La Cruz, F.	Mdl	Tex	7.19
T Barber, Brian	Lou	AmAs	7.13
Brammer, John	Clb	SAL	7.02
T Bishop, Joshua	BLT	Mid	6.79
Pincavitch, Kevin	SBr	Cal	6.78
*Barnes, Brian	Tol	Int	6.71
T Hackman, L.	Sal	Caro	6.58
T Jimenez, Miguel	Edm	PCL	6.56
T Kaufman, Brad	Mob	Sou	6.56
Ray, Ken	Oma	AmAs	6.37
T Paredes, Carlos	Lan	Mid	6.35
T Million, Doug	Sal	Caro	6.32

 # Switch-hitter
* Left-handed
T Player has been with more than one team; listed with last team.
(Players in major leagues are listed with last minor league club.)

PITCHING

PITCHING	W	L	ERA	G	SV	IP	H	R	ER	BB	SO
Byrd, Matt	3	2	6.00	28	0	45.0	58	31	30	21	38
Cather, Mike	5	2	4.34	22	1	37.1	37	18	18	7	29
Cortes, David	1	0	1.80	3	0	5.0	4	1	1	1	7
*Ebert, Derrin	11	8	4.10	27	0	175.2	191	95	80	48	101
Giard, Ken	3	0	1.96	25	6	36.2	30	9	8	11	39
Harvey, Bryan	1	1	5.18	22	0	24.1	23	15	14	16	18
*Hines, Rich	4	0	6.58	41	1	67.0	85	56	49	22	49
*Jacobs, Ryan	1	8	7.21	28	1	68.2	84	61	55	43	52
*King, Raymond	5	5	6.85	12	0	65.2	85	53	50	24	42
LeRoy, John	5	5	5.03	29	1	98.1	105	59	55	43	84
Ligtenberg, Kerry	3	1	2.04	31	16	35.1	20	8	8	14	43
Millwood, Kevin	3	5	4.11	11	0	61.1	59	37	28	24	61
*Moss, Damian	6	8	5.35	21	0	112.2	111	73	67	58	116
*Nelson, Erick	0	1	4.50	5	0	6.0	9	4	3	4	4
Olszewski, Eric	0	0	6.00	4	0	6.0	9	6	4	8	7
*Rocker, John	5	6	4.86	22	0	113.0	119	69	61	61	96
Rogers, Bryan	2	3	3.08	19	1	26.1	20	11	9	12	14
*Stewart, Chaad	1	2	8.50	6	0	18.0	20	18	17	12	11
*Wade, Terrell	0	2	4.97	8	0	12.2	15	10	7	8	14

Huntsville Stars (Athletics) AA

BATTING	AVG	AB	R	H	2B	3B	HR	RBI	BB	SO	SB
Ardoin, Danny, C	.231	208	26	48	10	1	4	23	17	38	2
#Castro, Jose, SS	.385	13	4	5	0	0	0	4	2	0	0
Christenson, Ryan, OF	.367	120	39	44	9	3	2	18	24	23	5
Coolbaugh, Mike, 3B	.308	559	100	172	37	2	30	132	52	105	8
*Cromer, D.T., 1B	.323	545	100	176	40	6	15	121	60	102	12
Deboer, Rob, DH	.243	288	55	70	16	1	18	48	60	111	8
*Grieve, Ben, OF	.328	372	100	122	29	2	24	108	81	75	5
Hernandez, Ramon, C	.193	161	27	31	3	0	4	24	18	23	0
Hughes, Troy, OF	.209	258	37	54	12	0	5	33	23	50	2
Martins, Eric, 2B	.259	205	33	53	10	3	3	31	23	31	2
Morales, Willie, C	.272	136	19	37	11	0	3	24	17	24	1
*Neill, Mike, OF	.340	486	129	165	30	2	14	80	72	113	16
*Newhan, David, 2B	.316	212	40	67	13	2	5	35	28	59	5
Ramirez, Roberto, OF	.318	66	7	21	4	0	0	6	0	16	2
#Smith, Demond, OF	.279	323	79	90	20	6	8	39	65	76	31
Tejada, Miguel, SS	.275	502	85	138	20	3	22	97	50	99	15
*Walker, Dane, 2B	.241	361	62	87	17	3	7	52	68	87	7

PITCHING	W	L	ERA	G	SV	IP	H	R	ER	BB	SO
*Baez, Benito	2	4	9.14	15	0	42.1	64	47	43	22	27
*Baxter, Bob	1	1	11.57	6	0	4.2	15	10	6	3	3
Bennett, Bob	4	3	7.17	23	1	42.2	64	38	34	15	32
Bradley, Bert	0	0	0.00	1	0	1.0	0	0	0	0	0
Bussa, Todd	2	1	4.22	19	7	21.1	20	13	10	12	27
Connelly, Steve	3	3	3.75	43	7	69.2	74	33	29	20	49
Dale, Carl	6	4	5.38	20	0	85.1	95	61	51	43	57
*Dunbar, Matt	1	0	5.40	5	0	5.0	8	3	3	1	7
Haught, Gary	0	1	5.59	6	0	9.2	15	6	6	2	6
Hollins, Stacy	5	4	5.37	32	2	114.0	110	77	68	72	68
Jimenez, Miguel	7	6	5.86	24	0	101.1	127	83	66	50	64
King, Bill	9	7	4.19	28	0	176.0	216	99	82	28	103
*Manning, Derek	1	2	5.93	21	2	44.0	57	31	29	12	27
Maurer, Mike	8	7	3.83	52	2	84.2	86	48	36	31	61
Nelson, Chris	9	3	4.97	20	0	99.2	116	60	55	25	71
Phoenix, Steve	0	3	5.80	29	9	35.2	43	25	23	11	21
Price, Jamey	9	3	5.30	20	0	110.1	153	71	65	38	80
*Rajotte, Jason	2	6	4.40	55	3	57.1	67	35	28	29	35
Rivette, Scott	3	1	6.69	7	0	39.0	52	29	29	19	33
Stein, Blake	3	2	5.71	7	0	34.2	36	24	22	20	25
*Wagner, Bret	0	0	20.25	3	0	2.2	7	11	6	6	3
*Weinberg, Todd	2	1	2.33	20	3	27.0	18	12	7	17	24

Jacksonville Suns (Tigers) AA

BATTING	AVG	AB	R	H	2B	3B	HR	RBI	BB	SO	SB
Almanzar, Richard, 2B	.243	387	55	94	20	2	5	35	37	43	20
#Barker, Glen, OF	.280	257	47	72	8	4	6	29	29	72	17
#Bream, Scott, 2B	.273	55	12	15	1	0	2	3	14	12	1
Bruno, Julio, 3B	.265	438	51	116	22	3	6	57	38	70	6
Conner, Decomba, OF	.208	154	22	32	6	3	4	17	30	45	5
Encarnacion, Juan, OF	.323	493	91	159	31	4	26	90	43	86	17
Garcia, Luis, SS	.268	456	55	122	19	1	5	48	10	59	3
Hurst, Jimmy, OF	.471	17	5	8	2	0	2	6	3	6	0
#Ibarra, Jesse, 1B	.283	441	73	125	24	1	25	91	55	85	3
Johnson, Earl, OF	.245	453	76	111	14	4	3	35	30	75	42

BATTING	AVG	AB	R	H	2B	3B	HR	RBI	BB	SO	SB
Lackey, Steve, 2B	.077	13	1	1	0	0	0	0	0	1	1
Lidle, Kevin, C	.151	186	18	28	7	0	1	16	17	77	0
Marine, Del, C	.238	328	45	78	22	1	12	43	48	92	0
*Marquez, Jesus, OF	.267	465	56	124	24	4	12	74	22	77	9
Miller, Orlando, SS	.364	11	2	4	1	0	1	3	1	1	0
*Roberts, David, DH	.296	415	76	123	24	2	4	41	45	62	23
Rodriguez, Adam, C	.200	5	0	1	0	0	0	0	2	0	0
Schmidt, Tom, 3B	.258	291	37	75	17	1	9	44	29	81	2
Smith, Ira, OF	.308	172	29	53	14	2	5	20	35	30	1

PITCHING	W	L	ERA	G	SV	IP	H	R	ER	BB	SO
Corey, Bryan	3	8	4.76	52	9	68.0	74	42	36	21	37
Drews, Matt	8	11	5.49	24	0	144.1	160	109	88	50	85
Drumright, Mike	1	1	1.57	5	0	28.2	16	7	5	13	24
*Duran, Roberto	4	2	2.37	50	16	60.2	41	19	16	39	95
Gallaher, Kevin	4	3	6.47	10	0	57.0	70	45	41	32	33
Gentile, Scott	1	5	5.23	43	2	63.2	69	41	37	21	52
Goldsmith, Gary	4	5	4.07	31	1	97.1	97	48	44	30	45
Greisinger, Seth	10	6	5.20	28	0	159.1	194	103	92	53	105
Marrero, Kenny	4	3	2.94	37	0	64.1	45	32	21	37	60
Melendez, Dave	6	4	5.33	12	0	72.2	77	47	43	24	55
Reed, Brandon	11	9	4.55	27	0	176.0	190	100	89	54	90
Roberts, Willis	6	15	6.28	26	0	149.0	181	120	104	64	86
Santana, Marino	4	1	3.28	39	1	74.0	55	28	27	43	98
Schroeder, Chad	0	0	0.00	2	0	3.2	1	0	0	1	4

Knoxville Smokies (Blue Jays) AA

BATTING	AVG	AB	R	H	2B	3B	HR	RBI	BB	SO	SB
Adriana, Sharnol, 2B	.236	314	50	74	11	1	6	39	47	66	9
*Candelaria, Ben, OF	.294	472	81	139	32	5	15	67	42	89	4
Cradle, Rickey, OF	.214	257	50	55	16	1	10	34	41	67	5
*Curl, John, DH	.207	29	0	6	1	0	0	1	3	6	0
DeLaCruz, Lorenzo, DH	.336	146	32	49	7	2	7	26	14	38	2
Diaz, Cesar, C	.200	15	2	3	1	0	1	3	5	2	0
Freel, Ryan, SS	.202	94	18	19	1	1	0	4	19	13	5
#French, Anton, OF	.333	6	2	2	0	1	0	1	0	2	0
Henry, Santiago, 2B	.291	196	25	57	10	1	5	26	4	35	3
Jones, Ryan, 1B	.256	328	41	84	19	3	12	51	27	63	0
#Melhuse, Adam, C	.230	87	14	20	3	0	3	10	19	19	0
Morgan, Dave, C	.273	44	6	12	2	0	0	4	10	14	0
Mosquera, Julio, C	.291	309	47	90	23	1	5	50	22	56	3
Ramirez, Angel, OF	.309	369	55	114	24	7	5	37	10	48	11
#Roberts, Lonell, OF	.190	21	5	4	0	1	0	0	2	3	0
Rodriguez, Luis, C	.269	78	6	21	3	1	0	6	3	20	0
Sanders, Anthony, OF	.266	429	68	114	20	4	26	69	44	121	20
Skett, Will, OF	.273	110	18	30	6	1	3	15	4	31	4
Solano, Fausto, SS	.265	378	52	100	24	4	10	56	37	47	8
#Soriano, Fred, 2B	.059	17	3	1	0	0	0	0	3	4	1
Strange, Mike, 2B	.095	21	1	2	0	1	0	0	3	4	0
Thompson, Andy, 3B	.286	448	75	128	25	3	15	71	63	76	0
*Witt, Kevin, 1B	.289	501	76	145	27	4	30	91	44	109	1

PITCHING	W	L	ERA	G	SV	IP	H	R	ER	BB	SO
Almanzar, Carlos	1	1	4.91	21	8	25.2	30	14	14	5	25
*Bogott, Kurtiss	2	1	3.90	35	2	64.2	66	32	28	25	77
*Brown, Chad	6	4	3.72	32	4	55.2	46	25	23	16	40
Czajkowski, Jim	2	2	6.47	25	5	32.0	43	27	23	11	33
Davey, Tom	6	7	5.83	20	0	92.2	108	65	60	50	72
Doman, Roger	7	3	3.67	48	4	100.2	99	46	41	29	71
Escobar, Kelvim	2	1	3.70	5	0	24.1	20	13	10	16	31
Folkers, Kenneth	1	0	0.00	1	0	4.1	1	0	0	0	4
Freeman, Chris	3	3	2.48	47	8	83.1	71	32	23	36	86
Gordon, Mike	2	3	5.33	33	2	72.2	91	46	43	40	64
Graterol, Beiker	2	1	5.40	3	0	16.2	24	12	10	9	11
Halladay, Roy	2	3	5.40	7	0	36.2	46	26	22	11	30
Harris, D.J.	1	1	1.64	2	0	11.0	6	2	2	6	8
Jarvis, Jason	0	2	9.78	4	0	19.1	28	24	21	9	11
*Lowe, Benny	3	1	5.54	18	0	26.0	33	21	16	14	29
*Lukasiewicz, Mark	2	0	3.65	27	7	37.0	26	17	15	14	43
McBride, Chris	4	4	3.71	10	0	60.2	61	30	25	14	33
Meiners, Doug	9	5	5.43	23	0	122.2	161	85	74	31	81
Meinershagen, Adam	0	0	3.71	7	0	17.0	16	8	7	6	7
Rhine, Kendall	0	0	10.32	8	0	11.1	13	13	13	15	6
Smith, Brian	0	0	0.00	1	0	1.0	0	0	0	1	1
Stevenson, Jason	12	9	4.27	26	0	149.2	166	88	71	43	101
*Veniard, Jay	3	8	5.85	17	0	75.1	97	59	49	37	54
Young, Joe	5	4	4.42	19	0	59.0	52	38	29	40	62

Pitching leaders across all leagues

(Cont'd from previous page)

LOW-HITTERS (0,1, 2, 3-HIT)

Player	Club	Lg.	LH
T Evans, Keith	WPB	FSL	4
T Guzman, D.	RC	Cal	3
*Krivda, Rick	Roc	Int	3
T Melendez, Dave	Jax	Sou	3
T Saipe, Mike	CSp	PCL	3

SO/9 IP RATIO (STARTERS)

Player	Club	Lg.	SO/9IP
O'Shaughnessy, J.	Sav	SAL	11.67
*Fuentes, Brian	Wsc	Mid	11.60
T Shoemaker, S.	CSp	PCL	11.49
Ortiz, Ramon	CR	Mid	11.19
*Chen, Bruce	Mac	SAL	11.19
T Wood, Kerry	Iwa	AmAs	11.04
Patterson, John	SBn	Mid	10.96
*Brester, Jason	SJ	Cal	10.88
Gregg, Kevin	VIS	Cal	10.61
*Lilly, Ted	SBr	Cal	10.56
T Stark, Dennis	Lnc	Cal	10.17
*Hamilton, Jimmy	Clb	SAL	10.02
T Guzman, D.	RC	Cal	10.00
*Bale, John	Hag	SAL	9.94
Lakman, Jason	Hck	SAL	9.78

AVERAGE AGAINST (STARTERS)

Player	Club	Lg.	BA
T Stark, Dennis	Lnc	Cal	.172
T Wood, Kerry	Iwa	AmAs	.181
Radlosky, Rob	FtM	FSL	.190
T Gorecki, Rick	SAn	Tex	.192
T Vazquez, Javier	Hrb	East	.200
T Shoemaker, S.	CSp	PCL	.201
Rodriguez, Nerio	Roc	Int	.203
*Fuentes, Brian	Wsc	Mid	.203
T*Blanco, Alberto	Kis	FSL	.206
O'Shaughnessy, J;	Sav	SAL	.207
*Coble, Jason	GBo	SAL	.208
Roberts, Grant	Clb	SAL	.208
Penny, Brad	SBn	Mid	.208
T Miller, Wade	Kis	FSL	.209
*Bowers, Cedrick	CSC	SAL	.209

Switch-hitter
* Left-handed
T Player has been with more than one team; listed with last team.
(Players in major leagues are listed with last minor league club.)

Pitching leaders across all leagues

(Cont'd from previous page)

SO/9 IP RATIO (RELIEVERS)

Player	Club	Lg.	SO/9IP
T Deschenes, M.	Kin	Caro	14.95
Sak, James	RC	Cal	14.39
*Duran, Roberto	Jax	Sou	14.09
T*Kubenka, Jeff	SAn	Tex	13.75
*Beasley, R.	Mac	SAL	12.87
T Service, Scott	Oma	AmAs	12.76
T Fleetham, Ben	Hrb	East	12.59
Kennison, Kyle	Wsc	Mid	12.55
T Hernandez, S.	Shr	Tex	12.51
Gonzalez, Lariel	Sal	Caro	12.47
T Kohlmeier, Ryan	Del	SAL	12.10
Molina, Gabe	Del	SAL	11.77
T Bussa, Todd	Hvl	Sou	11.70
T*Mullins, Greg	EIP	Tex	11.66
T Ligtenberg, K.	Rmd	Int	11.64

AVERAGE AGAINST (RELIEVERS)

Player	Club	Lg.	BA
T Fleetham, Ben	Hrb	East	.146
Robinson, Ken	Syr	Int	.158
Ryan, Matt	Car	Sou	.167
T*Young, Tim	Hrb	East	.168
T*Davis, Jason	Clw	FSL	.168
Sak, James	RC	Cal	.170
*Almanza, A.	PrW	Caro	.171
T Deschenes, M.	Kin	Caro	.173
Pisciotta, Marc	Iwa	AmAs	.175
T*Kubenka, Jeff	SAn	Tex	.176
T Dingman, Craig	GBo	SAL	.177
T Cortes, David	Grv	Sou	.180
T Winchester, S.	Ind	AmAs	.182
Molina, Gabe	Del	SAL	.183
T Kohlmeier, Ryan	Del	SAL	.183

Memphis Chicks (Mariners) AA

BATTING	AVG	AB	R	H	2B	3B	HR	RBI	BB	SO	SB
#Christian, Eddie, DH	.336	238	50	80	20	0	4	39	36	24	8
Cook, Jason, 2B	.216	162	23	35	7	0	0	19	21	24	2
#Correa, Miguel, OF	.260	250	33	65	13	0	6	31	16	49	2
#Dean, Chris, 2B	.253	237	24	60	11	5	3	18	25	37	3
Gipson, Charles, 3B	.247	320	56	79	9	4	1	28	34	71	31
Guevara, Giomar, SS	.263	228	30	60	10	4	4	28	20	42	5
*Jorgensen, Randy, 1B	.291	477	66	139	28	3	11	70	38	58	1
Lanza, Mike, 3B	.250	56	8	14	2	0	0	6	4	13	2
Maynard, Scott, C	.158	38	3	6	0	0	0	3	1	12	0
Millette, Joe, SS	.304	191	36	58	11	1	3	22	14	35	2
*Monahan, Shane, OF	.302	401	52	121	24	6	12	76	30	100	14
Saunders, Doug, 3B	.259	232	33	60	15	0	2	28	46	44	0
Sealy, Scot, C	.238	143	17	34	9	0	6	20	15	33	1
Seitzer, Brad, 3B	.329	70	14	23	8	1	2	13	6	13	1
Smith, Scott, OF	.249	453	58	113	19	2	14	67	44	132	4
*Sturdivant, Marcus, OF	.271	432	71	117	18	5	2	35	63	61	21
Thompson, Karl, C	.230	148	18	34	10	0	4	21	11	25	2
Torres, Paul, 3B	.344	218	40	75	8	3	6	55	38	30	3
#Wathan, Dusty, C	.268	149	20	40	4	1	4	19	19	28	1

PITCHING	W	L	ERA	G	SV	IP	H	R	ER	BB	SO
Apana, Matt	3	9	5.83	17	0	80.1	78	59	52	47	45
Beck, Chris	0	0	1.93	5	0	9.1	8	3	2	10	2
*Brosnan, Jason	2	3	2.53	40	5	53.1	44	16	15	11	62
Cloude, Ken	11	7	3.87	22	0	132.2	131	62	57	48	124
*Fernandez, Osvaldo	0	0	2.08	1	0	4.1	2	1	1	4	4
Franklin, Ryan	4	2	3.03	11	0	59.1	45	22	20	14	49
Harikkala, Tim	3	1	3.74	5	0	33.2	39	18	14	4	26
Hinchliffe, Brett	10	10	4.45	24	0	145.2	159	81	72	45	107
Holdridge, David	0	3	3.34	30	17	35.0	31	14	13	17	37
Luce, Robert	5	2	3.93	13	0	75.2	90	40	33	14	41
Manzanillo, Josias	0	0	3.00	2	0	3.0	1	1	1	0	6
Montane, Ivan	0	8	7.53	22	0	71.2	83	70	60	51	63
Pacheco, Alexander	1	1	3.75	9	0	12.0	7	5	5	9	13
Rivera, Rafael	0	0	2.57	6	0	7.0	7	3	2	7	8
*Simmons, Scott	8	4	3.28	40	1	90.2	77	40	33	40	85
Smith, Roy	0	0	10.38	4	0	4.1	6	5	5	1	6
Smith, Ryan	3	6	5.60	41	1	80.1	97	53	50	22	50
Thompson, John	3	2	4.62	45	4	60.1	59	33	31	48	44
*Whiteside, Sean	3	4	5.34	36	0	57.1	57	40	34	35	40
Wooten, Greg	11	10	4.47	26	0	155.0	166	91	77	59	98

Mobile Bay Bears (Padres) AA

BATTING	AVG	AB	R	H	2B	3B	HR	RBI	BB	SO	SB
Allen, Dustin, 1B	.253	475	85	120	28	4	17	75	81	116	1
Alvarez, Gabe, 3B	.300	427	71	128	28	2	14	78	51	64	1
*Bowie, Jim, DH	.241	54	4	13	2	0	1	10	10	5	0
Brinkley, Darryl, OF	.307	215	41	66	14	1	5	33	26	30	10
*Brown, Ray, 1B	.352	179	28	63	16	0	4	30	33	33	1
*Finley, Steve, OF	.500	4	1	2	0	0	1	2	1	2	0
Gama, Rick, 2B	.288	295	56	85	16	2	6	43	51	41	9
Gonzalez, Wikleman, C	.273	143	15	39	7	1	4	25	10	12	1
*Guiel, Aaron, OF	.385	26	9	10	2	0	1	9	5	4	1
Hills, Rich, 1B	.250	216	37	54	12	1	5	30	25	34	2
Keefe, Jamie, OF	.262	42	4	11	2	1	0	3	5	12	2
*Killeen, Tim, C	.202	168	23	34	8	1	5	21	53	60	0
LaRocca, Greg, 2B	.267	300	44	80	16	2	3	31	26	46	8
Mashore, Justin, OF	.238	281	53	67	10	5	11	41	32	70	11
#Matthews, Gary, OF	.244	90	14	22	4	1	2	12	15	29	3
#Melo, Juan, SS	.287	456	52	131	22	2	7	67	29	90	7
Poe, Charles, OF	.311	193	30	60	7	4	3	35	11	43	5
*Powers, John, 3B	.250	48	8	12	0	0	1	8	8	9	2
*Prieto, Chris, OF	.320	388	80	124	22	9	2	58	59	55	26
#Romero, Mandy, C	.320	222	50	71	25	0	13	52	38	31	0
#Schwenke, Matt, 1B	.000	1	0	0	0	0	0	0	0	0	0
#Tredaway, Chad, 2B	.083	12	2	1	0	0	0	0	2	1	0

PITCHING	W	L	ERA	G	SV	IP	H	R	ER	BB	SO
Anderson, Bill	0	0	1.86	7	0	9.2	8	3	2	6	6
*Baron, Jim	2	4	4.54	19	0	33.2	35	21	17	13	30
Castillo, Marino	0	1	4.32	8	1	8.1	14	4	4	5	10
Clayton, Craig	0	0	0.00	3	0	2.1	1	0	0	3	2
Clement, Matt	6	5	2.56	13	0	88.0	83	37	25	32	92
*Dixon, Bubba	7	2	3.45	56	1	75.2	67	31	29	37	88
Erdos, Todd	1	4	3.36	55	27	59.0	45	22	22	22	49

Switch-hitter
* Left-handed
T Player has been with more than one team; listed with last team.
(Players in major leagues are listed with last minor league club.)

PITCHING	W	L	ERA	G	SV	IP	H	R	ER	BB	SO
Kaufman, Brad	5	13	6.18	22	0	125.1	138	97	86	66	103
*Runyan, Sean	5	2	2.34	40	1	61.2	54	25	16	28	52
Skrmetta, Matt	2	3	5.23	21	1	32.2	32	21	19	21	30
Smith, Cam	3	5	7.03	26	1	79.1	85	70	62	73	88
Taylor, Kerry	2	1	4.85	5	0	26.0	27	14	14	13	30
Tollberg, Brian	6	3	3.72	31	0	123.1	123	60	51	24	108
VanDeWeg, Ryan	9	8	5.43	27	0	159.0	198	105	96	55	81
Veras, Dario	0	0	9.00	5	0	5.0	8	5	5	3	5
Walters, Brett	10	7	4.47	31	0	145.0	169	85	72	30	98
Wolff, Bryan	1	2	4.80	20	0	30.0	34	18	16	19	37
*Zancanaro, Dave	10	8	4.44	27	1	133.2	140	69	66	57	66

Orlando Rays (Cubs) AA

BATTING	AVG	AB	R	H	2B	3B	HR	RBI	BB	SO	SB
Ballara, Juan, C	.194	31	2	6	0	0	0	2	5	10	2
Cline, Pat, C	.255	271	39	69	19	0	7	37	27	78	2
Cox, Darron, C	.222	9	2	2	1	0	1	4	1	1	0
Devarez, Cesar, C	.281	96	13	27	4	1	5	17	8	15	1
Dowler, Dee, OF	.253	178	32	45	7	0	3	19	21	23	8
Ellis, Kevin, OF	.255	330	41	84	15	4	8	41	25	66	6
Font, Franklin, SS	.300	20	3	6	0	0	0	2	2	1	0
Forkerway, Trey, 2B	.199	166	19	33	6	0	1	10	25	30	4
Freeman, Ricky, 1B	.312	308	58	96	19	2	16	73	29	51	8
Gazarek, Marty, OF	.331	290	55	96	23	0	10	52	20	31	10
#Hightower, Vee, OF	.233	283	35	66	8	2	6	29	43	66	16
Joseph, Terry, OF	.277	452	80	125	22	11	11	68	59	87	17
#Livsey, Shawn, 2B	.267	30	6	8	2	0	1	2	7	4	2
Maxwell, Jason, SS	.279	409	87	114	22	6	14	58	82	72	12
*McCall, Rod, 1B	.300	70	11	21	2	0	6	20	10	24	0
*Micucci, Mike, C	.000	6	0	0	0	0	0	0	0	1	0
Molina, Jose, C	.172	99	10	17	3	0	1	15	12	28	0
*Morris, Bobby, 2B	.313	16	3	5	1	0	0	1	2	3	0
#Nelson, Bry, 3B	.288	382	51	110	33	2	8	58	45	43	5
Nunez, Raymond, 3B	.296	351	59	104	13	3	16	65	15	65	1
Orie, Kevin, 3B	.385	13	3	5	2	0	2	6	2	1	0
Porter, Bo, OF	.258	31	4	8	1	0	1	3	0	11	0
*Samuels, Scott, OF	.283	127	30	36	7	3	3	17	18	34	5
*Williams, Harold, 1B	.352	88	13	31	12	0	1	11	6	15	1
Wimmer, Chris, 2B	.275	371	62	102	15	3	2	28	23	37	23

PITCHING	W	L	ERA	G	SV	IP	H	R	ER	BB	SO
Barker, Richie	0	1	3.30	19	2	30.0	25	17	11	7	19
*Brown, Darold	0	0	4.20	18	0	30.0	28	15	14	18	24
*Byrne, Earl	5	5	3.95	32	0	130.0	102	62	57	73	128
Duncan, Courtney	2	2	3.40	8	0	45.0	37	28	17	29	45
Garcia, Al	4	4	3.48	12	0	72.1	87	39	28	23	27
Hammack, Brandon	0	6	7.29	39	8	42.0	58	43	34	28	36
*Hancock, Lee	0	2	16.62	3	0	4.1	12	13	8	4	2
Hart, Jason	0	1	6.62	14	0	17.2	20	13	13	2	21
Lyons, Curt	0	0	7.50	2	0	6.0	6	5	5	2	8
*McNichol, Brian	7	10	5.81	22	0	119.1	153	89	77	42	97
Moten, Scott	0	1	13.50	4	0	6.2	9	10	10	6	1
*Norton, Phillip	1	0	2.57	2	0	7.0	8	2	2	2	7
*Peterson, Mark	0	2	9.88	9	0	13.2	26	15	15	4	8
Pierce, Jeff	0	0	9.87	5	0	17.1	28	21	19	7	8
Pool, Matt	4	2	4.60	9	0	47.0	47	28	24	21	38
Rain, Steve	1	2	3.07	14	4	14.2	16	7	5	8	11
Ratliff, Jon	6	4	4.35	18	0	101.1	112	59	49	32	68
Ricketts, Chad	0	0	18.00	2	0	2.0	7	4	4	2	3
Russell, Lagrande	6	4	6.22	25	0	81.0	102	66	56	27	43
Speier, Justin	6	5	4.48	50	6	78.1	77	46	39	23	63
Stephenson, Brian	0	2	9.64	6	0	9.1	10	10	10	5	9
Tapani, Kevin	0	0	4.50	1	0	4.0	3	2	2	2	2
Telemaco, Amaury	1	0	2.25	1	0	8.0	9	2	2	2	6
*Twiggs, Greg	2	4	4.31	48	1	62.2	79	33	30	24	38
Walker, Wade	2	2	8.64	4	0	16.2	19	17	16	13	11
White, Rick	5	7	4.71	39	12	86.0	93	55	45	22	65
Wood, Kerry	6	7	4.50	19	0	94.0	58	49	47	79	106
*Worrell, Steve	7	4	3.47	44	2	62.1	52	25	24	20	54

Batting leaders by position

CATCHER

Player	Club	Lg.	BA
T Hinch, A.J.	Edm	PCL	.328
T Burke, Jamie	Van	PCL	.327
LoDuca, Paul	SAn	Tex	.327
T Foster, Jim	Bow	East	.317
LaRue, Jason	CWV	SAL	.315
Towle, Justin	Cng	Sou	.309
Roskos, John	Prt	East	.308
T Hernandez, R.	Hvl	Sou	.306
T#Curtis, Matt	LkE	Cal	.305
T King, Cesar	Tul	Tex	.304
T Kleiner, Stacy	Ark	Tex	.304
T#Meluskey, M.	NO	AmAs	.303
T Wilson, Tom	Nrw	East	.294
Torres, Jaime	Tam	FSL	.294
Moeller, Chad	FtW	Mid	.289

FIRST BASE

Player	Club	Lg.	BA
Lopez, Luis	Hag	SAL	.358
McCarty, Dave	Phx	PCL	.353
*Helton, Todd	CSp	PCL	.352
*Mitchell, Michael	RC	Cal	.350
*Wilson, Desi	Phx	PCL	.344
Millar, Kevin	Prt	East	.342
*Fick, Robert	WMi	Mid	.341
T*Ward, Daryle	NO	AmAs	.334
T*Lee, Travis	Tcn	PCL	.331
Mendez, Carlos	Wch	Tex	.325
Lee, Derrek	LVg	PCL	.324
*Cromer, D.T.	Hvl	Sou	.323
Freire, Alejandro	Lak	FSL	.323
Morman, Russ	Chr	Int	.319

Switch-hitter
* Left-handed
T Player has been with more than one team; listed with last team.
(Players in major leagues are listed with last minor league club.)

Batting leaders by position

(Cont'd from previous page)

SECOND BASE

Player	Club	Lg.	BA
Raabe, Brian	Tac	PCL	.352
*Counsell, Craig	CSp	PCL	.335
Matos, Francisco	Roc	Int	.324
Short, Rick	Fre	Caro	.319
*Harrison, Adonis	Wsc	Mid	.318
T Williams, Jason	Cng	Sou	.317
Doster, David	SWB	Int	.315
Tyler, Josh	Stk	Cal	.310
Abernathy, Brent	Hag	SAL	.309
T Merloni, Lou	Paw	Int	.305
T Betten, Randy	Van	PCL	.305
Meyers, Chad	Rkf	Mid	.301
Florez, Tim	Phx	PCL	.301

THIRD BASE

Player	Club	Lg.	BA
Kinkade, Mike	ElP	Tex	.385
Wilson, Todd	SJ	Cal	.345
Diaz, Eddy	Tcn	PCL	.329
T Torres, Paul	Tac	PCL	.323
Konerko, Paul	Abq	PCL	.323
Wood, Jason	Edm	PCL	.321
Ball, Jeff	Phx	PCL	.321
Lee, Carlos	W-S	Caro	.317
Beltre, Adrian	VB	FSL	.317
T Lowell, Mike	Col	Int	.315
#Tatis, Fernando	Tul	Tex	.314
T*Taylor, Jamie	NHv	East	.313
T Villalobos, C.	Lak	FSL	.312
T Liniak, Cole	Tre	East	.309
Coolbaugh, Mike	Hvl	Sou	.308

Texas League

Arkansas Travelers (Cardinals) AA

BATTING	AVG	AB	R	H	2B	3B	HR	RBI	BB	SO	SB
Almond, Greg, C	.203	158	23	32	4	1	0	16	29	38	0
Bell, David, 3B	.219	32	3	7	2	0	1	3	2	2	1
*Coughlin, Kevin, OF	.300	90	15	27	6	1	1	8	9	12	0
Dalton, Dee, 3B	.228	360	52	82	16	0	4	43	38	66	2
Difelice, Mike, C	.333	3	0	1	1	0	0	0	1	0	0
#Green, Scrbrgh., OF	.307	251	45	77	14	4	2	29	36	48	11
Kleiner, Stacy, C	.255	55	7	14	4	2	1	10	2	14	0
LaRiviere, Jason, OF	.274	372	50	102	24	5	6	60	33	69	4
Matvey, Mike, 3B	.221	136	16	30	4	0	1	9	21	33	1
McDonald, Keith, C	.240	233	32	56	16	0	5	30	31	56	0
McEwing, Joe, OF	.259	263	33	68	6	3	4	35	19	39	2
*Munoz, Juan, OF	.279	215	28	60	9	2	6	31	16	26	6
Ordaz, Luis, SS	.287	390	44	112	20	6	4	58	22	39	11
#Ozorio, Yudith, OF	.208	144	23	30	2	1	0	9	12	44	6
Pagnozzi, Tom, C	.317	63	8	20	0	0	5	17	4	8	0
Pecorilli, Aldo, 1B	.360	111	21	40	10	0	4	22	7	15	2
Polanco, Placido, 2B	.291	508	71	148	16	3	2	51	29	51	19
*Richard, Chris, 1B	.269	390	62	105	24	3	11	58	60	59	6
*Robinson, Kerry, OF	.321	523	80	168	16	3	2	62	54	64	40
Rupp, Brian, 3B	.295	122	18	36	9	0	1	15	13	16	0
Stefanski, Mike, C	.250	4	1	1	0	1	0	1	0	0	0

PITCHING	W	L	ERA	G	SV	IP	H	R	ER	BB	SO
Barber, Brian	0	1	10.47	3	0	16.1	28	19	19	5	15
Benes, Andy	1	0	1.29	1	0	7.0	2	1	1	2	6
Chavarria, David	3	6	4.50	28	2	90.0	85	56	45	41	62
Croushore, Rick	7	5	4.18	17	0	92.2	111	52	43	37	67
*Detmers, Kris	5	7	5.77	15	0	78.0	99	54	50	27	44
Garcia, Frank	1	3	6.63	28	0	38.0	43	38	28	24	25
Glauber, Keith	5	7	2.75	50	3	59.0	48	22	18	25	53
Heiserman, Rick	5	8	4.17	34	4	131.2	151	73	61	36	90
*Jarvis, Matt	8	5	1.91	50	2	80.0	70	24	17	45	52
King, Curt	2	3	4.46	32	16	36.1	38	19	18	10	29
Logan, Marcus	11	7	4.12	27	0	153.0	152	75	70	64	101
Looper, Braden	1	4	5.91	19	5	21.1	24	14	14	7	20
*Lovingier, Kevin	4	3	2.54	59	3	74.1	68	27	21	26	82
Politte, Cliff	4	1	2.15	6	0	37.2	35	15	9	9	26
Pote, Lou	0	0	1.54	7	0	23.1	15	10	4	8	21
Stein, Blake	8	7	4.24	22	0	133.2	128	67	63	49	114
Westbrook, Destry	0	2	2.74	14	0	23.0	16	11	7	17	16
Windham, Mike	3	3	5.48	19	0	88.2	107	61	54	37	44

El Paso Diablos (Brewers) AA

BATTING	AVG	AB	R	H	2B	3B	HR	RBI	BB	SO	SB
*Andreopoulos, Alex, C	.154	26	1	4	1	0	0	3	1	2	0
*Barker, Kevin, 1B	.277	238	37	66	15	6	10	63	28	40	3
Dobrolsky, Bill, C	.264	303	44	80	23	0	5	45	38	63	1
Felix, Lauro, 3B	.258	128	27	33	9	2	1	17	20	24	1
Groppuso, Mike, 3B	.345	87	15	30	6	2	8	23	10	19	1
Kinkade, Mike, 3B	.385	468	112	180	35	12	12	109	52	66	17
Klassen, Danny, SS	.331	519	112	172	30	6	14	81	48	104	16
Krause, Scott, OF	.361	474	97	171	33	11	16	88	20	108	13
Landry, Todd, 1B	.315	346	43	109	24	3	7	69	15	52	5
#Lopez, Mickey, 2B	.300	483	79	145	21	10	3	58	48	60	20
#Martinez, Greg, OF	.291	381	75	111	10	10	1	29	32	55	39
Nicholas, Darrell, OF	.315	518	79	163	47	5	14	68	27	116	17
O'Neal, Troy, C	.287	122	18	35	1	0	1	11	4	29	0
Perez, Richard, 3B	.300	30	5	9	2	1	0	4	5	1	0
#Rennhack, Mike, OF	.276	369	59	102	28	7	9	64	38	81	4
Rogue, Francisco, C	.125	24	3	3	1	0	0	1	1	5	0
Wachter, Derek, OF	.306	49	8	15	0	0	1	8	4	7	0
*Williams, Drew, 1B	.237	257	36	61	14	1	9	36	19	49	2

PITCHING	W	L	ERA	G	SV	IP	H	R	ER	BB	SO
Beck, Greg	1	5	6.52	18	0	48.1	75	46	35	15	37
Browne, Byron	0	1	7.50	1	0	6.0	8	5	5	3	3
*Dawsey, Jason	2	2	6.81	8	0	38.1	50	30	29	23	14
*Delossantos, Valerio	6	10	5.75	26	2	114.1	146	83	73	38	61
*Estrada, Horacio	8	10	4.74	29	1	153.2	174	93	81	70	127
Fieldbinder, Mick	2	3	5.73	6	0	37.2	55	32	24	12	20
Gardner, Scott	7	8	5.10	29	0	139.1	166	93	79	56	89
*Huber, Jeff	3	1	3.46	19	1	26.0	35	14	10	11	20
Huntsman, Scott	4	4	7.20	42	3	55.0	76	56	44	21	37

Switch-hitter
* Left-handed
T Player has been with more than one team; listed with last team.
(Players in major leagues are listed with last minor league club.)

PITCHING	W	L	ERA	G	SV	IP	H	R	ER	BB	SO
*Mullins, Greg	1	1	2.70	25	13	23.1	19	8	7	11	21
*Pace, Scotty	0	5	5.92	41	0	65.1	86	52	43	31	38
Rodriguez, Frankie	2	2	3.40	31	4	50.1	46	23	19	13	40
Rossiter, Mike	1	0	2.61	8	0	20.2	22	6	6	8	11
Sadler, Al	6	6	6.61	35	4	66.2	102	59	49	28	58
Smith, Travis	16	3	4.15	28	0	184.1	210	106	85	58	107
Wagner, Joe	1	2	9.32	19	1	28.0	32	35	29	32	19
Woodard, Steve	14	3	3.17	19	0	136.1	136	56	48	25	97

Jackson Generals (Astros) AA

BATTING	AVG	AB	R	H	2B	3B	HR	RBI	BB	SO	SB
*Abreu, Bob, OF	.167	12	2	2	1	0	0	0	1	5	0
Flora, Kevin, OF	.000	5	0	0	0	0	0	0	0	3	0
*Forkner, Tim, 3B	.261	398	52	104	23	1	7	46	60	68	4
Gonzalez, Jimmy, C	.254	342	49	87	18	0	14	58	37	91	2
#Guillen, Carlos, SS	.254	390	47	99	16	1	10	39	38	78	6
Hernandez, Carlos, 2B	.292	363	62	106	12	1	4	33	33	59	17
Lopez, Pedro, 1B	.295	88	9	26	5	0	2	13	4	16	0
*Martin, Jim, OF	.274	117	15	32	4	1	7	22	16	42	8
*McNabb, Buck, OF	.258	395	65	102	16	2	1	30	42	58	10
#Meluskey, Mitch, C	.340	241	49	82	18	0	14	46	31	39	1
Miller, Ryan, 2B	.200	55	6	11	0	2	1	8	5	10	1
*Mitchell, Donavon, OF	.256	477	64	122	17	6	5	44	61	48	22
Perez, Jhonny, OF	.253	154	16	39	7	0	3	17	12	26	4
*Peterson, Nate, OF	.301	143	19	43	11	0	4	24	17	21	2
Probst, Alan, C	.333	24	2	8	2	0	1	7	3	7	0
Robinson, Hassan, OF	.174	23	3	4	1	0	0	1	0	2	0
Rodriguez, Noel, OF	.235	85	12	20	3	0	4	17	11	18	0
Sanchez, Victor, OF	.211	175	22	37	4	0	8	35	23	42	1
*Saylor, Jamie, 2B	.254	205	23	52	12	3	5	21	18	43	3
*Trammell, Gary, OF	.264	314	38	83	10	1	2	28	24	53	0
*Ward, Daryle, 1B	.329	422	72	139	25	0	19	90	46	68	4

PITCHING	W	L	ERA	G	SV	IP	H	R	ER	BB	SO
Blanco, Alberto	1	0	2.57	1	0	7.0	5	2	2	3	4
Creek, Ryan	10	5	4.11	19	0	105.0	95	57	48	74	88
*DeClue, Jon	0	2	12.96	9	0	8.1	13	13	12	11	7
Diorio, Mike	1	3	9.53	8	1	11.1	18	17	12	6	9
Elarton, Scott	7	4	3.24	20	0	133.1	103	57	48	47	141
Grzanich, Mike	7	6	4.96	38	12	101.2	114	68	56	46	73
Gutierrez, Jim	4	4	2.93	52	5	89.0	96	33	29	23	51
Haas, David	1	1	5.03	13	0	19.2	23	14	11	4	5
Humphrey, Rich	0	1	32.40	3	0	1.2	7	9	6	3	0
Kester, Tim	4	6	5.23	47	2	82.2	107	53	48	26	50
*Lock, Dan	2	2	6.15	35	0	33.2	43	29	23	17	20
Lopez, Johann	6	8	4.38	35	1	133.2	131	79	65	57	109
Mlicki, Doug	4	4	5.36	9	0	48.2	69	36	29	20	35
*Mounce, Tony	8	9	5.03	25	0	145.0	165	91	81	66	116
O'Malley, Paul	0	2	6.45	28	0	44.2	53	32	32	21	25
*Peterson, Mark	0	0	5.40	6	0	5.0	7	3	3	2	6
Ramos, Edgar	0	2	4.82	4	0	18.2	24	12	10	7	12
*Rumer, Tim	1	2	3.89	7	0	34.2	32	21	15	10	31
Sikorski, Brian	5	5	4.63	17	0	93.1	91	55	48	31	74
Small, Mark	3	4	3.14	37	9	43.0	46	20	15	19	40
Springer, Russ	0	0	9.00	1	0	1.0	2	1	1	0	2
Walter, Michael	2	3	3.63	34	7	44.2	38	20	18	30	41

Midland Angels (Angels) AA

BATTING	AVG	AB	R	H	2B	3B	HR	RBI	BB	SO	SB
Betten, Randy, 3B	.291	220	39	64	13	3	3	24	22	45	7
*Bilderback, Ty, OF	.227	66	7	15	5	0	0	5	6	17	1
#Bolick, Frank, DH	.330	97	26	32	5	1	8	27	26	18	0
Burke, Jamie, 3B	.329	428	77	141	44	3	6	72	40	46	2
Buxbaum, Danny, 1B	.288	514	78	148	42	2	10	70	51	91	1
*Carter, Cale, OF	.167	24	3	4	0	0	0	2	3	7	1
Carter, Mike, OF	.277	65	9	18	3	1	0	2	2	8	5
Dalton, Jed, OF	.225	360	63	81	18	2	11	48	35	58	7
Davalillo, David, SS	.250	176	21	44	6	2	1	12	6	26	1
#Diaz, Freddie, SS	.267	135	21	36	9	0	2	18	18	30	0
*Guiel, Aaron, OF	.329	419	91	138	37	7	22	85	59	94	14
#Harkrider, Timothy, SS	.287	251	39	72	12	3	1	24	22	17	1
*Hemphill, Bret, C	.308	266	46	82	15	2	10	63	47	56	0
*Herrick, Jason, OF	.252	416	60	105	27	4	20	67	34	141	4
Johnson, Jack, C	.200	15	2	3	2	0	1	3	1	4	0
Luuloa, Keith, 2B	.273	421	67	115	29	5	9	59	36	59	7
Molina, Ben, DH	.330	106	18	35	8	0	6	30	10	7	0

Batting leaders by position

(Cont'd from previous page)

SHORTSTOP

Player	Club	Lg.	BA
Valette, Ramon	Day	FSL	.332
Klassen, Danny	EIP	Tex	.331
Collier, Lou	Cgy	PCL	.330
Shave, Jon	SLk	PCL	.329
Abreu, Dennis	Rkf	Mid	.321
Funaro, Joe	Bre	FSL	.319
T Martinez, R.	Shr	Tex	.315
Sheldon, Scott	Edm	PCL	.315
Howard, Matt	Col	Int	.312
T#Caruso, M.	W-S	Caro	.311
Eenhoorn, Robert	Van	PCL	.308
#Wilson, Enrique	Buf	AmAs	.306
Butler, Brent	Peo	Mid	.306
T#Ojeda, Augie	Roc	Int	.303
*Goligoski, Jason	HD	Cal	.300

OUTFIELD

Player	Club	Lg.	BA
Krause, Scott	EIP	Tex	.361
*Cruz, Jacob	Phx	PCL	.361
Stoner, Mike	HD	Cal	.358
T*Grieve, Ben	Edm	PCL	.350
*Darr, Mike	RC	Cal	.344
Miranda, Tony	Lan	Mid	.341
*Shockey, Greg	RC	Cal	.339
#Gibbs, Kevin	SAn	Tex	.335
Inglin, Jeff	Hck	SAL	.334
T*Guiel, Aaron	Mob	Sou	.333
T*Neill, Mike	Hvl	Sou	.333
*Gregg, Tommy	Rmd	Int	.332
T Gibson, Derrick	CSp	PCL	.332
Martinez, Manny	Cgy	PCL	.331
T#Christian, Eddie	Tac	PCL	.330

Switch-hitter
* Left-handed
T Player has been with more than one team; listed with last team.
(Players in major leagues are listed with last minor league club.)

Error leaders by position

CATCHER

Player	Club	Lg.	E
T Burke, Jamie	Van	PCL	29
Valencia, Victor	GBo	SAL	24
Phelps, Josh	Hag	SAL	21
T Gonzalez, J.	Jck	Tex	21
Diaz, Einar	Buf	AmAs	19
LaRue, Jason	CWV	SAL	19
Pachot, John	Hrb	East	19
Anderson, C.	CSC	SAL	19
Ortiz, Hector	Wch	Tex	18
Fauske, Joshua	Hck	SAL	17
T Hernandez, R.	Hvl	Sou	17

FIRST BASE

Player	Club	Lg.	E
*Pickering, Calvin	Del	SAL	27
#Durkac, Bo	HD	Cal	26
Coffee, Gary	Wil	Caro	23
T Torti, Michael	Pdt	SAL	22
Espinal, Juan	Sar	FSL	22
*Minor, Damon	Bak	Cal	22
*Yedo, Carlos	Tam	FSL	21
*Whitlock, Mike	Dun	FSL	20
*Burns, Kevin	QC	Mid	20
#LoCurto, Gary	Mch	Mid	19
Ashby, Chris	Nrw	East	19
*Pryor, Pete	W-S	Caro	18
*Cromer, D.T.	Hvl	Sou	18

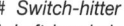

BATTING	AVG	AB	R	H	2B	3B	HR	RBI	BB	SO	SB
Norton, Chris, DH	.265	200	40	53	8	1	16	47	35	57	2
Ryder, Derek, C	.231	78	4	18	2	0	0	6	2	6	1
*Singleton, Duane, OF	.309	55	15	17	5	1	2	8	6	8	4
White, Derrick, DH	.189	37	2	7	2	0	0	3	5	6	1
Young, Kevin, OF	.284	338	64	96	23	6	6	53	49	40	6

PITCHING	W	L	ERA	G	SV	IP	H	R	ER	BB	SO
*Alvarez, Juan	4	1	8.27	24	0	37.0	63	42	34	22	27
*Beaumont, Matt	0	2	25.14	4	0	9.2	24	27	27	10	11
Bene, Bill	0	3	6.31	25	0	41.1	42	33	29	40	41
Bonanno, Rob	5	10	4.60	21	0	125.1	125	83	64	34	64
Bovee, Mike	8	2	4.24	20	0	102.0	117	53	48	23	61
Chavez, Anthony	1	2	4.21	33	6	47.0	53	23	22	15	35
Delacruz, Fernando	2	5	7.79	13	0	71.2	81	70	62	46	44
Freehill, Mike	0	7	7.05	35	10	37.0	46	33	29	20	32
*Gamez, Robert	7	2	5.10	51	0	47.2	62	37	27	20	46
*Harris, Bryan	0	2	11.29	10	1	18.1	28	26	23	15	15
Hook, Chris	1	4	7.07	22	2	35.2	41	34	28	19	24
Janicki, Pete	0	0	0.00	2	0	1.2	3	3	0	2	2
Knudsen, Kurt	0	4	8.68	35	0	57.0	88	63	55	25	35
Macey, Fausto	6	9	8.03	17	0	96.1	141	93	86	46	38
*Perisho, Matt	5	2	2.96	10	0	73.0	60	26	24	26	62
*Quirico, Rafael	3	3	6.91	20	0	54.2	73	47	42	22	37
*Schoeneweis, Scott	7	5	5.96	20	0	113.1	145	84	75	39	64
Skuse, Nick	0	0	6.27	30	16	33.0	31	26	23	15	30
*Washburn, Jarrod	15	12	4.80	29	0	189.1	211	115	101	65	146

San Antonio Missions (Dodgers) AA

BATTING	AVG	AB	R	H	2B	3B	HR	RBI	BB	SO	SB
Battle, Howard, 1B	.242	33	2	8	1	0	0	1	0	7	0
Cooney, Kyle, C	.290	252	39	73	16	2	8	49	7	44	4
*Cora, Alex, SS	.234	448	52	105	20	4	3	48	25	60	12
Davis, Eddie, OF	.209	206	30	43	8	2	11	34	15	69	2
*Durkin, Chris, OF	.272	125	18	34	11	0	4	18	13	33	8
#Gibbs, Kevin, OF	.335	358	89	120	21	6	2	34	72	48	49
Ingram, Garey, 2B	.299	348	68	104	28	7	12	52	37	50	16
Johnson, Keith, 2B	.268	298	43	80	9	3	9	52	17	48	7
*Kirkpatrick, Jay, 1B	.260	215	22	56	9	0	8	42	8	53	0
LoDuca, Paul, C	.327	385	63	126	28	2	7	69	46	27	16
*Melendez, Dan, 1B	.256	258	40	66	19	1	2	24	44	42	4
Richardson, Brian, 3B	.298	484	73	144	23	13	13	90	42	97	3
Richardson, Scott, OF	.283	304	49	86	15	1	7	38	46	54	6
Roberge, J.P., OF	.322	516	94	166	26	4	17	105	39	70	18
Romero, Willie, OF	.324	108	22	35	8	1	1	16	15	11	7
*Spearman, Vernon, OF	.279	136	31	38	3	3	1	7	19	25	9
Wingate, Ervan, 2B	.000	3	0	0	0	0	0	0	2	1	0

PITCHING	W	L	ERA	G	SV	IP	H	R	ER	BB	SO
Ahearne, Pat	4	5	4.50	14	0	84.0	109	48	42	13	45
Anderson, Mike	4	2	6.33	19	0	42.2	47	31	30	13	30
*Bland, Nate	3	2	7.02	10	0	41.0	47	34	32	24	30
Brown, Alvin	6	5	3.74	16	0	96.1	83	48	40	33	67
*Brunson, William	5	5	3.47	17	0	72.2	68	30	28	13	71
Flores, Ignacio	10	7	3.25	27	1	133.0	125	59	48	39	102
Garcia, Jose	3	1	3.15	10	1	20.0	19	8	7	4	14
Gorecki, Rick	4	2	1.39	7	0	45.1	26	8	7	15	33
Herges, Matt	0	1	8.80	4	0	15.1	22	15	15	10	12
Iglesias, Mike	6	2	3.64	42	8	59.1	51	25	24	26	55
Judd, Mike	4	2	2.73	12	0	79.0	69	27	24	33	65
*Kubenka, Jeffrey	3	0	0.70	19	4	25.2	10	2	2	6	38
Lagarde, Joe	4	4	3.76	53	17	69.1	68	34	29	31	65
Linares, Rich	2	1	7.23	18	0	23.2	37	21	19	6	11
Neal, Billy	2	4	6.10	25	0	31.0	35	25	21	16	12
*Reyes, Dennis	8	1	3.02	12	0	80.1	79	33	27	28	66
*Roach, Petie	7	4	3.73	13	0	82.0	76	39	34	35	56
Stone, Ricky	0	3	5.47	25	3	52.2	63	33	32	30	46
Urbina, Dan	0	0	3.86	9	0	14.0	19	8	6	13	6
*Watts, Brandon	0	0	9.00	1	0	1.0	2	1	1	0	2
Weaver, Eric	7	2	3.61	13	0	84.2	80	43	34	38	60
*Williams, Jeff	2	1	5.40	5	0	28.1	30	17	17	7	14

Shreveport Captains (Giants) AA

BATTING	AVG	AB	R	H	2B	3B	HR	RBI	BB	SO	SB
#Bess, Johnny, C	.143	28	1	4	3	0	0	6	3	5	0
Canizaro, Jay, 2B	.256	176	36	45	9	0	11	38	26	44	2
*Fick, Chris, OF	.000	5	1	0	0	0	0	0	1	4	0

Key

Switch-hitter
* Left-handed
T Player has been with more than one team; listed with last team.
(Players in major leagues are listed with last minor league club.)

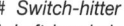

BATTING	AVG	AB	R	H	2B	3B	HR	RBI	BB	SO	SB
*Guzman, Edwards, 3B	.284	380	52	108	15	4	3	42	33	57	3
Kennedy, Darryl, C	.268	71	11	19	4	0	2	10	6	8	0
King, Brett, 3B	.218	193	28	42	6	1	6	20	30	55	4
Martinez, Ramon, SS	.319	404	72	129	32	4	5	54	40	48	4
*Mayes, Craig, C	.273	293	27	80	8	5	2	38	14	29	1
Murray, Calvin, OF	.272	419	83	114	25	3	10	56	66	73	52
Ramirez, Peto, C	.177	113	8	20	6	0	1	9	7	37	0
*Rios, Armando, OF	.289	461	86	133	30	6	14	79	63	85	17
*Sbrocco, Jon, 2B	.262	271	32	71	15	3	2	27	40	21	7
Simonton, Benji, 1B	.256	387	73	99	15	2	20	79	81	120	7
*Singleton, Chris., OF	.317	464	85	147	26	10	9	61	22	50	27
*Unrat, Chris, DH	.238	63	6	15	4	0	0	11	17	7	0
Williams, Keith, OF	.320	493	83	158	37	7	22	106	46	94	3
Woods, Ken, 2B	.300	293	41	88	14	2	2	32	28	40	6

PITCHING	W	L	ERA	G	SV	IP	H	R	ER	BB	SO
Barcelo, Lorenzo	2	0	4.02	5	0	31.1	30	19	14	8	20
Blood, Darin	8	10	4.33	27	0	156.0	152	89	75	83	90
*Brohawn, Troy	13	5	2.56	26	0	169.0	148	57	48	64	98
Corps, Edwin	5	3	4.35	43	6	72.1	66	38	35	35	24
Fontenot, Joe	10	11	5.53	26	0	151.1	171	105	93	65	103
Frontera, Chad	4	4	5.86	15	0	70.2	78	48	46	31	42
*Fultz, Aaron	6	3	2.83	49	1	70.0	65	30	22	19	60
*Hartvigson, Chad	1	0	3.55	4	0	12.2	11	8	5	5	9
Hernandez, Santos	1	1	2.30	11	6	15.2	13	4	4	3	14
Howry, Bob	6	3	4.91	48	22	55.0	58	35	30	21	43
Martin, Jeff	0	2	4.26	26	1	38.0	33	20	18	15	24
*Myers, Jason	1	0	0.75	7	0	12.0	14	7	1	0	12
*Oropesa, Eddie	7	7	3.92	43	0	124.0	122	58	54	64	65
Ortiz, Russ	2	3	4.13	12	0	56.2	52	28	26	37	50
Phillips, Randy	2	0	2.66	11	1	20.1	17	6	6	3	8
Schramm, Carl	1	0	6.43	3	0	7.0	10	6	5	0	5
Taulbee, Andy	4	8	5.17	14	0	85.1	104	59	49	32	46
Thurmond, Travis	0	1	6.00	2	0	6.0	10	9	4	9	4
Villano, Mike	3	1	6.29	30	2	34.1	41	25	24	20	26

Tulsa Drillers (Rangers) AA

BATTING	AVG	AB	R	H	2B	3B	HR	RBI	BB	SO	SB
*Barkett, Andy, 1B	.299	471	82	141	34	8	8	65	63	86	1
Bell, Mike, 3B	.285	123	17	35	11	0	8	23	15	28	0
*Blair, Brian, OF	.262	260	46	68	9	3	4	28	49	64	11
#Bokemeier, Matt, SS	.231	394	51	91	18	3	5	43	37	73	1
Burton, Essex, 2B	.206	63	8	13	2	1	0	2	3	7	3
#Cedeno, Domingo, SS	.444	9	0	4	0	1	0	0	0	3	0
Charles, Frank, C	.230	335	38	77	18	2	9	49	24	81	2
Christopherson, Eric, C	.244	123	26	30	9	0	6	34	25	22	1
Collier, Dan, DH	.257	389	60	100	20	0	26	79	44	134	1
Cossins, Tim, C	.296	108	11	32	5	1	4	17	8	24	2
Diaz, Edwin, 2B	.275	440	65	121	31	1	15	46	33	102	6
King, Cesar, C	.356	45	6	16	1	0	1	8	5	3	0
#Morillo, Cesar, SS	.264	288	38	76	18	1	1	23	28	53	0
Murphy, Mike, OF	.256	156	30	40	10	1	4	19	35	45	6
*Newson, Warren, OF	.143	7	1	1	0	0	1	2	2	1	0
O'Neill, Doug, OF	.277	412	69	114	21	0	20	64	49	122	12
Richards, Rowan, OF	.286	35	5	10	1	0	0	5	5	9	0
#Tatis, Fernando, 3B	.314	382	73	120	26	1	24	61	46	72	17
#Tettleton, Mickey, DH	.182	11	4	2	0	0	1	2	4	2	0
Vessel, Andrew, OF	.261	517	78	135	35	4	12	75	41	87	3

PITCHING	W	L	ERA	G	SV	IP	H	R	ER	BB	SO
Brower, Jim	5	12	5.21	23	0	140.0	156	99	81	42	103
Buckles, Bucky	2	2	7.00	34	1	45.0	59	38	35	20	29
Davis, Jeff	4	6	3.65	11	0	69.0	76	41	28	17	25
Dedrick, Jim	1	0	2.35	12	0	23.0	26	9	6	9	16
*Eddy, Chris	4	0	3.18	41	5	51.0	48	24	18	24	45
*Farrar, Terry	1	2	4.95	6	1	20.0	18	12	11	15	16
Glynn, Ryan	1	1	3.38	3	0	21.1	21	9	8	10	18
Hill, Ken	0	0	0.00	1	0	5.0	2	0	0	1	3
Johnson, Jonathan	5	4	3.52	10	0	71.2	70	35	28	15	47
*Kell, Rob	0	2	5.88	28	1	41.1	60	32	27	14	35
Knight, Brandon	6	4	4.50	14	0	90.0	83	52	45	35	84
*Kojima, Keiichi	1	8	8.83	13	0	53.0	83	55	52	18	40
Kolb, Danny	0	2	4.76	2	0	11.1	7	7	6	11	6
Manning, David	4	7	4.88	13	0	75.2	77	46	41	27	55
*Moody, Ritchie	2	4	5.88	30	0	49.0	52	41	32	41	38
Moore, Bobby	4	6	5.35	35	2	72.1	74	50	43	34	41
Patterson, Danny	0	0	4.50	2	0	2.0	5	4	1	0	0

Error leaders by position

(Cont'd from previous page)

SECOND BASE

Player	Club	Lg.	E
T Dallimore, Brian	Kis	FSL	46
#Smith, Rod	GBo	SAL	33
Spivey, Ernest	HD	Cal	33
Santana, Pedro	WMi	Mid	32
T#Dean, Chris	Mem	Sou	31
Henry, Santiago	Knx	Sou	30
Neal, Mike	Akr	East	29
*Anderson, M.	Rea	East	29
Edwards, Lamont	Pdt	SAL	29
T Jackson, D.	Ind	AmAs	28
Chamblee, J.	Mch	Mid	27
Owens, Eric	Ind	AmAs	27
Schreiber, Stan	Aug	SAL	27
*Bain, Tyler	CSC	SAL	27

THIRD BASE

Player	Club	Lg.	E
Kinkade, Mike	ElP	Tex	60
T Pellow, Kit	Wch	Tex	57
#Leon, Donny	GBo	SAL	40
Blake, Casey	Dun	FSL	39
Ramirez, Aramis	Lyn	Caro	39
#Norton, Greg	Nvl	AmAs	38
Beltre, Adrian	VB	FSL	37
Shatley, Andy	Hag	SAL	36
Minor, Ryan	Del	SAL	34
Lee, Carlos	W-S	Caro	34
T Garcia, Freddy	Car	Sou	34
Crede, Joe	Hck	SAL	33
#Nelson, Bry	Orl	Sou	33
Alvarez, Gabe	Mob	Sou	33
T Light, Tal	Sal	Caro	33

Switch-hitter
* Left-handed
T Player has been with more than one team; listed with last team.
(Players in major leagues are listed with last minor league club.)

383

Error leaders by position

(Cont'd from previous page)

SHORTSTOP

Player	Club	Lg.	E
Rivas, Luis	FtW	Mid	58
Ortiz, Jose	Mod	Cal	55
Klassen, Danny	ElP	Tex	50
Thoen, E.J.	CR	Mid	49
Delossantos, E.	CSC	SAL	42
Klee, Charles	Hck	SAL	41
Lugo, Julio	Kis	FSL	41
T Camilli, Jason	WPB	FSL	41
T#Caruso, M.	W-S	Caro	40
T#Guzman, C.	GBo	SAL	39
Abreu, Dennis	Rkf	Mid	39
Prieto, Alejandro	Wil	Caro	37
T Polanco, Enohel	Bng	East	37
Gonzalez, Alex	Prt	East	37

OUTFIELD

Player	Club	Lg.	E
Hermansen, C.	Car	Sou	39
#Failla, Paul	LkE	Cal	21
Goodell, Steve	Bre	FSL	21
T Asche, Mike	Lyn	Caro	19
Pointer, Corey	Aug	SAL	16
Jaime, Angel	SLu	FSL	16
T*Cotton, John	Nvl	AmAs	15
#Fonville, Chad	Abq	PCL	15
*Stenson, Dernell	Mch	Mid	14
Gomez, Ramon	W-S	Caro	14
Gonzalez, Raul	Wch	Tex	14
Walther, Chris	BLT	Mid	14
Briggs, Stoney	LVg	PCL	14
T Perez, Jhonny	Jck	Tex	14
Salinas, Hector	CSC	SAL	14

PITCHING	W	L	ERA	G	SV	IP	H	R	ER	BB	SO
Pavlik, Roger	0	0	3.60	1	0	5.0	3	2	2	2	4
Powell, John	4	3	2.56	43	5	63.1	54	22	18	23	56
Silva, Ted	13	10	4.09	26	0	171.2	178	88	78	42	121
*Smith, Dan	1	1	3.64	5	0	29.2	25	18	12	15	27
VanPoppel, Todd	3	3	5.06	7	0	42.2	53	27	24	15	26
*Venafro, Michael	0	1	3.45	11	1	15.2	13	12	6	12	13
York, Mike	0	0	5.06	1	0	5.1	7	3	3	2	2

Wichita Wranglers (Royals) AA

BATTING	AVG	AB	R	H	2B	3B	HR	RBI	BB	SO	SB
Brooks, Rayme, C	.229	140	19	32	5	0	4	16	19	45	2
Byington, Jimmie, OF	.235	196	30	46	8	0	2	16	15	39	5
Carr, Jeremy, OF	.306	340	76	104	19	1	8	40	50	53	39
*DeBerry, Joe, OF	.244	82	9	20	5	0	1	5	10	20	3
Diaz, Lino, 3B	.284	289	36	82	26	3	2	51	23	27	3
Fasano, Sal, C	.237	131	27	31	5	0	13	27	20	35	0
*Giambi, Jeremy, OF	.321	268	50	86	15	1	11	52	44	47	4
Gonzalez, Raul, OF	.285	452	66	129	30	4	13	74	36	52	12
Hatcher, Chris, OF	.262	42	7	11	0	0	5	7	4	16	1
Lopez, Mendy, SS	.232	357	56	83	16	3	5	42	36	70	7
McNally, Sean, 3B	.245	53	9	13	4	0	0	2	11	12	1
Medrano, Tony, 2B	.246	349	45	86	9	1	4	42	26	32	8
Mendez, Carlos, 1B	.325	507	72	165	32	1	12	90	19	43	4
#Merchant, Mark, DH	.340	147	27	50	9	0	9	38	23	35	0
*Myers, Rod, OF	.313	16	3	5	2	0	0	3	3	3	0
Nunez, Sergio, 2B	.277	137	18	38	1	1	1	11	6	17	12
Ortiz, Hector, C	.250	180	20	45	3	0	1	25	21	15	1
Pellow, Kit, 3B	.249	241	40	60	12	1	10	41	21	72	5
*Pledger, Kinnis, OF	.081	37	3	3	1	1	0	0	5	14	0
Quinn, Mark, OF	.375	96	26	36	13	0	2	19	15	19	1
Shirley, Al, OF	.271	240	31	65	10	1	4	25	21	92	9
Sisco, Steve, 2B	.286	182	34	52	8	2	3	24	24	29	3
*Smith, Matt, 1B	.227	176	19	40	7	1	1	15	13	37	1

PITCHING	W	L	ERA	G	SV	IP	H	R	ER	BB	SO
Bevil, Brian	0	0	5.63	4	0	8.0	11	8	5	4	10
Brewington, Jamie	2	5	6.71	10	0	51.0	68	43	38	28	31
Brixey, Dusty	0	4	6.98	5	0	19.1	23	15	15	9	5
Calero, Enrique	11	9	4.44	23	0	127.2	120	78	63	44	100
Evans, Bart	1	2	4.59	32	6	33.1	45	20	17	8	28
Flury, Pat	8	3	3.56	42	5	48.0	47	26	19	18	47
Gamboa, Javier	0	3	8.69	6	0	29.0	49	30	28	8	16
Grieve, Tim	3	1	3.38	17	1	37.1	30	15	14	21	36
Grundy, Phillip	9	11	5.70	28	0	156.1	194	108	99	53	117
*Haney, Chris	0	1	2.70	2	0	6.2	5	3	2	0	2
*McDill, Allen	0	1	3.12	16	3	17.1	18	7	6	7	14
Morvay, Joe	1	2	10.94	9	0	26.1	39	32	32	7	13
Mull, Blaine	1	2	6.65	8	0	44.2	66	41	33	23	16
Olsen, Steve	2	0	0.00	3	0	14.2	11	1	0	2	7
*Pennington, Brad	0	0	0.75	12	3	12.0	7	1	1	8	14
*Prihoda, Stephen	0	3	3.24	70	10	89.0	87	34	32	40	68
*Rawitzer, Kevin	5	1	5.75	44	0	97.0	125	68	62	44	75
Saier, Matt	7	5	4.90	17	0	101.0	112	66	55	48	53
Santiago, Jose	2	1	4.00	22	3	27.0	32	13	12	8	12
Smith, Toby	2	3	4.91	8	0	44.0	49	30	24	11	29
Telgheder, Jim	4	7	6.28	28	0	86.0	104	66	60	30	47
Toth, Robert	4	8	5.82	20	0	68.0	82	47	44	26	23
*Walker, Jamie	0	1	9.45	5	0	6.2	6	8	7	5	6
Wolff, Bryan	1	1	6.52	12	1	9.2	18	7	7	5	14
Zimmerman, Mike	1	2	3.67	11	0	27.0	21	14	11	17	11

Switch-hitter
* Left-handed
T Player has been with more than one team; listed with last team.
(Players in major leagues are listed with last minor league club.)

Clubhouse

1998 Baseball Weekly Almanac

- ▸Youth-league results
- ▸Little League
  World Series
- ▸Birmingham's
  Rickwood Field
- ▸Umpiring is kids' stuff
- ▸Youth-league
  directory

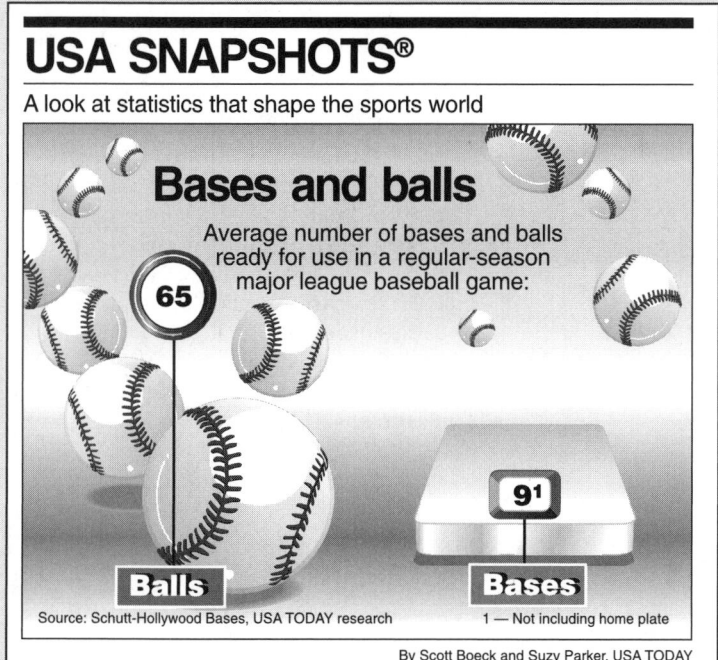

USA SNAPSHOTS®

A look at statistics that shape the sports world

Bases and balls

Average number of bases and balls ready for use in a regular-season major league baseball game:

65

91

Balls

Bases

Source: Schutt-Hollywood Bases, USA TODAY research

1 — Not including home plate

By Scott Boeck and Suzy Parker, USA TODAY

Little League World Series scores

▶**Little League (11-12):**
Guadalupe (Mexico) 5,
South Mission Viejo (Calif.) 4

▶**Junior League (13):**
Salem (N.H.) 4,
North Mission Viejo (Calif.) 1

▶**Senior League (13-15):**
San Francisco (Venezuela) 3,
Yucaipa (Calif.) 0

▶**Big League (16-18):**
Broward County (Fla.) 15,
Maracaibo (Venezuela) 3

PONY championship scores

▶**Mustang (9-10):**
Houston 7,
San Diego 1

▶**Bronco (11-12):**
West Covina (Calif.) 6,
Tampa 0

▶**Pony (13-14):**
Danville (Calif.) 7,
Hamilton (Ohio) 0

▶**Colt (15-16):**
Lutcher (La.) 11,
Levittown (Puerto Rico) 1

▶**Palomino (17-18):**
Sylmar (La.) 5,
Carolina (Puerto Rico) 3

Mexico rallies for Little League win

Determining when to remove a starting pitcher can be a wrenching decision for baseball managers at any level. When in doubt, major leaguers often go to a bullpen stocked with high-priced, hard-throwing specialists.

In Little League, where 12-year-olds play on fields with fences only 205 feet away, the stakes can be just as high. South Mission Viejo, Calif., manager Jim Gattis, who skippered independent minor league teams at Utica (N.Y.) and Salt Lake City in the 1980s, will never know if his footloose, beach-loving starter Gavin Fabian had enough left in the championship game at the 51st Little League World Series. Fabian was leading 4-1 and working on a no-hitter when he was removed after hitting a batter and walking another to start the final inning. Guadalupe, Mexico, then rallied for a 5-4 win in one of the most dramatic finishes in Series history.

After Fabian's exit, Gabriel Alvarez hit a three-run home run to tie it 4-4. After a walk and a sacrifice, Pablo Torres' line-drive single to center scored Javier de Isla when center fielder Ashton White bobbled the ball. "The team always plays hard until the last out. Today they did that," said Guadalupe manager Jaime Luna. Of Alvarez's blast, Luna said, "It was like a stick of dynamite."

Until this year, Monterrey's titles in 1957 and '58 had been the only ones in 13 previous appearances by Mexican teams. Guadalupe, located in the state of Nuevo León near Monterrey, knows the story of those titles. The '57 Monterrey team was Mexico's version of *Hoosiers*, an unheralded group of underdogs winning something big. A movie was made about them, too. In fact, the team from Guadalupe watched it—dubbed in Spanish—before the final.

Maybe it's time for a sequel. After all, Mexico seemed doomed with Fabian dominating. "He was difficult," said Torres. "He had a very good curveball. The curveball is our biggest weakness."

The heartbreaking loss left an imprint on Mission Viejo. "I told the kids we deserved to lose. I felt like we didn't play as a unit. We tried too hard," said Gattis. "There were a lot of personal failures." Asked if White could have thrown out de Isla had he not bobbled the ball, Gattis said, "I have no idea. I had no angle on it. That wasn't the issue."

Gattis made a huge decision when he removed Fabian in favor of Adam Sorgi, who allowed Alvarez's home run, and then Ryan O'Donovan, who gave up Torres' game-winning single. Fabian finished with no hits, eight

386

1998 BASEBALL WEEKLY ALMANAC

strikeouts and two earned runs. Alvarez saw his home run off Sorgi as redemption since he stood to be the losing pitcher. "I thought I would lose the game and we may not win the world championship," said Alvarez.

South Mission Viejo scored three runs in the fourth, helped by some Guadalupe sloppiness. White, the team's top hitter and son of 1979 Heisman Trophy winner Charles White, led off with a line-drive double to left field that bounced over the fence. Fabian then laid down a sacrifice bunt. Third baseman Ricardo Garcia had a play on White, caught between second and third, but threw the ball off the glove of shortstop Daniel Baca, who was covering third, and White scored. Then, with Nick Moore batting, Alvarez's pitch got away from catcher Luis Robles for a passed ball. Robles threw wildly to third trying to get Fabian, who then scored. Moore then homered for a 3-0 lead.

Guadalupe scored in the fifth when right fielder Greg Oates misplayed a soft line drive by Torres into a three-base error with one out. After Alejandro Robles struck out, third baseman Gary Gattis could not handle Adrian Luna's hard grounder for another error, scoring Torres. South Mission Viejo got the run back in the sixth on O'Donovan's leadoff double, a single by pinch-hitter Matt Cusick and a delayed double steal.

A crowd of 37,400 watched the championship game, bringing the week's total in Williamsport, Pa., to a record 182,358 for 15 games, topping the 156,000 attendance in '95. This year was the fourth consecutive time an international team has won the Series. The last U.S. winner was Long Beach, Calif., in '92 and '93.
—*by Peter Brewington*

Students bring oldest park into 21st century

The students at Mountain Brook Elementary School in Birmingham, Ala., learned about computers and baseball at the same time. They put together their own CD-ROM about Birmingham's Rickwood Field, listed on the National Register of Historic Places as America's oldest ballpark, with its Aug. 18, 1910, opening.

"One of the things I strive for is to give the kids a real-world experience," said Melinda Storey during the project. She is an enrichment teacher who works with gifted children in grades 4-6. "[We're] creating a multimedia interactive CD just like the ones you can buy. And this gets the kids to appreciate what's in their own backyard." The school was awarded a $2,400 grant from the Alabama Historical

NABF championship scores

▶**Freshman (11-12):**
East Cobb (Ga.) 12,
Oakland (Mich.) 2

▶**Sophomore (13-14):**
Norman (Okla.) 19,
Baltimore 2

▶**Junior (15-16):**
Bayside (N.Y.) 6,
Marietta (Ga.) 5

▶**High School (15-17):**
Indianapolis 10,
Suffolk County (N.Y.) 3

▶**Senior (17-18):**
Hammond (La.) 10,
Springfield (Ohio) 8

American Legion World Series scores

Sanford (Fla.) 11,
Medford (Ore.) 8

Babe Ruth championship scores

▶**Bambino (11-12):**
Amity (N.Y.) 6,
Willamette Valley (Ore.) 1

▶**13 year olds:**
Oakland (Calif.) 15,
Staten Island (N.Y.) 5

▶**13-15 year olds:**
Bakersfield (Calif.) 10,
Prince George (Md.) 6

▶**16 year olds:**
Satsuma (Ala.) 7,
South Shore (N.Y.) 3

▶**16-18 year olds:**
Antioch (Calif.) 5,
Tri Counties (Texas) 2

AABC champions

▶**Roberto Clemente (8 and under):** Dallas

▶**Willie Mays (10 and under):** Dallas

▶**Pee Wee Reese (12 and under):** Potros (Puerto Rico)

▶**Sandy Koufax (14 and under):** Memphis (Tenn.)

▶**Mickey Mantle (16 and under):** Orange County (Calif.)

▶**Connie Mack (18 and under):** Midland (Ohio) 13, Orange County (Fla.) 5

Commission to help underwrite the project, which was completed in April. Oddly, Storey got her idea in the spring of 1996 while buying shoes. "There was a pamphlet in the store about Rickwood Field," she said. "I thought this would make an interesting project."

The 100-page CD contains biographies of key players who have played at Rickwood Field, from Ty Cobb and Babe Ruth to Frank Thomas and Michael Jordan. The bios include former Negro leagues stars such as Satchel Paige and Josh Gibson, as well as Birmingham native Willie Mays, who grew up minutes from Rickwood and started in center field for the 1948 Black Barons, when he was 16 years old.

The CD includes a trivia challenge and "Wacky Baseball Stories" from Rickwood's 87 years. One of the children's favorites involves former outfielder Jimmy Piersall. "After he was ejected from a game, he climbed up to the roof of the stadium," fourth-grader Trey Merrill said. "He began to squirt people in the stands with a squirt gun."

The students devoted about four hours a week to the project. They researched the project by reading books and newspaper articles at the local library and by interviewing former Birmingham Barons players such as Walt Dropo and Fred Hatfield. They also visited Rickwood Field last summer. "The best part was the old [hand-operated] scoreboard," fifth-grader Abbie Wright said. "The guy let us put in the numbers. That was fun."

The students wrote all the copy in longhand. After their teacher edited it, the students typed it into the computer. The National Baseball Hall of Fame and Museum in Cooperstown, N.Y., helped by sending photos. "My favorite part is scanning in the pictures on a scanner we have at school," fifth-grader Christopher McSweeney said before the project's completion. "I've done about 50 so far, including Hank Aaron, Jackie Robinson, Lou Gehrig and Joe DiMaggio." After all the copy was written and photos dropped into place, the pages were linked and the CD completed.

The class produced about 100 copies of its CD. One was placed at the Rickwood Field museum, while others were sold to raise money for the Alabama Historical Commission.

The Birmingham Barons of the Class AA Southern League played at Rickwood through the 1987 season before moving to a modern stadium in suburban Hoover, Ala. The old ballpark was renovated three years ago for the films *Cobb* and *Soul of the Game*, complete with 1910-era signs and the hand-operated scoreboard in left field. The park currently hosts about

150 high school, college and recreation league games each year.
—by Bill Koenig

Young umpires learn game, gain respect

Kevin Curtin spends hours toiling under a hot sun, taking abuse from fans and players. What's an 11-year-old umpire to do? Talk back, he says. "I've had people say, 'That was a strike,' or, 'He was safe,'" he says. "I just tell them that I'm the umpire and I make the calls. Then they sit down."

Kevin's older brother, Brian, 13, is also an umpire. He calls games for 11-year-old Little Leaguers at Arrowhead Park in Naperville, Ill. The payoff is a little spending money—Brian makes $10 a game, Kevin makes $8—and both gain a greater understanding of the game. "Before, I didn't really know that if you catch a foul tip in the glove, runners can still go," says Brian, a catcher. "I threw a runner out at second base because I knew the rule. Otherwise, I would've just held the ball."

The boys took an umpiring course offered by Arrowhead Park last spring. Many parks and youth leagues offer courses. But be warned: The Curtin brothers had to memorize a book of rules—in Brian's case, that book was 76 pages in tiny type. "Studying how to umpire is nearly as hard as doing it," Brian says. "You have to know all the rules and know how and when to make the calls. In baseball, it seems like there are millions of rules."

Working behind the plate has helped the brothers develop new respect for major league umpires. "There's lots of traveling, and they have no home field," Brian says. "And there's long, hard, continuous work on the field in dark, hot clothes without a break for nine or more innings. Umpiring is a hard job, but professional umpires do a good job."

Adds Kevin: "Umpires have to know all the rules and make a call within a fraction of a second. Umpires make bad calls, but they make more good calls than bad ones."
—by Dana Heiss

Dixie championship scores

▶**Youth (11-12):**
Northeast Pensacola (Fla.) 8,
Hopemills (N.C.) 1

▶**Dixie 13 year old:**
Gonzales (La.) 3,
Phoenix City (Ala.) 2

▶**Dixie Boys (13-14):**
Hartsville (S.C.) 9,
Bossier City (La.) 1

▶**Pre-majors (15-16):**
Valdosta (Ga.) 7,
Bossier City (La.) 5

▶**Majors (15-18):**
Montgomery (Ala.) 13,
Petal (Miss.) 3

CLUBHOUSE

389

Who's playing the field

▶**American Amateur Baseball Congress:**
Founded in 1935. 12,895 teams, 257,900 players. Ages: 8-up.

▶**American Legion Baseball:**
Founded in 1925. 4,680 teams, 84,000 players. Ages: 16-18.

▶**Babe Ruth League Inc.:**
Founded in 1951. 5,800 leagues, 41,000 teams, 815,000 players in baseball; 3,500 teams, 70,000 participants in softball. Ages: 5-18.

▶**Continental Amateur Baseball Association:**
Founded in 1984. 1,379 leagues, 8,274 teams, approximately 124,110 players. Ages: 9-18.

▶**Dixie Baseball Inc. (includes Dixie Softball):**
Founded in 1956. 24,241 baseball teams, 363,615 players; 4,369 softball teams, 65,535 players (total 429,150 players, 11 states). Ages: 4-18.

▶**Little League Baseball Inc.:**
Founded in 1939. 196,000 teams, 2.7 million participants in the U.S., 3 million worldwide. Ages: 5-18.

▶**National Amateur Baseball Federation:**
Founded in 1914. 5,000 teams, 110,000 players (who advance into tournament competition). Ages: 12-up (including 30-and-over leagues).

▶**National Police Athletic League Baseball:**
Founded in 1960. 200,000 players in regional and national tournaments. Ages: 14-16.

▶**PONY Baseball/Softball Inc.:**
Founded in 1951. 28,500 teams, nearly 400,000 athletes in 45 states and 12 foreign countries. 2,000 softball teams. Ages: 5-18.

How to find a team

To find a team in your area, contact the national headquarters listed below for a regional reference.

▶**American Amateur Baseball Congress:**
118-19 Redfield Plaza, P.O. Box 467, Marshall, MI 49068; (616) 630-1213.

▶**American Legion:**
P.O. Box 1055, Indianapolis, IN 46206; (317) 630-1213.

▶**Babe Ruth League:**
1771 Brunswick Ave., P.O. Box 5000, Trenton, NJ 08638; (609) 695-1434.

▶**Continental Amateur Baseball Association:**
82 University St., Westerville, OH 43081; (614) 899-2103.

▶**Dixie Baseball:**
PO. Box 877, Marshall, TX 75671; (903) 927-2255.

▶**Little League:**
P.O. Box 3485, Williamsport, PA 17701; (717) 326-1921.

▶**National Amateur Baseball Federation:**
P.O. Box 705, Bowie, MD 20718; (301) 262-5005.

▶**National Police Athletic League:**
614 U.S. Hwy. 1, Ste. 20, North Palm Beach, FL 33408; (407) 844-1823.

▶**PONY Baseball/Softball:**
P.O. Box 225, Washington, PA 15301-0225; (412) 225-1060.

High school/ college baseball

▸**1997 Super 25 high schools**
▸**All-USA high school teams**
▸**1997 College World Series**

▸**1997 Top 25 college coaches' poll**
▸**1998 college preview**
▸**and more ...**

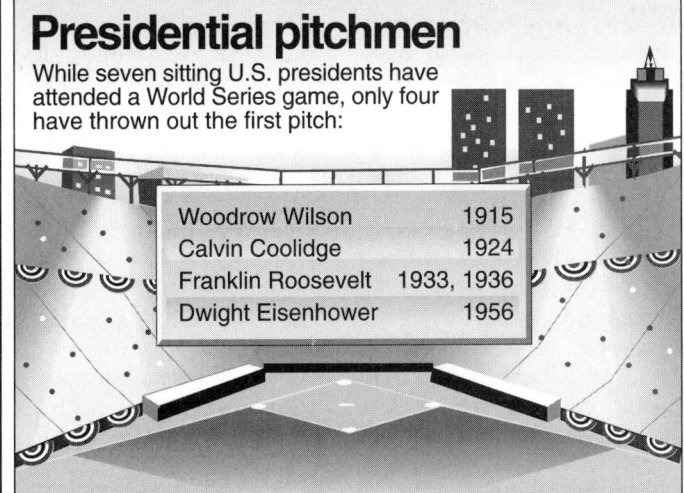

USA SNAPSHOTS®

A look at statistics that shape the sports world

Presidential pitchmen

While seven sitting U.S. presidents have attended a World Series game, only four have thrown out the first pitch:

Woodrow Wilson	1915
Calvin Coolidge	1924
Franklin Roosevelt	1933, 1936
Dwight Eisenhower	1956

Source: National Baseball Hall of Fame and Museum   By Scott Boeck and Suzan Deo, USA TODAY

USA TODAY Super 25:
Final 1997 high school rankings

▶**1. Clovis, Calif. (33-2)** Season recap: Won last 22 games and second Central Section Yosemite Division title. The team batted .330 and had a 1.82 ERA while setting a school record for wins. Lee Lambert was 8-0 with a 1.59 ERA and batted .383 with 41 RBI. Daryl Minugh was 13-1 with a 1.94 ERA and 130 strikeouts in 90⅓ innings.

▶**2. Hamilton, Ohio (29-2)** Season recap: Won last 20 games and second Division I title. Aaron Cook was 10-0 (and had a school-record 23 career victories) with a 1.23 ERA and batted .381 with 31 RBI. Curtis Moak was 7-1 with a 1.87 ERA and batted .403 with 13 doubles and 30 RBI.

▶**3. Jesuit, Tampa (32-3)** Season recap: Won last 16 games and second Class 4A title. Team batted .386 and had a 1.07 ERA. Geoff Goetz was 13-2 with a 0.68 ERA, striking out 149 and allowing 35 hits in 83 innings. He also batted .486 with a school-record 53 hits and 45 RBI. Josh Cervi batted .413 and Steven Shirley hit .385.

▶**4. Esperanza, Anaheim, Calif. (25-5)** Season recap: Won third Southern Section Division I title. Tommy Nicholson batted .456 with a school-record 47 hits and a record-tying 42 RBI. Nathan Choate was 13-0 with a 1.73 ERA. Rickey Leach was hit by a pitch a school-record 21 times.

▶**5. Westminster Christian, Miami (30-4-1)** Season recap: Won second consecutive Class 2A title, seventh overall. Harrison Boyd batted .436 with 43 runs and 31 RBI. Jason Moore batted .391 with 42 RBI and was 5-1 with a 0.64 ERA. Manny Crespo batted .406 with 11 home runs and 47 RBI.

▶**6. Rose, Greenville, N.C. (26-2)** Season recap: Won last 16 games and second Class 4A title. Monte Roundtree was 12-2 with a 0.69 ERA and 172 strikeouts in 98 innings and batted .488. Tutu Moye, who batted .505 with 46 RBI, made five errors in two years at shortstop.

▶**7. George Washington, New York City (44-2)** Season recap: Won last 18 games and second PSAL A Division title. Vicente Rosario batted .623 with 77 runs, 20 doubles, 16 home runs and 61 RBI. He was 89-for-92 in stolen base attempts, including taking home three times. Enmanuel Ulloa was 14-1 with a 0.87 ERA, striking out 127 and walking eight in 88 innings.

▶**8. Lake Brantley, Altamonte Springs, Fla. (30-5)** Season recap: Won first Class 6A title, second overall. Sophomore Justin Harris batted .500 with 22 RBI and 29 stolen bases. Junior Robbie Sitz (12-1, 1.13 ERA) threw two no-hitters.

▶**9. Barron Collier, Naples, Fla. (29-3)** Season recap: Won last 14 games and first Class 5A title, averaging a school-record 9.2 runs. Junior Dan Maurer was 13-2 with a 1.69 ERA and batted .464 with 46 runs and 36 RBI. Ryan Senkarik batted a school-record .490 with 36 RBI.

▶**10. Round Rock, Texas (32-6)** Season recap: Won last 11 games and first Class 5A title. Junior Ryan Langerhans, 11-1 with a 1.45 ERA, batted .427 with 44 runs and 36 RBI. Brian Gordon, 14-0 with a 1.44 ERA, batted .310 with seven home runs and 31 RBI. Junior Jeff Ontiveros batted .369 with nine home runs and 41 RBI.

▶**11. Harrison County, Cynthiana, Ky. (40-1)** Season recap: Won last 34 games and second state title. Bubba Hignite was 12-0 with a 1.65 ERA. Junior Will Renaker was 7-1 with a 2.13 ERA and batted .544 with 16 home runs and a school-record-tying 81 RBI. Sophomore Noochie Varner batted .507 with 12 home runs, 64 runs and 74 RBI, and his 71 hits tied a school record.

▶**12. Bishop Eustace, Pennsauken, N.J. (30-3)** Season recap: Won a school-record 30 games and fifth Parochial A title. Junior Marc Sauer was 12-1 with a 2.04 ERA and batted .489 with 19 RBI. Sophomore Mike Appalucci batted .409 with 44 runs and 44 RBI. Junior Craig Rutter batted .406 with 37 runs and 35 RBI.

▸**13. Central Dauphin, Harrisburg, Pa. (25-3)** Season recap: Won a school-record 25 games and first Class 3A title. Adam Belicic was 10-1 with a 2.30 ERA and batted .530 with 39 RBI. Steve Booker batted .424 with 43 runs and 18 stolen bases. Rich Powers batted .427 with 28 RBI.

▸**14. Grossmont, La Mesa, Calif. (29-5)** Season recap: Won third San Diego Section Division I title. Ryan Lehr batted .473 with 11 home runs and 49 RBI. Junior Beau Craig batted .395 with 34 runs and 49 RBI. Junior Kevin Correia was 7-0 with four saves and a 0.82 ERA.

▸**15. Schaumburg, Ill. (32-5)** Season recap: Won first Class 2A title as Mike Nall posted a 13-1 record with three saves and a 2.05 ERA. Tim Chambers batted .442 with 41 runs, 38 RBI and a school-record 58 hits.

▸**16. Iolani, Honolulu (23-1)** Season recap: Won seventh state title, setting school records for batting average (.425), home runs (35) and victories (23). Keoni DeRenne batted .519 with 42 runs and 33 RBI. Danny Kimura batted .534 with nine home runs (a state regular-season record) and 35 RBI and was 4-0 with two saves.

▸**17. Canyon, Anaheim, Calif. (25-6)** Season recap: Won first Southern Section Division III title. Jeff Leuenberger was 11-1 with a 2.69 ERA and batted .441 with 24 RBI, setting school records with 101 strikeouts as a senior and 34 victories in his career.

▸**18. Rochester, Mich. (36-2)** Season recap: Won a record 36 games and first Class A title. Andrew Good set school records with 12 victories (no losses), 95 strikeouts and a 0.62 ERA. Scott Loos batted .434 with 40 RBI.

▸**19. Greenbrier, Evans, Ga. (31-5)** Season recap: Won Class 3A title in first year of existence. Mark Thornhill batted .455 with 53 runs and 49 RBI. Mark Smith was 14-2 and batted .404 with 42 runs and 40 RBI.

▸**20. Christian Brothers, Memphis (35-5)** Season recap: Won fifth Class 3A title with a school-record 35 victories. Junior Kurt Evans led with a .429 batting average. Jay Fik led with 40 RBI and four home runs and was second with 41 runs.

▸**21. De La Salle, Concord, Calif. (25-3)** Season recap: Won third North Coast Section Class 3A title with a .342 team batting average. Jason Dennis was 11-1 with three saves and a 1.20 ERA, setting a school record with 25 career wins.

▸**22. Elk Grove, Calif. (31-4)** Season recap: Won second Sac-Joaquin Section Division I title. Mickey Kammeyer batted .441 with 47 runs and 33 RBI. Mike Tonis batted .398 with 47 RBI.

▸**23. Xaverian, Brooklyn, N.Y. (28-3)** Season recap: Won second New York City Catholic Athletic Association title, setting school records with 28 victories and 20 HRs. Junior Johnny Hernandez batted .462 with 28 RBI and 22 runs.

▸**24. Start, Toledo, Ohio (29-2)** Season recap: Division I runner-up with a young team, led by juniors Todd Moore (.480, 43 runs, 20 RBI); Mike Arbinger (.416, 45 runs, 36 walks, 39 RBI); and Jason Wanner (10-2, 1.95 ERA).

▸**25. Canyon del Oro, Tucson, Ariz. (27-6)** Season recap: Won Class 5A title with a young team. Junior Shelley Duncan was 6-2 with a 1.80 ERA and batted .477 with a school-record 13 home runs and 47 RBI in just 24 games.

—ranked by Dave Krider,
USA TODAY

1996 USA TODAY All-USA high school team

First team

▶Troy Cameron, SS

School: St. Thomas Aquinas (Ft. Lauderdale)
Ht.: 5-11 / **Wt.:** 180 / **Class:** Senior/ **B-T:** S-R
1997 statistics: Led team to a 28-2 record by batting .475, with six doubles, 14 HRs, 45 runs and 36 RBI. Walked 30 times and struck out just 13 times. Had a 1.075 slugging average. Was 2-1 pitching with two saves.
Coach Paul Herfurth says: "He carried us most of the season. The kids had a lot of confidence in him. He can turn a game around in a hurry. He is a perfectionist, and he dealt very well with the pressure."
The major league player I admire the most: "Alex Rodriguez. He's from this area, and I've met him a couple of times. He plays the position I play, is real young, and it didn't take him long to get up there."
Signed with: Atlanta Braves.

▶Michael Cuddyer, SS

School: Great Bridge (Chesapeake, Va.)
Ht.: 6-2 / **Wt.:** 190 / **Class:** Senior / **B-T:** R-R
1997 statistics: Batted .500, with 10 doubles, two triples, six HRs, 41 runs, 30 walks and 30 RBI. In 41 innings pitched, was 6-0 with two saves, struck out 48, allowed 28 hits and had a 2.39 ERA.
Coach Greg Jennings says: "He's the best high school hitter I've ever seen. He's one of the finest all-around young men I ever have met—the total package."
The major league player I admire the most: "Cal Ripken Jr. Obviously, he has tremendous talent, but he also has a lot of class. I like the way he handles himself on and off the field."
Signed with: Florida State.

▶Brett Groves, SS

School: Tampa Bay Tech (Tampa)
Ht.: 6-0 / **Wt.:** 175 / **Class:** Senior / **B-T:** S-R
1997 statistics: Set school records with 26 stolen bases and 22 walks. Batted .410, with eight doubles, two HRs, 34 runs and 15 RBI. Struck out five times in 73 at-bats.
Coach Larry Benton says: "He's an excellent defensive player with a great feel for the game. He has extraordinary range and is a big-play person. He has tremendous speed and gets a tremendous jump on stolen bases."
The major league player I admire the most: "Chipper Jones. I see myself as the same type of player. I'm a switch hitter and a good defen-

sive player. Plus, I get all the Braves games on TV."
Signed with: Florida State.

▶Jason Romano, 3B

School: Hillsborough (Tampa)
Ht.: 6-0 / **Wt.:** 190 / **Class:** Senior / **B-T:** R-R
1997 statistics: Batted .458, with 14 doubles, four triples, nine HRs, 31 runs and 40 RBI. Had 19 walks and 17 stolen bases and struck out nine times. Made only four errors at third base in 71 chances.
Coach Billy Reed says: "He has great determination and desire, good footwork, arm and instincts. He is equal to Gary Sheffield and Kiki Jones, who both played shortstop for me."
The major league player I admire the most: "Wade Boggs. He's proven he can play in the big leagues for so many years. He's a hometown hero around here, and he's a third baseman like me."
Signed with: Miami (Fla.).

▶Patrick Boyd, CF

School: Central Catholic (Clearwater, Fla.)
Ht.: 6-3 / **Wt.:** 195 / **Class:** Senior / **B-T:** S-R
1997 statistics: Set school records with 42 runs and 30 stolen bases. Batted .449, with eight doubles, three triples, seven HRs and 34 RBI. Made one error and had nine assists.
Coach Todd Vaughan says: "He can do everything. He's the only kid I've seen who can get on first and be on third after two pitches. He's real smart on the bases. He's the best player our school ever has had."
The major league player I admire the most: "Chipper Jones. I like the way he plays. He's a switch hitter, always gives 100 percent, and he's aggressive."
Signed with: Clemson.

▶Ryan Anderson, LHP

School: Divine Child (Dearborn, Mich.)
Ht.: 6-10 / **Wt.:** 215 / **Class:** Senior / **B-T:** L-L
1997 statistics: Had deceiving 5-3 record with two saves. In 59 2/3 innings, allowed just 10 hits, struck out 148 and had a 0.94 ERA. Walked 38 and allowed eight earned runs. Pitched three no-hitters; struck out 21 twice, 20 once and 19 once. (Anderson's league used a two-strike strikeout rule, with three balls for a walk.)
Coach Greg Green says: "Ryan is even more developed than Randy Johnson [was] when he was the same age. He throws 96 mph and is consistent at around 92."

The major league player I admire the most: "Randy Johnson. He's a power pitcher, and I see myself as a power pitcher. He's tall like me, and he's a forceful pitcher in the major leagues."
Drafted by: Seattle Mariners.

▶Darnell McDonald, CF

School: Cherry Creek (Englewood, Colo.)
Ht.: 5-10 / Wt.: 190 / Class: Senior / B-T: R-R
1997 statistics: First-team repeater played on three Class 5A baseball and three football state champions. Even though he was pitched around most of the year, he set a school record with a .606 batting average. Had eight doubles, 10 HRs, 37 runs, 14 walks, 35 RBI and 18 stolen bases. Struck out seven times. In six playoff victories, he was 13-for-17 with 11 runs, four doubles, five HRs and 15 RBI.
Coach Mark Johnson says: "He's the best big-gamer I ever saw. He had to hit many pitches that were not quality pitches. He hit a couple doubles on pitches a foot outside during the playoffs. I have coached seven first-round draft picks, and he is a level above every one."
The major league player I admire the most: "Ellis Burks. I am good friends with him. I like his work habits. He really works hard and prepares himself for the games."
Signed with: Texas, for football and baseball.

▶Rick Ankiel, LHP

School: Port St. Lucie, Fla.
Ht.: 6-3 / Wt.: 220 / Class: Senior / B-T: L-L
1997 statistics: Lost his final game to finish 11-1. Used 95-mph fastball and brilliant curve to strike out 162 and allow just 22 hits in 74 innings. Allowed five earned runs for a 0.41 ERA. Fired three no-hitters, giving him nine in his career, and had a 19-strikeout game. Batted .400, with seven HRs and 29 RBI.
Coach John Messina says: "I can't see there being a better high school athlete in the United States. He is a great outfielder and made some great plays this year. He is equal to Alex Fernandez."
The major league player I admire the most: "Ken Griffey Jr. I just like the way he hits the ball. Even though he's so young, he's had so much success."
Signed with: Miami (Fla.).

▶Vicente Rosario, CF

School: George Washington (New York City)
Ht.: 5-10 / Wt.:180 / Class: Senior / B-T: R-R
1997 statistics: Led team to 44-2 record and first New York City Public School Athletic League A Division title since 1973. Batted .623,

with 20 doubles, seven triples and 16 home runs. Scored 77 runs and drove in 61. Stole 89 bases in 92 attempts (including three steals of home) and was hit by a pitch 13 times.
Coach Steve Mandl says: "I compare him to Kenny Lofton and Devon White. This is the year of Jackie Robinson, and he is that kind of player. He is just a menace, because he can beat you in so many ways. I call him a 'home-sick kid.' He gets on base and gets home quick."
The major league player I admire the most: "Devon White. He steals a lot of bases, and I like his defense. He can beat you in a lot of ways. He's a real quiet guy and just goes out and does his job."
Drafted by: New York Mets.

▶Dane Sardinha, C

School: Kamehameha (Honolulu)
Ht.: 6-0 / Wt.: 200 / Class: Senior/ B-T: R-R
1997 statistics: Batted .443, with four doubles, four triples and six HRs. Scored 28 runs and drove in 36. Had .934 slugging percentage. Walked 17 times and struck out four times.
Coach Vern Ramie says: "He's one of the most complete players to come out of our state in a long time. He has all the tools to get to the major leagues."
The major league player I admire the most: "Ivan Rodriguez. He's not very big and has a strong arm. He's an all-around player with the total package."
Signed with: Pepperdine.

Coach of the year: James Patrick

School: Clovis (Calif.)
College: Graduate of Fresno State University, 1981. Played baseball at Fresno City College, 1977-78.
Family: Married 21 years to Cecilia; two children: Kevin, junior at Fresno City College; Chris, sophomore at Clovis. Both play baseball.
Coaching record: Two years (1983-84) as head coach at San Joaquin Memorial (34-14). In 1984, his team was 24-4 and ranked No. 1 in Division II in the state. Ten years (1988-97) as head coach at Clovis (222-74). 1997 record: 33-2; won second Central Section Yosemite Division title in last three years.
The major league manager I admire the most: "Tom Kelly. Very simply, every player on his team plays the right way. They always hustle, and he gets the most out of them."

Tigers roar once more

Louisiana State baseball coach Skip Bertman picked the perfect pregame video to show his troops before they took the field on June 7 against Alabama in the final of the 1997 College World Series championship in Omaha's Rosenblatt Stadium. It wasn't a video of Warren Morris' two-out, game-winning home run last year that won LSU its third title this decade. Nor was it highlights—make that lowlights—of the Tigers' 28-2 regular-season loss to Alabama, LSU's worst loss in school history. Instead, Bertman showed a montage of clips from the Tigers' three previous victories during the week, as Whitney Houston's Olympic anthem *One Moment in Time* played in the background. "I told them, 'This is their time,'" Bertman said.

After seeing the video, LSU defeated Southeastern Conference rival Alabama 13-6 to win its fourth college baseball championship in seven years. The all-SEC final made history: It was the first time that No. 1 and No. 2 seeds met in a Series finale. "It feels like a dream," said winning pitcher Doug Thompson. "I've always seen myself here doing things to win the national championship."

The victory also was historic for Bertman, who with four championships now trails only retired Southern Cal coach Rod Dedeaux (10) for most College World Series titles. "The reason we're here is two words: Skip Bertman," tournament MVP Brandon Larson said. "He's just done so much for this program." Bertman, known for getting the most out of his players, had just two regular position players return and a handful of pitchers. But LSU surprised everyone with a school-record 19-0 start. The new faces hit an NCAA-record 188 home runs, 10 in the College World Series. Dating back to Morris' home run in the 1996 championship, the Tigers have homered in 71 consecutive games. Shortstop Larson, a junior college transfer, led the way with a conference-record 40 home runs and 118 RBI. On June 3,

the Cincinnati Reds drafted him in the first round, with the 14th pick overall.

The final capped the best rivalry in college this season. Alabama, which won a school-record 56 games, is coached by Jim Wells, an LSU graduate-assistant coach under Bertman from 1987 to '89. And the two teams split their six meetings this year. LSU beat Alabama 6-4 to win the SEC regular-season title, but Alabama beat LSU to win the SEC tournament. Then, facing elimination in the Series after a second-round loss to Miami, Alabama won three games in four days to march into the second championship game in school history. In 1983 the Tide, led by Dave Magadan, lost 4-3 to Texas and Roger Clemens in the title game.

The Tigers, winners in 1991, '93 and '96, became the first team to win back-to-back titles since Stanford in 1987 and '88.

Playing before a record crowd—many wearing Mardi Gras beads and LSU purple and gold—the Tigers dominated Alabama from the beginning, taking the lead for good when leadoff batter Danny Higgins, 1-for-9 in the Series entering the game, homered on a 2-2 changeup. Before the first inning ended, LSU batted around and Higgins added a two-run single. The Tigers scored six runs on six hits and knocked out Alabama starter Michael Daniel. "We usually don't get out ahead that fast," Furniss said. "We usually have to come from behind. But we came out very focused and very relaxed."

LSU led 9-0 before Alabama scored two runs in the third and two in the fourth. Wells had just five pitchers available, and his fielders made three costly errors. "We couldn't turn two or even get one out sometimes," the Tide coach said. "You're just asking too much against LSU in a game of this magnitude when you keep giving them more and more outs."

In the final, Alabama looked tired in its third game in three days and missed key scoring opportunities. The backbreaker came in the fifth inning, when the Tide loaded the bases with one out before reliever Thompson struck out catcher Matt Frick and first baseman Robbie Tucker to get out of the inning. "It's been Alabama-LSU banging heads all year," Alabama catcher Matt Frick said. "It's disappointing. We came here to win the tournament. We didn't play well today, and I think that makes it hurt even more." There was one Tide highlight, though: Senior second baseman Joe Caruso set a Series record with 14 hits in the tournament.

"People said we couldn't win, but this team just refused to lose," Bertman said after the final. "I'm as proud of this team as of any LSU team I've ever coached in my career. This team is the guttiest, grittiest, battlingest team I've ever had."

—by Dana Heiss

batted .391 with 69 homers and 257 RBI in 200 games, setting nine school records and eight Atlantic Coast Conference records. Drew is also in the College World Series record books as the only player to homer three times in one game and hit four homers in one CWS (both in 1995, his freshman season).

Besides being extremely gifted at the plate, Drew has remarkable speed. His time in the 60-yard dash is 6.4 seconds, down from 6.77 a year ago. Drew, from Hahira, Ga., was considered the best college prospect in this year's draft. "He's the complete package," Martin says. "He hits with power, hits for average, throws well, has speed and he has really devoted himself to becoming a better defensive player. This guy will do very well on the next level."

—by Dana Heiss

FSU outfielder Drew a line to Howser award

What's the first thing to do when you're drafted second overall in the 1997 major league draft? If you're J.D. Drew, go fishing, of course. After putting together one of the greatest seasons ever in college baseball, Drew—Florida State's superstar junior outfielder—could afford some time off. Actually, he can afford lots of things now that the Philadelphia Phillies are willing to shell out millions of dollars to sign him.

Drew—the first 30-30 player in NCAA history, with 31 homers and 32 steals—is the winner of the 1997 Dick Howser Trophy, given to the Division I player of the year. He was selected for the honor by the American Baseball Coaches Association. The award was presented by *Baseball Weekly* and the St. Petersburg, Fla., Chamber of Commerce. Drew, who Florida State skipper Mike Martin calls the best hitter he's ever coached, batted .455 with 100 RBI this season. He had a team-best 34-game hitting streak and led the nation entering the College World Series with 110 runs scored and 84 walks.

In his three years in Tallahasee, Drew

Baseball Weekly/ABCA Top 25 college final poll

1. Louisiana State (57-13)
2. Alabama (56-14)
3. Miami (51-18)
4. Stanford (45-20)
5. Auburn (50-17)
6. Mississippi State (47-21)
7. UCLA (45-21-1)
8. Rice (47-16)
9. Florida State (50-17)
10. Southern Cal (42-20)
11. Georgia Tech (46-15)
12. Oklahoma State (46-19)
13. Arizona State (39-22)
14. Texas Tech (46-14)
15. Washington (46-20)
16. South Alabama (43-19)
17. Wichita State (51-18)
18. Florida (40-24)
19. Tennessee (42-19)
20. North Carolina State (43-20)
21. Oklahoma (39-20)
22. Texas A&M (39-22)
23. Fresno State (40-28)
24. Clemson (41-23)
25. Long Beach State (39-26)

1998 college preview: Top contenders

▶**Louisiana State** (57-13 in 1997): Coach Skip Bertman's knack for reloading gives LSU a solid chance to be the first team to three-peat since Southern Cal won an unprecedented five straight titles in the 1970s. Leading the Tigers' very successful swing-for-the-fences game plan (the Tigers hit an NCAA-record 188 last season) is senior first baseman Eddy Furniss, a 14th-round pick of the Twins who opted for school over pro baseball. Furniss batted .378 with 17 homers in '97.

▶**Alabama** (56-14): Coach Jim Wells may have assembled his best lineup yet. Among those providing the power are returning outfielder G.W. Keller (.369, 21 HR, 68 RBI), third baseman Andy Phillips (.366, 15 HR, 65 RBI) and catcher Matt Frick (.331, 16 HR, 55 RBI). Also returning to Alabama is 13-game winner Heath Henderson and two 10-game winners, Pete Fisher and Jarrod Kingrey.

▶**Stanford** (45-20): The time is now for Stanford's prospect-heavy squad to win it all, before the June amateur draft claims most of the Cardinal's junior class. The pitching staff is among the deepest in college baseball, featuring USA Baseball national-team alumnus right-hander Jeff Austin (5-2, 4.14 ERA); right-hander Chad Hutchinson, a two-sport star; and the Cape Cod League pitcher of the year, left-hander Brent Hoard.

▶**Miami** (51-18): Coach Jim Morris has taken the Hurricanes to Omaha in each of his first four seasons. He should make a fifth trip with an experienced Miami squad in '98. Joining star third baseman Pat Burrell (.409, 21 HR, 76 RBI) will be senior outfielder Jason Michaels, who surprised many by choosing to return to Miami. Right-handers Darin Spassoff (9-5, 4.61 ERA) and Alex Santos (9-3, 4.17) anchor a staff that includes closer Robbie Morrison (1.49 ERA).

▶**UCLA** (45-21-1): The Bruins stand out in the Pacific-10 Southern Division because of a terrific recruiting class, which includes eight incoming freshmen who were drafted in June. Its biggest name is shortstop Chase Utley, a second-round pick who turned down $500,000 from the Dodgers to attend college. Junior outfielder Eric Valent (27 HR, 91 RBI) is a top veteran.

▶**Southern California** (42-20): The Trojans were pleasantly surprised to learn that ace Seth Etherton (10-2, 2.96 ERA) was returning. Etherton, who led USC with 106 strikeouts last season, was drafted in the ninth round by St. Louis but came back to school. Senior closer Jack Krawczyk (3.20 ERA, 11 saves) also returns. Joining top catching prospect Eric Munson is senior second baseman Wes Rachels, perhaps USC's best player.

▶**Florida** (40-24): The Gators made it as far as the regionals in '97 and should go further this season behind three-way superstar Brad Wilkerson. The Gators' best hitter (.386, 23 HR, 76 RBI), Wilkerson also finished as the team's winningest pitcher (11-4, 4.56 ERA) while starting and relieving. Switch-hitting senior outfielder Derek Nicholson (.364) returns, as does junior reliever Josh Fogg (2.37 ERA, 8 saves, 84 K's).

▶**Florida State** (50-17): Jeremy Morris and J.D. Drew, who combined for 56 home runs and 216 RBI last season, are gone. But senior Brooks Badeaux, a switch-hitting shortstop, returns after hitting .365 in a injury-shortened '97 season. He's joined by catcher Jeremy Salazar (.297, 7 HR). FSU's outstanding recruiting class was heavy on pitching, with the most notable additions being left-handers Mike Smalley and Jason Hubbard.

▶**Auburn** (50-17): Coach Hal Baird believes he has his best offensive team ever in his 13 years at Auburn, led by senior left fielder Josh Etheredge (.342, 20 HR, 82 RBI), who should eclipse Frank Thomas' school records for homers and RBI before mid-season. There's also Utah transfer Scott Pratt, who hit 19 home runs last season, and All-SEC catcher Casey Dunn, who had a school-record 31-game hitting streak in '97. The question mark is pitching, as Auburn lost four of its six top pitchers.

Where are they now?

▶Sam McDowell,
  sports psychologist
▶Hit man Tony Oliva
▶The first black
  Red Sox player

▶McGregor now
  pitches prayer
▶The tragedy of
  Tony C.

USA SNAPSHOTS®

A look at statistics that shape the sports world

Major league records in stone

Most enduring major season batting records since 1901:

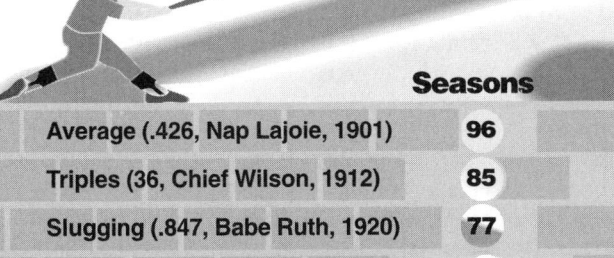

	Seasons
Average (.426, Nap Lajoie, 1901)	96
Triples (36, Chief Wilson, 1912)	85
Slugging (.847, Babe Ruth, 1920)	77
Base hits (257, George Sisler, 1920)	77
Total bases (457, Ruth, 1921)	76
Extra base hits (119, Ruth, 1921)	76

Source: USA TODAY research

By Scott Boeck and Julie Stacey, USA TODAY

McDowell pitches in to help others

One of the top left-handers of the 1960s, Sam McDowell was fast, man. Faster than a scalded cat. Randy Johnson fast.

"Sudden" Sam was a big man (6-foot-5, 190 pounds). In a 15-year career, spent mostly with the Cleveland Indians, he went 141-134 with a 3.17 ERA. He led the AL in strikeouts five times and led the league in innings pitched (304) in 1970 and in ERA (2.18) in 1965. In 1966 he became the first pitcher since Whitey Ford (1955) to toss back-to-back one-hitters. The question became, could he make it three in a row? "Even though Cleveland was in last place all the time . . . the networks changed their schedules to televise the game," McDowell says. "Well, I walked someone and gave up something like eight consecutive hits. I didn't get a single out. It wasn't humorous at the time, but I laugh about it now."

Despite his pitching success, McDowell had a drinking problem. After retiring in 1975 he got treatment and became a psychotherapist. Today McDowell runs the employee-assistance program and sports-psychology program for the Texas Rangers. He works with players and personnel at the major and minor league levels. McDowell also works with the Baseball Assistance Team, which takes care of anybody who was ever associated with baseball and could use some help. "We offer financial counseling and psychology, whatever is needed," McDowell says from his office in Pittsburgh, his hometown. "It's a 24-hour-a-day job."

McDowell's people receive an understanding ear. "In my own career I had serious difficulties early," he says. "I had talent but didn't know how to use it. I had trouble controlling my emotions and focus. That focus usually comes after several years of experience in the minors, but I only spent 1½ years in the minors."

As a player, McDowell didn't realize he was an alcoholic. "I was fortunate in that I had a family that was constantly on my case." McDowell sought help at the Gateway Rehabilitation Center in Pittsburgh.

After his recovery, McDowell came about his new career in a roundabout way.

"It was 1979, and troubled kids in Pittsburgh would come to me for help," he says. "I would take them to psychiatrist Abraham Tewerski. After a while he said, 'Sam, these kids are coming to see you.' He conned me into reading psychology books. Then I started taking classes at the University of Pittsburgh, Duquesne, and correspondence courses from Minnesota, the University of San Diego and Harvard Medical School."

McDowell eventually earned four associate degrees and was certified in 11 formal therapies. Today his son, Tim, 30, is one of four psychologists working with him. Soon Tim will receive a doctorate from Rice University. McDowell's daughter, Debbie Liebling, is his office manager.

When asked about changes in today's game, McDowell mentions the quality of relief pitchers. "When I played, the best four or five pitchers were the starters," he says. "The rest were relievers or fill-ins. So the starters didn't want to come out of the game. We didn't want to give it up to someone with lesser talent, especially in a one- or two-run game. Now, when someone like Dennis Eckersley or Lee Smith comes in, you know the game is sealed. That's a tremendous relief to a starter." He's not as impressed with the quality of the major league audience these days: "There are fewer baseball aficionados left. In the old days 50% of the fans in the stands knew the game. Today I'd bet it's less than 10%."

And about that Randy Johnson comparison? Who's faster? "There's no way to honestly compare how hard Randy Johnson throws to the way I threw," he says. "I've talked to people who've said that once a radar gun registers over 100, there's no telling. But there was a minor leaguer in the late 1950s or early 1960s, Steve Dalkowski. I could personally see the difference in *his* fastball. He could throw it 110 mph, but he couldn't keep the ball in the batting cage."

—by Chris Colston

Oliva's hot bat warmed up Minnesota

Oliva was one of the top AL hitters in the 1960s.

Sweet-swinging Tony Oliva hit .300 as easily as the snow piles up during a Minnesota winter. Oliva had a great career despite many injuries. He was the 1964 AL Rookie of the Year and led the league in batting three times. He played his entire 15-year career with the Minnesota Twins and still lives in Minneapolis.

"I was 20 years old when I first came here," says Oliva, a native of Pinar del Rio, Cuba, "and it's always been a special place for me. Everybody has treated me so nice. The winters are cold, but I learned to stay inside."

Oliva, 57, is under contract with the Twins as a minor league hitting instructor, traveling to their Class A Fort Myers club when they need him. He has a simple hitting philosophy. "I want to make hitting easy," he says. "You don't have that much time to think about it when the ball is coming at you. I don't put pressure on people, but they must be willing to work. A guy like Kirby Puckett, you never have to ask him to work."

Oliva spends a few weeks per year in Venezuela at a school for Twins prospects. "We have three or four people who recruit young players," he says. "I work with them, give them hitting advice." An outgoing sort, Oliva also makes public appearances for the ball club, visiting hospitals and speaking to youth groups.

He was the Twins' hitting instructor from 1976 to '78 and again from 1985 to '91. In between, he was a minor league hitting coach for the Twins. He'd love to return to the majors. "I'll be watching a game on TV and tell my wife, 'Honey, I miss being on the field. I want to get back in the big leagues!' and she says, 'You're crazy! You better retire!'"

He and Gordette have been together 34 years. They have three children: Anita, 29; Pedro, 27, who signed with the Twins and played one year before hurting his knee; and Rick, 21, a guitarist and songwriter in Minneapolis.

A lifetime .304 hitter, Oliva hit 220 home runs and led the AL in hits five times. Oliva holds the Twins' rookie records for batting average, games, at-bats, runs, hits and doubles and also has the Twins' single-season record for total bases. But his fondest baseball memory is of a team achievement, the Twins' 1965 season, when they won the pennant before losing the World Series in seven games to the Dodgers.

Oliva is somewhat disturbed by the quality of baseball's coaching. A lot of good baseball people are not in the game's teaching positions, he says. "When you are sick, you go to the best doctor you can find. But if you look in baseball, some of the best players aren't in coaching." On a related subject, learning, Oliva notes a difference with today's players: "When I was playing ball, I was never afraid of going to another player for advice. Once I was in a slump and I went to Ted Williams, who was the manager of the Washington Senators. I asked him what I was doing wrong, and he pointed out one little thing. That day I got three hits. So many players today are missing the boat. They're afraid of what someone will think."

—by Chris Colston

The last pioneer

Pumpsie Green never planned to be the first black player on the only team in baseball which had yet to integrate its roster. It wasn't his choice. But during the 1959 season, the Boston Red Sox purchased his minor league contract after snubbing him in spring training, and Green found himself in Chicago, facing that year's eventual Cy Young winner, Early Wynn of the White Sox. "I was fortunate to make contact," he says of his first major league at-bat. "I grounded out to Nellie Fox."

Green says he always felt the pressure that came with breaking the color barrier. He led the team in home runs and batting average in spring training in 1959. But Red Sox manager Mike Higgins, who was quoted as saying there would never be a black player on the team "as long as I have anything to say about it," sent Green to the minors. After a wave of protests, which included discrimination charges filed against the Red Sox, Higgins was fired. Green made his debut soon after. Higgins returned the next year and managed the team for the subsequent three years, some of which included Green.

In four seasons with Boston and one with the New York Mets, he hit .246 with 13 home runs and 74 RBI. Green, 64, has lived in the San Francisco area since his playing career ended. He retired last year from coaching, after 25 years at Berkeley High School.

Green says that as a player, he was never assaulted. Physically. "There was nothing but words," he says. "Unprintable things. Statements. Anything you could think of. Talking about my family, friends and relatives. You turn a deaf ear and try to hit the ball a little harder. If you let it, it could get to you."

Green is also remembered for a strange incident in 1962. While playing with the Red Sox, he and pitcher Gene Conley mysteriously disappeared on July 26, after a game with the Yankees. They left the team bus in traffic to use a restroom and didn't return. Rumor had it they planned to go to Israel for fun, but Green returned on July 28, and Conley came back the day after that. Conley had gone to the airport and tried to book a flight. He wasn't allowed to go because he didn't have a passport. Green insists he never planned to leave the country. "People are always asking me for 30 years about something I didn't do," Green says. "It never dies."

Green retired from baseball in 1965. He says he didn't "miss the hustle and the bustle or the bus rides. And the eating places and [hotels]—I had enough of that. Once I got out of baseball, I was all the way out." He got a physical education degree from San Francisco State and coached baseball. He says of his second career, "I didn't think I'd like coaching high school kids until I was an assistant coach. You get to know the kids . . . like the kids. They talk to me; they know I've been in the major leagues. They think I can help them."

Now he goes to the YMCA at 7 a.m. each morning to work out. "I've been keeping busy, trying to stay out of my wife's eyesight," Green says, laughing. He has two children—son Jerry, 38, is a mechanical engineer in nearby Fremont, Calif., and daughter Keisha, 26, lives in Los Angeles and works at a publishing company. Green and his wife, Marie, have been married for 40 years.

What about the name Pumpsie? That's what his mother called him—but he won't say why. "Everyone has always called me that," says the man born Elijah Jerry Green. He says he wouldn't have done anything differently in baseball. "I did it the way I wanted to do it, and the best I could. Now I just go and try go see if I can catch a few fishes."

—by Brian Breuhaus

From the pitching mound to the pulpit

Scott McGregor is making a different sort of pitch these days. The 43-year-old former Baltimore Orioles hurler left baseball for the ministry nearly nine years ago and now serves as the pastor at the Rock Church in Dover, Del. "After I got released in '88, I became a youth pastor in Baltimore," McGregor says from his Dover home. "Then we came to the church here about five years ago, in 1992."

McGregor spent more than four years in the Yankees farm system, but came to Baltimore with Rick Dempsey and Tippy Martinez in a 10-player deal in 1976 and was with the Orioles for his entire 13-year major league career, during which he went 138-108. He won 15 or more games four times and had an eight-year string of winning at least 13 games while having a winning percentage of .500 or better, from '78 through '85. He won 20 games in 1980, but his best season might have been in 1983, when he went 18-7 and led Baltimore to a World Series title.

"We had [Jim] Palmer, [Mike] Flanagan and myself, but 1983 was my year to shine," McGregor says. "I was the ace that season." Against the Philadelphia Phillies in the Series, he surrendered only nine hits and two runs in 17 innings, winning the final game with a five-hit shutout.

Never overpowering, McGregor struck out more than 100 batters only once, and he spent most of his career fooling opposing hitters with a variety of offspeed pitches. "When you throw 83 miles per hour, you'd better know how to pitch," he says. "I had good control and kept hitters off balance. At the end of my career I got down to the 70s, and then it was time to go."

The high visibility of a major league career is a far cry from the quiet life McGregor now enjoys with his wife, Kara; daughter Kate, 16; and son Michael, 10. His oldest son, Eric, 18, is a marketing major at Clemson. Eric continued the family tradition by landing an internship last summer with the Orioles.

McGregor maintains few connections to

McGregor was the Orioles' ace in their '83 title run.

403

his former career. He talks with old buddies Flanagan and Palmer, both Orioles broadcasters, and has participated in the team's fantasy camps. He occasionally offered advice when Flanagan was Baltimore's pitching coach in 1995, but he has no desire to return to the game. "After I was released, I didn't want to coach," he says. "Some guys never leave that atmosphere, but I didn't want to stick around. I like to be at home."

McGregor knew long before his career came to an end that he would follow a different path in his post-playing career. "I was born again in 1979 and got involved in the church," he says. "By the mid-'80s it became obvious that this was what I would be doing. I used to do the chapels in spring training. The atmosphere of professional sports, with all the pressure, will bring you to your knees. I knew there had to be more to life than baseball."

—by Scott Zucker

Courtesy of the Boston Red Sox

Conigliaro's powerful stroke and aggressive attitude at the plate were made for "The Green Monster."

Tony C. never recovered after beaning

It's a Friday evening in July at Fenway Park. A breeze is blowing in off the Charles River, and at first glance, it seems to be a perfect night for baseball—until you notice that the teams on the field, the hometown Red Sox and the visiting Angels, are the same as that tragic night. Once more, you're reminded that this sport can turn evil on any given pitch.

Just over 30 years ago, on Aug. 18, 1967, Red Sox slugger Tony Conigliaro was struck in the face by a pitch from the Angels' Jack Hamilton. In an instant, what promised to be a Hall of Fame career was almost over. Conigliaro suffered a fractured left cheekbone, dislocated jaw, scalp contusions and a severely bruised eye. The injury caused a cyst to form on the macula, a portion of the retina, resulting in a blurry blind spot. The eye injury would play havoc with his depth perception for the rest of his career, to the point

that he became a one-eyed batter. Even though Conigliaro did come back several times, he was never the same player.

Conigliaro lived life large—singing on *The Merv Griffin Show*, performing with Dionne Warwick and dating such socialites as Mamie Van Doren, Bo Belinsky's old flame. Conigliaro ranks as the second-youngest player to reach 100 career home runs, behind the Giants' Mel Ott. Until the beaning, it seemed only a matter of time until he hit 400, 500, even 600. "He might have been the guy to break [Babe] Ruth's and [Hank] Aaron's record," Hall of Famer Jim Palmer says.

The believer

There was something about the way Conigliaro carried himself that immediately won over Johnny Pesky. Pesky was the Red Sox manager in 1964 when

Conigliaro arrived. After seeing how the kid could hit the ball, Pesky lobbied hard to have Conigliaro on the major league roster when camp broke. "I put my neck out for him," Pesky says. "I knew he was the real thing."

On the first pitch of his initial at-bat at Fenway, Conigliaro, who was born in nearby Revere, proved Pesky a prophet, homering off Chicago's Joel Horlen. "He had the perfect swing for Fenway," says Red Sox pitcher Jim Lonborg. "But that swing made him vulnerable to getting hit." Before the tragic beaning in '67, Conigliaro already had suffered a broken finger, thumb, wrist, hand and shoulder blade—all from getting hit by a baseball. Despite missing six weeks because of injuries, he homered 24 times in 1964, the most in a season by any teenager in major league history.

Pesky was fired as the Red Sox manager after the 1964 season. "The night he was hurt, I was devastated," says Pesky, now 78. "If I live to be 100, I'll never forget Tony."

The rookie

Second baseman Mike Andrews was a rookie on the '67 Red Sox. He was one of the first to reach Conigliaro after the beaning, along with several teammates and manager Dick Williams. When Andrews ran to Conigliaro, Tony C. was motionless near the plate, blood coming from his nose and his left eye already beginning to swell. "Right then I knew that this was different than most injuries you see in baseball," says Andrews, now 54. "His eye was already swollen up."

Andrews finds it amazing that Conigliaro played baseball again. After missing the 1968 season, during which he first attempted to return as a pitcher, Conigliaro hit 20 home runs and got 82 RBI in 1969, and was named the American League's Comeback Player of the Year. In 1970, despite ongoing vision problems, he had 36 home runs and 116 RBI.

Even though Conigliaro remained tireless about his comeback, he became

reluctant to take center stage with a bat in his hands. He liked to take BP in private, wanting to get his stroke perfect. "That showed what kind of competitor Tony was," Andrews says. "He wasn't the same Tony. But that didn't stop him from trying. I learned a lot about tenacity and heart by watching him."

The brother

The night Conigliaro was hit, his younger brother Billy and his parents were at Fenway. Billy had been playing for the Red Sox's Class A team in Greenville, S.C., but his season had ended prematurely because of a torn hamstring. From the family seats, well back from the Red Sox dugout on the first base line, the beaning didn't seem that serious. "From where we were sitting, we didn't hear anything," Billy says.

Before the game, a slumping Tony told his brother that he was going to move back up on the plate for this game and start looking for something inside that he could pull. But he didn't react at all when Hamilton's pitch sailed high and inside. "Funny, you never go up there thinking you're going to be hit, and then in a fraction of a second you know it's going to happen," Tony later recalled in his autobiography, *Seeing It Through*. "When the ball was about four feet from my head, I knew it was going to get me. I knew that it was going to hurt because Hamilton was such a hard thrower."

To this day, Billy Conigliaro, who turned 50 three days before the anniversary of the beaning, hasn't forgiven Hamilton, the man who threw the pitch. "No doubt, that ball was thrown at his head," Billy says.

The pitcher

Thirteen years ago, the town of Branson, Mo., was nothing more than a wrinkle in the Ozarks. These days Branson draws 6 million visitors annually. With 30 music theaters, a 27-acre factory-outlet center and hotels, the traffic is bumper to bumper on Highway 76 through town.

And nobody is busier than Jack Hamilton, a Branson restaurateur since 1984.

"It's nice to know things work out for the best sometimes," says Hamilton, 58, who can be found at his restaurant, Pzazz, 12 hours a day, seven days a week. Hamilton's usually out front, greeting customers well into the night. When somebody from New England walks in, he invariably asks, "Aren't you the guy who hit Tony Conigliaro?" With a resigned look on his face, Hamilton will nod and talk about that pitch one more time.

Throughout the '67 season, it was rumored that Hamilton was throwing a spitball. In fact, early in the fateful game, Dick Williams complained to the umpires that Hamilton's pitches were behaving strangely. But the Angels' catcher that night, Buck Rodgers, denies that Hamilton was throwing a spitter. Rodgers remembers the pitch as "a fastball . . . that sailed."

Hamilton says Conigliaro was crowding the plate so much that his head was hanging over it. "No, I wasn't throwing a spitter," Hamilton says. "I had two outs in the inning. It was tied. Why would I want to hit anybody in that situation? I was just wild." (Over his career, Hamilton averaged more than five walks per nine innings.)

After Conigliaro went down, Hamilton stood on the mound with his arms folded, while many in the Fenway crowd of 31,027 booed. Hamilton started to walk toward home plate, but Rodgers, who had seen the condition Conigliaro was in, blocked his path. After the game, Hamilton tried to visit Conigliaro at the hospital. He says of the attempt, "They weren't letting people in. I never did talk with him. That's what really bothers me. I didn't get a chance to tell him that it was an accident."

The aftermath

The day after Conigliaro came home from the hospital, the Red Sox signed Ken "Hawk" Harrelson. The Hawk replaced Conigliaro in right field, col-

Tony C. was virtually a one-eyed batter after 1967.

lecting a league-high 109 RBI the following season.

In 1970, Conigliaro was traded to the Angels, where his eyesight continued to deteriorate. Midway through the 1971 season, Tony C. retired, at age 26. In 1975, he attempted one more comeback with his Red Sox. But it ended after 21 games, in which he hit only .123.

After broadcasting jobs on the West Coast, Conigliaro came home for the final time. In 1982, after he had auditioned for a broadcasting spot with the Red Sox, he suffered a heart attack. Although his heart recovered, his brain went too long without oxygen. He lived out the the rest of his days at a chronic-care hospital outside of Boston, where he required 24-hour care. Bumper stickers throughout New England read, "I pray for Tony C."

"I don't know how my mother and father did it," Billy Conigliaro says. "Each day was a struggle, and you just took it a day at a time. I know that's what killed my father. Seeing his son suffer like that."

Tony Conigliaro died on Feb. 24, 1990.

He was 45.

—by Tim Wendel

Courtesy of the Boston Red Sox

AMERICAN LEAGUE

ANAHEIM ANGELS

▶**Owner:** Gene Autry (75%), Disney (25%)
▶**General manager:** Bill Bavasi
▶**Ballpark:**
Edison International Field of Anaheim
2000 Gene Autry Way
Anaheim, Calif.
714-634-2000.
Capacity 45,054
Parking for 15,000 vehicles; public transportation available; family and wheelchair sections, elevators, ramps
▶**Team publications:** *Halo Insider Magazine,* media guide, yearbook
714-937-6700, ext. 7281
▶**TV, radio stations:**
KMPC 710 AM, KCAL Channel 9, Fox Sports West
▶**Camps and/or clinics:** Angels Clinic, on Saturdays during the season, 714-940-7204
▶**Spring training:**
Tempe Diablo Stadium
Tempe, Ariz.
Capacity 7,285
(9,785 including lawn)
602-438-4300

BALTIMORE ORIOLES

▶**Owner:** Peter Angelos
▶**General manager:** Pat Gillick
▶**Ballpark:**
Oriole Park at Camden Yards,
Baltimore, Md.
410-685-9800
Capacity 48,188
Public transportation available; disability seating, ramps, elevators, sound-amplification devices for the hearing-impaired
▶**Team publications:** *Orioles Magazine,* media guide
410-685-9800
▶**TV, radio stations:**
WBAL 1090 AM, WJZ Channel 13, Home Team, Sports Cable
▶**Camps and/or clinics:** Fantasy Camp (ages 30-plus), February,
410-799-0005
Cal Ripken Sr. Baseball School (ages 8-18), Mount St. Mary's, Emmitsburg, Md., late June and early July, 301-791-3512.
Elrod Hendricks Camp, Reisterstown, Md., July,
410-685-9800
Summer clinics, the Orioles region, during the season,
410-685-9800
▶**Spring training:**
Ft. Lauderdale Stadium
Ft. Lauderdale, Fla.
Capacity 8,346
954-776-1921

BOSTON RED SOX

▶**Owners:** JRY Corporation and John Harrington
▶**General manager:** Dan Duquette
▶**Ballpark:**
Fenway Park
4 Yawkey Way
Boston, Mass.
617-267-9440
Capacity 33,871
Public transportation available; family, wheelchair, and vision-impaired sections, ramps, sound- amplification and TDD ticket information for hearing-impaired
▶**Team publications:** Media guide, official scorebook, yearbook
617-267-9440
▶**TV, radio stations:**
WEEI 850 AM, WABU Channel 68, New England Sports Network Cable TV
▶**Spring training:**
City of Palms Park
Fort Myers, Fla.
Capacity 6,850
941-534-4799

CHICAGO WHITE SOX

▶**Owner:** Jerry Reinsdorf (chairman), Eddie Einhorn (vice-chairman) and a board of directors
▶**General manager:** Ron Schueler
▶**Ballpark:**
Comiskey Park
333 W. 35th St.
Chicago, Ill.
312-674-1000
Capacity 44,321
Parking for 7,000 vehicles; $10
Public transportation available; Kids Corner (with photo booth and uniforms for imitation baseball cards), elevators and seating for the handicapped, escalators, ramps, cash station, Hall of Fame
▶**Team publications:** Program, yearbook, media guide, calendar, team photos and player photos, 312-451-5300
▶**TV, radio stations:**
WMVP 1000 AM, WGN TV-9, SportsChannel Chicago
▶**Camps and/or clinics:** Chicago White Sox Training Centers
708-752-9225
▶**Spring training:**
Kino Veterans Memorial Sports Park
Tucson, Ariz.
Capacity 11,000
520-740-2680

CLEVELAND INDIANS

▶**Owner:** Richard E. Jacobs
▶**General manager:** John Hart
▶**Ballpark:**
Jacobs Field
2401 Ontario St.
Cleveland, Ohio
216-420-4200
Capacity 43,368
Downtown parking available; public transportation; handicapped seating; extremely accessible with escalators, elevators and ramps; all 38 bathrooms have diaper-changing areas; two unisex bathrooms for the physically challenged and kids.
▶**Team publications:** *Game Face Magazine, Tribe Talk*;
216-420-4200
▶**TV, radio stations:**
WKNR 1220 AM, WUAB Channel 43, SportsChannel Ohio

▶**Camps and/or clinics:** Cleveland Indians Fantasy Camp, January, 888-588-1975
▶**Spring training:**
Chain O'Lakes Park
Winter Haven, Fla.
Capacity 7,900
813-291-5803

DETROIT TIGERS

▶**Owner:** Michael Ilitch
▶**General manager:** Randy Smith
▶**Ballpark:**
Tiger Stadium
2121 Trumbull Ave.
Detroit, Mich.
313-962-4000
Capacity 46,945
Pay parking lot (independently owned); public transportation available; wheelchair section, ramps
▶**Team publications:** Scorebook/ program
▶**TV, radio stations:**
WJR 760 AM, WKBD
Channel 50, Fox Sports Director
▶**Camps and/or clinics:**
Tigers' Fantasy Camp
▶**Spring training:**
Marchant Stadium
Lakeland, Fla.
Capacity 7,100
941-688-9589

KANSAS CITY ROYALS

▶**Owner:** Greater Kansas Community Foundation, Board of Directors; David Glass, Chairman of the Board; Michael Hennan, President
▶**General manager:**
Herk Robinson
▶**Ballpark:**
Ewing Kauffman Stadium
1 Royal Way
Kansas City, Mo.
816-921-2200
Capacity 40,625
Pay parking lot; $6; public transportation available; wheelchair section and ramps, handicapped accessible
▶**Team publications:** Yearbook, scorecard, media guide
▶**TV, radio stations:**
KMBZ 980 AM, KCWB
Channel 29, Fox Sports Rocky Mountain
▶**Spring training:**
Baseball City Stadium
Baseball City, Fla.
Capacity 7,000 (1,000 on grass)
941-424-2500

MINNESOTA TWINS

▶**Owner:** Carl R. Pohlad
▶**General manager:** Terry Ryan
▶**Ballpark:**
Hubert H. Humphrey Metrodome
34 Kirby Puckett Place
Minneapolis, Minn.
612-375-1366
Capacity 48,678
Public transportation available; family and wheelchair sections, elevators
▶**Team publications:** *Twins Magazine*, 612-375-7458
▶**TV, radio stations:**
WCCO 830 AM, WCCO-TV Channel 4, Midwest Sports-Channel
▶**Camps and/or clinics:** Twins Clinics, weekends throughout the summer, 612-375-7498
▶**Spring training:**
Lee County Sports Complex
Fort Myers, Fla.
Capacity 7,500
813-768-4200

NEW YORK YANKEES

▶**Owner:** George Steinbrenner
▶**General manager:** Bob Watson
▶**Ballpark:**
Yankee Stadium
161st Street and River Avenue
Bronx, N.Y.
718-293-4300
Capacity 57,545
Parking (independently owned); $6 ; public transportation available; family and wheelchair sections, ramps, senior citizen discount ($2 tickets day of game), group discounts, monument park behind left center field with plaques honoring famous Yankees
▶**Team publications:** *Yankees Magazine,* media guide, score-card, yearbook, 718-293-4300
▶**TV, radio stations:**
WABC 770 AM, WPIX Channel 11, MSG Network
▶**Spring training:**
Legends Field
3802 Martin Luther King Blvd.
Tampa, Fla.
813-879-2244
Capacity: 10,382

OAKLAND ATHLETICS

▶**Owners:** Steve Schott and Ken Hofman
▶**General manager:** Billy Beane

▶**Ballpark:**
Oakland Coliseum
Nimitz Frwy & Hegenberger Rd.
Oakland, Calif.
510-568-5600
Capacity 43,662
Public transportation available; wheelchair sections and ramps, picnic areas
▶**Team publications:**
A's Magazine, media guide, 510-638-4900, ext. 2328
▶**TV, radio stations:**
KNEW 910 AM, KRON Channel 4, SportsChannel
▶**Spring training:**
Phoenix Municipal Stadium
Phoenix, Ariz.
Capacity 8,776
602-392-0074

SEATTLE MARINERS

▶**Owner:** Baseball Club of Seattle
▶**General manager:**
Woody Woodward
▶**Ballpark:**
The Kingdome
201 South King St.
Seattle, Wash.
206-628-3555
Capacity 59,856
Public transportation available; parking for 2,400 cars, 30,000 within a mile; family and wheelchair sections, birthday package, anniversary package
▶**Team publications:** *Mariners Magazine, Mariners Newsletter,* scorecard, media guide
206-346-4000
▶**TV, radio stations:**
KIRO 710 AM, KIRO Channel 7, Fox Sports Northwest Cable
▶**Spring training:**
Peoria Sports Complex
Peoria, Ariz.
Capacity 10,000
(3,000 on grass)
602-412-9000

TAMPA BAY DEVIL RAYS

▶**Owners:** Vincent J. Naimoli and a partnership
▶**General manager:** Chuck LaMar
▶**Ballpark:**
Tropicana Field
One Tropicana Drive
St. Petersburg, Fla.
813-825-3137
Capacity 45,200
Parking for 7,000 vehicles; public transportation available; family and wheelchair areas, elevators, ramps

- TV, radio stations:
  WFLA 970 AM, WWWB
  Channel 32, WTSP Channel 10,
  SportsChannel Florida
- Spring training:
  Al Lang Stadium
  St. Petersburg, Fla.
  Capacity 7,227

TEXAS RANGERS

Owners: J. Thomas Schieffer and
Edward W. Rose, managing
general partners
- General manager: Doug Melvin
- Ballpark:
  The Ballpark in Arlington
  1000 Ballpark Way
  Arlington, Texas
  817-273-5222
  Capacity 49,166
  Parking for 12,500 cars; $7; no
  public transportation; approxi-
  mately 480 wheelchair seats with
  additional handicapped seating;
  restrooms with diaper-changing
  areas; ramps, escalators and ele-
  vators to serve all areas
- Team publications: *On Deck
  Newsletter,* yearbook, *Program
  Magazine*
  817-273-5222
- TV, radio stations:
  KRLD-AM 1080, KXEB 910
  AM (Spanish), KXAS Channel 5,
  KXTX Channel 39, Fox Sports
  Southwest
- Camps and/or clinics: Texas
  Ranger Youth Summer Clinic
  (boys and girls), June;
  Coaches Clinic, April;
  Parent/Child Clinic, June,
  817-273-5222
- Spring training:
  Charlotte County Stadium
  Port Charlotte, Fla.
  Capacity 6,026
  813-625-9500

TORONTO BLUE JAYS

- Owners: Inter-Brew S.A.
  (Canadian Imperial Bank of
  Commerce owns 10%)
- General manager: Gord Ash
- Ballpark:
  SkyDome
  Toronto, Ontario
  416-341-1000
  Capacity 51,516
  Public transportation available;
  family and wheelchair sections,
  no-alcohol sections, ramps,
  Playland
- Team publications: *Scorebook
  Magazine* (Buzz Communica-

tions), 416-961-3319
- TV, radio stations:
  TSN, CBC CHUM AM 1050
- Spring training:
  Dunedin Stadium at Grant Field
  311 Douglas Ave.
  Dunedin, Fla.
  Capacity 6,218
  813-733-9302

ARIZONA DIAMONDBACKS

- Owners: Jerry Colangelo and a
  limited partnership
- General manager: J.Garagiola Jr.
- Ballpark:
  BankOne Ballpark
  201 E. Jefferson St.
  Phoenix, Ariz.
  602-514-8500
  Parking 1,500-car garage;
  18,600 spaces within 15-minute
  walk; wheelchair sections,ramps
- Team publications: Diamond-
  backs Quarterly
- TV, radio: KTAR 620 AM,
  KTVK Channel 3, Fox Sports
  Arizona
- Spring training:
  Tucson Electric Park
  Tucson, Ariz.

ATLANTA BRAVES

- Owner: Ted Turner
- General manager:
  John Schuerholz
- Ballpark:
  Turner Field
  P.O. Box 4064
  Atlanta, Ga. 30302
  404-522-7630
  Capacity 49,831
  Parking for 3,500 cars; $7; public
  transportation available by bus;
  family and wheelchair sections
- Team publications: *Fan
  Magazine,* 404-522-7630;
  *Chop Talk,*1-800-700-CHOP
- TV, radio stations: WSB 750 AM,
  WTBS Channel 17, Sport South
- Spring training:
  Disney's Wide World of Sports
  Orlando, Fla.

CHICAGO CUBS

- Owner: Tribune Company
- General manager: Ed Lynch
- Ballpark:
  Wrigley Field
  Clark and Addison Streets,
  Chicago, Ill.

773-404-2827
Capacity 38,884
Parking for 900; $10 and $15
(private lots available); public
transportation available; family
and wheelchair sections, ramps
and elevators
- Team publications: *Vineline,
  Scorecard Magazine, Cubs
  Quarterly,* 312-404-2827
- TV, radio stations:
  WGN 720 AM, WGN Channel 9
- Spring training:
  HoHoKam Park
  Mesa, Ariz.
  Capacity 12,500
  1-800-283-6372

CINCINNATI REDS

- Owners: Marge Schott and a
  limited partnership
- General manager:
  James G. Bowden
- Ballpark:
  Cinergy Stadium
  Pete Rose Way
  Cincinnati, Ohio
  513-421-4510
  Capacity 52,952
  Parking for 5,022 cars; $6;
  wheelchair locations, ramps
- Team publications: Media
  guide, yearbook/program, *Reds
  Report,* 1-800-760-2862
- TV, radio stations:
  WLW 700 AM, WSTR Channel
  64, SportsChannel-Ohio
- Spring training:
  Ed Smith Stadium
  Sarasota, Fla.
  Capacity 7,500
  941-954-4101

COLORADO ROCKIES

- Owner: Jerry McMorris
  (Colorado Baseball Partnership)
- General manager: Bob Gebhard
- Ballpark:
  Coors Field
  2001 Blake St.,
  Denver, Colo.
  303-762-5437
  Capacity 50,249
  Parking for 5,200 cars, 171
  permanent handicapped spaces,
  18,000 more spaces within a 15
  minute walk; public transporta-
  tion available; wheelchair section,
  family sections in all price ranges
- Team publications: Media
  guide, game program, yearbook
- TV, radio stations:
  KOA 850 AM, KWGN Channel 2
- Spring training:

Hi Corbett Field
Tucson, Ariz.
Capacity 9,500
602-327-9467

FLORIDA MARLINS

▶**Owner:** H. Wayne Huizenga
▶**General manager:**
David Dombrowski
▶**Ballpark:**
Pro Player Stadium
2267 N.W. 199th St.
Miami, Fla.
305-626-7400
Capacity 41,855
Parking 24,137 cars; $5; public
transportation available; wheel-
chair section, ramps and elevators
▶**TV, radio stations:**
WQAM 560 AM (English),
WCMQ 1210 AM (Spanish),
WBFS Channel 33, Sunshine
Network/Sports Channel
▶**Spring Training:**
Space Coast Stadium
Melbourne, Fla.
Capacity 7,200
407-633-9200

HOUSTON ASTROS

▶**Owner:** Drayton McLane Jr.
▶**General manager:**
Gerry Hunsicker
▶**Ballpark:**
Houston Astrodome
8400 Kirby Dr.
Houston, Texas
713-799-9500
Capacity 54,350
Parking for 26,000 cars; $4
(subject to change); public trans-
portation by bus; wheelchair
section and ramps
▶**Team publications:** *Astros
Magazine, Astros Media Guide,*
713-799-9600
▶**TV, radio stations:**
KILT 610 AM, UPN Channel
20, Fox Sports Southwest
▶**Camps and/or clinics:** Astros
Youth Clinics, during the sea-
son, 713-799-9877
▶**Spring training:**
Osceola County Stadium
Kissimmee, Fla.
Capacity 5,130
407-933-6500

LOS ANGELES DODGERS

▶**Owner:** Peter O'Malley
▶**General manager:** Fred Claire
▶**Ballpark:**
Dodger Stadium
1000 Elysian Park Ave.

Los Angeles, Calif.
213-224-1400
Capacity 56,000
Parking for 16,000 cars; $5;
wheelchair section and ramps
▶**Team publications:** Dodger
Yearbook, Dodger On-Line (bi-
monthly), *Dodger Magazine,*
media guide, *Line Drive*
▶**TV, radio stations:**
KISS 1150 AM, KWKW 1330
AM (Spanish), KTLA Channel
5, Fox Sports West
▶**Camps and/or clinics:** Twenty
clinics per year, 213-224-1435
▶**Spring training:**
Holman Stadium
Dodgertown
Vero Beach, Fla.
Capacity 7,000
407-569-4900

MILWAUKEE BREWERS

▶**Owner:** Allan H. (Bud) Selig
▶**General manager:** Sal Bando
▶**Ballpark:**
Milwaukee County Stadium
201 South 46th St.
Milwaukee, Wis.
414-933-4114
Capacity 53,192
Parking for approximately
11,000 cars; $5 or $7; public
transportation available; family
and wheelchair sections, ramps,
Designated Driver Program
including free taxi transporta-
tion for single ticket holders par-
ticipating in the DDP
▶**Team publications:** Media
guide, *Lead Off Magazine*
▶**TV, radio stations:**
WTMJ 620 AM, WVTV-TV 18
▶**Camps and/or clinics:** Gatorade
Youth Camp, during the season,
414-933-4114
Fantasy Camp, winter,
414-933-4114, 800-336-CAMP
▶**Spring training:**
Maryville Baseball Park
Maryville, Ariz.
Capacity 7,000
602-247-7177

MONTREAL EXPOS

▶**Owner:** Montreal Baseball Club
Inc., Claude R. Brochu
(president and general partner)
▶**General manager:** Jim Beattie
▶**Ballpark:**
Olympic Stadium
4549 Ave. Pierre-de-Coubertin,
Montreal, Quebec
514-253-3434

Capacity 46,500
Parking for 4,000 cars; $10;
public transportation available;
wheelchair sections, ramps,
extensive food concessions,
outfield bleachers
▶**Team publications:** Media
guide, *Expos Magazine,*
P.O. Box 500, Station M,
Montreal, Quebec H1V 3P2
▶**TV, radio stations:**
CIQC 600 AM, TSN (English);
CKAC 730 AM, FSRC-TV,
RDS TQS (French)
▶**Spring training:**
Roger Dean Stadium
4751 Main Street
Jupiter, Fla.
Capacity 7,000
561-775-1818

NEW YORK METS

▶**Owners:** Fred Wilpon (president
and CEO) and Nelson Double-
day (chairman of the board)
▶**President of baseball operations:**
Steve Phillips
▶**Ballpark:**
William A. Shea Municipal
Stadium
126th St. and Roosevelt Ave.
Flushing, N.Y.
718-507-METS
Capacity 55,777
Parking for 6,000 cars; $5; pub-
lic transportation available;
family and wheelchair sections,
ramps, elevators
▶**Team publications:** Yearbook,
scorecard, press guide,
919-688-0218
▶**TV, radio stations:**
WFAN 660 AM, WWOR
Channel 9, SportsChannel
▶**Camps and/or clinics:** Baseball
Heaven, 800-898-METS
▶**Spring training:**
Thomas J. White Stadium
Port St. Lucie, Fla.
Capacity 7,347
407-871-2100

PHILADELPHIA PHILLIES

▶**Owner:** Bill Giles
▶**General manager:** Lee Thomas
▶**Ballpark:**
Veterans Stadium
Broad St. and Pattison Ave.,
Philadelphia, Pa.
215-463-1000
Capacity 62,363
Parking for 10,000 cars; $5; pub-
lic transportation available;
wheelchair section and ramps,

TDD ticket information for hearing impaired (215-463-2998)
▶Team publications: Media guide, scorebook, *Phillies Magazine*
▶TV, radio stations:
WPHL Channel 17, WPHT 1210 AM Comcast Sportsnet
▶Spring training:
Jack Russell Memorial Stadium Clearwater, Fla.
Capacity 6,926
813-441-8638

PITTSBURGH PIRATES

▶Owner: Kevin McClatchy
▶General manager: Cam Bonifay
▶Ballpark:
Three Rivers Stadium
600 Stadium Circle
Pittsburgh, Pa.
412-323-5000
Capacity 47,972
Pay parking lot; $4; public transportation available; family and wheelchair sections, ramps, guest relations
▶Team publications: Yearbook, scorecard, *Info Guide, On Deck*
▶TV, radio stations:
KDKA 1020 AM, Fox Sports Pittsburgh
▶Camps and/or clinics: Youth Camps, 412-323-5098
▶Spring training:
McKechnie Field
Bradenton, Fla.
Capacity 6,562
941-747-3031

ST. LOUIS CARDINALS

▶Owner: St. Louis Cardinals LP
▶General manager: Walt Jocketty
▶Ballpark:
Busch Stadium
250 Stadium Plaza
St. Louis, Mo.
314-421-3060
Capacity 49,676 (includes 1,500 standing)
Parking for over 7,000 cars; $5; public transportation available; wheelchair section, ramps
▶Team publications: Media guide, *The Cardinals Magazine*, 314-982-7336
▶TV, radio stations:
KMOX 1120 AM, KPLR Channel 11, Fox Sports Midwest
▶Spring training:
Roger Dean Stadium
4751 Main Street
Jupiter, Fla.
Capacity 7,000
561-775-1818

SAN DIEGO PADRES

▶Owner: John Morris
▶General manager: Kevin Towers
▶Ballpark:
QualComm Park
9449 Friars Road
San Diego, Calif.
619-283-4494
Capacity 53,000 (approx.)
Parking for 18,751 cars; $6; public transportation available; wheelchair sections, ramps, pre-registration for telephone paging, ATM machines
▶Team publications: *Padre Magazine*, 619-881-6500
▶TV, radio stations:
KFMB 760 AM, XEXX AM (Spanish), KUSI Channel 51, Channel 4 Padres
▶Spring training:
Peoria Sports Complex
Peoria, Ariz.
Capacity 10,000 with grass seating
602-878-4337

SAN FRANCISCO GIANTS

▶Owner: Peter Magowan (president and managing general partner)
▶General manager: Brian Sabean
▶Ballpark:
3Com Park
Jamestown Ave. and Harney Way
San Francisco, Calif.
415-468-3700
Capacity 60,000
Parking for 17,000 cars; $6; public transportation available; family and wheelchair sections, ramps, battery charger plug-ins for wheelchairs, designated handicapped pick-up and drop-off sights
▶Team publications: *Giants Magazine, Giants Info Guide*, 415-468-3700, ext. 478
▶TV, radio stations:
KNBR 680 AM, KTVU Channel 2, KIQI (Spanish), Sports-Channel
▶Camps and/or clinics: Rob Andrews Baseball, June and July, 510-935-3505
▶Spring training:
Scottsdale Stadium
Scottsdale, Ariz.
Capacity 7,500 (plus 2,500 on outfield grass)
602-990-7972

Buffalo Bisons (Indians)
NorthAmeriCare Park
P.O. Box 450
Buffalo, NY 14205
(716) 846-2000
Capacity: 20,050
Charlotte Knights (Marlins)
Knights Castle
P.O. Box 1207
Fort Mill, SC 29716
(704) 357-8071
Capacity: 10,917
Columbus Clippers (Yankees)
Harold Cooper Stadium
1155 W. Mound St.
Columbus, OH 43223
(614) 462-5250
Capacity: 15,000
Durham Bulls (Devil Rays)
Durham Bulls Athletic Park
P.O. Box 507
Durham, NC 27702
(919) 687-6500
Capacity: 6,500
Indianapolis Indians (Reds)
Victory Field
1501 W 16th St.
Indianapolis, IN 46202
(317) 269-3545
Capacity: 15,400
Louisville Redbirds (Cardinals)
Cardinal Stadium
P.O. Box 36407
Louisville, KY 40233
(502) 367-9121
Capacity: 33,500
Norfolk Tides (Mets)
Harbor Park
150 Park Ave.
Norfolk, VA 23510
(804) 622-2222
Capacity: 12,000
Ottawa Lynx (Expos)
JetForm Park
300 Conventry Rd.
Ottawa, ON K1K 4P5
(613) 747-5969
Capacity: 10,000
Pawtucket Red Sox (Red Sox)
McCoy Stadium
P.O. Box 2365
Pawtucket, RI 02861
(401) 724-7300
Capacity: 7,002
Richmond Braves (Braves)
The Diamond
P.O. Box 6667
Richmond, VA 23230
(804) 359-4444
Capacity: 12,500

Rochester Red Wings (Orioles)
1 Morrie Silver Way
Rochester, NY 14608
(716) 454-1001
Capacity: 10,000
**Scranton/Wilkes-Barre
Red Barons (Phillies)**
P.O. Box 3449
Scranton, PA 18505
(717) 969-2255
Capacity: 10,800
Syracuse Sky Chiefs (Blue Jays)
P & C Stadium
Syracuse, NY 13208
(315) 474-7833
Capacity: 11,400
Toledo Mud Hens (Tigers)
Ned Skeldon Stadium
P.O. Box 6212
Toledo, OH 43614
(419) 893-9483
Capacity: 10,917

PACIFIC COAST LEAGUE-CLASS AAA

Albuquerque Dukes (Dodgers)
Albuquerque Sports Stadium
1601 Stadium Blvd. SE
Albuquerque, NM 87106
(505) 243-1791
Capacity: 10,510
Calgary Cannons (White Sox)
Burns Stadium
2255 Corwchild Trail NW
Calgary, AB T2M 4S7
(403) 284-1111
Capacity: 7,500
**Colorado Springs Sky Sox
(Rockies)**
Sky Sox Stadium
4385 Tutt Blvd
Colorado Springs, CO 80922
(719) 597-1449
Capacity: 6,130
Edmonton Trappers (Athletics)
Telus Field
10233 96th Ave.
Edmonton, AB T5K 0A5
(403) 429-2934
Capacity: 10,000
Fresno Grizzlies (Giants)
Beiden Field
1231 N St.
Fresno, CA 93740
(209) 442-1994
Capacity: 6,500
Iowa Cubs (Cubs)
Sec Taylor Stadium
350 SW 1st St.
Des Moines, IA 50309
(515) 243-6111
Capacity: 11,000

Las Vegas Stars (Padres)
Cashman Field
850 Las Vegas Blvd. N.
Las Vegas, NV 89101
(702) 386-7200
Capacity: 9,334
Memphis Redbirds (Cardinals)
Tim McCarver Stadium
800 Home Run Lane
Memphis, TN 38104
(901) 272-1687
Capacity: 10,000
Nashville Sounds (Pirates)
Herschel Greer Stadium
P.O. Box 23290
Nashville, TN 37202
(615) 242-4371
Capacity: 17,000
New Orleans Zephyrs(Astros)
Zephyr Field
6000 Airline Highway
New Orleans, LA 70003
(504) 734-5155
**Oklahoma City
Redhawks (Rangers)**
All-Sports Stadium
P.O. Box 75089
Oklahoma City, OK 73147
(405) 946-8989
Capacity: 15,000
Omaha Royals (Royals)
Rosenblatt Stadium
P.O. Box 3665
Omaha, NE 68103
(402) 734-2550
Capacity: 22,000
Salt Lake Buzz (Twins)
Franklin Quest Field
P.O. Box 4108
Salt Lake City, UT 84110
(801) 485-3800
Capacity: 15,000
Tacoma Rainiers (Mariners)
Cheney Stadium
P.O. Box 11087
Tacoma, WA 98411
(206) 752-7707
Capacity: 9,800
**Tucson Sidewinders
(Diamondbacks)**
Tucson Electric Park
P.O. Box 27045
Tucson, AZ 85726
(520) 325-2621
Capacity: 12,000
Vancouver Canadians (Angels)
Nat Bailey Stadium
4601 Ontario Street
Vancouver, BC V5V3H4
(604) 872-5232
Capacity: 6,500

EASTERN LEAGUE-CLASS AA

Akron Aeros (Indians)
Canal Park
300 S. Main St.
Akron, OH 44308
(330) 253-5151
Capacity: 10,000
Binghamton Mets (Mets)
Municipal Stadium
P.O. Box 598
Binghamton, NY 13902
(607) 723-6387
Capacity: 6,012
Bowie Baysox (Orioles)
Prince Georges Stadium
P.O. Box 1661
Bowie, MD 20717
(301) 805-6000
Capacity: 10,000
Harrisburg Senators (Expos)
Riverside Stadium
P.O. Box 15757
Harrisburg, PA 17105
(717) 231-4444
Capacity: 6,300
New Britain Rock Cats (Twins)
New Britain Stadium
P.O. Box 1718
New Britain, CT 06051
(860) 224-8383
Capacity: 6,146
New Haven Ravens (Rockies)
Yale Field
252 Derby Ave.
New Haven, CT 06516
(203) 782-1666
Capacity: 6,200
Norwich Navigators (Yankees)
Dodd Stadium
P.O. Box 6003
Yantic, CT 06389
(203) 887-7962
Capacity: 6,000
Portland Sea Dogs (Marlins)
Hadlock Field
P.O. Box 636
Portland, ME 04104
(207) 874-9300
Capacity: 6,000
Reading Phillies (Phillies)
Municipal Stadium
P.O. Box 15050
Reading, PA 19612
(610) 375-8469
Capacity: 7,500
**Trenton Thunder
(Red Sox)**
Waterfront Park
One Thunder Rd.
Trenton, NJ 08611
(609) 394-3000
Capacity: 6,341

1998 BASEBALL WEEKLY ALMANAC

SOUTHERN LEAGUE-CLASS AA

Birmingham Barons (White Sox)
Hoover Met
P.O. Box 360007
Birmingham, AL 35236
(205) 988-3200
Capacity: 10,000

Carolina Mudcats (Pirates)
Five County Stadium
P.O. Drawer 1218
Zebulon, NC 27597
(919) 269-2287
Capacity: 6,000

Chattanooga Lookouts (Reds)
Engel Stadium
P.O. Box 11002
Chattanooga, TN 37403
(423) 267-2208
Capacity: 7,500

Greenville Braves (Braves)
Municipal Stadium
P.O. Box 16683
Greenville, SC 29606
(864) 299-3456
Capacity: 7,027

Huntsville Stars (Athletics)
Joe W. Davis Stadium
P.O. Box 2769
Huntsville, AL 35804
(205) 882-2562
Capacity: 10,200

Jacksonville Suns (Tigers)
Wolfson Park
P.O. Box 4756
Jacksonville, FL 32201
(904) 358-2846
Capacity: 8,200

Knoxville Smokies (Blue Jays)
Bill Meyer Stadium
633 Jessamine St.
Knoxville, TN 37917
(615) 637-9494
Capacity: 6,412

Mobile Bay Bears (Padres)
Hank Aaron Stadium
P.O. Box 161663
Mobile, AL 36616
(334) 479-2327
Capacity: 6,000

Orlando Cubs (Mariners)
Tinker Field
287 Tampa Ave. S
Orlando, FL 32805
(407) 649-7297
Capacity: 5,104

West Tenn Diamond Jaxx (Cubs)
Stadium TBA
1861 N. Highland, Suite 1998
Jackson, TN 38305
(901) 664-2020
Capacity: 6,000

TEXAS LEAGUE-CLASS AA

Arkansas Travelers (Cardinals)
Ray Winder Field
P.O. Box 55066
Little Rock, AK 72215
(501) 664-1555
Capacity: 6,083

El Paso Diablos (Brewers)
Cohen Stadium
P.O. Drawer 4797
El Paso, TX 79914
(915) 755-2000
Capacity: 10,000

Jackson Generals (Astros)
Smith-Wills Stadium
P.O. Box 4209
Jackson, MS 39236
(601) 981-4664
Capacity: 5,200

Midland Angels (Angels)
Christensen Stadium
P.O. Box 51187
Midland, TX 79710
(915) 683-4251
Capacity: 5,000

San Antonio Missions (Dodgers)
Nelson Wolff Municipal Stadium
5757 Highway 90 W
San Antonio, TX 78227
(210) 675-7275
Capacity: 6,500

Shreveport Captains (Giants)
Fairgrounds Field
P.O. Box 3448
Shreveport, LA 71133
(318) 636-5555
Capacity: 6,200

Tulsa Drillers (Rangers)
Drillers Stadium
P.O. Box 4448
Tulsa, OK 74159
(918) 744-5998
Capacity: 10,995

Wichita Wranglers (Royals)
Lawrence-Dumont Stadium
P.O. Box 1420
Wichita, KS 67201
(316) 267-3372
Capacity: 6,058

CALIFORNIA LEAGUE-CLASS A

Bakersfield Blaze (Giants)
Sam Lynn Ballpark
P.O. Box 10031
Bakersfield, CA 93389
(805) 322-1363
Capacity: 4,300

High Desert Mavericks (Diamondbacks)
Maverick Stadium
12000 Stadium West
Adelanto, CA 92301
(619) 246-6287
Capacity: 3,808

Lake Elsinore Storm (Angels)
Lake Elsinore Diamond
P.O. Box 535
Lake Elsinore, CA 92531
(909) 245-4487
Capacity: 6,000

Lancaster Jethawks (Mariners)
The Hangar
45116 Valley Central Way
Lancaster, CA 93536
(805) 726-5400
Capacity: 7,000

Modesto A's (Athletics)
Thurman Field
P.O. Box 883
Modeston, CA 95353
(209) 572-4487
Capacity: 4,500

Rancho Cucamonga Quakes (Padres)
The Epicenter
P.O. Box 4139
Rancho Cucamonga, CA 91729
(909) 481-5000
Capacity: 6,500

San Bernardino Stampede (Dodgers)
San Bernardino Stadium
P.O. Box 1806
San Bernardino, CA 92402
(909) 888-9922
Capacity: 5,000

San Jose Giants (Giants)
Municipal Stadium
P.O. Box 21727
San Jose, CA 95151
(408) 297-1435
Capacity: 4,500

Stockton Ports (Brewers)
Billy Hebert Field
P.O. Box 8550
Stockton, CA 95208
(209) 944-5943
Capacity: 3,500

Visalia Oaks (Athletics)
Recreation Park
P.O. Box 48
Visalia, CA 93279
(209) 625-0480
Capacity: 2,000

CAROLINA LEAGUE-CLASS A

Danville 97's (Braves)
Dan Daniel Memorial Park
P.O. Box 3637
Danville, VA 24543

(804) 791-3346
Capacity: 2,588
Frederick Keys (Orioles)
Harry Grove Stadium
P.O. Box 3169
Frederick, MD 21705
(301) 662-0013
Capacity: 5,700
Kinston Indians (Indians)
Grainger Stadium
P.O. Box 3542
Kinston, NC 28502
(919) 527-9111
Capacity: 4,100
Lynchburg Hillcats (Pirates)
City Stadium
P.O. Box 10213
Lynchburg, VA 24506
(804) 528-1144
Capacity: 4,200
Prince William
Cannons (Cardinals)
Pfitzner Memorial Stadium
P.O. Box 2148
Woodbridge, VA 22193
(703) 590-2311
Capacity: 6,000
Salem Avalanche (Rockies)
Salem Mem. Baseball Stadium
P.O. Box 842
Salem, VA 24153
(540) 389-3333
Capacity: 6,300
Wilmington Blue Rocks (Royals)
Frawley Stadium
801 South Madison St.
Wilmington, DE 19801
(302) 888-2015
Capacity: 5,500
Winston-Salem Warthogs
(White Sox)
Ernie Shore Field
P.O. Box 4488
Winston-Salem, NC 27115
(910) 759-2233
Capacity: 6,280

FLORIDA STATE LEAGUE-CLASS A

Brevard County
Manatees (Marlins)
Space Coast Stadium
5600 Stadium Parkway
Melbourne, FL 32940
(407) 633-9200
Capacity: 7,200
Charlotte Rangers (Rangers)
Charlotte County Stadium
2300 El Jobean Rd.
Port Charlotte, FL 33948
(813) 625-9500
Capacity: 6,026
Clearwater Phillies (Phillies)
Jack Russell Stadium
P.O. Box 10336

Clearwater, FL 10336
(813) 441-8638
Capacity: 6,917
Daytona Cubs (Cubs)
Jackie Robinson Ballpark
P.O. Box 15080
Daytona Beach, FL 32114
(904) 257-3172
Capacity: 4,900
Dunedin Blue Jays (Blue Jays)
Dunedin Stadium
P.O. Box 957
Dunedin, FL 34697
(813) 733-9302
Capacity: 6,218
Fort Myers Miracle (Twins)
Lee County Complex
14400 Six Miles Cypress Pkwy.
Fort Myers, FL 33912
(941) 768-4210
Capacity: 7,500
Lakeland Tigers (Tigers)
Joker Marchant Stadium
P.O. Box 90187
Lakeland, FL 33804
(941) 688-7911
Capacity: 7,000
St. Lucie Mets (Mets)
Thomas J. White Stadium
525 N.W. Blvd.
Port St. Lucie, FL 34986
(561) 871-2100
Capacity: 7,350
St. Petersburg
Devil Rays (Devil Rays)
Al Lang Stadium
P.O. Box 12557
St. Petersburg, FL 33733
(813) 822-3384
Capacity: 7,004
Sarasota Red Sox (Red Sox)
Ed Smith Stadium
P.O. Box 2816
Sarasota, FL 34230
(941) 365-4460
Capacity: 7,500
Tampa Yankees (Yankees)
Legends Field
3802 W. Dr. MLK Blvd.
Tampa, FL 33614
(813) 875-7753
Capacity: 10,000
Vero Beach Dodgers(Dodgers)
Holman Stadium
P.O. Box 2887
Vero Beach, FL 32961
(407) 569-4900
Capacity: 6,500

MIDWEST LEAGUE-CLASS A

Beloit Snappers (Brewers)
Pohlman Field
P.O. Box 855
Beloit, WI 53512

(608) 362-2272
Capacity: 3,500
Burlington Bees (Reds)
Community Field
P.O. Box 824
Burlington, IA 52601
(319) 754-5705
Capacity: 3,500
Cedar Rapids Kernels (Angels)
Veterans Memorial Ballpark
P.O. Box 2001
Cedar Rapids, IA 52406
(319) 363-3887
Capacity: 6,000
Clinton Lumber Kings (Padres)
Riverview Stadium
P.O. Box 1295
Clinton, IA 52733
(319) 242-0727
Capacity: 3,400
Fort Wayne Wizards (Twins)
Memorial Stadium
4000 Parnell Ave.
Fort Wayne, IN 46805
(219) 482-6400
Capacity: 6,000
Kane County Cougars (Marlins)
Elfstrom Stadium
34W002 Cherry Ln.
Geneva, IL 60134
(630) 232-8811
Capacity: 5,900
Lansing Lugnuts (Royals)
Oldsmobile Park
505 E. Michigan Ave.
Lansing, MI 48912
(517) 485-4500
Capacity: 12,000
Michigan Battle Cats (Red Sox)
C.O. Brown Stadium
1392 Capital Ave. NE
Battle Creek, MI 49017
(616) 660-2287
Capacity: 6,200
Peoria Chiefs (Cardinals)
Pete Vonachen Stadium
1524 W. Nebraska Ave.
Peoria, IL 61604
(309) 688-1622
Capacity: 5,200
Quad City River Bandits (Astros)
John O'Donnell Stadium
P.O. Box 3496
Davenport, IA 52808
(319) 324-2032
Capacity: 5,500
Rockford Cubbies (Cubs)
Marinelli Field
P.O. Box 6748
Rockford, IL 61104
(815) 962-2827
Capacity: 4,300
South Bend Silver Hawks
(Diamondbacks)
Coveleski Stadium

P.O. Box 4218
South Bend, IN 46634
(219) 235-9988
Capacity: 5,000
West Michigan
Whitecaps (Tigers)
Old Kent Park
P.O. Box 428
Comstock Park, MI 49321
(616) 784-4131
Capacity: 5,500
Wisconsin Timber Rattlers
(Mariners)
Fox Cities Stadium
P.O. Box 464
Appleton, WI 54912
(414) 733-4152
Capacity: 5,200

SOUTH ATLANTIC LEAGUE-CLASS A

Asheville Tourists (Rockies)
McCormick Field
P.O. Box 1556
Asheville, NC 28802
(704) 258-0428
Capacity: 3,400
Augusta Greenjackets (Pirates)
Lake Olmstead Stadium
P.O. Box 3746 Hill Station
Augusta, GA 30904
(706) 736-7889
Capacity: 4,500
Cape Fear Crocs (Expos)
J.P. Riddle Stadium
P.O. Box 64939
Fayetteville, NC 28306
(910) 424-6500
Capacity: 3,200
Capital City Bombers (Mets)
Capital City Stadium
P.O. Box 7845
Columbia, S.C. 29202
(803) 256-4110
Capacity: 6,000
Charleston (S.C.) River Dogs
(Devil Rays)
Joseph P.Riley Jr. Park
P.O. Box 20849
Charleston, SC 29413
(803) 965-4096
Capacity: 5,900
Charleston (W.Va.)
Alley Cats (Reds)
Watt Powell Park
P.O. Box 4669
Charleston, WV 25304
(304) 344-2287
Capacity: 6,000
Columbus Redstixx (Indians)
Golden Park
P.O. Box 1886
Columbus, GA 31902
(706) 571-8866
Capacity: 4,000

Delmarva Shorebirds (Orioles)
Perdue Stadium
P.O. Box 1552
Salisbury, MD 21802
(410) 219-3112
Capacity: 5,200
Greensboro Bats (Yankees)
War Memorial Stadium
510 Yanceyville St.
Greensboro, NC 27405
(910) 333-2287
Capacity: 7,500
Hagerstown Suns (Blue Jays)
Municipal Stadium
P.O. Box 230
Hagerstown, MD 21740
(301) 791-6266
Capacity: 4,500
Hickory Crawdads (White Sox)
L.P. Frans Stadium
P.O. Box 1268
Hickory, NC 28603
(704) 322-3000
Capacity: 5,200
Macon Braves (Braves)
Luther Williams Field
P.O. Box 4525
Macon, GA 31208
(912) 745-8923
Capacity: 4,000
Piedmont Boll Weevils (Phillies)
Fieldcrest Cannon Stadium
P.O. Box 64
Kannapolis, NC 28082
(704) 932-3267
Capacity: 4,800
Savannah Sand Gnats (Rangers)
Grayson Stadium
P.O. Box 3783
Savannah, GA 31414
(912) 351-9150
Capacity: 8,000